The Law

of Business

Organizations

Sixth Edition

THE LAW OF BUSINESS ORGANIZATIONS

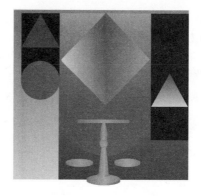

SIXTH EDITION

John E. Moye

THOMSON

DELMAR LEARNING

Australia Canada Mexico Singapore Spain United Kingdom United States

THOMSON
DELMAR LEARNING

WEST LEGAL STUDIES

THE LAW OF BUSINESS ORGANIZATIONS 6E
John E. Moye

Career Education Strategic Business Unit:
Vice President:
Dawn Gerrain

Director of Editorial:
Sherry Gomoll

Developmental Editor:
Melissa Riveglia

Editorial Assistant:
Sarah Duncan

Director of Production:
Wendy A. Troeger

Production Manager:
Carolyn Miller

Production Editor:
Betty L. Dickson

Director of Marketing:
Wendy Mapstone

Cover Design:
Rose Design

Cover Image:
Getty Images

Library of Congress Cataloging-in-Publication Data

Moye, John E.
   The law of business organizations / John E. Moye.— 6th ed.
       p. cm. — (West Legal Studies series)
Includes index
   ISBN 1-4018-2019-0
   1. Corporation law—United States.
   2. Partnership—United States. I. Title. II. Series.
KF1366.M68 2004
346.73'066—dc22

2004045494

NOTICE TO THE READER

To

Glenna McKelvy

with thanks for all you do

BRIEF CONTENTS

CONTENTS

TABLE OF FORMS

PREFACE

More than thirty years ago, I taught one of the pioneer paralegal courses in business organizations in the Continuing Legal Education Program of the University of Denver College of Law. The course materials were a compilation of examples of documents and certificates that were typically used by lawyers and their assistants to advise and represent business organizations. This book began in that classroom and has been developed through five previous editions to this newest and most complete sixth edition with the latest resources and examples and challenging problems that confront today's legal assistant, paralegal, and lawyer in representation of business clients. Previous editions of this book have been used extensively in paralegal training courses. They have also been used in several law schools and by practitioners who taught other lawyers in continuing legal education courses. This sixth edition is a greatly expanded version of the materials developed through all of those courses and through my own experiences counseling clients and teaching students over those thirty-plus years.

This book is designed to be used in two environments:

- It is a classroom teaching source for the training of paralegals and lawyers in the practical aspects of the law of business organizations.
- It is a useful how-to-do-it reference work for paralegals and attorneys in the practice of this field, with an explanation of the legal and ethical principles that must be observed in counseling an enterprise. As a reference work, it covers all of the issues that are typically encountered in working with business clients, and identifies resources to obtain forms and additional information.

In the classroom, the book provides the students with a variety of examples of the work in business organization law, including:

- Numerous sample clauses and forms sprinkled throughout the text to illustrate the legal rules described;
- Procedural checklists to study the array of tasks involved in accomplishing the client's objectives;
- Representative cases in each chapter to illustrate the manner in which courts interpret that area of business law;
- Problems illustrating the issues of each chapter, with expanded and practical problems to provide the real experiences of conducting research into the relevant facts and applying the facts to the legal task to be accomplished;
- Examples of the real forms being used by practitioners throughout the country.
- Resources on the Internet to review applicable local laws, to obtain forms, and to conduct further research on each topic;
- A glossary of legal terms used in this practice area with concise explanations of the terms and how they are used.

In the office, the book provides the practitioner with useful resources for the practice of business organization law, such as:

- How-to-do-it explanations of the steps involved in organizing, drafting, operating, and maintaining business entities, with state law variations highlighted and explained;

- Forms and checklists that are currently used in developing the documents required for business organization clients, including a Table of Forms for quick reference;
- Internet resources to download the most current forms in each state;
- The latest version of uniform laws and where to expect local state variations, together with Internet resources for quick reference to local laws;
- Sample clauses to use in drafting documents for clients;
- Identification of ethical issues that arise in representing business organization clients;
- Drafting techniques for business organization documents;
- Concise explanation and step-by-step review of registrations, reports, and documents required for public companies by the Securities Act of 1933, the Securities Exchange Act of 1934, and state securities laws.

Except for the sole proprietorship, business organizations are based upon statutory authority. To ensure national application of this book, the text explains the law based upon the following uniform laws and model acts (which are set forth in their entirety in Appendices A through I):

- the Uniform Partnership Act
- the Revised Uniform Partnership Act (1997)
- the Revised Uniform Limited Partnership Act with the latest amendments
- the Uniform Limited Partnership Act of 2001
- the Uniform Limited Liability Company Act
- the Model Business Corporation Act
- the Model Professional Corporation Act
- the Model Close Corporation Supplement

The limited liability partnership materials are based upon the states that have recently authorized the registration of such entities for limited liability purposes. All of these uniform laws and model acts have been extensively revised in the past few years, and state adaptations of these laws have variously combined the new model rules with existing state law. The text discusses both the revisions and the former approaches of the statutes, since many states' laws continue to be based upon some version of the pre-revision text. The revised organization and modern corporate concepts in the most current version of the Model Business Corporation Act are included as the basis of the corporate statutory rules. Important jurisdictional variations from these statutes are noted in footnotes in many cases, and the reader is regularly reminded to analyze the appropriate state law in practice.

The book begins with the most simple form of business enterprise, the sole proprietorship; progresses through general partnership, limited partnership, and limited liability partnership; describes the flexibility and operations of a limited liability company; and concentrates on the most complex business organization, the corporation. Chapter 7 considers issues relating to special corporate variations—public corporations, close corporations, and professional corporations.

Chapters 2, 3, and 4 contain discussions of frequently encountered problems in the organization and operation of sole proprietorship, and partnerships, including procedures for the formation and operation of the business, characteristics of the enterprise, liabilities of the associate parties, taxation issues, dissolution, and termination. The general partnership materials compare the original uniform version of the Uniform Partnership Act with the Revised Uniform Partnership Act. A paralegal or lawyer will eventually be working with the revised partnership law and will need to know modern thinking about partnership issues as they are addressed in the revised act. The materials on limited partnerships are based on the Revised Uniform Limited Partnership Act as amended in 1985, since that statute forms the basis of most states' limited partnership laws. The variations adopted in the Uniform Limited Partnership Act of 2001 are highlighted as the newest concepts in limited partnerships, which will likely be considered and adopted by various states during the next few years.

The limited liability company has become a very popular business form during the past decade. Most states have now adopted the Uniform Limited Liability Company Act with some variations; the text in Chapter 5 focuses on that uniform law with comparisons of the partnership and corporate forms. The chapter also highlights the drafting issues that are predictable from the various state statutes for a limited liability company. Logically, the limited liability company is a hybrid organization between partnerships and corporations, so the chapter concerning these entities follows partnerships and precedes corporations. It may be easier to understand the concepts of limited liability companies after a student first studies the basic forms of partnerships and corporations, since the LLC has characteristics of both.

The corporate materials are arranged somewhat chronologically as they usually will be met in practice. Following the identification of the intracorporate parties and a general discussion of the characteristics, powers, continuity, and taxation of the corporation, the remaining chapters consider formation procedures, meetings, development of the corporate financial structure, issues relating to publicly held corporations, dividends and corporate distributions, agreements affecting employment and share ownership, qualification and operation as a foreign corporation, modifications to the corporate structure, and dissolution. While these topics are organized in the sequence typically encountered in a functioning corporation, many of the subjects may be addressed in a different chronology and many of these matters also arise in the operation of a partnership or a limited liability company. For example, matters involving shareholder agreements may arise in the formation stage of a corporation; employment issues arise in all business entities; and cash distributions are made from all entities during business operations and upon dissolution. The material is all cross-referenced by footnotes for easy reference back and forth among the chapters.

Chapter 1 deals with the basic agency concepts that are applicable in every business entity and form the basis for the relationships between a business entity and its representatives. A general understanding of the law of agency is an important backdrop to describe the relationship of the people who operate business organizations. These concepts are directly related to the material on employment and compensation in Chapter 12, where the book covers the drafting and legal issues in formalizing the agency relationships through employment agreements. Chapter 12 appears in the corporate section of the book because it involves agreements that will be executed with key employees in corporate practice, and the discussions concerning pension and profit sharing plans, stock options, and insurance programs are almost exclusively corporate in nature. However, the remaining sections and particularly the discussion of agency law in the first chapter, are equally applicable to sole proprietorships, partnerships, and limited liability companies.

Chapter 13 discusses techniques in drafting shareholder buyout agreements, and the same concepts are often included in partnership agreements and operating agreements for limited liability companies. Again, these materials are useful in all business organizations and should be read in that context. Chapter 15 describes many of the new anti-takeover statutes and the lexicon of techniques that protect shareholders from hostile takeovers and minority shareholders from abusive corporate dissolutions. These sophisticated devices and techniques are becoming commonplace in the corporate world and are increasingly important to all practitioners of corporate law.

The practice of modern business organization law is being conducted increasingly over the Internet. Public officials who are required to accept formation and operational documents for these entities have been converting their files for electronic access and filing procedures, and they have been making forms and documents available to be downloaded from their Web sites. Similarly, computerized legal research is the modern way to verify and review local entity laws to ensure compliance with local statutory variations. This edition includes Internet resources with each topic, including sources for legal research into local statutes, sources for forms and information about the entity's operations, and sources for more sophisticated documents that are made available by various suppliers.

Having incorporated suggestions from the various teachers, practitioners, and students who have used the prior editions of this book, I am confident that this sixth edition covers the most current and important areas of enterprise practice. I commend it to the reader with the hope that I have created a usable manual for the assistance in or practice of the law of business organizations.

John E. Moye
Denver, Colorado

SUPPLEMENTAL TEACHING MATERIALS

- The **Instructor's Manual** is available on-line at *www.westlegalstudies.com* in the Instructor's Lounge under Resource. Written by the author of the text, the *Instructor's Manual* contains the following:
  - Suggestions for developing a course syllabus for courses of varying credit hours
  - Answers to the Problems within the text
  - Answers to the Review Questions within the text
  - Additional role-play problems with confidential facts
  - Synopses of the cases presented in the text
- The **WebTutor™** offers questions that augment those in the text and provides immediate feedback so that students know if their response is correct and know the reason if it is incorrect. Vocabulary is tested using "flashcards." Discussion questions challenge students to integrate and assimilate information. A brief introduction at the beginning of each section sensitizes students to what they should focus on.
- **Web page**—Come visit our Web site at *www.westlegalstudies.com,* where you will find valuable information such as hot links and sample materials to download, as well as other West Legal Studies products.
- **Westlaw®**—West's on-line computerized legal research system offers students "hands-on" experience with a system commonly used in law offices. Qualified adopters can receive ten free hours of Westlaw®. Westlaw® can be accessed with Macintosh and IBM PC and compatibles. A modem is required.
- **Survival Guide for Paralegal Students,** a pamphlet by Kathleen Mercer Reed and Bradene Moore covers practical and basic information to help students make the most of their paralegal courses. Topics covered include courses of study and note-taking skills.
- **West's Paralegal Video Library**—West Legal Studies is pleased to offer the following videos at no charge to qualified adopters:
  - *The Drama of the Law II: Paralegal Issues Video*
    ISBN: 0-314-07088-5
  - *The Making of a Case Video*
    ISBN: 0-314-07300-0
  - *ABA Mock Trial Video-Product Liability*
    ISBN: 0-314-07342-6
  - *Arguments to the United States Supreme Court Video*
    ISBN: 0-314-07070-2
- **Court TV Videos**—West Legal Studies is pleased to offer the following videos from Court TV for a minimal fee while supplies last:
  - *New York v. Ferguson—Murder on the 5:33: The Trial of Colin Ferguson*
    ISBN: 0-7668-1098-4
  - *Ohio v. Alfieri*
    ISBN: 0-7668-1099-2
  - *Flynn v. Goldman Sachs—Fired on Wall Street: A Case of Sex Discrimination?*
    ISBN: 0-7668-1096-8
  - *Dodd v. Dodd—Religion and Child Custody in Conflict*
    ISBN: 0-7668-1094-1
  - *In Re Custody of Baby Girl Clausen—Child of Mine: The Fight for Baby Jessica*
    ISBN: 0-7668-1097-6
  - *Fentress v. Eli Lilly & Co., et al—Prozac on Trial*
    ISBN: 0-7668-1095-x
  - *Garcia v. Garcia—Fighting over Jerry's Money*
    ISBN: 0-7668-0264-7
  - *Hall v. Hall—Irretrievably Broken—A Divorce Lawyer Goes to Court*
    ISBN: 0-7668-0196-9

- *Maglica v. Maglica—Broken Hearts, Broken Commitments*
  ISBN: 0-7668-0867-x
- *Northside Partners v. Page and New Kids on the Block—New Kids in Court: Is Their Hit Song a Copy?*
  ISBN: 0-7668-9426-7

Please note the Internet resources are of a time-sensitive nature and URL addresses may often change or be deleted.

Contact us at westlegalstudies@delmar.com

ACKNOWLEDGMENTS

I wish to express gratitude to some very special people who contributed significantly to the preparation of this work.

First I thank my partners at Moye Giles LLP for giving me the professional support and encouragement I needed to take the time to work on this book. I also thank our outstanding corporate paralegals at the firm for their excellence and proficiency in the practice of business organizations, much of which they will recognize in some of the forms and checklists used in the book.

I gratefully acknowledge the contributions of other authors, government officials, and corporate personnel for the forms and checklists used as examples.

I am indebted and grateful to Glenna McKelvy, my executive legal assistant, for her assistance and dedication in the preparation of the manuscript and in managing my schedule to accommodate my many clients while this edition was in process. Thanks to Gary Weitzel, our law firm Knowledge Manager, for his help with Uniform Acts and Web-based access to forms and statutes.

Last, but certainly not least, I thank my many family members, friends, and associates who appear as characters in the sample clauses throughout the book. Their assent to join the case of business personalities in the various transactions adds a flavor of realism and is sincerely appreciated.

REVIEWERS OF THE SIXTH EDITION

Susan Brewer
J. Sargent Reynolds College
Richmond, Virginia

Melody Brown
Idaho Technical College
Idaho Falls, Idaho

John Frank
Chippewa Valley Technical College
Eau Claire, Wisconsin

Janet Holt
Georgetown University
Washington, DC

Donna Kay Metz
Wharton College
Houston, Texas

Anthony Myers
Myers University
Cleveland, Ohio

Kathryn Myers
St. Mary of the Woods College
St. Mary of the Woods, Indiana

Carole Olsen
El Centro College
Dallas, Texas

AGENCY IN A BUSINESS ORGANIZATION

The law of agency is so basic to the operations of a business that it is important to understand the principles of agency to be able to appreciate the various structures in which an enterprise may operate. Management functions usually occur through agents in most organizations, and most of the legal relationships established in an enterprise occur through the law of agency.

The operations of every business enterprise are conducted by agents, either as employees or independent contractors, like consultants. Even in a sole proprietorship, the sole proprietor will hire other persons to perform certain duties, some as simple as cleaning up the premises and others as complex as managing the entire business. In a partnership, each partner is an agent for the partnership and for the other partners. In a limited liability company, the managers and members may all be agents of the business. And in a corporation, the firm can act only through agents. Although the corporation is a separate legal person, it can act, speak, and hear only through its directors, officers, or shareholders. Therefore, the law of agency plays a role in each business enterprise.

DEFINITION AND ELEMENTS OF AGENCY

An **agency** is a voluntary, consensual relationship between two persons. The relationship is created by law whenever one person, the **principal**, has a right to control the conduct of the **agent**, and the agent has the power to affect the legal relations of the principal. This relationship does not only occur in a business organization. Any time people ask other people to perform a task on their behalf, an agency relationship may be created. Your first experience with an agency relationship may have occurred when your mother asked you to go to the grocery store and buy a loaf of bread. In this context, your mother, as a principal, was authorizing you, as an agent, to perform a task for her, thereby giving you the authority to affect her legal relationship with the grocery store. In a business context, the legal relationship is more obvious. For example, the cashier at the counter in the local hardware store is an agent of the owner of the store and has the authority to perform legal obligations (and incur legal liability) on behalf of the owner.

Agency relationships can arise in several other situations. Whenever a client asks an attorney to represent the client, the attorney is an agent for the client. The same is true with accountants and other consultants who perform services for individuals and businesses at their request.

It is not necessary that the agency relationship be formalized by a written document, although frequently it is so formalized. Agency authority can be as informal as simply asking someone to perform a task, or as formal as an extensive written agreement that details all duties and obligations of the principal and the agent. For business entities, it is always advisable to use written documents to define and describe legal rights and obligations between the principal and the agent.

TYPES OF PRINCIPALS

The law of agency generally distinguishes three types of principals: disclosed, partially disclosed, and undisclosed. If an agent is conducting business for a principal, and the person with whom the agent is dealing knows the agent is acting for another and knows the person for whom the agent is acting, the principal is a **disclosed principal**. If a salesperson for IBM is selling hardware and software equipment to a purchaser, and the purchaser is aware that the salesperson is acting on behalf of IBM and that the equipment is manufactured and sold by IBM, IBM is a disclosed principal.

If an agent acts on behalf of a principal but does not disclose the identity of the principal, the principal is **partially disclosed**. In this case, the person dealing with the agent knows that a principal exists but does not know the identity of the principal. If Ned Giles wanted to purchase a new home in an exclusive subdivision but was concerned about everyone in the community knowing that he could afford a home in this subdivision, Ned might authorize an agent to make inquiries of prospective sellers without disclosing Ned's identity. Those agents would approach sellers of property, explaining that they were acting for another, but saying that they wanted to keep the identity of their prospective purchaser anonymous until a particular property was selected and a purchase contract was negotiated. In these cases, the sellers of the property would realize that they were dealing with an agent, but would know that the agent was not personally interested in purchasing the property. Nevertheless, they would not be aware of the identity of Ned Giles until the agent had disclosed Ned's identity after a contract had been completed.

Whenever an agent is acting on behalf of another but has not disclosed that fact or the identity of the person on whose behalf the agent is acting, the principal is **undisclosed**. If Ned Giles were worried that a prospective seller might learn his identity, he could authorize an agent to make inquiries concerning the purchase of property without disclosing that a principal was involved. In this case, the agent would be giving prospective sellers the impression that the agent was personally interested in purchasing the property, and the agent would negotiate a contract, according to Ned Giles's terms, without ever telling the sellers that Ned was the actual purchaser. The sellers would thus be dealing with an undisclosed principal, since the only person they know is the agent. An undisclosed principal may be found in many transactions and in many legal contexts. For example, a trustee who transacts business for the trust she represents may not disclose the existence of the trust but is creating legal rights and obligations on its behalf as an agent. When, as a teenager, you discreetly inquired on behalf of a friend whether a popular, attractive member of the opposite sex might have an interest in a date on Saturday night (pretending the friend knew nothing about this inquiry), you were an agent for an undisclosed principal.

TYPES OF AGENTS

The law of agency generally distinguishes among several types of agents: general or special agents, servants or independent contractors, and subagents or subservants. A **general agent** is a person who is continuously employed to conduct a series of transactions. The cashier at the hardware store is employed on a daily basis to greet customers, record their purchases, and collect their money. This person, who has ongoing responsibilities for a series of transactions on behalf of the principal, is regarded as a general agent.

A **special agent** is a person who is employed to conduct a single transaction or a limited number of transactions. When Ned Giles authorizes an agent to negotiate and purchase a piece of property, the agent's task is limited to negotiating for a single transaction (to purchase the property for Ned). Similarly, if a principal asked an agent to negotiate the purchase of several pieces of property, the agent's duties would be limited to the transactions involving designated properties in which the principal is interested. These agents, with limited authority and specific transactional duties, are regarded as special agents.

A **servant** is an agent who agrees to devote time to the principal's business and affairs and whose physical conduct, during the performance of the employment, is subject to the control of the principal. In modern business transactions, employees of a business are included within the traditional agency definition of servants. Whether the principal has a right to control the activities of the agent is usually interpreted from various factors, including the type of business of the principal, the type of activities performed for the principal by the agent, and agreements between the principal and agent that describe the agent's authority. The cashier at the hardware store is probably a servant. This person follows directives given by the owner of the hardware store concerning the manner in which customers are to be greeted, prices are to be ascertained, and cash is to be collected and handled. Most activities of the cashier are subject to the control of the owner and may be changed or modified frequently at the owner's whim and direction. Whenever a principal has a right to control the activities of an agent, the principal is called a **master**. In the law of agency, as described later, the "master/servant" relationship usually results in the master's liability for the acts of the servant that are performed within the scope of the servant's employment.

An **independent contractor** is a person who is conducting a transaction for the principal but is not subject to the control of the principal. These persons are expected to exercise independent judgment, usually within their own professional guidelines and responsibilities, and while they are acting on behalf of a principal, the principal does not have the right to tell them how to act or perform. The classic examples of independent contractors include attorneys, brokers, and consulting persons who have professional training and abilities that make them better able than the principal to accomplish a transaction. For instance, a client will explain to an attorney many facts and issues relating to litigation, and the attorney is expected to exercise professional judgment and to conduct the litigation on behalf of the client to achieve the outcome the client desires. Independent contractor status usually arises with agents who have specialized training, but it is not necessary that an independent contractor have specialized or professional training to serve in that capacity. The major factors used to distinguish an independent contractor from a servant are as follows:

Factor	Servant	Independent Contractor
Compensation	Salary	By the hour or project
Period of employment	Continuous	Project by project
Tools furnished by	Employer	Contractor
Place of work	Employer's premises	Contractor's office or shop
Quality of work	Unskilled/supervised	Skilled/unsupervised
Regularity of work	Part of normal business	Nonrecurring, unique projects

Whenever the relationship between a principal and an agent permits the agent to act individually according to the agent's own judgment, and particularly when an agent is hired for a specialized task that only the agent is capable of performing, an independent contractor status arises.

Whenever one agent hires another to assist in the performance of duties for the principal, the second agent becomes a **subagent**. A subagent is created only if the first agent is authorized to hire the second. An agent may be authorized to hire other agents, based upon the scope of the work that the agent has been requested to perform. The authority also may come from an express or implied agreement between the principal and the agent that grants authority to hire other persons to assist in the tasks the agent is expected to perform. For example, if the owner of a restaurant hired a manager to run the operations of the restaurant, the manager would have implied authority to hire a chef, dishwashers, waiters and waitresses, and other restaurant personnel. These persons would be subagents of the owner. If subagents are subject to the right of control by the principal, the subagents become subservants. Thus, if the owner of the restaurant can direct the activities of the chef who was hired by the manager, the chef becomes a subservant of the owner. Similarly, in the building of a house, an owner hires a general contractor, who has authority to hire a carpenter, plumber, electrician, and so forth. All of the subcontractors are subagents of the owner, and the term *subcontractor* should provide a clue that these persons are likely to be independent subcontractors, rather than subservants.

Duties and Obligations between the Principal and the Agent

The law of agency creates a **fiduciary relationship** between the principal and the agent. A fiduciary relationship means that the principal is placing trust or confidence in the agent to be faithful and loyal and to conduct the principal's business with care. When you deposit money with a stockbroker with instructions to buy stock in your name, the broker is in a position of trust and confidence, or a fiduciary position, with respect to your stock purchase transaction. Consequently, when a fiduciary relationship exists, the law implies certain duties that both parties must perform on behalf of the other, which may be amplified or supplemented by a written agreement.

The Agent's Duties to the Principal Agents generally owe their principals the duties of obedience, care, and loyalty. An agent has a duty to obey a principal and to perform all tasks the principal has directed, as long as those tasks are consistent with the engagement of the agent.

The agent's duty of obedience is an obligation to follow the principal's instructions and directions—essentially, an obligation to do what the principal tells the agent to do. If a principal authorizes an agent to buy goods for the principal's business and to pay for them with a check from the business checking account, it is a violation of this duty if the agent purchases the goods on credit from the supplier. The principal could recover the interest that the supplier charges on the credit account, since the agent did not precisely follow the principal's instructions.

Each agent is expected to use reasonable care and diligence to accomplish the principal's objectives. This means an agent should use personal skill and knowledge and perform all tasks diligently while working for the principal. For example, an attorney would be required to know the law to be applied in the client's case, and an insurance agent would be expected not to permit a policy of insurance to expire or terminate without appropriate notice to the policy owner. Even if an agent is performing without compensation, the agent owes the principal the obligation to use due care and prudence in performing all duties. Consistent with the duty of care is an agent's duty to act in a manner that will not embarrass the principal or bring the principal into disrepute, and an agent always has a duty to provide full information concerning any matters the principal would want to know in regard to the transaction undertaken by the agent.

The agent's duty of loyalty requires that the agent act solely for the interests of the principal while accomplishing the transactions for which the agent is employed. This duty requires the agent to report to the principal the amount of any profits received by the agent on the principal's behalf and to disclose fully any personal adverse or conflicting interests that would affect the agent's ability to act for the principal. Therefore, if an agent were engaged by a principal to find a particular parcel of property for the principal's business, and the agent also had an interest in acquiring a similar piece of property in the same area, the agent could not use negotiations for the principal to assist the agent in personal negotiations for the property, and the agent must disclose to the principal that the agent is also personally seeking a similar piece of property. An agent may not compete with the principal and must disclose all confidential information received on the principal's behalf.

The Principal's Duties to the Agent The principal also has obligations to the agent that are implied by law and that may be amplified or supplemented by an agreement. Generally, a principal is obligated to **compensate** an agent, according to the reasonable value of the agent's services, unless the agent has agreed to act without pay. The principal has a further obligation to provide the agent with the means to perform the agent's services, such as an office, samples of products the agent is expected to sell, transportation, or clerical assistance. The principal also may be obligated under an agreement with the agent to provide other benefits for the agent's service.

The principal has an additional obligation to **indemnify** the agent for any payments or liabilities incurred by the agent whenever the agent is performing a transaction on behalf of the principal. Since the agent is acting for the principal, any expenses or liabilities incurred belong to the principal, and the principal must pay them. Thus, if an agent incurs transportation costs or expenses entertaining the principal's customers, the principal must reimburse the agent under this duty.

The principal is also expected not to embarrass the agent or act in a manner that is harmful to the agent's reputation or self-esteem, and the principal must not interfere with the agent's performance by making the tasks more difficult or by sabotaging the agent's ability to perform the job. If the owner of the hardware store in the earlier example publicly berated the cashier in front of customers and other employees or refused to provide the cashier with a workable cash register to record customer purchases, the owner may have violated these duties to the cashier.

AGENCY AUTHORITY

Whenever a principal asks an agent to perform a task, the agent has authority to obligate the principal for legal rights and liabilities associated with that transaction. The law of agency has several distinctions concerning the types of authority the agent may enjoy and the rights and liabilities of the principal, the agent, and the other contracting parties whenever an agent negotiates a contract on the principal's behalf.

Actual Authority

An agent is always authorized to do what the principal has told the agent to do. The agent may reasonably infer authority to do acts required to perform the tasks assigned. General agents, who are engaged for a series of continuing transactions, usually may infer greater authority than special agents, who are limited to the authority necessary to accomplish a single assigned transaction. The authority usually and reasonably needed to complete an assigned task is called **actual authority**. For example, if a truck company hires a truck driver to make interstate deliveries of goods, the truck driver has actual authority to operate the truck and may reasonably infer authority to purchase gasoline and make repairs to the vehicle. However, the truck driver probably does not have actual authority to hire an assistant truck driver to help drive the truck, since that is not usually or reasonably inferred as being part of the truck driver's duties.

Actual authority typically is separated into two subcategories: express actual authority and implied actual authority. The *express actual authority* includes the statements that the principal made to the agent, orally or in writing. When the truck company tells the truck driver to drive the truck to South Dakota, the truck driver has express actual authority to do so. *Implied actual authority* is the additional authority the agent may infer from the express authority granted. The truck driver would have implied authority to purchase gasoline on the truck company's behalf while driving to South Dakota, even though the truck driver was not specifically instructed to do so.

Actual authority may be terminated in several ways. Since it is based upon the agent's understanding of the principal's directions and instructions to the agent, and on the reasonable inferences of authority from the principal's statements, an act or event that causes the agent to know or believe that the principal no longer desires the agent to act terminates the actual authority. The principal and agent may agree on the duration of the agency relationship in advance. If an employee is hired to work in a business for one month, the agreement engaging the employee establishes the length of the actual authority. At the end of the month, when the agreement terminates, the employee (agent) no longer has the actual authority to bind the employer (principal). In addition, the unilateral act of either the principal or the agent may terminate the actual authority. If the agent says, "I quit," or the principal says, "You're fired," the statement indicates that the agent no longer has authority to represent the principal. Similarly, when the principal's circumstances substantially change in a manner that should indicate to the agent that the principal would no longer want the agent to accomplish the assigned tasks, the actual authority to perform those tasks ends. For example, if the agent had been told to purchase new draperies for the principal's office, and before the agent had purchased the draperies, the office building in which the principal's office was located burned to the ground, the agent should realize that the purchase of draperies for the charred ruins of the principal's office would no longer be desired by the principal.

Actual authority also may be terminated by "operation of law" through events that eliminate the agent's ability or reason for acting on the principal's behalf. *Operation of law* means that statutes or case precedents have determined that upon certain events actual authority will cease even though neither the principal nor the agent might have contemplated those events in forming their relationship. Death or incapacity of either the principal or the agent, for example, terminates actual authority. Various legal techniques have been developed to avoid the unexpected termination of authority and, in some cases, to circumvent completely the problems caused by loss of authority. It is possible to extend an agent's authority beyond the death or incapacity of the principal by using a written instrument (that is expressly permitted under state law). In some states, such an instrument is called a *durable power of attorney;* this written document authorizes the agent to act for the principal even though the principal is dead or incapacitated. Such an extension of the principal's existence, however, must be authorized under state law.

E X A M P L E **Ways in Which Actual Authority Terminates**

- by agreement
- by the unilateral decision of either the principal or the agent
- by changed circumstances of which the agent is aware
- by operation of law
  —death or incapacity of the principal or agent
  —except for durable power of attorney when authorized under state law

---

Inherent Authority

Related to actual authority is the concept of **inherent authority**. This type of authority arises from the designation by the principal of a specific kind of agent who typically has certain powers. If the truck company hires a lawyer to negotiate a contract on its behalf, the lawyer has inherent authority to make legal statements and prepare legal documents on behalf of the company, even if the company has not given the lawyer specific directions or instructions concerning these tasks.

Apparent Authority

Even if the agent does not have actual authority, he or she may nevertheless obligate the principal in a transaction with a third party under the doctrine of **apparent authority**. Whenever conduct of the principal has caused a third party to believe that the agent has authority, the agent will have apparent authority to obligate the principal, even when the agent knows there is no such authority. As long as the third party reasonably believes that the agent has authority, from appearances created by the principal, the principal will be obligated to the third party. For example, if the cashier at the hardware store has been told by the owner not to accept any returned merchandise, the cashier knows that there is no actual authority to accept returned merchandise from customers. Nevertheless, if the owner does not take steps to inform customers that the cashier does not have this authority, the customers may reasonably believe that the cashier could accept returned merchandise on behalf of the store. If a customer returns a defective lawn mower and the cashier refunds the purchase price, the owner of the store is obligated by that act. The appearances created by the owner are that the cashier has the authority to make those decisions, and the third person could reasonably believe that the cashier has that authority. Similarly, in many businesses certain employees are responsible for purchasing raw materials and supplies. These purchasing agents may have specific instructions from their principal, the owner of the business, to purchase only certain types of materials and only on certain terms. However, the fact that the suppliers know that these persons are purchasing agents will provide apparent authority to deal with them (and to obligate the owner to pay for the goods purchased) even if the purchasing agents deviate from the specific instructions given by the owner.

Ratified Authority

If an agent did not have either actual or apparent authority, the principal may nevertheless **ratify** a transaction the agent has negotiated. Through ratification, the principal will become obligated as if authority existed at the time the transaction was negotiated. Assume that an alert real estate broker knows Ned Giles is looking for a new home. Without contacting Ned, the broker negotiates with several sellers for homes in an area where Ned would like to live. The broker is acting without any authority from Ned in negotiating these contracts. However, once the broker receives terms from a seller and presents those terms to Ned for his consideration, Ned can ratify the contract negotiated by the broker and agree to be obligated by that contract. Ratification requires that the principal have full knowledge of all material facts concerning the transaction, and the principal must indicate, through words or conduct, that he or she intends to be obligated in the transaction. In this case, even though the broker had no authority to negotiate on Ned's behalf, Ned's subsequent conduct in accepting the agreement would ratify the acts of the agent and obligate Ned to the contract.

TORTS COMMITTED BY AGENTS

The creation of an agency is an extension of the principal's existence. Consequently, the acts of the agent are often attributed to the principal. It is as if the principal committed the act himself. Whenever an agent commits a tort, or misdeed, while performing duties for a principal, the law may require that the principal be liable for the injuries created through the agent's actions. This concept is called **vicarious liability**. Another term for this concept is **respondeat superior**.

Liability of the Agent

The first rule is that the agent is personally liable for any injury caused by the agent's acts. If a truck driver negligently causes an accident at a busy intersection, the truck driver will be personally liable, even though the truck driver is acting as an agent for the trucking company. Similarly, if the cashier at the hardware store steals a customer's credit card and uses it for personal purchases, the cashier is personally responsible for those actions, even though the cashier is acting as an agent of the hardware store.

Liability of the Principal

It is possible that the principal may commit a tort in the selection or supervision of an agent, whether the agent is a servant or an independent contractor. For example, if a truck company hires a driver whose driving record indicates significant prior negligent and improper driving activities (such as convictions for speeding and careless driving), the truck company could be liable for negligent hiring if the driver subsequently causes an accident because of similar reckless driving.

In determining whether the principal will be liable for the acts of its agent, one must distinguish whether the agent is a servant or an independent contractor. Generally, the law requires that principals must be responsible for all acts of a servant, but not for the injuries caused by independent contractors.

Remember that a principal has the right to control the activities of a servant. In most employment relationships, the employer has the right to control the activities of an employee. Thus, if an employee negligently performs activities on behalf of the principal, the principal should have controlled the employee to be certain those activities did not cause harm. Consequently, if the truck driver injures a passenger in an automobile at an intersection, the owner of the trucking company will be liable if the owner had the right to control the truck driver's activities. The owner is responsible for giving the truck driver specific directions concerning driving in a busy intersection and for hiring truck drivers who are capable of driving correctly and safely. However, the owner is not responsible for every act of an employee. The employee must be performing duties within the scope of employment for the owner to be held responsible.

The scope of employment is determined by three factors: (1) the nature of the job the agent was engaged to perform, (2) time and space limitations concerning the agent's whereabouts and activities, and (3) whether the agent caused harm while performing duties that were intended to benefit the principal. For example, if the truck driver parked the truck overnight to rest in a motel and then left the motel without paying the bill, it is questionable whether the motel operator could recover from the trucking company. The truck driver was hired to drive a truck, not to stay in a motel, and consequently, the motel transaction may not have been within the scope of the truck driver's employment. However, if the truck driver's duties require several days of driving to accomplish the delivery, staying in the motel *may* be part of the scope of employment. On the other hand, if the cashier at the hardware store negligently drove into the side of a vehicle while leaving the parking lot at work, the owner of the hardware store should not be liable, since the duties of the cashier have nothing to do with driving an automobile, and driving a vehicle is not within the cashier's scope of employment.

Time and space limitations are imposed upon the agent's whereabouts and activities to determine whether the agent was performing duties within the scope of employment. If the truck driver decided to deviate from an assigned route to visit an aunt in a nearby city and caused an accident while driving to the aunt's house, the owner of the truck company should not be responsible because the truck driver was not on the assigned route at the time the accident occurred. This example raises an important distinction in the law of agency. The principal will be liable if the agent has merely "detoured" from the appointed tasks. As long as the agent is doing the assigned job, such as driving a truck, the owner may be liable wherever the agent is driving under the theory that the agent has merely detoured from the appointed route. On the other hand, if an agent "frolics," the principal will not be liable. An agent is frolicking when the agent's personal objectives become superior to the objectives of the principal. It could be argued that the truck driver's deviation from an assigned route to visit an aunt for personal purposes would make the trip a frolic, so that any accident occurring under those circumstances would not result in liability of the principal. Thousands of cases hinge on whether the agent was acting within the scope of employment, because the circumstances of any particular injury always provide compelling arguments about the three factors required to be proved to hold the principal liable. The most interesting cases usually involve an agent who stops to give aid and is negligent in parking or providing aid, when the agent had no authority or direction from the principal that stopping to give aid or assistance was part of the agent's assigned job.

EXAMPLE	**Scope of Employment**

- the nature of the agent's responsibilities
- time and space issues (frolic and detour)
- whether the agent's acts were intended to benefit the principal

AGENTS FOR A BUSINESS ENTERPRISE

The rules presented in this chapter apply to any situation in a business in which a person or entity authorizes another to perform a job or service. The employees of a sole proprietorship are governed by the agency rules. The directors, officers, and employees of a corporation are agents of the corporation. In a partnership, the partners are agents of each other and of the partnership. Limited liability companies also engage employees and hire managers who act under the agency principles.

Throughout the law of business organizations, the agency relationship of the parties is the underpinning of the business operations. A later chapter explores the employment agreements and other documents used to create formal agency relationships, but even without written instruments, the actions of agents define the legal relationships of the business enterprise.

KEY TERMS

agency	special agent	indemnify
principal	servant	actual authority
agent	master	inherent authority
disclosed principal	independent contractor	apparent authority
partially disclosed principal	subagent	ratification
undisclosed principal	fiduciary relationship	vicarious liability or respondeat
general agent	compensate	superior

CASES

RIVIELLO v. WALDRON
47 N.Y.2d 297, 418 N.Y.S.2d 300, 391 N.E.2d 1278 (1979).
FUCHSBERG, JUDGE

Plaintiff Donald Riviello, a patron of the Pot Belly Pub, a Bronx bar and grill operated by the defendant Raybele Tavern, Inc., lost the use of an eye because of what was found to be negligence on the part of Joseph Waldron, a Raybele employee. The jury having decided for the plaintiff, in due course the trial court entered a judgment in his favor for $200,000 plus costs and interest from the date of the verdict. . . .

As was customary, on the Friday evening on which Riviello sustained his injuries, only two employees manned the Pot Belly. One was the bartender. The other was Waldron, who, in this modest-sized tavern, wore several hats, primarily that of short-order cook but also the ones that went with waiting on tables and spelling the bartender. Though his services had been engaged by Raybele's corporate president in the main to improve business by introducing the sale of food, his testimony showed that the fact that,

as a local resident, he was known to most of the customers in this neighborhood bar figured in his hiring as well. There was also proof that, in the time he had been there, when not preparing or serving food or relieving the bartender, he would follow the practice of mingling with the patrons.

Nor was Riviello a stranger when he entered the premises that night. Living nearby, he had frequented the establishment regularly for some years. The two men knew one another and, after a while, Riviello gravitated to the end of the bar near the kitchen, where, during an interval when he had no food orders to fill, Waldron and another patron and mutual friend, one Bannon, were chatting. Riviello joined in the discussion, which turned to street crime in the neighborhood. In the course of the conversation, Waldron exhibited a knife, variously described as a pocketknife or, according to Bannon, a boy scout knife, containing a small blade and screwdriver attachment, which he said he carried for protection. At this point Waldron broke away to go to the kitchen to fill a food order for another patron. Several minutes later, while Waldron was returning from his chore to rejoin Bannon and Riviello, the latter suddenly turned and, as he did so, his eye unexpectedly came in contact with the blade of the knife which Waldron still had in his hand. On defendant's case, Waldron largely confirmed these facts, but added that he was "flipping" the knife, presumably as one might flip a coin, as he was coming from the direction of the kitchen and inadvertently struck the plaintiff. No one else so testified.

Applying the pertinent legal precepts to this factual framework, we first note what is hornbook law: the doctrine of *respondeat superior* renders a master vicariously liable for a tort committed by his servant while acting within the scope of his employment. . . . The definition of "scope of employment," however, has not been an unchanging one.

Originally defined narrowly on the theory that the employer could exercise close control over his employees during the period of their service, as in other tort law contexts . . . social policy has wrought a measure of relaxation of the traditional confines of the doctrine (see Restatement, Agency 2d, §219, Comment *[a]*). Among motivating considerations are the escalation of employee-produced injury, concern that the average innocent victim, when relegated to the pursuit of his claim against the employee, most often will face a defendant too impecunious to meet the claim, and that modern economic devices, such as cost accounting and insurance coverage, permit most employers to spread the impact of such costs (see Prosser, Torts [4th ed], §69; Seavey, Agency, §83).

So no longer is an employer necessarily excused merely because his employees, acting in furtherance of his interests, exhibit human failings and perform negligently or otherwise than in an authorized manner. Instead, the test has come to be " 'whether the act was done while the servant was doing his master's work, no matter how irregularly, or with what disregard of instructions' " . . .

Surely, the fact that Waldron, at the precise instant of the occurrence, was not plying his skills as a cook, waiter or bartender did not take him beyond the range of things commonly done by such an employee. The intermittent demands of his work meant that there would be intervals in which his function was only to stand by awaiting a customer's order. Indeed, except perhaps in a world of complete automation, as portrayed for instance in Charlie Chaplin's classic film "Modern Times," the busiest of employees may be expected to take pauses and, when they do, engage in casual conversation, even punctuated, as here, by the exhibition to others of objects they wear or carry on their persons.

* * *

Given all this, it was permissible to find as a fact that Raybele could have anticipated that in the course of Waldron's varied activities in the pursuit of his job, he might, through carelessness, do some injury. The specifics of the act, though it was not essential that they be envisaged, could be, as here, the product of an inattentive handling of the pocketknife he had described to Riviello and Bannon, or a similar mishandling of a paring knife he could have had in his hand as he left the kitchen, or perhaps a steak knife with which he was on his way to set a table. Or, perchance, instead of a knife, with equal non-malevolence it could in similar fashion have been a pen, a comb, a nail file, a pencil, a scissors, a letter opener, a screwdriver or some other everyday object that he was displaying. In any of these cases, an instant of inattention could render each an instrument of injury.

Further, since, as a result of our decision, this case will return to the Appellate Division for consideration of the facts, it is not amiss to add the following observations: Waldron's own testimony that he had "flipped" the knife (though not intending any injury) was no part of plaintiff's case. If it had been, it is not to be assumed that this kind of motion, any more than would the twirling of a chain containing sharp pointed keys or the tossing of a coin, or some other gesture, whether used as an aid to communication or an outlet for nervous energy, would be beyond the broad ambit of the employer's general expectation. For one employing men and women takes them subject to the kind of conduct normal to such beings.

* * *

LuPiano, J., dissenting.

As the record fails to provide a reasonable predicate for the conclusion that the negligent act was within the scope of Waldron's employment, it must be viewed as having occurred outside that employment as a matter of law. Waldron's unexpected knife flipping was not actuated by a purpose to serve Raybele. Assuming Waldron was available to prepare food for bar patrons at the time the accident occurred, he was not engaged in preparing or serving food when he flipped his own knife accidentally in plaintiff's eye. Indeed, Waldron was satisfying a personal desire to converse with friends. There is no explanation of his knife play which in any manner connects it with furthering the duties entrusted to him by his employer. Not only was this act dissimilar to any act he was authorized to perform, it was an act not commonly done by food preparers or foreseeable by his employer. . . .

LIND v. SCHENLEY INDUSTRIES, INC.

United States Court of Appeals, Third Circuit, 1960. 278 F.2d 79.
Biggs, Chief Judge

This is a diversity case. Lind, the plaintiff-appellant, sued Park & Tilford Distiller's Corp., the defendant-appellee, for compensation that he asserts is due him by virtue of a con-

tract expressed by a written memorandum supplemented by oral conversations as set out hereinafter. . . . The evidence, including Lind's own testimony, taking the inferences most favorable to Lind, shows the following. Lind had been employed for some years by Park & Tilford. In July 1950, Lind was informed by Herrfeldt, then Park & Tilford's vice-president and general sales-manager, that he would be appointed assistant to Kaufman, Park & Tilford's sales-manager for metropolitan New York. Herrfeldt told Lind to see Kaufman to ascertain what his new duties and his salary would be. Lind embarked on his new duties with Kaufman and was informed in October 1950, that some "raises" had come through and that Lind should get official word from his "boss," Kaufman. Subsequently, Lind received a communication, dated April 19, 1951, signed by Kaufman, informing Lind that he would assume the title of "District Manager." The letter went on to state: "I wish to inform you of the fact that you have as much responsibility as a State Manager and that you should consider yourself to be of the same status." The letter concluded with the statement: "An incentive plan is being worked out so that you will not only be responsible for increased sales in your district, but will benefit substantially in a monetary way." . . . In July 1951, Kaufman informed Lind that he was to receive 1% commission on the gross sales of the men under him. This was an oral communication and was completely corroborated by Mrs. Kennan, Kaufman's former secretary, who was present. On subsequent occasions Lind was assured by Kaufman that he would get his money. Lind was also informed by Herrfeldt in the autumn of 1952 that he would get a 1% commission on the sales of the men under him. Early in 1955, Lind negotiated with Brown, then president of Park & Tilford, for the sale of Park & Tilford's New Jersey Wholesale House, and Brown agreed to apply the money owed to Lind by reason of the 1% commission against the value of the goodwill of the Wholesale House. The proposed sale of the New Jersey Wholesale House was not consummated.

Notice to produce various records of Lind's employment was served on Park & Tilford but one slip dealing with Lind's appointment as district manager was not produced and is presumed to have been lost. The evidence was conflicting as to the character of the "incentive compensation" to be offered Lind in connection with his services as a district manager. Herrfeldt designated the incentive an "added incentive plan with a percentage arrangement." Kaufman characterized the plan as "bonuses and contests." Weiner, Park & Tilford's Secretary, said that the incentive was a "pension plan." Kaufman testified, however, that the pension plan had nothing to do with the bonus incentive he referred to.

The record also shows that Lind commenced his employment with Park & Tilford in 1941, that from 1942 to 1950 he worked on a commission basis, that on August 31, 1950, he became an assistant sales manager for the New York metropolitan area at $125 a week, which was raised to $150 a week on October 1, 1950, plus certain allowances. After Lind became district manager on April 19, 1951, he continued to receive the same salary of $150 a week but this was increased to $175 in January 1952. On February 1, 1952, Lind was transferred from New York to New Jersey to become state manager of Park & Tilford's business in New Jersey. He retained that position until January 31, 1957, when he was transferred back to New York.

* * *

The jury clearly found that Kaufman had apparent agency power to offer Lind the 1% commission and this verdict may be reversed only if there is no substantial evidence which could support the verdict.

* * *

The problems of "authority" are probably the most difficult in that segment of law loosely termed, "Agency." Two main classifications of authority are generally recognized, "actual authority," and "apparent authority." The term "implied authority" is often seen but most authorities consider "implied authority" to be merely a subgroup of "actual" authority. Mechem, Agency, §§ 51-60 (4th ed. 1952). An additional kind of authority has been designated by the Restatement, Agency 2d, § § 8A and 161(b) as "inherent agency." Actually this new term is employed to designate a meaning frequently ascribed to "implied authority."

"Actual authority" means, as the words connote, authority that the principal, expressly or implicitly, gave the agent. "Apparent authority" arises when a principal acts in such a manner as to convey the impression to a third party that an agent has certain powers which he may or may not actually possess. "Implied authority" has been variously defined. It has been held to be actual authority given implicitly by a principal to his agent. Another definition of "implied authority" is that it is a kind of authority arising solely from the designation by the principal of a kind of agent who ordinarily possesses certain powers. It is this concept that is called "inherent authority" by the Restatement. In many cases the same facts will support a finding of "inherent" or "apparent agency." Usually it is not necessary for a third party attempting to hold a principal to specify which type of authority he relies upon, general proof of agency being sufficient. Pacific Mut. Life Ins. Co. of California v. Barton, 5 Cir., 1931, 50 F.2d 362, certiorari denied 1931, 284 U.S. 647, 52 S.Ct. 29, 76 L.Ed. 550.

In the case at bar Lind attempted to prove all three kinds of agency; actual, apparent, and inherent, although most of his evidence was directed to proof of "inherent" or "apparent" authority. From the evidence it is clear that Park & Tilford can be held accountable for Kaufman's action on the principle of "inherent authority." Kaufman was Lind's direct superior, and was the man to transfer communications from the upper executives to the lower. Moreover, there was testimony tending to prove that Herrfeldt, the vice-president in charge of sales, had told Lind to see Kaufman for information about his salary and that Herrfeldt himself had confirmed the 1% commission arrangement. Thus Kaufman, so far as Lind was concerned, was the spokesman for the company.

It is not necessary to determine the status of the New York law in respect to "inherent agency," for substantially the same testimony that would establish "inherent" agency under the circumstances at bar proves conventional "apparent" agency. . . . There is some uncertainty as to whether or not the third person must change his position in reliance upon these manifestations of authority, but this is of no consequence in the case at bar since Lind clearly changed his position when he accepted the job of district manager with its admittedly increased responsibilities.

* * *

Testimony was adduced by Schenley tending to prove that Kaufman had no authority to set salaries, that power being exercisable solely by the president of the corpora-

tion, and that the president had not authorized Kaufman to offer Lind a commission of the kind under consideration here. However, this testimony, even if fully accepted, would only prove lack of actual or implied authority in Kaufman but is irrelevant to the issue of apparent authority.

* * *

The judgment of the court below will be reversed and the case will be remanded with the direction to the court below to reinstate the verdict and judgment in favor of Lind.

PROBLEMS

1. What is the difference between a servant and an independent contractor? Describe the facts you would consider important in making this distinction.

2. Describe a situation in which you acted as an agent of another. Indicate the type of authority you had, and describe the events that resulted from your use of that authority.

3. State the differences among the following agency relationships (for example, type of agent, type of authority, scope of employment issues, and so on):

a. an accountant to a client,
b. a secretary to an executive,
c. a nurse to a doctor,
d. a clerk to the owner of a retail store,
e. a real estate broker to a seller of property,
f. a real estate broker to a purchaser of property,
g. a director of a corporation to the shareholders,
h. an officer of a corporation to the directors,
i. a gardener to a homeowner, and
j. a paralegal to an attorney.

PRACTICE ASSIGNMENTS

1. Find a newspaper article about an agent acting on behalf of a principal. Describe the authority of the agent, and explain the duties the agent has to the principal based upon the story in the article.

2. Make a list of specific acts you would allow and limitations on authority you would give to your agent if you were using an agent to buy a car.

3. As you come and go from your class, identify the members of the faculty and staff that you see, and decide whether they are employee-servants or independent contractors. Think of a circumstance in which one of them could commit a tort, and imagine a circumstance in which one of them could obligate your

college/university in a contract. Describe the legal principles (and additional facts you might need to establish) that would be used to hold your college/university liable for their acts.

4. Go to a current movie and make a list of the principals and agents you see in the film. Describe whether the parties are entering into contractual relationships or committing torts, and indicate whether the principals will be liable for the acts of the agents and why. Also describe any disputes between principals and agents and indicate the fiduciary duties that may have been breached between them.

2

SOLE PROPRIETORSHIP

CHARACTERISTICS OF A SOLE PROPRIETORSHIP

The **sole proprietorship** (also called an "individual proprietorship") is the simplest and most common form of business enterprise. In the sole proprietorship organization, the individual proprietor owns all business properties and carries on business as sole owner. The typical individual proprietor is a merchant in a small retail store or corner grocery, but even a youngster who mows lawns during summer vacation is an individual proprietor. Some sole proprietorships may also become very large, successful businesses. The distinguishing characteristic of the sole proprietorship is that it is owned and managed by one person and thereby exists as an extension of that person. The single owner operating the business as an individual activity is a key element. If the business is conducted by co-owners, it is most likely a partnership. Unlike the corporation, a sole proprietorship requires no grant or charter from the state to exist as a going concern.

The greatest advantages to a sole proprietorship are the ease by which it may be formed and the degree of flexibility in managing the business. As sole owner, the individual proprietor may operate the business as he or she chooses. While the owner may hire employees and agents to assist in the operation of the business, he or she is vested with ultimate responsibility for all decisions affecting the business. Consequently, management is usually flexible and informal.

The disadvantages of the sole proprietorship all flow from the fact that the business has complete identity with the proprietor. As a practical matter, this individual's personal strengths and weaknesses are, necessarily, superimposed upon the business operations. Since management functions are vested in the proprietor, the proprietor's management ability has a direct effect on the success or failure of the business, which alone may explain why sole proprietorships are most frequently used for small limited businesses. The larger the scope of a business, the more that organization requires specialized business talent that few individuals could supply alone. Similarly, the identity of the individual with the business limits available business capital and thereby may limit the size of the business. Unlike a corporation, the sole proprietorship has no shares that can be sold to outside investors. The only available methods of obtaining funds for this form of business are personal contributions of the individual proprietor and loans from financial institutions or other private sources. Further, the proprietor's ability to borrow money is limited by the potential of the business and the extent of the proprietor's personal assets, which may have to be pledged as collateral to secure a loan.

LIABILITY OF THE SOLE PROPRIETOR

The law imposes certain disadvantages on the sole proprietorship, again equating the identity of the proprietor with the business. The proprietor is personally responsible for all business losses and must bear them to the full extent of available personal resources. The proprietor is personally liable for all business liabilities. In contrast with a corporate shareholder or a limited partner, a proprietor carries a financial risk that is not limited to his or her investment in the enterprise but may extend to all personal assets, including the proprietor's home, car, furniture, and similar property. This risk of **unlimited liability** may be diminished to some extent by insurance, but it may be impossible, and is at least costly and impracticable, to insure against every conceivable business hazard. In matters involving contracts with the sole proprietorship, it is possible to provide by agreement that any liability on the contract shall be limited to the business assets and shall not extend to the personal assets of the proprietor. Such an agreement provides little advantage, however, if the proprietor has contributed personal assets for use in the business or as collateral to secure business loans.

The unlimited liability of a sole proprietorship may be a severe disadvantage to an entrepreneur with extensive personal wealth who would prefer that he or she not be subjected to the risks of the business, since absent insurance or agreement to the contrary, all personal assets must be made available to satisfy business liabilities. The problem is further compounded if the business is unusually speculative or hazardous.

On the other hand, the individual proprietor has full control over the extent of the business liability by virtue of his or her individual right to manage the business. While the law permits all partners to obligate a partnership and the officers to obligate a corporation, only the proprietor, or individuals personally selected by the proprietor, may obligate the sole proprietorship.

TAXATION OF A SOLE PROPRIETORSHIP

The federal and state laws regarding taxation of a sole proprietorship may constitute an advantage in some cases. The law provides that all business income or loss will be treated as individual income or loss and taxed accordingly. The sole proprietor declares the business income on a separate schedule of an individual tax return. Once total income, including business income or loss, is computed, the individual income tax rates are applied. If the business is small and the owner has little income from other sources, the individual tax rates as applied to income from a sole proprietorship may be significantly lower than corporate tax rates. Similarly, if the business operates at a loss, the loss will be applied directly to offset other active personal income of the sole proprietor and will thereby result in direct tax savings.

Federal and state taxing authorities frequently change their tax rates for individuals and corporations to place greater burdens on or produce more desirable tax advantages for various business enterprises. For many years, certain individual tax rates were higher than corporate rates for larger amounts of income. The federal government has since increased the corporate rates so an individual's taxable income is almost always taxed at a lower rate than is a corporation's taxable income. Selections of a particular business entity requires careful tax planning to ensure that the income earned by the business will be taxed at rates that are not surprising to the owners. Effective business managers use the tax on income as a planning tool for determining both the sources of cash and the availability of deductions for predictable business expenses.

As a matter of tax planning, when individual rates are on a graduated basis so that they eventually reach or exceed corporate tax rates, it is possible to commence a business as a sole proprietorship to enjoy the lower tax rates or other tax benefits in the early stages of development, and to subsequently incorporate the business for more favorable tax rates as profits increase and as the graduated individual tax rates surpass the corporate rate. As long as the individual tax rates are less than the corporate rate, the tax incurred in a sole proprietorship will be less than the tax incurred in a corporation. Furthermore, corporate income may be subjected to *double taxation:* once as corporate income, and, if distributed as dividends to the shareholders, a second time as income to the shareholder.[1] Sole proprietors report the profits of their businesses on Schedule C to their personal federal income tax returns. (See Exhibit 2–1, Schedule C to Form 1040.)

In addition to tax benefits, which are a major consideration, many other factors should be considered in selecting a form of business enterprise.

FORMATION AND OPERATION OF A SOLE PROPRIETORSHIP

Virtually no formalities are required in the formation and operation of a sole proprietorship, which gives this form of business a distinct advantage over other forms. The sole proprietor

Exhibit 2–1.

Schedule C to Form 1040

SCHEDULE C (Form 1040)
Department of the Treasury
Internal Revenue Service (99)

Profit or Loss From Business
(Sole Proprietorship)
▶ Partnerships, joint ventures, etc., must file Form 1065 or 1065-B.
▶ Attach to Form 1040 or 1041. ▶ See Instructions for Schedule C (Form 1040).

OMB No. 1545-0074
2003
Attachment Sequence No. **09**

Name of proprietor .... Social security number (SSN)

A Principal business or profession, including product or service (see page C-2 of the instructions)
B Enter code from pages C-7, 8, & 9

C Business name. If no separate business name, leave blank.
D Employer ID number (EIN), if any

E Business address (including suite or room no.) ....
City, town or post office, state, and ZIP code

F Accounting method: (1) ☐ Cash (2) ☐ Accrual (3) ☐ Other (specify) ....
G Did you "materially participate" in the operation of this business during 2003? If "No," see page C-3 for limit on losses . ☐ Yes ☐ No
H If you started or acquired this business during 2003, check here . . . . ☐

Part I | Income

1	Gross receipts or sales. **Caution.** If this income was reported to you on Form W-2 and the "Statutory employee" box on that form was checked, see page C-3 and check here . . . . . . ☐	1	
2	Returns and allowances	2	
3	Subtract line 2 from line 1	3	
4	Cost of goods sold (from line 42 on page 2)	4	
5	**Gross profit.** Subtract line 4 from line 3	5	
6	Other income, including Federal and state gasoline or fuel tax credit or refund (see page C-3) . . .	6	
7	**Gross income.** Add lines 5 and 6 . . . . ▶	7	

Part II | Expenses. Enter expenses for business use of your home **only** on line 30.

8	Advertising	8		19	Pension and profit-sharing plans	19
9	Car and truck expenses (see page C-3)	9		20	Rent or lease (see page C-5):	
10	Commissions and fees . .	10			a Vehicles, machinery, and equipment .	20a
11	Contract labor (see page C-4)	11			b Other business property . .	20b
12	Depletion	12		21	Repairs and maintenance . .	21
13	Depreciation and section 179 expense deduction (not included in Part III) (see page C-4) . .	13		22	Supplies (not included in Part III) .	22
				23	Taxes and licenses	23
14	Employee benefit programs (other than on line 19) . . .	14		24	Travel, meals, and entertainment:	
					a Travel	24a
15	Insurance (other than health) .	15			b Meals and entertainment	
16	Interest:				c Enter nondeductible amount included on line 24b (see page C-5) .	
	a Mortgage (paid to banks, etc.) .	16a			d Subtract line 24c from line 24b .	24d
	b Other	16b		25	Utilities	25
17	Legal and professional services	17		26	Wages (less employment credits) .	26
18	Office expense	18		27	Other expenses (from line 48 on page 2)	27

28	**Total expenses** before expenses for business use of home. Add lines 8 through 27 in columns . ▶	28	
29	Tentative profit (loss). Subtract line 28 from line 7	29	
30	Expenses for business use of your home. Attach **Form 8829**	30	
31	**Net profit or (loss).** Subtract line 30 from line 29.		
	If a profit, enter on **Form 1040, line 12,** and **also** on **Schedule SE, line 2** (statutory employees, see page C-6). Estates and trusts, enter on Form 1041, line 3.	31	
	If a loss, you **must** go to line 32.		
32	If you have a loss, check the box that describes your investment in this activity (see page C-6).		
	If you checked 32a, enter the loss on **Form 1040, line 12,** and **also** on **Schedule SE, line 2** (statutory employees, see page C-6). Estates and trusts, enter on Form 1041, line 3.	32a ☐ All investment is at risk.	
	If you checked 32b, you **must** attach **Form 6198.**	32b ☐ Some investment is not at risk.	

For Paperwork Reduction Act Notice, see Form 1040 instructions.   Cat. No. 11334P   Schedule C (Form 1040) 2003 may simply commence business by the exercise of initiative. However, if the sole proprietor operates a regulated business that might require a license, hires employees, uses a **trade name**, or expands into other states, certain formalities are imposed.

If the proprietor intends to sell goods, a sales tax license is required in most jurisdictions. Any other license peculiar to the particular business also must be obtained. For example, doctors must be licensed to practice medicine, and a liquor license is required to sell alcoholic beverages.

If employees are contemplated, the sole proprietor must apply for a tax identification number from the Internal Revenue Service office and make arrangements to contribute to social security and unemployment compensation on behalf of the employees. The tax and employee benefit authorities require the business of a proprietor to be treated separately from the owner's personal tax affairs for payments to and withholding from employees. (See Exhibit 2–2, Application for Employer Identification Number.)

Exhibit 2–2.

Application for Employer Identification Number

Form SS-4
(Rev. December 2001)
Department of the Treasury
Internal Revenue Service

Application for Employer Identification Number

(For use by employers, corporations, partnerships, trusts, estates, churches, government agencies, Indian tribal entities, certain individuals, and others.)

See separate instructions for each line.   Keep a copy for your records.

EIN

OMB No. 1545-0003

Type or print clearly.

1 Legal name of entity (or individual) for whom the EIN is being requested

2 Trade name of business (if different from name on line 1)

3 Executor, trustee, "care of" name

4a Mailing address (room, apt., suite no. and street, or P.O. box)

5a Street address (if different) (Do not enter a P.O. box.)

4b City, state, and ZIP code

5b City, state, and ZIP code

6 County and state where principal business is located

7a Name of principal officer, general partner, grantor, owner, or trustor

7b SSN, ITIN, or EIN

8a **Type of entity** (check only one box)
☐ Sole proprietor (SSN)
☐ Partnership
☐ Corporation (enter form number to be filed)
☐ Personal service corp.
☐ Church or church-controlled organization
☐ Other nonprofit organization (specify)
☐ Other (specify)

☐ Estate (SSN of decedent)
☐ Plan administrator (SSN)
☐ Trust (SSN of grantor)
☐ National Guard   ☐ State/local government
☐ Farmers' cooperative ☐ Federal government/military
☐ REMIC   ☐ Indian tribal governments/enterprises
Group Exemption Number (GEN)

8b If a corporation, name the state or foreign country (if applicable) where incorporated

State

Foreign country

9 **Reason for applying** (check only one box)
☐ Started new business (specify type)
☐ Hired employees (Check the box and see line 12.)
☐ Compliance with IRS withholding regulations
☐ Other (specify)

☐ Banking purpose (specify purpose)
☐ Changed type of organization (specify new type)
☐ Purchased going business
☐ Created a trust (specify type)
☐ Created a pension plan (specify type)

10 Date business started or acquired (month, day, year)

11 Closing month of accounting year

12 First date wages or annuities were paid or will be paid (month, day, year). **Note:** If applicant is a withholding agent, enter date income will first be paid to nonresident alien. (month, day, year)

13 Highest number of employees expected in the next 12 months. **Note:** If the applicant does not expect to have any employees during the period, enter i-0-.i | Agricultural | Household | Other |

14 Check **one** box that best describes the principal activity of your business.
☐ Construction ☐ Rental & leasing ☐ Transportation & warehousing
☐ Real estate ☐ Manufacturing ☐ Finance & insurance
☐ Health care & social assistance ☐ Wholesale–agent/broker
☐ Accommodation & food service ☐ Wholesale–other ☐ Retail
☐ Other (specify)

15 Indicate principal line of merchandise sold; specific construction work done; products produced; or services provided.

16a Has the applicant ever applied for an employer identification number for this or any other business?   ☐ Yes   ☐ No
Note: If iYes,i please complete lines 16b and 16c.

16b If you checked "Yes" on line 16a, give applicant's legal name and trade name shown on prior application if different from line 1 or 2 above.
Legal name   Trade name

16c Approximate date when, and city and state where, the application was filed. Enter previous employer identification number if known.
Approximate date when filed (mo., day, year)   City and state where filed   Previous EIN

Third Party Designee

Complete this section **only** if you want to authorize the named individual to receive the entityis EIN and answer questions about the completion of this form.

Designee's name

Designee's telephone number (include area code)
(   )

Address and ZIP code

Designee's fax number (include area code)
(   )

Under penalties of perjury, I declare that I have examined this application, and to the best of my knowledge and belief, it is true, correct, and complete.

Applicant's telephone number (include area code)
(   )

Name and title (type or print clearly)

Applicant's fax number (include area code)
(   )

Signature   Date

For Privacy Act and Paperwork Reduction Act Notice, see separate instructions.   Cat. No. 16055N   Form **SS-4** (Rev. 12-2001)

A sole proprietor may conduct business under a name other than his or her own, and state statutes usually require registration of a trade (or assumed) name by the filing of an affidavit or certificate for that purpose with a court or public official. (See Exhibits 2–3, Assumed Business Name Registration, and 2–4, Certificate of Assumed Name.) These statutes usually also provide that the name used cannot be the same as, or deceptively similar to, another registered or well-known name, such as a trademark used by another. The circumstances under which a particular name must be filed are subject to some fine distinctions. Generally, a firm name that contains the proprietor's surname and does not imply that other owners are associated with the business need not be registered. For example, Smith Auto Parts or Lyons Retail Goods usually would not require filing. On the other hand, the use of the word *Company* or *Associates* implies other owners, and the name should be registered. State and local governments apply different rules and restrictions on trade names, and the local requirements must always be reviewed. In any questionable case, it is a good practice to register the name and avoid the problems associated with failure to file. Various penalties are prescribed for failure to register a trade name, but the usual sanction is refusal to allow the proprietor to pursue any litigation in state courts until filing has been accomplished. The filing procedure may vary by jurisdiction. Some states require a single

Exhibit 2–3.

Assumed Business Name Registration

SECRETARY OF STATE
Corporation Division
Business Registry
158 12th Street NE
Salem, OR 97310-0210
(503) 378-4166

ASSUMED BUSINESS NAME REGISTRATION
GENERAL INFORMATION

WHAT IS AN ASSUMED BUSINESS NAME?

An assumed business name is a name other than the real and true name of each person operating a business. A real and true name becomes an assumed business name with the addition of any words which **imply** the existence of additional owners. Examples include "Company," "Associates," and "Daughters."

A real and true name is the surname of an individual with the individual's given name(s) or initial(s), or a corporate name or limited partnership name already filed with Business Registry.

The Division **does not** register real and true names because they are not **assumed** business names.

WHY REGISTER AN ASSUMED BUSINESS NAME?

The purpose of registering an assumed business name is to let the public know who is transacting business under that business name.

Failure to register an assumed business name may preclude you from maintaining a lawsuit for the benefit of your business. Also, conviction for failure to register is punishable by a fine up to $100.

Registration of an assumed business name does not grant you the right to use or to exclude others from using any trademark, service mark, or tradename.

WHO MUST REGISTER AN ASSUMED BUSINESS NAME?

Any person who uses an assumed name to identify a business that the person transacts must register that name unless the real and true name of each person transacting the business is conspicuously disclosed.

WHAT IS TRANSACTING BUSINESS?

The term "transacting business" means to sell, lease, or purchase real estate, goods, intangible property, or services; to solicit an investment in or a donation to a business; or to apply for an extension of credit.

WHAT COUNTIES MUST BE REGISTERED?

An assumed business name must be registered in every county in which the business or a facility of the business is located or an employee is stationed.

RENEWAL OF YOUR REGISTRATION

Renewal applications are sent to the authorized representative. Therefore, you must amend your registration if there is a change in the address of the authorized representative. Your registration must be renewed two years from the date of registration and every two years thereafter.

ABN-1 (5/91)

Exhibit 2–3.

(continued)

Phone: (503) 986-2200
Fax: (503) 378-4381

Assumed Business Name—New Registration

Secretary of State
Corporation Division
255 Capitol St. NE, Suite 151
Salem, OR 97310-1327
FilingInOregon.com

REGISTRY NUMBER: _____

In keeping with Oregon Statute 192.410-192.595, the information on the application is public record.
We must release this information to all parties upon request and it may be posted on our website.

For office use only

Please Type or Print Legibly in **Black** Ink. Attach Additional Sheet if Necessary.

1) **ASSUMED BUSINESS NAME** (To be registered)

2) **DESCRIPTION OF BUSINESS** (Primary business activity)

4) **AUTHORIZED REPRESENTATIVE** (One name only)

3) **PRINCIPAL PLACE OF BUSINESS** (Address, city, state, zip)

5) **MAILING ADDRESS FOR BUSINESS**

6) **REGISTRANTS/OWNERS** (List name and **street** address of each person who will conduct or transact business under the assumed business name.)
(Attach a separate sheet if necessary.)

NAME	STREET ADDRESS	CITY/STATE/ZIP

7) **COUNTIES**

☐ ALL COUNTIES (Statewide)

☐ Baker	☐ Crook	☐ Harney	☐ Lake	☐ Morrow	☐ Union
☐ Benton	☐ Curry	☐ Hood River	☐ Lane	☐ Multnomah	☐ Wallowa
☐ Clackamas	☐ Deschutes	☐ Jackson	☐ Lincoln	☐ Polk	☐ Wasco
☐ Clatsop	☐ Douglas	☐ Jefferson	☐ Linn	☐ Sherman	☐ Washington
☐ Columbia	☐ Gilliam	☐ Josephine	☐ Malheur	☐ Tillamook	☐ Wheeler
☐ Coos	☐ Grant	☐ Klamath	☐ Marion	☐ Umatilla	☐ Yamhill

8) **EXECUTED/SIGNED BY:** (All registrants/owners must sign.)

FEES

Required Processing Fee $20
Confirmation Copy (Optional) $5

Processing Fees are nonrefundable.

Please make check payable to
"Corporaton Division."

NOTE:
Fees may be paid with VISA or MasterCard. The card number and expiration date should be submitted on a separate sheet for your protection.

9) **CONTACT NAME** (To resolve questions with this filing.)   **DAYTIME PHONE NUMBER** (Include area code.)

101 (Rev.10/03)

filing with a county or state official. Others, such as California, require filing plus publication once a week for four weeks in a local newspaper. The appropriate statute should be consulted for guidance on local procedure.

While more complex businesses, such as corporations, limited partnerships and limited liability companies, must register or "qualify" to do business in other states,[2] sole proprietorships are permitted to do business in more than one state without additional formalities for **qualification** to do business. Of course, local licensing and assumed name statutes must be observed.

The operation of a sole proprietorship is extremely flexible and personal to the individual. Governmental regulation of such a business is found only in licensing requirements and periodic reports that may be required for certain types of business. The individual proprietor personally determines the complexity or simplicity of the business records, the need for expansion and capital improvements, salaries, and other matters affecting the policy and daily operations of the business. Compared with owners in other forms of business, the sole proprietor has considerable freedom in these matters.

Exhibit 2–4.

Certificate of Assumed
Name (New York)

Certificate of Assumed Name
Pursuant to General Business Law, §130

NYS Department of State
Division of Corporations, State Records and UCC
41 State Street, Albany, NY 12231-0001
www.dos.state.ny.us

1. NAME OF ENTITY

1a. *FOREIGN ENTITIES ONLY.* If applicable, the fictitious name the entity agreed to use in New York State is:

2. NEW YORK LAW FORMED OR AUTHORIZED UNDER (CHECK ONE):

☐ Business Corporation Law   ☐ Limited Liability Company Law

☐ Education Law   ☐ Not-for-Profit Corporation Law

☐ Insurance Law   ☐ Revised Limited Partnership Act

☐ Other (specify law):

3. ASSUMED NAME

4. PRINCIPAL PLACE OF BUSINESS IN NEW YORK STATE (MUST BE NUMBER AND STREET. IF NONE, INSERT OUT-OF-STATE ADDRESS)

5. COUNTIES IN WHICH BUSINESS WILL BE CONDUCTED UNDER ASSUMED NAME

☐ ALL COUNTIES (if not, circle county[ies] below)

Albany	Clinton	Genesee	Monroe	Orleans	Saratoga	Tompkins
Allegany	Columbia	Greene	Montgomery	Oswego	Schenectady	Ulster
Bronx	Cortland	Hamilton	Nassau	Otsego	Schoharie	Warren
Broome	Delaware	Herkimer	New York	Putnam	Schuyler	Washington
Cattaraugus	Dutchess	Jefferson	Niagara	Queens	Seneca	Wayne
Cayuga	Erie	Kings	Oneida	Rensselaer	Steuben	Westchester
Chautauqua	Essex	Lewis	Onondaga	Richmond	Suffolk	Wyoming
Chemung	Franklin	Livingston	Ontario	Rockland	Sullivan	Yates
Chenango	Fulton	Madison	Orange	St. Lawrence	Tioga	

6. INSERT THE ADDRESS OF EACH LOCATION WHERE BUSINESS WILL BE CARRIED ON OR TRANSACTED UNDER THE ASSUMED NAME. Use a continuous sheet, if needed. (The address must be set forth in terms of a number and street, city, state and zip code. Please note that the address(es) reflected in paragraph 6 must be within the county(ies) circled in paragraph 5. If the entity does not have a specific location where it will conduct business under the assumed name please check the box.)

☐ No New York State Business Location

DOS-1338 (Rev. 5/03)

TERMINATION UPON DEATH OF THE PROPRIETOR

With very few exceptions specifically authorized by state statutes,[3] the sole proprietorship terminates by law upon the death of the proprietor. It is possible (but rare) to enter into an agreement with an employee or relative to buy and continue the business upon the death of the proprietor. The owner is also entitled to will the business to relatives or to an employee. But, absent such an agreement or estate planning, there is no assurance of continuity of the business after death. If the owner managed the business, and no relatives or associates are willing to continue, the business probably will be liquidated. Liquidation must be accomplished by a legal representative of the deceased owner, such as a trustee or an executor, and cannot be done by agents appointed by the owner during the owner's lifetime because, with the exception of a few administrative acts authorized by specific statutes,[4] agents are powerless to act after the death of their principal.[5] Since the business will be included in the personal estate of the deceased owner, a number of estate-planning considerations for the sole proprietor become essential. Generally, some authority must be granted to the proprietor's personal representatives to permit them to continue the business as necessary until it may be conveniently and profitably liquidated, to employ persons to assist in liquidation, and to execute all necessary documents incident to liquidation.[6] If the beneficiary of the deceased owner is willing to continue the business, a new sole proprietorship is created and will be governed by these same rules.

KEY TERMS

sole proprietorship	trade name	qualification
unlimited liability		

WEB RESOURCES

The primary issues in operating a sole proprietorship involve use of an assumed name, which probably will have to be registered in a public office, and licensing issues relating to professions and occupations upon which states have imposed licensing and regulatory requirements.

Access to state laws regarding licensing and regulatory requirements may be obtained through the Legal Information Institute maintained at the Cornell Law School:

<http://www.law.cornell.edu>

The National Association of Secretaries of State maintains links directly to the offices of the Secretaries of State in all states. Many of the state Web sites offer information concerning local treatment of sole proprietorships and issues relating to that business structure:

<http://www.nass.org>

The Small Business Administration offers on-line information and assistance in the formation, operation, and financing of the activities of a sole proprietorship:

<http://www.sba.gov>

The American Bar Association collects Internet sites that are important to lawyers. This site has links to and descriptions of the latest resources available to the legal profession:

<http://www.abanet.org>

Searching and locating trade names can be accomplished through various services offered on the Internet. Most of these services charge a fee for useful searches. They include the following:

<http://www.tmexpress.com>
<http://www.trademark-search-services.com>

CASES

SHELDON v. VERMONTY

1999 WL 1096043 (D.Kan.)
Nov. 29, 1999.
Lungstrum, District J.

Plaintiff Dave Sheldon brought this action against defendants alleging violations of the federal and state securities laws as well as various common law claims.

* * *

Presently before the court is the issue of dismissal of the plaintiff's case as set forth in the show cause order and plaintiff's amended motion for default judgment against defendants Power Phone, Inc., Noah Steinberg, Dr. Enrique R. Carrion, T.M.C. Agroworld, Inc., The Montecristi Group,

Manhattan Transfer Registrar Company, Princeton Research, Inc., and Jack Savage (doc. 85). For the reasons set forth below, plaintiff's motion is denied and the case is dismissed.

* * *

Defendant Hector Cruz opposes the entry of default judgment against Manhattan Transfer Registrar Company on the ground that, because Manhattan Transfer Registrar Company is a sole proprietorship of Hector Cruz, Mr. Cruz and Manhattan Transfer Registrar Company are not separate legal entities, but instead merely alter egos, and, therefore, an entry of default judgment against Manhattan Transfer Registrar Company would be improper and void on its face. The court agrees.

It is well-settled that "sole proprietors of unincorporated businesses . . . by definition, have no separate legal existence" from the proprietorship itself. *Vega v. National Life Ins. Servs., In* 188 F.3d 287, 294 (5th Cir.1999); *see also State v. ABC Towing,* 954 P.2d 575, 577 (Alaska Ct.App.1998) ("[A] sole proprietorship is not a legal entity. [It] has no legal significance apart from its sole proprietor. It cannot incur debts, conduct business, sue or be sued, or incur or pay taxes apart from its sole proprietor."); *Vernon v. Schuster* 688 N.E.2d 1172, 1776-77 (Ill.1997) ("It is well settled that a sole proprietorship has no legal identity separate from that of the individual who owns it"). As a result, a "default judgment entered against a sole proprietorship is void on its face." *Paul Revere Life Ins. Co. v. Rasul,* 1998 WL 259922 at *4 n. 3 (D.Md. May 18, 1998) (quoting *Dowis v. Watson,* 289 S.E.2d 558, 559 (Ga.App.Ct.1982)).

In the caption of his amended complaint, plaintiff lists the following persons and entities as defendants: Jay and Carmen Vermonty, Power Phone, Inc., Noah Steinberg, Gershon Tannenbaum, Dr. Enrique Reyes Carrion, T.M.C. Agroworld, Inc., The Montecristi Group, Manhattan Transfer Registrar Company, and Hector Cruz. Amended Compl. at 1-2. In his second and third amended complaints, plaintiff failed to list the defendants individually in the case caption, instead choosing to delineate the defendants as "Jay Vermonty et al."

In their original motion to dismiss plaintiff's amended complaint, citing Mr. Cruz's declaration dated August 12, 1998, defendants noted that "Manhattan Transfer Registrar Company, named as a defendant in the caption of this action, is a sole proprietorship of Defendant Cruz, has no separate legal existence, and is not a proper party to this action." Def. Mem. in Supp. Mtn. to Dismiss Amended Compl. at 1 n. 1. In his response to defendants' motion to dismiss the amended complaint, plaintiff did not oppose, contradict, or otherwise acknowledge this assertion. In their motion to dismiss plaintiff's third amended complaint, moving defendants Jay and Carmen Vermonty, Gershon Tannenbaum, and Hector Cruz reiterated their previous assertion that Manhattan Transfer Registrar Company is a sole proprietorship of defendant Cruz, and, as such, is not a proper party to this action. Def. Mem. in Supp. of Mtn. to Dismiss Third Amended Compl. at 2 n. 1. Nowhere in his third amended complaint does plaintiff set forth facts indicating that Manhattan Transfer Registrar Company was not a sole proprietorship, and plaintiff again failed to address this contention in his response to defendants' motion to dismiss plaintiff's third amended complaint. Thus, because plaintiff has failed to present any facts to indicate that Manhattan Transfer Registrar Company is not the sole proprietorship of defendant Hector Cruz, an entry of default judgment against Manhattan Transfer Registrar Company would be void on its face. Accordingly, plaintiff's motion for the entry of default judgment against Manhattan Transfer Registrar Company is denied.

STATE OF ALASKA v. ABC TOWING

954 P.2d 575
Feb. 20, 1998
MANNHEIMER, JUDGE

This case involves the law of "vicarious responsibility"—the law defining when one person can be held criminally responsible for the conduct of another. More specifically, this case presents the question of whether a business run by a sole proprietor is an "organization" under AS 11.16.130(a), a statute which declares that organizations are criminally responsible for certain acts of their agents. We hold that a sole proprietorship is not an "organization" for purposes of AS 11.16.130(a).

Rodney E. Lewis does business as "ABC Towing". When one of Lewis's employees discharged gasoline on the ground, the State brought criminal charges against both the employee and ABC Towing; both defendants were charged with violating an anti-pollution statute, AS 46.03.710.

Under Alaska law, organizations face broader vicarious criminal responsibility than do individuals. Generally speaking, an individual can be held criminally responsible for the conduct of another only if the individual asks or encourages the other person to commit the offense or if the individual helps to plan or commit the offense. *See* AS 11.16.110(2). The State presented no evidence that Lewis asked his employee to discharge the gasoline, or that Lewis aided or abetted the employee's act. However, an organization can be held accountable for criminal conduct that its owners, members, officers, or directors did not know about until afterwards. Under AS 11.16.130(a)(1), an organization is criminally responsible for an offense committed by one of its agents if the agent was acting in behalf of the organization and within the scope of the agent's employment, or if the organization subsequently ratified or adopted the agent's conduct. The State charged ABC Towing with the pollution violation, alleging that Lewis's employee had been acting within the scope of his employment, and in behalf of ABC Towing, when he discharged the gasoline on the ground.

The case against ABC Towing was tried to District Court Judge Natalie K. Finn on stipulated facts. The parties agreed that ABC Towing's employee had violated the antipollution statute and that the employee had been acting within the scope of his employment and in behalf of ABC Towing when he committed this violation. There was only one disputed issue, and that was an issue of law: was ABC Towing an "organization" for purposes of AS 11.16.130(a), so that it could be held liable for its employee's discharge of gasoline?

AS 11.81.900(b)(39) defines the term "organization" for purposes of Title 11. Under that definition, "organization" means:

> a legal entity, including a corporation, company, association, firm, partnership, joint stock company, foundation, institution, government, society, union, club, church, or any other group of persons organized for any purpose.

Lewis's attorney contended that ABC Towing was not an "organization" because it was a sole proprietorship—an unincorporated business owned solely by Lewis. In a well-reasoned opinion, Judge Finn concluded that this contention was correct—that sole proprietorships are not "organizations" under the statutory definition. Judge Finn wrote:

> [A] sole proprietorship is not a legal entity. [It] has no legal significance apart from its sole **proprietor.** It cannot incur debts, conduct business, sue or be sued, or incur or pay taxes apart from its sole proprietor. Legally, it makes no difference whether the business is named ABC Towing or Rodney E. Lewis. The accountability of ABC Towing is therefore no different from that of an individual. . . . This court finds that ABC Towing, a sole proprietorship, is not an organization within the meaning of AS 11.81.900(b)(39) and is therefore not legally accountable [for acts of its agents under] AS 11.16.130.

Judge Finn therefore dismissed the complaint against ABC Towing, and the State now appeals Judge Finn's decision.

Under AS 11.81.900(b)(39), "organization" (for purposes of Title 11) "means a legal entity." The statute does not define "legal entity" except by example, and the term "legal entity" is not further defined in Title 11 or, indeed, anywhere else in the Alaska statutes. However, the term "legal entity" does have a common-law meaning, and that meaning presumptively governs our interpretation of AS 11.81.900(b)(39). *See* AS 01.10.010 (the common law remains the rule of decision in this state unless it is inconsistent with the laws passed by the Alaska legislature or inconsistent with the federal or Alaska constitutions).

The concept of "legal entity" is a useful fiction employed by the law to distinguish an ongoing human endeavor from the people who presently own or control that endeavor. As Judge Finn correctly pointed out in her decision, the defining characteristic of a "legal entity" is its separate legal existence apart from its owners, officers, and directors.

At common law, sole proprietorships are not "legal entities." Neither are partnerships (for most purposes: *compare Pratt v. Kirkpatric* 718 P.2d 962, 967-68 (Alaska 1986)). Rather, sole proprietorships and partnerships are deemed to be merely the alter egos of the proprietor or the partners (as individuals). In a sole proprietorship, all of the proprietor's assets are completely at risk, and the sole proprietorship ceases to exist upon the proprietor's death.

* * *

With this background, we return to our definitional statute, AS 11.81.900(b)(39), and we find that it contains troublesome ambiguities. The statute declares that the term "organization" means a "legal entity." If the legislature had stopped there, then neither a sole proprietorship nor a partnership would be considered an "organization," because neither form of business is a legal entity. However, the statute then adds that the term "legal entity" includes "partnerships" as well as "associations," "societies," "clubs," and "any other group of persons organized for any purpose." This is a marked expansion of what the common law would recognize as a "legal entity" for other purposes (suing or being sued, holding title to property, employing workers, etc.).

The legislature undoubtedly has the authority to enlarge the definition of "legal entity" beyond its common-law boundaries *See State v. Erickson,* 574 P.2d 1, 15 (Alaska 1978) (in statutes regulating drugs, the legislature can define "narcotic" differently from its normal pharmacological meaning). It appears that AS 11.81.900(b)(39) was intended to modify the common-law definition of "legal entity" by broadening it to include partnerships, informal associations and clubs, and (in general) "any other group of persons organized for any purpose." However, the statutory roster of "legal entities" does not specifically include sole proprietorships.

The State argues that a sole proprietorship becomes a "firm" or an "association" or a "group" under AS 11.81.900(b)(39) whenever the sole proprietor hires other people to assist in the conduct of the business. We think that this is a strained interpretation of the statute.

Under the State's reading of the statute, an ice cream vendor or a house painter who employed a part-time helper during the summer would suddenly become a "firm," an "association," or a "group." In fact, under the State's wide-ranging construction of the phrase "group of persons organized for any purpose," home owners would seemingly become "organizations" whenever they hired someone to clean their house or maintain their lawn. Such a construction of the statute conflicts with the fact that employees generally do not direct the conduct of a business. Their contract of employment does not make them partners of the persons or entities who hire them, and they do not have the same legal rights and responsibilities as their employers. Based on the wording of AS 11.81.900(b)(39) and its legislative history, we doubt that the legislature intended the results advocated by the State.

Moreover, two rules of statutory construction counsel us to uphold the trial court's decision in this case. The first rule is that statutes in derogation of the common law should be construed strictly. That is, when courts are presented with a question involving the proper construction of a statute that modifies the common law, the normal rule of interpretation is that such statutes are construed so as to preserve the pre-existing common law unless the legislature has clearly indicated its purpose to change that law. *See Roeck* 885 P.2d at 1074; *University of Alaska v. Shanti,* 835 P.2d 1225, 1228 n. 5 (Alaska 1992). The second rule is that statutes imposing criminal liability should be construed narrowly. When the scope of a criminal statute is unclear, courts should normally construe the statute against the government—that is, construe it so as to limit the scope of criminal liability. *See Magnuson v. State,* 843 P.2d 1251, 1253 (Alaska App.1992).

The question in this appeal is whether sole proprietorships are to be treated as legal entities apart from their proprietors, so that the government can prosecute sole proprietorships for the acts of their agents under the theory of vicarious responsibility codified in AS 11.16.130(a). Under the common law, sole proprietorships are not legal entities. The expanded definition of legal entities in AS 11.81.900(b)(39) does not include a specific reference to sole proprietorships. The State has presented some inventive arguments as to why sole proprietorships should be viewed as "associations" or "firms" for purposes of Title 11, but in the end those arguments are only colorable, not convincing. On this point, the statute remains, at best, ambiguous.

This being so, we construe AS 11.81.900(b)(39) to preserve the pre-existing common law rule that sole proprietorships are not legal entities, and to narrowly construe the scope of vicarious criminal responsibility imposed by AS 11.16.130(a). We conclude that sole proprietorships are not "organizations" for purposes of AS 11.16.130(a). The district court therefore correctly granted the defendant's motion to dismiss.

CRANE CONSTRUCTION COMPANY v. KLAUS MASONRY, LLC

114 F.Supp.2d 1116
July 6, 2000
WESLEY E. BROWN, SENIOR DISTRICT JUDGE

This matter is before the court on the defendant's motion to dismiss the complaint. The motion raises a question of "successor liability." Specifically, the issue is whether the defendant Klaus Masonry, LLC, can be held responsible for an alleged liability of Klaus Masonry, a sole proprietorship that was owned by George Klaus until his death in 1994. The plaintiff alleges that Klaus Masonry, LLC is "a continuation of and successor to Klaus Masonry" and is liable for the alleged obligation. The defendant denies it can be held liable under this continuation theory and argues that plaintiff has failed to state a claim upon which relief can be granted. The court finds that oral argument would not assist in deciding the issues presented.

* * *

II. *Facts*
Crane is a general contractor that, in the early 1990's, was hired by Wal-Mart Stores, Inc., to build numerous stores throughout the southern United States. In 1992 Crane entered a contract with Wal-Mart to build a Sam's Club store located in Wichita, Kansas (the "Wichita Project"). Crane subcontracted the project masonry to an entity that identified itself as "Klaus Masonry." George Klaus, identified as the owner, signed the subcontract for Klaus Masonry. At that time, Klaus Masonry was a sole proprietorship owned by George Klaus.

In 1993, Crane sued Wal-Mart, alleging nonpayment on portions of the Wichita project and other projects. Wal-Mart counterclaimed, alleging defects in the construction on several jobs, including the Wichita project. The action was maintained in U.S. District Court in Memphis, Tennessee. In November of 1994, Crane notified Klaus Masonry of the suit and demanded, pursuant to an indemnity clause in the subcontract, that Klaus Masonry indemnify Crane for losses associated with Wal-Mart's claims.

* * *

George Klaus, the owner of Klaus Masonry, died on December 2, 1994. On December 19, 1994, Crane received notice of George Klaus's death in a letter sent by an insurance carrier. The letter identified Klaus Masonry as "a small family-operated concern," and identified George Klaus as "the company's president." The letter did not advise Crane that the company was a sole proprietorship or that Crane's claims needed to be pursued against the estate of George Klaus. Crane was not informed that Klaus Masonry was a sole proprietorship or that there were allegedly no assets in the estate of George Klaus until June of 1996, which was after the expiration of the non-claim statute.

In April of 1995, Michael Klaus, George Klaus's son, formed Klaus Masonry, LLC, a domestic limited liability company, headquartered in Hays, Kansas. The headquarters of the sole proprietorship had also been in Hays. Klaus Masonry, LLC, continued in the same business of masonry construction as the sole proprietorship, and assumed the trade name of the sole proprietorship. There was also a transfer of assets from the sole proprietorship to Klaus Masonry, LLC, including the goodwill of the sole proprietorship. Michael Klaus had been one of the principal employees of the sole proprietorship, and had performed some of the masonry work challenged by Wal-Mart.

In August of 1996 Crane and Wal-Mart settled their respective claims against each other. In November 1997, Crane commenced an action against "Klaus Masonry" in the

U.S. District Court for the District of Kansas, Case No. 97-1502-MLB (the "Klaus action"), based upon the indemnity clause in the subcontract. In that action, Crane alleged that Klaus Masonry was either a sole proprietorship or a partnership. Service of process was obtained on Mike Klaus at his place of business in Hays. An answer was filed on December 22, 1997, on behalf of "Klaus Masonry (actually George Klaus d/b/a Klaus Masonry)," and Klaus defended the action for nearly two years. On October 7, 1999, Judge Belot dismissed the claim, holding that Crane had sued the sole proprietorship, which was not a legal entity under Kansas law. [FN2 *See Crane Constr. Co. v. Klaus Masonry* 71 F.Supp.2d 1138, 1140 (D.Kan.1999). The court further found that Crane had not sued the estate of George Klaus, and that any such claim against the estate was now barred.

Crane filed the instant action against Klaus Masonry, LLC on November 19, 1999. The complaint alleges in part:

> 4. Klaus Masonry, LLC continued in the same business of masonry construction as Klaus Masonry and assumed the trade name and goodwill of Klaus Masonry. Upon information and belief, certain corporate assets, in addition to the corporate goodwill, passed from Klaus Masonry to Klaus Masonry, LLC.
> 5. Upon information and belief, Klaus Masonry, LLC paid no consideration for the use of Klaus Masonry trade name, corporate goodwill, or other assets.
> 6. Michael Klaus was a key employee of Klaus Masonry and supervised much of the masonry work at issue in this case.
> 7. The transfer of the trade name, goodwill, and other assets from Klaus Masonry to Klaus Masonry, LLC [affected] a dissolution of Klaus Masonry, such that claims of Klaus Masonry's creditors could not be paid. Accordingly, Klaus Masonry, LLC is the continuation of Klaus Masonry, a sole proprietorship. . . .

III. *Summary of Arguments*

The defendant contends that after George Klaus's death, Crane's exclusive remedy as an alleged creditor of the sole proprietorship was against Klaus's estate, and that any such claim is now barred. According to the defendant, Crane is attempting to circumvent the no-claim statute by asserting successor liability against the LLC. The defendant further argues that Crane's allegations fail to show there were common officers or directors between the sole proprietorship and the LLC, or that the transfer of the sole proprietorship's assets rendered it incapable of paying its creditors' claims because of dissolution, and that in the absence of such facts no claim of successor liability may be maintained.

For its part, Crane contends that successor liability may be imposed whenever the successor entity is merely a continuation of the predecessor, and that the only finding essential to such a claim is that "substantial continuity" exists between the two entities. Crane believes this presents a question of fact requiring an evaluation of numerous factors. According to Crane, liability may be imposed in the absence of common officers or directors because that is merely one factor to be weighed in the balance. Crane also asserts that it has adequately alleged that the transfer of assets to the LLC af-

fected a dissolution of the sole proprietorship such that claims by its creditors could not be paid. Crane thus contends it has stated a valid claim for relief against the defendant.

IV. *Discussion*

In *Comstock v. Great Lakes Distributing Co.,* 209 Kan. 306, 310, 496 P.2d 1308 (1972), the Kansas Supreme Court recognized the general framework governing successor liability of corporations:

> Generally, where one corporation sells or otherwise transfers all of its assets to another corporation, the latter is not liable for the debts and liabilities of the transferor, except: (1) where the purchaser expressly or impliedly agrees to assume such debts; (2) where the transaction amounts to a consolidation or merger of the corporation; (3) where the purchasing corporation is merely a continuation of the selling corporation; or (4) where the transaction is entered into fraudulently in order to escape liability for such debts.

Id. In this case, Crane contends the defendant is liable under the third exception as a "mere continuation" of the sole proprietorship operated by George Klaus under the trade name "Klaus Masonry."

* * *

The "mere continuation" rule is based upon the notion that corporate entities cannot escape valid claims merely by undergoing some insignificant change in form:

> The "mere continuation" of business exception reinforces the policy of protecting rights of a creditor by allowing a creditor to recover from the successor corporation whenever the successor is substantially the same as the predecessor. The exception is designed to prevent a situation whereby the specific purpose of acquiring assets is to place those assets out of reach of the predecessor's creditors. In other words, the purchasing corporation maintains the same or similar ownership but wears a "new hat." To allow the predecessor to escape liability merely by changing hats would amount to fraud. Thus, the underlying theory of the exception is that, if [a] corporation goes through a mere change in form without a significant change in substance, it should not be allowed to escape liability.
> Fletcher Cyc. Corp. § 7124.10 (Perm.Ed.1999).

Although these rules were designed to govern corporate liability, most courts have applied them "regardless of whether the predecessor or successor organization was a corporation or some other form of business organization."

* * *

Thus, the "mere continuation" exception has been applied where the predecessor was a sole proprietorship and the successor was a limited liability company. *LiButti,* 178 F.3d at 124.

* * *

When all of the elements are considered in view of the facts alleged by Crane, however, the court must conclude as a matter of law that Crane has failed to state a claim upon which relief can be granted. Three facts in particular combine to support this conclusion.

First, it is difficult to see how one could argue that the death of Mr. Klaus and his son's formation of an LLC to operate the masonry business was "a mere change in form without a significant change in substance" or that these two entities had "the same or similar ownership." *Cf.* Fletcher, *supra.* There is no allegation that the son had any ownership interest in the business prior to his father's death, and the transfer thus brought about a real and complete change in ownership. The *Stratton* court noted that "[t]he common identity of officers and shareholders in both predecessor and successor entities is a commonly cited criterion in determining the existence of continuity." *Id* 9 Kan.App.2d at 265, 676 P.2d 1. *See also Vernon V. Schuster* 179 Ill.2d 338, 228 Ill.Dec. 195, 688 N.E.2d 1172 (1997) (a majority of courts emphasize "a common identity of officers, directors, and stock between the selling and purchasing corporation as the key element of a 'continuation' "). Although sole proprietorships do not have officers, directors or stock as corporations do, at a minimum this element indicates that common ownership is significant in determining whether one entity is a mere continuation of another. Under the facts alleged by Crane, there was no common ownership between the two entities in this case. *Cf. Vernon,* supra (son who operated proprietorship after his father's death was not liable under a continuation theory).

A second factor weighing against Crane is that it can fairly be said it was Crane's failure to pursue a claim against the estate of George Klaus, rather than the fact of dissolution of the proprietorship and transfer of assets, that prevented Crane from recovering against the predecessor business. This is not a case of a transfer that left a creditor unprotected and without a remedy against the transferor entity. *Cf.* Fletcher, supra. Crane does not (and cannot) dispute that the law provided a claim against Klaus' estate and could have recovered against any assets found to properly belong to the estate. Given the availability of this remedy, the facts do not establish the fifth element of a "mere continuation" claim—i.e., that the transfer rendered the transferor incapable of paying its creditors' claims because it was dissolved in either law or fact. Assuming the claim was valid, Crane could have taken action to require the estate to pay the claim out of George Klaus' assets. *Cf. Gillespie v. Seymour,* 19 Kan.App.2d 754, 762, 876 P.2d 193, 200 (1994) (availability of other remedy weighed against finding of successor liability).

A third factor, related to the second, likewise weighs against Crane. Where a successor entity arises after the death of a **sole proprietor,** application of the "mere continuation" exception could conflict with the laws governing the administration of decedents' estates. As the defendant points out, a sole proprietorship has no legal significance apart from its sole proprietor. *See Sheldon v. Vermonty,* No. 98-2277-JWL, 1999 WL 1096043, *1 (D.Kan., Nov.29, 1999). When Crane contracted with "Klaus Masonry" it was in fact contracting with George Klaus, and when Mr. Klaus died Crane was a creditor with a contingent claim against Mr. Klaus' estate (including the assets of Klaus Masonry). Upon Mr. Klaus' death the probate laws governed Crane's right to assert a claim against Klaus' estate and his assets. Those laws clearly favor swift resolution of all claims against a decedent's estate. K.S.A. § 59-2239 provides in part that "No creditor shall have any claim against or lien upon the property of a decedent other than liens existing at the date of the decedent's death, unless a petition is filed for the probate of the decedent's will . . . or for the administration of the decedent's estate . . . within six months after the death of the decedent. . . ." Crane concedes that any claim against Klaus' estate is now barred because no such petition was filed. Nevertheless, Crane is attempting to follow the assets of the estate into the hands of the LLC, and to recover against the LLC because those assets were allegedly transferred from the estate without consideration. To recognize such a claim would, in the court's view, sanction an end-run on the nonclaim statute and would embroil the parties in a controversy over what assets belonged to the estate, whether Crane was a creditor with a valid claim against those assets, and whether the estate received adequate compensation upon the transfer of the assets. Such matters clearly could have—and should have—been addressed in a timely petition to probate George Klaus' estate. To litigate these issues now would circumvent the limitations of the probate code and would undermine the policy favoring swift resolution of claims against decedents' estates.

Under the circumstances, the court concludes that Crane's claim for successor liability against the defendant cannot be sustained and that the allegations fail to state a claim upon which relief can be granted.

PROBLEMS

1. Describe at least two ways to limit the personal liability of a sole proprietor.

2. Considering your local laws, which of the following names, if used by a sole proprietor named James M. Lyons, would require the filing of a trade name affidavit or registration of an assumed business name:

   James M. Lyons and Sons
   James M. Lyons and Daughters
   Lyons Company
   Lyons' Gas Station
   The Gas Station
   Lyons Limited

3. Describe at least two advantages and two disadvantages of operating a business as a sole proprietorship, and make recommendations concerning how the disadvantages can be mitigated.

PRACTICE ASSIGNMENTS

1. Prepare a list of appropriate and necessary documents for the formation and operation of a sole proprietorship in your state, county, and city. Assume this proprietorship is engaged in the hair salon and manicure business.

2. Obtain and prepare the following documents from the governmental authorities that require them:
   a. trade name affidavit or assumed business name registration;
   b. tax identification number application;
   c. sales or use tax license application; and
   d. application to operate a licensed business of your choice (such as a liquor store, beauty shop, bail bonds office, pharmacy, etc.).

3. Select a business that is operating as a sole proprietorship, interview the proprietor, and observe the business operation. List the advantages and disadvantages you observe in the following areas:
   a. management and control,
   b. personal liability exposure of the proprietor,
   c. the need for capital and the ability to raise it,
   d. continuity of the business, and
   e. taxation.

4. Prepare forms in Exhibits 2–5, Application for Registration of Fictitious Name; and 2–6, Application for Renewal of Fictitious Name. Use your best friend as your client.

Exhibit 2–5.

Application for Registration of Fictitious Name (Florida)

APPLICATION FOR REGISTRATION OF FICTITIOUS NAME
Note: Acknowledgements/certificates will be sent to the address in Section 1 only.

Section 1

1. _____
   Fictitious Name to be Registered (see instructions if name includes "Corp" or "Inc")
   _____
   _____
   Mailing Address of Business
   _____
   City   State   Zip Code

3. Florida County of principal place of business: _____
   _____
   (see instructions if more than one county)

4. FEI Number: _____   This space for office use only

Section 2

A. Owner(s) of Fictitious Name If Individual(s): (Use an attachment if necessary):

1. _____   2. _____
   Last   First   M.I.   Last   First   M.I.
   _____   _____
   Address   Address
   _____   _____
   City   State   Zip Code   City   State   Zip Code

B. Owner(s) of Fictitious Name If other than an individual: (Use attachment if necessary):

1. _____   2. _____
   Entity Name   Entity Name
   _____   _____
   Address   Address
   _____   _____
   City   State   Zip Code   City   State   Zip Code
   Florida Registration Number _____   Florida Registration Number _____
   FEI Number: _____   FEI Number: _____
   ☐ Applied for ☐ Not Applicable   ☐ Applied for ☐ Not Applicable

Section 3

I (we) the undersigned, being the sole (all the) party(ies) owning interest in the above fictitious name, certify that the information indicated on this form is true and accurate. In accordance with Section 865.09, F.S., I (we) understand that the signature(s) below shall have the same legal effect as if made under oath. (At Least One Signature Required)

_____   _____
Signature of Owner   Date   Signature of Owner   Date

Phone Number: _____   Phone Number: _____

CR4E001B (1/02)

Section 4

FOR CANCELLATION COMPLETE SECTION 4 ONLY:
FOR FICTITIOUS NAME OR OWNERSHIP CHANGE COMPLETE SECTIONS 1 THROUGH 4:

I (we) the undersigned, hereby cancel the fictitious name _____

_____, which was registered on _____ and was assigned

registration number _____

_____   _____
Signature of Owner   Date   Signature of Owner   Date

Mark the applicable boxes   ☐ Certificate of Status — $10   ☐ Certified Copy — $30
FILING FEE: $50

Exhibit 2–5.

(continued)

Instructions for Completing Application for Registration of Fictitious Name

Section 1:   **Line 1:** Enter the name as you wish it to be registered. A fictitious name may <u>not</u> contain the words "Corporation" or "Incorporated," or the abbreviations "Corp." or "Inc.," unless the person or business for which the name is registered is incorporated or has obtained a certificate of authority to transact business in this state pursuant to chapter 607 or chapter 617 Florida Statutes. Corporations are not required to file under their exact corporate name.

Line 2: Enter the mailing address of the business. This address does not have to be the principal place of business and can be directed to anyone's attention. DO NOT USE AN ADDRESS THAT IS NOT YET OCCUPIED. ALL FUTURE MAILINGS AND ANY CERTIFICATION REQUESTED ON THIS REGISTRATION FORM WILL BE SENT TO THE ADDRESS IN SECTION 1. An address may be changed at any future date with no charge by simply writing the Division.

Line 3: Enter the name of the county in Florida where the principal place of business of the fictitious name is located. If there is more than one county, list all applicable counties or state "multiple".

Line 4: Enter the Federal Employer Identification (FEI) number if known or if applicable.

Section 2:   **Part A:** Complete if the owner(s) of the fictitious name are individuals. The individual's name and address must be provided.

Part B: Complete if the owner(s) are not individuals. Examples are a corporation, limited partnership, joint venture, general partnership, trusts, fictitious name, etc. Provide the name of the owner, their address, their registration number as registered with the Division of Corporations, and the Federal Employer Identification (FEI) number. An FEI number must be provided or the appropriate box must be checked.

Owners listed in Part B must be registered with the Division of Corporations or provide documentation as to why they are not required to register. Examples would be Federally Chartered Corporations, or Legislatively created entities.

Additional owners may be listed on an attached page as long as all of the information requested in Part A or Part B is provided.

Section 3:   Only one signature is required. It is preferred that a daytime phone number be provided in order to contact the applicant if there are any questions about the application. Since the Department indexes fictitious names on a central database available on the internet, it is no longer required to advertise the intention to register a fictitious name.

Section 4:   **TO CANCEL A REGISTRATION ON FILE:** Provide fictitious name, date filed, and registration number of the fictitious name to be cancelled.

TO CHANGE OWNERSHIP OF A REGISTRATION: Complete section 4 to cancel the original registration. Complete sections 1 through 3 to re-register the fictitious name listing the new owner(s). An owner's signature is required in both sections 3 and 4.

TO CHANGE THE NAME OF A REGISTRATION: Complete section 4 to cancel the original registration. Complete sections 1 through 3 to re-register the new fictitious name. An owner's signature is required in both sections 3 and 4.

An acknowledgement letter will be mailed once the fictitious name registration has been filed.

If you wish to receive a certificate of status and/or certified copy at the time of filing of this registration, check the appropriate box at the bottom of the form. PLEASE NOTE: Acknowledgments/certificates will be sent to the address in Section 1. If a certificate of status is requested, an additional $10 is due. If a certified copy is requested, an additional $30 is due.

The registration and reregistration will be in effect until December 31 of the fifth year.

Send completed application with appropriate fees in the enclosed envelope to: Internet Address:
     Fictitious Name Registration   http://www.sunbiz.org
     PO Box 1300
     Tallahassee, FL 32302-1300

The fee for registering a fictitious name is $50. Please make a separate check for each filing payable to the Department of State. Application must be typed or printed in ink and legible.

Exhibit 2–6.

Application for Renewal of Fictitious Name (Florida)

FILE TO RENEW NOW:
FICTITIOUS NAME WILL EXPIRE ON 12/31/03

SECRETARY OF STATE   FLORIDA DEPARTMENT OF STATE
DIVISION OF CORPORATIONS

APPLICATION FOR RENEWAL OF FICTITIOUS NAME

REGISTRATION #

1. Name and Mailing Address

If above mailing address is incorrect in any way, line through incorrect information and enter correction in Block 2.

2. Mailing Address change if applicable:

Suite, Apt. #, etc.

City   State   Zip Code

CHECK HERE IF MAKING CHANGES

3. FEI Number

5. County of Principal Place of Business

4. Date Registered

6. Certificate of Status Desired

$10 Additional Fee Required

AN OWNER THAT IS A CORPORATION, LIMITED PARTNERSHIP OR OTHER BUSINESS ENTITY
MUST BE REGISTERED AND ACTIVE WITH THIS OFFICE.

7. CURRENT OWNER (S)		8. ADDITIONS / CHANGES TO OWNERS		
DOCUMENT #	DELETE	DOCUMENT #	Change	Addition
FEI #		FEI #		
NAME		NAME		
STREET ADDRESS		STREET ADDRESS		
CITY - ST - ZIP		CITY - ST - ZIP		
DOCUMENT #	DELETE	DOCUMENT #	Change	Addition
FEI #		FEI #		
NAME		NAME		
STREET ADDRESS		STREET ADDRESS		
CITY - ST - ZIP		CITY - ST - ZIP		
DOCUMENT #	DELETE	DOCUMENT #	Change	Addition
FEI #		FEI #		
NAME		NAME		
STREET ADDRESS		STREET ADDRESS		
CITY - ST - ZIP		CITY - ST - ZIP		
DOCUMENT #	DELETE	DOCUMENT #	Change	Addition
FEI #		FEI #		
NAME		NAME		
STREET ADDRESS		STREET ADDRESS		
CITY - ST - ZIP		CITY - ST - ZIP		

(CR4E003) 10/02

9. I (we) the undersigned, being the sole (all the) party(ies) owning interest in the above fictitious name, certify that the information indicated on this form is true and accurate. I (we) understand that the signature(s) below shall have the same legal effect as if made under oath. I further certify that the names of individuals listed on this form do not qualify for an exemption under section 119.07(3)(i), F.S. (At least one signature required)

Signature of Owner   Date   Signature of Owner   Date

Daytime Phone Number: _____   Daytime Phone Number: _____

Exhibit 2–6.

(continued)

MAKE CHECK PAYABLE TO DEPARTMENT OF STATE

FILING FEE $50.00

PLEASE READ ALL INSTRUCTIONS CAREFULLY BEFORE COMPLETING THE FORM. IF YOU NEED ASSISTANCE, PLEASE CALL (850) 488-9000.

INSTRUCTIONS FOR COMPLETING THE APPLICATION FOR RENEWAL

Block 1.   Block is preprinted with the fictitious name, the registration number, and mailing address of the business as it was originally registered with this office. The name of the business cannot be changed on the statement of renewal. A cancellation/reregistration must be filed. Please call (850) 245-6058 for the appropriate form.

Block 2.   If the mailing address printed in block 1 is incorrect, enter the correct mailing address in block 2. This address does NOT have to be the principal place of business and can be directed to anyone's attention. DO NOT USE AN ADDRESS THAT IS NOT YET OCCUPIED. ALL FUTURE MAILINGS AND ANY CERTIFICATION REQUESTED ON THIS RENEWAL FORM WILL BE SENT TO THE ADDRESS IN BLOCK 1 OR AS CHANGED IN BLOCK 2. WE WILL NOT SEND CERTIFICATION TO ANY OTHER ADDRESS OR REDIRECT MAIL RETURNED TO THIS OFFICE.

Block 3.   Block is preprinted with the Federal Employer's Identification (FEI) number. If blank, enter the FEI number if known. For FEI number assistance, call the IRS at (800) 829-1040.

Block 4.   Block is preprinted with the date filed in this office; if blank enter the correct file date, if known.

Block 5.   Block is preprinted with the county of the principal place of business. "MULTIPLE" may be preprinted if more than one county was reported when original registration was filed; change if necessary.

Block 6.   Should you desire a certificate of status, please check the box in block 6 and include an additional $10.00 with the filing fee. The certificate of status will be sent to address in block 1 or in block 2, if changed.

Block 7.   Block 7 contains the Fictitious Name owner(s), their addresses, document number and Federal Employer Identification Number (FEI) if applicable. (Due to space limitations only four owners are printed.) If there are additional owners, please list them on an attached sheet or in block 8 as additions. Do not make any changes in block 7 unless deleting an owner. Owners listed that are not individuals must be registered and active with this office or provide documentation as to why they are not required to register. Examples would be Federally Chartered Corporations or Legislatively created entities. NOTE: If the fictitious name indicated in block 1 contains the word(s) "corporation" or "incorporated", or the abbreviation "corp." or "Inc.", the owner(s) <u>must</u> be a corporation registered or incorporated with this state.

Block 8.   Block 8 is for changes or additions to the owners in block 7. Changes must be typed or printed in ink and legible. Owners that are not individuals must be registered and active with this office or provide documentation as to why they are not required to register. Examples would be Federally Chartered Corporations or Legislatively created entities. NOTE: If the fictitious name indicated in block 1 contains the word(s) "corporation" or "incorporated", or the abbreviation "corp." or "Inc.", the owner(s) <u>must</u> be a corporation registered or incorporated with this state.

Block 9.   This renewal must be signed in block 9 with an original signature by at least one owner that is listed in block 7, block 8 if a change, or on an attachment.

If this Application for Renewal of Fictitious Name is not filed on or before December 31, 2003, the fictitious name will be cancelled and removed from the records of the Department of State.

This renewal application must be post-marked by December 31, 2003.

After the Application for Renewal is filed, the effectiveness of the fictitious name registration is continued until December 31, 2008.

MAILING ADDRESS:
Fictitious Name Renewal
Division of Corporations
Post Office Box 1300
Tallahassee, Florida 32302-1300

Other Correspondence:
Division of Corporations
P.O.Box 6327
Tallahassee, Florida 32314

Courier Service Address:
Division of Corporations
409 East Gaines Street
Tallahassee, Florida 32399

Internet Address:
www.sunbiz.org

Phone Number: (850) 488-9000
Hearing/Voice Impaired may call (850) 245-6096 (TDD)

ENDNOTES

1. See "Taxation of Corporation" in Chapter 6.

2. See "Corporations in Foreign Jurisdictions" in Chapter 14.

3. Some states provide statutory authority for the continuity of a sole proprietorship by a proper testamentary distribution. E.g., McKinney Consol. Laws of N.Y.S.C.P.A. § 2108.

4. E.g., a bank is authorized to continue to pay checks of a deceased sole proprietor after death under U.C.C. § 4–405 until the bank learns about the death and has a reasonable opportunity to act on it.

5. See "Agency Authority" in Chapter 1.

6. See C. Rohrlich, Organizing Corporate and Other Business Enterprises § 13.02 (1967).

GENERAL PARTNERSHIP

CHARACTERISTICS OF A PARTNERSHIP

A **general partnership** is generally defined as an association of two or more persons to carry on as co-owners a business for profit. The business partnership is usually a contractual relationship between two or more persons whereby they agree to enter business together on their negotiated terms to produce a profit. The law partnership has deep roots in ancient law and is closely related to the law of agency,[1] in that each partner is an agent for the other partners and for the partnership business. The **partnership agreement** is the most important element of the partnership, since it governs all rights and responsibilities between the partners with respect to the business affairs of the firm. Partnerships are found in businesses as small as a local newsstand, and in businesses as large as some multistate enterprises.

Traditionally, the partnership has many of the legal characteristics of the sole proprietorship. It is distinguished from the proprietorship primarily in that it is owned by two or more persons, rather than a single individual. Thus, in the pure form of partnership, each partner is personally responsible for the liabilities of the firm; management of the business affairs is vested in all partners equally; the partnership is dissolved upon the death of a partner; and partnership profits and losses are taxed as though received individually by the partners. Each of these concepts, which are explored in greater detail later, presupposes that the partnership is nothing more than an aggregation of persons who join together to own and conduct a business. In this respect, the general partnership is clearly distinguished from the corporation, which has always been recognized as an entity, separate and distinct from its composite members.

Aggregate and Entity Theories of Partnership

Under modern commercial law, the **aggregate theory** of partnership has eroded in recognition of the commercial reality of the partnership enterprise. Most partnerships operate as business entities, the activities of which are separate from the activities of the individual partners. For example, the firm's delivery trucks are treated as belonging to the firm, not to the individual partners; the partners frequently are employed by the firm and are paid wages or salaries for their services; and the partnership conducts business and titles business property in the firm name.

The Uniform Partnership Act, which was originally adopted in 1914 and governs general partnerships, has been adopted in all but a few states.[2] The National Conference of Commissioners on Uniform Laws has drafted a new Uniform Partnership Act to clarify and modernize the statutory laws of partnerships. States gradually are converting their statutes on partnerships to conform to the revised act. The original Uniform Partnership Act treats partnerships as having both **entity** and aggregate characteristics; authorities dispute which theory prevails in most partnership problems. The revised statute, however, clearly states that "a partnership is an entity."[3] For purposes of this book, the question of when each of these theories applies is left to be resolved by those who consider the problem a serious one. The materials in this text concentrate on the elements, advantages, and disadvantages of partnership, and on problems in forming and conducting business under the partnership organization.

This chapter is concerned primarily with general partnerships. Another commonly recognized form of partnership is the limited partnership, in which some partners enjoy limited liability in exchange for limited control over the business. Many of the elements of a limited partnership are similar to those of a general partnership, but limited partnerships are discussed separately in the next chapter because of variations in their formation and operation. Many states have recently enacted statutes permitting either general or limited partnerships to register as limited liability partnerships and to thus insulate all partners from personal liability

States that have adopted Uniform Partnership Act of 1914	States that have adopted Revised Uniform Partnership Act of 1997
Alaska	Alabama
Arkansas	Alaska
Colorado	Arizona
Georgia	Arkansas
Illinois	California
Indiana	Colorado
Kentucky	Connecticut
Maine	Delaware
Massachusetts	District of Columbia
Michigan	Florida
Mississippi	Hawaii
Missouri	Idaho
Nevada	Iowa
New Hampshire	Kansas
New York	Maryland
North Carolina	Minnesota
Ohio	Montana
Pennsylvania	Nebraska
Rhode Island	New Jersey
South Carolina	New Mexico
Utah	North Dakota
Wisconsin	Oklahoma
	Oregon
	South Dakota
	Tennessee
	Texas
	Virgin Islands
	Washington
	West Virginia
	Wyoming

for partnership obligations. The registration process is separately discussed in "Registration as a Limited Liability Partnership" later in this chapter.

Definition of a Partnership

Under the Uniform Partnership Act, a partnership is defined as "an association of two or more persons to carry on as co-owners a business for profit."[4] A few words on each element are essential to an understanding of this business form.

The *association of persons* has been generally recognized to be a question of intent—the persons must voluntarily intend to associate together in a business relationship. Their intent is usually expressed in an agreement, either written or inferred from their conduct. Under the revised statute, however, a partnership can be created regardless of whether the partners intend to form one.[5] Consequently, partnerships may be very informal, perhaps even an oral understanding, but the better practice requires a comprehensive written agreement between the parties that clearly specifies their rights and responsibilities to each other and to the business.

The *persons* involved in a partnership must number two or more. A one-person business is a sole proprietorship. The persons need not be natural persons (human beings) under the Uniform Partnership Act. Partners may include corporations, other partnerships, and other associations. The Model Business Corporation Act complements this provision by permitting a corporation to be a partner.[6]

Partners must be *co-owners* of the business, which means they have not only joint ownership of specific tangible assets, but also joint rights to profit and control. The licenses and property of the partnership are held in a firm name or in the partners' names jointly. The partners share profits and losses and exercise joint management privileges, the details of which are usually described in the agreement. Absent provisions to the contrary in an agreement, profits, losses, and control are divided equally among the partners by law.[7]

By definition, a partnership must be engaged in carrying on a business for profit. *Carrying on* implies the continuation of the operations of the business for a period of time through many transactions. In contrast, a **joint venture** is formed for a single project or transaction. For example, if you and your friend purchased an apartment building intending to rent it to students attending your college or university, you would be engaged in the carrying on of a business for profit and would be partners. If you and your friend purchased the apartment building to sell it to another for a profit, you would have formed your association for a single project—buying and selling the building—and you would have formed a joint venture. The *business* part of this definition is broadly defined as "every trade, occupation or profession."[8] The *profit* element of the partnership definition is intended to exclude charitable, religious, and fraternal groups. The drafters of the Uniform Partnership Act could have realistically stated that the business also may be operated at a loss and still be a partnership, since many partnerships do lose money. In any case, if the other elements are satisfied and a business is organized in *expectation of profit,* the business is considered a partnership.

EXAMPLE

Characteristics of Partnership

- An association
- Two or more persons
- Co-owners
  —joint title to property
  —joint sharing of profit
  —joint control
- Carrying on a business
- With an expectation of profit

PARTNERSHIP PROPERTY

In a sole proprietorship, although the division may be informal, it is usually possible to distinguish business assets from personal assets of the proprietor. Since the business is an extension of the proprietor's personal life, segregation becomes important only in case of a contractual provision specifically limiting liability to the business assets of the firm. In the case of partnerships, however, a clear distinction between firm property and personal assets of the partners is necessary. Although the personal assets of the individual partners may be vulnerable to partnership obligations, the property should be clearly divided for operating purposes. For example, in a law firm that operates as a partnership, the partners may have purchased furniture, library books, computers, and supplies in the name of the partnership, and these assets belong to the firm. A partner may use her personal automobile in traveling to and from court in performing the business of the partnership, but her automobile is still her personal asset. Consequently, it is important to distinguish, preferably by agreement, which assets belong to the firm and which assets belong to the individual partner.

Partnership property is first acquired from contributions by the individual partners. The contributions of cash or property by partners are called their **capital contributions** and the value of these contributions is the value of the partner's equity in the partnership. Partners may contribute specific assets to the firm, such as land, buildings, furniture, or patents; upon contribution, the assets become partnership property. A partner may contribute cash, which is used to purchase specific assets; the cash and the assets so purchased also become firm property. The Uniform Partnership Act provides that "unless the contrary intention appears, property acquired with partnership funds is partnership property."[9] It should follow that property purchased on credit by the firm is partnership property. For the most part, it is not difficult to ascertain which property has been purchased with firm funds, but it may be difficult to identify property that has been contributed to the partnership unless the partnership agreement accurately reflects the intention of the parties. If a court were asked to decide whether certain property belongs to the firm or to the individual partner, it would test the intention of the parties as expressed in their agreement and through other overt acts.

The best guide to the intention of the partners is their written agreement. Thus, a complete description and agreed value of the property partners contribute is essential to good drafting. It is normal practice to describe the property contributed in a separate schedule, which is attached to the partnership agreement and incorporated by reference.

Contribution of Property

Glenna McKelvy shall contribute certain property valued at five thousand dollars ($5,000.00). Such property is described in Schedule A attached hereto.

EXAMPLE

The contribution of property to the partnership may have certain tax consequences, which are explored in detail later.[10]

Just as it is important to accurately and thoroughly describe the property contributed to the partnership, it is also important to specify which property is merely "loaned" to the partnership for its use, with the intention of retaining title in the individual partner's name. A clause covering this point should include the period of time the firm shall be permitted to use the property, unless indefinite; any restrictions on the owner that are desirable or necessary to ensure the use of the asset by the firm; and any compensation to be paid to the partner for the use of the asset.

| EXAMPLE | **Property Loaned to Partnership** |

Craig Carver, as the owner of one 2004 Chevrolet pick-up truck, agrees to contribute to the partnership the use of such truck, with the understanding that it shall remain his separate property, and not in any event become an asset of the partnership. It is agreed that until the termination of the partnership, or until the death or retirement of Craig Carver, he will not, without the consent of all other partners, sell, assign, pledge, or mortgage such property. Craig Carver further agrees that any money or rights occurring from the sale or assignment of the truck shall belong to the partnership during the term of the operation of the partnership. For the purpose of computation of profits, and not for participation in the distribution of the assets, the sum of twenty thousand dollars ($20,000.00) shall be included in Craig Carver's capital account to represent the value of the truck.

Thus, for property contributed at the commencement of the partnership, the intent of the parties with respect to ownership may be clearly expressed in the agreement.[11]

The Uniform Partnership Act assists in determining the partners' intentions with respect to property subsequently acquired by the firm by creating the presumption that property purchased with partnership funds is firm property. The firm also may hold property in its own name. Nevertheless, it is also possible to title partnership property in the names of the individual partners and, in such cases, the partner who holds the title can transfer the property on behalf of the partnership. In such cases the agreement should provide for this arrangement and indicate that the assets so titled are held as partnership property.

| EXAMPLE | **Title to Property** |

Partnership property (including real estate) may, by unanimous consent of the partners, be acquired and conveyed in the name of any partner or other person as nominee for the partnership. Such property shall be recorded as partnership property in the partnership accounts.

In addition to the specific provisions in the agreement, legal counsel should be sensitive to the need to provide other indicia of intent to determine ownership of partnership property. Partnership property should be formally transferred to the partnership by a bill of sale or an assignment document. It should be identified in the firm's books, and all expenses, including repairs, insurance, taxes, interest on a mortgage, and so forth, should be paid by the firm. To be consistent, the firm should deduct these payments as expenses on its income tax return. Careful drafting and planning will avoid confusion regarding ownership of partnership property.

Historically, partners joined together as co-owners of a business, and most jurisdictions considered all assets to be owned in a classification known as **tenancy in common**. In the pure sense, tenancy in common, as its name indicates, stands for common ownership, with each owner entitled to a fraction of full title, and with each owner entitled to **partition**, or to sever his or her fractional ownership and assign or sell it to another without the consent of the other co-owners. As the law of partnership developed, it modified this right of partition and imposed the limitation that partnership assets first be used for partnership purposes (including satisfying obligations of the firm). No partner could sell his or her fractional interest in the property until partnership debts were fully paid.

The Uniform Partnership Act continues the theory that partners are co-owners of partnership property, but it creates a new ownership classification called **tenancy in partnership**,[12] which better conforms to the reality that a partnership is a commercial entity using its own property for business purposes.[13] All partnership assets are held under this form of title, and while partners are said to be co-owners, they have very limited ownership rights. In general, a partner may not possess firm property for other than partnership purposes without the consent of the other partners; a partner may not sell firm property (or any fractional interest in the property) without the consent of the other partners; a partner's individual creditors cannot apply their claims against the partner to firm assets; and a partner's heirs have no interest in the partnership assets when the partner dies (the **surviving partners** are vested with the deceased partner's fractional ownership upon the partner's death). So, for example, if a three-person partnership owns a delivery truck that is used in the partnership's appliance business, no partner may use the truck to transport his family to a picnic without the other partners' consent. Similarly, all partners must agree to sell the truck; no single partner can sell his or her one-third interest in it. If one partner is being sued for a personal bill and refuses to pay, the creditor cannot use the truck to satisfy the judgment. Finally, if one partner dies, the truck belongs to the other two partners, and the deceased partner's heirs do not acquire the deceased partner's fractional ownership rights. The heirs are entitled to the deceased partner's "interest in the partnership," described below.

PARTNER'S INTEREST IN A PARTNERSHIP

Even though specific assets belong to the firm, and not to the individual partners, each individual partner is entitled to an **interest in the partnership**, which is best described as an intangible interest that includes a partner's proportionate share of the assets and liabilities together with an interest in profits and rights to management. With respect to assets and liabilities, for example, if an appliance partnership owns $1,000,000 in assets and owes $400,000 in liabilities, the total partnership interests equal $600,000. If the partnership agreement provides that each partner shares equally, each partner's interest in the firm is valued at $200,000. Thus, upon the death of one partner, the deceased partner's heirs are entitled to that partner's interest in the firm, meaning they have the right to be paid $200,000 from the two surviving partners. Typically, the partners purchase life insurance to pay the value of a deceased partner's interest in the partnership to the heirs of the deceased partner. Similarly, any living partner can **assign** her right to the $200,000 equity to any person outside the partnership who is willing to purchase it.

The partner's interest in the partnership is initially determined by the partner's capital contribution to the firm, which is one reason a value must be assigned to the contributions in the agreement. Thereafter, additional capital contributions increase the contributing partner's interest, and subsequent profits also increase the partner's interest, as they are distributed in the proportions specified in the agreement. Conversely, if a partner withdraws funds from the partnership, the interest is reduced.[14] To illustrate, suppose the partners in the appliance business began as follows:

> Smith contributed his delivery truck, valued at $50,000;
> Jones contributed $100,000 in cash to buy inventory and to lease a store; and
> Williams did not contribute tangible property but agreed to manage the store.

The agreement provided that the partners would share equally in profits and losses.

At this point, each partner's interest would be equal to his or her contribution. Williams had no interest, since she had yet to contribute anything.

During the year, Smith contributed a cash register valued at $4,000, and Jones withdrew $5,000 in cash for personal reasons. At the end of the year, the business showed a profit of $30,000.

The partners' respective interests in the partnership now would be as follows:

> Smith's interest would be $64,000, which includes the value of the truck and cash register, plus his share of profit;
> Jones's interest would be $105,000, which includes her initial cash contribution, plus her profit, less her withdrawal; and
> Williams's interest would be $10,000, all of which came from profit.

This intangible interest in the partnership is the partner's personal property right in the firm. It is considered to be a personal asset, which the partner owns just as one owns a home or other personal possessions. Consequently, this property interest passes to the partner's heirs

Know All Men by These Presents, that for and in consideration of the sum of One Dollar ($1) and other good and valuable considerations to me in hand paid, receipt of which is hereby acknowledged, I, _____, of _____, do hereby assign to _____, of _____, all of my right, title, and interest in and to a certain agreement of partnership bearing date the _____day of _____, 20__, made and entered into by and between _____, _____, and myself; and I do hereby authorize and direct _____ to account to and with for all profits, issues and income arising under the partnership agreement in the same manner and with the same force and effect as if such accounting were had and made with me personally.

In Witness Whereof, I have hereunto set my hand and seal this _____ day of _____, 20__.

_____[*Seal*]

upon death and may be reached by the partner's individual creditors for unpaid obligations. Similarly, a partner may assign this interest to an outsider and thereby confer his or her proportionate rights to profits and the value of the assets on the assignee.[15] (See Exhibit 3–1, Assignment of Partner's Interest in Firm.) Note that an assignment of a partner's interest in the firm does not make the assignee a partner, since no person may become a partner without the express or implied consent of all other partners.[16] Nor does the assignee acquire any right to interfere with the management of the business. The assignee's sole right is to receive the profits and assets to which the assigning partner is entitled.[17]

MANAGEMENT OF A PARTNERSHIP

Right to Manage

The right to manage and control the affairs of the partnership is governed by the Uniform Partnership Act and by the agreement of the partners. In the absence of an agreement to the contrary, all general partners have equal rights in the management and conduct of partnership business.[18] It is also possible (and perhaps desirable) to specify by agreement the specific management responsibilities and limitations for each partner.

Since each partner is an agent for the partnership, every act a partner performs on behalf of the firm must be an authorized act. Under the revised Uniform Partnership Act, any act of a partner, including the execution of documents in the partnership name, for apparently carrying on the business of the partnership in the usual way binds the partnership, unless the partner has no authority to act for the partnership and the person with whom the partner is dealing knows or has been notified that the partner lacks authority.[19] Actual authority of a partner may come from specific provisions in the agreement itself, or from the vote of the partners in the manner specified in the agreement or by law. The Uniform Partnership Act provides that decisions regarding ordinary matters of partnership business are to be made by a majority vote of the partners.[20] Each partner, regardless of that partner's contribution or share of profits, has one vote on such matters. Thus, under the statute, even though one partner has contributed 95% of the capital and is entitled to 95% of the profits, that partner has an equal voice with the other partners in management matters.

If the statutory management scheme—that is, equal rights in management and rule by majority vote—is deemed desirable by the partners, a clause reciting this scheme should be included in the agreement so the partners do not have to refer to the law to understand the management structure.

E X A M P L E   **Management**

All partners shall have equal rights in the management of the partnership business. Decisions shall be by majority vote, each partner having one vote, except as otherwise provided in this Agreement.

On the other hand, if not all partners will be actively engaged in the management of the business, it may be appropriate to appoint a managing partner or partners to control business affairs. In drafting such an appointment, it is good practice to specify the authority of the managing partners with reasonable detail and to provide a method for the resolution of disagreement between multiple managing partners.

Managing Partners

The management and control of the partnership business shall be vested in Martha Loomis, James Lyons, and Scott Charlton. Such managing partners shall have and are hereby given the sole power and authority:

a) to contract and incur liabilities for and on behalf of the partnership;

b) to borrow for and on behalf of the partnership from time to time such sum or sums of money which in their sole discretion is necessary to the conduct of the business of the partnership, and to mortgage, pledge, or otherwise encumber its assets to secure the repayment of such monies so borrowed;

c) to make all contracts for and on behalf of the partnership generally in the conduct of its business;

d) to employ and discharge all employees, including any of the other partners who may be so employed in respect to the transaction of the partnership business;

e) to otherwise carry on and transact or cause to be carried on and transacted, under their sole supervision and control, all of the other business of the partnership; and

f) to determine whether at any accounting period the profits, if any, of the partnership shall be apportioned and distributed, in whole or in part, to the partners, or retained and continued in use in the business of the partnership.

In the event of disagreement among the managing partners, a decision by the majority of them shall be binding upon the partnership. If any one or two of the managing partners shall die or retire from the partnership business or become unwilling or unable to act as a managing partner, the management and control of the partnership business shall be vested in the remaining partner or partners.

It is understood and agreed that the managing partners shall consult and confer with the other partners before taking any steps resulting in any substantial change in the operation or policies of the partnership affairs, or the sale of any portion of the partnership assets other than in the usual course of business, or in any manner affecting the partnership business unusually as judged by the ordinary operation of the partnership business.

The Uniform Partnership Act prohibits certain acts outside the ordinary course of business unless all partners consent. Historically, by law and in many existing partnership agreements adopting the law, these acts include assignment of partnership property in trust for creditors, sale of the goodwill of the business, confession of judgment against the firm, submission of a partnership claim to arbitration, and any other act that would make it impossible to carry on the partnership business. Managing partners cannot accomplish these acts unless all partners approve. The revised statute, however, takes a different approach to this issue. Instead of prohibiting certain transactions by statute, the new act permits the partnership to file a **statement of partnership authority** that identifies the partners authorized to perform certain acts (such as transferring real estate owned by the partnership) and describes the authority (or limitations on the authority) of the various partners.[21] (See Exhibit 3–2, Statement of Authority.) The revised act also permits the filing of a statement of denial by an individual partner to deny his or her authority or status as a partner.[22] (See Exhibit 3–3, Statement of Denial of Partnership Authority.) In any case, it is advisable to require the managing partners to refer unusual matters affecting the business to a committee of the whole for resolution rather than granting the managers unfettered discretion in these matters.

It is possible to provide by agreement what partners may *not* do without the unanimous consent of the other partners. Such a provision usually includes acts specifically prohibited by state law, in addition to other specific acts deemed appropriate by the partners.

Exhibit 3–2.

Statement of Partnership
Authority

STATEMENT OF PARTNERSHIP AUTHORITY

THIS STATEMENT OF PARTNERSHIP AUTHORITY, dated as of the _____ day of _____, 20____, pursuant to the Revised Uniform Partnership Act (hereinafter referred to as the "Act"), is presented to the office of the Secretary of State to state the authority and limitations upon authority of some or all of the partners to enter into transactions on behalf of the Partnership

FIRST: The name of the Partnership is Pyewacket General Partnership.

SECOND: The street address of the chief executive office of the Partnership is _____, Boise, Idaho.

THIRD: The names and addresses of all of the general partners of the Partnership are as follows:

Partner Name   *Partner Address*

_____   _____

                                       _____

                                       _____

_____   _____

                                       _____

                                       _____

                                       _____

_____   _____

                                       _____

FOURTH: The name and address of the Partnership's appointed agent for transaction of the Partnership's lawful business, including the transfer of real property, within the State of Idaho is:

Agent's Name   *Agent's Address*

_____   _____

                                       _____

                                       _____

FIFTH: The extent of the authority of the partners is granted and limited as follows;

[Here describe specific authority and limitations on authority, identifying the partner of agent who has authority to act on behalf of the Partnership. If authority to transfer real property on behalf of the Partnership is granted to a specific partner or agent, specifically identify the extent or limitations upon such authority.]

SIXTH: The foregoing Statement of Authority shall be effective upon the filing of this Statement of Authority with the office of the Secretary of State. If the foregoing authority includes the authority to transfer real property on behalf of the Partnership, this Statement of Authority for that purpose shall be effective upon filing of this Statement of Authority with the office of the clerk and recorder where real property transactions are recorded.

IN WITNESS WHEREOF, the undersigned General Partners of the Partnership are authorized to sign and deliver this Statement of Authority under the Partnership Agreement for the Partnership as of the _____ day of _____, 20____ .

PYEWACKET GENERAL PARTNERSHIP

By: _____
General Partner

By: _____
General Partner

Exhibit 3–2.

(continued)

STATEMENT OF DENIAL OF PARTNERSHIP AUTHORITY

THIS STATEMENT OF DENIAL OF PARTNERSHIP AUTHORITY, dated as of the _____ day of _____, 20____ , pursuant to Revised Uniform Partnership Act (hereinafter referred to as the "Act"), is presented to the office of the Secretary of State to deny and disaffirm authority of the undersigned person.

FIRST: The name of the Partnership is Pyewacket General Partnership.

SECOND: The street address of the chief executive office of the Partnership is_____, Boise, Idaho.

THIRD: The undersigned hereby denies that he/she is a partner in the Partnership, having withdrawn from the Partnership effective as of _____, 20____.

FOURTH: The undersigned hereby denies and disaffirms any of the following authority which was designated as his/her authority in a Statement of Authority filed by the Partnership with the office of the Secretary of State [and with the clerk and recorder of _____county]:

[Here describe specific authority that is being denied and disaffirmed.]

FIFTH: The foregoing Statement of Denial of Authority shall be effective upon the filing of this Statement of Denial of Authority with the office of the Secretary of State. If the foregoing authority includes the authority to transfer real property on behalf of the Partnership, this Statement of Denial of Authority for that purpose shall be effective upon filing of this Statement of Authority with the office of the clerk and recorder where real property transactions are recorded.

IN WITNESS WHEREOF, the undersigned person has signed and delivered this Statement of Denial of Authority as of the _____ day of _____, 20____.

_____
General Partner

Exhibit 3–3.

Statement of Denial of Partnership Authority

EXAMPLE

Limitations on Authority

Unless authorized by the other partners, one or more but less than all the partners have no authority to:

a) assign the partnership property in trust for creditors or on the assignee's promise to pay the debts of the partnership;

b) dispose of the goodwill of the business;

c) do any other act that would make it impossible to carry on the ordinary business of a partnership;

d) confess a judgment;

e) submit a partnership claim or liability to arbitration or reference;

f) make, execute, or deliver for the partnership any bond, mortgage, deed of trust, guarantee, indemnity bond, surety bond, accommodation paper, or accommodation endorsement;

g) borrow money in the partnership name or use partnership property as collateral;

h) assign, transfer, pledge, compromise, or release any claim of or debt owing to the partnership except upon payment in full;

i) convey any partnership real property;

j) pledge or transfer in any manner his or her interest in the partnership except to another partner; or

k) do any of the acts for which unanimity is required by other paragraphs of this Agreement.

Duties and Compensation

Partners are expected to devote their full time and attention to the activities of the partnership. This duty flows from a traditional reality that partners customarily participated in the conduct of the business, and it may have limited justification in modern practice. Moreover, the law denies partners the right to compensation for services performed on behalf of the firm,[23] since their remuneration is supposed to come from profits generated by their services and shared in a manner provided by the agreement.

If the parties desire a modification of the legal rule, matters such as salary and devotion to duty should be addressed in the partnership agreement.

EXAMPLE

Salaries and Duties

There shall be paid to each partner the following monthly salaries: To Anne Berardini, Two thousand dollars; to Michael Corrigan, One thousand five hundred dollars; etc. No increase in salaries shall be made without unanimous agreement. The payment of salaries to partners shall be an obligation of the partnership only to the extent that partnership assets are available therefor, and shall not be an obligation of the partners individually. Salaries shall, to this extent, be treated as an expense of the partnership in determining profits or losses.

EXAMPLE

Expense Allowance

An expense account, not to exceed Two thousand dollars ($2,000) per month, shall be provided for each partner for his or her actual, reasonable, and necessary expenses, in engaging in the business and pursuits of the partnership. Each partner shall be required to keep an itemized record of such expenses and shall be paid once each month upon the submission of such statements of records.

Devotion to duty may be covered by specifying the responsibilities of each partner. This is especially important if some or all of the partners have other employment or partnership obligations.

EXAMPLE

Devotion to Duty

Each partner shall devote his or her entire time and attention to the partnership business, except that each may devote reasonable time to civic, family, and personal affairs; and except that Peter McLaughlin shall be permitted to pursue the business of selling magazine subscriptions during his own time and at hours other than the business hours of the partnership business.

Standards of Conduct of Partners

Partners owe each other **fiduciary duties** because of their mutual agency relationship (principals to each other and agents of each other, as discussed in Chapter 1) and because of their joint control over the partnership's property and their joint authority over the partnership's affairs. These relationships traditionally have created a bundle of elaborate and frequently overlapping fiduciary duties. Justice Cardozo, one of the United States' preeminent jurists, once described the duties this way:

> Joint adventurers, like copartners, owe to one another . . . the duty of finest loyalty. Many forms of conduct permissible in a workaday world for those acting at arm's length, are forbidden to those bound by fiduciary ties. A trustee is held to something stricter than the morals of the market place. Not honesty alone, but the punctilio of an honor the most sensitive is then the standard of behavior. As to this there has developed a tradition that is unbending and inveterate. Uncompromising rigidity has been the attitude of courts of equity when petitioned to undermine the rule of undivided loyalty by the "disintegrating erosion" of particular exceptions. . . . Only thus has the level of conduct for fiduciaries been kept at a level higher than that trodden by the crowd. It will not consciously be lowered by any judgment of this court.[24]

The state statutes do not provide much statutory guidance regarding the scope of the fiduciary duties of a partner. The cases that have considered partner misconduct generally have concluded that partners must account for profits, care for partnership assets, not compete with the partnership business, faithfully serve the partnership business without diversions, fully disclose information relevant to partnership affairs, and act like reasonably prudent people in administering the partnership activities.[25] Careful drafters of partnership agreements address as many of these issues as possible to prevent any misunderstanding or confusion over the partners' rights and obligations to each other.

The Revised Uniform Partnership Act devotes statutory attention to the subject of fiduciary duties, presumably to avoid some of the traps for unwary lawyers in drafting partnership agreements, who have not read all of the cases under the original law. The revised statute provides that the only fiduciary duties a partner owes to the partnership and the other partners are the duties of loyalty and care.[26] The statute defines these duties as follows:

A partner's duty of loyalty to the partnership and the other partners is limited to the following:
  (1) to account to the partnership and hold as trustee for it any property, profit, or benefit derived by the partner, without the consent of the other partners, in the conduct and winding up of the partnership business or from a use or appropriation by the partner of partnership property or opportunity;
  (2) to refrain from dealing with the partnership in the conduct or winding up of the partnership business, as or on behalf of a party having an interest adverse to the partnership without the consent of the other partners; and
  (3) to refrain from competing with the partnership in the conduct of the partnership business without the consent of the other partners before the dissolution of the partnership.

A partner's duty of loyalty may not be eliminated by agreement, but the partners may by agreement identify specific types or categories of activities that do not violate the duty of loyalty, if not manifestly unreasonable.

A partner's duty of care to the partnership and the other partners in the conduct and winding up of the partnership business is limited to refraining from engaging in grossly negligent or reckless conduct, intentional misconduct, or a knowing violation of law.

A partner shall discharge the duties to the partnership and the other partners under this [act] or under the partnership agreement, and exercise any rights, consistent with the obligation of good faith and fair dealing. The obligation of good faith and fair dealing may not be eliminated by agreement, but the partners may by agreement determine the standards by which the performance of the obligation is to be measured, if the standards are not manifestly unreasonable.

A partner does not violate a duty or obligation under this [act] or under the partnership agreement merely because the partner's conduct furthers the partner's own interest. A partner may lend money to and transact other business with the partnership. The rights and obligations of a partner who lends money to or transacts business with the partnership are the same as those of a person who is not a partner, subject to other applicable law.

Interestingly, the new act reverses the drafting process lawyers traditionally used in representing partnership clients. Under the original Uniform Partnership Act, the careful drafter defined and crafted the fiduciary duties of a partner, but the revised act does not permit the agreement to eliminate the duty of loyalty or the obligations of good faith and fair dealing. The revised act only permits modifications of the duty of care that do not "unreasonably reduce" that duty.[27]

PROFITS AND LOSSES

Sharing of profit is an important element of co-ownership, the crux of the partnership. A partner is not entitled automatically to compensation for services performed for the partnership. It is hoped that the partner's reward is a rich share of profits from a successful business. Unfortunately, the right to enjoy profits carries with it the obligation to bear losses—perhaps the most distressing characteristic of co-ownership.

The agreement between partners usually states the proportion in which profits and losses will be shared, and these provisions may be as simple or as complex as the parties desire. If the partners have not specified any provision for profit sharing, the Uniform Partnership Act provides that profits shall be divided equally and losses shall be shared in the same proportion as profits.[28] For example, if the agreement provides that profits shall be shared in a 75%/25% proportion between two partners, losses will be shared in the same proportion. However, if the agreement provides that losses be shared in a 75%/25% proportion, and nothing is agreed as to the division of profits, profits will still be shared equally. (The agreement concerning the sharing of losses does not rebut the statutory presumption that profits are shared equally.)

There is no requirement that profit-loss sharing have any relationship to the respective capital contributions of the partners. For example, one partner may contribute all of the cash and property to the firm while the other contributes only services, but the partners may share profits and losses in any agreed proportion.

Unusual profit distribution formulas may be used in special cases. For example, the parties may agree that one partner should have a preference to profits for some compelling reason.

EXAMPLE

Preferential Distribution of Profit

As part of the consideration for Ted White joining the firm, it is understood that for a period of two years, in the annual distribution of profits, he shall receive a cumulative preference of ten percent on his share; that is, out of the annual profits, there shall first be a distribution to him up to ten percent on his share of the capital, and also to cover any deficiency from said ten percent in any previous years, and then a distribution pro rata to the other partners up to ten percent on their shares of the capital, and any surplus profits shall then be distributed among the partners according to their respective shares of the capital.

This example not only establishes a profit preference, but also requires that profit be distributed in the same proportions as capital contributions; note that although the partners are not required to distribute profits in the same proportion as they have contributed capital, they are permitted to do so if that is their agreement.

It is good practice to include provisions for computing **net distributable profit** to avoid later dispute among the partners, especially when the partnership is likely to incur unusual obligations that otherwise may not be included as expense items for profit computation.

Division of Profits and Losses and Computation

The net profits of the partnership shall be divided and the net losses of the partnership shall be borne in the following proportions: Pamela Owen, 25%; Michael Corrigan, 10%; etc. Net profits of the partnership for any period shall be made by deducting from the gross profits disbursements made by or on behalf of the partnership for the usual and customary expenses of conducting the business, taxes chargeable to and paid by the partnership, reserves for taxes accrued but not payable, interest on all interest-bearing loans of the partnership, salaries paid to employees and partners, reserves for depreciation of partnership property and contingencies, including bad debts, allowance for accruing liabilities, and any and all other disbursements made by the partnership during such period incidental to the conduct of the business, excepting, however, payments to the partners on account of partnership profits.

In drafting the partnership agreement, a distinction may be made between profits, losses, deductions, credits, and cash. All of these items may be allocated the same way among partners, but a **disproportionate allocation** may be appropriate among partners in some cases. First, although these allocable items are related to each other, they also are quite separate and distinct and have varying importance in the eyes of each partner. A business may operate "profitably" but, because of certain deductions (such as depreciation on buildings owned by the business), may incur losses for tax purposes, which are shared equally unless allocated differently in the agreement. Nevertheless, because revenues have exceeded expenses for which expenditures were required (depreciation not being such an expense since no cash need be expended until the depreciated property is actually replaced), there may be a surplus of cash in the business, which is available for distribution to partners. In addition, various tax credits might be available to the business, which are to be allocated and passed through to the partners.[29]

Add to these variations the preferences of the partners. Partner A may have contributed all or most of the capital of the partnership and may prefer to receive the contributed cash back as soon as possible with a disproportionately high allocation of distributable cash. Partner B may have a very low income and a high cash need, while Partner C may have a very high income and a low need for cash. Between them, it may be appropriate to give B more cash and profits and to give C more losses and credits, to maximize B's enjoyment of life and minimize the tax consequences C suffers because of C's high income. These disproportionate allocations are a method by which tax can be avoided, but the Internal Revenue Service is not in the dark about them. The service will not allow a disproportionate allocation without significant economic justification.[30]

For example, if Partner A contributed all of the cash to start the business, it may be justifiable economically to give A a preference to cash. If Partner B does most of the work managing the business, it may be justifiable economically to give B profits and cash in higher proportion than to the others. But what did Partner C do to justify the receipt of losses? There's the rub. *All* allocations must be justified or the Internal Revenue Service may reallocate items of profit, loss, deductions, and credits in a way that produces additional tax to the partners.

Examples of disproportionate allocations follow.

Allocations of Profits, Losses, Deductions, and Credits

Except as otherwise provided herein (dealing with the allocation of the proceeds upon sale or other disposition of the assets of the Partnership), ninety-five percent (95%) of the net profits and losses of the Partnership, and each item of income, gain, loss, deduction, or credit entering into the computation thereof, shall be allocated to the partners other than the managing General Partner in accordance with their respective capital contributions. Five percent (5%) of such net profits, and losses, and items of income, gain, loss, deduction, or credit entering into the computation thereof, shall be allocated to the Managing General Partner.

EXAMPLE	**Distribution of Cash**

One hundred percent (100%) of net cash, including amounts required to be retained by the Partnership pursuant to this Agreement, shall be allocated to the partners other than the Managing General Partner and no cash shall be allocated to the Managing General Partner until the partners other than the Managing General Partner have received cash distributions totaling $1,925,000. Thereafter, ninety-five percent (95%) of net cash shall be allocated to the partners other than the Managing General Partner and five percent (5%) of net cash shall be allocated to the Managing General Partner throughout the term of the Partnership. The Managing General Partner shall determine the net cash available for distribution after establishing a reasonable reserve for replacements, contingencies, and operating capital, and after satisfying other obligations of the Partnership then due and payable. The Managing General Partner shall distribute the next cash available for distribution no less frequently than quarterly.

LIABILITY OF PARTNERS

Like sole proprietorships, general partnerships suffer the disadvantage of unlimited liability for each partner. If the assets of the partnership are inadequate to pay partnership creditors, the personal assets of the individual partners may be reached to satisfy these obligations.[31] In one sense, there is an advantage to a partnership over a sole proprietorship because liabilities are apportioned to the partners pro rata and no one person is required to bear the full responsibility. On the other hand, since each partner has the capacity to bind the partnership, the potential risk of liability is proportionately increased.

The element of unlimited liability is a substantial disadvantage to hazardous and speculative enterprises, and it further imposes an unwelcome burden on a partner who enjoys substantially greater personal wealth than the other partners. It is possible, as with a sole proprietorship, to insure against potential liability whenever it may be anticipated. Moreover, the partnership may negotiate agreements with outsiders which provide that liability on the contract shall be limited to the partnership assets and will not extend to the individual assets of the partners. Additional protection for the partner's individual assets is provided by a rule called **marshaling of assets**, which requires that firm creditors must first look to firm property for satisfaction of their obligations, and that only if partnership assets are inadequate may they pursue the individual assets of the partners. Nevertheless, a partnership's potential unlimited liability, which cannot be completely circumscribed by insurance, agreement, or rule for priority of assets, limits the desirability of the partnership form of business enterprise.

Partly because of the significant disadvantage of personal liability in general partnerships and partly because of the availability of limited liability in new entities that function like partnerships, such as the limited liability company (discussed in Chapter 5), many states have now permitted general partnerships to register as limited liability partnerships to provide significant limited liability protection for general partners who choose to operate their businesses in the general partnership form. See "Registration as a Limited Liability Partnership" later in this chapter.

When a partner has been required to pay expenses or liabilities of the partnership personally, the Uniform Partnership Act creates an obligation of the partnership to **indemnify** a partner who has paid expenses or incurred liability in the ordinary course of partnership business.[32] Thus, if a particular partner uses individual assets to pay firm creditors, that partner is entitled to be reimbursed for the appropriate share of the other partners. Although the law grants this right of indemnification, the specific authority for indemnification should be specified in the agreement.

Indemnification

The partnership shall promptly indemnify each partner in respect of payments reasonably made and personal liabilities reasonably incurred by him or her in the ordinary conduct of its business, or for the preservation of its business or property.

A partner who leaves the firm, by retirement or withdrawal or for some other reason, remains individually liable for debts incurred while that partner participated in the firm.[33] As discussed in detail later, whenever a partner leaves the firm, a technical **dissolution** of the partnership occurs.[34] If the remaining partners are to continue the business, certain notice is necessary to persons who transacted business with the former firm in order to relieve the withdrawn partner from future liability. Personal notice must be given to persons or companies who extended credit to the firm while the retiring partner was a member (see Exhibit 3–4, Personal Notice of Dissolution of Partnership). Notice by publication will suffice for other persons who dealt with the firm (see Exhibit 3–5, Notice of Dissolution of Partnership by Publication).[35] Usually the remaining partners agree to indemnify the withdrawing partner from any further liability for firm obligations. An indemnification clause as provided in the preceding example creates the obligation to indemnify if included in the original partnership agreement.

The Revised Uniform Partnership Act handles the retirement or withdrawal of partners in a different manner than that in which they were treated in the original statute. Such persons are called **dissociated partners** and they remain liable for transactions entered into by the partnership while they were partners and for transactions entered into within two years after they have dissociated from the firm if the other party to the transaction reasonably believes that the dissociated partner is a partner at the time of the transaction and does not otherwise have notice of the partner's dissociation.[36] Notice can be accomplished by actual notice to the creditor that the partner has dissociated, by the filing of a limitation of the partner's authority to act in regard to the particular transaction, or by the filing of a "statement of dissociation" to warn creditors that the partner is no longer a member of the firm.[37] (See Exhibit 3–6, Statement of Dissociation.)

To: _____   Date: _____
    Please be advised that the partnership between A.B., C.D., and E.F. was dissolved on the _____ day of _____, 20__, and that E.F. is no longer a member of the firm. Your account, in the amount of $_____, according to our books, will be settled with A.B. and C.D. who will continue the business under the firm name of B. & D.

[Signatures of the partners]

Exhibit 3–4.

Personal Notice of Dissolution of Partnership

Notice is hereby given that the partnership between A.B., C.D., and E.F. was dissolved on the _____ day of _____, 20__, so far as relates to E.F. All debts due to the partnership, and those due by them, will be settled with and by the remaining partners who will continue the business under the firm name of B. & D.

[Date]   *[Signatures of the partners]*

Exhibit 3–5.

Notice of Dissolution of Partnership by Publication

Exhibit 3–6.

Statement of Dissociation
from a Partnership

THIS STATEMENT OF DISSOCIATION, dated as of the _____ day of _____, 20 ____, pursuant to the Revised Uniform Partnership Act (hereinafter referred to as the "Act"), is presented to the office of the Secretary of State to provide notice that the undersigned, a former general partner in the named Partnership, has dissociated from the Partnership.

FIRST:　The name of the Partnership is Pyewacket General Partnership.

SECOND:　The street address of the chief executive office of the Partnership is _____, Boise, Idaho.

THIRD:　The undersigned dissociated from the Partnership on _____, 20____. This Statement Dissociation shall be effective upon the filing of this Statement with the office of the Secretary of State.

IN WITNESS WHEREOF, the undersigned person has signed and delivered this Statement of Dissociation as of the _____day of _____, 20____.

_____
General Partner

Under both the original and the revised Uniform Partnership Acts, new partners to the firm are individually liable for obligations existing when they join only if they specifically agree to such liability. Absent an assumption of these obligations, their individual assets may not be reached to satisfy existing obligations. They are, however, liable to lose their investment in the firm for obligations of the firm that are asserted after they join the partnership and they are individually liable for any obligations incurred after they become partners.[38]

DISSOLUTION AND TERMINATION OF A PARTNERSHIP

Most state laws currently provide that the partnership enterprise is dissolved whenever any partner ceases to be associated with the partnership business. In this respect, a partnership is very much like a sole proprietorship, where the business entity expires when the proprietor retires, dies, or is otherwise disassociated from the business. However, the partnership is an association of two or more persons, which adds an element of continuity to the partnership business, since dissolution does not necessarily require termination of the business. In fact, the partnership may be technically dissolved, yet the remaining partners may continue the business without the partner who has been disassociated from the business. By a strict interpretation of partnership law, a new partnership is created immediately and is governed essentially by the terms of the original agreement. In many cases, however, dissolution of the partnership requires termination and **winding up** of the business.

The Revised Uniform Partnership Act acknowledges that a partner may dissociate from the firm without causing a dissolution, and the remaining partners may continue the business without dissolution by causing the dissociated partner's interest to be purchased at a buyout price determined by the statute, if the partners have not agreed to a different purchase price in their agreement.[39]

This section explores the circumstances that cause dissolution under current statutes and the specific statutory authority to continue the partnership business without winding it up. The partnership agreement plays an important role in these matters, and thus specific clauses are discussed.

Causes of Dissolution

Dissolution of partnership may result from a variety of causes. Since a partnership is created by agreement of the partners, it may also be dissolved by agreement. This agreement may state a specific date for termination of the business, or may provide that the business should be dissolved upon the happening of a contingent event.[40] For example, the parties may agree that the partnership will be dissolved on July 1, 2010, or if the business sustains operating losses for five consecutive months, whichever occurs first. The latter contingency may be a realistic agreement insofar as the parties usually seek to avoid operating a business at a loss. The former provision, specifying a date for dissolution, is unrealistic and uncommon, since most partnerships hope to generate profits from a continuing business and the abrupt termination because of a specific provision in the original agreement could result in considerable loss of "Going concern" values.

Dissolution Contingent upon Results of Operations   **EXAMPLE**

If the operation of the business over a period of five consecutive months or more discloses an average net monthly profit of less than $50,000, the managing partner is hereby authorized and empowered to negotiate a sale, exchange, or other disposition of the entire partnership business upon the best possible terms available at such time, and in the event of such disposition of the partnership business the proceeds derived therefrom after the payment of the necessary costs and expenses of such disposition of the business shall be applied first to the payment of the debts of the business according to their respective legal priority, and if any balance of such proceeds shall remain after the payment and satisfaction of the debts, obligations, and liabilities of the business, the same shall be divided equally between the partners. Either partner may become a purchaser of the business at any such sale.

Whether or not the original agreement contains any provision for dissolution, all partners may unanimously agree to dissolve the firm at any time.[41] Better practice requires that an agreement of the partners to dissolve the firm be reduced to writing.

Agreement to Dissolve   **EXAMPLE**

The partnership heretofore subsisting between us, the undersigned Michael Corrigan, Karen Burn, and Anne Berardini, under and pursuant to the within articles of partnership, is hereby dissolved, except so far as may be necessary to continue the same for the liquidation and settlement of the business thereof. The said Michael Corrigan [*or* each of the undersigned] is authorized to sign in liquidation. Dated _____, 20_____.

Signatures

Since a primary element of a partnership is that it be a "voluntary association" of persons, any partner who no longer desires to be associated with the firm may withdraw at will, and thereby cause a dissolution.[42] If the original agreement provided that the partnership would continue for a specified term, the willful withdrawal of a partner may result in liability to the other partners for breach of the agreement, but the partnership is nevertheless dissolved. However, if the original agreement between the partners was indefinite regarding the duration of the partnership, this right or power to withdraw at will may be fully exercised, without regard to the harm it may cause to the business or the other partners. The law does require that the withdrawing partner act in good faith to escape a surprise dissolution with impunity.

A partner may not have the choice of leaving the firm if the agreement provides that he or she may be expelled by the other partners. Such provisions may be drafted in the original agreement and usually are conditioned upon some misconduct by a party, such as neglecting the business, refusing to pay an assessment, and so on. The **expulsion** provision may be as

Exhibit 3–7.

Preliminary Notice of
Expulsion to Partner

To [*Name and address of partner*]

We hereby give you notice that we propose to exercise the power given to us by paragraph _____ of the agreement of partnership, dated the _____ day of _____, 20__, under which we are now carrying on business in partnership with you, of terminating the partnership so far as you are concerned on the ground that you have acted in a manner inconsistent with the good faith observable between partners [*or that you have been guilty of conduct such as would be a ground for an application to the court for a dissolution of the partnership*].

In order to afford you an opportunity of explaining and, if possible, satisfying us that no good cause of complaint exists, we hereby invite you to attend a meeting of the partners, to be held at _____, on _____ next, at _____ o'clock.

If you are unable to attend such meeting, we must ask you to arrange for another meeting with us, to be held at an early date and in any case within [*one week*] from the date of this notice.

Dated _____, 20__.   [*Signatures of partners*]

Exhibit 3–8.

Notice of Expulsion to
Partner

To [*Name and address of partner*]

Referring to our notice to you, dated the _____ day of _____, 20__, and to the meeting of the partners held pursuant to such notice on the _____ day of _____, 20__, [*or and in view of the fact that you neither attended the meeting to which we invited you in such notice nor have taken any other steps to meet us or explain matters*], we regret to inform you that we are unable to accept as satisfactory the explanations offered by you at such meeting after hearing from us exactly what was our cause of complaint against you, and accordingly, we hereby give you notice that in exercise of the power for this purpose given to us by paragraph _____ of the agreement of partnership, dated the _____ day of _____, 20__, under which we have heretofore carried on business in partnership with you, we hereby terminate the partnership so far as you are concerned as of the date of this notice on the ground generally that [*repeat the ground as stated in the preliminary notice and add*] and more particularly on the ground that [*state the facts relied on as constituting the general ground previously stated*].

Dated _____, 20__.   [*Signatures of partners*]

---

general and broad as the parties desire, but provisions permitting expulsion "without cause" or "in the best interests" of the partnership are rare. If an expulsion provision is included in the agreement, the "innocent" partners may cause a dissolution of the firm by exercising their right to expel a partner. (See Exhibit 3–7, Preliminary Notice of Expulsion to Partner, and Exhibit 3–8, Notice of Expulsion to Partner.)

Dissolution also may be required by operation of law. The partnership business may be declared unlawful, as was the case for liquor stores operated as partnerships when prohibition was imposed. More frequently, the partnership is dissolved when a partner dies or becomes individually bankrupt.[43] Both of these events cause dissolution because the partner's interest in the firm, which was once the partner's personal property, becomes the property of the partner's heirs or a trustee in bankruptcy, none of whom are partners. In both cases, the partner has withdrawn from the firm in a sense.

Finally, dissolutions may be decreed by a court whenever any partner becomes legally incompetent or incapable of furthering the partnership business, or if a partner acts in a manner so that it is impracticable to carry on the business, or in any other case that renders a dissolution equitable under the circumstances.[44] Thus, when partners simply cannot agree on the proper operation of the business and their constant disagreement is detrimental to the success of the business, a court may, on application by a partner, dissolve the partnership. In some cases of disagreement between partners, dissolution by a court may be the only available remedy, since even though a partner may terminate the partnership at will, that partner may be risking liability for breach of the partnership agreement by causing dissolution.

EXAMPLE

Causes of Dissolution of Partnership

- Agreement
  —definite time in advance
  —at the time of dissolution
- Termination by a partner at will
- Expulsion of a partner
- Operation of law
  —business unlawful
  —partner dies
  —partner is bankrupt
- Decree of court

Continuation of a Partnership Despite Dissolution

As a general rule, the dissolution of a partnership requires the winding up and termination of the business and the liquidation of the firm's assets. There are two major exceptions to this rule: The business may be continued by the remaining partners if the dissolution was wrongful or if the partners' original agreement so provided.[45]

A **wrongful dissolution** results when a partner causes a dissolution without having the right to do so. If a partner is expelled from the firm for misconduct or a violation of the partnership agreement, the resulting dissolution is wrongful, and the remaining partners are permitted to continue the business without liquidation. Similarly, a partner who causes a dissolution by withdrawing from the firm in violation of the agreement causes a wrongful dissolution. Whether withdrawal is wrongful depends upon whether the agreement specifies the duration of the partnership. The partner causing the wrongful dissolution will be entitled to the value of his or her interest in the partnership, less the damages caused by the wrongful dissolution.

Whenever the business is continued by the remaining partners following a wrongful dissolution, the remaining partners are required to compensate or to ensure compensation to the dissociated partner for that partner's interest in the firm and to indemnify the dissociated partner from partnership liabilities.[46]

Even when the dissolution is innocent, continuation of the partnership business may be desirable; for example, in the case of the untimely death of a partner, liquidation following dissolution might result in unnecessary adverse tax consequences and other economic loss to the remaining partners. Continuation following an innocent dissolution requires an agreement to that effect between the parties. The agreement may be concluded legally after dissolution has occurred, but it is far better to provide for continuation in the detached negotiations of the original agreement of the parties.

First, the agreement should contain a continuation provision authorizing the remaining partners to proceed with the business.

EXAMPLE

Right to Continue the Business

In the event of a dissolution caused by the retirement, death, withdrawal, permanent disability, or bankruptcy of a partner, the remaining partners shall have the right to continue the partnership business under the same name by themselves or with any other person or persons they may select, but they shall pay to the other partner or his or her legal representatives the value of his or her interest in the partnership as of the date of dissolution.

Second, a method for computing the value of the outgoing partner's interest and a method of payment should be specified. The various methods of providing for payment of outgoing interests, be they the result of death, withdrawal, or other act dissolving the partnership, have different tax consequences, which are sufficiently complex to be avoided here. An enterprising student may explore these various methods in detail by referring to other sources.[47] Frequently used methods of settling the payment of the outgoing interest include (1) the purchase of the interest of the outgoing partner by the continuing partners, and (2) liquidating distributions from the partnership to the outgoing partner, both of which, in effect, result in the sale of the partner's interest to the firm itself. The second method may provide for guaranteed periodic payments or payments out of partnership profits or partnership property.

EXAMPLE

Payments for Partnership Interest

For the interest of a retiring or deceased partner in the partnership property, including goodwill, the partnership shall pay to the retiring partner, or to the successor in interest of the deceased partner, $20,000 in each of the five years following the retirement or death of a partner, which amount may not be prepaid except with the consent of the payee. It is the intention of the partners that the payments provided under this paragraph shall qualify under 26 U.S.C.A. § 736(a), and shall constitute ordinary income to the recipient and reduce the taxable income of the continuing partners.[48]

The agreement will specify the methods to be used in disposing of the partner's interest and in computing the compensation to the partner. An example of a provision permitting the purchase of the outgoing partner's interest by the remaining partners follows.

EXAMPLE

Purchase of a Partner's Interest

Upon the death, withdrawal, or insolvency of either of the partners during the existence of the partnership, the surviving or remaining partner shall purchase all the right, share, and interest of the deceased, withdrawn, or insolvent partner in all the partnership business and property, and shall assume all the then existing liabilities of the partnership. The price to be paid for such purchase is hereby fixed and agreed upon as follows: It shall be the amount stated as the net value of the share in the partnership of the deceased, withdrawn, or insolvent partner in the balance sheet of the first of January next preceding his or her death or withdrawal or insolvency, together with interest thereon from the date of said balance sheet at the rate of ten percent per annum until paid. Such purchase price shall be paid as follows: fifty percent thereof within six months from the date of such death, withdrawal, or insolvency, and the remainder at such times and in such amounts as may suit the convenience of the surviving or remaining partner; provided, that the whole thereof shall be paid within two years. The estate of the deceased partner, or the withdrawing or insolvent partner, shall not be entitled to share in any increase or profits gained, nor be liable for any losses incurred, in the business after the first of January next preceding his or her death, withdrawal, or insolvency, but all such profits shall belong to, and such losses be borne by, the purchasing partner.

One other item must be considered in regard to the purchase of a deceased partner's interest: life insurance. If the partnership agreement provides for the purchase of a deceased partner's interest, life insurance funding ensures that money will be available to consummate the intention of the parties when a partner dies. Life insurance can also be purchased to compensate the partnership for the loss of revenue produced by a deceased partner. The partnership may apply for and purchase life insurance on the lives of the partners, or the partners may individually apply for and purchase insurance on each other. The former is commonly called an **entity purchase plan**, and the latter is referred to as a **cross purchase plan**. Such insurance agreements usually are executed separately and are not a part of the partnership agreement. However, since they are intended to fund the purchase of the deceased partner's interest, the provisions of the insurance agreement and the insurance acquired thereby should be consistent with the buy-out arrangements specified in the partnership agreement.[49]

In addition to permitting the continuation of the business and the disposition of the withdrawing or deceased partner's interest, a properly drafted agreement also should require the continuing partners to assume and pay all existing partnership obligations. Moreover, since creditors are likely to have extended credit to the firm before the partner's withdrawal, and the withdrawing partner may remain liable for future obligations unless proper notice is given, the agreement should specifically require such a notice.

Notice of Dissolution

EXAMPLE

Actual notice of dissolution shall be given to all persons who have had dealings with the partnership during the two years prior to dissolution.

Finally, it may be desirable to include a non-competition clause, to prevent, as much as possible, the withdrawing partner from competing against the firm or divulging the firm's trade secrets.

Noncompete Agreement

EXAMPLE

The retiring partner shall not for a period of two years from the date of his or her retirement, either alone, or jointly with or as agent for any person, directly or indirectly, set up, exercise, or carry on the trade or business of metal processing and plating within 500 miles from Denver, Colorado, and shall not set up, make, or encourage any opposition to the said trade or business hereafter to be carried on by the other party or his or her representatives or assigns, nor do anything to the prejudice thereof, and shall not divulge to any person any of the secrets, accounts, or transactions of or relating to the partnership.

It is recognized that damages, in the event of a breach by the retiring partner of the obligations and duties under this covenant, would be difficult to ascertain, and it is, therefore, agreed that the partnership in addition to, and without limiting any other power, remedy or right it may have, shall have the right to seek an injunction or other equitable relief in any court of competent jurisdiction, seeking to enjoin any such breach, and the retiring partner hereby waives any and all defenses he may have on the ground of lack of jurisdiction or competence of the court to grant such an injunction or other equitable relief. The existence of this right shall not preclude any other powers, rights, and remedies at law, in equity or otherwise which the partnership may have, but shall be in addition to, and cumulative with, any other remedy available to the partnership at law, in equity or otherwise.[50]

The continuation of a partnership business despite dissolution under the Revised Uniform Partnership Act involves many of the same considerations involved under the original law. An important additional feature of the revised act is **deferred dissolution**, which is a ninety-day period following a partner's withdrawal from the firm during which, if there is no agreement among the partners stating otherwise, the business of the partnership continues and the partner who is withdrawing may waive the right to have the partnership business wound up.[51] One can only imagine the pressure that might be placed on a withdrawing partner by fellow partners to encourage a waiver during the period. If there is no waiver during the ninety days, the partnership is regarded as dissolved, and its business must be wound up. During this deferred dissolution period, the withdrawing partner may not participate in management, is liable for obligations incurred (as though he or she were a "dissociated" partner), receives profits earned, and is charged with losses suffered (but only to the extent of the profits credited).[52]

Termination and Winding Up

In the event that the remaining partners do not desire to continue the business, a dissolution requires that the partnership be terminated and wound up. For these purposes, the remaining partners have the right to complete all pending partnership business and thereafter collect and dispose of the assets, pay the firm's creditors, and enjoy whatever is left. Depending upon the number of partners in the partnership, it may be desirable to appoint one partner to liquidate the business. Any remaining partner is eligible. If a liquidating partner is named in the original agreement, a successor should also be named in the event of that person's death. In any case, following a dissolution, a partner's authority to act for the partnership is limited to acts necessary to wind up the firm's affairs.[53]

State laws typically provide that in winding up a partnership, the partners must distribute the assets of the firm to pay the claims of

1. creditors other than partners;
2. partners other than for capital and profits;
3. partners in respect of capital; and
4. partners in respect of profits.[54]

The partners may agree to vary this distribution priority in any manner, except that partnership creditors, who are not bound by the terms of the partnership agreement, must always be completely satisfied before the partners are entitled to share the assets among themselves.

TAX CONSIDERATIONS OF A GENERAL PARTNERSHIP

A major consideration in the selection of the partnership as the appropriate form for a business enterprise is income taxation. The partnership itself pays no federal income tax. Instead, each partner is required to declare a share of the partnership income on his or her individual tax return. The partnership is thus treated as an aggregation of individuals for tax purposes, much like the sole proprietorship. The only difference is that the business income is divided among the partners in their respective proportions, rather than being applied completely to one person.

The partnership files an information tax return with the federal government on Form 1065. (See Exhibit 3–9, Form 1065.) The individual partners are furnished Schedule K-1 for their proportionate share of profits, losses, and other incidents of taxation. (See Exhibit 3–10, Schedule K-1.) These tax returns are used to ascertain whether the partners have declared and paid tax on their proportionate shares of income. It does not matter whether the profits have actually been distributed to the partners during the year. Even if profits are retained in the business, the partners must declare them as though they were distributed. When losses are considered, this rule can operate as an advantage of partnership taxation; all losses from the business are attributed personally to the partners and may be offset against personal income produced from other similar sources.

Because of the similarity of a partnership to a sole proprietorship for tax purposes, the sole proprietorship is not a viable alternative for tax advantage. A corporation, however, is taxed as an entity at special corporate rates, and a choice between a partnership and a corporation may depend on the tax differences. Under recent amendments to the Internal Revenue Code, a partnership could affirmatively elect to be taxed as a corporation (See Exhibit 3–11 Entity Classification Election), thus allowing it to achieve corporate tax advantages, such as the ability to accumulate profits to expand the business without requiring the individual partners to pay taxes on profits they have not received.[55] The comparison of corporate tax rates with individual tax rates is complicated because two or more persons are involved in the partnership. The business form that may be most desirable for one person may work as a disadvantage to the others. Each partner may have different incidents of taxation that are important in comparison to other partners who may not have the same types of income; for example, one partner may have significant amounts of income from other sources that are subject to minimum alternative taxes, or one partner may have substantial passive income that can be offset by passive losses from the partnership. Consequently, the only general statement that may be safely advanced regarding partnership tax considerations is that each case must be evaluated

Exhibit 3–9.

Form 1065

Form **1065**		**U.S. Return of Partnership Income**	OMB No. 1545-0099
Department of the Treasury Internal Revenue Service		For calendar year 2002, or tax year beginning ...., 2002, and ending ...., 20..... . See separate instructions.	**2002**

A Principal business activity	Use the IRS label. Other-wise, print or type.	Name of partnership	D Employer identification number
B Principal product or service		Number, street, and room or suite no. If a P.O. box, see page 14 of the instructions.	E Date business started
C Business code number		City or town, state, and ZIP code	F Total assets (see page 14 of the instructions) $

G Check applicable boxes: **(1)** ☐ Initial return **(2)** ☐ Final return **(3)** ☐ Name change **(4)** ☐ Address change **(5)** ☐ Amended return
H Check accounting method: **(1)** ☐ Cash **(2)** ☐ Accrual **(3)** ☐ Other (specify) ....
I Number of Schedules K-1. Attach one for each person who was a partner at any time during the tax year ....

Caution: Include **only** trade or business income and expenses on lines 1a through 22 below. See the instructions for more information.

Income

1a Gross receipts or sales	**1a**	
b Less returns and allowances	**1b**	**1c**
2 Cost of goods sold (Schedule A, line 8)		**2**
3 Gross profit. Subtract line 2 from line 1c		**3**
4 Ordinary income (loss) from other partnerships, estates, and trusts (attach schedule)		**4**
5 Net farm profit (loss) (attach Schedule F (Form 1040))		**5**
6 Net gain (loss) from Form 4797, Part II, line 18		**6**
7 Other income (loss) (attach schedule)		**7**
8 **Total income (loss).** Combine lines 3 through 7		**8**

Deductions (see page 15 of the instructions for limitations)

9 Salaries and wages (other than to partners) (less employment credits)		**9**
10 Guaranteed payments to partners		**10**
11 Repairs and maintenance		**11**
12 Bad debts		**12**
13 Rent		**13**
14 Taxes and licenses		**14**
15 Interest		**15**
16a Depreciation (if required, attach Form 4562)	**16a**	
b Less depreciation reported on Schedule A and elsewhere on return	**16b**	**16c**
17 Depletion **(Do not deduct oil and gas depletion.)**		**17**
18 Retirement plans, etc.		**18**
19 Employee benefit programs		**19**
20 Other deductions (attach schedule)		**20**
21 **Total deductions.** Add the amounts shown in the far right column for lines 9 through 20		**21**
22 **Ordinary income (loss)** from trade or business activities. Subtract line 21 from line 8		**22**

Sign Here

Under penalties of perjury, I declare that I have examined this return, including accompanying schedules and statements, and to the best of my knowledge and belief, it is true, correct, and complete. Declaration of preparer (other than general partner or limited liability company member) is based on all information of which preparer has any knowledge.

May the IRS discuss this return with the preparer shown below (see instructions)? ☐ Yes ☐ No

Signature of general partner or limited liability company member   Date

Paid Preparer's Use Only

Preparer's signature		Date	Check if self-employed ☐	Preparer's SSN or PTIN
Firm's name (or yours if self-employed), address, and ZIP code			EIN	
			Phone no. ( )	

For Paperwork Reduction Act Notice, see separate instructions.   Cat. No. 11390Z   Form **1065** (2002)

separately, based upon the potential profit or loss, the expected distributions from the business, and the individual financial positions and sources of income of the parties.

The sale of a partner's interest in the partnership usually results in a capital gain or loss much the same as does a shareholder's sale of corporate stock. When partnership property is sold, the capital gain or loss is attributable to the individual partner in the same proportion as are profits, unless altered by agreement. Since contributed property is partnership property, a special problem may arise with respect to its valuation for determining gain or loss. To illustrate the problem, consider the following case.

Murlin and Short formed a partnership with equal rights to profits. Murlin contributed $50,000 in cash and Short contributed a machine that had a fair market value of $50,000, but an adjusted basis (the cost to Short plus improvements by him) of $40,000. The basis of that

Exhibit 3–10.

Form K-1

SCHEDULE K-1 (Form 1065)	Partner's Share of Income, Credits, Deductions, etc.	OMB No. 1545-0099
Department of the Treasury Internal Revenue Service	See separate instructions. For calendar year 2002 or tax year beginning , 2002, and ending , 20	2002

Partner's identifying number | Partnership's identifying number

Partner's name, address, and ZIP code | Partnership's name, address, and ZIP code

A This partner is a ☐ general partner ☐ limited partner
☐ limited liability company member
B What type of entity is this partner? ....
C Is this partner a ☐ domestic or a ☐ foreign partner?

	(i) Before change or termination	(ii) End of year

D Enter partner's percentage of:
Profit sharing . . . . % .... %
Loss sharing . . . . % .... %
Ownership of capital . . . . % .... %
E IRS Center where partnership filed return:

F Partner's share of liabilities (see instructions):
Nonrecourse . . . . $ ....
Qualified nonrecourse financing . $ ....
Other . . . . $ ....

G Tax shelter registration number . ...

H Check here if this partnership is a publicly traded partnership as defined in section 469(k)(2) . . . . . . ☐

I Check applicable boxes: **(1)** ☐ Final K-1 **(2)** ☐ Amended K-1

J Analysis of partner's capital account:

(a) Capital account at beginning of year	(b) Capital contributed during year	(c) Partner's share of lines 3, 4, and 7, Form 1065, Schedule M-2	(d) Withdrawals and distributions	(e) Capital account at end of year (combine columns (a) through (d))
			( )	

(a) Distributive share item		(b) Amount	(c) 1040 filers enter the amount in column (b) on:
Income (Loss)	**1** Ordinary income (loss) from trade or business activities . . .	**1**	See page 6 of Partner's Instructions for Schedule K-1 (Form 1065).
	2 Net income (loss) from rental real estate activities	**2**	
	3 Net income (loss) from other rental activities	**3**	
	4 Portfolio income (loss):		
	a Interest	**4a**	Sch. B, Part I, line 1
	b Ordinary dividends	**4b**	Sch. B, Part II, line 5
	c Royalties	**4c**	Sch. E, Part I, line 4
	d Net short-term capital gain (loss)	**4d**	Sch. D, line 5, col. (f)
	e **(1)** Net long-term capital gain (loss).	**4e(1)**	Sch. D, line 12, col. (f)
	(2) 28% rate gain (loss)	**4e(2)**	Sch. D, line 12, col. (g)
	(3) Qualified 5-year gain	**4e(3)**	Line 5 of worksheet for Sch. D, line 29
	f Other portfolio income (loss) (attach schedule)	**4f**	Enter on applicable line of your return.
	5 Guaranteed payments to partner	**5**	See page 6 of Partner's Instructions for Schedule K-1 (Form 1065).
	6 Net section 1231 gain (loss) (other than due to casualty or theft)	**6**	
	7 Other income (loss) (attach schedule)	**7**	Enter on applicable line of your return.
Deductions	**8** Charitable contributions (see instructions) (attach schedule) . .	**8**	Sch. A, line 15 or 16
	9 Section 179 expense deduction	**9**	See pages 7 and 8 of Partner's Instructions for Schedule K-1 (Form 1065).
	10 Deductions related to portfolio income (attach schedule) . . .	**10**	
	11 Other deductions (attach schedule)	**11**	
Credits	**12a** Low-income housing credit:		
	(1) From section 42(j)(5) partnerships	**12a(1)**	Form 8586, line 5
	(2) Other than on line 12a(1)	**12a(2)**	
	b Qualified rehabilitation expenditures related to rental real estate activities	**12b**	
	c Credits (other than credits shown on lines 12a and 12b) related to rental real estate activities.	**12c**	See page 8 of Partner's Instructions for Schedule K-1 (Form 1065).
	d Credits related to other rental activities	**12d**	
	13 Other credits	**13**	

For Paperwork Reduction Act Notice, see Instructions for Form 1065.   Cat. No. 11394R   Schedule K-1 (Form 1065) 2002

machine to the partnership, for computing gain or loss, is the same as the basis to the individual: $40,000. If, during the year, the machine is sold at its fair market value of $50,000, the partnership receives a capital gain of $10,000, which is attributable to the partners in their respective proportions. Thus, both partners must claim a $5,000 capital gain that year. This should concern Murlin, who has now paid half the tax on Short's contributed asset. If Short had sold the machine when he owned it as an individual and contributed cash to the partnership, Short would have been individually responsible for the $10,000 gain.

Similarly, the rule may work a hardship on Short. Suppose the adjusted basis of the asset was $70,000 and Short contributed the machine when its fair market value was $50,000. When the machine is sold, the capital loss of $20,000 is shared between the partners. Murlin thereby acquires a tax benefit that Short really deserves.

Exhibit 3–11.

Form 8832
Entity Classification
Election

Form **8832**
(Rev. September 2002)
Department of the Treasury
Internal Revenue Service

Entity Classification Election

OMB No. 1545-1516

Type or Print

Name of entity

EIN

Number, street, and room or suite no. If a P.O. box, see instructions.

City or town, state, and ZIP code. If a foreign address, enter city, province or state, postal code and country.

1 **Type of election** (see instructions):

a ☐ Initial classification by a newly-formed entity.

b ☐ Change in current classification.

2 **Form of entity** (see instructions):

a ☐ A domestic eligible entity electing to be classified as an association taxable as a corporation.

b ☐ A domestic eligible entity electing to be classified as a partnership.

c ☐ A domestic eligible entity with a single owner electing to be disregarded as a separate entity.

d ☐ A foreign eligible entity electing to be classified as an association taxable as a corporation.

e ☐ A foreign eligible entity electing to be classified as a partnership.

f ☐ A foreign eligible entity with a single owner electing to be disregarded as a separate entity.

3 **Disregarded entity information** (see instructions):
a Name of owner
b Identifying number of owner
c Country of organization of entity electing to be disregarded (if foreign)

4 Election is to be effective beginning (month, day, year) (see instructions) ▸ _____ / _____ / _____

5 Name and title of person whom the IRS may call for more information

6 That person's telephone number
(   )

Consent Statement and Signature(s) (see instructions)

Under penalties of perjury, I (we) declare that I (we) consent to the election of the above-named entity to be classified as indicated above, and that I (we) have examined this consent statement, and to the best of my (our) knowledge and belief, it is true, correct, and complete. If I am an officer, manager, or member signing for all members of the entity, I further declare that I am authorized to execute this consent statement on their behalf.

Signature(s)	Date	Title

For Paperwork Reduction Act Notice, see page 4.

Cat. No. 22598R

Form **8832** (Rev. 9-2002)

In cases like this one, complicated matters arise in determining the fair allocation of depreciation on the asset between the parties. The Internal Revenue Code formerly offered a solution to the problem by permitting the parties to agree to the manner in which depreciation, depletion, gain, or loss of contributed property would be allocated between the partners to account for variations of this sort.[56] However, current tax law requires that all income, gain, loss, and deductions from property contributed to the partnership be shared among partners so as to account for variations between the basis of the property to the partnership and the property's fair market value at the time of contribution, regardless of the partners' desires as specified in the partnership agreement.[57] A clause in the agreement should address this issue so that partners are not surprised by the tax consequences that may result from contributed property.

EXAMPLE	**Allocation of Tax-related Items**

The partners understand that for income tax purposes the partnership's adjusted basis of property contributed by Maynard Short differs from the fair market value at which such property was accepted by the partnership at the time of its contribution. The partners recognize and understand that in determining the taxable income or loss of the partnership and the distributive share of each partner's depreciation or gain or loss with respect to such contributed property, the Internal Revenue Code requires that such items be shared among the partners so as to take account of the variation between the basis of the property to the partnership and its fair market value at the time of contribution.

Many other tax considerations apply to the partnership form, most of which are complicated because the partnership operates as an entity, acquiring property and earning money as an apparently separate legal unit, but is treated merely as an aggregation of individuals for tax purposes. Thus, the distribution of current assets or of assets during liquidation, the determination of the partnership's taxable year, and the transfer of partnership interests all pose unique tax problems that are beyond the scope of this text but are ably covered by other authors[58] (See Exhibit 3–11, Form 8832).

FORMATION AND OPERATION OF A GENERAL PARTNERSHIP

In many respects, the formation of a general partnership parallels the formation of a sole proprietorship. The obvious difference is the most important formality for the partnership: the agreement.

Selection of a Name

A partnership may operate under any name it chooses, provided the name is not deceptively similar to that of another company so as to constitute a deceptive trade practice. As with sole proprietorships, most states require registration of any fictitious partnership name under the assumed name statutes.[59]

If all of the partners' surnames are used in the firm name, the name is not considered to be fictitious; if fewer than all of the partners' names are used in the firm title, the name is fictitious. Thus, a partnership formed by Levine, Conviser, and Chess may use all names without registration, but if the firm name is Levine and Chess, registration is required. Similarly, the name Levine & Co. would require registration.

The sanctions imposed on a partnership for failure to file the assumed name information are the same as those imposed upon sole proprietors.[60]

Governmental Formalities

Partnerships may conduct any legal business in the same manner as may a natural person. Where state law imposes particular licensing requirements, the partnership must conform. Consequently, sales tax licenses must be obtained where appropriate, and the partnership must obtain any necessary licenses peculiar to the particular business conducted.

Tax identification numbers are necessary for partnerships, since informational returns are filed annually with federal and state authorities. If employees are hired, social security and unemployment compensation laws must be considered.

Interstate Business

Partnerships are not usually subject to any peculiar formalities for doing business in states other than the state in which the firm is formed. They must, however, comply with local licensing requirements, and the name of the firm must be registered appropriately with the foreign state. A few states, including California and New Hampshire, require qualification of a **foreign partnership**—a registered office and statutory agent (who accepts receipt of important documents, like service of process) must be present within the state, and a fee must be paid for the privilege of doing business in that state.[61] This qualification procedure is not popular, however, and is clearly a minority approach to interstate general partnership business.

The Agreement

Without the partnership agreement, the simple organizational formalities for the partnership would be extremely attractive. The partnership is organized in essentially the same manner as the sole proprietorship. It is even possible to form a partnership with nothing more than a handshake agreement to do business together. However, as the previous discussions of the nature of the partnership have demonstrated, that informality is usually a fatal oversight.

An old axiom states that one should never be a partner with a friend, recognizing the common tendency of human nature toward disagreement in business transactions. Eventually there will be some discord (or at least a friendly disagreement) between the parties, and an informal agreement offers no guidance whatever in the resolution of such disputes. Thus, the only proper practice requires the drafting of a comprehensive agreement between the parties, carefully specifying their purposes, contributions, management authority, voting powers, duties, rights, and responsibilities.

The partnership agreement, which is occasionally called the **articles of partnership**, must be tailored to the specific desires of the future partners. The following checklist with examples and references to the detailed discussions in this chapter may be used as a guide for preparing the agreement.[62]

Checklist

1. Names and addresses of the partners.

EXAMPLE

Agreement

Agreement made this ____ day of _____, 20____, between James A. Murlin, whose address is 526 Park Avenue, New York, New York, and Maynard P. Short, whose address is 1901 K Street, N.W., Washington, D.C., (hereinafter referred to as individuals or collectively as "Partners").

---

2. **Recitals**—The background of the partners' business relationship may be stated in order to explain the agreement. Recitals of such information are inserted at the beginning of the agreement. The recitals further serve to state the intent to form a partnership and may explain the business objectives of the enterprise. They recite the factual background of the agreement.

EXAMPLE

Recitals

WHEREAS, Murlin has acquired certain business expertise in the manufacturing and marketing of rubber bicycle tires; and

WHEREAS, Short has the financial ability to contribute certain sums of money for the manufacturing and marketing of rubber bicycle tires; and

WHEREAS the parties intend to operate a business for the manufacture and marketing of rubber bicycle tires and desire to do so under the form of a partnership;

NOW, THEREFORE, it is agreed:

---

3. **Name of the partnership**—If the firm name does not contain the surnames of the individual partners, a trade name affidavit is required (see "Selection of a Name" earlier in this section).

EXAMPLE

Name

The name of the Partnership shall be Shoylin Associates.

4. **Place of business**—The proposed offices of the firm should be stated, with permission for the partners to establish other offices as appropriate. If the firm will operate branch offices and their locations are known, those locations should be specified. If a multistate business is contemplated, the partners should have authority to establish offices in other states.

EXAMPLE

Place of Business

The principal place of business of the firm shall be located at 526 Park Avenue, New York, New York, or such other place as shall be designated by the partners from time to time. Branch offices may be located at 156 Cayuga Street, Ithaca, New York, and at a street address to be determined by agreement of the partners in Albany, New York. The partnership shall be authorized to conduct business and to establish offices in locations to be selected by agreement of the partners in the states of Connecticut, Rhode Island, and Pennsylvania.

5. **Purposes**—The description of the partnership business should be included in general terms, unless restrictive language is dictated by the partners' objectives. Any intended restrictions upon the scope of the partnership's business should be detailed, or, following a specific description of the contemplated purposes, the agreement may provide that the partnership will operate "no other business." Be certain to include a provision that allows the partners to *agree* to enter into other ventures so the agreement will not be unduly restrictive.

EXAMPLE

Nature of Business

The partnership shall engage in the business of manufacturing and marketing rubber bicycle tires, and in such other lawful business as is permitted in the jurisdiction of formation and as may be agreed upon from time to time by the partners.

[*or*]

The partnership shall engage in the business of manufacturing and marketing rubber bicycle tires, and shall not engage in any other business or activity except as shall be directly related and incident to such business or except as shall be agreed upon from time to time by the partners.

6. **Duration**—
   (a) The partnership may be formed for a definite term.
   (b) The partnership may be subject to termination by mutual agreement.
   (c) The partnership may be terminable at will when one partner gives the specified notice to the other partners.
   (d) The partnership may be terminated upon the completion of its purposes (e.g., the sale of a parcel of real estate).
   (e) The partnership may be terminated upon the happening of a contingent event (e.g., continuous losses for a specified period).
   (f) The partnership may be terminated under any combination of the preceding conditions.

EXAMPLE

Duration

The partnership shall begin on May 1, 2005, and shall continue for the term of ten years thereafter.

[*or*]

The partnership shall continue for the full term of five years from the date of this agreement, and thereafter until thirty days' written notice is given by any of the partners to the others.

7. **Capital**—The capital contributions of the partners should be described in detail. There are many possible variations of contributions (see "Partnership Property" and "Tax Considerations of a General Partnership" earlier in this chapter), but the following situations are most typical.

   (a) The partners' contributions will be cash. The agreement should specify the amount of the contribution and the time of payment.

Capital

The capital of the partnership shall be contributed in cash by the partners as follows:
James A. Murlin $50,000
Maynard P. Short $30,000
Such contribution shall be paid in full on or before May 10, 2005.

   (b) One or more of the partners will contribute services. The value of the services and the treatment of the respective capital accounts should be discussed.

Contribution of Services

James A. Murlin shall not be required to make a cash or property contribution to the partnership but shall devote his entire time to the partnership, and for such he shall be entitled to twenty percent (20%) of the profits to be divided [*term for division*] among the partners. In the event that his monthly share of the profits shall exceed thirty thousand dollars ($30,000), he shall contribute the excess to his capital account of business until the total amount of such contributions shall equal the capital contributions made by each of the other partners.

   (c) One or more of the partners will contribute tangible property. The agreed value of the property should be specified. Further, if the cost of the property to the contributing partner and the agreed value of the contribution are different, it is appropriate to consider and describe the tax consequences of the precontribution gain or loss in the agreement (see "Tax Considerations of a General Partnership" earlier in this chapter).

Contribution of Property

Maynard P. Short shall contribute property which the partners agree will be valued at ten thousand dollars ($10,000). Such property is described in Schedule A attached hereto.

   (d) The partners may be required to furnish additional capital. The agreement should specify the circumstances under which additional contributions may be assessed (e.g., in the event of continuous losses for a specified period, or upon the vote of the majority of the partners). The partners' respective proportions for additional contributions and the procedure by which the partners will be notified of the contributions should be specified.

Additional Capital Contributions

In the event that the cash funds of the partnership are insufficient to meet its operating expenses, the partners shall make additional capital contributions, in the same proportions in which they share the net profits of the firm.

The managing partner, after determining a cash deficit, shall notify the other partners in writing at least ten (10) days prior to the date upon which such cash funds are needed, and each partner shall be required to make such additional contributions on the date specified in the notice, or if none, on the tenth day after the date of the notice.

(e) Excess contributions may be construed as advances and may be treated as loans to the firm. The authority to make such loans comes from the agreement, which should specify the need for the consent of the other partners, the amount of the loan, and any desired restriction on the frequency of such advances.

EXAMPLE

Loans and Advances

Any of the partners may, from time to time, with the consent of all of the other partners, advance sums of money to the partnership by way of loan, and each such advance shall bear interest at the rate of twelve percent (12%) per annum.

(f) Profits may be accumulated as capital.

EXAMPLE

Accumulated Profits

Each of the partners shall be required to allow to remain in the business each year as a contribution to net worth of the partnership capital, an amount equal to thirty percent (30%) of the partnership profits which would otherwise be distributed to him or her. Such contributions shall be allocated to or reserved in accounts for each of the partners, and shall remain in the business and be employed as capital for the business subject to further direction and order of the partners.

(g) Capital may accumulate interest if the agreement so provides. If the partners agree that capital contributions should not accumulate interest, a statement to that effect should be included.

EXAMPLE

Interest on Capital

No interest shall be paid to the partners on any contributions to capital.
[*or*]
Each of the partners shall be entitled to interest at the rate of ten percent (10%) per annum on the amount of his or her respective contributions, payable semiannually, on June 1 and December 1, of each calendar year.

(h) If withdrawal of capital contributions is to be permitted, the agreement should detail the circumstances of withdrawal, limitations upon the amount of the withdrawal, if any, and any requirements for replenishing the capital account at specified times.

EXAMPLE

Withdrawal of Capital

Each of the partners may withdraw from the partnership, for his or her own use, a sum not exceeding seven thousand dollars ($7,000) per month. If, at the close of each fiscal year, it is found that any partner's share withdrawn by him or her is in excess of his or her distributive share for that fiscal year, he or she shall forthwith refund the difference within a period not exceeding five days from the time of such determination.

(i) If one partner allows profits to accumulate in a greater proportion than do the others, the excess may be described as a debt owed to that partner, and the agreement may provide an interest rate to be applied to the excess amount so that the partner is compensated for disproportionately leaving his or her profits to be invested in the business.

Individual Accumulation of Profit

All profits of the partnership during the year shall be allocated to the partners in their respective proportions in an income account which shall be subject to withdrawal by any partner from time to time. If a partner does not withdraw all of his or her income account during the year, the excess amount, not withdrawn, shall be treated as a loan to the partnership by the partner, and shall accumulate interest at the rate of ten percent (10%) per annum on the amount of the income account not withdrawn at the close of each calendar year, so long as such amount shall remain in the income account and is not withdrawn by the partner.

8. **Salaries and expenses—**
   (a) Since partners are not ordinarily entitled to remuneration for their services (see "Management of a Partnership"), the authority to pay salaries must be established by the agreement. Salaries may be contingent upon profits, or may be fixed by the agreement.

Salaries

There shall be paid to each partner the following monthly salaries: To James A. Murlin, three thousand dollars; to Maynard P. Short, five thousand dollars; *etc.* No increase in salaries shall be made without unanimous agreement. The payment of salaries to partners shall be an obligation of the partnership only to the extent that partnership assets are available therefor, and shall not be an obligation of the partners individually. Salaries shall, to this extent, be treated as an expense of the partnership in determining profits or losses.

   (b) Expense accounts are common in business partnerships. The agreement should establish a maximum periodic amount, a procedure for submitting expenses, and a procedure for reimbursement. The agreement also should specify that only expenses incurred in furtherance of the partnership business will be reimbursed.

Expenses

An expense account, not to exceed one thousand dollars ($1,000) per month, shall be provided for each partner for his or her actual, reasonable, and necessary expenses in engaging in the business and pursuits of the partnership. Each partner shall be required to keep an itemized record of such expenses and shall be paid once each month upon the submission of such statements of records.

9. **Profits, losses, deductions, and credits—**The agreement should establish a method for determining profit and loss. Simply providing for a determination of profit or loss by the partnership's accountant (or bookkeeper) using generally accepted accounting principles creates an objective standard for the determination that should avoid most disputes. However, the phrase "generally accepted accounting principles" sometimes baffles even the accountants who use it, if it is necessary for those accountants to justify the methods upon which they have determined financial information. It may be preferable to select a method of accounting, such as cash or accrual, and to specify that method as the partnership accounting procedure. Frequently, partnership agreements provide that income and loss will be determined on the same basis as that required for federal income tax purposes, so that accountants do not have to create separate financial statements for a partnership's internal use and for federal income tax reporting purposes. It may be desirable to allow for any partner to question a profit and loss determination by permitting another accountant (at the challenging partner's expense) to determine, independently, profits or

losses, and then permitting arbitration (or some other objective determination) if the results vary more than a stated percentage from the original amount.

In some cases, extraordinary expenses are involved, such as legal fees for litigation or unusual travel and entertainment in the start-up period of the business. These expenses may be detailed in the agreement and excluded from the normal profit and loss computation so that they may be shared in some other agreed proportion. Profits, losses, deductions (reductions of taxable income), and credits (reductions of tax) are usually shared in the same proportions, but not necessarily.[63] This clause is especially tailored to the desires of the partners. Some common schemes are as follows:

(a) sharing profits, losses, deductions, and credits equally;
(b) sharing profits, losses, deductions, and credits according to the proportion of capital contributions;
(c) allocating all items primarily to the partner who provides financial backing until he or she receives profits (or tax benefits) equal to the capital contributed, then making a primary allocation to the managing partner who is producing those profits;
(d) requiring that losses caused by the willful neglect or default of a partner be borne by that partner; and
(e) guaranteeing profits for certain partners, which usually requires the other partners to contribute any deficiency if the annual profit distribution does not exceed a certain amount.

EXAMPLE

Allocations of Profits, Losses, Deductions, and Credits

Seventy percent (70%) of the net profits and losses of the partnership, and each item of income, gain, loss, deduction, or credit entering into the computation thereof, shall be allocated to the partners other than the Managing General Partner in accordance with their respective capital contributions. Thirty percent (30%) of such net profits and losses, and items of income, gain, loss, deduction, or credit entering into the computation thereof, shall be allocated to the Managing General Partner.

---

10. **Cash distributions**—A partnership is a unique entity that allows for accumulations of cash when the business is actually producing a "paper" loss. For example, if the partnership operates an apartment building, depreciation and interest may reduce the profits of the partnership (and may actually produce a loss) even when rental receipts exceed operating expenses. The agreement should provide for distributions of cash to the partners in certain proportions, and this determination can be made separately from the distribution of profits, losses, deductions, and credits. Again, the specific desires of the partners should be observed. Some common methods of cash distribution include the following:
(a) in the same proportion as profits, losses, deductions, and credits are shared;
(b) to the partners who contributed cash or property as capital contributions, to the exclusion of any partner who is contributing only services, until a certain proportion of the contributed amount has been recovered;
(c) to the partner who needs it the most, at least for a period of time; and
(d) to the partner who will be required to pay the most taxes as a result of partnership operations, thereby permitting that partner to pay the taxes from the cash distributed.

EXAMPLE

Cash Distributions

One hundred percent (100%) of the net cash of the partnership shall be allocated to the partners other than the Managing General Partner in accordance with their respective capital contributions for the first three years of the operation of the business, and no cash shall be allocated to the Managing General Partner during that time. Thereafter, twenty percent (20%) of the net cash of the partnership shall be allocated to the partners other than the Managing General Partner, and eighty percent (80%) of the net cash shall be allocated to the Managing General Partner.

11. **Books and records—**

   (a) The **fiscal year** of the partnership must be established. The taxable year of the partnership is determined, for tax purposes, as though the partnership were a taxpayer. Normally this means that the taxable year must be the same for the partnership as for the partners who have an interest in the partnership profits and capital of greater than 50%. If the partners are individuals, that means the partnership's taxable year is the calendar year. The partnership can have a different taxable year only if it establishes a legitimate business purpose for a fiscal year different from the calendar year.

Fiscal Year

EXAMPLE

The fiscal year of the partnership shall be from November 1 until October 31.

[or]

The fiscal year of the partnership shall be the calendar year.

   (b) The method of accounting for the firm (accrual or cash) should be established. The agreement should provide that while generally accepted accounting principles will govern any matters not specifically covered by its terms, the method of accounting used for federal income tax purposes will be used for reports to partners. This avoids the cost of converting the accounting entries from the tax-basis reporting to generally accepted accounting principles when the accounting rules are different.

Method of Accounting

EXAMPLE

The partnership shall keep accounts on the accrual [*or* cash] basis. The accounts shall readily disclose items which the partners take into account separately for income tax purposes. As to matters of accounting not provided for in this agreement, generally accepted accounting principles shall govern.

   (c) The location of the firm's books and records must be established, and the partners' access to the books should be considered. Any restrictions upon a partner's right to inspect or copy books and records will be included here. For example, if an investment partner were also the owner of a supplying business, the agreement might limit that partner's access to the firm's vendor lists.

Location of Books

EXAMPLE

The partnership books shall be kept at the principal place of business of the partnership, and every partner shall at all times have access to and may inspect and copy any of them. [*Or,* all partners shall have access to such books and records only upon 72 hours prior written notice to the managing partner and during normal business hours.]

   (d) The bank accounts and other banking arrangements are stated in the agreement, including the persons authorized to sign checks, to borrow funds, and to otherwise conduct banking transactions on behalf of the firm.

Banking Arrangements

EXAMPLE

The partnership shall maintain such bank accounts as the partners shall determine. Checks shall be drawn for partnership purposes only and may be signed by any partner or partners designated by the partners. All moneys received by the partnership shall be deposited in such account or accounts.

(e) Provisions should be included for the rendering of periodic reports to partners (e.g., monthly, quarterly, semiannually, or annually). The partners may be required to sign and verify the reports, subject to objection for manifest errors within a specified period of time.

EXAMPLE

Reports of Operations

The managing partner shall provide reports of cash activity, profit or loss, and the current balance sheet of the partnership to each partner at least quarterly, within 15 days following the close of the calendar quarter of the partnership. Each partner shall be required to signify his or her receipt of such reports by signing a duplicate copy of the reports and returning the same to the managing partner within ten days following receipt of such reports. Any objections or questions concerning such reports must be addressed to the managing partner within 30 days following the receipt of the reports by each partner or the reports shall be deemed to be correct as to the matters presented therein.

(f) The person responsible for keeping the partnership books should be named.

EXAMPLE

Responsibility for Records

The managing partner shall be responsible for the partnership books and records and shall maintain the same at the principal place of business of the partnership. The managing partner may, upon notice to the other partners, delegate persons to assume the obligations of keeping the partnership records.

(g) An audit by independent certified public accountants may be appropriate for some financially complicated businesses, and the agreement will authorize such an audit.

EXAMPLE

Audit of Books and Records

As soon as practical after the close of the partnership's calendar year, the managing partner shall engage an independent certified public accountant to audit the partnership books and records, and shall provide copies of the audit report furnished by such accountant to each of the partners.

[or]

Each partner shall be entitled to engage the services of an independent certified public accountant to audit the books and records of the partnership following the close of the partnership's calendar year. The partner so desiring such audit shall pay all expenses and fees of the accountant, and no such expenses shall be assessed against the partnership, unless the results of the audit indicate a variance of over or under ten percent of the profit and loss reported to the partners by the managing partner in any calendar year, in which event the expenses of the audit shall be borne by the partnership as a partnership expense.

12. **Meetings**—Partners' meetings may be established on a regular basis by the agreement, specifying the time and place for such meetings. Special meetings may be called in accordance with the agreement. A clause authorizing special meetings should consider the parties who are entitled to call special meetings, the notice required, and whether the notice must specify the purpose of the meeting.

EXAMPLE

Meetings

Partners' meetings will be held on the second Tuesday of each month at 5:00 p.m. at the principal place of business of the partnership. No notice shall be required for the regular meetings of the partnership. A special meeting may be called by any partner upon giving three days' written notice to the other partners, specifying a time and place for the meeting and the purpose of the meeting.

13. **Management—**
(a) Method of management (see "Management of a Partnership" earlier in this chapter)—The management of the business affairs of the firm must be conducted in accordance with the agreement. One or more of the partners may have a specialized business skill, and this should not be overlooked. Many variations are possible for management activities, including the following:
   (1) Each partner has an equal voice in management.
   (2) Some partners (usually those with larger capital contributions) have a greater vote than others.
   (3) A committee of partners is established to make certain decisions.
   (4) A managing partner (or partners) is appointed to control the daily business affairs of the firm.
   (5) Some partners, usually called *dormant* or **silent partners**, have no management activities under the agreement.

Equal Management

EXAMPLE

Management and the conduct of the business of the partnership shall be vested in all partners, and no partner shall be solely responsible for management functions. The partners shall have an equal vote on all partnership matters, and all issues to be resolved in the partnership shall be determined by a majority vote.

Other-Than-Equal Management

EXAMPLE

Management and the conduct of the business shall be vested in all Partners, and no Partner shall be solely responsible for management functions. The Partners shall have the following votes on Partnership matters:

Peter J. McLaughlin	11
James T. Johnston	33
Steve Forness	11
John Anderson	11
Thomas Stubbs	33
Michael Theisen	1

A quorum shall be the presence at a meeting of 51 votes. No Partnership matter may be approved except at a meeting in which a quorum of votes is represented in the manner provided in this Paragraph, or as otherwise provided in this agreement.

(b) **Management duties—**
   (1) If a managing partner is used, the managing partner's duties should be specified in the agreement. Moreover, any management decisions that are to be referred to all of the partners should be described.

Duties of a Managing Partner

EXAMPLE

a) The affairs of the Partnership shall be managed and conducted by the Managing General Partner in accordance with the provisions of the Colorado Uniform Partnership Act, as amended, and subject to the terms and provisions of this Agreement.

b) The Managing General Partner shall devote such of his or her time as may be necessary to select, at his or her sole discretion, and to acquire master recordings for the Partnership; to retain a distributor for the recordings owned by the Partnership; to supervise the activities of the distributor and to hire replacement or additional distributors if deemed necessary by the Managing General Partner; to make inspections of any physical assets owned by the Partnership and to see to it that such assets are being properly maintained; to prepare or cause to be prepared all reports of operations which are to be furnished to the Partners or which are required by any government agencies; and to do all other things which may be necessary to supervise the affairs and businesses of the Partnership in a prudent and businesslike manner in the best interest of the Partners.

c) The Managing General Partner is hereby authorized, on behalf of the Partnership, to execute any contracts, notes, or other documents that may be required in connection with the acquisition, financing, and operation of the assets and business described in this Agreement.

d) The Managing General Partner, in addition to the other powers and rights granted to him or her and subject to the specific limitations imposed by this Agreement, shall have the right, upon such terms and conditions as he or she may deem proper, to (1)borrow money on the general credit of the Partnership for use in the Partnership business, including the right to borrow money from himself or herself and to charge the Partnership interest on funds so borrowed, provided the interest rate to be charged by the Managing General Partner for such borrowed funds shall not exceed the rate available from commercial lenders, and provided the Managing General Partner shall not further encumber any master recordings acquired by the Partnership after their initial acquisition, other than in the ordinary course of business, without the approval of the Partners; (2)purchase personal property for use in connection with the business of the Partnership and finance such purchases, in whole or in part, by giving the seller or any other person a security interest in the property purchased; (3)make reasonable and necessary capital expenditures and improvements with respect to the assets of the Partnership and take all action reasonably necessary in connection with the management thereof; (4)establish a reasonable reserve for contingencies and operating capital from available cash flow of the Partnership; (5)contract with himself or herself and affiliated persons on terms competitive with those which may be obtained in the open market for property or services required by the Partnership, provided, however, that the Managing General Partner shall not receive from himself or herself, or affiliated persons, or grant to himself or herself, or affiliated persons, any rebates, kickbacks, or give-ups, directly or indirectly, in such transactions or agreements; (6)make reasonable and necessary expenditures for the maintenance and operation of the assets of the Partnership; and (7)enter into agreements for the management of the assets of the Partnership.

e) The Managing General Partner shall assume a fiduciary responsibility for the safekeeping and use of all Partnership funds and assets, whether or not in his or her immediate possession or control, and shall not employ, or permit another to employ, such funds or assets in any manner except for the exclusive benefit of the Partnership. Partnership funds shall not be commingled with the funds of any other person or entity.

f) The Managing General Partner shall not cause the Partnership to purchase interests in other business organizations, underwrite the securities of any other businesses, offer Partnership interests in exchange for anything other than cash or notes, or make loans to other persons or entities.

g) Except where power or duties are reserved to the Managing General Partner, other Partnership matters shall be determined by the unanimous vote of the Partners.

Limitations on Powers of the Managing General Partner

The Managing General Partner shall have full, exclusive, and complete discretion in the management of and control over the affairs of the Partnership; provided, however, the Managing General Partner shall not take any of the following actions without the consent of all Partners:

a) sale, exchange, or other disposition of all or substantially all of the Partnership's assets other than in the ordinary course of business;

b) refinancing, recasting, increasing, modifying, or extending any loans secured in whole or in part by master recordings owned by the Partnership, other than in the ordinary course of business;

c) sale, assignment, or encumbrance of the Managing General Partner's interest in the Partnership;

d) admission of a Successor Managing General Partner to the Partnership;

e) admission of additional Partners to the Partnership;

f) engagement of the Partnership in a business other than that specified in this Agreement; and

g) amendment or modification of this Agreement unless that amendment or modification is otherwise permitted under this Agreement without action of all Partners.

(2) All partners are expected to devote their time and energies to the partnership business.[64] Any deviation from this rule must be detailed in the agreement.

Outside Activities

No partner shall engage in, or invest or deal in the securities of, any business that in any wise competes with that of this firm, nor shall he or she give any time or attention to any outside business, except that of bank director, without the written consent of his or her copartners.

(3) Each partner should be required, upon request, to account to the other partners regarding all transactions relating to the partnership business of which that partner has knowledge.

Reports of Activities

The managing partner shall, at least ten days prior to the regular meeting of the partnership, specify which of the partners are to report on areas of the partnership business within their control and responsibility. Such reports may be furnished orally at the meeting, unless the managing partner requires a written report in the notice, in which case a copy of the report shall be distributed to the partners at the meeting and appended to the minutes of the partnership meeting.

(4) The agreement may require certain partners to provide a bond for faithful performance of their management duties. For example, if certain partners were delegated the responsibilities of accounting for trust funds for clients of the partnership, it may be appropriate to insure against the possibility of their theft of the funds.

Fidelity Bond

The managing partner shall, at the expense of the partnership, acquire and maintain a fidelity bond in the amount of $1,000,000 with an insurance company acceptable to a majority of the partners. The bond shall provide for the payment upon such bond for any willful failure or neglect of the managing partner to perform his or her duties hereunder, upon defalcation or embezzlement by the managing partner, upon the loss to the partnership of any asset as a result of the negligence of the managing partner, and upon such other terms and conditions as may be required by the majority of the partners.

(c) **Management formula**—Depending upon the management method selected (e.g., equal voice, managing partner, etc.), the agreement will state a formula for determining partnership action. For example, if all partners have an equal voice, the formula may require a majority, two-thirds, or unanimous vote to carry action on behalf of the firm. The decision of a managing partner is usually final on matters within his or her control. In certain cases, unanimity of partners will be required by law.[65]

(d) **Disputes**—In case of a deadlocked dispute on management matters, the agreement usually requires submission of the dispute to an independent third party or to arbitration.

Arbitration

All disputes and questions whatsoever which shall, either during the partnership or afterwards, arise between the partners or their respective representatives, or between any partners or between a partner and the representative of any other or others, touching these articles, or the construction or application thereof, or any clause or thing herein contained, or any account, valuation, or division of assets, debts, or liabilities to be made hereunder, or as to any act, deed, or omission of any partner, or as to any other matter in any way relating to the partnership business or the affairs thereof, or the rights, duties, or liabilities of any person under these articles, shall be referred to a single arbitrator in case the parties agree upon one; otherwise to two arbitrators, one to be appointed by each party to the difference, or in case of their disagreement to an umpire, to be appointed by said arbitrators.

(e) **Prohibited activities—**[66]

(1) Certain matters affecting the partnership must be decided by all partners, including assignment of the partnership property in trust for creditors, sale of the goodwill of the business, confession of judgment against the firm, submission of a partnership claim to arbitration, and other acts that would make it impossible to carry out the partnership business.

EXAMPLE

Limitation on a Partner's Authority

No partner shall, without the unanimous consent of the other partners, do any of the following acts:
a) assignment of the partnership property in trust for creditors;
b) sale of the goodwill of the business or substantially all of the assets of the business;
c) confess a judgment against the partnership or its assets;
d) submit a partnership claim to arbitration; or
e) commit any other act that would make it impossible to carry out the partnership business.

---

(2) Partners may be further restricted in their power to bind the firm. An individual partner usually is not permitted to extend credit, pledge the partnership property, hire and fire employees, cause an attachment of firm property, or release debts without the appropriate consensus of the other partners.

EXAMPLE

Further Limitations on a Partner's Authority

No partner shall, without the consent of the others, borrow or lend money on behalf of the partnership; sell, assign, or pledge his or her interest in the partnership; or execute any lease, mortgage, security agreement, or endorsement on behalf of the partnership. No purchase or other contract involving a liability of more than five thousand dollars, nor any importation from abroad, shall be made, nor any transaction out of the usual course of the retail business shall be undertaken, by either of the partners without the previous consent and approval of the other partner.

---

(3) It may be desirable to govern the private lives of the partners in certain respects, for example, to forbid any partner from going into debt except for living necessaries, to restrict a partner's ability to deal in securities on margin, to demand that a partner discharge any filed liens against that partner's property within a thirty-day period, and so on.

EXAMPLE

Limitation on Extraordinary Debts

In order to protect the property and assets of the Partnership from any claim against any Partner for personal debts owed by such Partner, each Partner shall promptly pay all debts owing by him or her and shall indemnify the Partnership from any claim that might be made to the detriment of the Partnership by any personal creditor of such Partner.

---

(4) The partners may be restricted in their sale or assignment of any or all of their interests in the partnership.[67] Common restrictions include the requirement of consent by the other partners, or a right of first refusal for the other partners, permitting them to purchase the interest at the offered price.

Sale of a Partner's Interest

In the event that a Partner desires to sell, assign, or otherwise transfer his or her share of interest in the Partnership hereby created and has obtained a bona fide offer for the sale thereof made by some person not a member of this Partnership, he or she shall first offer to sell, assign, or otherwise transfer the said interest to the other Partners at the price and on the same terms as previously offered him or her, and each other Partner shall have the right to purchase his or her proportionate share of the selling Partner's interest. If any Partner does not desire to purchase the said interest on such terms or at such price, no other Partner may purchase any part of the interest, and the selling Partner may then sell, assign, or otherwise transfer his or her entire interest in the Partnership to the person making the said offer at the price offered. The intent of this provision is to require that the entire interest of a Partner be sold intact, without fractionalization. A purchaser of an interest of the Partnership shall not become a Partner without the unanimous consent of the nonselling Partners.

14. **Partnership property—**
    (a) The name in which partnership property will be titled is established by the agreement.

Title to Property

All assets of the partnership shall be titled in the name of the partnership, Shoylin Associates.

   (b) If any property is loaned to the firm by a partner, it should be separately described and the agreement should detail the duration of the loan, any restrictions upon the disposition of the property by the partner, and any compensation to be paid to the partner for the use of the asset.[68]

Loans of Property by a Partner

Maynard P. Short has loaned to the partnership, and by this agreement, agrees to the exclusive use of the partnership, all of the property listed and described on Exhibit B, attached to this agreement and incorporated herein by reference. The partnership shall have exclusive use and enjoyment of the property for a period of one year from the date of this agreement, and for successive annual periods, unless, prior to the expiration of an annual term, Mr. Short gives written notice of at least 30 days to the partnership of his intention to reacquire the possession and use of the property. So long as the partnership shall be in possession of the property, Mr. Short shall not assign, sell, encumber, or otherwise deal with such property, and any such action by Mr. Short shall be deemed to be a breach of this agreement. The partnership shall pay Mr. Short the sum of $10,000 per year in equal quarterly installments for the use of the property described on Exhibit B.

   (c) Accounting procedures for partnership property, including the treatment of depreciation, repairs, insurance, taxes, interest, and other expenses, should be considered.

Method of Accounting for Assets

All accounting for partnership assets shall be done according to generally accepted accounting procedures, using the most conservative methods of accounting for depreciation, investment tax credits, etc. The managing partner shall be directed to provide for depreciation, repairs, insurance, taxes, interest, and other reserves as necessary for partnership operations in order to meet such operating and capital expenses when they are incurred.

15. **Causes of dissolution—**[69]
    (a) **Retirement or withdrawal—**
        (1) The agreement may describe the circumstances under which a partner may retire. Most agreements permit the partner to retire and withdraw at any time after a certain date or after the partner has reached a certain age.

(2) Notice of retirement or withdrawal is usually required to be given to the other partners.

(3) A noncompetition clause may be appropriate to restrict the business activities of a retiring or withdrawing partner.[70]

(4) The agreement should provide for indemnification of the retiring or withdrawing partner for all existing liabilities if the remaining partners elect to continue the business.

(5) If the withdrawal of a partner is wrongful, any penalties to be imposed as a result of wrongful withdrawal should be specified in the agreement.

E X A M P L E

Retirement or Withdrawal

A Partner shall have the right, at any time during the continuance of this agreement and of the Partnership created hereby, to withdraw or retire from the said Partnership by giving three (3) months' notice to the other Partners at the Partnership's place of business.

Upon giving notice, the withdrawing or retiring Partner shall be entitled to payment of his or her interest in the Partnership, the amount of which and method of payment is determined by this agreement with reference to purchase of an expelled Partner's interest. Upon the receipt of such payment, the interest of the withdrawing or retiring Partner in the Partnership shall cease and terminate.

Notwithstanding the provisions above, if the remaining Partners shall decide not to continue the business upon withdrawal or retirement of a Partner, the remaining Partners may elect to terminate and dissolve the Partnership, in which case the withdrawing or retiring Partner shall only be entitled to his or her interest in liquidation, as stated in this agreement with reference to voluntary termination.

(b) **Expulsion of a partner—**
  (1) The circumstances justifying expulsion of a partner must be specifically detailed.
  (2) A method for deciding upon expulsion and a procedure for notifying the expelled partner should be established. If a hearing will be permitted, the procedure for conducting the hearing should be described.
  (3) The agreement should provide for indemnification of the expelled partner for all existing liabilities if the remaining partners elect to continue the business.

E X A M P L E

Expulsion

A partner of this partnership may, upon the affirmative vote of the other partners, be expelled for the following acts:
  a) committing a felony under the laws of the state in which this partnership is organized;
  b) failing to cure any default or breach of this agreement after receipt of a notice of such default or breach from the other partners in writing;
  c) committing an act that is deemed to be detrimental to the business or reputation of the partnership;
  d) adjudication of insanity of the partner; or
  e) competing with the business of the partnership for his or her personal account.

The partners so voting for expulsion shall give notice of expulsion, specifying the reasons therefor, to the expelled partner, who, upon receipt of such notice, shall have ten (10) days to request in writing a hearing on the matters specified in the notice. If a hearing is requested, the partner subject to expulsion shall appoint an impartial third party, and the other partners shall appoint an impartial third party, and each such third party shall appoint another impartial third party to hear such evidence or other matters as the expelled partner wishes to present on his or her behalf. Following such hearing, this panel shall determine whether the partner shall be expelled, and their decision shall be final.

The remaining partners may continue the business without the expelled partner and without liquidation of the partnership by paying the expelled partner his or her capital account, and by furnishing such indemnification and hold harmless documents as may be reasonably requested by the expelled partner for obligations of the partnership that come due following an expulsion.

(c) **Bankruptcy of a partner—**
  - (1) Provisions should be included for the continuance of the business in case of the bankruptcy of an individual partner.
  - (2) The purchase of the individual partner's interest in the partnership must be authorized.

Bankruptcy of a Partner

Upon the adjudication of bankruptcy of a partner, or the assignment by a partner for the benefit of his or her creditors, or the appointment of a receiver or conservator for the disposition of a partner's debts, the other partners shall have the right either to purchase the bankrupt partner's interest in the partnership or to terminate and liquidate the partnership business. If the remaining partners elect to purchase the bankrupt partner's interest, they shall serve notice of such election upon the trustee in bankruptcy, receiver, conservator, or assignees of the bankrupt partner within twenty (20) days following such event, and shall pay to such person or persons the value of the bankrupt partner's interest in the partnership determined as of the day before such event occurred. If the remaining partners do not elect to purchase the bankrupt partner's interest, and instead elect to terminate the business, they shall appoint a managing partner who shall proceed with reasonable promptness to sell the property of the partnership and to liquidate the business of the partnership. The bankrupt partner's estate shall thereafter share in the proceeds of liquidation in accordance with his or her pro rata share of the proceeds thereof.

(d) **Death of a partner—**
  - (1) Provisions should be included for the continuance of the business when one partner dies.
  - (2) If the deceased partner's estate is to participate in profits of the business, the agreement should describe the extent of participation. This clause should discuss the amount of profits to be distributed to the estate, the period during which such distributions are to be made, and whether profit distributions are guaranteed.
  - (3) The agreement should establish the authority for the purchase of life insurance on the partners. The partners may purchase life insurance on each other (cross-purchase plan) or the firm may purchase the insurance (entity purchase plan). The amount of the insurance to be maintained and the type of plan should be described in the agreement.
  - (4) If the life insurance plan is to be administered by a trustee, the trustee is named and his or her power and duties should be defined in the agreement.

Death of a Partner

Upon the death of any Partner, the surviving Partners shall have the right either to purchase the decedent's interest in the Partnership or to terminate and liquidate the Partnership business. If the surviving Partners elect to purchase the decedent's interest, they shall serve notice in writing of such election, within three (3) months after the death of the decedent, upon the executor or administrator of the decedent's estate, or if at the time of such election no legal representative has been appointed, upon any one of the known legal heirs of the decedent at the last known address of such heir. The closing of the purchase shall be within thirty (30) days of the notice of such election.

If the surviving Partners elect to purchase the decedent's interest, the purchase price and method of payment shall be as stated in this agreement with reference to purchase of an expelled Partner's interest, except in the event insurance is in effect with respect to decedent the method of payment is provided in this section. The period from the beginning of the fiscal year in which decedent's death occurred until the end of the calendar month in which his or her death occurred shall be the period used for purposes of calculating his or her share of Partnership profits and losses in the year of death. The decedent's share of profits and losses shall also include his or her share of profits and losses of the Partnership during the period between the end of the calendar month in which death occurred and the end of the calendar month preceding the closing of purchase.

EXAMPLE

If the surviving Partners do not elect to purchase the decedent's interest, and instead elect to terminate the business, they shall appoint a managing partner who shall proceed with reasonable promptness to sell the real and personal property owned by the Partnership and to liquidate the business of the Partnership. The surviving Partners and the estate of the deceased Partner shall share in their respective proportions stated during the period of liquidation, except that the decedent's estate shall not be liable for losses in excess of the decedent's interest in the Partnership at the time of his or her death. The managing Partner shall be entitled to reasonable compensation for services performed in liquidation. Except as otherwise stated herein, the procedure as to liquidation and distribution of the Partnership assets shall be the same as stated in this agreement with reference to voluntary termination.

The Partnership may contract for life insurance protection on the lives of each of the Partners, in any amount not disproportionate to the value of each Partner's interest. Each Partner may designate the beneficiary for such life insurance. In the event of death of a Partner, insurance proceeds paid to the Partnership will be used to purchase the decedent's interest, at the purchase price determined above, except that the payment of such price to the decedent's representatives or heirs shall be made within thirty (30) days following receipt of the insurance proceeds. Any surplus in insurance proceeds not required to purchase the decedent's interest shall be retained in the Partnership and proportionately added to the capital account of the surviving Partners. If the surviving Partners elect to liquidate the business in lieu of purchasing the decedent's interest, the proceeds of any life insurance shall be treated as an asset of the Partnership for liquidation.

    (e) **Other disabilities**—The partnership may be dissolved when an individual partner becomes disabled, insane, or otherwise incapable of continuing in the business relationship. These special incidents of dissolution should be considered in the agreement, with provisions for continuation of the business and purchase of the former partner's interest.

EXAMPLE

Disability of a Partner

In the event a partner becomes disabled, is adjudicated insane, or is otherwise unable to perform the duties required by this agreement, the remaining partners shall have the right either to purchase the disabled partner's interest in the partnership or to terminate and liquidate the disabled partner's interest in the partnership. If the surviving partners elect to purchase the disabled partner's interest, then the procedure described in this agreement for the purchase of a deceased partner's interest in the partnership shall apply. If the remaining partners elect to terminate and liquidate the business, they shall appoint a managing partner who shall proceed with reasonable promptness to terminate the business, sell the property of the partnership, and distribute the proceeds of such liquidation, after payment to creditors, in the manner provided for dissolution and liquidation in this agreement.

16. **Continuation of the business**—Following a dissolution, the remaining partners have the authority to continue the business if the dissolution was wrongful. In other cases of dissolution, the business may be continued only if the agreement so provides. A specific clause granting the remaining partners the right to continue business is appropriate. Notice of the intent to continue the business may be required to be given to the former partner or to the former partner's estate. In all cases, the withdrawing, retiring, or disabled partner or the estate of the deceased partner should be indemnified from business liabilities.

17. **Purchase of the partner's interest**—If a partner has caused a dissolution and the remaining partners intend to continue the business, the interest of the withdrawing, disabled, or deceased partner will be purchased by the firm or by the other partners.[71]
    (a) The agreement may provide that the former partner's interest will be purchased by the other partners jointly or individually in an established proportion.
    (b) The agreement may provide for liquidating distributions to the former partner, resulting in a purchase of that partner's interest by the firm.

(c) The value of the partner's interest should be ascertained in accordance with a formula specified in the agreement. Independent public accountants may be necessary to make the computations under the formula. The following typical alternatives are available:
   (1) a return of the capital contribution plus interest;
   (2) a stipulated value as described in the agreement;
   (3) a formula based upon historical earnings of the partnership (**earnings multiple formula**);
   (4) a formula based upon the value of the assets of the partnership (**book value formula**); and
   (5) an appraisal by an independent third party.[72]

(d) The extent to which goodwill is to be used to compute the value of the former partner's interest is established by the agreement. Goodwill may be ignored, or it may be considered an asset and appraised in determining the value of the interest.

(e) Payment terms should be established in the agreement. The period of time for installment payments, whether a promissory note is to be executed, and whether the obligation will be secured by assets of the partnership are appropriate topics for this provision.

(f) A fund may be withheld for a period of time for contingent claims arising before the dissolution.

(g) The treatment of the purchased interest should be discussed. The interest may be divided among partners in their remaining proportion of capital contributions, equally, or by some other formula.

Continuation of Business and Purchase of Partner's Interest

The Partners may elect to continue the business despite a dissolution of the partnership, by purchasing the deceased, disabled, expelled, or bankrupt Partner's interest; in such case, the purchase price shall be equal to the deceased, disabled, expelled, or bankrupt Partner's capital account as of the date of the notice required by this agreement, plus his or her income account as of the end of the prior fiscal year, increased by his or her share of Partnership profits, or decreased by his or her share of Partnership losses, computed to the date of the notice, and decreased by withdrawals such as would have been charged to his or her income account during the present year to the date of the purchase of his or her interest. The purchase price is subject to set-off for any damages incurred as the result of the expelled or bankrupt Partner's actions, and nothing in this paragraph is intended to impair the Partnership's right to recover damages for such reasons.

The date of the notice, referred to above, shall be the date personal notice is received, or the date the certified mail is postmarked, in the case of a breach of this agreement.

---

18. **Liquidation and winding up** (see "Dissolution and Termination of a Partnership" earlier in this chapter)—If the business will not be continued following dissolution, liquidation and winding up must follow in accordance with the agreement.

(a) A full and general account of the firm's assets, liabilities, and transactions should be authorized. An independent certified public accountant may be necessary for this purpose.

(b) A liquidating partner or committee of partners should be named. Since partners may receive remuneration for services in liquidation, the value of these services should be fixed by agreement.

(c) If the assets are capable of distribution to the partners, this may be authorized in the agreement, following the payment of business debts. Otherwise, the agreement should authorize the sale of the assets (usually in the discretion and good judgment of the liquidating partner) and the distribution of the cash received.

(d) The order of distribution of the assets is set by law.[73] If the order of distribution is to be altered, the agreement must specifically describe the new order of distribution.

(e) If the partnership has sustained a loss, so that one or more of the partners will be required to make additional capital contributions to facilitate distribution of assets, a period of time in which such payments are to be made and the manner of payment (cash, promissory note, etc.) should be specified.

| EXAMPLE | **Distribution on Termination** |

Upon termination of the Partnership, its affairs shall be concluded in the following manner:

a) The Managing General Partner shall proceed to the liquidation of the Partnership, and the proceeds of the liquidation shall be applied and distributed in the following order of priority:

1) to the payment of all debts and liabilities of the Partnership;

2) to the setting up of any reserve that the Managing General Partner shall deem reasonably necessary to provide for any contingent or unforeseen liabilities or obligations of the Partnership; provided, however, that at the expiration of such period of time as the Managing General Partner shall deem advisable, the balance of such reserve remaining after the payment of such contingency shall be distributed in the manner set forth in this section;

3) to the payment to the partners other than the Managing General Partner of an amount which, when added to any amount previously distributed to the partners other than the Managing General Partner pursuant to this agreement hereof, will equal their aggregate capital contributions to the Partnership;

4) any balance then remaining shall be distributed as follows:

    i) ninety percent (90%) of such balance to the partners other than the Managing General Partner;

    ii) ten percent (10%) of such balance to the Managing General Partner;

b) A reasonable time shall be allowed for the orderly liquidation of the assets of the Partnership and the discharge of liabilities to creditors; and

c) Each Partner shall be furnished with a statement certified by the Partnership's independent accountants which shall set forth the assets and liabilities of the Partnership as of the date of the complete liquidation.

REGISTRATION AS A LIMITED LIABILITY PARTNERSHIP

The most significant disadvantage to the general partnership form of doing business is the fact that the general partners have personal liability for partnership obligations. Many states have now authorized the formation of registered limited liability partnerships in which this personal liability can be avoided.[74] A **limited liability partnership** is an existing general partnership that is converted or a new partnership that is formed in which the individual partners are shielded from personal liability, except to the extent that the debt or liability arises from the partner's own conduct or as otherwise provided in the partnership agreement or a writing signed by the partner.

The partner causing the liability usually remains personally liable for the consequences of his or her actions. This is the same rule that applies to agents: the agent is personally liable for the agent's own conduct. The advantage of a limited liability partnership, therefore, is that the *other* partners will not be liable for the conduct of their fellow partners. Although agency and partnership law would attribute the liability of one partner to the others, the registration as a limited liability partnership cuts off the vicarious liability of the other partners.

In most states authorizing the limited liability partnership, a partner can still *agree* to be liable for the other partners' conduct, either in a written partnership agreement or otherwise. If a partner agrees to assume responsibility for partnership obligations, the limited liability feature of the entity is ignored because of the agreement. Thus, when an existing general partnership seeks to register for limited liability protection, counsel must be careful to review and amend the existing partnership agreement to eliminate any reference to individual liability or contributions if the partners are to receive the full benefits of limited liability.

Limited liability partnerships must file a registration statement with the Secretary of State or other state filing officer (see Exhibit 3–12, Certificate of Limited Liability Partnership) typically containing:

1. the name of the registered limited liability partnership (which must contain the words "registered limited liability partnership," "limited liability partnership," or the initials "L.L.P.," "LP," "R.L.L.P.," or "RLLP;"

Exhibit 3–12.

Certificate of Limited
Liability Partnership
(Maine)

Filing Fee $125.00

**DOMESTIC
LIMITED LIABILITY PARTNERSHIP**

STATE OF MAINE

**CERTIFICATE OF
LIMITED LIABILITY PARTNERSHIP**

(Mark box only if applicable)

☐ This is a professional limited liability partnership formed pursuant to 13 MRSA Chapter 22-A to provide the following professional services:

_____

_____
(type of professional services)

_____
Deputy Secretary of State

A True Copy When Attested By Signature

_____
Deputy Secretary of State

Pursuant to 31 MRSA ß822, the undersigned executes and delivers the following Certificate of Limited Liability Partnership:

FIRST: The name of the registered limited liability partnership is:

_____.
(The name must contain one of the following: "Limited Liability Partnership", "L.L.P." or "LLP"; ß803-A.1)

SECOND: The name of its Registered Agent, an individual Maine resident or a corporation, foreign or domestic, authorized to do business or carry on activities in Maine, and the address of the registered office shall be:

_____
(name)

_____
(physical location - street (not P.O. Box), city, state and zip code)

_____
(mailing address if different from above)

THIRD: The name and business, residence or mailing address of the contact partner is:

NAME   **ADDRESS**

_____   _____

FOURTH: Other provisions of this certificate, if any, that the partners determine to include are set forth in Exhibit _____ attached hereto and made a part hereof.

FORM NO. MLLP-6 (1 of 2)

2. the address of the partnership's principal office;
3. the address of the registered office and the name and address of a registered agent for service of process if the address at the principal office is not located in the state;
4. the date of formation of the partnership;
5. a description of the partnership's business; and
6. other matters required by statute or that the partnership wishes to include.

By filing the registration statement, the partnership will remain a registered limited liability partnership and the partners will enjoy limitations on their individual liability until the partnership elects to withdraw its registration statement or the registration is revoked by the state for failing to pay fees or file required reports.

Several state statutes provide that the limited liability for registered limited liability partnerships is to be treated and interpreted the same as the shield of limited liability for

Exhibit 3–12.

(continued)

PARTNER(S)*   DATED   _____

_____   _____
(signature)   (type or print name)

_____   _____
(signature)   (type or print name)

_____   _____
(signature)   (type or print name)

For Partner(s) which are Entities

Name of Entity _____

By _____   _____
(authorized signature)   (type or print name and capacity)

Name of Entity _____

By _____   _____
(authorized signature)   (type or print name and capacity)

Name of Entity _____

By _____   _____
(authorized signature)   (type or print name and capacity)

Acceptance of Appointment of Registered Agent

The undersigned hereby accepts the appointment as registered agent for the above-named limited liability partnership.

REGISTERED AGENT   DATED   _____

_____   _____
(signature)   (type or print name)

For Registered Agent which is a Corporation

Name of Corporation _____

By _____   _____
(authorized signature)   (type or print name and capacity)

Note: If the **registered agent does not sign**, Form MLLP-18 (ß807.2) must accompany this document.

_____

*Certificate **MUST** be signed by:
  (1) one or more **partners** who are authorized **OR**
  (2) any duly authorized person.
The execution of this certificate constitutes an oath or affirmation under the penalties of false swearing under Title 17-A, section 453.

Please remit your payment made payable to the Maine Secretary of State.

SUBMIT COMPLETED FORMS TO: CORPORATE EXAMINING SECTION, SECRETARY OF STATE,
101 STATE HOUSE STATION, AUGUSTA, ME 04333-0101
FORM NO. MLLP-6 (2 of 2) Rev. 7-1-2003   TEL. (207) 624-7740

corporations, including the application of corporate case law to determine the conditions and circumstances under which the limited liability veil can be pierced.[75]

To protect creditors, partners of a registered limited liability partnership are usually not entitled to receive distributions from the partnership unless the fair value of the partnership's assets exceed the liabilities of the partnership after giving effect to the distribution. Similarly, a partner is not entitled to receive a return of his or her capital contribution to the extent that a distribution reduces the partner's share of the fair value of the net assets below the value of the partner's undistributed contribution as of the date of the distribution. The consequence of these limitations is to require that the partnership retain enough assets in the business to be able to pay known creditors. Of course, if the partnership were to suffer a significant liability, such as from an unsuccessful lawsuit resulting from a defective product or negligence in providing a service, the victim may not be able to recover fully if the assets of the partnership

State of Utah
DEPARTMENT OF COMMERCE
Division of Corporations & Commercial Code

Non-Refundable Processing Fee
[ ]   New Filing $22.00

Exhibit 3–13.

Foreign Limited Liability
Partnership Application
(Utah)

Application for Foreign Limited Liability Partnership

Registration of this name does not guarantee exclusive right to disregard protection against unauthorized use of this name, (U.C.A. Section 48-1-42). When approved, your Limited Liability Partnership is registered for one (1) year. The last words of the name must be "Limited Liability Partnership" (LLP). An Original Certification of Fact or Good Standing from the Office of the Secretary of State, or other responsible Authority of the State in which the Limited Liability Partnership is formed, must accompany this application. Return fees with two (2) copies of this application.

1. Limited Liability Partnership name :_____
(Name of Limited Liability Partnership in the Home State)

2. Is a Limited Liability Partnership registered in the U.S.? If so, list state :_____

3. Registered on the _____ day of _____, ____.

4. Purpose of Limited Liability Partnership :_____

5. Principal Address:_____
Street Address Only   City   State   Zip

6. Minimum 2 Partners:_____   7. Phone Number:_____

8. Registered Agent: [   ] Check this box if the name on line 8 is the agent only.

_____   _____   _____
Print Name of Registered Agent   Signature of Registered Agent   Daytime Phone Number

_____   Utah   _____
Street Address   City   Zip

Authorized Partner(s) *attach additional pages if needed*:
Under penalties of perjury and as an authorized partner, I declare that this application, and if applicable, the statement of change of registered office and/or agent, has been examined by me and is, to the best of my knowledge and belief, true, correct, and complete.

_____   _____
Print Name   Signature

_____   _____
Street Address   City   State   Zip

_____   _____
Print Name   Signature

_____   _____
Street Address   City   State   Zip

The Limited Liability Partnership shall use as its name in Utah:_____.
Must be the same as number (1) unless the name is not available in Utah.

Where to file: You may file in person, by mail or by fax. Means of payment are, cash, check or money order payable to the "State of Utah". Please include one (1) self addressed envelope with application. **If you are faxing you must include, on cover sheet, the number of a Visa or MasterCard with the date of expiration.**

Mail In: PO Box 146705
Salt Lake City, UT 84114-6705
Walk In: 160 East 300 South, Main Floor
Information Center: (801) 530-4849
Toll Free: (877) 526-3994 (within Utah)
Fax: (801) 530-6438
Web Site: http://www.commerce.utah.gov

Revised 09/02

Under GRAMA {63-2-201}, all registration information maintained by the Division is classified as public record. For confidentiality purposes, the business entity physical address may be provided rather than the residential or private address of any individual affiliated with the entity.

are inadequate to pay the liability. Even if the partnership has not made distributions to the partners, it may not have enough money to pay a large liability. The creditor is not allowed to pursue the personal assets of the individual partners, however, if the partnership has registered as a limited liability partnership.

The election to register as a limited liability partnership usually requires the unanimous consent of the general partners, unless the partnership agreement provides otherwise.

When a limited liability partnership seeks to do business in states other than where it is formed, it is usually necessary to register and qualify the partnership in the other states in which business is to be conducted. By registering locally, the partnership is giving notice to the citizens of the other states that it is a limited liability partnership. (See Exhibit 3–13, Foreign Limited Liability Partnership Application.)

States that permit the formation of a Limited Liability Partnership

Alabama	Kentucky	North Carolina
Alaska	Louisiana	North Dakota
Arizona	Maine	Ohio
Arkansas	Maryland	Oklahoma
California	Massachusetts	Oregon
Colorado	Michigan	Pennsylvania
Connecticut	Minnesota	Rhode Island
Delaware	Mississippi	South Carolina
District of Columbia	Missouri	South Dakota
Florida	Montana	Tennessee
Georgia	Nebraska	Texas
Hawaii	Nevada	Utah
Idaho	New Hampshire	Virginia
Illinois	New Jersey	Washington
Indiana	New Mexico	West Virginia
Iowa	New York	Wisconsin
Kansas		

KEY TERMS

general partnership
partnership agreement
aggregate theory
entity theory
joint venture
capital contribution
tenancy in common
partition
tenancy in partnership
surviving partner
interest in partnership
assignment of interest

statement of partnership authority
statement of denial
fiduciary duty
net distributable profit
disproportionate allocation
marshaling of assets
indemnification
dissolution
dissociated partner
winding up
expulsion

wrongful dissolution
entity purchase plan
cross purchase plan
deferred dissolution
foreign partnership
articles of partnership
fiscal year
silent partners
earnings multiple formula
book value formula
limited liability partnership

WEB RESOURCES

The partnership agreement is the principal document required for the general partnership, and, to the extent that a limited liability partnership is desired, forms must be filed with a public filing officer, usually the Secretary of State, to register the limited liability partnership. Other issues in forming partnerships include the use of an assumed name, which will be registered in a public office, and licensing issues relating to professions and occupations upon which states have imposed licensing and regulatory requirements, such as law partnerships and medical practices.

Various sources exist for sample partnership agreements that may be tailored to the specific desires of the client. For example, partnership agreements can be found on the following sites:

<http://www.ilrg.com>
<http://www.law.com>
<http://www.lectlaw.com>
<http://www.legalwiz.com>
<http://www.findlaw.com>

Access to state laws regarding licensing and regulatory requirements may be obtained through the Legal Information Institute maintained at the Cornell Law School:

<http://www.law.cornell.edu>

The National Association of Secretaries of State maintains links directly to the offices of the Secretaries of State in all states. Most states requiring registration of limited liability partnerships provide forms for that purpose through the Secretary of State or Department of Commerce Web sites. These can be accessed through

<http://www.nass.org>

Tax forms, including the federal income tax returns and schedules, and the Classification of Entity tax elections may be accessed on line through

<http://www.irs.gov>

The Small Business Administration offers on-line information and assistance in forming, operating, and financing the activities of small partnerships:

<http://www.sba.gov>

Searching and locating trade names can be accomplished through various services offered on the Internet. Most of these services charge a fee for useful searches. They include

<http://www.tmexpress.com>
<http://www.trademark-search-services.com>

CASES

TARNAVSKY v. TARNAVSKY

147 F.3d 674
June 10, 1998
JOHN R. GIBSON, CIRCUIT JUDGE

I.

Before 1976, Mary Tarnavsky, with the help of her three sons, T. R., Morris, and Edward, controlled and operated a 2,840 acre ranch (Mary's ranch) in McKenzie County, North Dakota. Of these 2,840 acres, Mary individually owned 2,200 acres, Mary and Morris jointly owned 480 acres, and Edward owned 160 acres. In 1967, Mary, Morris, and T.R. jointly purchased 1,890 acres of adjoining land, referred to as the Christ place. Mary paid 50% of the purchase price as a down payment, and the parties assumed an existing contract for deed to the Christ place. T.R. and Morris opened a bank account, the Tarnavsky Brothers account, which was used to make payments on the Christ place contract for deed, to pay the Christ place property taxes, and to purchase cattle, equipment and related supplies and services under the partnership name. T.R. alleges that upon acquiring the Christ place, he and Morris orally agreed to form Tarnavsky Brothers partnership to operate the Christ place ranch with T.R. and Morris equally sharing the profits and losses of the partnership.

Since the acquisition of the Christ place in 1967, the parties have operated the entire 4,730 acres (the Christ place and Mary's ranch) as one unit, commingling cattle and farming operations. When cattle were sold, Mary received one-half the proceeds and T.R. and Morris received the other half. Grain proceeds were also distributed in this manner until 1973, the year Edward returned from college and began raising the grain on both ranches. At this point, Edward began receiving ten percent of grain proceeds, Mary received 45%, and Tarnavsky Brothers received 45%. On each of these occasions, Morris and T.R.'s share of the proceeds was deposited in the Tarnavsky Brothers bank account.

In 1980, Mary decided that she no longer wanted to receive proceeds from the sale of grain or cattle. Thereafter, Tarnavsky Brothers received 100% of the cattle proceeds, and 90% of the grain proceeds. Edward still did the farm work and received 10% of the grain proceeds.

Since 1967, Morris has worked full time on the ranch. In addition to handling other ranching responsibilities, Morris has been in charge of handling the livestock. Edward has worked full time on the ranch since he returned from college in 1973. Along with performing other tasks, Edward has been in charge of planting and harvesting grain on the ranch.

In 1967, T.R. lived in Bozeman, Montana, which is located about 500 miles from the ranch. In addition to occasionally working on the ranch, T.R. was in charge of bookkeeping. T.R. remained in Bozeman until 1977, when he and his wife moved to Sidney, Montana, which is about 75 miles from the ranch. At this point, T.R. spent more time working on the ranch, but the parties strongly dispute the amount of T.R.'s participation. In 1988, T.R.'s wife began to suffer severely from cancer. Thereafter, T.R. stopped being the "bookkeeper" and spent very little time working or participating in ranch activities.

After Mary's death in 1991, T.R. spent little or no time at the ranch. In March of 1992, Morris sent T.R. a Notice of Dissolution of Partnership. After attempts to settle the partners' accounts were unsuccessful, T.R. filed suit, claiming he and Morris had a partnership and requesting an accounting and payment of his partnership assets. The district court concluded that Morris and T.R. were partners, and ordered judgment of $220,000 in favor of T.R.

II.

On appeal, Morris and Edward argue that the district court erred in concluding that a partnership existed between T.R. and Morris. The existence of a partnership is a mixed question of law and fact. *See Frankel v. Hillier,* 16 N.D. 387, 113 N.W. 1067, 1070 (1907). There is no challenge to the district court's factual findings, and the ultimate conclusion of whether a partnership existed is a question of law, which we review de novo. *See In Matter of Newman,* 875 F.2d 668, 670 (8th Cir.1989).

Under North Dakota law, a partnership is "an association of two or more persons to carry on as co-owners a business for profit. *Gangl v. Gangl,* 281 N.W.2d 574, 579 (N.D.1979); N.D.Cent.Code. 45-13-01(4) (1997). "The existence of a partnership is not governed by one conclusive criterion but by the facts and circumstances of each case." *See Gangl* 281 N.W.2d at 579. However, certain elements are critical to the existence of a partnership. *Id.* These elements are: (1) an intention to be partners; (2) co-ownership of the business; and (3) profit motive. *Id.*

* * *

Morris and T.R.'s intent to be partners is established by the evidence. Although not determinative, it is uncontradicted that T.R. and Morris reported their farming activities on state and federal partnership income tax returns for over twenty years. From 1967 through 1987, T.R. prepared the "Tarnavsky Brothers" partnership tax returns, which Morris signed, showing a 50/50 allocation of profit and losses to T.R. and Morris. When Morris took the "bookkeeping" over from T.R. in 1988, he had an accountant prepare the "Tarnavsky Brothers Ranch" partnership tax returns for 1988, 1989, and 1990, which continued to show a 50/50 allocation of profit and losses to T.R. and Morris. This is strong evidence of Morris and T.R.'s intent to be partners. In addition to filing Tarnavsky Brothers partnership returns, appellants concede that Morris and T.R. opened a joint bank account entitled Tarnavsky Brothers. From this account, they made the Christ place property payments, purchased cattle, seed, and related supplies. Appellants also concede that T.R. and Morris purchased cattle and equipment and borrowed money under the name Tarnavsky Brothers. Furthermore, T.R. and Morris jointly engaged in a cow share arrangement with another farmer, and later jointly purchased his share of the calves. These actions by Morris and T.R. evidence their intent to be partners.

Co-ownership, the second element necessary for a partnership, includes the sharing of profits and losses as well as the power of control in the management of the business. *See Gangl* 281 N.W.2d at 580.

Morris and Edward argue that T.R. and Morris did not "share" profits because neither party took profit distributions from the Tarnavsky Brothers account. This argument is without merit. It is undisputed that after completing a sale of cattle or grain, the brothers would deposit their share of the income in their joint account. From this account, the brothers jointly paid expenses and used the remaining money (the profit) to purchase machinery, cattle, and make land payments on the Christ place property. Any remaining profit stayed in the joint ac count, accumulating over time. Although the money was not distributed, jointly purchasing land and machinery with profits is a form of profit sharing. *See Gangl,* 281 N.W.2d at 579. Further evidence that the brothers shared profits is that at the end of each year, Morris and T.R. would allocate the year's profits on the partnership income tax return equally between themselves, with each party being liable for his share of profits on his personal income tax return. This sharing of profits is further evidence that Morris and T.R. were partners. *See* N.D. Cent.Code § 45-14-02(3)(c) (Supp.1997).

Morris and Edward also argue that Morris and T.R. did not have the power of control over the management of the business. They argue that the Christ place was melded into the overall operation of the family ranch subject to Mary's control, and that the power to make decisions and to distribute income rested solely with Mary, and not with T.R. or Morris. This argument is also without merit.

Appellants concede that from the beginning purchase of the Christ place Morris and T.R. opened a joint bank account, took out joint partnership loans, and jointly purchased cattle and machinery in the partnership name. Appellants also admit in their brief that both Morris and T.R. were involved in working with banks to secure loans for cattle and equipment purchases, and that both T.R. and Morris handled "marketing the cattle" and performed various administrative functions, such as the discussion of rations. Furthermore, appellants state in their brief that Morris was "in charge" of livestock production and "administered" equipment purchases, and that T.R. was "in charge" of paperwork and finances. This is strong evidence that T.R. and Morris both had the power of control over management of the business. The argument that Mary controlled all business decisions is even less forceful for the period after 1980, when Mary's involvement in the ranch diminished, and all proceeds from grain and cattle were distributed either to the Tarnavsky Brothers account or the Tarnavsky Ranch account. Appellants make numerous arguments that any authority Morris and T.R. appeared to have was purely illusory, granted to T.R. and Morris by Mary so that Mary could accomplish certain objectives. These arguments were rejected by the district court. Although Mary may have been the lead figure in the "commingled" ranching operation until 1980, ample evidence illustrates that Morris and T.R. had the power to control business decisions relating to Tarnavsky Brothers partnership. Control, when combined with profit sharing, strongly suggests the evidence of a partnership. *See Gangl,* 281 N.W.2d at 580.

The final critical element of a partnership is profit motive, and there is no dispute that the farming business was operated with such motive.

We thus conclude that the district court's findings and the uncontested facts recited by appellants are sufficient to support a finding of the three critical elements necessary for the existence of a partnership. These facts, considered together, amply support the districts court's conclusion that T.R. and Morris were partners, and the district court did not err in so holding.

MACARTHUR COMPANY v. STEIN

282 Mont. 85, 934 P.2d 214
March 25, 1997
TRIEWEILER, JUSTICE

FACTUAL BACKGROUND

Karl Stein has operated Midland Roofing in Billings since 1974. Prior to July 1991, Midland Roofing was a sole proprietorship owned solely by Stein.

In the summer of 1991, several hail storms occurred in the Billings area. As a result, the demand for roofing services increased significantly in the late summer and fall of 1991. Stein recognized an opportunity to increase his profits because of the sudden demand for roofing services. He sought to take advantage of the business opportunity by seeking a line of credit at a local financial institution, but was unable to secure financing.

John L. Potter and Jesse Beebe approached Stein in late June or early July 1991 with the idea of expanding Stein's business to take advantage of the increase in roofing demand. Both Potter and Beebe were out-of-state businessmen who engaged in "storm tracking"—the business of traveling to areas where there was increased roofing activity due to storm damage. In early negotiations, Potter asserted that he could handle the general operation of a roofing business and that a third party, Bill Evans, could handle sales and material acquisition. In addition, Beebe represented that he had the ability to secure credit for the expanded business.

In early July, the parties entered into an agreement, some of which was in writing and some of which was not, but which was confirmed by subsequent actions of the parties. Pursuant to the agreement, Stein, Beebe, and Potter agreed to create a new entity which would operate under the name of Midland Roofing and Gutters. The parties expressly intended that the business name would be so similar to Stein's business name, Midland Roofing, that the public and customers would be unable to distinguish between the two businesses. In addition, both Midland Roofing and the new entity, Midland Roofing and Gutters,

were to use the same telephone number and all calls to that number were to be answered by employees of Midland Roofing and Gutters. The parties agreed that a record would be made of all telephone calls and that Stein would be given a first right to accept any potential roofing job. Midland Roofing and Gutters had the option to complete any other jobs.

As part of the parties' initial written agreement, Stein's compensation was equal to three percent of total gross charges for all "nail-on roofing" jobs and ten percent of gross charges for "hot roofing" jobs performed by Midland Roofing and Gutters. Midland Roofing and Gutters also agreed to pay one of Stein's employees a portion of his salary for inspection work and to set aside $.50 per roofing square to be set up in a two-signature account, which would bear the signatures of Stein and Beebe, to cover any warranty work necessary after Midland Roofing and Gutters ceased operation.

In August 1991, Jesse Beebe arranged a line of credit for Midland Roofing and Gutters from MacArthur Company. Stein had previously been denied credit by the company. His purchases from MacArthur were on a "cash only" basis. On the credit application, Beebe listed Midland Roofing and Gutters as the company seeking credit, and named himself as the "principal or officer." Neither Stein nor Midland Roofing was mentioned on the credit application, and MacArthur was not advised of Stein's association with Midland Roofing and Gutters. Based solely on Beebe's credit references, MacArthur granted Midland Roofing and Gutters a line of credit and supplied the company with materials from August 1991 through January 1992.

In January 1992, Jesse Beebe, John Potter, and Bill Evans departed the Billings area without notice, and left an unpaid balance to MacArthur Company in the amount of $39,75.27. On May 12, 1994, MacArthur Company filed a complaint in the Thirteenth Judicial District Court in Yellowstone County against Karl Stein, Midland Roofing, Midland Roofing and Gutters, and John Does 1 and 2. MacArthur alleged that each of the defendants, as partners in Midland Roofing and Gutters, was jointly and severally liable for the outstanding debt to MacArthur.

Following a hearing on January 11, 1995, the District Court concluded that Stein was a partner of Midland Roofing and Gutters at the time the debt to MacArthur was incurred. The District Court therefore concluded that, pursuant § 35-10-307, MCA, Stein was "jointly liable for all . . . debts and obligations of the partnership." Based on its conclusions, the court ordered Stein to pay $39,875.27, plus interest and attorney fees, for the debt owed to MacArthur by Midland Roofing and Gutters.

DISCUSSION

Section 35-10-201(1), MCA (1991), defines a partnership as "an association of two or more persons to carry on as co-owners a business for profit." Section 35-10-202, MCA (1991), provides:

In determining whether a partnership exists, these rules shall apply:

> (1) Except as provided by 35-10-308 persons who are not partners as to each other are not partners as to third persons.
> (2) Joint tenancy, tenancy in common, tenancy by the entireties, joint property, common property, or part ownership does not itself establish a partnership, whether such co-owners do or do not share any profits made by the use of the property.
> (3) The sharing of gross returns does not of itself establish a partnership, whether or not the persons sharing them have a joint or common right or interest in any property from which the returns are derived.
> (4) The receipt by a person of a share of the profits of a business is prima facie evidence that such person is a partner in the business, but no such inference shall be drawn if such profits were received in payment:
> (a) as a debt by installments or otherwise;
> (b) as wages of an employee or rent to a landlord;
> (c) as an annuity to a surviving spouse or representative of a deceased partner;
> (d) as interest on a loan, though the amount of payment varies with the profits of the business;
> (e) as the consideration for the sale of a goodwill of a business or other property by installments or otherwise.

This Court established the elements for the determination of the existence of a partnership in *Bender v. Bender* (1965), 144 Mont. 470, 480, 397 P.2d 957, 962; (1) the parties must clearly manifest their intent to associate themselves as a partnership; (2) each party must contribute something that promotes the enterprise; (3) each party must have a right of mutual control over the subject matter of the enterprise; and (4) the parties must agree to share the profits of the enterprise. We have consistently held that each of the four *Bender* requirements must be established in order to prove the existence of a partnership. [Citations omitted].

In this case, the District Court analyzed the alleged partnership of Stein, Beebe, Potter, and Evans pursuant to both § 35-10-202, MCA (1991), and the elements of partnership set forth in *Bender.* The court found that the parties' actions and conduct were sufficient to establish their intent to associate themselves as a partnership. In addition, the court found that each party had contributed something that promoted Midland Roofing and Gutters, that each had a joint proprietary interest and a right of mutual control over the enterprise, and that each had received a share of the profits of the enterprise. Based on its findings, the court concluded that Stein, Beebe, Potter, and Evans had created a partnership and that that partnership was in existence at the time the debt to MacArthur Company was incurred. The court therefore concluded that, as a partner in Midland Roofing and Gutters, Stein was liable "jointly for all . . . debts and obligations of the partnership," pursuant to § 35-10-307, MCA (1991).

The initial test for the determination of whether a partnership exists is the intent of the parties, *Antonick,* 236 Mont. at 284, 769 P.2d at 1242. At trial, Stein testified that he did not intend to create a partnership through his negotiations with Beebe and Potter. However, as this Court noted in *Truck Insurance Exchange v. Industrial Indemnity Co.* (1984), 212 Mont. 297, 300, 688 P.2d 1243, 1244-45:

> [I]f the facts bring the arrangement within the definition of a partnership, the parties cannot escape liability incident to that relationship merely by saying that no such thing exists. If the intended action of the parties creates a partnership in fact, what the parties call their arrangement or intend their arrangement to be is irrelevant.

(Citation omitted.) Therefore, where intent cannot be directly ascertained, it must be established from all the facts, circumstances, actions, and conduct of the parties. *Antonick, 236 Mont. at 284, 769 P.2d at 1242. In this case, then, it is not necessary that Stein intended to be a partner in Midland Roofing and Gutters; it is only necessary that he intended his actions and that his actions created a partnership in fact.*

In this case, the District Court found that, regardless of Stein's intentions, the parties had created a partnership in fact through their actions and conduct. Specifically, the court found that the remaining three elements *Bender*—contribution, joint interest and control, and the right to share profits—had been proven and were indicative of the parties' intent to establish a partnership.

Pursuant to *Bender,* in addition to the requirement of intent, each of the purported partners must contribute something that promotes the enterprise. *Bender,* 144 Mont. at 480, 397 P.2d at 962. In this case, the District Court found that each of the parties had made a contribution to Midland Roofing and Gutters sufficient to indicate the creation of a partnership. Specifically, the court found that Stein had contributed to Midland Roofing and Gutters the name of his business, his business license, and his goodwill in the community. In addition, the court noted that Stein had agreed to warrant work completed by Midland Roofing and Gutters. The other parties, the court found, had contributed roofing skills, start-up revenue, and sales skills. Based on the substantial contributions of each of the parties, the District Court found that the elements of contribution had been established.

The uncontroverted evidence at trial established that Stein lent his business name, his telephone number, his business leads, his good will, his business license, and his expertise to Midland Roofing and Gutters. We hold that such contribution was promotive of the enterprise of Midland Roofing and Gutters. We therefore conclude that the District Court's finding that the element of contribution had been established is supported by substantial, credible evidence and is not clearly erroneous.

A further requirement of *Bender* is that each party to an enterprise have a joint proprietary interest in, and right of control over the subject matter of the enterprise. *Bender,* 144 Mont. at 480, 397 P.2d at 962. In this case, the District Court found that Stein did have such interest and control. Specifically, the court found that, pursuant to the parties' agreement, Stein had the right to exercise quality control over the work performed by Midland Roofing and Gutters and, after inspection, could have required that the work conform with his standards. In addition, the court found that Stein had agreed to perform future warranty work for Midland Roofing and Gutters and had established a joint account for the payment for that work. Finally, the court found that Stein had reserved the right to discontinue the parties' arrangement and prohibit Midland Roofing and Gutters from using his telephone number and business license. Although the court noted that Stein did not specifically hire the employees of Midland Roofing and Gutters or arrange for their work schedule or payment, the court found that "there are sufficient indices of control and proprietary interest to determine that he was in fact a partner."

In addition to the District Court's specific findings regarding Stein's proprietary interest and right of control, the record reflects that Stein was involved in the oversight of the day-to-day workings of Midland Roofing and Gutters. Stein testified at trial that he visited Midland Roofing and Gutter job sites and gave advice on local building code requirements. In addition, Stein testified that he was in the offices of Midland Roofing and Gutters on a daily basis and answered the phones for that entity. Moreover, the evidence presented at trial established that Stein and Midland Roofing and Gutters worked together to contact the general public. This evidence was clearly indicative of Stein's interest in and control of Midland Roofing and Gutters. We therefore hold that the District Court's finding of Stein's right of mutual control and joint proprietary interest is supported by substantial credible evidence and is not clearly erroneous.

The final element of *Bender* requires that there must be an agreement to share profits in order to establish a partnership. *Bender,* 144 Mont. at 480, 397 P.2d at 962. In this case, the District Court found that Stein was entitled to receive a percentage of Midland Roofing and Gutters' profit. Specifically, the court noted that both the written agreement formalizing the parties' arrangement and its subsequent modification entitled Stein to a percentage of the gross revenue on all work done by Midland Roofing and Gutters. In addition, the court noted that, according to testimony at trial, Stein earned between $75,000 and $92,000 in both cash and materials from his agreement with Midland Roofing and Gutters. As the District Court correctly stated, "[t]he receipt by a person of a share of the profits of a business is prima facie evidence that such person is a partner in the business." Section 35-10-202(4), MCA (1991). Based on the evidence at the trial, which clearly established that Stein was entitled to share the profits of Midland Roofing and Gutters, we hold that the District Court's finding that the final element of *Bender* had been satisfied is not clearly erroneous.

Because we uphold the District Court's findings regarding the establishment of the four elements of a partnership, we hold that the court's conclusion that Stein, Beebe, Potter, and Evans had created a partnership is correct. The only remaining question, then, is whether Stein is liable, as a partner, for Midland Roofing and Gutters' debt to MacArthur Company.

Section 35-10-307(2), MCA (1991), provides that "[a]ll partners are liable . . . jointly for all . . . debts and obligations of the partnership." In this case, because we hold that Stein was a partner in Midland Roofing and Gutters, we further conclude he was jointly liable for the partnership's debt to MacArthur Company. We do not address the issue of whether that makes him individually liable for the entire partnership debt because that issue has been neither raised nor briefed by the parties. Furthermore, we reject Stein's contention that he is not liable to MacArthur because MacArthur was not aware of his relationship with Midland Roofing and Gutters when it extended credit to the company. Reliance is an element of partnership by estoppel; it is not necessary to the establishment of liability of a partner in fact. Therefore, we hold that the District Court was correct in its conclusion that, pursuant to § 35-10-307, MCA (1991), Stein was jointly liable for the partnership's debt to MacArthur Company.

We affirm the judgment of the District Court.

IN RE ESTATE OF JOHNSON
129 Ill.App.3d 22, 472 N.E.2d 72 (Ill.App. 1984)
TRAPP, JUSTICE

In 1942, Edmund Johnson and his brother, Wendell, became partners in a business known as Johnson & Johnson, which previously had been operated by their uncle. The partnership handled insurance, real estate, and a loan business. In 1943, the brothers reduced their partnership agreement to writing. [Article XII of the agreement, as amended, stated:

> "Upon the death of either partner, all interest of the deceased partner shall immediately be and become property of the surviving partner, and the surviving partner shall have the right to continue to operate the business as a sole proprietorship under the partnership name. In lieu of said partnership interest, the surviving partner shall be and he is hereby obligated to pay to the estate of the deceased partner the sum of $10,000 plus the amount, if any, payable to the deceased Partner, as shown by all ledger sheets for accounts of said deceased Partner with the partnership. Said payment shall be in full satisfaction for the interest of the deceased partner in the partnership business, property, and assets, and in full of all demands by the estate of said deceased partner, his executors, administrators, heirs, devisees, legatees, successors, or assigns.

> It is agreed that payment of said sum shall be an accounting in full to the executor or administrator of the estate of the deceased partner, for all interest of said deceased partner, and the surviving partner shall be relieved of any obligation for filing an inventory of the assets of the partnership in the Probate Court in which Letters are issued on the estate of the deceased partner."]

* * *

Besides the partnership business, both brothers maintained individual business interests. Edmund had a separate life insurance, appraisal, and income tax business. While he reported income from this business on his individual tax returns rather than partnership returns, records for the separate business were kept on the partnership ledgers. Wendell had comparable accounts kept on the partnership ledgers.

Edmund died on May 6, 1980, and was survived by his wife, Lois, and son, Steven. In accordance with his will, George Bauer and Wendell became the executors of Edmund's estate. Wendell paid the estate $10,000 plus an additional $20,963.60 for Edmund's individual business and partnership interests.

* * *

Defendants contend the trial court erred in holding that payment of $10,000 was sufficient to purchase the entire value of Edmund's interest in the partnership. They point out that Wendell received the entire good will of the business because he can continue to operate it under the name Johnson & Johnson. There is no valid reason, however, why partners cannot contract to transfer one partner's interest to the other for a set price, especially where no lack of mutuality or unconscionable conduct is present. (*In re Estate of Streck* (1962), 35 Ill.App.2d 473, 480, 183 N.E.2d 26, 30-31.) Partners may also provide by contract for the continuation of the business along with the purchase of the deceased partner's interests. *Keller v. Keller* (1972), 4 Ill.App.3d 89, 280 N.E.2d 281.

A partnership is controlled by the terms of the agreement under which it is formed. (*Harmon v. Martin* (1947), 395 Ill. 595, 612-13, 71 N.E.2d 74, 83.) Because a partnership is a contractual relationship, the principles of contract law fully apply to it. (*Allen v. Amber Manor Apartments Partnership* (1981), 95 Ill.App.3d 541, 549, 51 Ill.Dec. 26, 32, 420 N.E.2d 440, 446.) In construing an agreement, the court's primary objective is to ascertain the intent of the parties as evidenced by the language used. If the terms are unambiguous, then the intent of the parties must be ascertained solely from the words used; the agreement is not rendered ambiguous simply because the parties fail to agree upon its meaning. *Schoeneweis v. Herrin* (1982), 110 Ill.App.3d 800, 806, 66 Ill.Dec. 513, 518, 443 N.E.2d 36, 41.

The issue, therefore, is whether the partnership agreement is ambiguous. Ambiguity is a question of law for the court to decide. *URS Corp. v. Ash* (1981), 101 Ill. App.3d 229, 233, 56 Ill.Dec. 749, 753, 427 N.E.2d 1295, 1299.

Defendants assert article XII of the partnership agreement is ambiguous. Specifically, they contend the phrase "plus the amount, if any, payable to the deceased Partner, as shown by all ledger sheets for accounts of said deceased Partner with the partnership" creates an ambiguity. Defendants give conflicting interpretations to the phrase. At trial and in their briefs, they contended the brothers had intended to require the surviving partner to pay the deceased's estate $10,000 plus the value of the deceased's interest in the partnership, including the value of good will. At oral argument, they maintain the $10,000 represented payment for good will, but the survivor still had to pay for the deceased's capital interest in the partnership.

Plaintiffs contend the phrase plainly refers to accounts of the partners' individual business interests which were kept on the partnership books. They argue the agreement does not call for valuation of partnership assets, and the $10,000 fixed sum represents an easily ascertainable amount that allows the survivor to continue to operate the business.

Defendants first point to the third sentence in article XII, which says that surviving partner's payment shall be in full satisfaction of the deceased's interest in the partnership business. They conclude the payment is only for the partnership interest and cannot include non-partnership interest. Besides being in full satisfaction of a partner's interest in the partnership, however, the third sentence also states the payment shall be "in full of all demands by the estate of said deceased partner." This would include nonpartnership interest kept on the partnership books.

Defendants contend other articles of the agreement establish the partners' intent to require the survivor to pay the entire value of the deceased's partnership interest. Article X states:

> "Before either partner shall sell his interest in the partnership, the same shall be offered to the other partner or member of the firm, at the price the partner expects to sell his interest, and the other partner given a chance to purchase the same before any sale is made to an outsider."

Therefore, a partner had to pay the market value of the other's interest to buy him out during his lifetime. Defendants assert the same price should be paid at a sale caused by a partner's death. They conclude, therefore, the $10,000 figure is a minimum, not a fixed, price. Article X, however, was included in the original agreement. Under that agreement, a partner could purchase the deceased partner's interest for a flat sum. The brothers clearly differentiated between an *inter vivos* sale and a sale after a partner's death. The price for each sale was not to be calculated in an identical manner as defendants suggest.

* * *

Finally, defendants argue the $10,000 represents a fixed sum for the value of good will only. They maintain the phrase "accounts of said deceased partner" refers to the partner's share of the partnership capital. The partnership ledger sheets, however, could not show the firm's capital as payable to a deceased partner. Capital is partnership property, and thus it belongs to the partnership, not the individual partners. (*People v. Zangain* (1921), 301 Ill. 299, 304, 133 N.E. 783, 785.) A partner's interest in the partnership is his share of the profits and surplus. (Ill.Rev.Stat.1981, ch. 106 1/2, par. 26.) Capital, therefore, is payable only to the partnership, not to the individual partners.

The partnership agreement is not ambiguous. Article XII refers to accounts of the deceased partner with the partnership and not to partnership accounts. Although evidence extraneous to the agreement is necessary to determine the value of these accounts, the agreement clearly refers to accounts of a partner's individual business interests. Defendants are in effect asking for the payment of $10,000 plus one-half of the value of the partnership. To determine the value of the partnership, they desire an accounting of the partnership assets. Yet the second paragraph of article XII states the survivor is relieved of any obligation to account for the partnership assets. Rather, the partners intended the surviving partner to purchase the deceased's partnership interest for a flat sum of $10,000.

* * *

PROBLEMS

1. Under the Revised Uniform Partnership Act (in Appendix D), what are the elements of a partnership?

2. What is the difference between the "aggregate" theory and the "entity" theory in partnerships, and what difference does the use of one or the other make as a practical matter?

3. A has contributed $100,000 to a partnership; B has contributed $30,000 to the partnership; and C has contributed services in running the partnership business. There is no written agreement for the partnership, but the parties have agreed to run the business together. Answer the following questions:

   a. How are profits of the business shared?
   b. How are decisions made?
   c. How are losses of the business shared?
   d. What happens to the business if C dies?
   e. If the business is liquidated and $200,000 in assets remain after all creditors are paid, what distributions will be made to A, B, and C?

   f. How much is C entitled to be paid for the services rendered to the business?
   g. If B withdraws from the partnership when the business owes its creditors $50,000, for how much will B be personally liable?
   h. If D joins the partnership when the business owes its creditors $50,000, for how much will D be personally liable?

4. Name the three types of property typically associated with a partnership business. Describe what each type of property includes and explain how that property or the rights to that property may be transferred in the absence of any agreement.

5. State the differences, if any, between a partnership, a joint venture, and a sole proprietorship.

PRACTICE ASSIGNMENTS

1. Review your local statutes and find the law of partnerships. Compare the Revised Uniform Partnership Act (in Appendix D), with your local law and describe how your state's partnership rules vary from the uniform act.

2. A partnership agreement among A, B, C, D, E, and F was entered into on January 19, 2004, for a business to be known as "The Long Branch Investments." The location of the partnership's principal place of business is 1234 Main Street, Deadwood, South Dakota. In addition, the partnership will be carrying on certain activities in Houston, Texas. Prepare the appropriate documents to register the partnership's name.

3. Kathryn Blue, Pamela Owen, and Tory Church are opening an apparel store for high fashion clothing. Each partner will contribute $50,000 in cash and will work in the store. All partners want to be involved in major decisions. They are willing to share everything equally, but if one partner loans money to the business, they want the loan to be repaid before any profits are distributed. If a partner dies, is disabled, withdraws, or files for bankruptcy, the other partners want to be able to purchase that partner's interest for a fair value and

continue the business. The address of the partnership will be 8383 South Michigan Avenue, Chicago, Illinois. The name of the partnership will be "Blowtorch."

a. List the additional issues you would like to discuss with, and facts you would need to know from, Kathryn, Pamela, and Tory to be able to prepare their agreement based upon the sample form, Form I-1, in Appendix I.

b. Prepare a partnership agreement, using answers and facts you have assumed in (a), by tailoring the sample form, in Exhibit I-1, in Appendix I.

4. Jerry Jones, Kevin Burr, and Bill Schmatz are accountants and are partners in a partnership formed under the Uniform Partnership Act for their accounting practice, called "Jones, Burr and Schmatz, CPAs." Bill has lost his license to practice accounting because of tax fraud, and Jerry and Kevin intend to expel him from the partnership. Prepare the forms necessary or desirable to expel Bill from the partnership and to give notice of the dissolution of the partnership to the firm's creditors.

ENDNOTES

1. For general discussions of the law of agency and partnerships, see J.W. Callison, Partnership Law and Practice §§ 1.01, 1.02 (1992); J. Crane and A. Bromberg, Law of Partnership §§ 2, 49-56, 68-72 (1968); W. Seavey, Agency §§ 10A, 14A, 59 (1964); Chapter 1 of this volume.

2. 6 U.L.A. 1 (1969 and Supp. 1980). The Uniform Partnership Act (hereafter cited as U.P.A.) has not been adopted in Georgia and Louisiana.

3. Revised Uniform Partnership Act (R.U.P.A.) § 201.

4. U.P.A. § 6(1).

5. R.U.P.A. § 202(a).

6. Model Business Corporation Act (hereafter cited as M.B.C.A.) § 3.02(9).

7. U.P.A. § 18(a), (e).

8. U.P.A. § 2; R.U.P.A. § 101(1).

9. U.P.A. § 8(2).

10. See "Tax Considerations of a General Partnership" later in this chapter.

11. R.U.P.A. § 204 provides greater statutory clarity on the determination of property as partnership property:

WHEN PROPERTY IS PARTNERSHIP PROPERTY.

(a) Property is partnership property if acquired:

(1) in the name of the partnership; or

(2) in the name of one or more partners with an indication in the instrument transferring title to the property of the person's capacity as a partner or of the existence of a partnership, but without an indication of the name of the partnership.

(b) Property is acquired in the name of the partnership by a transfer to:

(1) the partnership in its name; or

(2) one or more partners in their capacity as partners in the partnership, if the name of the partnership is indicated in the instrument transferring title to the property.

(3) Property is presumed to be partnership property if purchased with partnership assets, even if not acquired in the name of the partnership or of one or more partners with an indication in the instrument transferring title to the property of the person's capacity as a partner or of the existence of a partnership.

(4) Property acquired in the name of one or more of the partners, without an indication in the instrument transferring title to the property of the person's capacity as a partner or of the existence of a partnership and without use of partnership assets, is presumed to be separate property, even if used for partnership purposes.

12. U.P.A. § 25.

13. R.U.P.A. § 203 provides that partnership property is owned by the partnership, rather than by the individual partners, which avoids the paradox found in the concept of "tenancy in partnership," which makes the partners nominal owners of partnership property but effectively negates the partners' ownership rights.

14. R.U.P.A. § 401(a) accomplishes these computations by requiring capital and income accounts to account for a partner's share of assets and profits. The section provides:

(a) A partnership shall establish an account for each partner which must be credited with an amount equal to the cash plus the value of any other property, net of the amount of any liabilities, the partner contributes to the partnership and the partner's share of the partnership profits. Each partner's account must be charged with an amount equal to the cash plus the value of any other property, net of the amount of any liabilities, distributed by the partnership to the partner and the partner's share of the partnership losses.

15. U.P.A. § 27.

16. U.P.A. § 18(g); R.U.P.A. § 401(i).

17. See R.U.P.A. § 503.

18. U.P.A. § 18(e); R.U.P.A. § 401(f).

19. R.U.P.A. § 301(1).

20. U.P.A. § 18(h); R.U.P.A. § 401(j).

21. R.U.P.A. § 303.

22. R.U.P.A. § 304.

23. U.P.A. § 18(f); R.U.P.A. § 401(h).

24. Meinhard v. Salmon, 249 N.Y. 458, 164 N.E. 545, 546 (1928).

25. See J. W. Callison, Partnership Law and Practice § 12.01 (1997).

26. R.U.P.A. § 404.

27. R.U.P.A. § 103(b).

28. U.P.A. § 18(a); R.U.P.A. § 401.

29. Partnership taxation is *pass-through* taxation, which means that each individual partner is taxed on the partner's pro rata share of each item of profit, loss, deductions, and credits. See "Tax Considerations of a General Partnership" later in this chapter.

30. Internal Revenue Code of 1986, 26 U.S.C.A. § 704(b). The regulations under section 704(b) of the code (adopted before the Tax Reform Act of 1976) outline several relevant considerations in making a determination in regard to whether a special allocation will be recognized for federal income tax purposes. Among these factors are (1) the presence of a business purpose for the allocation; (2) whether related items of income, gain, loss, deduction, or credit from the same source are subject to the same allocation; (3) whether the allocation was made without recognition of normal business factors; (4) whether it was made only after the amount of the specially allocated items could reasonably be estimated; (5) the duration of the allocation; and (6) the overall tax consequences of the allocation.

31. General partners are jointly and severally liable for damages caused by any tort or breach of trust committed by a partner within the scope of the partnership business. They are jointly liable for all other partnership obligations. U.P.A. § 15. Under R.U.P.A. § 306, all liability of partners is joint and several, and that change eliminates the creditors' efforts of finding and suing all partners for joint liability. Nevertheless, R.U.P.A. § 307(d) prevents execution of the assets of a partner to satisfy a judgment based upon a partnership claim without first

levying unsuccessfully against the partnership assets. This rule is called an "exhaustion" rule: individual partners are protected from personal liability until after firm assets have been "exhausted" to pay creditors.

32. U.P.A. § 18(b); R.U.P.A. § 401(c).

33. U.P.A. § 36(1).

34. See "Dissolution and Termination of a Partnership" later in this chapter.

35. U.P.A. § 35(1)(b).

36. R.U.P.A. § 703.

37. R.U.P.A. §§ 303(e), 703(b), 704.

38. U.P.A. § 17; R.U.P.A. § 309.

39. R.U.P.A. § 701. The "buyout" price under R.U.P.A. § 701(b) is the amount that would have been distributable to the dissociating partner if the assets of the partnership were sold at a price equal to the greater of the liquidation value or the value based upon a sale of the entire business as a going concern without the dissociated partner and the partnership were wound up as of that date. In either case, the sale price of the partnership assets must be determined on the basis of the amount that would be paid by a willing buyer to a willing seller, neither being under any compulsion to buy or sell, and with knowledge of all relevant facts. Damages caused by the dissociating partner can be offset against the buyout price. R.U.P.A. § 701(c).

40. U.P.A. § 31(1)(a).

41. U.P.A. § 31(1)(c). The R.U.P.A. similarly provides for dissolution and winding up by the "express will of all the partners." R.U.P.A. § 801(2)(ii).

42. U.P.A. § 31(1)(b)(2).

43. U.P.A. § 31(3), (4), (5).

44. U.P.A. §§ 31(6), 32. The R.U.P.A. provides, in section 801(5) and (6), that a partnership may be dissolved by a court under the following circumstances:

a. The economic purpose of the partnership is likely to be unreasonably frustrated;

b. Another partner has engaged in conduct relating to the partnership business that makes it not reasonably practicable to carry on the business in partnership with that partner;

c. It is not otherwise reasonably practicable to carry on the partnership business in conformity with the partnership agreement;

d. On the application by a transferee of a partner's transferable interest, whenever it is equitable to wind up the partnership business.

45. U.P.A. § 38(1).

46. U.P.A. § 38(2)(b). A dissociated partner is also entitled to indemnification from the continuing partnership under the R.U.P.A. for all liabilities incurred before the dissociation, except liabilities unknown to the part-

nership, and against all liabilities incurred after the dissociation, except liabilities caused by the dissociated partner. R.U.P.A. § 701(c).

47. See J. W. Callison, Partnership Law and Practice § 15.42 (1997).

48. Other examples of liquidating distributions may be found in article V, sections C and D, of the Complex Partnership Agreement, Form I-1, in Appendix I.

49. See also "Share Transfer Restrictions and Buyout Agreements" in Chapter 13.

50. See also "Trade Secret Protection" and "Covenants Not to Compete" in Chapter 11.

51. R.U.P.A. § 802.

52. R.U.P.A. § 802(c).

53. U.P.A. § 33; R.U.P.A. § 805.

54. U.P.A. § 50. The R.U.P.A. makes the distributions to partners more understandable by providing for "settlement of accounts" in R.U.P.A. § 808. The priority of distributions in that section provides:

a. Payments to discharge partnership obligations to creditors, including partners who are creditors;

b. Payment *to* the partners for any positive balances in their capital and income accounts (after allocating profits and losses resulting from the liquidation of assets); and

c. Payments *from* the partners who have a negative balance in their capital and income accounts (after allocating profits and losses resulting from the liquidation of assets).

55. Treas. Reg. § 301-7701-1 through 7701-8.

56. Internal Revenue Code of 1986, 26 U.S.C.A. § 704(c) (2).

57. Internal Revenue Code of 1986, 26 U.S.C.A. § 704(c).

58. See, e.g., J. W. Callison, Partnership Law and Practice §§ 4.01-.29 (1997).

59. Examples of trade name affidavits and certificates appear as forms in Chapter 2.

60. See "Formation and Operation of a Sole Proprietorship" in Chapter 2.

61. The qualification of a *foreign partnership* is patterned after the requirements for qualification of foreign corporations, discussed in Chapter 14.

62. Other helpful references include J. W. Callison, Partnership Law and Practice (1992); and M. Volz, C. Trower, and D. Reiss, The Drafting of Partnership Agreements, American Law Institute (1986).

63. See "Profits and Losses" earlier in this chapter.

64. See "Management of a Partnership" earlier in this chapter.

65. See "Management of a Partnership" earlier in this chapter.

66. See "Management of a Partnership" earlier in this chapter.

67. See "Partner's Interest in a Partnership" earlier in this chapter.

68. See "Partnership Property" earlier in this chapter.

69. See "Dissolution and Termination of a Partnership" earlier in this chapter.

70. See "Covenants Not to Compete" in Chapter 12.

71. See "Dissolution and Termination of a Partnership" earlier in this chapter.

72. See also "Share Transfer Restrictions and Buyout Agreements" in Chapter 13.

73. See "Dissolution and Termination of a Partnership" earlier in this chapter.

74. See Me. Rev. Stat. Ann § 31-804.2; Colo. Rev. Stat. §§ 7-60-102(7) and 7-60-144.

75. See Colo. Rev. Stat. § 7-60-153.

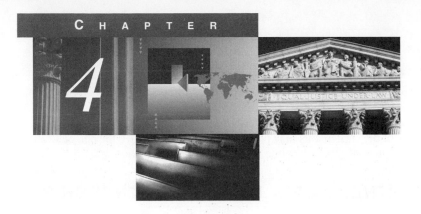

CHAPTER

4

LIMITED PARTNERSHIP

CHARACTERISTICS OF A LIMITED PARTNERSHIP

In many particulars, the **limited partnership** is the same as a general partnership. It is an association of two or more persons carrying on business as co-owners for profit with one or more general partners and one or more limited partners.[1] The limited partnership enjoys certain characteristics of a corporation insofar as the limited partners are concerned, since their investment and limited liability resemble those of a shareholder of a corporation. The general partners in a limited partnership are governed by all the rules of general partnership discussed in Chapter 3. A limited partnership, however, is a two-part business form, and the rights and responsibilities of the limited and general partners must be distinguished.

Most states have adopted a form of the Uniform Limited Partnership Act[2] to regulate the formation and operation of limited partnerships. The original Uniform Limited Partnership Act was approved in 1916, and a few states still use the act in its original form. A substantially revised act was approved by the commissioners in 1976 and several amendments were made in 1985. This Revised Uniform Limited Partnership Act (RULPA) has been adopted in most states and is currently the basis for most limited partnerships throughout the country. In 2001, the commissioners further modified the uniform law and published a Uniform Limited Partnership Act of 2001 (ULPA 2001), which further modernizes limited partnership law and removes some of the traps for the unwary practitioner that developed under the prior statutes. State legislatures are currently considering whether to adopt ULPA 2001. Consequently, at least three different approaches may be found in any local laws concerning the statutory basis for limited partnerships. This chapter refers primarily to the rules from RULPA, since it states the law that most states currently use, although it discusses unique issues that arose under the original act and important new changes that are being proposed in ULPA 2001 (for those who insist on knowing everything about limited partnership law throughout the country).

The most important statutory requirement under all versions of the act, the filing of a limited partnership certificate, is discussed in detail later in this chapter. It is important to note at the outset, however, that the limited partnership may be formed only with the formality prescribed in the statute and may not be born of a simple private agreement between the parties. Like a corporation, this form of business is formed by filing documents with a public filing office, usually the Secretary of State, and the fact that these documents disclose information about the operation of the business and the identity of the participants may pose additional problems for the person drafting the documents.

GENERAL PARTNERS OF A LIMITED PARTNERSHIP

Each limited partnership must have at least one general partner who faces the same risks and responsibilities as a partner in a general partnership. The liability exposure of limited partners is confined to their contributions, but the general partner suffers unlimited liability, meaning that his or her individual assets are vulnerable to firm creditors. In the previous chapter, you learned that in many states a partnership can be registered as a limited liability partnership to insulate the general partner from individual liability for partnership debts and obligations. Those same statutes also allow for limited partnerships to register to avoid the personal liability of the general partner.[3] The general partner also has full responsibility for management and control of the partnership affairs, since limited partners historically have been forbidden to participate in the control of the business if they are to maintain their limited liability status.[4]

One person may be both a general partner and a limited partner at the same time[5] simply by naming the person as a partner in both capacities in the partnership agreement and the certificate of limited partnership filed to form the partnership. This may produce some benefits for the person serving in both capacities. In a person's status as general partner, he or she is fully liable for firm obligations and has no limited liability. However, that person's contribution as a limited partner ranks with the priorities of other limited partners for dissolution purposes,[6] and his or her limited partnership interest is freely transferable without causing a dissolution of the partnership.[7]

If the limited partnership has two or more general partners, the rights and responsibilities between those general partners are the same as in any general partnership.

A partner's status is that of a general partner if that partner is identified as a general partner in the partnership agreement and named as a general partner in the certificate of limited partnership.[8] Once the original certificate of limited partnership has been filed, additional general partners may be admitted in the manner provided in the partnership agreement, or if the agreement is silent, with the written consent of all partners, both general and limited.[9]

There are several ways a general partner can dissociate or withdraw from the limited partnership, either intentionally or accidentally. The general partner "ceases to be a general partner of the partnership" whenever one or more of the following situations occur.

1. The general partner withdraws by giving notice to the other partners (this action may violate the partnership agreement and cause the general partner to be liable for damages).[10]
2. The general partner assigns the interest he or she owns in the partnership to another person who is not a partner. This action does not make the other person a partner in the partnership; it merely entitles that person to receive the distributions to which the general partner would be entitled. Nevertheless, the assignment causes the general partner to cease being a partner of the partnership.[11]
3. The general partner is expelled or removed as a general partner in accordance with the procedure described in the partnership agreement.[12]
4. The general partner admits personal insolvency (such as by filing a petition in bankruptcy or by agreeing to reorganization of his, her or its debts), but the general partner may continue being a partner if the partnership agreement excuses such an act.[13]
5. The general partner dies or is incompetent, or in the case of a general partner that is an association (such as a corporation, a trust, or another partnership), the association is terminated or dissolved.[14]

Recall that the withdrawal of a general partner has the effect of dissolving the partnership under general partnership law.[15] The same effect occurs under limited partnership law, with three major exceptions: (1) all of the partners may consent to the continued service of a general partner who has been subject to the foregoing events of withdrawal;[16] (2) another general partner may be permitted under the partnership agreement to continue the business even though a fellow general partner has withdrawn; (3) all of the partners may agree in writing within ninety days after the withdrawal of the general partner to continue the business by the appointment of one or more additional general partners.[17]

If the partnership agreement permits it, general partners have a right to vote (on a per capita or any other basis prescribed in the agreement) separately as general partners or together with the limited partners on any matter affecting partnership business.[18]

The remaining sections in this chapter deal with the limited partnership's unique variations from a general partnership. In all respects except those specifically set forth in the following sections, a limited partnership is governed by the same rules as a general partnership, including the general partner's fiduciary duties to account for profits, care for partnership assets, not compete with the partnership business, faithfully serve the partnership business without diversions, fully disclose information relevant to partnership affairs, and act in a reasonably prudent way in administering the partnership activities.[19]

LIMITED LIABILITY AND CONTRIBUTIONS

The most significant characteristic of the limited partnership is that limited partners are protected from full individual liability. The liability of the limited partner is limited to the amount of that partner's investment as stated in the partnership agreement,[20] and the limited partner's individual assets cannot be reached by partnership creditors for obligations of the limited partnership. In this respect, the limited partner is almost exactly like a shareholder of a corporation. This feature makes the limited partnership particularly attractive for persons with substantial private resources that they prefer not to risk in the business enterprise. The only potential loss is the investment.

The original Uniform Limited Partnership Act significantly restricted the limited partner's available source of contributions. That statute permitted contributions by a limited partner in cash or other property only. No contribution of services was permitted.[21] This rule was based, in part, on the prohibition against a limited partner's participation in management. Under the revised and new acts, partners may contribute cash, property, or services rendered, or may simply promise through a promissory note or other agreement to contribute cash or property or perform services in the future.[22] These expanded contribution rules reflect the attitude of the drafters of the revised act that persons who participate as limited partners in modern limited partnerships should be able to participate in some aspects of the management of the business without losing their limited liability protection. The management rights of the limited partner under the new statutory provisions are discussed in the next section of this chapter.

Partnership creditors are entitled to rely upon a limited partner's contribution as a source for payment of their obligations. Consequently, the limited partner's written promise in the partnership agreement to contribute assets or services to the partnership can be enforced by the creditors of the partnership. If a partner is unable to perform (because he or she has disposed of the asset promised to be contributed or is dead or disabled), that partner (or his or her estate) will be obligated to contribute cash equal to the value of the defaulted contribution.[23] The other partners of the partnership may be forgiving, however, and may, by a unanimous consent, agree to forgo any contribution not made by a limited partner. Nevertheless, any creditors who extended credit to the partnership before the other partners forgave the obligation may still be able to enforce the original obligation for the contribution against the limited partner.[24]

Historically, the law provided two limitations on the manner in which the limited partner's involvement in the partnership was projected to the outside world. Limited liability will only be observed provided the limited partner does not actively participate in the control of the business and does not knowingly permit the use of his or her name in the firm name (with some exceptions that are discussed later). The new act eliminates these restrictions on a limited partners activity. However, even with these restrictions under the laws currently in effect in most states, the limited partner would be liable to a person who reasonably believes, based upon the limited partner's conduct, that the limited partner is a general partner of the partnership. The limited partner could also be liable to creditors who extend credit to the partnership without actual knowledge that the limited partner is not a general partner.[25]

When a limited partner discovers that there is a possibility of personal liability and erroneously and in good faith believes that he or she is a limited partner in the partnership, that partner may avoid individual liability by filing the appropriate certificate or amendment to the certificate (if a creditor is asserting that the limited partnership was improperly formed or maintained). The limited partner may withdraw from future equity participation in the partnership by filing a certificate of withdrawal. By taking these actions, a limited partner would be liable only to a creditor who believed in good faith that the limited partner was a general partner of the partnership at the time of the transaction for which liability is claimed.[26] For example, suppose that Robbie Schwarz agreed to be a limited partner in a limited partnership formed with Michael Crouch as the general partner to operate an apartment building. Although the partnership agreement was signed by both Robbie and Michael, the limited partnership certificate was not filed properly, and, consequently, the limited partnership was not properly formed. A contractor was hired to construct some improvements to the apartment building and took instructions from Robbie because Michael was out of town when the work was begun. If the contractor's bill is not paid, the contractor might attempt to recover from both Michael and Robbie personally as partners. Robbie could avoid liability to the contractor by filing the certificate of limited partnership or filing a certificate of withdrawal *and* by showing that the contractor did not believe in good faith that Robbie was a general partner of the limited partnership.

MANAGEMENT AND CONTROL

The general partners of a limited partnership manage the business, and their management responsibilities and rights are the same in a limited partnership as they are in a general partnership.[27] The partnership agreement usually provides for the specific authority of the general partner and for any desired limitations on the general partner's authority. There are certain activities a general partner may never do without the consent of the limited partners, including acting in contravention of the agreement or interfering with the ordinary business of the partnership, possessing partnership property for other than business purposes, admitting another general partner, and confessing a judgment against the firm.[28] The general partner also has the fiduciary duties inherent in the partnership relationship and as any agent would have to the principal for whom the agent is conducting business.[29]

To preserve the limited partner's limited liability status, all management and control over partnership affairs should be vested in the general partner. Historically, this prohibition against management participation has caused some uncomfortable uncertainty in the limited partnership organization because it is difficult to predict the extent of participation that will defeat a limited partner's limited liability status.

Under most states' current law, limited partners are not permitted to participate in the control of the business if they wish to enjoy limited liability; however, a limited partner is not regarded as participating in the control of the business simply because he or she is involved in one or more of the following situations:

1. being a contractor for or agent or employee of the limited partnership or the general partner, or being an officer, director, or shareholder of the corporate general partner;
2. consulting with and advising the general partner regarding the business of the partnership;
3. acting as a surety for the partnership to guarantee or assume its specific obligations;
4. bringing a derivative action on behalf of the partnership;
5. requesting or attending a meeting of partners; or

6. proposing or voting on the firm's dissolution, a sale of substantially all of the firm's assets, the incurrence of debt outside the ordinary course of business, a change in the nature of the business, the admission or removal of a general or limited partner, amendments to the partnership agreement, transactions having a conflict of interest, or anything else that the partnership agreement permits the limited partners to decide by vote.

These activities described in the statutes are regarded as **safe harbor activities**, meaning that a limited partner may safely participate in these activities without risking the loss of limited liability. Most statutes even recognize that this is not a complete list of activities a limited partner may undertake. Because of the difficulty in applying the management rules to limited partners and the uncertainty created by the general standards stated in the statutes, the new uniform act assures limited partners of limited liability "even if the limited partner participates in the management and control of the limited partnership."[30] However, the issue of the limited partner's participation in the control of the business still remains an issue under most states' current laws.

Limited partners are always entitled to inspect and copy the books and to have an accounting of partnership affairs. They also have the right to be informed on all matters respecting the business of the firm, and may demand any information from the general partners as is just and reasonable.[31]

ADMISSION, SUBSTITUTION, AND WITHDRAWAL OF A LIMITED PARTNER

Unlike general partners, limited partners may freely come and go, with very few restrictions. If provisions are made in the partnership agreement and the certificate of limited partnership, additional limited partners may be admitted without the consent of the existing limited partners by complying with the procedures in the partnership agreement, and if necessary under local law, by filing an amendment to the certificate.[32] Similarly, a limited partner may withdraw from the partnership and receive a return of his or her capital contribution without causing a dissolution of the firm.[33] If the limited partner's contribution is essential to the continued operation of business, however, this right to withdraw may be restricted or denied by the agreement.

The law permits a limited partner to withdraw and demand the return of his or her contribution on the date specified for return of the contribution in the partnership agreement or upon giving six months' notice in writing.[34] The contribution also may be returned at any time if all partners, general and limited, consent to its return. However, the investment will be returned only if the firm's creditors have been paid or sufficient assets remain to pay them, which may mean that a limited partner will receive nothing if the partnership's debts are greater than its assets.[35] Unless the partnership agreement provides otherwise, or all partners consent, the limited partner has the right to demand only cash in withdrawal, even if other property was contributed to the partnership.[36] In many states, an amendment of the certificate must be filed to reflect the withdrawal.

The partnership agreement or certificate may grant to a limited partner authority to substitute a new limited partner in his or her place without the consent of the other partners. If the agreement does not contain such express authority, the transfer or assignment of a limited partner's interest has an effect similar to that of the assignment of a general partner's interest. The assignment grants to the assignee the right to receive the valuable characteristics of the limited partner's interest (the right to profits and other distributions—called the "limited partner's transferable interest" under the new law) but it does not make the transferee a new partner unless all the partners consent.[37] Any substitution of limited partners, by the power of agreement or by consent, may require an amendment to the certificate to reflect the change.[38] (See Exhibit 4–1, Assignment of a Limited Partner's Transferable Interest, and Exhibit 4–2, Consent to Substitution of a Limited Partner.)

Exhibit 4–1.

Assignment of a Limited
Partner's Transferrable
Interest

ASSIGNMENT OF A LIMITED PARTNER'S TRANSFERABLE INTEREST

For value received, I, the undersigned, of_____, hereby assign to_____, of _____, the whole of my interest in the limited partnership of _____, conducting business under a partnership agreement dated _____, 20___. Effective upon the signing of this instrument, the assignee shall be entitled to receive the transferable interest, including without limitations, the share of the profits or other compensation by way of income to which I would otherwise be entitled, and to the return of my contribution to the capital of the partnership. In the event that all the other members of the partnership consent thereto, the assignee shall be entitle to all the rights which I, as a limited partner, had in the partnership.

Dated_____, 20___.   *[Signature]*

[Acknowledgement]

Exhibit 4–2.

Consent to Substitution of a
Limited Partner

CONSENT TO SUBSTITUTION OF A LIMITED PARTNER

We, the undersigned, being all the members of the limited partnership of _____, except _____, who by an instrument dated _____, 20__, and duly acknowledged by her, has assigned her entire interest as a limited partner in this partnership to _____, of _____, do hereby consent that _____ be substituted as a limited partner in the place of _____, and entitled to all the rights which_____ had as a limited partner in this partnership pursuant to the terms of the partnership agreement dated _____, 20__.

Dated _____, 20__.   *[Signatures]*

DISSOLUTION OF A LIMITED PARTNERSHIP

Causes of Dissolution

Dissolution of limited partnerships is very similar to dissolution of general partnerships (discussed in Chapter 3). The major distinctions stem from the limited partner's typical position outside of the management of the business. A limited partner is usually a passive investor, like a shareholder of a corporation, and although the limited partner's demise, insanity, bankruptcy, or withdrawal may be a sad event, none of those things will affect the continuation of the business. Consequently, the incapacity of a limited partner does not cause dissolution. Similarly, the limited partner may withdraw his or her capital contribution (investment) and demand its distribution, and the partnership may continue without that partner. Most authorities agree, however, that misconduct by a limited partner, including any act that would adversely affect the business of the firm, would be grounds for dissolution by the other partners. In general, a limited partner has a contractual relationship with a limited partnership and is not regarded as an integral person for the operation of the business of the partnership. Nevertheless, the withdrawal by a limited partner before the termination of the partnership may be disruptive, at least, and a serious breach of the agreement, at worst. To guard against challenges to the permanence of estate planning limited partnerships, some states have amended their laws to prohibit limited partner withdrawal unless otherwise provided in the limited partnership agreement, and the new uniform act recognizes the limited partner's power to withdraw but permits the partnership agreement to eliminate it. If a limited partner withdraws from the partnership, rightfully or wrongfully, the business may continue, and any damages caused by the limited partner's withdrawal will simply be subtracted from the return of the limited partner's investment, as would be the case with any contract breach.

The limited partnership will be dissolved at the times for termination of the partnership specified in the certificate of limited partnership or in the partnership agreement. Furthermore, as with general partnerships, all partners of the limited partnership may consent to a dissolution at any time.[39]

Limited partners have only limited rights to ask for dissolution of the partnership if all other partners are not willing to dissolve the firm. A limited partner may have the right to request a dissolution by decree of court whenever it is not reasonably practical to carry on the business under the partnership agreement.[40] This is a very broad standard and probably incorporates most of the causes justifying dissolution under the original laws of limited partnership, such as incapacity of a general partner, misconduct or breach of the partnership agreement by a partner, or other business or legal reasons that would justify termination of the business based upon changed circumstances.[41] On the other hand, the limited partner may not be able to require a dissolution of the partnership for purely selfish reasons under the Revised Uniform Limited Partnership Act. For example, under the original act, it was possible for a limited partner to request a dissolution of the firm if the limited partner had rightfully demanded a return of a capital contribution but the demand had been ignored.[42] Under the revised act, the demanding limited partner is simply treated as an ordinary creditor of the partnership and may obtain a judgment for the amount of the unreturned contribution; and under the new uniform act, the limited partner is simply treated as a transferee of its own transferable interest in profits and other distributions.[43] In the formation of the partnership, however, limited partners can be granted the power to request dissolution under such circumstances and that right can be incorporated into the original partnership agreement.

The general partner is the only integral partner of the firm in the law of limited partnerships. A general partner will be deemed to have withdrawn from the limited partnership by resigning (through written notice); assigning his or her interest in the partnership to a third person; being removed in accordance with the agreement; becoming bankrupt (or taking action similar to bankruptcy); dying; becoming incompetent; or in the case of a general partner that is another business organization, ceasing to be a valid entity under law.[44] These **events of withdrawal** result in a dissolution of the partnership unless there is at least one other general partner and the partnership agreement permits the business to be carried on by the remaining general partner, or unless, within ninety days after the withdrawal, all partners agree in writing to continue the business and to the appointment of a new or additional general partner.[45] Although the various acts do not explicitly so state, acts of misconduct by the general partner that violate the partnership agreement but that do not result in removal of the partner probably still qualify as grounds for dissolution through court action on the request of either general or limited partners.[46]

Continuation of a Limited Partnership Following Dissolution

A disadvantage of a general partnership is the possibility that an accidental dissolution will trigger the obligation to wind up and liquidate the assets of the business at an inopportune time. The antiquated rules of general partnership permit a continuation of the business by the remaining partners only if the agreement anticipates the dissolution or if the dissolution is wrongfully caused.[47] Since the limited partnership is considered to be a useful business organization for modern transactions, and since limited partnership law has been revised several times in response to modern practices, the consequences of dissolution are much less drastic under limited partnership law than they are under general partnership law. As previously mentioned, the mere inability of the general partner to continue in that capacity does not eliminate the continuation of the partnership business. The partnership agreement may anticipate such an event and provide for the continuation of the business by another named general partner. Even if the partnership agreement is silent on this issue, the limited partners may, within ninety days after an event of withdrawal, agree in writing to continue the business without interruption.[48] Nevertheless, it is preferable to anticipate all potential events of dissolution and to provide in the partnership agreement for the procedure to continue the business. It is also best to name the person who will serve as a general partner if the original general partner is unable to continue to serve.

Termination and Winding Up

If a cause for dissolution occurs and the business is not continued, the limited partnership must be liquidated. The partnership agreement may (and should) anticipate the procedure for winding up by designating appropriate liquidators and giving them specific instructions concerning the procedure for liquidation. Limited partners were formerly prohibited from participating in the winding up of a limited partnership unless they obtained court permission.[49] Under the revised and new acts, unless the partnership agreement provides otherwise, limited partners may serve as liquidators, as may general partners who have not wrongfully dissolved the limited partnership.[50]

The original act prescribed a scheme of priorities for the distribution of assets of a limited partnership that created a substantial incentive for capital investment by limited partners. The effect of the original act was to prefer limited partners in the distribution of assets, so the general partners could be paid only after the limited partners were fully satisfied.

Under the current law there is no preference for limited partners unless the agreement creates one. The assets of the limited partnership are to be distributed as follows:

1. to creditors, including partners who are creditors, in satisfaction of liabilities of limited partnership, other than liabilities for distributions provided to the partners in the partnership agreement;
2. to all partners and former partners in satisfaction of any liabilities for distributions agreed under the partnership agreement; and
3. to all partners for the return of their contributions and, then, for their proportionate share of the excess assets (which constitute their share of profit.)[51]

Notice that general and limited partners rank at the same level for receipt of partnership distributions under the modern statutory provisions, but, as with general partnerships, it is still possible to provide for a different scheme of distributions in the partnership agreement, as long as business creditors are fully paid. Thus, a preference to distributions can be used as an incentive to obtain capital contributions of limited partners.

TAXATION OF A LIMITED PARTNERSHIP

Typically, a limited partnership is treated like a general partnership for tax purposes. Recall that the general partnership acts only as a conduit through which income is deemed to be distributed to each partner in the proportions specified in the agreement. The normal limited partnership has the same treatment, which may be an advantage to the limited partner seeking to declare losses to offset similar passive income from other sources.

This tax advantage from offsetting losses is one reason limited partnerships have become favored forms of organization for developing real estate and operating rental property. The accelerated depreciation allowances available for these enterprises produce paper losses, which are passed directly to the partners and shelter other income from taxation. More recent tax laws have significantly reduced this advantage, however, by requiring that losses from partnership investments (where a partner is not actively involved in the business of the partnership) be offset only against income from other passive investment sources. For example, if a limited partnership owned an apartment building and received income from rents, reduced by expenses of operation and depreciation of the building, any losses that resulted from the fact that expenses and depreciation exceeded the income could only be offset against other income from other rental properties. It is not possible to offset the "passive" partnership losses against income of a partner received from his or her employment. Federal law has developed a hostile attitude toward tax-sheltered investments of any type and has imposed significant restrictions on a partner's ability to offset income with losses and severe penalties for tax-motivated deductions that are not clearly authorized by the law. Consequently, the perception of a limited partnership as a tax-advantaged business enterprise has been considerably blurred. Most limited partnerships now promise significant real economic benefits to attract limited partners, rather than promising paper deductions and losses to tax-motivated investors.

Recently, the Internal Revenue Service issued new classification regulations[52] for taxation of business entities to replace the former rules and regulations, which had become extremely complex through the years of interpretation and forced limited partnerships to attempt to avoid corporate characteristics (such as free transferability of ownership interests, perpetual duration, etc.) to avoid being reclassified as a corporation for tax purposes.[53] Under the new regulations limited partnerships are treated as partnerships, even though the structure of the limited partnership may include many similarities to a corporation, unless the limited partnership affirmatively elects to be treated as a corporation for tax purposes. One reason that a limited partnership may want to be treated as a corporation is that the business will require significant capital accumulation for expansion, and the partners do not want to be taxed personally on the annual income of the business because they need to leave all of the available money in the business for expansion. Taxation as a corporation requires that the partnership pay corporate taxes on income, but the individual partners do not have to use other personal funds to pay individual taxes. Under the new regulations, a limited partnership is automatically taxed as a partnership if

1. the limited partnership is properly formed under state law as a business entity;
2. the limited partnership is not engaged in certain businesses that must be taxed as corporations, such as insurance companies, banks, and other businesses that are owned by governments; and
3. the limited partnership does not elect to be taxed as a corporation.

Limited partnerships formed prior to 1997 that have been taxed as partnerships will continue to be so taxed as long as there is a reasonable basis for that tax classification, the partners report their taxes under the partnership rules, and the Internal Revenue Service has not challenged the limited partnership's right to use the partnership classification for tax purposes.

FORMATION AND OPERATION OF A LIMITED PARTNERSHIP

With the singular, but extremely important, exception of the limited partnership certificate, the formation of a limited partnership is the same as the formation of a general partnership. Thus, licensing requirements have identical application to this form of business, and other state formalities must be observed. The agreement plays an even more important role in a limited partnership and should give special attention to the idiosyncrasies of the limited partnership.

Name

The revised statute governing the name of the limited partnership is very similar to statutes regulating corporate names. The name of the limited partnership must be stated in the limited partnership certificate (the public filing), and the name of the limited partnership must contain, without abbreviation, the words *limited partnership,* which should give notice to the world of the limited liability of certain of the firm's partners.[54] Some states permit the use of abbreviations, such as *L.P.* or *Ltd.,* although at least the latter may cause some confusion with corporate organizations, which are also permitted to use the words Limited or Ltd. If the limited partnership registers as a limited liability limited partnership to protect the general partner from personal liability for the partnership obligations, the name of the limited partnership must contain some acknowledgment that the partnership has full limited liability. An abbreviation of *registered limited liability limited partnership (R.L.L.L.P)* is usually required.

The name usually may not contain any word or phrase indicating or implying that the partnership is organized other than for a purpose stated in its agreement or certificate, and the name may not be the same as or deceptively similar to the name of any corporation or other limited partnership organized or qualified under the laws of the local jurisdiction.

The name of the limited partnership may be reserved by anyone attempting to organize the limited partnership or intending to qualify a foreign limited partnership in the state. (See Exhibit 4–3, Reservation of a Limited Partnership Name.) The normal period for the reservation of a

Exhibit 4–3.

Reservation of a Limited
Partnership Name

> Secretary of State
> _____
> _____
> _____
>
>   Re: Reservation of limited part-
>   nership name for [proposed
>   name]
>
> Ladies and Gentlemen:
>   Enclosed please find my check in the amount of $_____ to cover the
> cost of reserving the following limited partnership name for a period of 120 days
> in your records:
>   [_____]
>   I intend to organize a domestic limited partnership using said name.
>   Please acknowledge receipt of this reservation of limited partnership name
> and your acceptance of this reservation by receipting and returning to me the
> enclosed copy of this letter in the enclosed self-addressed envelope.
>   Thank you for your anticipated assistance.
>   Sincerely,
>
>   [Signature]

name is 120 days, and the reservation usually may be extended for an additional 60 days. More-over, similar to corporate law, limited partnership law allows the reserved limited partnership name to be transferred by an appropriate notice of transfer.[55]

Both the old and new laws contain a provision designed to avoid confusion of persons doing business with a partnership as to the identity of the general and limited partners. The use of a limited partner's surname in the name of the limited partnership is prohibited if the limited liability of that partner is to be maintained, unless (1) the partnership has a general partner with the same name, or (2) the business had been carried on under a name including the limited partner's surname before that person became a limited partner. Thus, a limited partnership composed of Ron Williams and Charlie Langhoff as general partners and Mary Williams, Scott Charlton, and Bob Thompson as limited partners could use the name "Williams and Langhoff, Limited Partnership," based on the first exception, even though Mary Williams is a limited partner. Similarly, if Charlie Langhoff subsequently became a limited partner, the firm could continue under the name "Williams and Langhoff, Limited Partnership," under the second exception. The new uniform act has removed that restriction and permits the use of a limited partner's name in the firm name.

The Partnership Agreement

The *partnership agreement* is defined in the current law as any valid agreement, written or oral, of the partners as to the affairs of the limited partnership and the conduct of business. (The agreement should be written, but the definition permits the use of an oral agreement.) The original act did not refer to the partnership agreement at all, and appeared to assume that all important matters would be set forth in the certificate of limited partnership. Under modern practice, however, it is common for partners to enter into a comprehensive partnership agreement, only part of which is included in the certificate, which is filed as a matter of public notice. The certificate has gained less and less importance in subsequent revisions of the law. The revised act originally provided that the certificate would be the source of public information concerning the addition and withdrawal of partners and capital and any other important issues concerning the structure of the partnership that might be important to creditors and others doing business with the partnership. In subsequent revisions to the revised act and in the new uniform act, the certificate is relegated to simply confirming the addresses and identity of the partnership and the general partners. All other issues are now left to be included in the partnership agreement.[56]

Preparation of the limited partnership agreement usually is based upon the expressed desires of the proposed general partners, since limited partners play a passive role in the formation and operation of the business. The basic form of the agreement resembles a general partnership agreement, since the limited partnership includes at least one general partner. All considerations specified in the checklist proposed for general partnerships (see "Formation and Operation of a General Partnership" in Chapter 3) should be considered in the drafting of the limited partnership agreement, especially when more than one general partner will manage the business.

Several special matters, raised by the specific statutory rules that govern limited partnerships, also should be addressed in the agreement. The following checklist is designed to be used in addition to that provided in Chapter 3 to draft a complete limited partnership agreement.

Checklist

1. Provide for the filing and recording of a certificate of limited partnership and other necessary documents in the appropriate places.

Certificate of Limited Partnership   **EXAMPLE**

A Certificate of Limited Partnership created hereby shall be recorded in accordance with the Limited Partnership Act in each state in which the Partnership may establish a place of business. In addition, the General Partner shall file and publish any other notices, certificates, statements, or other instruments required by any provision of any law of the state in which the partnership is organized or is qualified to do business.

---

2. State provisions for the admission of additional limited partners.

Admission of Additional Limited Partners   **EXAMPLE**

Subject to any other provision of this Agreement, after the formation of the Partnership, a person may be admitted as an additional Limited Partner with the written consent of the General Partner and the execution by the additional Limited Partner of a counterpart of this Agreement.

---

3. State provisions for the admission of transferees of limited partners.

Admission of Transferees of Limited Partners   **EXAMPLE**

Subject to the other provisions of this Agreement, a person who has received a valid written transfer of a partnership interest in this Partnership, including a transferee of a General Partner, may become a Limited Partner in the Partnership by a specific grant of authority from the transferor to the transferee of the right to become a Limited Partner in the Partnership. In addition, prior to admission of the transferee as a Limited Partner in the Partnership, the General Partner may require such opinions of counsel as are necessary or desired in the sole discretion of the General Partner, to determine that the transfer of the interest in the Partnership from the transferor to the transferee does not violate any federal or state securities law, or affect the tax consequences of the Partnership. The transferee shall also be required to execute a counterpart of this Agreement prior to admission as a Limited Partner.

---

4. Provide that any new partners must agree to be bound by the terms of the partnership agreement.

Additional Partners Bound by Agreement   **EXAMPLE**

Notwithstanding any other provisions of this Agreement, before any person is admitted or substituted as a Limited Partner, he or she shall agree in writing to be bound by all of the provisions of this Agreement.

---

5. Provide for additional capital contributions by limited partners if desired, and describe any restrictions or limitations on additional capital contributions.

EXAMPLE

Limitation on Additional Capital Contributions

After the initial capital contributions have been paid, Limited Partners may be required to contribute their proportionate share of the capital of this Partnership or such additional sums of money or property as shall be determined to be necessary by the General Partner to meet operating expenses of the Partnership when funds generated from Partnership operations are insufficient to meet such expenses. However, Limited Partners shall not be required to contribute more than twenty percent (20%) of their initial capital contributions as additional capital.

6. Describe the rights of limited partners to withdraw or reduce their capital contributions to the partnership. In addition, if limited partners will have the right to demand or receive property other than cash in return for a contribution, describe the circumstances under which such property would be distributed.

EXAMPLE

Withdrawal and Return of Capital

No Limited Partner shall have the right to withdraw or reduce his or her contribution to the capital of the Partnership without the consent of the General Partner. No Limited Partner shall have the right to bring an action for partition against the Partnership. No Limited Partner shall have the right to demand or receive property other than cash in return for his or her contribution. No Limited Partner shall have priority over any other Limited Partner, either as to the return of his or her contribution of capital or as to profits, losses, or distributions.

7. Although the modern uniform acts have become completely permissive concerning limited partner's participation in management of the business, current states' laws still usually restrict the limited partners from participation in the control of the business. To avoid any questions about the limited liability of a limited partner, it is best to restrict the limited partner's participation in typical management activities.

EXAMPLE

Role of Limited Partner

Except as otherwise provided in the Agreement, a Limited Partner shall have no part in or interfere in any manner with the conduct or control of the business of the Partnership, and shall have no right or authority to act for or by the Partnership. The Limited Partner of this Partnership will be permitted, if agreed by the General Partner, to perform the following acts on behalf of the Partnership:

1) acting as a contractor for or agent or employee of the Limited Partnership or of the General Partner or being an officer, director, or shareholder of the Corporate General Partner;

2) consulting with and advising the General Partner with respect to the business of the Limited Partnership;

3) acting as a surety for the Limited Partnership or guaranteeing or assuming one or more specific obligations of the Limited Partnership;

4) taking any action required or permitted by the laws of the state under which the Partnership was organized or qualified to bring or pursue a derivative action in the right of the Limited Partnership;

5) requesting or attending a meeting of partners; and

6) proposing, approving, or disapproving, by voting or otherwise, one or more of the following matters:

i) the dissolution and winding up of the Partnership;

ii) the sale, exchange, lease, mortgage, pledge, or other transfer of all or substantially all of the assets of the Limited Partnership;

iii) the incurrence of indebtedness by the Limited Partnership other than the ordinary course of its business;

iv) a change in the nature of the business;

v) the admission or removal of a General Partner;

vi) the admission or removal of a Limited Partner;

vii) a transaction involving an actual or potential conflict of interest between the General Partner and the Partnership or the Limited Partners;

viii) an amendment to the Partnership Agreement or Certificate of Limited Partnership;

ix) the approval of capital contributions in excess of $100,000; and

x) the location of the Partnership's offices within this state.

8. Describe in some detail the rights, powers, and obligations of the general partner, and the extent to which management may be delegated.

Rights, Powers, and Obligations of the General Partner

The management and control of the Partnership and its business and affairs shall rest exclusively with the General Partner who shall have all the rights and powers which may be possessed by a general partner by law, and such rights and powers as are otherwise conferred by law or are necessary, advisable or convenient, to the discharge of its duties under this Agreement and to the management of the business and affairs of the Partnership. Without limiting the generality of the foregoing, the General Partner shall have the following rights and powers:

a) to spend the capital and net income of the Partnership in the exercise of any rights or powers possessed by the General Partner hereunder;

b) to acquire, purchase, hold, and sell real estate and lease the same to third parties and to enter into agreements with others with respect to such activities, which agreements may contain such terms, provisions, and conditions as the General Partner in its sole and absolute discretion shall approve;

c) to borrow money to discharge the Partnership's obligations, or to protect and preserve the assets of the Partnership, or to incur any other indebtedness in the ordinary course of business and to pledge all or any of the Partnership's assets or income to secure such loans;

d) to employ a business manager or managers to manage the Partnership's affairs;

e) to execute leases, licenses, rental agreements, and use agreements, on behalf of the Partnership, of and with respect to all or any portion of the real property; and

f) to delegate all or any of its duties hereunder, and in furtherance of any such delegation to appoint, employ, or contract with any person it may in its sole discretion deem necessary or desirable for the transaction of the business of the Partnership, which persons may, under the supervision of the General Partner: administer the day-to-day operations of the Partnership; serve as the Partnership's advisers and consultants in connection with policy decisions made by the General Partner; act as consultants, accountants, correspondents, attorneys, brokers, escrow agents, or in any other capacity deemed by the General Partner necessary or desirable; investigate, select, and on behalf of the Partnership, conduct relations with persons acting in such capacities, and enter into appropriate contracts with, or employ, or retain services performed or to be performed by, all or any of them in connection with the real estate; perform or assist in the performance of such administrative or managerial functions necessary in the management of the Partnership and its business as may be agreed upon with the General Partner; and perform such other acts or services for the Partnership as the General Partner, in its sole and absolute discretion, may approve.

9. Describe any limitations or restrictions on the general partner's powers.

Limitations on General Partner's Powers

The General Partner shall not, without the written consent or ratification of the specific act by the Limited Partners:

a) make, execute, or deliver any assignment for the benefit of creditors, or sign any confession of judgment on behalf of the Partnership;

b) possess partnership property or assign its rights in specific partnership property for other than a Partnership purpose;

c) act in contravention of the Agreement;

d) conduct any act that would make it impossible to carry on the ordinary business of the Partnership;

e) admit a person as a general partner; or

f) permit a creditor who makes a nonrecourse loan to the Partnership to acquire any interest in profits, capital, or property of the Partnership other than as a secured creditor.

10. Describe the rights of limited partners, consistent with the limited partners' passive role in the partnership.

Rights of the Limited Partners

Limited Partners shall have the right to:
    a) have the Partnership books kept at the principal place of business of the Partnership or such other place as designated by the General Partner, and to inspect and copy any of them in accordance with this Agreement;
    b) obtain from the General Partner any information concerning the financial condition of the Partnership by requesting the same with 72 hours' written notice and meeting with the General Partner to obtain such information during normal business hours of the Partnership; and
    c) receive a copy of the Limited Partnership's federal, state, and local income tax returns for each year within 120 days after the close of the Partnership's fiscal year.

11. Describe any rights that will be granted to the limited partners to remove and replace the general partner. Since the limited partners cannot take active part in management without losing limited liability, their failure to designate a new general partner should require a liquidation of the partnership.

Removal of General Partner

Limited Partners shall have the right to remove the General Partner, by written vote or written consent signed and acknowledged by at least ninety percent (90%) of the then outstanding limited partnership interests, and given to the General Partner within thirty (30) days prior to the effective date of removal according to the following:
    a) removal of the General Partner shall be effective upon the substitution of the new General Partner.
    b) concurrently with notice of removal or within thirty (30) days thereafter by notice similarly given, the Limited Partners shall designate a new General Partner.
    c) substitution of a new General Partner shall be effective upon written acceptance of the duties and the responsibilities of General Partner hereunder. Upon effective substitution of a new General Partner, this Agreement shall remain in full force except for the change in General Partner, and the business of the Partnership shall be continued by the new General Partner. The new General Partner shall thereupon execute, acknowledge, file, and publish, as appropriate, amendments to the Certificate of Limited Partnership and Trade Name Affidavit.
    d) failure of the Limited Partners to designate a General Partner within the time specified herein or failure of a new General Partner so designated to execute written acceptance of the duties and responsibilities of General Partner hereunder within ten (10) days after such designation shall require the liquidation of the Partnership as provided in this Agreement.

12. For ease of management of the partnership, each limited partner may grant a power of attorney to the general partner to execute documents to maintain limited partnership status in his or her name. This practice avoids the nuisance of locating all limited partners to obtain their signatures for documents that need to be filed to properly maintain the partnership. Under the revised and new uniform acts, only general partners are required to sign the limited partnership certificate. However, most local laws are still based upon the original act and the unamended revised act, so administrative requirements such as these should be considered.

Power of Attorney

Each of the Limited Partners hereby irrevocably constitutes and appoints the General Partner as true and lawful attorney-in-fact for such Limited Partner with power and authority to act in his or her name and on his or her behalf in the execution, acknowledgment, filing, and recording of documents, which shall include the following:
    a) a Certificate of Limited Partnership and any amendment thereto, under the laws of the State of Colorado or the laws of any other state or other jurisdiction in which such certificate or any other amendment is required to be filed;

b) any other instrument that may be required to be filed or recorded by the Partnership under the laws of any state or by any governmental agency; or which, in the General Partner's discretion, it is advisable to file or record; and

c) any document that may be required to effect the continuation of the Partnership, the admission of an additional or substituted Limited Partner to the Partnership, or the dissolution and termination of the Partnership, provided that such documents are in accordance with the terms of the Partnership Agreement.

Such Power of Attorney (i) shall be a special power of attorney coupled with an interest, shall be irrevocable, and shall survive the death of the Limited Partner; (ii) may be exercised by the General Partner for each Limited Partner by a facsimile signature of the General Partner or by listing all of the Limited Partners executing any instrument with a single signature of the General Partner acting as attorney-in-fact for all of them; and (iii) shall survive the delivery of any assignment by the Limited Partner of the whole or any portions of his or her interest except that where the assignee of the whole thereof has been approved by the General Partner for admission to the Partnership as a substituted Limited Partner, the Power of Attorney shall survive the delivery of such assignment for the sole purpose of enabling the General Partner to execute, acknowledge, and file any instrument necessary to effect the substitution.

13. Describe any limitations to be placed on the transfer of limited partnership interests.

Transfer of Limited Partnership Transferable Interests

No heir, successor, donee, assignee, or other transferee (including a partner's spouse) of the whole or any interest in a Limited Partner's transferable interest in the Partnership shall have the right to become a substituted Limited Partner in place of his or her assignor unless all of the following conditions are satisfied:

a) Upon receipt of a bona fide offer to purchase a limited partnership transferable interest in an amount at least equal to or greater than the minimum subscription amount required by the securities laws in the respective states where the transferor and transferee reside, the holder of the transferable interest shall communicate the offer to the General Partner. The General Partner shall have a right of first refusal to purchase the transferable interest according to the price and terms of the bona fide offer, which option must be exercised within thirty (30) days from the date of first receipt of the notice of said bona fide offer. In the event that the General Partner fails to exercise its option hereunder, the Limited Partner may transfer his or her transferable interest upon the same terms as the offer and upon satisfaction of all other requirements of this Article.

b) The written instrument of assignment that has been filed with the Partnership is fully executed and acknowledged and sets forth the intention of the assignor that the assignee become a substituted Limited Partner in his or her place.

c) The assignor and assignee execute and acknowledge such other instruments as the General Partner may deem necessary or desirable to effect the substitution, including the written acceptance and adoption by the assignee of the provisions of the Agreement.

d) Recordation of an amendment to the Certificate of Limited Partnership in accordance with the Colorado Limited Partnership Act.

e) Payment by the transferor of all reasonable expenses of the Partnership connected with the transfer, including, but not limited to, legal fees and costs (which costs may include, for example, the cost of obtaining opinion of counsel as to the transferability of the interest or of filing any amendment to the Certificate of Limited Partnership).

f) The consent to the transfer in writing by the General Partner.

14. Describe any limitations to be placed upon partnership loans or other transactions of business with a limited partnership.

Limitations on Partnership Loans

No Partner, General or Limited, may lend money to the Partnership on a basis that is less favorable than the Partnership may obtain from independent financial institutions. All Partnership loans shall bear interest at a rate not to exceed the prime lending rate of the Partnership's principal financial institution, and shall provide for repayment no earlier than six months after the date of the loan.

15. Describe any voting procedures and rights that are desired for the various partners.

EXAMPLE

Voting Rights of Partners

The General Partners shall be permitted to vote on all matters respecting the business of the Partnership. The Limited Partners shall be entitled to vote on all matters that are referred to them by the General Partners for their approval. In any vote of the Partnership, the matters submitted to the vote of the Partners shall be approved by a majority of the vote of the General Partners, with the General Partners voting as a class, and a majority of the Limited Partners, with the Limited Partners voting as a class.

---

16. Provide for the admission of additional general partners, if desired, with a procedure that is different from the consent of all partners of the partnership.

EXAMPLE

Admission of General Partners

Additional General Partners may be admitted to the Partnership by the majority vote of the Limited Partners.

---

17. Provide for any limitations of the general partner's liability to the partnership or to the limited partners. It is not possible to limit the liability of the general partner to outsiders, but the partnership agreement may regulate claims among the partners.

EXAMPLE

Limitations on Liability of General Partner

The General Partner in this Partnership shall not be liable to the Partnership or to the Limited Partners except for acts of gross negligence and willful misconduct.

The Limited Partnership Certificate

A traditionally troublesome formality associated with the limited partnership is the certificate, which has to be properly filed and maintained to ensure limited liability for the limited partners. Failure to properly file and amend the certificate when necessary prevents recognition of the limited partnership, and all partners are treated as though they belonged to a general partnership. Recognizing that the failure to maintain the certificate of limited partnership could accidentally cause a change in the status of the partners, the drafters of the revised and new uniform acts substantially minimized the importance of the certificate in the most recent amendments. The policy of the revised act is to place greater emphasis on the terms of the partnership agreement, and to permit the certificate to be simply public notice of matters the general partners desire to make known and the public needs to know.

Content Many existing limited partnerships that were formed under the original Uniform Limited Partnership Act are operating with certificates of limited partnership that resemble a corporation's articles of incorporation (see Exhibit 4–4, Limited Partnership Certificate). These certificates, in some respects, are more specific and revealing about the structure of the agreement among the partners. In fact, in many cases, the partners simply filed the limited partnership agreement as the certificate of limited partnership.

Under current law, the information contained in the certificate of limited partnership is substantially simplified, requiring only the following (see Exhibit 4–5, Limited Partnership Certificate [Revised Uniform Limited Partnership Act]):

1. name of the limited partnership;
2. address of the office and name and address of the agent for service of process (discussed later in this section);

**COMMONWEALTH OF VIRGINIA
STATE CORPORATION COMMISSION**

LPA-73.11
(07/03)

CERTIFICATE OF LIMITED PARTNERSHIP

This certificate of limited partnership is presented for filing pursuant to § 50-73.11 of the Code of Virginia.

1. The name of the limited partnership is

_____.

2. The post office address, including the street and number, if any, of the specified office where the records
   shall be maintained pursuant to § 50-73.8 of the Code of Virginia is

_____
(number/street)

_____.
(city or town)   (state)   (zip)

3. A. The initial registered agent's name is _____.

   B. The registered agent is **(mark appropriate box):**

   (1) an **INDIVIDUAL** who is a resident of Virginia **and**
     [ ] a general partner of the limited partnership.
     [ ] an officer or director of a corporation that is a general partner of the limited partnership.
     [ ] a general partner of a general partner of the limited partnership.
     [ ] a member or manager of a limited liability company that is a general partner of the limited
        partnership.
     [ ] a trustee of a trust that is a general partner of the limited partnership.
     [ ] a member of the Virginia State Bar.
                       OR
   (2) [ ] a domestic or foreign stock or nonstock corporation, limited liability company or registered
        limited liability partnership authorized to transact business in Virginia.

4. The business address of the initial registered agent is:

_____
(number/street)

_____ VA _____,
(city or town)   (zip)

which is located in the [ ] city **or** [ ] county of _____.

5. The name, business address and SCC ID # (if assigned) of each general partner:

_____
(name and SCC ID #, if assigned)

_____
(street address)   (city or town)   (state)   (zip)

_____
(name and SCC ID #, if assigned)

_____
(street address)   (city or town)   (state)   (zip)

Check and complete if applicable:
[ ] The following general partner(s) is (are) serving, without more, as a general partner of, or as a partner in
a partnership which is a general partner of, a domestic or foreign limited partnership which does not
otherwise transact business in this Commonwealth pursuant to § 50-73.61 and/or § 13.1-757 of the Code
of Virginia:

_____

_____

[OVER]

3. name and business address of each general partner;
4. latest date upon which the limited partnership is to dissolve; and
5. any other matters the general partner has determined to include in the certificate of limited partnership.[57]

All states have some combination of the original act and the amended revised act as the local requirements for certificates of limited partnership. In each case, local law must be carefully reviewed to ensure that the certificate contains the required information.

Exhibit 4–4.

(continued)

6. The latest date upon which the limited partnership is to be dissolved and its affairs wound up is

_____.

7. Signature(s) of all general partner(s):

_____	_____	_____
(signature)	(printed name)	(date)
_____	_____	_____
(signature)	(printed name)	(date)
_____	_____	_____
(signature)	(printed name)	(date)

INSTRUCTIONS

The certificate must be in the English language, typewritten or printed in black, legible and reproducible. See § 50-73.17 of the Code of Virginia. The document must be presented on uniformly white, opaque paper, free of visible watermarks and background logos.

You can download this form from our website at **www.state.va.us/scc/division/clk/index.htm**.

The name of the limited partnership must contain the words "Limited Partnership" or "a Limited Partnership," the abbreviation "L.P." or "LP;" provided, however, that if the limited partnership is also applying for registered limited liability partnership status pursuant to § 50-73.132 of the Code of Virginia, the name must include either (1) (a) the words "limited partnership" or "a limited partnership," or the abbreviation "L.P." or "LP" and (b) the words "Registered Limited Liability Partnership" or "Limited Liability Partnership," the abbreviation "R.L.L.P." or "L.L.P." or the designation "RLLP" or "LLP," **or** (2) the words "Registered Limited Liability Limited Partnership" or "Limited Liability Limited Partnership," the abbreviation "R.L.L.L.P." or "L.L.L.P." or the designation "RLLLP" or "LLLP." See § 50-73.2 of the Code of Virginia.

The specified office is the location at which a current list of the full name and last known address of each general partner of the limited partnership is kept, as well as the other limited partnership information and records specified in § 50-73.8 of the Code of Virginia.

The address of the specified office must include a street address. A rural route and box number may only be used if no street address is associated with the specified office's location. A post office box is only acceptable for towns/cities that have a population of 2,000 or less if no street address or rural route and box number is associated with the specified office's location.

A registered limited liability partnership may not serve as its own registered agent.

The address of the registered agent's business office must include a street address. A rural route and box number may only be used if no street address is associated with the location of the registered agent's business office. A post office box is only acceptable for towns/cities that have a population of 2,000 or less if no street address or rural route and box number is associated with the location of the registered agent's business office. Set forth the name of the county or independent city in which the office is physically located. Counties and independent cities in Virginia are separate local jurisdictions.

This certificate <u>must</u> include the SCC ID # of each general partner that is of record with the State Corporation Commission.

This certificate must be signed by all of the general partners. Any person may sign a certificate by an attorney-in-fact. Each person signing this statement must set forth his printed name next to or beneath his signature. A person signing on behalf of a general partner that is a business entity should set forth the business entity's name, his or her printed name, and the capacity in which he or she is signing on behalf of the business entity. **As provided in § 50-73.15 C of the Code of Virginia, the execution of this certificate by a general partner constitutes an affirmation under the penalties of perjury that the facts stated herein are true.**

Submit the original, signed certificate to the Clerk of the State Corporation Commission, P.O. Box 1197, Richmond, Virginia 23218-1197, (Street address: 1300 East Main Street, Tyler Building, 1st floor, Richmond, Virginia 23219), along with a check for the filing fee in the amount of **$100.00**, payable to the State Corporation Commission. **PLEASE DO NOT SEND CASH.** If you have any questions, please call (804) 371-9733 or toll-free in Virginia, 1-866-722-2551.

Registered Office and Agent The benefit to the public and to local government agencies of a designated office for business records and an agent for service of process has long been recognized for corporations. An agent for service of process on the limited partnership must be an individual resident of the state and must be continuously maintained by the limited partnership. The limited partnership also must specify an office, which need not be its place of business in the state, where records of the partnership will be maintained.[58] At this office, the partnership is required to keep a current list of all partners in alphabetical order; a copy of the certificate of limited partnership and all amendments; copies of the partnership's financial statements and federal, state, and local income tax returns for three years; and copies of any effective written partnership agreement. The records maintained at the registered office must include a description of the capital contributions of each partner, the times when additional capital contributions will be required, the right of a partner to receive a distribution that may

(REVISED UNIFORM LIMITED PARTNERSHIP ACT)

We, the undersigned, for the purpose of forming a limited partnership pursuant to the Revised Uniform Limited Partnership Act as set forth in sections _____of the _____Code, hereby certify:

1. **Name.** The name of the partnership is _____.

2. **Character of Business.** The character of the business to be carried on is to engage in the business of _____.

3. **Address and Agent.** The address of the office of the partnership is , and the agent for service of process upon the partnership is _____.

4. **Members.** The name and the business address of each member of the partnership are as follows:

Name	Business Address	Type of Member
_____	_____	[General]
_____	_____	[Limited]
_____	_____	[Limited]

5. **Initial Contribution of Each Partner.** The amount of cash and a description and statement of the agreed value of other property or services contributed by each partner are as follows:

Name	Cash	Description of Property or Services	Agreed Value of Property or Services
_____	_____	_____	_____
_____	_____	_____	_____

6. **Additional Contributions.** The times or events that will require additional contributions to be made by each partner are as follows:_____

7. **Assignment of a Limited Partner's Interest.** Each limited partner is given the right to substitute an assignee as contributor in his or her place, provided that the assignment is approved by the general partners.

8. **Termination of Membership.** With sixty (60) days' written notice to the general partners, any member of the partnership may terminate his or her membership in the partnership and receive a full distribution of his or her partnership interest in cash, provided, however, that no such distribution shall be made unless the assets of the partnership exceed the liabilities of the partnership on a ratio of at least 2:1.

9. **Distributions.** The partners may receive from the partnership from time to time such property of the partnership, including cash, as may be agreed upon by the general partners.

10. **Return of a Capital Contribution.** The general partners may, from time to time, as they agree, distribute to the other partners such portions of the capital contributions of the other partners as the general partners may deem appropriate.

Exhibit 4–5.

(continued)

11. **Dissolution.** The partnership shall be dissolved and its affairs wound up upon the happening of any of the following:

    a. unanimous agreement by all members;

    b. death, insanity, disability, or retirement of a general partner without a successor general partner being elected within 90 days;

    c. sale or disposition of substantially all of the partnership property; or

    d. any event which, in the opinion of the general partners, prevents the partnership from carrying on its ordinary business.

12. **Continuation of Business.** Notwithstanding any event of dissolution, the remaining members of the partnership may continue the business of the partnership without liquidation of the partnership by electing a successor or replacement general partner within 90 days from the event that causes the dissolution.

13. **Other Matters.**_____

_____

_____

Date this _____day of _____, 20____.

                        [Signatures of general and limited partners]

Subscribed and sworn to before me this ____day of _____, 20____.

                                   _____

                                   Notary Public

include part of the contributions, and any events upon which the partnership will be dissolved. If these items are contained in the written partnership agreement, separate records do not have to be maintained for such matters. These records are subject to inspection and copying by any partner upon reasonable request during normal business hours.

Filing Most states designate the office of the secretary of state as the repository for the certificate. A few states require a single filing of the certificate in the office of the county clerk in the county in which the partnership's principal place of business is situated. Even fewer states require filing in both places. New York requires publication once a week for six weeks in two newspapers of general circulation in the county, one of which should be in the city in which the partnership is located. The appropriate state statue should be carefully reviewed in any case. Moreover, if the partnership intends to do business in more than one location, appropriate multiple filings should be made to avoid any question of compliance with these important provisions.

Amendments During the course of operating a limited partnership, several situations may require that the certificate be amended. Much information is required in the certificate of limited partnership under the original act, so amendments frequently are required under local laws following that statute.[59]

Under the revised and new law, the certificate may be amended at any time the general partners decide to add or delete information that is optionally included, and must be amended whenever a general partner is aware that a statement in the certificate is false or that circumstances have changed to make a statement inaccurate. An amendment must be filed within thirty days after a new general partner is admitted, an old general partner withdraws, or the business has been continued after a general partner has withdrawn.[60]

The amending statement (see Exhibit 4–6, Amendment of Limited Partnership Certificate) must state the name of the limited partnership, the filing date of the certificate, and the contents of the amendment. It must be signed by at least one general partner and by any new general partner. In jurisdictions that operate under the original act, signatures of limited partners are required on the amendment. To avoid the nuisance of locating and obtaining the signature of each limited partner (or of a new general partner), the partnership agreement may grant a

STATE OF DELAWARE
AMENDMENT TO THE CERTIFICATE OF
LIMITED PARTNERSHIP

The undersigned, desiring to amend the Certificate of Limited Partnership of _____

_____

pursuant to the provisions of Section 17-202 of the Revised Uniform Limited Partnership
Act of the State of Delaware, does hereby certify as follows:

FIRST: The name of the Limited Partnership is_____

_____.

SECOND: Article ____ of the Certificate of Limited Partnership shall be amended as
follows:_____

_____

_____.

IN WITNESS WHEREOF, the undersigned executed this Amendment to the Certificate
of Limited Partnership on this _____ day of _____, A.D._____.

By:_____

General Partner(s)

Name:_____

Print or Type

power of attorney to an existing general partner to enable that partner to sign amendments on
behalf of other partners.[61]

Even under the revised act, the amendment procedure is cumbersome and may be annoy-
ing. The details for which a limited partnership amendment is required are even more specific,
especially under the original statute, than the details for which a corporate amendment is required. For example, a corporation does not have to amend its articles of incorporation every
time it acquires a new shareholder or loses a director, but the limited partnership may be required to amend for analogous changes in personnel.

Cancellation of the Certificate When the limited partnership is dissolved and winding
up has commenced, or when there are no more limited partners, the certificate of limited partnership must be cancelled. Since the limited partnership was formed in a public manner by
filing the certificate, it should be dissolved with the same formality. A certificate of cancellation (see Exhibit 4–7, Statement of Cancellation) is provided for this purpose, and it must
be signed by all general partners.[62] If no certificate of cancellation is filed—as when, for example, limited partnership is insolvent and the partners have dispersed without observing dissolution formalities—the limited partnership may be administratively dissolved by the
secretary of state (for not filing annual reports, if required by local law) or simply remains as
a dormant business entity.

Exhibit 4–7.

Statement of Cancellation
(Idaho)

CERTIFICATE OF CANCELLATION OF LIMITED PARTNERSHIP

(Instructions on back of application)

1. The name of the limited partnership is: _____
   _____

2. The date its certificate of limited partnership was filed with the Secretary of State:
   _____

3. The limited partnership hereby cancels its certificate of limited partnership.

4. The effective date of cancellation, if other than the date of filing, is: _____
   (Leave blank if effective date is to be date of filing, or specify a **future** date.)

5. The reason for the cancellation is:

6. Other matters (optional):

7. Signatures of all general partners:

   Signature _____
   Typed Name _____
   Signature _____
   Typed Name _____
   Signature _____
   Typed Name _____
   Signature _____
   Typed Name _____

   g:\corp\forms\lp forms\cancellation LP.pm6
   Revised 1/2001

   Secretary of State use only

The certificate of cancellation is required when there is a dissolution of the partnership, but only if the partnership has commenced a procedure to wind up its affairs. A technical dissolution may occur under a number of situations, such as the death of a general partner; however, such a situation does not necessarily require that the partnership be liquidated. The agreement may allow the business to continue with an existing additional general partner or with the limited partners' appointment of another general partner. Consequently, only the commencement of the winding up of the partnership requires a certificate of cancellation. If the business is to be continued following a dissolution, a certificate of cancellation need not be filed.

Foreign Limited Partnerships

The modern uniform acts have borrowed a number of corporate rules providing for the qualification and registration of **foreign limited partnerships** in other states. Any foreign limited partnership (defined as a partnership formed under the laws of some other state) must register

DEAN HELLER
Secretary of State

202 North Carson Street
Carson City, Nevada 89701-4201
(775) 684 5708

**Application for
Registration of Foreign
Limited Partnership**
(PURSUANT TO NRS 88.570)

Office Use Only:

Important: Read attached instructions before completing form.

1.	**Name of Foreign Limited Partnership:**	
2.	**Name Being Registered with Nevada:** *(name under which this foreign limited partnership proposes to register and transact business in Nevada)*	
3.	**Date of Formation and State or Country in which Partnership was formed:**	Date Formed _____ State or Country where authorized
4.	**Resident Agent Name and Street Address:** *(must be a Nevada address where process may be served)*	Name _____ , **NEVADA** _____ Physical Street Address / City / Zip Code Additional Mailing Address / City / State / Zip Code This Foreign Limited Partnership hereby undertakes to keep a list of the names and addresses of the limited partners and their capital contributions at this office until its registration in Nevada is cancelled or withdrawn. In the event the above-designated Agent for Service of Process resigns and is not replaced or the agent's authority has been revoked or the agent cannot be found or served with exercise of reasonable diligence, then the Secretary of State is hereby appointed as the Agent for Service of Process.
5.	**Street Address of Principal Office:** *(or office required to be maintained in the domicile state by the laws of that state)*	Street Address / City / State / Zip Code
6.	**Names and Addresses of each General Partner:** *(attach additional pages if there are more than 2)*	1. _____ Name Street Address / City / State / Zip Code 2. _____ Name Street Address / City / State / Zip Code
7.	**Name and Signature of General Partner making Statement:**	Name _____ Signature _____ I hereby declare and affirm under the penalties of perjury that I am a General Partner in the above-named Foreign Limited Partnership and that the execution of this application for registration is my act and deed and that the facts stated herein are true.
8.	**Certificate of Acceptance of Appointment of Resident Agent:**	I hereby accept appointment as Resident Agent for the above named Foreign Limited Partnership. Authorized Signature of R.A. or On Behalf of R.A. Company Date

This form must be accompanied by appropriate fees. See attached fee schedule.

Nevada Secretary of State Form FOREIGNLPREG1999.01
Revised on: 12/11/02

with the secretary of state before transacting business in a new state (see Exhibit 4–8, Application for Registration of a Foreign Limited Partnership).[63]

An application for registration as a foreign limited partnership must contain the following items:

1. name of the foreign limited partnership and, if different, name under which that partnership proposes to register and transact business in the new state (including the words *Limited Partnership* as part of the name);
2. state and date of the partnership's formation;
3. name and address of any agent for service of process who is either a resident of the new state or an entity formed under the laws of and or qualified to do business in the new state;
4. appointment of the secretary of state of the new state as the agent of the foreign limited partnership if the otherwise appointed agent can no longer be found;
5. address of the partnership's office;
6. name and business address of each general partner; and

7. address of the office at which the list of names and addresses of the limited partners and their capital contributions may be found—The foreign limited partnership must commit to keep those records available until its registration in the foreign state is withdrawn.[64]

There are requirements for amendments to the registration certificate and for cancellation of registration when the partnership ceases to do business in the foreign state.[65]

A foreign limited partnership that transacts business without registration in a state operating under the modern acts is prohibited from maintaining any action, suit, or other proceeding in a court of that state until registration has occurred. However, mere failure to register does not affect any contract or act the foreign limited partnership conducts in the new state, nor does it affect the limited liability of limited partners in the new state.[66] For example, if the limited partnership between Michael Crouch, as general partner, and Robbie Schwarz, as limited partner, were formed in Delaware and bought and operated an apartment building in Maryland, it would be required to register to do business as a foreign limited partnership in Maryland. If Michael failed to register the partnership under the laws of Maryland, the partnership could not sue any of its tenants for past due rent in Maryland until it completed its registration in that state (and, if necessary, paid any fees or penalties assessed for failure to register). However, the contracts with its tenants, such as apartment leases, are valid under Maryland law, and Robbie's status as a limited partner and his right to limited liability are secure, notwithstanding the fact that the partnership has not properly registered in Maryland.

Derivative Actions

As you will learn in Chapter 6, stockholders of a corporation elect directors to manage the business and legal affairs of the corporation. In some cases, the directors may fail to act to enforce the legal rights of the corporation. In such circumstances, the stockholders may maintain a lawsuit to enforce the rights of their corporation. Because they are owners of the business, if the business has been legally injured, the owners may sue on behalf of the business to recover the damages suffered. Such an action is called a **derivative action,** since the stockholders are suing not for injury to themselves as individuals but rather to enforce rights derived from their ownership of the injured entity. A similar relationship exists in a limited partnership, where the general partner is expected to manage the business and legal affairs of the limited partnership for the benefit of all partners. However, a limited partner never expressly had the right to bring a derivative action under the original uniform act, and many cases have considered whether limited partners are entitled to bring derivative actions, with diverse results. The revised laws expressly permit a limited partner to bring an action in the right of the limited partnership to recover a judgment in its favor if the general partners with authority to do so have refused to bring the action or if an effort to cause the general partners to bring such an action is not likely to succeed.[67]

For example, in the limited partnership with Michael Crouch as general partner and Robbie Schwarz as limited partner, if Michael has leased one of the partnership's apartments to his fiancé, Heather, and Heather has failed to pay the rent for several months, the partnership has a right to collect the rent under the terms of Heather's lease. Michael, as general partner, should enforce the partnership's rights against Heather, but he may be reluctant to do so. Before the revised act, Robbie may not have been able to enforce the claim against Heather on behalf of the partnership and may have been limited to a claim against Michael for breaching his fiduciary duty as general partner to the partnership in not pursuing the partnership's rights. Under the revised act, however, Robbie, as a limited partner, may bring a lawsuit derivatively on behalf of the limited partnership to enforce the partnership's rights against Heather and recover the past due rent from her.

The provisions for derivative actions under the revised and new uniform acts are similar to those under state corporate laws. The partner bringing the action must have been a partner at the time of the transaction that is the subject of the lawsuit, and must be a partner at the time of bringing the action. The partner must attempt to have the general partners bring the action on behalf of the partnership, and must state with particularity in a complaint what actions were taken in that regard. If a partner is successful in prosecuting a claim on behalf of the partnership and obtains a judgment, compromise, or settlement of the claim, that partner may be awarded reasonable expenses, including attorneys' fees, for bringing the action.[68]

KEY TERMS

limited partnership	event of withdrawal	derivative action
safe harbor activities	foreign limited partnership	

WEB RESOURCES

The limited partnership agreement is the principal document required for the formation of a limited partnership. Like the general partnership, if the parties want to form a limited liability limited partnership, registration forms are available from a public filing officer, usually the Secretary of State, to register the limited liability limited partnership.

Various sources exist for sample partnership agreements that may be tailored to the specific desires of the client. In addition to the sites mentioned under "Web Resources" for General Partnerships in Chapter 3, limited partnership form templates are available on the following sites:

<http://www.partnershipkit.com>
<http://www.secure.uslegalforms.com>
<http://www.legaldocs.com>

Access to state laws regarding licensing and regulatory requirements may be obtained through the Legal Information Institute maintained at the Cornell Law School:

<http://www.law.cornell.edu>

The uniform laws of partnership, including the original Uniform Limited Partnership Act, the Revised Uniform Limited Partnership Act with Amendments, and the Uniform Limited Partnership Act of 2001 also can be accessed through the Legal Information Institute:

<http://www.law.cornell.edu>

The National Association of Secretaries of State maintains links directly to the offices of the Secretaries of State in all states. Most states requiring registration of limited liability limited partnerships provide forms for that purpose through the Secretary of State or Department of Commerce Web sites. These can be accessed through

<http://www.nass.org>

Tax forms, including the federal income tax returns and schedules, and the Classification of Entity tax elections may be accessed on line through

<http://www.irs.gov>

Searching and locating trade names can be accomplished through various services offered on the Internet. Most of these services charge a fee for useful searches. They include

<http://www.tmexpress.com>
<http://www.trademark-search-services.com>

CASES

ZEIGER V. WILF

333 N.J.Super. 258, 755 A.2d 608
July 19, 2000
LESEMANN, J.A.D.

This case offers a virtual primer in the Byzantine relationships among various forms of business organizations employed in a modern venture capital project. It includes a limited partnership, a corporation, a general partnership and several sophisticated individuals all involved in the proposed redevelopment of a hotel/office building in downtown Trenton. It also demonstrates the significance of limited individual liability which is a key reason for employing some of those entities, and the inevitable risk that anticipated rewards from such a venture may not be realized.

At issue here is an argument by which plaintiff, a seller of the property to be renovated, was to receive a "consultant fee" of $23,000 per year for sixteen years. The payments, however, ceased after two years. A jury found the redevelopers (a limited partnership and a corporation) liable for those payments, and an appeal by those entities has now been abandoned. As a result, the matter now focuses on plaintiff's claim that Joseph Wilf, the individual who led the various defendant entities, should be held personally liable for the consultant payments and that such liability should also be imposed on a general partnership owned by Wilf and members of his family.

There is no claim that Wilf personally, or his general partnership, ever guaranteed the consultant payments or that plaintiff ever believed Wilf had made such guarantees. Nor is there a claim that plaintiff did not understand at all times that he was contracting only with a limited partnership and/or a corporation, and not with Wilf personally or with his general partnership. For those reasons, and also because we find no merit in various other theories of individual liability advanced by plaintiff, we affirm the summary judgment entered in favor of Wilf individually, and we reverse the judgment against Wilf's family-owned general partnership.

The property in question was a rundown hotel on West State Street in Trenton located near several State government buildings. In or shortly before 1981, plaintiff Shelley Zeiger and his associate, Darius Kapadia, purchased the property with the intention of renovating and operating the hotel. They undertook some renovation and began operations but could not obtain sufficient financing to complete the project.

In or around March 1985, Steven Novick, an experienced developer, approached plaintiff concerning a possible purchase of the property. Novick believed the building could be successfully renovated and operated as an office building, (with perhaps some hotel facilities included), particularly if he could lease some or all of the office space to the State. Richard Goldberger, another experienced developer, soon joined Novick in the project, as did another associate, said to have considerable contacts within the State government. Plaintiff was also well known in Trenton governmental and political circles.

As the negotiations proceeded, Novick brought defendant Joseph Wilf into the picture. Wilf was described as a "deep pocket partner," whose financial means could help insure the success of the project. He was also a well known and successful real estate developer and soon became the leader and primary spokesman for the purchasing group. Novick and Goldberger generally deferred to Wilf during the negotiations and structuring of the transaction.

On February 17, 1987, the negotiations culminated in a contract with a purchase price of $3,840,000 for the real estate, a liquor license, and miscellaneous assets connected with the hotel's operation. The contract was signed by a corporation formed by the purchasers, known as Goldberger, Moore & Novick, Trenton, No. 2, Inc., (hereinafter, "Trenton, Inc." or "the corporation").

As the deal was finally struck, the parties also agreed that plaintiff would receive a "consulting fee" of $27,000 per year payable monthly for sixteen years. While plaintiff was to provide assistance when requested, it is clear that he was not expected to devote much time or effort to the project. The agreement specified he would not be required to spend more than two days per month in consultations. Plaintiff claims the consultation payments were, in reality, an additional part of the payment price, structured as they were to provide tax benefits to the Novick/Goldberger/Wilf group. In addition, plaintiff was to receive from the project two and one half percent of "annual net cash flow after debt service."

Closing took place on March 4, 1986. Trenton, Inc., was the purchaser and also signed the consultant agreement with plaintiff. The contract documents authorized the corporation to assign its property interests, as well as the consulting contract, to another entity, and on the day following closing the corporation did that by assignment to a limited partnership named Goldberger, Moore & Novick, Trenton, L.P., (hereinafter "Trenton L.P." or "the limited partnership").

The limited partnership then began the anticipated renovation and operation of the hotel/office building. Trenton, L.P. consisted of one general partner—the corporation just referred to (Trenton, Inc.), which owned 4.9 percent of the limited partnership. In addition, it had four limited partners: an entity known as Midnov, owned by Novick and Goldberger, which held a 42.7 percent interest; another entity known as Capitol Plaza Associates (CPA), controlled by Wilf and his family and described further below, which also owned 42.7 percent; George Albanese, a former State official, who held a 5.1 percent interest; and plaintiff Shelley Zeiger who owned a 4.9 percent interest.

The stock of Trenton, Inc., was owned fifty percent by Midnov (Novick and Goldberger's entity) and fifty percent by CPA (the Wilf family entity). Goldberger became president of Trenton, Inc.; Wilf was vice president; Novick was secretary/treasurer, and Bernadette Lynch was assistant secretary.

Thus, all of Wilf's interests in both the limited partnership and the corporation were held through his family entity, CPA. CPA was a general partnership and defendant Joseph Wilf was one of the general partners. While other family members were also general partners in CPA, Joseph Wilf was clearly its guiding and dominating force.

Shortly after closing, Trenton, L.P. began its attempts to secure both state leases for the property and a 9.5 million dollar mortgage to finance the required renovation. Wilf was the leader in that operation as he was in all aspects of the project. He maintains that in doing so, he was functioning as vice president of the corporation, which was the only general partner of the limited partnership. In substance, he claims that the limited partnership was operating (as it was required to do) through its general partner. Since that general partner was a corporation, the corporation was, in turn, operating in the only way that a corporation can operate: by the actions of its officers and agents. He maintains further that Goldberger and Novick soon abdicated most responsibility and simply stopped functioning as corporate officers—a claim not disputed by plaintiff. Thus, Wilf says, it was left to him to function as the responsible corporate officer.

Both the limited partnership and the corporation operated informally. There were few, if any, corporate meetings, resolutions or minutes. Wilf was less than meticulous in affixing his corporate title to documents or other papers which he says he signed as an officer of the corporate general partner. Significantly, however, plaintiff makes no claim that at any time he thought Wilf was operating in some other capacity, or that he believed Wilf or CPA were undertaking any personal responsibility or liability for any part of the project.

The limited partnership began making the monthly consultation payments to plaintiff in early 1986, and it continued to do so for approximately two years. In March 1988, however, the payments were stopped at Wilf's direction. An additional $12,000 was paid in May 1989 (which represented almost all the amount then due to plaintiff), but thereafter no further payments were made. Wilf said at the time that the money was needed for the renovation project and that (alone among all the participants), plaintiff was contributing nothing to the project. Plaintiff complained to Novick, and Novick promised to discuss the matter with Wilf. Novick did so, but Wilf continued to maintain that plaintiff should receive no further payments and thus, no further payments were made. Wilf subsequently acknowledged that he was not familiar with the terms of the consultation agreement or plaintiff's rights thereunder.

* * *

Eventually, the project failed. The limited partnership and the corporation filed bankruptcy, as did Novick individually. On July 19, 1993, plaintiff sued Wilf, claiming that Wilf had become the "surviving partner and owner of the partnership assets" pertaining to the "purchase and transfer of" the hotel, and that he was in default respecting payment of plaintiff's consulting fees.

* * *

[P]laintiff claims the limited partnership statute imposes general partner liability on Wilf because he functioned as the operating head of the parties' renovation project. We find the claim inconsistent with both the policy and the language of the statute.

A basic principle of the Uniform Limited Partnership Law (1976), *N.J.S.A.* 42:2A-1 to -72, is a differentiation between the broad liability of a general partner for the obligations of a limited partnership (*see N.J.S.A.* 42:2A-32b), and the nonliability of a limited partner for such obligations. *See N.J.S.A.* 42:2A-27a. Preservation of that distinction and protection against imposing unwarranted liability on a limited partner has been a consistent concern of the drafters of the Uniform Act on which our New Jersey statute is based, and has been described as "the single most difficult issue facing

lawyers who use the limited partnership form of organization." *See Revised Unif. Limited Partnership Act* Prefatory Note preceding § 101, U.L.A. (1976) (hereinafter "Commissioners' Report"). Indeed, the history of the Uniform Limited Partnership Act, and thus the evolution of our New Jersey statute, shows a consistent movement to insure certainty and predictability respecting the obligations and potential liability of limited partners. The framers of the Act have accomplished that by consistently reducing and restricting the bases on which a general partner's unrestricted liability can be imposed on a limited partner. Under the present version of the Uniform Act, the imposition of such liability (absent fraud or misleading) is severely limited. Our New Jersey statute (as discussed below) reflects that same philosophy in the provisions of *N.J.S.A.* 42:2A-27a.

The original version of the ULPA was adopted in 1916. That enactment dealt with the question of a limited partner's liability in one short provision. In Section 7 it said,

> A limited partner shall not become liable as a general partner unless, in addition to the exercise of his rights and powers as **limited partner,** he takes part in the **control** of the **business.**

In 1976, the original ULPA was substantially replaced by a revised version (on which the New Jersey statute is based) which "was intended to modernize the prior uniform law." *See* Commissioners Report Prefatory Note preceding Section 101. One of the ways that modernization was effected was by a new Section 303, which replaced the old Section 7, and was adopted virtually verbatim as Section 27 of the New Jersey statute. Section 303 reads as follows:

> [A] limited partner is not liable for the obligations of a limited partnership unless . . . , in addition to the exercise of his [or her] rights and powers as a **limited partner,** he [or she] takes part in the **control** of the **business.** However, if the **limited partner's** participation in **control** of the **business** is not substantially the same as the exercise of the powers of a general partner, he [or she] is liable only to persons who transact business with the limited partnership with actual knowledge of his participation in control.

The Commissioners' Report in the comment to Section 303 states:

> Section 303 makes several important changes in Section 7 of the 1916 Act. . . . The second sentence of Section 303(a) reflects a wholly new concept. . . . It was adopted partly because . . . it was thought unfair to impose general partner's liability on a **limited partner** except to the extent that a third party had knowledge of his participation in **control** of the business . . . , but also (and more importantly) because of a determination that it is not sound public policy to hold a limited partner who is not also a general partner liable for the obligations of the partnership except to persons who have done business with the limited partnership reasonably believing, based on the limited partner's conduct, that he is a general partner.

Following that 1976 version, more limitations on a limited partner's liability came in 1988, with a series of "Safe

Harbor" amendments, virtually all of which were adopted in New Jersey. *See N.J.S.A. 42:2A-27b.* The Commissioners' Report explained the reason for those additions to Section 303 of the Uniform Act:

> Paragraph (b) is intended to provide a "Safe Harbor" by enumerating certain activities which a **limited partner** may carry on for the partnership without being deemed to have taken part in **control** of the **business.** This "Safe Harbor" list has been expanded beyond that set out in the 1976 Act to reflect case law and statutory developments and more clearly to assure that limited partners are not subjected to general liability where such liability is inappropriate.

Although plaintiff argues that Section 27 of the New Jersey statute imposes a general partner's liability on Wilf (and CPA) because Wilf took "part in the control of the business," we are satisfied that the argument has no merit. To accept it, and impose such liability on the facts presented here, would reverse the evolution described above and create precisely the instability and uncertainty that the drafters of the ULPA (and the New Jersey Act) were determined to avoid.

Plaintiff's argument rests on Wilf's key role in the renovation project. Wilf acknowledges that role, but argues that his actions were taken as a vice president of Trenton, Inc.— the corporation which was the sole general partner of Trenton, L.P. Wilf argues that since the corporation is an artificial entity, it can only function through its officer *see Printing Mart- Morristown v. Sharp Electronics Corp.,* 116 *N.J.* 739, 761, 563 *A.*2d 31 (1989), and that is precisely what he was doing at all times when he acted concerning this enterprise. Wilf also points to the "Safe Harbor" provisions of *N.J.S.A.* 42:2A-27b to reinforce his claim that his actions here did not impose general partner liability upon him.

We agree with that analysis. As noted, the 1988 "Safe Harbor" provisions set out a number of activities which, under the statute, do not constitute participating in "the **control** of" a **business** so as to impose a general partner's liability on a **limited partner.** The provision to which Wilf particularly refers is subsection b(6) of section 27, which provides that,

> b. A **limited partner** does not participate in the **control** of the **business** within the meaning of subsection a. solely by[,]

> (6) Serving as an officer, director or shareholder of a corporate general partner;

That provision clearly applies here and essentially undercuts plaintiff's argument: while plaintiff claims that Wilf's activities constitute "control" of the activities of Trenton, L.P., the statute says, in just so many words, that those activities do not constitute the exercise of control.

In addition to the "Safe Harbor" protections, section 27a itself sharply limits the circumstances under which the exercise of "control" could lead to imposition of general partner liability on a limited partner. It first provides that if a limited partner's control activities are so extensive as to be "substantially the same as" those of a general partner, that control, by itself, is sufficient to impose liability: *i.e.,* if a limited partner acts "the same as" a general partner, he will be treated as a general partner. However, but for that extreme case, mere participation in control does not impose liability on a limited partner. Such liability may be imposed only as to "persons who," in essence, rely on the limited partner's participation in control and thus regard him as a general partner.

That limitation of liability to those who rely on a limited partner's exercise of control is critical to a sound reading of the statute. It is consistent with the series of amendments from 1916 to now, which have been designed to insure predictability and certainty in the use of the limited partnership form of business organization. To reject plaintiff's claim of liability would be consistent with that view of the statute. To accept the claim would inject precisely the instability and uncertainty which the statute is designed to avoid.

* * *

We are satisfied that, were we to find individual liability against Wilf because of his "control" here, we would be encouraging precisely the instability and uncertainty which are anathema to widespread use of the limited partnership as a business entity. The modern, sound view, epitomized by the ULPA, the New Jersey statute and the well reasoned decisions discussed above is in the other direction: to curtail the threat of personal liability unless there is some "reliance on the part of the outsider dealing with the limited partnership." There was no such reliance here, and there is no basis for imposing personal liability on Wilf.

EVANS v. GALARDI

546 P.2d 313 (Cal. 1976)
SULLIVAN, JUSTICE

The facts are not in dispute. El Dorado is a limited partnership formed for the purpose of owning and managing certain real property in the City of South Lake Tahoe, California, and of constructing, owning and managing a motel on the premises. Eventually, a motel known as the

Rodeway Inn was built. When the partnership was formed in June 1969, plaintiff and defendants were the limited partners and entitled to receive all of the partnership net profits. The general partner at all times material herein was a California corporation known as El Dorado Improvement Corporation which operated the motel and whose stock initially was owned entirely by plaintiff and defendants. Raymond Haley was the president of the corporate general partner and in this position was charged with the over-all management of the business and with the supervision of its large number of employees.

About September 15, 1970, plaintiff, defendants and El Dorado Improvement Corporation entered into a written contract whereby plaintiff agreed to sell and defendants agreed to purchase for the sum of $50,000 all of plaintiff's right, title and interest in the limited partnership and all of plaintiff's stock in the corporate general partner. Defendants executed and delivered to plaintiff their promissory note for the full amount of the purchase price. The respective obligations were undertaken by the parties as individuals, and not in their status as limited partners or shareholders of the corporate general partner. El Dorado was not a party to the agreement of purchase and sale and did not sign either the agreement or the promissory note. As a result of this transaction, defendants as limited partners in El Dorado each became entitled to 50 percent of its net profits, if any, and became the owners of all of the stock of the corporate general partner.

Defendants defaulted on the promissory note and about April 2, 1971, plaintiff brought an action against them in their individual capacity to recover on it. Ultimately judgment was entered in favor of plaintiff and against defendants individually in the sum of $60,008.15.

On May 9, 1973, plaintiff obtained a writ of execution for the full amount of the judgment, and instructed the Sheriff of El Dorado County to levy execution upon the Rodeway Inn and to place a keeper there to collect the receipts of the business until the judgment was satisfied.

* * *

Plaintiff does not dispute that the legal title to the Rodeway Inn and to the money receipts generated by the motel is vested in El Dorado. Rather, he asserts that since defendants in their capacities as limited partners are each entitled to one-half of the net profits, they together in fact own the entire equitable and beneficial interest in El Dorado's assets.

* * *

We begin our analysis by observing that as a general rule "[a]ll goods, chattels, moneys or other property, both real and personal, or any interest therein, of the judgment debtor, not exempt by law . . . are liable to execution." (Code Civ.Proc., § 688.) Thus, the initial and most important question confronting us is whether defendants, in their capacities as limited partners, have any interest in the assets of El Dorado as such which renders these assets potentially subject to execution in satisfaction of a personal judgment against defendants. In answering this question, we find it helpful to discuss briefly some of the basic principles underlying the law governing limited partnerships.

The form of business association known as a "limited partnership" was not recognized as common law and is strictly a creature of statute. [Citations omitted] It can generally be described as a type of partnership comprised of one or more general partners who manage the business and who are personally liable for partnership debts, and one or more limited partners who contribute capital and share in the profits, but who take no part in running the business and incur no liability with respect to partnership obligations beyond their capital contribution. (Corp. Code, § 15501; 2 Barrett & Seago, Partners and Partnerships, Law and Taxation, *supra,* Limited Partnerships, § 1. p.482; 2 Rowley on Partnership, *supra,* Limited Partnerships, § 53.0, p.549.) The obvious purpose underlying legislative recognition of this type of business entity was to encourage trade by permitting "a person possessing capital to invest in business and to reap a share of the profits of the business, without becoming liable generally for the debts of the firm, or risking in the venture more than the capital contributed, provided he does not hold himself out as a general partner, or participate actively in the conduct of the business." (*Skolny v. Richter, supra,* 124 N.Y.S. 152, 155; see also *Clapp v. Lacey* (1868) 35 Conn. 463, 466.)

The California Legislature first legitimated limited partnerships in this state in 1870 by enacting a "special partnership" statute (Stats.1869–1870, ch. 129, p.123). These provisions were subsequently repealed in 1929, when the Legislature adopted the Uniform Limited Partnership Act. Among other things, this act sets forth with considerable specificity the rights and obligations of the general and the limited partners, including a detailed description of their proprietary interest in the business. With certain specified limitations, the general partner has all of the rights and powers enjoyed by partners in "non-limited" partnerships. (§ 15509.) Thus, by reference to the Uniform Partnership Act (§ 15001 et seq.), his property rights include: "(1) *his rights in specific partnership property,* (2) his interest in the partnership, and (3) his right to participate in the management." (§ 15024, italics added.) In sharp contrast, the limited partner is given no property interest in the specific partnership assets as such. Rather, he is entitled, among other things, "to receive a share of the profits or other compensation by way of income, and to the return of his contribution as provided in Sections 15515 and 15516." (§ 15510, subd. 2.)

This unwillingness on the part of the Legislature to grant the limited partner a property interest in the specific assets owned by the partnership, while at the same time providing for such an interest in the general partner, compels the conclusion that the limited partner has no interest in the partnership property by virtue of his status as a limited partner. Thus, such assets are not available to satisfy a judgment against the limited partner in his individual capacity. (Code Civ.Proc., § 688.)

While our research has disclosed no reported California decision which has considered this question, we note that our conclusion in this regard finds ample support in the decisions of our sister states and of the federal courts as well as in various treatises and other legal authorities. [Citations omitted]

Thus, in a case substantially identical to the one at bench, the New York Court of Appeals held that a sheriff lacked the power and jurisdiction to sell property owned by a limited partnership in execution of a judgment against a limited partner. In so holding, the court reasoned: "The interest of Harris [the limited partner] in the property of a limited partnership can hardly be said to be an interest in the property of the firm. He advanced to the firm a sum of money, which he is entitled to receive back, with interest, at the termination of the partnership; he is also entitled to a share in the profits; but he is to no further extent the owner of the property. Upon payment of these claims, the property would belong to the general partners." (*Harris v. Murray, supra,* 28 N.Y. 574, 86 Am.Dec. 268, 270.)

Quite apart from the lucid statutory language and the overwhelming weight of authority, the very nature of the limited partner's relationship with the business organization indicates that he has no property interest in the specific partnership assets which would render them available to his personal creditors. The limited partner is, primarily, an investor, who contributes capital and thereby acquires the right to share in the business profits. (See Uniform Limited Partnership Act, Official Comment, § 1.) His contribution must be in the form of cash or other property, may not consist of services (§ 15504), and must be specified as to amount in the partnership certificate. (§ 15502.) His surname may not be used as part of the firm name. (§ 15505.) He may not actively participate in the conduct of the business. (§ 15507.) Assuming that he complies with these conditions, he is not liable as a general partner on business debts and obligations, except to the extent of his capital contribution. (§§ 15501, 15507.) His death or withdrawal will not dissolve the partnership (§§ 15519, 15520, 15521), and he is not a proper party to proceedings by or against the firm. (§ 15526). In sum, "[t]he most striking feature of the relation of a special partner to the copartnership is its detached and impersonal character which accentuates sharply its dissimilarity from the relations of a general partner." (*Skolny v. Richter, supra,* 124 N.Y.S. at p.155.)

In the instant case, it is undisputed that plaintiff's action on the promissory note and the ensuing judgment were against defendants as individuals, and that El Dorado was not named as a party to the action or as a judgment debtor. Furthermore, there is no question but that the cash receipts of the Rodeway Inn constitute an asset owned by El Dorado. Therefore, under the principles heretofore discussed, defendants in their capacities as limited partners had no property interest in these receipts; accordingly, the receipts were improperly levied upon in execution of plaintiff's judgment against defendants.

* * *

PROBLEMS

1. Why would a person want to be both a general and a limited partner at the same time?

2. Compare your state's limited partnership law with the Revised Uniform Limited Partnership Act of 1976 with 1985 amendments (R.U.L.P.A.) and the Uniform Limited Partnership Act of 2001 (U.L.P.A. 2001) and answer the following questions:

   a. What may be contributed as capital
      (1) by a general partner under your local law?
      (2) by a limited partner under your local law?
      (3) by a general partner under the R.U.L.P.A.?
      (4) by a limited partner under the R.U.L.P.A.?

   b. What must a limited partner do to withdraw from the partnership under your state law, the R.U.L.P.A., and the U.L.P.A. 2001? What does a limited partner get when he or she withdraws under the respective acts?

   c. What can a limited partner do if he or she learns that a limited partnership has not been created and the limited partner wants to avoid personal limitability

   for partnership debts under your state law, the R.U.L.P.A., and the U.L.P.A. 2001?
      (1) If you were a limited partner in this circumstance, would you prefer to be governed by your state law, the R.U.L.P.A., or the U.L.P.A. 2001, and why?
      (2) Is it easier to avoid limited liability under your state law, the R.U.L.P.A., or the U.L.P.A. 2001 under this circumstance and why?

3. Review section 303 of the R.U.L.P.A. and section 303 of the U.L.P.A 2001, and review the facts and holding of *Zeiger v. Wilf* as it applies to Wilf. Under which statute would you prefer to argue that Wilf *is* liable because of his activities on behalf of the partnership?

4. Review sections 701 through 703 of the U.L.P.A. 2001. How, if at all, will this statute change or confirm the result of *Evans v. Galardi?*

5. How many general partners and how many limited partners are required for a limited partnership?

PRACTICE ASSIGNMENT

1. Review the Revised Uniform Partnership Act of 1976 with 1985 amendments (R.U.L.P.A.). Section 101(9) permits an oral agreement to form a limited partnership. Make a list of the provisions in the R.U.L.P.A. that require a "written" agreement to implement or amend.

2. Contact your local public filing office for limited partnerships (e.g., secretary of state or local corporate/partnership recording office). Obtain your local forms for a certificate of limited partnership and an amendment of the certificate of limited partnership. Complete the certificate form for a partnership that has your mother as the general partner, your father and you as the limited partners, and your address as the principal place of business of the partnership. Then amend the certificate to reflect the fact that your cousin just bought your father's interest as a limited partner and has been substituted in his place.

3. The investors of Post Petroleum Exploration-93, a limited partnership formed in January 1993 to engage in the exploration and drilling of oil and gas, were recently concerned to hear of the death of Roy C. Post, founder and chair of the board of directors of Post Petroleum, Inc., the corporate general partner of the partnership. The corporation assured the investors that the partnership would continue its activities as before and that, in fact, the remaining members of the board of directors had decided to expand the drilling activities of the partnership and would require additional cash contributions from each of the limited partners. All limited partners agreed to contribute an amount equal to their initial contribution of $50,000, except Paul Fogelberg who said he would like to assign his interest in the partnership to his daughter-in-law, Connie Hendrickson, in Minnetonka, Minnesota, who would be willing to contribute the additional cash. Prepare the necessary documents to accomplish all transactions described that require documentation, including any documents that would normally be filed for public record.

4. Jeb Pitkin and Winifred Alexis have asked you to prepare the limited partnership documents for their new enterprise, a summer camp for gifted children. The camp will be called "Camp Runamuck." At least $250,000 is needed to open the camp and pay the initial expenses. Jeb and Winifred expect to find ten or fewer investors to contribute that capital. Jeb and Winifred will serve as the general partners and will contribute cash equal to 5% of the amount contributed by the limited partners when the partnership is formed. They are willing to pay all cash generated by the business to return the capital contributions to the limited partners with a cumulative return of 10% per year before any amounts are paid to them as general partners, including their annual salaries of $50,000. Jeb and Winifred will retain 60% of the profits of the business, and the limited partners will be entitled to 40% of the profits after initial capital contributions have been returned in full. If both Jeb and Winifred are unable to continue as general partners for any reason, they want the partnership dissolved and liquidated, regardless of the desires of the limited partners at the time. Use the sample form, Form I-2, in Appendix I, and prepare the documents necessary to form this limited partnership.

ENDNOTES

1. Uniform Limited Partnership Act (hereafter cited as U.L.P.A.) § 1; Revised Uniform Limited Partnership Act (hereafter cited as R.U.L.P.A.) § 101(7). U.L.P.A. 2001 § 102(11).

2. 6 U.L.A. 561 (2003). Louisiana has its own laws based upon the civil code for a "Partnership in Commendam," the equivalent of a limited partnership. The references to the uniform laws are confusing: "U.L.P.A." or "original act" refers to the original uniform act; "R.U.L.P.A." or "revised act" refers to the 1976 revised act with 1985 amendments; and "U.L.P.A. 2001" or "new act" refers to the 2001 revision to the uniform law.

3. See "Registration as a Limited Liability Partnership" in Chapter 3.

4. U.L.P.A. § 7; R.U.L.P.A. § 303(a); U.L.P.A. 2001 § 303 now permits limited partners to participate in the management and control of the limited partnership without losing limited liability protection for partnership debts.

5. U.L.P.A. § 12; R.U.L.P.A. § 404; U.L.P.A. 2001 § 113.

6. See "Dissolution of a Limited Partnership" later in this chapter.

7. U.L.P.A. § 19(1); R.U.L.P.A. § 702; U.L.P.A. 2001 § 702.

8. R.U.L.P.A. § 101(5); U.L.P.A. 2001 § 201.

9. U.L.P.A. § 9(1)(e); R.U.L.P.A. § 401; U.L.P.A. 2001 § 401.

10. R.U.L.P.A. §§ 402(1), 602; U.L.P.A. 2001 § 603.

11. R.U.L.P.A. §§ 402(2), 702; U.L.P.A. 2001 § 603.

12. R.U.L.P.A. § 402(3); U.L.P.A. 2001 § 603.

13. R.U.L.P.A. § 402(4); U.L.P.A. 2001 § 603.

14. R.U.L.P.A. § 402(6)–(10); U.L.P.A. 2001 § 603.

15. See "Dissolution and Termination of a Partnership" in Chapter 3.

16. R.U.L.P.A. § 402; U.L.P.A. 2001 § 605.

17. R.U.L.P.A. § 801(4); U.L.P.A. 2001 § 801.

18. R.U.L.P.A. § 405; U.L.P.A. 2001 § 406.

19. U.L.P.A. § 6(2); R.U.L.P.A. § 1105, and see "Management of a Partnership—Standards of Conduct of Partners" in Chapter 3. U.L.P.A. 2001 departs from the historical approach of linking the limited partnership law to the general partnership act to fill any gaps in the rules for limited partnership, but U.L.P.A. 2001 incorporates into its sections many of the Revised Uniform Partnership Act rules that would apply to partners in a limited partnership. With respect to fiduciary duties, U.L.P.A. 2001 provides that the only fiduciary duties that a general partner has to the limited partnership and the other partners are the duties of care and loyalty, including the duty to account, to refrain from dealing with adverse parties and to refrain from competing. U.L.P.A. 2001 § 408.

20. U.L.P.A. § 7; R.U.L.P.A. § 303(a); U.L.P.A. 2001 § 303.

21. U.L.P.A. § 4.

22. R.U.L.P.A. § 501; U.L.P.A. 2001 § 501.

23. R.U.L.P.A. § 502(b); U.L.P.A. 2001 § 502.

24. R.U.L.P.A. § 502(c); U.L.P.A. 2001 § 502(c).

25. R.U.L.P.A. § 303.

26. R.U.L.P.A. § 304; U.L.P.A. 2001 § 306.

27. R.U.L.P.A. § 403; U.L.P.A. 2001 § 406.

28. U.L.P.A. § 9; R.U.L.P.A. § 403. U.L.P.A. 2001 requires the consent of the limited partners to amend the partnership agreement, amend the certificate of limited partnership to add or delete a statement that the limited partnership is a limited liability limited partnership, and to sell, lease, exchange, or otherwise dispose of all, or substantially all, of the partnership's property other than in the usual and regular course of the partnership's business. U.L.P.A. 2001 § 406.

29. See "Types of Agents—Duties and Obligations between the Principal and the Agent" in Chapter 1 and "Standards of Conduct of Partners" in Chapter 3.

30. U.L.P.A. 2001 § 303. Compare R.U.L.P.A. § 303(a).

31. U.L.P.A. § 10; R.U.L.P.A. § 303; U.L.P.A. 2001 § 304.

32. U.L.P.A. § 8; R.U.L.P.A. § 301(a); U.L.P.A. 2001 § 301.

33. U.L.P.A. § 16; R.U.L.P.A. § 603.

34. U.L.P.A. § 16; R.U.L.P.A. § 603. Under the original act, notice must be given to "all members"; under the revised act, notice is given to "each general partner." U.L.P.A. 2001 § 602 provides that upon the dissociation of a limited partner, the limited partner ceases to have rights of a partner, but is in the same position of a transferee of the limited partner's transferable interest—namely, entitled to receive distributions of profits and assets, but not allowed to withdraw capital from the partnership.

35. U.L.P.A. § 16; R.U.L.P.A. § 607.

36. U.L.P.A. § 16(3); R.U.L.P.A. § 605.

37. U.L.P.A. § 19(4); R.U.L.P.A. §§ 301(2), U.L.P.A. 2001 § 602(3).

38. U.L.P.A. § 19; R.U.L.P.A. § 301(b). The revised act abandons the terminology of a "substituted" limited partner. Instead, the revised act refers to an assignee who has been granted the right to become a limited partner. Amendment of the certificate is discussed in "Formation and Operation of a Limited Partnership" later in this chapter.

39. U.L.P.A. §§ 9(1) (g), 20; R.U.L.P.A. § 801; U.L.P.A. 2001 § 801.

40. R.U.L.P.A. § 802; U.L.P.A. 2001 § 802.

41. See U.L.P.A. § 10(c); U.P.A. § 32.

42. U.L.P.A. § 16(4) (a).

43. R.U.L.P.A. § 606; U.L.P.A. 2001 § 603(3).

44. R.U.L.P.A. § 402. U.L.P.A. 2001 § 603. See "General Partners of a Limited Partnership" earlier in this chapter.

45. R.U.L.P.A. § 801(3).

46. The misconduct of a general partner would cause dissolution to be "equitable and proper" under U.L.P.A. § 10(c) and presumably would be an event that makes it reasonably impracticable "to carry on the business in conformity with the partnership agreement" under R.U.L.P.A. § 802 and U.L.P.A. 2001 § 802.

47. See "Dissolution and Termination of a Partnership" in Chapter 3.

48. R.U.L.P.A. § 801(4); U.L.P.A. 2001 § 801. An example of an agreement to continue the business appears in clause 26 of the sample limited partnership agreement, Exhibit I-2, in Appendix I.

49. U.L.P.A. § 10(c).

50. R.U.L.P.A. § 803; U.L.P.A. 2001 § 803.

51. R.U.L.P.A. § 804; U.L.P.A. 2001 § 812.

52. Treas. Reg. §§ 301.7701-1 through 301.7701-3 (*1996, as amended).

53. See Treas. Reg. § 3-1.7701-2 (1960, as amended) specifying corporate characteristics that would affect the tax status of limited partnerships.

54. R.U.L.P.A. § 102; U.L.P.A. 2001 § 108.

55. R.U.L.P.A. § 103; U.L.P.A. 2001 § 109.

56. R.U.L.P.A. § 101(9); U.L.P.A. 2001 §§ 102(13), 110.

57. R.U.L.P.A. § 201; U.L.P.A. 2001 § 201.

58. R.U.L.P.A. § 104.

59. Under the original act, amendments are required whenever there is a change in the name of the partnership, amount or character of the limited partners' contributions; the character of the business; or the time for dissolution or return of contributions. Amendments also are required on the admission of any partner; on the substitution of a limited partner; for the continuation of the business after withdrawal, death, or insanity of a general partner; or in any case where there is a need to correct an erroneous statement in the certificate or to represent accurately the agreement between partners. U.L.P.A. § 24.

60. R.U.L.P.A. § 202; U.L.P.A. 2001 § 202.

61. R.U.L.P.A. § 204; U.L.P.A. 2001 § 204.

62. R.U.L.P.A. § 203; U.L.P.A. 2001 § 203.

63. R.U.L.P.A. §§ 101(4), 902; U.L.P.A. 2001 § 902.

64. R.U.L.P.A. § 902; U.L.P.A. 2001 § 902.

65. R.U.L.P.A. §§ 905, 906; U.L.P.A. 2001 §§ 905, 906.

66. R.U.L.P.A. § 907; U.L.P.A. 2001 § 907.

67. R.U.L.P.A. § 1001; U.L.P.A. 2001 § 1002.

68. R.U.L.P.A. §§ 1002–1004; U.L.P.A. 2001 §§ 1003–1005.

LIMITED LIABILITY COMPANY

For many years, the primary business entities in use in the United States were sole proprietorships, general and limited partnerships, and corporations. The limited liability company has been rapidly accepted and is one of the more popular forms of business organizations today. Rarely has a new form of organization been so accepted for widespread use.

The limited liability company combines the operational flexibility and favorable tax treatment of partnerships with the limited liability feature of a corporation. The initial statutes authorizing the formation of limited liability companies have borrowed heavily from the Model Business Corporation Act and the Revised Uniform Limited Partnership Act, incorporating the most desirable features of each act. The first limited liability company statute was enacted in Wyoming in 1977. Florida followed Wyoming's example five years later. Rapidly, states adopted variations of these initial and analogous uniform statutes. A Uniform Limited Liability Company Act that was drafted in 1995 and modified in 1996, has been the basis for recent amendments to and initial adoptions of statutes authorizing limited liability companies. All states now have a limited liability company act.[1]

The limited liability company may elect to have pass-through tax advantages, like Subchapter S corporations and partnerships, but may avoid several restrictive and burdensome requirements of the Subchapter S election.[2] A Subchapter S corporation may not have more than seventy-five shareholders, and those shareholders cannot include other corporations, nonresident aliens, general or limited partnerships, trusts, pension plans, or charitable organizations; but a limited liability company is not restricted to a specific number of members, nor are the members limited to individual citizens. A Subchapter S corporation may not own more than eighty percent of the stock of another corporation,[3] while a limited liability company can own any percentage or all of the stock in a corporation. The limited liability company also allows flexibility in distributions and special allocations to members, as compared with the one class of stock limitation imposed upon a corporation electing to be taxed under Subchapter S.[4]

All members of a limited liability company are granted limited liability protection from debts of the business. In partnership law, all general partners in a general partnership are individually liable for the debts and obligations of the partnership. A limited partnership exposes at least one partner, the general partner, to liability, even though personal liability may be avoided by using a corporate general partner. Historically, tax rules impose requirements that the corporate general partner must have a minimum owner-ship interest in the partnership and a substantial capitalization (so that there are assets of the general partner available for creditors of the partnership). Only the limited partners of a limited partnership are afforded the benefits of limited liability, and even the limited part-ners may risk losing this protection if they actively participate in control of the business of the partnership. It is now possible to form partnerships (both general and limited) that per-mit limited liability for the partners and the recently adopted Uniform Limited Partnership Act has eliminated liability exposure for limited partners who are participating in manage-ment activities of the partnership. However, potential liability of partners is always a source of concern in the planning and operation of any partnership.[5]

CHARACTERISTICS OF A LIMITED LIABILITY COMPANY

A limited liability company is recognized as a separate legal entity apart from the owners who own the membership interest, similar to the separate existence of a corporation.[6] A limited liability company is also entitled to exercise statutory powers very similar to the powers of a corporation. Under the Uniform Act, limited liability companies have the same powers as an individual to do all things necessary or convenient to carry on its busi-ness or affairs.[7]

While the limited liability company can function only in accordance with the power given to it by statute and the authority granted in its articles of organization by the members of the company, it should be obvious that the statutory power under the Uniform Act is very broad and extensive, encouraging the participation of limited liability companies in nearly any busi-ness transaction.

Many state statutes predate the Uniform Act and still provide similar, yet diverse, rules for the formation and operation of the limited liability company. Eventually, the Uniform Act will be used as the basis for amendments to these statutes. In the meantime, however, it is very im-portant to review the specific state statutes to detect local variations and idiosyncracies that will affect the operation of such a company formed in that state. For example, many statutes provide that the limited liability company can only be formed for a certain duration, such as 30 years. This feature was initially required primarily to accommodate tax issues when the reg-ulations would not permit the entity to have "continuity of life" for tax purposes.[8] Under the Uniform Act, a limited liability company may last for any period of time desired (such as "100 years from the date of filing the articles of organization"), but if the articles of organization do not specifically so state, the duration of the company is "at will," meaning the withdrawal of any member will potentially dissolve the company.[9]

In either case, the limited liability company is not appropriate for certain types of busi-nesses. For example, any business that desires longevity through many generations could not operate as a limited liability company if the statute required that it have a limited duration. Similarly, businesses that require long-term lending arrangements, such as public utilities and real estate investment businesses, could not operate under this business form because they typ-ically borrow money over a period longer than the statutory period would permit and the length of time in which they pay back their loans exceeds the authorized duration of the entity. Un-der most current state statutes and the Uniform Act, it is now possible to carefully draft the or-ganizing documents for a limited liability company to make it adaptable to most businesses, but it takes some thought and creativity to maneuver through the statutory variations to shape the organization to fit all the needs of the business.

The operations of a limited liability company are also governed by rules and regulations adopted by the organizers of the business. The articles of organization and the operating agree-ment (both discussed in detail later) are used to impose rules for operation and structure for the company.

The limited liability company is often used in businesses or ventures where limited liabil-ity and pass-through tax consequences are particularly desirable. For example, professional service businesses (such as those of lawyers or physicians) can benefit substantially from this form of business organization where so permitted under state law. Businesses that are expected to mature and prosper with only a few owners for the predictable future are also appropriately organized as limited liability companies. While it would be possible to have a publicly owned limited liability company, the fact that all members have some rights and obligations that are similar to partners in a partnership would make the operations of a publicly owned limited liability company unwieldy. The company is also particularly adaptable to businesses that require unique provisions for sharing of profits and losses or cash and management structures that can accommodate a single manager or no managers at all.

In summary, the limited liability company is an attractive alternative to conventional partnerships and corporations. It grants limited liability, favorable tax treatment, and operational flexibility without many of the restrictive requirements imposed on corporations and limited partnerships. It is treated as a legal entity, distinct from the members who own and manage it. Under the Uniform Act, the lawyer or paralegal is free to alter most of the statutory provisions in the organizing documents; thus, the entity can be nearly any form and shape desired with unique features to accommodate any client. These are all the reasons why this form of business organization is becoming very popular for closely held businesses.

STATUTORY POWERS OF A LIMITED LIABILITY COMPANY

The limited liability company obtains power to operate its business from the authority of the state statute. Because this form of business organization is intended to be a rational alternative to partnerships and corporations, the powers of a limited liability company are typically quite broad. For example, the Uniform Act grants a limited liability company the power to

(a) sue and be sued, and defend in the company name;

(b) purchase, receive, lease, or otherwise acquire, and own, hold, improve, use, and otherwise deal with real or personal property, or any legal or equitable interest in property, wherever located;

(c) sell, convey, mortgage, grant a security interest in, lease, exchange, and encumber or dispose of all or any part of its property;

(d) purchase, receive, subscribe for, or otherwise acquire, own, hold, vote, use, sell, mortgage, lend, grant a security interest in, or otherwise dispose of and deal in and with shares or other interests in or obligations of any other entity;

(e) make contracts and guarantees, incur liabilities, borrow money, issue its notes, bonds, and other obligations, which may be convertible into or include the option to purchase other securities of the limited liability company, and secure any of its obligations by a mortgage on or a security interest in any of its property, franchises, or income;

(f) lend money, invest and reinvest its funds, and receive and hold real and personal property as security for repayment;

(g) be a promoter, partner, member, associate, or manager of any partnership, joint venture, trust, or other entity;

(h) conduct its business, locate offices, and exercise the powers granted by this Act within or without the State;

(i) elect managers and appoint officers, employees, and agents of the limited liability company, define their duties, fix their compensation, and lend them money and credit;

(j) pay pensions and establish pension plans, pension trusts, profit sharing plans, share bonus plans, share option plans, and benefit or incentive plans for any or all of its current or former members, managers, officers, employees, and agents;

(k) make donations for the public welfare or for charitable, scientific, or educational purposes; and

(l) make payments or donations, or do any other act, not inconsistent with law, that furthers the business of the limited liability company.[10]

Notice the similarity between the foregoing powers and the powers granted to business corporations in Chapter 6. The drafters of the limited liability statutes obviously borrowed the rules of corporate statutes in defining the power to do business in a limited liability company.

The limited liability company is given power necessary and convenient to effect all of the "business" for which it is organized.[11] The business purposes of the company, which are described in the statute, are typically broad. For example, a limited liability company usually can conduct any lawful business. Delaware, in its inimitable simplicity, broadly grants limited liability companies "all the powers and privileges granted" by the enabling statute, any other law, or its operating agreement, "together with any powers incidental thereto, so far as such powers and privileges are necessary or convenient to the conduct, promotion or attainment of the business, purposes or activities of the limited liability company."[12]

Any desired restrictions on the power of a limited liability company can be placed in its articles of organization or operating agreement. The articles of organization are filed in a state filing office, usually the Secretary of State, and are available for public inspection and information. The operating agreement is a private agreement among members of the limited liability company and is accessible only to the members and managers of the company unless it is voluntarily disclosed to others.

The purposes of the limited liability company are usually described in the articles of organization, which delineate the business objectives the company intends to pursue, such as owning and operating an apartment building, practicing law, selling and leasing equipment, or any other defined business operation. With appropriate drafting of articles of organization and operating agreement, counsel can tailor the specific features of the limited liability company to the precise powers and purposes that the organizers desire for its operation.[13]

Because of the similarity between the statutory powers of a limited liability company and the statutory powers of a corporation, it is expected that corporate cases interpreting corporate powers will be applicable by analogy to the powers of a limited liability company.[14]

OWNERSHIP AND MANAGEMENT OF A LIMITED LIABILITY COMPANY

The owners of a limited liability company, called **members**, are analogous to partners in a partnership and to shareholders in a corporation. Under the Uniform Act and in many states it is now possible to have a single-member limited liability company, in which only one person forms the company and is its only member. This allows a sole proprietor, for example, who prefers the sole ownership and management of his or her business to achieve limited liability from obligations of the business by forming a limited liability company and transferring the sole proprietorship's assets to it. The possibility of a single-member company also makes the limited liability company more adaptable than a partnership, since any form of partnership requires at least two members.

The members' contribution may consist of tangible or intangible property or other benefit to the company, including money, promissory notes, services performed, or other obligations to contribute cash or property, or contracts for services to be performed.[15] Like corporate shareholders, the members of a limited liability company may be passive investors whose contributed capital is used for the operation of the business, and whose opinion is solicited only for certain significant decisions required to be made by the members by statute, such as the admission of new members or the dissolution of the company. It is also possible to provide that the members will manage the business; and like partners, they are integral to the operation of the business insofar as their death, retirement, or resignation will cause a dissolution of the company.[16] The specific rights and obligations of the members and their participation in the business are defined in the articles of organization or the operating agreement.

Right to Vote

Members have certain statutory voting rights, including typically the right to vote for managers of the company,[17] the right to approve amendments to the articles of organization and the operating agreement, the admission of a new member to the company, transfers of member-ship interests by other members,[18] and consent to dissolve the company.[19] Several statutory variations of these voting rights exist. In some states, the members are the managers unless managers are specifically provided in the structure of the company as described in the articles of organization.[20] In Maryland, the members are the agents of the company and can obligate the company even if managers are appointed.[21] In some states, the transferee of a membership interest may become a member automatically upon the transfer without the consent of the other members.[22] In the Uniform Act and all states, the members have the right to vote on any matter as provided in the operating agreement, subject to any statutory provisions that require a majority or unanimous vote, consent, or agreement of the members.[23]

Admission and Dissociation

A member may **dissociate** from a limited liability company at any time by giving written no-tice of his or her resignation to the other members. However, if the resignation violates the op-erating agreement, the company may recover damages from the resigning member for a breach of the operating agreement or for resigning before the expiration of the term of the company.[24] A resigning member is entitled to receive any distribution to which the member is entitled un-der the operating agreement; if the operating agreement is silent on this subject, the member is entitled to receive fair value of the membership interest in the company as of the date of res-ignation (minus damages caused by his or her breach of the agreement).[25] A member may also dissociate involuntarily by death, bankruptcy, or expulsion from the company as provided in the operating agreement.[26] In order to protect creditors, in most states the member (or the member's estate) may not receive any distributions from the company if the company's assets do not exceed its liabilities.[27] If a member has received any part of the contribution in viola-tion of the operating agreement or the statute, the member is liable for the amount of the con-tribution wrongfully returned. Even if a member has received the contribution consistently with the operating agreement or the statute, the member must be prepared to return the distri-bution to the extent necessary to discharge the company's liabilities to creditors.[28] The Uni-form Act refers to the payments to a dissociated member as a **distributional interest**, the fair value of which can be determined by a court, if necessary, considering the going concern value of the company, any agreement among the members specifying a formula for determining value, or the recommendations of an appraiser appointed by the court.[29]

   In the Uniform Act and states that attribute partnership characteristics to limited liability companies, new members cannot be admitted to a limited liability company without the writ-ten consent of all existing members.[30] Similarly, in many states, the death, retirement, resig-nation, expulsion, bankruptcy, or dissolution of a member or any other event that terminates the continued membership of a member in the company causes a dissociation of the member and a dissolution of the company unless the company purchases the distributional interest of the dissociated member.[31] In modern practice, where the underlying state statute so permits, the operating agreement addresses the consequences of the withdrawal of a member by death or some other event, and provides for the membership interest of the withdrawn member to be purchased by the company or other members upon terms and conditions that will not disrupt the ongoing operations of the business.

Right to Remove Manager

If the company has managers, the manner in which the managers can be removed is usually covered in the operating agreement. However, if the operating agreement does not provide for the removal of managers, some state statutes provide that the managers may be removed with or without cause by a vote of the majority of the members entitled to vote for an election of the managers.[32]

Right to Information

Members of a limited liability company have a right to inspect and copy records as provided by the statute and to obtain from the managers, subject to any reasonable standards set forth in the operating agreement, true and full information regarding the state of the business and financial condition of the limited liability company. The members also are entitled to receive from the managers any other information regarding the affairs of the company and to have the federal, state, and local income tax returns for each year. The operating agreement may provide for access and dissemination of other information to members as well. In the Uniform Act, members are entitled to all information concerning the company's business or affairs "reasonably required for the proper exercise of the member's rights and performance of the member's duties under the operating agreement."[33] In some states, members are entitled, like partners in a partnership, to a "formal accounting" of affairs whenever circumstances render it "just and reasonable."[34]

Meetings

Some of the more elaborate statutes authorizing limited liability companies describe corporate-type provisions for meetings and membership action. In states that do not have specific statutory requirements, the articles of organization or the operating agreement should address any issues relating to meetings of members.

In a statutory scheme, member's meetings may be held at any place stated or fixed in the operating agreement; and if the agreement does not address the place of the meeting, the meeting is held at the registered office of the company. Annual and special meetings are authorized by most statutes, and special meetings may be called by any persons so authorized in the articles of organization, the operating agreement, or the statute.[35]

Notice of meetings is required by some statutes, similar to notice for corporate meetings. The notice usually must be sent within a certain time period prior to the meeting, and must specify the type of business to be conducted for a special meeting of the members.[36]

Unless otherwise provided in the articles of organization or the operating agreement, a majority of the members entitled to vote will be quorum at a meeting of members. If a quorum is present, the affirmative vote of the majority of the members represented at the meeting and entitled to vote on the subject matter will bind the members. The articles of organization or the operating agreement can increase to the size of the quorum or the vote required.[37]

The Uniform Act and most states permit members of limited liability companies, like stockholders in corporations, to take action by signing a unanimous written consent instead of attending a meeting.[38]

The specific procedures and requirements for formal meetings of limited liability companies and corporations are discussed in more detail in Chapter 10.

MANAGERS

General Powers

The management of the business and affairs of a limited liability company may be conducted by the members or, if the members agree, may be vested in a **manager** or managers. In some states, managers are called a *board of governors* or *directors,* and in some states, the company is required to have at least one *chief manager.*[39] These persons act in a manner similar to the general partners of a limited partnership and the directors of a corporation. The articles of organization or the operating agreement of the limited liability company may apportion management responsibility and voting powers among the various named managers.[40]

Since a limited liability company generally is operated in the same manner as a partnership, it is possible to specify, in the operating agreement or the articles of organization, particular duties for managers and certain issues on which the managers are required to act as a group. The limited liability company structure permits maximum flexibility in granting or restricting the authority of individual managers or the group of managers collectively.

Election and Term

A limited liability company may operate with a single manager or several managers, as determined by the organizers in the articles of organization or the operating agreement. The number of initial managers is normally fixed in the articles of organization; and if the operating agreement does not provide otherwise, the number stays the same as that provided in the articles of organization.[41]

Similar to a board of directors of a corporation, the initial managers hold office until the first annual meeting of the members or until their successors have been elected and qualified.[42]

The managers are elected by a majority of the members, unless the operating agreement provides for a different method of appointment of managers.[43]

Like the corporate model, the structure of the limited liability company makes it possible to stagger or classify managers so that the entire group of managers does not have to be re-elected each year. Typical statutory authority on staggering or classification permits a division of the managers into either two or three classes, so that each class is elected in successive years. For example, if there are nine managers and the group of managers is classified into three classes, three managers serve until the first annual meeting, three managers serve until the second annual meeting, and three managers serve until the third annual meeting. Each year, the company elects three new managers to join the six managers whose terms have not yet expired.[44]

It is also possible to describe a method of election of managers in the operating agreement so that individual managers represent a constituency of members who elect them. Because the operating agreement (like a partnership agreement) generally may include any provision agreed to by the members, the members may allocate representation among the managers in any way they wish.

Qualifications

A manager usually must be a natural person, but in some states a manager can be another entity such as a corporation, partnership, or trust. States that require natural persons have adopted the philosophy that individual management decisions are appropriate in operating a business under the limited liability company structure. Managers may have to be a certain age[45] but usually do not have to be members of the limited liability company.[46] The articles of organization or the operating agreement may provide other qualifications desired by the members.[47]

Vacancies

If a vacancy occurs in the group of managers, either because of the death, removal, or retirement of a manager or by an amendment increasing the number of managers, the vacancy can be filled by a majority of the remaining managers.[48] At least one state requires a written agreement among the managers in order to fill such a vacancy.[49]

A manager selected to fill a vacancy serves the unexpired term of the predecessor manager or, if the vacancy results from an increase in the number of managers, until the next annual meeting of members when a successor is elected and qualified.[50]

Removal

Managers, like directors of corporations, serve at the pleasure of the members of the limited liability company. Their positions are not as secure as general partners in a partnership (whose expulsion must be specifically described in the partnership agreement). A manager may be removed with or without cause, as provided in the operating agreement, or if the operating agreement is silent, by the vote of the majority of members who would have been entitled to elect the manager.[51]

Duties

Managers are agents of the limited liability company. In fact, the Uniform Act and some statutes specifically describe the manager's duties as those of an agent.[52] As agents, they are authorized to conduct the business of the limited liability company in the usual way consistent with the purposes described in the articles of organization and consistent with the authority granted to the managers in the operating agreement. As long as a manager is acting within the scope of his or her authority and the business purposes of the company, the acts of the manager legally bind the limited liability company.[53]

Under some statutes, the manager is required to perform specific duties. For example, only the managers of the company may be able to contract for debts of the company[54] or to execute instruments and documents provided for the acquisition, mortgage, or disposition of real or personal property of the company.[55] Managers generally are expected to perform duties similar to those of a director of a corporation.[56] Thus, managers generally are required to act in good faith, in a manner reasonably believed to be in the best interests of the company, and with such care as an ordinarily prudent person in a like position would use under similar circumstances.[57] Most statutes permit managers to rely upon information obtained from employees or other agents, attorneys or other professional advisers, or committees of the managers in making decisions on behalf of the company.[58]

The Uniform Act describes two fiduciary duties of managers: a duty of care and a duty of loyalty. The manager's duty of care is limited to refraining from engaging in grossly negligent or reckless conduct, intentional misconduct, or a knowing violation of law.[59] The duty of loyalty requires a manager to account to the company and hold "as trustee" for it property, profit, or benefits derived by a manager in the conduct or winding up of the company's business or derived from any use by the manager of the company's property, including the appropriation of an opportunity in which the company would be interested in exploiting; to refrain from dealing with people having an interest adverse to the company; and to refrain from competing with the company's business.[60] Although not described as a fiduciary duty of a manager, the Uniform Act also requires managers to perform their duties consistently with the obligation of good faith and fair dealing.[61]

The manager's duties may be expanded or contracted in the articles of organization or the operating agreement; indeed, like a partnership agreement, the operating agreement should specify the manager's duties in detail so that the structure of the business can be tailored specifically to the desires of the organizers. The articles of organization and the operating agreement are binding on managers, and the managers must scrupulously follow the duties and obligations imposed upon them by those documents.[62]

Like directors of a corporation but unlike general partners of a partnership, managers of a limited liability company are not liable for any obligations of the company.[63] Under most limited liability company statutes, managers are entitled to be indemnified for expenses or liabilities suffered for claims made against them because of acts done in their "official capacities" as managers on behalf of the limited liability company.[64] The indemnification method generally follows the scheme used by a corporation to indemnify its officers and directors and is often confirmed and amplified in the operating agreement.[65]

TRANSFERABILITY OF MEMBERSHIP INTEREST

The ownership interest in a limited liability company is an interesting blend of ownership of stock in a corporation and ownership of an interest in a partnership. The Uniform Act calls the member's ownership interest in the company the "distributional interest."[66] On the one hand, the membership interest is personal property of the member, like stock in a corporation, and may be transferred or assigned in the manner provided in the operating agreement.[67] Consequently, the operating agreement typically provides for the basis upon which membership interest can be transferred, and may impose any agreed-upon restrictions or conditions to the transfer of membership interest.[68]

In some states and in the Uniform Act, on the other hand, a feature of partnership is superimposed on the ability of members to sell a membership interest. If all other members of the limited liability company do not approve of a proposed transfer by unanimous written consent, the purchaser of a membership interest has no right to participate in the management or business affairs or to become a member.[69] This rule is based on the concept that a member of a limited liability company is an integral part of the company, which is a carryover of the concept that a partner is an integral part of the partnership. No new members are permitted unless all other members agree. If the other members do not agree to a transfer of a membership interest, the purchaser is entitled only to the share of profits or other compensation and the return of contributions to which the selling member would have been entitled.[70] If all other members consent to a transfer of membership interest, however, the purchaser becomes a substituted member and has all the rights of the member from whom the interest is purchased or received.[71]

FINANCE

Contributions

The contributions of capital to a limited liability company can be made tangible or intangible property or other benefit to the company (such as a guaranty of the company's indebtedness), including money, promissory notes, services performed, or other obligations to contribute cash or property, or contracts for services to be performed.[72] Most statutes anticipate that the articles of organization and the operating agreement will address this subject by placing restrictions on or defining the types of consideration that can be received in exchange for membership interest. In some elaborate statutory schemes, provisions for contributions to a limited liability company are defined in considerable detail. For example, in Minnesota, the statute provides the following details concerning these contributions:

1. The board of governors (the Minnesota name for "managers") accepts the contribution on behalf of the limited liability company, describing the contribution, including terms of future performance, and stating the value of the contribution.
2. The determination of the board of governors as to the amount or fair value of the contribution and the terms of payment or performance must be made in good faith and on the basis of accounting methods or a fair valuation or other method reasonable in the circumstances.
3. The governors who intentionally or without reasonable investigation accept a consideration that is unfair to the company or overvalue property or services received will be liable to the company for the damage caused to the members.
4. The types of membership interests may be set by the articles of organization, and may include more than one class of membership interest with various terms, including the right of the company to redeem membership interests, entitling the members to preferential distributions, entitling the members to convert from one class of membership interest to another, and having various voting rights on various matters.
5. A "would-be contributor" must sign a written contribution agreement.
6. The contribution agreement is irrevocable for six months.
7. The contribution agreement must be paid or performed in full at the times or in the installments specified in the contribution agreement or, if there is no such provision, as determined by the board of governors uniformly among all contributors for membership interest of the same class.
8. If a would-be contributor fails to perform a contribution agreement, the company may sue to recover the amount due or may declare a forfeiture of the contribution agreement and cancel it.
9. Upon forfeiture of a contribution agreement, the membership interest is offered for sale by the company, and any excess net proceeds realized by the company over the amount owed by the delinquent would-be contributor are paid to the delinquent would-be contributor. If the membership interest does not sell for more than the amount due, the company may cancel the contribution agreement and retain a portion of the price paid up to ten percent of the price stated in the contribution agreement.
10. If a new contribution is received by a limited liability company subsequent to another contribution, the board must restate the value of the old contribution.[73]

Distributions

Members of a limited liability company are entitled to receive distributions from the company at the times and on the events specified in the articles of organization or operating agreement, as the managers (if any) specify, or as the members shall agree.[74] These distributions, like those of a partnership, include allocations of profits, losses, deductions, credits, and cash. The operating agreement or the articles of organization may specify the manner in which the distributions will be shared; and some statutes contain a "default provision," stating that distributions and allocations will be made on the basis of the members' capital value if no contrary provisions appear in the organizing documents.[75] A dissociating member, like a resigning or withdrawing partner in a partnership, is entitled to receive distributions to which he or she is entitled under the operating agreement or articles of organization; and if this situation is not addressed in those documents, the member is entitled to receive the fair value of the member's membership interest in the company as of the date of dissociation.[76] Members are entitled to receive distributions from the company in cash; unless otherwise provided in the operating agreement or articles of organization, members may not be compelled to accept distributions of any assets in kind that would have to be shared with other members entitled to distributions from the company.[77]

When a member becomes entitled to receive a distribution, that member, similar to a shareholder in a corporation, has the status of and is entitled to all remedies available to a creditor of the company for the amount of the distribution.[78] However, most states impose the same restrictions on distributions of limited liability companies that are imposed on those of corporations: the company must be able to pay its debts as they become due in the usual course of business, and the company's assets must exceed its liabilities.[79]

Members who receive distributions in violation of the statutory restrictions are liable for the return of those distributions if the assets are needed to pay creditors.[80] Similarly, any managers who vote for distributions in violation of the statute may be liable to the company, like directors of corporations who are liable for improperly distributed corporate dividends.[81]

CONTINUITY OF EXISTENCE AND DISSOLUTION

Statutory Term

The statutes permitting the formation of limited liability companies provide that the articles of organization must set forth whether the duration of the company is for a specified term, and, if so, the period specified.[82] Today, most state statutes and the Uniform Act allow a limited liability company to last indefinitely if no period of duration is specified in the articles of incorporation. When limited liability companies were first authorized, many were formed with a limited duration, so that organizers could ensure that the company received pass-through taxation. The tax rules governing this issue were based on partnership taxation, and the regulations required that such an entity must lack certain corporate characteristics, one of which is **continuity of life**.[83] New tax regulations now allow a limited liability simply to elect to be treated as a partnership, and the term of existence of the company does not affect its tax status.[84] Imposing any limitation on the term of existence should be carefully considered in preparing a limited liability company for a client, since it is not possible to extend the limited liability company beyond its term. At the expiration of the term, it is necessary to dissolve the company, convert it into a new entity, or transfer its assets to a different organization to continue conducting its business; either option may have significant tax consequences.[85]

Dissolution

A limited liability company is dissolved under circumstances similar to those under which a partnership is dissolved. A dissolution typically occurs by

1. an event specified in the operating agreement;
2. consent of the number or percentage of members specified in the operating agreement;
3. the expiration of the term of duration;

4. an event that makes it unlawful for all or substantially all of the business of the company to be continued, but any cure of illegality within 90 days after notice to the company of the event is effective retroactively;

5. a court order on application by a member or a dissociated member or a transferee of a member of an at-will company that the economic purpose of the company is likely to be unreasonably frustrated; it would be not reasonably practicable to carry on the company's business because of the acts of a member; if the company failed to purchase a dissociated member's distributional interest; or the managers or members in control of the company have acted, are acting, or will act in a manner that is illegal, oppressive, fraudulent, or un-fairly prejudicial to the member.[86]

States have taken different approaches to the issue of dissolution upon the dissociation of a member because of death, retirement, resignation, expulsion, bankruptcy, or dissolution (of an entity member). Some statutes require an "absolute" dissolution of the company and require that dissociation will *always* lead to dissolution, unless the members, by unanimous consent given after the dissolution, elect to continue the business.[87] Other states have "flexible" statutory rules and permit members to provide in the organizing documents that such events will not result automatically in dissolution of the company.[88] In the latter situation, the drafter of the articles of organization or the operating agreement must consider whether the flexibility of continuation of the business is desirable considering the personal contribution to the company that each member is making. If a member's managerial expertise is critical to the operation of the business, it may be preferable to require dissolution upon a dissociation of that member. On the other hand, if the member's participation in the business is merely that of an investor or can easily be replaced by other persons, the dissolution should be avoided to ensure continuity of the business.

When a dissolution occurs by a member's dissociation, if the remaining members elect to continue the business of the company without liquidating its affairs, the company must purchase the distributional interest of the dissociated member, less any damages caused by the member's untimely dissociation or breach of the operating agreement.[89] However, if the members do not have the authority (or the will) to continue the business once a dissolution has occurred, the company must begin to wind up its affairs, usually commencing with filing a statement of intent to dissolve the company with the state.[90] This statement is intended to notify creditors that the company will be liquidating its assets and distributing them to creditors and members.

In settling accounts after dissolution, the assets of the limited liability company are distributed using a scheme similar to that used in partnership distributions. First, creditors must be paid. Then, depending upon the provisions of the operating agreement, assets are distributed to members to return their contributions and to share any profits of the business.[91]

Once the liabilities of a dissolving company have been paid or provided for and the remaining assets have been distributed to the members, the company must file articles of dissolution or **articles of termination** with the state.[92]

CONVERSION OF OTHER ENTITIES AND MERGER

A unique feature of limited liability companies is the right granted under some state statutes to convert general or limited partnerships into limited liability companies by filing articles of organization that meet the requirements of the statutes. This statutory authority is unique, because rarely is it possible to convert one type of business organization into another by simply filing an additional document. Normally, substantial documentation must be prepared to convert the ownership of a sole proprietor into a partnership or to convert a partnership into a corporation.

The Uniform Act permits conversion of a partnership or a limited partnership into a limited liability company.[93] Several states have adopted statutes permitting conversion of a partnership to a limited liability company. In Virginia, for example, conversion is accomplished by filing articles of organization and a document that names the partnership and describes the date and place of filing of the original certificate of partnership.[94]

One of the hybrid corporate features enjoyed by limited liability companies in the Uniform Act and several states is the authority to **merge** or consolidate one limited liability company with another or to merge limited liability companies with limited partnerships or corporations.[95] Partnerships cannot be merged in most states, and a merger of a partnership with a corporation also is not normally authorized. Consequently, the enabling legislation for the merger of limited liability companies with other companies, partnerships, or corporations is novel. The procedure for merger and **consolidation**, when authorized, is very similar to that for corporations, described in Chapter 15.

TAXATION OF A LIMITED LIABILITY COMPANY

The taxation of a limited liability company has been uncertain and confusing in the early development of the entity. The Internal Revenue Service initially suggested that the limited liability company formed under the Wyoming statute—the first enabling statute—be taxed as a corporation. The draft regulations to that effect were withdrawn after significant criticism from tax specialists. Following an extensive study, the Internal Revenue Service ruled in 1988 that a limited liability company under the Wyoming statute would be treated as a partnership for tax purposes.[96]

Taxation as a partnership is a significant advantage of the limited liability company. Before 1997, most cautious practitioners relied only on private or public letter rulings from the Internal Revenue Service that interpret and compare the local statutes to their predecessors.[97] In 1997, the Internal Revenue Service adopted new regulations that permit limited liability companies to elect the tax status for the entity. Thus, a limited liability company could elect to be taxed like a corporation (if the organizers preferred to accumulate income for expansion and did not want the members to be taxed on income they do not receive), or it automatically will otherwise be taxed like a partnership.[98] A single-member limited liability company will automatically be taxed as a sole proprietorship—that is, the income is attributable to the member and may be reported on his or her personal tax return. Most states authorizing the formation of a limited liability company tax it as a partnership.[99]

FORMATION AND DOCUMENTATION OF A LIMITED LIABILITY COMPANY

The formation of a limited liability company involves the drafting of documents that are similar to partnership agreements and the documents required for the formation of a corporation. The articles of organization parallel the articles of incorporation for corporations; the operating agreement contains issues that typically are addressed in partnership agreements and in the bylaws of corporations.

Name

All states that permit the formation of limited liability companies impose restrictions on the names of the companies. The name must include the words "Limited Liability Company" or some authorized abbreviation such as "L.L.C." or "L.C." (these vary from state to state). Limited liability companies are authorized to use assumed business names in some states, provided they make appropriate filings under the assumed business name statutes.[100] The name of the limited liability company cannot be deceptively similar to any other registered corporate, partnership, or limited liability company name. It can be reserved and registered in advance like a partnership or corporate name. (See Exhibit 5–1, Reservation of Limited Liability Company Name.)

Limitation on Purposes

Although most states permit limited liability companies to be organized for any lawful purpose, some enabling statutes restrict the activities of these companies. Wyoming and Nevada

W. Fox McKeithen
Secretary of State

**RESERVATION OF CORPORATE/LIMITED LIABILITY
COMPANY NAME**
(R.S. 12:23, 12:204, 12:303, 12:1307 & 12:1344)

Enclose $25 filing fee
Make remittance payable to
Secretary of State
Do Not Send Cash

Return to: Commercial Division
P. O. Box 94125
Baton Rouge, LA 70804-9125
Phone (225) 925-4704
Web Site: www.sec.state.la.us

The Secretary of State, State of Louisiana is requested to reserve the following name for use as a

corporate/limited liability company name:

_____

Said name is requested to be reserved on behalf of _____

_____ , for a period of sixty days from the date of

your receipt of this application.

_____
Name

_____
Address

_____
City/State/Zip

_____
Area code/phone number

Submitted by:

_____
Date

If the requested name is not available, please return this application and the filing fee to the above.

398 Rev. 03/03   (see instructions on back)

Exhibit 5–1.

Reservation of Limited
Liability Company Name
(Louisiana)

prohibit them from participating in banking and insurance industries.[101] Many states allow the use of partnerships and corporations for professional services, such as the practice of law, medicine, or accounting, and have recently amended this statutory authority to include limited liability companies.[102] Unless a local statute or rule permits the practice of professional services in a limited liability company, the formation of a limited liability company to render such services is not allowed. Often, local statutes provide that even if professional practices may occur in a limited liability company structure, the person rendering the services remains personally liable for all acts or omissions causing damage to a client or patient.[103] In such cases, the only advantage of forming a limited liability company for a professional practice is that the professional's colleagues will not be liable for his or her malpractice.

Exhibit 5–2.

Articles of Organization
(Oklahoma)

FILING FEE: $100.00

FILE IN DUPLICATE

PRINT CLEARLY

ARTICLES OF ORGANIZATION
OF AN
OKLAHOMA LIMITED LIABILITY COMPANY

TO: OKLAHOMA SECRETARY OF STATE
2300 N Lincoln Blvd., Room 101, State Capitol Building
Oklahoma City, Oklahoma 73105-4897
(405) 522-4560

The undersigned, for the purpose of forming an Oklahoma limited liability company pursuant to the provisions of 18 O.S., Section 2004, does hereby execute the following articles:

1.   The name of the limited liability company (**Note:** The name <u>must</u> contain either the words **limited liability company** or **limited company** or the abbreviations **LLC, LC, L.L.C**. or **L.C**. The word limited may be abbreviated as Ltd. and the word Company may be abbreviated as Co.):

_____

_____

2.   The street address of its principal place of business, wherever located:

_____
Street address   City   State   Zip Code

3.   The name and street address of the resident agent in the state of Oklahoma:

_____
Name   Street Address   City   State   Zip Code
(P.O. Boxes are **not** acceptable.)

4.   The term of existence: _____

Articles of organization <u>must</u> be signed by at least one person who need not be a member of the limited liability company.

Dated: _____

Signature: _____

Type or Print Name: _____

Address: _____

(SOS FORM 0073-11/99)

Interstate Business

Theoretically, a limited liability company is entitled to do business in any state in addition to the state in which the company is formed. Like partnerships and sole proprietorships, the company is required to comply with any local licensing and filing requirements. Provisions for qualification of foreign limited liability companies, which are similar to the requirements for qualification of foreign corporations, must be followed.[104]

Articles of Organization

The creation of a limited liability company depends on the filing of **articles of organization** with an appropriate filing officer, usually the secretary of state. The articles of organization must state certain matters required by statute, and may contain other rules for the operation of the company that are desired by the organizers. (See Exhibit 5–2, Articles of Organization).

The juxtaposition of the articles of organization and the operating agreement in a limited liability company deserves special comment, considering the rules that apply to corporations, which are discussed in detail later. The articles of organization are filed with a public office and can be amended only by a formal procedure that requires a filing of an amendment to the articles of organization. The formal procedure usually involves a recommendation of the amendment by the managers (if the company is managed by managers) and a vote by the members to approve the amendment. The membership vote required to approve an amendment is usually a majority, unless the articles of organization or operating agreement increase the percentage vote required for amendments. On the other hand, the operating agreement, which also contains rules for the operation of the business, is an agreement among *all* members. Consequently, an amendment to the operating agreement can probably be accomplished only by the unanimous consent of all members unless otherwise expressly provided in the agreement. Thus, in a limited liability company, rules desiring permanence should be included in the operating agreement, and those rules that may be expected to change from time to time should be placed in the more easily amended articles of organization. The converse is true for corporations: articles of incorporation can be amended only by a cumbersome formal voting procedure, while bylaws may be informally amended by directors or shareholders.[105]

The items that are to be addressed in the articles of organization and the operating agreement should be determined in an early conference with the organizers of the company when all statutory requirements and other drafting issues for the formation of the entity are discussed. A checklist for this conference is Exhibit I–3 in Appendix I.

According to the Uniform Act, the articles of organization must set forth the following:

1. The name of the company;
2. The address of the initial designated office;
3. The name and street address of the initial agent for service of process;
4. The name and address of each organizer;
5. Whether the duration of the company is for a specified term and, if so, the period specified;
6. Whether the company is to be manager-managed, and, if so, the name and address of each initial manager;
7. Whether the members of the company are to be liable for its debts and obligations.

The articles of organization *may* set forth the following:

1. Provisions permitted to be set forth in an operating agreement; or
2. Any other matters not inconsistent with law.[106]

The specific requirements of the applicable state statute should be carefully reviewed, since the acts permitting the formation of limited liability companies vary widely. Typical requirements are discussed briefly here.

Name

The articles of organization must contain the name of the company, which usually cannot be deceptively similar to any other corporate, partnership, or assumed business name in the state. The name may be previously reserved, but the filing of the articles of organization permanently reserves the name for the duration of the company.

Name

EXAMPLE

The name of the limited liability company is Independent Enterprises, Limited Liability Company.

Initial Designated Office or Principal Place of Business

The initial designated office or principal place of business of the company must be stated. Under most statutes, the initial designated office or principal place of business may be either within or outside of the state of organization of the company.

EXAMPLE

Principal Place of Business

The principal place of business of the Limited Liability Company is 423 W. 54th St., New York, New York.

Duration

If the limited liability company will have a stated term, the latest date upon which the limited liability company is to dissolve and other events of dissolution must be stated in the articles of organization. If no duration is stated, under the Uniform Act, a limited liability company is an at-will company.

EXAMPLE

Duration

This Limited Liability Company shall dissolve and terminate 30 years from the date of filing these Articles of Organization with the Secretary of State.

Registered Office and Agent

Like a corporation and some limited partnerships, the limited liability company must maintain a registered office and agent for receipt of official notices and legal matters. The registered agent usually can be any person or entity maintaining an office within the state, although some statutes describe specific qualifications for registered agents. Each statute should be consulted separately to determine the appropriate requirements.

EXAMPLE

Registered Agent

The registered agent of this Limited Liability Company in this state is Glenna McKelvy, and the business address of the registered agent is 303 Hopkins Boulevard, Minneapolis, Minnesota 55102.

Initial Managers

If the company is to be managed by managers, instead of the members, the names and business addresses of the initial managers usually must be stated in the articles of organization. Managers generally must be natural persons, but in some states, they may be other entities such as partnerships, corporations, or other limited liability companies. The articles of organization can impose qualifications for managers if the organizers so desire.

EXAMPLE

Initial Managers

The names and business addresses of the initial Managers who are to serve as Managers until the first annual meeting of the Members or until their successors are elected and qualified are as follows:

Name	Address
Boutrous Archibald	1156 Humboldt Street, Denver, Colorado 80218
Sally Endive	1968 Jasmine Street, Denver, Colorado 80220

Classification of Managers

Some states permit the staggering or **classification** of managers, sometimes depending on the number of managers (e.g., six or more). Classification of the managers provides continuity of management, since the entire group of managers is not reelected at each annual meeting.

Instead, a few of the managers are elected each year. A provision for the staggering or classification of managers should be included in the articles of organization.

Classification of Managers

The Managers shall be divided into three classes, each class to be three Managers, and the term of the office of Managers of the first class will expire at the first annual meeting of Members after their election. The term of the office of Managers of the second class will expire at the second annual meeting after their election. The term of the Managers of the third class will expire at the third annual meeting after their election. At each annual meeting after such classification, the number of Managers equal to the number of the class whose term expires at the time of such meeting shall be elected to hold office until the second succeeding annual meeting, if there are two classes, or until the third succeeding annual meeting, if there are three classes. No classification of Managers shall be effective prior to the first annual meeting of Members.

Members

In many states, if the members are to manage the business (instead of managers), the articles of organization must state the names and addresses of the initial members. Many states and the Uniform Act now authorize single-member limited liability companies; other statutes require that there be at least two members of the limited liability company upon formation, and that fact should be stated in the articles of organization. The articles of organization also may state any qualifications for membership, such as professional licensure, residence, age, and similar qualifications.

Members

There will be at least two Members of this Limited Liability Company upon formation.

Initial Members

The names and business addresses of the initial Members of the Company who will manage the Company, instead of Managers, are as follows:

Name	Address
Edward M. Giles	1225 Seventeenth Street Suite 2900 Denver, Colorado 80202
Edward F. O'Keefe	1225 Seventeenth Street Suite 2900 Denver, Colorado 80202

Qualifications of Members

The members of this limited liability company shall be limited to attorneys licensed to practice law in the state of Colorado who are residents of Colorado and are at least 32 years of age or older.

Purposes

Many states permit a limited liability company to be organized for any lawful purpose. If any restrictions are desired on the business objectives of the company, they should be stated in the articles of organization. Similarly, any statutory restrictions that may apply to the company's business should be observed. For example, in some states, these companies cannot engage in the businesses of insurance or banking.

Purposes

The purposes for which this Limited Liability Company is formed are to own and operate apartment buildings within the city limits of Denver, Colorado; and to engage in any other lawful business.

Indemnification of Managers

Managers, especially those who are not members, may need protection from liability and expenses incurred in their position as managers, which can be provided by indemnification. The provisions allowing indemnification by limited liability companies vary widely from state to state, and specific statutory authority for indemnification should be carefully reviewed.

Indemnification

The Managers of this Company shall be entitled to the full indemnification provided by law and the Company shall be obligated to indemnify and hold harmless a Manager who is subject to any claim while a Manager of the Company, or who is or was serving at the Company's request as a director, officer, partner, trustee, employee or agent of any other foreign or domestic corporation, partnership, joint venture, trust, limited liability company, or employee benefit plan so long as the Manager qualifies for such indemnification under the terms of this Operating Agreement or by law.

Right to Continue Business

Since under many statutes the limited liability company dissolves as a result of the death, retirement, resignation, expulsion, bankruptcy, or dissolution of a member, the articles of organization should address the manner in which the business may be continued and the circumstances under which members must consent to the continuation. Similarly, the purchase of the distributable interest owned by the deceased, retired, resigned, expelled, or bankrupt member should be described.

Right to Continue Business

Upon the death, retirement, resignation, expulsion, bankruptcy, or dissolution of a Member or the occurrence of any other event that terminates the continued Membership of a Member ("Dissolution Event") in the Limited Liability Company, the business of the Limited Liability Company may be continued as long as there are at least two remaining Members and all Members consent to the continuation of business. The Managers of the Limited Liability Company shall call a special meeting of Members within ninety (90) days after the Dissolution Event for purposes of determining whether the business should be continued.

Upon the occurrence of a Dissolution Event, the Company shall purchase the Membership Interest owned by the deceased, retired, resigned, expelled, or bankrupt Member by paying to him or her the fair value of his or her Membership in the Limited Liability Company in cash within ninety (90) days following the Dissolution Event. A "fair value" shall be the value determined and agreed upon by the Company and the Member owning the Membership Interest, or if no agreement can be reached, the value determined by the accountant then engaged by the Limited Liability Company, whose determination shall be conclusive for all purposes.

Optional Provisions

The articles of organization may contain any other provision, not inconsistent with law, that the members elect to set out for the regulation of the internal affairs of the limited liability company. These optional provisions usually may include any provisions required or permitted to be set forth in the **operating agreement**. However, since the existing statutes authorizing limited liability companies are not based upon the Uniform Act but have been drafted, in many cases, through the collective ideas of various state legislators, they are less than precise on the placement of certain important provisions in the company's operations documents. In many cases, the statutes state that certain provisions may be included in the operating agreement, but fail to state that similar provisions may be included in the articles of organization. Conversely, some provisions that must be included in the articles of organization are not allowed to be included in the operating agreement. The drafter of the articles of organization and the operating agreement for a limited liability company must review carefully the local statutes and observe the statutory requirements for placement of operational rules in the appropriate documents.

Operating Agreement

The operating agreement for a limited liability company is similar to a partnership agreement for a partnership. In fact, all the issues typically addressed in a partnership agreement should be addressed in the operating agreement, since the relationship among members of a limited liability company is very similar to that of partners in a partnership. Like a partnership agreement, the operating agreement of a limited liability company can change most statutory rules that the organizers desire to modify for the structure of the business. At least two important distinctions, however, differentiate the operations of a limited liability company from those of a partnership:

1. The decisions of the limited liability company may be made by managers elected by members, and if that structure is desired, a procedure for the administration of the activities of both managers and members must be included; and
2. The articles of organization are also a governing document that provides rules for the operations of the business. Consequently, the operating agreement must be consistent with the articles of organization.

Under the Uniform Act, the operating agreement may vary all statutory "default" provisions, except that the operating agreement may not

1. unreasonably restrict a member's right to information or access to records;
2. eliminate the duty of loyalty, but the agreement may identify specific types or categories of activities that do not violate the duty of loyalty (if not manifestly unreasonable) and specify the number or percentage of members or disinterested managers that may authorize or ratify, after full disclosure of all material facts, a specific act or transaction that otherwise would violate the duty of loyalty;
3. unreasonably reduce the duty of care;
4. eliminate the obligation of good faith and fair dealing, but the agreement may determine the standards by which the performance of the obligation is to be measured (if the standards are not manifestly unreasonable);
5. vary the right to expel a member;
6. vary the requirement to wind up the company's business in case of certain dissolutions;
7. restrict rights of third parties as provided in the statute.[107]

For the drafter, the preparation of documents for a limited liability company is quite a challenge, since almost all of the clauses that would be used in a partnership agreement and in corporate articles of incorporation and bylaws need to be included to cover thoroughly all the issues that may arise in the operations of the limited liability company.

Some state statutes describe the items that are to be addressed in the operating agreement. For example, Maryland states that the operating agreement may include provisions establishing

1. the manner in which the business and affairs of the limited liability company shall be managed, controlled, and operated, which may include the grant of exclusive authority to manage, control, and operate the limited liability company to persons who are not members;
2. the manner in which the members will share the assets and earnings of the limited liability company;

3. the rights of the members to assign all or a portion of their interest in the limited liability company;

4. the circumstances in which any assignee of a member's interest may be admitted as a member of the limited liability company;

5. the member's right to have a certificate evidencing the member's interest in the limited liability company, and the procedure by which the certificate is to be issued by the company;

6. the procedure for assignment, pledge, or transfer of any interest represented by a member's interest; and

7. the method by which the operating agreement may from time to time be amended.[108]

The operating agreement must be tailored to the specific desires of the organizers and members. The following checklist with examples and references to the detailed discussions of this chapter may be used as a guide for preparing the agreement.

Checklist

1. Acknowledge the articles of incorporation and provide for conflicts between the articles of organization and the operating agreement.

EXAMPLE

Articles of Organization and Conflicts

This Company is organized pursuant to the provisions of the Limited Liability Company Laws of the State of Colorado, pursuant to Articles of Organization filed with the Secretary of State on February 10, 2005, and the rights and obligations of the Company and the Members shall be provided in the Articles of Organization and this Operating Agreement. If there is any conflict between the provisions of the Articles of Organization and this Operating Agreement, the terms of [the Articles of Organization] or [this Operating Agreement] shall control.

---

2. **Contributions**—Provide for the initial and additional capital contributions by the members for the purchase of their membership interest.

EXAMPLE

Contributions

The capital contributions to be made by the Members with which the Company shall begin business are as follows:

Member Name	Contribution
Susan Bartic	$10,000 in cash
Glenna McKelvy	$25,000 in cash
Brent Karasiuk	$15,000 in property as described on Schedule A.

EXAMPLE

Additional Capital Contributions

In the event that the cash funds of the Company are insufficient to meet its operating expenses or to finance new investments deemed appropriate to the scope and purpose of the Company as determined by the Managers, the Members shall make additional capital contributions in the proportion of their capital contributions. The amount of the additional capital required by the Company and the period during which such additional capital shall be retained by the Company shall be determined by the Managers.

---

3. **Loans**—If the Company is to be authorized to borrow money, provisions authorizing the loans and providing for any restrictions on the authority of the Managers or Members with respect to such loans should be stated.

Loans

In lieu of voting an additional assessment of capital to meet operating expenses or to finance new investments, the Company may, as determined by the Managers, borrow money from one or any of the Managers, Members, or third persons. In the event that a loan agreement is negotiated with a Manager or Member, he or she shall be entitled to receive interest at a rate and upon such terms as determined by the Managers, excluding the Manager making said loan, if applicable, and said loan shall be repaid to the Manager or Member, with unpaid interest, if any, as soon as the affairs of the Company permit. The loan shall be evidenced by a promissory note obligating the assets of the Company. Such interest and repayment of the amounts so loaned are to be entitled to priority of payment over the division and distribution of capital contributions and profit among Members.

4. **Establishment of capital and income accounts**—A limited liability company financial structure is similar to a partnership, providing for **capital accounts** for members and their membership interest. Similarly, an income account should be established to reflect distributions of profits, losses, gains, deductions, and credits.

Capital Accounts

A separate capital account shall be maintained for each Member. The capital accounts of each Member shall initially reflect the amounts specified as initial capital to be contributed by each member, and if a Member has merely promised to contribute such amounts, the Company shall maintain a corresponding subscription receivable on behalf of that Member. No Member shall withdraw any part of his or her capital account, except upon the approval of the Managers. If the capital account of a Member becomes impaired, or if he or she withdraws from said capital account with approval of the Managers, his or her share of subsequent Company profits shall be credited first to his or her capital account until that account has been restored, before such profits are credited to his or her income account. During the period when a Member's capital account is impaired or he or she has withdrawn funds therefrom as hereinbefore provided, if an additional contribution is required of the Members for purposes specified in this Operating Agreement, the Member with the withdrawn or impaired capital account shall be required to contribute his or her proportionate share of the additional capital contribution and restore the deficiency then existing in his or her capital account, so as to return the capital accounts to the same proportion existing as of the date of the additional contribution. No interest shall be paid on any capital contributions to the Company.

Income Accounts

A separate **income account** shall be maintained for each Member. Company profits, losses, gains, deductions, and credits shall be charged or credited to the separate income accounts annually unless a Member has no credit balance in his or her income account, in which event losses shall be charged to his or her capital account. The profits, losses, gains, deductions, and credits of the Company shall be distributed or charged to the Members as provided in this Operating Agreement. No interest shall be paid on any credit balance in an income account.

5. **Allocations to members**—The ratio for sharing profits, losses, deductions, credits, and cash among the members should be specified.

Allocations among Members

The profits, gains, and cash of the Company shall be divided and the losses, deductions, and credits of the Company shall be borne in the following proportions:

Susan Bartic 20%
Glenna McKelvy 50%
Brent Karasiuk 30%

6. **Distributions of assets**—The limitations on distributions of assets and the allocations among members should be stated clearly in the operating agreement. The statutes provide

the conditions upon which distributions may be made and the circumstances under which a member has a right to receive a distribution from the company in kind. The operating agreement should be clear on these issues.

EXAMPLE

Distributions of Assets

(1) All distributions of assets of the Company, including cash, shall be made in the same allocations among Members as described in this Operating Agreement.

(2) The Managers shall determine, in their discretion, whether distributions of assets of the Company should be made to the Members; provided, however, that no distribution of assets may be made to a Member if, after giving effect to the distribution, all liabilities of the Company, other than liabilities to Members on account of their capital and income accounts, would exceed the fair value of the Company assets.

(3) A Member has no right to demand and receive any distribution from the Company in any form other than cash.

7. **Admission of members**—The circumstances under which additional members may be admitted to the company should be described.

EXAMPLE

Admission of New Members

Additional Members may be admitted upon the unanimous written consent of all Members.

8. **Voting members**—The circumstances under which members are entitled to vote and matters upon which their votes will be solicited should be described. The agreement should provide the percentage of the members' votes required to approve any issues.

EXAMPLE

Voting of Members

A Member shall be entitled to one vote on any matter for which Members are required to vote. A Member may vote in person or by proxy at any meeting of Members. All decisions of the Members shall be made by a [majority] or [unanimous] vote of the Members at a properly called meeting of the Members at which a quorum is present, or by unanimous written consent of the Members.

9. **Meetings of members**—Most state statutes do not describe a procedure for meetings for members. Consequently, the rules desired by the organizers and the members should be described in the operating agreement.

EXAMPLE

Meetings of Members

(1) Meetings of Members may be held at such time and place, either within or without the State of Colorado, as may be determined by the Managers or the person or persons calling the meeting.

(2) An annual meeting of the Members shall be held [on the 5th day of March in each year] or [at such time and place as shall be determined by a resolution of the Managers during each fiscal year of the Company].

(3) Special meeting of the Members may be called by the Managers and by at least one-tenth of all of the Members entitled to vote at the meeting.

(4) Written notice stating the place, day, and hour of the meeting and, in the case of a special meeting, the purpose for which the meeting is called, shall be delivered not less than ten days nor more than fifty days before the date of the meeting, either personally or by mail, by or at the direction of the Managers or any other person calling the meeting, to each Member of record entitled to vote at the meeting. A waiver of notice in writing that is signed by the Member before, at, or after the time of the meeting stated in the notice shall be equivalent to the giving of such notice.

EXAMPLE

(continued)

(5) By attending a meeting, a Member waives objection to the lack of notice or defective notice unless the Member, at the beginning of the meeting, objects to the holding of the meeting or the transacting of business at the meeting. A Member who attends a meeting also waives objection to consideration at the meeting of a particular matter not within the purpose described in the notice unless the Member objects to considering the matter when it is presented.

Quorum and Adjournment

EXAMPLE

A majority of the Members entitled to vote shall constitute a quorum at the meeting of Members. If a quorum is not represented at any meeting of the Members, the meeting may be adjourned for a period not to exceed sixty days at any one adjournment; provided, however, that if the adjournment is for more than thirty days, a notice of the adjourned meeting shall be given to each Member entitled to vote at the meeting.

10. **Powers of managers—**The operating agreement may broaden or restrict the powers of the managers. Most state statutes do not limit the authority of managers in any way; if the members desire any limitations, they should specifically describe them. Managers may be authorized by the members to do any or all acts to manage the company.

General Powers

EXAMPLE

Management and the conduct of the business of the Company shall be vested in the Managers. The Managers may adopt resolutions to govern their activities and the manner in which they shall perform their duties to the Company.

Duties of Managers

EXAMPLE

(1) The Managers shall have the duties and responsibilities as described in the Colorado Limited Liability Company Act, as amended from time to time [with the following limitations and restrictions:].

(2) The Managers, or any one of the Managers designated by resolution of the Managers, shall execute any instruments or documents providing for the acquisition, mortgage, or disposition of the property of the Company.

(3) Any debt contracted or liability incurred by the Company shall be authorized only by a resolution of the Managers, and any instruments or documents required to be executed by the Company shall be signed by the Managers or by any one of the Managers designated by resolution of the Managers.

(4) The Managers may designate to any one of the Managers or delegate to an employee or agent the responsibility for daily and continuing operations of business affairs of the Company. All decisions affecting the policy and management of the Company—including the control, employment, compensation, and discharge of employees; the employment of contractors and subcontractors; the control and operation of the premises and property including the improvement, rental, lease, maintenance, and all other matters pertaining to the operation of the property of the business—shall be made by the Managers.

(5) Any Manager may draw checks upon the bank accounts of the Company and may make, deliver, accept, or endorse any commercial paper in connection with the business affairs of the Company.

11. **Qualifications of managers—**Any qualifications required by the statute or desired by the organizers should be stated in the operating agreement.

Qualifications of Managers

EXAMPLE

Managers shall be natural persons eighteen years of age or older and shall be residents of the State of Colorado.

12. **Number, election, and term**—Provisions should state the number of managers, how they will be elected, and the term of their office.

EXAMPLE

Number, Election, and Term

(1) The number of Managers shall be three. The number of Managers shall be increased or decreased by the vote or consent of the Members.

(2) The initial Managers shall hold office until the first annual meeting of Members and until their successors have been elected and qualified. Thereafter, each Manager elected by the Members shall hold office for a one-year term or until his or her successor has been elected and qualified.

(3) Managers shall be elected by a vote or consent of the Members at an annual meeting or at a special meeting called for that purpose.

13. **Meeting and voting of managers**—Only a few statutes provide a statutory scheme for the meetings and voting of managers. The operating agreement should address these issues.

EXAMPLE

Meetings and Voting

(1) Meetings of the Managers may be held at such time and place as the Managers by resolution shall determine.

(2) Written notice of meetings of the Managers shall be delivered at least twenty-four hours before the meeting, personally or by telecopier or mail actually delivered to the Manager within the twenty-four-hour period. A waiver of notice in writing that is signed by the Manager before, at, or after the time of the meeting stated in the notice shall be equivalent to the giving of such notice.

(3) By attending a meeting, a Manager waives objection to the lack of notice or defective notice unless the Manager, at the beginning of the meeting, objects to the holding of the meeting or the transacting of business at the meeting.

(4) A majority of the Managers entitled to vote shall constitute a quorum at the meeting of Managers.

(5) All decisions of the Managers shall be made by a [majority] or [unanimous] vote of the Managers at a properly called meeting of the Managers at which a quorum is present, or by unanimous written consent of the Managers.

14. **Devotion to duty**—The operating agreement should provide that each manager, like the partners in a partnership, must devote reasonable time and attention to the duties of the company.

EXAMPLE

Devotion to Duty

At all times during the term of a Manager, each Manager shall give reasonable time, attention, and attendance to, and use reasonable efforts in the business of, said Company; and shall, with reasonable skill and power, exert himself or herself for the joint interest, benefit, and advantage of said Company; and shall truly and diligently pursue the Company's objectives.

15. **Books and records**—Provisions concerning access, inspection, copying, and methods of accounting in regard to the books and records of the company should be described in the operating agreement. Each state statute is different in terms of the financial information that must be available to the members. The applicable statute should be reviewed carefully to be certain that all information required to be communicated by the statute is included in the operating agreement.

EXAMPLE

Location of Records

The books of the Company shall be maintained at the principal office of the Company or at such other place as the Managers by vote or consent shall designate.

Access to Records and Accounting

EXAMPLE

Each member shall at all times have access to the books and records of the Company for inspection and copying. Each Member shall also be entitled:

(1) to obtain from the Managers upon reasonable demand for any purpose such information reasonably related to the Member's Membership Interest in the Company;

(2) to have true and full information regarding the state of the business and financial condition and any other information regarding the affairs of the Company;

(3) to have a copy of the Company's federal, state, and local income tax returns for each year promptly after they are available to the Company; and

(4) to have a formal accounting of the Company affairs whenever circumstances render an accounting just and reasonable.

Accounting Rules

EXAMPLE

The books shall be maintained on the cash basis. The fiscal year of the Company shall be the calendar year. Distributions to income accounts shall be made annually. The books shall be closed and balanced at the end of each calendar year, and if an audit is determined to be necessary by vote or consent of the Managers, it shall be made as of the closing date. The Managers may authorize the preparation of year-end profit and loss statements, balance sheets, and tax returns by a public accountant.

16. **Dissolution**—The causes of dissolution and the circumstances under which the business may be continued should be described in the operating agreement.

Causes of Dissolution

EXAMPLE

The Company shall be dissolved upon the occurrence of any of the following events:
(1) at any time by unanimous agreement of the Members;
(2) upon the expiration of the period fixed for the duration of the Company in its Articles of Organization; or
(3) upon the death, retirement, resignation, expulsion, bankruptcy, or dissolution of a Member.

Continuation of Business

EXAMPLE

Notwithstanding a dissolution of the Company, the Members may elect to continue the business of the Company, as long as there are at least two Members remaining who then consent to do so, by purchasing the deceased, retired, resigned, expelled, or bankrupt Member's ("Withdrawn Member") Membership Interest.

17. **Provisions for purchase of a withdrawn member's membership interest**—If the business is to continue after a member withdraws from the company, the provisions should state the basis upon which the withdrawn member's interest in the company will be purchased.

Purchase of Withdrawn Member's Membership Interest

EXAMPLE

(1) If the Members elect to continue the business, the purchase price of the Withdrawn Member's Membership Interest shall be equal to the Withdrawn Member's capital account as of the Effective Date, plus his or her income account as of the end of the prior fiscal year, decreased by his or her share of the Company losses, deductions, and credits computed to the Effective Date, and decreased by withdrawals such as would have been charged to his or her income account during the present year to the Effective Date. The purchase price is subject to set-off for any damages incurred as a result of the Withdrawn Member's actions, and nothing in this paragraph is intended to impair the Company's right to recover

damages for the Withdrawn Member's wrongful dissolution of Company by reason of the Withdrawn Member's expulsion, retirement, resignation, or bankruptcy.

(2) The purchase price shall be paid to the Withdrawn Member in cash within ninety (90) days from the Effective Date.

(3) The "Effective Date" shall be the date of death of a deceased Member; the date personal notice is received, or the date the certified mail is postmarked, in the case of a retired, resigned, or expelled Member; or the date the notice is delivered to a Withdrawn Member, or to the place of business of the Company in the case of bankruptcy of a Member.

18. **Distribution of assets**—If the business is not continued, the operating agreement should provide for the basis upon which assets of the company will be distributed.

Distribution of Assets If Business Is Not Continued

In the event of dissolution of the Company and if the Members do not elect to or are unable to continue the business of the Company following dissolution, the Managers shall proceed with reasonable promptness to sell the real and personal property owned by the Company and to liquidate the business of the Company. Upon dissolution, the assets of the Company business shall be used and distributed in the following order:

(1) any liabilities and liquidating expenses of the Company shall be paid;

(2) the reasonable compensation and expenses of the Managers in liquidation shall be paid;

(3) the remaining amount shall be paid to and divided among the Members in accordance with the statutory scheme for distribution and liquidation of the Company under the Colorado Limited Liability Company Act, as amended from time to time.

19. **Expulsion**—The circumstances justifying expulsion of a member should be specifically detailed, and the procedure for expulsion should be stated.

Causes of Expulsion

A Member shall be expelled from the Company upon the occurrence of any of the following events:

(1) if a Member shall violate any of the provisions of this Agreement;

(2) if a Member's Membership Interest is subject to a charging order or tax lien that is not dismissed or resolved to the satisfaction of the Managers of the Company within thirty days after assessment or attachment; or

(3) if a Member is caught picking his or her nose.

Notice of Expulsion

Upon the occurrence of an event justifying Expulsion, written notice of Expulsion shall be given to the violating Member either by serving the same by personal delivery or by mailing the same by certified mail to his or her last known place of residence as shown on the books of said Company. Upon the receipt of personal notice, or the date of the postmark for certified mail, the violating Member shall be considered expelled and shall have no further rights as a Member of the Company, except to receive the amounts to which he or she is entitled under this Operating Agreement for the purchase of the violating Member's Membership Interest.

20. **Bankruptcy**—Provisions should be included for the continuation of the business in case of bankruptcy of a member and the basis upon which the member's membership interest will be purchased.

Bankruptcy Defined

A Member shall be considered "bankrupt" if the Member files a petition in bankruptcy (or an involuntary petition in bankruptcy is filed against the Member and the petition is not dismissed within sixty (60) days) or makes an assignment for the benefit of creditors or otherwise enters into any proceeding or agreement for compounding his or her debts other than by the payment of them in the full amount thereof, or is otherwise regarded as insolvent under any Colorado Insolvency Act.

Effective Date for Bankruptcy

The Effective Date of a Member's bankruptcy shall be the date that the Managers, having learned of the Member's bankruptcy, give notice in writing, stating that the Member is regarded as bankrupt under this Agreement. Such notice is to be served personally or by leaving the same at the place of business of the Company. As of the Effective Date, the bankrupt Member shall have no further rights as a Member of the Company, except to receive the amounts to which he or she is entitled under this Operating Agreement for the purchase of the violating Member's Membership Interest.

21. **Retirement or withdrawal**—The circumstances under which a member may retire and the consequences of the retirement should be described. A noncompetition clause to restrict the business activities of the withdrawing member also may be appropriate.

Right to Retire or Resign

A Member shall have the right, at any time, to retire or resign as a Member of the Company by giving three (3) months' notice to the Company at the Company's place of business.

Consequences of Retirement or Resignation If the Business Is Continued

Upon giving notice of an intention to retire or resign, the Withdrawn Member shall be entitled to have his or her Membership Interest purchased as provided in this Operating Agreement, if the remaining Members elect to continue the business of the Company. Upon the receipt of notice of the remaining Members' election to continue the business, the Membership Interest of the Withdrawn Member in the Company shall cease and terminate, and the Withdrawn Member shall be entitled only to the payments provided for the purchase of the Withdrawn Member's Membership Interest.

Consequences of Retirement or Resignation If the Business Is Not Continued

If the remaining Members elect not to continue the business upon retirement or resignation of a Member, or are unable to do so by law, the Withdrawn Member shall be entitled only to his or her interest in liquidation, as stated in this Operating Agreement, subject to any set-off or damages caused by the Member's retirement or resignation.

22. **Death of a member**—The death of a member should allow the remaining members to continue the business and purchase the deceased member's membership interest. A provision should be included to authorize the purchase of life insurance to fund the purchase of the deceased member's interest.

Death of a Member

Upon the death of a Member, the deceased Member's rights as Member of the Company shall cease and terminate except as provided in this Article.

EXAMPLE

Consequences of Death If Business Is Continued

If the surviving Members elect to continue the business, the Managers shall serve notice in writing of such election, within three (3) months after the death of the decedent, upon the executor or administrator of the decedent's estate, or if at the time of such election no legal representative has been appointed, upon any one of the known legal heirs of the decedent at the last known address of such heir. The Company shall purchase the Membership Interest of the deceased Member, and the closing of such purchase shall be within thirty (30) days of the notice of such election, except in the event the Company has life insurance on the decedent, in which event the amount and method of payment for the Membership Interest of the deceased Member will be as provided in the following paragraph.

EXAMPLE

Insurance

The Company may contract for life insurance on the lives of each of the Members, in any amount not disproportionate to the value of each Member's Membership Interest. In the event of death of a Member, insurance proceeds paid to the Company will be used to purchase the Membership Interest of the deceased Member, and the purchase price shall be the greater of the amount determined for purchase of a Withdrawing Member's Membership Interest or the amount of insurance proceeds received by the Company. The payment of the purchase price to the decedent's representatives or heirs shall be made within thirty (30) days following receipt of the insurance proceeds by the Company. If the surviving Members do not elect to continue the business of the Company, or are unable to do so by law, the proceeds of any life insurance shall be treated as an asset of the Company for liquidation.

EXAMPLE

Consequences of Death If the Business Is Not Continued

If the surviving Members do not elect to continue the business, or are unable to do so by law, the deceased Member shall be entitled only to his or her interest in liquidation as stated in this Operating Agreement.

23. **Restriction on sale of membership interests**—Any provisions restricting the sale of membership interests should be included in the operating agreement. Similarly, any outside indebtedness that may result in an involuntary sale of a membership interests (such as a loan or nonpayment of debts to individual creditors) should be addressed.

EXAMPLE

Provisions Restricting Sale of Membership Interests

In the event that a Member desires to sell, assign, or otherwise transfer his or her Membership Interest in the Company and has obtained a bona fide offer for the sale thereof made by some person not a member of this Company, he or she shall first offer to sell, assign, or otherwise transfer the Membership Interest to the other Members at the price and on the same terms as previously offered him or her, and each other Member shall have the right to purchase his or her proportionate share of the selling Member's Membership Interest. If any Member does not desire to purchase the Membership Interest on such terms or at such price and the entire Membership Interest is not purchased by the other Members, no other Member may purchase any part of the Membership Interest, and the selling Member may then sell, assign, or otherwise transfer his or her entire Membership Interest in the Company to the person making the said offer at the price offered. The intent of this provision is to ensure that the entire Membership Interest of a Member will be sold intact, without fractionalization. A purchaser of a Membership Interest of the Company shall not become a Member without the unanimous consent of the nonselling Members, but shall be entitled to receive the share of profits, gains, losses, deductions, credits, and distributions to which the selling Member would be entitled.

> **Member's Personal Debts**
>
> In order to protect the property and assets of the Company from any claim against any Member for personal debts owed by such Member, each Member shall promptly pay all debts owing by him or her and shall indemnify the Company from any claim that might be made to the detriment of the Company by any personal creditor of such Member.

EXAMPLE

> **Alienation of Membership Interest**
>
> No Member shall, except as provided in this Operating Agreement, sell, assign, mortgage, or otherwise encumber his or her Membership Interest in the Company or in its capital assets or property; or enter into an agreement of any kind that will result in any person, firm, or other organization becoming interested with him or her in the Company; or do any act detrimental to the best interests of the Company.

EXAMPLE

Filing Procedure

The articles of organization are filed with the secretary of state or some other designated public official (such as a corporation commission), and the filing scheme generally follows the procedure required for articles of incorporation for corporations. In some states, after the filing officer determines that the articles of organization have been properly prepared and all fees have been paid, the filing officer issues a certificate of organization for the company.

It is not necessary to file the operating agreement with any public office. To the extent that the company is engaged in real estate transactions or other businesses in which public records generally are maintained, it may be appropriate to file excerpts of the operating agreement for public information. For example, information regarding the duties of the managers may be important to creditors and third parties with whom the company is doing business, and the filing of the statement of those duties gives public notice of the authority of the managers. In addition, to the extent that other licensing statutes require organizational documents to be filed (e.g., statutes regarding organization of professional service corporations for lawyers, accountants, or physicians), the operating agreement and the articles of organization should be filed with the appropriate licensing authorities in order to comply with those rules.

Organizational Meetings of Managers

If the limited liability company will be managed by managers, it is appropriate to document the actions of the managers in the same manner as the actions of directors of a corporation are documented. An organizational meeting of the managers should be held to formally adopt certain actions on behalf of the company.[109] Exhibit 5–3 illustrates the business that typically would be conducted at the first meeting of the managers of a Colorado limited liability company.

KEY TERMS

membership	continuity of life	articles of organization
members	at-will company	classification
dissociate	articles of termination	operating agreement
distributional interest	merge	capital account
manager	consolidation	income account

Exhibit 5–3.

Unanimous Consent of
Managers (Colorado)

Unanimous Consent of Managers

The undersigned, being all of the managers of a Colorado Limited Liability Company, do hereby consent to, approve, and adopt the following resolutions:

ADOPTION OF ARTICLES OF ORGANIZATION

RESOLVED, that the Articles of Organization of the Limited Liability Company as filed in the office of the Secretary of State of Colorado are hereby accepted and approved, and that said Articles of Organization shall be placed in the records of the Limited Liability Company.

ADOPTION OF OPERATING AGREEMENT

RESOLVED, that the Operating Agreement in the form reviewed by the Managers and attached hereto is hereby accepted and adopted as the Operating Agreement of this Limited Liability Company.

MEMBERSHIP CERTIFICATE

RESOLVED, that the form of membership certificate as reviewed by the Managers is hereby approved and adopted as the form of membership certificate of the Limited Liability Company.

PAYMENT OF ORGANIZATIONAL EXPENSES

RESOLVED, that the Limited Liability Company is hereby authorized and directed to pay all fees and expenses reasonably necessary for the organization of the Limited Liability Company and to reimburse those persons who have advanced said fees and expenses on behalf of the Limited Liability Company.

ACCEPTANCE OF MEMBER'S SUBSCRIPTION AGREEMENTS

RESOLVED, that the Limited Liability Company hereby accepts the Subscription Agreements offered by Members on behalf of the Limited Liability Company in the forms attached to this Consent and incorporated herein by reference.

FURTHER RESOLVED, that the Limited Liability Company shall hereby execute and deliver to the Members whose Subscription Agreements have been accepted certificates representing the Membership Interests represented thereby.

BANK ACCOUNT

RESOLVED, that the resolutions relating to the establishment of a bank account at Women's Bank, N.A., Denver, Colorado, attached hereto are hereby approved and adopted.

LOAN TRANSACTION

WHEREAS, the Limited Liability Company has need of funds in addition to the equity capital currently contributed by the Members; and

WHEREAS, Glenna McKelvy has expressed a willingness to lend the Limited Liability Company $55,000 on the terms set forth in Exhibit A attached hereto; and

WHEREAS, the Managers believe that it is in the best interest of the Limited Liability Company to enter into such loan arrangements;

NOW, THEREFORE, BE IT RESOLVED, that the Limited Liability Company hereby approves and agrees to pay the loan described and the Managers are hereby authorized and directed to enter into and execute appropriate documents required to obtain such loan.

EMPLOYMENT CONTRACTS

RESOLVED, that the Employment Contracts on behalf of the Limited Liability Company with Susan Bartic and Brent Karasiuk in the form attached hereto are hereby approved and accepted.

FOREIGN QUALIFICATION

RESOLVED, that the Limited Liability Company is authorized to take such action as may be necessary and appropriate to obtain and maintain on behalf of the Limited Liability Company a Certificate of Authority to transact business in the states of Oklahoma and Nevada.

OTHER BUSINESS

[State other business desired to be included in the Consent.]

_____
Manager

_____
Manager

WEB RESOURCES

The articles of organization and the operating agreement are the principal documents required for the formation of a limited liability company.

The forms for articles of organization are available from the Secretary of State or Department of Commerce offices where they are required to be filed. The National Association of Secretaries of State maintains links directly to the offices of the Secretaries of State in all states. These can be accessed through

<**http://www.nass.org**>

Various sources exist for sample operating agreements that may be tailored to the specific desires of the client. In addition to the sites mentioned under "Web Resources" for General Partnerships in Chapter 3, operating agreement form templates are available on the following sites:

<**http://www.paralegal-plus.com**>
<**http://www.alberty.com**>
<**http://www.legaldocs.com**>
<**http://www.findlegalforms.com**>

Access to state laws regarding licensing and regulatory requirements may be obtained through the Legal Information Institute maintained at the Cornell Law School:

<**http://www.law.cornell.edu**>

The Uniform Limited Liability Company Act of 1996, and links to state statutes for states that have based local law on the Act also can be accessed through the Legal Information Institute:

<**http://www.law.cornell.edu**>

Tax forms, including the federal income tax returns and schedules, and the Classification of Entity tax elections may be accessed on line through

<**http://www.irs.gov**>

Searching and locating trade names can be accomplished through various services offered on the Internet. Most of these services charge a fee for useful searches. They include

<**http://www.tmexpress.com**>
<**http://www.trademark-search-services.com**>

CASES

BONNER et al. v. BRUNSON et al.
—- S.E.2d ——, 3 FCDR 2407
(Ga. Ct. App. ____, 2003)
ANDREWS, PRESIDING JUDGE

Fred Bonner and Bonner Roofing & Sheet Metal Company, Inc. (collectively Bonner) sued T.I. Brunson, LLC and Thomas I. Brunson, individually, to collect over $288,000 claimed due for roofing work done pursuant to a subcontract with the LLC on a condominium construction project on which the LLC acted as the general contractor. At issue is Bonner's claim that Thomas Brunson (the owner and controlling member of the LLC) is personally liable for the alleged debt of the LLC because he abused the form of the LLC and is therefore no longer protected by the veil of a separately maintained LLC. Because we find no evidence in the record to support this claim, we

conclude Brunson was not personally liable and affirm the trial court's grant of summary judgment in favor of Brunson, individually.

Just as the so-called "corporate veil" protects an individual shareholder of a corporation from personal liability for the debts of the separate corporate entity (so long as the corporate forms are maintained) so is a member of a limited liability company (LLC) "veiled" from personal liability for the debts of the separately maintained LLC entity. *Yukon Partners v. Lodge Keeper Group,* 258 Ga.App. 1. 5-6, 572 S.E.2d 647 (2002); OCGA §§ 14- 11-303; 14-11-1107(j). In order to **pierce** this veil and hold Brunson personally liable for the alleged debt of the LLC, there must be evidence that he abused the forms by which the LLC was maintained as a separate legal entity apart from his personal business. *Fuda v. Kroen,* 204 Ga.App. 836, 837, 420 S.E.2d 767 (1992). A court may disregard the separate LLC entity and the protective veil it provides to an individual member of the LLC when that member, in order to defeat justice or perpetrate fraud, conducts his personal and LLC business as if they were one by commingling the two on an interchangeable or joint basis or confusing otherwise separate properties, records, or control. *Stewart Bros., Inc. v. Allen,* 189 Ga.App. 816, 377

S.E.2d 724 (1989); *Bone Constr. Co. v. Lewis,* 148 Ga.App. 61, 250 S.E.2d 851 (1978); *Clark v. Cauthen,* 239 Ga.App. 226, 228, 520 S.E.2d 477 (1999).

Bonner contends that various conduct by the LLC and Brunson supports piercing the LLC veil and holding Brunson personally liable.

Bonner argues that construction loan draw requests submitted to the lender through December 1999 on behalf of the LLC showed work done by Bonner, but that none of the money was paid to Bonner and excessive sums were paid to a Brunson-owned corporation, which was a subcontractor for heating and air work on the project.

* * *

There is nothing in the draw request evidence that shows the LLC form was abused or that Brunson commingled or confused his personal affairs with the business of the LLC.

Bonner claims Brunson commingled LLC funds with his personal funds by taking a $360,000 check from the LLC.

* * *

The uncontradicted evidence shows that the LLC's money was paid to Brunson and repaid by him to the LLC under an agreement which maintained the LLC and its property as separate from Brunson's personal account.

Bonner contends Brunson treated LLC funds as his own when Brunson's wife, the LLC's bookkeeper, wrote 16 LLC checks to cash totaling about $3,700. The record shows that the seven checks which Bonner specifically cites to in the record provided cash to pay for casual labor or security services for the project.

* * *

Bonner claims Brunson used LLC funds to have work done on his house. Brunson's affidavit shows that one of the subcontractors on the LLC's project also did personal work for Brunson at his house. The subcontractor submitted a single bill for $1,080 for all the work, and the LLC mistakenly paid the entire bill which included $408 for the work at Brunson's house. When the error was discovered, it was corrected and Brunson was billed by the LLC for the $408. There was no evidence of abuse of the LLC form or commingling of properties.

Finally, Bonner contends that at least six payments made by the LLC to Brunson's separate corporation (a heating and air subcontractor on the project) were not related to heating and air work on the project. Even if there was evidence that the payments showed an abuse of the separate LLC and corporate forms, this would have no bearing on Bonner's claim that Brunson abused the forms legally separating the LLC from his personal affairs. *Fuda,* 204 Ga.App. at 838–839, 420 S.E.2d 767. In any event, we decline to consider the payments at issue. In support of this contention, Bonner argues only that there is an absence of evidence showing what the payments were for and cites to a 28-page list of checks in the record showing about a thousand checks written by the LLC for various purposes on the project, apparently hoping we will sift through all the checks to find and address the six or more payments. See Court of Appeals Rule 27(c)(3).

In the absence of any evidence that Brunson abused the form of the LLC by commingling or confusing LLC business with his personal affairs, the trial court correctly granted summary judgment dismissing the claim that Brunson was personally liable for the alleged debt of the LLC. *Stewart Bros.,* 189 Ga.App. 816, 377 S.E.2d 724; *Bone Constr. Co.,* 148 Ga.App. 61, 250 S.E.2d 851; *Clark,* 239 Ga.App. at 228, 520 S.E.2d 477.

Judgment affirmed.

MEYER v. OKLAHOMA ALCOHOLIC BEVERAGE LAWS ENFORCEMENT COMMISSION

890 P.2d 1361 (Okla. Ct. App. 1995)
STUBBLEFIELD, JUDGE

This is an appeal from the district court's reversal of the declaratory ruling of the Oklahoma Alcoholic Beverage Laws Enforcement Commission (ABLE) that a newly created form of business entity, a limited liability company (LLC), is not entitled to receive and hold a retail package store license. Wanda L. Meyer, holder of a retail package store license, initiated these proceedings when she petitioned ABLE requesting a declaratory judgment that she could

hold the license as an LLC, a business entity authorized by the Oklahoma Legislature in 1992 through the adoption of the Oklahoma Limited Liability Company Act (OLLC Act). . . . ABLE denied the petition, thus holding that an LLC is not eligible to hold a retail package store license.

Meyer, pursuant to the provisions of the Administrative Procedures Act, 75 O.S.1991 §§ 250–323, appealed the ABLE decision to the district court. That court focused on two provisions of the law: (1)The Oklahoma constitutional provision, which only prohibits licensing of "corporations, business trusts, and secret partnerships," Okla. Const. art. 28, § 10; and, (2)The provision in the LLC Act that authorized LLCs to "conduct business in any state for any lawful purpose, except the business of banking and insurance," 18 O.S.Supp.1992 §

2002 (emphasis added) (footnote omitted). Based upon those provisions, and a conclusion that the provisions of the Oklahoma Alcoholic Beverage Control Act "do not prohibit an LLC from holding a package store license," the trial court reversed the ABLE ruling and ordered it to "issue such license to petitioner as a limited liability company."

ABLE appeals, claiming that the order of the lower court is contrary to law in that an LLC is not authorized to hold a package store license.

* * *

The issue is one of first impression—whether an LLC, created pursuant to the OLLC Act, is eligible for issuance of a retail package store liquor license. Indeed, the issue could only have arisen after the 1992 legislative creation of the new form of business entity. LLCs were not a recognized business entity in this state at the time of adoption of our Constitution or at the time of adoption of the Oklahoma Alcoholic Beverage Control Act. However, both the Constitution and the Oklahoma Alcoholic Beverage Control Act do address qualifications of an applicant for a package store license. We conclude that the constitutional directives do prohibit the holding of a license by an LLC and, thus, the lower court did err in its conclusion. The pertinent constitutional provisions are Okla. Const. art. 28, §§ 4 and 10. Section 4, in pertinent part, provides:

> Not more than one retail package license shall be issued to any person or general or limited partnership.

Section 10, in pertinent part, provides:

> No retail package store or wholesale distributor's license shall be issued to:
> (a) A corporation, business trust or secret partnership.
> (b) A person or partnership unless such person or all of the copartners including limited partners shall have been residents of the State of Oklahoma for at least ten (10) years immediately preceding the date of application for such license.
> (c) A person or a general or limited partnership containing a partner who has been convicted of a violation of a prohibitory law relating to the sale, manufacture, or the transportation of alcoholic beverages which constituted a felony or misdemeanor.
> (d) A person or a general or limited partnership containing a partner who has been convicted of a felony.

It is true, as noted by the trial court in its decision, that the specific constitutional prohibitions regarding license holders includes only corporations, business trusts, and secret partnerships. Of course, neither the framers nor amenders of the Constitution could have addressed the qualification or disqualification of LLCs as retail package store licensees, because the business entity did not exist in this state until 1992. Indeed, the testimony before ABLE indicated that the business form did not exist in this country until 1977. However, the Constitution did address all of the business formats as they existed at the time of adoption of the article on alcoholic beverage laws and enforcement and,

significantly, section 4 names only individuals and partnerships as those entities to which a license may be issued.

Likewise, it is true that the Oklahoma Alcoholic Beverage Control Act does not prohibit an LLC from holding a license. However, what the Act does or does not prohibit is not dispositive because the Act does not purport to address the nature of the applicant—a matter controlled by the constitutional provisions. The Act does restate some of the disqualifications set forth in section 10 of the Constitution regarding residency, criminal conviction, etc., but does not purport to prohibit the licensing of corporations, business trusts and secret partnerships, which are specifically prohibited as licensees by the Constitution. It appears that qualification as a license holder, with regard to types of business entities, was left to the constitutional pronouncement.

When the legislature adopted the OLLC Act, it provided that "[a] limited liability company may be organized under this act and may conduct business in any state for any lawful purpose, except the business of banking and insurance." 18 O.S.Supp.1992 § 2002 (footnote omitted). Of course, such a legislative enactment could not countermand a constitutional prohibition, even if that had been the legislative intent. However, we do not believe the language of section 2002 indicates a legislative intent to extend the authority of LLCs in ways specifically prohibited elsewhere by statute, and particularly not to an act prohibited by the Oklahoma Constitution. Thus, we do not view section 2002 of the OLLC Act as sanction for the operation of a retail package store by an LLC.

If we interpreted section 2002 as argued by Meyer, then it could, in some respects, negate specific declarations of Okla. Const. art. 28, § 10. An LLC—neither a person, corporation nor partnership—is not specifically named in section 10 and, thus, if eligible as a licensee, its members would not be subject to the same restrictions regarding residence, violations of the liquor laws and status as a felon, which are imposed upon members of other permissible business entity licensees. Even the similar prohibitions in 37 O.S.1991 § 527, are not drawn with this new business entity in mind and would not clearly apply to LLC members. Meyer apparently recognized this fundamental problem with the LLC business entity and by company rule restricted membership in keeping with the prohibitions of the Constitution and section 527. However, these restrictions are set out in fully amendable articles. 18 O.S.Supp.1992 § 2011. Furthermore, the question is not whether the members of this particular LLC are eligible applicants because those members are not the applicants. The applicant is the LLC, and the question is whether the business entity is a permissible license holder.

Meyer argues that an LLC is essentially a partnership. However, the act creating the business form is in Title 18, which is entitled "Corporations." Furthermore, a provision in our Uniform Partnership Act states that "any association formed under any other statute of this state . . . is not a partnership under this act, unless such association would have been a partnership in this state prior to adoption of this act." 54 O.S.1991 § 206(2).

Meyer claims that its expert witness, the only witness in all the proceedings, testified that an LLC was a partnership. However, contrary to Meyer's contention, the witness's testimony was not so unequivocal. The totality of the testimony was that an LLC is a hybrid that has attributes of both corporations and partnerships. The witness indicated an LLC is more like a partnership, but noted the primary difference is that all owners/members have limited liability in an LLC—something not found in partnerships. We conclude that the limitation of liability of all LLC members is a substantial difference especially relevant to the provisions of our liquor laws.

Our examination of the pertinent constitutional provisions leads us to conclude that their evident purpose was the assignment of personal responsibility for compliance with the liquor laws. Thus, business forms that did not insure such personal responsibility were excluded from eligibility for licensing.

The OLLC Act does exactly what its name indicates. It creates a form of business that has as its most important feature the limitation of liability of its members. This liability limitation is also a shield from the very responsibility and accountability that the constitutional provisions regarding alcoholic beverage laws and enforcement sought to impose. The trial court reversed the ABLE decision as contrary to law. Based upon the foregoing analysis, we conclude that there was no such error and that the trial court erred in reversing the ABLE decision. Because of our ruling, we do not need to address ABLE's contention that the trial court erred in ordering it to grant a license when an application had not been made. The judgment of the trial court is REVERSED.

GOODMAN, P. J., and REIF, J. (sitting by designation), concur.

JM AVALON INVESTMENTS, LLC v. NISCHAN

1997 WL 133939 (Conn. Super. 1997)
SKOLNICK, J.

On February 6, 1996, the plaintiffs, JM Avalon Investments, LLC (Avalon) and William J. Gaspero, filed a seven-count complaint alleging conversion, fraud, negligence, two counts of breach of loan agreements, and two counts in unjust enrichment against the defendants, Michel and Lori Nischan. The plaintiffs allege the following facts in their complaint. On January 27, 1994, Avalon was formed with Gaspero and Lori Nischan as its members, for the purpose of operating a restaurant in Stamford, Connecticut known as "Miche Mache." Michel Nischan, the husband of Lori Nischan served as the chef and general manager of Miche Mache, and was assisted in the management by Lori Nischan. The plaintiffs also allege that the defendants converted cash and property of Miche Mache; fraudulently failed to transfer the trade name "Miche Mache" to Avalon; negligently damaged the plaintiffs' property including the company car; and refused to repay loans made by Gaspero and Avalon in the amounts of $34,000 and $24,000.

On January 15, 1997, the defendants filed an amended motion to dismiss . . . in which they argue that the court lacks subject matter jurisdiction on the ground that Avalon lacks standing to sue.

* * *

The defendants contend that the court lacks subject matter jurisdiction because Avalon was not authorized to bring suit against the defendants, and because Avalon ceased to exist by operation of law when Lori Nischan tendered her resignation on August 30, 1995.

"Standing is the legal right to set judicial machinery in motion. One cannot rightfully invoke the jurisdiction of the court unless he has, in an individual or representative capacity, some real interest in the cause of action . . . [O]nce the question of lack of [standing] is raised, [it] must be disposed of no matter in what form it is presented . . . [A] court must have jurisdiction to determine its own jurisdiction once that has been put in issue." (Citation omitted)

The defendants argue that Gaspero brought this action on behalf of Avalon without the consent of Lori Nischan, a fifty percent owner of Avalon. The plaintiffs maintain that they have authority to bring this action pursuant to General Statutes 34-100 et. seq. General Statutes 34-186 provides that "[s]uits may be brought by or against a limited liability company in its own name." General Statutes 34-187(a) provides in pertinent part that "[e]xcept as otherwise provided in an operating agreement, suit on behalf of the limited liability company may be brought in the name of the limited liability company by: (1) Any member or members of a limited liability company, whether or not the articles of organization vest management of the limited liability company in one or more managers, who are authorized to sue by the vote of a majority in interest of the members. . . ."

The defendant, Lori Nischan, argues that she is fifty percent owner, and that she did not give her consent to bring suit in the name of Avalon. However, 34-187(b) provides that "[i]n determining the vote required under section 34-142 for purposes of this section, the vote of any member or manager who has an interest in the outcome of the suit that is adverse to the interest of the limited liability company shall be excluded." The plaintiff's complaint, with the exception of two counts, alleges tortious conduct and breach of a loan agreement by Lori Nischan against Avalon. Therefore, the court believes that her interests in the outcome of the suit are adverse to those of Avalon. If Nischan is excluded from voting, the only remaining member of Avalon is Gaspero. Accordingly, the court finds that Gaspero has the authority to bring an action in the name of Avalon.

The defendants also contend that Lori Nischan resigned as a member of Avalon on August 30, 1995, thereby dissolving Avalon by operation of law, leaving it without standing to sue. Nevertheless, General Statutes 34-208(a) provides in relevant part that "[e]xcept as otherwise provided in writing in the operation agreement, the business and affairs of the limited liability corporation may be wound up (1) by the members or managers who have authority pursuant to section 34-140 to manage the limited liability company prior to dissolution . . ." General Statutes 34-140(a) provides that "[s]ubject to any provisions of sec-

tions 34-100 to 34-242, inclusive, or the articles of organization, the business, property and affairs of a limited liability company shall be managed by its members.

Since Lori Nischan resigned on August 30, 1995, that left Gaspero as the only member with authority to wind up Avalon. Section 34-208(b) provides in pertinent part that "[t]he persons winding up the business and affairs of the limited liability corporation may, in the name of, and for and on behalf of, the limited liability company: (1) Prosecute and defend suits. . . ."

The court finds, based on the relevant statutes, that Avalon has standing to bring suit. Gaspero has authority to bring suit in the name of Avalon because of Lori Nischan's adverse interest in the outcome of the action, and because she resigned as a member of Avalon. . . . Accordingly, the defendants' motion to dismiss is denied.

PROBLEMS

1. Describe three advantages of a limited liability company over a general partnership. Describe three disadvantages of a limited liability company compared with a general partnership.

2. Describe three advantages of a limited liability company over a limited partnership. Describe three disadvantages of a limited liability company compared with a limited partnership.

3. List two corporate characteristics of a limited liability company, and explain why they are advantages or disadvantages for operation of the business.

4. Is it better to draft operational rules that require permanence into the articles of organization or into the operating agreement, and why?

5. What makes a limited liability company more flexible for tax purposes than a Subchapter S corporation?

6. If the organizers of a company want all participants to have limited liability, what makes a limited liability company easier to form than a limited partnership?

PRACTICE ASSIGNMENTS

1. Select a limited liability company statute in your state or a state near you, and determine the answers to the following questions based upon that statute:
   a. What is the longest permissible period of duration for the limited liability company?
   b. Is the company managed by members or managers?
      (1) If the company is managed by managers, how are they elected?
      (2) If the company is managed by members, how do they meet and vote on management matters?
   c. Can a membership interest be transferred without the consent of the other members? If consent is required, what percentage of members must approve a transfer of a membership interest?
   d. What type of consideration is permitted for the purchase of a membership interest?

   e. What types of business may the limited liability company lawfully conduct?
   f. Under what circumstances will the limited liability company dissolve? Can the members continue the business after dissolution?

2. Using the same statute and assuming that a client wants to change the statutory rules for the operations of the business, make a list of those matters that may be changed only in the articles of organization, those that may be changed only in the operating agreement, and those that may be changed in either document.

3. Susan Rogers, Ed Naylor, and Adam Golodner are starting an environmental waste disposal business in Richmond, Virginia. The business will be called "Recycled Refuse," and each of them will be involved in managing

and operating the business. Susan will be the primary administrator of the business, Ed will be the salesperson, and Adam will handle the financial affairs. They will each contribute $50,000 to begin the business, and they expect to share all benefits from the business equally. None of them will receive a salary, but each of them would like to draw $5,000 advances monthly against the profits of the business, and they will agree to return any draws in excess of their respective share of profits within 30 days of the end of each year (when their annual share of profits is finally determined). The offices of the company will be located at 98076 Ridge Road, Richmond, Virginia. Susan will be the registered agent of the company.

a. Prepare articles of organization for a limited liability company to be formed to operate this business.

b. Prepare an operating agreement for the company, using sample Exhibit I–4 in Appendix I.

4. Paul Lewis is a sole proprietor of a business known as "Lewis Mens Wear and Storm Door Company." Lewis wants to solicit new capital from his uncle, Louis Lewis, and his aunt, Lois Lewis, to expand his business and open two new stores. Prepare a memorandum to Paul describing the advantages of using a limited liability company for the receipt of capital from Louis and Lois and for the continued operations of the business.

ENDNOTES

1. See C. Bishop and D. Kleinberger, Limited Liability Companies, Tax and Business Law, Warren, Gorham & Lamont (2004).

2. See "Taxation of a Corporation—Subchapter S Election" in Chapter 6.

3. Internal Revenue Code (hereafter I.R.C.) of 1986, 26 U.S.C.A. § 1361(b) (2) (A). Since a limited liability company is treated as a partnership for tax purposes, a Subchapter S corporation would be able to own more than 80% of a limited liability company without losing the Subchapter S status. A limited liability company could be used as a vehicle for a combination of Subchapter S corporations. See Rev. Rul. 77-220, 1977-1 C.B. 263.

4. I.R.C. § 1361(b) (1) (D).

5. See "Limited Liability and Contributions" and "Management and Control" in Chapter 4.

6. See Uniform Limited Liability Company Act ("U.L.L.C.A.") § 201.

7. U.L.L.C.A. §112.

8. See "Taxation of a Limited Liability Company" in this chapter.

9. See, U.L.L.C.A. §§ 101(2) and 203(a)(5).

10. U.L.L.C.A. § 112.

11. U.L.L.C.A. § 112(b)(12).

12. Del. Code Ann. tit. 6, § 18-106.

13. Under U.L.L.C.A. § 103(a) the operating agreement is intended to regulate the affairs of the company and the conduct of its business and to govern relations among the members, managers, and the company. The operating agreement may vary almost all of the provisions of the statute to suit the desires of the members and managers, with only a few limitations stated in U.L.L.C.A. § 103(b).

14. See "Statutory Powers of a Corporation" in Chapter 4.

15. U.L.L.C.A. § 401; and see Okla. Stat. Ann. tit. 148, § 2023, permitting cash, property, services rendered, or a promissory note or other obligation to contribute cash or property or to perform services.

16. See Va. Code § 13.1-1046.

17. See "Managers" in this chapter; U.L.L.C.A. § 404(b)(3)(i) and Colo. Rev. Stat. § 7-80-402(2).

18. See U.L.L.C.A. § 404(c) and Colo. Rev. Stat. § 7-80-702(1). If the other members do not unanimously approve the transfer, the transferee will have no right to participate in the management.

19. U.L.L.C.A. § 404(c) and 801(b)(2).

20. McKinney's Cons. Laws. N. Y. Ann. Ch. 34 § 401.

21. See Md. Code Ann. § 4A-401.

22. See Tex. Corps. & Ass'ns Code Ann. tit. 605, § 4.07(A)(1).

23. U.L.L.C.A.   404 and Colo. Rev. Stat. § 7-80-706(1).

24. U.L.L.C.A. §§ 601(1) and 602.

25. U.L.L.C.A. § 701.

26. U.L.L.C.A. § 601.

27. See Colo. Rev. Stat. § 7-80-606.

28. See Colo. Rev. Stat. § 7-80-607.

29. U.L.L.C.A.§ 702.

30. U.L.L.C.A. § 404(c)(7) and see Colo. Rev. Stat. § 7-80-701.

31. U.L.L.C.A. § 801.

32. See, e.g., Colo. Rev. Stat. § 7-80-405.

33. U.L.L.C.A. § 408(b)(1).

34. See. e.g., Va. Code § 13.1-1028(B) (2).

35. Colo. Rev. Stat. § 7-80-707.

36. See Colo. Rev. Stat. § 7-80-709; "Corporate Meetings—Shareholder Meetings—Notice" in Chapter 10.

37. See Colo. Rev. Stat. § 7-80-708; "Corporate Meetings—Shareholder Meetings—Quorum and Voting of Shares" in Chapter 10.

38. U.L.L.C.A. § 404(d).

39. See Minn. Stat. Ch. 322B § 322B.67.

40. U.L.L.C.A. § 103(a), and see Delaware Stat. Ann. § 6-18-404.

41. See Colo. Rev. Stat. § 7-80-402.

42. See Colo. Rev. Stat. § 7-80-402(1); "Business Corporation—Ownership and Management of a Corporation—Directors" in Chapter 6.

43. Colo. Rev. Stat. § 7-80-402(1).

44. See Colo. Rev. Stat. § 7-80-403; "Business Corporation—Ownership and Management of a Corporation—Directors" in Chapter 6.

45. Colo. Rev. Stat. § 7-80-401(2).

46. See Mass. Gen Laws ch. 156C § 25.

47. See Colo. Rev. Stat. § 7-80-401.

48. Minn. Stat. § 322B-613.

49. Colo. Rev. Stat. § 7-80-404.

50. Colo. Rev. Stat. § 7-80-404.

51. Colo. Rev. Stat. § 7-80-405.

52. U.L.L.C.A. § 301(b)(2) and see Utah Code Ann. § 48-2b-125(2).

53. See U.L.L.C.A. § 404(b)(1).

54. Colo. Rev. Stat. § 7-80-407.

55. Colo. Rev. Stat. § 7-80-408.

56. See "Ownership and Management of a Corporation—Director's Duties" in Chapter 8.

57. See Ohio Rev. Stat. § 1705.29(B).

58. See Minn. Stat. § 322B.620.

59. U.L.L.C.A. § 409(c) and 409(h)(2).

60. U.L.L.C.A. § 409(b) and 409(h)(2).

61. U.L.L.C.A. § 409(d) and 409(h)(2).

62. Colo. Rev. Stat. § 7-80-406(3).

63. Colo. Rev. Stat. § 7-80-705.

64. Colo. Rev. Stat. § 7-80-410.

65. See Me. Ann. Laws §31-13-654 and "The Articles of Incorporation—Optional Provisions—Indemnification of Officers and Directors" in Chapter 6.

66. U.L.L.C.A. § 101(5).

67. U.L.L.C.A. § 501(b) and see Colo. Rev. Stat. § 7-80-702(1). The Uniform Act also provides that the distributional interest can be evidenced by a certificate, like a stock certificate in a corporation. U.L.L.C.A. § 501(c).

68. See "Share Transfer Restrictions and Buyout Agreements" in Chapter 13.

69. See U.L.L.C.A. § 502; "A Partner's Interest in a Partnership" in Chapter 3.

70. See U.L.L.C.A. § 502.

71. See U.L.L.C.A. § 503(a).

72. See U.L.L.C.A. § 401.

73. See Minn. Stat. §§ 322B.40-42.

74. See Ill. Rev. Stat. ch. 805, § 25-1.

75. R.I. Gen. Laws §§ 7-16-26, 7-16-27.

76. U.L.L.C.A. §§ 603(a)(2) and 701(a)(2); and see Ill. Rev. Stat. ch. 805, § 25-10.

77. R.I. Gen. Laws § 7-16-30.

78. Ill. Rev. Stat. ch. 805, § 25-20.

79. Minn. Stat. § 322B.54.

80. Minn. Stat. § 322B.55.

81. See Minn. Stat. § 322B.56 and "Corporate Dividends and Other Distributions—Cash and Property Dividends" in Chapter 11.

82. See U.L.L.C.A. § 203(a)(5).

83. See Treas. Reg. § 301.7701-2.

84. See "Taxation of a Limited Liability Company" in this chapter.

85. See "Taxation of a Limited Liability Company" in this chapter.

86. See U.L.L.C.A. § 801.

87. See, e.g., Ark. Code Ann. § 4-32-802.

88. See, e.g., Tex. Corps. & Ass'ns Code Ann. tit. 605, § 6.01(A) (5); Kan. Stat. § 17-776116.

89. See U.L.L.C.A. § 701.

90. See Colo. Rev. Stat. § 7-80-801(2).

91. See U.L.L.C.A. § 808 and Colo. Rev. Stat. § 7-80-805. The Uniform Act provides that if the operating agreement does not specify otherwise, members receive the return of their contributions and any surplus is distributed to them equally. U.L.L.C.A. § 808(b).

92. See U.L.L.C.A. § 805 and Colo. Rev. Stat. § 7-80-806.

93. See U.L.L.C.A. § 902.

94. Va. Code Ann. § 13.1-1010.1.

95. See U.L.L.C.A. § 904 and Va. Code Ann. § 13.1-1070 to 13.1-1073.

96. Rev. Rul. 88-76, 1988-2 C.B. 360.

97. See I.R.C. 88-76 (relating to the classification of a Wyoming limited liability company as a partnership for federal income tax purposes); Priv. Ltr. Rul. 8937010 (relating to the classification of a Florida limited liability company as a partnership for federal income tax purposes).

98. See Treas. Reg. §§ 301-7701-1 through 7701-8 (1996).

99. Florida treats a limited liability company as an "artificial entity," which formerly placed it within the corporate tax rules, but recently Florida has applied partnership tax rules to limited liability companies. Fla. Stat. § 608.471.

100. See the tradename affidavits and certificates for assumed business names under "Formation and Operation of a Sole Proprietorship" in Chapter 2.

101. Nev. Rev. Stat. § 86.141; Wyo. Stat. § 17-15-103.

102.Utah specifically authorizes professional services to be formed as limited liability companies in the limited liability company statute. See Utah Code Ann. § 48-2b-102(7).

103. See Utah Code Ann. § 48-2b-111.

104. See "Corporations in Foreign Jurisdictions" in Chapter 14.

105. See "Formation of a Corporation—The Articles of Incorporation" in Chapter 8.

106. U.L.L.C.A. § 203.

107. U.L.L.C.A. § 103.

108. Md. Corps. & Ass'ns Code Ann. § 4A-402(a).

109. See "Formation of a Corporation—Formalities After Formation of the Corporation—Organizational Meetings" in Chapter 8; "Corporate Meetings—Requirements for Organizational Meetings" in Chapter 10.

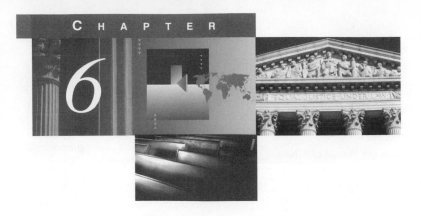

BUSINESS CORPORATION

The **business corporation** is the most complex form of business enterprise, and the remainder of this book is concerned primarily with doing business as a corporation. This chapter defines the legal characteristics of the corporation, the interaction of the corporation's owners and agents in the management of its business, and the recognized advantages and disadvantages of the corporate business form. Later chapters discuss problems of formation and organization, corporate finance, internal agreements, distributions of cash and property, qualification of foreign corporations, corporate structural changes, and dissolution.

The term *business corporation* excludes the many other types of corporations that may be formed under federal or state law. For example, most states authorize the formation and operation of special-purpose corporations, such as religious and charitable corporations and municipal corporations, all of which have peculiar characteristics that are not discussed in this work. The **professional corporation**, formed for the purpose of practicing learned professions such as law, medicine, and accounting, is considered in the next chapter.

ENTITY CHARACTERISTICS OF A CORPORATION

The characteristic that historically distinguished a corporation from other forms of business enterprise is that the corporation is considered by the law to be a separate legal **entity**, a separate "person." The business, therefore, exists quite apart from its aggregate owners. A sole proprietorship is no more than an extension of the personal life of the proprietor, its owner. A partnership has historically been regarded as an aggregation of individuals, and, although modern partnership statutes treat the partnership as an entity, it remains, for the most part, an extension of the individuality of the respective partners, as evidenced by rules that prohibit the addition of a partner without the unanimous consent of the other partners and that require dissolution whenever a partner leaves the firm. Similar limitations are imposed upon limited liability companies, which are recognized as separate entities but which are dependent upon the continued participation of their original members. A corporation, however, exists alone and detached. **Shareholders** (its owners) may come and go without affecting its legal status. Continuing this theme, the corporation is liable for its own obligations, and the individual assets of its owners usually may not be reached for satisfaction of those obligations. This concept of separateness creates special advantages (and occasionally disadvantages) for the corporation as compared with other business organizations.

Since the corporation is treated as a legal entity, it is a legal person created by statute. It obtains life from the applicable state law, which authorizes corporate powers, prescribes rules and requirements for the regulation of the corporation's business affairs, and controls the internal relationships between shareholders and management. State statutes vary considerably in their approach to corporations, and thus the corporate structure in one state is often quite different from the corporate structure in another state. For example, a Delaware corporation may have a one-person board of directors, while many states require at least three members on the board.[1] Similarly, in some states the initial bylaws of the corporation are adopted by the board of directors, while a few states permit the shareholders to adopt bylaws.[2] Such details are dictated by local corporate statutes, which authorize the formation and operation of the corporation as a business form. Consequently, analysis of these statutory requirements and strict compliance with them are the touchstones of a successful corporate practice. A few words about the statutory variations and their history follow.

The law of corporations was developed by each state to regulate the internal affairs of the corporations that state had chartered to do business within its boundaries. As American businesses expanded, interstate operations became commonplace, and organizers of a corporation could shop around for a state in which corporation laws were permissive, so that the formation and operation of the corporation would be an easy exercise. The more strict and complex a state's regulations, the less attractive that state became to those establishing a corporation. Since it is possible to do business in one state and be incorporated in another, and since a state acquires certain benefits by having businesses incorporated under its laws (not the least of which is the authority to levy taxes), state legislatures recognized they could attract corporate businesses by adopting flexible and permissive statutory provisions. New Jersey was the first state to liberalize its laws for this purpose, and Delaware followed closely. Delaware has remained the consistent leader in "parenting" corporations, and its statute is considered by many to be the most modern, most permissive, and most sympathetic to the problems of corporate organization and operation.[3]

In 1950, the American Bar Association Committee on Corporate Laws prepared a Model Business Corporation Act, which was initially patterned after Illinois law. The act has been revised extensively, with a view toward permissiveness and flexibility, and has been used as a model by many states in their own revisions of corporate statutes. The discussion of corporate law in this book concentrates on the provisions of the Model Business Corporation Act, but unusual variations from important states are separately noted and discussed. No state has adopted the Model Business Corporation Act in its most current form verbatim; consequently, there is no substitute for full and complete analysis and understanding of the particular requirements of the state statute under which incorporation is contemplated.

In addition to statutory regulations, rules and regulations adopted by the persons forming the business govern corporate operations. The **articles of incorporation** and the **bylaws** (both discussed in detail later) are adopted by the corporate owners and directors and govern the corporation's activities throughout its operation.[4] Most state statutes are very broad in their descriptions of corporate powers, because each statute is designed to cover every conceivable corporate form and every type of business. The articles of incorporation may contain only the essential information required by statute, or they may elaborate on specific matters to govern internal corporate affairs. If the articles are general, the bylaws should provide specific rules for regulation of corporate activities. A properly formed corporation will have no conflict between the bylaws, the articles, and the appropriate state law; rather, the bylaws and articles will refine and elaborate upon the concepts embodied in the state statute, thereby providing a comprehensive and workable scheme for the regulation of the corporation. Bylaws are adopted and modified by internal action of the corporation, and consequently, the rules contained therein are easily changed. The articles of incorporation, which are filed with the secretary of state as public notice of the existence and structure of the corporation, may be amended only by a cumbersome amendment procedure. The most flexible regulation of internal affairs results from drafting the rules for corporate activities in the easily amended bylaws.

In summary, a properly formed corporation exists as a legal entity and is treated for all practical purposes as an individual person, separate and distinct from the persons who own and manage it. Its formation and operation are governed by specific state statutes and by its own articles of incorporation and bylaws, as adopted to suit the particular needs of its business.

STATUTORY POWERS OF A CORPORATION

Each state's law grants a corporation the necessary powers to conduct business, and to conduct any other activities necessary to the business in which it is engaged. Most statutes granting corporate powers permit the corporation to do almost everything a private individual could do. Section 3.02 of the Model Business Corporation Act enumerates corporate powers as follows

> Unless its articles of incorporation provide otherwise, every corporation has perpetual duration and succession in its corporate name and has the same powers as an individual to do all things necessary or convenient to carry out its business and affairs, including without limitation, power:
>
> (1) to sue and be sued, complain and defend in its corporate name;
>
> (2) to have a corporate seal, which may be altered at will, and to use it, or a facsimile of it, by impressing or affixing it or in any other manner reproducing it;
>
> (3) to make and amend bylaws, not inconsistent with its articles of incorporation or with the laws of this state, for managing the business and regulating the affairs of the corporation;
>
> (4) to purchase, receive, lease, or otherwise acquire, and own, hold, improve, use, and otherwise deal with, real or personal property, or any legal or equitable interest in property, wherever located;
>
> (5) to sell, convey, mortgage, pledge, lease, exchange, and otherwise dispose of all or any part of its property;
>
> (6) to purchase, receive, subscribe for, or otherwise acquire; own, hold, vote, use, sell, mortgage, lend, pledge, or otherwise dispose of, and deal in and with shares or other interests in, or obligations of, any other entity;
>
> (7) to make contracts and guarantees, incur liabilities, borrow money, issue its notes, bonds and other obligations (which may be convertible into or include the option to purchase other securities of the corporation), and secure any of its obligations by mortgage or pledge of any of its property, franchises, or income;
>
> (8) to lend money, invest and reinvest its funds, and receive and hold real and personal property as security for repayment;
>
> (9) to be a promoter, partner, member, associate, or manager of any partnership, joint venture, trust, or other entity;
>
> (10) to conduct its business, locate offices, and exercise the powers granted by this Act within or without this state;
>
> (11) to elect directors and appoint officers, employees, and agents of the corporation, define their duties, fix their compensation, and lend them money and credit;
>
> (12) to pay pensions and establish pension plans, pension trusts, profit sharing plans, share bonus plans, share option plans, and benefit or incentive plans for any or all of its current or former directors, officers, employees, and agents;
>
> (13) to make donations for the public welfare or for charitable, scientific, or educational purposes;
>
> (14) to transact any lawful business that will aid governmental policy;
>
> (15) to make payments or donations, or do any other act, not inconsistent with law, that furthers the business and affairs of the corporation.

Remember that the foregoing powers are conferred by statute, and a corporation is permitted to do all things authorized in these powers. The attorney may, in his or her discretion, deem it appropriate to grant broad powers (consistent with local law) or to restrict powers in the articles of incorporation.

EXAMPLE

Powers

To do everything necessary and proper for the accomplishment of any of the purposes, or the attainment of any of the objects, or the furtherance of any of the powers hereinbefore set forth, either alone or in association with other corporations, firms, or individuals, and to do every other act or acts, thing or things, incidental to or growing out of or connected with the aforesaid business or powers, or any part or parts thereof; provided, the same is not inconsistent with the laws under which this corporation is organized.

In most cases, however, the articles of incorporation and the bylaws of the corporation will refine the statutory powers to tailor the corporate structure to the incorporators' needs.

Notice that the description of some statutory powers encourage or require further elaboration in the articles of incorporation or bylaws. For example, the articles of incorporation or bylaws must define the duties of officers,[5] and may predetermine the maximum interest rate at which the corporation may borrow funds.[6]

EXAMPLE

Power to Borrow

To borrow money, and to make and issue notes, bonds, debentures, obligations, and evidences of indebtedness of all kinds, whether secured by mortgage, pledge, or otherwise, without limit as to amount, but with interest not to exceed 12 per cent per annum, and to secure the same by mortgage, pledge, or otherwise, and generally to make and perform agreements and contracts of every kind and description.

It is also good practice to elaborate upon the corporation's power to conduct business in other states and countries.

EXAMPLE

Power to Qualify in Foreign Jurisdictions

The company shall have power to conduct and carry on its business, or any part thereof, and to have one or more offices, and to exercise all or any of its corporate powers and rights, in the State of New York, and in the various other states, territories, colonies, and dependencies of the United States, in the District of Columbia, and in all or any foreign countries.

Thus, the general grant of power under the state statute represents the maximum limits of corporate power. If incorporators or organizers intend to restrict this power, the modifications are drafted into the articles of incorporation and bylaws.

Subsection (15) of section 3.02 of the Model Business Corporation Act grants power to do any act that is not inconsistent with law and that furthers the business and affairs of the corporation. The extent of the business and affairs of the corporation is defined in the articles of incorporation as the corporate purposes. The **corporate purposes** are the particular business objectives that the incorporators direct their corporation to pursue, such as operating a restaurant, owning and leasing real estate, and so forth. These purposes should be specified in the articles of incorporation, are drafted in accordance with the objectives of the incorporators, and guide corporate management in the type of business to be conducted.[7] The permitted purposes are also regulated by statute, but this is one place where permissiveness is rampant. The Model Business Corporation Act and most states permit business corporations to be organized for "any lawful business," subject to other state statutes that may regulate certain industries, such as banking and insurance. Consequently, if the incorporators adopt very broad corporate purposes and authorize the corporation to transact any lawful business, the statutory corporate powers, permitting power to do any act that furthers the business and affairs of the corporation, will grant the corporation as much power as any individual would have in conducting a business.

The corporate powers enumerated and described in the Model Business Corporation Act are typical of the powers contained in most state statutes. There are, however, some important variations and details pertaining to certain powers, which are discussed here.

Power to Exist Perpetually

The vast majority of states allow a corporation to exist indefinitely and also permit the existence of a corporation to be limited to a specific period of time if such a restriction is deemed important by the incorporators. Most statutes require that the articles of incorporation recite the period of corporate existence, and if none is stated, the corporation will be deemed to exist perpetually. Based upon antiquated notions that indefinite and permanent legal structures are undesirable, a few states do not permit perpetual existence and specifically limit the duration of a corporation. For example, Mississippi limits the duration of a corporation to ninety-nine years.

Power to Own and Deal with Real Property

Every state permits a corporation to acquire and hold real property in the corporate name. In several jurisdictions, however, this power is limited to property necessary to further corporate purposes.[8] Thus, if a restaurant corporation were to acquire a larger building than it actually needed for its restaurant business, there would be a question about its power to do so. However, if the corporation could show that the larger building was purchased with a view to future expansion of the restaurant business or is otherwise convenient and appropriate to its specified corporate purposes, its ownership of that building would be authorized. A specific power clause on this point in the articles of incorporation may help.

EXAMPLE

Power to Deal in Property

To the same extent as natural persons might or could do, to purchase or otherwise acquire, and to hold, own, maintain, work, develop, sell, lease, exchange, hire, convey, mortgage, or otherwise dispose of and deal in lands and leaseholds, and any interest, estate, and rights in real property, and any personal or mixed property, and any franchises, rights, licenses, or privileges necessary, convenient, or appropriate for any of the purposes herein expressed.

Power to Lend Money to Assist Employees

These provisions vary considerably among the states. Most states have no statutory power for corporate loans to employees, directors, or officers. Because of the possibility of improper self-dealing by management, some states completely prohibit loans to officers and directors. Those that do grant such power usually impose certain restrictions on it. Shareholder approval of a loan is frequently required; and in some cases, the directors must be able to show that the transaction will be of some benefit to the corporation or advance notice to shareholders may be required.[9]

Power to Make Donations

Statutes authorizing corporate power to make donations specify various purposes for which donations may be made, different procedures for internal authorization of donations, and certain limitations on the amount. Usually donations may be made for charitable, educational, religious, public welfare, and scientific purposes.[10] In most states, the decision to donate would be made by the board of directors, but shareholder approval can be required in the articles of incorporation or bylaws to restrict the authority. Some states permit charitable donations "irrespective of benefit to the corporation."[11] Several states impose limitations on the amount donated; in some states, the limitations are flexible, such as a "reasonable sum" in New Jersey, and in some they are specific, such as five percent of net income before taxes in Virginia.

Power to Be a Partner or Member of Another Enterprise

Early law prohibited a corporation from having the power to become a partner in a separate enterprise, but nearly all states now grant this power through statutory authority. (The judicial attitude toward the power had become increasingly favorable even without statutory support.) In most cases and in some statutes, this power is limited to permit a corporation to become a partner or member of another enterprise conducting a business that could be authorized in the corporate purposes—that is, a business the corporation could lawfully conduct on its own.[12]

Power to Engage in Transactions to Aid Government Policy

The Model Business Corporation Act has always permitted the corporation to engage in transactions that aid government policy. Theoretically, this power can be broadly interpreted to include the making of a profit, since that will cause taxes to be collected, which certainly is an important government policy. Theoretically, this power also may allow the corporation to sell arms privately to foreign governments, provided that would be consistent with the policy of the administration. This power is treated differently in various states. In some jurisdictions, the corporation has this power only in a time of war or national emergency. Other jurisdictions require that the government must request a corporation's aid before the corporation is authorized to assist.

Power to Establish Pension Plans

Almost all states permit the corporation to establish pension, profit sharing, and other benefit plans for certain employees. The Model Business Corporation Act permits these plans to benefit any current or former directors, officers, employees, and agents of the corporation. A few states permit these benefits to extend to such persons serving a subsidiary corporation.[13] Not all states grant the power to adopt such benefit plans for all persons who service the corporation. Only a few states permit the payment of pensions to agents such as the Model Business Corporation Act provides.[14]

Emergency Powers

Although the corporation is a separate legal entity, it can act only through its directors and officers. Directors are required to function at a properly called meeting or by written consent with an appropriate number of directors present for that purpose; however, if, because of some catastrophic event, the directors were unable to assemble according to the regular rules of the corporation, the corporation could not function. Accordingly, the Model Business Corporation Act and nearly half the states have provided separate **emergency powers** in case of a disaster or other event that would otherwise prevent the corporation from taking action.

Originally, the Model Business Corporation Act limited the use of emergency powers to situations involving an attack on the United States or a nuclear or atomic disaster. Now those powers may be exercised whenever there is a "catastrophic event." In such situations, the board of directors of the corporation may modify lines of succession to accommodate incapacitated corporate employees; relocate the principal office (presumably to get it out of the way of whatever catastrophe is occurring); have a meeting with directors who can be reached by any practical manner; and promote officers into directors, if necessary, to achieve a quorum of the board. Since it is likely that corporate action will be taken quickly and furiously under these circumstances, the statute further provides that any action taken in good faith will bind the corporation, but may not be used to impose liability on corporate employees who had to make the decisions. Even in states that provide enabling statutory rules for this power, organizers of a corporation typically include appropriate emergency provisions in the bylaws of the corporation so that some guidance is available under these circumstances, assuming that the corporate employees will have the time, and the inclination, to locate those bylaws.

OWNERSHIP AND MANAGEMENT OF A CORPORATION

The corporation departs significantly from the sole proprietorship, the partnership and the limited liability company in the areas of ownership and management of the business enterprise. The sole proprietor is the owner and manager of his or her own business. In the general partnership, each partner is an owner, and each partner is vested with the responsibilities of management. More analogous to a corporation, a limited partnership has investors with restrictions on their management control who merely contribute cash or property to the capital of the business while the general partners are responsible for management. A limited liability company is more closely aligned with a corporation, especially in those states permitting management of the company by managers who are selected or appointed by the members. Corporate business is managed by a board of directors and by officers that the board has appointed. The owners of the business are the shareholders, who contribute cash, property, or services in exchange for their ownership rights, evidenced by shares of stock in the form of share certificates. It is possible for a shareholder to also be a director and an officer, but the rights and responsibilities of each intracorporate group are clearly segregated in corporate law, and each capacity must be separately considered.

Incorporators

The **incorporators** are responsible for filing the articles of incorporation and securing preincorporation agreements and share subscriptions. The incorporators are usually the **promoters** of the corporation who work closely with counsel in drafting the appropriate documents to comply with the statutory requirements. The main tasks of the incorporators are to prepare and sign the articles of incorporation and to file those articles with the secretary of state. Attorneys or their staff who are forming the corporation may act as the incorporators (sometimes referred to as "dummy" incorporators), since the act of incorporation is primarily a technical legal function. In a normal case, the promoters will make arrangements for the business to be conducted in the preincorporation stage, hiring employees, negotiating leases and purchases of property and equipment, and researching the market for the business. The promoters will hire a lawyer to prepare the necessary documents according to the structure they envision for the business functions they require. Of course, it is good practice to require the promoters to review, understand, and approve all of the terms of the articles of incorporation before the articles are filed with the appropriate filing office. The lawyer or a paralegal will often sign and file the articles of incorporation for the business simply for efficiency so that the promoters do not have to make an extra trip to the law firm to sign the organizing documents.

The necessary number of incorporators and their qualifications are specified by statute. The original provision of the Model Business Corporation Act required that three or more incorporators were needed to incorporate properly and that such persons must be over the age of twenty-one. In keeping with the trend toward permissive corporate statutes, the act has been amended to require one or more incorporators without mention of age or other qualifications.[15] Most states require adult natural persons to incorporate, and only a small minority of states have state residency requirements for the incorporators.[16] Some states require that the incorporators subscribe for shares. The modern trend is to permit any one person to act as an incorporator; most states have adopted statutes permitting a single incorporator.

Directors

General Powers Section 8.01 of the Model Business Corporation Act states that the business and affairs of a corporation shall be managed by a board of **directors**, which shall exercise all powers of the corporation unless otherwise provided in the statute or in the articles of incorporation. Thus, the board of directors is the governing body of the corporation and is responsible for managing the shareholder's enterprise. The directors usually determine corporate policies, manage the affairs of the business, and select and supervise the officers who handle the detailed business matters.

The Model Business Corporation Act vests all corporate power in the directors "subject to any limitation set forth in the articles of incorporation." In addition, section 8.01(c) provides that a corporation having fifty or fewer shareholders may dispense with or limit the authority of a board of directors by describing in the articles of incorporation the persons who will perform some or all of the duties of the board. Therefore, in any corporation, the incorporators (or shareholders at a later date) may limit the authority of the board of directors by placing restrictions on the board's authority in the articles of incorporation. Similarly, a corporation with only a few shareholders may eliminate or minimize the authority of the board and provide that the shareholders will have the management power. Such provisions are found most frequently in close corporations, which are discussed in detail in the next chapter.

Election and Term Since directors act as the primary governing body for a shareholder-owned business, it is appropriate that the shareholders be entitled to elect the directors. The first directors of the corporation must be named in the articles of incorporation in most states, and this initial board serves until the shareholders meet to elect their successors. If the initial directors are not named in the articles of incorporation, an organizational meeting of the shareholders is necessary to elect a board. After the initial board is elected, subsequent elections should occur at each annual shareholders' meeting, the directors so elected usually serving until the next directors are elected. Although the directors' terms expire at the next annual shareholders' meeting following their election, directors continue to serve until successors are elected and qualified or until the number of directors is decreased by official corporate action.

It is possible to **stagger** or **classify** the board of directors to ensure continuity of corporate management. This procedure avoids the election of a complete new board every year by varying the term of office for each director. Section 8.06 of the Model Business Corporation Act authorizes as many as three classes if the board has more than nine members. Thus, if the board has twelve members and three classes, four directors would serve until the first annual meeting, four would serve until the second annual meeting, and four would serve until the third annual meeting. When the four new directors are elected at the first annual meeting, they would serve for three years, until the fourth annual meeting, and the process would repeat itself. Thus, shareholders would elect four new directors every year, and those new directors would join a board of eight continuing experienced directors, who presumably are familiar with existing corporate policy and will ensure continuity in management principles. The staggering procedure is treated differently in state statutes, but most states permit it. The number of classes and the necessary size of the board before staggering is permitted are the major variants. The following chart illustrates how the staggering process works to elect a portion of the board of directors each year:

Total Directors (12)	Appointed in Articles of Incorporation	Elected in Year 2	Elected in Year 3	Elected in Year 4
1st staggered group (4 directors)	X (for one year)	X (for three years)		
2nd staggered group (4 directors)	X (for two years)		X (for three years)	
3rd staggered group (4 directors)	X (for three years)			X (for three years)

In another classification technique permitted by section 8.04 of the Model Business Corporation Act, if the shares of stock of a corporation are divided into classes, the articles of incorporation may authorize the election of certain directors by the holders of certain classes of shares. This feature permits shareholders to elect a representative to the board of directors even if those shareholders hold only a minority of the total outstanding shares of stock. For example, if a corporation has a board of directors consisting of three members, it can classify its board of directors, by an amendment to the articles of incorporation, to designate one director position for a new class of stock it hopes to sell to investors. Those investors could purchase only a small number of shares of the new class, but would always be assured of electing a representative to the board of directors, because one director position has been designated to be elected by that class alone.

Qualifications Any person may be a director of a corporation, and only a few states require that a director be of "full" or "legal" age.[17] The Model Business Corporation Act specifically provides that directors do not have to be shareholders of the corporation or residents of the state unless the articles of incorporation or the bylaws so require.[18] No state requires share ownership by a director, but a few impose residency requirements on at least a fraction of the board.[19] The articles of incorporation or the bylaws may impose residency or share ownership requirements as necessary qualifications to hold the office of director. Moreover, these documents may prescribe any other reasonable qualifications for directors, such as a minimum or maximum age or United States citizenship.

Number of Directors In most states, the board of directors must consist of at least three members; the exact number is fixed in the articles of incorporation or the bylaws. The Model Business Corporation Act was amended in 1969 to require only one director if the incorporators or shareholders feel that is appropriate.[20] The "one director" provision is also found in a majority of states, including Delaware. In some states, three directors are required unless there are fewer than three shareholders, in which case the corporation may have the same number of directors as shareholders. Thus, if a corporation has only one shareholder, only one director is required; if it has two shareholders, two directors are required; and if it has three or more shareholders, at least three directors are required.

A corporation usually may have an unlimited number of directors, but the greater the number of persons on the board, the more difficult it becomes to make corporate decisions. Practically speaking, the larger the group the more difficult it will be to convene a meeting, and more diverse points of view expressed always complicate the process of reaching a decision. The number of directors, as fixed in the articles of incorporation or bylaws, may be increased or decreased by an appropriate amendment thereto, but the amendment may never authorize less than the minimum number of persons required by the state statute.

Vacancies If any vacancy occurs in the board, either by death, removal, or retirement of a director or by an amendment increasing the number of directors, the vacancy may be filled under the Model Business Corporation Act either by the shareholders or by the affirmative vote of a majority of the remaining directors.[21] This is the only time a director is not elected by the shareholders, and some states expressly reserve to shareholders the power to fill the vacancy, especially if the vacancy has been created by the shareholders' removal of a director.[22] A director selected to fill a vacancy serves for the remaining term of the previous director, and a new director is elected at the next meeting of shareholders.

A director may resign at any time by delivering written notice to the other members of the board or to the corporation. The resignation is effective when the notice is delivered unless a later effective date is specified in the notice. During the period before the effective date of the resignation, a replacement director may be selected, but the new director may not take office until the resignation is effective and the vacancy occurs.[23]

Removal Directors serve at the pleasure of the shareholders. As owners of the corporate business, the shareholders probably have their most important power in their control over the positions of corporate directors. Section 8.08 of the Model Business Corporation Act amplifies this power by permitting the shareholders to remove a director with or without cause, unless the articles restrict that power to removal for cause only. Therefore, according to the act, whether or not a director is guilty of misconduct, the shareholders may remove the director at will and for whatever reason. Further, the shareholders' purge is not limited to one director at a time; the shareholders may vote to remove the entire board if that is deemed appropriate.[24]

The required vote for removal of a director is usually a majority of the shares that were entitled to vote for the election of the same director. Consequently, if a director was elected by a special voting group of shareholders, such as where the director position was classified, only the shareholders of that voting group may vote to remove the director. A recent revision to the act at least removes the element of surprise from this decision. If a director is to be removed by the shareholders, the notice of the meeting must state that the purpose of the meeting is to consider the removal of that director.

Duties   The board of directors takes action on behalf of the corporation at regular or special meetings at which the directors consider and adopt resolutions of corporate policy. These meetings are called in accordance with the corporate bylaws and are discussed in greater detail in Chapter 10.

Generally, the board of directors is empowered to make all corporate decisions, but realistically its actions are concerned with certain special important matters. The day-to-day activities of the corporation are left to the officers. Directors are considered by the law to be **fiduciaries**, which means that all of their actions should be directed to further and protect the interests of the corporation they serve. Note that the director's duty is owed to the corporation, a separate legal entity, and the business objectives of the corporation may not necessarily be consistent with the objectives of the shareholders who own the corporation. Thus, the directors' fiduciary capacity requires that they act independently, and they are not bound by the will of the shareholders who elect them. Of course, a director who ignores the desires of his or her constituents, the shareholders, runs the risk of being removed from office or losing reelection at the next shareholder meeting. Apart from this realistic possibility of losing his or her job by acting too independently, a director is only required to act in the best interests of the corporation by using independent discretion. More specifically, a director is required to use his or her best judgment in determining corporate policy and in authorizing corporate action, and to avoid any act that is in conflict with the director position or that will cause a personal profit to the director to the detriment of the corporation.

Because of the substantial increase in shareholder litigation against directors in recent years, most state statutes now specify guidelines for directors to follow in making corporate decisions. Section 8.30 of the Model Business Corporation Act instructs a director to perform the duties "in good faith," "with the care an ordinarily prudent person would exercise under similar circumstances," and "in a manner he reasonably believes to be in the best interests of the corporation." The director is also entitled to rely upon information, opinions, reports, or statements prepared by officers believed to be reliable and competent in such matters, professional advisers in their expert capacities, and committees of the board if their recommendations merit confidence. A director will not be liable for corporate action taken as long as the director complies with these standards. Some states are even more protective of their directors. Indiana will permit a director to be liable only if breach of the director's duty "constitutes willful misconduct or recklessness,"[25] and Delaware and several other states permit the articles of incorporation to eliminate or limit the personal liability of a director for monetary damages for breach of a fiduciary duty.[26]

Any transaction with the corporation in which a director has a personal interest will be tainted by a potential conflict of interest. If the director personally owns a piece of real estate that the corporation desires to acquire, the director is obviously in a superior bargaining position, knowing of the corporation's interest in the property and being a part of the decision-making body that will eventually approve the transaction. Consequently, shareholders or creditors of the corporation may object to transactions in which a director has a personal interest unless those transactions have been approved by independent persons. Section 8.31 of the Model Business Corporation Act provides that a director will have a personal interest in such a transaction if the director is personally involved in the transaction (such as the purchase of the director's own property) or if another entity that the director has a material financial interest in or manages is involved in the transaction (such as when another corporation sells the property, but the director of the buyer is also a director of the seller). In such cases, the statute provides a scheme by which the transaction may be approved so that it will not be voidable as a result of the conflict of interest. Approval may be obtained by doing one of the following:

1. disclosing all material facts of the transaction to other members of the board who independently approve it. For this purpose, the interested director's vote cannot count for approval, and a majority of the disinterested directors will constitute a quorum (even though they otherwise may not be sufficient for a quorum of the directors at a meeting). If only one director is not interested in the transaction, that person alone may not approve the transaction.

2. disclosing all material facts of the transaction to the shareholders, who approve the transaction by a majority vote. Similarly, if the director is also a shareholder, the director's vote may not count to approve the transaction. A majority of the shares held by shareholders who are not interested in the transaction may be a quorum for this purpose, although this majority may not otherwise qualify as a quorum of shareholders in a normal meeting.

Directors also have fiduciary duties to observe the rules and standards set in the corporation's articles or incorporation, bylaws, and official resolutions. These rules establish the structure and direction of the corporation, and each director is bound to follow them in making decisions on behalf of the corporation. Directors also have a duty not to unfairly compete with the corporation and not to exploit personally business opportunities that the corporation may expect to pursue. For example, if a corporation were in the business of buying and leasing apartment buildings, it would be inappropriate for a director to purchase an apartment building that the corporation could afford to buy and to try to lease it at rental rates that are substantially less than the rental rates charged by the corporation for its apartments. This could be both a usurpation of a corporate opportunity and unfair competition by the directors.

FIDUCIARY DUTIES OF DIRECTORS

— Duty of Care
— Duty to Observe Rules in the Articles of Incorporation, Bylaws, and Resolutions
— Duty of Loyalty

Duty not to have a conflict of interest
Duty not to compete unfairly
Duty not to take corporate opportunities personally

It is common to address these issues in the articles of incorporation to warn prospective directors and shareholders about the standards to be applied in approving transactions in which a director or officer may have a potential conflict of interest.

EXAMPLE

Transactions with an Interested Director or Officer

No contract or other transaction between this corporation and one or more of its directors, officers, or stockholders or between this corporation and any other corporation, firm, or association in which one or more of its officers, directors, or stockholders are officers, directors, or stockholders shall be neither void or voidable (1) if at a meeting of the board of directors or committee authorizing or ratifying the contract or transaction there is a quorum of persons not so interested and the contract or other transaction is approved by a majority of such quorum, or (2) if the contract or other transaction is ratified at an annual or special meeting of stockholders, or (3) if the contract or other transaction is just and reasonable to the corporation at the time it is made, authorized, or ratified.

A director also may have a conflict of interest in approving a loan from the corporation to the director. Section 8.32 of the Model Business Corporation Act permits such a transaction to be approved by a majority vote of the shareholders (not counting the votes of the benefitted director-shareholder) or by a decision of the corporation's board of directors determining that the loan benefits the corporation. Remember that the other directors must make an independent determination, using their best judgment, that the corporation would be benefitted by a loan to a director, so any resolution authorizing such a transaction should specifically state all the reasons why such a benefit will result.

Delegation of Duties   Although directors generally are vested with primary responsibility for management decisions, their powers may be delegated to officers or to an executive committee unless such a delegation is prohibited by the articles of incorporation or bylaws.

Executive Committee   EXAMPLE

The Board of Directors may, by resolution or resolutions passed by a majority of the whole Board, designate one or more committees, each committee to consist of two or more of the directors of the Corporation, which, to the extent provided in said resolution or resolutions, shall have and may exercise the powers of the Board of Directors in the management of the business and affairs of the Corporation, and may have power to authorize the seal of the Corporation to be affixed to all papers that may require it. Such committee or committees shall have such name or names as may be determined from time to time by resolution adopted by the Board of Directors.

The articles of incorporation or bylaws may restrict the authority of any committee created by the board of directors to consider certain corporate matters. However, even if the articles or bylaws are silent on this subject, there are some specific matters upon which the directors are required to act as a board and not through committees.

Selection of Officers   Section 8.40 of the Model Business Corporation Act provides that the officers shall be described in the bylaws or appointed by the board of directors as prescribed by the bylaws. Many important jurisdictions, including Massachusetts, have adopted statutes permitting the articles of incorporation or bylaws to allow for the election of certain officers by the shareholders. Since the officers are selected by the directors in most cases, and are required to be appointed by the directors in jurisdictions following the Model Business Corporation Act, the directors are under a duty to supervise the officers. The directors may be liable for failure to use due care in the appointment or supervision of an officer.

Determination of Management Compensation   The board of directors fixes executive compensation, including that of the officers and that of the directors themselves, but the articles of incorporation or bylaws may require shareholder approval.

Management Compensation   EXAMPLE

No salary or other compensation for services shall be paid to any director or officer of the corporation unless the same has been approved in writing or at a duly held stockholders' meeting by stockholders owning at least seventy-five percent in amount of the capital stock of the corporation then outstanding.

Bylaws   In most states and under the Model Business Corporation Act, the initial bylaws of the corporation are adopted by the board of directors if the incorporators have not already prepared and adopted bylaws.[27] The directors also retain, concurrently with the shareholders, the power to alter, amend, or repeal the bylaws or to adopt new bylaws, but the articles of incorporation may reserve these rights exclusively to the shareholders. In either case, the articles should be specific on the authority desired.

Adoption, Amendment, or Repeal of Bylaws

The directors shall also have power, without the assent or vote of the stockholders, to adopt, amend, or repeal bylaws relating to the business of the corporation, the conduct of its affairs, and the rights or powers of its shareholders, directors, or officers.

Initiation of Extraordinary Corporate Matters Extraordinary corporate matters, such as amendments of the articles of incorporation, sale or lease of all the corporate assets not in the regular course of business, merger, consolidation, and so forth, are usually initiated by the board of directors and approved by the shareholders. These matters are beyond the scope of day-to-day management and may have considerable ramifications on the ownership rights of the shareholders. Consequently, the shareholders must approve such an action by an appropriate vote after the action has been initiated by the board of directors.[28] The articles of incorporation should contain provisions respecting the directors' powers in such cases.

Disposition of Assets

The directors shall also have power, with the consent in writing of a majority of the holders of the voting stock issued and outstanding, or upon the affirmative vote of the holders of a majority of the stock issued and outstanding having voting power, to sell, lease, or exchange all of its property and assets, including its good will and its corporate franchises, upon such terms and conditions as the Board of Directors deem expedient and for the best interests of the corporation.

Declaration of Distributions Distributions are paid to shareholders from time to time as a return on their investment. The determination of whether distributions are to be paid is a decision for the board of directors. Broad discretion is reserved to directors in this area.[29] A committee of the board of directors may not assume this responsibility, except within limits specifically prescribed by the board of directors.[30]

Issuance of Stock and Determination of Value The articles of incorporation must state the number of shares of stock the corporation is authorized to issue. It is most unusual for a corporation to issue all of the **authorized shares** at the beginning of its corporate existence. Consequently, the subsequent determination to issue stock is a decision for the board of directors. The articles of incorporation may reserve to the board of directors the right to set **preferences**, limitations, and relative rights of classes of shares so that the corporation has the flexibility to fix the rights to accommodate the particular needs of a potential investor.[31]

Reacquisition of Shares The corporation has the power to repurchase its own shares; the board of directors must make the decision to do so.[32]

Officers

Officers usually are appointed by and receive their power from the board of directors.[33] Corporations traditionally were required to have a president, a secretary, and a treasurer; and many states still require these offices. However, modern corporate law is beginning to recognize that there is little advantage to specifying particular offices in a statute. In fact, such statutes may create problems of implied or apparent authority and cause confusion with other offices created by corporations that are not specifically authorized by statute. Long before the offices of chief executive officer and chief financial officer started creeping into state statutes as authorized positions, many corporations used those titles and asked lawyers to draft specific descriptions of the authority of those offices in the articles or bylaws. Many states that require certain offices in the statute prohibit one person's holding certain different offices, such as the offices of president and secretary.

The new Model Business Corporation Act does not require any specific officers, and permits the corporation to describe in its bylaws the officers it desires, or to grant to the board of directors the authority to appoint officers in accordance with the procedure described in the bylaws. The same individual may simultaneously hold more than one office in any corporation, and officers are permitted to appoint additional officers if they are authorized to do so by the bylaws or the board of directors. The only statutory duty the officers must perform is to prepare minutes of the directors' and shareholders' meetings and to confirm the validity of records of the corporation.[34]

The authority and responsibility of the officers is a very broad topic. Generally, officers perform whatever duties have been delegated to them by the board of directors or the bylaws,[35] and the officers are responsible for managing the day-to-day affairs of the corporation. In addition, state statutes frequently require officers to perform certain administrative tasks. These typically include the execution of articles of merger, articles of consolidation, articles of amendment, and articles of dissolution[36] by appropriate officers of the corporation. Similarly, the officers usually must sign the certificates representing the shares of the corporation.

Officers are subject to removal at the pleasure of the board of directors, although some states require the directors to establish that the best interests of the corporation will be served by removing an officer. The revised Model Business Corporation Act permits the board of directors to remove any officer at any time with or without cause.[37] However, if the officer negotiated an employment contract with the corporation, removing that officer before the term of the contract expires may subject the corporation to a lawsuit for breach of contract.[38] Considering the potential liability of the corporation, the removal of an officer under an employment contract must be supported by a very good reason, even if the directors have authority to remove an officer without cause.

An officer may resign at any time by delivering a notice to the corporation. The resignation is effective when the notice is delivered, unless the notice specifies a later effective date. The board of directors may fill a vacancy before the effective date, but the successor may not take office until the effective date.[39]

Officers are generally subject to the same standard of conduct as are directors. They are entitled to rely on information, reports, or statements that justify reliance or are based upon professional competence. But even though this standard appears to be the same for officers and directors, keep in mind that officers are more familiar than directors with the daily activities of the corporation; and consequently, an officer's reliance on reports and information prepared or submitted by others may be less justified than a director's reliance on such information, depending on the circumstances.[40]

Shareholders

The shareholders are the owners of the corporation. They contribute capital for investment in the business, and receive in exchange stock certificates representing their ownership interest. For purposes of most state statutes, shareholders are defined as "holders of record of shares in a corporation." The words **holder of record** deserve some explanation. A corporation maintains a stock transfer ledger, in which the names of the owners of shares of the corporation are registered. The persons listed in the ledger are the holders of record. Whenever shares are transferred, the new owner's name is entered on the stock transfer ledger and that person becomes the holder of record. The holder of record is entitled to vote the shares, to receive distributions, and to receive a proportionate share of assets in dissolution, depending on the voting, distribution, and dissolution characteristics of the stock.[41] Thus, if you own shares of stock in a corporation, your name will be registered as the owner in the corporate records. If you sell your shares to a friend, you will still be the holder of record until your friend submits the transferred stock certificate to the corporation so that the transfer of shares can be registered in the corporate records. Until that happens, you will still receive notices of meetings and distributions of dividends, and you will be entitled to exercise all rights of a shareholder, even though you no longer own the shares.

Corporations and **stock transfer agents** have long worried that someday the proliferation of shareholders and the number of certificates transferred on stock exchanges would result in an unbreakable logjam of paperwork, which would eventually cause the system of delivering stock certificates to collapse. Accordingly, the law has been amended in many states to permit shares in a corporation to be represented by **uncertificated securities**, meaning that the corporation records the ownership of shares on its books and records, but does not issue to the shareholder a certificate representing the shares. To accommodate this modern approach to stock ownership, the Model Business Corporation Act recognizes that a shareholder can be "a person in whose name shares are registered in the records of the corporation or the **beneficial owner** of shares to the extent of the rights granted by a **nominee certificate** on file with the corporation."[42] Consequently, the recognition of shareholder status depends upon whether the records of the corporation reflect the shareholder as an owner. Shareholders may be "beneficial owners" of shares subject to voting trust agreements (discussed in detail later). A "nominee certificate" is a certificate held by a stockbroker or other financial institution to represent shares held by many shareholders. These nominee arrangements may allow for individual owners to be considered shareholders for corporate purposes, even though shares are not actually registered in their names.

As owners of the corporation, shareholders enjoy certain ownership rights, but not in the same sense as a sole proprietor owns a proprietorship, or even as a general partner has ownership rights in a partnership. Rather, the shareholder's rights as an owner are strictly limited by the state corporation statute. Generally, the shareholders' ownership rights include only their right to vote, their right to a return on their investment by way of distributions if the directors declare such distributions, and their right to share in the assets if the business is liquidated. Shareholders have little or no voice in the day-to-day management of the corporation. However, they do have the power to elect the directors, who are responsible for the appointment and supervision of the officers, who in turn are responsible for the daily corporate activities. Thus, shareholders indirectly control corporate policy and activity by electing directors who are sympathetic to their desires. Moreover, the law requires that shareholders be consulted whenever the governing body, the board of directors, intends to modify or transform the character of the business in any manner that will materially affect the shareholders' ownership interests. These "fundamental" corporate changes are described in this book as extraordinary changes in corporate structure, and they include such matters as amendments to the articles, merger, consolidation, exchange of stock, sale or exchange of assets not in the ordinary course of business, and dissolution. Shareholder control is limited, therefore, to the shareholders' rights to vote in the selection of the corporate management and rights to be consulted in matters that may modify the character of their investment in the business. These indirect ownership rights are explored here in some detail.

Right to Elect and Remove Directors The initial directors of the corporation may be named in the articles of incorporation. These directors usually serve until the first annual shareholders' meeting, at which time shareholders elect new directors. The new directors serve for the prescribed term, usually until the next annual shareholders' meeting. Directors are subject to removal with or without cause by an appropriate vote of the shareholders, as prescribed by state statute. If the statute does not specifically provide for removal without cause, a clause to that effect in the articles of incorporation or bylaws is necessary if that right is deemed important.

EXAMPLE

Removal of Directors

The stockholders of the Corporation may, at any meeting called for the purpose, remove any director from office, with or without cause, by a vote of a majority of the outstanding shares of the class of stock that elected the director; provided, however, that no director shall be removed if votes of a sufficient number of shares are cast against his or her removal, which if cumulatively voted at an election of the entire board of directors would be sufficient to elect him or her.

In corporate law, there is a special procedure for the election of directors, called **cumulative voting**. This procedure is designed to enable minority shareholders to elect a representative to the board of directors, even though they hold fewer than a majority of shares of the corporation's stock. For example, if Amanda owns 301 shares of stock and Alexis owns 300 shares of stock, the three directors of the corporation will always be selected by Amanda since she outvotes Alexis for each position on the board. Cumulative voting, if authorized, permits Alexis to "cumulate" all of the votes she can cast for directors, and to vote all of her votes for a director she prefers. Alexis may cast 900 votes (300 shares × 3 directors) for her favorite director, leaving Amanda to apply 903 votes among two other candidates she prefers. Alexis' candidate will thus be elected, even though Alexis is a minority shareholder.[43] Cumulative voting may or may not be in effect in a particular corporation, depending on the appropriate state law and the articles of incorporation. Some states guarantee cumulative voting by constitutional provision.[44] Other states have statutes that require cumulative voting to be used unless the procedure is specifically denied in the articles of incorporation.[45] And other states, including Delaware, do not grant cumulative voting unless the articles of incorporation specifically authorize it.[46] The Model Business Corporation Act offers still another variation on this issue. Under the revised act, shareholders do not have a right to cumulate their votes unless the articles of incorporation so provide, and cumulative voting may not be used unless

1. the notice for the meeting to elect directors says that cumulative voting will be permitted; or
2. a shareholder who has the right to cumulate votes gives notice to the corporation within forty-eight hours before the time set for the meeting of an intention to cumulate votes at the election. In the second case, if one shareholder gives proper notice, all other shareholders will have the right to cumulate their votes without further notice.[47]

As with most specific points of corporate law, it is very important to review the appropriate state statute to determine the manner by which cumulative voting is authorized, and to state the desired procedure in the articles of incorporation.

Cumulative Voting

At all elections for directors each stockholder shall be entitled to as many votes as shall equal the number of his or her shares of stock multiplied by the number of directors to be elected, as he or she may cast all of such votes for a single director, or may distribute them among the number to be voted for, or any two or more of them, as he or she may see fit.

Right to Amend the Articles of Incorporation The articles of incorporation may be amended upon the recommendation of the board of directors to the shareholders and, in some states, upon the suggestion of a certain percentage of shareholders. In any case, the proposed amendment must be submitted to a vote of the shareholders, either at an annual meeting or at a special meeting called for that purpose. Shareholders' approval of such amendments to the basic "charter" or organizing document of their corporation is consistent with their rights as owners.[48]

Right to Take Other Extraordinary Corporate Action Shareholder approval is required for certain **extraordinary corporate matters**, such as merger, consolidation, exchange of shares, sale or exchange of assets out of the ordinary course of business, and dissolution of the corporation. Since such an action may significantly alter the character of the investment, a shareholder objecting to the action may have his or her stock appraised and purchased. As a simple rule of thumb, any matter that may have a substantial impact on the operation of the business or the ownership rights of the shareholders requires shareholder approval. Even without a statutory mandate for shareholder approval, a sensible board of directors will request shareholder approval of major corporate decisions, perhaps for no other reason than to gauge shareholder sentiment regarding the directors' activities.

Right to Inspect A corollary to the shareholder's voting right is the shareholder's right to check up periodically on management and inspect corporate records. Most states have statutes that permit the shareholder a qualified right to inspect and copy books and records, including minutes of shareholders' meetings and other shareholder records. To avoid the problems created by recalcitrant persons who simply buy shares to harass corporate management, these statutes establish certain criteria as a condition to the shareholder's right to inspect. The original Model Business Corporation Act and most states, for example, require the demanding shareholder to have share ownership for at least six months preceding a demand of inspection or to be a holder of record of at least five percent of all the outstanding shares of the corporation. Thus, the demanding shareholder must be established as a shareholder or must purchase a significant block of stock in order to have the right to inspect. Moreover, all the statutes require that the demand for inspection state the purpose of the inspection and that the stated purpose be "proper," and not for a reason conflicting with the best interests of the corporation. In states following these procedures, it may also be a good idea to grant the directors power to control inspection times and procedures in the bylaws.

EXAMPLE   **Inspection by Shareholders**

The directors from time to time may determine at what times and places, and under what conditions and regulations, the accounts and books of the Corporation shall be open to the inspection of the stockholders.

The modern trend in corporate statutes is to permit any shareholder of a corporation to inspect the corporation's books and records under certain conditions. The shareholder must give written notice of an intention to inspect at least five business days before the date of inspection. The shareholder must state the purpose of the inspection, and the records the shareholder desires to inspect must be directly connected with that purpose. Upon meeting these requirements, a shareholder will be entitled to inspect and copy minutes of meetings, accounting records, and the record of shareholders.[49] Unlike most current state statutes, the Model Business Corporation Act does not permit the articles or bylaws to abolish or limit the shareholders' inspection rights on the theory that a shareholder's right to information is a fundamental right of an owner of the company.

Preemptive Rights The shareholders' **preemptive rights** are their rights to purchase newly issued shares of the corporation in the same proportions as their present share ownerships before outsiders may purchase them. For example, suppose XYZ Corporation has three shareholders—Judi Wagner, who owns 100 shares; Gail Schoettler, who owns 200 shares; and Pamela Owen, who owns 300 shares—and the corporation determines that it will issue 1,500 new shares of stock. If the shareholders have preemptive rights, Wagner has the right to buy 250 shares (one-sixth) of the new issue, Schoettler has the right to buy 500 shares (one-third) of the new issue, and Owen has the right to buy 750 shares (one-half) of the new issue. If the shareholders fail to buy their allocated number of shares, the shares then may be sold to outsiders.

Preemptive rights began as a common law theory designed to protect shareholders' proportionate interests and to preserve their proportionate control over the corporation. In the previous example, Wagner, Schoettler, and Owen would suffer complete loss of control if the 1,500 shares were sold to a single outsider. If control is not important, the shareholders can choose not to purchase their proportionate amount of the new issue, in which case the shares will be sold to other investors. To visualize this concept consider the following chart:

Shareholder	Preemptive rights to purchase 1,500 new shares of stock	Shares actually purchased by existing shareholders	Shares available to sell to a new shareholder
Judi Wagner 100 shares (16%)	Can purchase 250 shares to maintain 16% ownership	0	250
Gail Schoettler 200 shares (33%)	Can purchase 500 shares to maintain 33% ownership	0	500
Pamela Owen 300 shares (50%)	Can purchase 750 shares to maintain 50% ownership	750	0

Thus, in this example, the corporation will sell 750 shares to a new shareholder, and will have a total of 2,100 shares outstanding after the transaction. Owen will still own 50% of the outstanding stock; the new shareholder will own 36% of the outstanding stock; Wagner will own 5% of the outstanding stock; and Schoettler will own 10% of the outstanding stock. Wagner and Schoettler have been **diluted** because they did not exercise their preemptive rights to purchase the new shares. Owen has maintained her same percentage ownership by exercising her preemptive rights.

Most states now treat preemptive rights specifically in their corporate statutes. Some states provide that preemptive rights are granted automatically by law unless the articles of incorporation specifically deny them.[50] Other states, including Delaware, provide that the articles of incorporation must specifically grant preemptive rights or those rights do not exist.[51] The new Model Business Corporation Act has adopted the latter position.[52]

Preemptive rights are important to shareholders of closely held corporations and a nuisance to shareholders of large, publicly held corporations. If Microsoft Corporation had to offer a proportionate right to purchase to each of its millions of shareholders, for example, the procedural problems and expense would be overwhelming. To maintain the flexibility of incentive compensation programs, it is a good idea to exclude employee stock option plans from preemptive rights. The articles of incorporation should specify the corporate policy with respect to preemptive rights.

Preemptive Rights

EXAMPLE

No holder of any stock of the Corporation shall be entitled, as a matter of right, to purchase, subscribe for, or otherwise acquire any new or additional shares of stock of the Corporation of any class, or any options or warrants to purchase, subscribe for, or otherwise acquire any such new or additional shares, or any shares, bonds, notes, debentures, or other securities convertible into or carrying options or warrants to purchase, subscribe for, or otherwise acquire any such new or additional shares.

Distributions In addition to voting, inspection, and preemptive rights, shareholders are entitled to a return on their investment by way of **dividend** distributions if the corporation makes a profit, and if the directors in their discretion and good judgment deem such a distribution desirable. The shareholder's primary objectives are to receive dividend distributions and realize capital appreciation when the value of the stock increases.

As owners of the corporation, shareholders may share in the assets of the corporation when the business is dissolved and the corporate creditors have been paid. The remaining assets are divided among the shareholders proportionately and in accordance with any preferential rights created in the articles of incorporation for the particular class of stock.[53]

LIMITED LIABILITY

An attractive characteristic of the corporation is that the investors risk only the amount of their investment and are not individually responsible for corporate obligations. This **limited liability** advantage flows from the recognition by the law that the corporation is a separate legal person, and its debts and liabilities are personal to it.

Limited liability for the corporate debts and obligations can be contrasted with the full individual liability of a partner in a partnership or an owner in a sole proprietorship. The limited partnership and the limited liability company borrow this characteristic of limited liability from the corporation in protecting limited partners and members. The shareholder, who is the owner of the corporation, risks only the amount contributed for shares of the corporation. Although the shareholder may lose the amount of money he or she paid for the shares, personal assets of the shareholder are not exposed if the corporation incurs excessive liability. Similarly, the persons who manage the corporation—the directors, officers, and other corporate executives—are not personally liable for corporate obligations unless they have exceeded their authority or breached their fiduciary duties of using good judgment and due care in incurring those obligations.

The protection of limited liability offered by corporations is a principal reason for choosing the corporate form over others, and the theory of limited liability is well established in judicial decisions. There are, however, two limitations on the principle, one practical and the other legal.

When a new corporation has been formed, usually it has not matured to an established business, and while it may own certain assets and have good prospects for future profit, its ability to generate profits is untested. Consequently, potential creditors are understandably wary of extending credit to a new corporation. If the business is not as good as predicted or if the directors and officers are not as capable as they think they are, the corporation may not prosper, and a creditor may be forced to look only to the corporate assets for satisfaction of the obligation. Anticipating this problem, sophisticated creditors of the corporation will attempt to obligate all available parties for the repayment of the obligation—just in case something goes wrong. In such a case, the shareholders and directors may personally agree to pay corporate obligations in order to persuade outsiders to advance credit to their corporation, in which case they may offer a **guaranty** for the corporate debts and become individually responsible for the obligation. For example, if Robbie Schwarz and Michael Crouch form a new corporation to operate a travel agency and negotiate a loan from their local bank to finance the operations of the business for the first few months, the bank will likely require that Robbie and Michael sign personally and be individually obligated to repay the loan, since the money will be spent for daily expenses and the corporation's assets are inadequate in the early stages of operation to assure repayment. Thus, practical realities may cause the limited liability protection to be diminished by agreement.

The legal problem associated with limited liability is a theory called **piercing the corporate veil.** The courts that have imposed personal liability on shareholders under this theory have recognized the corporate organization as offering a "shield" of limited liability for shareholder protection. Upon finding abuse of this protection, courts have been perfectly willing to pierce the shield, disregard the corporate entity, and hold shareholders responsible for the acts of the corporation. Implicit in the finding of abuse of this protection is a finding that the shareholders have neglected to comply with the statutory requirements for proper operation of a corporation. It is possible, therefore, to advise a client in advance of ways to avoid this problem.

Typical abuses of the corporate form that appear consistently in piercing the corporate veil cases are failure by the shareholders to supply the corporation with adequate financial resources to support its operations and failure to observe corporate formalities, such as holding meetings for shareholders and directors, keeping separate books of the corporation, distinguishing personal assets from corporate assets, and issuing stock. In addition, if a corporation is used to perpetrate fraud or for other illegal purpose, a court will pierce the corporate veil and hold the individual shareholders responsible, whether or not the corporation was properly funded or the formalities were observed.

These problems are more likely to arise in a closely held corporation than in one of the industrial giants. The entrepreneur who has formed a corporation for its limited liability benefits is most vulnerable to the theory of piercing the veil. If this person uses the family computer to compose business letters, uses excess family furniture in the office, commingles personal funds with corporate funds, and ignores formal meetings in making corporate decisions, the corporate protection is weak. Recognize, however, that if the entrepreneur's corporate assets are substantial, this piercing problem may never arise, even with the suggested transgressions. The piercing doctrine is a judicial theory used to resolve litigation if necessary. If a corporation is sued by a business creditor or a victim who slipped on its snow-covered sidewalk and the corporate assets are adequate to pay the claim, there is no need to pierce the corporate veil to reach the shareholders' personal resources. On the other hand, if a creditor or victim suffers because of an inadequately financed corporation, the courts tend to reach behind the corporate shield to require the shareholders to pay.

As a precautionary measure, all corporate clients should be advised to observe the following four principal objectives.

1. The formalities of corporate procedure, including the holding of share-holders' and directors' meetings and the keeping of minute books, should be observed.
2. The corporation should be operated as a separate business and financial unit, with separate books and accounts, without any intermingling or confusing of its funds, affairs, and transactions with those of the shareholders (whether individuals or corporations), officers, directors, or affiliated corporations in disregard of the corporate entity.
3. No representation or other holding out should be made by any corporate agents that would lead outsiders to believe that the business is being conducted as a sole proprietorship or as a partnership (with the assurance of personal liability to those forms).
4. The corporation should have adequate capital to meet its obligations and such contingencies as are reasonably to be expected in its business.[54]

The theory of piercing the corporate veil is a frequent problem with parent-subsidiary corporations. If a large, profitable corporation is seeking to enter a risky enterprise, it may be imprudent to risk all of the corporation's profit and other assets for one questionable venture. The solution is to form a separate corporation (called a **subsidiary**), whose stock is primarily or wholly owned by the large corporation (called a parent corporation), and the only risk, if the subsidiary corporation's shield of liability is observed, is the subsidiary's assets. The questions in these cases are substantially the same as those detailed earlier. If the subsidiary is undercapitalized and the separation between the parent and subsidiary is not clear-cut, the parent may be required to respond to all liabilities and obligations of the subsidiary.

CONTINUITY OF EXISTENCE AND DISSOLUTION

A corporation has the power to exist perpetually under most state statutes and, therefore, is unaffected by the death of an owner or manager or by the transfer of ownership interests. The definitive term of a sole proprietorship, which ends when the proprietor dies, and of a partnership, which is technically dissolved upon the death, withdrawal, or other incapacity of a partner, was deemed to be a disadvantage to those forms of business. Similarly, the limited liability company may be required to adopt a short duration and to dissolve upon the loss of one of its members.[55] The corporation, on the other hand, does not suffer from this infirmity. It is assured indefinite life by statute, and its ownership interests (shares) can be freely transferred without impairing its continuity.

Continuity of existence is an extremely important characteristic for a large corporation, since any abrupt termination of existence could result in financial tragedy. On the other hand, the continuity of a corporation may work a hardship on a minority shareholder who is dissatisfied with the investment and can find no market for his or her shares. This shareholder will be unable to terminate the corporate entity in order to withdraw the investment, and may simply be forced to continue in shareholder status at the mercy of the majority shareholders and management.

Dissolution of a corporation may be accomplished by agreement of the appropriate intracorporate group (incorporators or shareholders) as provided by statute. These voluntary dissolutions are cumbersome and require the consensus of at least a majority of the appropriate incorporators, directors, or shareholders, as required, to carry a resolution for dissolution.[56] A corporation also may be dissolved administratively by the secretary of state (or other filing official) for failure to file periodic reports or by a court upon request of the attorney general whenever the corporation has failed to comply with statutory requirements, has procured its articles by fraud, or has otherwise abused its authority. In addition, many modern corporate statutes have provisions for involuntary dissolution for the benefit of minority shareholders who are being unfairly prejudiced by those in control of the corporation,[57] and the Model Business Corporation Act permits a judicial dissolution if the directors or those in control are acting in a manner that is illegal, oppressive, or fraudulent.[58] It is hoped that these court-ordered dissolutions will remain rare.

TAXATION OF A CORPORATION

Corporations, like natural persons, are subject to taxation by the federal, state, and local governments based on the amount of income they earn each year. Consistent with the separate corporate personality, the corporation is regarded as a separate taxable entity for most federal and state tax purposes. The corporation files its own tax return (see Exhibit 6–1, U.S. Corporation Income Tax Return) and is taxed on separate corporate tax rates. This separate entity taxation is a significant distinguishing characteristic of the corporation from the sole proprietorship, partnership, and limited liability company, where income is merely funneled to the individuals who make up the business organization and is declared as individual income for tax purposes.[59] Taxation of corporations has advantages and disadvantages, all of which must be carefully considered by the attorney in advising the client that the corporate form is the proper organization for a proposed business.

Double Taxation

The greatest disadvantage of corporate taxation is the concept of **double taxation**. Income received by the corporation is taxed at the corporate level according to the corporate rates then in effect. The profit remaining after taxes is available for distribution to shareholders as dividends; and if dividends are distributed, the distribution is taxed again as personal income to the shareholder.

Federal and state governments set different individual and corporate tax rates. Individual tax rates have been graduated from a low of approximately 14% to a high of over 50% on ordinary income. Corporate tax rates also have been adjusted regularly to accomplish various tax policies and have been graduated from a low of approximately 15% to a high of approximately 46%, depending on total taxable income. Regardless of the level of tax rates in effect, certain tax planning principles are relevant to the taxation of a corporation. Some hypothetical situations are reviewed here to illustrate how double taxation is a significant disadvantage to the corporate business form.

Whenever corporate tax rates are higher than individual tax rates, no tax advantage can be achieved for ordinary income in the corporate form, since every dollar earned by the corporation will be taxed at a higher rate than any dollar earned by the individual. Consequently, since sole proprietorships and partnerships are taxed based on individual rates, fewer after-tax dollars will be available for any business that is operating under the corporate form.

Even when the corporate tax rates for ordinary income are lower than individual tax rates, the concept of double taxation places the corporation at a disadvantage. For example, suppose the corporate tax rate is 20% and the individual tax rate is 30%. At first glance, it would appear that the business profit produced by the corporation will result in less tax than the same

Exhibit 6–1.

U.S. Corporation Income Tax Return

Form **1120**

Department of the Treasury
Internal Revenue Service

U.S. Corporation Income Tax Return

For calendar year 2002 or tax year beginning ...., 2002, ending ...., 20....
Instructions are separate. See page 20 for Paperwork Reduction Act Notice.

OMB No. 1545-0123

2002

A Check if a:
1 Consolidated return (attach Form 851) ☐
2 Personal holding co. (attach Sch. PH) ☐
3 Personal service corp. (as defined in Regulations sec. 1.441-3(c)— see instructions) ☐

Use IRS label. Otherwise, print or type.

Name

Number, street, and room or suite no. (If a P.O. box, see page 7 of instructions.)

City or town, state, and ZIP code

B Employer identification number

C Date incorporated

D Total assets (see page 8 of instructions)

E Check applicable boxes: (1) ☐ Initial return (2) ☐ Final return (3) ☐ Name change (4) ☐ Address change $

Income

1a	Gross receipts or sales _____ **b** Less returns and allowances _____ **c** Bal	1c
2	Cost of goods sold (Schedule A, line 8)	2
3	Gross profit. Subtract line 2 from line 1c	3
4	Dividends (Schedule C, line 19)	4
5	Interest	5
6	Gross rents	6
7	Gross royalties	7
8	Capital gain net income (attach Schedule D (Form 1120))	8
9	Net gain or (loss) from Form 4797, Part II, line 18 (attach Form 4797)	9
10	Other income (see page 9 of instructions—attach schedule)	10
11	**Total income.** Add lines 3 through 10	11

Deductions (See instructions for limitations on deductions.)

12	Compensation of officers (Schedule E, line 4)	12
13	Salaries and wages (less employment credits)	13
14	Repairs and maintenance	14
15	Bad debts	15
16	Rents	16
17	Taxes and licenses	17
18	Interest	18
19	Charitable contributions (see page 11 of instructions for 10% limitation)	19
20	Depreciation (attach Form 4562) ... 20	
21	Less depreciation claimed on Schedule A and elsewhere on return ... 21a	21b
22	Depletion	22
23	Advertising	23
24	Pension, profit-sharing, etc., plans	24
25	Employee benefit programs	25
26	Other deductions (attach schedule)	26
27	**Total deductions.** Add lines 12 through 26	27
28	Taxable income before net operating loss deduction and special deductions. Subtract line 27 from line 11	28
29	**Less:** a Net operating loss (NOL) deduction (see page 13 of instructions) 29a	
	b Special deductions (Schedule C, line 20) 29b	29c

Tax and Payments

30	**Taxable income.** Subtract line 29c from line 28	30
31	**Total tax** (Schedule J, line 11)	31
32	**Payments:** a 2001 overpayment credited to 2002 32a	
b	2002 estimated tax payments 32b	
c	Less 2002 refund applied for on Form 4466 32c ( ) **d Bal** 32d	
e	Tax deposited with Form 7004 32e	
f	Credit for tax paid on undistributed capital gains (attach Form 2439) 32f	
g	Credit for Federal tax on fuels (attach Form 4136). See instructions 32g	32h
33	Estimated tax penalty (see page 14 of instructions). Check if Form 2220 is attached ☐	33
34	**Tax due.** If line 32h is smaller than the total of lines 31 and 33, enter amount owed	34
35	**Overpayment.** If line 32h is larger than the total of lines 31 and 33, enter amount overpaid	35
36	Enter amount of line 35 you want: **Credited to 2003 estimated tax** _____ **Refunded**	36

Sign Here

Under penalties of perjury, I declare that I have examined this return, including accompanying schedules and statements, and to the best of my knowledge and belief, it is true, correct, and complete. Declaration of preparer (other than taxpayer) is based on all information of which preparer has any knowledge.

Signature of officer _____ Date _____ Title _____

May the IRS discuss this return with the preparer shown below (see instructions)? ☐ **Yes** ☐ **No**

Paid Preparer's Use Only

Preparer's signature	Date	Check if self-employed ☐
Firm's name (or yours if self-employed), address, and ZIP code		

Preparer's SSN or PTIN

EIN

Phone no. (   )

Cat. No. 11450Q

Form **1120** (2002)

---

business profit produced by an individual proprietor or a partnership. However, if the only way the corporation can distribute cash to its shareholders is through distributions of dividends, those distributions must be paid from after-tax corporate dollars. (Dividends distributed to shareholders are not deductible by the corporation as an expense.) Consequently, when the corporation earns $1.00 of profit, that profit is immediately reduced to $0.80 through the corporate tax rate. When the dividend is paid to the shareholder, the shareholder must pay ordinary income tax on the dividend received. The $0.80 is thus reduced by an additional $0.24, leaving $0.56 as the net after-tax available cash. If the same business were conducted as a partnership or sole proprietorship, only the individual tax rate would be applied to each dollar of profit, leaving $0.70 available after taxes were paid.

When tax rates are graduated (when they increase as the level of income increases) for both corporations and individuals, the double taxation problem can be considerably worse for successful corporations owned by successful shareholders. For example, if the highest corporation tax rate is 40% for all corporate profit over $100,000, and the highest individual tax rate is 50% for all income earned over $100,000, almost all profit that is earned by the corporation and distributed to the shareholder will be paid to the federal and state taxing authorities. Every corporate dollar earned over $100,000 will be reduced $0.40 at the corporate taxation level. If the remaining $0.60 is distributed to a shareholder who is taxed in the 50% bracket, it is taxed an additional $0.30. Thus, the corporate dollar is reduced a total of $0.70 in taxes, leaving the shareholder with $0.30 cash to spend!

With parent-subsidiary corporations, there may even be triple taxation—the subsidiary pays its corporate tax and distributes remaining profits to the parent as dividends, which are taxed as the parent's corporate income; and then the dividends are distributed to the parent corporation's shareholder, who is taxed at individual tax rates.

Double taxation is recognized as a distinct disadvantage for the corporation as compared with other business forms, especially if a significant portion of the corporate income will be paid to the shareholders as dividend distributions. Large corporations with many stockholders simply accept the disadvantage, since the corporate form offers many advantages that are essential to the operation of a large business. In small, closely held corporations, double taxation may be minimized by several options. Whenever shareholders are officers or employees of the corporation, as is frequently the case in small organizations, they may be paid salaries, which are deductible as a corporate expense. The shareholder-employee is thereby compensated, and since the corporate tax is not imposed on the salary, double taxation is avoided. Furthermore, anticipating this problem, a small corporation may be structured so that much of its capital comes from loans to the business, rather than from shareholder investment. Having established sufficient equity capital (money paid through shareholder investment), the corporation may raise the remaining funds needed for the business through interest-bearing loans, and the interest is deductible to the corporation as an expense. The interest paid to the creditor (investor) is income, which substitutes for dividends and is not subject to double taxation. Similarly, shareholders of closely held corporations may purchase property and equipment and lease it to their corporation, receiving rental payments, which are treated as expenses to the corporation and are taxed only as rental income to the shareholder-lessors.

Another practical approach to double taxation is to leave the corporate profits in the business and not distribute dividends. Then only corporate tax rates are applied, and while the retained profits will increase the value of the stock, resulting in a capital gains tax when the stock is sold, no individual income tax is applied to the profits themselves. This solution is too simple to be effective, however, since the taxing authorities have devised a penalty that encourages corporations to distribute earnings to the shareholders rather than accumulate them. The accumulated earnings tax is applied to income unreasonably retained by the corporation. The company must pay a penalty tax of 27.5% on the first $100,000 of accumulated earnings (for which no adjustments are available) and 38.5% of the accumulated taxable income in excess of $100,000.[60] The corporation has the burden of establishing adjustments to the accumulated earnings tax for certain transactions that might qualify for adjustments, or the corporation must prove that income has been accumulated for the reasonable needs of the business in order to avoid the penalty.

Subchapter S Election

The Internal Revenue Code provides that a "small business corporation" may elect not to be taxed at the corporate level but to have its income (whether distributed or not) passed through and taxed pro rata to its shareholders as ordinary income.[61] This election effectively treats the corporation as a sole proprietorship or partnership for tax purposes, and all profits are attributed proportionately to the persons who own the business. Similarly, corporate losses generally may be offset against other personal income of the shareholders. The election is particularly beneficial to shareholders whose tax rates are significantly lower than the corporate tax rate, or when it is expected that most of the corporate profits will be distributed to the shareholders. The election avoids two disadvantages of corporate taxation: the profits are not double taxed, and when a shareholder actively participates in the business, corporate losses may be taken as ordinary losses, thereby reducing the personal income of the shareholder.

To be classified as a small business corporation for the **Subchapter S** election, a corporation must meet the following requirements:

1. There may be no more than seventy-five shareholders (spouses are treated as one shareholder, regardless of how the stock is held).
2. Shareholders must be natural persons, and cannot be another corporation or partnership, but may be an estate of a natural person or certain trusts.
3. The corporation may have only one class of stock (although different classes are permitted provided the only difference among them is voting rights).
4. The corporation cannot have a nonresident alien as a shareholder.

The election of a small business corporation refers to the number of shareholders, as indicated in the listed requirements for qualification, and has nothing to do with the size of the corporation in terms of its assets, revenue, or earnings. These requirements effectively limit the Subchapter S election to close corporations.[62]

Under the Subchapter S election, corporate profits, whether distributed or not, must be claimed as taxable income by each shareholder in the proportion of ownership interest held, and consequently, shareholders must consent to the election. Each shareholder should sign a separate statement of consent acknowledging the effect of the election (see Exhibit 6–2, Shareholder's Statement of Consent as to Taxable Status under Subchapter S). The statement is submitted with the form electing taxation under Subchapter S.

The election to be taxed under Subchapter S is made on Form 2553 of the Internal Revenue Service (see Exhibit 6–3, Election of Subchapter S Taxation), and it may be made for any taxable year at any time during the previous taxable year or at any time before the fifteenth day of the third month of the taxable year (March 15 for calendar year corporations).[63]

The Subchapter S election may be terminated in one of several ways. The most common termination results from the corporation ceasing to qualify as a small business corporation under the requirements listed earlier, as, for example, when it acquires a seventy-sixth shareholder. It also may be terminated if the majority of the shareholders consent to revocation of the election. Finally, the election may be terminated whenever the corporation has received more than twenty-five percent of its gross income during three consecutive taxable years from passive sources, such as royalties, rents, dividends, interest, annuities, and sales or exchanges of stock or securities.[64] The election cannot be terminated by a new shareholder who does not affirmatively consent to tax treatment under Subchapter S, unless the new shareholder is the seventy-sixth shareholder of the corporation, or unless the new shareholder purchases a majority of the stock and then affirmatively revokes the election.

The Subchapter S election is particularly desirable when the corporation is expected to incur losses during the first few years of operation, when shareholders' individual tax rates are lower than the corporate rates, or when corporate profits are regularly expected to be

---

_____, the undersigned, as a stockholder of _____CORPORATION, hereby consents and agrees to the Corporation's election under Section 1372(a) to be treated as a "Small Business Corporation" for income tax purposes. It has been explained to me that the taxable income of the Corporation, to the extent that it exceeds dividends distributed in money out of earnings and profits of the taxable year, will be taxed directly to shareholders (rather than to the Corporation) to the extent that it would have constituted a dividend if it had been distributed on the last day of the Corporation's taxable year.

_____
Shareholder

Exhibit 6–2.

Shareholder's Statement of Consent as to Taxable Status under Subchapter S

Exhibit 6–3.

Election of Subchapter S
Taxation

Form **2553** (Rev. December 2002)	**Election by a Small Business Corporation** (Under section 1362 of the Internal Revenue Code)	
Department of the Treasury Internal Revenue Service	See Parts II and III on back and the separate instructions. The corporation may either send or fax this form to the IRS. See page 2 of the instructions.	OMB No. 1545-0146

Notes:
1. *Do not* file **Form 1120S**, U.S. Income Tax Return for an S Corporation, for any tax year before the year the election takes effect.
2. This election to be an S corporation can be accepted only if all the tests are met under **Who May Elect** on page 1 of the instructions; all shareholders have signed the consent statement; and the exact name and address of the corporation and other required form information are provided.
3. If the corporation was in existence before the effective date of this election, see **Taxes an S Corporation May Owe** on page 1 of the instructions.

Part I	**Election Information**	

Please Type or Print	Name of corporation (see instructions)	**A** Employer identification number
	Number, street, and room or suite no. (If a P.O. box, see instructions.)	**B** Date incorporated
	City or town, state, and ZIP code	**C** State of incorporation

D   Check the applicable box(es) if the corporation, after applying for the EIN shown in **A** above, changed its name ☐ or address ☐

E   Election is to be effective for tax year beginning (month, day, year) . . . .   /   /

F   Name and title of officer or legal representative who the IRS may call for more information
G Telephone number of officer or legal representative
(   )

H   If this election takes effect for the first tax year the corporation exists, enter month, day, and year of the **earliest** of the following: (1) date the corporation first had shareholders, (2) date the corporation first had assets, or (3) date the corporation began doing business . . . .   /   /

I   Selected tax year: Annual return will be filed for tax year ending (month and day) . . . .
If the tax year ends on any date other than December 31, except for a 52–53-week tax year ending with reference to the month of December, you **must** complete Part II on the back. If the date you enter is the ending date of a 52–53-week tax year, write "52–53-week year" to the right of the date.

J Name and address of each shareholder; shareholder's spouse having a community property interest in the corporation's stock; and each tenant in common, joint tenant, and tenant by the entirety. (A husband and wife (and their estates) are counted as one shareholder in determining the number of shareholders without regard to the manner in which the stock is owned.)	**K** Shareholders' Consent Statement. Under penalties of perjury, we declare that we consent to the election of the above-named corporation to be an S corporation under section 1362(a) and that we have examined this consent statement, including accompanying schedules and statements, and to the best of our knowledge and belief, it is true, correct, and complete. We understand our consent is binding and may not be withdrawn after the corporation has made a valid election. (Shareholders sign and date below.)		**L** Stock owned		**M** Social security number or employer identification number (see instructions)	**N** Share-holder's tax year ends (month and day)
	Signature	Date	Number of shares	Dates acquired		

Under penalties of perjury, I declare that I have examined this election, including accompanying schedules and statements, and to the best of my knowledge and belief, it is true, correct, and complete.

Signature of officer	Title	Date

For Paperwork Reduction Act Notice, see page 4 of the instructions.   Cat. No. 18629R   Form **2553** (Rev. 12-2002)

distributed to shareholders as dividends. Note that the election and maintenance of Subchapter S treatment increase the burdensome formalities required for corporate existence, as well as the legal and accounting costs of corporate operation. This is one reason why the limited liability company has such current popularity. The limited liability company automatically provides for the use of individual tax rates of the owners for any company profits, and the complicated restrictions of Subchapter S concerning the number and type of owners, uniform ownership rights among owners, and ownership by and of other entities do not apply to limited liability companies.

State Income Tax

Corporations operating within any given state are subject to state income tax. The general rule is that a state may tax a corporation operating within its borders in a reasonable relation to the

Form 2553 (Rev. 12-2002)   Page **2**

Part II   **Selection of Fiscal Tax Year** (All corporations using this part must complete item O and item P, Q, or R.)

O Check the applicable box to indicate whether the corporation is:
    1. ☐ A new corporation adopting the tax year entered in item I, Part I.
    2. ☐ An existing corporation retaining the tax year entered in item I, Part I.
    3. ☐ An existing corporation changing to the tax year entered in item I, Part I.

P Complete item P if the corporation is using the automatic approval provisions of Rev. Proc. 2002-38, 2002-22 I.R.B. 1037, to request **(1)** a natural business year (as defined in section 5.05 of Rev. Proc. 2002-38) or **(2)** a year that satisfies the ownership tax year test (as defined in section 5.06 of Rev. Proc. 2002-38). Check the applicable box below to indicate the representation statement the corporation is making.

    1. Natural Business Year ☐ I represent that the corporation is adopting, retaining, or changing to a tax year that qualifies as its natural business year as defined in section 5.05 of Rev. Proc. 2002-38 and has attached a statement verifying that it satisfies the 25% gross receipts test (see instructions for content of statement). I also represent that the corporation is not precluded by section 4.02 of Rev. Proc. 2002-38 from obtaining automatic approval of such adoption, retention, or change in tax year.

    2. Ownership Tax Year ☐ I represent that shareholders (as described in section 5.06 of Rev. Proc. 2002-38) holding more than half of the shares of the stock (as of the first day of the tax year to which the request relates) of the corporation have the same tax year or are concurrently changing to the tax year that the corporation adopts, retains, or changes to per item I, Part I, and that such tax year satisfies the requirement of section 4.01(3) of Rev. Proc. 2002-38. I also represent that the corporation is not precluded by section 4.02 of Rev. Proc. 2002-38 from obtaining automatic approval of such adoption, retention, or change in tax year.

Note: *If you do not use item P and the corporation wants a fiscal tax year, complete either item Q or R below. Item Q is used to request a fiscal tax year based on a business purpose and to make a back-up section 444 election. Item R is used to make a regular section 444 election.*

Q Business Purpose—To request a fiscal tax year based on a business purpose, you must check box Q1. See instructions for details including payment of a user fee. You may also check box Q2 and/or box Q3.

    1. Check here ☐ if the fiscal year entered in item I, Part I, is requested under the prior approval provisions of Rev. Proc. 2002-39, 2002-22 I.R.B. 1046. Attach to Form 2553 a statement describing the relevant facts and circumstances and, if applicable, the gross receipts from sales and services necessary to establish a business purpose. See the instructions for details regarding the gross receipts from sales and services. If the IRS proposes to disapprove the requested fiscal year, do you want a conference with the IRS National Office?
    ☐ Yes ☐ No

    2. Check here ☐ to show that the corporation intends to make a back-up section 444 election in the event the corporation's business purpose request is not approved by the IRS. (See instructions for more information.)

    3. Check here ☐ to show that the corporation agrees to adopt or change to a tax year ending December 31 if necessary for the IRS to accept this election for S corporation status in the event (1) the corporation's business purpose request is not approved and the corporation makes a back-up section 444 election, but is ultimately not qualified to make a section 444 election, or (2) the corporation's business purpose request is not approved and the corporation did not make a back-up section 444 election.

R Section 444 Election—To make a section 444 election, you must check box R1 and you may also check box R2.

    1. Check here ☐ to show the corporation will make, if qualified, a section 444 election to have the fiscal tax year shown in item I, Part I. To make the election, you must complete **Form 8716**, Election To Have a Tax Year Other Than a Required Tax Year, and either attach it to Form 2553 or file it separately.

    2. Check here ☐ to show that the corporation agrees to adopt or change to a tax year ending December 31 if necessary for the IRS to accept this election for S corporation status in the event the corporation is ultimately not qualified to make a section 444 election.

Part III   **Qualified Subchapter S Trust (QSST) Election Under Section 1361(d)(2)***

Income beneficiary's name and address	Social security number
Trust's name and address	Employer identification number

Date on which stock of the corporation was transferred to the trust (month, day, year) . . . .   / /

In order for the trust named above to be a QSST and thus a qualifying shareholder of the S corporation for which this Form 2553 is filed, I hereby make the election under section 1361(d)(2). Under penalties of perjury, I certify that the trust meets the definitional requirements of section 1361(d)(3) and that all other information provided in Part III is true, correct, and complete.

_____   _____
Signature of income beneficiary or signature and title of legal representative or other qualified person making the election   Date

*Use Part III to make the QSST election only if stock of the corporation has been transferred to the trust on or before the date on which the corporation makes its election to be an S corporation. The QSST election must be made and filed separately if stock of the corporation is transferred to the trust after the date on which the corporation makes the S election.

✪   Form **2553** (Rev. 12-2002)

Exhibit 6–3.

Election of Subchapter S Taxation *(continued)*

business activity conducted within the state. Thus, a corporation incorporated in Colorado is automatically subject to the Colorado state tax if it does business there or has Colorado source income, because it was originally formed in that state. If the corporation then does business in Wyoming and Nebraska, those states may also tax its income in relation to the business conducted within their borders. The domestic or domicile state, in this case Colorado, usually allows a tax credit for taxes paid to other states.

Various formulas are employed by the states to determine a proper allocation of tax on local business activity. As a practical matter, states attempt to devise formulas that will maximize tax revenue from business activity. For example, a state with very little localized industry usually has a formula based on sales made within the state rather than on corporate assets located within the state. On the other hand, a state with a heavy industrial population will probably tax on a percentage of total assets located within the state.

In addition to state and federal income taxes, corporations are frequently subject to other special taxes, which may result in the corporation bearing a greater tax burden than other forms of business enterprise. **Franchise taxes**, organization and capital taxes, original issue taxes for the issuance of shares of stock, and taxes on transfers of shares and other corporate securities are the most common. Proper planning in the selection of a business organization requires an analysis of the myriad charges imposed by various states on the corporations operating within their boundaries.

Section 1244 Stock

The foregoing discussion has been primarily concerned with income taxes assessed against a corporation and its shareholders. The other tax ramifications of a corporation include **capital gains and losses** associated with the purchase or sale of stock. Each share of stock is a capital asset, and if it is sold after appreciating in value, a taxable gain is realized. Similarly, when stock is sold after depreciating in value, a capital loss is claimed. Capital losses for individuals may be used only to offset capital gains, if there are any, or deducted from ordinary income up to a maximum limitation. For example, suppose a shareholder invested $5,000 in the stock of a corporation, which then became bankrupt, thus making the stock worthless and resulting in a capital loss of $5,000. If the stockholder had no capital gains that year, the stockholder may not be able to deduct the loss. There are certain carry-forward provisions for individual losses, but it would be preferable to be able to claim the full $5,000 against ordinary income for that taxable year. **Section 1244** of the Internal Revenue Code provides this effect for stock that qualifies as small business stock.[65]

The definition of a small business is different for Section 1244 stock than for a Subchapter S election. In this case, the qualification of a corporation as a small business depends upon the amount of money to be raised by a plan to sell Section 1244 stock and the existing equity capital of the corporation. The amount of stock that is offered under the plan and intended to qualify under Section 1244, and the amounts received by the corporation as contributions to capital or paid in surplus, cannot exceed $1,000,000. Any property contributed for stock (other than money) is valued at the adjusted basis of the property to the corporation, less any liability against the property assumed by the corporation.

For example, suppose the Lyons Corporation adopts a Section 1244 plan to offer stock for an amount not in excess of $500,000. If its equity capital were $600,000 at the time the plan was adopted, $100,000 of the stock would not qualify under Section 1244 because the equity capital plus the aggregate amount offered would exceed $1,000,000. In such a case, the maximum amount that would qualify under the plan would be $400,000. The corporation has a right to designate which stock shall qualify. However, suppose the Lyons Corporation was newly formed when it adopted the plan. In its first year, it sold $400,000 in stock, and business successes deposited $800,000 into equity capital. This does not destroy the qualification of the stock because the equity capital test includes only amounts paid for contributions to capital, not revenues from operations.

To qualify for Section 1244 stock, the corporation must acquire most of its income (more than fifty percent) from sources other than royalties, rents, dividends, interest, annuities, and transactions in stock for five years preceding the loss.[66] The effect of the plan will be lost if the business does not comply with this source-of-income provision after the stock is issued and for five years before the investor sustains a loss.

The former requirement that the Section 1244 stock be issued pursuant to a written plan has been repealed. Nevertheless, it is good practice to prepare a written plan or corporate resolution to indicate clearly that the shares are being sold pursuant to Section 1244 (see Exhibit 6–4, Resolution Authorizing Issuance of Section 1244 Stock, and Exhibit 6–5, Plan for Issuance of Section 1244 Stock).

If all requirements of the statute are met, all stock issued pursuant to the plan will receive ordinary loss treatment if a loss is incurred when the stock is sold. This means that the selling shareholders may use any loss on the stock to offset ordinary income during the taxable year, rather than treating the loss as a capital loss with its limited and deferred tax treatment.

Whereas, the Corporation is authorized to offer and issue 500 shares of common stock, no par value, none of which has yet been issued, and the directors desire to hereafter issue 100 shares of said common stock for $20,000;

Whereas, A_____ B_____ and C_____ D_____ have expressed the wish that each be permitted to subscribe for 50 shares of said common stock at a price of $200 a share; and

Whereas, the Corporation is a domestic corporation meeting the definition of a "small business corporation" contained in section 1244(c)(2) of the Internal Revenue Code of 1954;

Upon motion duly made, seconded, and unanimously carried, it was

Resolved, that the Corporation hereby adopts a plan, effective this date, to offer 50 shares of common stock, no par value, each to A_____ B_____ and C_____ D_____ in consideration of $10,000 to be paid by each only in money and property acceptable to the Corporation (other than stock or securities), provided, however, that said A_____ B_____ and C_____ D_____ shall within two weeks after the date of adoption of this plan notify the Corporation in writing of the acceptance of this offer, and during the said two-week period the Corporation shall offer and issue only such common stock. The maximum amount to be received by the Corporation in consideration of the stock to be issued pursuant to this plan shall be $20,000. It is the intention of the officers and directors of the Corporation to comply in every respect with section 1244 of the Internal Revenue Code of 1954 pertaining to "Losses on Small Business Stock," and any questions concerning the interpretation or operation of this plan shall be resolved in such manner as will qualify the plan under said law. The officers of the Corporation are hereby authorized, empowered and directed to do and perform any and all acts and deeds necessary to carry out the plan.

Exhibit 6–4.

Resolution Authorizing Issuance of Section 1244 Stock

Qualified Small Business Stock

As part of the small business incentives under the Revenue Reconciliation Act of 1993, the Internal Revenue Code was amended to permit individual shareholders who hold "qualified small business" stock for more than five years to exclude half of any gain from the sale or exchange of the shares.[67] The remaining half of the gain is taxed at a capital gain rate, and, thus, the effective tax rate for the sale of shares is one-half of the capital gain rate.

A "qualified small business" must have less than $50 million of aggregate capital as of the date the shares were issued and have at least eighty percent of the value of corporate assets used in an active "qualified trade or business." Generally, a qualified trade or business would not include a corporation where the principal asset of the business is the reputation or skill of one or more of its employees. Consequently, corporations formed to practice a profession, such as law, medicine, architecture, accounting, and similar services, will not qualify for this favorable tax treatment.

Other Tax Advantages of a Corporation

Tax authorities allow a corporation to deduct certain "necessary" expenses incurred in providing fringe benefits to employees to encourage their continuous faithful performance. There are also tax advantages to the employee under "qualified" incentive plans. If these employees are also shareholders, the deductibility of such expenses is unaffected. Incentive benefits with tax advantages include share options; medical and dental reimbursement plans; qualified pension and profit sharing plans; and life, health, and accident insurance programs.[68]

Incentive compensation programs give employees the right to participate in the success of the business, while enjoying significant tax breaks on the compensation received under the plan. For example, a qualified profit sharing plan permits a corporate deduction of profits

Exhibit 6–5.

Plan for Issuance of Section 1244 Stock

1. The corporation shall offer and issue under this Plan, a maximum of _____ shares of its common stock at a maximum price of _____ ($_____) per share.

2. This offer shall terminate, unless sooner terminated by _____, upon:

(a) complete issuance of all shares offered hereunder, or

(b) appropriate action terminating the same by the Board of DIrectors and the Stockholders, or

(c) the adoption of a new Plan by the Stockholders for the issuance of additional stock under Section 1244, Internal Revenue Code.

3. No increase in the basis of outstanding stock shall result from a contribution to capital hereunder.

4. No stock offered hereunder shall be issued on the exercise of a stock right, stock warrant, or stock option, unless such right, warrant, or option is applicable solely to unissued stock offered under the Plan and is exercised during the period of the Plan.

5. Stock subscribed for prior to the adoption of the Plan, including stock subscribed for prior to the date the corporation comes into existence, may be issued hereunder, provided, however, that said stock is not in fact issued prior to the adoption of the Plan.

6. No stock shall be issued hereunder for a payment which, alone or together with prior payments, exceeds the maximum amount that may be received under the Plan.

7. Any offering or portion of an offer outstanding that is unissued at the time of the adoption of this Plan is herewith withdrawn. Stock rights, stock warrants, stock options, or securities convertible into stock that are outstanding at the time this Plan is adopted are likewise herewith withdrawn.

8. Stock issued hereunder shall be in exchange for money or other property except for stock or securities. Stock issued hereunder shall not be in return for services rendered or to be rendered to, or for the benefit of, the corporation. Stock may be issued hereunder, however, in consideration for cancellation of indebtedness of the corporation, unless such indebtedness is evidenced by a security or arises out of the performance of personal services.

9. Any matters pertaining to this issue not covered under the provisions of this Plan shall be resolved in favor of the applicable law and regulations in order to qualify such issue under Section 1244 of the Internal Revenue Code. If any shares issued hereunder are finally determined not to be so qualified, such shares, and only such shares, shall be deemed not to be in this Plan, and such other shares issued hereunder shall not be affected thereby.

10. The sum of the aggregate amount offered hereunder plus the equity capital of the corporation amounts to $_____.

11. The date of adoption of this Plan is _____, 20____.

accumulated for employees under the plan, but the employee is not taxed until he or she receives payment. Qualified pension plans are similarly treated for tax purposes.

Insurance plans may provide a direct economic benefit to employees, who may also be shareholders, without tax on the proceeds of the insurance. The corporation may deduct the expense of paying insurance premiums for employees as an ordinary business expense. Hospital, accident, health, and disability insurance plans may be maintained by the corporation with very few limitations. Group life insurance, with maximum dollar limitations per employee, may be maintained by the corporation, with the premiums treated as an expense of the corporation but not taxable to the employee.

These special insurance and incentive compensation plans, with their attendant tax advantages, are unique to the corporation, with its separate legal personality. Partnerships and sole proprietorships do not enjoy the separate entity characteristic and, therefore, do not obtain tax advantages through these devices.

KEY TERMS

business corporation	classify	preemptive rights
professional corporation	fiduciaries	dilution
entity	authorized shares	dividend
shareholder	preferences	limited liability
articles of incorporation	officer	guaranty
bylaws	holder of record	piercing the corporate veil
corporate purposes	stock transfer agent	subsidiary corporation
emergency powers	uncertificated securities	double taxation
incorporator	beneficial owner	Subchapter S corporation
promoter	nominee certificate	franchise tax
director	cumulative voting	capital gains and losses
stagger	extraordinary corporate matter	Section 1244 stock

WEB RESOURCES

General information concerning formation and operation of corporations is available on every state Secretary of State's (or Department of Commerce) Web site, most of which offer forms that are required for filing to form and maintain corporations. The National Association of Secretaries of State maintains links directly to the offices of the Secretaries of State in all states. These can be accessed through

<http://www.nass.org>

Access to state corporate laws may be obtained through the Legal Information Institute maintained at the Cornell Law School:

<http://www.law.cornell.edu>

The specific sections of a state's corporate law may be located by a search site that directly ties to the corporate laws of the state. This search may be accessed at

<http://www.megalaw.com>

Tax forms, including the federal income tax returns and schedules necessary to elect Subchapter S and to report federal income tax for Subchapter S and Subchapter C corporations are available on line at

<http://www.irs.gov>

Various resources are available for sample forms and information about the formation and the operation of corporations, including the following:

<http://www.toolkit.cch.com>
<http://www.findlaw.com>
<http://www.lectlaw.com>
<http://www.ilrg.com>

CASES

UNION BANK v. ANDERSON

232 Cal. Rptr. 823 (Cal.App. 5 Dist. 1991)
ARDAIZ, ACTING PRESIDING JUSTICE

[Sam Hamburg Farms, Inc. (SHF, Inc.) was a California corporation owning approximately 6200 acres of farming property in Merced and Fresno Counties. In 1975, John Anderson and Henry Stone negotiated to purchase the 6200 acres, intending to buy the land as an investment, farm it, then break it up and sell it. In order to comply with Federal Bureau of Reclamation requirements for federal water rights on the property, Anderson and Stone decided to buy the stock of SHF, Inc., and thereby acquire the control of the land, buildings, equipment, crops, and water rights. The purchase price was paid by a promissory note for $2,650,000, payable in ten annual installments commencing in January 1977, and the note was secured by a deed of trust on the real estate. Anderson and Stone failed to pay the promissory note and claimed they could not be sued for the difference between the value of the land and the amount of the note because of California Code of Civil Procedure section 580b, which stated:

> "No deficiency judgment shall lie in any event after any sale of real property for failure of the purchaser to complete his contract of sale, or under a deed of trust, or mortgage, given to the vendor to secure payment of the balance of the purchase price of real property, or under a deed of trust, or mortgage, on a dwelling for not more than four families given to a lender to secure repayment of a loan which was in fact used to pay all or part of the purchase price of such dwelling occupied, entirely or in part, by the purchaser."]

* * *

It appears both Anderson and Stone acknowledge the instant transaction could only fall within section 580b protection as a variation on the standard purchase money transaction. The question presented is whether a sale of all of the *stock* of an existing farming corporation, whose tangible assets consisted of real property, buildings, equipment, growing crops and other assets, secured by a note and attendant subordinate deeds of trust executed by the shareholders of the corporation on the corporation's real property, constitutes a variation on the standard purchase money transaction? Anderson maintains "[equitable] ownership of the real property was transferred" and that "[i]n their analysis of CCP § 580b, the courts have repeatedly disregarded the form of the transaction to determine its true substance." Stone agrees and maintains "[t]he transaction was a real property purchase money transaction."

* * *

Anderson and Stone's arguments and case authority fail under these facts. It is well recognized that a corporation is a legal entity having an existence separate from that of its shareholders. (*Merco Constr. Engineers, Inc. v. Municipal Court* (1978) 21 Cal.3d 724, 729, 147 Cal. Rptr. 631, 581 P.2d 636.) When shareholders purchase stock in a corporation, and the corporation includes certain holdings in real property, the shareholders do not acquire an ownership interest in the real property. A share is simply a unit of proprietary interest which the shareholder holds in the corporation. (*Kohl v. Lilienthal* (1889) 81 Cal. 378, 385, 22 P. 689; Corp.Code, § 184.) That is, the shareholders are *not* the owners of corporate prop-

erty; the whole title is in the corporation. (*Barnett v. Lewis* (1985) 170 Cal.App.3d 1079, 1088, 217 Cal. Rptr. 80; *Baker Divide Mining Co. v. Maxfield* (1948) 83 Cal.App.2d 241, 248, 188 P.2d 538.) "The shareholders of a corporation do not have legal title to the assets or capital of the corporation, have no right to the possession thereof, may not transfer or assign the properties or assets of the corporation nor apply corporation funds to personal debts." (*In re Mercantile Guaranty Co.* (1968) 263 Cal.App.2d 346, 352, 69 Cal.Rptr. 361.) Even upon dissolution, the shareholder is not entitled to a proportionate share of the property held by the corporation, only the assets left after liabilities of the corporation are adequately provided for or paid. (Corp. Code, § 2004.)

While Stone is correct in his assertion that "[t]he factual situations in which purchase money transactions occur . . . are limited only by the creative imaginations of the participants *in real property sales,*" here there was no real property sale. Indeed, Anderson and Stone's then-attorney, during negotiations in 1975, acknowledged to the Department of the Interior that the transaction was " 'strictly a stock acquisition. . . .' "

Parties to a sale of stock cannot simply disregard the corporate form of the acquisition, no matter what the "intent" of the parties to the sale might have been at one time. While Anderson and Stone may have initially negotiated to buy real property, eventually they knowingly purchased only the stock of SHF, Inc.

* * *

Anderson and Stone specifically purchased all the outstanding shares of stock because it enabled them to retain federal water rights on all of the acreage, which a buy up of the corporation (and acquisition of its real property) would not have provided. Simply put, they bought out the shares of a corporation. The corporation owned the property. Their note was for the purchase of personal property (shares in the corporation). The fact that it may have been secured by real property does not render the transaction a purchase money transaction for real property. This is not a situation where they purchased the land from the corporation; they simply purchased all the shares of the corporation which owned the land. We conclude section 580b does not apply to the note.

* * *

ICELAND TELECOM, LTD. v. INFORMATION SYSTEMS AND NETWORKS CORPORATION

268 F.Supp.2d 585 (2003)

WILLIAMS, DISTRICT JUDGE

Iceland Telecom, Ltd. ("Plaintiff") brought this diversity action against Arvin Malkani ("Malkani"), ISN Global Communications, Inc. ("ISNGC"), and Information Systems and Networks Corporation ("ISN")(collectively, "Defendants") alleging in two counts breach of contract and unjust enrichment.

* * *

ISNGC was a telecommunications company incorporated in 1998 under the laws of the State of Delaware. The company was founded by Malkani. ISN was founded in 1980 and its CEO/President and sole-owner is Malkani's mother, Roma Malkani. Iceland Telecom is a telecommunications service provider in Iceland. Iceland Telecom owns Skima, Ltd. ("Skima"), which provides internet telephone services.

Arvin Malkani was the sole-owner, sole stockholder, CEO, and president of ISNGC. The three directors of the company were Malkani, his mother Roma, and his sister Sabrina Malkani. Malkani claims that ISNGC provided "internet telephony service." ISNGC was headquartered in the same building as ISN in Bethesda, Maryland. The building was owned by another separate company, which Roma Malkani also owned. ISNGC also did business in New York. ISNGC was not, however, registered to do business in either Maryland or New York. Plaintiff also asserts that ISNGC never paid state or federal taxes during its two-year existence. Defendants do not directly dispute this assertion; Malkani stated in his deposition that he "thinks" ISNGC paid taxes.

ISNGC never held a stock-holder meeting, nor did it ever hold a meeting of corporate directors. Roma Malkani stated in her deposition that she did not know that she was a member of the board and she also posited that her daughter, Sabrina, would also not be aware that she was on the board of ISNGC.

All indications point to the fact that ISNGC was a subsidiary of ISN. ISN gave one million dollars in start-up funds to ISNGC. ISNGC's letter-head stated that ISNGC was an "ISN Company". A description-of-business form stated that ISN was its "parent company." Additionally, it is not in dispute that Roma Malkani and ISN were directly involved in the day-to-day operations of ISNGC. The pay stubs for ISNGC's president, Malkani, indicate that he was paid salary by ISN. ISN also reviewed ISNGC's expenses and reimbursed many of them. Time sheets for IS-NGC employees were submitted to ISN. Other ISNGC expenses were picked up by ISN: (1) ISNGC travel expenses (2) Malkani's ISNGC business dinners (3) magazine subscriptions; (4) petty cash and lunches; and (5) other invoices for services provided to ISNGC by other companies.

Additionally, ISN and ISNGC shared the same office space. There is nothing in the record to suggest that any payments were made by ISNGC to ISN for the "leased" space. ISNGC used ISN's overhead, including phone numbers and office furniture. It appears also that some of the staff for ISN did work for ISNGC.

In early 1999, ISNGC and Plaintiffs entered into negotiations. The negotiations were carried out by Skima for Iceland Telecom and by Malkani. The communications between the parties indicate that Plaintiff thought that it was dealing with ISN. Malkani did not disabuse Plaintiff of this notion. In fact, he appears to have added to the confu-

sion. For example, he wrote an email to Skima stating that he would be gone the following week, but that in his absence Plaintiff should contact an ISN employee.

Malkani also faxed a non-disclosure agreement to Plaintiffs. The fax cover sheet was from ISN. In the email correspondence, Plaintiff repeatedly referred to ISNGC as ISN. The parties then entered into an agreement, which was signed only by ISNGC and Plaintiff. Eventually, a payment dispute arose between the parties. ISNGC "ceased to exist" in 2001.

* * *

The issue presented in Defendants' motion for partial summary judgment is whether Arvin Malkani, individually, and/or ISN can be sued by Plaintiff for the alleged breach of contract of ISNGC. Plaintiff does not dispute that neither ISN nor Malkani were party to the contract. Plaintiff nevertheless argues under two theories for why the Court should hold those non-parties liable for the obligations of ISNGC: (1) the Court should pierce the corporate veil under an instrumentality/alter ego theory; and/or (2) the Court should hold that ISNGC acted as an agent for Malkani or for ISN. Defendants argue that no grounds exist to hold the non-parties liable either under the "piercing the corporate veil" doctrine or under a doctrine of agency.

A) *Piercing the Corporate Veil: Maryland Law*

The oft-stated rule on piercing the corporate veil in Maryland is that "although courts will, in a proper case, disregard the corporate entity and deal with substance rather than form, as though a corporation did not exist, shareholders are generally not held individually liable for the debts and obligations of a corporation except where it is necessary to prevent fraud or enforce a paramount equity." *Bart Arconti & Sons, Inc. v. Ames-Ennis, Inc.,* 275 Md. 295, 310, 340 A.2d 225 (1975) (internal citations omitted); *Residential Warranty Corp. v. Bancroft Homes Greenspring Valley, Inc.,* 126 Md.App. 294, 306, 728 A.2d 783 (1999); *Dixon v. Process Corp.,* 38 Md.App. 644, 654, 382 A.2d 893 (1978). Much like individual stockholders, a corporate parent also will not be liable for the debts/obligations of its subsidiary absent the showing of the same two factors. *See Dixon,* 38 Md.App. at 654, 382 A.2d at 899 (court would not pierce the corporate veil absent fraud or the need to enforce a paramount equity even when the two corporations were found not to be separate entities). The Maryland state courts have emphasized the difficulty faced by a Plaintiff seeking to hold a parent liable for the obligations of the subsidiary stating, "woe unto the creditor who seeks to rip away the corporate facade in order to recover from one sibling of the corporate family what is due from another in the belief that the relationship is inseparable, if not insufferable, for his is a herculean task." *Id.* at 645, 382 A.2d 893.

While it is clear that a showing of fraud will often suffice to pierce the corporate veil, it is less clear what other situations give rise to the liability of individual stockholders. "Despite the proclamation that a court may pierce the corporate veil to enforce a paramount equity, arguments that have urged the piercing of the corporate veil 'for reasons other than fraud' have failed in Maryland courts." *Residential Warranty,* 126 Md.App. at 307, 728 A.2d at 789 (citing *Travel Committee, Inc. v. Pan American World Airways, Inc.,* 91 Md.App. 123, 138, 603 A.2d 1301 (1992)). "Notwithstanding its hint that enforcing a paramount equity might suffice as a reason for piercing the corporate veil, the Court of Appeals to date has not elaborated upon the meaning of this phrase or applied it in any case of which we are aware." *Travel Committee,* 91 Md.App. at 138, 6093 A.2d at 1318.

In *Travel Committee,* the Court of Special Appeals hinted that a court should look to the Fourth Circuit opinion in *DeWitt Truck Brokers v. W. Ray Flemming Fruit Co.,* 540 F.2d 681 (4th Cir.1976) for guidance in analyzing whether the court should look beyond the corporate fiction, holding individual stockholders liable. The Fourth Circuit, applying South Carolina law, stated that on occasion courts should pierce the veil even absent fraud:

> But when substantial ownership of all the stock of a corporation in a single individual is combined with other factors clearly supporting disregard of the corporate fiction on grounds of fundamental equity and fairness, courts have experienced 'little difficulty' and have shown no hesitancy in applying what is described as the 'alter ego' or 'instrumentality' theory in order to cast aside the corporate shield and to fasten liability on the individual stockholder.

DeWitt, 540 F.2d at 685. The *Travel Committee* court appeared to cite *DeWitt* with approval for a list of factors to be considered by courts faced with arguments for piercing the corporate veil:

> These include: whether the corporation was grossly under-capitalized, the corporation's failure to observe corporate formalities, non-payment of dividends, the debtor's corporation's insolvency, the dominant stockholder's siphoning of corporate funds, the non-functioning of other officers or directors, the absence of corporate records, and the corporation's status as a facade for the stockholder's operations.

* * *

Were the Court to apply the *DeWitt* factors to the case at bar, it would be hard pressed to conclude that equity does not demand the piercing of the corporate veil. Arvin Malkani was the sole owner and stockholder of ISNGC. Furthermore, all other factors indicate that ISNGC was a mere "instrumentality." ISNGC appears to have disregarded all corporate formalities. The company never had a board of directors meeting, nor was there ever a meeting of stockholders. ISNGC never registered to do business in the two places that it was doing business, New York and Maryland. It also appears that ISNGC never paid taxes to those two states or to the federal government. In his deposition,

Malkani stated that he "thinks" ISNGC paid taxes, but no proof was provided in support of that assertion. The Court has before it no corporate records from ISNGC; it also has no record of why ISNGC "ceased to exist."

On top of all that, the overlap between ISN and ISNGC is telling of the "instrumentality" nature of the relationship. ISN paid salaries to employees at ISNGC including Malkani himself. When expenses were charged to ISNGC, they were reimbursed by ISN. The start-up money for ISNGC came from ISN, and when ISNGC was short on money, Roma Malkani "loaned" the company between one-hundred and two-hundred thousand dollars. No record exists of any repayment of that loan. Above and beyond all that, and drawing all inferences in favor of the non-movant, ISNGC appears to have been grossly under-capitalized.

In many other jurisdictions, this plethora of evidentiary facts would support the Court's denying of this partial summary judgment motion and its piercing of the corporate veil so that Plaintiff could hold Malkani and ISN liable for the debts and obligations of ISNGC. Whatever may be said about other jurisdictions, however, the law in Maryland leads this Court to conclude that Plaintiff's argument must fail for the following reasons. First, for however persuasive the *DeWitt* opinion may sound—and, in fact, its reasoning has been applied in other jurisdictions—it is only that: persuasive. It has no binding effect on this Court because it was applying the law of South Carolina. Second, all binding precedent from the state courts of Maryland, while referencing other factors, give this Court no example of when a Court should pierce the corporate veil absent a showing of fraud; in fact, the cases demonstrate that Maryland has a markedly restrictive approach to piercing the corporate veil. In *Bart Arconti,* the high court of Maryland stated that even if a sham corporation was set-up for the *sole* purpose of evading legal obligations, a court should not use its equitable powers to pierce the corporate veil. *Bart Arconti,* 275 Md. at 309, 340 A.2d at 233-34. Similarly, in *Dixon,* the Court stated that even if a subsidiary was a mere "instrumentality"—which the *Dixon* Court had concluded was established in that case—it would still not suffice to hold the parent liable. *Dixon,* 38 Md.App. at 655, 382 A.2d at 900. As for the failure to abide by corporate formalities, it was clear in *SS Vedalin* that Chief Judge Northrop had serious doubts about the validity of the corporation. He seemed convinced that the corporation used by the individual investors to shield themselves from liability was a fiction, calling evidence that it wasn't a mere "alter ego . . . tenuous at best." He refused, however, to disregard the corporate entity. *SS Vedalin,* 346 F.Supp. at 1181.

Plaintiff strenuously argues that the Court should ignore this overwhelming binding precedent, applying the *DeWitt* factors enumerated by the Fourth Circuit. But the Court would apparently then become the first federal court sitting in diversity in Maryland to pierce the corporate veil upon a theory of the need to enforce a paramount equity, expanding the breadth of the law substantially. The Maryland courts that have spoken on the issue have cautioned against piercing the corporate veil. It is not the province of this Court, but rather the state courts of Maryland, to flesh out and expand the factual scenarios that could warrant a court's piercing of the corporate veil. For those reasons, the Court will not pierce the corporate veil to hold Malkani or ISN liable for the debts of ISNGC.

* * *

PROBLEMS

1. Describe the duties owed to the corporation by the board of directors.

2. Who elects or appoints the following persons in a corporate structure?
   a. the officers
   b. the directors
   c. the employees
   d. the incorporator

3. State at least three ways a corporation can distribute money to its shareholders without having the money taxed at the corporate level.

4. State two reasons why limited partners in a limited partnership are more likely to have limited liability than shareholders in a corporation.

5. State the basis upon which the corporation's "veil" can be pierced to impose personal liability upon the shareholders.

6. Review the Model Business Corporation Act in Appendix E. State at least three things a corporation formed under that act does not have the power to do.

PRACTICE ASSIGNMENTS

1. Write a memorandum about the position in the corporation (incorporator, director, officer, or shareholder) that has the most power to
   a. determine long-term business policies of the business.
   b. establish rules for the relationships among the intra-corporate groups.
   c. determine management philosophy.
   d. control financial activities of the corporation.
   e. hire and fire employees.
   f. produce a profit by the daily management of the company's business.

2. Select a local corporation that is known to you and design an organizational chart for the corporation, showing all management, operational, and financial personnel. Be sure to include the shareholders.

3. Terry and Perry Gorrell formed a corporation with Eddy and Betty O'Keefe in 1989. Terry and Perry own 50% of the outstanding stock and Eddy and Betty own 50% of the outstanding stock. Terry, Perry, Eddy, and Betty are all members of the board of directors, and they are officers of the corporation as follows:

   Terry—President
   Eddy—Vice-President
   Betty—Secretary
   Perry—Treasurer

   Today, Terry and Perry cannot stand Eddy and Betty, and the feeling is mutual. They have not been able to agree on anything for the past year. The operations of the corporation are at a standstill because of their personal attitudes toward each other. What could you recommend so this corporation could become functional again?

4. Based upon current federal tax rates, at what point will income in a corporation be taxed less than income taxed at individual tax rates?

ENDNOTES

1. See "Ownership and Management of a Corporation" later in this chapter.

2. See "Ownership and Management of a Corporation" later in this chapter.

3. Many states advertise the advantages of incorporation under their laws. Delaware sends the following synopsis of its permissive corporate laws to persons requesting information regarding incorporation:

The outstanding advantages of incorporating in Delaware are as follows: The fees payable to the State of Delaware are based upon the number of shares of authorized capital stock, with the no par shares fee one-half the par shares fee. The franchise tax compares favorably with that of any other State. Shares of stock owned by persons outside of the State are not subject to taxation. Shares of stock which are part of the estate of a non-resident decedent are exempt from the State Inheritance Tax Law. The policy of Delaware courts has always been to construe the corporation law liberally, to interpret any ambiguities or uncertainties in the wording of the Statutes so as to reach a reasonable and fair construction. This causes the careful investor to have confidence in the security of the investment. The corporation service companies throughout the nation consider the Delaware corporation law among the most attractive for organization purposes and the State of Delaware a valuable jurisdiction in which to organize new companies.

4. See "The Articles of Incorporation" and "Bylaws" in Chapter 8.

5. Model Business Corporation Act (hereafter M.B.C.A.) § 3.02(11); see "Bylaws" in Chapter 8. Also see the sample bylaws, Exhibit I–10 in Appendix I.

6. M.B.C.A. § 3.02(7).

7. Examples of specific corporate purposes appear in the discussion of the articles of incorporation in Chapter 8.

8. This restriction may appear in the state constitution, as in Oklahoma (Okla. Const. art. XXII, § 2), or in the state corporation statutes, as in New Hampshire (N.H. Rev. Stat. Ann. § 293-A.4(V)).

9. Colo. Rev. State § 7-108-501(4).

10. See M.B.C.A. § 3.02(13).

11. E.g., New Jersey, N.J. Stat. Ann. § 14A:3-4.

12. E.g., Delaware, 8 Del. Code Ann. § 122(11).

13. E.g., Tennessee, Tenn. Code § 48-13-102(12).

14. E.g., New Jersey, N.J. Stat. Ann. § 14A:3-1(1)(1).

15. M.B.C.A. § 2.01.

16. E.g., South Dakota, S.D. Comp. Laws. Ann. § 47-2-4.

17. E.g., Pennsylvania, 15 Pa. Stat. §§ 1401, 1402.

18. M.B.C.A. § 8.02.

19. E.g., Hawaii requires that at least one member of the board be a resident of the state (Hawaii Rev. Stat. § 415.35).

20. M.B.C.A. § 8.03(a).

21. M.B.C.A. § 8.10.

22. E.g., Wisconsin, Wis. Stat. Ann. § 180.34.

23. M.B.C.A. §§ 8.07, 8.10.

24. However, if cumulative voting is in effect for the election of directors, the same procedure must be followed in the removal of a director. See "Shareholder Business and Vote Required" in Chapter 10.

25. Ind. Code. Ann. § 23-1-35-1.

26. See, e.g., 8 Del. Code Ann. § 102(b) (7).

27. M.B.C.A. § 2.06.

28. See "Amendment of the Articles of Incorporation," "Merger, Consolidation, and Exchange," and "Sale, Mortgage, or Other Disposition of Assets" in Chapter 15.

29. M.B.C.A. § 6.40. Corporate distributions and dividends are fully discussed in Chapter 11.

30. M.B.C.A. § 8.25(e) (1).

31. M.B.C.A. § 6.02. Characteristics of corporate stock are discussed fully in Chapter 9.

32. M.B.C.A. § 6.31.

33. M.B.C.A. § 8.41.

34. M.B.C.A. § 8.40.

35. See the sample bylaws, Exhibit I–10 in Appendix I.

36. These documents are required to accomplish extraordinary corporate actions and are discussed in Chapter 15.

37. M.B.C.A. § 8.43(b).

38. See "Employment Agreements" in Chapter 12; M.B.C.A. § 8.44.

39. M.B.C.A. § 8.43(a).

40. M.B.C.A. § 8.42.

41. These characteristics are discussed in "Common Stock Rights" and "Preferred Stock Rights" in Chapter 9.

42. M.B.C.A. §§ 1.40(21) and 7.23.

43. Cumulative voting is discussed in detail in "Shareholder Business and Vote Required" in Chapter 10.

44. E.g., Illinois, Ill. Const. Transition Schedule § 8.

45. E.g., Texas, Tex. Stat. Ann. § 2.29.

46. E.g., 8 Del. Code Ann. § 214.

47. M.B.C.A. § 7.28.

48. The procedure for accomplishing amendments to the articles is more fully explored in "Amendment of the Articles of Incorporation" in Chapter 15.

49. M.B.C.A. § 16.02.

50. E.g., Minnesota Minn. Stat. Ann. § 302A-413.

51. E.g., Delaware, 8 Del. Code Ann. § 102(b) (3).

52. M.B.C.A. § 6.30.

53. Dividend distributions are discussed in Chapter 11; distributions in dissolution are considered in Chapter 15.

54. R. Deer, The Lawyers Basic Corporate Practice Manual § 1.02 (1971).

55. See "Limited Liability Companies—Continuity of Existence and Dissolution and Taxation of a Limited Liability Company" in Chapter 5.

56. Precise elements and the procedure for dissolution are discussed in Chapter 15.

57. E.g., Minnesota, Minn. Stat. Ann. § 302A-751.

58. M.B.C.A. § 14.30.

59. See "Taxation of a Sole Proprietor" in Chapter 2; "Tax Considerations of a General Partnership" in Chapter 3; and "Taxation of a Limited Liability Company" in Chapter 5.

60. Internal Revenue Code (hereafter I.R.C.) of 1986, 26 U.S.C.A. § 531.

61. I.R.C. of 1986, 26 U.S.C.A. §§ 1361–1379.

62. Close corporations are specifically discussed in "Close Corporations" in Chapter 7.

63. I.R.C. of 1986, 26 U.S.C.A. § 1362(b).

64. I.R.C. of 1986, 26 U.S.C.A. § 1244(c) (3).

65. I.R.C. of 1986, 26 U.S.C.A. § 1244(c) (3).

66. I.R.C. of 1986, 26 U.S.C.A. § 1244(c) (1) (C).

67. I.R.C. of 1986, 26 U.S.C.A. § 1202.

68. See Chapter 12 for a full discussion of incentive benefit plans.

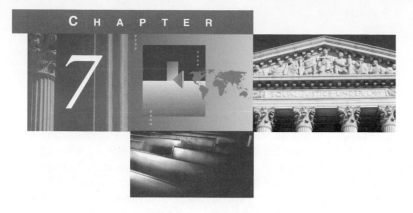

VARIATIONS ON THE CORPORATE FORM

The corporate model described in the previous chapter is typical of most American business corporations. Some important variations on the typical corporate model are used to raise capital (as in public corporations), to ensure control for the shareholders (as in close corporations), and to practice professional services (as in professional corporations). These various corporate forms require the lawyer and paralegal to be familiar with significant additional statutory and practical rules, legal techniques, and documentation.

PUBLIC CORPORATIONS

A corporation that has sold its shares to investors through public stock markets is referred to as a **public corporation**. Although thousands of corporations are formed annually throughout the United States, only a few of these corporations will ever sell shares to the public and become public corporations. Nevertheless, public corporations are the most prominent and well-known corporations in the world. The activities of these corporations are reviewed regularly by the press, and governmental regulations require complete disclosure of all their business activities and financial information.

The public corporation is the epitome of capitalism. Promoters develop an idea for a new business venture and form a corporation to develop the business opportunity. After the necessary initial capital is invested by the founders, also called the first **inside shareholders**, the corporation begins the research and development of the business or product and attracts the interest of business analysts and investment bankers who recognize the opportunity to attract a broad base of investors for a business of this type. When the corporation's stock is offered though public markets, any person can buy that stock for the public offering price of a few dollars per share. Small and large investors who purchase shares of a public corporation wisely can buy the stock at a low price and sell the stock at a higher price to make a profit. The corporation has the benefit of a substantial amount of capital through the public investment in its stock, and the investor has an opportunity to make a profit without having to invest large sums of capital and wait long periods of time for the business to develop, become profitable, and distribute eventually the fruits of its business. The purchase and sale of public corporation shares can make and break fortunes. Most private individuals own shares of publicly traded corporations, and the economic impact of publicly traded corporations on the U.S. economy is significant.

It should be noted that the sale of securities to the public does not only apply to stock in corporations, although the corporate form is the most adaptable business organization to widespread ownership of securities. Limited partnerships with public investors are used frequently in the telecommunications business to develop television and communication equipment, and publicly held real estate investment trusts are prolific during economic cycles in which real estate investments are profitable. Other entities, such as a limited liability company, are best used for privately owned businesses that can use the flexibility of this business form to the best advantage.

Any corporation can become a public corporation if its directors and shareholders decide to issue shares to the public through a publicly traded market and if the company business is sufficiently unique or innovative to attract investors. Corporations that issue their securities to the public are subject to substantial federal and state governmental regulation concerning the registration of the offering and sale of securities and public disclosure that must be made to the investors who are willing to risk their money by investing in the stocks or bonds of the corporation.

As we will see in Chapter 9, the securities of a corporation include shares of stock (equity securities) and loans to the corporation (debt securities or bonds).[1] If these securities are offered, sold, or delivered to interstate commerce, such as publicly traded markets, mail, telephone calls, the Internet or other multistate communications, these investment transactions are a **public offering** that is regulated under the Securities Act of 1933[2] and the regulations interpreting the statute adopted by the Securities and Exchange Commission (SEC). In addition, publicly traded securities are regulated by state securities commissioners under state securities laws and regulations. If the sale of securities is offered only to residents within a particular state, without using interstate commerce, only the regulations in the state in which such an offering is made would apply to an **intrastate offering**. The time and effort of management, lawyers, and accountants required to comply with the governmental regulations associated with a public offering of securities are enormous, and the costs are substantial. These efforts and costs are justified by the economic advantages of being a public corporation. The advantages of going public include access to a much broader base of available capital, since the sale of shares to the public injects substantial amounts of money into the business and, if the corporation becomes popular among investors in public markets, the value of the securities will increase through market forces, rather than simply the accumulation of corporate assets. Particularly in times of successful market trading, investors are anxious to invest in companies with unique and promising products and services, and the investment markets provide substantial liquidity for investors who can buy and sell their shares on a daily basis. These securities are almost like currency; they can be purchased and sold through brokerage houses and can be used as valuable collateral for loans. In smaller, nonpublic corporations, the shareholders rarely have a market for their shares until the company itself is sold. Another advantage of a publicly held corporation is the ability to attract highly qualified management personnel, who tend to apply their talents in public companies because compensation packages involving public stock are offered to them. For example, executive incentive compensation in a public corporation usually includes options to purchase the corporation's public shares at a price that is lower than the market value of the stock at the time the option is exercised.

On the other hand, the decision to go public may have a significant impact on existing shareholders. The shareholders who were involved in the organization of the corporation will usually lose voting control when corporation shares are sold to the public. The registration process required to sell the shares in a public market itself is very costly. In addition, the disclosure and communication obligations for the corporation as required under federal and state law to keep public shareholders fully informed about the activities of the corporation are extensive and expensive. Finally, since the value of the corporation's shares will depend upon the price investors are willing to pay for them through the markets, the value of the shares does not necessarily represent the true value of the company. The market may control the success or failure of the investment (and thereby the success or failure of the company) regardless of how effectively management operated the business. While the value of a share of stock depends upon the profitability or future prospects of the corporation, its market price depends upon how much other people are willing to pay for it based upon their evaluation of these prospects.[3]

The Process of Becoming a Public Corporation

All public corporations are formed as corporations under state statutes like any other corporation. If the directors and principal shareholders of the corporation, through the advice of their professional advisors, determine that additional capital is available and desired through public markets, the corporation will begin to negotiate with investment bankers concerning the market potential and terms and conditions of an **initial public offering**, commonly referred to as an "IPO."

Corporations in earlier days sold securities to agents who sold them to investors on a commission basis. These agents eventually matured into an industry of investment banker businesses and brokerage houses that offer various services to corporations to reach the public capital markets, including development of a plan and method to be pursued to raise the money, the assumption by the investment bankers of some of the risks of the offering, and the distribution of the securities to the shareholders. These investment bankers are known as **underwriters**. They enter into underwriting agreements with the corporation to provide for various services of the underwriter and terms that will apply to the public offering. Underwriters often form an underwriting group that is sometimes called a **pool** or **syndicate** to share the underwriting risk and to more widely distribute the shares to the investing public. Usually one investment banking firm is the **manager** who will be responsible for the supervision of compliance with the registration requirements and will primarily distribute the securities to investors. The other firms are called **selected dealers** and they are responsible for selling the securities to their customers to broaden the distribution and ownership of the securities.

The terms of the underwriting relationship are defined by an underwriting agreement that may take many forms. Usually, underwriters will offer securities to the public on either a firm commitment or a best-efforts basis. The **firm commitment** transaction involves the purchase by the managing underwriter of all shares to be sold to the public by the corporation. The underwriter will then resell these securities to the investors. This is actually a purchase and sale arrangement by which the underwriter assumes the entire risk for placement of the stock. Since the underwriter has purchased the securities, the underwriter must be able to sell the securities to investors for at least as much as the underwriter has paid. In addition to other negotiated fees and expenses, the underwriter can make a profit on the difference between the amount the underwriter pays the corporation for the securities and the amount the underwriter receives when the securities are resold to an investor. The **best-efforts** transaction involves the underwriter's agreement to use its best efforts to sell the securities as an agent for the corporation. If investors purchase the securities, the corporation will receive the funds; if investors are not interested in the shares, the offering is terminated. In a best-efforts transaction, the corporation assumes the risk that the offering will not be successful.

The managing underwriter, in turn, enters into selected dealer or selling agreements with other investment bankers and brokerage companies who will either buy the securities from the corporation or the managing underwriter on a firm commitment basis or use their best efforts to market the securities to their customers.

Trading of Securities

The securities of public corporations are "traded" through purchases and sales from one investor to another in a market for the securities. The facilities through which securities are traded are called a **stock exchange**, or the "market." An exchange is defined by law to be "an organization, association or group of persons . . . which constitutes, maintains or provides a market place or facilities for bringing together purchasers and sellers of securities . . . and includes the market place and the market facilities maintained by such exchange."[4] The largest securities market in the United States is trading in bonds (or debt securities) issued by federal and state governments and large corporations. The bond markets primarily attract institutional investors such as banks and insurance companies. The most well-known securities markets are markets for common stocks. The New York Stock Exchange and the American Stock Exchange are well-known trading facilities for the purchase and sale of public shares. These businesses operate physical facilities in which all orders for purchase and sale of the securities offered by the exchange are directed and accomplished. These exchanges adopt their own rules to impose qualification requirements for companies to be listed on the exchange so that their securities can be traded there. In addition, strict rules are enforced to ensure standardization of stock certificates, amounts of commissions to be charged in purchase and sale transactions, and other requirements that ensure the rapid and consistent flow of securities as they are purchased and sold through the exchange. Securities that are traded on an exchange can only be traded by persons who are admitted as members of the exchange, and a particular public corporation's securities are sold by a specialist who acts as a dealer for that particular security. Any person wishing to buy the securities must purchase them through the specialist.

The **over-the-counter** market is much less structured and involves the trading of securities through computer communications among brokers buying and selling stock. Any number of investment bankers may act as "dealers" or "market makers" in a particular stock and may deal directly with the investors. If the underwriting firm has been involved as a manager or selected dealer in the offering of the securities to the public, it usually also acts as a dealer or market maker from whom those securities are available to other investors who want to purchase them after the initial public offering is sold. If an investor places an order through a broker who is not a dealer in the stock, the broker will find another broker who is and will purchase the shares for the investor from that dealer/broker. The National Association of Securities Dealers Automatic Quotation system (NASDAQ) reports the market prices of many securities traded over-the-counter, and brokers use other quotation systems, such as the Internet Trading System, the National Securities Trading System, and reports that are referred to as *pink sheets* by the brokerage industry to track the most current purchase (or "bid") and sale (or "ask") price of the securities. The access to public stock markets provided through the Internet has substantially increased the volume of trading and the number of investors. The "day-trader," an investor who buys his or her own stocks in the morning and sells them in the afternoon, has emerged during the past decade as a force in the public markets. Even after-hours market purchases and sales are available with Internet access and the appropriate accounts, and overnight quotations can be as meaningful as the regular market movement during the day. In summary, the investors who are participating in the markets in publicly traded stocks have increased substantially over the years, and have had a significant impact on the values of corporations that have their stocks available in such markets.

Regulation of Securities

The purchase and sale of securities among public investors are regulated by both federal and state laws that were enacted primarily as a response to the tragic decline in public securities values created by the Great Depression. The Securities Act of 1933 and the Securities and Exchange Act of 1934, both administered by the Securities and Exchange Commission (SEC) that was established in 1934, are the principal federal statutes that govern these transactions.

The Securities Act of 1933 (the 1933 Act) deals mostly with the registration, sale, and initial distribution of securities by a corporation selling shares to the public. Under the 1933 Act, no security may be offered or sold through interstate commerce without compliance with the registration and disclosure requirements contained in the statute unless the security or the transaction in which the security is sold is exempt. Generally, the sale of a public corporation's securities to investors through an exchange will require the registration and disclosure specified in the 1933 Act.

The 1933 Act does exempt a number of types of securities from its registration requirements[5] and there are several exemptions for certain types of transactions in securities.[6] If neither the security nor the transaction is exempt, in order to sell its securities to the public, a corporation must register the shares under Section 5 of the 1933 Act. Section 5 requires the filing of a **registration statement** with the SEC before the securities may be sold to public investors.[7]

A registration statement is a disclosure describing all the information that might be necessary or desirable for a public investor to make an informed investment decision about the corporation. The registration statement has two parts: the **prospectus** and additional information. The prospectus must be furnished to every purchaser of the securities, and the additional information will be on file with the SEC for public inspection by anyone who cares to review the information. Usually the additional information will include all of the important corporate documents, such as the articles of incorporation, bylaws, and other important agreements among the corporation, its management, shareholders, underwriters, and persons and entities with which it does business.

The registration statement may be filed on one of many forms prescribed by the SEC. The basic form for registration is Form S-1, which is used in all public offerings for which no other specialized form is prescribed. (See Exhibit 7–1, Form S-1 Registration Statement under the Securities Act of 1933). Other registration forms are available for companies that have already registered with the SEC or companies undertaking specialized offerings, such as Form SB2, which can be used to publicly market shares of a "small business issuer which is defined as a company with annual revenues of less than $25,000,000."[8]

The registration statement is filed with the SEC with an appropriate fee, and the SEC staff begins to review the registration statement soon after it is filed. Prior to filing the registration statement, the corporation will have undertaken preliminary negotiations to enter into the underwriting agreement with the managing underwriter concerning the terms of the offering and to define the selected dealer selling group. Following the filing of the registration statement and before the SEC has completed its review of the information (called the **waiting period**) the corporation or the underwriters can make oral offers to sell the securities but cannot make any written confirmations of sales. During the waiting period, copies of a preliminary prospectus can be distributed. This preliminary prospectus is called a **red herring** because of the red ink marginal notation on its cover that indicates it is only preliminary, has not yet been approved by the SEC, and does not yet contain the price of the securities. (See Exhibit 7–2, Preliminary Prospectus.) Also during the waiting period, **tombstone ads** describing the number of shares, the company offering the securities, the price and the selling group can be printed to publicize the forthcoming sale of the public securities. (See Exhibit 7–3, Tombstone Ad.)

According to the 1933 Act, the registration statement automatically becomes effective 20 days after the complete registration statement is filed with the SEC.[9] When the registration statement becomes effective, the company is then authorized to sell its registered securities to public investors. The SEC can delay or suspend the effective date if it does not feel that the prospectus adequately discloses all the material information necessary about the company. In practice, lawyers and paralegals working on a registration statement file a registration with the SEC anticipating that the SEC staff will comment on the adequacy of the disclosure in the statement. The SEC does not approve or disapprove of the securities or whether they will be a good or bad investment, but it does determine whether the proposed prospectus discloses adequate material information necessary for a public investor to make an informed decision about whether to invest. The letters of comment from the SEC staff will recommend additional matters to be disclosed or expanded upon, and only after the additional disclosure has been added and approved will the SEC permit the registration statement to become effective and the sale of the securities to commence. In practice, lawyers and paralegals working on the registration statement normally wait until the last comments

Exhibit 7–1.

Form S-1 Registration
Statement under the
Securities Act of 1933

OMB APPROVAL	
OMB Number:	3235-0065
Expires:	February 28, 2006
Estimated average burden hours per response . . . 432.00	

UNITED STATES
SECURITIES AND EXCHANGE COMMISSION
Washington, D.C. 20549

FORM S-1

REGISTRATION STATEMENT UNDER THE SECURITIES ACT OF 1933

_____
(Exact name of registrant as specified in its charter)

_____
(State or other jurisdiction of incorporation or organization)

_____
(Primary Standard Industrial Classification Code Number)

_____
(I.R.S. Employer Identification Number)

_____
(Address, including zip code, and telephone number,
including area code, of registrantís principal executive offices)

_____
(Name, address, including zip code, and telephone number,
including area code, of agent for service)

_____
(Approximate date of commencement of proposed sale to the public)

If any of the securities being registered on this Form are to be offered on a delayed or continuous basis pursuant to Rule 415 under the Securities Act of 1933 check the following box: ☐

If this Form is filed to register additional securities for an offering pursuant to Rule 462(b) under the Securities Act, please check the following box and list the Securities Act registration statement number of the earlier effective registration statement for the same offering. ☐

If this Form is a post-effective amendment filed pursuant to Rule 462(c) under the Securities Act, check the following box and list the Securities Act registration statement number of the earlier effective registration statement for the same offering. ☐

If this Form is a post-effective amendment filed pursuant to Rule 462(d) under the Securities Act, check the following box and list the Securities Act registration statement number of the earlier effective registration statement for the same offering. ☐

Persons who are to respond to the collection of information contained in this form are not required to respond unless the form displays a currently valid OMB control number.

SEC 870 (10-03)

from the SEC staff have been received and responded to and, in consultation with management of the corporation and the managing underwriter, make a final "price amendment" to the registration statement. The price amendment states the actual price of the securities to be offered to the public; it is the last piece of information required by the registration statement. Twenty days after filing that amendment (or earlier if the SEC staff will permit) the registration can become effective. The final prospectus thus contains all of the information the SEC required to be disclosed about the company and the price of its securities to be offered to the public.

When the registration statement becomes effective, underwriters and dealers may sell these securities to any investor willing to purchase them. The final prospectus must be delivered contemporaneously with the investor's purchase of securities. Of course, any material changes in the status of the corporation during the period that the securities are being

Exhibit 7–2.

Preliminary Prospectus

Subject to completion, dated October 23

PROSPECTUS
dated

2,000,000 SHARES

COMMON STOCK

Of the 2,000,000 shares of Common Stock offered hereby, 1,600,000 shares are being issued and sold by Novoste Corporation ("Novoste" or the "Company") and 400,000 shares are being offered by certain shareholders of the Company (the "Selling Shareholders"). See "Principal and Selling Shareholders." The Company will not receive any proceeds from the shares being sold by the Selling Shareholders.

The Common Stock is traded on The Nasdaq National Market under the symbol "NOVT." On October 21, 1997, the last sale price of the Common Stock on The Nasdaq National Market was $18.625 per share. See "Price Range of Common Stock."

This Offering involves a high degree of risk and should be considered only by persons who can afford to lose their entire investment. See "Risk Factors" beginning on page 7 for a discussion of certain factors that should be considered by prospective investors.

THESE SECURITIES HAVE NOT BEEN APPROVED OR DISAPPROVED BY THE SECURITIES AND EXCHANGE COMMISSION OR ANY STATE SECURITIES COMMISSION NOR HAS THE SECURITIES AND EXCHANGE COMMISSION OR ANY STATE SECURITIES COMMISSION PASSED UPON THE ACCURACY OR ADEQUACY OF THIS PROSPECTUS. ANY REPRESENTATION TO THE CONTRARY IS A CRIMINAL OFFENSE.

	Price to Public	Underwriting Discount(1)	Proceeds to Company(2)	Proceeds to Selling Shareholders
Per Share	$	$	$	$
Total(3)	$	$	$	$

(1) The Company and the Selling Shareholders have agreed to indemnify the Underwriters against certain liabilities, including under the Securities Act of 1933. See "Underwriting."

(2) Before deducting offering expenses payable by the Company estimated at $350,000.

(3) The Company and two Selling Shareholders have granted the Underwriters a 30-day option to purchase up to an aggregate of 300,000 shares of Common Stock solely to cover over-allotments, if any, at the Price to Public less the Underwriting Discount. If the Underwriters exercise this option in full, the total Price to Public, Underwriting Discount, Proceeds to Company and Proceeds to Selling Shareholders will be $, $, $ and $, respectively. See "Underwriting."

The shares of Common Stock are offered by the Underwriters subject to prior sale when, as, and if delivered and accepted by the Underwriters and subject to their right to reject orders in whole or in part. It is expected that delivery of the certificates representing the shares of Common Stock will be made at the offices of Piper Jaffray Inc. in Minneapolis, Minnesota on or about

PIPER JAFFRAY INC.

COWEN & COMPANY

NATIONSBANC MONTGOMERY SECURITIES, INC.

sold to the public must be disclosed. A prospectus may be updated to reflect current information by filing a **sticker** amendment to the registration statement with the SEC. The sticker is attached to each final prospectus as it is delivered to an investor purchasing the securities.

After the initial public offering has been fully sold to the investors, further public disclosure is accomplished through compliance with the Securities and Exchange Act of 1934.[10]

Liability for Failure to Comply with Securities Act

In the registration process, persons who sign or contribute information for the registration statement have a duty to provide complete and accurate information or they will be liable under Section 11 of the 1933 Act for any damages resulting from a purchaser being

Exhibit 7–3.

Tombstone Ad

This announcement is neither an offer to sell nor a solicitation of an offer to buy and of these Securities.
The offer is only made by the Prospectus.

New Issue

MEDicalSONICS
The Key to Life

5,000,000 Shares

Common Stock

———

Price $9 Per Share

———

Copies of the Prospectus may be obtained in any State from only such of
the undersigned as may legally offer these Securities in compliance
with the securities laws of such State.

Bank Republic Michaels   **Underwriters Unique, Inc.**

Hambone & Whist   **Clammesst Inc.**   **Hover Albert Scott & Co.**

Raymond Johns & Associates, Inc.   **The Johnson-Johnson Company**

misled by an inadequate or incorrect registration statement.[11] Liability under Section 11 extends to

- any person who signed the registration statement;
- any person who is a director (or a person in a similar capacity) of the corporation at the time of filing the registration statement;
- any person who is named in the registration statement as a person about to become a director or a person performing similar functions;
- any professional person (accountant, engineer, appraiser, etc.) who has been named in the registration statement as having prepared or certified a portion of it; and
- any underwriter involved in the sale of the security.

This liability can be avoided by persons who can show that they have, after reasonable investigation, had reasonable grounds to believe and did believe the information in the registration statement to be true and accurate. In practice, lawyers, paralegals, and other professionals who are involved in the preparation of a registration statement review all records and information applicable to the corporation that are described or mentioned in the registration statement so as to be able to show that they had a reasonable basis to believe that the information contained in the registration statement was accurate. This very time-consuming and expensive process of reviewing all company records and information is known as a **due diligence** investigation; it is one of the reasons why the public offering of securities is so costly. The devotion of time and effort to review all of this information by persons billing their time at high hourly rates is extensive.

Any other fraudulent conduct in connection with securities transactions may result in lia-bility under Section 17 of the 1933 Act.[12] This section prohibits any fraudulent conduct in con-nection with the sale or an offer to sell securities and broadly covers any activity that may constitute fraud or failure to adequately disclose information other than or in addition to prob-lems with the registration statement.

Regulation After a Public Offering

After a corporation has registered a public offering and sold its shares to the public, the sec-ondary distribution of securities (where buyers and sellers purchase and sell the corporation's shares in the markets) is regulated by the Securities Exchange Act of 1934 (the 1934 Act).[13] This statute governs, among other things, the filing by registered companies of annual and pe-riodic reports with the SEC and with any stock exchange where the stock is being traded, reg-ulation of proxy solicitations for shareholder voting of registered securities, limitations on insider trading of securities of public corporations, and prohibition of fraud and manipulation in connection with the purchase and sale of registered securities. Generally, the 1934 Act pro-tects investors from fraud and other abuses that might affect the market value of their securi-ties. The 1934 Act also regulates the securities markets and brokers and dealers who trade shares in them.

Registration Requirements

Any company that has a class of securities traded on a national securities exchange must reg-ister with the SEC under Section 12 of the 1934 Act.[14] This is a different type of registration from the registration of an offering of securities by filing a registration statement under the 1933 Act. The latter is for the purpose of determining the adequacy of disclosure in connec-tion with the information distributed to potential investors who are being offered securities that are *about to be* publicly traded; the former is designed for periodic reporting of information concerning a corporation that has completed a public offering and its securities are being pub-licly traded. A corporation that is registered with the SEC under the 1934 Act would still need to file a registration statement with the SEC under the 1933 Act for a new public offering of its securities.

Each company that has registered with the SEC under Section 12 of the 1934 Act must file periodic and other reports with the SEC.[15] Such companies must also follow the rules for so-licitation of proxies from their shareholders for shareholder meetings.[16] The 1934 Act also pro-hibits insider trading by officers, directors, and shareholders owning more than ten percent of the shares of a corporation. These persons must report any purchase and sale of the shares of the company to the SEC and will be required to turn over to the corporation any profit earned by them from purchases and sales of the corporation's securities in a six-month period.[17]

Periodic Disclosure Requirements

The 1934 Act is designed to ensure that the investors who have purchased publicly traded se-curities have adequate disclosure of financial information and other material facts about a pub-lic corporation to make an informed investment decision of whether to buy, retain, or sell the securities. A corporation initially files a detailed registration statement when it first registers under the 1934 Act, and thereafter the corporation must file annual, quarterly, and current re-ports as the law and SEC regulations may require. These reports are an annual report on Form 10-K, a quarterly report on Form 10-Q, and current reports on Form 8-K for any month in which a significant material event may occur within the public corporation.

Annual Report (Form 10-K) The annual report of a public corporation is called a Form 10-K. (See Exhibit 7–4, Form 10-K.) This form must be filed with the SEC within 90 days after the end of the corporation's fiscal year. Most of the information required to be described in Form 10-K is the same as the information required in the original registration statement filed for the public of-fering under the 1933 Act. Form 10-K is expected to update and disclose the same type of infor-mation on a current basis. Much of the information in Form 10-K may be incorporated by

OMB APPROVAL	
OMB Number:	3235-0063
Expires:	July 31, 2006
Estimated average burden hours per response . . 2,1960.00	

UNITED STATES
SECURITIES AND EXCHANGE COMMISSION
Washington, D.C. 20549

(Mark One)   **FORM 10-K**

[ ] ANNUAL REPORT PURSUANT TO SECTION 13 OR 15(d) OF THE SECURITIES EXCHANGE ACT OF 1934

For the fiscal year ended_____

or

[ ] TRANSITION REPORT PURSUANT TO SECTION 13 OR 15(d) OF THE SECURITIES EXCHANGE ACT OF 1934

For the transition period from _____ to _____

Commission file number _____

_____
(Exact name of registrant as specified in its charter)

State or other jurisdiction of incorporation or organization	(I.R.S. Employer Identification No.)

_____
(Address of principal executive offices)   (Zip Code)

Registrant's telephone number, including area code _____

Securities registered pursuant to Section 12(b) of the Act:

Title of each class	Name of each exchange on which registered

Securities registered pursuant to section 12(g) of the Act:

_____
(Title of class)

_____
(Title of class)

Indicate by check mark whether the registrant (1) has filed all reports required to be filed by Section 13 or 15(d) of the Securities Exchange Act of 1934 during the preceding 12 months (or for such shorter period that the registrant was required to file such reports), and (2) has been subject to such filing requirements for the past 90 days.   ☐ Yes   ☐ No

Indicate by check mark if disclosure of delinquent filers pursuant to Item 405 of Regulation S-K (§ 229.405 of this chapter) is not contained herein, and will not be contained, to the best of registrant's knowledge, in definitive proxy or information statements incorporated by reference in Part III of this Form 10-K or any amendment to this Form 10-K.   ☐

Persons who respond to the collection of information contained in this form are not required to respond unless the form displays a currently valid OMB control number.

SEC 1673 (8-03)

reference to the corporation's annual report to its shareholders. Public corporations engage public relations and marketing personnel to present favorably the company's image to its shareholders in the annual report. Of course, the financial and other factual information contained in the annual report is also designed to advise shareholders about the current status of the company. To the extent that the annual report includes the information required to be presented in Form 10-K, the corporation can simply reference the material in the annual report in its report to the SEC.

Form 10-K requires a report of any significant changes that may have occurred in the company during the previous fiscal year and a summary of the operations of the company for the previous five years (or since the company was formed if less than five years). The report also identifies the principal shareholders of the corporation and transactions involving the purchase or sale of significant percentages of the corporation's securities.

Exhibit 7–5.

Form 10-Q

OMB APPROVAL	
OMB Number:	3235-0070
Expires:	March 31, 2006
Estimated average burden hours per response . . . 192.00	

**UNITED STATES
SECURITIES AND EXCHANGE COMMISSION
Washington, D.C. 20549**

FORM 10-Q

(Mark One)

[ ] QUARTERLY REPORT PURSUANT TO SECTION 13 OR 15(d) OF THE SECURITIES EXCHANGE ACT OF 1934

For the quarterly period ended _____

or

[ ] TRANSITION REPORT PURSUANT TO SECTION 13 OR 15(d) OF THE SECURITIES EXCHANGE ACT OF 1934

For the transition period from _____ to_____

Commission File Number: _____

_____
(Exact name of registrant as specified in its charter)

_____
(State or other jurisdiction of incorporation or organization)   (I.R.S. Employer Identification No.)

_____
(Address of principal executive offices)   (Zip Code)

_____
(Registrant's telephone number, including area code)

_____
(Former name, former address and former fiscal year, if changed since last report)

Indicate by check mark whether the registrant (1) has filed all reports required to be filed by Section 13 or 15(d) of the Securities Exchange Act of 1934 during the preceding 12 months (or for such shorter period that the registrant was required to file such reports), and (2) has been subject to such filing requirements for the past 90 days.   ☐ Yes ☐ No

Indicate by check mark whether the registrant is an accelerated filer (as defined in Rule 12b-2 of the Exchange Act).   ☐ Yes ☐ No

APPLICABLE ONLY TO ISSUERS INVOLVED IN BANKRUPTCY
PROCEEDINGS DURING THE PRECEDING FIVE YEARS:

Indicate by check mark whether the registrant has filed all documents and reports required to be filed by Sections 12, 13 or 15(d) of the Securities Exchange Act of 1934 subsequent to the distribution of securities under a plan confirmed by a court.   ☐ Yes ☐ No

SEC 1296 (08-03)   **Potential persons who are to respond to the collection of information contained in this form are not required to respond unless the form displays a currently valid OMB control number.**

4

Many corporations use their own internal personnel who are familiar with the financial and business aspects of the business to prepare Form 10-K. The corporation's lawyers, paralegals, and accountants conduct a final review of the form to ensure compliance with the disclosure requirements of the statute. The form must be signed by an authorized person on behalf of the corporation, by its principal executive, by financial and accounting officers, and by a majority of the board of directors. The corporation and its personnel will be subject to civil and criminal sanctions if the information reported is inaccurate or otherwise misleading.[18]

Quarterly Report (Form 10-Q) The quarterly report of a public corporation is called Form 10-Q. This report contains primarily financial information regarding the corporation, including its shareholder equity positions and whether the corporation has sold any other securities during the reporting period. To the extent that the information required in a Form 10-Q is contained in a company-produced quarterly report to its shareholders, the quarterly report can be incorporated by reference. At the end of the corporation's fiscal year, the fourth quarter report is included in

Form 8-K

UNITED STATES
SECURITIES AND EXCHANGE COMMISSION
Washington, D.C. 20549

FORM 8-K

CURRENT REPORT
Pursuant to Section 13 OR 15(d) of The Securities Exchange Act of 1934

Date of Report (Date of earliest event reported) _____

_____

(Exact name of registrant as specified in its charter)

| (State or other jurisdiction | (Commission | (IRS Employer |
| of incorporation) | File Number) | Identification No.) |

_____

(Address of principal executive offices)   (Zip Code)

Registrant's telephone number, including area code _____

_____

(Former name or former address, if changed since last report.)

GENERAL INSTRUCTIONS

A. Rule as to Use of Form 8-K.

Form 8-K shall be used for current reports under Section 13 or 15(d) of the Securities Exchange Act of 1934, filed pursuant to Rule 13a-11 or Rule 15d-11 and for reports of nonpublic information required to be disclosed by Regulation FD (17 CFR 243.100 and 243.101).

B. Events to be Reported and Time for Filing of Reports.

1. A report on this form is required to be filed upon the occurrence of any one or more of the events specified in Items 1-4, 6 and 10 of this form. A report of an event specified in Items 1-3 is to be filed within 15 calendar days after the occurrence of the event. A report of an event specified in Item 4, 6 or 10 is to be filed within 5 business days after the occurrence of the event; if the event occurs on a Saturday, Sunday, or holiday on which the Commission is not open for business then the 5 business day period shall begin to run and include the first business day thereafter. A report on this form pursuant to Item 8 is required to be filed within 15 calendar days after the date on which the registrant makes the determination to use a fiscal year end different from that used in its most recent filing with the Commission. A registrant either furnishing a report on this form under Item 9 or electing to file a report on this form under Item 5 solely to satisfy its obligations under Regulation FD (17 CFR 243.100 and 243.101) must furnish such report or make such filing in accordance with the requirements of Rule 100(a) of Regulation FD (17 CFR 243.100(a)). A report on this form pursuant to Item 11 is required to be filed not later than the date prescribed for transmission of the notice to directors and executive officers required by Rule 104(b)(2) of Regulation BTR (§245.104(b)(2) of this chapter).

SEC 873 (6-03)   **Potential persons who are to respond to the collection of information contained in this form are not required to respond unless the form displays a currently valid OMB control number.**   1 of 8

Form 10-K. In the three prior quarters during the year, Form 10-Q must be filed with the SEC within 45 days of the close of the corporation's fiscal quarter. (See Exhibit 7–5, Form 10-Q.)

Current Reports (Form 8-K) If any material or significant event occurs within the business or operations of a public corporation, then the corporation must file Form 8-K with the SEC within ten days after the close of the month in which such a significant event occurred. The types of events that must be reported on this form include changes in control of the company, purchases or sales of a substantial percentage of the company's assets outside of the ordinary course of business, significant legal proceedings, changes in any of the rights of the security holders, a material default under any promissory notes or senior equity securities (such as not paying dividends on a preferred stock), increases and decreases in outstanding shares, and the issuance or grant of a substantial number of options to purchase the corporation's securities. This report is designed to alert public shareholders quickly if there are events occurring within the company that may have an effect on the value of their securities. (See Exhibit 7–6, Form 8-K.)

Proxy Regulation

Public corporations that are registered under the 1934 Act are prohibited from soliciting proxies from their shareholders for shareholder meetings unless they comply with the statute and regulations concerning proxy disclosure.[19] The SEC enforces detailed regulations that describe the form of the proxy and the information that must be delivered to the shareholders prior to the meeting. Before every meeting of the shareholders, the corporation must furnish a **proxy statement** containing the information specified in Schedule 14(A) of the 1934 Act regulations, together with the form of the proxy upon which the security holder can state his or her approval or disapproval of each proposal to be presented at a meeting.

Publicly traded securities are often held by a shareholder in his or her account with a brokerage company or a bank. In such cases, the brokerage company is actually the registered owner of the securities so the brokerage company can freely buy and sell the shares upon instructions from its various customers. The shareholder/customer owns the right to the value of his or her proportion of the total shares registered in the name of the brokerage company through the specific account maintained by the broker. This is called holding shares in **street name**. The securities are registered in the broker's name but the shareholder is the **beneficial owner**. The corporation has the obligation to ensure that the proxy statement reaches its shareholders. Thus, the corporation must distribute enough copies of the proxy statement to the brokerage companies and banks so that the proxy statement can be further distributed to the beneficial owners, the public investors.

If the matters to be considered at the meeting for which the proxy is being solicited simply involve typical annual shareholder meeting issues, such as the election of directors and approval of accountants, the proxy statement and the form of proxy must be filed with the SEC at the time they are first mailed to the security holders. These are routine matters and the SEC is not likely to find any fault with the factual disclosures relating to these issues. If any other matters are to be considered at the meeting, such as an amendment to the articles of incorporation, approval of executive compensation plans, or a material change in the corporation's business direction, the proxy statement and form of proxy must be filed with the SEC 10 days before being mailed to security holders, permitting the review of the proxy statement by the SEC staff to determine the adequacy of the disclosures about these issues. Again, the SEC staff does not judge the merit of the issues the security holders will be voting upon but determines whether the disclosure concerning those issues will allow the shareholders to make an informed decision about how to vote on them.

If the proxies are being solicited for an annual meeting for the election of directors, the proxy statement must include comparative financial statements of the corporation. This way the shareholders can assess whether the directors they are electing are managing the company properly and profitably.

The form of proxy must indicate in bold face type whether the proxy is being solicited on behalf of management or on behalf of other persons who want the shareholders to vote a particular issue at a meeting. The form must also indicate clearly whether a particular matter has been proposed by management or proposed by the shareholders. The form has a place for a date and must provide a place for the shareholder to approve or disapprove the action. When a board of directors is being elected at the meeting, the proxy states the names of the nominees and provides for the shareholder to vote or withhold a vote for each nominee. The proxy usually also provides discretionary authority for any other matters that may be considered at the meeting and states that a corporate officer, such as the corporate secretary, is authorized to cast the shareholder's vote for those matters in the officer's discretion. (See Exhibit 7–7, Proxy Form.)

Shareholders are allowed to propose issues to be considered and voted upon at a shareholder meeting, and if a shareholder gives timely notice to corporate management of an intention to present a proposal at a meeting, the management must include the proposal with the shareholder's short statement (not more than 500 words) concerning the proposal in the proxy statement. Shareholders often propose changes to a public corporation's policies concerning the environment, civil rights, and, in such industries as the tobacco and drug industries, judgmental resolutions that may

Exhibit 7–7.

Proxy Form

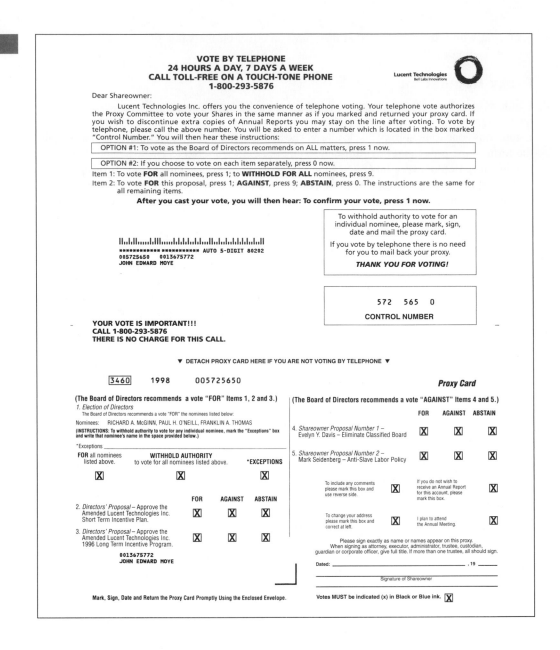

directly affect the company's business. The rules concerning the shareholder's proposals have caused significant controversy since management generally prefers not to be bothered with such proposals.[20]

Distribution of a misleading proxy statement may cause several liability or criminal penalties to be invoked under the 1934 Act.[21]

Insider Trading Provisions

Each officer and director of a public corporation and each owner of more than ten percent of any class of stock of a public corporation are subject to the rules against insider trading of the corporation's securities in Section 16 of the 1934 Act.[22]

Such officers, directors, and shareholders must file an initial report with the SEC showing their security holdings in the public corporation. They must also then file a report in each month in which they buy or sell any securities in their public corporation. Any profits realized by such a person in connection with the purchase and sale or sale and purchase of the corporation's securities within a six-month period may be recovered by the corporation. Profits made by these persons during the six month period are commonly called **short-swing**

profits. This rigid rule discourages corporate insiders from taking advantage of their access to inside information about the activities of the corporation to make a profit by buying and selling the corporation's securities. For example, if an officer of a public corporation has just received a report that the corporation's oil exploration activities have discovered a significant oil deposit that the corporation will be able to exploit profitably, it is not fair to the public shareholders who do not have that information if the officer purchases the corporation's stock before the information is released to the public. Similarly, an officer who learns that the corporation is about to suffer substantial liability for some transgression that has not yet been made public should not be able to sell his or her shares of the corporation's stock before the stock price plummets.

Since a public corporation's securities are traded on an exchange, the insider who takes advantage of inside information can buy or sell the securities through a broker transaction. In these cases, it is not possible to determine who bought the securities sold by the insider or who sold the securities purchased by the insider. Thus, it is not possible to provide for a direct recovery by the investor injured when an insider takes advantage of inside information in a public corporation. Similarly, it is very difficult to prove that an insider actually was acting upon inside information in making an investment decision. Members of corporate management should be encouraged to buy shares of their corporation's stock, and significant shareholders are expected to trade the shares as a matter of their own investment objectives. The 1934 Act approaches the potentially abusive insider transaction simply by assuming that an insider who makes a profit on the corporation's securities in a six-month period must have been acting on some information that gave the insider an advantage. It does not matter whether the insider actually acted upon material information that would make a difference to the market; the rule is simply applied to take away the insider's profits if the profit is made during a six-month period. The law simply destroys the incentive for insiders to manipulate their holdings of the corporation's securities with inside information.

It should also be noted that Section 16 of the 1934 Act is designed to prevent the unfair use of inside information, but it does not reach all potential abuses. It only allows recovery of specific amounts from a specific combination of transactions by specified individuals during the specified six-month period. The SEC requires that insiders file reports disclosing their transactions, but it is up to the corporation to recover the profits from its officers, directors, or shareholders.

Other Antifraud Provisions

As one would imagine, whenever investor funds are available to capitalize a corporation, unscrupulous people have devised all types of schemes to encourage investors to part with their money. The federal and state statutory and regulatory framework deals with this problem by placing civil and criminal penalties in the way of people who mislead the public about investments. The most important and far-reaching antifraud rule is contained in the 1934 Act. Thousands of pages of cases and text have been written concerning SEC Rule 10(b)5, promulgated under the authority of Section 10(b) of the 1934 Act. This rule makes unlawful any deceptive or manipulative device or contrivance, including fraud or deceit in connection with the purchase or sale of any security whether or not listed on an exchange, in interstate commerce, through the mails, or through a national securities exchange facility.

Most 10(b)5 violations involve an untrue statement of material fact or an omission to state a material fact necessary to make the statements made, in the light of the circumstances under which they were made, not misleading in connection with the purchase and sale of any security.[23] The broad application of the rule reaches all types of frauds. If a promoter lies to an investor about the prospects of an investment in a company, the rule would be violated. Similarly, telling an investor that the company has a new product with great promise of profitability, but omitting to disclose that the product has been patented by another company, which has not granted a license for its use, would be prohibited by the rule. The rule also would cover transactions by persons who are aware of material information about a company that might enhance or diminish the value of its securities and who fail to disclose such information when buying or selling its securities. It could also be a violation of Rule 10(b)5 to misstate information in a registration statement filed under the 1933 Act or in a proxy statement filed under the 1934 Act.

Rule 10(b)5 and similar antifraud provisions in state securities laws are the regulatory guardians of truthful and complete disclosure to investors who invest in a company's securities.

Regulation of Professional Advisors to Public Companies

In recent years, public companies have become ever more obsessed with reporting successful operations and earnings in order to satisfy the investors who demand high returns on their investments. Public pressure for high profits and expansion caused directors and officers to search for ways to improve their company's currency in the markets, even if it meant using accounting and other financial tricks to impress brokers and their investors. Enron Corporation used limited partnerships to handle some of its more risky or less profitable operations, in order to keep those results off of its publicly filed financial statements. Other large companies have been accused of recording transactions that did not occur and hiding liabilities and expenses in subsidiary entities so they would not depress the market price of the stock. In a reaction to these market abuses, the federal government adopted the Sarbanes-Oxley Act of 2002 to regulate the directors and officers of these corporations who have actively caused a fraud on the markets, but more importantly, the law also extends to the accountants and lawyers advising the public corporations who are guilty of such activities.[24] Generally, the statute requires that professional advisors who sense that their clients are pursuing such illegal or improper activities will have a duty to disclose this information to the Securities and Exchange Commission, as well as to the supervisors to whom the allegedly guilty management persons report. In summary, the statute creates a mandatory "whistle-blowing" disclosure whenever a professional advisor, including a lawyer or paralegal, is involved in a situation that could potentially violate the securities laws.

State Securities Regulation

While the federal securities regulation of public corporations is most widely used to register and sell securities to the public and regulate transactions in securities, its application results from the fact that most such transactions occur in interstate commerce. Each state also has statutory and regulatory authority over securities transactions that occur within its borders. In the case of an intrastate offering, in which securities are purchased and sold only within the boundaries of a particular state, the state regulations alone may govern the offering of the securities, since the transaction is exempt under federal law.

States have been regulating securities transactions long before the 1933 Act and 1934 Act were ever adopted. The state statutes and rules are commonly referred to as **blue-sky laws**. The origin of the phrase "blue sky" has been variously attributed. In folklore, the phrase originated on the floor of the Kansas legislature when a state legislator was proposing an antifraud law to "keep intruders from coming to Kansas to sell our citizens a piece of the blue sky." A Supreme Court case also used the term in ruling against "speculative schemes which have no more basis than so many feet of blue sky."[25]

The state regulatory scheme for public corporation securities is compatible with the federal regulations. The state laws require registration of securities before they may be sold to public investors within the state, but in most cases, registration with the SEC satisfies the state requirements for registration. When a public offering is registered with the SEC, the offering may be simultaneously registered with applicable states in which the securities will be offered and sold. Depending upon the operating history of the corporation offering the securities, the registration may occur at the state level through **registration by filing** (for corporations that have been operating in the United States for at least three years, are registered under the 1934 Act with the SEC, and have minimum net worth and trading volume requirements) or **registration by coordination** (for other companies that are registering with the SEC but have not registered under the 1934 Act and may not meet the net worth and trading requirements). In each case, the corporation offering its securities files the statements required by the state laws and regulations with the applicable state securities commission, and the filing includes the registration materials filed with the SEC as the necessary disclosure to satisfy state laws. If a corporation were undertaking a purely intrastate offering within the boundaries of a particular state, its securities would be registered at the state level using **registration by qualification**, a procedure substantially similar to registration under the 1933 Act, but the filing and the disclosure evaluation occurs only at the state level.

State statutes also have antifraud provisions to prevent securities fraud. State statutes will be applicable to any securities transactions within a state. Thus, the sale of securities of a New York company to a resident of Georgia will be subject to Georgia securities laws. Similarly, the New York laws will apply since the company selling the securities is located there. And, of course, since the transaction between New York and Georgia will occur in interstate commerce, the 1933 Act, the 1934 Act, and federal regulations will apply as well.

CLOSE CORPORATIONS

Corporations whose shares are not traded on an exchange and are owned by a small group of shareholders are called **close corporations**. The shareholders of a close corporation frequently are related closely by blood or at least by friendship. In most jurisdictions, these corporations are distinguishable from other business corporations only in that their share ownership is restricted to a select few persons who are intimately involved with the business and who operate the corporation with substantial shareholder participation. A significant characteristic of the close corporation is that the shareholders actively participate in the management of the business. Thus, unlike a large, publicly held corporation, the close corporation has a mixture of management and ownership, and this unique relationship among the shareholders usually results in a guarded interest in maintaining ownership control through internal shareholder agreements and restrictions on the transfer of equity securities. These corporate objectives accurately suggest that the operation of a close corporation resembles the operation of a partnership or a member-managed limited liability company. An examination of any close corporation should reveal a person or group of persons who might as well have been a sole proprietor or partners in a partnership, but instead selected the corporate form for its limited liability and tax advantages. The volume of business or the number of employees has nothing to do with whether a corporation might be a close corporation. It is simply a matter of whether the shareholders desire to retain control of the corporation and participate in the management of its business. Some prominent corporations, such as Ford Motor Company and Hallmark Corporation, were once successfully operated as close corporations.

The attorney's greatest challenge in the formation and operation of a close corporation is the drafting of the various agreements among shareholders that are designed to perpetuate management and ownership control through voting power and share transfer restrictions. These intricate agreements are considered in detail in a later chapter.[26] For now, the primary concern is the manner in which the structure and operation of close corporations differ from those of other corporations.

Many jurisdictions have no separate close corporation statute and require that close corporations be formed and operated under the normal corporation code. In these states, any desired informality and owner management must be achieved by procedures or agreements that comply with the normal statutory requirements. The modern trend toward permissiveness in corporate statutes, however, has provided the close corporation with statutory authority for the desired flexibility and informality. For example, formal shareholder meetings may be avoided under section 7.04 of the Model Business Corporation Act. Instead, action by shareholders may be taken without a meeting if all shareholders entitled to vote at the meeting sign a written consent to the action. To enable the shareholders of a close corporation to maintain tight personal control over corporate activities, section 7.25 of the act permits greater-than-normal voting requirements for shareholder action to be drafted into the articles of incorporation. If the statute normally permitted shareholder action by the vote of the majority, the articles could specify a two-thirds, three-fourths, or even unanimous voting requirement to increase individual control. The act further authorizes an important adjustment in management functions for the close corporation by providing that a corporation with fifty or fewer shareholders may provide in its articles of incorporation the persons who will perform the duties of a board of directors, and may thereby limit the authority of a board of directors or even dispense with the board of directors completely.[27] Shareholder management authority, therefore, may be specified in the articles of incorporation to the extent desired by corporate personnel. Some states, notably New York and North Carolina, allow shareholder agreements to impinge on management functions that are usually reserved to the board of directors. Thus, persons seeking the control desired in a close corporation and use of close corporation procedures may be accommodated under several modern corporate statutes that permit flexibility in operation and control of corporations.

A few jurisdictions have adopted more sophisticated statutory authority for close corporations by adding in the regular corporation statute separate sections specifically directed to the unique operations of close corporations.[28] Separate forms for formation of the close corporation are occasionally provided. (See Exhibit 7–8, Article of Incorporation for a Close Corporation.) The Model Business Corporation Act has adopted a close corporation supplement to provide for flexible rules for the operation of a close corporation. The purpose of these statutory provisions is to avoid the expense of drafting an elaborate set of specially tailored close corporation documents. The statutory provisions would be particularly useful for a small business that is likely to remain a closely held business, all or most of whose shareholders are active in the business; a corporation of professional practitioners, such as lawyers or accountants, whose shareholders wish to be taxed as a corporation but would prefer to operate internally as a partnership; or a wholly owned subsidiary corporation, which may be created and operated with a very simple corporate structure.

Definition

A statutory close corporation is a corporation whose articles of incorporation contain a statement that the corporation is intended to be a "statutory close corporation." A corporation having fifty or fewer shareholders may become a statutory close corporation by amending its articles to say that it is a statutory close corporation.[29] Some states define close corporations as those whose shares are not "publicly traded." This provision is concerned with a public offering, which requires registration under state and federal securities laws. Any corporation whose shares are not publicly traded is usually permitted to elect close corporation status under these statutes.[30]

Usually, a warning that the corporation is a close corporation must be placed on each share certificate. For example, the Model Business Corporation Act requires a legend on the stock certificate stating the following:

> The rights of shareholders in a statutory close corporation may differ materially from the rights of shareholders in other corporations. Copies of the articles of incorporation and bylaws, shareholder agreements, and other documents, any of which may restrict transfers and affect voting and other rights, may be obtained by a shareholder on written request to the corporation.[31]

Provisions Relating to Shares

One traditional feature of a close corporation is that the stock issued to shareholders is subject to certain restrictions on transfer. Restrictions can be established by a shareholder agreement (under the regular corporation law), or they may be automatic (as in a statutory close corporation). The Model Business Corporation Act provides that shareholders of a close corporation may transfer their shares to other shareholders, members of their immediate families, and persons who have been approved in writing by all the holders of the corporation's shares having general voting rights. In addition, transfers are permitted to executors and administrators when a shareholder dies, to trustees (as in the case of bankruptcy of a shareholder), in mergers or other business combinations where shares are normally exchanged, or as collateral for a loan.[32] Otherwise, any person who wishes to transfer shares in a close corporation must offer them first to the corporation. The corporation then has an opportunity to purchase the shares if the shareholders authorize the purchase. If the corporation purchases the shares, it may allocate

DEAN HELLER
Secretary of State

206 North Carson Street
Carson City, Nevada 89701-4201
(775) 684 5708

Articles of Incorporation of

_____
(Name of Close Corporation)

A Close Corporation
(PURSUANT TO NRS 78A)

(Name of corporation _MUST_ appear in the above heading)

Important: Read attached instructions before completing form.   ABOVE SPACE IS FOR OFFICE USE ONLY

1. **Name of Close Corporation:**

2. **Resident Agent Name and Street Address:** *(must be a Nevada address where process may be served)*

Name

Physical Street Address   City   **NEVADA**   Zip Code

Additional Mailing Address   City   State   Zip Code

3. **Shares:** *(no. of shares corporation authorized to issue)*

Number of shares with par value: _____   Par value: $____   w   Number of shares ithout par value: _____

4. **Governing Board:** *(check one; if yes, please complete below)*

This corporation is a close corporation operating with a board of directors_____ **Yes** / or_____ **No**

Names, Addresses, Number of Board of Directors: *(if more than two directors, please attach additional pages)*

1._____   _____
Name

Street Address   City   State   Zip Code

2._____   _____
Name

Street Address   City   State   Zip Code

5. **Purpose:** *(optional/See Instructions)*

The purpose of this Corporation shall be:

6. **Names, Addresses and Signatures of Incorporators:** *(if more than two incorporators, please attach additional pages)*

Name   Signature

Address   City   State   Zip Code

Name   Signature

Address   City   State   Zip Code

8. **Certificate of Acceptance of Appointment of Resident Agent:**

I hereby accept appointment as Resident Agent for the above named corporation.

Authorized Signature of R.A.   or   On Behalf of R.A. Company   Date

This form must be accompanied by appropriate fees. See attached fee schedule.   Nevada Secretary of State Form 78A ARTS.2003
Revised on: 09/29/03

some or all of the shares to the other shareholders. If the corporation and the selling shareholder cannot agree upon the price or terms of purchase, the shareholder is free to sell the shares to an outsider.[33] The outsider must be eligible to become a shareholder without affecting the corporation's tax status.[34] If a shareholder attempts to transfer shares in violation of these restrictions, the transfer is ineffective.[35]

If the articles of incorporation of a close corporation so provide, the corporation is required to purchase shares of a deceased shareholder.[36] The procedure in case of death is similar to the procedure for voluntary transfer. After receiving notice of the shareholder's death and a request that the corporation purchase the shares, the corporation, if authorized to do so by its shareholders, makes a purchase offer for the shares, accompanied by recent financial statements. The price and other terms may be fixed in advance by provisions in the articles of incorporation, by-laws, or a written agreement. If the corporation fails to make an offer for a compulsory purchase, a court may order the corporation to purchase the shares at a fair value.[37]

Shareholder Management

Recall that the owner-manager characteristics of a business are usually found in partnerships and limited liability companies. In a close corporation, it is possible to adopt shareholder management provisions that effectively structure the operation of the business to be like that of a partnership or a limited liability company. Under the Model Business Corporation Act, in any corporation with fifty or fewer shareholders, provisions may be adopted that dispense with or limit the authority of a board of directors and permit shareholders to perform those duties.[38] All shareholders may agree in writing concerning the management of the affairs of the corporation, and the agreement can eliminate a board of directors, restrict the power of the board of directors, cause the corporation to be treated as a partnership, and permit partner-type relationships among shareholders.[39] For example, a shareholder agreement can state when distributions are to be made from the corporation and who the corporate officers will be. An agreement also can provide that the corporation will be dissolved whenever a shareholder dies or is bankrupt. These are typical partnership characteristics, but shareholders of a close corporation may have legitimate reasons for using such rules to operate their business.

If the corporation has a board of directors, it would be unfair to permit a shareholder agreement to reserve management power to the shareholders and still expose the board of directors to liability for shareholders' decisions. Consequently, any agreement that restricts the discretion of the board of directors also relieves the directors from liability for such matters, and places the liability on the people who are making the decisions.[40] It is possible to completely eliminate the board of directors if the articles of incorporation so states.[41] When this happens, the powers of the corporation are exercised by the shareholders, and the rules that normally apply to the directors apply to the shareholders. If an official demands evidence of director action, the shareholders of a close corporation without directors may appoint a shareholder (or several shareholders) to sign documents as a "designated director."[42] As with a designated hitter in baseball, this person ought to be someone who is particularly talented at fulfilling this privileged capacity.

Anticipating that the shareholders of a close corporation will address management issues in their agreement, certain formalities are relaxed in the statute. For example, it is not necessary to have bylaws (if the normal provisions are contained in the articles or a shareholder agreement),[43] and an annual meeting need not be held unless a shareholder demands it.[44]

Fundamental Changes

Statutory close corporations may participate in mergers and share exchanges, and may transfer all of their assets of the corporation with shareholder approval, just as regular corporations do. However, these transactions must be approved by at least a two-thirds vote of the shares, based upon the policy that shareholders will more actively participate in such decisions in a close corporation.[45] Another major departure from typical corporate law is the authority for any shareholder to dissolve the corporation at will or upon the occurrence of a specified event or contingency.[46] This provision, which acknowledges the integral position played by each shareholder in a close corporation is similar to the right of a partner to terminate the partnership enterprise at will, a right that is particularly important in a close corporation, where a deadlock may occur easily if the shareholders cannot agree on the operation of the business.

Judicial Supervision

A corporation with an independent elected board of directors is usually managed by sophisticated, intelligent, and judicious individuals. These directors usually seek legal advice to be certain they are exercising their judgment and management duties correctly, and they are willing to compromise and make reasonable business judgments in order to make the business successful. In a close corporation, where the owners-shareholders are entitled to manage the business, petty disputes and selfish decisions are more likely to occur. Consequently, a close corporation may be subject to extensive judicial review if the shareholders begin to squabble among themselves.

Any shareholder may ask for judicial relief if the persons in control of the corporation are acting in an illegal, oppressive, fraudulent, or unfairly prejudicial manner toward the shareholder. Similarly, a court may be asked to break a deadlock that injures the business affairs of the corporation.[47] Upon finding that such allegations are justified, a court may order practically anything to remedy the situation, including changing the action adopted by management, canceling articles or bylaws, removing officers or directors, or appointing a custodian to manage the business. The court also has broad power in a situation in which it finds that a shareholder has asked for court help to harass the other members of the corporation. The court may award all attorneys' fees and expenses against the shareholder if it finds the action has been brought arbitrarily, vexatiously, or not in good faith.[48] If the court believes the situation cannot be reconciled, it may order the corporation to dissolve or to purchase the shares of the complaining shareholder at fair value.[49]

Protection from Piercing the Corporate Veil

Remember that a classic remedy of creditors who are unable to satisfy their claims against the corporation is the right to pierce the corporate veil when corporate formalities have not been properly observed.[50] A close corporation may be operated without much formality at all, and thus would seem always to be vulnerable to a claim that the corporation was merely operating as the alter ego of the shareholders without observing normal statutory formalities. To avoid that result, the Model Business Corporation Act provides that the failure of the close corporation to observe the usual corporate formalities will not be a basis for imposing personal liability on the shareholders for liabilities of the corporation.[51]

Alternatives to Close Corporations

With the increasing popularity of limited liability companies and the amendments to the Uniform Partnership Act, it will be increasingly difficult to distinguish the desirability of a close corporation from that of alternative business forms in selecting an appropriate structure of organization for a client. The close corporation was developed at a time when the choices were more obvious. Partnership law historically was based upon an antiquated statute, and the relationships among partners had to be developed from scratch through elaborate agreements. Now the Revised Uniform Partnership Act and the Uniform Limited Partnership Act of 2001 provide more definition and clarity to the management and operation of partnerships, and the statutory framework for both general and limited partnerships provides substantially greater certainty for the resolution of issues among partners. Persons desiring active participation in management may more safely consider the partnership form today and do not have to resort to a renovated corporate model like the close corporation to achieve their preferred management structure.

Similarly, it was not previously possible to ensure limited liability for all persons who desired to be active participants at all levels of a business (as owners, managers, employees, and agents) without using a close corporation form. Today, the limited liability company is a natural alternative, since its structure makes it possible to protect against individual liability and provides partner-type management and ownership features that permit active participation in all business relationships.[52] However, many states still impose certain limitations on limited liability companies regarding longevity of the business form and transferability of ownership interests that may be onerous and unwelcome.[53] On the other hand, the limited liability company permits pass-through taxation of income to the owners without their observation of the strict restrictions imposed upon corporations using Subchapter S tax status,[54] and the internal relationships among the members-managers of a limited liability company can be created in any manner desired without compliance with the rules regarding distinctions among directors, officers, and shareholders that still pervade the operations of a close corporation. For example, the shareholders of a close corporation cannot share income, losses, tax credits, tax deductions, and cash distributions disproportionately without using elaborate agreements, and in some cases, without forcing relationships among the shareholders (such as having a shareholder purchase the corporate building and act as a landlord to receive rental income and to deduct the depreciation on the building). Each shareholder of a close corporation is supposed to receive his or her share of these items based exclusively upon his or her proportionate ownership of shares, while in a limited liability company or a partnership, disproportionate allocations are common and are limited only by the drafter's imagination and some basis in economic reality.[55]

Nevertheless, the continued utility of close corporations is not likely to be threatened by the partnership statutory revisions and the new interest in limited liability companies. In fact, lenders and sophisticated business people are often wary of the flexibility of new partnerships with limited liability and the variations permitted in the structures of limited liability companies, and complex business or financing transactions are often complicated by the need to explain (and in some cases, to agree to waive the advantages of) these entities in order to accomplish the business objectives of the company. There always will be clients who prefer the certainty of the corporate form based on the statutes and case interpretations, and who have management and operational objectives that are best served by a close corporation.

PROFESSIONAL CORPORATIONS

The "learned" professions, such as law, medicine, and accounting, traditionally were prohibited from operating as corporations. State law defines these professions, usually in statutes or rules that require licenses to practice them, and the same statutes or rules also address whether the practice of the profession is permitted in a corporate entity. The policy reasons behind this interdiction were never clearly defined but probably grew out of desire to limit the association of persons engaged in such professions to duly licensed practitioners and out of concern that professional persons should not be allowed to shield themselves from liability through the use of the corporate form. The obvious disadvantage to professionals who were required to practice as sole proprietors or partners was that they could not use favorable corporate tax rates and fringe benefit plans unique to corporations. Some states recognized this disadvantage and enacted professional corporation statutes in 1961, but it was not until 1969 that the Internal Revenue Service conceded that a professional organization should be treated like any other corporation for income tax purposes. In 1979, the Model Business Corporation Act finally adopted the Model Professional Corporation Supplement,[56] referred to in this text as the Model Professional Corporation Act.

Some states now permit professionals to form professional associations, which are really partnerships with a number of corporate characteristics such as continuity of life, centralized management, and transferability of ownership interests that allow them to be taxed like corporations.[57] Other states permit the formation of either an association or a corporation for professionals.[58] This section is concerned primarily with the professional corporation.[59]

The statutory authority for professional corporations varies widely from state to state. Several states include the authority to incorporate with other statutes regulating the particular profession (such as licensing and qualification statutes), and these states have no single professional corporation law. The Model Professional Corporation Act has not been adopted in its entirety in any state. In a few jurisdictions, the authority for professional legal corporations for attorneys is contained in a Supreme Court rule rather than in a statute.[60] In states where the professional corporation has been added as an adjunct to the business corporation statutes, the business corporation statutes control except for the specific provisions of the professional corporation section. Occasionally, separate forms are provided for the formation of a professional corporation. (See Exhibit 7–9, Guide for Articles of Incorporation for a Professional Corporation.)

All states now allow the creation of professional corporations, including those composed of attorneys, doctors, and dentists. Accountants, veterinarians, psychologists, engineers, and architects usually are included, and a few states permit corporate practice by registered nurses, physical therapists, pharmacists, and marriage counselors.

The structural variations of the professional corporation from the business corporation are treated differently in the individual state statutes, but most states have adopted certain general modifications that are the same as the provisions of the Model Professional Corporation Act.

Exhibit 7–9.

Guide for Articles of
Incorporation for a
Professional Corporation

SCC544
(05/02)

COMMONWEALTH OF VIRGINIA
STATE CORPORATION COMMISSION

ARTICLES OF INCORPORATION
PROFESSIONAL CORPORATION

The undersigned, pursuant to Chapters 7 and 9 or 10 of Title 13.1 of the Code of Virginia, state(s) as follows:

1. The name of the professional corporation is:

    _____.

2. The professional corporation is organized for the sole and specific purpose of rendering the professional

    services of: _____.

3. The number (and classes, if any) of shares the professional corporation is authorized to issue is (are):

    Number of shares authorized   **Class(es)**

    _____   _____

    _____   _____

4. A. The name of the professional corporation's initial registered agent is

        _____.

    B. The initial registered agent is **(mark appropriate box):**
        (1) an <u>individual</u> who is a resident of Virginia **and**
            [ ] an initial director of the professional corporation.
            [ ] a member of the Virginia State Bar.
                OR
        (2) [ ] a domestic or foreign stock or nonstock corporation, limited liability company, or registered
                 limited liability partnership authorized to transact business in Virginia.

5. A. The professional corporation's initial registered office address, which is the business office of the
        initial registered agent, is:

        _____, VA _____.
        (number/street)   (city or town)   (zip code)

    B. The registered office is physically located in the [ ] city **or** [ ] county of _____.

6. The first board of directors shall have _____ member(s).

7. The initial directors are:
        NAME(S)   **ADDRESS(ES)**

    _____   _____
                                          _____
    _____   _____
                                          _____

8. The undersigned INCORPORATOR(s) is (are) duly licensed <u>**or**</u> legally authorized to render the listed
    professional services, and at least one incorporator is so licensed or legally authorized in Virginia.

    _____   _____

    _____   _____
        SIGNATURE(S)   **PRINTED NAME(S)**

                See instructions on the reverse.

Scope

Under the Model Professional Corporation Act, organizations in professions in which a service is rendered lawfully only by persons licensed under provisions of a state licensing law may become "professional corporations." Some state statutes under which professional persons are permitted to incorporate cover all licensed services and are not restricted to persons who are otherwise prohibited from incorporating under the business corporation law. Other state statutes limit those who may incorporate to members of specific professions described in a single statute or in a series of similar statutes each applicable to one profession. The definition in the Model Professional Corporation Act restricts the use of the act to the practice of the professions; however, rather than listing designated professions, the act follows the precedent set by many state statutes of defining professional services as licensed services that may not be rendered by a corporation organized under the business corporation law.[61]

Purposes, Powers, and Prohibited Activities

Most state statutes have limited the purposes of a professional corporation to the practice of a single profession because of the ethical proscriptions placed upon joint practice of various professions. The Model Professional Corporation Act permits the practice of various professional services and ancillary services within a single profession, but also permits a joint practice of various professions if this combination of professional purposes is permitted by the licensing laws of the local state.[62] For example, doctors and nurses could practice together in a clinic under a professional corporation structure so long as the licensing law for both professions allowed a professional practice under the corporate form. In most states, lawyers and paralegals are allowed to practice law in the same professional corporation.

A professional corporation formed under the Model Professional Corporation Act would be permitted all the powers enumerated in the Model Business Corporation Act, except that the professional corporation may not be a promoter, general partner, or entity associated with a partnership, joint venture, trust, or other enterprise unless it is engaged only in rendering professional services or carrying on a business permitted by the corporation's articles of incorporation. Similarly, the professional corporation can engage only in the professions and businesses permitted by its articles of incorporation. The professional corporation act, however, permits the investment of funds in real estate, mortgages, stock, bonds, and any other types of investments made as part of the activities of a professional corporation.[63]

Name

State statutes vary in the terms required to be included in the corporate name as designations for a professional corporation. The Model Professional Corporation Act permits the designations *professional corporation, professional association,* or *service corporation,* or the abbreviations *P.C., P.A.,* or *S.C.*[64] As with other corporate statutes, the name of a professional corporation should not be the same as or deceptively similar to the name of any other corporation; however, the act makes an exception if similarity results from the use in the corporate name of personal names of shareholders who are or were associated with the organization or if written consent of the other corporation using a similar name is filed with the secretary of state.[65] These special provisions are intended to make allowance for the similarity of personal names used by professional practitioners in their practices and are based on the assumption that the public is not likely to be confused significantly if professional corporations have similar names that are personal to those who practice as members of the corporation.

Share Ownership

Shares in professional corporations may be owned only by persons who are authorized to render the professional services permitted by the articles of incorporation. The Model Professional Corporation Act and a few states permit shares to be owned by partnerships and other professional corporations that are authorized to render the professional services permitted by the articles of incorporation and by persons licensed outside of the state of incorporation.[66]

No shares of a professional corporation can be transferred or otherwise disposed of except to persons who are qualified to hold shares issued by the professional corporation. The intent of these provisions is to require that the shares of a professional corporation be held only by persons who are licensed to practice the particular profession, so that any transfer of the shares to persons who are not so licensed will be void, against public policy, and in violation of the statute.[67] To accomplish this objective, each certificate representing shares of a professional corporation should state conspicuously on its face that the shares are subject to restrictions upon transfer imposed by the statute and by the licensing authority that supervises the profession.

If a shareholder dies or becomes disqualified (for example, by losing his or her license to practice the profession), the shares should be transferred to a qualified shareholder or purchased by the corporation within a specified period of time following the shareholder's death or disqualification. The Model Professional Corporation Act requires payment of fair value for such shares if the corporation does not establish an alternative method, and the procedure for determining fair value is analogous to the procedure of the Model Business Corporation Act with respect to the determination of rights of dissenting shareholders.[68] If shares of a deceased or disqualified shareholder have not been transferred or purchased within ten months after the death or five months after disqualification, the shares are canceled and the shareholder's interest becomes a creditor's claim against the corporation.[69]

Liability for Professional Activities

The principal excuse for refusing corporate status to professional service organizations was that each practitioner should be individually responsible for all professional acts, and that no professional person should be able to hide behind the corporate shield of limited liability when professional services are improperly rendered. However laudatory that policy may be, there is a chilling corollary: in an unincorporated practice, such as a general partnership, the other partners are personally liable for those professional mistakes as well, even though they were not involved in the event causing damage to a patient or a client. The imposition of liability on all other owners is an example of "vicarious liability," in which a person or entity is liable for the act of another. All state statutes concerning professional corporations include some provision about professional liability or professional responsibility. Most enabling statutes specifically provide that the professional person shall be personally liable for improper acts performed by that person or under that person's supervision. In some cases, limited liability is allowed when the corporation maintains a minimum amount of liability insurance. Most states are silent about the vicarious liability of shareholders of a professional corporation, although some statutes clearly provide that shareholder liability is limited as it would be in a business corporation. In other words, if a doctor commits malpractice in a professional corporation, that doctor may be personally liable for his or her own malpractice, but fellow shareholders of the professional corporation will not be liable individually for their colleague's malpractice. A few other states expressly state that the shareholders are jointly and severally liable for obligations of the corporation. Most states simply provide that the statute does not modify any law applicable to the relationship between a person furnishing professional services and a person receiving such services, including liability arising out of professional services.

The Model Professional Corporation Act affirmatively states rules for liability of the professional corporation, its employees, and its shareholders resulting from negligence in the performance of professional services. A professional employee is responsible only for his or her personal negligence, and the corporation may be liable for the conduct of professional employees within the scope of their employment or within their apparent authority.[70] The Model Professional Corporation Act proposes three alternative provisions in regard to the liability of shareholders of professional corporations:

1. limited liability as in a business corporation;
2. vicarious personal liability as in a partnership; and
3. personal liability limited in amount and conditioned on financial responsibility in the form of malpractice or negligence insurance or a surety bond.[71]

Most state statutes and the Model Professional Corporation Act specifically provide that any relationship of confidence that exists between a professional person and a client or patient is preserved notwithstanding the use of the corporate form. For example, any confidential communications between a client and a lawyer are protected by an attorney-client privilege— meaning the lawyer must keep the communication confidential and may not disclose it without the client's consent. In fact, any privilege applicable to communications with a professional person extends to the professional corporation.[72]

Directors and Officers

Most states express a preference that all directors and officers be licensed to practice the particular profession involved. Where lay directors are permitted, they usually are not allowed to exercise any authority over professional matters. The Model Professional Corporation Act requires that not less than one-half the directors of a professional corporation and all the officers other than the secretary and the treasurer should be qualified persons (licensed to practice the particular profession) with respect to the corporation.[73]

Fundamental Changes

Professional corporations are capable of normal fundamental corporate acts, such as amendment of the articles of incorporation, merger, consolidation, share exhange, and dissolution. Most state statutes and the Model Professional Corporation Act provide enabling legislation to permit such activities by professional corporations, provided the professional status and purposes of the corporation and the qualifications of shareholders are always observed. For example, section 40 of the Model Professional Corporation Act permits mergers and consolidations among professional corporations and business corporations as long as every shareholder of each corporation is qualified to be a shareholder of the surviving or new corporation.

If a professional corporation ceases to render professional services, the Model Professional Corporation Act permits the corporation to amend its articles to delete the rendering of professional services from its purposes and to conform to the requirements of the Model Business Corporation Act regarding its corporate name. The corporation may then continue in existence as a corporation under the Model Business Corporation Act.[74] This section would avoid the forced dissolution of a professional corporation whose shareholders have died or become disqualified. The corporation could continue in business, under the Model Business Corporation Act, to invest its funds or conduct any other business lawfully permitted under the local law.

Foreign Professional Corporation

Many professional practices are conducted in more than one state by individuals licensed to practice in more than one state or by partnerships whose members are licensed to practice in various states. Few state statutes contain any provisions concerning **foreign professional corporations**, but the Model Professional Corporation Act has specifically provided for the admission, qualification, and authority of professional corporations to do business among states.

The professional corporation that seeks to practice the profession in a new state is not entitled to avoid the professional corporation laws of the state in which it carries on its practice by incorporating in a state with more lenient professional corporation requirements. Foreign corporations must comply with the domestic state law requirements concerning corporate purposes and the qualifications of shareholders, directors, and officers.[75] A foreign corporation may render professional services only through persons permitted to render such services in the state.[76] Responsibility for professional services and security for professional responsibility is made applicable to foreign corporations as well as domestic corporations, and foreign corporations also are subject to regulation by the local licensing authority to the same extent as are domestic corporations.[77]

A professional corporation must obtain a **certificate of authority** if the corporation maintains an office in a state.[78] The application for a certificate of authority of a foreign professional corporation would include information required for normal business corporations, and a statement that all the shareholders, not less than one-half the directors, and all the officers other than the secretary and treasurer are licensed to render a professional service described in the statement of purposes of the corporation.[79]

Under the state statutes that permit a professional corporation and under the Model Professional Corporation Act, professional persons are entitled to the advantages of the corporate business form. Although one important advantage of corporateness—limited liability—is lost to the professions, and although the statutory requirements for shareholder-director-officer qualification and operation are strict and must be rigidly observed, the tax advantages and operating flexibility of the corporate organization make the professional corporation an attractive business form.

KEY TERMS

public corporation	stock exchange	street name
inside shareholders	over the counter	beneficial owner
public offering	registration statement	short-swing profits
intrastate offering	prospectus	blue-sky laws
initial public offering	waiting period	registration by filing
underwriter	red herring	registration by coordination
pool or syndicate	tombstone ad	registration by qualification
manager	sticker	close corporation
selected dealers	due diligence	foreign professional corporation
firm commitment	proxy statement	certificate of authority
best efforts		

WEB RESOURCES

Information concerning public companies and the regulations that applies to them, including forms for registration of shares with the Securities and Exchange Commission and the other public reports and forms for registration and maintenance of a public corporation, can be located on the Securities and Exchange Commission Web site:

<http://www.sec.gov>

Access to the filings with the Securities and Exchange Commission on line is available through the EDGAR system on the following sites:

<http://www.freeedgar.com>
<http://www.edgar-online.com>
<http://www.pwcglobal.com>

The text of the federal and state securities laws may be reviewed at the following sites:

<http://www.seclaw.com>
<http://www.law.cornell.edu>

Information about the operation of stock exchanges for a public corporation's shares can be accessed through the exchange Web sites:

<http://www.nyse.com>
<http://www.amex.com>
<http://www.nasdaq.com>

Forms for professional corporations are often available from the Secretary of State (or Department of Commerce) where formation documents are filed. The National Association of Secretaries of State maintains links directly to the offices of the Secretaries of State in all states. These can be accessed through

<http://www.nass.org>

Access to state corporate laws may be obtained through the Legal Information Institute maintained at the Cornell Law School:

<http://www.law.cornell.edu>

Resources for sample forms and information about the formation and operation of professional and close corporations include the following:

<http://www.toolkit.cch.com>
<http://www.findlaw.com>
<http://www.lectlaw.com>
<http://www.ilrg.com>

CASES

AKERMAN v. ORYX COMMUNICATIONS, INC.

810 F.2d 336 (7th Cir. 1987)

MESKILL, CIRCUIT JUDGE

* * *

This case arises out of a June 30, 1981, initial public offering of securities by ORYX, a company planning to enter the business of manufacturing and marketing abroad video cassettes and video discs of feature films for home entertainment. ORYX filed a registration statement and an accompanying prospectus dated June 30, 1981, with the Securities and Exchange Commission (SEC) for a firm commitment offering of 700,000 units. Each unit sold for $4.75 and consisted of one share of common stock and one warrant to purchase an additional share of stock for $5.75 at a later date.

The prospectus contained an erroneous pro forma unaudited financial statement relating to the eight month period ending March 31, 1981. It reported net sales of $931,301, net income of $211,815, and earnings of seven cents per share. ORYX, however, had incorrectly posted a substantial transaction by its subsidiary to March instead of April when ORYX actually received the subject sale's revenues. The prospectus, therefore, overstated earnings for the eight month period. Net sales in that period actually totaled $766,301, net income $94,529, and earnings per share three cents. ORYX'S price had declined to four dollars per unit by October 12, 1981, the day before ORYX revealed the prospectus misstatement to the SEC. The unit price had further declined to $3.25 by November 9, 1981, the day before ORYX disclosed the misstatement to the public. After public disclosure, the price of ORYX rose and reached $3.50 by November 25, 1981, the day this suit commenced.

Plaintiffs allege that the prospectus error rendered ORYX liable for the stock price decline pursuant to sections 11 and 12(2) of the Securities Act of 1933. In July 1982, ORYX moved for summary judgment on the grounds, inter alia, that the misstatement was not material for purposes of establishing liability under section 11 and that the misstatement had not actually caused the price decline for purposes of damages under section 11. ORYX also moved for summary judgment on the section 12(2) claims, again arguing that the error was immaterial and also that plaintiffs lacked "privity," as required under section 12(2), to maintain a suit against ORYX as an issuer because the offering was made pursuant to a "firm commitment underwriting." In December 1982, plaintiffs brought the underwriters into the suit. The underwriters subsequently moved for summary judgment, making substantially the same arguments as had ORYX.

* * *

Section 11(a) of the 1933 Act imposes civil liability on the signatories of a registration statement if the registration statement contains a material untruth or omission of which a "person acquiring [the registered] security" had no knowledge at the time of the purchase[1] . . . Plaintiffs in the Akermans' situation, if successful, would be entitled to recover the difference between the original purchase price and value of the stock at the time of suit. . . . A defendant may, under section 11(e), reduce his liability by proving that the depreciation in value resulted from factors other than the material misstatement in the registration statement. . . . A defendant's burden in attempting to reduce his liability has been characterized as the burden of "negative causation.". . .

The district court determined that plaintiffs established a prima facie case under section 11(a) by demonstrating that the prospectus error was material "as a theoretical matter.". . . The court, however, granted defendants' motion for summary judgment on damages under section 11(e), stating: "[Defendants] have carried their heavy burden of proving that the [ORYX stock price] decline was caused by factors other than the matters misstated in the registration statement.". . . The precise issue on appeal, therefore, is whether defendants carried their burden of negative causation under section 11(e).

1. Section 11(a) provides in pertinent part:

In case any part of the registration statement, when such part became effective, contained an untrue statement of a material fact or omitted to state a material fact required to be stated therein or necessary to make the statements therein not misleading, any person acquiring such security (unless it is proved that at the time of such acquisition he knew of such untruth or omission) may, either at law or in equity, in any court of competent jurisdiction, sue—

(1) every person who signed the registration statement:

. . . .

(5) every underwriter with respect to such security. 15 U.S.C.s 77k(a).

Defendants' heavy burden reflects Congress' desire to allocate the risk of uncertainty to the defendants in these cases. . . . Defendants' burden, however, is not insurmountable; section 11(e) expressly creates an affirmative defense of disproving causation. . . . The Akermans' section 11(a) claim survived an initial summary judgment attack when the court concluded that the prospectus misstatement was material. . . . We note, however, that the district court held that the misstatement was material only "as a theoretical matter.". . . As described below, this conclusion weighs heavily in our judgment that the district court correctly decided that the defendants had carried their burden of showing that the misstatement did not cause the stock price to decline.

The misstatement resulted from an innocent bookkeeping error whereby ORYX misposted a sale by its subsidiary to March instead of April. ORYX received the sale's proceeds less than one month after the reported date. The prospectus, moreover, expressly stated that ORYX "expect[ed] that [the subsidiary's] sales will decline.". . . Indeed, Morris Akerman conceded that he understood this disclaimer to warn that ORYX expected the subsidiary's business to decline. . . . Thus, although the misstatement may have been "theoretically material," when it is considered in the context of the prospectus' pessimistic forecast of the performance of ORYX's subsidiary, the misstatement was not likely to cause a stock price decline. . . . Indeed, the public not only did not react adversely to disclosure of the misstatement, ORYX's price actually rose somewhat after public disclosure of the error.

The applicable section 11(e) formula for calculating damages is "the difference between the amount paid for the security (not exceeding the price at which the security was offered to the public) and . . . the value thereof as of the time such suit was brought.". . . The relevant events and stock prices are:

Date	ORYX Stock Event	Price
June 30, 1981	Initial public offering	$4.75
October 15, 1981	Disclosure of error to SEC	$4.00
November 10, 1981	Disclosure of error to public	$3.25
November 25, 1981	Date of suit	$3.50

The price decline before disclosure may not be charged to defendants. . . . At first blush, damages would appear to be zero because there was no depreciation in ORYX's value between the time of public disclosure and the time of suit. The Akermans contended at trial, however, that the relevant disclosure date was the date of disclosure to the SEC and not to the public. Under plaintiffs' theory, damages would equal the price decline subsequent to October 15, 1981, which amounted to fifty cents per share. Plaintiffs attempted to support this theory by alleging that insiders privy to the SEC disclosure—ORYX's officers, attorneys and accountants, and underwriters and SEC officials—sold ORYX shares and thereby deflated its price before public disclosure. . . . The district court attributed "at least possible theoretical validity" to this argument. . . . After extensive discovery, however, plaintiffs produced absolutely no evidence of insider trading. . . . Plaintiffs' submissions and oral argument before us do not press this theory.

The Akermans first attempted to explain the public's failure to react adversely to disclosure by opining that defendant-underwriter Moore & Schley used its position as market maker to prop up the market price. This theory apparently complemented the Akermans' other theory that insiders acted on knowledge of the disclosure to the SEC to deflate the price before public disclosure. The Akermans failed after extensive discovery to produce any evidence of insider trading and have not pressed the theory on appeal.

The district court invited statistical studies from both sides to clarify the causation issue. Defendants produced a statistical analysis of the stocks of the one hundred companies that went public contemporaneously with ORYX. The study tracked the stocks' performances for the period between June 30, 1981 (initial public offering date) and November 25, 1981 (date of suit). The study indicated that ORYX performed at the exact statistical median of these stocks and that several issues suffered equal or greater losses than did ORYX during this period. . . . Defendants produced an additional study which indicated that ORYX stock "behaved over the entire period . . . consistent[ly] with its own inherent variation.". . .

Plaintiffs offered the following rebuttal evidence. During the period between SEC disclosure and public disclosure, ORYX stock decreased nineteen percent while the over-the-counter (OTC) composite index rose five percent (the first study). During this period, therefore, the OTC composite index outperformed ORYX by twenty-four percentage points. Plaintiffs also produced a study indicating that for the time period between SEC disclosure and one week after public disclosure, eighty-two of the one hundred new issues analyzed in the defendants' study outperformed ORYX's stock. Plaintiffs' first study compared ORYX's performance to the performance of the OTC index in order to rebut a comparison offered by defendants to prove that ORYX's price decline resulted not from the misstatement but rather from an overall market decline. . . . The parties' conflicting comparisons, however, lack credibility because they fail to reflect any of the countless variables that might affect the stock price performance of a single company. . . . The studies comparing ORYX's performance to the other one hundred companies that went public in May and June of 1981 are similarly flawed. The studies do not evaluate the performance of ORYX stock in relation to the stock of companies possessing any characteristic in common with ORYX, e.g., product, technology, profitability, assets or countless other variables which influence stock prices, except the contemporaneous initial offering dates.

* * *

Granting the Akermans every reasonable, favorable inference, the battle of the studies is at best equivocal; the studies do not meaningfully point in one direction or the other. . . . Defendants met their burden, as set forth in section 11(e), by establishing that the misstatement was barely material and that the public failed to react adversely to its disclosure. With the case in this posture, the plaintiffs had to come forward with "specific facts showing that there is a genuine issue for trial.". . . Despite extensive discovery, plaintiffs completely failed to produce any evidence, other than unreliable and sometimes inconsistent statistical studies and theories, suggesting that ORYX's price decline actually resulted from the misstatement. . . . Summary judgment was properly granted.

SECTION 12(2) CLAIMS AGAINST ORYX

The Akermans also appeal the district court's holding that they lack privity to maintain a suit against ORYX under section 12(2) of the Securities Act of 1933. Section 12(2) imposes liability on persons who offer or sell securities and only grants standing to "the person purchasing such security" from them. . . . This provision is a broad antifraud measure and imposes liability whether or not the purchaser actually relied on the misstatement.

The offering here was made pursuant to a "firm commitment underwriting," as the prospectus indicated. Title to the securities passed from ORYX to the underwriters and then from the underwriters to the purchaser-plaintiffs. ORYX, therefore, was not in privity with the Akermans for section 12(2) purposes. . . .

The Akermans nonetheless contend that ORYX may be held liable under section 12(2) as a participant in the offering. It is true that a person who makes a misrepresentation may be held liable as a "participant" even though he is not the immediate and direct seller of the securities. This is true, however, only if there is proof of scienter. . . . The Akermans completely failed to make a showing that ORYX possessed scienter. Therefore, summary judgment was proper.

We affirm the judgment on the plaintiffs' section 11 and section 12(2) claims and . . . remand to the district court for further proceedings.

BIREN, v. EQUALITY EMERGENCY MEDICAL GROUP, INC.
102 Cal.App.4th 125, 125 Cal.Rptr.2d 325

In 1988, emergency room physicians Biren, Kenneth Corre, Emanuel K. Gordon, David Kalmanson, and Michael Vitullo formed Equality Emergency Group, Inc. to provide emergency room services to hospitals under contract. Each physician owned 20 percent of the corporation's shares, was a member of the board of directors, and served as a corporate officer. In 1991, Biren became the chief financial officer and later assumed responsibility for oversight of patient billing. In 1995, the physicians formed E.E.M.G.-SIMI, Inc. to segregate accounting and billing for Simi Valley Hospital from other hospitals that Equality serviced. The shareholder physicians treated the two corporations as one business.

On November 14, 1990, the five physicians entered into a written Agreement detailing their relationship and governing management of Equality. Paragraph 3.06 of the Agreement provided: "The following corporate actions shall require the prior written consent of Shareholders holding a majority of Shares entitled to vote on matters affecting the Corporation: . . . (ii) Entry into contracts for the provision of the following services to the Corporation: . . . B. Billing."

Shortly thereafter, the shareholders amended Paragraph 3.06 to delete the formality of a writing. The amendment conformed to the shareholders' practice of voting orally on important matters, including engaging a billing company. Although Paragraph 5.11 of the Agreement required amendments to be in writing, the shareholders did not execute a written amendment.

In 1994, Equality transferred its patient and insurance billing to Gottlieb Financial Services (Gottlieb) in Florida.

Timely and accurate billing of Equality's physician services was vital to the cash flow and profitability of the business, which employed other physicians and office personnel. At trial, expert witness Daryl Favale testified that "huge [and] not insignificant differences" exist among billing companies and that performances "can be off 30 percent, 40 percent."

In early 1997, Biren learned that Gottlieb had fallen significantly behind in billing for Equality. Biren's and Equality's office manager, Liz Lopez, met with Gottlieb's vice-president, Randy Wilson, to discuss the problem. Wilson assured them that Gottlieb was "going to turn [the backlog] around" by adding employees to service the Equality account and by opening an office on the west coast.

* * *

On August 14, 1997, Biren terminated Gottlieb and orally authorized PHSS to process Equality's billing. She stated to Lopez that "it was an emergency crisis situation and . . . as CFO . . . it was her fiduciary responsibility to maintain the financial stability of the [business] and make a quick and emergency decision." Biren did not obtain prior shareholder approval for terminating Gottlieb and contracting with PHSS; she stated that she acted alone because the other directors were either on vacation or otherwise unavailable.

* * *

On November 20, 1998, a majority of Equality directors and shareholders voted to remove Biren as an officer and director and to redeem her shares for contracting with PHSS without prior shareholder approval, among other things. The directors relied upon Paragraph 3.06 of the

Agreement regarding the necessity for shareholder consent to billing contracts and Paragraph 2.09 regarding a shareholder's material breach of the Agreement.

* * *

Biren's Breach of the Agreement and the Business Judgment Rule

Equality contends the trial court's findings establish that Biren breached the Agreement and her fiduciary duties as a director and officer of Equality. It argues that she violated her fiduciary duties by (1) unilaterally dismissing Gottlieb and contracting with PHSS, and (2) not notifying the Equality shareholders and directors of the PHSS contracts and Gottlieb's performance.

The court's finding that Biren "reasonably relied" on information she believed to be correct was tantamount to a finding she acted in good faith. Biren learned that Gottlieb had stopped billing, which in turn affected Equality's cash flow and payroll. Lopez told Biren that she learned of a "mass exodus" of Gottlieb employees and that Gottlieb would not commit to "catch up" on months of delayed billings. She learned from Weitz that his office was experiencing similar billing problems with Gottlieb. From this evidence, the court could find that Biren reasonably believed Gottlieb could not service the accounts. Moreover, because Weitz advised her that Sing had strong references the court could find that Biren reasonably believed that PHSS could service them.

" '[A] director is not liable for a mistake in business judgment which is made in good faith and in what he or she believes to be the best interests of the corporation. . . .' " (*Barnes v. State Farm Mut. Automobile Ins. Co.* (1993) 16 Cal.App.4th 365, 378, 20 Cal.Rptr.2d 87). "The business judgment rule sets up a presumption that directors' decisions are made in good faith. . . ." (*Lee v. Interinsurance Exchange* (1996) 50 Cal.App.4th 694, 715, 57 Cal.Rptr.2d 798, italics omitted.)

Equality argues that assuming Biren's good faith, the business judgment rule does not protect her because she did not obtain board approval prior to engaging PHSS. "But the [business judgment] rule . . . protect [s] well-meaning directors who are misinformed, misguided, and honestly mistaken." (*F.D.I.C. v. Castetter* (9th Cir. 1999) 184 F.3d 1040, 1046). Her breach of the Agreement resulted from her mistaken belief that as a director and officer she had the authority to act on behalf of Equality. She stated to office assistant Lopez that "it was an emergency crisis situation and . . . as CFO . . . it was her fiduciary responsibility to maintain the financial stability of the [business] and make a quick and emergency decision." That Biren violated the Agreement by not obtaining prior board approval for the billing contract did not by itself make the business judgment rule inapplicable. (Cf. *F.D.I.C. v. Benson* (S.D. Tex.1994) 867 F.Supp. 512, 522 [F.D.I.C. alleged that directors allowed officers to make improper loans without obtaining the required board approval. But directors were protected by the business judgment rule unless they knew their acts were illegal or they "knowingly committed acts outside the scope of their authority"]; 3A Fletcher, Cyc. Corp. (Perm. ed.2001 supp.) § 1128 at pp. 55–56.)

Larger corporations often have formal board committees to recommend the approval of a variety of contracts. But small corporations like Equality conduct much of their official business informally. (See Friedman, Cal. Practice Guide: Corporations 2 (The Rutter Group 2002) ¶¶ 6:174-6:181, pp. 6-32–6:34; Corp.Code, § 300, subd. (e).) "[I]t is well known that corporations which include only a few shareholders do not often act with as much formality as larger companies. This is especially so where the members of the board personally conduct the business of the corporation." (2 Fletcher, Cyc. Corp. (Perm. ed.1998) § 394.10, pp. 246-247, fn. omitted.) The practice of allowing officers to approve contracts is so prevalent in some close corporations, for example, that they bind the entity even though the officer should have obtained board approval. (2 Fletcher, Cyc. Corp., *supra,* § 444, pp. 368–369.)

Equality was a small corporation run informally by physicians who themselves worked 12-hour shifts in hospital emergency rooms. The Agreement states Equality was a close corporation, although it did not comply with the requirements to establish a close corporation. It delegated most of the billing responsibility to Biren, who relied upon Equality office personnel. Unlike larger corporations, there were no distinct lines between management levels. Biren was given a large responsibility and Equality did not prove she intentionally usurped her authority. (*F.D.I.C. v. Benson, supra,* 867 F.Supp. at p. 522.) The court could reasonably infer that Biren remained within the protection of the business judgment rule because Equality did not prove her actions were anything more than an honest mistake. (*Lee v. Interinsurance Exchange, supra,* 50 Cal.App.4th at p. 715, 57 Cal.Rptr.2d 798).

Biren's Breach of the Agreement

Biren contends the trial court erroneously found that she materially breached the Agreement. She points out that in practice, the shareholders never consented in writing to a billing company contract and their Agreement did not provide for oral consent. Biren contends that the oral amendment of Paragraph 3.06, deleting the requirement of written approval for billing contracts, was invalid because the Agreement requires amendments thereto to be written. She also relies upon the trial judge's remarks that she had "a good argument that she didn't have to follow" the Agreement regarding written consent.

The court found Biren materially breached the Agreement by, among other things, not obtaining prior approval for dismissing Gottlieb and engaging PHSS. Although Paragraph 3.06 requires prior written shareholder approval for billing contracts, the shareholders orally amended the provision to allow oral approval.

Biren's argument rests upon assumptions that are not correct. She assumes the shareholders could not orally amend the Agreement because amendments require a writing according to Paragraph 5.11. But "the parties may, by their conduct, waive such a provision" where evidence shows that was their intent. (*Frank T. Hickey, Inc. v. Los Angeles Jewish Community Council* (1954) 128 Cal.App.2d 676, 682-683, 276 P.2d 52.) The court found that in the past, the shareholders took oral votes on billing company contacts. The court reasonably could infer that amendment of the written approval requirement showed the shareholders' intent to conform to practice. Biren's acts also show an intent to treat the written approval provision as if it never existed. Because she "behaved in a manner antithetical" to it, she may not now rely on it. (*Wagner v. Glendale Adventist Medical Center* (1989) 216 Cal.App.3d 1379, 1388, 265 Cal.Rptr. 412.)

Moreover, the trial court found, with sufficient evidentiary support, that Biren's breach was material. It stated that Biren did not give other shareholders an opportunity to discuss or evaluate PHSS. It found that had she let the board decide "it is more likely than not that Equality would not have terminated Gottlieb. . . ."

* * *

SELECTIVE INSURANCE COMPANY OF AMERICA V. MEDICAL ALLIANCES, LLC

362 N.J. Super.392, 827 A. 2d 1188 (2003)

Selective alleges that the practice structure of Medical Alliances, LLC, Prema, LLC, and Neurological Testing Services, LLC is contrary to longstanding jurisprudence in this state, and elsewhere, holding that professional services such as law and medicine may not be practiced in a corporate format, except pursuant to specific, legislative or regulatory exceptions.[FN1]

FN1. The Legislature has carved several statutory exceptions from this common law ban against the corporate practice of professional services to permit hospitals, nursing homes and certain other "ambulatory care" facilities to operate as general business corporations. *See N.J.S.A.* 26:2H-2a; *see generally,* A. Wilcox, *Hospitals and the Corporate Practice of Medicine,* 45 *Cornell L.O.* 432, at 466-85. The rationale for this exception is that the adverse influences and countervailing interests peculiar to a business corporation are minimized and overshadowed by their public necessity, by a public need to assure institutional continuity, and by the fact that such entities are regulated and inspected by the State Department of Health and Senior Services, *see,* e.g. *N.J.A.C.* 8:43G-1.1 (licensing standards for hospitals), *N.J.A.C.* 8:43A-1.1 (standards licensing "ambulatory care facilities"), *N.J.A.C.* 8:43C-1.1 (regulations governing public health centers, health maintenance organizations, ambulatory care facilities and rehabilitation faculties), thus providing similar protections otherwise provided by the regulations of the State Board of Medical Examiners, *N.J.A.C.* 13:35-6.16(f)(4), which limit the ability of its licensees to be shareholders or employees of a general business corporation to five settings.

In 1968, New Jersey adopted the New Jersey Business Corporation Act, *N.J.S.A.* 14A:1-1 to -9. Under this act, "[a] corporation may be organized . . . for any lawful business purpose or purposes except to do in this State any business for which organization is permitted under any other statute of this State unless such statute permits organization under this act." *N.J.S.A.* 14A:2-1. The foregoing statute makes is clear that in order to lawfully incorporate as a general business corpora-

tion, the entity must not be permitted to incorporate under an alternative statute unless the alternative statute permits the entity to also incorporate as a general business corporation.

In 1969, New Jersey adopted The Professional Service Corporation Act, *N.J.S.A.* 14A:17-1 to 18 (the "Act"), which states that "[i]t is the legislative intent to provide for the incorporation of an individual or group of individuals to render the same professional service to the public for which such individuals are required by law to be licensed or to obtain other legal authorization." *N.J.S.A.* 14A:17-1. The Legislature defined the term "[p]rofessional service" to mean "any type of personal service to the public, which requires as a condition precedent to the rendering of such service the obtaining of a license or other legal authorization. . . ." *N.J.S.A.* The Legislature identified chiropractors as individuals rendering a service coming within the definition of "[p]rofessional service," as defined by the statute. *Ibid.* Importantly, the Legislature specifically noted that chiropractors could not lawfully render services in the corporate form prior to the passage of The Professional Service Corporation Act. The Legislature stated that "prior to the passage of this act and by reason of law [chiropractic] could not be performed by a corporation." *Ibid.*

The Professional Service Corporation Act states, in essence, that a group of individuals who must be licensed to perform their service must be incorporated as a professional corporation, rather than incorporated as a general business corporation, with certain exceptions. Thus, this Act prohibits chiropractors from incorporating as a general business corporation since they must be licensed by the State to perform chiropractic treatment. *See N.J.S.A.* 14A:17-3. The Act does not permit alternative incorporation, for example by way of a general business corporation.

Although the present action deals partly with limited liability companies ("LLCs"), rather than general business corporations, the underlying issues are the same. Like a general business corporation, the members of a limited liability company do not have to be licensed professionals nor do they have to obtain and maintain malpractice insurance as physicians do. *N.J.S.A.* 45:9-19.17a. Members of a professional corporation, on the other hand, all have to be licensed professionals. Unlike a general corporation, or an LLC, a lay person cannot become a member of a professional corporation as The Professional Corporation Act provides that only licensed professionals may hold a shareholder interest in a professional service corporation. *See N.J.S.A.* 14A:17-10. Thus, unlike a general business corporation or an LLC, if a managing member loses his license to perform chiropractic, he would no longer be permitted by law to control or be a member of the professional service corporation.

In fact, whenever a shareholder of a professional service corporation shall cease to hold his or her professional license, the shareholder is then required to sever all ties with the professional service corporation and, if he does not do so, the corporation is automatically "converted into . . . a [general] business corporation. . . ." *See N.J.S.A.* 14A:17-11 and -13(b). Accordingly, since the Act does not permit alternative incorporation as, for example, a general business corporation, chiropractors are barred from forming a general business corporation even if all members were licensed in New Jersey and complied with various regulations adopted in New Jersey.

Although an exception has been created for attorneys by the New Jersey Supreme Court with regard to LLCs, *see R.* 1:21-1B, [FN2] no such exception has been carved out by the Legislature for chiropractors or physicians. The Board of Medical Examiners and Board of Chiropractor Examiners have never adopted a rule permitting or prohibiting LLCs.

> FN2. Notably, a limited liability company formed for the practice of law must "obtain and maintain in good standing one or more policies of lawyers' professional liability insurance which shall insure the limited liability company against liability imposed upon it by law for damages resulting from any claim made against the limited liability company by its clients arising out of the performance of professional services by attorneys employed by the limited liability company in their capacities as attorneys." *R.* 1:21-1B(a)(4).

There is nothing in the LLC Act or its legislative history to indicate that, when authorizing LLCs, the Legislature meant to displace existing statutes governing board licenses. In the event that the Legislature were to specifically permit licensed medical personnel or entities to form an LLC, they certainly would prescribe many conditions, such as ownership, as the Supreme Court did with lawyers in adopting *R.*

1:21-1B. Thus, the only legal way to form a corporation of chiropractors is to form a professional service corporation, as detailed in the statute or possibly an LLC with all members being duly licensed. In addition, if an LLC were permitted to be formed by chiropractors and/or physicians or medical facilities and lay persons, then a lay person could have control over the actions of chiropractors, physicians and medical facilities and reap the financial benefits.

* * *

These concerns are the basis for the general prohibition of the practice of law by corporations. Although there is no reported decision of a New Jersey court extending the rationale of *Unger* or *In re Co-operative Law Co.* to the professions of medicine and chiropractic, our courts have recognized that a similarly confidential relationship exists between a physician and his or her patient. "[T]he relationship between a doctor and his patient is of . . . a confidential and vital nature. . . ." *Lopez v. Sawyer,* 115 *N.J.Super.* 237, 251, 279 *A.2d* 116 (App.Div.1971), *aff'd,* 62 *N.J.* 267, 300 *A.2d* 563 (1973). The New Jersey State Board of Chiropractic Examiners ("Board") has also recognized that a similar relationship of trust and confidence exists between a chiropractor and his or her patient.

* * *

New Jersey's health care statutes prescribe requirements for obtaining a chiropractic license, which can only be obtained by an individual, as opposed to a general business corporation or an LLC. *See N.J.S.A.* 45:9-41.1 to -11. These statutes indicate that an applicant for a chiropractic license must be an individual, not a corporate entity. This distinction is significant in light of the fact that a general business corporation or an LLC is an entity which is separate and distinct from its shareholders. *Lyon v. Barrett,* 89 *N.J.* 294, 300, 445 *A.2d* 1153 (1982).

In adopting the statute permitting LLCs, the Legislature never considered whether licensed professionals (or lay persons) could form and practice in that capacity.

[The Court ruled that Selective would be entitled to additional discovery to determine if the LLCs were truly owned by medical doctors, chiropractors, corporations, or lay persons and whether they were actually practicing in New Jersey.]

PROBLEMS

1. Use <http://www.sec.gov> to locate the full text and instructions of Form 8K and determine which of the following events would require a filing of a Form 8-K report for the company:

   a. The resignation of the Chief Executive Officer.

   b. The hiring of new certified public accountants.

   c. A bank makes a loan to a shareholder who acquires fifteen percent of the company's outstanding stock with the money from the loan.

   d. The sale of the company's manufacturing plant in Pittsburgh, which accounted for twenty-two percent of the company's total sales.

e. The resignation of a director, who delivers a letter stating that she disagrees with the current management policies and thinks the company is doomed.

f. The change in the fiscal year of the company from January 1–December 31 to July 1–June 30.

2. Write a memorandum to the client indicating the important differences between a best-efforts underwriting and a firm commitment underwriting. Include in the memorandum the difference it would have made in the *Akerman* case at the end of this chapter had the underwriting been a best-efforts underwriting.

3. Describe the advantages and disadvantages of providing for supermajority voting (e.g., seventy-five percent, ninety percent, or unanimous) for shareholders of a close corporation.

4. Mark Foster is a corporate paralegal in the law firm of Jones, Smith and Cohen, P.C. Mark acted as incorporator to form the professional corporation for the firm. Review the Model Professional Corporation Supplement in Appendix G and answer the following questions concerning Mark:

a. What officer position(s) may he hold in the professional corporation?

b. May he be a director?

c. May he be a shareholder?

d. Is he liable for his own negligence?

e. Is he liable for the negligence of the senior attorney who supervises his work?

f. Is he liable for the lease of the office space that has been entered into with the professional corporation?

5. Describe the advantages and disadvantages of using a limited liability company instead of a close corporation as a business structure.

6. If a doctor is licensed to practice medicine in Connecticut and forms a professional corporation for that practice, can she qualify the corporation to do business in New Hampshire and practice medicine there without obtaining a license to practice medicine in New Hampshire? Why or why not?

PRACTICE ASSIGNMENTS

1. Join one or two classmates and develop a list of issues that must be resolved in order to form a close corporation among you. Use the Model Statutory Close Corporation Supplement in Appendix F as your guide. Determine how you, as potential shareholders, want to structure your relationship for the operation of the business.

2. Review your local statutes that authorize the formation of professional corporations or associations and determine the following:

a. Which professions are authorized to conduct business as professional corporations?

b. Find at least three differences in the statutory authority to form and operate a professional corporation among the professions so authorized and explain the policy reasons behind the variations.

c. What names are permitted in your state for professional corporations or associations? Do they differ among professions, and if so, why?

d. To what extent does the existence or nonexistence of insurance affect the individual liability of the shareholders of a professional corporation or association? Does it differ among professions, and if so, why?

3. Review Exhibit I–5 (concerning a close corporation) and Exhibit I–6 (concerning a professional corporation) in Appendix I. Which provisions of these documents would not be necessary to form a close corporation or a professional corporation under the model acts in Appendixes G and H? Which additional clauses would be required in these documents in order to comply with the model acts?

4. Assume that you are working for a law firm that represents ORYX Communications, Inc. (the defendant in the *Akerman* case at the end of this chapter). You have been told about the problem with the earnings and sales of the company *before* the final registration statement and prospectus have been prepared.

a. Write a paragraph of disclosure that you believe would be necessary to disclose the problem fully to the public investors.

b. Write a "Risk Factor" that can be included in the prospectus to warn investors that such problems may arise in the future as well.

c. Using the http://www.sec.gov Web site, locate the Attorney Conduct Rule adopted by the Securities and Exchange Commission under the Sarbanes-Oxley Act of 2002. With the information you have been furnished about the problem with the earnings and sales of the company, what obligations would you (and your supervising attorney) have under the Attorney Conduct Rule?

ENDNOTES

1. See "Types of Corporate Securities" in Chapter 9.

2. 15 U.S.C.A. § 77(a) *et. seq.*

3. See D. L. Ratner, *Securities Regulation in a Nutshell,* Sixth Edition (West 2002).

4. Securities Exchange Act of 1934, § 3(a)(1), 15 U.S.C.A. § 78c(a)(1).

5. Generally, the types of securities that are exempt from the registration requirements of the 1933 Act include:

    a. securities of domestic governments and banks;

    b. commercial paper involving financing for current transactions with a maturity not longer than nine months;

    c. securities of charitable organizations;

    d. securities of building and loan associations and farmer's cooperative associations;

    e. securities of transportation carriers where the issuance is subject to the Interstate Commerce Commission;

    f. certificates issued by receivers or trustees in bankruptcy with court approval;

    g. insurance policies and annuity contracts issued by corporations subject to the supervision of a state regulatory agency;

    h. an exchange of one security by the corporation with its shareholders for another security owned by them without any commission or remuneration;

    i. securities issued in a reorganization of a corporation with court or other governmental approval; and

    j. securities sold only to persons residing within a single state (an intrastate offering).

Securities Act of 1933 § 3(a), 15 U.S.C.A. § 77c.

6. The important exemptions for transactions in securities include:

    a. transactions by any person other than the selling corporation, an underwriter, or dealer;

    b. transactions by the selling corporation not involving a public offering;

    c. transactions among dealers not involving the sale to customers;

    d. offerings of not more than $5,000,000 made solely to "accredited investors."

Securities Act of 1933 § 4, 15 U.S.C.A. § 77d.

7. Section 5 of the Securities Act of 1933 provides:

    a. Unless a registration statement is in effect as to a security, it shall be unlawful for any person, directly or indirectly

    (1) to make use of any means or instruments of transportation or communication in interstate commerce or of the mails to sell such security through the use or medium of any prospectus or otherwise; or

    (2) to carry or cause to be carried through the mails or in interstate commerce, by any means or instruments of transportation, any such security for the purpose of sale or for delivery after sale.

Securities Act of 1933 § 5, 15 U.S.C.A. § 77e.

8. Other commonly used registration forms are Form S-2 for any company that has been filing reports under the Securities and Exchange Act of 1934 for at least three years; Form S-4 for mergers and acquisitions among corporations; Form S-8 for employee stock purchase plans; and Form S-11 for sale of securities of real estate investment companies.

9. Securities Act of 1933 § 8(a) 15 U.S.C. A. § 77e.

10. 15 U.S.C.A. §§ 78a–78jj. See "Regulation After a Public Offering" in this chapter.

11. Securities Act of 1933 § 11 (a), 15 U.S.C.A. § 77k.

12. Securities Act of 1933 § 17; 15 U.S.C.A. § 77q.

13. 15 U.S.C.A. §§ 78a–78jj.

14. Securities Exchange Act of 1934 § 12; 15 U.S.C.A. § 77l. Registration is also required for companies that have a certain amount of total assets (over $1,000,000.00) and a large number of shareholders (500 or more). However, exemptions from registration exist for a privately held company with total assets of less than $10,000,000.00.

15. Securities Exchange Act of 1934 § 13; 15 U.S.C.A. § 78m.

16. Securities Exchange Act of 1934 § 14; 15 U.S.C.A. § 78n.

17. Securities Exchange Act of 1934 § 16; 15 U.S.C.A. § 78p.

18. Both civil and criminal penalties are provided under the 1934 Act. *See* Securities and Exchange Act of 1934 §§ 18, 20, 26, and 32; 15 U.S.C.A. §§ 78r, t, z and dd.

19. Securities Exchange Act of 1934 § 14; 15 U.S.C.A. § 78n. See "Shareholder Meetings" in Chapter 10.

20. Rule 14(A)(8)(c) Securities Exchange Act 1934, permits management to exclude a proposal if, among other things, it:

    a. is under a governing state law not a proper subject for action by security holders;

    b. would require the company to violate any laws;

    c. is contrary to the SEC proxy rules;

    d. relates to redress of a personal claim or grievance;

    e. relates to operations which account for less than 5% of the company's business;

    f. is beyond the company's power to effectuate;

    g. deals with the company's ordinary business operations;

    h. relates to an election to office;

    i. is counter to a management proposal;

    j. has been rendered moot;

    k. is duplicative of another proposal included in the proxy statement; or

    l. is substantially similar to a proposal previously submitted during the past five years which received affirmative votes less than a required percentage of the shares to approve the proposal.

21. Securities Exchange Act of 1934 § 18; 15 U.S.C.A. § 78r.

22. Securities and Exchange Act of 1934 § 16; 15 U.S.C.A. § 78p.

23. Rule 10(b)5, Securities Exchange Act of 1934 § 10(b); 15 U.S.C.A. § 78j(b).

24. The Sarbanes-Oxley Act of 2002 directed the Securities and Exchange Commission to adopt rules regulating conduct of corporate officers and directors of public companies and professional advisors to public companies, including accountants and lawyers. The standards for professional conduct for lawyers and paralegals is contained in 17 C.F.R. 205, and provides for attorneys and paralegals to report evidence of material violations of the securities laws to higher corporate officials and to the SEC.

25. See *Hall v. Geiger-Jones,* 242 U.S. 539 (1917).

26. See Chapter 13. An agreement between shareholders organizing a close corporation appears as Exhibit 1–5 in Appendix I.

27. Model Business Corporation Act (hereafter M.B.C.A.) § 8.01(c).

28. E.g., Delaware, Del. Code Ann. tit. 8, §§ 341–56.

29. Model Statutory Close Corporation Supplement (hereafter M.S.C.C.S.) § 3. The text of the M.S.C.C.S. is reproduced in Appendix G.

30. E.g., Delaware, Del. Code Ann. tit. 8, §§ 342, 343.

31. M.S.C.C.S. § 10(a).

32. M.S.C.C.S. § 11.

33. M.S.C.C.S. § 12.

34. M.S.C.C.S. § 12(b). Remember that Subchapter S has strict requirements relating to the number of shareholders and their status as individual citizens. A new shareholder must meet the qualifications to avoid disturbing the corporation's tax status. See "Taxation of Corporations—Subchapter S Election" in Chapter 6.

35. M.S.C.C.S. § 13. In states that have no statutory provisions restricting the transfer of shares in close corporations, the same result can be reached through an agreement among shareholders. See "Share Transfer Restrictions and Buyout Agreements" in Chapter 13.

36. M.S.C.C.S. § 14.

37. M.S.C.C.S. §§ 15–17.

38. M.B.C.A. § 8.01(c).

39. M.S.C.C.S. § 20(b).

40. M.S.C.C.S. § 20(c).

41. M.S.C.C.S. § 21(a).

42. M.S.C.C.S. § 21(c) (5).

43. M.S.C.C.S. § 22.

44. M.S.C.C.S. § 23.

45. M.S.C.C.S. § 30.

46. M.S.C.C.S. § 33.

47. M.S.C.C.S. § 40.

48. M.S.C.C.S. § 41.

49. M.S.C.C.S. §§ 43, 44.

50. See "Limited Liability" in Chapter 6.

51. M.S.C.C.S. § 25.

52. See "Ownership and Management of a Limited Liability Company" in Chapter 5.

53. See "Continuity and Transferability of Interests" in Chapter 5.

54. Compare "Taxation of a Limited Liability Company" in Chapter 5 with "Taxation of a Corporation—Subchapter S Election" in Chapter 6.

55. See "Taxation of a Partnership" in Chapter 3 and "Taxation of a Limited Liability Company" in Chapter 5.

56. The text of the Model Professional Corporation Supplement (1984) to the Model Business Corporation Act is reproduced in Appendix H.

57. E.g., Pennsylvania, 15 Pa. Stat. Ann. §§ 12601—19. Forms for the formation of a professional association may be found in West's Modern Legal Forms §§ 6461—66.

58. E.g., Texas, Tex. Rev. Civ. Stat. Ann. arts. 1528(e), 1528(f) (West).

59. Articles of incorporation of a professional medical corporation and its application for registration appear as Exhibits I-6 and I-7 in Appendix I.

60. E.g., Colorado, 7A Colo. Rev. Stat. ch. 22, rule 265.

61. Model Professional Corporation Supplement to the Model Business Corporation Act (hereafter M.P.C.A.) § 3(7).

62. M.P.C.A. § 11(b).

63. M.P.C.A. §§ 12(b), 14(b).

64. M.P.C.A. § 15(a).

65. M.P.C.A. § 15(b).

66. M.P.C.A. § 20.

67. M.P.C.A. § 22.

68. See M.P.C.A. § 23–26; M.B.C.A. §§ 13.01–28.

69. M.P.C.A. § 27.

70. M.P.C.A. § 34(a), (b).

71. M.P.C.A. § 34(c).

72. M.P.C.A. § 33.

73. M.P.C.A. § 30.

74. M.P.C.A. § 41.

75. M.P.C.A. § 50(b) (2).

76. M.P.C.A. § 50(b) (3).

77. M.P.C.A. § 64.

78. M.P.C.A. § 50(a).

79. M.P.C.A. § 51.

FORMATION OF
A CORPORATION

PREINCORPORATION RESPONSIBILITY

The embryo of a corporation is the business idea conceived by an individual or group of individuals. The idea may be fresh, as with entrepreneurs who simply decide to begin a business, or it may evolve from an established commercial enterprise that will continue under the corporate form. Regardless of the genesis of the idea, the attorney is consulted for the purpose of forming the appropriate structure for operation of the business. If limited liability, flexible capital structure, and tax advantages are desired, the corporate organization may be most desirable. The organizers rely upon the attorney to properly consider the advantages and disadvantages of the various business forms and to advise them of the most beneficial organization.[1]

At this point, the organizers are private individuals with a business idea, and good practice suggests that they agree among themselves in writing about certain important matters regarding the corporation to be formed. The relationship between these organizers or **promoters** resembles a **joint venture,** which is like a partnership. Even without a written agreement, the law imposes certain rights and responsibilities upon the relationship, including duties to disclose important information to each other and to avoid any conflict of interest that might interfere with their participation in the project. However, to avoid disputes and to facilitate the smooth incorporation of their business, a written agreement between the organizers is appropriate (see Exhibit 8–1, Agreement Between Promoters).

The organizers or promoters are responsible for investigating the particular business opportunity and assembling the property, cash, and personnel to accomplish the business objectives. Generally, the promoters will look for a suitable business establishment; negotiate a lease or purchase of that establishment; and contract for necessary furniture, fixtures, and so forth. They will search for capable employees, if needed, and may negotiate employment contracts with them. If the business opportunity is unique, patents, copyrights, or trademarks must be obtained. A common denominator to each of these activities is that the promoters are acting as individuals in a joint venture relationship on behalf of a corporation yet to be formed. They cannot bind the corporation to the contracts they are negotiating because the corporation does not exist. In some respects, they are agents acting on behalf of a principal that has yet to be created. Consequently, the promoters usually are required to obligate themselves individually on those contracts. After the corporation is formed, it may adopt the contracts through appropriate action by the board of directors, but the promoters who have signed the contracts in their individual capacities usually remain obligated for performance of the contracts. Promoters considering the corporate form should always be advised of these ramifications of preincorporation agreements, but they should not be deterred by these facts from forming a corporation, since they would not escape individual liability by using any alternative business form.

Exhibit 8–1.

Agreement Between Promoters

AGREEMENT BETWEEN PROMOTERS

Agreement, made this _____day of _____, 20___, between A_____ B_____ of _____, and C_____ D_____ of _____.

Whereas, the parties desire to form a corporation upon the terms and conditions set forth in this agreement.

Now, therefore, it is agreed:

1. **Formation of the Corporation.** The parties shall as soon as possible form a corporation under the laws of the State of _____.

2. **Certificate of Incorporation.** The certificate of incorporation shall provide substantially as follows:

(a) The name of the corporation shall be _____, or if this name is not available such other name as the parties shall select.

(b) The principal office or place of business of the corporation shall be located at _____. The name and address of its resident agent shall be _____.

(c) The purpose of the corporation shall be the manufacture and wholesale distribution of textile fabrics. The corporation shall have such powers as may be appropriate in connection with such a business.

(d) The names and places of residence of each of the incorporators are:

_____   _____

_____   _____

_____   _____

(e) The corporation shall have perpetual existence.

(f) The minimum amount of capital with which the corporation shall commence business is $1,000.

(g) The total number of shares of stock shall be 1,000, divided into two classes as follows:

Common Stock, $10 par value	500 shares
Preferred Stock, $100 par value	500 shares

(h) The designations; the powers, preferences, and rights; and the qualifications, limitations, or restrictions of such stock are: [*Here describe*].

3. **Subscriptions of Parties.** The parties subscribe for shares of stock of the proposed corporation, as follows:

(a) Within one week after the certificate of incorporation has been filed and recorded the corporation shall issue to A_____ B_____ _____shares of common stock of the corporation, $10 par value, in consideration of the simultaneous execution and delivery to the corporation of a deed transferring marketable title to the following described real property, free and clear of liens: [*Here describe*].

(b) Within one week after the certificate of incorporation has been filed and recorded the corporation shall issue to C_____ D_____ shares of preferred stock of the corporation, $100 par value, in consideration of the simultaneous payment by C_____ D_____ to the corporation of the sum of $_____ in cash.

4. **Agreement to Purchase Additional Stock.** C_____ D_____ shares of preferred stock of the corporation, $100 par value, in consideration of the simultaneous payment by C_____ D_____ agrees to purchase additional preferred stock not to exceed $_____ in par value if during the first two years of the operation of the corporation its net profits do not equal at least $_____.

Exhibit 8–1.

(continued)

5. **Stock to Promoter for Services.** The corporation shall issue to_____ of _____, _____shares of common stock of the corporation, par value $, in consideration for his services in organizing the corporation.

6. **First Directors of Corporation.** The directors of the corporation for the first year shall be _____, _____, and _____.

7. **Employment Contracts.** The corporation shall employ A_____ B_____ as president and general manager and C_____ D_____ as secretary-treasurer, each for a term of 5 years, at a salary of $_____ per year for A_____ B_____ and $_____ per year for C_____ D_____. Their employment shall not be terminated without cause and their salary shall not be increased or decreased without unanimous approval of all directors. Written employment contracts shall be entered into with A_____ B_____ and C_____ D_____ wherein they agree to devote their time and best efforts exclusively to the business and interests of the corporation.

8. **Restrictions on Transfer of Stock.** Each of the parties agrees not to transfer, sell, assign, pledge, or otherwise dispose of his or her shares of stock of the corporation without first obtaining the written consent of the other parties to the sale or other disposition, or without first offering to sell the shares to the corporation at a value to be determined by a board of 3 appraisers, one of whom shall be appointed by each of the parties, A_____ B_____, and C_____ D_____. The offer shall be in writing and shall remain open for 30 days. If the corporation fails to accept the offer within that period, a second offer also is writing shall then be made to sell the shares on similiar terms to the other parties to this agreement pro rata. If the offer be not accepted by either the corporation or the other parties, the shares shall thereafter be freely transferable.

9. **Designation of Incorporators.** The parties appoint and designate _____and _____to act as the incorporators of the corporation and to take whatever steps are necessary to organize the corporation in accordance with the applicable laws of the State of _____. The authority which is hereby granted shall extend to the preparation, execution, and filing of such documents and other papers as are necessary in the incorporation process to carry out the terms and conditions of this agreement.

10. **Organization Expenses.** Each of the parties shall advance to _____his or her pro rata share of the funds which shall be necessary to pay the expenses and costs of incorporation. As soon as practicable after it commences business, the corporation shall reimburse each of the parties for such advances.

11. **Arbitration.** All disputes, differences, and controversies arising under or in connection with this agreement shall be settled and finally determined by arbitration in the City of _____according to the Rules of the American Arbitration Association now in force or hereafter adopted.

12. **Nonassignability of Agreement.** This agreement shall not be assignable by any party without the written consent of the other parties.

13. **Subchapter S Election.** Each of the undersigned who make the capital contribution required under section 3 of this agreement further agree to elect to be shareholders in a corporation taxed under Subchapter S of the Internal Revenue Code of 1986, as amended, and to sign and file Form 2553 with the Internal Revenue Service for that purpose.

14. **Persons Bound.** The terms and conditions of this agreement shall be binding upon the parties and their respective legal representatives, successors, and assigns. However, if one of the parties dies prior to the time the corporation comes into existence, this agreement shall automatically terminate.

Executed in triplicate on the date first above written.

A_____   B_____

C_____   D_____

When soliciting capital for the corporation, the promoters' activities are governed by a different set of rules. Operating capital may be obtained through loans or by the sale of stock in the corporation to be formed. Loans negotiated before the formation of the corporation are treated as ordinary preincorporation agreements, with the promoters risking individual liability for repayment. Sales of stock are accomplished by a preincorporation share subscription.

PREINCORPORATION SHARE SUBSCRIPTIONS

Share subscriptions are offers from interested investors to purchase shares of a corporation. **Preincorporation share subscriptions** are, as the name indicates, offers to purchase shares when the corporation is subsequently formed. These share subscriptions may be necessary to the proper formation of a corporation for several reasons.

In a practical sense, every corporation needs capital to commence business, and investors must be identified and promises to purchase shares must be secured before the new enterprise is launched. In addition, from a strictly legal standpoint, some state statutes require the use of preincorporation share subscriptions in various stages of the formation procedure. One such provision, not found in the Model Business Corporation Act, is that the incorporators must also be subscribers.[2] In states with this provision, a prospective incorporator must tender a preincorporation share subscription in order to qualify as an incorporator. Several other states require that a corporation must have a minimum amount of **paid-in capital** before it may commence business (see Exhibit 8–2, Certificate of Paid-in Capital);[3] and in these jurisdictions, preincorporation share subscriptions are used to solidify promises to contribute the amount required by statute, since the corporation will not be allowed to commence business without the requisite capital. Thus, preincorporation share subscriptions are used in most cases for practical or legal reasons to secure promises to purchase shares once the corporation is formed.

A preincorporation share subscription may be executed by anyone who has decided to invest in the company. The terms of the subscription describe an offer to purchase shares. The subscription may also contain any other contractual terms desired, such as restrictions on the transferability of the shares once they are issued to the shareholders. If the corporation accepts the offer, a binding contract is created. A few states require written, signed subscriptions, and it is good practice to obtain a written offer in any case. A single subscription may be executed by several subscribers, or each subscriber may execute his or her own subscription.

EXAMPLE

Share Subscription for Several Subscribers

We, the undersigned, hereby severally subscribe for the number of shares of the capital stock of Trouble, Inc., set opposite our respective names. The Corporation is to be organized under the laws of the State of Delaware, with an authorized capital stock of $50,000.00 consisting of 5,000 shares of common stock, $10.00 par value. We further agree to pay the amount subscribed in cash on demand of the treasurer of the said Corporation as soon as it is organized [*or* at such times and in such amounts as may be prescribed by the Board of Directors of the Corporation].

Dated July 1, 2000.

Names	*Addresses*	*Shares Subscribed*	*Amount Subscribed*
___	___	___	___
___	___	___	___

Form C-109—10-31-61 5 M

Filing $5.00
Recording $2.00
Total $7.00

Certificate of Payment of Capital Stock

of the .... Company.

The location of the principal office in this State is at No. .... Street,

in the .... of .... County of ....

The name of the agent therein and in charge thereof, upon whom process against this corporation may be served, is ....

In accordance with the provisions of Section 14:8-16 of the Revised Statutes, we ....

.... President,

and .... Secretary of the

.... Company,

a corporation of the State of New Jersey, do hereby certify that ....

.... dollars, being the ....

....

of capital stock of said company, as authorized by its Certificate of Incorporation filed in the

Department of State on the .... day of ....

A. D. 19 ...., has been fully paid in: ....

dollars thereof by the purchase of property and ....

dollars thereof in cash. The capital stock of said company previously paid and reported is

$ .... of Common Stock and .... of Preferred Stock.

WITNESS our hands the .... day of ....

A. D. 19 ....

.... *President.*

.... *Secretary.*

STATE OF ....

COUNTY OF .... } ss.

.... President,

and .... Secretary of the

.... Company.

Being severally duly sworn, on their respective oaths depose and say that the foregoing certificate by them signed is true.

Subscribed and sworn to before me,

this ....

day of .... A. D. 19 ....

.... *President.*

.... *Secretary.*

Exhibit 8–2.

Certificate of Paid-in Capital (New Jersey)

Share Subscription for a Single Subscriber

The Dillon Manufacturing Company to be incorporated under the laws of the State of Michigan.

Capital Stock $1,000,000.00   Shares $100.00 par value

I, the undersigned, hereby subscribe for 100 shares of the capital stock of the Dillon Manufacturing Company to be incorporated and agree to pay in cash for said stock the sum of $10,000.00 on demand of the Board of Directors of the Corporation.

This agreement is made upon the condition that eighty percent of the capital stock of the Corporation is subscribed in good faith by solvent persons on or before the 1st day of July, 2005, and the Corporation is incorporated within 30 days thereafter.

Dated May 1, 2005.

These subscriptions are also assignable. Therefore, in jurisdictions where incorporators are required to be subscribers by law, the incorporators must subscribe, but if they do not intend to invest, they may assign their preincorporation share subscriptions to outsiders who have acknowledged a desire to invest.

The law presumes that the corporation is formed in reliance upon the offers of subscribers to purchase shares, especially when the statute requires minimum paid-in capital as a condition to commencing business. Under common law, share subscriptions were revocable until the corporation had been formed and had accepted them by agreeing to issue shares for the amount of the subscriptions. Modern statutes provide that the preincorporation share subscriptions are irrevocable for a period of time. Section 6.20 of the Model Business Corporation Act states that a preincorporation subscription of shares of a corporation is irrevocable for a period of six months unless otherwise provided in the terms of the subscription agreement or unless all of the subscribers consent to the revocation. The period of irrevocability varies among the state statutes from three months to one year.[4] A few states specify the period to be a stated time after the certificate of incorporation is issued.[5] If a corporation is formed during the period of irrevocability, it may accept the subscription and require the subscriber to purchase the shares for the amount stated therein. In most jurisdictions, acceptance occurs by action of the board of directors after the corporation is formed,[6] but Pennsylvania makes acceptance automatic upon the filing of articles of incorporation,[7] and a few states make acceptance automatic upon the issuance of a certificate of incorporation.[8] When the subscription is accepted by the corporation or automatically under the statute, the subscriber is usually required to pay the amount in full, but the board of directors may permit payment in installments.

Call of Subscription

August 1, 2005

To: James Lyons

[Address]

Dear Sir:

At a regular meeting of the Board of Directors of Trouble, Inc., held on July 30, 2005, a resolution was duly adopted fixing the amount of calls on stock issued as partly paid and the date of payment of each call.

You are hereby notified that the first call on your subscription for partly paid stock amounts to $500.00, which sum is due and payable at the office of the Corporation on August 15, 2005.

Trouble, Inc.

By _____, Secretary

If a subscriber defaults on the subscription contract and refuses to pay any installment when due, the corporation may sell the shares to another investor, and the defaulting subscriber may be liable for breach of contract. Moreover, under the Model Business Corporation Act, a subscriber may forfeit any right to the shares if the amount due is not paid within twenty days after a written demand has been made.[9]

Demand for Payment and Notice of Forfeiture

September 1, 2005

To: James Lyons
[*Address*]

   You are hereby notified that at a regular meeting of the Board of Directors of Trouble, Inc., the following resolution was duly adopted:

   "Resolved, that the entire [or _____ percent of the] unpaid balance on all subscriptions to the common stock of this Corporation is hereby called for payment forthwith, and the Secretary is hereby directed to demand payment from each subscriber having an unpaid balance, by mailing to him [or her], at his [or her] last known address, a written demand requiring payment within 20 days from receipt of such notice, in default of which his [or her] shares and all previous payments thereon will be forfeited."

   Demand is hereby made upon you for payment in accordance with the provisions of the above resolution, and you are hereby notified that, in default of payment within 20 days from receipt of this notice and demand, your shares and previous payments thereon will be forfeited.

Trouble, Inc.

By _____, Secretary

   Most statutes permit the bylaws to prescribe other penalties for failure to pay in accordance with the subscription.

SELECTION OF JURISDICTION

Preceding sections have discussed the variations in corporate statutes and the trend toward permissiveness and flexibility in the jurisdictional approach to corporate problems. Moreover, states approach corporate taxation differently, and they subject corporations doing business outside the boundaries of their domestic or home states to special procedures when qualifying them to do business.[10] These factors play an important role in the selection of the jurisdiction in which to incorporate. (See Exhibit 8–3, Nevada's Advertisement for Corporations.)

   A corporation formed within the state is known as a **domestic corporation,** and one formed in some other state is called a **foreign corporation.** Each state's statute has provisions regulating domestic corporations and special provisions for foreign corporations. If a particular state's statute contains flexible and advantageous provisions for its domestic corporations but contains restrictive and cumbersome procedures for foreign corporations, that state should be considered a good candidate for incorporation (domestication). The converse is also true. There are other considerations as well, such as whether the state corporation law has been well tested by court decisions so as to be capable of accurate interpretation; whether the state's taxation structure is acceptable; and whether the state laws will permit all desired corporate features. This last consideration requires an analysis of all important points of corporate law in each jurisdiction to be considered (see Exhibit 8–4, Checklist for Selection of Jurisdiction).

   Having perused the checklist, you may be reeling at the thought of the monumental task of comparing all of those points for each of fifty states, and also wondering how a corporation is ever formed if that much research is required as a preface. A couple of observations may decrease your anxiety.

   First, a corporation should not consider incorporating in a state where it does not intend to do business. To domesticate the corporation in a state where no business activity will be conducted only complicates the corporate structure, increases the cost of organizational expenses, and may result in double taxation. The exceptional case may arise when a permissive jurisdiction, such as Delaware, is particularly attractive for some special reason.[11] Thus, incorporators of a restaurant business in Santa Fe, New Mexico, would not consider incorporating outside the state unless an extremely attractive feature of another state is deemed particularly important for their corporate structure. Consequently, the first predisposition in the selection of jurisdiction is to incorporate in the state where the corporation will conduct

Exhibit 8–3.

Nevada's Advertisement for Corporations

Dean Heller
Nevada Secretary of State

Corporate Information

Why Incorporate in Nevada?

- No Corporate Income Tax
- No Taxes on Corporate Shares
- No Franchise Tax
- No Personal Income Tax
- No I.R.S. Information Sharing Agreement
- Nominal Annual Fees
- Minimal Reporting and Disclosure Requirements
- Stockholders are not Public Record

Additional Advantages

- Stockholders, directors and officers need not live or hold meetings in Nevada, or even be U.S. Citizens.
- Directors need not be Stockholders
- Officers and directors of a Nevada corporation can be protected from personal liability for lawful acts of the corporation.
- Nevada corporations may purchase, hold, sell or transfer shares of its own stock.
- Nevada corporations may issue stock for capital, services, personal property, or real estate, including leases and options. The directors may determine the value of any of these transactions, and their decision is final.

SOS Contact Information

★ SOS Home   ★ Legislature   ★ Nevada Home

http://sos.state.nv.us/../comm_rec/whyinc.htm   10/7/2003

(1) Are there express provisions for preincorporation share subscriptions?

(2) May a corporation be formed for perpetual or limited duration?

(3) How restrictive are the provisions concerning corporate names?

(4) Are there express provisions permitting use of a similar corporate name with the consent of the existing corporation? In the case of affiliated corporations? Otherwise?

(5) Is reservation of a corporate name possible? By express statutory provisions? By administrative courtesy?

(6) For what period may a corporate name be reserved?

(7) What renewals of reservation of corporate name are possible?

(8) Is a single incorporator permissible?

(9) Are there any requirements that the incorporator(s) subscribe for shares? What are the qualifications required of the incorporator(s) with respect to: Residence? Citizenship? Age? Otherwise?

(10) May a corporation serve as an incorporator?

(11) Are there express provisions for informal action by the incorporator(s)?

(12) For what purposes may a corporation be incorporated?

(13) Are broad purposes permissible?

(14) Must specified purposes be set forth in the articles of incorporation?

(15) Are there any constitutional or statutory restrictions on corporate ownership of real property? Agricultural land? Personal property? Shares in other corporations? Are there any constitutional or statutory debt limitations?

(16) Are there express provisions on the **ultra vires doctrine?**

(17) How broad are the statutory general corporate powers? Do they include power to make charitable contributions irrespective of corporate benefit? To carry out retirement, incentive, and benefit plans for directors, officers, and employees? To be a partner? To adopt emergency bylaws? Must the statutory general corporate powers be set forth in the articles of incorporation?

(18) What are the fees for filing or recording the articles of incorporation?

(19) What are the organization taxes? Other initial taxes?

(20) Do such taxes discriminate against shares without par value?

(21) Are filings subject to close administrative scrutiny and conservatism, with resulting delays?

(22) Is there a state stamp tax on the issuance of securities?

(23) Are **"blue-sky" law requirements** burdensome?

(24) What, if any, is the minimum authorized or paid-in capital requirement? Must evidence of compliance be filed? Who will be liable, and to what extent, for noncompliance?

(25) What qualitative and quantitative consideration requirements apply to par value shares? To shares without par value? With respect to the valuation of property or services, does the "true value" or "good faith" rule apply? Do preincorporation services satisfy such consideration requirements?

(26) To what extent may a portion of the consideration received for shares be allocated to capital surplus? Within what period after the issuance of the shares may this be done?

(27) May partly paid shares be issued? May certificates for partly paid shares be issued?

(28) Are there express provisions for fractions of shares? **Scrip?**

(29) What provisions may be made with respect to dividend preferences? Liquidation preferences?

(30) When two or more classes of shares are authorized, must the provisions concerning them be stated or summarized on the share certificates?

Exhibit 8–4.

Checklist for Selection of Jurisdiction

Exhibit 8–4.

(continued)

(31) Are express provisions made for issuing preferred or other "special" classes of shares in series? What are the limitations on permissible variations between series of the same class?

(32) To what extent may preferred shares be made **redeemable?** To what extent may common shares be made redeemable?

(33) To what extent may shares be made **convertible?**

(34) What are the record date provisions? Are bearer shares permissible? What rights attach to them?

(35) What are the express statutory provisions for, and judicial and administrative attitudes toward, close corporations?

(36) To what extent may voting rights of shareholders be denied or limited? Absolutely? Contingently? May shares carry multiple votes? Fractional votes?

(37) What are the minimum quorum requirements for shareholder action?

(38) Are there express provisions permitting greater-than-normal requirements for: Shareholder quorum? Shareholder vote?

(39) Are there express provisions for holding shareholder meetings outside the state? On dates to be set by board of directors? What are the notice requirements?

(40) Are there express provisions for informal action by shareholders? Unanimously? By required percentages?

(41) Is cumulative voting permissive or mandatory?

(42) What are the provisions for shareholder class voting for directors?

(43) Are there express provisions for shareholder voting agreements?

(44) Are there express provisions permitting shareholder control of directors?

(45) Are there express provisions for **irrevocable proxies?**

(46) Are there express provisions for voting trusts, permitting closed voting trusts and renewals?

(47) Are there express provisions for purchase and redemption by the corporation of its own shares, including use of stated capital if the purchase is made for specified purposes?

(48) Are there provisions concerning the validity and enforceability of agreements by the corporation to purchase its own shares?

(49) Is insolvency, in either the equity or the bankruptcy sense, a limitation on the redemption or purchase by the corporation of its own shares?

(50) Are there express provisions for rights and options to purchase shares, including the issuance of shares, and the share certificates therefor, even partly paid, to directors, officers, and employees? What are the judicial attitudes with respect thereto?

(51) Is shareholder approval required for the issuance of share options, either generally or to directors, officers, and employees?

(52) Do preemptive rights exist or not exist absent provision in the articles of incorporation? Are they adequately defined? May they be denied, limited, amplified, or altered in the articles of incorporation?

(53) What is the minimum number of authorized directors?

(54) What are the qualifications required of directors with respect to: Residence? Citizenship? Shareholding? Age? Otherwise?

(55) May the board of directors be classified? Staggered?

(56) What are the minimum quorum requirements for board of directors action?

(57) Are there express provisions permitting greater-than-normal requirements for: Board of directors quorum? Board of directors vote?

(58) Are there express provisions for holding board of directors meetings outside the state?

Exhibit 8–4.

(continued)

(59) Are there express provisions for informal action by the board of directors? By means of conference telephone or some comparable communication technique?

(60) What are the provisions for removal of directors? For cause? Without cause?

(61) Are there express provisions for filling vacancies on the board of directors? By shareholder action? By board of directors action?

(62) Are there provisions for increasing the size of the board of directors? By shareholder action? By board of directors action?

(63) Are there provisions for filling newly created directorships? By shareholder action? By board of directors action?

(64) Are there express provisions for executive committees of the board of directors? Other committees of the board of directors? Informal action by committees? What powers may be exercised by committees? What is the minimum number of committee members?

(65) Are there express interested directors/officers provisions?

(66) What corporate officers are required?

(67) May the same person hold more than one office?

(68) What are the required qualifications of the various officers with respect to: Residence? Citizenship? Shareholding? Being a director? Age? Otherwise?

(69) Are there provisions for the election of officers by shareholders? For the removal of officers by shareholders?

(70) To what standards are directors and officers held accountable? Standard of care? Fiduciary standards? Statutory duties? What are the possible liabilities of directors? Officers?

(71) To what extent may directors immunize themselves from liability by filing their written dissents? By reliance on records?

(72) What are the express provisions for deadlock, arbitration, and dissolution, and the judicial attitudes concerning the same?

(73) Are cash and property dividends payable out of surplus? Capital surplus? Earned surplus? Net profits?

(74) Is insolvency, in either the equity or the bankruptcy sense, a limitation on cash or property dividends?

(75) Are unrealized appreciation and depreciation recognized in computing surplus? Capital surplus? Earned surplus?

(76) Are there express **"wasting assets"** corporation dividend provisions?

(77) Are there express provisions for share dividends? Share splits? Other share distributions?

(78) To what extent do statutory requirements of notice or disclosure to shareholders apply in the event of: Cash or property dividends or other distributions from sources other than earned surplus? Share distributions? Reduction of stated capital by cancellation of reacquired shares? Reduction of stated capital made by board of directors? Elimination of deficit in earned surplus account by application of capital surplus ("quasi-reorganization")? Conversion of shares? Who will be liable for noncompliance? Corporation? Directors or officers for subjecting corporation to liability?

(79) What are the provisions for shareholder class voting for extraordinary corporate matters? May filings effecting extraordinary corporate matters have delayed effective dates?

(80) What shareholder approval is required for a sale, lease, exchange, or other disposition of corporate assets?

(81) What shareholder approval is required for a corporate mortgage or pledge?

(82) What shareholder approval is required for a corporate guaranty?

Exhibit 8–4.

(continued)

(83) Do the statutory provisions provide for expeditious amendment of the articles of incorporation? Including elimination of preemptive rights? Elimination of cumulative voting? Elimination of cumulative preferred dividend arrearages? Making nonredeemable shares redeemable? Are there provisions for "restated" articles of incorporation?

(84) What are the statutory provisions permitting merger or consolidation?

(85) Are there provisions for short-merger of a subsidiary into a parent corporation? Of a parent into a subsidiary corporation?

(86) What are the statutory provisions concerning nonjudicial dissolution?

(87) What are the statutory provisions concerning judicial dissolution?

(88) How extensive are the appraisal remedies afforded dissenting shareholders? To what extent are appraisal remedies exclusive?

(89) What are the express provisions relating to shareholder derivative actions?

(90) Are there express provisions for derivative actions by a director? By an officer? By a creditor? By others?

(91) Is there statutory differentiation between shareholder derivative actions and other actions brought by shareholders?

(92) What are the provisions for indemnification for litigation expenses of directors? Of officers? Of other corporate personnel? Are there provisions for insurance?

(93) Are the statutory indemnification provisions exclusive or not with respect to directors? Officers? Other corporate personnel?

(94) What books and records must be kept within the state?

(95) What are the requirements with respect to annual and other reports?

(96) What are the annual franchise tax rates?

(97) What are the state share transfer tax rates?

(98) Are nonresident security holders subject to local taxes? Personal property taxes? Inheritance taxes?

(99) Are there express provisions to accommodate small business investment companies?

(100) Are there express provisions to accommodate open-end investment companies ("mutual funds")?

(101) To what extent are foreign corporations doing business in the state subject to the corporate statute's regulatory provisions? Local "blue sky" laws? Local fees and taxes?

(102) To what extent has the corporate statute been construed by the courts? Are judicial and administrative attitudes sympathetic?

(103) Does the state have a statute or regulations similar to Subchapter S?[12]

most of its business. If business is to be conducted in only one state, that state should be the prime candidate for incorporation.

Second, when a corporation intends to conduct relatively equal amounts of business in several jurisdictions, a state-by-state comparison of all of the checklist items will yield a net result of advantages and disadvantages for each state, and a coin-toss decision may be appropriate. The permissive jurisdictions will stand out in relative advantages and flexibility, and they should always be considered when extensive interstate business is contemplated. Remember, however, that flexibility and ease of formation and operation are frequently costly. Most states with permissive corporate laws are seeking to attract corporate business—so they can impose taxes. Make certain that the choice of a permissive state is worth the cost.

Other than the foregoing rules, perhaps the most accurate statement that can be made regarding jurisdiction selection is that the choice depends upon the circumstances of each case. The particular needs and desires of the client on each of the enumerated points in the checklist must be considered, and the decision will depend upon the weight assigned to each element of the corporate structure.

SELECTION AND RESERVATION OF CORPORATE NAME

Most states require that every corporation must have a name that indicates it is a corporation. Even in the states that do not require a corporate "catchword" as part of the name, it is recommended that organizers adopt one so that the corporate name clearly indicates to outsiders that it is a corporate entity. The selection and determination of the availability of the name should come at an early stage in the incorporation procedure. The Model Business Corporation Act specifically requires that all names of corporations contain the words "Corporation," "Company," "Incorporated," "Limited," an abbreviation of one of those words, or an abbreviation of similar meaning in another language.[13] This requirement is common to most jurisdictions. A few states will not permit "Limited" or "Company" and other statutory restrictions specify certain names and titles that may not be used in a corporate name.[14] Many state statutes also prohibit a corporate name that contains any word or phrase indicating that the corporation is organized for any purpose other than the purposes stated in its articles of incorporation. Moreover, most jurisdictions forbid a corporate name that is the same as, or deceptively similar to, the name of any other domestic corporation existing under the laws of the state or any foreign corporation authorized to transact business in the state.[15] This last requirement is a response to unfair competition and is designed to avoid the use of one organization's name and reputation by another in order to induce public patronage. For example, the Great Atlantic and Pacific Tea Company, which operates A & P Food Stores, prevented a separate corporation from using the name A & P Trucking Corporation because of the possible public confusion in the names.

The prohibition against deceptive similarity has several ramifications. On the negative side, care must be taken to avoid the selection of a name that is dangerously close to that of another well-known company or individual. Moreover, if the new corporation intends to do business in several states, the name cannot approximate a well-known name in any of those states, even if the similar name is recognized only regionally and would be unknown in all the other states. If a name has been registered as a **trademark** under federal trademark registration laws, there are substantial civil penalties for using a deceptively similar name to the trademark even if the trademark is not used in the state where the corporation is formed. On the positive side, the selected corporate name should be one the state courts will protect against infringement by others. For example, descriptive names, such as Janitorial Service, Inc., or Builders Supply Company are very vulnerable to infringement because of their general application. Similarly, Jones and Smith, Inc., could not expect complete protection because of the courts' reluctance to prohibit other Joneses and Smiths from using their own names. On the other hand, coined names that are selected arbitrarily, such as Gazorninplat Corporation, Jello, Inc., or Sunkist Fruit Co., will receive the greatest protection from infringement by a competitor.

The selection of the name is another of those individual matters for the client to decide. However, the problems of similarity, overstating corporate purposes, and statutory requirements must be considered in making that decision.

Availability of Name

To determine whether the proposed corporate name is available for use in a particular state, counsel should consult the state agency designated as the repository of corporate names, which is usually the secretary of state. That office will review the records to determine if the name has been used or if it is deceptively similar to the name of another corporation. The decision regarding availability is usually discretionary with the state authorities, and those authorities will refuse to accept a reservation of name or the articles of incorporation if they feel the name is too similar to another in use. Sometimes this issue may be negotiated if the name is important to the client, and the addition of an extra word to the name

Exhibit 8–5.

Application for Reservation
of Corporate Name
(Mississippi)

F0016 - Page 1 of 1   **OFFICE OF THE MISSISSIPPI SECRETARY OF STATE**
P.O. BOX 136, JACKSON, MS 39205-0136   (601) 359-1333
Reservation of Name

1. Type of Corporation ('X' in one only)

☐ Mississippi Profit   ☐ Mississippi Nonprofit   ☐ Mississippi Limited Partnership

☐ Foreign Limited Partnership   ☐ Foreign Profit   ☐ Foreign Nonprofit

2. Name to reserve

3. (For Foreign Corporations and Limited Partnerships ONLY) - Name elected to use in Mississippi

4. Applicant's name and address

Address

City, State, ZIP5, ZIP4   -

Signature
of Owner/
Applicant   (Please keep writing within blocks)

Rev. 01/96

---

may be enough to obtain permission to use the desired name. According to legend, one secretary of state once refused the use of the name Westwind Corporation because another corporation was using it, but permitted the new corporation to be formed under the name Westwind Corporation Jr. The addition of one word—Jr.—was enough to distinguish the names. Both corporations (apparently operating different types of businesses) operated happily ever after.

Since the name will appear on all corporate documents, the choice of the name and its **reservation** must come early in the incorporation procedure.

Reservation of Name

If the proposed corporate name is available, it should be reserved while the corporate papers are being prepared (see Exhibit 8–5, Application for Reservation of Corporate Name, and Exhibit 8–6, Certificate of Reservation of Corporate Name). Nothing is more frustrating and embarrassing than learning that a name is available, and preparing all corporate documents using that name, only to learn upon filing that the name has just been taken by another organization. Most states permit reservation of a corporate name for a limited period of time (from thirty days to twelve months) for a small fee,[16] and a few states allow extension of the reservation for another limited period. Reservation holds the particular name for the exclusive use of the corporation for the specified period.

Under the Model Business Corporation Act, a corporate name may be reserved by any person intending to organize a corporation, domestic or foreign; any foreign corporation intending to qualify to do business within the state; or any organized domestic or foreign corporation

businesses and, probably, the imagination of the drafter.[26] Details of the financial structure that must be described in the articles of incorporation in order to authorize the issuance of equity securities typically include the following:

1. the number of shares of each class and series that the corporation is authorized to issue,
2. if the shares are to be divided into classes or series:
   (a) the designation of each class
   (b) a statement of the preferences limitations and relative rights of the shares of each class or series;
3. the authority of the board of directors to issue shares in series and to determine variations in the rights and preferences between series.[27]

The articles of incorporation must authorize one or more classes of shares that have unlimited voting rights at any given time and one or more classes of shares that are entitled to receive the net assets of the corporation upon dissolution at any given time.[28] For example, a corporation could have a class of stock with voting rights on certain issues and another class with certain voting rights on other issues, so long as some group of shareholders will be able to vote on all potential issues that may arise at any time. Similarly, one class could have unlimited voting rights for a period of time (e.g., the first five years of the corporation's existence) and another class could have unlimited voting rights thereafter, so long as some shareholders could vote on any issue at any point in time. The same is true for the distribution of assets upon dissolution of the corporation: there must be some shareholder to whom the assets may be distributed at any given time. In addition, the revised Model Business Corporation Act provides certain guidance concerning the permissible variations of shares among classes, which are as follows:

1. shares that have special, conditional, or limited voting rights, or no right to vote;
2. shares that are redeemable or convertible at the option of the corporation, the shareholder, or another person, or upon the occurrence of a designated event; for cash, indebtedness, securities, or other properties; in a designated amount or in an amount determined in accordance with the designated formula;
3. shares that entitle the holders to distributions calculated in any manner, including dividends that may be cumulative, noncumulative, or partially cumulative; and
4. shares that have a preference over other shares with respect to distributions, including dividends and distributions upon dissolution of the corporation.[29]

The share authorization clause in the articles of incorporation may be very simple, as when the corporation intends to issue only one class of common stock, or quite complex, as when multiple classes of stock are to be issued with varying rights and preferences among the classes.

E X A M P L E

Capital Stock

The amount of the total authorized capital stock of the Corporation shall be 50,000 shares of common stock of the par value of $1.00 per share.

The capital stock structure is developed after studying many financial and practical matters, all of which are discussed in detail later.[30] Briefly, the decision to issue par value or **no par value** shares depends upon the consideration (money, property, or services) expected to be given in exchange for the shares, the organizational taxes imposed by the state, and the accounting ramifications of each value approach. Par value shares may not be sold for less than par value,[31] which means that a share of $100 par value stock can be issued only in exchange for cash, property, or services valued at $100 or more. No par value shares may be sold at their **stated value,** which is determined from time to time by the board of directors.[32] The no par feature adds some flexibility to the sale of shares, since the board of directors may exert control over the going price of the shares.

EXAMPLE

Capital Stock

a) The total authorized capital stock of this Corporation shall be divided into one thousand (1000) shares of which five hundred (500) shares shall be preferred stock and shall be issued at a par value of One Hundred Dollars ($100) each; and five hundred (500) shares shall be common stock which shall be issued without par value and shall be sold at One Dollar ($1) per share.

b) The holders of the shares of preferred stock shall be and are entitled to receive and shall so receive dividends on the value of such stock at the rate of six percent (6%) per annum, which shall be cumulative and which shall be set aside and paid before any dividend shall be set aside or paid upon the shares of common capital stock.

c) The voting power of the shares of capital stock in this Corporation shall be vested wholly in the holders of the shares of common capital stock. The preferred capital stock shall have no voting power whatever.

d) In the event of the liquidation or dissolution, or the winding up of the business affairs of the Corporation, the holders of the preferred shares of capital stock shall be and are entitled to be paid first for the full and determined value of their shares, together with unpaid dividends up to the time of the payment; after the payment to the preferred stockholders, the remaining assets of the Corporation shall be distributed among the holders of the common capital stock to the extent of their respective shares.

e) This Corporation shall have the right at its option to retire the preferred stock upon ten (10) days notice, by a resolution of its Board of Directors, by paying for each share of preferred stock One Hundred Two Dollars ($102) in cash, and in addition thereto all unpaid dividends accrued thereon to the date fixed for such redemption.

Organizational taxes are imposed in some jurisdictions on the total aggregate value of the authorized capital stock structure, and the distinction between par value and no par value shares is important for tax computation. To compute the total aggregate value, state statutes usually place a value on no par shares. For example, suppose the state imposes a $10 tax for each $10,000 aggregate authorized capital stock, and places a $100 value on each no par share. A corporation could authorize 100 shares with no par value for a tax of $10; it could also set par value of $1 per share and authorize 10,000 shares for the same tax. A few jurisdictions with organization taxes based upon the capital stock structure try to discourage no par shares by placing a high valuation on them for tax computation purposes.[33]

Finally, accounting principles require that the par value of issued shares must be placed in an account called stated capital, and that account is restricted so that no dividends may be paid from it. However, the consideration for no par shares may be allocated to an account called **capital surplus,** and those funds may be available in special circumstances for distribution to shareholders or for repurchase of corporate shares.[34] Thus, if the corporation issued $100 par value shares for $100 cash, all of the funds must go to the restricted stated capital account; however, if it issued no par shares for the same amount, some or all of the $100 could be placed in capital surplus, a more flexible account. These accounting ramifications may be important to a corporation that requires the flexibility to be able to distribute its equity accounts before it has accumulated profits to distribute.

The decision to issue several classes of equity securities is usually based upon the attractiveness of the securities to potential investors. If shares of common stock will sell well enough to raise the needed capital, there is usually no reason to authorize other classes of stock. However, if some investors insist that their stock must have special preferences to dividends, voting, or liquidation, then separate classes of securities will be necessary.

All special features of equity securities should be described in the articles of incorporation. Conversion privileges, redemption provisions, and restrictions on the sale of stock also should be specifically described in the articles of incorporation as part of the capital stock structure.[35]

Registered Office and Agent The corporation must maintain a **registered office** and a **registered agent** within the state so that all legal or official matters pertaining to its corporate existence may be addressed there. The registered office does not have to be the principal place of business of the corporation, although it frequently is. The registered agent may be any natural person or entity located at that office.

The registered office serves many functions and is referred to throughout state corporate laws. For example, most statutes require notices to the corporation to be addressed to the registered office, and many states require the corporation to keep the stock transfer record at the registered office.

The registered agent has the primary responsibility for receiving notices of litigation (service of process) for the corporation. If the corporation has no available registered agent, the secretary of state (or another specified state office) receives process on behalf of the corporation. Under the Model Business Corporation Act, the failure to maintain a registered agent for sixty days is grounds for an administrative dissolution of the corporation.[36]

Every state except California and Connecticut requires a registered office; but several states, including New York, Pennsylvania, and Minnesota, do not require a registered agent. The corporate statute of the jurisdiction in which incorporation is contemplated should be carefully studied for this purpose.

Registered Office and Agent

EXAMPLE

The registered office of the corporation shall be at 730 Seventeenth Street, Suite 600, Denver, Colorado, 80202, and the name of the initial registered agent at such address is Nancy A. Stober. Either the registered office or the registered agent may be changed in a manner provided by law.

The registered agent may be required to consent to his or her appointment as such. (See Exhibit 8–16, Consent to Appointment by Registered Agent.)

Incorporators The incorporators are named in the articles of incorporation, and they sign the articles. Usually the incorporators must be adults of "legal age," and they may have to meet other qualifications such as citizenship, residency, or share subscription requirements.[37]

Permissive Provisions

The preceding material considers certain provisions that are required to be enumerated in the articles of incorporation under the Model Business Corporation Act. Many other provisions must be included in the articles of incorporation under specific state statutes, and *may* be included under the Model Business Corporation Act.

Initial Directors The Model Business Corporation Act permits the articles of incorporation to name the initial board of directors and to give their addresses.[38] Regarding the structure of the board of directors, the articles of incorporation may do one of three things: (1) specify the number of directors who will constitute the board; (2) specify a formula or procedure by which to determine the desired number; or (3) delegate this determination to the bylaws.

Initial Board of Directors

EXAMPLE

The initial board of directors of the corporation shall consist of three directors, and the names and addresses of the persons who shall serve as directors until the first annual meeting of shareholders or until their successors are elected and shall qualify are as follows:

Name	Address
_____	_____
_____	_____
_____	_____

Exhibit 8–16.

Consent to Appointment by
Registered Agent
(Wyoming)

SECRETARY OF STATE
State of Wyoming
The Capitol
Cheyenne, WY 82002

CONSENT TO APPOINTMENT
BY REGISTERED AGENT

I, _____ , voluntarily consent to serve as the

registered agent for _____ on the date shown

below.

The registered agent certifies that he is: (circle one)

(a)   An individual who resides in this state and whose business office is identical with the registered office;

(b)   A domestic corporation or not-for-profit domestic corporation whose business office is identical with the registered office; or

(c)   A foreign corporation or not-for-profit foreign corporation authorized to transact business in this state whose business office is identical with the registered office.

Dated this _____ day of _____ , 19___ .

_____
Signature of Registered Agent

Revised: 7/1/96

EXAMPLE

Number of Directors

The number of directors of the corporation shall be fixed and may be altered from time to time as may be provided in the bylaws. In case of any increase in the number of directors, the additional directors may be elected by the directors or by the stockholders at an annual or special meeting, as shall be provided in the bylaws.

No particular qualifications are required for directors under the Model Business Corporation Act, although some states require legal age, share ownership, or state citizenship.[39] Moreover, the act permits a single director, but many states require three or more. If specified in the articles of incorporation, the initial directors hold office until the shareholders meet to elect their successors. The written consent of the initial board of directors to serve as directors may be necessary under state law and may be a desirable procedure in any case, since these persons will be assuming fiduciary duties to the corporation being formed. It is prudent to obtain their consent to assume those responsibilities.

Period of Duration If the issue of duration is addressed in the articles of incorporation (as it must be in many states), the articles usually state that the corporation shall exist perpetually. It is possible to establish a specified period after which the corporate existence will automatically terminate, but such a provision may cause an unnecessary burden in that an amendment to the articles of incorporation would be required if the owners should subsequently decide to continue the business. If perpetual existence is specified in the articles of incorporation, the corporation will terminate only if dissolved according to the statutory procedure.[40]

Period of Duration	EXAMPLE

This corporation shall exist perpetually [or shall terminate on December 31, 2020], unless dissolved according to law.

Corporate Purposes The corporation may engage in any lawful business, unless the articles of incorporation restrict the corporate purposes, and then the corporation may do only acts that are within the scope of its stated authorized purposes. **Corporate purposes** should be distinguished from **corporate powers,** which are discussed in "Statutory Powers of a Corporation" in Chapter 6. The purposes are the business objectives of the corporation, and the powers are the means by which those objectives are achieved. For example, the incorporators may form a corporation to purchase and rent apartment buildings. Their corporate *purposes* would specify real estate investment, management, operation, lease, and so on. Their statutory *powers* would provide that the corporation has the power to purchase and hold property, make contracts, borrow money, and so on. The powers, therefore, are the enabling authority for the corporation to pursue its purposes.

The modern trend of corporate law is either to eliminate the need to address purposes in the articles of incorporation or to permit the incorporators to adopt broad corporate purposes and thereby authorize the corporation to do any legal act. Most states allow the formation of a corporation for any lawful purposes, except banking and insurance. Several states, including Delaware and Pennsylvania, permit the articles of incorporation to authorize "any lawful activity."

In the drafting stages, the incorporators describe the general nature of the contemplated business, such as operating a bookstore, manufacturing bicycles, conducting environmental services, and so forth. After formation, however, the management of the corporation may decide to invest in real estate with its merchandising profits, or to open a cafeteria next to its bookstore, and the scope of the designated purposes in the articles of incorporation then becomes a critical consideration.

The purpose clauses of the corporation usually specify a particular type of business, as shown in the following examples.

Purposes for a Cherry Fruit Business	EXAMPLE

To buy and sell, and otherwise deal in, at both wholesale and retail, all kinds and brands of cherries; to brine and preserve maraschino cherries of every nature and character; to engage in the canning and pitting of cherries and to prepare cherries for every possible purpose and use; to engage in the buying, selling, and otherwise dealing with and in the canning, preservation, and preparation of all kinds of fruits of every nature, character, and description; and generally to do all acts reasonable and necessary for the furtherance of the foregoing business.

Purposes for a Jewelry Store	EXAMPLE

To carry on business as jewelers, gold and silver smiths; as dealers in china, curiosities, coins, medals, bullion, and precious stones; as manufacturers of and dealers in gold and silver plate, plated articles, watches, clocks, chronometers, and optical and scientific instruments and appliances of every description; and as bankers, commission agents, and general merchants.

These limited purposes, however, would not allow the corporations to operate a restaurant, or to manufacture bicycles, or to invest in real estate. When the incorporators anticipate additional activities but wish to specify purposes in the articles of incorporation, additional purpose clauses must be added.

If the state statute is sufficiently permissive to allow the articles of incorporation to authorize "any lawful activity" without further specification and the incorporators want broad purposes, the drafting of the purpose clauses is simple. However, if the state requires specificity of corporate purposes, or if the incorporators desire to restrict the corporate purposes, the drafter's job becomes more difficult. Counsel must pay close attention to detail to ensure that the drafted purpose clauses in the articles of incorporation will permit the corporation to do everything necessary to operate the intended business. The purpose clauses must anticipate expansion and give the corporation room to do everything it might be expected to do in the near future, but they must not be so overbroad that management has no business guidance. The incorporators may restrict the corporate purposes to direct management toward specific business objectives.

The law provides implied power for the corporation to conduct any necessary act consistent with its stated purposes, but the law does not allow the corporation to exceed its purposes if those purposes are restricted in the articles of incorporation. Admittedly, this is a delicate distinction. Consider the cherry fruit business described in the preceding example. The corporate *powers* would permit the corporation to buy a cannery to conduct its canning and pitting operations, and they might allow it to buy an adjacent building if expansion was contemplated. However, the corporate *purposes* would not allow it to buy the adjacent building for investment purposes. Consequently, under modern statutes, it is best to state the corporate purposes as broadly as possible. The drafter should attempt to prepare a statement of corporate purposes that is sufficiently specific to avoid excursions into unauthorized areas of business but sufficiently broad to allow expansion of the contemplated business without amendment of the articles of incorporation.

A word about the dangers lurking in the statement of corporate purposes: A corporation is not permitted to exceed its stated corporate purposes; if it does, it is said to have committed an *ultra vires* act. The law protects the shareholders from such abuses of corporate authority by allowing application by the shareholders to a court to have the unauthorized act stopped. The attorney general may protect the interests of the state by suing to stop the act or to dissolve the corporation for committing unauthorized acts. Moreover, directors and officers who have caused the corporation to venture forth into the unauthorized business activities may be held personally liable for any loss occasioned by the transactions.[41]

Preemptive Rights The articles of incorporation may contain a statement regarding shareholders' preemptive rights. A shareholder's preemptive right is the common law right to maintain a proportionate ownership interest in the corporation. If the corporation intends to issue additional shares of stock, the existing shareholders have the right to buy their proportionate shares of the new stock. Some states require preemptive rights for the shareholders unless such rights are specifically denied in the articles of incorporation.[42] Other statutes provide that preemptive rights do not exist unless specifically granted in the articles of incorporation.[43] It is good practice to always specify the desires of the incorporators on this point.

The articles of incorporation may simply deny or grant preemptive rights without further elaboration.

EXAMPLE

Preemptive Rights

No holder of any stock of the Corporation shall be entitled, as a matter of right, to purchase, subscribe for, or otherwise acquire any new or additional shares of stock of the corporation of any class, or any options or warrants to purchase, subscribe for, or otherwise acquire any such new or additional shares, or any shares, bonds, notes, debentures, or other securities convertible into or carrying options or warrants to purchase, subscribe for, or otherwise acquire any such new or additional shares.

The articles also may distinguish preemptive rights among specified classes of equity securities.

Preemptive Rights among Classes

Holders of preferred stock shall have the right to subscribe for and purchase their pro rata shares of any new preferred stock that may be issued by the Corporation, but shall have no such preemptive rights with respect to new shares of common stock that may be issued. Holders of common stock shall have the right to subscribe for and purchase their pro rata shares of any new common stock that may be issued, but shall have no such preemptive rights with respect to new shares of preferred stock that may be issued.

EXAMPLE

In addition, it is possible to limit, define, or expand preemptive rights in the articles of incorporation. For example, preemptive rights may be limited to stock issued only for cash and may be excluded from employee stock option plans. It is also good practice to specify the scope of preemptive rights with respect to **treasury shares** (stock repurchased by the company that may be subsequently resold).[44]

Cumulative Voting If shareholders are to be permitted to cumulate their shares in elections of directors, a statement to that effect in the articles of incorporation is appropriate and may be required. Cumulative voting is treated like preemptive rights in the various state statutes; that is, some states grant the right unless it is specifically denied, and others deny it unless specifically granted.[45] The articles should always reflect the corporate policy either way.

Cumulative Voting

At all elections for directors each stockholder shall be entitled to as many votes as shall equal the number of his or her shares of stock multiplied by the number of directors to be elected, and each stockholder may cast all such votes for a single director, or may distribute them among the number to be voted for, or any two or more of them, as he or she may see fit.

EXAMPLE

Optional Provisions

The Model Business Corporation Act allows the articles of incorporation to contain any provision for the regulation of internal affairs of the corporation that might ordinarily be set forth in the bylaws, as long as those provisions are not inconsistent with the statute.[46] By virtue of this broad statutory authority, the articles of incorporation may contain any number of various rules and regulations pertaining to the operation of the company. However, remember that provisions in the articles are more permanent than are bylaw provisions, since the amendment procedure for articles of incorporation is considerably more difficult.[47] The drafter should begin with this inflexibility in mind when considering miscellaneous optional provisions for the articles of incorporation.

Generally, the articles of incorporation may contain any regulation of internal affairs that is not inconsistent with the law. If the incorporators have devised a procedure for distributing keys to the corporate restrooms, for example, the procedure can be posted on a bulletin board, written into the bylaws, or given special dignity (and public notice) by being drafted into the articles of incorporation. In this case, the inflexibility of the articles could become painfully obvious if it were later discovered that the specified procedure did not cover certain corporate executives, and those executives had to wait for keys to the restroom until an amendment could be adopted.

There are, however, several instances in the Model Business Corporation Act and other corporate statutes where the articles of incorporation may modify the statutory rules, but a bylaw provision is ineffective for that purpose. Therefore, if the incorporators desire a modified approach to their corporate structure, certain additional optional provisions must be included in the articles of incorporation. The following statutory rules of the act and other corporation codes may be modified or amplified only by a special provision in the articles of incorporation.

Directors Several procedures regulating the conduct of directors must be addressed in the articles of incorporation in order for those procedures to be changed from the normal statutory scheme. The Model Business Corporation Act permits the board of directors to be dispensed with entirely under certain circumstances, and the directors' activities may be limited or restricted by provisions in the articles of incorporation.[48] Limitations may be placed on the directors' ability to fix their own compensation.[49] Several provisions may be included concerning the election and terms of the directors, requiring a vote greater than a plurality,[50] providing for directors to be elected by specific classes of shares,[51] and staggering directors' terms so that all directors are not elected in the same year.[52] Shareholders' power over the removal of directors may be restricted or eliminated,[53] and the power to fill vacancies on the board of directors may be limited to a decision by the shareholders.[54]

All of these provisions should be discussed in detail with the organizers of the corporation to determine the specific corporate structure that will best suit their needs. If these issues are not addressed in the articles of incorporation, the statutory provision concerning the resolution of these matters will govern the issues. For example, if the organizers want the board of directors to be removed only upon the vote of the holders at least ninety percent of the shares entitled to vote, a provision to that effect must be drafted in the articles of incorporation to be effective under the Model Act. If such a provision were drafted in the bylaws, it would not be effective, and the Model Act default rule, that a majority vote to remove a director is sufficient, would govern.

Limitation on Director Liability During the past decade, a combination of factors caused sharp increases in the cost of **director and officer liability insurance** (typically called "D&O insurance"), and led in many cases to its unavailability at any price. Several court decisions also eroded the confidence of members of corporate boards of directors by imposing liability for damages based upon decisions made by the directors using their business judgment (or lack of it). Many directors became concerned about their potential liability, including the nonmonetary costs of litigation such as damage to their reputations, loss of time, and distraction from other activities. Consequently, many outside directors of corporations (particularly of public corporations) resigned or declined to be elected to the board because of potential financial exposure.

Several state legislatures quickly adopted legislation to solve the problem, and most states now have adopted some form of legislation aimed at limiting the exposure of directors (and in some cases, officers) to personal liability for money damages. These limited liability statutes fall into three categories:

1. authorization for a provision in the articles of incorporation eliminating or limiting personal liability for money damages, with stated exceptions ("optional statutes");
2. elimination of personal liability for money damages, with certain exceptions ("self-executing statutes"); and
3. limitation on the amount of personal liability for money damages, with certain exceptions ("damage limitation statutes").

Delaware was the first state to enact an "optional statute," and most states have followed its lead. In these states, a corporation may adopt a provision eliminating or limiting the personal liability of a director to the corporation or its stockholders for monetary damages for breach of fiduciary duty as a director.[55] In most states, the limitation of liability does not apply to suits by third parties who are not shareholders, such as creditors of the corporation.[56] The organizers should decide whether such a limitation on the liability of directors would be appropriate for the operations of the corporation to be formed.

> ## Limitation on Director Liability
>
> The directors of this corporation shall not be liable to the corporation or its shareholders for money damages for any action taken, or any failure to take any action, as a director, except liability for (a) the amount of a financial benefit received by a director to which the director was not entitled; (b) an intentional infliction of harm on the corporation or the shareholders; (c) improper distributions from the corporation as prohibited by statute; or (d) an intentional violation of criminal law.

EXAMPLE

The principal difference among the optional statutes is found in their exceptions, which generally state the standard that a plaintiff must meet in order to impose personal liability for money damages upon a director. For example, many states do not permit the director to be relieved from liability for breach of the director's duty of loyalty to the corporation or to its stockholders, acts or omissions not in good faith, intentional misconduct, knowing violation of law, improper distributions, or any transaction from which the director derived an improper personal benefit.[57]

The most radical legislative approach to director liability is the self-executing statutes, which impose liability on a director only if the director has breached or failed to perform duties in compliance with the statutory standard of care *and* "the breach or failure to perform constitutes willful misconduct or recklessness."[58] In these states, a director would have to commit a damaging act intentionally or with careless regard for the consequences to be liable. A person seeking to hold a director responsible under such a standard would have a substantial burden to prove that the director's act justified liability.

The third approach, the damage limitation statutes, combines a provision in the articles of incorporation with a statutory limit on liability. In Virginia, for example, the damages that may be assessed against an officer or director are limited to a monetary amount specified in the articles of incorporation or the bylaws or a statutory amount based upon the compensation received by the officer or director during the previous twelve months.[59]

Indemnification of Officers and Directors   The corporation has the power to **indemnify** its management personnel from any liability or expenses incurred by reason of litigation against them in their capacities as directors, officers, or employees of the corporation. The Model Business Corporation Act specifically confers this power in sections 8.50 through 8.58. These complex provisions generally grant the right to indemnification if the individual was not negligent in the performance of his or her duties to the corporation and if the director was acting in good faith and in a manner he or she reasonably believed to be in the best interests of the corporation. In addition, if a director is acting outside of the director's "official capacity" (which would include service for any other corporation or any partnership, joint venture, trust, employee benefit plan, or other enterprise), the director may be indemnified if the director's conduct was not opposed to the best interests of the corporation. For example, suppose a director of a corporation is also a real estate developer, and she borrowed money from the local bank for her real estate investments. The real estate has declined in value, forcing the director to declare bankruptcy personally to avoid the debt. This fact is highly publicized in the local newspapers because the director is such a prominent citizen. A shareholder of the corporation sues the director, claiming that the director's conduct in becoming overextended financially has embarrassed the corporation and caused it to lose money. The director could not show that her actions in borrowing the money and filing bankruptcy were in the best interests of the corporation—they actually had little to do with the corporation's interests at the time. But the director could obtain indemnification for expenses and liability in the lawsuit if she could show that her actions were *not opposed to* the best interests of the corporation.

In jurisdictions adopting the act's provision, the statutory authority for indemnification obviates any need to grant such power in the articles of incorporation; but in most jurisdictions, the statutory right to indemnification is considerably limited.[60] Many persons would not agree to serve as a director, officer, or employee unless they knew that the corporation would stand behind them for litigation fees, expenses, and liability incurred as a result of their employment. Consequently, the articles of incorporation should establish the scope of indemnification for corporate personnel.

EXAMPLE

Indemnification

The Corporation shall indemnify any director, officer, or employee, or former director, officer, or employee of the Corporation, or any person who may have served at its request as a director, officer, or employee of another corporation in which it owns shares of capital stock, or of which it is a creditor, against expenses actually and necessarily incurred by him or her in connection with the defense of any action, suit, or proceeding in which he or she is made a party by reason of being or having been such director, officer, or employee, except in relation to matters as to which he or she shall be adjudged in such action, suit, or proceeding to be liable for negligence or misconduct in the performance of duty. The Corporation may also reimburse to any director, officer, or employee the reasonable costs of settlement of any such action, suit, or proceeding, if it shall be found by a majority of a committee composed of the directors not involved in the matter in controversy (whether or not a quorum) that it was to the interests of the corporation that such settlement be made and that such director, officer, or employee was not guilty of negligence or misconduct. Such rights of indemnification and reimbursement shall not be deemed exclusive of any other rights to which such director, officer, or employee may be entitled under any bylaws, agreement, vote of shareholders, or otherwise.

[*or*]

(1) *Definitions.* The following definitions shall apply to the terms as used in this Article:

(a) "Corporation" includes this corporation and any domestic or foreign predecessor entity of the corporation in a merger, consolidation, or other transaction in which the predecessor's existence ceased upon consummation of the transaction.

(b) "Director" means an individual who is or was a director of the corporation and an individual who, while a director of the corporation, is or was serving at the corporation's request as a director, officer, partner, trustee, employee, or agent of any other foreign or domestic corporation or of any partnership, joint venture, trust, other enterprise, or employee benefit plan. A director shall be considered to be serving an employee benefit plan at the corporation's request if his or her duties to the corporation also impose duties on or otherwise involve services by him or her to the plan or to participants in or beneficiaries of the plan. "Director" includes, unless the context otherwise requires, the estate or personal representative of a director.

(c) "Expenses" includes attorney fees.

(d) "Liability" means the obligation to pay a judgment, settlement, penalty, fine (including an excise tax assessed with respect to an employee benefit plan), or reasonable expense incurred with respect to a proceeding.

(e) "Official capacity," when used with respect to a director, means the office of director in the corporation, and, when used with respect to a person other than a director, means the office in the corporation held by the officer or the employment or agency relationship undertaken by the employee or agent on behalf of the corporation. "Official capacity" does not include service for any other foreign or domestic corporation or for any partnership, joint venture, trust, other enterprise, or employee benefit plan.

(f) "Party" includes an individual who was, is, or is threatened to be made a named defendant or respondent in a proceeding.

(g) "Proceeding" means any threatened, pending, or completed action, suit, or proceeding, whether civil, criminal, administrative, or investigative, and whether formal or informal.

(2) *Indemnification for Liability.*

(a) Except as provided in paragraph (d) of this section (2), the corporation shall indemnify against liability incurred in any proceeding any individual made a party to the proceeding because he or she is or was a director or officer if:

(I) he or she conducted himself or herself in good faith;

(II) he or she reasonably believed:

(A) in the case of conduct in his or her official capacity with the corporation, that his or her conduct was in the corporation's best interests; or

(B) in all other cases, that his or her conduct was at least not opposed to the corporation's best interests; and

(III) in the case of any criminal proceeding, he or she had no reasonable cause to believe his or her conduct was unlawful.

(b) A director's or officer's conduct with respect to an employee benefit plan for a purpose he or she reasonably believed to be in the interests of the participants in or beneficiaries of the plan is conduct that satisfies the requirements of this Section (2). A director's or officer's conduct with respect to an employee benefit plan for a purpose that he or she did not reasonably believe to be in the interests of the participants in or beneficiaries of the plan shall be deemed not to satisfy the requirements of this Section (2).

(c) The termination of any proceeding by judgment, order, settlement, or conviction, or upon a plea of nolo contendere or its equivalent, is not of itself determinative that the individual did not meet the standard of conduct set forth in paragraph (a) of this Section (2).

(d) The corporation may not indemnify a director or officer under this Section (2) either:

(I) in connection with a proceeding by or in the right of the corporation in which the director or officer was adjudged liable to the corporation; or

(II) in connection with any proceeding charging improper personal benefit to the director or officer, whether or not involving action in his or her official capacity, in which he or she was adjudged liable on the basis that personal benefit was improperly received by him or her.

(e) Indemnification permitted under this Section (2) in connection with a proceeding by or in the right of the corporation is limited to reasonable expenses incurred in connection with the proceeding.

(3) *Mandatory Indemnification.*

(a) Except as limited by these Articles of Incorporation, the corporation shall be required to indemnify a director or officer of the corporation who was wholly successful, on the merits or otherwise, in defense of any proceeding to which he or she was a party against reasonable expenses incurred by him or her in connection with the proceeding.

(b) Except as otherwise limited by these Articles of Incorporation, a director or officer who is or was a party to a proceeding may apply for indemnification to the court conducting the proceeding or to another court of competent jurisdiction. On receipt of an application, the court, after giving any notice the court considers necessary, may order indemnification in the following manner:

(I) If it determines the director or officer is entitled to mandatory indemnification, the court shall order indemnification under paragraph (a) of this Section (3), in which case the court shall also order the corporation to pay the director's or officer's reasonable expenses incurred to obtain court-ordered indemnification.

(II) If it determines that the director or officer is fairly and reasonably entitled to indemnification in view of all the relevant circumstances, whether or not he or she met the standard of conduct set forth in paragraph (a) of Section (2) of this Article or was adjudged liable in the circumstances described in paragraph (d) of Section (2) of this Article, the court may order such indemnification as the court deems proper; except that the indemnification with respect to any proceeding in which liability shall have been adjudged in the circumstances described in paragraph (d) of Section (2) of this Article is limited to reasonable expenses incurred.

(4) *Limitation on Indemnification.*

(a) The corporation may not indemnify a director of officer under Section (2) of this Article unless authorized in the specific case after a determination has been made that indemnification of the director or officer is permissible in the circumstances because he or she has met the standard of conduct set forth in paragraph (a) of Section (2) of this Article.

(b) The determination required to be made by paragraph (a) of this Section (4) shall be made:

(I) by the board of directors by a majority vote of a quorum, which quorum shall consist of directors not parties to the proceeding; or

(II) A quorum cannot be obtained, by a majority vote of a committee of the board designated by the board, which committee shall consist of two or more directors not parties to the proceeding; except that directors who are parties to the proceeding may participate in the designation of directors for the committee.

(c) If the quorum cannot be obtained or the committee cannot be established under paragraph (b) of this Section (4), or even if a quorum is obtained or a committee designated if such quorum or committee so directs, the determination required to be made by paragraph (a) of this Section (4) shall be made:

(I) by independent legal counsel selected by a vote of the board of directors or the committee in the manner specified in subparagraph (I) or (II) of paragraph (b) of this Section (4) or, if a

E X A M P L E

quorum of the full board cannot be obtained and a committee cannot be established by independent legal counsel selected by a majority vote of the full board; or

(II) by the shareholders.

(d) Authorization of indemnification and evaluation as to reasonableness of expenses shall be made in the same manner as the determination that indemnification is permissible; except that if the determination that indemnification is permissible is made by independent legal counsel, authorization of indemnification and evaluation as to reasonableness of expenses shall be made by the body that selected said counsel.

(5) *Advance Payment of Expenses.*

(a) The corporation shall pay for or reimburse the reasonable expenses incurred by a director, officer, employee, or agent who is a party to a proceeding in advance of the final disposition of the proceeding if:

(I) the director, officer, employee, or agent furnishes the corporation a written affirmation of his or her good faith belief that he or she has met the standard of conduct described in subparagraph (I) of paragraph (a) of Section (2) of this Article;

(II) the director, officer, employee, or agent furnishes the corporation a written undertaking, executed personally or on his or her behalf, to repay the advance if it is determined that he or she did not meet such standard of conduct; and

(III) a determination is made that the facts then known to those making the determination would not preclude indemnification under this Section (5).

(b) The undertaking required by subparagraph (II) of paragraph (a) of this Section (5) shall be an unlimited general obligation of the director, officer, employee, or agent, but need not be secured and may be accepted without reference to financial ability to make repayment.

(c) Determinations and authorizations of payments under this Section shall be made in the manner specified under Section (4) hereof.

(6) *Reimbursement of Witness Expenses.* The corporation shall pay or reimburse expenses incurred by a director in connection with his or her appearance as a witness in a proceeding at a time when he or she has not been made a named defendant or respondent in the proceeding.

(7) *Insurance for Indemnification.* The corporation may purchase and maintain insurance on behalf of a person who is or was a director, officer, employee, fiduciary, or agent of the corporation or who, while a director, officer, employee, fiduciary, or agent of the corporation, is or was serving at the request of the corporation as a director, officer, partner, trustee, employee, fiduciary, or agent of any other foreign or domestic corporation or of any partnership, joint venture, trust, other enterprise, or employee benefit plan against any liability asserted against or incurred by him or her in any such capacity or arising out of his or her status as such, whether or not the corporation would have the power to indemnify him or her against such liability under the provisions of this Article. Any such insurance may be procured from any insurance company designated by the Board of Directors of the corporation, whether such insurance company is formed under the laws of Colorado or any other jurisdiction of the United States of America, including any insurance company in which the corporation has equity or any other interest, through stock or otherwise.

(8) *Notice of Indemnification.* Any indemnification of or advance of expenses to a director in accordance with this Article, if arising out of a proceeding by or on behalf of the corporation, shall be reported in writing to the shareholders with or before the notice of the next shareholders' meeting.

(9) *Indemnification of Officers, Employees, and Agents of the Corporation.* The Board of Directors may indemnify and advance expenses to an officer, employee, or agent of the corporation who is not a director of the corporation to the same or greater extent as to a director if such indemnification and advance expense payment is provided for in these Articles of Incorporation, the Bylaws, by resolution of the shareholders or directors, or by contract, in a manner consistent with the Colorado Corporation Code.

Purchase of Corporate Shares Although the Model Business Corporation Act has been amended to eliminate statutory restrictions on purchases of corporate shares,[61] many state statutes permit the corporation to repurchase its own shares from investors, thereby creating *treasury shares.* These statutes, however, limit the source of funds for such purchases to unreserved and unrestricted earned surplus, which means that the corporation may repurchase its own shares from investors only with accumulated profits that have not been designated for any other purpose. Under these statutes, if no profits have accumulated, the corporation may not repurchase its own stock. However, the articles of incorporation may provide that capital surplus (the excess amount collected over par value, or the amount collected and designated capital surplus for no par value shares) may be used in addition to earned surplus for this purpose. There are many reasons supporting this flexibility. For example, management may desire to reduce the number of shares outstanding so as to increase the earnings-per-share figures, or it may wish to reacquire outstanding shares to hold for employee stock purchase plans. Counsel should remember that an appropriate clause in the articles of incorporation is necessary to open the capital surplus account for the repurchase of shares.

The provisions of the articles of incorporation may have a negative impact on the corporation's purchase of its own securities. The articles may restrict management by requiring that all corporate shares repurchased by the corporation be canceled and not resold or reissued. Management is not bound to cancel such shares, however, without an express provision to that effect in the articles of incorporation.

EXAMPLE

Repurchase of Corporate Shares

The corporation shall have the power to repurchase its shares of cumulative preferred stock with any surplus then in existence that has not been otherwise reserved or restricted. [Check statutory authority for the type of surplus that may be permitted for repurchase of shares.]

[*and*]

Upon repurchase of shares of the corporation, the corporation shall cancel and retire the same, and such shares shall not be held as treasury shares or reissued to shareholders under any circumstances.

Reservation of the Right to Fix Consideration for Shares to the Shareholders

Many matters that are ordinarily determined by the directors may be reserved to the shareholders by an appropriate clause in the articles of incorporation. This is one of them. Section 6.21 of the Model Business Corporation Act vests in directors the power to determine the price of shares and proper consideration for the issuance of those shares, but the shareholders may exercise this power if the articles of incorporation so provide.

EXAMPLE

Right to Fix Consideration for Shares

The shareholders of the corporation at a meeting duly called for such purpose shall fix and determine the stated value of the shares of the corporation.

Stock Rights and Options The corporation may create **stock options** or stock rights that entitle the holder of the option or right to buy shares at a designated price. The articles of incorporation may restrict management in creating such options or rights and may also elaborate upon the terms of those options or rights, including time of exercise and price. A restrictive provision in the articles of incorporation would be necessary only if the incorporators wanted to narrow management's broad statutory authority to create such options, as is contained in section 6.24 of the Model Business Corporation Act.

EXAMPLE

Restrictions on the Issuance of Stock Rights and Options

The board of directors may not, without the express approval of at least the majority of the then outstanding shares of the corporation at a meeting duly called for such purpose, create or issue rights or options entitling the holders thereof to purchase from the corporation shares of any class or classes. Further, even upon such approval by the shareholders, the board of directors shall not create and issue such rights or options that shall provide for a price less than fifty percent (50%) of the then market value of such shares, determined by an independent certified public accountant of the corporation, or upon terms that would permit the holder of such options or rights to pay the purchase price of such shares over a period longer than six months.

Quorum and Vote of Shareholders and Directors A majority of the shares entitled to vote is a **quorum** for shareholder meetings, and the affirmative vote of the majority of the quorum carries action on behalf of the shareholders under section 7.25 of the Model Business Corporation Act. The articles of incorporation may vary these requirements in any manner, but most states still provide that a quorum may never be less than one-third of the shares entitled to vote. Thus, the articles of incorporation can provide that a quorum shall be forty percent of the shares entitled to vote and shareholder action requires an affirmative vote of seventy-five percent of the shares represented, or that a quorum requires eighty percent of the shares entitled to vote and shareholder action requires eighty percent of the shares represented, and so forth.

The articles of incorporation may similarly modify the quorum and vote necessary for director action under section 8.24. However, a quorum or vote of directors usually may not be reduced below a majority, and the voting or quorum requirements may be increased only by the articles of incorporation. The Model Business Corporation Act permits the quorum of a board of directors to be reduced to as low as one-third of the directors in office.[62]

EXAMPLE   **Quorum and Vote of Shareholders**

The quorum of the shareholders of this corporation for each annual or special meeting of the shareholders shall be one-third of the shares then outstanding and entitled to vote. No resolution of the corporation at any meeting of the shareholders shall be adopted except by the vote of at least seventy-five percent (75%) of the shares represented in a properly called meeting at which a quorum of the shares is present.

EXAMPLE   **Vote of Directors**

No resolution of the corporation at any meeting, whether regular or special, shall be adopted except by the unanimous vote of the three directors duly elected as provided herein.

Directors are permitted by statute to take action without a meeting by signing a consent to action in writing.[63] The articles of incorporation may deny this power, however, if the incorporators want their directors to act only in formal session.

Shareholder Control of Bylaws The initial bylaws of the corporation are adopted either by the incorporators or the board of directors at an organizational meeting, and the normal statutory rule is that the board of directors has the power to alter, amend, or repeal the bylaws.[64] This power may be reserved to the shareholders in the articles of incorporation.

EXAMPLE   **Amendments to the Bylaws**

The bylaws of this corporation shall not be amended, modified, or altered except by the vote of the shareholders of the corporation at a meeting of the shareholders, duly called, at which a quorum is present.

The articles of incorporation may also reserve to the shareholders the right to adopt or amend a bylaw that provides for greater quorum or voting requirements for the shareholders than are required by statute.[65] With this authority placed in the articles of incorporation, the shareholders may, from time to time, amend and modify their own quorum and voting requirements by simply changing the bylaws.

Distribution Provisions The board of directors has full discretion under the Model Business Corporation Act for the payment of **dividends** to shareholders.[66] The articles of incorporation may restrict this discretion, and may establish certain conditions that must be satisfied before dividends may be declared. Conversely, in most states the articles of incorporation may expand the corporation's ability to distribute cash or property to shareholders by expressly authorizing such distributions out of capital surplus.[67] Moreover, the articles of incorporation for a corporation whose principal business is the exploitation of natural resources, as in timber operations, oil wells, and mines, may authorize the payment of dividends from **depletion reserves,** an account that reflects the reduction of the natural resources available to the corporation.[68]

Restriction on Payment of Dividends

The board of directors of the corporation may not pay or declare a dividend during the first two years of the corporation's operation of its business. Thereafter, the board of directors may, from time to time, declare and pay dividends in accordance with the law provided that the corporation has adequate cash reserves at all times to meet six months' projected operating expenses.

EXAMPLE

Distributions from Capital Surplus

The board of directors of the corporation may, from time to time, distribute to the shareholders out of capital surplus of the corporation a portion of the assets of the corporation, in cash or property, provided:

a) no such distribution shall be made at a time when the corporation is insolvent or when the distribution would render the corporation insolvent;

b) no such distribution shall be made to the holders of any class of shares unless all cumulative dividends accrued on all preferred classes of shares entitled to preferential dividends have been fully paid;

c) no such distribution shall be made to the holders of any class of shares that would reduce the remaining net assets of the corporation below the aggregate preferential amount payable in the event of an involuntary liquidation to the holders of shares having preferential rights to the assets of the corporation in the event of liquidation; and

d) such distribution, when made, shall be identified as a distribution from capital surplus and the amount per share disclosed to shareholders receiving the same concurrently with the distribution thereof.

EXAMPLE

Payment of Dividends from Depletion Reserves

The board of directors may, from time to time, declare and the corporation may pay dividends in cash from the depletion reserves earned by the corporation through its business of exploiting natural resources, but such reserves and the amount per share paid from such reserves shall be disclosed to the shareholders receiving the same concurrently with the distribution thereof.

EXAMPLE

Transactions with Interested Directors A director owes a strict fiduciary duty of loyalty to the corporation and, in exercising his or her responsibilities, must strive to represent the corporation without any conflict of interest. The common law looked askance at any contract formed between a director's corporation and the director in a personal capacity or between the director's corporation and another corporation for which the same person also served as a director. When the same director appeared in the negotiations for both sides of the transaction, either personally or as a director to another corporation, the transaction was always vulnerable to a court test and would be upheld only upon a showing that it was eminently fair despite the apparent conflict.

In modern corporations, common, or **interlocking,** directors appear frequently, and it is good practice to include in the articles of incorporation a clause that describes the corporation's position on transactions where a conflict of interest may be implied. The clause should provide that such transactions will not be considered automatically invalid, but also should not completely exculpate the directors involved. The conflict of interest protection should be preserved for the rare cases where a director has compromised the corporation for personal gain.

EXAMPLE

Transactions with Interested Directors

No contract or other transaction between the corporation and any other corporation, whether or not a majority of the shares of the capital stock of the other corporation is owned by the corporation, and no act of the corporation shall in any way be affected or invalidated by the fact that any of the directors of the corporation are pecuniarily or otherwise interested in, or are directors or officers of, the other corporation. Any director individually, or any firm of which the director may be a member, may be a party to, or may be pecuniarily or otherwise interested in, any contract or transaction of the corporation, provided that the fact that the director of the firm is so interested shall be disclosed to or is known by the Board of Directors or a majority thereof, and provided that any director of the corporation who is also a director or officer of the other corporation, or who is so interested, may be counted in determining the existence of a quorum at any meeting of the Board of Directors of the corporation to authorize such contract or transaction, and may vote at that meeting to authorize such contract or transaction, with like force and effect as if he or she were not the director or officer of the other corporation or not so interested.

Classification, Compensation, and Qualifications of Directors   The articles of incorporation may provide for staggered terms for directors to ensure continuity of management policies. A staggered board of directors will always have some "seasoned" members.[69] Section 8.06 of the Model Business Corporation Act permits classification of directors only if the entire board consists of nine or more members. A sample classification clause for the articles of incorporation follows.

EXAMPLE

Classification of Directors

At the first annual meeting of the shareholders, the members of the Board of Directors shall be divided into three classes of three members each. The members of the first class shall hold office for a term of one year; the members of the second class shall hold office for a term of two years; the members of the third class shall hold office for a term of three years. At all annual elections thereafter, three directors shall be elected by the shareholders for a term of three years to succeed the three directors whose terms then expire, provided that nothing herein shall be construed to prevent the election of a director to succeed himself or herself.

As long as the articles of incorporation are touching upon some matters relating to directors, qualifications may also be covered. Under the Model Business Corporation Act, directors need not have any particular qualifications to serve as such,[70] but the articles of incorporation or the bylaws may impose qualifications for directors. It may be desirable to require that directors be shareholders, for example, or that they be over thirty-five years of age, or perhaps under thirty-five years of age. Director qualifications should be tailored to the desires of the incorporators.

FILING AND OTHER FORMALITIES

Filing Procedure

The articles of incorporation are filed with the secretary of state or other designated public official, and the Model Business Corporation Act requires an original and a conformed (exact) copy to be filed.[71] Several states also require that the articles be filed with certain designated county offices in which the corporation has its registered office, and the corporation is not properly formed unless the articles of incorporation are filed in all places required by statute.[72] After determining that the articles of incorporation are in proper form and that all fees have been paid, the secretary of state will return the duplicate copy of the articles of incorporation with the certificate of incorporation. Many states are now providing on-line filing of articles of incorporation and other entity documents through Internet access. Where on-line filing is permitted, it is also possible to download a certificate confirming that the document has been filed appropriately.

Miscellaneous Formalities

Each state statute treats the execution and filing of the articles of incorporation differently. All jurisdictions require that the articles of incorporation must be signed by the incorporator. The Model Business Corporation Act states simply that the incorporators sign the document, but acknowledgment (a procedure whereby the signatures of the incorporators must be notarized) is required in the New York statute and in several other states.[73] County recording of the articles of incorporation is a common formality. Some states require approval of the state corporation commission,[74] filing with a probate judge,[75] or publication of the articles of incorporation in a newspaper of general circulation in the county where the corporation has its registered office.[76] Finally, a state may require certain other documents to be filed with the articles of incorporation. For example, California requires the filing of an application for a permit to issue stock with the commissioner of corporations, and many states that require payment of a minimum amount of paid-in capital also require an affidavit of subscription or payment to accompany the articles of incorporation.

Careful analysis of the particular state statute under which the corporation is to be formed is absolutely necessary to ensure strict compliance with its provisions.[77]

Payment of Capital

The Model Business Corporation Act formerly required that a certain amount of capital must be collected before a corporation may commence business, and many states have preserved this rule. In those states, the payment of the preincorporation share subscriptions in the prescribed amount is a formality that must be satisfied before the corporation may commence business.

CORPORATE EXISTENCE

Modern statutes have adopted simple incorporation procedures, the principal features of which are the preparation and filing of the articles of incorporation and, in most cases, the subsequent issuance of the certificate of incorporation (see Exhibit 8–17, Certificate of Incorporation). In most states, corporate existence begins when the secretary of state, after reviewing the articles of incorporation, issues the certificate of incorporation.[78] The Model Business Corporation Act and several jurisdictions, including Maine, Michigan, New York, Delaware, and California, provide that corporate existence begins when the articles of incorporation are *filed* with or endorsed by the appropriate state official.[79]

The point at which the corporation is born is used to circumscribe shareholder and promoter liabilities for corporate obligations and to establish the beginning of corporate characteristics, such as taxation as a separate entity. When the certificate of incorporation is issued, or, in the appropriate case, when the articles are filed, the corporation is said to be a **de jure corporation,** or a corporation by law, and it acquires all power to act in accordance with the statute under which it is organized.

Exhibit 8–17.

Certificate of Incorporation
(North Dakota)

FORMALITIES AFTER FORMATION OF A CORPORATION

Although the corporation is formed when the articles of incorporation are filed or when a certificate of incorporation is issued, several other matters should precede commencement of the corporate business.

Organizational Meetings

Organizational meetings of the incorporators and the initial directors are usually required as one of the first matters of corporate business. Because organizational meetings are quite routine, counsel may draft the minutes in advance and use the predrafted minutes as an agenda for the meetings. The particular statute of each state should be consulted to determine which of the corporate groups (incorporators, directors, or shareholders) are required to hold an organizational meeting. The Model Business Corporation Act requires an organizational meeting of the incorporators if initial directors are not named in the articles of incorporation. If initial directors are named in the articles of incorporation, the initial directors are to hold the organizational meeting.[80] Several states require only an organizational meeting of the incorporators.[81] Florida, Hawaii, New Jersey, and most other states require only an organizational meeting of the directors. In addition, there is nothing wrong with holding an organizational meeting for a corporate group that is not required to meet by statute.

Organizational meetings assist in establishing the air of formality that must be continually observed in corporate operations. The important point, however, is the corporation's need to hold the statutory organizational meetings so as to be considered a properly formed corporation. Even if corporate existence begins when the certificate of incorporation is issued or the articles are filed, a failure to observe the statutory formalities following these events may destroy the protection and special privileges of the corporation.

An organizational meeting of the incorporators may consider acceptance of the certificate of incorporation or articles of incorporation and acknowledgment of the payment of taxes, election of initial directors (if they are not named in the articles of incorporation) and resignation of any accommodation (dummy) directors, authorization of the board of directors to issue shares, adoption of bylaws, transfers of any subscriptions from accommodation (dummy) incorporators, and transaction of any other business appropriate for incorporators to consider.

An organizational meeting of the board of directors will consider many of the same matters, and if an organizational meeting of incorporators has been held, the board usually reviews and approves the business conducted there. In addition, the board of directors will decide other matters of corporate business, such as the issuance and transfer of shares, ratification of preincorporation agreements, banking arrangements, the election of officers, qualification as a foreign corporation, and tax plans.[82] The organizational meeting will be discussed in more detail in Chapter 10.

Corporate Supplies

The attorney's office usually orders the corporation's supplies for the newly formed business. The corporation must maintain a **minute book** and a **stock transfer ledger,** and it must have share certificates and a **corporate seal.** Corporation kits containing these supplies are available from many local printers and those who advertise in legal periodicals.

BYLAWS

Bylaws complement the state statute and the articles of incorporation by prescribing rules to regulate the internal affairs of the corporation. The bylaws must be consistent with the articles of incorporation and the statute. Rules that are for the internal management and are intended to be flexible are best described in the bylaws, since they are most easily amended. On the other hand, rules that require permanence should be placed in the articles of incorporation. Interchangeability between the articles and bylaws is facilitated by the statutory rule that any provision that is required or permitted to be set forth in the bylaws may also be included in the articles of incorporation.[83] The converse is not true.

The authority to adopt bylaws is contained in the state statute, which may also suggest certain matters that should be contained in the bylaws.[84] Most states and the Model Business Corporation Act simply provide that the bylaws may contain any provision for the regulation and management of the corporation's affairs that is not inconsistent with statutory law or the articles of incorporation.[85] In these jurisdictions, the bylaws may be either simple or complicated. Certain provisions usually appear in the bylaws, such as the place of holding meetings of shareholders and the time of the annual meeting of shareholders; the number of directors, except the first board of directors; the notice to be given for directors' meetings; the procedure for the election and appointment of officers; and a description of the officers' duties.

The bylaws should not be complicated with intricate procedures for corporate operation, because a complicated bylaw provision may become a trap for the unwary, rather than a useful guide to corporate management. However, the bylaws should be as extensive and thorough as necessary to ensure that the procedures for internal management of the corporation are fully described in writing for the officers and directors.

Initial Bylaws

The adoption of the initial bylaws is the responsibility of the incorporators, the shareholders, or the board of directors, depending upon the jurisdiction involved. In New York, the incorporators adopt the initial bylaws. The bylaws are then approved by the board of directors at its organizational meeting. In a few jurisdictions, the shareholders adopt the initial bylaws.[86] The Model Business Corporation Act provides that the incorporators or the board of directors (if the initial board is named in the articles of incorporation) will adopt the initial bylaws of the corporation.[87] Most jurisdictions and the act provide for the adoption of the initial bylaws by the board of directors, but the articles of incorporation may reserve this power to the shareholders.[88]

The bylaws are prepared by counsel, with guidance from the incorporators and the initial directors, and they are presented at the organizational meeting for the approval of the appropriate intracorporate group.

Content of Bylaws

Standard bylaw provisions deal with the following matters:

1. Offices
   (a) Location of the principal office of the corporation
   (b) Location of the registered office of the corporation
   (c) Authority to change the address of the registered office by the board of directors

---

EXAMPLE

Offices

The principal office of the Corporation in the State of South Dakota shall be located in the City of Deadwood, County of Lawrence. The Corporation may have such other offices, either within or without the State of South Dakota, as the Board of Directors may designate or as the business of the Corporation may require from time to time.

The registered office of the Corporation required by the South Dakota Business Corporation Act to be maintained in the State of South Dakota may be, but need not be, identical with the principal office in the State of South Dakota, and the address of the registered office may be changed from time to time by the Board of Directors.

---

2. Shareholders[89]
   (a) Time of the annual meeting

EXAMPLE

Annual Meeting

The annual meeting of the shareholders shall be held on the first Tuesday in the month of May in each year, beginning with the year 2005, at the hour of 9:00 A.M., for the purpose of electing directors and for the transaction of such other business as may come before the meeting. If the day fixed for the annual meeting shall be a legal holiday in the State of South Dakota, the meeting shall be held on the next succeeding business day. If the election of directors shall not be held on the day designated herein for any annual meeting of the shareholders, or at any adjournment thereof, the Board of Directors shall cause the election to be held at a special meeting of the shareholders as soon thereafter as is convenient.

(b) Procedure for calling special meetings of shareholders

Special Meetings

Special meetings of the shareholders, for any purpose or purposes, unless otherwise prescribed by statute, may be called by the President or by the Board of Directors, and shall be called by the President at the request of the holders of not less than one-tenth of all the outstanding shares of the corporation entitled to vote at the meeting.

(c) Place of the shareholder meetings

(d) Authority for waiver of notice to be signed by shareholders entitled to vote at the meeting—This procedure permits a cure of defective notice or failure to give notice by obtaining written waivers from shareholders entitled to notice.

Place of Meeting and Waiver of Notice

The Board of Directors may designate any place, either within or without the State of South Dakota, as the place of meeting for any annual meeting or for any special meeting called by the Board of Directors. A waiver of notice signed by all shareholders entitled to vote at a meeting may designate any place, either within or without the State of South Dakota, as the place for the holding of such meeting. If no designation is made, or if a special meeting be otherwise called, the place of meeting shall be the principal office of the Corporation in the State of South Dakota.

(e) Procedure for sending notice of meeting and the time period within which notice is given.

Notice of Meeting

Written notice stating the place, day, and hour of the meeting, and in case of a special meeting, the purpose or purposes for which the meeting is called, shall be delivered not less than ten nor more than fifty days before the date of the meeting, either personally or by mail, by or at the direction of the President, or the Secretary, or the persons calling the meeting, to each shareholder or record entitled to vote at the meeting. If mailed, such notice shall be deemed to be delivered when deposited in the United States mail, addressed to the shareholder at his or her address as it appears on the stock transfer books of the corporation, with postage thereon prepaid.

(f) Procedure for determining the shareholders entitled to notice or entitled to vote or entitled to receive dividends—This procedure states a particular time that the stock transfer books will be closed in order to determine the holders of record.

Determination of Shareholders Entitled to Notice or Vote

For the purpose of determining shareholders entitled to notice of or to vote at any meeting of shareholders or any adjournment thereof, or shareholders entitled to receive payment of any dividend, or in order to make a determination of shareholders for any other proper purpose, the Board of Directors of the Corporation may provide that the stock transfer books shall be closed for a stated period but not to exceed, in any case, fifty days. If the stock transfer books shall be closed for the purpose of determining shareholders entitled to notice of or to vote at a meeting of shareholders, such books shall be closed for at least ten days immediately preceding such meeting. In lieu of closing the stock transfer books, the Board of Directors may fix in advance a date as the record date for any such determination of shareholders, such date in any case to be not more than fifty days, and in case of a meeting of shareholders, not less than ten days, prior to the date on which the particular action, requiring such determination of shareholders, is to be taken. If the stock transfer books are not closed and no record date is fixed for the determination of shareholders entitled to notice of or to vote at a meeting of shareholders, or shareholders entitled to receive

EXAMPLE

(continued)

payment of a dividend, the date on which notice of the meeting is mailed or the date on which the resolution of the Board of Directors declaring such dividend is adopted, as the case may be, shall be the record date for such determination of shareholders. When a determination of shareholders entitled to vote at any meeting of shareholders has been made as provided in this section, that determination shall apply to any adjournment thereof except where the determination has been made through the closing of the stock transfer books and the stated period of closing has expired.

(g) Procedure for preparation of **voting lists**

(h) Provision for examination of voting lists

EXAMPLE

Voting Lists

The officer or agent having charge of the stock transfer books for shares of the Corporation shall make a complete list of the shareholders entitled to vote at each meeting of shareholders or any adjournment thereof, arranged in alphabetical order, with the address of and the number of shares held by each. The list shall be produced and kept open at the time and place of the meeting and shall be subject to the inspection of any shareholder during the whole time of the meeting.

(i) Number of shares required to constitute a quorum, and number of shares required to adjourn the meeting of shareholders

EXAMPLE

Quorum

A majority of the outstanding shares of the Corporation entitled to vote, represented in person or by proxy, shall constitute a quorum at a meeting of shareholders. If less than a majority of the outstanding shares are represented at a meeting, a majority of the shares so represented may adjourn the meeting from time to time without further notice. At an adjourned meeting at which a quorum is present or represented, any business may be transacted that might have been transacted at the meeting as originally notified. The shareholders present at a duly organized meeting may continue to transact business until adjournment, notwithstanding the withdrawal of enough shareholders to leave less than a quorum.

(j) Authorization for voting by proxy

EXAMPLE

Proxies

At all meetings of shareholders, a shareholder may vote in person or by proxy executed in writing by the shareholder or by his or her duly authorized attorney in fact. Such proxy shall be filed with the secretary of the Corporation before or at the time of the meeting. No proxy shall be valid after eleven months from the date of its execution, unless otherwise provided in the proxy.

(k) Voting entitlements of each class of stock

EXAMPLE

Voting of Shares

Each outstanding share entitled to vote shall be entitled to one vote upon each matter submitted to a vote at a meeting of shareholders.

(l) Authorization to vote by representatives of the holder of record (e.g., administrator, executor, agent of another corporation, etc.)

Voting of Shares by Certain Holders

Shares standing in the name of another corporation may be voted by such officer, agent, or proxy as the bylaws of that corporation may prescribe or, in the absence of such provision, as the board of directors of that corporation may determine.

Shares held by an administrator, executor, guardian, or conservator may be voted by that person, either in person or by proxy, without a transfer of the shares into his or her name. Shares standing in the name of a trustee may be voted by him or her, either in person or by proxy, but no trustee shall be entitled to vote shares held by that trustee without a transfer of the shares into his or her name.

Shares standing in the name of a receiver may be voted by the receiver, and shares held by or under the control of a receiver may be voted by the receiver without the transfer thereof into his or her name if such authority is contained in an appropriate order of the court by which the receiver was appointed.

A shareholder whose shares are pledged shall be entitled to vote the shares until the shares have been transferred into the name of the pledgee, and thereafter the pledgee shall be entitled to vote the shares so transferred.

Neither shares of its own stock held by the Corporation, nor those held by another corporation if a majority of the shares entitled to vote for the election of directors of the other corporation are held by the Corporation, shall be voted at any meeting or counted in determining the total number of outstanding shares at any given time for purposes of any meeting.

(m) Informal action by the shareholders

Informal Action by Shareholders

Any action required to be taken at a meeting of the shareholders, or any action that may be taken at a meeting of the shareholders, may be taken without a meeting if a consent in writing, setting forth the action so taken, shall be signed by all of the shareholders entitled to vote with respect to the subject matter thereof.

(n) Cumulative voting rights

Cumulative Voting

At each election for directors, every shareholder entitled to vote at the election shall have the right to vote, in person or by proxy, the number of shares owned by that shareholder for as many persons as there are directors to be elected and for whose election that shareholder has a right to vote, or to cumulate his or her votes by giving one candidate as many votes as the number of the directors multiplied by the number of his or her shares shall equal, or by distributing the votes on the same principles among any number of candidates.

3. Board of directors
   (a) Authorization for the board of directors to manage the business[90]

General Powers

The business and affairs of the Corporation shall be managed by its Board of Directors.

(b) The number, tenure, and qualifications of directors

Number, Tenure, and Qualifications

The number of directors of the Corporation shall be nine. Each director shall hold office until the next annual meeting of shareholders and until his or her successor has been elected and qualified. Directors need not be residents of the State of South Dakota or shareholders of the Corporation.

(c) Classification of directors (if desired)[91]

EXAMPLE

Classification of Directors

At the first annual meeting of the shareholders, the members of the Board of Directors shall be divided into three classes of three members each. The members of the first class shall hold office for a term of one year; the members of the second class shall hold office for a term of two years; the members of the third class shall hold office for a term of three years. At all annual elections thereafter, three directors shall be elected by the shareholders for a term of three years to succeed the three directors whose terms then expire; provided that nothing herein shall be construed to prevent the election of a director to succeed himself or herself.

(d) Time and place for regular meetings[92]

EXAMPLE

Regular Meetings

A regular meeting of the Board of Directors shall be held without other notice than this Bylaw immediately after, and at the same place as, the annual meeting of shareholders. The Board of Directors may provide, by resolution, the time and place, either within or without the State of South Dakota, for the holding of additional regular meetings without other notice than such resolution.

(e) Procedure for calling special meetings

EXAMPLE

Special Meetings

Special meetings of the Board of Directors may be called by or at the request of the President or any two directors. The person or persons authorized to call special meetings of the Board of Directors may fix any place, either within or without the State of South Dakota, as the place for holding any special meeting of the Board of Directors called by them.

(f) Procedure for giving notice of special meetings
(g) Authorization to waive notice of any meeting

EXAMPLE

Notice and Authorization to Waive Notice

Notice of any special meeting shall be given at least two days previously thereto by written notice delivered personally or mailed to each director at his or her business address, or by telegram. If mailed, such notice shall be deemed to be delivered when deposited in the United States mail so addressed, with postage thereon prepaid. If notice is given by telegram, such notice shall be deemed to be delivered when the telegram is delivered to the telegraph company. Any director may waive notice of any meeting. The attendance of a director at a meeting shall constitute a waiver of notice of that meeting, except where a director attends a meeting for the express purpose of objecting to the transaction of any business because the meeting is not lawfully called or convened. Neither the business to be transacted at, nor the purpose of, any regular or special meeting of the Board of Directors need be specified in the notice or waiver of notice of the meeting.

(h) The number of directors for a quorum and to adjourn the meeting

EXAMPLE

Quorum

A majority of the number of directors fixed by these Bylaws shall constitute a quorum for the transaction of business at any meeting of the Board of Directors, but if less than such majority is present at a meeting, a majority of the directors present may adjourn the meeting from time to time without further notice.

(i) The number of directors required to approve a certain matter

Manner of Acting

The act of the majority of the directors present at a meeting at which a quorum is present shall be the act of the Board of Directors.

[or]

No resolution of the corporation at any meeting, whether regular or special, shall be adopted except by the unanimous vote of the directors duly elected as provided herein.

(j) Informal action by the board of directors

Action without a Meeting

Any action that may be taken by the Board of Directors at a meeting may be taken without a meeting if a consent in writing, setting forth the action to be taken, is signed before the action by all the directors.

(k) Procedure for filling vacancies and removing directors[93]

Vacancies

Any vacancy occurring in the Board of Directors may be filled by the affirmative vote of a majority of the remaining directors though less than a quorum of the Board of Directors. A director elected to fill a vacancy shall be elected for the unexpired term of his or her predecessor in office. Any directorship to be filled by reason of an increase in the number of directors may be filled by election by the Board of Directors for a term of office continuing only until the next election of directors by the shareholders.

Removal

The stockholders of the Corporation may, at any meeting called for the purpose, remove any director from office, with or without cause, by a vote of a majority of the outstanding shares of the class of stock that elected the director; provided, however, that no director shall be removed if the votes of a sufficient number of shares are cast against the director's removal, which if cumulatively voted at an election of the entire board of directors would be sufficient to elect that director.

(l) Compensation and payment of expenses

Compensation

By resolution of the Board of Directors, each director may be paid his or her expenses, if any, of attendance at each meeting of the Board of Directors, and may be paid a stated salary as a director or a fixed sum for attendance at each meeting of the Board of Directors or both. No such payment shall preclude any director from serving the Corporation in any other capacity and receiving compensation therefor.

(m) Presumption of assent when the director is present at a meeting

Presumption of Assent

A director of the Corporation who is present at a meeting of the Board of Directors at which action on any corporate matter is taken shall be presumed to have assented to the action taken unless that director's dissent shall be entered in the minutes of the meeting or unless that director shall file his or her written dissent to such action with the person acting as the secretary of the meeting before the adjournment thereof or shall forward such dissent by registered mail to the Secretary of the Corporation immediately after the adjournment of the meeting. Such right to dissent shall not apply to a director who voted in favor of such action.

    4. Executive committees[94]

        (a) Authority for the appointment of executive committees and the delegation of authority

---

EXAMPLE

Appointment

The Board of Directors, by resolution adopted by a majority of the full board, may designate two or more of its members to constitute an Executive Committee. The designation of such committee and the delegation thereto of authority shall not operate to relieve the Board of Directors, or any member thereof, of any responsibility imposed by law.

EXAMPLE

Authority

The Executive Committee, when the Board of Directors is not in session, shall have and may exercise all of the authority of the Board of Directors except to the extent, if any, that such authority shall be limited by the resolution appointing the Executive Committee and except also that the Executive Committee shall not have the authority of the Board of Directors in reference to amending the Articles of Incorporation; adopting a plan of merger or consolidation; recommending to the shareholders the sale, lease, or other disposition of all or substantially all of the property and assets of the Corporation otherwise than in the usual and regular course of its business; recommending to the shareholders a voluntary dissolution of the Corporation or a revocation thereof; or amending the Bylaws of the Corporation.

        (b) Tenure and qualifications of members of the executive committee

---

EXAMPLE

Tenure and Qualifications

Each member of the Executive Committee shall hold office until the next regular annual meeting of the Board of Directors following his or her designation and until his or her successor is designated as a member of the Executive Committee and is elected and qualified.

        (c) Time and place for regular meetings of the executive committee

        (d) Procedure for calling special meetings of the executive committee

        (e) Procedure for giving notice of a meeting to the executive committee

---

EXAMPLE

Meetings

Regular meetings of the Executive Committee may be held without notice at such times and places as the Executive Committee may fix from time to time by resolution. Special meetings of the Executive Committee may be called by any member thereof upon not less than one day's notice stating the place, date, and hour of the meeting, which notice may be written or oral, and if mailed, shall be deemed to be delivered when deposited in the United States mail addressed to the member of the Executive Committee at his or her business address. Any member of the Executive Committee may waive notice of any meeting, and no notice of any meeting need be given to any member thereof who attends in person. The notice of a meeting of the Executive Committee need not state the business proposed to be transacted at the meeting.

        (f) Number of the members of the committee necessary to constitute a quorum, and vote required of the committee to authorize certain acts

Quorum

A majority of the members of the Executive Committee shall constitute a quorum for the transaction of business at any meeting thereof, and action of the Executive Committee must be authorized by the affirmative vote of a majority of the members present at a meeting at which a quorum is present.

(g) Informal action by the executive committee

Action without a Meeting

Any action that may be taken by the Executive Committee at a meeting may be taken without a meeting if a consent in writing, setting forth the action to be taken, is signed before such action by all the members of the Executive Committee.

(h) Procedure for filling vacancies, accepting resignations, and removing members of the executive committee

Vacancies

Any vacancy in the Executive Committee may be filled by a resolution adopted by a majority of the full Board of Directors.

Resignation and Removal

Any member of the Executive Committee may be removed at any time with or without cause by resolution adopted by a majority of the full Board of Directors. Any member of the Executive Committee may resign from the Executive Committee at any time by giving written notice to the President or Secretary of the corporation, and unless otherwise specified therein, the acceptance of such resignation shall not be necessary to make it effective.

(i) Procedure for conducting executive committee meetings

Procedure

The Executive Committee shall elect a presiding officer from its members and may fix its own rules of procedure which shall not be inconsistent with these Bylaws. It shall keep regular minutes of its proceedings and report the same to the Board of Directors for its information at the meeting thereof held next after the proceedings have been taken.

5. Officers[95]
   (a) Number of officers

Number

The officers of the Corporation shall be a President, one or more Vice Presidents (the number thereof to be determined by the Board of Directors), a Secretary, and a Treasurer, each of whom shall be elected by the Board of Directors. Such other officers and assistant officers as may be deemed necessary may be elected or appointed by the Board of Directors. Any two or more offices may be held by the same person, except the offices of the President and Secretary.

(b) Procedure for election and term of office

Election and Term of Office

The officers of the Corporation to be elected by the Board of Directors shall be elected annually by the Board of Directors at the first meeting of the Board of Directors held after each annual meeting of the shareholders. If the election of officers shall not be held at such meeting, such election shall be held as soon thereafter as is convenient. Each officer shall hold office until that officer's successor has been duly elected and has qualified or until that officer's death or until that officer shall resign or shall have been removed in the manner hereinafter provided.

(c) Removal and the filling of vacancies

Removal

Any officer or agent may be removed by the Board of Directors whenever in its judgment the best interests of the Corporation will be served thereby, but such removal shall be without prejudice to the contract rights, if any, of the person so removed. Election or appointment of an officer or agent shall not of itself create contract rights.

Vacancies

A vacancy in any office because of death, resignation, removal, disqualification, or other reason may be filled by the Board of Directors for the unexpired portion of the term.

(d) Responsibilities of the officers

Officers

President. The President shall be the principal executive officer of the Corporation and, subject to the control of the Board of Directors, shall in general supervise and control all of the business and affairs of the Corporation. The President shall, when present, preside at all meetings of the shareholders and of the Board of Directors. The President may sign, with the Secretary or any other proper officer of the corporation thereunto authorized by the Board of Directors, certificates for shares of the corporation, any deeds, mortgages, bonds, contracts, or other instruments which the Board of Directors has authorized to be executed, except in cases where the signing and execution thereof shall be expressly delegated by the Board of Directors or by these Bylaws to some other officer or agent of the corporation, or shall be required by law to be otherwise signed or executed; and in general shall perform all duties incident to the office of President and such other duties as may be prescribed by the Board of Directors from time to time.

Vice Presidents. In the absence of the President or in the event of his or her death, inability, or refusal to act, the Vice President (or if there is more than one, the Vice Presidents in the order designated at the time of their election or, in the absence of any designation, in the order of their election) shall perform the duties of the President and, when so acting, shall have all the powers of and be subject to all of the restrictions upon the President. Any Vice President may sign, with the Secretary or an assistant Secretary, certificates for shares of the Corporation; and shall perform such other duties as from time to time may be assigned to him or her by the President or by the Board of Directors.

Secretary. The Secretary shall: (a) keep the minutes of the proceedings of the shareholders and of the Board of Directors in one or more books provided for that purpose; (b) see that all notices are duly given in accordance with the provisions of these Bylaws or as required by law; (c) be custodian of the corporate records and of the seal of the Corporation and see that the seal of the Corporation is affixed to all documents the execution of which on behalf of the Corporation under its seal is duly authorized; (d) keep a register of the post office address of each shareholder which shall be furnished to the Secretary by such shareholder; (e) sign with the President, or a Vice President, certificates for shares of the Corporation, the issuance of which shall have been authorized by resolution of the Board of Directors; (f) have general charge of the stock transfer books of the Corporation; and (g) in general perform all duties incident to the office of Secretary and such other duties as from time to time may be assigned to him or her by the President or by the Board of Directors.

Treasurer. The Treasurer shall: (a) have charge and custody of and be responsible for all funds and securities of the Corporation; (b) receive and give receipts for moneys due and payable to the Corporation from any source whatsoever, and deposit all such moneys in the name of the Corporation in such banks, trust companies, or other depositories as shall be selected in accordance with the provisions of these By-laws; and (c) in general perform all of the duties incident to the office of Treasurer and such other duties as from time to time may be assigned to the Treasurer by the President or by the Board of Directors. If required by the Board of Directors, the Treasurer shall give a bond for the faithful discharge of his or her duties in such sum and such surety or sureties as the Board of Directors shall determine.

Assistant Secretaries and Assistant Treasurers. The Assistant Secretaries, when authorized by the Board of Directors, may sign with the President or a Vice President certificates for shares of the Corporation the issuance of which shall have been authorized by a resolution of the Board of Directors. The Assistant Treasurers shall respectively, if required by the Board of Directors, give bonds for the faithful discharge of their duties in such sums and with such sureties as the Board of Directors shall determine. The Assistant Secretaries and Assistant Treasurers, in general, shall perform such duties as shall be assigned to them by the Secretary or the Treasurer, respectively, or by the President or the Board of Directors.

(e) Salaries

Salaries

The salaries of the officers shall be fixed from time to time by the Board of Directors, and no officer shall be prevented from receiving such salary by reason of the fact that he or she is also a director of the Corporation.

[*or*]

No salary or other compensation for services shall be paid to any director or officer of the corporation unless the same has been approved in writing or at a duly held stockholders' meeting by stockholders owning at least seventy-five percent in amount of the capital stock of the corporation then outstanding.

6. Authorization for executing contracts and other written matters on behalf of the corporation—These provisions permit the board of directors to authorize any officer to contract on behalf of the corporation, and they may further restrict the ability of management to contract loans or other indebtedness. It is common to specify here which persons must sign checks, drafts, and other evidences of indebtedness issued in the name of the corporation, and where the funds of the corporation will be deposited.

Authorization

Contracts. The Board of Directors may authorize any officer or officers, agent or agents, to enter into any contract or execute and deliver any instrument in the name of and on behalf of the Corporation, and such authority may be general or confined to specific instances.

Loans. No loans shall be contracted on behalf of the Corporation and no evidences of indebtedness shall be issued in its name unless authorized by a resolution of the Board of Directors. Such authority may be general or confined to specific instances.

Checks, Drafts, etc. All checks, drafts, or other orders for the payment of money, notes, or other evidences of indebtedness issued in the name of the corporation, shall be signed by such officer or officers, agent or agents of the Corporation and in such manner as shall from time to time be determined by resolution of the Board of Directors.

Deposits. All funds of the Corporation not otherwise employed shall be deposited from time to time to the credit of the Corporation in such banks, trust companies, or other depositories as the Board of Directors may select.

7. Matters involving the certificates of shares and their transfer[96]—These provisions usually permit the board of directors to determine the form of the share certificates and prescribe which of the corporate officers will be required to sign them. Section 6.25 of the Model Business Corporation Act requires that if certificates are used by the corporation, each certificate representing shares shall set forth on its face that the corporation is organized under the laws of the particular state; the name of the person to whom issued; and the number and class of shares represented. In addition, if the corporation is authorized to issue different classes of shares, the certificates should specify the designations, preferences, limitations, and relative rights of the shares of each class. These statutory requirements need not be restated in the bylaws. If the incorporators wish to restrict the board of directors' use of uncertificated shares, a prohibitive provision to that effect should be stated in the bylaws. Any other special provisions respecting the transfer of shares and the method of keeping the stock transfer ledger should also be included under this bylaw section.

EXAMPLE

Certificates for Shares

Certificates representing shares of the Corporation shall be in such form as shall be determined by the Board of Directors. Such certificates shall be signed by the President or a Vice President and by the Secretary or an Assistant Secretary and sealed with the corporate seal or a facsimile thereof. The signatures of such officers upon a certificate may be facsimiles if the certificate is countersigned by a transfer agent, or registered by a registrar, other than the Corporation itself or one of its employees. All certificates for shares shall be consecutively numbered or otherwise identified. The name and address of the person to whom the shares represented thereby are issued, with the number of shares and date of issue, shall be entered on the stock transfer books of the Corporation. All certificates surrendered to the Corporation for transfer shall be canceled and no new certificate shall be issued until the former certificate for a like number of shares shall have been surrendered and canceled, except that in case of a lost, destroyed, or mutilated certificate, a new one may be issued therefor upon such terms and indemnity to the Corporation as the Board of Directors may prescribe.

The board of directors shall not be permitted to issue "uncertificated" shares without the express approval of at least two-thirds of the then outstanding stock entitled to vote.

EXAMPLE

Transfer of Shares

Transfer of shares of the Corporation shall be made only on the stock transfer books of the Corporation by the holder of record thereof or by his or her legal representative, who shall furnish proper evidence of authority to transfer, or by his or her attorney thereunto authorized by power of attorney duly executed and filed with the Secretary of the Corporation, and on surrender for cancellation of the certificate for such shares. The person in whose name shares stand on the books of the corporation shall be deemed by the Corporation to be the owner thereof for all purposes.

EXAMPLE

Transfer Agent

The Secretary of the Corporation shall act as Transfer Agent of the certificates representing the shares of common stock and preferred stock of the Corporation. That person shall maintain a Stock Transfer Book, the stubs in which shall set forth, among other things, the names and addresses of the holders of all issued shares of the Corporation, the number of shares held by each, the certificate numbers representing such shares, the date of issue of the certificates representing such shares, and whether or not such shares originate from original issue or from transfer. The names and addresses of the stockholders as they appear on the stubs of the Stock Transfer Book shall be conclusive evidence as to who are the stockholders of record and as such entitled to receive notice of the meetings of stockholders; to vote at such meetings; to examine the list of the stockholders entitled to vote at meetings; to receive dividends; and to own, enjoy, and exercise any other property or rights deriving from such shares against the Corporation. Each stockholder shall be responsible for notifying the Secretary in writing of any change in his or her name or address, and failure to do so will relieve the Corporation and its directors, officers, and agents from liability for failure to direct notices or other documents, or pay over or transfer dividends or other property or rights, to a name or address other than the name and address appearing on the stub of the Stock Transfer Book.

8. The fiscal year of the corporation—The corporation is a separate legal person and, as such, can adopt a fiscal year for its business other than the calendar year. This allows the corporation to select any twelve-month period to account for its operations. Its tax returns must be filed within 75 days after the close of its fiscal year. A Subchapter S corporation must use the calendar year as its fiscal year because its shareholders declare its profits on their personal tax returns and those must be filed based upon a calendar year.

Fiscal Year

EXAMPLE

The fiscal year of the Corporation shall begin on the first day of January and end on the thirty-first day of December in each year.

9. Authority of the board of directors to declare and pay distributions on the outstanding shares of the corporation[97]

Distributions

EXAMPLE

The Board of Directors may from time to time declare, and the Corporation may pay, dividends on its outstanding shares in the manner and upon the terms and conditions provided by law and its Articles of Incorporation.

10. Description of the corporate seal

Seal

EXAMPLE

The Board of Directors shall provide a corporate seal that shall be circular in form and shall have inscribed thereon the name of the Corporation, the state of incorporation, and the words "Corporate Seal."

11. Provisions for adopting emergency bylaws and the term for which those bylaws will be in effect

Emergency Bylaws

EXAMPLE

The Emergency Bylaws provided in this Article shall be operative during any emergency in the conduct of the business of the Corporation resulting from a catastrophic event, notwithstanding any different provision in the preceding Articles of the Bylaws or in the Articles of Incorporation of the Corporation or in the Business Corporation Act. To the extent not inconsistent with the provisions of this Article, the Bylaws provided in the preceding Articles shall remain in effect during such emergency and upon its termination the Emergency Bylaws shall cease to be operative.

During any such emergency:

a) A meeting of the Board of Directors may be called by any officer or Director of the Corporation. Notice of the time and place of the meeting shall be given by the person calling the meeting to such of the Directors as it may be feasible to reach by any available means of communication. Such notice shall be given at such time in advance of the meeting as circumstances permit in the judgment of the person calling the meeting.

b) At any such meeting of the Board of Directors, a quorum shall consist of [*here insert the particular provision desired*].

c) The Board of Directors, either before or during any such emergency, may provide, and from time to time modify, lines of succession in the event that during such an emergency any or all officers or agents of the Corporation shall for any reason be rendered incapable of discharging their duties.

d) The Board of Directors, either before or during any such emergency, may, effective in the emergency, change the head office or designate several alternative head offices or regional offices, or authorize the officers so to do.

EXAMPLE

(continued)

No officer, Director, or employee acting in accordance with these Emergency Bylaws shall be liable except for willful misconduct.

These Emergency Bylaws shall be subject to repeal or change by further action of the Board of Directors or by action of the shareholders, but no such repeal or change shall modify the provisions of the next preceding paragraph with regard to action taken prior to the time of such repeal or change. Any amendment of these Emergency Bylaws may make any further or different provision that may be practical and necessary for the circumstances of the emergency.

12. Provisions for amending, altering, or repealing the bylaws or adopting new bylaws

EXAMPLE

Amendment

These Bylaws may be altered, amended, or repealed and new Bylaws may be adopted by the Board of Directors at any regular or special meeting of the Board of Directors.

Sample bylaws for a Delaware corporation appear as Exhibit I–10 in Appendix I.

KEY TERMS

promoters	trademark	treasury shares
joint venture	reservation of corporate name	director and officer liability
preincorporation share subscription	transfer of corporate name	insurance
common stock	registration of corporate name	indemnify
par value	"name-saver corporation"	stock option
preferred stock	assumed name	quorum
paid-in capital	articles of incorporation	dividend
domestic corporation	equity securities	depletion reserve
foreign corporation	debt securities	interlocking director
ultra vires doctrine	no par value	de jure corporation
"blue-sky" requirements	stated value	organizational meeting
scrip	capital surplus	minute book
redeemable shares	registered office	stock transfer ledger
convertible shares	registered agent	corporate seal
irrevocable proxies	corporate purposes	voting list
"wasting assets" provisions	corporate powers	

WEB RESOURCES

Forms and information concerning the formation of corporations are available from the Web sites of the various Secretaries of State and the Departments of Commerce where corporate documents are filed. Nearly every office offers incorporation forms and guidance on their local filing and documentation rules. These state sites may be accessed through links on the National Secretary of State Association site:

<http://www.nass.org>

Access to state corporate laws may be obtained through the Legal Information Institute maintained at the Cornell Law School:

<http://www.law.cornell.edu>

A variety of business forms and articles are available as Law Commerce™, a member of the LexisNexis Group. Several research pages and best selling forms and agreements are available in an electronic marketplace at

<http://www.lawcommerce.com>

Various resources are available for sample forms and information about the formation and the operation of corporations, including the following:

<http://www.toolkit.cch.com>
<http://www.findlaw.com>
<http://www.tannedfeet.com>
<http://www.lectlaw.com>
<http://www.ilrg.com>

Information on international corporations and transnational business research may be reviewed at

<http://www.hg.org>

Delaware corporate law, including selected filings and opinions in corporate and other business litigation in the Delaware Court of Chancery is available through a project with the Widener University School of Law and Stanford University School of Law. This information is located at

<http://www.corporate-law.widener.edu>

The Small Business Administration provides a number of forms, advice, and guidance to small businesses. Information on business law, regulations, and financing can be accessed at

<http://www.sba.gov>

CASES

CHARLES A. TORRENCE COMPANY v. CLARY

121 N.C.App. 211, 464 S.E.2d 502 (1995)
GREEN, JUDGE

The undisputed facts show that plaintiff provided services to Clary, Martin, McMullen & Associates, Inc. (the Corporation), between 24 April 1991 and 26 March 1992, upon which there remains an account balance of $14,230.49, plus interest. The Corporation's charter was suspended on 17 November 1989, pursuant to N.C.Gen.Stat. § 105-230, for failure to pay franchise taxes and remained in a state of suspension through the date of the trial of this action. The defendant, a shareholder, president and director of marketing of the Corporation, did not learn of the corporate charter suspension until September 1992. All invoices and statements for monies due to plaintiff were sent to the Corporation and not to any of its owners, including defendant. The defendant did not guarantee any of the Corporation's debt owed to plaintiff. The trial court concluded that because the defendant had no knowledge that the charter had been suspended at the time the debt was incurred, the defendant could not be held personally liable for the Corporation's debt to plaintiff.

The dispositive issue is whether an officer of a corporation whose charter has been suspended has any personal liability for debts incurred by the corporation during the period of suspension.

Our legislature has provided that any person who "shall exercise or by any act attempt to exercise any powers, privileges, or franchises under articles of incorporation or certificate of authority after the same are suspended . . . shall pay a penalty." N.C.G.A. § 105-231 (1992). Our statutes are silent on whether the shareholders, directors and officers have any personal liability for debts incurred on behalf of a corporation during the time the charter is suspended. The general rule is that the shareholders of a corporation whose charter has been suspended "are not made individually liable for its debts incurred during the suspension." 19 Am.Jur2d *Corporations* § 2887 (1986). "The 'corporate veil' is not pierced, because the suspension was only designed to put 'additional bite' into the collection of franchise taxes, but not to deprive the shareholders of the normal protection of limited liability." *Id.* On the other hand, directors and officers are personally liable for corporate obligations incurred by them on behalf of the corporation, or by others with their acquiescence, if at that time they were aware that the corporate charter was suspended. *Id.; Pierce Concrete, Inc. v. Cannon Realty & Constr. Co.,* 77

N.C.App. 411, 414, 335 S.E.2d 30, 31-32 (1985); *see* N.C.G.S. § 55-8-30(c) (1990); N.C.G.S. § 55-8-42(c) (1990). Shareholders, directors and officers "of a pretended corporation which is neither a *de jure* nor a *de facto* corporation are generally held personally and individually liable . . . for the debts of the pretended corporation . . . without any reference to whether the persons sought to be held liable, actively participated in contracting the debt." *Guilford Builders Supply Co. v. Reynolds,* 249 N.C. 612, 616, 107 S.E.2d 80, 83 (1959).

In this case, the evidence is that the defendant was an officer of a lawful corporation but had not knowledge, at the time the debt was incurred on behalf of the Corporation, that the corporate charter was suspended. Accordingly, the defendant has no personal liability for the Corporation's debt to the plaintiff and the trial court correctly dismissed the complaint.

Affirmed.

MARK D. MARTIN and McGEE, JJ., concur.

MURPHY v. CROSLAND

886 P.2d 74 Utah (1994)

JACKSON, JUDGE

Crosland Industries, Inc. (CI) was properly incorporated in Utah on January 28, 1986. At all times relevant to this appeal, Todd Crosland was president, a director, and principal shareholder of CI, while Jeff Crosland was vice president and a director.

On March 1, 1987, CI's certificate of incorporation was suspended pursuant to Utah Code Ann. § 16-10-88.2 (1987) (repealed 1992) for failure to file its annual report.

The Murphys owned Granny's Buns, a cinnamon roll store in Las Vegas, Nevada. On January 8, 1988, the Murphys entered into a contract to sell Granny's Buns to Arnold Swenson. On that date, Mr. Swenson executed a promissory note in the Murphys' favor for a principal amount of $70,000. On that same date, and during the period of its suspension, CI agreed to guarantee Mr. Swenson's performance on both the sales contract and the note. Todd Crosland negotiated the guarantees on CI's behalf, and Jeff Crosland executed the guarantees in his capacity as an officer of CI.

Subsequently, Mr. Swenson defaulted under the terms of both the sales contract and the note, and CI failed to honor its guarantees. Having failed to remedy its suspended status and to restore its good standing, CI was involuntarily dissolved on March 1, 1988, pursuant to Utah Code Ann. § 16-10-88.2 (1987) (repealed 1992).

On July 27, 1989, the Murphys obtained a default judgment against CI in the amount of $72,987.46 plus interest, resulting from CI's failure to honor the guarantees. The Murphys then brought the present suit seeking to hold Todd and Jeff Crosland jointly and severally liable, under Utah Code Ann. § 16-10-139 (1987) (repealed 1992), for the judgment against CI. The Murphys claimed that by negotiating, authorizing, and executing CI's guarantees while the corporation was suspended, the Croslands "assumed to act as a corporation without authority so to do" in violation of Utah Code Ann. § 16-10-139.

* * *

ANALYSIS

I. Development of the MBCA

"In the United States the granting of corporate franchises has been regarded from the beginning as a prerogative of the legislature. The early American corporations were chartered by special acts of state legislatures." Model Business Corp. Act Ann., § 1 cmt., at 2 (1971). Later, "A procedure for incorporating under laws of general application was developed." *Id.* at 2-3.

The general laws enacted throughout the country shared similarities, but varied from state to state in scope and structure. Indeed, several states began to take advantage of these differences, enacting competitive statutes intended to induce corporations to organize in their jurisdictions. *Id.* at 3.

In addition, several common law concepts developed in the area of corporate law, supplementing the statutes. For example, "[a]t common law, corporations could be either de jure, de facto, or by estoppel." *American Vending Servs., Inc. v. Morse,* 881 P.2d 917, 920 (Utah App.1994).

> A de jure corporation is ordinarily thought of as one which has been created as the result of compliance with all of the constitutional or statutory requirements of a particular governmental entity. A de facto corporation, on the other hand, can be brought into being when it can be shown that a bona fide and colorable attempt has been made to create a corporation, even though the efforts at incorporation can be shown to be irregular, informal or even defective. Corporations by estoppel come about when the parties thereto are estopped from denying a corporate existence. In other words, the parties may, by their agreements or conduct, estop themselves from denying the existence of the corporation. [Citations omitted]

Beginning in the late 1920s, the states began to modernize their corporation laws by enacting entirely new statutes. Model Business Corp. Act Ann., § 1 cmt., at 3 (1971). As part of this revisionary movement, a committee of the American Bar Association drafted the Model Business Corporation Act (MBCA), first published as a complete act in 1950. *Id.* "The MBCA strove to codify a uniform set of laws regarding corporations and to provide some clarity and bright-line tests to previously clouded areas." *Morse,* 881 P.2d at 921. Furthermore, the MBCA eliminated the common law concepts of de facto corporations, de jure corporations, and corporations by estoppel. *See* 3A William M. Fletcher, Fletcher Cyclopedia of the Law of Private Corporations § 1229 (1990) (Fletcher).

* * *

Accordingly, the MBCA contemplated three relevant periods in the life of a corporation: (1) the preincorporation period—during which those who assumed corporate powers would be held personally liable under the MBCA, thereby negating the doctrines of de facto corporation and corporation by estoppel; (2) the incorporation period—during which the corporation enjoyed all the powers, rights, and privileges conferred by law; and (3) the postdissolution period—for which no statutory change was made because the common law already held personally liable those who carried on the business in an unauthorized manner. The MBCA's scheme did not include corporate suspension as a step prior to dissolution; hence, the MBCA's drafters had no need to consider the effect of any of the Act's provisions on a corporation that had been suspended.

* * *

We conclude that corporate suspension under UBCA section 16-10-88.2 resulted in suspension of a corporation's authority to conduct business as usual. A corporation suspended under this statute could engage only in activities necessary to wind up its affairs or to remedy its suspension. UBCA section 16-10-139 applies to a suspended corporation; anyone acting on the corporation's behalf who exceeds the corporation's remaining authority is jointly and severally liable for debts and liabilities incurred as a result.

CONCLUSION

Todd and Jeff Crosland exceeded their suspended corporation's authority in negotiating and executing guarantee agreements for CI. Thus, they are jointly and severally liable for the default judgment entered against CI because the judgment represents corporate liability arising from the Crosland's unauthorized actions. We affirm the trial court's grant of summary judgment. . . .

BILLINGS and GREENWOOD, JJ., concur.

PROBLEMS

1. When the corporate veil is pierced, who are the persons held liable for the debt or injury?

2. ABC Corporation has 103 shares issued and outstanding. If Renee Crumb owns 30 shares, Mary Hanko owns 35 shares, Susan Stroud owns 38 shares, and there are seven directors to be elected, how many votes will be needed to elect one director? How many directors may Susan Stroud elect?

3. What is the difference between corporate "purpose" and corporate "powers"? Which is easier to change?

4. What are the qualifications of an incorporator under the model act?

5. What is the difference between a "staggered" board of directors and a "dummy" board of directors?

6. If the articles of incorporation do not identify the initial board of directors, who must hold an organizational meeting and what business must be conducted?

7. What is the difference between articles of incorporation and bylaws? Which is easier to change and why?

PRACTICE ASSIGNMENTS

1. Review your local corporation statute and make a list of the following:
   a. the items required to be specified in the articles of incorporation;
   b. the items permitted to be modified by the articles of incorporation alone;
   c. the items permitted to be modified by the articles of incorporation or the bylaws; and

   d. the items that could not be modified by the articles or bylaws even if a contrary provision were included in the document.

2. Find a friend or relative who is involved with a corporation. Ask them to show you copies of their articles of incorporation or bylaws and to explain their business to you. Review the articles of incorporation and bylaws

and either critique or justify the provisions based upon the unique requirements of the business and your local corporation statute.

3. Steven Levine owns a lumber business, which he founded thirty years ago. His business, Emperor Lumber Company, has business offices at 200 West 14th Avenue, New York, New York; a lumber yard and mill in Atlanta, Georgia; and sells retail lumber to consumer customers. The business has been improving, and presently nets approximately $450,000 per year before taxes. Levine has operated the business as a sole proprietor with seven full-time employees, including an employee-manager of the lumber yard, Rick Duffy. Levine's son, Magic Levine, has been working with the business since he graduated from high school. Magic is presently 18 years old. In addition to his lumber business, Steven owns other investments and nonbusiness property that afford him approximately $100,000 per year in income.

Steven is exploring several possibilities for the direction of the business, and he is excited about the possibility of adding a retail hardware inventory to his retail lumber business. The addition of a hardware line would require approximately $650,000 in capital, the addition of a new store at another location, and hiring approximately ten to fifteen new employees.

Steven says he has the following alternatives: (1) he may continue the business alone and eventually give it or will it to his children; or (2) he may add his employee-manager as a partner to the business, with a contribution of approximately $300,000 in capital by the employee-manager; or (3) he may consider incorporating the business if you so advise.

If a partnership is to be formed, Steven would contribute the lumber mill valued at $500,000, timber lands worth $150,000, and inventory items worth approximately $120,000. The goodwill of the business is valued at approximately $250,000. In a partnership arrangement with Duffy, the employee-manager, Levine is willing to share profits fifty-fifty.

If a corporation is to be formed, Levine suggests that his son and his employee-manager join him as the directors of the business. It is extremely important to Levine that these three people maintain complete control over the business. Although his son does not have any individual capital to contribute, Levine would like him to maintain an ownership interest in the corporation.

Recognizing the need for capital to begin the retail hardware business, Steven has located three potential outside investors who will provide capital no matter what form the business assumes. These people include Donna Skibbe and Richard Conviser, each of whom will contribute or invest $150,000, and are interested in a minimum annual return of ten percent and capital appreciation. Neither Skibbe nor Conviser have any interest in management or control, but they insist on some sort of protection should they fail to receive their desired return on investment for any substantial period of time. A third investor, Stanley Chess, will contribute or invest up to $250,000 provided he receives a guaranteed fifteen percent minimum annual return. He is not concerned about control or capital appreciation. Levine is willing to meet all these demands, but Levine wants to be able to retire or redeem any business obligations that might make subsequent investment or acquisition of outside capital unattractive.

a. Prepare a memorandum on the advantages of incorporation or partnership for this business.

b. Prepare a skeletal structure for both a partnership and a corporation and a list of questions and issues you think would be appropriate to discuss with Levine during your second interview.

c. Draft all documents necessary to form a corporation for Levine's business under your local corporation code.

ENDNOTES

1. The advice must consider the particular needs of the business, including ownership rights, management responsibilities, duration, need for capital, potential liability, and taxation. If a corporation is selected as the appropriate business form, certain special information must be obtained from the organizers. A preincorporation checklist appears as Exhibit I–8 in Appendix I.

2. E.g., Pennsylvania, 15 Pa. Stat. Ann. §§ 1201 1204(8).

3. Several states require $1,000 minimum paid-in capital (e.g., Texas, Tex. Bus. Corp. Act Ann. § 3.02(7)). A few states require that if an initial amount of capital is desired, it must be stated in the articles of incorporation (e.g., Ohio, Ohio Rev. Code § 1701.04 [Baldwin]).

4. E.g., New York, three months, N.Y. Bus. Corp. Law § 503 (McKinney); and Louisiana, one year, La. Rev. Stat. Ann. § 12:71 (West).

5. E.g., New Jersey, six months or sixty days after filing certificate of incorporation, N.J. Stat. Ann. § 14A:7-3 (West).

6. See Model Business Corporation Act (hereafter M.B.C.A.) § 6.20.

7. 15 Pa. Stat. § 1207.

8. Oklahoma, Okla. Stat. Ann. tit. 18, § 1010.

9. M.B.C.A. § 6.20(d).

10. See Chapter 14.

11. Reprinted with permission from H. Henn and J. Alexander, Handbook of the Law of Corporations and Other Business Enterprises 179–185 (3d ed. 1983) (copyright 1983 by West Publishing Company).

12. For example, it may be particularly important for management to be able to declare dividends out of current profits even if the corporation did not have an "earned surplus." This is permitted in Oklahoma. Okla. Stat. Ann. tit. 18, § 1049. It would not be permitted in Texas. Tex. Bus. Corp. Act. Ann. art. 2.38.

13. M.B.C.A. § 4.01.

14. See 1 Prentice-Hall, Corporation Reporter, Corporation Checklists ¶ 9002, subparagraph 14 under each state.

15. See, e.g., M.B.C.A. § 4.01(b). Some jurisdictions and the Model Business Corporation Act allow the use of a similar corporate name, provided the written consent of the holder of the name is obtained and a distinguishing word is added to the name.

16. Many states use a thirty-day period for reservation of corporate names (e.g., Maryland, Md. Corps. & Ann. art. 23, § 6; and Massachusetts, Mass. Gen. Laws Ann. ch. 155, § 9(a)).

17. M.B.C.A. § 4.02.

18. M.B.C.A. § 4.03.

19. See Chapter 14 on the qualification of foreign corporations.

20. E.g., Colorado, Colo. Rev. Stat. § 7-71-101.

21. The Model Business Corporation Act and most jurisdictions use the term *articles of incorporation.* M.B.C.A. §§ 1.40(I), 2.02.

22. See "Amendment of the Articles of Incorporation" in Chapter 15.

23. M.B.C.A. § 2.02.

24 Examples of articles of incorporation appear as Exhibits I–6 and I–9 in Appendix I.

25. See "Selection and Reservation of Corporate Name" earlier in this chapter.

26. The details and flexibility of the corporate financial structure are discussed more fully in Chapter 9.

27. This summary paraphrases the requirements of M.B.C.A. § 6.01, except that the act does not require any statement concerning par value of shares. Most states still require this designation for shares.

28. M.B.C.A. § 6.01(b).

29. M.B.C.A. § 6.01(c).

30. See Chapter 9.

31. See "Par Value or No Par Value" and "Consideration for Shares" in Chapter 9.

32. M.B.C.A. § 6.21 permits shares to be issued at a price set by the board of directors, and the price set is entirely at the directors' discretion if par value is not required in the articles of incorporation. See M.B.C.A. § 2.02.

33. E.g., Alabama places a value of $50 on each no par share for computation of the initial taxes. In this state, a corporation can authorize fifty times as many $1 par value shares as no par shares for the same tax.

34. See "Sources of Funds for Distribution" in Chapter 11.

35. See "Preferred Stock Rights" in Chapter 9 and "Share Transfer Restrictions and Buy-out Agreements" in Chapter 13.

36. See M.B.C.A. § 14.20; "Involuntary Dissolution" in Chapter 15.

37. See "Ownership and Management of a Corporation" in Chapter 6.

38. M.B.C.A. § 2.02(b)(1).

39. See "Ownership and Management of a Corporation" in Chapter 6.

40. See "Voluntary Dissolution" and "Involuntary Dissolution" in Chapter 15.

41. M.B.C.A. § 3.04.

42. E.g., New York, N.Y. Bus. Corp. Law § 622 (McKinney).

43. E.g., Delaware, Del. Code Ann. tit. 8, § 102(b)(3).

44. Treasury shares are defined in most corporation statutes. On preemptive rights and treasury shares, see clause 9 in Delaware Articles of Incorporation, Exhibit I–9, in Appendix I.

45. See "Ownership and Management of a Corporation" in Chapter 6; "Shareholder Business and Vote Required" in Chapter 10.

46. M.B.C.A. § 2.02(b)(3).

47. See "Amendment of the Articles of Incorporation" in Chapter 15.

48. M.B.C.A. § 8.01.

49. M.B.C.A. § 8.11.

50. M.B.C.A. § 7.28.

51. M.B.C.A. § 8.04.

52. M.B.C.A. § 8.06.

53. M.B.C.A. § 8.08.

54. M.B.C.A. § 8.10.

55. Del. Code Ann. tit. 8, § 102(b)(7).

56. 15 Pa. Stat. Ann. § 1713.

57. Del. Code Ann. tit. 8, § 102(b)(7).

58. Ind. Code Ann. § 23-1-35-1(e). In Indiana, Florida, and Maine, the limitation on liability applies to suites by third parties as well as by shareholders, and there is no provision for a corporation formed in any of these three states to eliminate the statutory limitation of liability even if the corporation's shareholders so desire.

59. Va. Code Ann. § 13-1.692.1(A) (Michie). The Virginia limitation is the greater of (1) $100,000, or (2) "the amount of cash compensation received by the officer or director from the corporation during the 12 months immediately preceding the act or omission for which liability was imposed;" but the statute permits the shareholders to reduce or eliminate (but not increase) this limit to "monetary amounts specified" in a provision of either the articles of incorporation or the bylaws.

60. E.g., California, Cal. Corp. Code § 317 (West).

61. M.B.C.A. § 6.31.

62. M.B.C.A. § 8.24.

63. M.B.C.A. § 8.21.

64. M.B.C.A. § 10.20.

65. M.B.C.A. § 10.21.

66. M.B.C.A. § 6.40; see "Sources of Funds for Distribution" and "Cash and Property Dividends" in Chapter 11.

67. See, e.g., Delaware, Del. Code. Ann. tit. 8, § 170.

68. See, e.g., Delaware, Del. Code. Ann. tit. 8, § 170(b).

69. See "Ownership and Management of a Corporation" in Chapter 6.

70. M.B.C.A. § 8.02.

71. M.B.C.A. § 55.

72. E.g., Delaware, Del. Code. Ann. tit. 8, § 103(c)(5).

73. N.Y. Bus. Corp. Law § 402(a) (McKinney).

74. E.g., Arizona, Ariz. Rev. Stat. Ann. § 10-055.

75. Alabama, Ala. Bus. Corp. Act § 10-2B-1.25.

76. E.g., Pennsylvania, 15 Pa. Stat. Ann. § 205.

77. The myriad variations of filing requirements may be easily reviewed by consulting 1 Prentice-Hall, Corporation Reporter, Corporation Checklists, ¶ 9002 *et seq.*

78. E.g., Nevada, Nev. Rev. Stat. § 78.050.

79. M.B.C.A. § 2.03.

80. M.B.C.A. § 2.05.

81. E.g., New York, N.Y. Bus. Corp. Law § 404 (McKinney).

82. Checklists and a full discussion of organizational meetings are contained in Chapter 10.

83. See M.B.C.A. § 2.02(b)(3).

84. Some state statutes prescribe certain specific matters that must be contained in the bylaws. E.g., California, Cal. Corp. Code § 212 (West).

85. See M.B.C.A. § 2.06.

86. E.g., Nebraska, Neb. Rev. Stat. § 21-2026.

87. M.B.C.A. § 2.05.

88. E.g., Kentucky, Ky. Rev. Stat. Ann. § 271A.145 (Baldwin).

89. See "Shareholder Meetings" in Chapter 10.

90. See "Ownership and Management of a Corporation" in Chapter 6.

91. The Model Business Corporation Act requires that a classification provision ap-pear in the articles of incorporation, and a bylaw provision would be ineffective. See M.B.C.A. § 2.01; "Filing and Other Formalities" earlier in this chapter. However, several states permit classification of the board of directors to be accomplished in the by-laws. E.g., New York, N.Y. Bus. Corp. Law § 704 (McKinney); Pennsylvania, 15 Pa. Stat. Ann. § 403.

92. See "Directors' Regular and Special Meetings" in Chapter 10.

93. See "Taxation of a Corporation" in Chapter 6.

94. See M.B.C.A. § 2.15.

95. See "Ownership and Management of a Corporation" in Chapter 6.

96. See Certificate for Shares" earlier in this chapter; "Share Transfer Restrictions and Buy-out Agreements" in Chapter 13.

97. See "Cash and Property Dividends" and "Share Dividends" in Chapter 11.

CORPORATE FINANCIAL STRUCTURE

GENERALLY

Corporate capital is obtained principally from investors, creditors, and shareholders, who exchange money, property, or services for securities issued by the corporation. The attractiveness of shares as an investment is an important advantage to the corporate form of business enterprise. In addition to corporate equity securities, or shares, a corporation may contract for various types of debt financing, transactions whereby the corporation borrows money from outsiders who are willing to lend funds to the corporation. Unlike shareholders, these creditors are not owners of the company, but their loans are generally considered to be a more conservative investment than an investment in shares. The corporation is obligated to repay a loan from a debt investor, but there is no obligation to repay the funds invested by shareholders, who risk the loss of some or all of their funds.

The corporate financial structure has great flexibility, and corporate securities may have a number of features that increase the quality and attractiveness of the investment. The capitalization may be limited only to common stock, or may be some combination of equity securities, including separate classes and series, and debt securities.

TYPES OF CORPORATE SECURITIES

The term **securities** has a special meaning in the law. It generally refers to a contractual-ownership obligation that exists between a business enterprise and an investor. For purposes of the federal and state securities acts, the term may include any one of several different forms of investment obligations. In the corporate sense, securities fall into two classes:

1. *debt securities,* which evidence a corporate obligation to repay money borrowed from a creditor and are also typically called *bonds;* and
2. *equity securities,* which evidence a shareholder's ownership interest in the corporation and are usually referred to as *shares.*

When a corporation borrows money, it executes a document or bond that represents the obligation of the corporation to repay the borrowed funds. Bonds may be unsecured or secured for payment with property of the corporation. An unsecured obligation, the corporate equivalent of a personal signature loan, is called a **debenture.** Secured bonds may be called **mortgage bonds.**

Bonds always state a principal amount owed by the corporation, a date when repayment of the principal amount is due, and a provision for interest, which is usually paid periodically. Debt securities may be marketed at a higher price than the principal amount if the attractiveness of the investment creates a demand, in which case it is said that they are sold at a **premium,** or if the investment is not all that attractive, at a lower price than the principal amount, in which case they are sold at a **discount.** Debt securities usually do not have voting rights in the corporate affairs. Instead, they represent a loan obligation in the strict business sense and the holders are merely creditors. As a practical matter, debt securities are often issued under an agreement executed by the corporation, the outside lender, and a trustee who is usually a financial institution. The agreement is called an **indenture,** and it includes the terms of the obligation, the rights of the security holders and the trustee, and any conditions upon which the bonds are issued. Debt securities issued by large corporations are freely sold on an open market, and the price of a bond depends upon the quality of the investment. Bonds frequently have several advantageous features that make them a desirable investment, such as a high interest rate, a provision allowing conversion into common shares at a specified price, and redemption features.

Equity securities are distinguished from debt securities by the relationship between the investor and the corporation. A purchaser of equity securities, a shareholder, becomes a part owner of the corporation. The proportion that the shareholder's shares bear to the total number of shares outstanding represents the shareholder's fractional ownership interest. When shares are issued, the corporation, instead of creating a liability, creates a capital account, which represents the equity of the corporation. Unlike a debt security, the corporation is under no obligation to repay a shareholder, and the return of the investment is usually strictly dependent upon the shareholder's ability to sell his or her shares to another investor. The income paid on equity securities is usually a distribution of the profit of the corporation and is called a *dividend.* The frequency and amount of these distributions are determined within the discretion of the board of directors. An equity investment is attractive if it appears that the corporation's business will expand and be profitable, thereby increasing the value of the equity security and likely resulting in dividend distributions to the shareholders. Shareholders also have the right to a proportionate distribution of corporate assets upon dissolution of the corporation.

Imaginative entrepreneurs have developed all sorts of variations on the two basic types of corporate securities, and most state corporation statutes encourage inspired financial configurations by imposing very few restrictions upon the corporate financial structure. However, since some unscrupulous entrepreneurs have duped investors with worthless securities, it should be noted that the issuance and sale of corporate securities is strictly regulated by federal and state securities laws. Any public sale of corporate shares or bonds is subject to the disclosure requirements of the **Securities Act of 1933**[1] or the applicable state blue-sky laws. These acts and the **Securities Exchange Act of 1934**[2] are generally designed to fully inform a potential investor of the character and quality of the investment, and to avoid untrue statements and misleading omissions about the security that may affect a decision to purchase or sell. The requirements of the securities acts are discussed in Chapter 7.[3]

EQUITY SECURITIES

Equity securities grant the shareholder a three-pronged ownership interest in the corporation. A shareholder is entitled to a proportionate share of earnings, distributed as dividends at the discretion of the board of directors; a proportionate share of assets in corporate dissolution; and a vote on all shareholder matters, which gives indirect control over management activities. Ignoring special classes of equity securities for a moment, a common stock shareholder is entitled to share in the earnings and assets of the corporation in the proportion of the number of shares owned compared against the total number of shares outstanding. Each common shareholder is also entitled to one vote for each share. Every state authorizes by statute the issuance of a certain number of shares, and the division of those shares into classes, allowing preferences, limitations, and other special rights as specified in the articles of incorporation. The Model Business Corporation Act grants this general authority in section 6.01.

STAGES OF EQUITY SECURITIES

The articles of incorporation must state the number of shares the corporation will have the authority to issue.[4] This number will be determined by the incorporators and counsel, considering the anticipated capital requirements of the corporation. Having established the authority, the corporation may issue up to the specified number of shares without any requirement for an amendment to the articles of incorporation. Thus, the first step in the issuance of corporate equity securities is the creation of the authority to issue them by describing the characteristics of the securities and specifying the number of shares in the articles of incorporation. The shares described in the articles of incorporation are the **authorized shares** of the corporation.

It is not necessary to issue all of the authorized shares of the corporation, and it is sometimes undesirable to do so. It is necessary to issue the number of shares required for the minimum paid-in capital, if that is a requirement under the applicable state statute,[5] and to issue enough shares for sufficient capital to commence business even if no minimum capital requirements exist. Other authorized shares should be saved to allow for additional capital financing in future corporate operations. Shares that have been authorized and sold are issued to the holders and are described as **issued** and **outstanding shares.** Thus, a shareholder holds authorized, issued, and outstanding shares of the company.

Shares that have been sold to investors may be reacquired by the corporation by one of several methods. The shareholder may donate or resell them to the company, or the corporation may, if so authorized in the articles of incorporation, redeem the shares or convert them to other shares. When shares are reacquired by the corporation, they are called treasury shares.[6] Treasury shares are authorized and issued but are not outstanding, since they are held by the corporation and not by investors.

The issuance and sale of shares is initiated by the decision of the board of directors to obtain additional capital for the corporation. The board of directors may not issue more shares than have been authorized in the articles of incorporation. It also must observe the present shareholders' preemptive rights, if they exist, by offering newly issued shares to existing shareholders in their respective proportions of share ownership before selling the shares to other investors.[7] In addition, there may be other statutory limitations on the authority of the board of directors to issue shares. For example, section 6.21 of the Model Business Corporation Act requires a shareholder vote to approve any issuance of shares that comprises more than 20% of the voting power of the corporation and also allows all decisions concerning the consideration for the issuance of shares to be reserved to the shareholders in the articles of incorporation.

The distinction between the stages of equity securities is important for several reasons. For equity securities to be fully active (including entitlement to vote, receipt of a proportionate share of earnings, and receipt of a proportionate share of assets upon dissolution), shares must be authorized, issued, and outstanding. Treasury shares are usually not counted for determining a quorum and are not entitled to a vote.[8] They also may not be entitled to any dividend distributions.[9]

Another distinguishing feature involves the consideration for shares. If shares are authorized and are being issued and sold, they usually must be sold for an amount no less than the par value if they have par value, or for the stated value if they are no par value shares. Thus, if shares bear a $10 par value, the corporation may not sell them for less than $10 per share. If the corporation sells shares for less than that amount, the consideration is inadequate and the shares become **watered,** or **discount, shares.** Shareholders who purchase watered shares can be assessed for the full amount of unpaid consideration. On the other hand, shares that are authorized, issued, and outstanding and are reacquired and held by the corporation as treasury shares may be sold again for any consideration fixed by the board of directors, whether or not the consideration is equal to or less than par value. For example, if a shareholder agreed with the corporation to purchase 1,000 shares of stock with a $10 par value for a price of $7,000, the shares would be "watered" stock if the corporation is issuing them from the authorized but unissued shares available under the authorized capital in the articles of incorporation. The shareholder is liable to pay the additional $3,000 to the corporation because the shares were sold for less than the par value. On the other hand, if the corporation had repurchased the 1,000 shares from a former shareholder and held the shares in the corporate treasury, the corporation could sell the shares for any agreed amount, and the shareholder is not required to pay any more than $7,000.

PAR VALUE OR NO PAR VALUE

Several jurisdictions still require a statement in the articles of incorporation indicating whether shares are to be issued for a stated par value or for no par value. The Model Business Corporation Act and many states are now taking the position first propounded by California that it is not necessary to state whether shares have a par value.[10] The corporation always has a choice between no par or par value shares, except in Nebraska, where all shares must have a par value.[11] The distinction between these provisions relates to the value required to be given for the purchase of shares and to the rates of capital franchise fees that must be paid in some states upon incorporation. In addition, shares with no par value permit greater flexibility in allocating the amount received in exchange for the shares to certain surplus accounts in the corporate books.

Shares with a par value may be issued only for such consideration expressed in dollars, not less than the par value, as may be fixed from time to time by the board of directors. This provision is common in most state statutes. It means that shares with a $10 par value may be issued for $20 if someone is willing to pay that amount, but in no case may they be issued for less than $10. A handful of states make exceptions to this rule if the board of directors can justify the reason for selling below par value.

Shares without par value may be issued for whatever consideration may be fixed from time to time by the board of directors,[12] although many states provide that the articles of incorporation may reserve the right to fix the consideration for no par value shares to the shareholders.[13] A few jurisdictions reverse this authority—they grant it to the shareholders unless it is reserved to the directors in the articles of incorporation. Thus, shares without par value may be issued for any amount set by the board of directors or shareholders in their good judgment. The only limitation on this authority to fix the amount of no par value shares is that the shares must be issued for approximately the same amount of consideration at approximately the same time.

Major variations in prices of no par value shares within a short time period raise a question of breach of the director's duty of due care in dealing with shareholders. For example, suppose a corporation intended to sell no par value shares to three investors: Burn, Bush, and Bradford. In private discussions with the three investors, it was determined that Burn and Bush would pay approximately $10 per share, but Bradford could be persuaded to pay $15 per share. If 100 shares were simultaneously issued to each investor at those prices, Bradford would have immediate grounds for complaint. Bradford's shares were immediately "**diluted**" with the sales to the other two investors because the board of directors effectively reduced the stated value by $5 per share. However, if Burn and Bush purchased their shares in January, and Bradford's purchase at $15 per share occurred in September, it may be said that the shares increased in value enough to warrant the increase in price. The dilution problem results when no par value shares are sold at substantially lower prices at about the same time as other no par value shares, to undercut the contribution of an investor. Notwithstanding the foregoing, if the board of directors can establish that the varying prices were set for a good business reason, the board will be permitted to rapidly adjust the prices on shares without par value.

The par value-no par value distinction has other ramifications in states that exact annual **franchise fees** based upon the aggregate authorized capital of the corporation. In some states, the franchise fee is computed upon the amount stated in the articles of incorporation as the total aggregate value of authorized shares. To compute this fee, shares without par value are assigned an arbitrary value. For example, if an arbitrary value of $1 per share were placed on each no par share to compute the franchise fee for a state, the franchise fee would be the same for a corporation authorized to issue 10,000 shares at $5 par value as it would be for a corporation authorized to issue 50,000 shares at no par value in that state. States that discourage the use of no par value shares impose a high statutory valuation on those shares to compute the fee. It then becomes more advantageous to set a lower par value and to authorize more shares.[14]

Certain accounting classifications also depend upon the distinction between par value and no par value shares. In some cases it may be desirable to create a capital surplus account for the corporation in the early stages of corporate existence—assuming, for example, that the incorporators predict the desirability of repurchasing some of the shares issued by the corporation. Many statutes, and formerly the Model Business Corporation Act, permit the corporation to repurchase its own shares only if it has a surplus account from which it may make the purchase.[15]

The creation of a surplus account occurs in different ways. The typical surplus accounts are **earned surplus** and **capital surplus.** Earned surplus is created when the corporation accumulates profits from operations. Capital surplus is an account created for surplus funds received from the sale of stock. If the corporation issues $10 par value stock for $30 per share, $10 must be placed in stated capital, and $20 may be placed in capital surplus. Any consideration in excess of par value may be placed in capital surplus, and with no par stock, any part of the consideration may be placed in capital surplus.[16]

If there is a need for a surplus account in the early stages of the corporate operations, the par value or no par value characteristic of the stock is important. For example, if a corporation has issued shares with $10 par value, and those shares are sold for exactly $10 each, that amount of money must be placed in an account called **stated capital.** There would be no capital surplus, and if the corporation had not yet earned profits to hold as retained earnings, there would be no earned surplus. In such a case, the corporation would not be able to repurchase its own shares, since there would be no surplus account. On the other hand, if a corporation has sold shares with no par value for $10 a share, it can divert any portion of that consideration to a capital surplus account. The board of directors may allocate, usually within sixty days after no par value shares have been issued, a portion of the consideration to capital surplus. Capital surplus could receive $9 per share, for example, and stated capital the other $1 per share. The corporation could then use the amount of capital surplus to repurchase its own shares, provided the articles of incorporation authorize the use of capital surplus for this purpose.

Dividends and other distributions to shareholders are subject to similar rules. Most states limit the payment of distributions to funds available from earned surplus, with a few exceptions. The corporation is permitted to distribute cash or property to its shareholders out of capital surplus under certain circumstances.[17] If management intends to make a distribution to shareholders before there is sufficient earned surplus to declare a dividend, the creation of a capital surplus account is essential. No par value stock will ensure that the board of directors will be able to create the account immediately upon issuance of the first shares.

CERTIFICATES FOR SHARES

The shares of the corporation are generally represented by **certificates** (see Exhibit 9–1, share certificate). Share certificates are **negotiable,** meaning that they are like a form of currency. If a person possesses a share certificate with an appropriate endorsement—the signature of the owner of the certificate transferring the shares—that person is entitled to enforce the rights to the shares even if the transfer of the certificate was wrongful, such as by theft

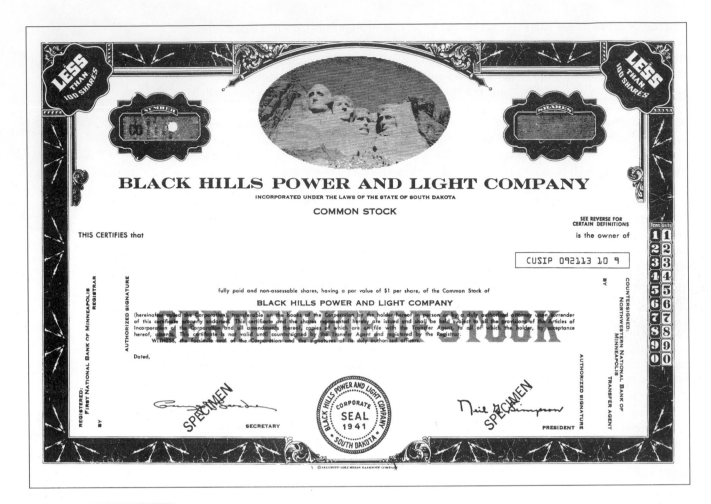

Exhibit 9–1.

Share Certificate

or other fraud. Thus, shareholders of corporations are wise to keep their share certificates in a secure place. The Model Act and the Uniform Commercial Code permit a corporation to provide by resolution that some or all of the classes and series of shares shall be *uncertificated,* which means that the ownership of the shares is recorded in the corporate records, but the shares are not represented by a certificate. The rights and obligations of the holders of uncertificated shares and the rights and obligations of the holders of certificates representing shares of the same class and series are identical under corporate law. The primary purposes of the uncertificated provision is to accommodate the modern trend of transferring share ownership by computer communications and to avoid the paper crunch anticipated as more and more corporations issue certificates for shares and those certificates are rapidly traded on over-the-counter and national stock exchanges. The uncertificated system is intended to simplify the transfer of ownership in a corporation by eliminating the need for transfer of a piece of negotiable paper as part of that transaction. It is also intended to guard against the loss or theft of the negotiable piece of paper (the certificate) representing ownership in the corporation.

When certificates are used, all states prescribe the content of the certificate representing shares, and the requirements of the Model Business Corporation Act are typical:

> Each share certificate (1) must be signed (either manually or in facsimile) by two officers designated in the bylaws or by the board of directors and (2) may bear the corporate seal or its facsimile.[18]

The statute further provides that the signature of any person who was an officer and ceased to be such before the certificate is issued will have the same effect as if that person were still

BLACK HILLS POWER AND LIGHT COMPANY

Notice: The Corporation will furnish to any shareholder upon request and without charge, a full statement of the designations, preferences, limitations, and relative rights of the shares of each class of stock authorized to be issued, and a like full statement relative to any preferred or special class of stock in series which the Corporation is or may be authorized to issue, or has issued, as to the variations in the relative rights and preferences between the shares of each such series so far as the same have been fixed and determined and the authority of the Board of Directors to fix and determine the relative rights and preferences of subsequent series.

The following abbreviations, when used in the inscription on the face of this certificate, shall be construed as though they were written out in full according to applicable laws or regulations:

TEN COM—as tenants in common

TEN ENT —as tenants by the entirety

JT TEN —as joint tenants with right of survivorship and not as tenants in common

UNIF GIFT MIN ACT—_____Custodian_____
        (Cust)   (Minor)
under Uniform Gifts to Minors
Act_____
      (State)

Additional abbreviations may also be used though not in the above list.

For Value Received, _____ *hereby sell, assign and transfer unto*

PLEASE INSERT SOCIAL SECURITY OR OTHER
IDENTIFYING NUMBER OF ASSIGNEE

(PLEASE PRINT OR TYPEWRITE NAME AND ADDRESS OF ASSIGNEE)

_____ *Shares*

of the Stock represented by the within certificate and do hereby irrevocably constitute and appoint

_____ *attorney,*

to transfer the same on the books of the within-named Corporation, with full power of substitution in the premises.

Dated _____

Notice: The signature to this assignment must correspond with the name as written upon the face of the certificate in every particular, without alteration or enlargement or any change whatever.

SIGNATURE GUARANTEED BY:

THIS SPACE MUST NOT BE COVERED IN ANY WAY

an officer as of the date of the issuance.[19] Each certificate representing shares must state upon its face

1. the name of the corporation and that the corporation is organized under the laws of the particular state;
2. the name of the person to whom the shares are issued; and
3. the number and class of shares and the designation of the series, if any, represented by the certificate.

The major variations among the state statutes with respect to requirements for share certificates are what officers are required to sign the certificates, the circumstances under which facsimile signatures may be used, the need for a corporate seal, and whether the certificate must state that the shares are fully paid. In all states, if the shares have a par value, the amount of the par value must be stated on the certificate.

If the corporation is authorized to issue only one class of stock, its share certificates need contain only the bare statutory requirements. A corporation may adopt a more complex financial structure and choose to issue shares in various classes or in series; in such a case, each certificate must describe the particular elements of each class or series. Section 6.25 of the Model Business Corporation Act requires that every share certificate of a corporation authorized to issue shares of more than one class shall set forth a full statement of the designations, preferences, limitations, and relative rights of the shares of each class authorized to be issued (or, as is more common, state conspicuously that the corporation will furnish to any shareholder upon request and without charge). Further, if the corporation is authorized to issue preferred or special classes in series, the variations between the shares so far as they have been determined and the authority of the board of directors to fix the relative rights of the shares must be stated on the certificate (see Exhibit 9–2, Preferred Stock Certificate). If the latter procedure is used, it is not necessary to amend or otherwise modify the certificates representing shares whenever the corporate financial structure is changed. The classes and series of shares are explored in detail in the next section of this chapter.

CLASSIFICATIONS OF SHARES

The articles of incorporation may authorize the issuance of only one class of shares (i.e., common stock), in which case the shareholders of the common stock are entitled to all of the voting rights, all of the dividends, and all of the net assets in a dissolution distribution. In a Subchapter S corporation, it is possible to have another class of shares with different voting rights but no other differences. However, other corporate financial structures may be more complicated.

Classes of Shares

The equity securities of the corporation may be divided into several classes of shares. Common stock is the basic class, and additional classes may be authorized to grant certain shareholders a preferred right to dividends or a preferred right to assets in case of corporate dissolution. Various classes of securities may also have different voting rights, such as no vote, or two votes per share, or any other formula. When more than one class is to be authorized, the articles of incorporation must set forth the designations, preferences, limitations, and relative rights of each class.

EXAMPLE	**Classes of Stock**

Classes of Stock

The total number of shares of all classes of stock which the Corporation shall have authority to issue is 500,000, of which 100,000 shares shall be Class A common stock without par value and 400,000 shares shall be Class B common stock without par value. There shall be no distinction between the two classes, except that the holders of the Class B common stock shall have no voting power for any purpose whatsoever and the holders of the Class A common stock shall, to the exclusion of the holders of the Class B common stock, have full voting power for all purposes.

The share certificate must either contain this information or contain a conspicuous statement that the corporation will provide this information without charge to any shareholder requesting it.

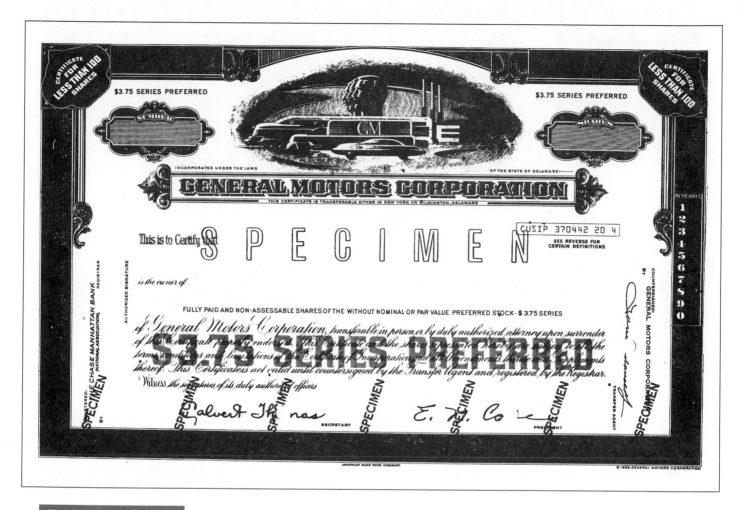

Exhibit 9–2.

Preferred Stock Certificate

It may be helpful to consider the circumstances under which authority to issue preferred shares is used. The general principle is that certain investors may insist upon a superior ownership position in the corporation, and in order to obtain necessary financing, it may be necessary to *prefer* those investors over others. For example, suppose Hopkins and Conner plan to form a corporation for the operation of a restaurant. Hopkins intends to run the business and to invest his available personal capital of $25,000, and Conner is capable of investing $100,000. Assume further that no other shareholders are contemplated at this point. Conner may be willing to take a greater proportion of common stock for his $100,000 investment, but that will give him 80% of the common stock to Hopkins, 20%. Conner clearly would have shareholder control in such a case, and Hopkins' may be thereby hampered in his efforts to run the business. Hopkins will be aware of Conner's potential control, and may object to this posture.

It is possible, however, to issue each investor $25,000 in common stock (with voting rights) and to issue nonvoting preferred shares, with dividend and liquidation preferences, to Conner for his $75,000 excess investment. With this arrangement, Conner and Hopkins have equal voting rights and an equal investment in the basic equity of the corporation. Conner's excess investment is protected by his preferred status, ensuring that Conner will receive the first distributions of profit through his dividend preference, and the first distribution of assets in

Exhibit 9–2.

(continued)

GENERAL MOTORS CORPORATION

The following abbreviations, when used in the inscription on the face of this certificate, shall be construed as though they were written out in full according to applicable laws or regulations:

TEN COM — as tenants in common	UNIF GIFT MIN ACT —
TEN ENT — as tenants by the entireties	
JT TEN — as joint tenants with right of survivor- ship and not as tenants in common	_____ Custodian _____ (Cust) (Minor) under Uniform Gifts to
	Minors Act_____ (State)

Additional abbreviations may also be used though not in the above list.

THE CORPORATION WILL FURNISH WITHOUT CHARGE TO EACH STOCKHOLDER WHO SO REQUESTS A STATE-MENT OF THE RIGHTS, PRIVILEGES, RESTRICTIONS, VOTING POWERS, LIMITATIONS AND QUALIFICATIONS OF THE SEVERAL CLASSES OF STOCK OF THE CORPORATION. REQUESTS MAY BE DIRECTED TO THE TRANSFER AGENT, GENERAL MOTORS CORPORATION, 767 FIFTH AVENUE, NEW YORK, NEW YORK 10022.

FOR VALUE RECEIVED, THE UNDERSIGNED HEREBY SELLS, ASSIGNS AND TRANSFERS THE SHARES OF THE CAPITAL STOCK REPRESENTED BY THE WITHIN CERTIFICATE AS FOLLOWS:

PLEASE INSERT SOCIAL SECURITY OR OTHER
IDENTIFYING NUMBER OF ASSIGNEE

_____ UNTO _____

SHARES   FULL NAME AND ADDRESS (INCLUDING ZIP CODE) OF ASSIGNEE SHOULD BE TYPEWRITTEN OR PRINTED LEGIBLY

AND HEREBY IRREVOCABLY CONSTITUTES AND APPOINTS

_____ ATTORNEY

TO TRANSFER THE SAID STOCK ON THE BOOKS OF THE WITHIN-NAMED CORPORATION WITH FULL POWER OF SUBSTITUTION IN THE PREMISES.

DATED_____

SIGN HERE_____

SIGNATURE MUST CORRESPOND WITH NAME ON FACE OF CERTIFICATE

SIGNATURE GUARANTEED

NOTICE: THE SIGNATURE TO THIS ASSIGNMENT MUST CORRESPOND WITH THE NAME AS WRITTEN UPON THE FACE OF THE CERTIFICATE IN EVERY PARTICULAR WITHOUT ALTERATION OR ENLARGEMENT OR ANY CHANGE WHATEVER.

THIS SPACE MUST NOT BE COVERED IN ANY WAY

dissolution through the liquidation preference. Thereafter, Conner and Hopkins share equally, just as though each had invested only $25,000.

Similar problems arise when a third investor is considered. Suppose Carver has offered to invest $50,000, but has no expertise in the restaurant business, and no interest in management and control. However, Carver is concerned about two things: a high return on his investment and a right to assert a vote if the business is being managed improperly. A separate class of securities can be created for Carver's investment. He may receive first dividend preference, even over Conner's preferred status, and his preference may be at a higher rate and may be cumulative to ensure an accumulated high return on his investment every year. His securities would have no voting rights until the happening of a contingent event, such as when the gross receipts from the business drop below a certain amount for several consecutive months.

The possibilities for variations in preferred shares are endless, and each class can be structured to fit the peculiar needs of the investors.

The statutory authority for issuance of shares in classes usually specifies the manner in which those shares may differ from common shares. For example, section 6.01 of the Model Business Corporation Act provides that a corporation may issue shares of preferred or special classes that

1. have special, conditional, or limited voting rights, or no right to vote, except to the extent provided by the statute;
2. are redeemable or convertible as specified in the articles of incorporation at the option of either the shareholder, the corporation, or other persons, or on the occurrence of a designated event; for cash, indebtedness, securities, or other property; in a designated amount or in any amount determined in accordance with a designated formula or by reference to other events;
3. entitle the holders to distributions calculated in any manner, including dividends that may be cumulative, noncumulative, or partially cumulative; and
4. have preference over any other class of shares with respect to distributions, including dividends and distributions upon the dissolution of the corporation.

These variations among the shares are not considered to be exhaustive; the Model Business Corporation Act permits additional variations as long as they do not conflict with other statutory rules.[20] In any case, one or more classes of shares must have unlimited voting rights, and one or more classes of shares must be entitled to receive the net assets of the corporation upon dissolution. These rules are designed to ensure that someone will be entitled to exercise the shareholders' voting rights (even if that entitlement shifts among classes from time to time or on certain events) and that someone will be entitled to receive the assets of the corporation if the corporation is dissolved and liquidated.[21] However, the articles of incorporation may limit or deny the voting rights or provide special voting rights for certain classes under the authority of section 7.21. The individual variations in these rights are explored in detail in "Preferred Stock Rights" later in this chapter.

Shares in Series

The articles of incorporation may authorize the division and issuance of any class of shares in series.[22] The principle behind **series shares** is a refinement of the theory behind preferred shares. Classes of preferred shares meet the particular needs and demands of certain investors, and series shares do the same thing. However, all authority to issue shares comes from the articles of incorporation. Thus, for a special class of shares to be issued, the articles of incorporation must authorize that class and define its designations, preferences, limitations, and relative rights. If the articles of incorporation do not specifically authorize the issuance of a particular class of shares, the articles must be amended to grant this authority, and an amendment requires a board of directors' resolution, the approval of the shareholders, and the appropriate filing with the secretary of state.[23] The corporate officials attempting to raise capital may thus be hindered by a cumbersome, time-consuming amendment procedure in tailoring the corporate securities to the requirements of potential investors. This procedure may be particularly frustrating when prompt action is essential, such as when the corporation is negotiating to acquire desirable property in exchange for its preferred shares.

Series shares are designed to avoid this problem. The board of directors may be authorized (by the articles of incorporation) to fix the terms of a series of preferred shares, without requiring a formal amendment to the articles or shareholder approval. This board authority to vary the terms of the stock is the source of the common name, **blank stock,** for series shares. With this authority, the Model Business Corporation Act permits directors to issue shares that vary from other shares of the same class as long as the board of directors determines the preferences, limitations, and relative rights before the issuance of any shares of that class. The board of directors may thus set any rights for any series of shares within the boundaries of the various rights provided by the statute.[24] For example, the articles of incorporation could authorize the creation of an additional class of shares at the discretion of the board of directors, stating that the shares may have a preferential dividend over all other shares and all other rights would be the same as the common shares. The board could then issue these series shares by resolution, providing that the first series will have a $2.00 per share dividend preference and the second series will have a $4.00 per share dividend preference, and so on. The board is allowed to set the preference for dividends as the board deems appropriate, since the articles authorize any variation with respect to dividends for shares issued from the series.

Most states permit the creation of series shares, but are more specific than the Model Business Corporation Act in identifying the types of rights that may be granted within the series. In most states, the series shares may differ from other shares of the same series in the following particulars: (1) the rate of dividend; (2) the price at and the terms and conditions upon which shares may be redeemed; (3) the amount payable upon shares in the event of voluntary or involuntary liquidation; (4) **sinking fund** provisions, if any, for the redemption or purchase of shares; (5) the terms and conditions upon which shares may be **converted;** and (6) voting rights. In all other respects, the shares of the series must be the same as other shares of the same class.

The scope of the directors' authority to establish series shares is defined by the articles of incorporation. The articles may state that the board of directors has full authority to divide classes of shares into series and to determine the variations in the relative rights.

EXAMPLE

Shares in Series

The preferred stock of the Corporation shall be issued in one or more series as may be determined from time to time by the Board of Directors. In establishing a series the Board of Directors shall give to it a distinctive designation so as to distinguish it from the shares of all other series and classes, shall fix the number of shares in such series, and the preferences, rights, and restrictions thereof. All shares of any one series shall be alike in every particular. All series shares shall be alike except that there may be variation as to the following: (1) the rate of dividend, (2) the price at and the terms and conditions on which shares shall be redeemed, (3) the amount payable upon shares in the event of involuntary liquidation, (4) the amount payable upon shares in the event of voluntary liquidation, (5) sinking fund provisions for the redemption of shares, and (6) the terms and conditions on which shares may be converted if the shares of any series are issued with the privilege of conversion.

The articles also may limit the authority to vary series shares to certain characteristics, such as conversion privileges or dividend preferences.

The procedure for establishing a series is considerably less formal than that for establishing a formal amendment to the articles of incorporation. The directors adopt a resolution stating the designation of the series and fixing the rights of the series shares. A statement, which the Model Act refers to as the articles of amendment,[25] is filed with the secretary of state or other authorized public filing office (see Exhibit 9–3, Statement with Respect to Shares). This statement is effective without shareholder action. It quotes the resolution and acknowledges that the resolution was adopted by the board of directors on a certain date. In some states, franchise taxes and fees will be due upon the establishment of the series shares. The amendment to the articles, as filed, should contain the following information:

1. the name of the corporation;
2. the text of the resolution determining the terms of the class or series of shares;
3. the date the resolution was adopted; and
4. a statement that the amendment was officially adopted by the board of directors.

Exhibit 9–3.

Statement with Respect to Shares (Pennsylvania)

**PENNSYLVANIA DEPARTMENT OF STATE
CORPORATION BUREAU**

Statement with Respect to Shares
Domestic Business Corporation
(15 Pa.C.S. ß 1522)

Entity Number

Name

Address

City   State   Zip Code

Document will be returned to the name and address you enter to the left.

Fee: $52

Filed in the Department of State on _____

_____
Secretary of the Commonwealth

In compliance with the requirements of 15 Pa.C.S. ß 1522(b) (relating to statement with respect to shares), the undersigned corporation, desiring to state the designation and voting rights, preferences, limitations, and special rights, if any, of a class or series of its shares, hereby states that:

1. The name of the corporation is:

2. *Check and complete one of the following:*

____ The resolution amending the Articles under 15 Pa.C.S. ß 1522(b) (relating to divisions and determinations by the board), set forth in full, is as follows:

____ The resolution amending the Articles under 15 Pa.C.S. ß 1522(b) is set forth in full in Exhibit A attached hereto and made a part hereof.

3. The aggregate number of shares of such class or series established and designated by (a) such resolution, (b) all prior statements, if any, filed under 15 Pa.C.S. ß 1522 or corresponding provisions of prior law with respect thereto, and (c) any other provision of the Articles is _____ shares.

Exhibit 9–3.

(continued)

DSCB:15-1522-2

4. The resolution was adopted by the Board of Directors or an authorized committee thereon on:

_____

5. *Check, and if appropriate complete, one of the following:*

____ The resolution shall be effective upon the filing of this statement with respect to shares in the Department of State.

____ The resolution shall be effective on: _____ at _____.
                                              Date   Hour

IN TESTIMONY WHEREOF, the undersigned corporation has caused this statement to be signed by a duly authorized officer thereof this

_____ day of _____,_____.

_____
Name of Corporation

_____
Signature

_____
Title

Department of State
Corporation Bureau
P.O. Box 8722
Harrisburg, PA 17105-8722
(717) 787-1057
web site: www.dos.state.pa.us/corp.htm

Instructions for Completion of Form:

A. Typewritten is preferred. If not, the form shall be completed in black or blue-black ink in order to permit reproduction. The filing fee for this form is $52 made payable to the Department of State.

B. A separate form shall be submitted for each class or series of shares affected. If a number of classes or series of shares are affected at the same time, consideration should be given to filing form DSCB:15-1915/5915 (Articles of Amendment-Domestic Corporation).

C. The effective date in Paragraph 5 may not be prior to the filing date, but the resolution may state a prior effective date "for accounting purposes only."

D. If the corporation was incorporated on or after October 1, 1989, the words "or corresponding provisions of prior law" may be omitted from Paragraph 3.

E. This form and all accompanying documents shall be mailed to the address stated above.

F. To receive confirmation of the file date prior to receiving the microfilmed original, send either a self-addressed, stamped postcard with the filing information noted or a self-addressed, stamped envelope with a copy of the filing document.

FRACTIONS OF SHARES AND SCRIP

In some cases the corporation may need to issue fractions of shares of stock, and the authority for the issuance of a **fractional share** must come from the appropriate state statute. For example, fractional shares may be required when a corporation has declared a stock dividend entitling the holders of 100 shares of stock to receive one additional share as a dividend. In that case, the holder of 150 shares of stock would be entitled to one and one-half shares. If the state statute permits fractional shares, the corporation may issue a certificate for a one-half share. Many statutes authorize the issuance of scrip in lieu of fractional shares. *Scrip* is a separate certificate representing a percentage of a full share. It entitles a shareholder to receive a certificate for one full share when the shareholder has accumulated scrip aggregating a full share.

The Model Business Corporation Act provides that a corporation may, but is not obligated to, issue a certificate for fractional share or scrip in lieu thereof. Other alternatives include disposition of fractional interests, as by finding two shareholders who are each entitled to one-half share and arranging for a sale from one to the other so a whole share will be issued, or payment to the shareholder of cash equal to the fair value of the fractional interest.[26] If a certificate for a fractional share is issued, the holder is entitled to exercise a fractional voting right, to receive a fractional share of dividends, and to participate accordingly in the corporate assets in the event of liquidation.[27] Unless otherwise provided by the board of directors, a holder of scrip is usually not entitled to these rights. The board of directors may provide that scrip will become void if not exchanged for full certificates before a specified date.

State statutes take divergent positions with respect to fractional shares and scrip, and the individual statutes should be consulted. Most states authorize one or more of the options specified in the Model Business Corporation Act.

CONSIDERATION FOR SHARES

The consideration required for shares depends in part upon whether the shares have a par value or are without par value.[28] Shares with a par value usually may be issued for no less than the par value, and shares with no par value receive a stated value as fixed from time to time by the board of directors or the shareholders, as provided by statute and the articles of incorporation. Thus, in the quantitative sense, the consideration given in exchange for shares must at least equal the par value or the stated value for no par shares, whichever the case may be.

When the consideration for shares is cash, the quantity valuation is obvious. When property is transferred or services are performed in exchange for shares, the law has developed at least three rules for appraising the consideration. The first rule, the **true value rule,** requires that the property or services have, at the time of the issuance of shares, an actual value that is no less than par value or no less than the stated value for no par shares. This means that the property or services must be appraised and the actual value compared with the minimum requirements for the particular type of stock. Most jurisdictions follow the second rule, the **absence of fraud rule,** which requires that the property or services be evaluated and deemed adequate by the board of directors, who must determine in good faith that the consideration received has a value at least equal to the minimum requirements and whose determination of value will be conclusive in the absence of fraud. The third, and most flexible, rule is contained in the Model Business Corporation Act, and simply provides that "the board of directors must determine that the consideration received or to be received for shares to be issued is adequate."[29] The determination by the board of directors will be conclusive in determining the adequacy of the consideration. When the second or third rule is used, the board of directors, in determining the value of the offered consideration, should carefully document and support its evaluation. These rules are used to determine whether the amount of consideration received for shares is legally adequate.

Statutes also dictate the types of consideration that may be given in exchange for stock in terms of quality. Historically, the permissible consideration was limited to money; other property, tangible or intangible; or labor or services actually performed for the corporation.[30] Many states prohibited the issuance of stock for promissory notes.[31] There is some authority to the effect that preincorporation services—the services performed by the promoters and incorporators are not really performed for the corporation because the corporation does not yet exist. Consequently preincorporation services are not generally considered adequate consideration for stock.[32]

The Model Business Corporation Act developed a trend toward greater permissiveness in the financial provisions for the issuance of shares. Acceptable consideration for shares now includes any tangible or intangible property (including benefits the corporation may receive from a contract or other instrument), cash, promissory notes, services already performed for the corporation and contracts for services to be performed, and other securities of the corporation that may be exchanged for newly issued shares.[33]

These rules give the board of directors great flexibility in accepting items of value in exchange for shares, and place the corporation on a more equal footing with the limited partnership and limited liability company in accepting almost anything that is offered by an investor in exchange for ownership interest. However, to protect the interests of the existing shareholders, section 6.21 of the Model Business Corporation Act provides two important limitations on the board of director's discretion to accept non-cash consideration for shares: (1) if the shares are issued for consideration other than cash or cash equivalents, the shareholders must approve the transaction by a majority vote; and (2) the determination of adequacy of the consideration that is normally decided by the board of directors, may be reserved to the shareholders by the articles of incorporation.

Notice that a potential shareholder may not be obligated to give any current value in exchange for shares. The promise to pay money in the future through a promissory note or the promise to perform services at a later time under a contract are both recognized as valuable consideration, and a shareholder may receive shares immediately upon the issuance of the note or the execution of the contract. To be certain the shareholder will perform these promises, the corporation may place the issued shares in possession of an escrow agent or independent third party to deliver to the shareholder when the services are performed or the money has been contributed. If the promises are never performed, the shares that are escrowed or restricted may be canceled.[34]

When the corporation receives the consideration for which the board of directors has authorized the issuance of shares, the shares are considered fully paid and **nonassessable.** If shares that are not fully paid are issued, the shareholders may be liable to the creditors of the corporation for the deficiency, and the shares are **assessable.** In such a case, the directors who vote to issue shares that are not fully paid and fail to place those shares in escrow or to restrict their transfer have probably violated their fiduciary duty to the corporation and other shareholders, and may be personally liable.

COMMON STOCK RIGHTS

The corporation organized with only one class of stock has only common stock, which is best described as shares of the corporation without any special features. To authorize the issuance of common stock, the articles of incorporation need only describe the number of shares authorized and, if desired or required by statute, their par value, or contain a statement that the shares have no par value. Common stock has the following rights under most state statutes.

Distribution Rights

Distributions may be declared from time to time at the discretion of the board of directors, and may be paid in cash, property, or other shares of the corporation, provided the corporation is solvent. Common stockholders receive distributions in the same proportion that their individual shares bear to the total number of common shares outstanding. The common stockholder's right to declared distributions is limited only by the solvency of the corporation (so creditors cannot be harmed by a distribution of assets as a dividend from an insolvent corporation) and by preferred stockholders' rights to distributions, which must be paid before the common shares are entitled to distributions. The rules relating to these distributions are discussed in detail in a later chapter.[35]

Voting Rights

The one-vote-per-share rule is codified in section 7.21 of the Model Business Corporation Act. At a meeting of the shareholders, each outstanding share regardless of class is entitled to one vote, and each fractional share is entitled to a corresponding fractional vote on each matter submitted to a vote. The statute further provides, however, that the voting rights of any class may be limited or denied by the articles of incorporation. These voting rules are common to most jurisdictions. If the corporation has only one class of stock, which is not divided into series, the single class must have full voting rights. If the corporation's financial structure includes several classes or series of securities, one or more of those classes or series may have limited or expanded voting rights.

The voting right of a shareholder may be the most important right in the corporation, since it permits the shareholder to express his or her views concerning the performance of management. If several corporations have **circular holdings,** where one corporation owns a majority of the stock in a subsidiary, and the subsidiary also owns a majority of the stock in the parent, the minority stockholders of both corporations would always be outvoted, since the same board of directors may be voting the majority shares in both corporations. For example, if X Corporation owns 60% of the stock of Y Corporation, and thereby elects all of the members of Y Corporation's board, and if Y Corporation also owns 60% of the stock of X Corporation, and thereby elects all of the members of X Corporation's board, the minority stockholders of both corporations will have nothing to say in the election of directors. To counter that problem, the Model Business Corporation Act provides that unless there are "special circumstances," the shares of a corporation may not be entitled to vote if they are owned by a second corporation and the first corporation owns a majority of the shares entitled to vote for the directors of the second corporation. If a court decided that there was no abuse as a result of this circular ownership, it could allow the shares owned by the respective corporations to be voted for the election of directors. Otherwise, those shares must be silent and the minority stockholders will be entitled to control the vote for the respective corporations.[36]

Depending upon the statutory requirements and the provisions in the articles of incorporation, cumulative voting may be authorized for shares of common stock.[37]

Liquidation Rights

After a decision has been made to dissolve the corporation, corporate officials are required by law to collect and dispose of the assets, and to satisfy all liabilities and obligations. Thereafter, the remaining assets in cash or property are distributed to the shareholders according to their respective interests. If the corporation has a single class of common stock, those shareholders will receive a proportionate interest in all of the net assets following dissolution and liquidation. The liquidation rights of common stock may be subordinated by the issuance of additional classes of securities that have a preference to the assets in dissolution. For example, if a corporation is being liquidated and has $1,000,000 in cash available to distribute to the shareholders after all creditors and obligations have been paid, the common shareholders with 1,000 shares will be entitled to receive $100 per share in liquidation. If this corporation has 100 shares of a preferred class that are entitled to a liquidation preference of $2,500 per share, this preferred class would receive $250,000, the preference amount, and the common shareholders would receive only $75 per share in liquidation.

Preemptive Rights

Depending upon the state statute, preemptive rights may exist unless denied, or may not exist unless granted, in the articles of incorporation. The Model Business Corporation Act uses the latter approach in section 6.30. The preemptive right of a shareholder is the right to purchase a pro rata share of newly issued stock before that share may be offered to outsiders.[38]

PREFERRED STOCK RIGHTS

Preferred stock is a class of stock that has been granted a preference to one or more of the normal shareholder rights; that is, preferred stock usually has a preference to distributions, to assets in liquidation, or to both. Issuance of preferred stock must be authorized by the articles of incorporation, and the terms of the articles must contain the designation of each class and a statement of the preferences, limitations, and relative rights of the shares issued in each class. Moreover, if management intends to issue the shares of a preferred class in series, the designation of each series and a statement of the variations in the rights and preferences between series must be contained in the articles of incorporation. The articles also must describe any authority to be vested in the board of directors to establish the series and to determine the variations in the relative rights of the series.

Preferred stock is customarily preferred in the following ways.

Distribution Preference

A common attraction to preferred stock is a distribution preference, if and when the board of directors declares a distribution. Preferred shareholders may have a mandatory priority to distributions, in a predetermined amount, before the corporation may pay any distributions to the holders of any other class of stock. A distribution preference may be cumulative, noncumulative, or a compromise of the two, and may also include a participation provision.

Cumulative A **cumulative distribution preference** means that preferred stockholders will accrue an entitlement to distributions each year, whether or not the distributions are declared and paid. If the distributions are not paid during a certain year, they accumulate in the prescribed amount, and when the board of directors finally declares a distribution, all accumulated distributions on the preferred stock must be paid before distributions may be paid on any other stock. For example, suppose preferred stock is entitled to a cumulative distribution of $4 per share and Alexis Levine owns 100 shares. In the first and second years the corporation pays no distributions, so Alexis's stock accumulates distributions of $400 per year to a total amount of $800. In the third year management declares a distribution on all classes of stock. The corporation must first pay Alexis $1200 on her shares ($800 accumulated plus $400 for the present year) before it may pay any distributions to other classes of stock.

A statement of a cumulative distribution preference follows.

E X A M P L E

Cumulative Preferred Distributions

The holders of the preferred stock shall be entitled to receive, when and as declared by the Board of Directors, out of the assets of the Corporation legally available therefor, cash distributions at the rate of $8.40 per share per year, and no more, payable quarterly on the first days of January, April, July, and October in each year, prior to the payment of any distributions of the common stock. Such distributions shall be cumulative from the date of original issue.

Noncumulative Noncumulative preferred stock is entitled to receive a distribution preference in any given year, but if distributions are not paid during the year, the preferred shareholders lose their right to those distributions (just as common shareholders have no right to undeclared distributions). Using the same example of Alexis, if the preferred stock is entitled to a $4 per share **noncumulative distribution,** when the corporation fails to pay in the first and second year, Alexis loses the right to the $400 preference she would have had during each of those years. In the third year, if management decides to pay distributions, it must pay her $400 (that year's preferred amount) before it can pay other shareholders.

EXAMPLE

Noncumulative Preferred Distributions

The holders of the preferred stock shall be entitled to receive out of the surplus or net profits of the Corporation, in each fiscal year, distributions at such rate or rates, not exceeding 8.4 percent per annum, as shall be determined by the Board of Directors in connection with the issue of the respective series of said stock and expressed in the stock certificates therefor, before any distributions shall be paid upon the common stock, but such distributions shall be noncumulative. No distributions shall be paid, declared, or set apart for payment on the common stock of the Corporation, in any fiscal year, unless the full distribution on the preferred stock for such year shall have been paid or provided for. However, if the Directors in the exercise of their discretion fail to declare distributions on the preferred stock in a particular fiscal year, the right of such stock to distributions for that year shall be lost even though there was available surplus or net profits out of which distributions might have been lawfully declared.

Other Provisions for Distribution Preferences   Preferred stock may have a "**cumulative to the extent earned**" preference to distributions, permitting distributions to accumulate on preferred stock if the corporation earned money and could have declared distributions in a given year, but the board of directors decided not to declare distributions that year. On the other hand, if the corporation did not earn or accumulate enough profit to declare a distribution that year, the distribution would be lost and would not carry forward.

Another common provision is the right of the preferred stockholder to **participate** in other distributions declared, in addition to the preference. For example, if Alexis's stock provided for a $4 per year preference, noncumulative but participating, then in the third year when the corporation determined to pay distributions, Alexis would be entitled to $400 as a preference, and she also would be entitled to share on a pro rata basis with all other securities in the remaining distributions that were to be declared and paid.

Liquidation Preference

Holders of preferred stock are frequently granted a preference upon dissolution and liquidation of the corporation. The terms of the stock usually recite the right for the preferred stockholder to be paid a specified amount, plus any accrued distributions that have not been paid, before any other equity security holder is entitled to share in the assets upon liquidation. The preferred shareholder is thus placed in a position analogous to that of a priority creditor. A liquidation preference is the best guarantee that can be arranged to ensure that shareholders will recoup their investment in case of liquidation. Although the preferred shareholders are subordinate to corporate creditors, they are paid before any other investor, and are entitled to be fully satisfied before any other shareholder receives a distribution in liquidation.

Liquidation preferences may be determined at a fixed percentage of par value.

EXAMPLE

Liquidation Preference at a Fixed Percentage of Par Value

In the event of any liquidation, dissolution, or winding up of the Corporation, either voluntary or involuntary, or in the event of any reduction of capital of the Corporation resulting in a distribution of assets to its stockholders, the holders of preferred shares shall be entitled to receive out of the assets of the Corporation, without regard to capital or the existence of a surplus of any nature, an amount equal to one hundred percent (100%) of the par value of such preferred shares, and, in addition to such amount, a further amount equal to the distributions unpaid and accumulated thereon to the date of such distribution, whether or not earned or declared, and more, before any payment shall be made or any assets distributed to the holders of the common shares. After the making of such payments to the holders of the preferred stock, the remaining assets of the Corporation shall be distributed among the holders of the common stock alone, according to the number of shares held by each. If the assets of the Corporation distributable as aforesaid among the holders of the preferred stock shall be insufficient to permit of the payment to them of said amounts, the entire assets shall be distributed ratably among the holders of the preferred stock.

Liquidation rights also may be based on a fixed sum, with participation rights.

EXAMPLE

Liquidation Preference Based on a Fixed Sum, with Participation Rights

In the event of any liquidation, dissolution, or winding up of the corporation, whether voluntary or involuntary, the holders of the preferred stock of the Corporation shall be entitled, before any assets of the Corporation shall be distributed among or paid over to the holders of the common stock, to be paid in full $100.00 per share of preferred stock, together with all accrued and unpaid distributions and with interest on said distributions at the rate of fifteen percent (15%) per annum. After payment in full of the above preferential rights of the holders of the preferred stock, the holders of the preferred stock and common stock shall participate equally in the division of the remaining assets of the Corporation, so that from such remaining assets the amount per share of preferred stock distributed to the holders of the preferred stock shall equal the amount per share of common stock distributed to the holders of the common stock.

Voting Rights

Each corporation must have one or more classes of shares that have full voting rights, so at least some shareholder will be entitled to vote on all matters submitted to the shareholders.[39] A corporation with multiple classes of stock may have one class with full voting rights in shareholder matters, and another class with no voting rights at all. It is also permissible to grant more than one vote per share to one class while retaining the single vote per share for another class. These provisions are designed to establish voting control in one of the classes of securities. A typical application of these rules may involve shareholders of a corporation who wish to retain their control, but need to issue additional shares to secure new capital. With the establishment of a new class of nonvoting shares, the issuance of new shares will not dilute present voting control.

Modifications to voting rights are described in the articles of incorporation, and they may be expanded, denied, or granted subject to a contingency. For example, preferred shares may have no voting rights unless they have not received distributions for a specified period of time, in which case they will be entitled to vote.

EXAMPLE

Modifications to Voting Rights

The holders of the preferred stock shall not have any voting power whatsoever, except upon the question of selling, conveying, transferring, or otherwise disposing of the property and assets of the Corporation as an entirety, provided, however:

In the event that the Corporation shall fail to pay any distribution upon the preferred stock when it regularly becomes due, and such distribution shall remain in arrears for a period of six (6) months, the holders of the preferred stock shall have the right to vote on all matters in like manner as the holders of the common stock, during the year next ensuing, and during each year thereafter during the continuance of said default until the Corporation shall have paid all accrued distributions upon the preferred stock. The holders of the common stock shall have the right to vote on all questions to the exclusion of all other stockholders, except as herein otherwise provided.

If no modifications of voting rights appear in the articles, the Model Business Corporation Act and most states grant each outstanding share (including preferred shares) one vote on each matter submitted to a vote at the meeting of the shareholders.[40] The articles of incorporation may reconfirm the statutory voting scheme.

EXAMPLE

Reconfirmation of Statutory Voting Rights

The preferred stock and common stock shall have equal voting powers and the holders thereof shall be entitled to one vote in person or by proxy for each share of stock held. The common stock, however, to the exclusion of the preferred stock, shall have the sole voting power with respect to the determination of whether the preferred stock shall be redeemed, as hereinafter provided

If voting rights are denied to a particular class of shares, the holders of shares in that class are not entitled to vote on typical shareholder business. A potential problem lurks in this rule. Consider that the structure (including distribution and liquidation entitlements) of the nonvoting securities is specified in the articles of incorporation and that this structure may be changed by an amendment to the articles that is approved by the shareholders. If the holders of the nonvoting classes were never entitled to vote, even on such matters, they would be at the mercy of the voting shareholders, who could vote to amend away the advantageous features of their stock. Consequently, corporate statutes uniformly provide for class voting on matters that may affect the rights of the class.

Section 7.25 of the Model Business Corporation Act permits shares to vote as a **separate voting group** and to take action in a meeting when a quorum of the separate voting group is present. The separate voting group may be one or more classes of stock that are entitled to vote on certain matters, either because the articles of incorporation provide for a vote of the separate group, or the statute requires such a vote.

Section 10.04 of the act provides that a class will be entitled to vote as a separate voting group on any proposed amendment that would affect the rights of that class.[41]

Redemption Rights

The terms of preferred stock may include provisions for the **redemption** of the shares. A corporation may have the right to redeem or reacquire its shares if redemption terms are included in the description of the class. The redemption feature is a greater advantage to the corporation than to the shareholders. For example, suppose the corporation issued 20% cumulative redeemable preferred stock to acquire needed capital. The distribution percentage would make this stock very attractive, but management would prefer not to continue paying a high cumulative distribution any longer than necessary. The redemption feature would permit the corporation to retire the securities when it had generated enough capital from operations to do so.

A proper redemption provision should spell out the terms of the "forced" sale from the preferred shareholders to the corporation and the procedure that must be followed to accomplish the sale. A redemption clause must appear on the articles of incorporation and on the share certificate; it typically includes

1. a date upon which the stock will be redeemable by the corporation;
2. a price at which the stock is redeemable, usually with a provision to the effect that an amount equal to accrued and unpaid distributions will be added to the price;
3. a period of notice preceding the date of redemption and the persons to whom notice must be given;
4. a place at which payment is to be made, and the person who will make payment;
5. a time at which payment is to be made and whether the board of directors has a right to accelerate the payment date;
6. provisions regarding the surrender of share certificates and the cancellation of all rights of the shareholder upon redemption; and
7. provisions covering the possibility that a shareholder will not surrender shares for cancellation in accordance with the redemption right.

EXAMPLE

Redemption of Shares

The preferred stock may be redeemed in whole or in part on any quarterly dividend payment date, at the option of the Board of Directors, upon not less than sixty (60) days' prior notice to the holders of record of the preferred stock, published, mailed, and given in such manner and form and on such other terms and conditions as may be prescribed by the bylaws or by resolution of the Board of Directors by payment in cash for each share of the preferred stock to be redeemed of one hundred two percent (102%) of the par amount thereof and in addition thereto all unpaid dividends accrued on such share.

From and after May 1, 1995, the Board of Directors shall retire not less than 1,000 shares of preferred stock per annum; but the Board of Directors shall first set aside a reserve to provide full dividends for the current year on all preferred stock that shall be outstanding after such purchase or retirement, and provided further that no such purchase or retirement shall be made if the capital of the Corporation would thereby be impaired.

If less than all the outstanding shares are to be redeemed, such redemption may be made by a lot or pro rata as may be prescribed by resolution of the Board of Directors; provided, however, that the Board of Directors may alternatively invite from shareholders offers to the Corporation of preferred stock at less than One hundred two dollars ($102.00), and when such offers are invited, the Board of Directors shall then be required to buy at the lowest price or prices offered, up to the amount to be purchased.

From and after the date fixed in any such notice as the date of redemption (unless default shall be made by the Corporation in the payment of the redemption price), all dividends on the preferred stock thereby called for redemption shall cease to accrue and all rights of the holders hereof as stockholders of the Corporation, except the right to receive the redemption price, shall cease and determine.

Any purchase by the corporation of shares of its preferred stock shall not be made at prices in excess of said redemption price.

[or]

By a unanimous vote of a full board of directors of the number fixed by the stockholders at their last annual meeting, all or any shares of common stock of the Corporation held by such holder or holders as may be designated in such vote may be called at any time for purchase, or for retirement or cancellation in connection with any reduction of capital stock, at the book value of such shares as determined by the Board of Directors as of the close of the month next preceding such vote. Such determination, including the method thereof and the matters considered therein, shall be final and conclusive.

Not less than 30 days prior to the day for which a call of common stock for purchase or for retirement or cancellation is made, notice of the call shall be mailed to each holder of shares of stock called at his or her address as it appears upon the books of the Corporation. The Corporation shall, not later than said day, deposit with a bank to be designated in such notice, for the account of such holder, the amount of the purchase price of the shares so called. After such notice and deposit, all shares so called shall be deemed to have been transferred to the Corporation, or retired or canceled as the case may be, and the holder shall cease to have, in respect thereof, any claim to future dividends or other rights as stockholder, and shall be entitled only to the sums so deposited for his or her account. Any shares so acquired by the Corporation may be held and may be disposed of at such times, in such manner, and for such consideration as the Board of Directors shall determine.

The redemption of corporate securities requires large disbursements of cash and may be impossible to absorb in normal corporate operations. To plan for eventual redemption, therefore, management should consider a sinking fund for the payment of the purchase price. The objective of the sinking fund is the same as that of a holiday savings plan. By faithfully depositing a certain amount at periodic intervals, depositors can ensure that a lump sum will be available at the projected date of need. A clause establishing redemption of preferred stock with a sinking fund might look like this.

The Model Business Corporation Act repealed its statutory restrictions on redemption of shares several years ago. Many state statutes are still based on the former act provisions, however, and continue to restrict the redemption right in two important areas: (1) redemption or purchase of shares is prohibited when the corporation is insolvent or would be rendered insolvent by the redemption; and (2) redemption is forbidden if the transaction would reduce the net assets below the aggregate amount payable to the holders of shares having prior or equal rights to the assets of the corporation upon involuntary dissolution.

Sinking Fund

a) There shall be a sinking fund for the benefit of the shares of the preferred stock. As long as there shall remain outstanding any preferred stock, the Corporation shall set aside annually, on or before October 15, 1995, and on or before October 15th in each year thereafter, as and for such sinking fund for the then current year, an amount in cash equal to the lesser of either $25,000 or 2.7% of the Consolidated Net Earnings of the Corporation and its subsidiaries for the preceding calendar year (computed as hereinafter provided). As long as dividends on the preferred stock for any past quarterly dividend payment date shall not have been fully paid or declared and a sum sufficient for the payment thereof set apart, the date for the setting aside of any amounts for the sinking fund shall be postponed until all such dividends in arrears shall have been paid or declared and a sum sufficient for the payment thereof set aside, and no amounts shall be set aside for the sinking fund while such arrears shall exist. In addition to the aforesaid sinking fund payments, the Corporation shall pay out of its general funds all amounts paid in excess of $103 per share (for commissions or as, or based upon, accrued dividends) upon any purchase or redemption of preferred stock through the sinking fund, as hereinafter provided.

b) The moneys set aside for any annual installment for the sinking fund (with any amounts remaining unexpended from previous sinking fund installments), may, at the option of the Corporation, be immediately applied (but not earlier than the October 15th on or before which such installment is required to be set aside), as nearly as possible, to the redemption of shares of preferred stock at the redemption price of $103 per share plus dividends accrued thereon to the date of redemption, in the manner provided herein for the redemption of preferred stock; provided, however, that if at the time any such annual installment is set aside (but not earlier than the October 15th on or before which such installment is required to be set aside), any holder of preferred stock shall hold 5% or more of the then outstanding shares of preferred stock, then there shall promptly be redeemed from such holder the number of whole shares of preferred stock (and no more) that shall bear, as nearly as practicable, the same ratio to the total number of shares which could be redeemed pursuant to this subdivision with such moneys, as the number of shares of preferred stock then owned by such holder shall bear to the total number of shares of preferred stock then outstanding.

c) Any moneys set aside for the sinking fund, as hereinabove required, and not applied to the redemption of preferred stock as provided in the preceding clause (b) (with any amounts remaining unexpended from previous sinking fund payments) shall be applied from time to time by the Corporation to the purchase, directly or through agents, of preferred stock in the open market or at public or private sale, with or without advertisement or notice, as the Board of Directors shall in its discretion determine, at prices not exceeding $103 per share plus accrued dividends and plus the usual customary brokerage commissions payable in connection with such purchases. If at the expiration of a full period of 90 days following the date each such amount is set apart during which the Corporation shall have been entitled hereunder to purchase shares of preferred stock with such funds, there shall remain in the sinking fund amounts exceeding $5,000 in the aggregate which shall not have been expended during such periods, then the Corporation shall promptly select and call for redemption at $103 per share plus dividends accrued thereon to the date of redemption, in the manner herein provided for the redemption of preferred stock such number of shares of preferred stock as is necessary to exhaust as nearly as may be all of said moneys, except that no shares shall then be allocated for redemption from any holder if the pro rata share of the then current sinking fund payment shall have been applied to the redemption of shares of such holder as hereinabove in paragraph (b) of this subdivision provided. Anything herein to the contrary notwithstanding, no purchase or redemption of shares of preferred stock with any moneys set aside for the sinking fund shall be made or ordered unless full cumulative dividends for all past quarterly dividend payment dates have been paid or declared and a sum sufficient for the payment thereof set aside upon all shares of preferred stock then outstanding. When no shares of preferred stock shall remain outstanding, any balance remaining in the sinking fund shall become part of the general funds of the Corporation.

The last provision deserves an illustration. Suppose the corporation has $1,000,000 in assets, $700,000 in liabilities, and three classes of stock outstanding (1,000 shares of 8% noncumulative preferred stock with a $105 liquidation preference; 2,000 shares of 10% noncumulative preferred stock redeemable at $100 per share; and 100,000 shares of common stock). The net assets of the corporation (assets minus liabilities) total $300,000. The corporation could not redeem all 2,000 shares of the 10% preferred stock, since that would require $200,000 and payment of that amount would reduce net assets to $100,000. The remainder would be insufficient to pay the 8% preferred shareholders' liquidation preference of $105,000.

Exhibit 9–4.

Cancellation of
Redeemable Shares

Form **BCA-9.05**
(Rev. Jan. 2003)

STATEMENT OF CANCELLATION
of
NON-REISSUABLE SHARES

File #

Jesse White
Secretary of State
Department of Business Services
Springfield, IL 62756
Telephone (217) 782-1831
http://www.cyberdriveillinois.com

Remit payment in check or money order, payable to "Secretary of State."

SUBMIT IN DUPLICATE

This space for use by Secretary of State
Date

Filing Fee $ 5.00

Approved:

---

1. CORPORATE NAME: _____

2. **The corporation has acquired and cancelled its own shares, and the articles of incorporation prohibit the re-issuance of such shares.**

3. Number of shares cancelled and redemption or purchase price:

Class	Series	Par Value	Number of Shares Cancelled	Redemption or Purchase Price	Date of Cancellation
____	____	_____			

	BEFORE CANCELLATION				AFTER CANCELLATION		
	Class	Series	Par	Number	Class	Series	Par	Number
4. Number of authorized shares:								
5. Number of issued shares:								
6. Paid-in capital:	$ _____				$ _____			

7. The undersigned corporation has caused this statement to be signed by a duly authorized officer who affirms, under penalties of perjury, that the facts stated herein are true. (All signatures must be in **BLACK INK**.)

Dated _____ , _____   _____
          (Month & Day)   *(Year)*   *(Exact Name of Corporation)*

_____
(Any Authorized Officer's Signature)

_____
(Type or Print Name and Title)

Redeemed shares are usually canceled and restored to authorized status, just as if they have never been issued. Under the current Model Business Corporation Act, the restoration of the shares to this status is automatic unless the articles of incorporation provide that the shares shall not be reissued, in which case the redeemed shares are eradicated by reducing the total authorized shares.[42] A statement of **cancellation** must be filed upon redemption, describing the name of the corporation; the reduction in the number of authorized shares, itemized by class and series; and the total number of authorized shares remaining after the reduction (see Exhibit 9–4, Cancellation of Redeemable Shares). The act regards this statement as an amendment to the articles of incorporation without shareholder action.

Conversion Privileges

Certain classes of stock may be entitled to a **conversion** privilege whereby a holder of those shares may convert the shares of one class for shares of another class at a specified rate and time. A conversion feature enhances the marketability of conservative classes of stock, because the holder has the best of both worlds. A holder of preferred shares with a conversion privilege, for example, enjoys the preferences and conservative investment protection of the preferred stock while maintaining the option to convert to common stock if its growth rate is attractive. The shareholder who owns convertible preferred stock, therefore, receives the security of preferred shares plus the right to elect an interest in the basic equity growth of the company.

A conversion clause should appear in the articles of incorporation and on the share certificates. A conversion privilege provision should include

1. a conversion rate specifying the number of shares of common stock (or another class) into which each share of preferred stock is convertible;
2. provisions respecting the issuance of fractional shares, since the conversion may result in a fractional share problem;[43]
3. a procedure for the method of conversion, detailing the written notice required to convert the shares and a period of time following the election that the conversion will become effective;
4. provisions for the adjustment of conversion rates in case a stock dividend, stock split, or other corporate action changes the character of the shares into which the preferred stock can be converted;
5. requirement of notice to preferred shareholders when the conversion rate is adjusted; and
6. reservation of an adequate number of shares of common stock, in case all conversion privileges are exercised.

Remember that a corporation must have authority to issue common stock in its articles of incorporation, and enough common shares must be reserved to allow the preferred shareholders to exercise their conversion privilege.

Conversion of Shares

EXAMPLE

The preferred stock of this Corporation of $100 par value may, at the option of the holder thereof, at any time on or before January 10, 2005, be converted into common stock of this Corporation of $100 par value upon the following terms:

a) Any holder of such preferred stock desiring to avail himself or herself of the option for conversion of that stock shall, on or before January 10, 2005, deliver, duly endorsed in blank, the certificates representing the stock to be converted to the Secretary of the Corporation at its office, and at the same time notify the Secretary in writing over the holder's signature that the holder desires to convert his or her stock into common stock of $100 par value pursuant to these provisions.

b) Upon receipt by the Secretary of a certificate or certificates representing such preferred stock and a notice that the holder desires to convert the same, the Corporation shall forthwith cause to be issued to the holder one share of common stock for each share of preferred stock surrendered, and shall deliver to such holder a certificate in due form for such common stock.

c) One hundred thousand shares of common stock of this Corporation shall be set aside and such shares shall be issued only in conversion of preferred stock as herein provided.

d) Shares of preferred stock that have been converted shall revert to the status of unissued shares and shall not be reissued. Such shares may be eliminated as provided by law.

e) If, at any time the convertible preferred stock of this Corporation is outstanding, the Corporation increases the number of common shares outstanding without adjusting the stated capital of the corporation, the conversion rate shall be adjusted accordingly, so as to make each share of preferred stock convertible into the same proportionate amount of common stock into which it would have been convertible without such adjustment to the common stock. Each preferred shareholder shall be notified in writing of the adjusted conversion rate within thirty (30) days of such action by the Corporation.

f) These provisions for conversion of preferred stock of this Corporation shall be subject to the limitations and restrictions contained in the Business Corporation Law.

TRANSFER AGENTS

Many public corporations employ **transfer agents** and **registrars** to keep track of the record holders of corporate securities. In a close corporation, where share certificates are exchanged only rarely, corporate officers or counsel usually serve this function. By statute, a stock transfer ledger must be maintained either at the place of business of the corporation or at the office of its transfer agent or registrar,[44] which is normally a bank or other financial institution that has a separate division for the explicit purpose of maintaining such records for corporations. The transfer agent is responsible for issuing new stock certificates. Blank certificates are usually kept in bulk at the agent's office; the statutory signatures are usually printed on the certificates, since the Model Business Corporation Act permits a **facsimile signature** of the officers.[45] If a registrar as well as a transfer agent is used, the transfer agent delivers newly prepared certificates to the registrar for registration and countersignature. The registrar returns the registered and signed certificates to the transfer agent, who then issues them. The registrar's responsibilities include recording all certificates representing shares of stock in the corporation. If the transfer agent and registrar are separate individuals, all entries made in the stock transfer ledger are made by the registrar, and the ledger is kept at the registrar's office. Transfer agents and registrars receive corporate authority by resolution of the board of directors (see Exhibit 9–5, Appointment of Transfer Agent and Registrar).

In addition to a specification of authority to act as transfer agent or registrar, such a resolution may also include a statement that the officers of the company are authorized and empowered to give instructions to the transfer agent and to the registrar and to take any other action they deem necessary to effect the issuance of the common stock.

DEBT SECURITIES (BONDS)

Every state empowers a corporation to borrow funds for corporate purposes. Debt securities represent loans to the corporation, and a debt security holder is a creditor of the corporation. A debt holder usually enjoys no right to participate in management and also has no right to receive profits. A debt security holder is, however, entitled to the repayment of the loan with the prescribed interest, and if the debt remains unpaid at the time of dissolution, repayment of the debt may be obtained from the available assets. Furthermore, debt security holders enjoy greater security for their investment than do equity security holders, since debt holders are creditors and thus are entitled to be satisfied from the available assets before equity holders are paid.

Debt securities state a principal amount, a maturity date, and a periodic interest rate. The interest is the return on the investment, and usually determines the attractiveness of a debt security. State statutes do not strictly regulate debt obligations, and as a matter of law these securities are considered to be individual agreements between the debt security holder and the corporation, containing negotiated terms. The terms of debt securities (bonds) issued by public corporations are fixed and are not subject to negotiation or modification. For example, Peoples Energy Corporation may issue bonds in the amount of $25,000,000, with interest set at 5.34% per year and a maturity date of 2020. Investors who wish to purchase these bonds simply buy them from a broker on those terms. However, in closely held corporations, debt securities may contain a variety of terms that are negotiated between the creditor-investor and the corporation. When Local Pharmacy, Inc., decides to raise money by borrowing funds, it may negotiate with various investors in the community to reach acceptable terms for their investment. It may issue a bond to one investor for $10,000 with interest at 8% per year to be paid in 3 years and another bond to a different investor for $25,000 with interest at 12% per year to be paid in 2 years, and so on. Nevertheless, it is possible to generalize about the typical features of debt securities.

Exhibit 9–5.

Appointment of Transfer
Agent and Registrar

Appointment of   TRANSFER AGENT
                               REGISTRAR

_____
                        (Name of Corporation)
    Resolved, that The_____Bank_____is
hereby appointed [sole] [Transfer Agent] [Registrar] for all of the shares
                                   of the_____Preferred stock, and
[_____shares]
[all of the shares]

                                         of the_____Common stock
of this Company, to act in accordance with its general practice and with the
regulations set forth in the pamphlet submitted to this meeting entitled "Regulations of The_____Bank_____
for the Transfer and Registration of Stock," which pamphlet the Secretary is
directed to mark for identification and file with the records of the Company.
    I, the undersigned, Secretary of the above-named Corporation, do hereby
certify that the foregoing is a true and correct copy of a resolution duly adopted
by the Board of Directors of said Corporation at a meeting thereof duly called
and held on_____, 20___, at which a quorum were present, and that said
resolution has not been in any wise rescinded, annulled, or revoked but the same
is still in full force.
    And I do further certify to the following facts:
    The authorized and outstanding stock of the Corporation is as follows:

Class	Par Value	Authorized	Outstanding
_____	_____	_____	_____
_____	_____	_____	_____

The address of the Corporation to which notices may be sent is_____
    The below-named persons have been duly elected and qualified as, and this
day are, officers of the Corporation, holding the respective offices set opposite
their names, and the signatures set opposite their names are their genuine
signatures.

_____President_____
_____Vice-President_____
_____Vice-President_____
_____Treasurer_____
_____Assistant Treasurer_____
_____Secretary_____
_____Assistant Secretary_____

_____
    The name and address of legal counsel for the Corporation is_____
    The names and addresses of all of the Transfer Agents and Registrars of the
stock of the Corporation are as follows:

Class of Stock	Transfer Agent(s)	Registrar(s)
_____	_____	_____
_____	_____	_____

    Witness my hand and the seal of the Corporation this_____day of,
20_____.

                                                    _____
                                                    Secretary

[Corporate Seal]

TYPES OF CORPORATE DEBT SECURITIES

Unsecured Debt

A corporate debt obligation may be set out in a simple **promissory note,** the terms of which include the amount of the debt, a promise to pay the principal at a certain time, and a promise to pay interest.

E XAMPLE

Promissory Note

$50,000.00   November 1, 2006

One year after date, for value received, Happiness, Inc., promises to pay to Jeb P. Owen or order, payable at 1216 Charlotte Avenue, Austin, Texas, the sum of Fifty thousand DOLLARS, with interest thereon at the rate of 15 percent, per annum from date, payable monthly until paid.

Failure to pay any installment of principal or interest when due shall cause the whole note to become due and payable at once, or the interest to be counted as principal, at the option of the holder of this note, and it shall not be necessary for the holder to declare the same due, but he may proceed to collect the same as if the whole was due and payable by its terms.

Presentment for payment, notice of dishonor, and protest are hereby waived by the maker or makers, and endorser or endorsers, and each endorser for himself or herself guarantees the payment of this note according to its terms. No extension of payment shall release any signer or be paid by the parties liable for the payment of this note.

Happiness, Inc., By: Susan Powers President

Alternatively, it may be a lengthy, complex debenture obligation:

E XAMPLE

18% Twenty-Year Debenture Due August 1, 2025

$1,000   No._____

Trouble, Inc., a Colorado corporation (hereinafter called the "Company," which term includes any successor corporation under the Indenture hereinafter referred to), for value received, hereby promises to pay to the bearer, or, if this Debenture be registered as to principal, to the registered holder hereof, on August 1, 2025, the sum of One Thousand Dollars and to pay interest thereon, from the date hereof, semi-annually on June 1 and December 1 in each year, at the rate of Eighteen (18) percent per annum. Payment of the principal of (and premium, if any) and interest on this Debenture will be made at the office or agency of the Company maintained for that purpose in Denver, Colorado, in such coin or currency of the United States of America as at the time of payment is legal tender for payment of public and private debts.

This Debenture is one of a duly authorized issue of Debentures of the Company designated as its 18% Twenty-Year Debentures Due August 1, 2025 (hereinafter called the "Debentures"), limited in aggregate principal amount to $1,500,000.00, issued and to be issued under an indenture dated August 1, 2005 (hereinafter called the "Indenture"), between the Company and Glorious Trust Company as Trustee (hereinafter called the "Trustee," which term includes any successor trustee under the Indenture), to which Indenture and all indentures supplemental thereto reference is hereby made for a statement of the respective rights thereunder of the Company, the Trustee and the holders of the Debentures and coupons, and the terms upon which the Debentures are, and are to be, authenticated and delivered.

If an Event of Default, as defined in the Indenture, shall occur, the principal of all the Debentures may be declared due and payable in the manner and with the effect provided in the Indenture.

The Indenture permits, with certain exceptions as therein provided, the amendment thereof and the modification of the rights and obligations of the Company and the rights of the holders of the

Debentures under the Indenture at any time by the Company with the consent of the holders of $66\frac{2}{3}\%$ in aggregate principal amount of the Debentures at the time outstanding, as defined in the Indenture. The Indenture also contains provisions permitting the holders of specified percentages in aggregate principal amount of the Debentures at the time outstanding, as defined in the Indenture, on behalf of the holders of all the Debentures, by written consent to waive compliance by the Company with certain provisions of the Indenture and certain past defaults under the Indenture and their consequences. Any such consent or waiver by the holder of this Debenture shall be conclusive and binding upon such holder and upon all future holders of this Debenture and of any Debenture issued in exchange herefor or in lieu hereof whether or not notation of such consent or waiver is made upon this Debenture.

No reference herein to the Indenture and no provision of this Debenture or of the Indenture shall alter or impair the obligation of the Company, which is absolute and unconditional, to pay the principal of (and premium, if any) and interest on this Debenture at the times, place, and rate, and in the coin or currency, herein prescribed.

This Debenture is transferable by delivery, unless registered as to principal in the name of the holder in the Debenture Register of the Company. This Debenture may be so registered upon presentation hereof at the office or agency of the Company in any place where the principal hereof and interest hereon are payable, such registration being noted hereon. While registered as aforesaid, this Debenture shall be transferable on the Debenture Register of the Company by the registered holder hereof, upon like presentation of this Debenture for notation of such transfer hereon, accompanied by a written instrument of transfer in form satisfactory to the Company and the Debenture Registrar duly executed by the registered holder hereof or his or her attorney duly authorized in writing, all as provided in the Indenture and subject to certain limitations therein set forth; but this Debenture may be discharged from registration by being in like manner transferred to bearer, and thereupon transferability by delivery shall be restored. This Debenture shall continue to be subject to successive registrations and transfers to bearer at the option of the bearer or registered holder, as the case may be. Such registration, however, shall not affect the transferability by delivery of the coupons appertaining hereto, which shall continue to be payable to bearer and transferable by delivery. No service charge shall be made for any such registration, transfer, or discharge from registration, but the Company may require payment of a sum sufficient to cover any tax or other governmental charge payable in connection therewith.

The Company, the Trustee, and any agent of the Company may treat the bearer of this Debenture, or, if this Debenture is registered as herein authorized, the person in whose name the same is registered, and the bearer of any coupon appertaining hereto, as the absolute owner hereof for all purposes, whether or not this Debenture or such coupon be overdue, and neither the Company, the Trustee, nor any such agent shall be affected by notice to the contrary.

The Debentures are issuable as coupon Debentures, registrable as to principal, in the denomination of $1,000 and as registered Debentures without coupons in denominations of $1,000 and any multiple thereof. As provided in the Indenture and subject to certain limitations therein set forth, Debentures are exchangeable for a like aggregate principal amount of Debentures of a different authorized kind or denomination, as requested by the holder surrendering the same, upon payment of taxes and other governmental charges.

Unless the certificate of authentication hereon has been executed by the Trustee by the manual signature of one of its authorized officers, neither this Debenture, nor any coupon appertaining hereto, shall be entitled to any benefit under the Indenture, or be valid or obligatory for any purpose.

In witness whereof, the Company has caused this Debenture to be duly executed under its corporate seal, and coupons bearing the facsimile signature of its Treasurer to be hereto annexed. Date: December 15, 2005

Trouble, Inc.
By: Teresa Thrailkill
President

Attest:
Jerrold Glick
Secretary

Exhibit 9–6.

Debenture Certificate

(See Exhibit 9–6, Debenture Certificate, and Exhibit 9–7, Debenture Certificate with Coupons on page 324.)

In any case, these are unsecured obligations, meaning that the corporation simply borrows money on the strength of its own ability to repay. The characteristic common to the simple promissory note and the debenture bond is that there is no specific corporate property to which the creditor will be entitled if the corporation defaults.

Secured Debt

The unsecured debenture or promissory note should be contrasted with a mortgage bond or **secured** note in which the corporation pledges certain property as collateral to secure repayment of the obligation. If there is a default, the creditor may reach the collateral to satisfy the debt. Mortgage bonds usually have corporate land as collateral. The obligation between the creditor and the corporation is represented by a mortgage bond, or note, and a mortgage agreement, which specifies the terms under which the property will be held for the benefit of the creditor. A mortgage agreement usually requires the mortgagor (corporation) to insure the property, maintain it in good order, and keep it free from other liens or obligations so that the creditor will have its full benefit, if necessary. Secured debt obligations may also involve personal property collateral, including equipment, inventory, accounts, and so on. Personal property security interests are governed by the Uniform Commercial Code, which has been adopted in every state. The code requires a security agreement between the debtor and cred-

Exhibit 9–6.

(continued)

AMERICAN TELEPHONE AND TELEGRAPH COMPANY

This Debenture is one of a duly authorized issue of Debentures of the Company, designated as set forth on the face hereof (herein referred to as the "Debentures"), limited to the aggregate principal amount of $1,569,327,000, all issued or to be issued under and pursuant to an indenture dated May 18, 1970 (herein referred to as the "Indenture"), duly executed and delivered by the Company to Chemical Bank, Trustee (herein referred to as the "Trustee"), which Indenture and all indentures supplemental thereto are hereby incorporated by reference in and made a part of this instrument and are hereby referred to for a description of the rights, limitation of rights, obligations, duties and immunities thereunder of the Trustee, the Company and the holders (the words "holders" or "holder" meaning the registered holders or registered holder) of the Debentures.

In case an Event of Default, as defined in the Indenture, shall have occurred and be continuing, the principal hereof may be declared, and upon such declaration shall become, due and payable, in the manner, with the effect and subject to the conditions provided in the Indenture.

The Indenture contains provisions permitting the Company and the Trustee, with the consent of the holders of not less than 66-2/3% in aggregate principal amount of the Debentures at the time outstanding, evidenced as in the Indenture provided, to execute supplemental indentures adding any provisions to or changing in any manner or eliminating any of the provisions of the Indenture or of any supplemental indenture or modifying in any manner the rights of the holders of the Debentures; provided, however, that no such supplemental indenture shall (i) extend the fixed maturity of any Debentures, or reduce the principal amount thereof, or reduce the rate or extend the time of payment of interest thereon, or reduce any premium payable upon the redemption thereof, without the consent of the holder of each Debenture so affected, or (ii) reduce the aforesaid percentage of Debentures, the consent of the holders of which is required for any such supplemental indenture, without the consent of the holders of all Debentures then outstanding. It is also provided in the Indenture that, under certain circumstances, the holders of a majority in aggregate principal amount of the Debentures at the time outstanding may on behalf of the holders of all of the Debentures waive any past default under the Indenture and its consequences, except a default in the payment of the principal (or premium, if any) or interest on any of the Debentures. Any such consent or waiver by the holder of this Debenture (unless revoked as provided in the Indenture) shall be conclusive and binding upon such holder and upon all future holders and owners of this Debenture and of any Debenture issued in exchange or substitution therefor, irrespective of whether or not any notation of such consent or waiver is made upon this Debenture or such other Debenture.

No reference herein to the Indenture and no provision of this Debenture or of the Indenture shall alter or impair the obligation of the Company, which is absolute and unconditional, to pay the principal of (and premium, if any) and interest on this Debenture at the place, at the respective times, at the rate and in the coin or currency herein prescribed.

The Debentures are issuable as registered Debentures without coupons in denominations of $100 and any multiple of $100. At the office or agency of the Company referred to on the face hereof and in the manner and subject to the limitations provided in the Indenture, Debentures may be exchanged without a service charge for a like aggregate principal amount of Debentures of other authorized denominations.

The Debentures may be redeemed, at the option of the Company, as a whole or from time to time in part (selected by lot or otherwise in such manner as the Trustee may deem appropriate and fair), on or after May 15, 1975 and prior to maturity, upon the notice referred to below, at the following redemption prices (expressed in percentages of the principal amount): during the 12 months' periods ending May 14:

1976	107.00%	1983	104.55%	1990	102.10%
1977	106.65%	1984	104.20%	1991	101.75%
1978	106.30%	1985	103.85%	1992	101.40%
1979	105.95%	1986	103.50%	1993	101.05%
1980	105.60%	1987	103.15%	1994	100.70%
1981	105.25%	1988	102.80%	1995	100.35%
1982	104.90%	1989	102.45%		

and thereafter, 100%, together in each case with accrued interest to the date fixed for redemption. As provided in the Indenture, notice of redemption to the holders of Debentures to be redeemed as a whole or in part shall be given by mailing a notice of such redemption not less than thirty nor more than ninety days prior to the date fixed for redemption to their last addresses as they shall appear upon the register kept for that purpose.

Upon due presentment for registration of transfer of this Debenture at the above-mentioned office or agency of the Company, a new Debenture or Debentures, of authorized denominations, for a like aggregate principal amount, will be issued to the transferee as provided in the Indenture. No service charge shall be made for any such transfer, but the Company may require payment of a sum sufficient to cover any tax or other governmental charge that may be imposed in relation thereto.

The Company, the Trustee, any paying agent and any Debenture registrar may deem and treat the holder hereof as the absolute owner hereof (whether or not this Debenture shall be overdue and notwithstanding any notation of ownership or other writing hereon) for the purpose of receiving payment of or on account of the principal hereof (and premium, if any) and, subject to the provisions on the face hereof, interest hereon, and for all other purposes, and neither the Company nor the Trustee nor any paying agent nor any Debenture registrar shall be affected by any notice to the contrary.

No recourse shall be had for the payment of the principal of (or premium, if any) or the interest on this Debenture, or for any claim based hereon, or otherwise in respect hereof, or based on or in respect of the Indenture or any indenture supplemental thereto, against any incorporator, shareholder, officer or director, as such, past, present or future, of the Company or of any successor corporation, either directly or through the Company or any successor corporation, whether by virtue of any constitution, statute or rule of law or by the enforcement of any assessment or penalty or otherwise, all such liability being, by the acceptance hereof and as part of the consideration for the issue hereof, expressly waived and released.

The following abbreviations shall be construed as though the words set forth below opposite each abbreviation were written out in full where such abbreviation appears:

TEN COM – as tenants in common
TEN ENT – as tenants by the entireties
JT TEN – as joint tenants with right of survivorship and not as tenants in common

(Name) CUST (Name) UNIF (Name) as Custodian for (Name) under the
GIFT MIN ACT (State) (State) Uniform Gifts to Minors Act

Additional abbreviations may also be used though not in the above list.

FOR VALUE RECEIVED, the undersigned sells, assigns and transfers unto

PLEASE PRINT OR TYPE
TAXPAYER-IDENTIFYING NUMBER

NAME AND ADDRESS INCLUDING ZIP CODE OF ASSIGNEE

RESERVED FOR A.T.&T. CO. USE			
RIN			
TRANS CODE	DEB NOTE	TOWN CODE	CLASS NON-DOM.
61 NA 1			
CC 2			4

the within Debenture of AMERICAN TELEPHONE AND TELEGRAPH COMPANY and hereby irrevocably constitutes and appoints

_____ Attorney
to transfer said Debenture on the books of said Company with full power of substitution in the premises.

Dated _____

THE SIGNATURE(S) TO THIS ASSIGNMENT MUST CORRESPOND WITH THE NAME(S) AS WRITTEN UPON THE FACE OF THE DEBENTURE IN EVERY PARTICULAR WITHOUT ALTERATION OR ENLARGEMENT OR ANY CHANGE WHATEVER. THE SIGNATURE(S) SHOULD BE GUARANTEED BY A COMMERCIAL BANK OR TRUST COMPANY, OR BY A NEW YORK, BOSTON, MIDWEST, PHILADELPHIA-BALTIMORE-WASHINGTON OR PACIFIC COAST STOCK EXCHANGE MEMBER OR FIRM WHOSE SIGNATURE IS KNOWN TO THE TRANSFER OFFICE.

---

itor (see Exhibit 9–8, Security Agreement under the Uniform Commercial Code on page 326).[46] Further, a financing statement that meets the statutory requirements[47] must be recorded in the appropriate state or county offices (see Exhibit 9–9, Uniform Commercial Code—Financing Statement on page 328).[48]

TRUST INDENTURE

When numerous bonds are issued at once, a trustee is usually appointed to act on behalf of the holders of the security in case of default by the corporation. The appointment of a trustee is particularly desirable for secured debt obligations because it will be necessary for someone to take the necessary action to recover the collateral pledged to secure the bond and distribute the proceeds of its sale to the bondholders. If the corporation defaults, the trustee will act on behalf

of the creditors to recover the property securing the obligations. The trustee is usually a financial institution, and is appointed by the execution of a **trust indenture,** an agreement that specifies the rights and responsibilities of the corporation, the rights and responsibilities of the trustee, and the rights of the security holders. If the bonds are to be sold to the public, the indenture must comply with the requirements of the **Trust Indenture Act of 1939,** the federal Securities Act of 1933,[49] and perhaps state securities statutes. The document that evidences the obligation, the bond itself, merely refers to the trust indenture for all details of the obligation. Trust indentures are unconscionably lengthy documents, and most experienced financial institutions have standard indentures for the use of their corporate customers.[50]

Exhibit 9–7

(continued)

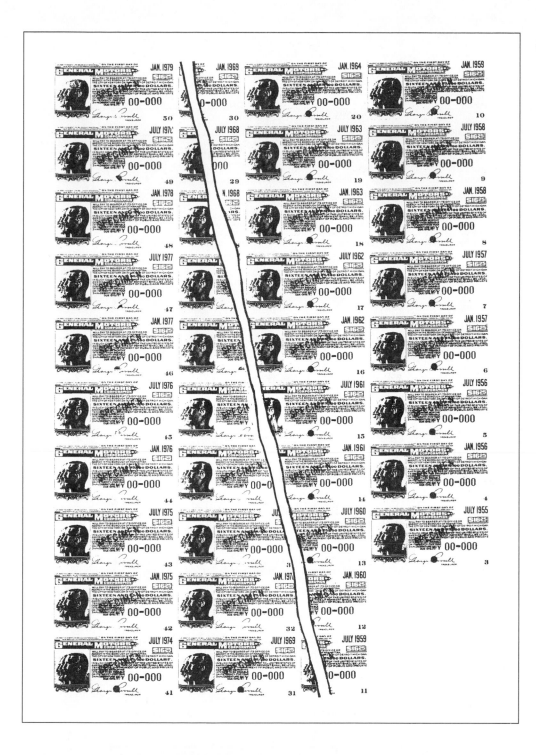

COMMON PROVISIONS IN DEBT SECURITIES

As with stock, it is possible to introduce into debt securities various privileges that make the investment more attractive. Debt securities may also have redemption or conversion provisions, and the terms of the obligation may contain a subordination feature, which establishes a priority of one debt security over another. The investment objectives of a debt security holder are twofold: repayment of the principal and receipt of the periodic interest. The security may become more or less attractive depending upon the circumstances under which it may be redeemed (terminating the interest), converted (altering the character of the investment), or subordinated (endangering repayment of the principal).

Exhibit 9–8.

Security Agreement under the Uniform Commercial Code

SECURITY AGREEMENT

Debtor:
Name: _____
(Exact Legal Name Required)
Address:
Residence: _____
(Street, City, State, Zip)
Business: _____
(Street, City, State, Zip)
Secured Party:
Name: _____

Address: _____
(Street, City, State, Zip)

Debtor, for consideration, hereby grants to Secured Party a security interest in the following property, and any and all property of like type now owned or hereafter acquired by Debtor, together with all additions, accessions, substitutions, proceeds and products therefrom, including natural increase of livestock, all herein called the "Collateral":

To secure payment of the indebtedness evidenced by _____ certain promissory note _____ of even date herewith, payable to the Secured Party, or order, as follows:

and all other liabilities of Debtor to Secured Party, absolute or contingent, due or to become due, now existing or hereafter arising, including liabilities arising because of funds advanced in the future at the option of Secured Party, all herein called the "OBLIGATIONS."

DEBTOR EXPRESSLY WARRANTS AND COVENANTS:

The Collateral is used or bought primarily for:

☐ Personal, family or household purposes;

☐ Use in farming operations;

☐ Use in business.

That Debtor's residence, state of organization or chief executive office is as stated herein, and the Collateral will be kept at

Location _____ County _____ State _____.
If any of the Collateral is oil, gas, or minerals to be extracted or timber to be cut, or goods which are or are to become fixtures, said Collateral concerns the following described real estate situate in the _____ County of _____ and State of Colorado, to-wit:

The undersigned acknowledge receipt of a copy of this Security Agreement on date hereof, and agree that it includes and is subject to the ADDITIONAL PROVISIONS on the reverse side hereof, the same being incorporated herein by reference.

Debtor:

_____
Debtor's state of organization, or if not a registered organization, chief executive office

_____   _____
Debtor's State Identification No.

_____   Dated this _____ day of _____, 20_____.

No. 651. Rev. 8-01. SECURITY AGREEMENT (Page 1 of 2)

Redemption

Bonds may be redeemable at the option of the board of directors at a specified time and a specified price. Redemption provisions are usually included in bonds that have very high interest rates (making them attractive to investors) but the corporation does not want to pay such high interest rates any longer than necessary. Consequently, bonds have a redemption provision allowing the corporation to buy them from the investor before maturity and eliminate the remaining interest payments. The redemption price for bonds is usually stated in terms of a

Exhibit 9–8.

(continued)

ADDITIONAL PROVISIONS

FURTHER WARRANTIES AND COVENANTS OF THE DEBTOR. The Debtor hereby warrants and covenants that:

1.   Except for the security interest granted hereby, the Debtor is, or to the extent that this agreement states that the Collateral is to be acquired after the date hereof, will be, the owner of the Collateral free from any prior lien, security interest or encumbrance; and the Debtor will defend the Collateral against all claims and demands of all persons at any time claiming the same or any interest therein.

2.   Irrespective of whether the Secured Party claims a security interest in proceeds hereunder, the Debtor will not sell or offer to sell or otherwise transfer or encumber the Collateral or any interest therein without the prior written consent of the Secured Party. The Collateral will be located at and kept at the location shown on the reverse side hereof and shall not be removed without the prior written consent of the Secured Party.

3.   The Debtor will pay all taxes and assessments of every nature which may be levied or assessed against the Collateral.

4.   The Debtor will keep the Collateral at all times insured against risks of loss or damage by fire (including so-called extended coverage), theft and such other casualties as the Secured Party may reasonably require, including collision in the case of any motor vehicle, all in such amounts, under such forms of policies, upon such terms, for such periods, and written by such companies or underwriters as the Secured Party may approve, losses in all cases to be payable to the Secured Party and the Debtor as their interest may appear. All policies of insurance shall provide for at least ten days' prior written notice of cancellation to the Secured Party; and the Debtor shall furnish the Secured Party with certificates of such insurance or other evidence satisfactory to the Secured Party as to compliance with the provisions of this paragraph. The Secured Party may act as attorney for the Debtor in making, adjusting and settling claims under or cancelling such insurance and endorsing the Debtor's name on any drafts drawn by insurers of the Collateral.

5.   The Debtor will not permit or allow any adverse lien, security interest or encumbrance whatsoever upon the Collateral, and will not permit the same to be attached or replevined.

6.   The Collateral is in good condition, and the Debtor will, at the Debtor's own expense, keep the same in good condition and from time to time, forthwith, replace and repair all such parts of the Collateral as may be broken, worn out, or damaged without allowing any lien to be created upon the Collateral on account of such replacement or repairs, and the Secured Party may examine and inspect the Collateral at any time, wherever located.

7.   The Debtor will not use the Collateral in violation of any applicable statutes, regulations or ordinances.

ADDITIONAL RIGHTS OF PARTIES. At its option, but without obligation to the Debtor, the Secured Party may discharge taxes, liens, or security interests or other encumbrances at any time levied or placed on the Collateral, may place and pay for insurance thereon, may order and pay for the repair, maintenance and preservation thereof and may pay any necessary filing or recording fees. The Debtor agrees to reimburse the Secured Party on demand for any payment made or any expense incurred by the Secured Party pursuant to the foregoing authorization. Until default the Debtor may have possession of the Collateral and use it in any lawful manner, and upon default the Secured Party shall have the immediate right to the possession of the Collateral.

Borrower hereby waives all right of homestead exemption in the Collateral, including that granted by §38-41-201.6, C.R.S. and waives any other statutory exemptions, including those granted by §13-54-102, C.R.S., insofar as such exemptions pertain to the Collateral described in this Security Agreement.

THE DEBTOR SHALL BE IN DEFAULT under this agreement upon the happening of any of the following events or conditions:

(a)   default in the payment or performance of any obligation, covenant or liability contained or referred to herein or in any note evidencing the same;

(b)   the making or furnishing of any warranty, representation or statement to the Secured Party by or on behalf of the Debtor which proves to have been false in any material respect when made or furnished.

(c)   loss, theft, damage, destruction, sale or encumbrance to or of any of the Collateral, or the making of any levy, seizure or attachment thereof or thereon;

(d)   death, change of name, dissolution, merger, termination of existence, insolvency, business failure, appointment of a receiver of any part of the property of, assignment for the benefit of creditors by, or the commencement of any proceeding under any bankruptcy or insolvency laws of, by or against the Debtor or any guarantor or surety for the Debtor.

UPON SUCH DEFAULT and at any time thereafter, or if it deems itself insecure, the Secured Party may declare all Obligations secured hereby immediately due and payable subject to any notice required by law or agreement, and shall have the remedies of a secured party under Article 9 of the Colorado Uniform Commercial Code. The Secured Party may require the Debtor to assemble the Collateral and deliver or make it available to the Secured Party at a place to be designated by the Secured Party which is reasonably convenient to both parties. Expenses of retaking, holding, preparing for sale, selling or the like shall, subject to any applicable limits set forth in the Colorado Uniform Consumer Credit Code, include the Secured Party's reasonable attorneys' fees and legal expenses (including the allocated fees and expenses of in-house counsel) and such portion of the Secured Party's overhead as it may in its reasonable judgment deem allocable to and includable in such expenses. Unless the Collateral is perishable or the Secured Party in good faith believes that the Collateral threatens to decline speedily in value or is of a type customarily sold on a recognized market, the Secured Party will give the Debtor reasonable notice of the time and place of any public sale thereof or of the time after which any private sale or any other intended disposition thereof is to be made. The requirements of reasonable notice shall be met if such notice is mailed, postage prepaid, to the address of the Debtor shown at the beginning of this Agreement at least ten days before the time of the sale or disposition. As respects crops covered by this Security Agreement, upon such default, it is agreed by the parties hereto that said crops are perishable or may decline speedily in value, and that the Secured Party may protect, cultivate, care for, harvest, or process said crops at the expense of the Debtor and may sell and dispose of said crops at private or public sale as the same mature or are harvested, at the price then available. [Where the Collateral is livestock, it is agreed that a commercially reasonable means of disposing of the Collateral shall include sale of such Collateral in the customary manner on the Denver, Colorado, livestock market or through a licensed livestock sales ring in Colorado. Sale of such livestock may be otherwise as permitted by law. It is expressly agreed also that it will not be necessary, after default and before the sale of any livestock Collateral, to collect said livestock or to have the same present at the place of sale.] In the event the Secured Party institutes legal proceedings to regain possession of the Collateral, Debtor knowingly and voluntarily waives his or her right to a hearing prior to losing possession of the Collateral by means of a court order, and agrees that the Secured Party may obtain an order for possession prior to hearing as provided in C.R.C.P. 104(d)(4).

No waiver by the Secured Party or any default shall operate as a waiver of any other default or of the same default on a future occasion. The taking of this security agreement shall not waive or impair any other security the Secured Party may have or hereafter acquire for the payment of the Obligations, nor shall the taking of any such additional security waive or impair this security agreement; but the Secured Party may resort to any security it may have in the order it may deem proper, and notwithstanding any Collateral Security, the Secured Party shall retain its rights of setoff against the Debtor.

All rights of the Secured Party hereunder shall inure to the benefit of the Secured Party's heirs, personal representatives, successors or assigns; and all promises and duties of the Debtor shall bind the Debtor's heirs, personal representatives, successors or assigns. If there be more than one Debtor, their liabilities hereunder shall be joint and several.

Should any provision of this Security Agreement violate any federal, state or local law or ordinance, that provision shall be deemed amended to so comply with such law or ordinance, and shall be construed in a manner so as to comply.

No. 651. Rev. 8-01. SECURITY AGREEMENT (Page 2 of 2)

---

percentage of the principal amount, and it may be determined by a declining percentage from the date of issue to maturity or a fixed percentage figure throughout. For example, a bond may be redeemable during the first year at 110% of the principal amount, during the second year at 109.5%, during the third year at 109%, and so forth. As the bond nears maturity, the redemption price will approach 100%. The declining percentage is designed to protect the bondholder's expectation of high interest payments by discouraging early redemption by the corporation.

Exhibit 9–9.

Uniform Commercial
Code—Financing
Statement

UCC FINANCING STATEMENT
Filing Fee: $15
Follow Instructions (front and back) Carefully

A. NAME & PHONE OF CONTACT (optional)

B. SEND ACKNOWLEDGMENT TO: (Name and Address)

[   ]

[   ]
ABOVE SPACE FOR FILING OFFICE USE ONLY

1. DEBTOR'S EXACT FULL LEGAL NAME – insert only one debtor name (1a or 1b) – do not abbreviate or combine names

OR   1a. ORGANIZATION'S NAME

1b. INDIVIDUAL'S LAST NAME	FIRST NAME	MIDDLE NAME	SUFFIX

1c. MAILING ADDRESS	CITY	STATE	POSTAL CODE	COUNTRY

1d. TAX ID#: SSN OR EIN (OPTIONAL: **NOT REQUIRED**)	ADD'L INFO RE ORGANIZATION DEBTOR	1e. TYPE OF ORGANIZATION	1f. JURISDICTION OF ORGANIZATION	1g. ORGANIZATIONAL ID#, if any ☐ NONE

2. ADDITIONAL DEBTOR'S EXACT FULL LEGAL NAME – insert only one debtor name (2a or 2b) – do not abbreviate or combine names

OR   2a. ORGANIZATION'S NAME

2b. INDIVIDUAL'S LAST NAME	FIRST NAME	MIDDLE NAME	SUFFIX

2c. MAILING ADDRESS	CITY	STATE	POSTAL CODE	COUNTRY

2d. TAX ID#: SSN OR EIN (OPTIONAL: **NOT REQUIRED**)	ADD'L INFO RE ORGANIZATION DEBTOR	2e. TYPE OF ORGANIZATION	2f. JURISDICTION OF ORGANIZATION	2g. ORGANIZATIONAL ID #, if any ☐ NONE

3. SECURED PARTY'S NAME (or NAME of TOTAL ASSIGNEE of ASSIGNOR S/P) – insert only one secured party name (3a or 3b)

OR   3a. ORGANIZATION'S NAME

3b. INDIVIDUAL'S LAST NAME	FIRST NAME	MIDDLE NAME	SUFFIX

3c. MAILING ADDRESS	CITY	STATE	POSTAL CODE	COUNTRY

4. This FINANCING STATEMENT covers the following collateral:

5.   ALTERNATIVE DESIGNATION (if applicable): ☐ LESSEE/LESSOR   ☐ CONSIGNEE/CONSIGNOR   ☐ BAILEE/BAILOR
                                                 ☐ SELLER/BUYER   ☐ AG LIEN   ☐ NON-UCC FILING

6. ☐ This FINANCING STATEMENT is to be filed (for record) in the REAL ESTATE RECORDS   7. Check to REQUEST SEARCH REPORT(S) on Debtor(s) (Optional)
                                                                                              ☐ All Debtors   ☐ Debtor 1   ☐ Debtor 2

8. OPTIONAL FILER REFERENCE DATA

No. 602. Rev. 7-01. UCC FINANCING STATEMENT (UCC1) - COLORADO

The terms of bond redemption provisions are similar to the redemption clauses for shares enumerated earlier in the "Preferred Stock Rights" section of this chapter, including the authority to create a sinking fund for redemption. An example of a fixed percentage redemption provision follows.

E X A M P L E

Redemption Provisions

The company may at its option redeem this debenture at any time hereafter upon payment of the principal amount hereof, plus a premium of five percent (5%) of such principal amount, plus any unpaid interest payable for any fiscal year ended prior to the date of redemption, plus interest at the rate of five percent (5%) per annum upon such principal amount for the period from the first day of the fiscal year in which redemption is so made to the date of redemption, provided that notice of such redemption, stating the time and place of redemption, shall be published at least once each week for four (4) successive

Exhibit 9–9.

(continued)

Instructions for UCC Financing Statement-Colorado (Form UCC1)

Please type or laser-print this form. Be sure it is completely legible. Read all Instructions, especially Instruction 1; correct Debtor name is crucial. Follow Instructions completely.

Fill in form very carefully; mistakes may have important legal consequences. If you have questions, consult your attorney. Filing office cannot give legal advice.

Do not insert anything in the open space in the upper portion of this form; it is reserved for filing office use.

When properly completed, send Filing Office Copy, with required fee, to filing office. If you want an acknowledgment, complete item B and, send Acknowledgment Copy; otherwise detach. If you want to make a search request, complete item 7 (after reading Instruction 7 below) and send Search Report Copy, otherwise detach. Always detach Debtor and Secured Party Copies.

If you need to use attachments, use 8-1/2 X 11 inch sheets and put at the top of each sheet the name of the first Debtor, formatted exactly as it appears in item 1 of this form; you are encouraged to use Addendum (Form UCC1Ad).

A. To assist filing offices that might wish to communicate with filer, filer may provide information in item A. This item is optional.

B. Complete item B if you want an acknowledgment sent to you. If filing in a filing office that returns an acknowledgment copy furnished by filer, present simultaneously with this form a carbon or other copy of this form for use as an acknowledgment copy.

1. **Debtor name:** Enter only <u>one Debtor name in item 1</u>, an organization's name (1a) **or** an individual's name (1b). Enter Debtor's <u>exact full legal name</u>. Don't abbreviate.

1a. <u>Organization Debtor</u>. "Organization" means an entity having a legal identity separate from its owner. A partnership is an organization; a sole proprietorship is not an organization, even if it does business under a trade name. If Debtor is a partnership, enter exact full legal name of partnership; you need not enter names of partners as additional Debtors. If Debtor is a registered organization (e.g., corporation, limited partnership, limited liability company), it is advisable to examine Debtor's current filed charter documents to determine Debtor's correct name, organization type, and jurisdiction of organization.

1b. <u>Individual Debtor</u>. "Individual" means a natural person; this includes a sole proprietorship, whether or not operating under a trade name. Don't use prefixes (Mr., Mrs., Ms.). Use suffix box only for titles of lineage (Jr., Sr., III) and not for other suffixes or titles (e.g., M.D.). Use married woman's personal name (Mary Smith, not Mrs. John Smith). Enter individual Debtor's family name (surname) in Last Name box, first given name in First Name box, and all additional given names in Middle Name box.
For both <u>organization and individual Debtors</u>: Don't use Debtor's trade name, DBA, AKA, FKA, Division name, etc. in place of or combined with Debtor's legal name; you may add such other names as additional Debtors if you wish (but this is neither required nor recommended).

1c. An address is always required for the Debtor named in 1a or 1b.

1d. Debtor's taxpayer identification number (tax ID # — social security number or employer identification number — this item is optional and is only required for EFS filings).

1e,f,g. "Additional information re organization Debtor" is always required. Type of organization and jurisdiction of organization as well as Debtor's exact legal name can be determined from Debtor's current filed charter document. Organizational ID #, if any, is assigned by the agency where the charter document was filed; this is different from tax ID #; this should be entered preceded by the 2-character U.S. Postal identification of state of organization if one of the United States (e.g., CA12345, for a California corporation whose organizational ID # is 12345); if agency does not assign organizational ID #, check box in item 1g indicating "none."

Note: If Debtor is a trust or a trustee acting with respect to property held in trust, enter Debtor's name in item 1 and attach Addendum (Form UCC1Ad) and check appropriate box in item 17. If Debtor is a decedent's estate, enter name of deceased individual in item 1b and attach Addendum (Form UCC1Ad) and check appropriate box in item 17. If Debtor is a transmitting utility or this Financing Statement is filed in connection with a Manufactured-Home Transaction or a Public-Finance Transaction as defined in applicable Commercial Code, attach Addendum (Form UCC1Ad) and check appropriate box in item 18.

2. If an additional Debtor is included, complete item 2, determined and formatted per Instruction 1. To include further additional Debtors, or one or more additional Secured Parties, attach either Addendum (Form UCC1Ad) or other additional page(s), using correct name format. Follow Instruction 1 for determining and formatting additional names.

3. Enter information for Secured Party or Total Assignee, determined and formatted per Instruction 1. If there is more than one Secured Party, see Instruction 2. If there has been a total assignment of the Secured Party's interest prior to filing this form, you may either (1) enter Assignor S/P's name and address in item 3 and file an Amendment (Form UCC3) [see item 5 of that form]; or (2) enter Total Assignee's name and address in item 3 and, if you wish, also attaching Addendum (Form UCC1Ad) giving Assignor S/P's name and address in item 12.

4. Use item 4 to indicate the collateral covered by this Financing Statement. If space in item 4 is insufficient, put the entire collateral description or continuation of the collateral description on either Addendum (Form UCC1Ad) or other attached additional page(s).

5. If filer desires (at filer's option) to use titles of lessee and lessor, or consignee and consignor, or seller and buyer (in the case of accounts or chattel paper), or bailee and bailor instead of Debtor and Secured Party, check the appropriate box in item 5. If this is an agricultural lien (as defined in applicable Commercial Code) filing or is otherwise not a UCC security interest filing (e.g., a tax lien, judgment lien, etc.), check the appropriate box in item 5, complete items 1-7 as applicable and attach any other items required under other law.

6. If this Financing Statement is filed as a fixture filing or if the collateral consists of timber to be cut or as-extracted collateral, complete items 1-5, check the box in item 6, and complete the required information (items 13, 14 and/or 15) on Addendum (Form UCC1Ad).

7. This item is optional. Check appropriate box in item 7 to request Search Report(s) on all or some of the Debtors named in this Financing Statement. The Report will list all Financing Statements on file against the designated Debtor on the date of the Report, including this Financing Statement. There is an additional fee for each Report. If you have checked a box in item 7, file Search Report Copy together with Filing Officer Copy (and Acknowledgment Copy).

8. This item is optional and is for filer's use only. For filer's convenience of reference, filer may enter in item 8 any identifying information (e.g., Secured Party's loan number, law firm file number, Debtor's name or other identification, state in which form is being filed, etc.) that filer may find useful.

No. 602. Rev. 7-01. UCC FINANCING STATEMENT (UCC1) - COLORADO

E X A M P L E

weeks prior to the redemption date in a daily newspaper of general circulation published in Cook County, Illinois. Thereupon this debenture shall become due and payable at the time and place designated for redemption in such notice, and payment of the redemption price shall be paid to the bearer of this debenture upon presentation and surrender thereof and of all unpaid interest coupons annexed hereto. Unless default shall be made in the redemption of this debenture upon such presentation, interest on this debenture shall cease from and after the date of redemption so designated. If the amount necessary to redeem this debenture shall have been deposited with the Abraham Lincoln Trust Company and if the notice of redemption shall have been duly published as aforesaid, this debenture shall be conclusively deemed to have been redeemed on the date specified for redemption, and all liability of the Company hereon shall cease on such date and all rights of the holder of this debenture, except the right to receive the redemption price out of the moneys so deposited, shall cease and terminate on such date.

The notice required by the redemption provision could be worded as follows:

EXAMPLE

Notice of Redemption

Notice is hereby given that the Ten-Year Convertible Income Debentures due November 30, 2010, of the Nobles Corporation have been called for redemption at 110% of the principal amount thereof and will be redeemed at the office of the Abraham Lincoln Trust Company, 1198 West Adams Street, Chicago, Illinois, on May 15, 2005. From and after May 15, 2005, the holders of said Debentures will have no conversion rights or any other rights, except to receive the redemption price.

Conversion

Debt securities may be convertible into equity securities, and this convertibility further enhances the value of a bond. The bond conversion feature will specify the number of shares of stock into which the bond is convertible, the procedure for conversion, a reservation of an appropriate number of common shares, and adjustments and other matters that concern the conversion privilege.

EXAMPLE

Conversion Provisions

As provided in the indenture with Abraham Lincoln Trust Company, this bond is convertible at the option of the holder thereof, at any time prior to maturity (or, if this bond is at any time called for redemption, then at any time before the date fixed for redemption), upon surrender of this bond for that purpose at the office of the Nobles Corporation, Chicago, Illinois. Conversion shall be made into common shares of the Nobles Corporation upon the basis of one common share for each $100 of principal sum of this bond, subject to the provision of the indenture as to interest on bonds converted and dividends on shares received therefor, and as to change in the conversion basis or substitution of other shares, securities, or property in the event of consolidation, merger, conveyance of assets, recapitalization, or the issuance of additional shares.

Priority and Subordination

Management of the corporation may desire to **subordinate** the existing debt securities in order to secure additional financing at a later time. If the bondholders agree to accept second or third place to other creditors for certain purposes, the subordination of their debt should assist in obtaining the maximum borrowing capacity for the corporation. The subordination feature would apply only if the bonds were not paid. If the corporation defaults on the obligation, the subordination clause will determine which creditors have prior rights to corporate assets to enforce their respective rights against the corporation.

When a bond issue is already outstanding and management is attempting to obtain additional financing, subordination may be an afterthought. Corporate officials may approach existing bondholders and solicit their agreement to subordinate their debt. On the other hand, subordination may be a condition precedent to the bond obligation. For example, an investor may be willing to invest in the corporation and purchase a bond, or lend the money, provided the corporation will subordinate any future borrowing to this debt security. Subordination provisions always include the amounts that will be subordinated (principal only, principal and interest, interest only, etc.), and they always describe the senior obligations to which the bond is subordinated.

EXAMPLE

Subordination Provisions

The rights of the holder hereof to the principal sum or any part thereof, and the interest due thereon, are and shall remain subject and subordinate to the claims as to principal and interest of the holders of 7¾% First Mortgage Bonds of the corporation, and upon dissolution or liquidation of the corporation no payment shall be due or payable upon this debenture until all claims of the holders of said bonds shall have been paid in full.

Voting Rights

A rare privilege accorded to bondholders in only a few jurisdictions is the right to vote on corporate matters, if so authorized in the articles of incorporation.[51] If holders of debt securities are permitted to vote in corporate elections, they are treated like a separate class of voting shareholders.

IMPORTANT CONSIDERATIONS REGARDING DEBT AND EQUITY

In planning the capitalization of the corporation, the drafter has tremendous flexibility. The necessary capital may be raised in any number of ways and represented by any of the myriad debt or equity securities, depending upon the expectations of the investors and the selected corporate capitalization structure. However, certain practical matters should be considered in choosing between debt and various classes of equity securities.

Anticipation of Later Financing

If the capital structure of the corporation is simple in the beginning, management will have greater flexibility in the raising of money in the future. If the initial corporate structure has several classes of stock and various debt securities, it will be considerably more difficult to create new classes of stock later, since new classes will probably affect the rights of the existing shareholders, whose approval must be acquired for any such amendments to the articles of incorporation. It is important, therefore, to consider the future capital needs of the business at the outset, and to plan the initial capital structure with those predictions in mind.

Advantages to Common Shareholders through the Use of Senior Securities

Preferred stock and bonds are commonly called **senior securities** because of their special preferential rights. Preferred shareholders are usually entitled to a dividend preference and liquidation preference, ensuring a return on and a return of their investment. Similarly, holders of debt securities have a right to interest and a right to repayment of their obligation upon maturity. Recall that the common shareholders have no special rights to distributions, and they are entitled to share in the assets in liquidation only after the holders of debt securities and the holders of preferred stock have been satisfied. However, the common shareholders may gain an advantage through the use of senior securities when the expected profit return on capital each year exceeds the payments that must be made, either in distributions or in interest, to the holders of senior securities. The converse is also true. If the expected profit return on capital each year is less than the payments that must be made to the holders of senior securities, the common shareholders are at a disadvantage.

These principles are illustrated in the following example. Suppose Trouble, Inc., needs $100,000 capital for the operation of its business and can reasonably predict profits after taxes of $20,000 or more each year. Assuming a hypothetical federal income tax rate of 30%, the profit before taxes must be $28,572 or more. The securities that will be issued in exchange for the $100,000 capital may be any combination of common stock, preferred stock, and debt. The profit return on capital after taxes is now estimated to be 20% or more each year. If 1,000 shares of common stock are issued to raise the $100,000 capital, the earnings per share are computed as follows, assuming the estimated profit is realized.

Profit before taxes	$28,572
Federal income tax (30%)	8,572
Profit after taxes	$20,000
Earnings per share of common stock (1,000 shares)	$20.00

Now assume that investors are found who are willing to take preferred stock with $100 par value and a preferred dividend rate of 16%. The $100,000 capital may be raised by issuing 500 shares of 16% preferred stock for $50,000, and 500 shares of common stock for $50,000. The common stock earnings per share are computed as follows:

Profit before taxes	$28,572
Federal income tax (30%)	8,572
Profit after taxes	$20,000
Preferred dividends (16% of $50,000)	8,000
Profit after preferred dividends	$12,000
Earnings per share of common stock (500 shares)	$ 24.00

Next assume that instead of preferred stock, debt securities with the same interest rate (16%) are issued for the $50,000 capital. The interest paid on debt securities is deductible as an expense before taxes, which further improves the common shareholders' earnings. The statement looks like this:

Profit before interest	$28,572
Interest (16% of $50,000)	8,000
Profit before taxes	$20,572
Federal income tax (30%)	6,172
Profit after taxes	$14,400
Earnings per share of common stock (500 shares)	$28.80

A combination of all three securities will be even better for the common shareholders. Suppose $40,000 capital is raised by the sale of 400 common shares, $30,000 by the sale of 300 shares of 16% preferred stock, and $30,000 by 16% debt securities. The result is as follows:

Profit before interest	$28,572
Interest (16% of $30,000)	4,800
Profit before taxes	23,772
Federal income tax (30%)	7,132
Profit after taxes	$16,640
Dividends for preferred stock (16% of $30,000)	$4,800
Profit after preferred dividends	$11,840
Earnings per share of common stock (400 shares)	$29.60

The common stock takes the full risk that profits will reach or exceed expectations. The illustrated advantage depends upon the profits after taxes being a greater percentage of capital than the percentage return required to be paid to the senior securities. Watch what happens to the last example if profits dip to $15,000 (before deducting interest) rather than the predicted $28,572 or more. The statement looks like this:

Profit before interest	$15,000
Interest (16% of $30,000)	4,800
Profit before taxes	$11,200
Federal income tax (30%)	3,360
Profit after taxes	$7,840
Dividends on preferred stock (16% of $30,000)	4,800
	$3,040
Earnings per share of common stock (400 shares)	$7.60

Contrast this earnings figure with the one in the following statement based on the original capital structure by which the whole amount of $100,000 is raised by the sale of $1,000 shares of common stock.

Profit before taxes	$15,000
Federal income tax (30%)	4,500
Profit after taxes	$11,500
Earnings per share of common stock (1000 shares)	$11.50

In the last situation, the common shareholders would benefit more from complete common stock capitalization than from combinations of common stock, preferred stock, and debt.

Taxes

The concept of double taxation and its erosion of corporate profits is discussed in "Taxation of a Corporation" in Chapter 6. Debt securities avoid double taxation, since the interest paid on the debt is deductible as an expense to the corporation, rather than being taxed as corporate profit. In this respect, debt securities enjoy a tax advantage over equity securities, since distributions to shareholders in the form of dividends are taxed first as corporate profit and again as individual income.

The solution, you might propose, would be to issue as many debt securities and as few equity securities as possible. The tax authorities of the federal government have thought of this. A disproportionate debt-to-equity ratio is called **thin incorporation.** When thin incorporation exists, the tax authorities may characterize interest payments on debt securities as dividends on equity securities for tax purposes, disallowing the interest expense deduction and requiring tax to be paid on the resulting increased profits. This restructuring has been upheld in severe cases, such as where the majority shareholder loaned considerable sums to a corporation in return for separate debt securities, and where all shareholders loaned disproportionately large amounts to a corporation with very little investment represented in common stock. A good debt-to-equity ratio should not exceed 4:1 to avoid problems of thin incorporation.

KEY TERMS

securities	certificates	participation
debenture	negotiable	separate voting group
mortgage bonds	series of shares	redemption of shares
premium	blank stock	cancellation of redeemable shares
discount	sinking fund	conversion of stock
indenture	conversion of stock	transfer agent
Securities Act of 1933	fractional share	registrar
Securities Exchange Act of 1934	true value rule	facsimile signature
authorized shares	absence of fraud rule	unsecured debt
issued shares	nonassessable	promissory note
outstanding shares	assessable	secured debt
watered, or discount, shares	circular holdings	trust indenture
diluted shares	cumulative distribution preference	Trust Indenture Act of 1939
franchise fee	noncumulative distribution	subordination of bonds
earned surplus	preference	senior securities
capital surplus	"cumulative to the extent earned"	thin incorporation
stated capital	distribution preference	

WEB RESOURCES

Access to state laws regarding issuance of stock and bonds, creation and perfection of security interests, and the other local issues related to stockholder and bondholder rights may be obtained through the Legal Information Institute maintained at Cornell Law School:

<http://www.law.cornell.edu>

The National Association of Secretaries of State maintains links directly to the offices of the Secretaries of State in all states. Forms for each state's filing requirements with respect to the corporate financial structure are available from that state's Web site in most cases:

<http://www.nass.org>

The specific sections of a state's corporate law may be located by a search site that directly links to the corporate laws of the state. The search may be accessed at

<http://www.megalaw.com>

Access to the filings with the Securities and Exchange Commission on line is available through the EDGAR system on the following sites:

<http://www.freeedgar.com>
<http://www.edgar-online.com>
<http://www.pwcglobal.com>

The text of the federal and state securities laws may be reviewed at the following sites:

<http://www.seclaw.com>
<http://www.law.cornell.edu>

Information about the operation of stock exchanges for a public corporation's shares can be accessed through the exchange Web sites:

<http://www.nyse.com>
<http://www.amex.com>
<http://www.nasdaq.com>

Forms for promissory notes and debentures are available from

<http://www.sbaonline.sba.gov>
<http://www.ilrg.com>

Forms for stock certificates are available from

<http://www.corpkit.com>
<http://www.uslegalforms.com>
<http://www.goesstockcertificates.com>
<http://www.stocktransfer.com>

An explanation of generally accepted accounting principles (GAAP) in the United States and the financial accounting standards bulletins (FASBs) may be accessed at

<http://www.cpaclass.com/gaap/>

Information on stock transfer agents, including comparison reports and surveys, is at

<http://www.stockholderconsulting.com>
<http://www.stocktransfer.com>

Application for a CUSIP number (Standard and Poors' identification number for issuers of publicly held securities) can be submitted at

<http://www.stocktransfer.com>

CASES

STROH v. BLACKHAWK HOLDING CORPORATION

48 Ill. 2d 471, 272 N.E.2d 1 (1971)
DAVIS, JUSTICE

[Blackhawk Holding Corporation was organized under Illinois law in November 1963. The articles of incorporation authorized the issuance of 3,000,000 shares of Class A stock with a par value of $1, and 500,000 shares of Class B stock without par value. The articles of incorporation provided that Class B stock was not entitled to any dividends.]

* * *

The only issue before this court is the validity of the 500,000 shares of Class B stock, which by the articles of incorporation of Blackhawk were limited in their rights by the provision "none of the shares of Class B stock shall be entitled to dividends either upon voluntary or involuntary liquidation or otherwise." It is the plaintiffs' contention that because of the foregoing limitation—depriving the Class B shares of the "economic" incidents of shares of stock, or of the proportionate interest in the corporate assets—the Class B shares do not in fact constitute shares of stock.

* * *

A corporation is a creature of statute. (Craig v. Sullivan Machinery Co., 344 Ill. 334, 336, 176 N.E. 353.) It is a legal entity which owes its existence to the fiat of law. Its being and powers are from the sovereign State as its will is expressed through legislative enactment. (Chicago Title and Trust Co. v. Central Republic Trust Co., 299 Ill. App. 483, 492, 20 N.E.2d 351.) The articles of incorporation of an Illinois corporation constitute a contract, threefold in nature. It is a contract between the corporation and the State and it creates powers and limitations, rights and duties as between the corporation and its shareholders, as well as between the shareholders themselves. The powers and limitations of a corporation are found in its articles of incorporation, the provisions of its stock certificates, its by-laws, and in the constitutional and statutory provisions in force when the articles of incorporation were adopted. [Citations omitted] The articles of incorporation of Blackhawk purport to create a Class B stock that possesses no rights in the assets or in the earnings of the corporation. Whether this can be done, and whether such shares have the requisite attributes of a valid share of stock, must be determined in accordance with the constitution of the State, the provision of the Business Corporation Act, and the common law of the State.

Under the Illinois constitution of 1870, a stockholder in an Illinois corporation is guaranteed the right to vote based upon the number of shares owned by him. (Ill. Const. art. XI, sec. 3, S.H.A.) Section 14 of the Business Corporation Act (Ill.Rev.Stat.1969, ch. 32, par. 157.14) provides that shares of stock in an Illinois corporation may be divided into classes,

> "with such designations, preferences, qualifications, limitations, restrictions and such special or relative rights as shall be stated in the articles of incorporation. The articles of incorporation shall not limit or deny the voting power of the shares of any class.
>
> Without limiting the authority herein contained, a corporation when so provided in its articles of incorporation, may issue shares of preferred or special classes:
>
> * * * * * *
>
> (c) Having preference over any other class or classes of shares as to the payment of dividends.
>
> (d) Having preference as to the assets of the corporation over any other class or classes of shares upon the voluntary or involuntary liquidation of the corporation."

Section 41 of the Act, relating to the power of the board of directors to declare dividends, provides that no dividends may be declared or paid contrary to any restrictions in the articles of incorporation. Ill. Rev.Stat.1969, ch. 32, par. 157.41(h).

Section 2.6 of the Act, in defining "shares" states, " 'Shares' means the units into which the proprietary interests in a corporation are divided." (Ill.Rev.Stat.1969, ch. 32, par. 157.2-6.)

* * *

To the plaintiffs, "proprietary," as used in the definition of shares, means a property right, and shares must then represent some economic interest, or interest in the property or assets of the corporation. However, the word "proprietary" does not necessarily denote economic or asset rights, although it has been defined as synonymous with ownership or to denote legal title (Evans v. United States, D.C., 251 F. Supp. 296, 300; Asch v. First National Bank in Dallas, Tex.Civ.App., 304 S.W.2d 179, 183; The American Heritage Dictionary of the English Language (1969)), and "proprietary rights" have been defined as those conferred by virtue of ownership of a thing (Colten v. Jacques Marchais, Inc., Mun.Ct., 61 N.Y.S.2d 269, 271; Black's Law Dictionary, 4th Ed.Rev., 1968). In *Colten,* the court

defined "proprietary" as meaning ownership, exclusive title or dominion, and implying possession and physical control of a thing.

In Millar v. Mountcastle, 161 Ohio St. 409, 119 N.E.2d 626, 632, the Supreme Court of the State of Ohio discussed the meaning of ownership as represented by holding shares of stock. The court said that by reason of ownership of a share of corporate stock, one becomes the owner of intangible property comprised of various relationships which are determined by the terms of the stock certificate, the articles of incorporation, and the internal regulations of the corporation, and the statutes and common law of the State of incorporation. The court stated that the ownership comprising the relationship might include "one or more" of several specified rights, including the right to vote.

The meaning of ownership may vary depending upon the subject matter of the ownership, the place of the ownership, and any particular restraints placed thereon by contract or law. Both the plaintiffs and the defendants stress that section 2.6 of the Business Corporation Act, in defining shares in terms of a proprietary interest, did not change the prior statutory definition of shares as the "right to participate in the control of the corporation, in its surplus or profits, or in the distribution of its assets." Both parties find comfort in the grammatical construction of the prior definition.

We agree with the defendants' construction. We interpret this statutory definition to mean that the proprietary rights conferred by the ownership of stock may consist of one or more of the rights to participate "in the control of the corporation, in its surplus or profits, *or* in the distribution of its assets." The use of the disjunctive conjunction "*or,*" indicates that one or more of the three named rights may inure to a stockholder by virtue of his stock ownership. A series of phrases in the disjunctive does not require that each phrase be separated by the word "or," as the plaintiffs suggest; more commonly and correctly each phrase except the last is preceded only by a comma, and the last is preceded by the word "or." The absence of the disjunctive "or" preceding the phrase "in its surplus or profit," is too thin a reed to support the construction urged by the plaintiffs. The phrases in the series represent alternatives (People v. Vraniak, 5 Ill.2d 384, 389, 125 N.E.2d 513; Central Standard Life Insurance Co. v. Davis, 10 Ill.App.2d 245, 254, 255, 134 N.E.2d 653), and we so construe them. This conclusion, however, is not dispositive of this litigation.

We must here decide the extent to which economic attributes of shares of stock may be eliminated. This must be determined from the intent of the legislature which, in no small part, can be gathered from the language and words it chose to express that intent. The statutory definition of "shares" is of particular importance in that it governs the meaning of the word as used throughout the Business Corporation Act and controls in its construction. The legislature has the power to make any reasonable definition of the terms in a statute and such definition for the purposes of the Act, will be sustained. Modern Dairy Co. v. Department of Revenue, 413 Ill.55, 66, 108 N.E.2d 8.

Section 14 of the Act clearly expresses the intent of the legislature to be that parties to a corporate entity may create whatever restrictions and limitations they may want with regard to their corporate stock by expressing such restrictions and limitations in the articles of incorporation. These rights and powers granted by the legislature to the corporation to make the terms of its contract with its shareholders are limited only by the proviso that the articles may not limit or deny the voting power of any share. This section of the Act expressly confers the right to prefer a class of shares over another with regard to dividends and assets. Section 2.6 defines shares as "The units into which the proprietary interests in a corporation are divided."

In seeking the intent of the legislature, a statute should be construed as a whole and its separate parts considered together. Our present constitution requires only that a shareholder not be deprived of his voice in management. It does not require that a shareholder, in addition to the management aspect of ownership, must also have an economic interest.

Thus, section 14, like the constitution, limits the power of a corporation only as to the voting aspect of ownership. It confers upon the corporation the "power to create and is-sue the number of shares stated in its article of incorporation;" it expressly permits the shares to be subject to "such designations, preferences, qualifications, limitations, restrictions, and such special or relative rights as shall be stated in the articles of incorporation;" it also suggests that "Without limiting the authority herein contained, a corporation, when so provided in its articles of incorporation, may issue shares of preferred or special classes," which classes are delineated therein.

Section 41 of the Act recognizes that while the power to declare dividends with respect to shares is in the board of directors, this power is limited, among other things, by any restrictions in the articles of incorporation.

When the relevant sections of the Act are read together with the constitution, it seems apparent that it was the intent of the legislature that the proprietary interests represented by the shares of stock consist of management or control rights, rights to earnings, and rights to assets. There are other rights which are incidental to these. Under our laws, the rights to earnings and the rights to assets—the "economic" rights—may be removed and eliminated from the other attributes of a share of stock. Only the management incident of ownership may not be removed.

* * *

[The Class B stock was held to be valid under the statute.]

STAAR SURGICAL COMPANY v. WAGGONER

588 A.2d 1130 (Del. 1991)
MOORE, JUSTICE

In this latest dispute between the parties we determine the validity of two million shares of STAAR Surgical Company ("STAAR") common stock issued to STAAR's former President and CEO, Thomas R. Waggoner and his wife, Patricia Waggoner "Waggoner" or "Waggoners").

* * *

STAAR was facing severe financial difficulties in 1987. At that time, STAAR had an open line of credit with the Bank of New York ("BONY") secured by certain of STAAR's account receivables and inventory. In September, 1987, STAAR's accountants caused the company to write-down its accounts receivables. The write-down left the BONY line of credit undercollateralized by almost two million dollars.

At approximately the same time, certain STAAR shareholders were concerned about the financial performance of the company. The stockholders conferred in November 1987, and later that month discussed their concerns directly with Waggoner. On December 13, 1987, the shareholders met with the STAAR directors in New York City. STAAR's outside counsel, Elliot Lutzker, informed the shareholders at the meeting that among other things, STAAR was overdrawn on its BONY line of credit and that BONY had "demanded" Waggoner's personal guarantee to secure all of STAAR's debt to the bank. The shareholders were outraged and demanded Waggoner's immediate resignation. The STAAR board and the shareholders reached a compromise providing for the election of two new outside directors.

The STAAR board then formally convened after the meeting on December 13, 1987. Waggoner told the board that BONY had demanded his personal guarantee of STAAR's debts. Waggoner advised the board that he would guarantee the debts only if he was given voting control of the company while the guarantees were outstanding. Waggoner and the board generally concluded at the end of the meeting that STAAR would issue some type of convertible securities to Waggoner in exchange for his guarantee. The two sides did not formally adopt or memorialize their understanding.

BONY then sent a formal letter to Waggoner three days later, on December 16, 1987, requesting his "immediate attention" to the matter of a personal guarantee. The letter required Waggoner to respond no later than noon on December 18, 1987. Lutzker informed both Waggoner and Lamar T. Laster, STAAR's Chief Financial Officer, that BONY could shut STAAR down if it did not receive Waggoner's personal guarantee.

Waggoner then called a special board meeting for December 17, 1987 to consider BONY's "demand." The meeting was hastily summoned and poorly organized. We previously described the meeting in *Waggoner I,* quoting the trial court's finding that:

> The December 17 meeting was conducted by telephone with little or no advance notice, and lasted for approximately 25 minutes. Dr. Utrata, a Board member of only four days' standing, participated between performing surgical operations. Mr. Ford, a trial attorney, participated while speaking from his car phone and while traveling between court appearances. According to the minutes, Mr. Silverman was absent for a portion of the discussion, and Mr. Sodero, a fourth director, intended to (and did) resign at the conclusion of that meeting, to be replaced by Dr. Brown.

[citation omitted]

* * *

The minutes of the December 17, 1987 STAAR Board meeting also state that the board formally adopted the following resolution:

> RESOLVED, that pursuant to the authority granted to the Board of Directors in the Certificate of Incorporation, as amended, the Board hereby authorizes the creation of a series of Convertible Preferred Stock, all of which shall be held by Tom Waggoner, or his designees, which shall be converted into two million shares of Common Stock after January 16, 1988, unless all of the personal guarantees and stock pledges of Common Stock by Tom Waggoner now or hereafter in effect are removed, or a binding agreement to such effect is in place by January 16, 1988. In the event that all of the Waggoner guarantees are removed by January 16, 1988, all of the shares of Convertible Preferred Stock shall be redeemed by the Company at $.01 per share. In the event that the two million shares of Common Stock are issued to Tom Waggoner, all of the remaining Convertible Preferred and stock pledges are removed. Holders of the Convertible Preferred Stock shall be entitled to elect a majority of the Company's directors and to otherwise vote a majority of the Shares of Common Stock outstanding at any time. The shares of Convertible Preferred Stock, in accordance with the provision of the SEC's safe-harbor rule, shall have a liquidation preference however, [sic] not entitle the holder to any dividends.
> [Citation omitted]

In fact, the trial court found, and we affirmed in *Waggoner I,* that the board *never formally adopted* the resolution and only Waggoner signed the minutes.

After the board meeting, Lutzker prepared a certificate of designation pursuant to 8 *Del.C.* § 151(g), at some time between December 18, 1987 and December 24, 1987. The certificate allegedly established the rights, powers and preferences of the convertible preferred shares pursuant to the December 17, 1987 "resolution." The certificate also recited that it included the December 17, 1987 board resolution. The certificate was six pages long and contained detailed, comprehensive language regarding the voting, conversion and redemption rights of the preferred shares not mentioned in the December 17 resolution. [Citation omitted] Furthermore, like the December 17 "resolution," the STAAR board never *formally adopted the certificate of designation.* STAAR actually issued the preferred shares to Waggoner on December 18, 1987.

Some STAAR board members were dissatisfied with the terms of the preferred stock transaction and called a board meeting for January 11, 1988. At that meeting, the board attempted to delay the conversion feature of the preferred stock. On January 19, 1988, however, Waggoner exercised his conversion option and received two million shares of STAAR common stock. Allegedly, Waggoner's action was authorized pursuant to the resolution and the certificate of designation because STAAR failed to replace Waggoner's guarantee within the prescribed time limits.

In August, 1989, the Waggoners attempted to exercise the voting provisions of the remainder of their preferred shares by removing STAAR's board. The directors, aided by two shareholders, contested the election under 8 *Del.C.* § 225. On October 24, 1989, the Court of Chancery ruled that the super voting provisions of the preferred shares were invalid. *See Laster,* slip op. at 39-40. We affirmed that decision. *See Waggoner I,* 581 A.2d at 1137-38.

The Waggoners then filed an action pursuant to 8 *Del.C.* § 211 to compel STAAR to convene a shareholders meeting. STAAR answered the Waggoners' § 211 claim denying that the Waggoners even owned the two million STAAR shares. The Waggoners then moved pursuant to 8 *Del.C.* § 227(a) for an order determining their right to vote the disputed shares. On March 15, 1990, the Court of Chancery ruled that even though the Waggoners' preferred shares were invalid, they were entitled as a matter of equity to own and vote the disputed two million common shares which were derived from the invalid preferred stock. *See Waggoner II,* slip op. at 15-16.

* * *

We start with basic and clearly applicable provisions of the Delaware General Corporation Law. A corporation can issue more than one class of stock, including preferred shares with a conversion feature. *See, e.g.,* 8 *Del.C.* §§ 151(a), (e) & (g). The powers, preferences, rights and other characteristics of such shares must be fixed in either the certificate of incorporation or through a board resolution adopted pursuant to an explicit grant of authority in the certificate of incorporation. *See* 8 *Del.C.* §§ 102(a)(4), 151(a). There is no dispute that the STAAR certificate of incorporation authorized the board to issue, by resolution, "blank check" preferred stock with such terms and conditions, including:

> [T]he rights, if any, of holders of the shares of the particular series to convert the same into shares of any other series or class or other securities of the corporation. . . .

The Delaware General Corporation Law mandates adoption of a board resolution, when such new shares of so-called "blank check" preferred, are issued. Section 151(a) of the General Corporation Law requires, in part, that all new stock voting powers, designations, preferences and other special rights must either be in the certificate of incorporation or:

> [I]n the resolution or resolutions providing for the issue of such stock *adopted* by the board of directors pursuant to authority expressly vested in it by the provisions of its certificate of incorporation. 8 *Del.C.* § 151(a) (emphasis added).

Section 151(e), which specifically authorizes a company to issue convertible securities, requires, in part, that the corporation issue the new shares:

> [A]t such price or prices or at such rate or rates of exchange and with such adjustments as shall be stated in the certificate of incorporation or in the resolution or resolutions providing for the issue of such stock *adopted by the board of directors as hereinabove provided.* 8 *Del.C.* § 151(e) (emphasis added).

Finally, Section 151(g) requires a corporation to file a certificate of designation when the certificate of incorporation permits the board to issue new securities through a resolution "adopted by the board." The statute provides:

> When any corporation desires to issue any shares of stock of any class or of any series of any class of which the powers, designations, preferences and relative, participating, optional or other rights, if any, or the qualifications, limitations or restrictions thereof, if any, shall not have been set forth in the certificate of incorporation or in any amendment thereto but shall be provided for in *a resolution or resolutions adopted by the board* of directors pursuant to authority expressly vested in it by the certificate of incorporation or any amendment thereto, a *certificate of designations setting forth a copy of such resolution* or resolutions and the number of shares of stock of such class or series as to which the resolution or resolutions apply shall be executed, acknowledged, filed, recorded and shall become effective, in accordance with § 103 of this title. . . . 8 *Del.C.* § 151(g) (emphasis added).

Waggoner concedes that the STAAR board never formally adopted either the board resolution on December 17, 1987, or the certificate of designation. Finally, the trial court found in *Laster* that the certificate of designation did not "set forth" a copy of the December 17, 1987 resolution. Slip op. at 11-12. Indeed, the court ruled that the certificate of designation contained materially different language from that in the resolution. *Id.* at 11 n. 5.

The parties' arguments seem to pass like two ships in the night. STAAR contends that the board's failure to adopt the resolution or the certificate of designation rendered the preferred shares void, thus invalidating the common stock. STAAR relies on *Triplex Shoe Co. v. Rice Hutchins, Inc.,* Del.Supr., 152 A. 342 (1930), for the proposition that illegally issued stock is void and, regardless of the equities, cannot be transferred or voted. The Waggoners, in contrast, focus on the common stock and not the preferred shares. They assert that even if the board failed to technically conform to the clear corporate law, the STAAR directors all agreed at the December 1, 1987 board meeting to issue Waggoner two million shares of common stock as compensation for his guarantee of the BONY loans. Therefore, Waggoner claims, it was clear to all of the parties that he would eventually receive the two million shares if STAAR could not find alternate financing for the loan.

The Waggoners also contest STAAR's interpretation of *Triplex,* claiming that it is distinguishable on its facts. The Waggoners argue that the certificate of incorporation in *Triplex,* and the then current corporate law, did not authorize the board to issue new shares of a certain type of stock. Therefore, they contend, the stock in *Triplex* was void and subsequent board action could not have validated those shares. In contrast, the Waggoners argue that the STAAR certificate of incorporation at all times authorized the board to issue new shares of common stock and thus *Triplex* is not dispositive.

We must reject the Waggoners' attempt to separate the common shares from the preferred stock. We also reject their very limited interpretation of *Triplex.* Stock issued without authority of law is void and a nullity.

It is undisputed that Waggoner could not receive his common stock without exercising the conversion option of at least one preferred share. The December 17, 1987 resolution and the certificate of designation purportedly authorized the issuance of the preferred shares. Without validly issued preferred stock, there was simply no other legal mechanism by which the common shares could be issued. Simply stated, if the preferred shares were void, as the Court of Chancery assumed, then the common stock could not be created out of whole cloth.

Based on the trial court's findings, it is clear that the preferred convertible shares originally issued to the Waggoners were invalid and void under Delaware law. There was no compliance with the terms of 8 *Del.C.* § 151. The directors never formally adopted either the December 17, 1987 resolution or the certificate of designation.

The Waggoners' attempt to trivialize the unassailable facts of this case as mere "technicalities" is wholly unpersuasive. The issuance of corporate stock is an act of fundamental legal significance having a direct bearing upon questions of corporate governance, control and the capital structure of the enterprise. The law properly requires certainty in such matters.

There are many interacting principles of established law at play here. First, it is a basic concept that the General Corporation Law is a part of the certificate of incorporation of every Delaware company. *See* 8 *Del.C.* § 394. Second, a corporate charter is both a contract between the State and the corporation, and the corporation and its shareholders. *See Lawson v. Household Finance Corp.* Del.Supr., 152 A. 723, 727 (1930). The charter is also a contract among the shareholders themselves. *See Morris v. American Public Utilities Co.,* Del.Ch., 122 A. 696, 700 (1923). When a corporation files a certificate of designation under § 151(g), it amends the certificate of incorporation and fundamentally alters the contract between all of the parties. *See* 8 *Del.C.* §§ 104, 151(g). A party affecting these interrelated, fundamental interests, through an amendments to the corporate charter, must scrupulously observe the law.

Finally, it is a basic concept of our corporation law that in the absence of a clear agreement to the contrary, preferred stock rights are in derogation of the common law and must be strictly construed. [Citations omitted]

This principle of "strict construction" applies with equal force to the creation of preferred stock and its attendant rights, powers, designations and preferences. Accordingly, a board's failure to adopt a resolution and certificate of designation, amending the fundamental document which imbues a corporation with its life and powers, and defines the contract with its shareholders, cannot be deemed a mere "technical" error.

Thus, we must reject the trial court's authorization of the two million shares of common stock on equitable grounds. Stock issued in violation of 8 *Del.C.* § 151 is void and not merely voidable.

* * *

The judgment of the Court of Chancer is
REVERSED.

PROBLEMS

1. The 3N Corporation has developed its financial structure during the past decade by issuing and selling the following securities: (1) 500 bonds, with a principal amount of $1,000 each, interest at 6% plus .0025% of profit per year, without security, each exchangeable for 200 shares of common stock at the holder's option. The money received from the bonds has been used exclusively to purchase equipment for the corporation; (2) 500 shares of preferred stock, $1 par value, with a 5% dividend preference and no voting rights; and (3) 1,000 shares of common stock, $5 par value. Answer the following questions concerning this financial structure:

   a. Are the bonds best described as
      (1) 6% convertible equipment bonds;
      (2) income bearer equipment bonds;
      (3) registered participating redeemable debentures; or
      (4) participating convertible debentures?
   b. What is the minimum amount required for the corporation's stated capital account?
   c. What additional rights would be given to the preferred stock under the corporation statute in your state?
   d. Would the bonds have any preemptive rights to buy additional shares of common stock under the corporation statute in your state?

   e. Would the preferred stock have any preemptive rights to buy additional shares of preferred stock under the corporation statute in your state?
   f. If the corporation issues 5,000 additional shares of common stock, what adjustments will be required to the terms of the bonds or the preferred stock, if any, to keep the bondholders and preferred stockholders in the same positions they now occupy?

2. Review the corporation statute in your state and answer the following questions:
   a. What are the rights of each holder of the common stock?
   b. What variations are permitted for classes of stock?
   c. Do redeemed shares have to be canceled?
   d. May bondholders vote?

3. What is the difference between repurchased and redeemed shares? What funds may be used for each purpose under the corporation statute in your state?

4. If you had your choice among a debenture, a share of preferred stock, or a share of common stock from the largest corporation in your city, which would you select and why?

PRACTICE ASSIGNMENTS

1. Write to a publicly traded corporation of your choice. Request a statement of preferences and rights associated with that company's various shares of stock and bonds. Write a report concerning the policy considerations used in developing the equity and debt structure, and analyze the advantages and disadvantages of "senior securities."

2. Draft a capital stock structure that will meet the following client needs:

   a. Three director-shareholders want to maintain complete control over the corporation. They will contribute capital in the amount of $50,000 each.

   b. Two outside investors are willing to contribute $50,000 each and are primarily interested in capital appreciation and return on investment (10% minimum is required). They are willing to leave control to the director-shareholders, but insist upon some right of contingent control if business is not prospering (for example, if it is unable to pay any dividends).

   c. An outside investor is willing to contribute $75,000 to the business and requires a minimum of 15% return on invested capital. She is not interested in capital appreciation and does not want to be bothered with any control.

   d. The director-shareholders anticipate finding additional investors and want to be able to tailor the securities to be issued to each investor as necessary to attract the investor without having to consult anyone. They also want to be able to retire any corporate obligations that might make subsequent investment by others unattractive.

3. Review section 6.21 of the Model Act. Assume a corporation has 25,000 shares of common stock with a par value of $5 per share. Is there any legal way that the corporation could sell these shares at $4 per share? Prepare a memorandum.

4. The Nobles Company has raised capital in the following amounts with the following securities: (1) $50,000 by issuing 5,000 shares of common stock at $10 per share; and (2) $50,000 by issuing 1,000 shares of 6% cumulative preferred stock at $50 per share. Prepare a memorandum for management that answers the following questions:

   a. Why is it more beneficial to the common shareholders to have the senior (preferred) securities if the business is successful?

   b. What is the approximate profit-point at which it would cease to be beneficial to the common shareholders to have senior securities?

   c. Why would the common shareholders be in a better position if 6% debt securities had been issued instead of the preferred stock?

ENDNOTES

1. Securities Act of 1933, 15 U.S.C.A. §§ 77a–77aa.

2. Securities Exchange Act of 1934, 15 U.S.C.A. §§ 78a–78m.

3. See "Public Corporations" in Chapter 7 and see J. Seligman and L. Loss, Fundamentals of Securities Regulation, 4th Edition (2002).

4. See Model Business Corporation Act (hereafter M.B.C.A.) § 6.01; "The Articles of Incorporation" in Chapter 8.

5. See "Filing and Other Formalities" in Chapter 8.

6. See Del. Code Ann. tit. 8, § 160.

7. See "Ownership and Management of a Corporation" in Chapter 6.

8. See, e.g., Ill. Compiled Statutes § 5/7.40.

9. E.g., New York, N.Y. Bus. Corp. Law § 510 (McKinney).

10. See M.B.C.A. § 2.02 (b); also see "The Articles of Incorporation" in Chapter 8.

11. Neb. Rev. Stat. § 21-2018.

12. See M.B.C.A. § 6.21 (b).

13. E.g., Arkansas, Ark. Bus. Corp. Act § 4-27-601.

14. "The Articles of Incorporation" in Chapter 8.

15. E.g., Idaho, Idaho Code § 30-1-6.

16. See, e.g., New York, N.Y. Bus. Corp. Law § 506 (McKinney).

17. Dividends and other distributions are discussed in detail in Chapter 11.

18. M.B.C.A. § 6.25 (d).

19. M.B.C.A. § 6.25 (e).

20. M.B.C.A. § 6.01.

21. M.B.C.A. § 6.01 (b).

22. See M.B.C.A. § 6.02.

23. See "Amendment of the Articles of Incorporation" in Chapter 15.

24. M.B.C.A. § 6.02.

25. M.B.C.A. § 6.02 (c).

26. M.B.C.A. § 6.04 (a).

27. M.B.C.A. § 6.04 (c).

28. See "Par Value or No Par Value" earlier in this chapter.

29. M.B.C.A. § 6.21.

30. E.g., Missouri, Mo. Ann. Stat. § 351.160 (Vernon).

31. E.g., Colorado Const. Article XV, § 9.

32. However, the corporation could ratify the obligation to pay for services performed by promoters, and thereby cause such services to be valid consideration for stock. See "Agency Authority—Ratified Authority" in Chapter 1.

33. M.B.C.A. § 6.21.

34. M.B.C.A. § 6.21 (e).

35. See Chapter 11.

36. M.B.C.A. § 7.21(b).

37. See "The Articles of Incorporation" in Chapter 8.

38. See "Ownership and Management of a Corporation" in Chapter 6; "The Articles of Incorporation" in Chapter 8.

39. M.B.C.A. § 6.01 (b).

40. M.B.C.A. § 7.21 (a).

41. M.B.C.A. § 10.04 provides that class voting is required for any amendment that would:

    1. effect an exchange or reclassification of all or part of the shares of the class into shares of another class;

    2. effect an exchange, or create a right of exchange, of all or any part of the shares of another class into the shares of the class;

    3. change the preferences, limitations, or relative rights of the shares of the class;

    4. change the shares of the class into a different number of shares of the same class;

    5. create a new class of shares having rights and preferences prior or superior to the shares of the class;

    6. increase the rights and preferences or the number of authorized shares of any class having rights and preferences prior or superior to the shares of the class;

    7. limit or deny any existing preemptive rights of the shares of the class; or

    8. cancel or otherwise affect distributions or dividends on the shares of the class that have accumulated but have not been declared.

42. M.B.C.A. § 6.31.

43. See "Fractions of Shares and Scrip" earlier in this chapter.

44. See M.B.C.A. § 16.01.

45. See M.B.C.A. § 6.25 (d).

46. Uniform Commercial Code (hereafter U.C.C.) § 9-201-9-206.

47. U.C.C. § 9-502.

48. U.C.C. § 9-501.

49. Securities Act of 1933, 15 U.S.C.A. §§ 77a–77aa; Trust Indenture Act of 1939, 15 U.S.C.A. §§77aaa–77bbbb.

50. A skeletal trust indenture, including articles, section, and subsection headings, is Exhibit I–11 in Appendix I.

51. E.g., Delaware, Del. Code Ann. tit. 8, § 221.

MEETINGS

TYPES AND PURPOSES OF MEETINGS

Corporate activity is conducted through meetings of the internal corporate groups: the incorporators, the directors, and the shareholders. Under the common law of corporations, the directors of a corporation do not act individually, but may act only as a board collectively convened. Shareholder and incorporator activities are somewhat more individual, but the democratic rule that the majority will control the minority is applied to both groups. Traditionally, corporate action may not be taken unless it has been approved by one of these groups duly convened at a meeting. In theory, then, any action taken by the corporation requires an approving resolution by the appropriate intracorporate group. In reality, however, it would be much too cumbersome to hold a meeting of one of these groups for daily business decisions. Instead, the board of directors delegates authority for the everyday business affairs of the corporation to the officers, and the board is responsible for the supervision of officer activities. Nevertheless, a corporate decision of any magnitude should be made at a directors' meeting with an appropriate resolution set forth in the minutes, and some major corporate decisions require shareholder approval.[1]

Depending upon the structure of a limited liability company, the internal operations of the company may involve formal meetings of the members and managers, similar to the typical meetings held in corporations. The various features of the limited liability company are discussed in Chapter 5. If the business is to be managed by managers elected by the members, the operating agreement of the limited liability company will frequently describe the types and regularity of meetings of both the managers and members; and in some states, statutory provisions for such meetings, similar to corporate statutes, prescribe the formalities for notice, determination of the members who are entitled to vote, and manner of taking action for the intracompany groups. Similarly, limited liability partnerships may conduct business through formal meetings of the partners. In part, the formality of such meetings supports the treatment of these organizations as entities, which justifies their limited liability feature. Although the remainder of this chapter describes the intricacies of corporate meetings, the same rules and procedures may apply to the operations of a limited liability company and limited liability partnerships as well.

Four types of meetings may be held by the intracompany groups described here: organizational meetings, annual meetings, regular meetings, and special meetings. State statutes often detail the circumstances that require such meetings, authority to call them, the notice required, and time and place for the meetings.

REQUIREMENT FOR ORGANIZATIONAL MEETINGS

The corporation is formed by the filing of articles of incorporation or the issuance of a certificate of incorporation, depending upon the law of the particular jurisdiction.[2] Thereafter, certain organizational meetings must be held, and each state statute should be consulted to determine the parties to the meeting and the business that must be conducted. The organizational meetings are, by most statutes, a required condition that should be satisfied before the corporation commences business operations.[3] Some states require only an organizational meeting of the incorporators; others require only an organizational meeting of the directors. Still other states permit either group to hold an organizational meeting, and a few also require the shareholders to have an organizational meeting.[4] Section 2.05(a) of the Model Business Corporation Act provides as follows:

> After incorporation:
> (1) if initial directors are named in the articles of incorporation, the initial directors shall hold an organizational meeting, at the call of a majority of the directors, to complete the organization of the corporation by appointing officers, adopting bylaws, and carrying on any other business brought before the meeting.
> (2) if initial directors are not named in the articles, the incorporator or incorporators shall hold an organizational meeting at the call of a majority of the incorporators:
> (i) to elect directors and complete the organization of the corporation; or
> (ii) to elect a board of directors who shall complete the organization of the corporation.

DIRECTORS' ORGANIZATIONAL MEETING

The Model Business Corporation Act provides that the directors' organizational meeting may be called by a majority of the directors named in the articles of incorporation, or a majority of the incorporators if no initial directors were named in the articles. Several states have adopted this rule.

Notice

In many states, at least three days' notice must be given to the directors by mail. Some states and the Model Business Corporation Act require no notice, and Pennsylvania prescribes five days' notice.[5] It is common practice, however, to either give notice or secure a waiver of notice from the initial directors to avoid the observance of the notice period.

EXAMPLE

Waiver of Notice of Organizational Meeting

We, the undersigned, constituting all of the directors of Happiness, Inc., a corporation organized under the laws of the State of Colorado, do hereby severally waive notice of the time, place, and purpose of the first meeting of directors of said corporation, and consent that the meeting be held at the corporate offices, and on the 10th day of June, 2005 at 8:30 A.M., and we do further consent to the transaction of any and all business that may properly come before the meeting.

Dated June 10, 2005

_____
_____
_____

Nominal Directors

If initial directors are named, the articles of incorporation need only contain the names of the persons who will serve as directors until the first meeting of shareholders and until their successors have been elected and qualified. If the persons named are the actual directors of the corporation, they may transact all necessary director business at their organizational meeting. On the other hand, if the directors named in the articles of incorporation are only **nominal,** or **dummy, directors**, they should not be expected to conduct any more than the formal statutory business, such as adopting bylaws and electing officers. Other corporate business should be reserved for the consideration of the actual directors elected by the shareholders. If multiple meetings are undesirable, it is possible to have the nominal directors submit their resignations one by one at the organizational meeting, with the board of directors adopting by resolution the resignation of each dummy director and electing the actual director to fill the vacancy. The actual director will then serve for the period of the predecessor dummy director, or until the next shareholder meeting when a successor will be elected.

EXAMPLE

Resignation of a Dummy Director

To the Board of Happiness, Inc.
I regret that, owing to other business commitments, I am no longer able to act as a director, and I hereby tender my resignation as a director of Happiness, Inc., to take effect as and from the 10th day of June, 2005.

Edward O'Keefe

EXAMPLE

Acceptance of the Resignation of a Director

RESOLVED, that the resignation of Edward O'Keefe as director of this Corporation be accepted to take effect on June 10, 2005, and the secretary is hereby directed to notify Edward O'Keefe of such acceptance.

If the directors are not named in the articles of incorporation, they are elected at an organizational meeting of the incorporators. The elected directors then hold an organizational meeting after their election.

INCORPORATORS' ORGANIZATIONAL MEETING

If the state statute requires an organizational meeting of the incorporators, it also may require a period of notice preceding the meeting and usually will specify the business to be conducted at the meeting. The statutory requirements must be strictly followed. Even if the statute does not specify the business that must be conducted, certain matters are normally considered at all organizational meetings.

BUSINESS CONDUCTED AT ORGANIZATIONAL MEETINGS

Most state statutes describe specific matters that must be on the agenda of an organizational meeting. In the Model Business Corporation Act, the organizational meeting must consider the adoption of the bylaws and the election of officers. The statute further provides that the organizers should consider "carrying on any other business brought before the meeting."[6] The following discussion considers the chronological order of business at an organizational meeting and includes examples of the way in which the minutes should reflect the actions taken.

Determination of a Quorum and Election of a Chair and Secretary

Counsel (or the person who is initially presiding) should be certain to determine the presence of a quorum according to the rules stated in the articles of incorporation or the statute. If a quorum is present, the fact should be noted in the minutes, and the persons present and absent should be named in the minutes.

A chair and a secretary should be elected as the first order of business at an organizational meeting. The secretary is responsible for the minutes of the meeting. The minutes are frequently prepared in advance by counsel and may serve as an agenda for the meeting, but the secretary should review them for accuracy and add any necessary new material. The chair is responsible for an orderly meeting.

EXAMPLE

Recital of Quorum, and Election of Chair and Secretary

The following directors named in the articles of incorporation were present: Edward Giles, Gary Nakarado, and Terryl Gorrell. The following directors named in the articles of incorporation were absent: Richard Vermeire and Adam Golodner.

The presence of the foregoing directors constituted a quorum. By unanimous vote of the directors, Edward Giles was elected Chair of the meeting and Gary Nakarado was elected Secretary of the meeting.

Notice of Waivers of Notice

If the appropriate notice has been given to the members of the group, a copy of the notices should be presented at the meeting and attached to the minutes. If waivers of notice of the meeting have been obtained from those present, the waivers should be presented at the meeting and affixed to the minutes as an attachment.

EXAMPLE

Recognition of Notice

The Secretary presented the waiver of notice of the meeting signed by all of the directors, which was ordered filed with the minutes of the meeting.

Determination of Actual Directors

If the directors named in the articles of incorporation are the actual directors of the corporation, no further action regarding their status is required at the organizational meeting. Some states do not require the naming of the initial directors, and all states permit dummy directors to be named in the articles of incorporation.

Election of the actual directors occurs at the incorporators' organizational meeting if no directors are named in the articles of incorporation. If the directors are named but are only nominal directors, the incorporators may obtain the resignations of the nominal directors and replace those directors with actual directors at the incorporators' organizational meeting.

The directors' organizational meeting should be conducted by actual directors. Therefore, if nominal directors are named in the articles of incorporation and there is no meeting of incorporators to elect actual directors, the nominal directors may be replaced by the procedure suggested earlier in this chapter under "Directors' Organizational Meeting."

The resignations of nominal directors should be affixed to the minutes of the meeting during which they were replaced.

Determining Actual Directors

The Secretary announced that resignations had been received from Richard Vermeire and Adam Golodner, who were nominal directors of the corporation named in the articles of incorporation.

Thereupon, upon motion duly made, seconded, and unanimously adopted it was

RESOLVED, that the resignations of Richard Vermeire and Adam Golodner as directors of this corporation be accepted to take effect on the date of this meeting, and the Secretary is hereby directed to notify Mr. Vermeire and Mr. Golodner of such acceptance, and to affix to the minutes of this meeting the original written resignations of these directors.

FURTHER RESOLVED, that Edward Naylor and James Burghardt shall be appointed to fill the vacancies created by the resignations of these directors, and shall be directors of this corporation to serve until the first annual meeting of the shareholders or until their successors are otherwise elected and qualified.

Presentation of Articles of Incorporation

The articles of incorporation, returned by the secretary of state (or other designated filing officer) with the certificate of incorporation (if one has been issued under local law), should be presented to the meeting and affixed as an attachment to the minutes of the meeting. It is not necessary to have a resolution approving the articles of incorporation, but the minutes should reflect that the articles were presented to the meeting, and the secretary should be instructed to insert the articles and the certificate of incorporation in the minute book.

Presentation of the Articles of Incorporation

The Chair submitted to the meeting a copy of the Articles of Incorporation of the corporation and an original receipt showing payment of the statutory organization taxes and filing fees. The Chair reported that the original of these Articles of Incorporation had been filed in the office of the Secretary of State, State of Nebraska, on November 1, 2005. Thereupon, upon motion duly made, seconded, and unanimously adopted, it was:

RESOLVED, that the Articles of Incorporation as presented be, and they hereby are, accepted and approved and that said Articles of Incorporation, together with the original receipt showing payment of the statutory organization taxes and filing fees, be placed in the minute book of the corporation.

Approval of Action Taken at Previous Meetings

When the incorporators have held an organizational meeting and the board of directors subsequently conducts an organizational meeting, it is customary for the board to approve, ratify, and confirm all of the actions taken at the incorporators' meeting. This procedure has the effect of making the actions of the incorporators the actions of the board of directors. For example, if the incorporators have adopted the bylaws, this resolution grants approval of the same by the board of directors. The minutes of the board of directors' meeting may be abbreviated in this fashion:

Acceptance of Incorporators' Action

The Secretary presented to the meeting the minutes of the first meeting of incorporators of the Corporation together with a copy of the Bylaws adopted by the incorporators at their meeting held November 10, 2005.

On motion duly made and seconded, it was unanimously

RESOLVED, that the minutes of the first meeting of the incorporators of the Corporation held on November 10, 2005, be hereby in all respects ratified, approved, and confirmed.

FURTHER RESOLVED, that the Bylaws adopted by the incorporators at the first meeting are hereby adopted by this Board as the Bylaws of this Corporation.

Approval of Bylaws

Counsel should have drafted the bylaws pursuant to the instructions of the incorporators before the organizational meeting. The bylaws are presented to the organizational meeting of the appropriate group for approval. The minutes must contain a resolution that the bylaws have been approved, and the secretary should be instructed to insert a copy of the bylaws in the minutes.

Acceptance of Bylaws

EXAMPLE

RESOLVED, that the Bylaws submitted to the meeting be and are adopted as the Bylaws of the Corporation, and that the Secretary is instructed to insert a copy of such Bylaws, certified by the Secretary, in the minute book immediately following the Certificate of Incorporation with affixed duplicate original of the Articles of Incorporation.

Approval of Corporate Seal

As a part of the corporate supplies, counsel should have obtained a corporate seal designed to the specifications of the incorporators. Even in states that make the use of the corporate seal optional, in many formal transactions, such as the purchase or sale of real estate, corporate officers will be expected to affix the corporate seal to certain documents, such as the deed or mortgage. It is customary to adopt a resolution to the effect that the seal is accepted as the corporate seal, and to affix the seal to the margin in the minute book page. If any regulation of the use of the seal is contemplated, the regulation should be specified in the resolution.

Acceptance of the Seal

EXAMPLE

RESOLVED, that the seal now produced by the secretary, an impression whereof is now made in the minute book of the Company, be adopted as the seal of the Company, and that such seal shall not be affixed to any deed or instrument of any description, except in the presence of an officer, or director, and the secretary of the Company, who shall respectively sign said deed or instrument.

Approval of Share Certificates

Share certificates are obtained as part of the corporate supplies, and a specimen certificate should be presented at the meeting and attached to the minutes for filing in the minute book. The share certificate should contain all appropriate legends if share transfer restrictions are contemplated, and all other matters unique to the particular corporation or the particular class of stock.[7] The share certificate is accepted by resolution at the organizational meeting, and the secretary should insert the specimen in the minute book.

Acceptance of Share Certificate

EXAMPLE

RESOLVED, that the form of share certificate presented at this meeting is adopted as the form of share certificate for this Corporation; and the Secretary of the meeting is instructed to append a sample of the certificate to the minutes of this meeting.

Authorization to Issue Shares

At their organizational meeting, the incorporators authorize the board of directors to issue the shares of the company. The incorporators' resolution granting such authorization should be contained in the minutes of their meeting. The directors may adopt such a resolution at their organizational meeting authorizing the appropriate officers (as specified by statute) to issue the certificates.

EXAMPLE

Authority to Issue Shares

RESOLVED, that the President and Secretary of this Corporation be, and they are, hereby authorized to issue certificates for shares in the form as submitted to this meeting and ordered attached to these minutes.

Acceptance of Transfers of Share Subscriptions from Dummy Incorporators

Some states require that an incorporator subscribe for shares as a condition to qualification as an incorporator.[8] To satisfy this rule, incorporators frequently subscribe for shares they do not intend to purchase. In such cases, the incorporators may assign their preincorporation **share subscriptions** to actual investors in the company, and these subscription transfers are presented at the organizational meeting of the board of directors for the directors' approval. A resolution reflecting the directors' approval should be included in the minutes.

EXAMPLE

Transfer of Subscription

Dated, Kearney, Nebraska, October 31, 2005
FOR VALUE RECEIVED, I, Charles Luce, hereby sell, assign, and transfer unto William Callison all my right, title, and interest as subscriber to the shares of common stock of Happiness, Inc., which subscription was executed by me on the 3rd day of October 2005, and, when accepted, entitles me to receive 500 shares of the common stock of Happiness, Inc., and I hereby direct said corporation to issue certificates for said shares of stock to and in the name of the aforesaid assignee, or his nominees or assigns.

Charles Luce

EXAMPLE

Adoption of Assignment

RESOLVED, that the assignment and transfer of a stock subscription from Charles Luce to William Callison, dated October 31, 2005, is hereby approved and accepted on behalf of the Corporation.

Acceptance of Share Subscriptions

The preincorporation share subscriptions are offers to the corporation to buy shares when the corporation is formed.[9] Once formation has been accomplished, the board of directors should accept the offers on behalf of the corporation and thereby obligate the subscribers to pay for the shares they have offered to purchase. The acceptance of the share subscriptions is accomplished by a resolution, and each subscription should be listed therein, specifying the number of shares the subscriber has offered to purchase, the class of the security, the par value, and the price at which the offer was tendered.

If cash has been offered for share purchases, the resolution accepting the offer need only state the amount offered when describing the consideration.

EXAMPLE

Acceptance of Cash Subscriptions

RESOLVED, that the written offers dated March 23, 2005, pertaining to the issuance of shares of the Corporation, to wit:

Name	Number of Shares	Consideration
John O'Brien	100	$ 100
Dwight Shellman	1000	$1000
Kevin Burr	750	$ 750

be, and the same hereby are, in all respects accepted for and on behalf of the Corporation.

If property or services are offered to the corporation in exchange for shares, the board of directors must evaluate the property and services consistently with the valuation rule of the particular jurisdiction. Some states require that an actual market value be determined and used by the board in appraising property or services, but most states permit the board of directors to determine the value of the property or services in good faith considering the best interests of the corporation. The directors' determination of value is then conclusive in the absence of fraud. The Model Business Corporation Act requires a directors' determination of adequacy of consideration in section 6.21. This determination of value is critical to the issuance of par value securities, since those securities cannot be sold for less than par value. Thus, if a corporation receives an offer to transfer certain land in exchange for 300 shares that each have a $100 par value, the board of directors must appraise the land, by the appropriate valuation rule, at an amount equal to or greater than $30,000. The resolution in the minutes should state the valuation determination.

Acceptance of Property Subscription

EXAMPLE

RESOLVED, that this Corporation hereby accepts the offer of Marcia Kearney and Stephen Roark, as joint owners, to sell and convey to it good and marketable title to the fee of the premises known as 3590 E. Nobles Road, Littleton, Colorado, 80122, together with the buildings thereon, and all personal property belonging to them used in connection with the premises free and clear of all liens and encumbrances, in consideration of this Corporation's issuing and delivering to Stephen Roark, or his nominee, certificates for 150 of its fully paid and nonassessable shares of its 5½% preferred shares, $100 par value, and of its issuing and delivering to Marcia Kearney, or her nominee, certificates for 150 of its fully paid and nonassessable 5½% preferred shares, $100 par value. The Board of Directors does hereby adjudge and declare that said property is of the fair value of $30,000, and that the same is necessary for the business of the corporation.

If the cash or property is not immediately tendered with the offer, it is appropriate for the directors to adopt a resolution to assess or **call** the consideration due. Unless otherwise stated in the subscription agreement, the offer is payable in full upon acceptance, but the board of directors may permit payment by installments.[10]

Partial Call of Subscriptions

EXAMPLE

RESOLVED, that a call of fifty percent is hereby made upon each and every share of the capital stock of the Company subscribed for, and same is to be paid by each subscriber to the treasurer of the Company, on or before the 30th day of November, 2005 (and that the president and secretary issue certificates of fully paid stock therefor).

Full Call of Subscriptions

EXAMPLE

RESOLVED, that a full call is hereby made upon each and every share of the capital stock of the Company subscribed for, and the same is to be paid by each subscriber to the treasurer of the Company, on or before the 30th day of November, 2005 (and that the president and secretary issue certificates of fully paid stock therefor).

Authorization to Issue Shares

The board of directors should authorize the officers of the company to issue the shares represented by the accepted share subscriptions. The resolution generally states that the company will issue and deliver the prescribed number of shares to the subscriber when full consideration has been received for the shares. The resolution should further state that the officers are authorized to sign stock certificates and to register the shares in the names of the subscribers.

EXAMPLE

Authorization to Issue Shares

RESOLVED, that the Corporation issue and deliver to those persons upon receipt of the consideration therefor, pursuant to the terms of the aforesaid offer, certificates representing the subscribed shares of the Corporation, each such shares to include the shares originally subscribed for by the subscribers to the capital stock of the Corporation, and subsequently assigned to the officers; and

FURTHER RESOLVED, that the officers of the Corporation be, and they hereby are, authorized, empowered, and directed to take any and all steps, and to execute and deliver any and all instruments, in connection with consummating the transaction contemplated by the aforesaid offer and in connection with carrying the foregoing resolutions into effect; and

FURTHER RESOLVED, that upon the delivery to this Corporation of proper instruments of conveyance, assignment, and transfer, in such form as counsel for this Corporation may approve and the proper officers of this Corporation may approve, the proper officers of this Corporation be, and they hereby are, authorized and directed to issue to Ms. Kearney an appropriate certificate for 150 of its $5\frac{1}{2}\%$ preferred shares, $100 par value, which when issued as provided in the foregoing resolutions shall be fully paid and nonassessable.

If the shares are being issued in excess of par value, or if no par value shares are being sold in excess of stated value, the board of directors should adopt a resolution to allocate the excess consideration to the capital surplus account if they want the corporation to be able to use any of the contributed funds for distributions to shareholders later.

EXAMPLE

Allocation to Capital Surplus

RESOLVED, that since the corporation's common stock has a par value of $.50 per share, and the same is being sold for $1.00 per share, the excess amount over par value shall be allocated to the capital surplus account of the corporation;

AND FURTHER RESOLVED, that seventy-five percent (75%) of the consideration received for the company's no par value stock shall be allocated and applied to the capital surplus account of the corporation.

Since the Model Business Corporation Act now permits shares to be issued for promissory notes and services to be performed, the board of directors may authorize the issuance of shares in such cases, but should take steps to protect the corporation in the event the promissory note is not paid or the contract is not performed. Section 6.21(e) of the act suggests that the corporation may place shares in escrow or otherwise restrict the transfer of shares until the entire purchase price has been received. Provisions concerning the disposition of the shares, in the event that the payment or performance does not occur, should also be included.

EXAMPLE

Escrow of Shares

RESOLVED, that the corporation issue and deliver in escrow to the First Interstate Bank certificates representing the subscribed shares of the corporation, no par value, in exchange for the subscriptions by the subscribers to the capital stock of the corporation which have not been fully performed, including promissory notes and contracts to perform future services; and

FURTHER RESOLVED, that the officers of the corporation be, and they hereby are, authorized, empowered, and directed to collect all promissory notes and require the performance of all contracts for services, and to notify the First Interstate Bank as escrow agent of the collection of the promissory note or the performance of the contracts for services; and

FURTHER RESOLVED, that upon the payment of the promissory note or the performance of contracts for services, that the officers of the corporation shall release the escrow of shares with First Interstate Bank, and cause the share certificates to be delivered to the subscribers; and

E X A M P L E

(continued)

FURTHER RESOLVED, that in the event that the promissory notes are not fully paid or the contracts for services are not fully performed, that the officers of the corporation shall notify First Interstate Bank as escrow agent of the default on such notes and contracts, and to take any and all steps, and to execute and deliver any and all instruments or documents necessary to cancel those shares that have not been paid.

Reimbursement of Fees

The authority to pay expenses in connection with the formation of the corporation emanates from the board of directors in its organizational meeting. The treasurer is authorized to pay all taxes, fees, and other expenses incurred and to be incurred in connection with the organization of the company and to reimburse any persons who have made expenditures on behalf of the company during the formation procedure. Legal fees are included here, which usually makes this resolution very important.

E X A M P L E

Authorization to Pay Expenses

FURTHER RESOLVED that the President of this Corporation be, and hereby is, authorized to pay all charges and expenses incident to or arising out of the organization of this Corporation, including the bill of Chesley Culp III, Esq., for legal services in connection therewith in the sum of $2,500, and to reimburse any person who has made any disbursement therefor.

Adoption of Preincorporation Agreements

Before formation of the corporation, the incorporators may have entered contracts on behalf of the corporation to ensure that the necessary resources for conducting business would be available when the corporation was formed. For example, they may have leased office space or they may have purchased equipment on credit. An earlier section discussed the general resolution by which the board of directors adopts the acts of the incorporators.[11] Any preincorporation agreements that were intended to benefit the corporation should be adopted by a separate, specific resolution during the board of directors' organizational meeting so that it is clear in the corporate minutes that the specific agreement has been adopted by the corporation. The resolution should summarize the terms of the agreements and clearly express the directors' approval of the transactions.

E X A M P L E

Adoption of Preincorporation Agreements

RESOLVED, the board of directors has reviewed and considered an agreement on behalf of the corporation, a copy of which is attached to these minutes as Exhibit A and incorporated herein by reference. This agreement was entered into prior to the existence and formation of the corporation, and the board of directors, having considered the agreement on behalf of the corporation, does hereby adopt and accept the agreement according to its terms, and agrees that the corporation shall perform all of its obligations and be entitled to all of its rights as specified therein.

Election of Corporate Officers

The officers of the corporation are elected by the board of directors, and this election is one of the prescribed matters to be considered at the directors' organizational meeting. The resolution for the election usually states that the officers will serve for a stated period of time or at the discretion of the board of directors, and fixes the officers' compensation.

EXAMPLE

Election and Compensation of Officers

The meeting then proceeded to the election of officers to serve until the next annual meeting of stockholders or until their successors are elected and qualified. The following nominations were made and seconded:

President	Glenna McKelvy
Vice President	Bill Bradford
Secretary	Mary Matthies
Treasurer	Dave Herrenbruck

There being no further nominations, the foregoing persons were unanimously elected to the office set opposite their respective names.

RESOLVED, that until further action by the Board of Directors, the annual salaries of the officers are fixed in the following amounts, effective as of January 1, 2006, and payable in twelve equal monthly installments:

President	$50,000.00
Vice President	$45,000.00
Secretary	$25,000.00
Treasurer	$20,000.00

Bank Resolution

The bank resolution prescribes the authority for the maintenance of a bank account and names the persons who have authority to obligate the corporation in banking matters. The treasurer of the corporation is often authorized to sign bank documents and in some states may be required to sign for certain banking transactions, such as mortgages or promissory notes. The appropriate persons to sign checks and other routine banking papers is a question of security and the preferences of the directors and officers. It is good practice to require more than one signature on transactions involving significant sums of money. Every bank supplies a form for a banking resolution, which should be completed and attached to the minutes of the meeting. The minutes contain a directors' resolution that authorizes the opening of the bank account, and adopts by reference the provisions in the attached bank form. The directors' resolution looks like this:

EXAMPLE

Acceptance of Bank Resolution

RESOLVED that the funds of the Corporation be deposited in the Central City Bank of Kearney, 6th Avenue Branch, and that the printed resolutions supplied by that bank, as filed at this meeting, be attached to the minutes of this meeting and be deemed resolutions of this Corporation duly adopted by the Board of Directors.

A sample of a bank resolution follows.

Bank Resolution[12]

. . . .
(Name of Corporation)

I HEREBY CERTIFY TO . . . . ,
that at a meeting of the Board of Directors of . . . . , a corporation organized under the laws of the State of . . . . duly called (a quorum being present) and held at the office of said corporation, No . . . . in the
city of . . . . State of . . . . on the . . . . day .
. . . . , 20 ., the following resolutions were duly adopted and are now in
full force and effect:

Depositary and Signing Resolution

RESOLVED, that the above bank be designated as a depositary of this corporation and that funds of this corporation deposited in said Bank be subject to withdrawal upon checks, notes, drafts, bills of exchange, acceptances, undertakings of
other orders for the payment of money when signed on behalf of this corporation by
any . . . . of its following officers to wit:

(Number)

RESOLVED, that the above bank, is hereby authorized to pay any such orders
and also to receive the same for credit of or in payment from the payee or any other
holder without inquiry as to the officer or tendered in payment of his individual obligation.

Borrowing Resolution

RESOLVED, that . . . .
. . . .
be and they hereby are authorized to borrow from time to time on behalf of this
corporation from the above bank sums of money for such period or periods of time,
and upon such terms, rates of interest and accounts as may to them in their discretion seem advisable, and to execute notes or agreements in the forms required by said
Bank in the name of the corporation for the payment of any sums so borrowed.

That said officers are hereby authorized to pledge or mortgage any of the bonds,
stocks or other securities, bills receivable, warehouse receipts or other property real
or personal of the corporation, for the purpose of securing the payment of any moneys so borrowed; to endorse said securities and/or to issue the necessary powers of
attorney and to execute loan, pledge or liability agreements in the forms required by
the said bank in connection with same.

That said officers are hereby authorized to discount with the above bank any bills
receivable held by this corporation upon such terms as they may deem proper.

That the foregoing powers and authority will continue until written notice of revocation has been delivered to the above bank.

RESOLVED, that the secretary of this corporation be and he or she hereby is authorized to certify to the above bank, the foregoing resolutions and that the provisions thereof are in conformity with the charter and by-laws of this corporation.

I FURTHER CERTIFY that there is no provision in the charter or by-laws of said
corporation limiting the power of the board of directors to pass the foregoing resolutions and that the same are in conformity with the provisions of said charter and
by-laws.

I further certify that the following are the genuine signatures of the persons now
holding office in said company as indicated opposite their respective signatures.

. . . . (Title)
. . . . (Title)
. . . . (Title)

Application for Qualification as a Foreign Corporation

If management contemplates doing business in another jurisdiction, the board of directors
must adopt an appropriate resolution authorizing the officers of the corporation to apply for
admission and qualification of the corporation as a foreign corporation in any other jurisdiction in which it plans to do business.

Authorization of Foreign Qualification

RESOLVED, that the officers of the Corporation be authorized and directed to qualify the Corporation as a foreign corporation authorized to conduct business in the State of Kansas, and in connection therewith to appoint all necessary agents or attorneys for service of process and to take all other action that may be deemed necessary or advisable.

Appointment of Resident Agents and Office

The articles of incorporation name the resident agents, but the appointment of those agents should be *ratified* by a resolution of the board of directors. Similarly, the establishment of a principal office of the corporation may be resolved at the organizational meeting.

Principal Office and Agent

RESOLVED, that the Articles of Incorporation correctly state the principal office of the corporation and that the person named therein as registered agent shall remain registered agent until subsequently changed by a resolution of the board of directors.

Designation of Counsel and Auditors

The board of directors may designate a certain attorney to act as the general counsel of the company, if appropriate, and also may specify the persons to be retained as the corporation's auditors.

Appointment of Counsel and Auditors

RESOLVED, that Patrick Meyer be hereby appointed to act as attorney for the Company, and that he be paid the ordinary professional charges for his services as attorney.

RESOLVED, that Bert Bondi & Co. be hereby appointed auditors of the Company for the ensuing year, and that the remuneration for their services as such auditors be the sum of $10,000.00

Authority to Use Assumed Name

Some states permit the corporation to conduct business under an assumed name as long as that name is not deceptively similar to another reserved or registered name. Usually the corporation must file a statement of assumed name with the appropriate state official.[13] The authority to use such a name and to file the statement comes from a resolution of the directors.

Adoption of an Assumed Name

RESOLVED, that the corporation may use the name "Black, Inc." as an assumed business name to carry out its purposes and objectives in the state of Oregon, and that the officers of the corporation as required by the statute are authorized to execute such documents as are necessary to accomplish the registration of the corporation's assumed business name.

Adoption of Section 1244 Plan

The Small Business Tax Revision Act added Section 1244 of the Internal Revenue Code to offer special loss protection for shareholders of a small corporation. Losses on Section 1244 stock are fully deductible as business losses up to certain dollar limits per year, instead of being treated as capital losses (which are only allowed to offset capital gains). (The substantive rules of Section 1244 stock are explained in detail in "Taxation of a Corporation" in Chapter 6.) To qualify to issue Section 1244 stock, a corporation must be a small business corporation, as defined by the statute.[14]

A **Section 1244 plan** permits a new corporation that qualifies as a small business corporation and issues Section 1244 stock to cause shareholder losses from the sale of the shares to be treated as ordinary losses and not capital losses, so the shareholder may offset the lost value against ordinary income, such as the shareholder's wages, interest, dividends, and so on. Unless the shares qualify under Section 1244, any such losses offset only capital gains and, to a very limited extent, ordinary income.

Although the statutory requirement of a written plan has been eliminated, it is good practice to clearly indicate the intention to qualify for this special protection by adopting a resolution and plan in the minutes of the organizational meeting. A proper resolution adopting a Section 1244 plan should restate the statutory requirements. Thus, it should recite that the payment of the shares will be in cash or other property but not securities or services, and it should provide that the stock will be offered for sale at a price not lower than the par value of the shares and not higher than an aggregate of $1,000,000.

EXAMPLE

Section 1244 Plan

A plan was read and (unanimously) adopted for the issuance of common stock of the corporation to qualify the same as "small business corporation" stock under the provisions of Section 1244 of the Internal Revenue Code of 1986 as amended. The Secretary was directed to place a copy of the Plan immediately following these minutes.

Plan for Issuance of Stock

1. The corporation shall offer and issue under this Plan, a maximum of 50,000 shares of its common stock at a maximum price of ten dollars ($10.00) per share.

2. This offer shall terminate by:
   (a) complete issuance of all shares offered hereunder,
   (b) appropriate action terminating the same by the Board of Directors and the Stockholders, or
   (c) the adoption of a new Plan by the Stockholders for the issuance of additional stock under Section 1244, Internal Revenue Code.

3. No increase in the basis of outstanding stock shall result from a contribution to capital hereunder.

4. No stock offered hereunder shall be issued on the exercise of a stock right, stock warrant, or stock option, unless such right, warrant, or option is applicable solely to unissued stock offered under the Plan and is exercised during the period of the Plan.

5. Stock subscribed for prior to the adoption of the Plan, including stock subscribed for prior to the date the corporation comes into existence, may be issued hereunder, provided, however, that the said stock is not in fact issued prior to the adoption of such Plan.

6. No stock shall be issued hereunder for a payment which, along or together with prior payments, exceeds the maximum amount that may be received under the Plan.

7. Any offering or portion of an offer outstanding that is unissued at the time of the adoption of this Plan is herewith withdrawn. Stock rights, stock warrants, stock options, or securities convertible into stock that are outstanding at the time this Plan is adopted are likewise herewith withdrawn.

8. Stock issued hereunder shall be in exchange for money or other property except for stock or securities. Stock issued hereunder shall not be in return for services rendered or to be rendered to, or for the benefit of, the corporation. Stock may be issued hereunder, however, in consideration for cancellation of indebtedness of the corporation, unless such indebtedness is evidenced by a security or arises out of the performance of personal services.

9. Any matters pertaining to this issue not covered under the provisions of this Plan shall be resolved in favor of the applicable law and regulations in order to qualify such issue under Section 1244 of the Internal Revenue Code. If any shares issued hereunder are finally determined not to be so qualified, such shares, and only such shares, shall be deemed not to be in the Plan, and such other shares issued hereunder shall not be affected thereby.

10. The sum of the aggregate amount offered hereunder plus the equity capital of the corporation amounts to $500,000.00.

11. The date of adoption of this Plan is November 15, 2005.

This plan should be copied directly into the minutes.

Subchapter S Election

To elect taxation under Subchapter S, the corporation must again qualify as a small business corporation, but the Subchapter S definition of a small business corporation is different from the section 1244 definition.[15] Under a **Subchapter S election**, the income of the corporation is treated as ordinary income of the shareholders, and thus the problem of double taxation of corporation income is avoided.[16] If the shareholders desire to be taxed under Subchapter S, the board of directors should adopt a resolution that provides that the corporation has elected to be taxed as a small business corporation so that the corporate records will reflect that the corporation will file the election and tax returns under Subchapter S and provide shareholders the information necessary to file their tax returns to report their proportionate share of the corporate income. It also may be appropriate to obligate the corporation to distribute to the shareholders the funds necessary to pay the tax on the corporate income they are required to report on their personal tax returns. The resolution should also state that the corporation meets the statutory requirements for Subchapter S corporations.

EXAMPLE

Subchapter S Election

WHEREAS, the corporation qualifies as a small business corporation under Section 1361(b) of the Internal Revenue Code of 1986, as amended (the "IRC"); and

WHEREAS, the board of directors deems it to be in the best interests of the corporation and the shareholders to elect to be taxed as a small business corporation under the IRC, it is

RESOLVED, that the election to be so taxed be submitted to the shareholders for their consent, and that, upon obtaining said consent, the officers of the corporation shall prepare and submit the necessary documents and forms to accomplish said election under Section 1362 of the IRC.

FURTHER RESOLVED, that the corporation shall distribute to the shareholders on or before April 1 of each fiscal year cash in the amount of 40% of the corporation's net profit for the previous fiscal year to provide funds to the shareholders to pay the federal and state income taxes applicable to the corporation's net profit.

The shareholder consent, duly signed, together with a copy of Form 2553 filed with the Internal Revenue Service, should be attached to the minutes.

EXAMPLE

Shareholder Consent to Subchapter S

_____ 20 ___

We, the undersigned, being all of the stockholders in Happiness, Inc., a Nebraska corporation, hereby consent to the election under Section 1361 of the Internal Revenue Code of 1986 as amended, to be treated as a small business corporation for income tax purposes, and submit the following information:
Name and Address of Corporation: Happiness, Inc., 200 West 14th Avenue, Kearney, Nebraska

Name and Addresses of Stockholders	No. of Shares	Date Acquired
_____	_____	_____
_____	_____	_____
_____	_____	_____

Dates of Meetings

The bylaws usually permit the directors to establish regular meetings for their board, and a resolution establishing dates and times is appropriate at the organizational meeting. The resolution also usually identifies the place for the meeting.

> **Place of Regular Meetings**
>
> RESOLVED, that regular meetings of the Board of Directors be held at the office of the Corporation at 200 West 14th Avenue, Kearney, Nebraska, on the third Wednesday of the months of February, May, September, and December, and that a regular meeting also be held in April immediately following the annual meeting of shareholders. No notice shall be required to be given of any of these regular meetings.

EXAMPLE

Delegation of Authority to the Officers

The board of directors may adopt a resolution defining the authority of the officers. These resolutions are usually drafted broadly, and they are not necessary if the officers' duties are described in the bylaws. They may be useful, however, as a written record that the directors have delegated the authority. The typical text of the resolution includes grants of authority to the president and vice-president to conduct all business on behalf of the corporation, to sign all documents necessary in the ordinary course of business in the corporate name, and to perform other necessary managerial acts on behalf of the corporation. The secretary is authorized to procure and maintain necessary corporate books and records, and to open and maintain a stock transfer ledger in accordance with the statute and bylaws. The treasurer is always authorized to pay and discharge any obligations of the corporation, and to perform all other acts necessary and proper within the financial structure of the corporation. The authority of the officers is specified in the bylaws,[17] however, and by approving the bylaws, the directors accomplish the same delegation of authority.

> **Delegation of Authority to Officers**
>
> The authority of the officers of the corporation was discussed, and upon motion made and unanimously approved, the following authority is granted to the officers of the corporation, until subsequently modified by appropriate resolution of the Board of Directors:
>
> *President.* The President shall be the principal executive officer of the Corporation and, subject to the control of the Board of Directors, shall in general supervise and control all of the business and affairs of the Corporation. The President shall, when present, preside at all meetings of the shareholders and of the Board of Directors. The president may sign, with the Secretary or any other proper officer of the corporation thereunto authorized by the Board of Directors, certificates for shares of the corporation, any deeds, mortgages, bonds, contracts, or other instruments that the Board of Directors has authorized to be executed, except in cases where the signing and execution thereof shall be expressly delegated by the Board of Directors or by the Bylaws to some other officer or agent of the corporation, or shall be required by law to be otherwise signed or executed; and in general shall perform all duties incident to the office of President and such other duties as may be prescribed by the Board of Directors from time to time.
>
> *The Vice-Presidents.* In the absence of the President or in the event of the President's death, or inability or refusal to act, the Vice-President (or in the event there be more than one Vice-President, the Vice-Presidents in the order designated at the time of their election, or in the absence of any designation, then in the order of their election) shall perform the duties of the President, and when so acting, shall have all the powers of and be subject to all the restrictions upon the President. Any Vice-President may sign, with the Secretary or an Assistant Secretary, certificates for shares of the Corporation; and shall perform such other duties as from time to time may be assigned to him or her by the President or by the Board of Directors.
>
> *The Secretary.* The Secretary shall: (a) keep the minutes of the proceedings of the shareholders and of the Board of Directors in one or more books provided for that purpose; (b) see that all notices are duly given in accordance with the provisions of the Bylaws or as required by law; (c) be custodian of the corporate records and of the seal of the Corporation and see that the seal of the Corporation is affixed to all documents the execution of which on behalf of the Corporation under its seal is duly authorized; (d) keep a register of the post office address of each shareholder, which shall be furnished to the Secretary by such stockholder; (e) sign with the President, or a Vice-President, certificates for shares of the Corporation, the issuance of which shall have been authorized by resolution of the Board of Directors; (f) have general charge of the stock transfer books of the Corporation; and (g) in general perform all duties incident to the

EXAMPLE

office of Secretary and such other duties as from time to time may be assigned to him or her by the President or by the Board of Directors.

The Treasurer. The Treasurer shall: (a) have charge and custody of and be responsible for all funds and securities of the Corporation; (b) receive and give receipts for moneys due and payable to the Corporation from any source whatsoever, and deposit all such moneys in the name of the Corporation in such banks, trust companies, or other depositaries as shall be selected in accordance with the provisions of the Bylaws; and (c) in general perform all of the duties incident to the office of Treasurer and such other duties as from time to time may be assigned to him or her by the President or by the Board of Directors. If required by the Board of Directors, the Treasurer shall give a bond for the faithful discharge of his or her duties in such sum and with such surety or sureties as the Board of Directors shall determine.

Assistant Secretaries and Assistant Treasurers. The Assistant Secretaries, when authorized by the Board of Directors, may sign with the President or a Vice-President certificates for shares of the Corporation, the issuance of which shall have been authorized by a resolution of the Board of Directors. The Assistant Treasurers shall, if required by the Board of Directors, give bonds for the faithful discharge of their duties in such sums and with such sureties as the Board of Directors shall determine. The Assistant Secretaries and Assistant Treasurers, in general, shall perform the duties assigned to them by the Secretary and the Treasurer, respectively, or by the President or the Board of Directors.

Adjournment, Signatures, and Attachments

After all the business has been conducted, the minutes should close with the statement, "There being no further business the meeting is adjourned."

Normally, the secretary, who is in charge of complete and accurate minutes, will sign the minutes of the organizational meeting. It is also permissible to have the chair and the other directors, after their review, sign the minutes of the meeting, signifying their approval.

The **attachments to the minutes** of the meeting are important. A typical organizational meeting will have at least the following attachments, which should be referred to in the minutes and labeled as exhibits:

1. notice or waiver of notice of the meeting;
2. articles of incorporation and certificate of incorporation;
3. minutes and attachments of incorporators' meeting, if appropriate;
4. bylaws;
5. all promoter or incorporator contracts approved by the board of directors;
6. specimen share certificates;
7. written stock subscriptions;
8. bills for organizational expenses;
9. bank resolution; and
10. (if Subchapter S has been elected) Internal Revenue Service form 2553, Election of a Small Business Corporation by the Shareholders.

DIRECTORS' REGULAR AND SPECIAL MEETINGS

Directors' meetings are not strictly regulated by statute. The Model Business Corporation Act states that the directors may meet at regular or special meetings, either within or without the state, and defers to the bylaws most details such as notice and frequency of the meetings.[18] Since the statutes contain little guidance for directors' meetings, the bylaw provisions should be carefully drafted to specify any desired procedures or notice for these meetings.[19] Even in states where the statutes specify certain rules regulating directors' meetings, the rules usually may be changed in the bylaws.

Matters Provided by Statute

The quorum of directors required for action by the board is specified in section 8.24 of the Model Business Corporation Act to be the majority of the number of directors fixed by the bylaws or stated in the articles of incorporation, but either of these documents may provide that a greater number than a majority is required for a quorum.

The articles of incorporation or bylaws also may reduce the quorum of the board of directors to as low as one-third of the directors. If the corporation has a variable-size board (such as when a provision in the articles states that the board of directors shall be between nine and fifteen members), a quorum is a majority of the directors in office immediately before the meeting begins. Section 8.24 further provides that a board of director action will be approved by a majority vote of the directors present, unless the articles of incorporation or bylaws state that a greater-than-majority vote is required.

These director quorum and voting provisions are common to most jurisdictions. To observe how they work, suppose the corporation has a nine-member board of directors. If five members are present, they constitute a quorum and may conduct business. The affirmative vote of three members will carry action for the board, since the three members are more than half of those present even though they represent only one-third of the total board.

Most state statutes and the Model Business Corporation Act provide that the attendance of a director at a meeting shall constitute a waiver of notice of the meeting unless the director attends for the express purpose of objecting to the transaction of any business because the meeting is not lawfully convened. To make such an objection successfully, the director must object at the beginning of the meeting (or promptly upon arrival) and may not vote on or assent to any action taken at the meeting.[20] The procedures for sending notice and the content of the notice are subjects to be determined in the bylaws.

Section 8.20 of the Model Business Corporation Act authorizes directors to participate in any meeting by conference telephone or by other communication devices by which all directors may simultaneously hear each other during the meeting. Most modern corporate statutes are now including this meeting technique to take advantage of modern electronic technology so that not all directors have to travel to a single meeting place. Whether or not communication devices are used, directors must have an interchange of ideas, as if they were in a single room discussing the issues, so it is necessary that the directors be able to participate in the meeting by hearing all comments of all directors and communicating their comments to all others.

Matters Contained in Bylaws or Resolutions

Place of Regular Meetings The place for the directors' **regular meeting** may be specified in the bylaws or may be left to the determination of the board of directors from time to time. If the bylaws leave the decision to the board members, a resolution should be adopted at each meeting of the board of directors specifying where the next regular meeting will be held.[21]

Call and Procedure for Special Meetings Certain rules for **special meetings** of the board of directors should be detailed in the bylaws, such as the persons authorized to call such a meeting and the notice that must be given. The place for special meetings of the board also may be established in the articles of incorporation bylaws, but, if the local statute permits, it is preferable to defer the selection of a meeting place to the person calling the meeting.

Notice of a Directors' Special Meeting

EXAMPLE

To Jerry Jones, Stephen Hess, and Randall Wilson, Directors:

Pursuant to the power given me by the Bylaws of Happiness, Inc., I hereby call a special meeting of its Board of Directors to be held at the corporate offices, on the 20th day of July, 2005 at 4:00 P.M., for the purpose of considering the advisability of authorizing the officers of the Company to renew the lease on the offices now occupied by them, and for such other action in regard thereto as the Board may deem advisable.

_____ President

The undersigned hereby admit receipt of a copy of the foregoing notice and consent that the meeting may be held as called.

_____

_____

_____

Directors

Notice Whether notice should be required for regular directors' meetings depends upon the size of the board, the directors' involvement in other corporate affairs, their proximity to the corporate offices, and their personal preferences. For example, formal notice is probably not required for a small group of directors who are also key employees of the corporation. However, notice may be necessary for a large board composed of advisory directors whose only corporate function is attendance at board meetings. Courtesy reminders should be given in any case. If formal notice is deemed desirable, the bylaws should specify the manner of giving notice and the period of time within which notice must be given.

EXAMPLE

Notice of a Directors' Regular Meeting

To: [*Name and address of director*]

You are hereby notified that the regular quarterly meeting of the Board of Directors of Happiness, Inc., will be held at the principal office of said Company at 200 West 14th Avenue, Kearney, Nebraska, on the 1st day of August, 2005, at 2:00 P.M.

[*Date*]

_____ , Secretary

EXAMPLE

Notice of a Directors' Special Meeting

To: [*Name and address of director*]

You are hereby notified that a special meeting of the Board of Directors of Happiness, Inc., has been called by the president of the Company, to be held at the principal office of the Company at 200 West 14th Avenue, Kearney, Nebraska, on Monday, the 9th day of September, 2005, at 10:00 A.M., to consider the question of selling the corporate stock of Trouble Corporation, and of authorizing the officers of this Company to make the transfer.

[*Date*]

_____ , Secretary

Unless required by the bylaws or state law, the notice need not specify the purpose of the meeting. The Model Business Corporation Act requires two days' notice for special directors' meetings, but permits the articles or bylaws to specify a different notice period and to state whether the purpose of the meeting must be given in the notice.[22] It is common to provide a short period of notice for special meetings, since such meetings are usually called to consider urgent matters and a cumbersome notice procedure is likely to be detrimental to the best interests of the corporation.

The notice requirements are nullified somewhat by the statutory provisions that attendance at a meeting by a director constitutes waiver of notice, unless the director attends only for the purpose of objecting to the call for the meeting. In addition, most state statutes provide that whenever any notice is required to be given, a waiver of notice in writing signed by the person entitled to the notice, whether executed before or after the time stated therein, shall be equivalent to the giving of such notice. The Model Business Corporation Act contains this rule in section 8.23.

EXAMPLE

Waiver of Notice

We, the undersigned, directors of Happiness, Inc., a Nebraska corporation, do hereby waive any and all notice required by the statutes of Nebraska, or by the Articles of Incorporation or Bylaws of said Corporation, of a meeting to be held on the 10th day of August, 2005, at 4:00 P.M., for the purpose of authorizing the officers of said Corporation to execute a trust deed for the benefit of creditors.

Dated August 10, 2005.

[*Signatures of all directors*]

Method of Voting Voting by directors is usually conducted in an informal manner, but formal records should be kept, particularly regarding matters on which there is disagreement among directors. There is no particular statutory regulation of director voting, but directors must vote in person and are not permitted to vote by proxy. The bylaws may prescribe any desirable voting procedure. It is good practice to specify a voting procedure for large boards. Directors express their vote by voice or written ballot on each resolution presented to the meeting, and the secretary of the meeting is responsible for recording the votes. If the vote is not unanimous on any particular issue, each director's position should be stated in the minutes of the meeting in case an issue of liability arises from the board's action. For example, suppose a board of directors consisting of Ed Naylor, Pat Linden, and Sheri Visani are voting on whether the corporation should leave its current offices and lease new space. Visani is concerned that the corporation will breach its existing lease with its landlord if it abandons the current office, and she votes against the proposal. Her negative vote on this issue should be expressed in the minutes. If the corporation is later sued by the landlord and the directors are accused of breaching their fiduciary duties to the corporation for causing it to move too soon, Visani will be able to use the minutes to defend herself from these allegations.

SHAREHOLDER MEETINGS

Frequency

Shareholders' meetings are more strictly regulated by statute than are directors' meetings, to protect the shareholder voice in corporate matters. Moreover, shareholders have the responsibility of electing directors, which is usually done on an annual basis. Consequently, the Model Business Corporation Act provides that an annual meeting of the shareholders *shall* be held at the time and place that is fixed in the bylaws.[23] This statutory provision clearly indicates that a shareholder meeting must be held every year. The act further provides that if the annual meeting is not held within six months after the end of the corporation's fiscal year or within fifteen months of the last annual meeting, any shareholder may apply to a court to summarily order a meeting to be held.

The various state statutes approach this issue differently. Nearly all states require annual meetings of shareholders, but failure to call such a meeting triggers various consequences. A few jurisdictions and the Model Business Corporation Act allow shareholders to apply to a court to order the meeting.[24] Most states permit a certain number of the holders of the voting shares to call a meeting.[25] All states agree that a failure to hold the shareholders' meeting does not invalidate the acts of the corporation, constitute grounds for dissolution, or otherwise impair the corporation's business operations.

In addition to the regular annual meeting, the Model Business Corporation Act states that special meetings of the shareholders may be called by the board of directors or the holders of not less than one-tenth of all the shares entitled to vote at the meeting. Furthermore, the articles of incorporation or bylaws may authorize any other person to call a special shareholders' meeting.[26] The call is usually addressed to the secretary of the corporation, who is responsible for giving notice of the meeting.

Call of a Special Shareholders' Meeting   **EXAMPLE**

To Judi Wagner, Secretary:

We, the undersigned, Stockholders of Happiness, Inc., owning the number of shares of stock opposite our names, pursuant to provisions of the Bylaws, do hereby call a special meeting of the Stockholders of said Company to be held at the corporate offices, on the 15th day of July, 2005, at 3:00 P.M. for the purpose of removing Charles Miser as a director and for the transaction of any or all business that may be brought before the meeting, and we hereby authorize and direct that you notify the Stockholders of such meeting in accordance with the provisions of the Bylaws.

Dated_____ , 20___ .

Signature of Stockholders   *Number of Shares*

_____   _____

_____   _____

_____   _____

State statutes specify different persons who are entitled to call a special meeting, and they particularly differ on the number of shareholders who must join in the call of their own special meeting. For example, the Ohio statute requires holders of 25% of the voting shares to join, and the articles of incorporation may require the concurrence of up to 50% of the voting shares to call a special meeting in that state.

Location

The bylaws may fix a particular place for the shareholders' meeting or they may authorize the board of directors to determine the meeting place from time to time. The latter authority facilitates a decision by the board of directors to hold the annual shareholders' meeting near the beaches of Florida if it is a winter meeting, or in the cool mountains of Colorado if it is scheduled in the summertime. State statutes usually provide that if the bylaws are silent on the matter, the meetings will be held at the principal office of the corporation.

Notice

Shareholders must receive notice of all shareholder meetings, and the statutory notice procedure may be burdensome, especially if the shareholder population is large. State statutes protect the shareholders by prescribing rules for determining the persons who are entitled to receive notice and setting the periods within which notice must be sent.

Persons Entitled to Receive Notice

To determine the shareholders entitled to receive notice of the meeting, the board of directors may set a date at which the corporation's stock transfer books will be closed. All persons listed in the stock record at that time are identified as **holders of record**, and those holders will be entitled to notice of the meeting. Instead of closing the stock transfer books, the board of directors may set a record date in advance of the meeting, and a list of shareholders entitled to receive notice will be prepared that day. Alternatively, the directors may simply direct that the notices will be mailed on a specified date, and all shareholders as of the close of business the day before that date will receive notice.[27] Since these determinative dates are all before the meeting, a person holding shares at the time the notice lists are prepared could sell those shares and no longer be a shareholder at the time of the annual meeting. Nevertheless, that person will receive the notice of the meeting and will be entitled to vote at the meeting. The voting determination procedure is founded on the proposition that the corporation must draw the line somewhere; in the interests of orderly procedure, the statute merely suggests a cutoff date.

The various state statutes have a few principal differences in determining the persons who are entitled to notice and to vote at the meeting. In some states, directors determine which shareholders are entitled to notice of a meeting by closing the stock transfer books before the meeting. In this procedure, the books must be closed during a period up to fifty days before a meeting, and the books may be closed for at least ten days immediately preceding the meeting. Thus, there is a period from ten to fifty days preceding the meeting within which the stock transfer books may be closed.

Instead of closing the stock transfer books, the bylaws of the board of directors may fix a **record date** for determination of the shareholders entitled to notice. That date may simply be a certain number of days before the date of the shareholders' meeting. Under the record date procedure, the transfer books are not closed, but an arbitrary date is fixed—say, thirty days before the scheduled meeting—and all persons who own shares as of that date will receive notice and be entitled to vote. Section 7.07 of the Model Business Corporation Act limits the period for setting the record date to seventy days before the meeting. In addition, section 7.05 requires that notice of the meeting must be given no fewer than ten nor more than sixty days before the meeting date.

A final alternative is allowed: If the stock transfer books are not closed and no record date is set, the day before the date that the notice is mailed to the shareholders will be considered to be the record date for determination of shareholders. Since the notice must be delivered no less than ten and no more than sixty days before the meeting,[28] roughly the same time periods apply to this alternative. Thus, the board of directors or bylaws may simply direct that notices will be sent on the thirtieth day preceding the meeting, and the thirty-first day before the meeting is then the record date. This last procedure is realistically feasible only if the notices are prepared and sent the same day.

The major variant in these provisions among the states is the period within which the books may be closed or the record date set. The Delaware statute allows the board of directors to fix a record date not more than sixty nor less than ten days before the meeting and, like the Model Business Corporation Act, states that if no record date is fixed, the record date will be determined to be the close of business on the day preceding the day on which the notice is given. Most states have a minimum period of ten days. The longest maximum period for identifying holders of record is ninety days preceding the meeting in Maryland.

Advance Notice Notice of the shareholder meeting must be written under most statutes, and should be written anyway. It must state the place, day, and hour of the meeting, and for a special meeting, it usually must also indicate the purposes for which the meeting is called.[29] A few states require that notices for any meeting must state the purpose of the meeting.[30]

Notice for the meeting may be delivered to the shareholder either personally or by mail. If mailed, the notice is deemed to be delivered when deposited in the United States mail with postage prepaid and addressed to the shareholder at the shareholder's address as it appears on the stock transfer books of the corporation.

Notice of Annual Shareholders' Meeting

EXAMPLE

To the Stockholders of Happiness, Inc.:

The Annual Meeting of the Stockholders of Happiness, Inc., will be held in the office of the Company, at 200 West 14th Avenue, Kearney, Nebraska, on Monday, September 9, 2005, at twelve o'clock noon, for the election of three directors and for the transaction of such other business as may properly come before the meeting.

The stock transfer books of the Company will not be closed, but only stockholders of record at the close of business on August 20, 2005, will be entitled to vote.

_____, Secretary

Dated_____, 20___.

Notice of Special Shareholders' Meeting

EXAMPLE

To the Stockholders of Happiness, Inc.:

Pursuant to vote of the Board of Directors, a special meeting of the Stockholders of Happiness, Inc., is hereby called to be held on Wednesday, November 8, 2005, at 10:00 A.M., at the principal office of the Corporation at 200 West 14th Avenue, Kearney, Nebraska, for the following purposes:

1. To consider and act upon the question of increasing the authorized capital stock of the Corporation and of amending the Certificate of Incorporation of the Corporation accordingly, as set forth in the following resolutions of the Board of Directors passed at a meeting of said Board held on the 3rd day of October, 2005, viz.:

"Resolved, that it is advisable that the amount of the authorized capital stock of this Corporation be increased, by amendment of the Certificate of Incorporation, so as to authorize 100,000 additional shares of the common stock, of the par value of $1.00 each, and that for this purpose Article V of said Certificate of Incorporation should be amended by striking out the first two sentences thereof and substituting in lieu of said first two sentences the following, viz.: 'The total amount of the authorized capital stock of the Corporation is $500,000, divided into 500,000 shares, of the par value of $1.00 each. Of such authorized capital stock, 100,000 shares, amounting at par to $100,000, shall be preferred stock, and 400,000 shares, amounting at par to $400,000, shall be common stock.' Said Article V in all other respects to remain unchanged.

"Further resolved, that a special meeting of the stockholders be called to be held at the principal and registered office of the Corporation, to wit, at the office of 200 West 14th Avenue, Kearney, Nebraska, on November 8, 2005, at 10:00 A.M. to take action on the foregoing resolution."

E X A M P L E

(continued)

2. To transact any other business that may properly come before the meeting. The transfer books of the Corporation will be closed at the close of business on October 20, 2005, and reopened at 10:00 A.M. on November 8, 2005.

By order of the Board of Directors.

Dated _____ , 20 _____ . _____ , Secretary

If you are unable to be present at the above meeting, please sign and return the enclosed proxy.

Under the Model Business Corporation Act, the notice must be given not less than ten nor more than sixty days before the meeting.[31] Although this time period is similar to the record date period used in many states, the rule is different from the one stated earlier for the determination of shareholders entitled to receive notice and to vote. The shareholders entitled to notice must first be determined, and then their notice must be properly delivered. Section 1.41 of the Model Business Corporation Act provides that written notice is effective at the earliest of: when received by the shareholder, five days after its deposit in the mail (if mailed postpaid and correctly addressed), or upon the date shown on a written receipt (if sent by registered or certified mail, return receipt requested). Thus, for example, the board of directors is permitted to set a record date for determining shareholders entitled to receive notice anytime up to seventy days before the meeting, and it could legally establish the record date on the eleventh day before the meeting. However, if some notices were not received by the shareholders until the ninth day before the meeting, the delivery rule would be violated.

The time period within which the notice must be delivered varies by jurisdiction. The shortest statutory period for delivery of notice is five days' personal notice in Pennsylvania, and the earliest period prescribed is ninety days in Maryland. A few states say nothing about the time for notice, and Delaware allows the period to be changed in the bylaws.

Several jurisdictions have special notice rules if certain unusual matters are to be considered at the meeting. These statutes usually specify a longer minimum time within which the notice must be given, apparently so the shareholders will have a longer period of time to consider their vote. For example, many states still follow the original rules of the Model Business Corporation Act, which require a minimum of twenty days' notice when the shareholders' meeting is being called for the purpose of considering a plan of merger or consolidation or approval of the sale of assets not in the ordinary course of business.[32]

Having waded through the notice provisions and determined the precise procedure and timing of the notice, the giving of proper notice in practice can be a fulfilling event. But if one becomes mired in these rules, one may ask, and not necessarily rhetorically, "What happens if we just ignore this requirement and hold the meeting anyway?"

Failure to give proper notice renders the meeting invalid and vulnerable to the challenge of any shareholder who did not receive proper notice. However, there are some saving provisions. Section 7.06 of the Model Business Corporation Act permits written waiver of notice by any shareholder entitled to receive such notice. The waiver may be signed before or after the event. Also, a procedure for obtaining written consent to action is discussed in "Action without a Meeting" later in this chapter; it may be a solution to the inadequate notice problem for small corporations. As in the rule for directors' meetings,[33] a shareholder may attend a meeting for which no notice was given, and the attendance waives objection to the lack of notice unless the shareholder objects at the beginning of the meeting to the holding of the meeting without notice. If notice is given but does not state the purposes of the meeting, a shareholder may object to any consideration of a matter that was not mentioned in the notice.

Shareholders' Waiver of Notice

The undersigned, a shareholder of Happiness, Inc., hereby waives any and all notice required by the statutes of Nebraska, or the articles of incorporation or bylaws of said corporation, for a meeting to be held on the 24th day of November, 2005 at 3:00 P.M. at the corporate offices for the purposes of increasing the authorized capital stock of the corporation and amending the certificate of incorporation of the corporation accordingly.

Dated November 24, 2005.

[Signature of the Shareholder]

Voting Lists

After the record date has been established, the corporation is required to prepare an alphabetical list of names of all of its shareholders who will be entitled to notice of the shareholders' meeting. This list is to be arranged by voting group, and must show the address of and number of shares held by each shareholder. The list is available for inspection by any shareholder, beginning two business days after notice of the meeting is given, and the list must be available at the corporations's principal office or another place identified in the notice. All shareholders are entitled to inspect the list during regular business hours. The purpose of the voting list is to permit shareholders to learn the identities of the other shareholders so they may discuss issues that are likely to arise at the meeting to see if all shareholders share the same concerns or are interested in voting their shares in a certain manner.

Proxies

Shareholders who are unable to be present at the shareholders' meeting may vote by proxy. A **proxy** is a written authorization by a shareholder directing the proxy holder to vote the shareholder's shares on behalf of the shareholder. The proxy holder is bound to vote the shares in the manner directed by the shareholder in the proxy.

Proxies, like any other agreement, may contain any limiting or expanding provisions that the shareholder desires. The proxy form is usually furnished by the management and conforms to a standard form for general authorization to vote. The Model Business Corporation Act and other statutes regulating proxies require that they be written and signed by the shareholder. The act also permits the proxy to be signed by the shareholder's attorney-in-fact.[34]

A general proxy authorizes the proxy holder to vote on all matters properly presented to the shareholder meeting.

General Proxy for a Specified Meeting

I hereby constitute and appoint Ezra Brooks or Jack Daniels, or either one of them, and in place of either, in case of substitution, his substitute, attorneys and agent for me and in my name, place, and stead, to vote as my proxy at the next Annual Meeting, and at any adjournment or adjournments thereof, of the Stockholders of Happiness, Inc., upon any question that may be brought before such meeting, including the election of directors, according to the number of votes I should be entitled to vote if then personally present, with full power to each of my said attorneys to appoint a substitute in his place.

Dated _____ , 20 _____ .

The proxy may have a stated duration, in which case it is valid for the period of time stated. If no period is stated, it automatically expires after eleven months from the date of execution under the Model Business Corporation Act.

EXAMPLE

Continuing General Proxy

The undersigned hereby constitutes and appoints Jack Daniels, Bud Weiser, and John Walker, or any two of them acting jointly, as his, her, or their proxy to cast the votes of the undersigned at all general, special, and adjourned meetings of the Stockholders of Happiness, Inc., from time to time and from year to year, when the undersigned is not present at any such meeting or, if present, does not elect to vote in person. This proxy shall be effective for two years from the date hereof unless sooner revoked by written notice to the Secretary of the Corporation.

Dated _____ , 20 _____ .

_____

The statutory period of duration varies among the jurisdictions, but proxies are revocable at will, unless they are "coupled with an interest," such as when stock is pledged to a creditor to secure repayment of a loan, and a proxy to vote the shares is given to the creditor for the duration of the security interest. Section 7.22 of the Model Business Corporation Act recognizes that proxies may be made irrevocable in favor of a creditor (to whom the shares have been pledged), a person who has purchased the shares, an employee of the corporation who required the proxy as part of the employment contract, or a party to a voting agreement.

Proxies are most frequently used for large, publicly held corporations, where many shareholders will not be able to attend the meeting. The federal Securities Exchange Act of 1934 strictly regulates the solicitation of proxies for shareholders of a publicly held corporation.[35] A proxy in compliance with that act must satisfy special requirements as to wording and form.

EXAMPLE

Public Corporation Proxy

Happiness, Inc.
Proxy Solicited by Management for Special Meeting
of Stockholders, October 10, 2005

P   The undersigned hereby appoints Jack Daniels, Bud Weiser, and John Walker and each or any of them, attorneys, with powers the undersigned would possess if personally present, to vote all shares of Com-

R   mon Stock of the undersigned in Happiness, Inc. at the Special Meeting of its Stockholders to be held October 10, 2005, at 2:00 P.M., Central Daylight Saving Time, at Kearney, Nebraska, and at any ad-

O   journment thereof, upon the proposed amendment to the Certificate of Incorporation of the Company, which amendment is set forth in the Proxy Statement and has been declared advisable by the Board of

X   Directors, and upon a split of each outstanding share of Common Stock of the par value of $5 into two shares of Common Stock of the par value of $5 each, and upon other matters properly coming before the

Y   meeting.

(Continued, and to be signed on the other side.)

(Continued from the other side.)   Proxy No.

The directors favor voting FOR the proposed amendment to the Certificate of Incorporation.

The vote for the undersigned is to be cast (please indicate)

FOR   ☐   AGAINST   ☐

the proposed amendment to the Certificate of Incorporation and the split of each outstanding share of Common Stock of the par value of $5 into two shares of Common Stock of the par value of $5 each.

UNLESS OTHERWISE DIRECTED THE VOTE OF THE UNDERSIGNED IS TO BE CAST "FOR" THE PROPOSED AMENDMENT TO THE CERTIFICATE OF INCORPORATION AND THE SPLIT OF EACH OUTSTANDING SHARE OF COMMON STOCK.

Receipt of Notice of Special Meeting of Stockholders and the accompanying Proxy Statement is acknowledged.

Date _____ 20 _____

[Name and address of stockholder]

_____

_____

_____

Please sign above as name(s) appear(s) hereon.

(When signing as attorney, executor, administrator, trustee, guardian, etc., give title as such. If joint account, each joint owner should sign.[36]

Quorum

The Model Business Corporation Act states that the majority of shares entitled to vote (represented in person or by proxy) will constitute a **quorum** at a shareholder meeting unless otherwise provided in the articles of incorporation.[37] Most states have similar provisions and permit the articles of incorporation to modify the quorum. In most states, the quorum may not be reduced to less than one-third of the shareholders entitled to vote at the meeting, although Louisiana permits reduction to as low as one-quarter of the voting shares. The reduction-in-quorum requirements may be contained in the bylaws in some states.[38]

Voting of Shares

Unless the articles of incorporation provide otherwise, each outstanding share, regardless of class, is entitled to one vote according to the provision in section 7.21 of the Model Business Corporation Act, and most states take this approach to shareholder voting. A few jurisdictions extend voting to fractional shares, permitting a corresponding fractional vote on each matter submitted to the shareholders.[39]

Shareholder voting may be altered and concentrated through several devices. The articles of incorporation may provide that shares of different classes will have more or less than one vote per share—a principle called **weighted voting**.[40] To concentrate voting power, shareholders may predetermine how their shares will be voted by using a pooling agreement or voting trust.[41]

In most cases, the affirmative vote of the majority of shares present at the meeting and entitled to vote constitutes the act of shareholders, although this provision may be modified by the articles of incorporation or bylaws. Thus, if the corporation has 100,000 shares of voting stock outstanding, 50,001 shares constitute a quorum for a meeting, and shareholder action would be taken if 25,001 shares were voted in favor of the proposition. The articles of incorporation could provide that one-third of the shares entitled to vote would constitute a quorum, in which case 33,334 shares could hold a meeting and 16,668 shares could decide any issue. In both of these cases, the shares that carry the action are less than the majority of all shares entitled to vote. Conversely, if the articles of incorporation required that 80% of the voting shares must be represented to constitute a quorum, and 80% of the represented shares must vote affirmatively to carry an issue, an affirmative vote by a minimum of 64,000 shares would be required to constitute shareholder action. The rule is to apply the appropriate percentage to the shares represented once a quorum is present.

The Model Business Corporation Act and modern corporate statutes recognize that shareholders may be grouped together (other than simply divided among classes) into separate **voting groups**, which are entitled to vote and be counted together on certain specific corporate issues. For example, the articles of incorporation could designate Class A and Class B shareholders as a single voting group for purposes of approving a transaction involving a merger, but state that Class A, Class B, and Class C shareholders would be a single voting group to decide whether the corporation should dissolve. The voting group must be described in the articles of incorporation,[42] then the quorum and voting requirements are applied based upon each voting group. For example, if Class A and Class B shareholders are a voting group for purposes of approving a merger, the majority of those shareholders, counted together, would be required for a quorum, and a majority vote among the voting group of both Class A shareholders and Class B shareholders would be required to approve the action.[43]

A word of caution: A statute may require greater than a majority vote on certain matters. The necessary shareholder vote on individual issues is specified in the following section dealing with shareholder business.

The method of voting at a shareholder meeting is not generally prescribed by statute. Although any method is acceptable, including voice vote or written ballot, written ballot is the preferable procedure to provide a record of the shares voted in favor and against a proposal. A ballot may be required for the election of directors. Moreover, shareholder action is taken by a specified percentage of shares represented at the meeting. A voice vote or show of hands indicates the shareholders' vote for each person, but if there is any disagreement, a ballot will be necessary to determine the number of *shares* (not shareholders) voting in favor of the proposition. A ballot should specifically describe the matter being submitted to shareholder vote, and the secretary of the meeting is responsible for tallying the votes. Some states permit the appointment of impartial judges of election if requested by the shareholders or required in the bylaws.[44] These judges are responsible for determining whether the required shareholder vote has been received.

EXAMPLE

Ballot

For voting at a meeting of the Shareholders of Happiness, Inc., on November 24, 2005.

ISSUE NO. _____

RESOLVED, [*here state resolution to be acted upon*]

Please record my vote:

_____ FOR

_____ AGAINST

_____ ABSTAIN

_____
Signature of Shareholder
[optional]

_____
Number of Shares

SHAREHOLDER BUSINESS AND VOTE REQUIRED

Shareholders have an indirect voice in management and, except in a close corporation, have very little direct control over the daily business affairs of the corporation. Their meetings, therefore, generally focus on receiving information about corporate business and taking action on matters that are within the ambit of shareholder control as specified in the statute, the articles of incorporation, and the bylaws.

The most important shareholder business is the election of directors. Through their right to elect directors, shareholders indirectly control the management policies and direction of their corporation. Moreover, shareholders are expected periodically to review management activities, and they may ratify and approve management acts at their annual shareholders' meeting. Most statutes also grant shareholders the right to vote directly on major decisions involving modifications in the structure of their corporation. These major fundamental changes usually significantly affect the ownership rights of the shareholder. It is also possible for the incorporators to grant greater control to the shareholders by special provisions in the articles of incorporation or bylaws. Shareholder involvement in each area of shareholder control depends on the particular structure of the corporation and the voting requirements imposed by the statute.

The agenda of a shareholder meeting, therefore, varies considerably from corporation to corporation. Certain shareholder business, however, may be expected to be conducted in every case.

Special Matters over Which Shareholders Have Control

The articles of incorporation or bylaws may reserve to the shareholders certain items of business that would otherwise be determined by the directors. The reservation of control may be as extensive as allowing complete control over all management activities, as is permitted under the close corporation statutes enacted in Delaware and elsewhere,[45] or as limited as allowing the shareholders to amend and repeal bylaws. Depending upon the local statutory authority to place control with the shareholders, the articles of incorporation or bylaws may grant shareholders the right to select officers; fix compensation; determine the stated value of no par stock; adopt, amend, and repeal bylaws; and so forth. However, there are obvious practical limitations on shareholder control in these areas. If shareholders are cohesive and few, they may comfortably be vested with these responsibilities. On the other hand, the larger the group of shareholders, the more cumbersome it becomes to take action in these management areas.

The shareholders' vote necessary to carry action on matters reserved to their control is governed by statute and may be altered by the articles of incorporation or bylaws. The Model Business Corporation Act provides that shareholder action on a matter will be approved if the votes cast by the shareholders (or within a voting group, if one is designated) favoring the action exceed the votes cast opposing the action.[46] There is a subtle distinction here that is not found in most state statutes. Most states require that shareholder matters must be approved by a majority vote of the shareholders present constituting a quorum. For example, if 100 shares were entitled to vote on a matter, and 51 shares were represented at a meeting, a quorum would be present. Under most state statutes, 26 of those shares present must vote affirmatively to approve action by shareholders. Under the Model Business Corporation Act, however, fewer than a majority could approve the action if some shareholders abstained. Thus, if 20 shares voted in favor of the action, 19 shares voted against the action, and 12 shares abstained, the matter would be approved under the act, but would not be approved under most state statutes.

Election of Directors

The election of directors is usually an item of business at each annual shareholders' meeting, since the term of office for directors is generally until the next succeeding annual shareholders' meeting and until the successor directors have been elected and qualified.[47] Even if the board of directors is classified or staggered, a certain percentage of the board will be elected each year.

Shareholders may be able to cumulate their votes in the election of directors, depending upon the local statute and articles of incorporation. Some jurisdictions require the use of the cumulative voting procedure in the election of directors as a constitutional right of the shareholder. Others have statutes requiring cumulative voting unless the articles of incorporation specifically deny it. Delaware and other states deny cumulative voting under the corporation statute, but permit the articles of incorporation to grant it. The Model Business Corporation Act also takes this approach.[48]

Cumulative voting is a procedure for voting shares in the election of directors that is designed to secure representation of the minority shareholders on the board of directors. With straight voting, the holders of a majority of the stock should be able to elect the directors who will represent their interests, and if the interests of the majority are inconsistent with the interests of the minority, the minority group may suffer without representation on the board. With cumulative voting, each share carries as many votes as there are vacancies to be filled on the board of directors, and each shareholder is permitted to distribute the votes for all his or her shares among any candidates the shareholder desires to elect.

For example, suppose Bilko Building Company has three directors to be elected every year, and has 500 shares of stock outstanding, of which Anderson owns 300 shares, Bonner owns 100 shares, and Carlyle owns 100 shares. With straight voting, each person votes his or her shares for the candidates one at a time. Suppose three directors are to be elected at the meeting. If Anderson nominates Davis, Everett, and Ford as directors, and the minority shareholders nominate Girtler to represent their interests, the votes will probably be tallied as follows with straight voting.

Anderson's 300 shares	*Bonner's 100 shares*	*Carlyle's 100 shares*
X Davis	Davis	Davis
X Everett	X Everett	X Everett
X Ford	X Ford	X Ford
Girtler	X Girtler	X Girtler

The total votes for each candidate are as follows:

Davis	300
Everett	500
Ford	500
Girtler	200

Thus, Davis, Everett, and Ford are elected to fill the three director positions, and the minority shareholders have lost in their bid to elect Girtler.

Contrast the result of this election with a result using the cumulative voting procedure. Each shareholder is entitled to as many votes as shares owned, multiplied by the number of vacancies to be filled. Thus, Anderson has 900 votes (300 shares × 3 vacancies); Bonner has 300 votes (100 × 3); and Carlyle has 300 votes (100 × 3). Each shareholder may cast his or her available votes in any manner, including applying all of them to one candidate. Therefore, if Bonner and Carlyle want to be certain to elect Girtler as their director, they may apply all of their votes for that purpose. Anderson cannot prevent Girtler's election no matter how Anderson votes. A cumulative voting ballot will look like this:

Anderson's 300 shares (900 votes)	Bonner's 100 shares (300 votes)	Carlyle's 100 shares (300 votes)
300 Davis	0 Davis	0 Davis
300 Everett	0 Everett	0 Everett
300 Ford	0 Ford	0 Ford
0 Girtler	300 Girtler	300 Girtler

The total votes for the candidates are as follows:

Girtler	600
Davis	300
Everett	300
Ford	300

Thus, Girtler is elected, and a runoff election is necessary to determine the two remaining positions between Anderson's three nominees. Anderson could have applied 601 votes for one of the other candidates, thereby ensuring that one of those candidates would beat Girtler, but that would have left Anderson with only 299 shares for another candidate, and Girtler still would have been elected.

Notice that cumulative voting ensures minority representation on the board only if the minority shareholders are cohesive and determined in electing a representative. If Bonner and Carlyle could not have agreed on a suitable candidate to represent the minority, they may have lost the success of their combined vote.

Directors may be removed with or without cause by vote of the shareholders. If a director were elected to represent the minority interests under a cumulative voting procedure, the protection of cumulative voting could be nullified if the majority shareholders could remove the minority director after the election. Consequently, state statutes usually specify that if cumulative voting is in effect for the election of directors, no director may be removed unless the same cumulative voting procedure is used in the removal action. The director cannot be removed if the votes cast against the removal would be sufficient to elect the director if cumulatively voted at an election of the entire board of directors.[49] Thus, Bonner and Carlyle could vote cumulatively *against* Girtler's removal and prevent the removal in the same manner in which they elected Girtler.

Finally, many states permit the board of directors to be classified or staggered, so that not all directors are elected each year.[50] When this classification procedure is combined with cumulative voting, it may neutralize the protective effect of cumulative voting. Suppose that in the previous example, the corporation's three directors are staggered over a three-year period. Only one director would be elected each year. Thus, cumulative voting, which authorizes the number of votes equal to the number of shares times the number of vacancies to be filled, gives

Anderson 300 votes (300 shares $\times$ 1 vacancy); Bonner 100 votes (100 $\times$ 1); and Carlyle 100 votes (100 $\times$ 1). Anderson, therefore, can always defeat Bonner and Carlyle with 300 votes to their 200, just as with straight voting. For this reason, several states permit staggering of the board only if the board consists of nine or more members.[51] That way, at least three directors will be elected each year, and the effect of cumulative voting is preserved.

The ballot for the election of directors should present all nominees and, if cumulative voting is used, should explain how to use it.

E X A M P L E

Ballot for the Election of Directors Using Straight Voting

[STRAIGHT VOTING]

Annual Meeting of the Shareholders of Happiness, Inc., November 24, 2005.

The following persons have been nominated for the Board of Directors of Happiness, Inc., to serve until the next annual meeting of the Shareholders or until their successors have been elected and qualified.

<u>Slate of Directors</u>

[Nominee]

[Nominee]

[Nominee]

[Nominee]

Other nominations

_____

_____

[write in]

FOUR DIRECTORS ARE TO BE ELECTED. PLEASE CHECK ONLY FOUR SELECTIONS. IF MORE THAN FOUR SELECTIONS ARE MADE, THIS BALLOT WILL BE VOIDED [*or* ONLY THE FIRST FOUR SELECTIONS WILL BE COUNTED].

Please enter the number of shares you own: _____ Shares

Voted for	*Name of Nominee*
_____	[Nominee]
_____	[Nominee]
_____	[Nominee]
_____	[Nominee]
_____	[write in]
_____	[write in]

_____

Signature of Shareholder

[optional]

E X A M P L E

Ballot for the Election of Directors Using Cumulative Voting

[CUMULATIVE VOTING]

Annual meeting of the Shareholders of Happiness, Inc., November 24, 2005.

The following persons have been nominated for the Board of Directors of Happiness, Inc., to serve until the next annual meeting of the Shareholders or until their successors have been elected.

<u>Slate of Directors</u>

[Nominee]

[Nominee]

[Nominee]

[Nominee]

Other nominations

_____

_____

[write in]

EXAMPLE

(continued)

FOUR DIRECTORS ARE TO BE ELECTED. YOU ARE ENTITLED TO CUMULATE YOUR VOTES IN THIS ELECTION. PLEASE COMPUTE THE NUMBER OF VOTES TO WHICH YOU ARE ENTITLED AS FOLLOWS:

Number of shares owned _____ × 4 = _____

Number of Votes

You may cast these votes for any or all of the nominees, by writing the number of votes you wish to cast for each nominee next to the name of the nominee. THE TOTAL VOTES CAST MAY NOT EXCEED THE NUMBER OF VOTES COMPUTED ABOVE. IF YOU CAST MORE VOTES THAN YOU ARE ALLOWED, OR IF THE <u>NUMBER</u> OF VOTES IS NOT ENTERED BELOW, THIS BALLOT WILL BE VOIDED.

Number of votes
cast [write number]   *Name of Nominee*

_____   [Nominee]

_____   [Nominee]

_____   [Nominee]

_____   [Nominee]

_____   [write in]

Total votes cast

_____   _____

               Signature of Shareholder
                   [optional]

Approval of Extraordinary Matters

Certain structural changes of a corporation require the approval of the shareholders because the shareholders' ownership rights as investors may be materially affected by the action. These changes may involve major modifications to the organization or financial structure of the corporation, disposition of the corporation's assets, adjustments in the ownership characteristics of the shares, or termination of business.

The most frequent structural change in the corporation is the amendment of its articles of incorporation. The organization of the corporation is described in the articles of incorporation, and any amendment to those provisions modifies the structure and probably affects the ownership characteristics of the shareholders in some manner. An amendment as minor as changing the corporate name usually must be approved by the shareholders through the amendment procedure, although the actual effect on shareholder rights may be imperceptible. Other changes may have a more obvious effect on the character of the investment, such as amending the corporation's period of duration or diminishing the scope of the business it will conduct. Other typical changes directly concern the shares themselves. These include amendments to change the aggregate number of shares the corporation has authority to issue; to exchange, divide, reclassify, redesignate, or cancel shares; to create new classes, with special preferences; to modify preferences or change the authority of the board of directors to establish series of shares; to cancel or otherwise affect accumulated distributions; and to limit, deny, or grant preemptive rights of shareholders.

Recognizing the cumbersome procedure required to approve amendments to the articles of incorporation, the Model Business Corporation Act has begun a trend of permitting the board of directors to make certain changes without shareholder approval. The relaxed rules permit the board alone to extend the duration of the corporation, delete the names and addresses of directors and the registered agent, authorize a stock split or dividend by increasing the total number of shares, and make certain changes in the corporation's name.[52] In most states, however, any amendment to the articles of incorporation must be submitted to a vote of the shareholders.[53]

Merger, share exchange, or **consolidation** of the corporation and disposition of corporate assets other than in the ordinary course of business also require special shareholder approval. In a merger, one corporation joins another, the merging corporation ceases to exist, and the surviving corporation continues business with the assets, liabilities, and shareholders of both corporations. In a share exchange or consolidation, two corporations join to form a new corporation, and both of the original corporations may cease to exist. The ownership rights of the shareholders of the constituent corporations will be modified in these transactions. The corporation that is the survivor to the merger will probably issue new shares of stock to the shareholders of the merged corporation, which may dilute the ownership interests of the shareholders in the survivor corporation. The shareholders of the merged corporation will likely have exchanged their stock for shares of the survivor corporation. In a share exchange procedure, one corporation exchanges its shares for all or part of another corporation, or two corporations form a new corporation and the new corporation resulting from the combination will issue new securities to shareholders of both old corporations. The shareholders should have some say in these matters. Similarly, if the directors of the corporation intend to sell or otherwise dispose of substantially all of the assets of the corporation, it may be necessary to obtain shareholder approval. Such approval is not necessary, however, when the corporation merely sells goods from inventory, such as when a department store sells television sets to its customers. However, when the sale of assets is outside the scope of the ordinary course of business, as when the department store sells its display counters, cash registers, and substantially all of its inventory in one transaction with another department store, the shareholders should be asked for their approval.

Finally, the shareholders' ownership rights certainly will be affected by a dissolution of their corporation. The directors are not vested with the authority to dissolve the corporation at will if shares have been issued; voluntary dissolution is regarded as a fundamental change requiring shareholder approval. Similarly, if the shareholders have approved dissolution of their corporation, the directors may not revoke the dissolution proceedings without affirmative shareholder approval of the revocation.

The specific procedures for the approval of these corporate structural modifications are discussed in a later chapter,[54] but the vote necessary for shareholder approval is discussed here. The Model Business Corporation Act originally provided that shareholder action on these matters would be carried by the affirmative vote of the holders of two-thirds of the shares entitled to vote on the issue. If a particular class was entitled to vote on the issue as a class,[55] the two-thirds affirmative vote of that class was also required. Many states still require this percentage of shareholder vote to approve structural modifications to the corporation. The Model Business Corporation Act, however, now merely requires a majority vote by the appropriate shares for approval, in order to comply with "contemporary practice in similar institutional matters." The act, like other jurisdictions that permit approval by the majority, allows the articles of incorporation to require a greater proportion of shareholder votes, if the extra shareholder protection is desired in these special areas. When a two-thirds vote is required for approval of the fundamental corporate changes, the minority shareholders holding more than one-third of the voting stock can successfully block such actions by the majority. Since the majority shareholders may be at odds with the minority, and there are cases where the majority stands to profit from such transactions, the extra protection for the minority shareholders may be important.

ACTION WITHOUT A MEETING

Notwithstanding the foregoing discussion intimating that shareholder and director meetings are necessary for effective corporate action, state law usually prescribes a written consent procedure for these intracorporate groups to take action without a formal meeting. The Model Business Corporation Act permits written consent by shareholders in section 7.04 and by directors in section 8.21. The act further provides that the articles of incorporation or bylaws can deny this written consent procedure for directors, but it does not allow restrictions on the written consent procedure by shareholders. All states now have comparable provisions.

The statutory requirements for taking action without a meeting are that the proposed action would have been proper to submit to a regular meeting, and that consent in writing setting forth the proposed action must be obtained for all shareholders or all directors, as the case may be. Thus, unanimous consent is required for written action without a meeting.

EXAMPLE

Unanimous Consent to Action of the Board of Directors

Pursuant to the provisions of the Nebraska Corporation Code, the following action is taken by the board of directors of Happiness, Inc., by unanimous written consent as if a meeting of the board of directors had been properly called pursuant to notice and all directors were present and voting in favor of such action.

RESOLVED, that the salary of the vice-president be increased from the sum of $150,000.00 per year to the sum of $200,000.00 per year.

IN WITNESS WHEREOF, we have executed this unanimous Consent of Action on the dates set forth after our respective names, effective November 10, 2005.

_____	_____
[Director]	Date
_____	_____
[Director]	Date
_____	_____
[Director]	Date

EXAMPLE

Unanimous Consent to Action of the Shareholders

Pursuant to the provisions of the Nebraska Corporation Code, the following action is taken by the shareholders of Happiness, Inc., by unanimous written consent, as if a meeting of the shareholders had been properly called pursuant to notice and all shareholders entitled to vote on the matters presented herein had been present and voting in favor of such action.

There are 100,000 shares entitled to vote on the matters presented herein, and the undersigned shareholders are the holders of record of all such shares on the date of this Unanimous Consent of the Shareholders.

RESOLVED, that the action of the officers and directors of this corporation in making an investment in securities of Trouble, Inc., as set forth in the report that the corporation mailed to all stockholders of record on May 1, 2005, be and the same hereby is ratified.

IN WITNESS WHEREOF, the undersigned, constituting all of the shareholders of the corporation entitled to vote on the matters presented herein, have executed this unanimous Consent to Action of the Shareholders on the dates set forth after our respective names, effective November 10, 2005.

_____	_____
[Shareholder] [Number of shares]	[Date]
_____	_____
[Shareholder] [Number of shares]	[Date]
_____	_____
[Shareholder] [Number of shares]	[Date]
_____	_____
[Shareholder] [Number of shares]	[Date]

[etc.]

The only major variations among the statutes with consent-to-action provisions are whether the articles of incorporation or bylaws may deny this procedure for directors' meetings, and the percentage of shareholders required to file written consent in order to carry the shareholder action. Most states do not authorize a limitation on the directors' rights to file written consent and act without a meeting. The Model Business Corporation Act, Delaware, and New Jersey allow the certificate or articles of incorporation or bylaws to alter this provision.

Delaware allows for less-than-unanimous approval for shareholder consent. The statute provides that the holders of outstanding stock having at least the minimum number of votes that would be necessary to approve such action at a meeting may consent in writing and thereby bind the shareholders. The remaining shareholders are then entitled to notice of the action so taken.[56] Other states authorize the articles of incorporation or bylaws to prescribe a less-than-unanimous number for shareholder written consent.[57] Otherwise, most states provide that all of the shareholders must file written consent to act without a meeting.

The use of shareholder consent without a meeting should be limited to small, close corporations. The requirements of unanimity and of obtaining the signatures of all shareholders make the procedure impracticable for larger groups of shareholders and impossible for a publicly held corporation.

MINUTES

There is no mandatory procedure for conducting meetings of shareholders and directors. In many cases, these meetings are conducted in an informal manner, but they usually become more formal as the group becomes larger. The science of conducting a corporate meeting for a large intracorporate group has been described with forms and guidelines in various publications that are available to corporate secretaries,[58] so formal meeting procedures escapes further elaboration here.

It is always necessary to follow the statutory requirements, such as notice, voting, and solicitation of proxies, for every meeting. Consequently, the minutes of the meeting should always reflect that the statutory requirements have been observed. The minutes of the meeting constitute the permanent written record of the corporate history, and all matters considered at a meeting must be carefully recorded in order to trace the origin of all corporate actions. (See Exhibit 10–1, Special Meeting of the Board of Directors, and Exhibit 10–2, Special Meeting of the Shareholders.)

Exhibit 10–1.

Special Meeting of the Board of Directors

A Special Meeting of the Board of Directors of _____, Inc., was held at _____, _____, _____ on the _____ day of _____, 20 ___, at ____ o'clock.

The meeting was called pursuant to section _____ of the _____ Corporation Code [and] [or] article ____ of the Articles of Incorporation of the corporation [and] [or] section ____ of the Bylaws of the corporation.

The following directors were present:_____.
The following directors were absent:_____.

The presence of the foregoing directors constitutes a quorum. The following other persons were also present:_____.

The meeting was held pursuant to notice addressed to each director in accordance with the statute, the Articles of Incorporation, and the Bylaws of the corporation. A copy of the notice, together with the Secretary's certificate that such notice was properly mailed or delivered, is attached to the minutes of the meeting.

[or]

The meeting is held pursuant to Waiver of Notice from each director, a copy of which is attached to the minutes of the meeting.

The minutes of the meeting of the Board of Directors on _____, 20 ___, were approved as read.

The President stated that the purpose of the meeting was to [here describe purpose in narrative form].

Following full discussion, upon motion duly made, seconded and unanimously adopted it was

RESOLVED, [here describe substance of resolution]

[or]

Following full discussion, upon motion duly made by _____, seconded by _____, the following directors voted in favor: __[names]__ ; and the following directors voted against: __[names]__ ; the following resolution:

RESOLVED, [here describe substance of resolution].

The Treasurer of the corporation reported on the financial condition of the corporation, a copy of which is attached to these minutes.

The Board of Directors informally discussed [here describe] and no action was taken at this time.

There being no further business, the meeting was adjourned.

_____
Secretary

Exhibit 10–2.

Special Meeting of the
Shareholders

A Special Meeting of the Shareholders of _____, Inc., was held at _____, _____, _____on the day of _____, 20_____, at _____o'clock.

The meeting was called pursuant to section _____of the _____Corporation Code [and] [or] article _____of the Articles of Incorporation [and] [or] section _____of the Bylaws of the corporation, by the [President] [Secretary] [The holders of ___% of the shares entitled to vote] [other].

[A copy of the call of the meeting dated _____, 20_____, addressed to the Secretary of the corporation and signed by the holders of _____% of the shares entitled to vote, is attached to the minutes of this meeting.]

The meeting was held pursuant to notice addressed to each shareholder in accordance with the statute, the Articles of Incorporation, and the Bylaws of the corporation. A copy of the notice, together with the Secretary's certificate that such notice was properly mailed or delivered to each Shareholder, is attached to the minutes of the meeting.

The Board of Directors, by resolution dated _____, 20_____, set _____, 20_____, as the record date for the determination of the Shareholders entitled to vote at this meeting, and only Shareholders of record on that date are entitled to vote.

[or]

The meeting was held pursuant to Waiver of Notice from each Shareholder, a copy of which is attached to the minutes of this meeting.

Shareholders holding _____Shares of record were present at the meeting. Shareholders holding _____Shares of record were represented by proxy at the meeting, and their shares were voted by _____, duly constituted proxy in their names.

The minutes of the Shareholder meeting on _____, 20_____, were approved as read.

The President stated that the purpose of the meeting was to [here describe purpose in narrative form].

Following full discussion, upon motion duly made, and seconded, _____Shares voted in person in favor; _____Shares voted by proxy in favor; _____Shares voted in person against; and _____Shares voted by proxy against the following resolution:

RESOLVED, [here describe substance of resolution].

The Treasurer of the corporation reported on the financial condition of the corporation, a copy of which is attached to these minutes.

Several questions were raised by the Shareholders concerning [here describe informal discussion and questions]. No action was taken on these matters.

There being no further business, the meeting was adjourned.

_____
Secretary

The secretary of the corporation is usually given the privilege of keeping the minutes. The only guidelines for recording minutes are that the secretary must comply with instructions given by the board of directors and by the chair of the meeting, and the secretary must compose the minutes in such a way that they constitute an accurate and complete transcription of the action taken by the intracorporate group at the particular meeting recorded. Otherwise, the secretary has broad discretion in the manner in which the minutes will be kept. Counsel may assist the secretary in establishing a corporate minute policy after formation of the corporation. As a general guide, all minutes should include at least the following:

1. name of the corporation;
2. date;
3. place where the meeting is held;
4. special statutory, articles of incorporation, or bylaw authority under which the meeting is called;

5. persons present, persons absent, or shares represented in person or by proxy;
6. statement that the meeting is held pursuant to a notice or waiver that is attached to the minutes;
7. nature of the meeting (regular or special);
8. approval of minutes of previous meetings;
9. substance of the issues presented at the meeting, and description of how they were submitted and by whom;
10. decision and vote of the intracorporate group on each issue, in resolution form;
11. presentation of all reports, with copies attached if a report is written and a summary of the report if it is oral;
12. summary of the other business before the meeting; and
13. statement that the meeting was properly adjourned and the time of adjournment.

If the meeting is a directors' meeting, the directors present and absent should be named. It is important to report correctly the directors' vote on each resolution. If the vote is unanimous, that should be stated. If any director abstains or dissents, that director's name and vote should be stated, particularly if there is any possibility that the issue of personal liability of directors for the action taken may arise. For example, if the director were voting on the issuance of a dividend but funds were not legally available for payment of the dividend, the recording of a dissent may be necessary to relieve the director from liability for illegally declared dividends. If a director is "interested" in the particular action, as when the contract being considered by the board of directors is with another corporation in which the director is financially interested, it should be noted that the interested director did not vote or left the room during the discussion.[59]

The names of the shareholders present at a shareholder meeting and the number of shares they hold may be noted if the group is small. Otherwise, the number of shares represented in person and by proxy should be listed.

Informal activity that occurs during a meeting should not be described in unnecessary detail. It is not necessary to record all activities or conversations that occur at a meeting. However, informal information about tentative corporate plans and current business conditions may be reported if it was discussed at the meeting. In this regard, if the chair obtains the informal consensus of the group on any particular matter, the minutes should express the affirmative reaction of those present.

SPECIAL PREPARATION FOR PUBLIC COMPANY SHAREHOLDER MEETINGS

For a publicly held corporation, there may be months of preparation by counsel and the corporate secretary to establish an orderly schedule to ensure that the meeting will run smoothly. The first step in organizing the annual meeting is to prepare and adhere to a schedule or checklist of tasks to be completed prior to the meeting, often referred to as a **timetable**. The timetable establishes deadlines for tasks to be performed prior to the meeting, assigns responsibility for the performance of the tasks, and serves as a checklist of the tasks completed. The timetable must take into account the time periods necessary to prepare, file, and distribute the proxy statement and proxy forms to the shareholders.[60]

A typical timetable includes deadlines for the following:

1. shareholder proposals (Shareholders are permitted to propose issues to be voted upon at shareholder meetings, and these proposals must be described in the proxy statement sent to all shareholders before the meeting. These issues often usually involve issues of environmental, civil rights, or social policy and are presented by shareholders who want to change or challenge the corporation's policies on such matters. These shareholders are often called *corporate gadflies*);
2. the ordering of envelopes for mailing and stock for proxy and proxy statements;
3. preparation and distribution of the officers' and directors' questionnaires for the proxy materials (soliciting individual and financial information required for disclosure in the proxy

materials since it will be necessary to disclose information about management and their share ownership in the proxy statement);

4. preparation of the preliminary proxy materials;
5. determination of the availability of nominees (persons who are designated in the proxy materials as nominees to vote the proxies);
6. reservation of the meeting place;
7. setting the record date for determination of shareholders entitled to vote at the meeting;
8. notifying exchanges, depositaries, brokers, banks, proxy agents and other nominees of the record date;
9. mailing of "search cards" to brokers and others so the proxy statement materials can be distributed to all shareholders;
10. committee or board approval of the proxy materials;
11. mailing preliminary copies of documents and filing fees to the Securities and Exchange Commission, allowing time for the Commission's comments and approval;
12. mailing proxy material and annual reports to the shareholders, brokers, bank, depositaries, proxy agents and other nominees, the appropriate stock exchanges, and the Securities and Exchange Commission;
13. mailing of any follow-up correspondence or making of follow-up telephone calls;
14. holding the annual meeting; and
15. sending postmeeting reports to the shareholders.[61]

A word of caution about the use of a timetable is appropriate. It should not be a rigid document that must be slavishly followed. The schedule may be exhaustive and unrealistic, and counsel must revise it as often as necessary to ensure that all of the important tasks will be completed and the time available will be used effectively.

The presiding officer of the meeting should be selected in accordance with the bylaws, or if the bylaws do not designate the chair of the meeting, the board of directors should appoint a chair in advance of the meeting. The annual meeting is a unique opportunity for management to meet and impress shareholders on a personal basis. The chair should be a person skilled as a "master of ceremonies" and as a "facilitator." Usually the Chairman of the Board and Chief Executive Officer share the duties of chairing the meeting (whether or not they have such skills). The function of the chair is to preside over the meeting and to defer to or call on others to provide expert information regarding the operations of the corporation.

In selecting the location of the meeting, consideration should be given to the corporate policy of attempting to reach as many shareholders as possible. Some corporations prefer to have their meeting at the same location each year so that the company is familiar with the setting of its meeting, which minimizes the unexpected problems that can result from unfamiliarity with new locations. Other corporations prefer to have meetings in various locations, so that shareholders in different parts of the country or world will be able to attend the meeting at some time. The facilities for the meeting should be capable of accommodating a crowd. Most meeting planners seriously consider the acoustics, sound equipment, lighting, ventilation, seating capacity, parking facilities, availability of caucus rooms, and expense of the various facilities under consideration. Many statutes, including the Model Business Corporation Act, permit corporations with geographically diverse shareholders to use telecommunications innovations that allow closed circuit or satellite meetings in remote locations simultaneously with the principal meeting. Some corporations make their annual meeting an important social and public relations event.

A script usually is prepared for the chair and other participants in the meeting to ensure that all necessary items are considered and acted upon appropriately. A "background binder" or "fact book" is also prepared to summarize important background information regarding the various areas of the corporation's business. Such documents as the articles of incorporation, bylaws, recent reports to the Securities and Exchange Commission, recent annual reports to the shareholders, and proxy statements usually are included in this book. Counsel should anticipate questions that are likely to be presented by shareholders and summarize the questions and answers in the information book. Likely topics include questions that have been asked at previous shareholder meetings and controversial issues that have been contained in the company's annual report. The script should include a complete text of anticipated comments to be made by the chair, other officers, and any scheduled speakers. However, the chair should be allowed to remain flexible and should use the script only as a guide. Depending upon the reaction of the shareholders, the chair may need to change the agenda or deviate from the script to manage the meeting appropriately.

The script should identify by name or title each person who must make a required response at the meeting. An occasional anxious moment will occur at a meeting when a question is asked or a response is required and no one is designated in the script to respond. Counsel should be prepared to nudge a nearby officer or director to solicit a response if the script has not anticipated a situation. Skilled managers may freeze if they have been told to follow a script and the script does not say they should speak. The script is only for the internal use of management participating in the meeting; it is never distributed to the shareholders in attendance.

The shareholders receive a printed agenda in advance of the meeting; the agenda usually is prepared by counsel. A typical agenda includes the following:

1. call to order;
2. announcements and introductions;
3. declaration of a quorum;
4. voting on directors;
5. voting on auditors;
6. voting on stockholders' proposals;
7. remarks by management;
8. presentation of reports of election inspectors who monitor the counting of votes and proxies;
9. discussions and questions; and
10. adjournment.[62]

Note the position of the "discussion" section of the meeting on the agenda. By placing general discussion toward the end of the agenda, the chair is able to curtail unwanted general discussions by the shareholders on any of the prior topics, such as election of directors. The chair may deviate from the agenda, however, if it is appropriate to do so.

KEY TERMS

nominal, or dummy, directors	Subchapter S election	quorum
share subscription	attachments to minutes	weighted voting
cash subscription	regular meetings	voting groups
property subscription	special meetings	merger
call for consideration due	holder of record	share exchange
escrow of shares	record date	consolidation
Section 1244 plan	proxy	timetable

WEB RESOURCES

Access to specific provisions of state laws regarding shareholder and director meetings may be obtained through the Legal Information Institute maintained at the Cornell Law School:

<http://www.law.cornell.edu>

Forms for resolutions, notices, and text of other documents relevant to shareholder and director meetings are available at

<http://www.uslegalforms.com>

Topics of interest to corporate secretaries, including information about stock exchanges, financial information, investor relations, corporate governance, news, and Internet search and navigational tools (including links to further resources) may be accessed at

<http://www.ascs.org>
<http://www.corpgov.net>

Explanation of the terminology applicable to the position of corporate secretary and the duties associated with the position is available at

<http://www.chasemellon.com>

The text of the proxy regulations and the federal and state securities laws that apply for public solicitation of shareholders at a meeting may be reviewed at the following sites:

<http://www.sec.gov>
<http://www.seclaw.com>
<http://www.law.cornell.edu>

CASES

UNITED STATES v. FALCONE

934 F.2d 1528 (1991)
PER CURIAM

[Robert and Sandra Falcone were convicted of federal bank fraud because they opened accounts with a federal bank in the name of a Florida corporation, Ocean General Agency, Inc. (OGA) and obtained money by stamping the signature of the corporate treasurer, Wellington "Duke" Peay on checks drawn on the account. The corporate records of OGA required two signatures on each check, Robert Falcone's and either Edwin Rillo's or Duke Peay's.]

Robert Falcone argues that the evidence was insufficient to support his section 1344(a)(2) convictions for obtaining money from Orange State with the checks stamped with Peay's signature without Peay's authorization. Falcone points out that OGA's articles of incorporation provided that the shareholders, not a board of directors, would manage the corporation; the articles, moreover, did not specifically require that the shareholders act as a majority or quorum when they exercised their management power. He contends, therefore, that Sandra Falcone, as a minority shareholder, could, without the knowledge or consent of the other shareholder/directors or officers of the corporation, validly define permitted uses for and use the signature stamp, especially as no corporate resolution expressly forbade or limited use of the stamp. That Peay himself did not authorize the use of the stamp on the checks, according to Falcone, is irrelevant, because Peay was not a shareholder and thus had no power to take corporate action. Falcone concludes that Sandra Falcone's use of the stamp, or his own use pursuant to her authorization, could not be a false or fraudulent representation. We disagree.

In Florida, the board of directors of a corporation generally manage the company, and the shareholders are "without power, aside from that which is delegated to them as agents, to represent the corporation or act for it in relation to its normal business." [Citations omitted.] Florida corporation law in effect when OGA was incorporated, however, did permit a corporation, in its articles of incorporation, to provide that the shareholders, rather than the board, would manage the corporation. *See id.* Thus, Falcone is correct that, under OGA's articles of incorporation, the shareholders retained management power.

Falcone cites no law in support of the proposition that when a corporation's articles provide that the shareholders will manage the corporation but do not expressly provide that they must act collectively or by majority vote, any minority shareholder may, without the assent or knowledge of the other shareholders, make management decisions and act for the corporation. It is perhaps arguable that such a clause in the articles, if the shareholders make no further provision—in the bylaws or otherwise—defining the way in which they will exercise their management power, allows each shareholder unilaterally to function as a general manager of the corporation—essentially turning the corporation into a partnership. In that case, each shareholder would have the power to act individually for the corporation, constrained only by their fiduciary duty to the corporation and the other shareholders. We note, however, that such a result, in a corporation with several shareholders, might lead quickly to anarchy.

We do not decide, however, whether Falcone's interpretation of this clause in OGA's articles is correct under Florida law, because the shareholders of OGA, exercising their management power, chose, in early 1985, to elect themselves (plus Wayne Dent) as a board of directors. Essentially, the shareholders decided that they would manage the corporation collectively, acting as a board of directors; they therefore defined the manner in which they intended to exercise the general management powers granted them by the articles. As board members, the shareholders could act collectively by majority vote taken at a meeting or by unanimous written consent to action taken without meeting, or, because OGA was a close corporation, in limited circumstances by an informal meeting or discussion of all shareholder/directors, *see Etheredge v. Barrow,* 102 So.2d 660,

663 (Fla.Dist.Ct.App.1958). Each shareholder/director could not, however, act for the corporation individually unless a majority of the shareholder/directors, acting as a board, had given the individual shareholder general management power or express or implied authority to act. 5 W. Fletcher, Cylopedia of the Law of Private Corporations § 2101, at 527 (rev. perm. ed. 1987) ("[t]he directors . . . of a corporation are vested with its management, not as individuals, but as a board and, as a general rule, they can act so as to bind the corporation only when they act as a board and at a legal meeting").

Acting collectively, the shareholder/directors appointed officers (Rillo, as president and treasurer; Peay, as vice president; and Sandra Falcone, as secretary) to run OGA's day-to-day business. They also passed a corporate resolution requiring two signatures on OGA's banking transactions at Orange State.

Contrary to Falcone's assertion, therefore, Peay could authorize the use of, and define permitted uses for, the signature stamp. Pursuant to the corporate banking resolution, validly passed by the shareholders acting as a board of directors, Peay was a required signor on the Orange State accounts. As such, he could sign OGA checks individually or authorize an agent to affix his signature, either by hand or by the use of a signature stamp. He testified, at trial, that he did authorize the use of such a stamp for limited purposes. *See supra* note 10.

After the shareholders decided to manage the corporation as a board and appointed officers, Sandra Falcone could act for the corporation in two capacities, as one member of the board of directors or as secretary. As a board member, she could not act individually, and there is no evidence that the board ever expressly or impliedly granted her the power to circumvent the requirement that Peay sign (and, thus, authorize) all checks. *See* 5 W. Fletcher, *supra* p. 1543, § 2101, at 527.

As secretary, likewise, she had no authority inherent in her office to expand the permitted uses of the stamp, or to use it in a manner that Peay had not authorized. Under Florida law, "[t]he Secretary of a corporation, merely as such, is a ministerial officer, without authority to transact the business of the corporation upon his volition and judgment." *Ideal Foods, Inc. v. Action Leasing Corp.,* 413 So.2d 416, 417 (Fla.Dist.Ct.App.1982). A secretary "has none of the powers of a general or managing agent," 2A W. Fletcher, *supra* p. 1543, § 637, at 182, and "has no power by virtue of his office to execute . . . checks," *id.* § 641, at 191. Although the Secretary, "[l]ike every other corporate agent," "may have more extensive functions than those ordinarily incident to the office," *Ideal Foods,* 413 So.2d at 417 n. 1, there is no evidence in this case that Sandra Falcone's power as secretary was more extensive than the norm or that the board ever granted her express or implied authority to designate new uses for the stamp or to use it without Peay's authorization; indeed, the testimony at trial indicated that she had very little to do with the day-to-day operation and management of the company.

In neither of her roles, therefore, did Sandra Falcone have the authority or power, either inherent in her position or expressly or impliedly granted by the shareholder/directors, individually to authorize the use of the stamp or Peay's signature for purposes beyond the limited ones he had approved or to stamp checks with Peay's signature without his authorization.

* * *

MYHRE v. MYHRE
554 P.2d 276 (Mont. 1976)
BENNETT, DISTRICT JUDGE

[Eric Myhre sued his mother and father, Gertrude and Thor Myhre, concerning an agreement to transfer stock in the family advertising company, alleging that his father wrongfully removed him as vice-president of the company. The trial court held that Eric was entitled to the stock he had been promised, and the court enjoined the corporation from removing Eric as vice-president. Thor Myhre appealed, arguing, among other things, that Eric had been properly fired.]

* * *

In his letter dismissing Eric from employment by the corporation, Thor made it clear he was not attempting to alter Eric's status as either a vice president or a member of the board. There is no evidence of a written contract or agreement between Eric and the board as to Eric's employment by the company. Uncontradicted testimony and pleadings by Eric established he did not receive any compensation as vice president or director; he was employed as manager of the Great Falls office and in the year 1974 his salary was increased by Thor without board action. The whole record shows this was a closely held family corporation with Thor acting as head of the corporation as well as the family and carrying on the corporate operations pretty much as he wished with the approval of the board. Finally, the owners of the majority of the stock were aware of Thor's move, both before and after it was made, and they ratified it at the next board of directors meeting.

We conclude from this that Eric wore three hats vis-a-vis the corporation: he was a director, an officer and an employee. (As to divisibility of status, see 2 Fletcher Cyclopedia Corporations, Section 266, p. 15, Perm.Ed., 1969). He was discharged as an employee and not as director or officer. As an employee, he had no enforceable contract of employment with the board. As president, acting for the chairman of the board, Thor Myhre had authority to hire and fire employees. His dismissal of Eric was informally approved at the time by directors with control of a majority of the corporation's stock and formally ratified at the next meeting of the board of directors. Where the directors of a corporation are the only stockholders, they may act for the corporation without formal meetings. Formal meetings can also be waived by custom or general consent, which seems

to have been the case with the Myhre Corporation. See 2 Fletcher Cyclopedia Corporations, Section 394 at pp. 236, 237 and discussion and cases 19 Am.Jur.2d Corporations, §§ 1121 and 1122.

For the above reasons, the award of damages to the plaintiff should be set aside, as should the injunction against removal of Eric from employment.

* * *

PROBLEMS

1. Notice for a shareholder's meeting for a Model Act corporation must be sent how many days before the meeting? How early before the meeting may notice be sent?

2. ABC Corporation has 20,000 shares of common stock authorized, 2,000 of which are treasury shares and 1,000 of which are issued and outstanding:
   a. What is the minimum number of shares required to constitute a quorum under your state statute?
   b. What is the minimum number of shares that may constitute a quorum if the articles of incorporation so provide?
   c. What is the maximum number of shares that may constitute a quorum if the articles of incorporation so provide?
   d. What number of shares are required to be voted affirmatively to pass shareholder action if a bare quorum is present under (a), (b), or (c)?

3. Which of the following statements(s) is (are) true under the Model Act? A voting list of shareholders:
   a. must be kept available for inspection for 10 days at the meeting place.
   b. only lists record holders entitled to vote at the meeting.
   c. must be prepared on the record date.
   d. is subject to challenge by any shareholder.

4. What is the statutory minimum number of directors to constitute a quorum in your local corporation law?

5. What is the statutory maximum number of directors to constitute a quorum if the articles of incorporation so provide in your local corporation law?

6. Everready Corporation has 2,000 authorized voting shares, of which 100 shares are treasury shares and 1,900 shares are outstanding. If persons owning 1,000 shares were present and voting at a meeting and cumulative voting were used:
   a. How many votes would be needed to be certain to elect one of three directors?
      (1) 251
      (2) 751
      (3) 1434
      (4) 1501
   b. How many shares would be necessary to elect one of nine directors?
      (1) 101
      (2) 191
      (3) 251
      (4) 901

7. On normal shareholder matters, which of the following statement(s) about Everready Corporation (see problem 6, above) is (are) correct?
   a. The articles of incorporation could lower the quorum of shareholders to as low as 667 shares.
   b. An affirmative vote of 1,001 shares is necessary for shareholder approval.
   c. If the articles of incorporation are silent, a quorum would be 951 shares.
   d. If the articles of incorporation are silent, the minimum affirmative vote for shareholder approval would be 501 shares.

PRATICE ASSIGNMENTS

1. Review the Model Act sections concerning shareholder and director meetings and prepare the following:
   a. a timetable for the directors' regular meeting;
   b. a timetable for the shareholders' annual meeting;
   c. a notice for the directors' regular meeting;
   d. a notice for the shareholders' annual meeting; and
   e. a waiver of notice for a director.

2. Join members of your family or friends and conduct an organizational meeting of a hypothetical corporation you are forming. Make up all of the facts you need to

complete resolutions and to conduct the business required. Prepare minutes of the meeting.

3. Contact a publicly owned company in your area, and ask to receive a copy of their latest annual report and proxy statement. Prepare resolutions for adoption by their board of directors for the transactions described in the proxy statement to be voted upon at the annual meeting.

ENDNOTES

1. See Chapter 15.

2. See "Corporate Existence" in Chapter 8.

3. See Model Business Corporation Act (hereafter M.B.C.A.) § 2.05 (organizational meeting of incorporators or initial directors).

4. See "Formalities after Formation of a Corporation" in Chapter 8.

5. E.g., Pennsylvania, 15 Pa. Stat. Ann. § 1310.

6. M.B.C.A. § 2.05.

7. See "Certificates for Shares" in Chapter 9.

8. See "Ownership and Management of a Corporation" in Chapter 6; "Preincorporation Share Subscriptions" in Chapter 8.

9. See "Preincorporation Share Subscriptions" in Chapter 8.

10. M.B.C.A. § 6.20.

11. See "Approval of Action Taken at Previous Meetings" earlier in this section.

12. DeLano Service, Allegan, Mich. Form R-10.

13. See "Selection and Registration of Corporate Name" in Chapter 8.

14. Internal Revenue Code of 1986, U.S.C.A. § 1244(c) (3).

15. See "Taxation of a Corporation" in Chapter 6.

16. Substantive elements of the Subchapter S election are discussed in "Taxation of a Corporation" in Chapter 6.

17. See "Bylaws" in Chapter 8.

18. M.B.C.A. § 8.20.

19. See the sample bylaw provisions regulating directors' meetings in "Bylaws" in Chapter 8 and Exhibit I–10 in Appendix I.

20. See M.B.C.A. § 8.23.

21. See the bylaw provisions in "Bylaws" in Chapter 8 and Exhibit I–10 in Appendix I, and the directors' resolution in "Directors' Regular and Special Meetings" earlier in this chapter.

22. M.B.C.A. § 8.22.

23. M.B.C.A. § 7.01.

24. E.g., Nebraska, Neb. Rev. Stat. § 21–2053 (application to a court after fifteen months without a meeting).

25. In Massachusetts, the holders of one-tenth of the voting shares may call a special meeting if the annual meeting has not been held. Mass. Gen. Laws Ann. ch. 156B, § 33 (West).

26. M.B.C.A. § 7.02.

27. See M.B.C.A. §§ 7.05 (d), 7.07.

28. M.B.C.A. § 7.05.

29. M.B.C.A. § 7.05.

30. E.g., New Jersey, N.J. Stat. Ann. § 14A:5–4 (West).

31. M.B.C.A. § 7.05.

32. For further elaboration on voting procedures for these transactions, see "Merger, Consolidation, and Exchange" and "Sale, Mortgage, or Other Disposition of Assets" in Chapter 15.

33. See "Directors' Regular and Special Meetings" earlier in this chapter.

34. M.B.C.A. § 7.22.

35. Securities Exchange Act of 1934, 15 U.S.C.A. § 78n, and the rules promulgated thereunder. See "Public Corporations" in Chapter 7.

36. This proxy must be accompanied by a special notice and a proxy solicitation statement, prepared in accordance with the Securities Exchange Act of 1934.

37. M.B.C.A. § 7.25.

38. E.g., New York, N.Y. Bus. Corp. Law § 608 (McKinney).

39. M.B.C.A. § 6.04(c).

40. Variations in voting rights between classes of shares are discussed in "Common Stock Rights" and "Preferred Stock Rights" in Chapter 9.

41. These shareholder agreements are most frequently found in close corporations. See "Concentration of Voting Power" in Chapter 13.

42. M.B.C.A. § 1.40(26).

43. M.B.C.A. §§ 7.25, 7.26.

44. E.g., California, Corp. Code § 707 (West); New York, N.Y. Bus. Corp. Law § 610 (McKinney).

45. See "Close Corporation" in Chapter 7.

46. M.B.C.A. § 7.25.

47. M.B.C.A. § 8.05.

48. M.B.C.A. § 7.28 (b); see "The Articles of Incorporation" in Chapter 8.

49. M.B.C.A. § 8.08.

50. See "Ownership and Management of a Corporation" in Chapter 4; "The Articles of Incorporation" in Chapter 8.

51. E.g. California, Cal. Gen. Corp. Law § 301.5.

52. M.B.C.A. § 10.05

53. Further elaboration on the procedure to amend the articles of incorporation is contained in "Amendments of the Articles of Incorporation" in Chapter 15.

54. See Chapter 15.

55. See "Preferred Stock Rights" in Chapter 9.

56. Del. Code Ann. tit. 8, § 228.

57. E.g., New York, N.Y. Bus. Corp. Law § 615 (McKinney) (certificate of incorporation): Pennsylvania, 15 Pa. Stat. Ann. § 1766 (by-laws).

58. See CCH Corporate and Finance Group, Corporate Secretaries Guide (2003) supplemented monthly and available through <http://www.onlinesotre.cch.com>.

59. See M.B.C.A. § 8.31.

60. See "Public Corporations" in Chapter 7.

61. V. Futter, Shareholder Meetings, reprinted in Shareholder Meetings and Shareholder Control in Today's Securities Markets 489, 492–94 (P.L.I. 1985).

62. R. F. Balotti and J. Finkelstein, 2 Delaware Law of Corporation and Business Organizations § 7.53 (2000).

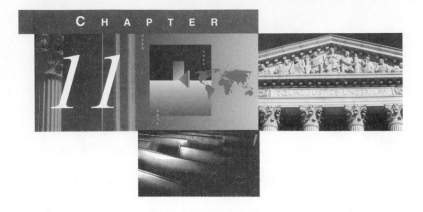

CORPORATE DIVIDENDS AND OTHER DISTRIBUTIONS

TYPES OF CORPORATE DISTRIBUTIONS

One investment objective of share ownership is the receipt of profit distributions or dividends. The attractiveness of a stock investment is measured by this yield in addition to the projected value appreciation of the shares as the corporate business prospers. Shares are also entitled to receive a proportionate share of the assets of the corporation when the business is dissolved and liquidated. These distributions to shareholders are the subject matter of this chapter.

The revised Model Business Corporation Act has developed a series of financial provisions governing distributions from the corporation to its shareholders. Section 1.40 defines a **distribution** as a "direct or indirect transfer of money or other property (except its own shares) or the incurrence of an indebtedness by a corporation to or for the benefit of its shareholders in respect of any of its shares. A distribution may be in the form of a declaration or payment of a dividend; a purchase, redemption or other acquisition of shares; a distribution of indebtedness; or otherwise." Modern corporate practice is to refer to all of these payments to shareholders as distributions, regardless of whether they represent a distribution of corporate profits or a distribution of assets in liquidation. The term *dividends,* which represents the distribution of corporate profits to a corporation's shareholders, is being phased out of corporate parlance. However, this chapter uses the term *dividends* to describe distributions of corporate profit to shareholders, and reserves the term *distributions* to describe payments made to shareholders for other reasons.

The board of directors is vested with the authority and the discretion to declare dividends from time to time. Dividends may be paid in cash, property, or shares of the corporation, but most states restrict payment to certain available funds or prohibit payment unless certain financial tests are met.[1] Generally, if the appropriate funds are available or if the financial condition of the corporation is satisfactory, the directors may distribute all sorts of desirable things to the shareholders.

Cash is always welcome, and the cash dividend is the most common corporate distribution. Cash dividends are declared by director resolution, which usually specifies a dollar amount per share and directs payment of the dividend to all shareholders entitled to receive it.

Property dividends are less common, but are equally available for use by the board of directors. If the corporation markets a desirable product, the product itself may be a dividend distribution. For example, R.J. Reynolds Tobacco Company once distributed a specially prepared package of its tobacco products to its shareholders as a dividend, and one famous corporate case involved a scramble to purchase shares of a distillery corporation that was reported to be preparing to issue a property dividend of its liquor products during World War II when liquor was scarce.[2] The 3M Company of Minnesota used to send its shareholders its sponge, tape, and paper products. (Now it offers to sell them at a discount to shareholders as gift packages for the holidays.) Property dividends occasionally include shares of stock of a subsidiary corporation owned by the parent corporation. There is no restriction on the type of property that may be distributed. If a corporation had a surplus of janitorial supplies, it could distribute them as dividends, subject to the approval of the shareholder public relations department.

Dividends may consist of more shares of the same corporation. Share dividends increase the number of shares owned by the receiving shareholder, but do not affect the shareholder's proportionate ownership interest. For example, the directors may declare a dividend of 1 share of common stock for every 100 shares outstanding. Each shareholder will receive 1 extra share of stock per 100 as a corporate distribution. Fractional shares[3] become relevant here. If Mary Smith owns 125 shares and a one-for-one-hundred stock dividend is declared, she will be entitled to receive 11/4 shares in the dividend. The corporation may issue a stock certificate, scrip, or an uncertificated entry in the corporate records representing the fraction. Or it may pay the fair value of the quarter share in cash, or it may arrange for the sale of the fractional interest to another shareholder similarly situated.

Dividend distributions to shareholders do not necessarily come at regularly scheduled intervals. The board of directors may declare as many or as few dividends as it deems appropriate. Directors who declare frequent dividends are usually popular with the shareholders. Large corporations with established dividend policies usually declare a regular quarterly dividend on the corporate shares, as profits permit.

A **dissolution distribution** is usually a one-time distribution to shareholders when the corporate assets are liquidated and business is terminated. Partial liquidations are possible, however, if the corporation ceases to operate one phase of its business and distributes assets from the discontinued operations to shareholders, but continues other active business operations thereafter.

The most important legal considerations regarding corporate distributions are the authority to declare or demand distributions; the legally available funds out of which distributions are paid; and the tax ramifications of distributions.

SOURCES OF FUNDS FOR DISTRIBUTION

All state statutes regulate the manner in which a corporation may distribute its assets to its shareholders, and each statute either places statutory restrictions on the effect of a dividend payment or identifies particular accounts from which a distribution may be made. Common sources of dividend funds are earned surplus or **retained earnings** or profits. The Model Business Corporation Act permits dividends from any source as long as the corporation remains solvent and its total assets remain greater than its total liabilities (plus any amounts payable as liquidation preferences).[4] Many state statutes use "unreserved and unrestricted earned surplus" as the main source for dividend distributions, and also allow dividends to be paid from other more specialized accounts. Understanding of the law of corporate distributions requires a grasp of the distinctions between sources of funds for distributions and the accounting principles used in creating these accounts. Consider the following types of accounts (and their definitions in many state statutes):

1. **Net assets**—the amount by which the total assets of a corporation exceed the total debts of the corporation.

2. **Stated capital**—at any particular time, the sum of (a) the par value of all shares of the corporation having a par value that have been issued; (b) the amount of the consideration received by the corporation for all shares of the corporation without par value that have been issued, except such part of the consideration therefor as may have been allocated to capital surplus in a manner permitted by law; and (c) increases caused by issuance of new shares (e.g., a share dividend) and reductions.

3. **Surplus**—the excess of the net assets of a corporation over the corporation's stated capital.

4. **Earned surplus**—the portion of the surplus of a corporation equal to the balance of its net profits, income, gains, and losses after deducting distributions to shareholders and transfers to stated capital and capital surplus to the extent such distributions and transfers are made out of earned surplus. Earned surplus includes also any portion of surplus allocated to earned surplus in mergers, consolidations, or acquisitions of all or substantially all of the outstanding shares or of the property and assets of another corporation, domestic or foreign.

5. **Capital surplus**—the entire surplus of a corporation other than its earned surplus.

Now review the following corporate **balance sheet** with these definitions in mind.

THE NOBLES COMPANY

BALANCE SHEET

December 31, 2005

ASSETS			
Current Assets:			
Cash	$5,000		
Marketable Securities			
Apex Telephone Company, at cost	8,000		
Accounts Receivable	2,000		
Inventory	5,000	$20,000	
Total Current Assets			$20,000
Property Plant and Equipment			58,000
Total Assets			$78,000
LIABILITIES AND EQUITY			
Current Liabilities:			
Accounts Payable	$3,000		
Accrued Expenses Payable	3,000		
Total Current Liabilities		$ 6,000	
Bonds, First Mortgage 13 1/2% Interest		20,000	
Total Liabilities			$26,000
Equity			
Stated Capital			
Common Shares, $1 par value; 50,000 authorized, 5,000 issued and outstanding	$5,000		
Preferred Shares, 5% cumulative, $100 par value; 100% or par liquidation preference; 10,000 authorized, 50 issued and outstanding	5,000		
Total Stated Capital		$10,000	
Capital Surplus		20,000	
Earned Surplus		22,000	
Total Equity			52,000
Total Liabilities and Equity			$78,000

Following the statutory definitions, net assets is the amount by which the total assets, $78,000, exceed the total debts, $26,000. Thus, the net assets of the corporation in this case are $52,000.

Stated capital in this example equals the par value of the 5,000 common shares plus the par value of the 50 preferred shares. The capital surplus results from the excess consideration for which the par value shares were sold. For example, the balance sheet shows capital surplus of $20,000, which could have resulted from selling the 5,000 common shares at $4 a share, allocating the $3 per share in excess of par to capital surplus, and selling the preferred shares at $200 per share, allocating the $100 per share excess to capital surplus.

Earned surplus represents accumulated corporate profits that have been earned during preceding accounting periods and retained in the corporation. The term *surplus* refers to the total amount of earned surplus and capital surplus. Thus, the total surplus of this corporation is $42,000. The entire equity section of the balance sheet is also called **net worth**.

There is one other important definition for analyzing the legality of corporate distributions. A corporation is **insolvent** when it is unable to pay its debts as they become due in the usual course of business.[5] This corporation is solvent under this test, since it has cash of $5,000 and marketable securities that could be sold for at least $8,000, which could pay its current liabilities (debts that are coming due) of $6,000.

The application of these terms becomes more clear through consideration of the statutory provisions regulating corporate distributions.

CASH AND PROPERTY DIVIDENDS

A dividend is a distribution of cash, other property, or shares to the stockholders of the corporation in the proportion of their share ownership. Recall that various classes of stock may be treated differently with respect to dividends. **Dividend preferences** are common in complex corporate financial structures, and preferences must always be observed. There is also a rule that dividends must be uniform within each class or series, meaning that each share of a given class or series will receive the same distribution as the other shares of that class or series. By way of illustration, consider the Nobles Company capital structure that was described previously with 5,000 shares of common stock and 50 shares of 5% cumulative preferred with $100 par value. Suppose the directors decided to issue a dividend and to distribute $2,000 in cash to the shareholders. The preferred shareholders are entitled to be paid their preferential dividends (5% of $100 per share), so they would receive $250 in dividends first. This leaves $1,750 for distribution to the common shareholders, who should receive $0.35 per share. Each shareholder of the particular class must be treated equally. The directors could not order a distribution of $0.50 per share to some common shareholders and $0.20 per share to others.

Shareholders' Rights to Dividends

The decision to distribute dividends is within the sole discretion of the board of directors, and no shareholder has a right to dividends until the board of directors authorizes it or unless the shareholders successfully challenge the business judgment of the board of directors.[6] Cumulative preferred stock will accumulate dividends annually until they are finally paid, but even preferred shareholders have no right to dividends until they are authorized by the board of directors. In the Nobles Company example, the 5% cumulative preferred stock will accumulate a dividend entitlement of five dollars per share per year, and if the board of directors ever authorizes a dividend, the arrearage must be paid before the common shareholders may receive dividends.

Once the board of directors has authorized a dividend through an appropriate resolution, the shareholders have a right to the dividend and it becomes a debt from the corporation to the shareholders.

Section 6.40(f) of the Model Business Corporation Act makes this indebtedness to the shareholders equal to the corporation's indebtedness to other general, unsecured creditors, unless a shareholder has specifically agreed to subordinate the right to receive dividends to the claims of other creditors. The procedure for authorizing a dividend is discussed after the next section regarding the restrictions on sources of funds for dividends.

Restrictions on Payment of Dividends

Corporate statutes usually restrict the payment of dividends to funds contained in specified corporate accounts. There are also certain restrictions on payment even if funds appear to be available in the prescribed accounts. Section 6.40 of the Model Business Corporation Act prohibits the payment of dividends if the corporation is insolvent, or if the authorization or payment would be contrary to any restriction contained in the articles of incorporation.[7] If the organizers intend to restrict the directors' ability to authorize and pay dividends, the law honors their restraints.

The act further provides that dividends may be authorized only if the corporation's total assets exceed total liabilities and (unless provided otherwise in the articles of incorporation) the amounts payable to preferred shares having a preference to assets in liquidation. In the case of the Nobles Company, this excess is $47,000: total assets ($78,000) less total liabilities ($26,000) and amounts payable in liquidation to the preferred shares (100% of par, or $5,000). The asset and liabilities values are determined from the balance sheet or based on some other reasonable and fair valuation. Thus, if the Nobles Company's stock in Apex Telephone Company were valued in the market at $20,000, an additional $12,000 would be available for dividends.

In deciding whether the corporation would violate the rules restricting payment of dividends, the board of directors may rely upon the financial statements, fair market appraisals, or any other reasonable determination of value of the assets of the corporation. In measuring whether a dividend has the effect of causing insolvency or the reduction of net assets below the threshold amounts, the date the dividend is authorized is generally the date the determination is made. However, if the dividend is paid more than 120 days after the authorization of the dividend, the date of payment will be the relevant date for this determination.

Many states continue to permit dividends to be paid in cash or property only out of the unreserved and unrestricted earned surplus of the corporation, with a few exceptions, which are discussed in a moment. In those states, therefore, a corporation may pay dividends from available funds in its earned surplus account, and in the case of the hypothetical Nobles Company, $22,000 would be available for payment of dividends. However, there may be practical restrictions on the payment of such dividends. A glance at the balance sheet reveals that payment of a $22,000 dividend is unrealistic considering the relatively low cash position of the corporation and considering that the corporation's total liquid assets, including cash, securities, inventory, and accounts receivable, total only $20,000. The corporation would be unable to pay a full $22,000 dividend without liquidating part of its plant and equipment, even though the funds are legally available under statute for dividends up to $22,000. Thus, in every case, the maximum legal limits on dividends will be tempered by business advisability. The directors determine the latter within the bounds of the former.

Some states, including Delaware, provide that in addition to the funds from earned surplus, dividends may be declared and paid out of the unreserved and unrestricted "net earnings for the current fiscal year and the next preceding fiscal year taken as a single period." This means that if the corporation has no historical earned surplus, but has earnings (profits) for the past two fiscal years, dividends may legally be paid from the profit funds, without regard to the balance in the earned surplus account.

In California, the availability of funds for dividends depends on a ratio of current assets to current liabilities, and management is allowed to *anticipate* receipts and expenses for the next year to make the computation.

Earned surplus generally represents the accumulated profits from corporate operations as determined by accepted accounting principles. Earned surplus or earnings may be restricted in several ways. Suppose a corporation has borrowed money from a bank or other financial institution, and the terms of the loan agreement require that earned surplus be maintained at a minimum level of $10,000 for the duration of the loan. In accordance with the loan agreement, that amount of earned surplus should be restricted, and may not be used for the payment of dividends. A restriction also would be imposed when the corporation purchases its own shares from outside investors to hold as treasury shares. Most statutes require that the amount of earned surplus used to purchase treasury shares be restricted for as long as the shares remain treasury shares.[8] Many statutes ignore the distinction between ordinary surplus and reserved or restricted surplus and permit dividends to be authorized and paid without such restrictions.

Sometimes dividends may be paid out of the **depletion reserves** of a corporation engaged in exploiting natural resources, such as minerals, oil, gas, and timber. The articles of incorporation must expressly authorize such dividends.[9]

Cash and property dividend provisions vary extensively among the states. Most states couch their restrictions on legally available funds in terms of solvency: assets minus liabilities (including preferences to be paid in liquidation) or whether the corporation can pay its debts in the usual course of business. Others use earned surplus or earnings during a prescribed period. Several other states add further restrictions to prohibit dividends from unrealized appreciation and depreciation.[10]

Procedure for Authorization, Payment, and Accounting

The board of directors has sole discretion to determine the amount to be paid as dividends by the corporation. Notice, however, that in the Nobles Company financial structure, the directors must pay $5 per share for 50 shares of preferred stock as a cumulative dividend before any dividends may be paid to the common shares. If the directors authorized a dividend of $3,000, they would first resolve to distribute $250, or $5 per share, to the preferred shares, and would then distribute the remaining $2,750 in a dividend of $0.55 per share for the common stock.

The decision to authorize the dividend is made at a directors' meeting and is recorded as a resolution in the minutes.

EXAMPLE

Resolution to Authorize a Cash Dividend

RESOLVED, that a dividend of $5 per share be authorized and paid on the preferred stock and a dividend of $.55 per share be authorized and paid on the common stock of this corporation out of the unreserved and unrestricted earned surplus to the holders of stock as shown by the records of the corporation on the 15th day of June, 2005, distributable on the 1st day of July, 2005, and that the treasurer is directed forthwith to mail checks for the same to the stockholders of record.

An example of a resolution for a property dividend follows.

EXAMPLE

Resolution to Authorize a Property Dividend

From the report furnished the meeting on the financial condition of the Company for the fiscal year ended December 31, 2005, and for each of the subsequent months, it appeared that the Company was in a position to authorize and pay a dividend in property upon its outstanding shares of common stock.

Thereupon, after discussion it was on motion duly made, seconded, and unanimously adopted by the affirmative vote of the directors present:

RESOLVED, that a dividend on the outstanding shares of common stock of this Corporation be and it hereby is authorized and ordered to be paid in property of this Corporation, to-wit, shares of common stock of Apex Telephone Company owned by this Corporation at the rate of ten shares of common stock of said Apex Telephone Company for each share of common stock of this Corporation issued and outstanding. Said dividend to be payable on September 1, 2006, to the holders of record of said common stock of this Corporation at the close of business on August 10, 2006, from the net surplus of this Corporation as at the close of business on December 31, 2005, or from the net profits of this Corporation for its current fiscal year; and

FURTHER RESOLVED, that the proper officers of the Corporation be and they hereby are authorized and directed in the name and on behalf of the Corporation to do or cause to be done all acts or things necessary or proper to carry out the foregoing resolution.

Notice that the resolution sets a record date for a determination of stockholders who will be entitled to receive dividends. Nearly every state statute has certain rules to follow in fixing the record date, and in most states the rules are exactly the same as those regarding shareholder voting described earlier.[11] These rules permit the stock transfer books to be closed before the dividend is paid. Alternatively, the directors may set a record date to determine which stockholders are entitled to receive dividends. If the books are not closed and if no date is set, the date for determining shareholders of record is the date that the board of directors adopts the resolution authorizing the dividend. The Model Business Corporation Act gives the directors authority to fix a record date for determining shareholders entitled to a dividend, but if the directors fail to do so, the record date will be on the date the board of directors authorizes the distribution of the dividend. The dividend will be paid to the shareholder of record on the record date, even if that shareholder has sold the shares before the dividend is disbursed. When a dividend has been declared by the board of directors but has not yet been paid, the shares are commonly described as **ex-dividend**, meaning any person who purchases the shares before the dividend is paid will not receive the dividend. It will be paid to the former owner of the shares.

When the dividend is paid in cash, both the cash account and the earned surplus account are reduced by $3,000, which maintains the balance on the balance sheet. If the dividend is paid in other property, such as the securities described in the foregoing property dividend example (which appear as current assets on the balance sheet), and if the securities distributed are valued at $3,000, both the earned surplus and the marketable securities accounts are reduced by that amount. The value of the property distributed and charged to earned surplus is determined by the **book value,** which is the value shown on the balance sheet.

Tax Ramifications of Cash or Property Dividends

In an earlier discussion of the corporate form, it was observed that one disadvantage of corporate existence is the problem of double taxation. Dividends are at the heart of that problem. The corporation is taxed on its profits, and if the after-tax profits are distributed to shareholders as dividends, the dividends are income to the shareholders and are also taxed at the individual shareholder's rate. A corporation may avoid the problem of double taxation by paying salaries or consulting expenses to its shareholders wherever possible, since these items are deductible as expenses and the money thus expended is not taxed at the corporate level. Salaries are a viable alternative to dividends when the shareholders are employees of the corporation, as is frequently the case in small, close corporations. In large corporations, however, dividends that are subject to double taxation are necessary to provide the shareholders a return on their investment.

Cash dividends are declared on a shareholder's income tax return as income in the actual amount distributed. Property dividends are subject to a special rule. When property is distributed as a dividend, the shareholders must report as income the **fair market value** of the property received, even though the book value of the property may be less.[12] For example, if the distributed marketable securities of the Apex Telephone Company have a fair market value of $4,000, even though their book value is $3,000, the shareholder must report $4,000 as ordinary income.

Corporations that pay dividends aggregating more than $10 to any one person during the calendar year must file certain reports with the Internal Revenue Service, which uses those **informational reports** to determine whether the shareholders have reported the dividends on their individual income tax returns.

Shareholders of a Subchapter S corporation must report and pay taxes upon their proportionate share of the corporation's entire income, regardless of whether they have received distributions of cash equivalent to their share of income. The advantage (or perhaps disadvantage) of a Subchapter S corporation is that the shareholder's proportionate share of corporate income is attributable to each shareholder as individual income.

SHARE DIVIDENDS

A share dividend is a corporation's distribution of its own shares. The number of shares owned by the shareholders is increased, but the proportionate stock ownership of each shareholder does not change. A share dividend requires no modification in any of the characteristics of the shares, and it adds nothing to a shareholder's ownership interest; instead, it simply dilutes the shareholder's ownership interest by dividing the same investment into more shares. From a business and public relations perspective, a corporation issuing a share dividend has achieved the best of all possible results: it has distributed a valuable dividend to its shareholders (because the new shares distributed will have value) and it has not depleted any of its assets. The shareholders are actually receiving part of the value they already had in the stock they already owned. The new shares distributed have value only because they dilute the value of the existing shares.

Legal Restrictions

Most states permit share dividends from two sources: the corporation's treasury shares, if shares have been purchased and held in the treasury; and authorized-but-unissued shares. In either case, the earned surplus account must contain available funds, and it will be adjusted to reflect the dividend.

When authorized-but-unissued shares are used for share dividends, a transfer from surplus to stated capital occurs. The Model Business Corporation Act formerly required such a transfer, and many states still follow the rule.[13] If the shares have a par value, they must be issued at an amount equal to or greater than the par value. An amount of surplus equal to the aggregate par value of the dividend shares must then be transferred to stated capital at the time the dividend is paid. If the dividend shares have no par value, the shares are issued at a stated value fixed by a resolution of the board of directors, and stated capital receives an amount of surplus equal to the aggregate stated value. Further, the amount of surplus so transferred to stated capital must be disclosed to the shareholders when the dividend is paid.

To avoid dilution of one class in favor of another class, there is usually an additional restriction. No dividend payable in shares of any class may be paid to the holders of shares of any other class unless doing so is authorized by the articles of incorporation *or* by the affirmative vote or the written consent of the holders of at least a majority of the outstanding shares of the class in which the payment is to be made.

Using the Nobles Company as an example, note that the balance sheet reflects that 10,000 preferred shares with $100 par value are *authorized,* but only 50 of these shares are *issued and outstanding.* There are, therefore, 9,950 preferred shares authorized but unissued. The directors may consider issuing one share of preferred stock for each share of common stock as a share dividend, but they have two hurdles to jump: the authority to issue a share dividend to holders of one class in shares of another class, and the legally available funds for the dividend. If 5,000 shares of preferred were distributed to the common shareholders, the present holders of the 50 preferred shares would have their ownership interests severely diluted. Accordingly, either the articles of incorporation must authorize such a share dividend, or the preferred shareholders must approve the dividend. The second hurdle is insurmountable in this case, since each of the preferred shares has a par value of $100, and that amount must be transferred from surplus to stated capital for each distributed share. The surplus of the Nobles Company—the excess of net assets and stated capital—is only $42,000. To issue 5,000 shares of $100 par value stock, $50,000 in surplus must be transferred to stated capital. Consequently, this total share dividend could not be distributed; the greatest number of shares of preferred stock that could be distributed is 4,200. Note that a share dividend of one class of shares to the holders of another class is rare. Usually a share dividend will be paid to holders of each class in shares of the same class.

If the corporation has no treasury shares and all of the authorized shares have been issued, the articles of incorporation must be amended to supply additional authorized shares before a share dividend may be declared.

Procedure for Authorization, Payment, and Accounting

The decision to declare a share dividend is made by the board of directors, which adopts a resolution specifying the number of shares to be distributed, the proportion of distribution, record and payment dates for the persons to receive dividends, and, if necessary under local law, the authority for the transfer of surplus to stated capital.

EXAMPLE

Resolution to Declare a Stock Dividend

WHEREAS, there has been accumulated from undistributed profits of the company a surplus of $22,000, which in the opinion of the board of directors can be advantageously used for the benefit of stockholders.

RESOLVED, that a stock dividend be and the same hereby is declared payable to stockholders of record as of the 10th day of July, 2005, one share of common stock of the par value of $1 per share to be distributed as such stock dividend to the holder of each outstanding share of common stock, and a like amount to the holder of each share of preferred stock of the par value of $100 each, said stock dividend to be extra and additional to any cash dividend now or hereinafter declared; and

FURTHER RESOLVED, that $5,050 of said surplus be transferred to capital to accomplish said stock dividend, and 5,050 shares of common stock of the par value of $1 per share be issued and disbursed as hereinbefore provided.

On the record date, the shareholders entitled to receive the shares are identified, and on the payment date, certificates are executed and distributed to those persons.

All accounting entries reflecting a stock dividend occur in the shareholders' equity section of the balance sheet, because the *payment* (the value of the shares) is transferred from the surplus accounts to the stated capital account. Stated capital receives the amount of the par value of the shares if the shares have a par value, or an amount determined by the board of directors for no par shares. For example, if the Nobles Company declared a one-share-per-ten common stock dividend, 500 new shares at $1 par common stock would be issued as a dividend to the holders of the 5,000 outstanding shares. The stated capital would be increased by $500, the amount equal to the par value per share times the number of shares distributed as a dividend. The earned surplus account would be reduced by $500, since payment is theoretically made from there.

The New York Stock Exchange imposes a special accounting rule for stock dividends from companies listed on the exchange, and generally accepted accounting principles require the use of the rule for other corporations as well. Stated simply, the accounting for a stock dividend must recognize the fair market value of the shares being distributed. In the preceding Nobles Company distribution, suppose the 500 common shares, with $1 par value, have a fair market value of $10 per share. If the same shares were sold, $500 would be entered in stated capital and $4,500 would be transferred to capital surplus. When the shares are distributed as a stock dividend, the proper accounting entries are $500 to stated capital, $4,500 to capital surplus, and $5,000 from earned surplus.

Study of these accounting entries illustrates why the issuance of a stock dividend adds nothing to the true economic interests of the shareholder. The shareholder's ownership interest in the corporation is represented by the shareholders' equity section of the balance sheet, including stated capital, capital surplus, and earned surplus. In issuing a stock dividend, the corporation is merely transferring funds within the shareholders' equity accounts, and not distributing any assets of the corporation. For that reason, the Model Business Corporation Act and many states have removed the statutory requirements of legally available funds as they relate to share dividends. While it is important to understand the accounting concepts to understand the source of a share dividend, the transaction has no effect on creditors or the financial well-being of the corporation. The advantage of a stock dividend lies in the future; if the business continues to prosper, the value of each share of stock will increase. The hope of shareholders is that all stock, including shares distributed as stock dividends, will appreciate in value, and the shareholders will realize huge capital gains when the stock is sold.

Tax Ramifications of Share Dividends

The tax ramifications of a stock dividend for shareholders are simple on their face but complicated in their application. The dividend itself is a nontaxable transfer, since the shareholder receives no distribution of value from the stock dividend. Rather, the ownership interest is simply divided into more shares. Thus, no tax need be paid when a stock dividend is received. The tax problem comes later.

When the shares are sold, the shareholder must compute the **basis for the shares**—that is, their cost to the shareholder—in order to compute the capital gains. Stated very simply, if shares were purchased for $5 per share, and subsequently sold for $8 per share, the basis is the cost of the shares and the capital gain is $3 per share. Stock dividends complicate this computation, because they require an adjustment to the basis of the original shares. For example, suppose a shareholder purchased 100 shares of Nobles Company common stock at $5 per share, and subsequently received a one-for-ten stock dividend, resulting in a total of 110 shares for the original investment of $500. The shareholder's basis per share is now $4.545 per share, and that figure will be used to compute capital gains when the shares are sold. Further complications are apparent if the shareholder had purchased 10 shares in 2000 for $5 per share, 50 shares in 2001 for $6 per share, 25 shares in 2002 for $6.50 per share, and 15 shares in 2003 for $6.75 per share. When this shareholder later receives a ten-share stock dividend, all of these figures must be adjusted. A stock dividend may be most popular with the shareholder's accountant because of these confusing tax computations.

STOCK SPLITS

A **stock split** is similar to a stock dividend inasmuch as it results in a greater division of the same ownership interest for each shareholder. However, a typical stock split usually involves some modification of the capital stock structure itself. If the corporation's shares have a par value, a split is normally accomplished by reducing the par value of the shares so that the aggregate stated capital of the corporation is unaffected by the distribution. If the shares have no par value, the stock split effects a reduction of the stated value of each share.

The generally accepted distinction between stock splits and stock dividends stems from the mechanics of effecting the distribution. A stock *dividend* traditionally involves a transfer of surplus to stated capital within the shareholders' equity section of the balance sheet. When taken from surplus and added to capital, the stock dividend may be considered to be a type of earnings distribution, although no value is actually distributed to the shareholders. A stock *split,* on the other hand, simply changes the total number of shares outstanding, and the stated capital remains the same. There are no shifting of funds and no distributions of earnings. This distinction between stock dividends and stock splits has little practical effect, with the singular exception that in some states a true stock split requires an amendment to the articles of incorporation.

Like a share dividend, a stock split involves the issuance of a certain number of shares for each share currently held. Splits may be two-for-one, three-for-one, or even one-hundred-for-one. Under the Model Business Corporation Act, there is no distinction in the corporate formalities required to issue a share dividend or to declare a stock split. In section 6.23, the board of directors has the authority to issue a share dividend by simply authorizing one. Under section 10.05, the board of directors also has the authority to amend the articles of incorporation to change the total number of issued shares into a greater number of shares. There are two separate procedures for accomplishing a split. If the shares have a par value, a modification of the par value of the shares is a common method. In a two-for-one split, the par value is halved, and twice as many shares are issued for the same amount of stated capital. In the case of the common shareholders of the Nobles Company, a two-for-one stock split reduces the par value of the common shares to $0.50 per share, and results in a distribution of 5,000 additional shares for the 5,000 shares presently outstanding. There are then 10,000 shares of common stock issued and outstanding represented by the same $5,000 in stated capital. The shareholders' equity section of the balance sheet is changed only to indicate that there are 10,000 shares issued and outstanding, and that the par value is now $0.50 per share. An amendment to the articles of incorporation is necessary to reflect the new par value in the capital structure. The amendment may also require an increase in the authorized stock of the particular class. If the Nobles Company sought to issue an eleven-for-one stock split, the presently authorized shares would be insufficient for the distribution, since 55,000 shares would be needed. The extra shares may be authorized in the same amendment that changes par value.

Shares without par value may be involved in a split, in which case an amendment to the articles may not be necessary since such shares remain without par value after the split. An amendment is required, however, if additional authorized shares are needed to accomplish the split. The initiative for the stock split begins with a resolution by the board of directors for an amendment to the articles of incorporation:

EXAMPLE

Resolution to Amend the Articles for a Stock Split

RESOLVED, that Article Fourth of the Articles of Incorporation be and the same is hereby amended as follows:

"FOURTH: One hundred thousand (100,000) shares shall be common stock with a par value of $.50 per share."

At the time this amendment becomes effective, and without any further action on the part of the corporation or its stockholders, each share of common stock of a par value of $1.00 per share then issued and outstanding shall be changed and reclassified into two fully paid and nonassessable shares of common stock of a par value of $.50. The capital account of the corporation shall not be increased or decreased by such change and reclassification. To reflect the said change and reclassification, each certificate representing shares of common stock of a par value of $1.00 theretofore issued and outstanding shall be canceled, and the holder of record of each such certificate shall be entitled to receive a new certificate representing two shares of common stock of a par value of $.50, so that upon this amendment becoming effective, each holder of record of a certificate representing theretofore issued and outstanding common stock of the corporation will be entitled to certificates representing in the aggregate two shares of common stock of a par value of $.50 authorized by this amendment for each share of common stock of a par value of $1.00 per share of which he or she was the holder prior to the effectiveness of this amendment.[14]

In many states, this recommendation for an amendment to the articles of incorporation must be submitted to the shareholders for an appropriate vote. Section 10.05 of the Model Business Corporation Act permits the board of directors to simply increase the total number of shares of a particular class without obtaining the approval of the shareholders.

The second method of declaring a stock split is the same procedure used to issue a share dividend. Instead of modifying the par value of the shares by an amendment to the articles of incorporation, the board of directors may authorize the issuance of new shares from the available authorized but unissued shares. In states that still impose restrictions on legally available funds, an amount must be transferred from surplus to stated capital, and the new shares may be issued for the increased stated capital. For example, the Nobles Company could accomplish a two-for-one split by transferring $5,000 from surplus to capital, thereby increasing stated capital to $10,000 and covering the issuance of 5,000 additional shares at the same par value. Although this is technically a distribution of earnings and is more appropriately described as a share dividend, it is generally referred to as a split because of the doubling of shares held by each shareholder. An amendment to the articles of incorporation may still be necessary if the remaining authorized but unissued shares are fewer than the additional shares required in the split.

In addition to the amendment procedure and transfer of surplus to capital methods of accomplishing stock splits, other rules may require **capitalization of earnings** in a stock distribution. The phrase "capitalization of earnings" refers to the second procedure of transferring surplus to stated capital. The rules of the New York Stock Exchange and the Securities Exchange Act of 1934 should be consulted for the circumstances requiring capitalization of earnings in a stock split.[15]

In all other respects, stock splits are treated the same as share dividends. Upon appropriate resolution of the board of directors, and amendment of the articles of incorporation, if necessary, new certificates are issued to shareholders reflecting the additional shares of the split. The tax ramifications for the shareholders are identical to the tax treatment of share dividends.

CORPORATION'S PURCHASE OF ITS OWN SHARES

The corporation may purchase its own shares from its shareholders if the board of directors authorizes the purchase and the applicable state statute so permits. There are many reasons why a corporation may repurchase its shares from the shareholders. It might be required to do so under a shareholder agreement that requires the repurchase of shares when a shareholder retires or dies. It might have business reasons for reducing the number of its shareholders, such as eliminating its public corporation status by "going private" and repurchasing shares owned by public investors. Or it might simply negotiate with a shareholder to repurchase the shares with the objective of selling them at a higher price to another investor.

The Model Business Corporation Act authorizes the repurchase of shares in section 6.31, and section 6.40 treats a repurchase as a distribution to shareholders, so that the same restrictions placed upon dividends also apply here. Most states regulate the repurchase of shares as dividends are regulated, so funds used to purchase the shares are subject to solvency restrictions under the Model Act: the corporation must be able to pay its debts, and its assets must exceed its liabilities (including liquidation preferences) after payment of the purchase price. In states that use capital accounts to determine the legality of a purchase of shares the funds used to purchase the shares are limited to unrestricted and unreserved earned surplus, although usually capital surplus may be used if authorized by the articles of incorporation or by a majority vote of the shareholders.

The corporation's purchase of its own shares is a distribution to shareholders, since the corporation exchanges cash for shares. The law refuses permission to purchase shares if the corporation is insolvent or would be rendered insolvent by the purchase. However, there are some generally recognized exceptional cases when the corporation may reacquire its own shares without making a distribution subject to statutory regulation. These include the purchase of corporate shares to eliminate fractional shares,[16] to compromise or collect an indebtedness to the corporation, to pay dissenting shareholders entitled to payment under the law,[17] and to retire redeemable shares.

Consider the purchasing ability of the Nobles Company. Under the Model Business Corporation Act approach, the corporation may make a distribution only if it will be able to pay its debts as they come due and if total assets exceed (and after the distribution occurs will continue to exceed) total liabilities plus the amount payable to preferred shares as a liquidation preference.[18] The balance sheet of the Nobles Company shows total assets of $78,000, total liabilities of $26,000, and a liquidation preference for preferred shares of $5,000. Thus, the corporation has a total of $47,000 in legal purchasing power, subject to its ability to pay debts as they come due. In states that use the earned surplus and capital surplus tests, the Nobles Company would have less purchasing power. The balance sheet shows unreserved and unrestricted earned surplus of $22,000, and that amount could be used by the board of directors to purchase shares. The balance sheet also shows $20,000 in capital surplus, which could be used if the articles of incorporation or the holders of the majority of voting shares authorized the action. However, the liquidity of the company may be a practical barrier to the purchase of shares. The corporation will be limited by the relatively low cash position shown on the balance sheet under both tests.

The shares purchased by the corporation may be returned to the status of authorized-and-unissued shares, canceled, or, in some states, held by the corporation as treasury shares. Section 6.31 of the Model Business Corporation Act anticipates that the shares would be either

Exhibit 11–1.

Statement of Cancellation
of Non-Reissuable Shares
(Illinois)

Form **BCA-9.05**	**STATEMENT OF CANCELLATION**	
(Rev. Jan. 2003)	**of**	File #
	NON-REISSUABLE SHARES	

Jesse White
Secretary of State
Department of Business Services
Springfield, IL 62756
Telephone (217) 782-1831
http://www.cyberdriveillinois.com

Remit payment in check or money order, payable to "Secretary of State."

SUBMIT IN DUPLICATE

This space for use by Secretary of State
Date

Filing Fee $ 5.00

Approved:

1.   CORPORATE NAME: _____

2.   **The corporation has acquired and cancelled its own shares, and the articles of incorporation prohibit the re-issuance of such shares.**

3.   Number of shares cancelled and redemption or purchase price:

Class	Series	Par Value	Number of Shares Cancelled	Redemption or Purchase Price	Date of Cancellation
_____	_____	_____	_____	_____	_____

	BEFORE CANCELLATION				**AFTER CANCELLATION**			
	Class	Series	Par	Number	Class	Series	Par	Number
4. Number of authorized shares:								
5. Number of issued shares:								
6. Paid-in capital:	$ _____				$ _____			

7.   The undersigned corporation has caused this statement to be signed by a duly authorized officer who affirms, under penalties of perjury, that the facts stated herein are true. (All signatures must be in **BLACK INK**.)

Dated _____ , _____   _____
      (Month & Day)   *(Year)*   *(Exact Name of Corporation)*

                                    _____
                                    (Any Authorized Officer's Signature)

                                    _____
                                    (Type or Print Name and Title)

returned to authorized-but-unissued status or, if so provided in the articles of incorporation, permanently cancelled. The accounting treatment of the purchase requires that the amount paid for the shares is deducted from the asset side of the balance sheet, and the amount of the stated capital and capital surplus used to purchase the shares is deducted from the equity portion of the balance sheet.

When treasury shares are permitted by statute, most states require that the surplus used to purchase the shares must be restricted in the amount required for the purchase, and the restriction must remain in effect as long as the shares are held as treasury shares. If the shares are subsequently sold or canceled, the restriction may be removed. To illustrate, assume that the Nobles Company repurchased 1,000 shares of its common stock to hold as treasury shares at a price of $3 per share, using $3,000 of the earned surplus for the purchase. The earned surplus account would reflect $19,000 in available earned surplus and $3,000 in restricted earned surplus, representing the 1,000 shares of common stock held in the treasury. Thereafter, the corporation may resell the treasury shares for any price (including a price below par value). When resold, the shares are no longer treasury shares and the restriction is lifted. If the corporation sells the shares for $2.50 per share, then only $2,500 will be added back to earned surplus, and the loss of $500 will be permanently subtracted from that account. These transactions show that the corporation in this situation would suffer a loss by investing in its own shares.

Sections 6.31 and 10.05 of the Model Business Corporation Act prescribe a streamlined procedure for canceling the purchased shares. In many states, the board of directors adopts a resolution authorizing the **cancellation** of shares and a statement of cancellation is filed with the secretary of state (see Exhibit 11–1, Statement of Cancellation of Non-Reissuable Shares). Under the Model Act procedure, the board of directors (without shareholder approval) adopts an amendment to the articles of incorporation to reflect the reduction in the number of authorized shares, and the total number of authorized shares after the reduction. When the cancellation is completed, the equity section of the balance sheet is adjusted. If capital and surplus accounts are used, the stated capital account is reduced to reflect the cancellation, and the earned surplus is adjusted to show that only the par value of the shares has been realized by the company. Thus, if the 1,000 shares reacquired by the Nobles Company for $3,000 were recorded as treasury shares first and later canceled, the stated capital account would show 4,000 common shares issued and outstanding with $4,000 stated capital. The earned surplus account would be adjusted as follows:

After purchase, before cancellation:

	Earned surplus	
	Unrestricted	$19,000
	Restricted	3,000
	Total	$22,000

Cancellation:

	Remove restriction—	
	Add par value of canceled shares	$ 1,000
	Subtract purchase price of shares	(3,000)
	Net reduction	$ (2,000)

After cancellation:

	Earned surplus	
	Unrestricted	$20,000

Remembering that with dividend distributions, all shareholders of the same class must be treated equally, a relevant question at this point might be, Is the corporation required to purchase the entire class of stock if it intends to purchase any shares? The answer is no. The corporation may purchase all or any part of a particular class, and theoretically may select the shareholders from whom the purchase is made. However, there is a taint of unfairness if the selling shareholders happen to be the directors who authorized the purchase, and the plot thickens if the corporate business suddenly takes a turn for the worse right after the sale. There are laws that protect the other shareholders in such a case. Traditional common law principles of fraud apply here, and the shareholders are further protected through the fiduciary duties owed them by management. If the board of directors voted to purchase their own shares in the corporation, they may be liable to the shareholders for self-dealing—entering into an unfair transaction in which they have a personal financial interest. Finally, federal securities laws regulate insider trading by management, and those laws also may resolve the harm. Nevertheless, the corporate statutes do not require that all shareholders of a particular class be treated equally when the corporation purchases its own shares.

PARTIAL LIQUIDATIONS

A **partial liquidation** is a combination of a distribution of assets, usually cash, and the purchase of the corporation's own shares. In fact, any purchase of shares by a corporation is a partial liquidation. The concept of partial liquidation became popular when certain tax advantages were allowed for partial liquidations that qualified for special favorable tax treatment. The favorable tax consequences for partial liquidations have been eliminated in the federal tax law, but the term *partial liquidation* is still used whenever an identifiable segment of a business is distributed to the shareholders; for example, when a particular division of a corporation is closed and the trade conducted by that division is terminated. After creditors are paid, the assets can be distributed as a partial liquidation to the stockholders. A partial liquidation also may result from a contraction of the corporation's business, such as the closing of certain selected manufacturing plants.

As an illustration of a partial liquidation, suppose the Nobles Company could sell a portion of its plant and equipment, and liquidate the cash received in a distribution to the shareholders in exchange for stock. The transaction could occur as follows: The company sells $13,000 in plant equipment and continues its reduced business with the remaining plant and equipment available, and the net cash from the sale is distributed to the stockholders in exchange for a proportionate amount of stock. Since the $13,000 in plant and equipment equals approximately one-fourth of the net assets, the corporation may reacquire approximately one-quarter of the total outstanding stock in exchange for the distribution. The corporation has accomplished a purchase of stock by distributing cash assets received in a partial liquidation.

The procedure for a partial liquidation begins with a resolution of the board of directors.

EXAMPLE

Resolution to Partially Liquidate

Whereas, this Corporation presently is the owner of sundry producing and undeveloped oil and gas leases, drilling equipment, oil payments, and miscellaneous properties;

Whereas, the Board of Directors deem it good business and advisable to make a partial liquidation of the Corporation and to pay out certain properties of the Corporation as a dividend in kind ratably to the stockholders of record on the 10th day of December, 2004; and

Whereas, the payment of a partial liquidating dividend will not impair the capital stock of the Corporation.

Now, therefore, be it resolved, that a partial liquidating dividend be declared and paid as of January 2, 2005, said dividend to be paid in properties in kind and consisting of the following described properties: *[Here describe.]*

Be it further resolved, that the Certificate of Incorporation of this Corporation be amended, reducing the capital stock of the Corporation from 5,000 shares of common stock of the par value of $1 per share to 3,750 shares of common stock of the par value of $1 per share, and from 50 shares of preferred stock of the par value of $100 per share to 37.5 shares of preferred stock of the par value of $100 per share; and that of the net book value of the assets paid out as a liquidating dividend, $1,250 of such amount be charged against the stated capital of the common shares and $1,250 of such amount be charged against the stated capital of the preferred shares, and the remainder be charged against the capital surplus account.

DISSOLUTION AND LIQUIDATION

Distributions to shareholders also are involved in a complete dissolution of the corporation, since the shareholders are entitled to receive their proportionate ownership interests in the assets after corporate creditors have been paid. Shareholders of record are identified and notice is given to creditors, permitting a reasonable period for filing claims.[19]

All shareholders participate ratably in the net assets of the corporation after payments to creditors, unless the articles of incorporation provide otherwise. The articles may authorize a capital stock structure with various classes or series of shares, one or more of which may be entitled to a preference to assets in liquidation. The preference will be honored before other classes of stock are entitled to their proportionate shares of assets.

Liquidation preferences are usually fixed as a percentage of par value or a specified dollar amount, and preferred shares, while entitled to the first priority to the assets, are limited to the liquidation amount specified. For example, observe that the preferred shares of the Nobles Company are entitled to a liquidation preference of 100% of par value per share. If dissolution occurred when the financial status of the corporation was as described earlier in the balance sheet, the net assets of the corporation would be $52,000 at dissolution. The preferred shares would be entitled to receive $5,000 of the assets (100% of $100 par value for 50 shares). The remaining $47,000 in assets would be distributed to the common shareholders, and the preferred shareholders would not share in this distribution. It is possible, however, to create participating preferred shares, so the preferred shareholders participate in the distribution of assets after receiving their preference. To illustrate, suppose that in addition to the 100% par value preference in liquidation, the articles of incorporation further provided that the preferred shares would participate equally with the common shares in liquidation. The preferred shares would still receive the first $5,000, and the remaining $47,000 would be distributed equally among 5,050 shares (5,000 common and 50 preferred). Each share of each class would receive $9.31 in liquidation in the second distribution. Thus, the total liquidation distribution to the preferred shareholders would be $109.31 per share.

Classes of preferred stock that are entitled to cumulative *dividend* preferences may also have a preferred claim in liquidation to the extent of the **dividend arrearages**. This issue has undergone some tortured construction in litigation and is not firmly settled. However, interpretation problems can be avoided by careful drafting of the articles of incorporation. Again consider the example of the Nobles Company. Its preferred shares are entitled to a 5% cumulative dividend preference, meaning that dividends of $5 per share (5% of $100 par value) accumulate annually. When a dividend is finally declared, the total arrearage must be paid to the cumulative preferred shareholders before any other shareholders may receive dividends. Suppose the Nobles Company has not declared dividends for five years and is now being dissolved and liquidated. The dividends for the preferred shares have accumulated in the amount of $25 per share. The question is whether the preferred shareholders are entitled to receive their dividend arrearages as a preference in liquidation before other classes of stock are permitted to share the assets. The articles of incorporation can provide either way, but should be specific in any case. If it is intended that the preferred shares will be entitled to a liquidation preference for unpaid cumulative dividends, the articles should so specify, and should also define a dividend arrearage or accumulation as including unpaid amounts regardless of whether the corporation has ever declared a dividend or has had funds available for a declaration of a dividend. To negate the liquidation preference for unpaid cumulative dividends, the articles should specifically state that the right to unpaid accumulated dividends is lost if the corporation is dissolved and liquidated.

KEY TERMS

distribution	balance sheet	informational reports
dissolution distribution	net worth	basis for shares
retained earnings	insolvent	stock split
net assets	dividend preference	capitalization of earnings
stated capital	depletion reserve	cancellation of repurchased shares
surplus	ex-dividend	partial liquidation
earned surplus	book value	liquidation preference
capital surplus	fair market value	dividend arrearages

CASES

DODGE v. FORD MOTOR CO.

204 Mich. 459, 170 N.W. 668 (1919)
OSTRANDER, C.J.

[The Dodge brothers were minority shareholders of the Ford Motor Company. Henry Ford, president of the company, owned a majority of the shares, and the company was not paying dividends to the shareholders. The Dodge brothers sued to force the company to pay dividends.]

* * *

When plaintiffs made their complaint and demand for further dividends, the Ford Motor Company had concluded its most prosperous year of business. The demand for its cars at the price of the preceding year continued. It could make and could market in the year beginning August 1, 1916, more than 500,000 cars. Sales of parts and repairs would necessarily increase. The cost of materials was likely to advance, and perhaps the price of labor; but it reasonably might have expected a profit for the year of upwards of $60,000,000. It had assets of more than $132,000,000, a surplus of almost $112,000,000, and its cash on hand and municipal bonds were nearly $54,000,000. Its total liabilities, including capital stock, was a little over $20,000,000. It had declared no special dividend during the business year except the October, 1915, dividend. It had been the practice, under similar circumstances, to declare larger dividends. Considering only these facts, a refusal to declare and pay further dividends appears to be not an exercise of discretion on the part of the directors, but an arbitrary refusal to do what the circumstances required to be done. These facts and others call upon the directors to justify their action, or failure or refusal to act. In justification, the defendants have offered testimony tending to prove, and which does prove, the following facts: It had been the policy of the corporation for a considerable time to annually reduce the selling price of cars, while keeping up, or improving, their quality. As early as in June, 1915, a general plan for the expansion of the productive capacity of the concern by a practical duplication of its plant had been talked over by the executive officers and directors and agreed upon; not all of the details having been settled, and no formal action of directors having been taken. The erection of a smelter was considered, and engineering and other data in connection there-

with secured. In consequence, it was determined not to reduce the selling price of cars for the year beginning August 1, 1915, but to maintain the price and to accumulate a large surplus to pay for the proposed expansion of plant and equipment, and perhaps to build a plant for smelting ore. It is hoped, by Mr. Ford, that eventually, 1,000,000 cars will be annually produced. The contemplated changes will permit the increased output.

The plan, as affecting the profits of the business for the year beginning August 1, 1916, and thereafter, calls for a reduction in the selling price of the cars. It is true that this price might be at any time increased, but the plan called for the reduction in price of $80 a car. The capacity of the plant, without the additions thereto voted to be made (without a part of them at least), would produce more than 600,000 cars annually. This number, and more, could have been sold for $440 instead of $360, a difference in the return for capital, labor, and materials employed of at least $48,000,000. In short, the plan does not call for and is not intended to produce immediately a more profitable business, but a less profitable one; not only less profitable than formerly, but less profitable than it is admitted it might be made. The apparent immediate effect will be to diminish the value of shares and the returns to shareholders.

It is the contention of plaintiffs that the apparent effect of the plan is intended to be the continued and continuing effect of it, and that it is deliberately proposed, not of record and not by official corporate declaration, but nevertheless proposed, to continue the corporation henceforth as a semi-eleemosynary institution and not as a business institution. In support of this contention, they point to the attitude and to the expressions of Mr. Henry Ford.

Mr. Henry Ford is the dominant force in the business of the Ford Motor Company. No plan of operations could be adopted unless he consented, and no board of directors can be elected whom he does not favor. One of the directors of the company has no stock. One share was assigned to him to qualify him for the position, but it is not claimed that he owns it. A business, one of the largest in the world, and one of the most profitable, has been built up. It employs many men, at good pay.

"My ambition," said Mr. Ford, "is to employ still more men, to spread the benefits of this industrial system to the greatest possible number, to help them build up their lives and their homes. To do this we are putting the greatest share of our profits back in the business."

"With regard to dividends, the company paid sixty per cent. on its capitalization of two million dollars, or $1,200,000, leaving $58,000,000 to reinvest for the growth of the company. This is Mr. Ford's policy at present, and it is understood that the other stockholders cheerfully accede to this plan."

He had made up his mind in the summer of 1916 that no dividends other than the regular dividends should be paid, "for the present."

> "Q. For how long? Had you fixed in your mind anytime in the future, when you were going to pay? A. No."
> "Q. "That was indefinite in the future? A. That was indefinite; yes, sir.""

The record, and especially the testimony of Mr. Ford, convinces that he has to some extent the attitude towards shareholders of one who has dispensed and distributed to them large gains and that they should be content to take what he chooses to give. His testimony creates the impression, also, that he thinks the Ford Motor Company has made too much money, has had too large profits, and that, although large profits might be still earned, a sharing of them with the public, by reducing the price of the output of the company, ought to be undertaken. We have no doubt that certain sentiments, philanthropic and altruistic, creditable to Mr. Ford, had large influence in determining the policy to be pursued by the Ford Motor Company—the policy which has been herein referred to.

. . . There should be no confusion (of which there is evidence) of the duties which Mr. Ford conceives that he and the stockholders owe to the general public and the duties which in law he and his codirectors owe to protesting, minority stockholders. A business corporation is organized and carried on primarily for the profit of the stockholders. The powers of the directors are to be employed for that end. The discretion of directors is to be exercised in the choice of means to attain that end, and does not extend to a change in the end itself, to the reduction of profits, or to the nondistribution of profits among stockholders in order to devote them to other purposes.

There is committed to the discretion of directors, a discretion to be exercised in good faith, the infinite details of business, including the wages which shall be paid to employees, the number of hours they shall work, the conditions under which labor shall be carried on, and the price for which products shall be offered to the public.

It is said by appellants that the motives of the board members are not material and will not be inquired into by the court so long as their acts are within their lawful powers. As we have pointed out, and the proposition does not require argument to sustain it, it is not within the lawful powers of a board of directors to shape and conduct the affairs of a corporation for the merely incidental benefit of shareholders and for the primary purpose of benefiting others, and no one will contend that if the avowed purpose of the defendant directors was to sacrifice the interests of shareholders, it would not be the duty of the courts to interfere.

We are not, however, persuaded that we should interfere with the proposed expansion of the business of the Ford Motor Company. In view of the fact that the selling price of products may be increased at any time, the ultimate results of the larger business cannot be certainly estimated. The judges are not business experts. It is recognized that plans must often be made for a long future, for expected competition, for a continuing as well as an immediately profitable venture. The experience of the Ford Motor Company is evidence of capable management of its affairs. It may be noticed incidentally, that it took from the public the money required for the execution of its plan, and that the very considerable salaries paid to Mr. Ford and to certain executive officers and employees were not diminished. We are not satisfied that the alleged motives of the directors, in so far as they are reflected in the conduct of the business, menace the interests of shareholders. It is enough to say, perhaps, that the court of equity is at all times open to complaining shareholders having a just grievance.

Assuming the general plan and policy of expansion and the details of it to have been sufficiently, formally, approved at the October and November, 1917, meetings of directors, and assuming further that the plan and policy and the details agreed upon were for the best ultimate interest of the company and therefore of its shareholders, what does it amount to in justification of a refusal to declare and pay a special dividend or dividends? The Ford Motor Company was able to estimate with nicety its income and profit. It could sell more cars than it could make. Having ascertained what it would cost to produce a car and to sell it, the profit upon each car depended upon the selling price. That being fixed, the yearly income and profit was determinable, and, within slight variations, was certain.

* * *

Defendants say, and it is true, that a considerable cash balance must be at all times carried by such a concern. But, as has been stated, there was a large daily, weekly, monthly, receipt of cash. The output was practically continuous and was continuously, and within a few days, turned into cash. Moreover, the contemplated expenditures were not to be immediately made. The large sum appropriated for the smelter plant was payable over a considerable period of time. So that, without going further, it would appear that, accepting and approving the plan of the directors, it was their duty to distribute on or near the 1st of August, 1916, a very large sum of money to stockholders.

* * *

The decree of the court below fixing and determining the specific amount to be distributed to stockholders is affirmed.

* * *

ANACOMP, INC. v. WRIGHT

449 N.E.2d 610 (Indiana 1983)

RATLIFF, JUDGE

[F. Thomas Wright negotiated with Anacomp to become an executive with that company. In the negotiations, Anacomp agreed to sell Wright 3,060 shares of common stock, and Wright bought the stock and paid for it. His employment negotiations were not successful, and during the negotiation period, Anacomp issued cash dividends and stock dividends, and declared a stock split. Wright's original 3,060 shares had become 6,603 shares through the additional stock issued in dividends and splits. When negotiations broke off, Anacomp tried to cancel the 3,543 extra shares Wright had received during the negotiations.]

* * *

The law provides that the right to receive dividends is an incident of stock ownership which applies equally to stock and cash dividends. 19 Am.Jur.2d *Corporations* § 890 at 370 (1965). The general rule is stated that "whoever owns the stock in a corporation at the time a dividend is declared owns the dividend also. . . ." *Bright v. Lord,* (1875) 51 Ind. 272, 276; 6 I.L.E. *Corporations* § 102 at 506 (1958); 19 Am.Jur.2d *Corporations* § 890 at 371 (1965). In the words of another authority, "[s]tock dividends, like cash dividends, belong, in the absence of an agreement to the contrary, to the holders of stock at the time when the dividend is payable, and without regard to the source from which, or the time during which, the funds to be divided among the stockholders were acquired." (Footnote omitted.) 11 W. Fletcher, *Cyclopedia of Corporations* § 5359 at 739 (Perm.Ed.1971).

* * *

We note that Anacomp raises no question with respect to Wright's entitlement to the cash dividends in this appeal. Although Anacomp distinguishes at great length the completely different natures of cash and stock dividends as far as tax and trust cases are concerned, we are not convinced that there is any reason to distinguish between the two in this case. The trial court found correctly, according to the law, that Anacomp was not entitled to a return of the dividends, be they cash or stock.

Anacomp also posits the argument that even if Wright is entitled to the additional shares of stock represented by the stock dividends, he is not entitled to those shares which he accumulated as a result of stock splits. Anacomp asserts that there is a distinction between stock dividends and stock splits. We agree. Stock dividends suggest a capitalization of earnings or profits together with a distribution of the added shares which evince those assets transformed into capital. 19 Am.Jur.2d *Corporations* § 808 at 284 (1965). Stock splits, on the other hand, connote a mere increase in the number of shares evincing ownership without altering the amount of capital, surplus, or segregated earnings. *Id.* A stock split, therefore, is essentially a matter of form and not of substance in that it does not change the stockholder's proportionate ownership or participating interest in the corporation. *Id.; Rogers Walla Walla, Inc. v. Ballard,* (1976) 16 Wash.App. 81, 553 P.2d 1372, 1376. Courts have recognized, however, that what is denominated by a corporation as a stock dividend may in truth be a stock split and vice versa. *Rogers Walla Walla.* Thus, while the corporation's denomination of an issue of stock to shareholders as a stock dividend or a stock split may be useful and definitive for certain purposes, courts, where necessary, will look behind that denomination to the essence of the corporate transaction to determine whether the dividend was in actuality issued as a result of a transfer of accumulated earnings into capital or as a mere increase in the number of shares of stock. *See, e.g., Rogers Walla Walla; Geier v. Mercantile-Safe Deposit & Trust Co.,* (1974) 273 Md. 102, 328 A.2d 311.

Despite Anacomp's insistence that stock certificate numbers 33684 and 41552 were issued as a result of stock splits, the court found, and the corporate minutes in the record support the finding, that

> "upon the declaration of each of the stock dividends, as stated above, Anacomp transferred additional 'earned surplus', or 'capital surplus' into its common stock account; and that although each shareholder, unless he sold some of his stock, would maintain the same proportion of stock equity in the corporate assets, the value thereof would not remain the same because the dividend stock thus issued represented part of the profits earned by Anacomp from the use of its stock investor's cash payments including the $25,625.00 paid by Wright."

Record at 53. Thus, we find no basis in fact or at law to support Anacomp's position that somehow the stock split shares should be treated differently from the other dividends declared and issued to Wright.

* * *

PROBLEMS

1. XYZ Corporation has the following balance sheet at the end of 2006:

ASSETS

Cash	$ 45,000
Equipment	10,000
Building	100,000
Stock	10,000
	$165,000

LIABILITY AND EQUITY

Accounts Payable	$100,000
Capital Surplus	20,000
Earned Surplus	25,000
Stated Capital	
(Common Stock)	
$2 par value	
10,000 shares	20,000
authorized, issued	
and outstanding	
	$165,000

a. What is the maximum cash dividend that could be legally declared in your state?

b. If the XYZ Corporation purchased 1,000 shares at par value to be held as treasury shares, what would be the amounts in the following accounts?
Assets/Stock $_____
Stated Capital $_____
Capital Surplus $_____

2. The financial statements of Slumbertele Corporation indicate negative retained earnings for 2003 in the amount of $(10,500), and earnings of $20,150 in 2004

and $15,600 in 2005. The Company has authorized, issued and outstanding 1,000 shares of 4% cumulative nonparticipating prior preferred shares with $100 par value; 1,500 shares of 5% nonparticipating preferred shares with $10 par value; and 2,000 common shares with $100 par value. During 2001, the Company paid a $4 dividend per share to the 4% prior preferred, a $.50 dividend per share to the 5% preferred, and a $6 dividend per share to the common shares. It paid a $4 dividend per share in 2002 and a $2 dividend per share in 2003 to the 4% prior preferred. No other dividends have been paid.

a. During 2006, which of the following is correct?
   (1) The directors may not declare a dividend for the common shares.
   (2) The directors may not declare a dividend because there is no surplus.
   (3) The directors must pay the 4% cumulative preferred holders their total dividend arrearage before any other dividends may be paid.
   (4) None of the above.

b. If the directors pay the maximum amount legally available in dividends in 2006, which of the following will be the dividend that is distributed?
   (1) $10 to the 4% prior preferred; $.50 to the 5% preferred; $7.25 to the common.
   (2) $14 to the 4% prior preferred; $2.50 to the 5% preferred; $3.75 to the common.
   (3) $10 to the 4% prior preferred; $2 to the 5% preferred; $6.125 to the common.
   (4) $14 to the 4% prior preferred; $.50 to the 5% preferred; $5.25 to the common.

PRACTICE ASSIGNMENTS

1. Prepare a memorandum to advise the board of directors of Trouble, Inc., of the maximum dividend that can be declared for holders of common stock this year.

2. Prepare all documents necessary to accomplish a two-for-one stock split of the preferred stock.

TROUBLE, INC.

BALANCE SHEET

ASSETS

Cash		$ 8,500.00
Accounts Receivable		
Current	$ 2,000.00	
Over 30 days	1,200.00	3,200.00
Office Equipment	8,000.00	
Less Accumulated Depreciation	(1,000.00)	7,000.00
Supplies		650.00
Land and Buildings	32,000.00	
Accumulated Depreciation	(7,000.00)	25,000.00
		44,350.00

LIABILITIES

Accounts Payable		
Current	6,000.00	
Over 30 days	1,000.00	$ 7,000.00
Insurance Payable		500.00
Long-Term Debt		25,000.00
		32,500.00

SHAREHOLDERS' EQUITY

Stated Capital:		
Common stock		
50,000 shares authorized, no par value; 1,000 shares outstanding	1,000.00	
Preferred stock		
6% cumulative dividends; 10,000 authorized; $100 par value; 50 shares outstanding	5,000.00	
Capital Surplus	1,000.00	
Earned Surplus	4,850.00	
	11,850.00	11,850.00
		$44,350.00

ENDNOTES

1. See Model Business Corporation Act (hereafter M.B.C.A.) § 6.40.

2 Park & Tilford v. Schulte, 160 F.2d 984 (2d Cir. 1947).

3 See "Fractions of Shares and Scrip" in Chapter 9.

4 M.B.C.A. § 6.40.

5. See M.B.C.A. § 6.40(c).

6. See M.B.C.A. § 6.40(c).

7. Dividend restrictions in the articles of incorporation are suggested as important considerations at the drafting stage. See "The Articles of Incorporation" in Chapter 8.

8. See "Corporation's Purchase of Its Own Shares" later in this chapter.

9. E.g., New York, N.Y. Bus. Corp. Law § 510 (McKinney).

10. E.g., California, Cal. Corp. Code § 500 (West).

11. See "Shareholder Meetings" in Chapter 10.

12. Internal Revenue Code of 1986, 26 U.S.C.A. § 301.

13. The Model Business Corporation Act has eliminated the concepts of treasury shares, stated capital, and surplus.

14. The procedure to amend the articles of incorporation is detailed in "Amendment of the Articles of Incorporation" in Chapter 15.

15. See Rule 10(b)-12, Securities Exchanges Act of 1934, 15 U.S.C.A. § 78(j).

16. See "Fractions of Shares and Scrip" in Chapter 9.

17. See "Rights of Dissenting Shareholders" in Chapter 15.

18. See "Preferred Stock Rights" in Chapter 9.

19. The dissolution procedure is more fully discussed in "Voluntary Dissolution," "Involuntary Dissolution," and "Liquidation" in Chapter 15.

EMPLOYMENT AND COMPENSATION

The first chapter discusses the principles of agency. These rules are the foundation of the operations of a business enterprise. Sole proprietors must hire employees and agents to perform duties in the business if they want help in their daily operations. Partners are agents for their partnership and for the other partners. A limited liability company may employ managers and other agents to administer its affairs. In a corporation, the business acts only through directors and officers, who are agents of the corporation. Agency is the underlying basis for most of the internal legal relationships of an enterprise.

The agency rules can apply to any situation in which a person authorizes another to perform a task. In a business organization, those tasks usually relate to the operations of the business, such as performing the duties of a cashier or truck driver or acting as the attorney or accountant for the business.

Because of the significant obligations created under agency law, all business relationships that involve an agent should be reduced to writing and clearly defined so that the obligations and rights of the principal and the agent can be clearly understood and interpreted. Within a business organization, employees are agents and their duties and rights are generally based upon the principles of agency law. Most of these rules may be defined and supplemented by agreements, and both the employer and the employee generally desire a clear understanding concerning the nature of the employment, the duties to be performed, and the compensation and benefits to which the employee will be entitled. Other issues also may be addressed in employment agreements to clearly define the rights and responsibilities of the agent and the principal.

A corporation offers the most flexible employment and compensation possibilities of any form of business. Managerial talent may be widely distributed in the corporate structure, from directors and officers to other management executives and supervisory personnel, and the compensation schemes are equally varied, particularly because of the many tax advantages available through the corporate entity. However, much of what is said here also applies to employees of proprietorships, partnerships, and limited liability companies whose business structures approach the complexity of a corporation and whose employees may be entitled to similar compensation and tax-advantaged incentive programs.

Most employees are hired on an informal basis, without any written contract, and they perform duties for a stated compensation, in salary or wages, until their employment is terminated. Certain personal motives may induce the employee's performance and provide compensatory incentives. The company may be a family business, and the employee, as a member of the family, may have a kindred incentive to do the job well. The employee may be a shareholder and, therefore, have a pecuniary interest in his or her own performance; if the employee's performance contributes to business successes, the employee's stock becomes more valuable. These informal employee relationships do not require much planning or counsel and, because of their simplicity, are appropriate arrangements for most proprietorships and many partnerships, limited liability companies, and corporations. However, they do not take advantage of the special methods of preserving talent and compensation available through more elaborate employment agreements.

These traditionally informal employment arrangements have become more complicated through various state and federal laws that have been enacted to protect employees' rights and to ensure fairness in hiring and firing practices.

EMPLOYMENT AT WILL

As a matter of contract law in most states, employees are presumed to be employed as **employees at will** unless they have agreements that they will be employed for a specified term or may be terminated only for specified causes.[1] At-will employees are not employed for any set period of time. They may resign or their employer may fire them at any time, with or without cause and without advance notice, procedures, or formality.

There are a few exceptions to the freedom employers generally enjoy regarding at-will employees. Employers may not terminate employees, including at-will employees, as a result of illegal discrimination. In addition, certain large employers must give advance notice before laying off a significant number of workers.[2]

Prohibited Employment Discrimination and Required Conduct

There are several areas in which employers must comply with federal equal employment laws and regulations, including many areas for which it is wise to have personnel policies. Employers must comply with equal employment opportunity laws and may not discriminate against applicants or employees based on: race, color, religion, sex, or national origin under Title VII of the Civil Rights Act of 1964[3] and the Equal Pay Act of 1963[4]; age (employees 40 or more years old under the Age Discrimination in Employment Act);[5] or disabilities under the Americans with Disabilities Act.[6] Employers also may not engage in and should not tolerate sexual harassment or harassment based on an employee being, or perceived to be, a member of a protected class.[7]

Most private employers also must meet federal requirements for employee compensation (e.g., minimum wage, overtime, withholding and record-keeping[8]) and employee rights to leave of absence (for pregnancy,[9] jury duty,[10] military service,[11] and, for large employers, medical and family needs[12]).

Many states have employment discrimination laws that parallel the federal laws and impose additional restrictions and requirements, such as prohibiting discrimination based on marriage and requiring leaves for voting. An increasing number of local governments have nonsmoking ordinances employers must follow. Many jurisdictions prohibit discrimination based on employees' sexual preference.

To help avoid or minimize problems, employers are well advised both to avoid the prohibited discrimination considered above and to have personnel policies about at-will employment, equal employment, pay, overtime, leaves, harassment, and sexual harassment. The personnel policies may be stated in an employee manual (discussed later in this chapter) or simply used as guidelines that are followed by the persons responsible for human resource problems in the company. In addition, all employers must post notices in a conspicuous place about

- equal employment (federal and state antidiscrimination laws)
- minimum wage

- overtime
- child labor
- job safety
- workers' compensation
- unemployment insurance benefits
- protection from lie detector tests
- smoking

Depending on their size and business, employers must also post other notices or distribute policies. For instance, companies with more than 50 employees must post notices about leaves under the Family and Medical Leave Act, and certain industries, such as those that employ interstate drivers or whose workers may be exposed to hazardous materials, are required to have notices and policies about drug screening and testing or hazardous materials.

Employee Records

Employers must comply with certain laws and keep records of their compliance with the laws covering the following areas:

- immigration (Form I–9 and proof of each employee's citizenship)
- wages and overtime (payroll and employee identification data; hours all nonexempt employees worked; pay and means of pay calculation, including all additions or deductions and the value of any nonmonetary compensation; and documents describing any benefit and premium payments for employee benefits)
- leave (leave notices, employer leave policies)
- personnel records (job advertisements; employment applications; records regarding hiring, employment agreements, training, testing, promotion, demotion, or transfer; total employee count for each month, states of residency and states where they worked for the employer; performance evaluations; any disciplinary action taken or considered; any employee disputes; any harassment or sexual harassment complaint or discrimination charge or action, investigation and result; layoffs or termination, including all reasons for separation; references received and given; and any medical certifications or records, which must be kept in separate, confidential files)

The time such records must be kept varies. The maximum requirement applies to wages and personnel information, for which employers must preserve records for five years.

Wages and Overtime

Any business with gross annual sales or business totaling $500,000 or more or that has two or more employees who engage in interstate commerce is covered by the federal Fair Labor Standards Act (the "FLSA"). The FLSA and many similar state or local wage laws specify that employers must pay a minimum wage. Wages must be paid in cash or its equivalent; employees cannot be paid in merchandise, products, or other coupons or paper that allows employees to purchase products from the employer. Employees must be paid at least monthly and employees earning hourly wages must be paid within ten days after the end of a pay period.

Most federal and state employee laws distinguish between exempt employees and nonexempt employees in describing the mandatory pay and benefits to which employees are entitled.

Exempt employees are paid according to their salary and are not entitled to overtime payments. These persons are professional and managerial personnel who are expected (and paid) to work until they have accomplished the tasks that have been assigned to them. **Nonexempt employees** are entitled to be paid overtime for all hours worked over forty hours in any work week, which is typically defined as a set period of seven consecutive days. Overtime is usually paid at 1 1/2 times each nonexempt employee's regular rate of pay. *Pay* for overtime purposes includes all remuneration nonexempt employees receive for their labor. "Pay" does not include compensation through retirement or profit-sharing plans, bonuses that are entirely discretionary, travel or other expense reimbursement, holiday pay or occasional gifts such as on holidays that are not related to hours worked, or compensation based upon production or efficiency. Under most current laws, employers may not provide nonexempt employees with time off or **comp time** to avoid paying overtime.

Workers' Compensation and Unemployment Insurance Compensation

All states have workers' compensation insurance to cover employees' work-related injuries. This type of insurance is mandatory and, provided it is in force when an accident occurs, is the exclusive remedy for employees who are injured on the job.

Unemployment insurance is also created and governed by the laws of the state in which employees perform services for their employers. In general, employees who are terminated involuntarily are eligible for unemployment insurance benefits. Many unemployment insurance schemes disqualify employees whose terminations are "for cause," provided the reason for termination corresponds with any reason on a list of serious misconduct (such as theft, violence, gross insubordination, or continued unexcused absences from work).

Employers should verify the workers' compensation and unemployment insurance requirements of each state in which they have employees. Typically, employers must register with state offices that administer these benefits and obtain required levels of coverage from state insurance funds or approved private insurers.

Disadvantages of Employee at Will Status

Employee at will status gives the employee the right to stop working at any time and gives the employer the right to terminate employment at any time. In addition to the uncertainty caused by spontaneity of the relationship, there are employment benefits that an employee might desire from his or her employment. Unless employers commit to any of the following through an express contract, or through their words or conduct that form a promise or create an implied contract, there is generally no legal requirement to provide any of the following:

- pay for time not worked, including severance pay, paid vacations, holidays, or sick leave (except that some jury duty must be paid);
- holidays or vacation (except earned vacation time);
- rest periods (with some exceptions for certain hazardous jobs);
- limits on the work time or hours worked, such as involuntary overtime, weekend, holiday, or night work;
- pay raises or bonuses;
- premium pay for weekends or holidays;
- benefits (other than unemployment and workers' compensation);
- advance notice or reasons for termination, layoffs, or schedule changes (except large employers must give layoff notices); or
- access to personnel records.

As the company structure becomes larger and more employees are needed, managerial talent becomes more important. **Key employees** become an integral part of the organization, and their compensation and incentives assume greater significance. The company must ensure that these people will remain employees in order to guarantee a smooth reliable business organization. Key employees are not necessarily executives. They include salespersons, research and development personnel, and any other employees with special skills. The objectives of the company in retaining these people are selfish on two counts: first, with a loss of key employees, the business may suffer mild to serious reversals until they are replaced; and second, if key employees decide to work for the corporation's competitors, the company not only loses valuable talent but also risks the loss of important trade secrets and processes.

The employees also have some stake in their employment arrangements. Theirs is a question of job security, advancement, and compensation. These complementary objectives of a continuing employment relationship may be satisfied through many combinations of employee agreements, incentive compensation plans, and fringe benefits.

EMPLOYMENT AGREEMENTS

An employee's job security objectives may be ensured by an **employment agreement** or **contract** in which the company promises to keep the employee employed for a period of time and the employee promises to perform the specified duties diligently for the specified period. Employment contracts provide considerably greater protection for the employee than for the employer, in part because courts generally refuse to force a person to perform against that person's will. Consequently, if the employee quits before the expiration of the employment term, the employer cannot successfully petition a court to order the employee to continue working involuntarily. On the other hand, if the employer fires the employee before the expiration of the agreement, the employee may recover the compensation he or she would have received had he or she been allowed to perform the agreement, unless the employer can prove good cause for termination. Nevertheless, an employer may gain some benefits from the employment contract insofar as the contract's terms prescribe incentive compensation to encourage the faithful continued performance of the employee. Further, the agreement may include noncompetition clauses that prohibit the employee's entry into a competing business upon termination, or it may reserve to the company any developments or ideas discovered by the employee during employment.

Like the documents used in many other areas of the law of business organizations, employment contracts must be tailored to the particular needs of the parties. It would be unrealistic to attempt to cover every possibility, but there are certain general rules basic to each agreement. A typical employment agreement should contain clauses describing the employee's responsibilities and duties; provisions for compensation and reimbursement of expenses; a description of the duration of the agreement; provisions for termination of the agreement; and, in many cases, noncompetition clauses, death and disability clauses, and provisions for company rights to discovery and development during employment.

Employee Duties

The contractual language that details the duties and responsibilities of the employee always depends on the particular needs of the employer, the talent and position of the employee, and the needs of the business. The definition of duties is extremely important, considering the possibility of later disputes. Not only must the employee know what the employer expects, but the employer must have some definitive guidelines upon which to measure the employee's performance. If the employee is terminated involuntarily before the expiration of the term of the agreement, the employer must be prepared to show that the employee failed to perform the specified duties under the contract. If the duties described in the agreement are ambiguous or otherwise ill-defined, this proof may be impossible.

The description of duties for top-level management positions necessarily must be broad. It would be difficult to detail all the duties expected of a company executive, since this person is hired to run the business. A general statement of management duties is unavoidable here.

Duties of a Manager

EXAMPLE

The Manager shall well and faithfully serve the Employer in such capacity as aforesaid, and shall at all times devote his or her whole time, attention, and energies to the management, superintendence, and improvement of said business to the utmost of his or her ability, and shall do and perform all such services, acts, and things connected therewith as the Employer shall from time to time direct that are of a kind properly belonging to the duties of a Manager.

More specific provisions may be used for positions with definable boundaries. Consider the following example regarding the duties of a research chemist.

EXAMPLE   **Duties and Inventions of a Research Chemist**

The Corporation hereby employs the Employee as a research chemist. The Employee's duties shall include the application of his or her skill and knowledge as a chemist toward devising new pharmaceutical products and improving existing formulas, processes, and methods employed by the Corporation. All inventions, discoveries, and improvements devised or discovered by the Employee while in the employ of the Corporation shall become and remain the sole and exclusive property of the Corporation, whether discovered during or after regular working hours.

A manager of a merchandising outlet could have duties prescribed as follows:

EXAMPLE   **Duties of a Merchandising Outlet Manager**

The duties of the Manager shall be such as are assigned to him or her by the Company. Initially there shall be included among his or her duties and authority the selection of a stock of merchandise for this venture, schedule of purchases to be submitted and subject to advance approval by the Company, and copies of proposed orders to be submitted to the Company to be passed upon and approved. Selections for current replacements for stock and purchases for new season requirements shall likewise be made by the Manager subject to prior approval by and submission of orders to the Company, in the same manner as is above provided for the initial stock. The Manager shall also keep a perpetual inventory of merchandise on hand and take a monthly physical inventory. The Manager likewise shall have full authority to employ and discharge employees of the business, subject to approval of the Company. The Manager will refer all disputed claims, not allowed by him or her for adjustments or returns on complaints, to the Company. The duties and authority hereby conferred are subject to change at the pleasure of the Company.

In preparing a description of duties, the employer (or, in some cases, the employee) shall prepare a statement of job description that includes all the specific items the employee is expected to do as part of employment. The initial job description prepared by the employer or the employee may then be modified to include other items related to the types of specific duties the employee will perform for the employer. The list of duties should begin with the most specific duties anticipated, and the duties should become more general as the list grows longer. It is important to attempt to identify all potential duties the employee is expected to perform and to highlight technical duties that are unique to this particular employee. In addition, each description of duties must be tailored to the specific employee and to the position the employee will hold.

In representing the employer, it is advisable to include a phrase that permits additional duties to be assigned to the employee from time to time. For example, a duties clause may provide that the employee will perform certain duties and "all other matters connected therewith as the employer shall from time to time direct, and that are of a kind properly belonging to the duties of an employee of this type." Similarly, the duties clause may include a statement that says "the duties and authority hereby conferred are subject to change at the pleasure of the company." These catchall provisions are desirable from the employer's viewpoint in order to ensure that the talents of the employee may be directed to changing employment opportunities, and also to permit the employer to assign specific duties that may not have been contemplated at the time the agreement was negotiated, but which will better define a breach of the agreement should an employee fail to perform them.

Catchall provisions in a statement of duties work to the disadvantage of the employee, unless certain limits are placed upon them. On behalf of an employee, it would be important to provide that any additional duties assigned are to be "of a type that properly belongs to the duties of an employee in a particular position," or "reasonable duties." In this manner, the employee may avoid the assignment of duties that are not consistent with the overall employment or the assignment of inappropriate or distasteful duties to force the employee to breach the agreement.

The duties clause of the employment agreement also may serve to restrict authority and responsibility of the employee. Any limitations on the scope of the employee's authority should be clearly defined. Remember that the business will be liable for any transactions the employee is authorized to undertake, and the principal source of an employee's authority is the description of the employee's duties in the employment agreement. The agreement may reserve certain decisions or transactions to employees at a higher level for organizational purposes. The duties clause may define territories, as in the case of sales personnel, or impose any other restrictions consistent with the employment relationship.

Limitations on Authority of District Manager

EXAMPLE

The District Manager shall possess no authority not herein expressly granted and is not authorized on behalf of the Company to make, alter, or discharge contracts or binders, except as may be directed in writing by the Company, nor to waive forfeitures, grant permits, guarantee in dividends, if any, name extra rates, extend the time of payment of any premium, waive payment in cash, or to write receipts except for first premiums, or make any endorsements on the policies of the Company, and shall receive no further remuneration for any service except as herein provided. It is expressly stipulated and agreed that the District Manager is not authorized to incur any indebtedness or liability in the name or in behalf of the Company for any advertising, office rent, clerk hire, or any other purposes whatsoever or to receive any moneys due or to become due the Company exclusive of the first premium, except as may be specifically directed by the Company, and the powers of the District Manager shall extend no farther than are herein expressly stated.

Restriction

EXAMPLE

The District Manager shall not make or permit to be made by any agent, any use of the radio or insert any advertisement respecting the Company in any paper, or other matter, magazine, newspaper, periodical, or other publication or issue any circular or paper referring to the Company without the written consent of the Company.

Reservation of Right to Reject Orders

EXAMPLE

No order shall be deemed binding upon the company until accepted by the company in its principal office in writing, and the company reserves the right to reject any order, or to cancel the same or any part thereof after acceptance, for credit or any other reason whatsoever deemed by the company to be sufficient.

Compensation

The **compensation** clauses of an employment contract deserve special attention. In the first place, any ambiguity here is certain to become a matter of dispute, since financial matters are of utmost concern to both parties to the agreement. Moreover, the compensation provisions of the contract offer the best opportunity for the employer to ensure continued faithful performance by the employee. Recall that courts are generally unwilling to force an employee to return to the job following a breach of an employment contract. Carefully planned incentive compensation provisions will motivate the employee to remain with the company. Finally, the compensation provisions may permit certain tax advantages for all parties, and these matters should be explored and explained to the client.

At this point the discussion is limited to basic compensation schemes, applicable to all types of business organizations, and to current incentive provisions that encourage immediate, rather than long-term, performance. The exclusively corporate compensation schemes, such as stock options, and the long-term incentive provisions, such as deferred compensation and profit sharing, are discussed separately in later sections.

The most basic type of compensation for an employee is a **salary** arrangement, and contractual terms should specify at least the amount and frequency of payment.

EXAMPLE

Salary Compensation

In consideration of the service so to be performed, the Employer agrees to pay to the Employee the sum of $100,000.00, payable in equal monthly installments for twelve consecutive months at the end of each month, until the termination of this agreement.

A **current incentive** may supplement the salary agreement to encourage diligent performance by the employee.

EXAMPLE

Current Incentive Compensation

The Employer shall pay to the Manager a salary of $120,000.00 per annum, payable by monthly installments of $10,000.00 on the tenth day of each month and shall also pay to the manager a commission of two percent per annum on the net profits of said business, such commission to be paid within ninety days after the year accounts have been certified by the accountants employed by the employer, whose certificate as to the amount of such net profits shall be conclusive.

A percentage compensation agreement, a **commission**, is probably the best current incentive provision. The rate of compensation is based directly upon the employee's own performance, and the commission technique is used most effectively when applied to individual activities. However, this scheme also may be used to compensate management or supervisory employees whose performance depends in part on the efforts of others they control. For management employees, the percentage is frequently based upon profits produced under their direction. A clause must be included to define profits for application of the percentage. Moreover, since a determination of profits usually is not made until the close of the business year, the employee usually is permitted to withdraw specified sums in advance for current living expenses until the employee's percentage share has been determined. Examples of provisions for executive compensation follow:

EXAMPLE

Executive Commission Compensation

The Company shall pay to the Manager as compensation for his or her services one-third of the net profits arising from the Chicago business.

EXAMPLE

Net Profits

In arriving at what shall be deemed the net profits arising from the Chicago business, the following items shall be paid out of the gross profits, viz.: the rents of the premises wherein the Chicago business shall be conducted and all repairs and alterations of the same, all taxes and payments for insurance, all salaries and wages of clerks and employees other than the Manager employed in or about the Chicago business, and all charges and expenses incurred in or about the same, all debts or other moneys that shall be payable on account of the Chicago business, the interest on the capital for the time being advanced by the Company, and all losses and damages incurred in or about the Chicago business.

Drawing Account

The Manager shall have the right to draw out for his or her own use the sum of $7,500.00 per month on account of his or her salary. The balance of his or her one-third share in the net profits shall not be withdrawn by him or her until after the annual general account hereinafter mentioned shall have been made and signed.

Commission provisions for an individual employee's performance require a similar approach. However, instead of profit, the percentage is usually applied to sales obtained for the company by the employee, and that criterion creates another definitional problem. The sale of goods involves at least four transactional stages: the order is signed, the order is approved by the company, the goods are shipped, and the customer pays. One of these four stages, or some other reasonably ascertainable point, should be selected as the time the commission is earned. If any intermediate stage is selected, the company may further specify that the commission will be withdrawn or reduced if the customer fails to pay.

Compensation and Basis for Computing Commissions

In consideration of your services, we agree to pay you a commission of five percent on all sales during the term of your employment made to customers located in the territory covered by you. Such commissions shall be calculated on the net amount of sales, after deducting returns, allowances, freight charges, discounts, bad debts, and similar items, and shall be deemed to be earned and payable only as and when orders have been shipped and actually paid for by customers. The prepayment of commissions shall not be deemed to be a waiver of the foregoing provisions, and in all cases in which commissions have been paid in advance of payment by the customer, or where returns or allowances are subsequently made, such appropriate adjustment as may be necessary shall thereafter be made.

Drawing Account and Traveling Expenses

You shall be entitled to receive and we agree to pay you a drawing account of $2,000.00 per week, which sum shall be applied against and deducted from commissions then or thereafter due you. You personally shall pay all traveling and other expenses incurred by you in connection with your employment.

To be effective, current incentive programs should be directly related to the performance of the employee or of the persons under the employee's supervision. The employee has no control over unrelated performance and thus has no opportunity (or incentive) to improve it.

Current incentive programs pose special drafting problems to ensure absolute clarity. In the foregoing examples, the percentages, time for payment, formula for determining the amount to which the percentage is applied, and application of draws against earned compensation are all well defined. Each of these items must be unambiguous if the compensation provisions are to be effective. Some additional suggestions may be helpful:

1. A date or periodic date should be specified for the payment of incentive compensation. For example, if the incentive compensation is computed on an annual basis, it should be specified that payment will be made on a specific date of the following year, or within a certain number of days from the close of the business year. The exact date permits the employee to plan the receipt of income, and allows the employer to plan cash flow.
2. If accounting terms are used, such as *net profit* or *net sales,* they should be defined in the agreement. Specific expense items should be named if they are to be deducted from gross profit to reach net profit, or from gross sales to reach net sales. Moreover, the provisions should define profit as before or after income taxes are deducted, whichever represents the agreement of the parties.
3. The person or persons who determine the base amount against which the percentage is applied should be named. If the company retains independent public accountants to audit its

records, the accountants should be specified as the persons who will make these determinations, and it is common practice to specify that their determination is to be based upon "generally accepted accounting principles." However, keep in mind that generally accepted accounting principles are not well-defined rules, even for accountants. To avoid any disputes concerning computations in an employment agreement, it is preferable to provide that the amount will be determined "by the accountant then engaged by the company in the accountant's sole and exclusive judgment, which will be a conclusive determination for all purposes."

4. If the employee is permitted to **draw** against the incentive compensation, the agreement should cover the contingency that the draws may exceed the earned compensation. For example, suppose the manager is to receive one-third of the profits as determined at the end of the year, and the manager has drawn $36,000 during the year. If the profits total $99,000 when tallied, will the manager be required to repay the company $3,000, or will that amount accrue to be applied against the following year's profits, or will it be forgiven and deemed to be an expense of the company? The agreement should provide an answer.

5. If the incentive compensation is based upon periodic performance such as annual profits, the employee's commencement and termination during the period should be considered. A relatively small number of employees are hired on the first day of the business year. (A few more may quit on the last day, however, considering that the arduous task of taking inventory may be looming in the immediate future.) Nevertheless, some formula must be inserted for the employee who has not worked for the entire period upon which incentive compensation is based. A formula for this purpose may be drafted on any reasonable basis. For example, the employee's percentage may be applied to profit computed for the period of the year during which the employee actually worked. If the employee began working August 1, the actual profit would be computed from August 1 to December 31, and the percentage applied against that figure. Alternatively, the formula may specify a pro rata determination of profit for the entire year. Here, the entire year's profit would be reduced to five-twelfths, the fraction of the year from August 1 to December 31, and the percentages would be applied to that amount. Finally, a separate special formula for years of commencement and termination may be stated, such as one-sixth of the profit for these years, or no profit percentage if the employee works for less than half of any year, and so forth.

6. If the incentive compensation is based upon an event, such as the sale of the employer's products or services, the event that will cause the compensation to be payable should be specified. The event could be
   (a) when the salesperson enters into the contract to provide products or services;
   (b) when the company accepts the order;
   (c) when the products are shipped or the services are performed; or
   (d) when the company is paid by the customer.
   All of these events are negotiable between the employee and the employer, but the applicable event should be clearly specified in the agreement.

Closely related to the percentage compensation is a **bonus plan** based upon minimum performance of the employee, or the employee's division or department. The agreement may establish certain sums to be paid at a specified time following the close of the business year if the employee's individual performance or the employee's section of the organization produces results above a specified minimum. The bonus amounts may be periodically increased to reward continued performance. For example, the agreement with a manager of a retail store may provide that the manager shall receive a bonus of $1,000 the first year that net profits before taxes from the store exceed $10,000; $2,000 the second consecutive year that profits exceed that amount; and $3,000 the third and subsequent consecutive years that profits continue to exceed $10,000. The drafting considerations detailed earlier are equally applicable here. The agreement should define net profit or any other selected criterion, should specify the person who will determine the base figures, should provide for termination during the year, and should specify a date the bonus will be paid.

The bonus plan may be limited to an incentive for continuous employment, without considering the specific performance of the employee. For example, the agreement may discourage voluntary termination during the year.

Compensation and Bonus

EXAMPLE

The Employee shall receive a weekly salary of $1,000. In addition, the Company shall pay to the Employee at the end of each year of the term a year-end bonus of not less than $10,000 (less withholding taxes, social security, and other required deductions); but no part of said bonus shall be payable if the Employee shall be in default under this agreement or shall not then be in the employ of the Company.

The compensation section of the employment agreement is also an appropriate place to describe incidental financial benefits, such as reimbursement for expenses, vacation pay, and so forth.

Expense Reimbursement

EXAMPLE

Employer shall also pay to the Salesperson his or her reasonable expenses of traveling, board and lodging, postage, and other expenses reasonably incurred by him or her as such Salesperson in or about the business of the Employer.

Vacations

EXAMPLE

The Employee shall be entitled to vacations with pay in accordance with the established practices of the Company now or hereafter in effect for supervisory personnel.

The foregoing compensation plans are common to most employment agreements. Continued faithful performance of the employee also may be reasonably ensured by use of the special compensation techniques discussed in subsequent sections.

Term of the Agreement

The duration of the employment agreement should be specific and, as a general rule, should be reasonably short for the company's protection. If a continuing employment relationship is contemplated, it is far better to provide for options to renew the agreement than to leave the term indefinite.

The basic term of the agreement is always simple.

Duties and Term

EXAMPLE

The Employee agrees to give his or her undivided time and service in the employ of the Employer in such capacity as the Employer may direct, for the period of one year from and after the 1st day of December, 2005.

Renewal provisions may be drafted in one of three ways. First, the option to renew the agreement may be granted to the employer, with appropriate advance notice to the employee of the election to renew. Second, the option to renew may be vested with the employee, with appropriate advance notice to the employer of the election to renew. Third, the agreement may be automatically renewed for specified periods unless appropriate notice is given by either party to the other of the intention not to renew. The last provision is most common, and most adaptable to a continuing employment relationship.

Option to Renew

Employee grants Employer the option to renew this contract for a period of two years upon all the terms and conditions herein contained, except for the option to renew for a further period. This option may be exercised by Employer by giving Employee notice in writing at least thirty days prior to the expiration hereof; and such notice to Employee may be given by delivery to Employee personally or by mailing to Employee at the last known address.

Initial Term and Automatic Renewal

The term of this employment shall commence February 1, 2005, and shall continue for a period of two years until January 31, 2007, and thereafter shall be deemed to be renewed automatically, upon the same terms and conditions, for successive periods of one year each, until either party, at least thirty days prior to the expiration of the original term or of any extended term, shall give written notice to the other of intention not to renew such employment.

Provisions for notice should be tailored for specific circumstances. Written notice should always be required, and should be sent to a specified address of each party. For the employee, the address may be specified as "the last known address," or "the address on the records of the company." The time period for notice should be longer for a more specialized employee so that the employee may search for other employment if necessary, or so that the company may search for a replacement.

Termination of the Agreement

The employment agreement should be terminated or terminable upon the happening of certain contingent events. In many cases, salary continuation protection for an employee may be appropriate upon the happening of one of these events, and in cases where the event is also defined by an insurance policy, the employment agreement should use the definition from the insurance policy to be certain there is no conflict between the two definitions.

The following contingent events should be considered as potential causes for termination:

1. the employee is disabled for a period of time;
2. the employee is bankrupt;
3. the employee has been convicted of a crime;
4. the employee is incarcerated;
5. the employee is mentally disabled or otherwise unable to perform duties;
6. the employee is suffering from substance-abuse disabilities;
7. the employee breaches the agreement;
8. the portion of the business in which the employee is employed is discontinued for any reason;
9. the business is insolvent or bankrupt;
10. a substantial portion of the business assets are destroyed;
11. the business is sold, merged, or dissolved for any reason;
12. majority ownership of the business changes; or
13. any other matter arises that, considering the special duties of the employee, may constitute cause for termination under the agreement.

Termination of Manager with Cause

In the event of the illness of the Manager or other cause incapacitating him or her from attending to his or her duties as manager for six consecutive weeks, the Employer may terminate this agreement without notice upon payment to the Manager of $5,000.00 in addition to all arrears of salary and commission when ascertained up to the date of such termination. In the event of a breach of this agreement or of an act of bankruptcy on the part of the Manager, the Employer may terminate this agreement without notice or payment of salary or commission as hereinbefore provided.

Termination with Cause

This agreement shall terminate in the event of the dissolution of the firm by death or otherwise, the appointment of a receiver or trustee in bankruptcy or the filing of a petition to reorganize under the Bankruptcy Act, or the destruction by fire of the firm's warehouse at South Bend, Indiana, notwithstanding the full term of one year may not, at the happening of any of said events, have fully expired.

Finally, it is possible to agree to termination without cause with due notice.

Termination without Cause

The employment of the Employee may be terminated at any time (during the said period of two years) by either party giving to the other two calendar months' notice in writing of its or his or her intention to terminate the same, or by the Company upon its paying to the Employee a sum equal to two months' salary at the rate aforesaid in lieu of such notice.

Severance Compensation

Most current employment agreements for senior executives in business provide for **severance compensation** upon termination of the agreement, especially when the company chooses to terminate the agreement. When an employment agreement provides for the consequences of termination in terms of compensation to the terminated employee, the likelihood of litigation alleging wrongful termination is reduced (since agreement usually provides that receipt of the severance compensation is a release of any claims for wrongful termination) and the payments are regarded by both the employer and the employee as a form of agreed damages to compensate the employee for the difficulty and burden of looking for new employment. High-level managers are not freely marketable; they will require some time to find new positions that match their talents and meet their compensation requirements. Severance packages are customarily called "**golden parachutes**," and they provide for continuation of salary or lump sum payments of future expected salary, continuation of employee benefits for a period of time, and, in some cases, the repurchase of stock or ownership interests in the business owned by the executive.

The variations of golden parachute provisions are endless and depend entirely upon the executive's ability to negotiate his or her termination provisions upon accepting employment. Usually, the value of the severance package varies according to whether the company terminates the employee with or without cause or whether the employee elects to terminate the employment to leave for greener pastures. In some cases, the employee is entitled to severance payments if the employee elects to resign because his or her duties have substantially changed through a modification of company policies by the board of directors or through a transfer of the control of the business to another entity. The duration of the compensation and benefits often depends upon the employee's obligations under a covenant not to compete or similar employment restriction imposed by the employment agreement.

EMPLOYEE HANDBOOKS AND MANUALS

Although the definition of the employment relationship in a written contract is the best method of ensuring the legal responsibilities and rights of the parties, most employees do not have written agreements with their employers and serve as employees at will. Written employment agreements usually are used for senior management and key administrative persons in whom the employer has a significant business interest, to protect the employer by contractually ensuring the employees' availability for services with the company.

It has become customary for large businesses to publish and distribute **employee handbooks** or **manuals** governing the employment relationship between the employee and the employer. The information in these documents helps to ensure uniform administration of employment relations and personnel policies and to describe standards for the performance of duties and conduct of the employees. Common provisions include specific obligations assumed by the employer, such as compensation increases, benefit program coverage, vacation and sick leave benefits, and workplace accommodations and etiquette. The handbook usually describes expectations of the employer and permissible conduct of the employee on issues of absenteeism, dishonesty, insubordination, and disloyalty. Because of the proliferation of employment-related civil rights and discrimination legislation and judicial interpretations during the past decade, employers have found it necessary and desirable to state certain policies of the business in a published manual to advise all employees of the company's position on these important issues. For example, issues such as sexual harassment, which is considered under federal law as a form of discrimination, and other issues relating to discrimination are frequently addressed in policies describing the types of employee behavior that are unacceptable, the consequences for engaging in such behavior, and complaint and hearing procedures for resolution of any such incidents. Finally, the manual often sets forth progressive disciplinary and appeal steps to be followed in the event of employee misconduct or nonperformance, and states the method by which the employment relationship will be terminated.

In summary, the employee handbook provides a means by which an employer can explain the rules and policies concerning employment with the company and show that the company subscribes to a policy of fairness and equal treatment in employment matters covering a broad range of employee issues and disputes.

Employee handbooks are usually prepared internally by the company's human resources staff or personnel department, since they describe the specific employment issues that have been encountered in the company's history. The handbook should always be reviewed by the company's lawyer for legal sufficiency and to detect inadvertent (and costly) commitments to employees. Generally, the handbook will include the following topics:

1. Organization and administration of the company, describing the history, culture, ethics, and structure of the firm. The supervisory hierarchy of the company, including the management configuration and personnel-related committees, are normally described here. This section usually contains a statement concerning equal employment opportunity and the company's policy concerning discrimination or harassment issues.
2. Employee benefits and policies. This section describes the company's policies concerning holidays, vacation, sick time, leaves of absence, insurance, retirement plans, and other miscellaneous benefits, such as continuing education, legal services, direct banking arrangements available to employees, and the like. The description of benefits and policies should always provide for the employer to change the benefits and policies with appropriate notice to the employees.
3. General personnel policies. This section describes the procedures for payment of compensation, overtime, advances, and bonuses; procedures for updating personal information in the company's files; policies concerning promotions and lateral transfers; procedures for reporting accidents, soliciting fellow employees, expressing grievances, and personnel reviews; and policies concerning nepotism, alcoholism or drug abuse, and other work-related impairment issues. This section also usually describes the policies and procedures to be followed upon termination of employment, including voluntary resignation, disciplinary action, compensation upon termination, and policies regarding letters of reference.
4. General office procedures. This section covers topics such as working hours, personal conduct, facilities maintenance and use, completion of reports, and communication procedures within the company.

5. Administrative services. This section describes the services and facilities available to the employees and the methods by which their uses are regulated or limited. The use of the company's Internet Access, telephones, mail services, records, supplies, copy equipment, and other available items is a typical issue in this section.

6. Accounting and expense services. This section usually states the method by which disbursements are made, expenses are reimbursed, and accounting procedures are imposed.

7. Security and emergency procedures. This section deals with the rules of employee and company security and describes the procedures to be followed in an emergency.

Each employment manual is tailored to the specific policies and activities of the company, so only general statements concerning content can be made here. The employer should strive to include all items of policy or procedure about which there is a possibility of an employee misunderstanding or dispute. The rules must be written with clarity and precision to avoid confusion and uncertainty. On the other hand, the manual should be an expression of the business's guidelines and should be flexible enough for individual application in unique situations.

Employers historically distributed handbooks freely without concern that the statements or policies in the manuals had any legal significance. The guidelines were regarded as the employer's unilateral rules, freely modifiable by the employer (unless actually incorporated into a written employment agreement) and unsupported by any legal consideration, since the employee usually did not decide to accept employment based upon the rules in the manual and, in some cases, did not even learn about the manual until after being hired and completing a probationary employment period. However, recent employment cases have demonstrated that handbooks carelessly drafted without careful consideration of employment laws can create significant legal problems for the employer.[13]

The modern approach to employment manuals assumes that the manuals may become contracts of employment. Most courts considering the issue have imposed an objective test to determine whether an employee has a contractual right to enforce what is written in the employee manual: Would a reasonable person looking at the objective manifestations of the parties' intent find that they intended the manual to be a contract between them? Based upon this test, it is possible that not all statements contained in employee handbooks would be found to have created contractual rights and duties. For example, a statement that "an employee will be treated fairly and with dignity" is not likely to form the basis for a contractual obligation. Unspecific job security provisions, such as "an employee can expect a high degree of job security," are too vague to be actionable.[14] However, statements concerning compensation and specific procedures for discipline and discharge may be enforceable by a disgruntled employee. Courts also may impose an **implied covenant of good faith and fair dealing** in the employment relationship and use the statements in the employee handbook as the baseline measure of whether the employer has acted in good faith and fairly. In addition, the policies and procedures in the handbook may be used as a basis for discrimination allegations. For example, if the handbook states that an employee may return to the company in an equivalent position following a leave of absence, a returning employee who is demoted following medical treatment for pregnancy may use the manual provisions to show discrimination.

The most common dispute to surface concerning employee manuals regards limitations on an employer's right to discharge an employee. A handbook contractually limits an employer's right to discharge an employee if the book contains a provision that is an express limitation to that effect, such as a statement that "an employee will only be terminated for cause." If an employee is able to identify a written provision in the manual in which the employer has expressly agreed to limit its rights to discharge the employee, a court will likely enforce the limitation. Even in the absence of an express provision, some courts have used the policies and procedures published in the book as a basis for an implied contract imposing limitations on termination. If the manual sets forth a disciplinary procedure by which an employee receives first an oral warning, then a written warning, and then discharge, the employer will be required to follow that procedure. If the employer attempts to discharge an employee on the spot, even for extreme misconduct or insubordination, the employer could be liable for wrongful termination of the employment relationship. Similarly, if the manual describes a hearing and appeal procedure accompanying the discharge of an employee, the company must follow the procedure and ensure that the employee's hearing and appeal is substantive and fair.

Most benefits promised to employees by an employer in an employee handbook are enforceable by the employees. If the employer states that after retirement the employer will pay severance benefits or continue to pay life insurance premiums for the employee, the employer is legally bound to observe those promises. If any flexibility is desired by the employer, the handbook must contain an unambiguous and prominently displayed reservation-of-rights clause, permitting the employer to amend or cancel the described benefits at the employer's discretion. Most careful benefit administrators ask employees to sign a personnel form expressing their understanding of the company's right to modify its benefits and compensation arrangements at any time.

Counsel should review the company's employee handbook and ascertain carefully whether the statements contained in the book create express or implied promises upon which an employee could bring a claim against the employer. Several practices have developed in response to the recent proliferation of cases concerning these manuals to protect the employer from unwanted and unexpected legal liability. First, the book should not be distributed without a prominent, conspicuous statement that no contractual relationship is intended by the issuance and delivery of the manual. The book should state the employer's intention to create only an employment relationship at will. It also is usually advisable to include a similar statement in the company's application for employment form. Any waivers or disclaimers concerning benefit plans must be carefully drafted to comply with laws and regulations governing employee benefits, such as the **Employment Retirement Income Security Act (ERISA)**, discussed later in this chapter.[15]

To protect the employer and the employee from misunderstandings concerning the purpose and the legal enforceability of the handbook, the manual should begin with an explanation of the employer's intentions and the purpose of the book.

EXAMPLE

Beginning Disclaimer in Employer Handbook

Although we hope our relationship will be long and mutually beneficial, it should be recognized that neither you nor the Company has entered into any contract of employment, express or implied. Your relationship with the Company is and will always be "at will," which means your employment with the Company is voluntary, and you are free to resign at any time. Similarly, the Company is free to terminate your employment at any time, for any reason, with or without cause.

The information contained in this employee handbook is subject to change or elimination at any time by management without notice as business conditions and needs change.

Neither this handbook nor any other communication by any company representative, either written or oral, made before or when you are hired is intended in any way to create an employment contract. During your employment, no employee, officer, or other representative of the Company is authorized to give you any oral or written assurance of continued employment or of any other term or condition of employment, and you may not rely on any written or oral assurance of continued employment or any other term or condition of employment unless you receive any such assurance in writing from the Board of Directors.

It is also advisable to include an acknowledgment concerning the utility and purpose of the handbook on the employee's application for employment.

Application of Employment Acknowledgment

Acknowledgment

I acknowledge that I have received a copy of the Company's employee handbook dated _____, and I agree to familiarize myself with the handbook and to comply with the information the handbook contains.

I understand that my employment with the Company is and always will be "at will" and may be terminated, with or without cause, by me or by the Company at any time and for any reason. I also understand that no employee, officer, or other representative of the Company is authorized to make any oral or written assurance of continued employment, and that I may only rely on any such assurance if it is in writing to me from the Board of Directors.

I understand the handbook is intended to serve only as a guide to the Company's policies and procedures, and that the policies and procedures are subject to change or elimination without notice and at any time in the Company's sole discretion, as business conditions and needs change. I also understand that nothing in the handbook and no custom or practice of the Company is intended to be nor will they constitute a contract of any kind between the Company and me, including any contract regarding the length of my employment or any term or condition of my employment with the Company.

I understand I have an obligation to inform my supervisor, in writing, of any changes in the information I provided in my employment application, including my address, telephone number, and any change in my marital status and number of dependents for insurance and withholding purposes.

DATED:_____, 20_____.

_____
(Employee Signature)

_____
(Witness)

RESTRICTIVE AND PROPRIETARY COVENANTS

Although an employer may be unsuccessful in persuading a court to order an employee to continue to work for the company against the employee's will, the employer may prevent the employee from exploiting the company by appropriating ideas that were developed during the employment for the employee's own benefit; leaving with trade secrets, specialized confidential knowledge, or customer lists; or working for competitors. Certain **restrictive** or **proprietary covenants** in the employment agreement or signed by an employee at will as a condition of hiring may protect the employer from such abuse, and if properly drafted, these covenants will receive court protection.

The covenants generally cover three areas of possible employee exploitation: (1) competing with the company after employment; (2) maintaining confidentiality of business secrets during and after employment; and (3) using developments, inventions, and ideas that the employee produced during the course of employment. Without an agreement on each of these points, under common law the employer risks the loss of significant market advantages through the acts of unfaithful employees.

No former employee is prohibited from competing against a former employer without a specific agreement to that effect. The law has always favored fair and free competition, and there is nothing implicit in an employment relationship that requires the employee to withdraw from the marketplace after the employment is terminated. That is not to say, however, that the employee would be allowed to duplicate the former employer's secret practices and processes in future competition.

The law protects **trade secrets**, even without an agreement prohibiting their use, but the protection is somewhat elusive and unsatisfactory if left to common law resolution alone. First, it is difficult to determine which practices, procedures, and other matters are truly trade secrets entitled to protection. The employer has the burden to prove that the company is the "owner" of the secret, meaning the secret was developed by or for the company, is not used by others, and is sufficiently unique so as to deserve legal protection. Further, the employer must show that the secret is known only to company employees in whom it must be confided for business purposes. Even if the matter were shown to be a trade secret, a court would have to be convinced that the employee's exploitation should be prohibited. The court would have to find that the employee's use or publication of the secret could cause irreparable harm to the employer. An agreement restricting the employee's use of trade secrets is essential for certainty of protection in this area.

The common law is also unpredictable on the question of an employer's rights in an employee's original ideas and developments discovered during the course of employment. Certainly, if the employee is hired to do research and create inventions, the employer has ownership rights in any productive research while the employee is on the job. But what happens if the employee dreams up an invention that is unrelated to the employer's research, or if the employee quits before research is productive and subsequently produces an invention for the personal benefit of the employee? Specific provisions in the agreement may anticipate and resolve these problems.

EMPLOYER'S RIGHT TO EMPLOYEE WORK PRODUCT

The employer may have hired the employee for the express purpose of developing new products or business innovations. Certain specialized skills, such as research chemistry or engineering, are widely sought for this purpose, and the employment relationship is directed to the production of inventions. The employee also may be hired to develop certain business practices and procedures that will increase efficiency and utilization of other employees' skills. These common cases should be distinguished by the test of a **work product** that can be legally protected. In the first case, an invention from the original thought of an engineer may be patentable and thereby have certain proprietary interests attached to it. In the second case, a particular procedural system devised by a time-and-motion expert may be unique, but will not be such a unique, original creative product that a patent or copyright could be obtained. The employer's interest in each may be indistinguishable, however. The company obviously wants to retain proprietary rights in patentable inventions, and management may be equally concerned about reserving newly devised business procedures to themselves for the associated competitive advantages. The clauses suggested here will protect the company's rights to the patentable inventions, but they may not be adaptable to protection of other unpatentable work products. Rather, in the second case it would be more appropriate to describe the developed business procedure as a trade secret in the agreement and thereby ensure some confidentiality, or to prohibit the development of a similar system for a competitor through a noncompetitive covenant with the employee.

Work product clauses are most effective for inventions and other original creations that are so unique that they are capable of being patented or copyrighted. A work product clause should include at least the following general components:

1. a specific grant from the employee to the employer of the right to use the work product;
2. a statement that the clause applies to any use to which the employer chooses to make of the work product;
3. a statement that the clause applies to inventions, designs, procedures, and other matters in both their unperfected and improved states;
4. a statement that the clause applies to inventions, designs, and other matters developed or obtained by the employee alone or severally or jointly with other persons;
5. a statement that the clause applies to the entire period of the employment with the employer;
6. a specific description of the employee's talents out of which inventions and designs are expected to be produced;
7. a specific description of the type of inventions, designs, and other matters the employee is expected to develop;

8. a general statement that other inventions or designs, and other matters that relate to the employee's product will be covered by the clause;

9. a release by the employee of any legal or equitable right to the work product;

10. a promise by the employee that all necessary documents for assigning and transferring ownership will be executed and delivered to the employer on demand;

11. a representation by the employee that the work product will not infringe upon any patents or protected rights of others;

12. any special compensation arrangements that have been negotiated with the employee for subsequent use of the invention, design, or work product;

13. an agreement that the work will be protected by statutes governing trade secrets to protect against its publication before a patent, copyright, or other protected proprietary rights may be obtained; and

14. the relief or remedies to which the employer may be entitled for a breach of the clause, such as injunctions, liquidated damages, a constructive trust on all profits produced, and so forth.

The scope of these provisions is usually determined by the nature of the employment. For example, if an employee is hired for the broad purpose of researching and developing improvements in elevators, a broad protective grant of a license would be appropriate.

Grant of License

EXAMPLE

The Employee hereby grants to the Employer the exclusive license to manufacture, sell, and deal in all inventions, designs, improvements, and discoveries of the Employee, whether now perfected or whether invented, improved, and discovered subsequent hereto, which pertain or relate to elevators and their appliances, or are capable of use in connection therewith.

If the employment objective is more specific, such as the research and development of a valve and starter plug to improve elevator control, the clause may be more specific.

Inventions Designated as the Property of the Employer

EXAMPLE

The Employee agrees that all inventions, improvements, ideas, and suggestions made by him or her and patents obtained by him or her severally or jointly with any other person or persons during the entire period of his or her employment, and any written renewal thereof made by him or her with the Employer, with relation to said valve and its appurtenances, including present starting plug, or method of elevator control, and all inventions of elevator valves, plugs, or methods of elevator control and valve appliances, and to machinery for manufacturing the same, are and shall be the sole property of the Employer, free from any legal or equitable title of the Employee, and that all necessary documents for perfecting such title shall be executed by the Employee and delivered to the Employer on demand.

The specificity of the clause may be a matter for negotiation between the parties. The employee in the second example may have insisted upon the narrow description so that his or her subsequent development of an elevator door, for example, would not belong to the employer. However, the employee may be willing to consent to the broader provision for increased compensation. The employer's objective is to make the subject matter of the clause all-inclusive.

Work product protection clauses should always require the execution of any necessary documents for perfecting the employer's title to the inventions, as shown in the second example. This requirement may obviate any need for an interpretation of the contract before the employer can market the invention, and the clause will place the employee in breach of the agreement if the employee fails to cooperate fully with the employer. It is also desirable to contract for trade secret protection of the invention to protect against the invention's publication before a patent may be obtained. A clause on these points follows.

EXAMPLE

Execution of Further Documents

I further agree, without charge to said company, but at its expense, to execute, acknowledge, and deliver all such further papers, including applications for patents, and to perform such other acts as I lawfully may, as may be necessary in the opinion of said company, to obtain or maintain patents for said inventions in any and all countries and to vest title thereto in said company, its successors and assigns; and I further agree that I will not divulge to others any information I may obtain during the course of my employment relating to the formulas, processes, methods, machines, manufacturers, compositions, or inventions of said company without first obtaining written permission from said company to do so.

It may be appropriate (and necessary, if the employee skillfully negotiates the agreement) for the employer to compensate the employee based upon the profitable inventions the employee has created for the company. The percentage compensation scale can be tailored to the demands of the parties, and might look like this:

EXAMPLE

Compensation for Inventions

In order to recompense the above employee (hereinafter called the Employee) for meritorious inventions, the Company agrees on its part to examine the inventions disclosed to it by the Employee, and where said inventions, in the sole opinion of the Company, warrant such action, to cause United States patent applications to be filed through its attorneys covering the same, but without assuming any responsibility for the prosecution or defense of such patent applications, and further agrees to give to the Employee in any cases where it decides to license said inventions, applications, or patents to others, a percentage of any money royalties that it may receive from such licenses upon the following scale:

Of the first $10,000 or part thereof collected in any one calendar year—40%
Of the next $20,000 or part thereof collected in any one calendar year—30%
Of the next $30,000 or part thereof collected in any one calendar year—20%
Of the next $50,000 or part thereof collected in any one calendar year—15%
Of all further sums collected in any one calendar year—10%

It is understood and agreed, however, that the question of when, how, and to whom licenses shall be granted shall be in the sole discretion of the Company, and that in cases where the Company shall grant licenses involving, in addition to the Employee's inventions, the inventions of others, the Company shall have the sole right and authority to apportion the royalties received, and the Employee shall receive the above percentage on the proportion awarded to his or her inventions.

TRADE SECRET PROTECTION

Beginning with the truism that various companies have various secrets, some more important than others, trade secret protection must always be drafted to fit the particular needs of the company. A discount retail merchant may consider its supplier list to be a trade secret; a manufacturing company may consider the assembly process to be a trade secret; and a computer firm would treat its programs and techniques for interpretation as trade secrets. In each business, the "secret" is an integral part of the competitive advantage, and confidentiality is deemed to be crucial to continued success of the operation. In part, this mystery is a result of using well-drafted employment agreements (or **nondisclosure agreements**) and never completely disclosing the secret process to anyone (see Exhibit 12–1, Nondisclosure Agreement).

NON-DISCLOSURE AGREEMENT

_____

NON-DISCLOSURE AGREEMENT
Covering Inventions, Discoveries, and Confidential Matter

In consideration of my employment, or my continued employment, as the case may be, by _____, a Delaware corporation (hereinafter called the Company), I agree with the Company as follows:

So long as I shall remain in the employ of the Company I will devote my whole time and ability to the service of the Company in such capacity as it shall from time to time direct, and I will perform my duties faithfully and diligently.

I will not, during my employment or thereafter, use or disclose to others without the written consent of the Company, any trade secrets, secret "know-how", confidential or secret technical information or other confidential information relative to your business obtained by me while in the employ of the Company. Upon leaving the employ of the Company I will not take with me any confidential data, drawings, or information obtained by me as the result of my employment, or any reproduction thereof. All such Company property will be surrendered to the Company on termination or at any time on request.

I will disclose to the Company and, upon the Company's request, assign to it, without charge, all my right, title and interest in and to any and all inventions and discoveries which I may make solely or jointly with others, while in the employ of the Company which relate to or are useful or may be useful in connection with business of the character carried on or contemplated by the Company, and all my right, title and interest in and to any and all domestic and foreign applications for patents covering such inventions and discoveries and any and all patents granted for such inventions and any and all reissues and extensions of such patents; and upon request of the Company whether during or subsequent to this employment I will do any and all acts and execute and deliver such instruments as may be deemed by the Company necessary or proper to vest all my right, title and interest in and to said inventions, applications, and patents in the Company and to secure or maintain such patents, reissues and/or extensions thereof. Any inventions and discoveries relating to the Company's business made by me within one year after termination of my employment with the Company shall be deemed to be within this provision, unless I can prove that the same were conceived and made following said termination. All necessary and proper expenses in connection with the foregoing shall be borne by the Company, and if services in connection therewith are performed at the Company's request after termination of employment, the Company will pay reasonable compensation for such.

Attached hereto is a list of patent applications and unpatented inventions made prior to my employment by the Company, which I agree is a complete list and which I desire to remove from the operation of this agreement.

This Agreement shall enure to the benefit of the Company, its subsidiaries, allied companies, successors and assigns or nominees of the Company, and I specifically agree to execute any and all documents considered convenient or necessary to assign, transfer, sustain and maintain inventions, discoveries, applications and patents, both in this and foreign countries.

IN WITNESS WHEREOF, I have hereunto signed my name and affixed my seal, this ____ day of _____, 20__.

Witness:

_____ _____(SEAL)

_____ _____(DEPT.)

Distribution: Execute in triplicate – White copy for Department, yellow copy for Employer; and pink copy for Personnel Relations Department.

Exhibit 12–1.

Nondisclosure Agreement

Several important rules should be followed in drafting trade secret clauses for employment contracts. First, the promise to keep the secrets should bind the employee during the employment and after termination of employment. Second, the clause should cover not only specific secrets that the employee uses in performing duties under the agreement, but also secrets the employee may have learned from alert observations or from other employees. Third, the agreement should broadly prohibit divulging any "trade secrets, procedures, processes, or knowledge of operations," and should specifically itemize particular matters that are to be protected. Fourth, because of the difficulty of proving actual damages from the publication of a trade secret, an agreed damage clause, or **liquidated damages**, should be considered. A clause with all of these ingredients follows.

EXAMPLE

Trade Secrets

The Salesperson further covenants not to communicate during the continuance of this agreement, or at any time subsequently, any trade secrets, processes, procedures, or business operations, specifically including but not limited to information relating to the secrets of the traveling, advertising, and canvassing departments, nor any knowledge or secrets he or she then had or might from time to time acquire pertaining to other departments of the business of the Employer, to any person not a member of the Employer's firm, except as requested in writing by the Employer. In case of violation of this covenant, the Salesperson agrees to pay the Employer or its successors the sum of $5,000 as liquidated damages, but such payment is not to release the Salesperson from the obligations undertaken, or from liability for further breach thereof.

It also would be advisable to prohibit the employee's use of the secret as an individual, or the employee's direct or indirect benefit from the use of the secret, such as when a shareholder, partner, employee, consultant, creditor, or other participant in another business learns about or adopts the secret from the employee. It is also customary to agree that the employer will be entitled to injunctive relief against the person using the trade secret to stop such use and avoid irreparable harm to the employer's business.

Customer lists commonly are covered in trade secret clauses, since courts are not likely to construe customer lists as a business secret under common law so as to shelter them without an agreement. However, in highly competitive businesses, the secrecy of customer lists is an important competitive advantage. A competitor who obtains them will be spared considerable time and expense in locating interested customers. Depending upon the nature of the business, customer list protection may not need to extend indefinitely after termination of employment. The list may change significantly within a year or two, and the contractual provision may be so limited.

EXAMPLE

Customer Lists

The Employee further agrees that during the period of one (1) year immediately after the termination of his or her employment with the Employer, he or she will not, either directly or indirectly, make known or divulge the names or addresses of any of the customers or patrons of the Employer at the time he or she entered the employ of the Employer or with whom he or she became acquainted after entering the employ of the Employer, to any person, firm, or corporation, and that he or she will not, directly or indirectly, either for himself or for herself or for any other person, firm, company, or corporation, call upon, solicit, divert, or take away, or attempt to solicit, divert, or take away any of the customers, business, or patrons of the Employer upon whom he or she called or whom he or she solicited or to whom he or she catered or with whom he or she became acquainted after his or her employment with the Employer.

The Employee hereby consents and agrees that for any violation of any of the provisions of this agreement, a restraining order and/or an injunction may issue against him or her in addition to any other rights the Employer may have.

In the event that the Employer is successful in any suit or proceeding brought or instituted by the Employer to enforce any of the provisions of this Agreement or on account of any damages sustained by the Employer by reason of the violation by the Employee of any of the terms and/or provisions of this Agreement to be performed by the Employee, the Employee agrees to pay to the Employer reasonable attorneys' fees to be fixed by the Court.

COVENANTS NOT TO COMPETE

Unlike the foregoing restrictive provisions governing the employer's ownership rights to the employee's work product and the protection of trade secrets and other confidential information, a **covenant not to compete** does not endeavor to solidify the company's ownership rights. Rather, this covenant is designed to prevent the employee from using personal talents (which were probably developed or improved during the employment) against the employer. Although an employer is entitled to protection from an employee's competition *while em-*

ployed by the employer under common law principles of fiduciary duty and theft of the employer's business opportunities, covenants not to compete are often included in an employee's agreement prohibiting competition during employment so that the employee's loyalty is clearly defined and easily enforced according to the terms of the agreement. These covenants are most often enforced against former employees who have left the employer's business and are attempting to compete against the employer based upon what they have learned while working there.

The negative objective causes some problems. Consider the plight of a research chemist who is an expert in industrial cleaning solutions. If he is a party to an employment contract that contains a clause forbidding future employment with any other industrial cleaner manufacturer, upon termination of his employment, he will lose his livelihood. His specialized technical knowledge significantly reduces his professional flexibility, and he must either breach the agreement or develop a new expertise. The company's objective is to prevent the employee from using his or her technical abilities to benefit a competitor, and the more specialized the skill, the more important it is for the company to discourage its marketability after termination. There is a bit of a tug of war here. If the restriction is too severe, a court simply will not enforce it; if it is too loose, the company cannot enforce it.

Many courts are very reluctant to enforce noncompetition agreements for several reasons. First, a noncompetition agreement is a restraint of trade, which is normally illegal both in common law and under state and federal antitrust statutes. However, limited noncompetition covenants are lawful and enforceable if they are agreed in conjunction with an otherwise legitimate agreement. Generally, a reasonable noncompetition agreement will be enforced if it is necessary for the protection of the employer, imposes no undue hardship on the employee, and does not injure the general public. Because courts are frequently reluctant to enforce noncompetition agreements, many states have adopted statutes that severely restrict the use of such covenants. In some states, all restrictive competition covenants are void except when given in connection with the sale of a business or the dissolution of a partnership.[16] Other states permit such clauses in employment contracts, but limit the effectiveness to certain justifying characteristics, such as training or advertising expenses, a license to practice, executive or management personnel, or specific territory limitations.[17]

Almost uniformly, the enforceability of a covenant not to compete depends upon whether the covenant is "reasonable," the determination of which includes consideration of the following:

1. the legitimate needs of the employer for such protection;
2. the interest of society in preventing monopolies or other excessive restrictions on competition;
3. the burden placed upon the employee;
4. whether the employee has had frequent contacts with customers or clients of the employer;
5. whether the employer's business relies to a substantial degree on trade secrets to which the employee had access;
6. whether the employer provided training to the employee;
7. whether the employer's business is highly technical or complex;
8. whether the employer's business is highly competitive;
9. whether the employee, while employed, was a key employee, such as a manager or executive;
10. whether the employee provided unique services while employed by the employer;
11. whether the covenant exceeds boundaries of time, space, and type of activity that are reasonably required to give the employer the protection to which the employer is entitled;
12. whether there is a clear disparity of bargaining power between the employer and the employee; and
13. whether the employee understood the nature of the covenant at the time it was signed.

The drafting of a noncompetition clause with these considerations in mind is a delicate operation.

One rule is absolute: a noncompetition clause may never prohibit the employee from engaging in competitive activity indefinitely. The protection of the clause must have a reasonable basis in fact, and no employer will be able to convince a court that competitive activity by a certain employee will forever cause irreparable harm to the business. Consequently, the clause should be limited to a specified period during which the company will be justified in keeping the employee out of the market to preserve a competitive advantage.

From the employer's standpoint, the agreement should also provide that the employee is prohibited from competition upon termination "for any reason whatsoever." An employee who has left to work for a competitor before the expiration of the agreement cannot expect much sympathy from a court. However, an employee who has been fired and must now refrain from marketing personal talents is in a different position. Without the language suggested above, a court may narrowly construe an employee's termination and enforce the noncompetition clause only when termination results from the employee's initiative.

To enforce a noncompetitive agreement, the employer may have to show a court that the former employee's competitive activities are causing irreparable harm to the company. The difficulties of producing such proof may be avoided by exacting a consent to injunctive relief against the employee should the employee violate the agreed provisions.

Finally, the competitive activities that are to be prohibited and the geographical limits of the prohibition should be specified with accuracy and clarity. If the provision is overly broad, it is less likely to be enforced in litigation involving its breach. Moreover, any ambiguity will always be resolved against the drafter, meaning the employer. For example, a provision that prohibits the employee from working in "the retail sales industry" is useless. A description of "retail sales of men's wear" is better but questionable because it is so broad. Equally unenforceable is a provision that prohibits the employee's competition in the "western part of the United States." The "South Dakota area" may be enforceable but requires a great deal of interpretation and undoubtedly would be limited to the boundaries of the state. The defined activities and geographical area should be consistent with the activities and market of the employer and should be specific. Consider the strengths and weaknesses of the following examples.

EXAMPLE

Agreement Not to Compete

I also agree that I will not work for any competitive company or for myself to sell directly or indirectly milk or milk products in the same territory covered by me either as route salesman or foreman of routes for a period of at least one year after termination of my employment, voluntarily or involuntarily, with this Company.

EXAMPLE

Covenant Not to Compete

It is further agreed by the Employee that the sale of the Employer's petroleum products in the trading area hereinbefore referred to is a valuable asset to the Employer, and in order to promote the sales of petroleum products in said trading area, the Employer will make expenditures through advertising and otherwise, and in consideration of the covenants and agreements herein contained, the Employee agrees that in the event of the termination of this contract for any reason, with or without cause, the Employee will not engage in the sale of gasoline, fuel oils, or petroleum products, directly or indirectly, either on her own account, or as an employee for any other person, firm, or corporation, in the city of Chicago, Cook County, Illinois, for a period of five (5) years following the termination of this contract.

Agreement and Covenant Not to Compete

The Employee further covenants and agrees that at no time during the term of this employment, or for two (2) years immediately following termination thereof (regardless of whether such termination is voluntary or involuntary), will he for himself or in behalf of any other person, partnership, corporation, or company, engage in the pest control business or any business engaged in the eradication and control of rats, mice, roaches, bugs, vermin, termites, beetles, and other insects within the territory known as cities of Spearfish and Belle Fourche, South Dakota, and a radius of 25 miles of each of said cities, nor will he directly or indirectly for himself, or in behalf of or in conjunction with any other person, partnership, corporation, or company, solicit or attempt to solicit the business or patronage of any person, corporation, company, or partnership within the said territory for the purpose of selling a service for the eradication and control of rats, mice, roaches, bugs, vermin, termites, beetles, and other insects, and such other incidental business and service now engaged in by the Company, nor will the Employee disclose to any person whatsoever any of the secrets, methods, or systems used by the Company in and about its business.

The Employee hereby consents and agrees that for any violation of any of the provisions of this agreement, a restraining order and/or an injunction may issue against him in addition to any other rights the Employer may have.

It is better practice to specifically define the boundaries in which competition is prohibited. For example, describing county lines or city limits is preferable to providing a point from which a radius will be computed. The larger the geographical area, the less likely it is that the covenant will be enforced. If the employer is engaged in the sale of goods within a particular city, it would be inadvisable to define noncompetition to include the entire state, even if the employer plans to expand operations to the entire state, since a court will be more concerned with the actual needed protection at the time the covenant was signed than with speculation about expansion and potential competitive problems in the future.

The clause should provide that the employee understands the nature of the covenant and consents to the covenant's prohibition of the employee's activities that may compete with the employer. Further, the covenant should specify that the employee understands that the clause is necessary for the employer's protection, and that the employee agrees that any violation of the clause will do irreparable harm to the employer.

The employee should be prohibited from directly or indirectly competing with the employer as an owner, manager, operator, or controlling person, or through being employed by, participating in, or being connected in any manner with the ownership, management, operations, or control of a competitor, including holding a position as a creditor. A classic avoidance technique for these covenants involves former employees who loan money to a new corporation that will compete with the former employer. In exchange for the loan, these "creditors" receive convertible debentures that will be converted to common stock (and majority ownership of the corporation) the day after the former employees' covenants not to compete expire.

If the covenant will be regulated by a statute in the jurisdiction in which it is to be enforced, the specific statutory reason for the covenant (such as because the employee was trained by the employer, or because the employee is a member of the management or executive personnel) should be stated in the covenant.

The clause should contain **severability provisions**, which allow for the removal of any objectionable portion of the clause without affecting the enforcement of the remainder of the clause for the employer's protection.

Consideration should be given to penalties other than injunctive relief or damages, such as loss of accrued but unpaid commissions, loss of retirement or profit sharing incentives, and similar penalties that discourage but do not forbid one from entering into competition.

The fair objective of restrictive covenants in employment contracts is to protect the legitimate interests of the company without unduly restricting the activities of the employee.

Properly drafted restrictions never exceed the limits of necessary company protection and are firm and thorough on those points, thereby affording a better opportunity to have them do what they are supposed to do.

INCENTIVE COMPENSATION PLANS

Employee incentive is a key element to current performance and continued employment with the company. Individual incentive compensation terms for individual employment contracts have been discussed previously.[18] It may be desirable, however, to use **group incentive plans** in lieu of or in addition to individual incentive provisions in each agreement. As the number of beneficiaries to an incentive compensation plan grows larger, however, the plan becomes less effective as a true incentive. For example, an individual salesperson can be easily motivated by a personal incentive based directly on individual sales, but personal motivation is more tenuous if the entire sales division, comprising many salespersons, is rewarded for the aggregate performance of all.

As with personal incentive plans, a cardinal rule for the effectiveness of a group incentive plan is that the compensation must be related directly to the performance of an ascertainable division of the company. In practice, these incentive plans are usually directed to key employees, since key employees motivate other employees to concentrate their efforts toward the employer's growth and profits, and further provide an incentive for other employees to remain with the company.

A group plan is properly administered under the direction of a committee, which, in the case of a corporation, may be, but does not have to be, composed of the directors. Persons who are entitled to compensation under the plan should not be members of the committee. The committee is usually vested with some discretion to determine the amount of the incentive awards and the recipients from among those eligible to participate in the plan.

The written plan should begin with a statement of purpose, which usually indicates an intent to provide incentives to certain employees by enabling those employees to participate in the success of the company. The eligible participants in the plan must be clearly defined, as should the base accounts from which the amounts awarded under the plan will be determined. For example, if the participants under the plan are to receive a certain percentage of *profits*, that word must be defined, specifying whether taxes, allocations of overhead, contingent or unusual expenses, and so on are to be deducted. The formula for compensation under the plan may refer to multiple accounts, such as a percentage of the extent to which profits exceed capital, and all stated accounts should be clearly defined.

The membership of the committee is set forth in the plan, and the committee's duties and term of membership should be prescribed. If the committee is to have discretion in granting the incentive awards, a procedure for determination of the recipients, with specified guidelines for merit, may be provided. Alternatively, a formula may be drafted that makes the application of the awards a mechanical task for the committee, but the use of such a formula minimizes the flexibility of the plan by removing the committee's discretion from the incentive characteristics. True merit may be rewarded at the committee's discretion, but a formula may not account for that.

A method for determining the amount of the fund must be included in the plan. A percentage of the defined revenue or profits is the most simple method; the complex formulas of other methods defy the imagination. The fund is usually set aside in an incentive compensation reserve account, awaiting the directions of the committee.

The payments under a corporate incentive plan may be made in cash or a stock equivalent, based upon the current market price of stock. If the stock is reported on a national exchange, a method is prescribed to compute market price, such as "the average daily opening price on the exchange during the calendar month preceding the month of award." The committee may decide whether the award is to be in cash or stock, and the committee also should have the authority to pay the award immediately or to defer payment in whole or in part. If deferral is permitted, separate accounts must be maintained for that purpose. The deferral of the award may provide certain tax benefits to the employees.[19]

Additional incentive thrust results from imposition of conditions upon payment of the compensation. For example, the terms of the plan may refuse payment to an eligible participant if that employee resigns during the year without the consent of the company. The plan may further deny deferred payments if a former employee is subsequently employed by a competitor of the company. It is also common to provide for forfeiture of any award if the employee is discharged for misconduct. The plan should specifically state that the employee has no claim or right to be granted an award under the plan, and the plan should not be construed as granting the participant a right to be retained in the employ of the company.

The company management should be granted authority to modify or suspend the plan at their discretion, but only prospectively so as not to affect any rights of employees working in reliance on the incentive benefits under the plan. Management should not be able to retroactively affect the rights of employees with respect to unpaid awards previously granted. Finally, a corporate incentive plan should be approved by the shareholders, especially if it contemplates the issuance of stock as an incentive award.[20]

DEFERRED COMPENSATION

Key employees and executives may be plied with an incentive to remain with the company by a **deferred compensation plan**. These plans are designed to meet two important objectives in the employment relationship: (1) income for the employee is deferred until the employee retires or becomes incapacitated, providing necessary security and allowing receipt when the employee's income is taxed in a lower bracket; and (2) the employee is given an incentive to remain with the company to receive accumulated retirement benefits. The agreement for a deferred plan may be incorporated into an employee agreement or may be executed separately after a period of satisfactory employment.

The amounts of compensation to be deferred may be determined by a number of methods. A portion of base salary may be deferred, or a percentage of salary in addition to normal base salary may be used. The deferral provisions also may be tied to bonus or incentive plans, such as those described in the preceding section.

The deferred income is retained in a fund for the employee until payment at the prescribed time, usually following retirement or disability. Payment may be in a lump sum or in installments over a period of years.

Retirement Date   **EXAMPLE**

The Company agrees that Patricia Smith may retire from the active and daily service of the Company upon the first day of the month nearest her sixty-fifth birthday.

Retirement Compensation   **EXAMPLE**

The Company agrees that commencing with the date of such retirement, it will pay to Patricia Smith the sum of $36,000.00 per annum payable in equal installments of $3,000.00 each, payable upon the first business day of each calendar month. The Company agrees that it will continue to make such payments to Patricia Smith during her lifetime, and with no liability to make payments to her legal representatives, for ten (10) years and until Patricia Smith shall have received one hundred twenty (120) monthly payments of $3,000.00 each; subject, however, to the conditions and limitations hereinafter set forth.

The incentive to continue with the company results from the continual increase in the deferred fund and from the terms of the agreement, which typically conclude all rights and obligations under the agreement if the employee voluntarily terminates the employment relationship without the consent of the company.

EXAMPLE

Termination of Employment

If Patricia Smith shall voluntarily terminate her employment during her lifetime and prior to her said retirement, or if her employment shall be terminated for sufficient cause as determined by the Board of Directors of the Company, this Agreement shall automatically terminate and the Company shall have no further obligation hereunder.

These agreements also frequently prescribe a **forfeiture** of all benefits under the plan if the employee subsequently engages in competition with the company.

EXAMPLE

Covenant Not to Compete

Patricia Smith agrees that during such period of receipt of monthly payments from the Company, she will not directly or indirectly enter into or in any manner take part in any business, profession, or other endeavor either as an employee, agent, independent contractor, owner, or otherwise in the City of Fort Lauderdale, Florida, that in the opinion of the directors of the Company shall be in competition with the business of the Company, which opinion of the directors shall be final and conclusive for the purposes hereof.

EXAMPLE

Forfeiture

Patricia Smith agrees that if she fails to observe any of the covenants hereof and continues to breach any covenant for a period of thirty (30) days after the Company has requested her to perform the same, or if she has entered any business described in the preceding paragraph and continues therein, either directly or indirectly, as aforesaid for a period of fifteen (15) days after the Company has notified her in writing at her home address that the directors of the Company have decided that such business is in competition with the Company; then, any of the provisions hereof to the contrary notwithstanding, Patricia Smith agrees that no further payments shall be due or payable by the Company hereunder either to Patricia Smith or to her spouse, and that the Company shall have no further liability hereunder.

In addition to their incentive character, the forfeiture clauses serve another useful purpose. The tax benefits from a deferred compensation plan may be generally stated to be that the company may deduct the payments to the deferred fund when paid, but the employee need not declare the payments as income until those payments are received. The latter rule is based upon the condition that the employee does not "constructively receive" the payments earlier—that is, the employee does not earn a vested right to the payments before they are paid. The conditions described earlier avoid the **constructive receipt** problem, since the employee's continuous performance and prohibition against competition are superimposed upon the employee's right to payment and prevent any vesting of the employee's interest until the conditions are satisfied.

The deferred compensation plan should divert the payment of the deferred income to the employee's heirs in the case of the employee's death.

EXAMPLE

Payments to Spouse If Employee Dies after Retirement

The Company agrees that if Patricia Smith so retires but dies before receiving the said one hundred twenty (120) monthly payments, it will continue to make such monthly payments, to Fred Smith, her spouse, if he survives Patricia Smith, until the total payments made to Patricia Smith and her spouse equal $180,000.00; provided that if Fred Smith survives Patricia Smith but dies before the said amount is paid by the Company, the Company shall have no liability to continue any payments hereunder beyond the first day of the month in which Fred Smith died.

Death of Spouse after Retirement

> EXAMPLE

If Patricia Smith so retires and her spouse does not survive her, the Company shall not be required to continue any payments hereunder beyond the first day of the month in which Patricia Smith dies.

Payments to Spouse If Employee Dies before Retirement

> EXAMPLE

If Patricia Smith dies before the aforesaid retirement date and her spouse survives her, the Company agrees to make the said monthly payments hereinbefore described to the said Fred Smith, commencing with the first day of the month following the month in which Patricia Smith dies and ending when one hundred twenty (120) monthly payments have been made to Fred Smith or until and including the first day of the month in which Fred Smith dies, whichever event shall first occur.

Death of Employee before Retirement with No Spouse Surviving

> EXAMPLE

If Patricia Smith dies before the said retirement date, the Company shall not be required to make any payments hereunder.

PENSION AND PROFIT SHARING PLANS

Pension and **profit sharing plans** are deferred compensation plans, but they may produce additional tax benefits for the employer and the employee if they qualify under the Internal Revenue Code.[21] Whether a particular plan qualifies under the Internal Revenue Code depends upon compliance with complicated tax rules that are discussed later in this section. Both pension and profit sharing plans accumulate and defer income until some future date. The employer's objective is to induce the employee to remain with the company to receive accumulated retirement benefits. The profit sharing plan also adds a current performance incentive, since the amount contributed to the plan is based upon profits produced by the employee and the employee's coworkers.

Both profit sharing and pension plans are directed toward retirement or disability income and faithful performance. However, each plan reaches the objective by different means. The profit sharing plan is based upon profits, and the employer's contribution to the fund is couched in terms of a percentage of annual profit. From the employer's standpoint, a profit sharing plan is less onerous than a pension plan. It is subject to special tax rules, since the obligation to contribute depends upon the profitable operation of the business, and there is no fixed obligation to contribute annually. The contribution requirements reflect the economic cycles of the business, and as a result the plan is more flexible than a pension plan. The size of the fund will depend entirely upon the profits contributed throughout the duration of the plan. Allocation of the fund to individual employees is usually based upon employees' compensation during their periods of employment. These factors result in a minimal burden for the employer and, if incentives are taken seriously, greater benefit to the employees. Young, aggressive employees who intend to remain with the company will particularly benefit. Their efforts in producing profit increase their compensation under the plan, and as they remain with the company, their share of the profits distributed to the fund will increase as their base compensation increases. Finally, it is possible to provide for periodic withdrawals from the profit sharing accounts in addition to distribution upon retirement, death, or disability.

Pension plans, on the other hand, are specifically directed toward retirement income, and the employer is usually obliged to contribute the necessary funds on an annual basis. Pension plans may be either defined benefit plans (where the exact benefits upon retirement are specified and contributions must be made to reach the specified benefits) or defined contribution plans (where a certain contribution is made by the employer each year and the benefits depend on the total funds available upon retirement). The benefits of the plan provide a specified income for the employee after retirement, and the employer contributions are fixed by an amount necessary to provide income for the specified period. The employer contributions are a fixed annual obligation and are not related to profits in any way. The contribution is, therefore, a charge on operations that must be considered in estimating costs and pricing. Moreover, the contribution is usually directly based upon the employee's length of service and age, since the contribution for an older employee must be higher to accumulate enough funds for that employee's specified retirement income under the plan. The allocation of funds among eligible employees under the plan will be in accordance with the prescribed pension, and young, aggressive employees are not particularly rewarded for their enthusiastic business achievements. However, the fixed obligation to contribute to the pension plan has some employee advantages that are not available with a profit sharing plan. The pension plan permits recognition of employment before the establishment of the plan, and accommodates immediate pensions for employees who have already reached retirement age when the plan is adopted.

The general distinction between types of plans can be summarized as follows:

Defined Benefit Plan	*Defined Contribution Plan*
Includes pension plans	Includes profit sharing, qualified deferred compensation, and employee stock ownership plans
Benefits calculated by a formula based upon years of service and average compensation	Each participant has an account that includes contributions, investment income, and forfeitures of terminated participants
Benefits cannot exceed the lesser of (i) 100% of the participant's average earnings in the three best-paid years of employment or (ii) a dollar amount specified in the statute	Contributions to an account cannot exceed the lesser of (i) 25% of the participant's compensation (15% for a profit sharing plan) or (ii) a dollar amount specified in the statute
Forfeitures cannot increase benefits to any participant (must be used to pay expenses)	Forfeitures may be allocated to the account of the remaining participants
Minimum funding required	No minimum funding required
Best for older employees since benefits can be funded over a shorter time	Best for younger employees since higher benefits will result over a longer period of time

The choice among the types of plans depends on many factors, the most important of which include the ability of the company to make the required contributions, the desired stimulation of incentive, and the characteristics of the employee group. A combination of both plans may be used to benefit all employees.

Tax Ramifications

The tax treatment of profit sharing and pension plans is complicated and should be thoroughly studied before a plan is recommended or drafted. Only a few of the most important provisions are covered here.

Tax-favored plans must be qualified, meaning they must satisfy the statutory requirements prescribed in the Internal Revenue Code.[22] A qualified plan results in tax benefits for both the employer and the employee. Subject to certain statutory limitations, the employer is permitted to deduct contributions to the plan in the year made, just as normal compensation would be deducted as an expense, even though the compensation is not actually paid to the employee during that year.[23] Therefore, the employer suffers no tax disadvantage by paying compensation to the plan, rather than paying directly to the employee. The funds paid into the plan may be accumulated and invested during the holding period, but the income earned on the investment is exempt from any tax.[24] The funds thereby increase much faster than if they were invested by the corporation without a qualified plan or by the individual employee. The employee-beneficiary of the plan is not taxed on any of the funds until those funds are distributed.[25] Thus, an executive who receives a substantial salary that elevates his or her tax bracket at the height of his or her earning power will not lose a proportionate amount of the compensation under the plan by having to pay tax on this deferred income in the years he or she is employed. Rather, the employee will pay tax on distributed amounts received in years of retirement, when his or her other income is likely reduced and his or her tax bracket is much lower. Finally, the amounts contributed by the company and paid to heirs or beneficiaries upon the death of the employee can pass free of estate tax, since the employee may specify direct payment to named beneficiaries and the funds will not be included in the employee's estate.

The foregoing tax benefits increase the desirability of these plans as a part of the employee compensation scheme. Qualified plans permit the employer to minimize cost while maximizing employee compensation.

Qualification

The requirements of federal law, regulations of the Department of Labor, and the rulings thereunder are a maze of intricate rules with myriad exceptions, definitions, inclusions, and exclusions—all designed to describe the **qualification** procedure and standards of profit sharing and pension plans. The purpose of the plan, amounts of benefits, participation, entitlement to benefits, operation, contributions, and reporting must be structured in accordance with the statutory rules.

Few rules of life have changed as frequently as the rules regarding qualified profit sharing and pension plans. The Internal Revenue Code has been modified hundreds of times in an attempt to balance the interests of the employer and the employee in providing tax-advantaged compensation plans that are fair, effective, and legitimate. Frequently, the rules will be modified on a prospective basis to encourage employment of certain classes of persons, such as persons over or under a certain age, persons with underemployed talents, persons involved in certain industries or professions, and so on. The rules that follow are general rules that may have changed or become subject to exceptions by the time you read them, but they generally illustrate the approach of the tax qualification procedures and the requirements necessary for qualified plans.

A qualified plan must be adopted for the purpose of offering the employees a share of the profits or income of the employer or for providing a fund that will be distributed to the employees or their beneficiaries after retirement. The plan must be established and maintained by the employer for the exclusive benefit of the employees. The funds cannot be diverted for any use other than the specified purposes.

The plan may not be qualified if it is intended to benefit only a few select employees. Section 401(a) of the Internal Revenue Code is extremely forceful in insisting that the qualified plan may not discriminate in favor of employees who are officers, shareholders, or highly compensated employees. Generally, the contributions to the plan should be allocated in proportion to and benefits awarded in relation to the total current compensation of the participants of the plan. It is possible to base contributions and benefits on less than all compensation of the employees as long as the plan remains nondiscriminatory.

Participation in the plan depends upon compliance with two general statutory tests: age and service requirements, and coverage requirements.

The material in this section describes these requirements, discusses how **vesting** affects the age and service requirements, outlines certain limitations on contributions to qualified plans, and explains the formalities associated with establishing a qualified plan.

Age and Service Requirements Concerning the minimum age and service conditions, the qualified plan must permit participation for employees who have completed at least 1 year of service with the employer or who have reached age 21, whichever is later. One year of service means a 12-month period during which the employee works at least 1,000 hours. A part-time employee who works for more than a year but only logs 18 hours a week can be safely excluded under a qualified plan. But a full-time employee who works 40 hours a week and takes a 25-week vacation must be permitted to participate (unless the vacation turns out to be permanent and the vesting rules permit a forfeiture for the terminated employee). If the plan provides that benefits will not be subject to forfeiture, or vested, immediately for employees who participate, an employer may provide for an eligibility waiting period (such as 2 years after employment begins). Older employees cannot be excluded from the plan simply because of age unless the plan is a defined (or target) benefit plan and an employee begins employment within 5 years of the normal retirement age specified in the plan. This last rule permits an employer to hire an employee who is near retirement without having to contribute large sums to the plan to provide the defined benefit amount when the employee retires during the next 5 years.

Coverage Requirements The rules for participation of certain classes of employees in a qualified plan are even more involved. Generally, a plan must pass one of four tests: a percentage test, a fair-cross-section test, a ratio test, or an average benefits test.

The **percentage test** requires that the plan cover either

1. 70% or more of all employees; or
2. 80% or more of all eligible employees, provided 70% or more of all employees are eligible.

The **fair-cross-section test** permits the plan to cover a classification of employees that is determined by the Internal Revenue Service not to be discriminatory in favor of officers, shareholders, or highly compensated employees. The test anticipates that the Internal Revenue Service will review the employees who are covered, make a determination that the plan is fair and not discriminatory, and approve the plan for qualification.

The **ratio test** compares highly compensated employees against non–highly compensated employees. The percentage of non–highly compensated employees covered must be at least 70% of the percentage of highly compensated employees covered by the plan.

The **average benefits test** combines the fair-cross-section test and the ratio test. The plan may benefit certain employees under a classification that the Internal Revenue Service has determined does not discriminate, and the average benefit percentage for non–highly compensated employees must be at least 70% of the average benefit for highly compensated employees.

A complex illustration may serve to explain these otherwise simple rules. Suppose a corporation has 80 regular employees who work full-time, and 5 part-time employees who work less than 1,000 hours in a 12-month period. The 80 regular employees may be classified as follows:

Age	Served over 5 Years	Served 3–5 Years	Served 1–3 Years	Served Less Than 12 Months
Over 60	7	2		
21–60	42	7	5	1
Under 21	3	4	2	7
	52	13	7	8

First, a determination is made regarding who will be potentially excludable under the age and service rules. The plan may exclude the 5 part-time employees, because they work too few hours, and may exclude the 8 full-time employees who have served less than 12 months. The other 9 full-time employees who have not reached age 21 may be excluded. The plan also could exclude the 2 employees who are over 60 and who have served less than 5 years, but only if they began their employment when they were older than a specified age (say 60), *and* if the normal age of retirement is not more than 5 years older (say 65), *and* if the plan is a defined benefit plan where benefits are set in a certain amount after retirement and the employer would have to rapidly contribute great quantities of money for these employees in order to meet those benefits upon retirement.

As for coverage, the percentage test requires that a qualified plan must cover 70% of *all* employees or 80% or more of all *eligible* employees, provided 70% or more of all employees are eligible. In this case the plan must cover at least 56 employees (based upon 70% of all employees). It has already been determined that the plan excludes the 5 part-time employees, the 8 full-time employees who do not meet minimum service requirements, and the 9 full-time employees who are under age 21. This leaves 63 employees who meet the minimum age and service requirements (adequate to meet the 70% test). Under the second part of the percentage test, the plan also could be qualified if only 80% of all eligible employees are covered, as long as 70% of all employees are eligible. Thus, since 63 employees are eligible, as few as 51 (80% of those eligible) could be covered and the plan would still qualify for tax advantages.

If the plan provided that only employees who earned more than $30,000 per year would be included as participants, and if only 40 employees qualified under that test, the plan would not be qualified under the first part of the percentage test because of the participation formula rules. However, the plan might qualify under the fair-cross-section test if the Internal Revenue Service determines that even though only 40 employees are covered, the plan does not discriminate in favor of officers, shareholders, or highly compensated employees. This decision would require a determination that enough employees make substantially more than $30,000 per year that the threshold salary does not meet the "highly compensated" standard.

Suppose the corporation adopts a plan designed to cover only employees who work in a specified place, and only 20 employees meet that test. All is not lost even though the plan dismally fails the percentage test. The plan could still obtain special approval of the Internal Revenue Service if it is found not to be discriminatory in favor of officers, shareholders, or highly compensated employees. However, if the service learned that the "specified place" is corporate headquarters where management offices are located, the special classification would not be likely to succeed.

Try another example. Suppose the 80 regular employees are further classified as follows:

	Highly Compensated Employees	Non–Highly Compensated Employees
Eligible Employees	13	46
Noneligible Employees	4	17
Ratio of Eligible to Noneligible Employees	76%	73%

Using the ratio test, the plan would be qualified with the proportions of the employees specified in the table, since the non–highly compensated employees covered must be at least 70% of the highly compensated employees covered by the plan. Seventy-six percent of the highly compensated employees are eligible, and 73% of the non–highly compensated employees are eligible. This is a 96% ratio (70% to 73%).

The average benefits test compares the average benefits paid to non–highly compensated employees with the average benefits paid to highly compensated employees, based upon a classification approved by the Internal Revenue Service. Again in this case, the Internal Revenue Service reviews the average benefits paid to the respective groups and makes a determination whether the plan discriminates in favor of the highly compensated employees.

One final question to test the reader's keen awareness of these rules: Could the corporation qualify a plan that covered only the 63 employees who work full-time, are over 21 years of age, and have worked at least 3 full years with the corporation? The answer is, yes. The plan meets the 70% test. Minimum age and service requirements are also met *if* the plan provides for immediate vesting.

Vesting   Vesting is the employer's incentive hammer. As long as the benefits under the plan have not vested, the employer can reasonably expect that the employee will continue to work for the employer, hoping to enjoy vesting of the benefits one day. If the benefits have vested, the employee is absolutely entitled to them, and the incentive to remain with the company may be diminished. Consequently, most employers prefer to defer vesting as long as possible. The vesting schedules state the *maximum* periods of time the plans may defer vesting and still be qualified.

The qualified plan may meet one of two alternative vesting schedules under section 411 of the Internal Revenue Code. The first alternative is called **five-year cliff vesting**. The plan may provide that no benefits will vest until five years of service have been completed, and then the benefits must be 100% vested and nonforfeitable. Under the second alternative, the plan may provide for three- to seven-year vesting. The employee may be required to complete at least three years before any benefits become vested. At the end of three years, 20% of the benefits vest, and each year 20% more of the benefits vest until the seventh year, when the benefits are 100% vested and nonforfeitable.

Limitations on Contributions Section 415 of the Internal Revenue Code places certain limitations on the benefits and contributions to qualified plans that must be strictly observed. A defined benefit plan is generally limited to the lesser of $90,000 or 100% of the participant's average compensation for his or her highest three years. This $90,000 is adjusted for cost-of-living increases by the Treasury Department annually, and the limitation is also modified depending upon the age and years of service for each employee. The defined contribution plan is limited to the lesser of $30,000 or 25% of the participant's compensation for the annual contribution to the plan. This amount is also adjusted for cost-of-living increases, and employee contributions are taken into account in making the computation.

Formalities The statutory formalities demand that the plan be permanent, in writing, and communicated to the employees. Its terms must contemplate a continuing program of contributions by the employer and distributions to the employees. Although the plan may be terminated for business exigencies not within the employer's control, termination is always subject to careful scrutiny by the Internal Revenue Service to determine whether the plan was truly intended to be continuous at inception. Thus, there must be a valid business reason, unforeseeable when the plan was adopted, for the plan to be terminated. The written plan may be distributed to the employees; or, at least, a pamphlet describing the salient provisions of the plan should be available to the employees.

Finally, the operation of the plan is an important element to its qualification. The plan must be funded. The **funding** arrangements may be accomplished by a trust, requiring contributions from the employer to an institutional trustee, who invests the funds and distributes them in accordance with the trust agreement. The funds also may be used to purchase insurance contracts or other investment contracts for the benefit of the employee plan. In sum, there must be a formal contribution and investment arrangement, distinguishable from normal corporate activities by contractual provisions, preferably with an independent third party, to operate and administer the plan.[26]

INCENTIVE STOCK OPTIONS

Stock options that are offered as additional employee compensation may perform an incentive function with tax advantages. However, rather than monetary remuneration, a stock option is designed to give the optionee-employee an ownership interest in the corporation-employer (the optionor).

A stock option is a written instrument in which a corporation offers the right to purchase stock in the corporation to an individual at a predetermined price at any time during a stated period. The individual is under no obligation to accept the offer to purchase. As you may expect, to benefit the recipient, the option offers the stock to the optionee at a price other than the market price. This feature has considerable incentive value, much as the carrot in front of the donkey does. The price is set at an amount higher than market price at first, encouraging the employee to produce profits so the market price will rise above the option price, at which time the employee will have the option to purchase the stock at the discount option price. The incentive factor continues even after the employee exercises the option, since the value of the stock purchased should increase as the profits of the granting corporation increase.

An employee compensated by stock options should be motivated to work very hard on behalf of the corporation, since the employee will eventually profit by holding the option until the market value of the stock exceeds the option price. By exercising the option, the employee makes a discount purchase of the stock and becomes a shareholder who has a pecuniary interest in the corporation's performance. Moreover, by using stock options, the corporation is compensating an employee without incurring any immediate expense, because the issuance of an option requires no direct payment to the employee. The ownership interest of existing shareholders is affected by stock options, since the exercise of the option dilutes their proportionate ownership of the company, but if the stock option motivates employees to continually strive for profits, the existing shareholders also benefit from the resulting increase in stock values.

As a part of its compensation program, a corporation may adopt a stock option plan to benefit certain employees. Options granted under the plan give the recipients the right to purchase stock of the corporation at a specified price, the **option price**, for a specified period of time. The offer of stock to the employee may be accepted only during this period, and the act of acceptance is the exercise of the option. Upon payment of the option price to the corporation, the employee is entitled to receive certificates for the stock.

Tax Ramifications

Incentive stock options (ISOs) may receive special tax treatment under the Internal Revenue Code.[27] An incentive stock option is an option granted by a corporation to an individual based upon the individual's employment with the corporation.

When a corporation grants an incentive stock option to an employee, the employee does not realize any income at the time of the receipt of the option (even though the option may have value). If the corporation were to give the employee a cash payment equivalent to the value of the option, the payment would be treated as ordinary income and taxed immediately. Instead, with an incentive stock option plan, the employee will be taxed only when stock acquired through the exercise of the option is sold. This could be several years later, after the stock has substantially appreciated in value.

To obtain the benefits of an incentive stock option plan, the employee must not dispose of the stock for at least two years from the date the option was granted, and the employee must hold the stock for at least one year after purchasing it through the option. (These periods do not apply if the employee dies.) The employee also must remain employed by the corporation from the time the option is granted until three months before the option's exercise. These factors explain why these plans are regarded as incentive plans, since the employee must stay employed in order to realize the benefit of the stock option, the stock purchased, and the tax consequences.

When stock is purchased under an incentive stock option plan, the amount by which the fair market value of the stock at the time the option is exercised exceeds the option price is an item of **tax preference**. Tax preference income is subject to a surtax of an additional percentage. This additional tax does not constitute an onerous burden on most employees, since the tax preference surtax is charged only against employees who receive substantial benefits from the exercise of the option. To illustrate, consider Shelley Roberts, an employee of the Nobles Company, who has an option to buy 1,000 shares of corporate stock at $10 per share. When she exercises the option, the market price of the stock is $50 per share. In that year, she has tax preference income of $40,000, the difference between the market value and the option price. Further suppose that Shelley's tax preference income is taxed at 15%. The tax preference surtax is $6,000 in the year the option is exercised. If she holds the stock for more than three years, and sells it at $60 per share, her gain is $50,000, since she purchased the stock at $10 per share. The tax preference surtax does not diminish the desirability of the incentive stock option as a form of compensation. Shelley will have paid $6,000 in extra tax in the hypothetical transaction, but she also has profited $50,000. Who would complain about that?

Qualification

The Internal Revenue Code specifies several requirements for the qualification of tax-favored incentive stock option plans,[28] and like qualified pension and profit sharing plans, the incentive stock option plan must accord strictly with the statutory rules. Generally, these requirements are concerned with the adoption and content of the option plan, the duration of the plan, the exercise of the option, the option price, and the employees covered by the plan.

An incentive stock option plan must state the number of shares that may be issued under the plan, and must describe the classes of employees who are eligible to receive options. The identification of shares to be issued under the plan should include the description of the shares from the articles of incorporation. The number may be specific, or a formula may be prescribed to establish the total number of shares that may be issued under the plan.

EXAMPLE

Shares Subject to the Plan

The Committee, from time to time, may provide for the option and sale in the aggregate of up to 100,000 shares of Common Stock of the Company. Shares shall be made available from authorized and unissued or reacquired Common Stock.

For the tax benefits of the qualified stock option to be enjoyed, the option must be granted to a person employed at the time of the grant. Individuals who are employed by a parent or subsidiary corporation of the granting corporation would qualify, but a prospective employee would not. Moreover, the optionee must remain an employee at all times during the period from the date the option is granted to three months before the date the option is exercised. The continuous employment requirement does not apply to a deceased employee, but is strictly observed in all other cases. The plan may include this limitation in its provisions.

EXAMPLE

Rights in Event of Termination of Employment

In the event of termination of employment for any cause other than death, a participant's option shall expire within three months after his or her employment terminates. Nothing contained in the Plan shall confer upon any participant any right to be continued in the employ of the Company or any subsidiary of the Company or shall prevent the Company or any subsidiary from terminating the participant's employment at any time, with or without cause.

It is possible to state in the plan that the stock options granted under the plan will expire immediately upon termination of employment; the Internal Revenue Code simply provides that the option may not extend beyond three months after termination to qualify for the advantageous tax treatment. The estate of a deceased employee is not so limited unless the option specifically so provides, and it may.

EXAMPLE

Rights in the Event of Death

In the event of the death of a participant while in the employ of the Company or a subsidiary, or within three months after termination of such employment, the option theretofore granted the participant shall be exercisable, in whole or in part, within the next three months succeeding the participant's death, if and to the extent the participant could have exercised it at the date of his or her death, by such person as shall have acquired the right to exercise such option by will or by the laws of descent and distribution.

The identification of employees covered by the plan may be satisfied by reasonably specific descriptions—for example, "supervisory employees," "all salaried employees," or "all employees of the corporation." The board of directors, or its delegates, usually has the power to determine the number of shares to be optioned to each employee within those described in the plan. Employees who own 10% or more of the voting stock of the corporation immediately before the option is granted are ineligible, unless the option price is at least 110% of the fair market value of the stock at the time the option is granted and the option terms require that the option must be exercised within a five-year period.

Participants

The Committee shall determine and designate from time to time those key employees (including employees who are also officers or directors) of the Company and its subsidiaries (as defined in section 425(f) of the Internal Revenue Code of 1986, as amended) to whom options are granted and who thereby become participants in the Plan. In selecting the individuals to whom options shall be granted, as well as in determining the number of shares subject to each option, the Committee shall weigh the positions and responsibilities of the individuals being considered, the nature of their services, their present and potential contributions to the success of the Company, and such other factors as the Committee shall deem relevant to accomplish the purpose of the Plan. No option shall be granted to an employee who, immediately before such option is granted, owns stock possessing more than 10 percent of the total combined voting power or value of all classes of stock of the Company or its subsidiaries. Each grant of an option shall be evidenced by an option agreement which shall contain such terms and conditions as may be approved by the Committee and shall be signed by an officer of the Company and the employee.

An incentive stock option plan must be approved by the stockholders of the granting corporation within twelve months before or after the date the plan is adopted. A plan is usually adopted by an appropriate resolution of the board of directors.

Resolution to Adopt a Qualified Stock Option Plan

WHEREAS, it is the belief of the Board of Directors of this Corporation that its key employees would be interested in acquiring a part of the capital stock of this Corporation, and that ownership of stock of this Corporation by its key employees would be to the advantage of this Corporation, and

WHEREAS, by the recent increase in capital stock of this Corporation, there is available for further subscriptions a total of one hundred thousand (100,000) shares of the common stock of this Corporation,

BE IT RESOLVED, That the Board of Directors do hereby adopt the Incentive Stock Option Plan, a copy of which is made a part of this resolution, subject to the approval of the common stockholders at their next regular meeting, and

RESOLVED FURTHER, That the Board of Directors of this Corporation do hereby recommend to the stockholders that they authorize the Board of Directors to set aside a total of ten thousand (10,000) shares of the common stock of this Corporation for sale to its key employees under said Incentive Stock Option Plan.

The date of the resolution adopting the plan will be the date used to determine whether shareholder approval has been obtained within the statutory period. The required shareholder approval may come within twelve months before or after the adoption of the plan by the board of directors. Consequently, the shareholder action may be the impetus that causes the board to adopt a plan. As long as shareholder approval and board adoption occur within a twelve-month period, the plan may be qualified.

The federal tax law requires only that the plan be approved by the affirmative vote of the holders of the majority of the voting stock of the corporation. The vote is taken at a regular or special stockholders' meeting, and the normal shareholder voting provisions of the state corporate statute apply.[29] Further, there may be other requirements for shareholder action in the statute, articles of incorporation, or bylaws to obtain a waiver of any preemptive rights in the stock issued under the option. Shareholder approval of the plan must comply with those requirements.

An incentive stock option must be granted within ten years from the date on which the plan is adopted or the date on which the plan is approved by stockholders, whichever is earlier. Accordingly, the plan should contain an expiration date within the ten-year period. The expiration of the plan has no effect upon any options previously granted pursuant to the plan's terms.

EXAMPLE

Termination

The Plan shall terminate ten years after its effective date, or on such earlier date as the Board of Directors may determine.

The option may not be exercised after the expiration of ten years from the date it is granted. The plan should so state, and each option should recite a specified period for exercise within this limitation.

EXAMPLE

Option Period

The term of each option shall be such period as the Committee may determine, but not more than ten years from the date the option is granted.

Some quick mathematics should reveal that the period from first grant to last exercise under any qualified stock option plan may not exceed twenty years. If an option were granted just before the expiration of the ten-year period following adoption and shareholder approval of the plan, it would remain exercisable for ten additional years. Thus, the last option may be exercised almost twenty years after the plan takes effect.

The option price may not be less than the fair market value of the stock on the date the option is granted for the plan to qualify for special tax treatment. Thus, the employee can benefit only from the appreciation in the value of the stock following the grant of the option. This feature increases the incentive value of the option, since the employee's performance will be directed toward increasing the market value of the stock over the option price. The tax benefits of an incentive stock option are lost if the option price is less than the market price when the option is granted.

The determination of the option price is generally the responsibility of the board of directors or its appointed committee, and only a general statement regarding option price need be included in the option plan. It is absolutely necessary to specify that the option price will be not less than the market value of the stock on the date the option is granted. If the stock subject to the option has a par value, the option price also must be at least par value.

EXAMPLE

Option Price

Shares of Common Stock of the Company shall be offered from time to time at a price to be determined by the Stock Option Committee, which price shall be not less than the fair market value of the stock on the day the option is granted.

Fair market value shall be the mean between the highest and lowest selling prices on the New York Stock Exchange on the valuation date. If there are no sales on such date, the value shall be determined by taking the mean between the highest and lowest sales upon the last preceding date on which such sales occurred. In no event shall the option price be less than the par value.

The remaining statutory requirements for qualification limit the employee-shareholder's ability to exercise other outstanding options, the ability to transfer the option to others, and the percentage ownership interest in the corporation and its affiliated corporations. The first rule is that an option may not be exercisable while there is outstanding an employee stock option previously granted to the same employee. This rule prevents the successive issuance of options at lower amounts when the market value of the company's stock is declining. The plan should recognize this limitation in its terms.

Prior Options

A subsequent option may not be exercised by a participant while that participant has outstanding any other prior stock options under this or prior stock option plans that entitle him or her to purchase stock of the same class in the Company at a price higher than the option price of such subsequent option.

The Internal Revenue Code also states that an incentive stock option may not be transferable by the employee—it may be exercised only by that employee. The singular exception to this rule is that transfers are permitted upon the death of the employee by the employee's will or by the laws of descent and distribution. The terms of the option should so state.

Nonassignability

Options are not transferable otherwise than by will or the laws of descent and distribution, and are exercisable during a participant's lifetime only by the participant.

Finally, the Internal Revenue Service frequently places various limitations on the amount of stock that may be subject to the option. Sometimes it states those limitations in terms of a **grant limitation**, so that an incentive stock option plan will not qualify if an employee is granted incentive stock options in excess of a certain amount (e.g., $100,000) in a calendar year. Sometimes those limitations are stated in terms of **exercise limitations**, so that an employee may not exercise incentive stock options in excess of a certain amount (e.g., $100,000) in any calendar year. Any limitations in the Internal Revenue Code must be observed. When a limitation is changed, the prior limitation usually applies for all options granted while the prior limitation was in effect, and the new limitations apply only to options granted thereafter. Sometimes the machinations of the Internal Revenue Service can be a significant advantage to an employee. For example, an employee who is granted an option for $100,000 of stock in 1996 (when grant limitations applied) and is also granted an option for an additional $100,000 of stock in 2004 (when exercise limitations applied) may be able to purchase $200,000 of stock in 2004, since both the grant and exercise limitation rules for the applicable options are met.

Administration of the Plan

The terms of the plan will describe the persons who are to administer it. The board of directors can serve in this capacity, but it may delegate administration authority to a committee appointed by the board. The terms of the plan should prescribe a procedure for the administrators' actions, and the authority granted or restricted in the administration of the plan.

Administration

The Plan shall be administered by a Stock Option Committee (herein called the Committee) consisting of three or more members of the Board of Directors of the Company who are not eligible to receive options under the Plan or who have waived their rights to receive options during such time as they are members of the Committee. The Committee shall be appointed annually by the Board of Directors, which may from time to time appoint additional members of the Committee or remove members and appoint new members in substitution for those previously appointed and fill vacancies however caused. A majority of

EXAMPLE

the Committee shall constitute a quorum and the acts of a majority of the members present at any meeting at which a quorum is present, or acts approved in writing by all of the members, shall be deemed the action of the Committee. Subject to the provisions of the Plan, the Committee is authorized to interpret it; to prescribe, amend, and rescind rules and regulations relating to it; and to make all other determinations necessary or advisable for its administration. It is intended that all options granted under the Plan be "incentive stock options" under the Internal Revenue Code of 1986, as amended.

EXAMPLE

Allotment of Shares

The Committee shall determine the number of shares to be offered from time to time to each participant except that the maximum number of shares offered to any one participant upon the initial offering at the inception of the Plan shall not exceed 2,000 shares, and the maximum number of shares that any participant may purchase pursuant to the initial offering and all subsequent offerings under the Plan shall not exceed 5,000 shares. The Committee also may prescribe a minimum number of shares that may be purchased at any one time, and the time or times shares will be issued pursuant to the exercise of options. In any offering after the initial offering, the Committee may offer available shares to new participants or to then participants or to a greater or lesser number of participants, and may include previous participants in accordance with such determination as the Committee shall make from time to time.

The administrators should have authority to adjust the provisions of the option to account for subsequent capital adjustments in the corporation. For example, a stock split or stock dividend will reduce the market price, and may cause the option price to be unrealistic. An adjustment to the option will preserve its viability.

EXAMPLE

Adjustment upon Changes in Capitalization

In the event there is any change in the Common Stock of the Company by reason of stock dividends, stock split-ups, recapitalization, reorganizations, mergers, consolidations, combinations or exchanges of shares, or otherwise, the number of shares available for option and the shares subject to any option shall be appropriately adjusted by the Committee.

The plan should carefully limit the authority of the administration to modify its terms. If an amendment to the plan violates any of the statutory requirements for qualification, the qualified status of the plan and the options granted under it will be lost, and the tax benefits will be eliminated. Consequently, only technical amendments should be permitted, and the authority to amend should prohibit the types of changes that would result in a substantive modification affecting qualification.

EXAMPLE

Amendment

The Board of Directors may at any time suspend, rescind, or terminate the Plan and may amend it from time to time in such respects as it may deem advisable, provided, however, that no such amendment shall, without further approval of the stockholders of the Company, except as provided herein, (a) increase the aggregate number of shares as to which options may be granted under the Plan either to all individuals or any one individual; (b) change the minimum option purchase price; (c) increase the maximum period during which options may be exercised; (d) extend the termination date of the plan; or (e) permit the granting of options to members of the Committee. No option may be granted during any suspension of the Plan or after the Plan has been rescinded or terminated, and no amendment, rescission, suspension, or termination shall, without the participant's consent, alter or impair any of the rights or obligations under any option theretofore granted to that participant under the Plan.

In granting a stock option, the corporation is offering to issue securities that may have to be registered under federal and state securities laws. If the securities have been registered, the corporation should have no problem issuing the stock under the option. However, if the securities are not registered, it is important to obtain a representation from the employees that the stock is being purchased only for investment and not for distribution and resale to the general public. The sale of securities to key employees may be exempt from the registration requirements of the securities laws, but severe penalties are prescribed for sale of unregistered stock to the general public. The representation by the employee not to resell to the public is designed to protect against these liabilities. The plan may contain a clause acknowledging the purpose of the purchase.

Purchase for Investment

All stock of the company purchased pursuant to any option must be purchased for investment and not with the view to the distribution or resale thereof. Each option will be granted on the understanding that any shares purchased thereunder will be so purchased, and each employee to whom an option is granted shall be required to deliver to the company a written representation and agreement to that effect.

EXAMPLE

Finally, the plan should recite the requirements of payment and other consideration to be given by the employee for the receipt and the exercise of the option. The plan may exact a promise from the employee that the employee will remain employed with the company for a period of time as a condition to the privilege of receiving the option.

Consideration for Option

Each participant shall, as consideration for the grant of the option, agree to remain in the continuous employ of the Company or one or more of its subsidiaries for at least two years from the date of the grant of such option.

EXAMPLE

Payment for Stock

Full payment for shares purchased shall be made at the time of exercising an option in whole or in part. No shares shall be issued until full payment therefor has been made, and a participant shall have none of the rights of a stockholder until shares are issued to him or her.

EXAMPLE

LIFE INSURANCE PROGRAMS

Various programs of life insurance coverage are available to a corporation for the benefit of its employees. Some of these programs have unique income tax advantages under the Internal Revenue Code, and all of them are intended to benefit the beneficiaries of an employee upon the employee's death with little or no cost to the employer.

Death benefit compensation programs are frequently used by corporations. Typically, the employer will promise to pay a portion of the employee's salary to the heirs for a period of time after death in consideration of the employee's continuous faithful performance. The corporation will normally apply for life insurance on the employee to cover this contingent liability, and will use the proceeds of the insurance to pay the agreed amounts to the heirs. For the employee, a death benefit agreement is like an insurance policy for the family, and the insurance is completely without cost to the employee.

Split-dollar insurance is another common plan used to benefit key personnel. The corporation and the employee join in the purchase of a life insurance policy on the life of the employee, and the employer-corporation pays a share of the premium, usually equal to the annual increase in the cash value of the policy. The employee pays the remaining premium. The corporation is named beneficiary to receive the amount of the premiums it has paid, and the employee will designate a beneficiary for the balance. When the employee dies, the corporation receives a return of all premiums paid, and the employee's beneficiary receives the remaining face value of the policy. The advantage to the employee is that the beneficiary will receive a considerable sum while the employee's share of the premiums has been minimal. The corporation will recover all it has paid and will have no out-of-pocket costs to provide the insurance benefit.[30]

EMPLOYEE EXPENSE REIMBURSEMENT PLANS

Many companies have instituted self-insured plans for employees as a method of supplementing group hospital insurance plans, major medical insurance, and other forms of reimbursement that may be provided to all employees. The variety of employee benefit plans is limited only by the imagination and generosity of the employer. Employers provide free transportation, buffet lunches, health and athletic club memberships, and a variety of other **expense reimbursement** provisions that encourage employees to remain loyal and dedicated to their work.

The Internal Revenue Code recognizes certain statutory benefit plans that provide reimbursement of expenses to employees, and permit tax benefits for the company for payment on the plans. These plans include accident and health plans, qualified group legal services plans, educational assistance programs, dependent care assistance programs and cafeteria plans, where the employee may select the particular benefit he or she desires.

Comprehensive nondiscrimination rules are applied to benefit plans for which there are tax advantages. These rules generally are designed to avoid a "top heavy" plan that provides benefits to only highly compensated employees to the exclusion of other employees. For a plan to provide tax-free benefits, it must meet certain tests to determine whether participation in the plan is permitted on a nondiscriminatory basis, whether the benefits received from the plan are provided on a nondiscriminatory basis, and whether the plan is valid. While similar in intent, the rules are different from the nondiscrimination rules relating to pension and profit sharing plans.[31]

Administration of the Plan

These employee plans and the nondiscrimination provisions that apply to them are administered by companies specializing in employee benefit administration. Rarely does the lawyer or paralegal become involved in making the necessary computations and applying the eligibility or benefit rules to determine if the plan will achieve the tax-advantaged objectives. The primary task of legal counsel is to draft a plan that complies with the statutory rules and regulations and requires compliance in the future with the various nondiscrimination provisions.

Drafting a Valid Plan

To avoid taxation of employer-provided benefits, the company must adopt a plan that meets at least five requirements:

1. the plan must be in writing;
2. the plan must provide employees with reasonable notification of benefits available under the plan;
3. the plan must be maintained for the exclusive benefit of employees, or spouses and dependents of employees where permissible;
4. the employee's rights under the plan must be legally enforceable (which means that benefits under the plan may not be discretionary with the employer); and
5. the employer must have intended to maintain the plan indefinitely when the plan was established.

The following checklist should be followed for preparation of a plan.

Checklist

1. An introduction to the plan should recite the plan's purpose, the plan's effective date, and the manner in which the plan will be administered.

Purpose, Effective Date, and Administration

MEDICAL AND DENTAL EXPENSE REIMBURSEMENT PLAN (the "Plan") has been established by Sickness and Health, Inc., a corporation (the "employer"), to provide for reimbursement of certain medical and dental expenses incurred by its eligible employees and their dependents.

Effective Date
The "effective date" of the Plan is July 1, 2005. The Plan year shall be the calendar year.

Administration of the Plan
The Plan will be administered by the employer. Any documents required to be filed with the employer will be given or filed properly if delivered or mailed by registered mail, postage prepaid, to the employer at 7561 South Cedar Street, Atlanta, Georgia.

---

2. The membership should be defined in accordance with the rules against discrimination.

Membership

Each employee of the employer will become a member in the Plan on the effective date, or on the first day of any calendar month during which the employee meets all of the following eligibility requirements, if such employee is not employed or does not meet such requirements, on the effective date:

a) The employee is customarily employed by the employer on a full time (customarily fifteen (15) hours or more per week) and permanent (customarily five (5) months or more per calendar year) basis;

b) The employee has attained the age of twenty-one (21); and

c) The employee has completed six (6) months of service with the employer. However, if the employer has not been in existence for such period upon meeting the other requirements hereof, then the employee shall qualify if such employee has been employed for the lesser period in which the employer has been in existence.

---

3. The plan benefits should be stated, with a maximum dollar limit.

Plan Benefits

Subject to the conditions and limitations of the Plan, each calendar year, beginning on the effective date, each member will be entitled to reimbursement from the employer of the medical care costs (as defined herein) incurred during that year with respect to that member's family unit (as defined herein) to the extent that such costs do not exceed an amount equal to the lesser of:

a) the total medical care costs of the family unit paid during that calendar year; or

b) $10,000.

---

4. A definition of medical care costs should be included.

Medical Care Costs

The term "medical care costs" as used in the Plan means amounts paid by a member (or any other individual included in that member's family unit) for:

a) diagnosis, cure, mitigation, treatment, or prevention of disease, or for the purpose of affecting any structure or function of the body;

b) transportation primarily for and essential to medical care referred to in subparagraph (a) above;

c) insurance covering medical care referred to in subparagraphs (a) and (b) above; and

d) any other amounts paid that are included within the meaning of "medical care" as defined in section 213 of the Internal Revenue Code of 1986, or any comparable provision of any future legislation that amends, supplements, or supersedes that section.

5. The beneficiaries under the plan should be defined.

EXAMPLE

Family Unit

The term "family unit" as applied to any member means the member, the member's spouse, and such other persons as are dependents within the meaning of section 152 of the Internal Revenue Code of 1986, or any comparable provision of any future legislation that amends, supplements, or supersedes that section.

---

6. The manner of making payments under the plan should be described.

EXAMPLE

Manner of Making Payments

By the end of each calendar year or within thirty (30) days thereafter, the employer shall reimburse each member for the portion of the member's family unit's medical care costs incurred during the year that is payable to that member, provided that by the end of that year or within thirty (30) days thereafter, the employer receives evidence acceptable to it that such medical care costs have been paid by the member or any other individual included in the member's family unit.

---

7. Provisions should be recited to avoid duplication of payments for the same expenses.

EXAMPLE

Nonduplication of Benefits

A member shall not be reimbursed for medical care costs under this Plan to the extent that such costs are paid to or for the benefit of the member, or to or for the benefit of any other individual included in the member's family unit, under the provisions of any public plan of health insurance or under the provisions of any other plan or insurance policy, the costs or premiums of which are directly or indirectly paid, in whole or part, by the employer.

---

8. If the employer is to pay all of the benefits under the plan, that should be stated.

EXAMPLE

Financing Plan Benefits

Subject to the provisions of [Amendment and Termination], the employer expects and intends to pay the entire cost of the benefits provided by this Plan. No member will be required or permitted to make contributions under the Plan.

---

9. The items required by the employer to document the charges should be described.

EXAMPLE

Information to Be Furnished by Members

Members must furnish to the employer such documents, evidence, data, or information as the employer considers necessary or desirable for the purpose of administering the Plan or for the employer's protection. The benefits of the Plan for each member are on the condition that the member furnish full, true, and complete data, evidence, or other information, and that the member will promptly sign any documents related to the Plan requested by the employer.

10. Any implication that the plan provides a continuing right of employment should be eliminated.

EXAMPLE

Employee Rights

The Plan does not constitute a contract of employment, and participation in the Plan will not give any member the right to be retained in the employ of the employer, nor will participation in the Plan give any member any right or claim to any benefit under the Plan, unless such right or claim has specifically accrued under the terms of the Plan.

11. Someone (usually the employer) should be able to interpret the plan, with that person's decision being final.

EXAMPLE

Provision That Employer's Decision Is Final

Any interpretation of the Plan and any decision on any matter within the discretion of the employer made by the employer in good faith is binding on all persons. A misstatement or other mistake of fact shall be corrected when it becomes known, and the employer shall make such adjustments on account thereof as it considers equitable and practicable.

12. Provisions for terminated participating employees should be included.

EXAMPLE

Benefits of Terminated Participating Employees

If a member's employment by the employer is terminated by reason of the member's resignation or dismissal, then any amount payable to that member under the Plan immediately prior to the member's termination shall be paid to the member. If a member's participation in the Plan is terminated by reason of the member's death, then any amount that has become payable to the member under the Plan as of the date of his or her death shall, in the discretion of the employer, be paid to either the member's spouse or the member's estate.

13. Amendment and termination provisions should describe the manner in which an amendment occurs, the causes of termination, and provisions for notice of either.

EXAMPLE

Amendment and Termination

General. While the employer expects to continue the Plan, it must necessarily reserve and does reserve the right to amend the Plan from time to time or to terminate the Plan.

Amendment. If the employer exercises its right to amend the Plan, any amount that has become payable under the Plan to any person prior to the date on which such amendment is adopted shall be paid by the employer in accordance with the terms of the Plan in effect prior to that date.

Termination. The Plan will terminate on the first to occur of the following:

a) the date it is terminated by the employer;

b) the date the employer is judicially declared bankrupt or insolvent; or

c) the dissolution, merger, consolidation, or reorganization of the employer, or the sale by the employer of all or substantially all of its assets, except that in any such event arrangements may be made whereby the Plan will be continued by any successor to the employer or by any purchaser of all or substantially all of the employer's assets, in which case the successor or purchaser will be substituted for the employer under the Plan.

If the Plan is terminated in accordance with subparagraph (a) or (c) above, any amount that has become payable under the Plan to any person prior to the date of termination shall be paid by the employer in accordance with the terms of the Plan in effect prior to its termination.

Notice of Amendment or Termination. Members will be notified of an amendment or termination within a reasonable time.

Variations on Employee Retirement Plans

Individual Retirement Accounts An individual income earner may establish his or her own plan for retirement using an Individual Retirement Account (IRA). The individual establishes an account with a bank or financial institution into which he or she makes contributions that are deductible from the individual's taxable income in the year of contribution. An individual may use an IRA only if he or she is not covered under any other qualified plan. The deductibility of income decreases as one's income grows and is eventually phased out completely over a certain threshold of income. Penalties will be imposed if the funds are withdrawn before the individual reaches age $59\frac{1}{2}$ and the funds are taxed when they are distributed. Distributions must be made before the individual reaches age $70\frac{1}{2}$.

SEP-IRA Self-employed individuals may adopt a Simplified Employee Pension (SEP) plan to make annual contributions for retirement up to the lesser of 15% of the individual's compensation or a ceiling amount (e.g., $30,000). If the self-employed individual employs other persons, such as an assistant or a paralegal, contributions may be made to this SEP plan by them as well. The contributions are tax deductible and the earnings in the account will not be taxed until the funds are withdrawn. A penalty will be imposed if the funds are withdrawn before the individual reaches age $59\frac{1}{2}$, and the funds are taxed when they are distributed. Distributions must be made before the individual reaches age $70\frac{1}{2}$.

Roth IRA A variation on this theme of Individual Retirement Accounts is the Roth IRA, which permits contributions of funds to a retirement account from income that has already been subject to income tax. The amount of the contributions to a Roth IRA are not deductible, so the employee must pay tax on the income before contributing funds to this account. However, earnings on investments made in the account will not be taxed, and distributions after the employee has reached age $59\frac{1}{2}$ are not taxable. These funds do not have to be withdrawn when an individual reaches age $70\frac{1}{2}$, allowing the account to be retained as part of the individual's estate for his or her heirs. There are limitations on the individuals who are entitled to use a Roth IRA. Generally, persons earning more than a specified ceiling of taxable income (e.g., $110,000 for a single individual) are not eligible for this plan.

SIMPLE A SIMPLE (Savings Incentive Match Plan for Employees) is a plan that can be used by small employers to begin a retirement program for employees. The plan is usually structured as an Individual Retirement Account into which employees may contribute an amount of their annual income. A SIMPLE-IRA allows the employee to contribute more than would ordinarily be allowed to be contributed by an Individual Retirement Account (See Exhibit 12–2, Form 5304-SIMPLE).

401(k) Plans Section 401(k) of the Internal Revenue Code provides for retirement plans that consist mostly of contributions by the employees that are tax advantaged for purposes of saving for retirement. These plans are favored by smaller companies because they allow for annual employee contributions (up to a certain threshold amount) in an account set aside as a 401(k) account. The employee contributions may be made from deductions from the employee's compensation and are not taxed at the time the compensation is paid. The employer may contribute up to the amount contributed by the employee. The amount saved in the 401(k) account may be invested by the plan administrator or sponsor. The profits earned on those investments are not taxed until the money is withdrawn, when the employee is retiring and in a lower individual income tax bracket. Contributions that were made by the employer may not be withdrawn unless the employee reaches age $59\frac{1}{2}$, is disabled, suffers some hardship, or retires. If an employee changes his or her place of employment, the 401(k) account can be brought to the new employer and continued.

Exhibit 12–2.

Form 5304-SIMPLE

Form **5304-SIMPLE** (Rev. March 2002) Department of the Treasury Internal Revenue Service	**Savings Incentive Match Plan for Employees of Small Employers (SIMPLE)—Not for Use With a Designated Financial Institution**	OMB No. 1545-1502 **Do not** file with the Internal Revenue Service

_____ establishes the following SIMPLE
Name of Employer

IRA plan under section 408(p) of the Internal Revenue Code and pursuant to the instructions contained in this form.

Article I—Employee Eligibility Requirements *(complete applicable box(es) and blanks—see instructions)*

1 General Eligibility Requirements. The Employer agrees to permit salary reduction contributions to be made in each calendar year to the SIMPLE IRA established by each employee who meets the following requirements (select either 1a or 1b):

a ☐ **Full Eligibility.** All employees are eligible.

b ☐ **Limited Eligibility.** Eligibility is limited to employees who are described in both (i) and (ii) below:

    (i) Current compensation. Employees who are reasonably expected to receive at least $ _____ in compensation (not to exceed $5,000) for the calendar year.

    (ii) Prior compensation. Employees who have received at least $ _____ in compensation (not to exceed $5,000) during any _____ calendar year(s) (insert 0, 1, or 2) preceding the calendar year.

2 Excludable Employees.

    ☐ The Employer elects to exclude employees covered under a collective bargaining agreement for which retirement benefits were the subject of good faith bargaining. **Note:** *This box is deemed checked if the Employer maintains a qualified plan covering only such employees.*

Article II—Salary Reduction Agreements *(complete the box and blank, if applicable—see instructions)*

1 Salary Reduction Election. An eligible employee may make an election to have his or her compensation for each pay period reduced. The total amount of the reduction in the employee's compensation for a calendar year cannot exceed the applicable amount for that year.

2 Timing of Salary Reduction Elections

a For a calendar year, an eligible employee may make or modify a salary reduction election during the 60-day period immediately preceding January 1 of that year. However, for the year in which the employee becomes eligible to make salary reduction contributions, the period during which the employee may make or modify the election is a 60-day period that includes either the date the employee becomes eligible or the day before.

b In addition to the election periods in 2a, eligible employees may make salary reduction elections or modify prior elections _____ _____. If the Employer chooses this option, insert a period or periods (e.g. semi-annually, quarterly, monthly, or daily) that will apply uniformly to all eligible employees.

c No salary reduction election may apply to compensation that an employee received, or had a right to immediately receive, before execution of the salary reduction election.

d An employee may terminate a salary reduction election at any time during the calendar year. ☐ If this box is checked, an employee who terminates a salary reduction election not in accordance with 2b may not resume salary reduction contributions during the calendar year.

Article III—Contributions *(complete the blank, if applicable—see instructions)*

1 Salary Reduction Contributions. The amount by which the employee agrees to reduce his or her compensation will be contributed by the Employer to the employee's SIMPLE IRA.

2a Matching Contributions

    (i) For each calendar year, the Employer will contribute a matching contribution to each eligible employee's SIMPLE IRA equal to the employee's salary reduction contributions up to a limit of 3% of the employee's compensation for the calendar year.

    (ii) The Employer may reduce the 3% limit for the calendar year in (i) only if:

        (1) The limit is not reduced below 1%; **(2)** The limit is not reduced for more than 2 calendar years during the 5-year period ending with the calendar year the reduction is effective; and **(3)** Each employee is notified of the reduced limit within a reasonable period of time before the employees' 60-day election period for the calendar year (described in Article II, item 2a).

b Nonelective Contributions

    (i) For any calendar year, instead of making matching contributions, the Employer may make nonelective contributions equal to 2% of compensation for the calendar year to the SIMPLE IRA of each eligible employee who has at least $ _____ (not more than $5,000) in compensation for the calendar year. No more than $200,000* in compensation can be taken into account in determining the nonelective contribution for each eligible employee.

    (ii) For any calendar year, the Employer may make 2% nonelective contributions instead of matching contributions only if:

        (1) Each eligible employee is notified that a 2% nonelective contribution will be made instead of a matching contribution; and

        (2) This notification is provided within a reasonable period of time before the employees' 60-day election period for the calendar year (described in Article II, item 2a).

3 Time and Manner of Contributions

a The Employer will make the salary reduction contributions (described in 1 above) for each eligible employee to the SIMPLE IRA established at the financial institution selected by that employee no later than 30 days after the end of the month in which the money is withheld from the employee's pay. See instructions.

b The Employer will make the matching or nonelective contributions (described in 2a and 2b above) for each eligible employee to the SIMPLE IRA established at the financial institution selected by that employee no later than the due date for filing the Employer's tax return, including extensions, for the taxable year that includes the last day of the calendar year for which the contributions are made.

* For 2003 and later years, this amount is subject to annual cost-of-living adjustments. The IRS announces the increase, if any, in a news release, in the Internal Revenue Bulletin, and on the IRS's internet web site at **www.irs.gov.**

For Paperwork Reduction Act Notice, see page 6.   Cat. No. 23377W   Form **5304-SIMPLE** (Rev. 3-2002)

Exhibit 12–2.

(continued)

Form 5304-SIMPLE (Rev. 3-2002)   Page **2**

Article IV—Other Requirements and Provisions

1   **Contributions in General.** The Employer will make no contributions to the SIMPLE IRAs other than salary reduction contributions (described in Article III, item 1) and matching or nonelective contributions (described in Article III, items 2a and 2b).

2   **Vesting Requirements.** All contributions made under this SIMPLE IRA plan are fully vested and nonforfeitable.

3   **No Withdrawal Restrictions.** The Employer may not require the employee to retain any portion of the contributions in his or her SIMPLE IRA or otherwise impose any withdrawal restrictions.

4   **Selection of IRA Trustee.** The employer must permit each eligible employee to select the financial institution that will serve as the trustee, custodian, or issuer of the SIMPLE IRA to which the employer will make all contributions on behalf of that employee.

5   **Amendments To This SIMPLE IRA Plan.** This SIMPLE IRA plan may not be amended except to modify the entries inserted in the blanks or boxes provided in Articles I, II, III, VI, and VII.

6   **Effects Of Withdrawals and Rollovers**

a   An amount withdrawn from the SIMPLE IRA is generally includible in gross income. However, a SIMPLE IRA balance may be rolled over or transferred on a tax-free basis to another IRA designed solely to hold funds under a SIMPLE IRA plan. In addition, an individual may roll over or transfer his or her SIMPLE IRA balance to any IRA after a 2-year period has expired since the individual first participated in any SIMPLE IRA plan of the Employer. Any rollover or transfer must comply with the requirements under section 408.

b   If an individual withdraws an amount from a SIMPLE IRA during the 2-year period beginning when the individual first participated in any SIMPLE IRA plan of the Employer and the amount is subject to the additional tax on early distributions under section 72(t), this additional tax is increased from 10% to 25%.

Article V—Definitions

1   **Compensation**

a   **General Definition of Compensation.** Compensation means the sum of the wages, tips, and other compensation from the Employer subject to federal income tax withholding (as described in section 6051(a)(3)) and the employee's salary reduction contributions made under this plan, and, if applicable, elective deferrals under a section 401(k) plan, a SARSEP, or a section 403(b) annuity contract and compensation deferred under a section 457 plan required to be reported by the Employer on Form W-2 (as described in section 6051(a)(8)).

b   **Compensation for Self-Employed Individuals.** For self-employed individuals, compensation means the net earnings from self-employment determined under section 1402(a), without regard to section 1402(c)(6), prior to subtracting any contributions made pursuant to this plan on behalf of the individual.

2   **Employee.** Employee means a common-law employee of the Employer. The term employee also includes a self-employed individual and a leased employee described in section 414(n) but does not include a nonresident alien who received no earned income from the Employer that constitutes income from sources within the United States.

3   **Eligible Employee.** An eligible employee means an employee who satisfies the conditions in Article I, item 1 and is not excluded under Article I, item 2.

4   **SIMPLE IRA.** A SIMPLE IRA is an individual retirement account described in section 408(a), or an individual retirement annuity described in section 408(b), to which the only contributions that can be made are contributions under a SIMPLE IRA plan and rollovers or transfers from another SIMPLE IRA.

Article VI—Procedures for Withdrawal *(The employer will provide each employee with the procedures for withdrawals of contributions received by the financial institution selected by that employee, and that financial institution's name and address (by attaching that information or inserting it in the space below) unless: (1) that financial institution's procedures are unavailable, or (2) that financial institution provides the procedures directly to the employee. See Employee Notification on page 5.)*

Article VII—Effective Date

This SIMPLE IRA plan is effective _____ . See instructions.

*   *   *   *   *

_____   By: Signature   Date
Name of Employer

_____   _____
Address of Employer   Name and title

Form **5304-SIMPLE** (Rev. 3-2002)

KEY TERMS

employment at will	salary	golden parachute provision
exempt employees	current incentive program	employee handbook/manual
nonexempt employees	commission	implied covenant of good faith and
comp time	draws against compensation	fair dealing
key employee	bonus plan	Employment Retirement Income
employment agreement/contract	renewal provision	Security Act (ERISA)
compensation	severance compensation	restrictive or proprietary covenant

trade secrets
work product protection clause
nondisclosure agreement
liquidated damage clause
covenant not to compete,
    noncompetition agreement
severability provision
group incentive plan
deferred compensation plan
forfeiture clause

constructive receipt
pension plan
profit sharing plan
qualification of plan
vesting
percentage test
fair-cross-section test
ratio test
average benefits test
five-year cliff vesting

funding of plan
stock option, incentive stock option
option price
tax preference
grant limitation
exercise limitation
death benefit compensation program
split-dollar insurance
employee expense reimbursement plan
Revenue Act of 1978

WEB RESOURCES

For research on federal and state minimum wage laws and the Fair Labor Standards Act, access

<http://www.dol.gov>

Employment resources at federal and state levels, including business laws and regulatory assistance and complete texts of the current federal regulations may be obtained from

<http://www.sba.org>
<http://www.access.gpo.gov>
<http://www.osha.gov>

Forms for incentive compensation plans are available from

<http://www.techagreements.com>

Forms for SIMPLE Plans are available from

<http://www.irs.ustreas.gov>

Information concerning Employee Retirement Income Security Act (ERISA) filings, IRS approved rollovers, public pension funds, administrative providers, tax exempt organizations, SEC filings, and other useful information about tax-deferred plans and programs is available at

<http://www.freeerisa.com>

Form employment agreements, employment manuals and handbooks, and other employer-employee related notices and documents are available free or at a moderate cost from

<http://www.lawdepot.com>
<http://www.uslegalforms.com>
<http://www.easyemploymentagreements.com>
<http://www.vcaonline.com>
<http://www.techagreements.com>
<http://www.weblawresources.com>

CASES

CLAY v. ADVANCED COMPUTER APPLICATIONS, INC.

536 A.2d 1375 (Pa. Super. 1988)
MONTEMURO, JUDGE

Appellants, Jeffrey Clay and Mary Clay, challenge the dismissal of their claims against appellees, Bjorn J. Gruenwald and Richard Baus. We affirm in part and reverse in part the order of the Bucks County Court of Common Pleas.

The Clays filed this action to recover damages for wrongful discharge, breach of an implied contract of em-

ployment and intentional infliction of emotional distress. In their complaint, they alleged that Bjorn Gruenwald had terminated their employment with Advanced Computer Applications, Inc. solely because Mary Clay had rebuffed the sexual advances of Richard Baus, a management-level employee. The complaint named as defendants (1) Advanced Computer; (2) Bjorn J. Gruenwald, both individually and as president of Advanced Computer, and (3) Richard Baus.

* * *

In support of their breach of contract claim, the Clays alleged that Advanced Computer hired them "on a regular full time basis for the purpose of long-term employment and career advancement." The Clays also allege that they "accepted the positions offered" and "ceased . . . looking for other gainful employment" in reliance upon "oral statements of the Defendant corporation." More specifically, they claimed that several months after they began working for Advanced Computer they informed Mr. Gruenwald of their plan to purchase a new home. Mr. Gruenwald, according to the Clays, not only encouraged the purchase but represented that "there were no problems with job security." The Clays insist that these facts are sufficient to show an "implied in fact" employment contract. They apparently believe that this "contract" overcomes the presumption of at-will employment. We disagree.

Pennsylvania courts have long recognized the rule that an employer may discharge his or her employees at any time for any or no reason, absent a statutory or contractual provision to the contrary. [Citations omitted]

* * *

Although we have questioned the viability of this belief given the more regulated environment of modern employment relationships, we have repeatedly reaffirmed the at-will rule in recent years. [Citations omitted] The rule has become so thoroughly woven into the fabric of our law and our commerce that only a legislative mandate will completely abolish it. [Citations omitted]

Nevertheless, as with any hoary principle of law, the at-will rule has spawned judicial exceptions. The discharged employee can now seek relief through an action in tort for wrongful discharge. A discharge is "wrongful" when it transgresses a clearly-articulable public policy or when the employer intends to harm the employee. [Citations omitted] In addition to the wrongful discharge action, the employee can, as always, defeat the at-will presumption by establishing that he or she contracted for an employment other than one terminable at will. Courts in our sister states increasingly have recognized that this kind of contract can arise from such sources as employee handbooks. [Citations omitted] This court, however, has repeatedly refused to recognize contractual modification of the at-will rule absent a clear expression of the parties' intent. [Citations omitted] The need for clarity is not unique to at-will employment cases. A party who wishes to enforce a contract must plead every element of that contract specifically, and clarity is particularly important when the alleged contract is oral. [Citations omitted] We cannot give legal significance to vague promises or to statements that reflect only the aspirations or hopes of the employer, whether written or spoken. The ordinary language of friendship and collegiality should not usually bind the speaker or writer as an enforceable obligation. In this case, none of the words or actions that the Clays attribute to their former employer even approach a clear impression of intent to contract away the at-will rule.

* * *

Purchasing a new home and foregoing other employment opportunities are detriments that "all manner of salaried professionals" incur in reliance upon their employment. The facts alleged by the Clays simply do not suggest that they "brought to the employment so substantial a benefit, or incurred so detrimental a hardship in taking the job, that [they] should be accorded treatment any different from the typical at-will employee."

Even if the Clays somehow did plead the necessary elements to prove a contract of definite duration, they have failed to allege any facts that would render either Mr. Gruenwald or Mr. Baus liable for breach. In fact, the complaint indicates that the Clays "were hired by the Defendant corporation." It also indicates that the Clays relied upon representations of "the Defendant corporation" when they "ceased looking for other gainful employment" and that they informed "the corporation," through its president Mr. Gruenwald, of their intent to buy a new home. The Clays nowhere allege that either Mr. Gruenwald or Mr. Baus was party to the employment agreement between the Clays and Advanced Computer. If neither Mr. Gruenwald nor Mr. Baus entered into the contract with the Clays, they could not have breached that contract.

[The Court found that the Clays could not recover for breach of an implied employment contract.]

WORTH v. HUNTINGTON BANCSHARES, INC.

540 N.E.2d 249 (Ohio 1989)

WRIGHT, JUSTICE

In February 1981, appellant, Paul E. Worth, commenced employment as Assistant Vice President with the Energy Division of Union Commerce Bank ("UCB"), a wholly owned subsidiary of Union Commerce Corporation ("UCC"). In June of that year appellee, Huntington Bancshares, Inc. ("Huntington"), contacted UCC officials and expressed an interest in combining the two bank holding companies' systems. When UCC declined the invitation, Huntington began acquiring stock in UCC, and by December 1981 it owned approximately five percent of UCC's voting stock.

In response to Huntington's proposed takeover attempt, UCC executed several employment agreements of the type commonly known as "golden parachutes" with several key employees, including Worth. Worth's employment agreement, the pertinent parts of which are fully set forth below, provided that in the event of a change of control of UCC, Worth would be entitled to resign within two years and receive certain economic benefits if he in good faith believed that his status or responsibilities had diminished following the takeover. The agreement also provided that Worth would be entitled to recover attorney fees incurred in defense of the agreement's validity, and that UCC would establish an irrevocable standby letter of credit of $500,000 for such fees. The enforceability of this provision for indemnification of legal expenses was upheld in an earlier decision of this court. Worth v. Aetna Cas. & Sur. Co. (1987), 32 Ohio St.3d 238, 513 N.E.2d 253. Huntington subsequently completed its acquisition of UCC, having obtained more than fifty percent of the stock therein by November 1982. The UCC chairman, chief executive officer, and some directors were replaced, and the name of UCB was changed to Huntington Bank of Northeast Ohio ("HBNO"). UCC was merged into Huntington and ceased to exist as a separate entity.

Worth continued in the employ of HBNO until May 31, 1983, at which time he exercised his option under the employment agreement and resigned. Huntington refused to pay Worth the economic benefits provided therein, and on July 22, 1983, Worth brought this action to enforce the agreement.

* * *

Section 2 listed numerous benefits to which Worth would be entitled if his employment were terminated involuntarily within one year following a change in control. These benefits included two times his annual salary, payable in monthly installments over a two-year period; two times the amount he was to receive under the company's Incentive Compensation Plan; comprehensive medical coverage for two years, or the cost thereof; payment for two years of club dues and special assessments; monthly payments for rental of an automobile; lump-sum cash payment for purchase of an annuity, or the benefits to which he has a vested right under the company's pension plan; and the option to surrender his stock to the company for cash.

Section 3 of the agreement provided as follows:

"3. Resignation Within Two Years. In the event that Employee should determine in good faith that his status or responsibilities with the Company or UCB has or have diminished subsequent to a change in control, and shall for that reason resign from his employment with the Company or UCB within two years after such change in control, Employee shall be entitled to receive all of the payments and enjoy all of the benefits specified in Section 2 hereof."

* * *

This case presents the court with its first opportunity to address the enforceability of corporate employment agreements commonly known as "golden parachutes." In general, "golden parachutes" are defined as "agreements between a corporation and its top officers which guarantee those officers continued employment, payment of a lump sum, or other benefits in the event of a change of corporate owner-

ship." Schreiber v. Burlington Northern, Inc. (1985), 472 U.S. 1, 3, fn. 2, 105 S.Ct. 2458, 2460, fn. 2, 86 L.Ed.2d 1.

Much has been written about this form of agreement, principally as to its use as a defense against hostile takeovers. See 2 Winter, Stumpf & Hawkins, Shark Repellants and Golden Parachutes: A Handbook for the Practitioner (1985) 432, fn. 1. Proponents of such contracts identify at least three primary benefits: (1) attraction and retention of competent managerial personnel, (2) promotion of executive objectivity by ensuring continued financial security, and (3) effective deterrence of hostile takeover attempts. Opponents argue that these potential benefits are illusory, and that golden parachutes operate solely for the benefit of executives and at the expense of shareholders. [Citations omitted]

Recent decisions contain numerous arguments against the enforceability of golden parachute agreements, including: (1) that such contracts are void as against public policy; (2) that they are unenforceable for lack of consideration; (3) that the benefits provided are penalties and not valid liquidated damages; and (4) that such contracts bear the taint of a conflict of interest in favor of the managerial beneficiaries and to the detriment of shareholders. In some early cases courts reached a decision on procedural issues, such as standing, without reaching the merits of these arguments. [Citations omitted] However, in a few recent cases where the merits have been considered, golden parachute agreements have been upheld. [Citations omitted]

Since these agreements will vary greatly, we can make no broad pronouncement as to their validity other than to say that an agreement such as the one executed by UCC and Worth is most certainly not void as against public policy. A corporation's decision to enter into a golden parachute agreement is, like all other matters dealing with compensation of corporate executives, within the sound discretion of the corporation's board of directors. The court of appeals here specifically found that Worth's agreement was neither excessive nor tainted by executive self-dealing or conflict of interest. [Citations omitted] We see nothing in the record to cause us to disturb these findings. It is certainly not for this court to second-guess the business judgment of corporate executives. Thus we hold that an agreement between a corporation and its officer which guarantees to the officer continued employment or economic benefits following a change in corporate ownership is not void as against public policy. Accordingly, we hold that the employment agreement at issue is valid and enforceable.

* * *

The real crux of Worth's argument lies in his claim that the court should have completely deferred to Worth's subjective determination that his status and responsibilities had diminished and that he resigned for that reason. The fact that the contract provided certain benefits upon

Worth's "good faith" determination required the trial court to examine the subjective bases of Worth's decisions. However, this does not require the court to ignore evidence which conflicts with Worth's claimed reasoning. In some situations lack of good faith is synonymous with "bad faith," a term more frequently defined. However, this is certainly not true in all situations. See, *e.g.,* Kalain v. Smith (1986), 25 Ohio St.3d 157, 159, 25 OBR 201, 202–203, 495 N.E.2d 572, 574 (construing R.C. 1343.03[C] and holding that, "A party may have 'failed to make a good faith effort to settle' even when he has not acted in bad faith."). Moreover, in all cases a "good faith determination" requires at least to some extent that the determination be informed. Where a contract provides that entitlement to benefits thereunder is contingent on a party's good faith determination, a court reviewing that party's good faith determination should consider not only the party's subjective reasoning but also the facts and circumstances surrounding the determination. An individual claiming to make a good faith decision cannot ignore the surrounding circumstances which ought to bear on that decision. Here, there is ample evidence to support the conclusion reached below that Worth's purported reasons

for determining that his status and responsibilities had diminished were both speculative and uninformed.

In any event, the trial court's conclusion that Worth resigned for reasons other than a determination that his status had diminished is amply supported by the record. The evidence reveals several other reasons for the resignation: (1) a desire to leave the banking industry; (2) a desire to return to Massachusetts and commence an energy consulting business; and (3) a recognition that his continued employment with HBNO would no longer be guaranteed under Section 2 of his employment agreement, as the one-year protection provided therein was to end shortly after the day he tendered his resignation. The trial court's findings in this regard are supported by competent, credible evidence, and we will not overturn these findings.

Accordingly, we conclude that, because Worth did not resign because he in good faith determined that his status and responsibilities had diminished following the takeover, Worth was not entitled to the benefits provided in paragraphs two and three of his employment agreement.

* * *

PROBLEMS

1. Oswald Manufacturing Company has 250 employees, including 40 persons who are shareholders owning more than 5% of the company's stock or who earned more than $80,000 during last year. The company's benefit package for its employees is valued at $1,000,000 per year, $450,000 of which apply to the 40 owner/executive employees. Does the company meet the nondiscriminatory benefits requirements of the Internal Revenue Code for its benefit program?

2. The employee's work product (i.e., inventions) should be protected while the proprietary interest of the employer is being perfected (e.g., patented) by
   a. a consent to an injunction against the employee in the agreement;
   b. a covenant not to compete with respect to that particular invention;
   c. an assignment agreement for the invention from the employee to the employer;
   d. a trade secret clause covering the invention.

3. Which of the following statements are true about qualified stock option plans?
   a. The plan must be approved by the shareholders before the option may be granted.

   b. The grant may be conditioned upon shareholder approval within six months.
   c. The shareholders may approve the plan within twelve months either side of the board of directors' adoption of the plan.
   d. none of the above
   e. a and b but not c
   f. a and c but not b

4. Assume you are representing the employee in negotiating an employment contract. Select the clause that would be most beneficial to the employee in the duties section of the agreement:
   a. Employee's duties shall be such as are from time to time assigned by the company.
   b. Employee's duties shall be strictly limited to those duties specified in this agreement.
   c. Employee's duties shall include those duties that are reasonable and consistent with the other duties specified in this agreement.

5. Assume you are representing the employer in negotiating the employment contract. Select the clause in question 4 that would be most beneficial to the employer.

PRACTICE ASSIGNMENTS

1. Write an employment agreement for your last job *from your employer's point of view.* Include a specific description of your duties, any restriction upon your authority, and clauses that your employer probably would have desired to govern your employment relationship.

2. Prepare a memorandum concerning the relevant issues in drafting clauses in employment contracts for the following benefits:
   a. access to a day care center;
   b. college tuition program;
   c. reimbursement of medical expenses for executive personnel;
   d. incentive compensation for senior managers based upon their areas of responsibility;
   e. disability salary continuation policy; and
   f. a profit sharing plan for a business with young, entrepreneurial employees.

3. Timberline Lumber Company would like to negotiate an employment contract with its employee-manager. Draft the agreement, making certain that the following important particulars are covered.
   a. Compensation will be on a salary with some incentive feature.
   b. The duties should be sufficiently broad to allow the employee-manager to do anything for the business.
   c. The contract should be terminable if the store fails to gross $10,000 for four consecutive months.
   d. The employee-manager should have an expense allowance.
   e. Provide for a noncompetition clause (5 years, radius of 500 miles from your city).

4. Prepare an incentive stock option plan that will qualify with the Internal Revenue Service.

ENDNOTES

1. For an extensive discussion of the law relating to human resource practices and employment law see J. Paddock, *Employment Law and Practice,* West 1998.

2. Worker Adjustment and Retraining Notification Act, 29 U.S.C.A. §§ 2101–2109.

3. 42 U.S.C.A. §§2000e, et seq.

4. 29 U.S.C.A.§ 206(d).

5. 29 U.S.C.A. §§ 621–34.

6. 42 U.S.C.A. § 12102.

7. Civil Rights Act of 1991, 29 C.F.R. § 1604.11.

8. Fair Labor Standards Act, 29 U.S.C. §§ 201–219.

9. Pregnancy Discrimination Act of 1978, 42 U.S.C.A.§ 2000e(k).

10. Protection of Juror's Employment Act, 28 U.S.C. § 1875.

11. 38 U.S.C. §§ 4301-07; §§ 28-3-506, 28-3-609–611.

12. Family and Medical Leave Act, 29 C.F.R. § 825.303.

13. See Johnson v. National Beef Packing Co., 220 Kan. 52, 4551 P.2d 779 (1976); Wooley v. Hoffmann-LaRoche, Inc., 99 N.J. 284, 491 A.2d 1257, *modified* 101 N.J. 10, 499 A.2d 515 (1985); Toussaint v. Blue Cross & Blue Shield, 408 Mich. 579, 292 N.W. 2d 880 (1980); see Shaw and Rosenthal, *Employment Law Deskbook,* Lexis/Nexis (1989 Supp. 2003).

14. Pine River State Bank v. Mettille, 333 N.W. 2d 622, 626 (Minn. 1983).

15. See "Employee Expense Reimbursement Plans" later in this chapter.

16. E.g., Cal. Bus. & Prof. Code §§ 16600–02 (West).

17. See Colo. Rev. Stat. § 8-2-113; Fla. Stat. Ann. § 542.33 (West); S.D. Codified Laws Ann. § 53-9-8.

18. See "Employment Agreements" earlier in this chapter.

19. See "Deferred Compensation" later in this chapter.

20. Forms for incentive compensation plans can be obtained from <http://www.techagreements.com>.

21. Internal Revenue Code (hereafter I.R.C.) of 1986, 26 U.S.C.A. § 401.

22. I.R.C. of 1986, 26 U.S.C.A. § 401.

23. I.R.C. of 1986, 26 U.S.C.A. § 404.

24. I.R.C. of 1986, 26 U.S.C.A. §§ 401, 501.

25. I.R.C. of 1986, 26 U.S.C.A. § 402.

26. Several firms act as administrators of pension and profit sharing plans. A list of administrators may be found at <http://www.freeerisa.com>.

27. I.R.C. of 1986, 26 U.S.C.A. § 422.

28. I.R.C. of 1986, 26 U.S.C.A. § 422.

29. The Model Business Corporation Act and most states require the affirmative vote of the holders of a majority of the voting stock to approve such action. See M.B.C.A. § 7.25; "Shareholders Meetings—Voting of Shares" in Chapter 10.

30. The tax treatment of split-dollar arrangements has recently been modified by the Internal Revenue Service. The arrangement may be treated either as (1) a loan by the employer to the employee for the amount of the premiums paid by the employer or (2) a taxable benefit to the executive equal to the cost of the insurance plus the net cash value available to the executive.

31. Nontaxable Insurance, Health, and Fringe Benefit Plans are authorized generally in the I.R.C. of 1986 §§ 101–140. Each section contains particular eligibility, participation, and coverage requirements for qualified plans, and should be reviewed for the current requirements.

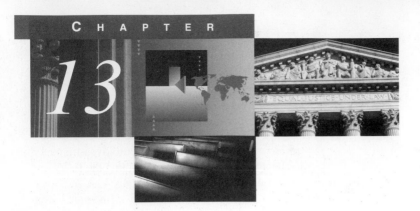

AGREEMENTS REGARDING OWNERSHIP

PURPOSES AND LEGAL SUPPORT

The close corporation has been discussed in a previous chapter.[1] The close corporation is usually owned by a small group of shareholders, who also may be the acting management of the corporation. The control exercised by the shareholders is a significant characteristic of this special corporate form, and this exclusive control may be protected by various provisions and agreements that prevent the sale of stock to persons outside of the select shareholder group. **Share transfer restrictions** are designed to preserve present ownership interests. These restrictions may be drafted as a limitation upon the capital stock structure in the articles of incorporation or may be the subject matter of a shareholder agreement to which all of the shareholders and the corporation are parties.

Agreements among members in a limited liability company and among partners in a partnership also may involve ownership and transfer of the equity interests of the entity or association. Although this chapter is concerned primarily with ownership agreements among shareholders, the principles and drafting techniques described here may be used with partnerships and limited liability companies as well.

Restrictions on the transfer of shares are recognized as a viable and legal way to retain ownership control among a closed group of people, with one important limitation. Since corporate shares are personal property of the shareholder, and since the law will not enforce an agreement that completely nullifies property rights, an agreement restricting the transfer of shares may not completely and irrevocably prohibit the sale of the stock. An agreement may, however, impose all sorts of restrictions that discourage sale to outsiders, and it may require that the shares must first be offered to the corporation or the other shareholders before they may be sold elsewhere. Although the selling shareholder must be able to sell the stock in the end, the shareholder may be required to satisfy a maze of conditions before doing so.

There are also shareholder agreements designed to concentrate voting power, with a group of shareholders pooling their votes under a contract that prescribes in advance how their shares will be voted on certain matters. Whatever control can be wielded by the concerted action of the total shares represented by the agreement will be applied to a vote on the specified corporate issues. The typical issues covered by shareholder voting agreements include the election of directors, amendments to the articles of incorporation, mergers, share exchanges, dissolution, and sales or other disposition of assets. Although these agreements are not unique to close corporations, they may be used in that setting to establish a predetermined voting position on matters such as salaries and dividends, especially where the shareholders also are employees of the corporation and are receiving salaries in lieu of dividends.

Shareholder voting agreements are commonly used to protect minority shareholders from abusive action by the majority shareholders. Recall that there are other provisions, statutory and by agreement, that protect the minority shareholders from the dangers of oppressive majority control. Cumulative voting is specifically designed to ensure minority shareholder representation on the board of directors (but an agreement among minority shareholders may be necessary to effectively utilize cumulative voting).[2] The articles of incorporation may require greater-than-majority voting requirements for shareholder action. For example, if the articles of incorporation require a 90% affirmative vote on all shareholder matters, an 11% minority shareholder could effectively veto any unwanted action. However, the majority shareholders may not appreciate this, and the incorporators must consider the potential dissatisfaction of majority shareholders when the articles are drafted. After all, the majority shareholders do invest the majority of capital. Some state statutes require a greater-than-majority vote for major changes in the corporate structure, such as amendments to the articles of incorporation, merger, and so forth,[3] and the minority shareholders receive some protection against modifications to their ownership interests in the corporation. Finally, judicial decisions support a cause of action by the minority shareholders against majority shareholders for oppression of the minority interest, but it is far more desirable to avoid that oppression through concentrated voting power rather than by litigation.

The Model Business Corporation Act grants statutory authority for shareholder voting agreements. Section 7.31 states that such agreements shall be valid and specifically enforceable according to their terms, meaning that a court may order a party to the agreement to perform his or her obligations under the agreement. Common law has long recognized the ability of shareholders to predetermine their position by agreement on normal shareholder business, such as electing directors. A rule has developed, however, that discourages any shareholder agreement that impinges on the statutory rules or usurps the power of the board of directors. For example, shareholders cannot agree that a quorum for shareholder meetings shall be one-fourth of the total voting shares, since the minimum allowable by statute is one-third in most jurisdictions.[4] Similarly, a shareholder agreement that a particular person will be continuously maintained as an officer of the corporation may be ineffective because the authority to select officers belongs to the directors. The Model Act and several states have adopted statutory rules that would permit the latter agreement, but further add that the shareholders must bear full responsibility for managerial acts governed by their agreement.[5]

Leaving aside agreements that encroach upon director discretion or regulate other managerial acts, there is no question that shareholders may agree regarding the manner in which their shares will be voted on issues normally requiring shareholder action.

CONCENTRATION OF VOTING POWER

In addition to the statutory and chartered rules that protect the minority interest (cumulative voting and greater-than-majority voting requirements), shareholders may pool their votes in an agreement executed among themselves, and thereby concentrate their aggregate voting power on each shareholder issue. There are formal ways and informal ways to do this. The formal voting trust ensures a more reliable concentration of power, since it prevents the possibility of a divided position from a shareholder who subsequently decides to act independently, but the voting trust must comply with the requirements of state corporate statutes. The informal voting or pooling agreement is much easier to use and may exist for longer periods of time, but it may not be as effective to control voting.

The following chart describes the important distinctions between voting trusts and pooling agreements:

Voting Trust	Pooling Agreement
Must be in writing	May be informal, but most statutes require a written agreement
Separates legal and beneficial ownership of shares	Each shareholder remains the legal owner of the shares
Must be a limited time (usually ten years)	May agree to last any period of time
A copy must be deposited with the corporation for the trust to be effective	No requirement for deposit with the corporation (may be a secret)
Ensures voting control because the trustee is the person who will cast the vote for all shares represented	Will require court action to enforce the agreement if a shareholder votes in violation of the agreement

Voting Trust

The formal approach to the concentration of shareholder voting power is a device called the **voting trust.** Voting trusts are permitted under the Model Business Corporation Act and in most jurisdictions, and the statutory requirements must be strictly followed. The voting trust is a trust arrangement in every sense of the term. The shares represented by this agreement are placed in trust, out of the hands of the shareholders, and a designated voting trustee is directed to vote the shares represented by the trust in accordance with the terms of the agreement. The duration of a voting trust is limited to a period of ten years under the Model Business Corporation Act.[6] A few states increase the term to fifteen years,[7] and a couple permit a twenty-one-year period.[8] Extensions for an additional period of ten years are permitted in the Model Business Corporation Act and in several jurisdictions. The shareholders who are parties to a voting trust surrender their shares to the trust and the voting trustee becomes the record owner of those shares, thereby ensuring that the trustee is notified of every shareholder meeting and that the trustee will have the legal right to vote the shares at such meetings. This is the "legal ownership" interest. The shareholder is issued a voting trust certificate representing the shares of stock he or she once held and is entitled to receive all distributions from the shares. This is the "beneficial ownership" interest. Voting trust certificates may be as transferable as the stock certificates themselves, although the purchaser takes them subject to the terms of the trust, which are stated on the certificate. The certificate also states the name of the trustee and other important matters respecting the agreement.

Under the Model Business Corporation Act, a voting trust becomes effective on the date that the first shares subject to the trust are registered in the trustee's name.[9] To meet the specific statutory requirements of most states and the act, the trust must be established as follows:

1. A written trust agreement must be prepared specifying the terms and conditions of the trust and conferring upon the trustee the right to vote the shares represented by the trust;
2. The shares represented must be transferred to the trustee in return for voting trust certificates;
3. The term of the agreement shall not be more than the statutory period, usually ten years;
4. The trustee must keep a record of all beneficiaries (shareholders) with their names and addresses and the number of shares deposited with the trust; and
5. A counterpart of the trust agreement and the record of beneficiaries must be deposited with the corporation at its principal office.

Several jurisdictions omit the requirement that the trustee maintain a record of beneficiaries.

The voting trust agreement must strictly observe the statutory requirements; a failure to do so may invalidate the trust. The agreement should specify its duration (within the statutory limit) and may provide for termination at any time by a prescribed vote of the beneficiaries. The designation of the trustees should state any qualifications the parties intend to impose, such as requiring the trustees to be shareholders or prohibiting any director of the corporation from acting as trustee. The description of authority should carefully detail the power of the trustees to vote the stock, naming specific issues if the trust is so limited, or granting total voting power of the stock to the trustees. The decisions of the trustees may be based upon the trustees' good judgment, or the agreement may require that the trustees obtain the consensus of a certain percentage of the beneficiaries before casting the trust vote. The trustees should be excused from liability for their actions, except for gross negligence, and should be indemnified for expenses and liabilities incurred in the exercise of their trust power. The procedure for the transfer and issuance of voting trust certificates must be detailed. Finally, ministerial duties of the trustees in receiving and paying dividends of the stock, filing documents with the corporation, and recording voting trust certificates may be specified.

A sample voting trust agreement with a voting trust certificate is Exhibit J–12 in Appendix I.

Stock Voting Agreement

Another agreement designed to concentrate shareholder voting power is a voting or pooling agreement, which may accomplish the same purpose as the voting trust, but usually is not subject to the same statutory regulation. Several shareholders join together and pool their respective voting interests, predetermining the manner in which the shares will be voted by the agreement.

Stock voting agreements may be quite informal and may vary depending upon the desires of the parties, since there is virtually no statutory regulation governing their formation and interpretation. Section 7.31 of the Model Business Corporation Act simply states that "two or more shareholders may provide for the manner in which they will vote their shares by signing an agreement for that purpose." Voting agreements that are created under section 7.31 are not subject to the rules concerning voting trusts in section 7.30. In principle, then, a stock voting agreement can last indefinitely, as contrasted with the voting trust, which has a limited term. The voting agreement also may be a secret, if that is desirable, since no evidence of the agreement need be deposited with the corporation.

Stock voting agreements have traditionally suffered from one serious deficiency: a lack of enforceability. Unlike voting trust agreements, stock voting agreements do not require shareholders to deposit their shares with anyone. The shareholders merely agree to vote the shares, which they still control, in the same manner as do the other parties to the agreement. Suppose Wagner, Naylor, and Shaklee enter into a stock pooling agreement that they will vote the same way on shareholder matters and that the manner in which they vote will be determined by a majority vote among them. Suppose further that on a given issue Wagner and Naylor want the votes cast one way, but Shaklee dissents. If Shaklee refuses to abide by the decision, he may still cast the votes he controls in any way he wants. The other parties may be able to sue him for breach of the pooling agreement, but the most important objective, the concentrated voting power, has been lost on that issue. This situation cannot occur with a formal voting trust. In an effort to solve this problem, the Model Business Corporation Act provides that a voting agreement will be specifically enforceable, meaning that a shareholder can be required by a court to cast his or her vote in conformity with the agreement. Several states have also adopted this provision.

Another problem unique to the voting agreement arises if one of the parties to the agreement decides to sell the stock. The concentrated voting power is lost if the purchaser is not obliged to abide by the agreement. A typical response to this problem is to impose a restriction on the transfer of stock held by the parties to the agreement, requiring that an offer to sell the stock be directed to the other parties before the shares may be sold to a nonparty investor.

Restriction on Transfer of Stock

EXAMPLE

Neither party will sell any shares of stock in the corporation to any other person whomsoever, without first making a written offer to the other party hereto of all of the shares proposed to be sold, for the same price and upon the same terms and conditions as in such proposed sale, and allowing such other party a time of not less than 180 days from the date of such written offer within which to accept same.

The stock voting agreement requires joint action of the participants in exercising their voting rights. The joint action may be required on all matters submitted to the vote of the shareholders, or may be limited to certain issues where concentration of voting power is deemed to be important, such as amendments to the articles, election of directors, and so forth. An example of a joint action clause covering all shareholders' matters looks like this:

EXAMPLE | **Joint Action**

In exercising any voting rights to which either party may be entitled by virtue of ownership of stock held by them in the corporation, each party will consult and confer with the other, and the parties will act jointly in exercising the voting rights in accordance with such agreement as they may reach with respect to any matter calling for the exercise of the voting rights.

The determination of how the votes will be cast is made by agreement of the participants; if there are more than two parties to the agreement, a formula should be prescribed for this determination. For example, the agreement can require the unanimous vote of the shareholders represented by the agreement, although this criterion may be impossible to satisfy. A provision allowing the determination of position to be made by a majority of the shares represented by the agreement is more practicable. If a deadlock is possible under the agreement, as it might be if only two shareholders are parties, a provision regarding arbitration or another settlement mechanism, such as mediation, is appropriate.

EXAMPLE | **Arbitration**

In the event the parties fail to agree with respect to any matter covered by the preceding paragraph, the question in disagreement shall be submitted for arbitration to D. S. Charlton, of Montgomery, Alabama, as arbitrator, and his decision thereon shall be binding upon the parties hereto. Such arbitration shall be exercised to the end of ensuring good management for the corporation. The parties may at any time by written agreement designate any other individual to act as arbitrator in lieu of said D. S. Charlton.

Duration and termination provisions should be included, reflecting the desires of the parties as to such matters.

EXAMPLE | **Duration**

This agreement shall be in effect from the date hereof and shall continue in effect for a period of twenty years unless sooner terminated by mutual agreement in writing by the parties hereto.

Agreements to Secure Director Representation

Since corporate management is vested in the board of directors and the board of directors is elected by the shareholders, the board is usually elected by the majority shareholders, particularly when cumulative voting is not in effect. Even if cumulative voting is used in the election of directors, the minority shareholders may have to unite to secure representation of the board.[10] Consequently, the minority shareholders frequently are not represented on the board of directors.

An assurance of minority representation on the board may be accomplished by agreement in two ways. With the first method, using the concentration of minority voting power, a shareholder voting agreement or voting trust may predetermine the manner in which the parties to the agreement will vote at the election of the directors. The terms of this agreement would provide that all parties to the agreement (or the trustee) would vote for a person who, according to a majority of the persons represented by the agreement (or other formula determination), would best represent the interests of the parties. With the second method, there would be an agreement among all shareholders that certain positions on the board of directors would be reserved to the nominee of the minority shareholders, and that all shareholders would vote to elect the **minority nominee** to the board at each election.

Agreement to Segregate the Board of Directors

That the number of the members of the Board of Directors of Trouble, Inc., be reduced from five, as it now is, to the number of four, that the number of members of said Board of Directors shall be maintained at four in number, of which at all times two thereof shall be such persons as shall be nominated or designated by the said parties of the first part and the other two thereof shall be such persons as shall be nominated or designated by the said party of the second part. And it is further mutually agreed between the parties that at all stockholders' meetings of the said Trouble, Inc., held for the purpose of election of directors or director (in case of vacancy of the Board of Directors), that all of the said shares of stock of parties of the first part and also of party of the second part and also any additional shares of stock of Trouble, Inc., which may be subsequently acquired by the said parties or either of them, shall be voted in such manner and for such person or persons as will keep and maintain the Board of Directors four in number, of which two thereof shall be such persons as shall be nominated or designated by said parties of the first part and two thereof shall be such persons as shall be nominated or designated by the said party of the second part.

Instead of the general description "minority nominee," it is possible to name a certain person in the shareholder agreement and agree that he or she will be continually elected as a director to represent the specialized shareholder interests. However, these agreements have been subjected to careful scrutiny by the courts and have been declared invalid if they fail to leave room for the defeat of an incompetent director. On the other hand, a shareholder agreement will be enforceable if it states that a named director will be maintained in office as long as that person faithfully and conscientiously performs the duties of that office. Therefore, it is good practice to include a **savings clause,** making the election of a particular director obligatory only if that person is competent to serve in that position.

Agreements Concerning Management Issues

Although the traditional rule of corporate law is that the shareholders cannot enter into agreements that may interfere with or usurp the authority of the board of directors, modern corporate statutes acknowledge that the shareholders should be entitled to enter into agreements among themselves about certain management issues of particular importance to them. Certainly partners in partnerships and members of limited liability companies can agree on management issues (and, in fact, are expected to address such issues in their agreements), so it is reasonable that the shareholders of closely held corporations should be allowed to do the same.

Section 7.32 of the Model Act provides statutory guidance for shareholder agreements on certain management issues. That section specifically authorizes agreements that

1. eliminate the board of directors or restricts its power;
2. authorize distributions to the shareholders (which may be disproportionate to the ownership of shares but subject to the solvency limitations on distributions);
3. determine the identity and terms of the directors and officers (and how they will be selected or removed);
4. govern how voting will occur among shareholders and directors;
5. establish terms and conditions of any agreement involving property or services among the corporation and its shareholders, directors, or employees;
6. transfer to a shareholder or other person corporate authority under certain described circumstances;

7. require dissolution of the corporation at the request of a shareholder or on a specified event;
8. otherwise govern the exercise of corporate powers or management of the business, so long as it is not contrary to public policy.

For such an agreement to be valid, it must be set forth in the articles of incorporation or bylaws and approved unanimously by all shareholders or must be in a written agreement that is signed by all shareholders. Thus, like partners who are parties to a partnership agreement or members who enter into an operating agreement for a limited liability company, the shareholders of a closely held corporation may agree on their management structure and responsibilities differently than the normal rigid corporate divisions of authority. The Model Act adjusts other corporate rules for that privilege, however, and provides that any such agreement that limits the discretion or powers of the board of directors shall relieve the directors of any liability for decisions made pursuant to the agreement. There is also a limitation on the duration of such agreements (ten years) unless the agreement expressly provides otherwise. Further, the existence of such an agreement must be conspicuously noted on the certificates for shares to warn purchasers of such shares that the structure of the corporation has been changed by the agreement. If the notation on the certificate was omitted and a purchaser of shares was not aware of the agreement, the purchaser can rescind the purchase of shares on that basis.

SHARE TRANSFER RESTRICTIONS AND BUYOUT AGREEMENTS

Shareholder agreements frequently are concerned with restrictions on the transfer of shares. These restrictions are not necessarily directed to the protection of special shareholder stock voting agreements. Usually the restrictions on transfer are intended to protect all shareholders who desire to avoid alienation or interference with corporate control. Minority shareholders could suffer greatly if majority shareholders were allowed to sell their shares and the associated control of the corporation to an outsider who is not sympathetic to the minority interest. Similarly, majority shareholders could suffer from the sale of even one share to a recalcitrant, argumentative shareholder, particularly in a close corporation where all of the shareholders must work closely to further the enterprise.

Restrictions on transfer of shares may be imposed in the articles of incorporation, the bylaws, or separate shareholder agreements. The corporation is usually a party to the restrictive agreement because the agreement usually grants the corporation the right to repurchase shares if a shareholder wants to sell them. The thrust of most restrictive agreements is to prohibit the transfer of shares to an outsider without first offering them for sale to the corporation or to the other shareholders.

Agreements affecting share ownership may specify **mandatory buyout or sellout arrangements,** directed to the corporation and the shareholders, but the objectives here are opposite from those of the share transfer restrictions. While share transfer restrictions are intended to discourage the transfer of shares, mandatory buyout or sellout arrangements are designed to require the transfer of shares. The intracorporate groups may prefer to prohibit share ownership by a person who is not actively engaged in the business, and a mandatory sellout agreement may satisfy this objective. On the other hand, a shareholder may wish to ensure the existence of a market in which to sell his or her shares, which can be accomplished through a mandatory buyout agreement. In small, closely held corporations, the shares may not be marketable, and without a mandatory buyout agreement, a shareholder has no choice but to hold the shares indefinitely with no prospect of receiving a return of invested capital until the corporation is dissolved. Finally, a mandatory buyout agreement also ensures that a deceased shareholder's heirs will receive the agreed value of the shares when a shareholder dies.

Restrictive Agreements

Section 6.27 of the Model Business Corporation Act provides statutory authority for an agreement among shareholders concerning restrictions on the transfer of shares of the corporation.

The restrictions may be contained in the articles of incorporation, the bylaws, or a separate agreement. The share transfer restriction is authorized

1. to maintain the corporation's status when that status is dependent on the number or identity of the corporation's shareholders (such as when a corporation makes a Subchapter S election for tax purposes);
2. to preserve exemptions under federal or state laws (such as when a corporation offers shares privately to shareholders and does not register the shares with the Securities and Exchange Commission so the restriction prevents shares from being transferred to the public); and
3. to accomplish any other reasonable purpose.

The validity of a share transfer restriction depends, in part, upon the nature and structure of the business. The restriction must be adopted for a lawful purpose, and it may be necessary to show that there is a special need for a share transfer restriction in the particular type of business or in the particular relationship between shareholders. This burden should not be onerous, but it should be considered when a share transfer restriction is adopted by the parties. There is ample reason to support the restriction in small, close corporations, but in any case, the agreement should recite that its purpose is to further harmonious relations between the parties and to promote the best interests of the business.

The most effective way to ensure that no outsider will be admitted to a select shareholder group would be to completely and forever prohibit the sale of the stock to any person at any time. Such a complete prohibition on transferability is certainly restrictive, but it is also unenforceable and against public policy. Agreements that indefinitely prohibit the exercise of personal rights are presumed to be unfair, and it is virtually impossible to muster any rational reason to support such a severe restriction.

The most common restriction used to control the transfer of shares grants the corporation or the other shareholders the first option to purchase shares before those shares may be sold to an outsider.

Events Triggering the Restriction   A stock transfer restriction is normally triggered when a selling shareholder has received a valid and sincere offer to purchase his or her shares. If the agreement does not provide for some method of determining whether an offer is valid and sincere, a shareholder may manipulate the agreement. If the shareholder gives notice of an intention to sell the shares, the corporation and the other shareholders must either buy the stock or run the risk that the stock will be free from any transfer restriction. Thus, some definition of a **good faith offer** to purchase should be included in every restriction. Several possibilities exist for establishing the validity of an offer:

1. The agreement should provide that the offer to purchase the shares from an outside investor should be in writing.
2. The agreement may provide that the good faith offer must be supported by an earnest-money deposit.
3. The agreement may provide that the good faith offer must be supported by an escrow of the total purchase price, the terms of which would provide that in the event the corporation or the other shareholders fail to purchase their proportionate share of the selling shareholder's stock, the escrow proceeds would be distributed automatically to the selling shareholder and the stock would be deemed to have been purchased at that time.
4. The agreement may or may not provide for the disclosure of the identity of the good faith purchaser. On the one hand, disclosure of the identity of the purchaser will affirm the existence of a real purchaser and help the other shareholders to decide if they are comfortable having the purchaser as a fellow shareholder. On the other hand, if the corporation and the other shareholders know the identity of the purchaser, they might attempt to thwart the sale or sell other shares to the identified purchaser, thereby discouraging the purchase from the proposed selling shareholder.

Bona Fide Offer

Upon receipt of a bona fide offer to purchase the shares by a person not a shareholder of the corporation, a selling shareholder must follow the restrictions contained in this article prior to selling any shares of stock to the offeror. A bona fide offer shall require that the offeror place an amount equal to the purchase price of the stock in escrow, the terms of which shall require the release of said funds for the purchase of the stock if the corporation and other shareholders do not exercise their options hereunder, and contain an agreement from the offeror to be bound by the terms of these restrictions upon purchase of such shares.

Other events also may be the subject of a stock transfer restriction that prevents the free transferability of shares under certain conditions. For example, the restriction may require that on the death of a shareholder, the heirs or representatives of the deceased shareholder must offer the shares to the corporation or to the other shareholders. Similarly, retirement, disability, bankruptcy, or loss of a professional or occupational license necessary to the business of the corporation (as in a professional corporation) may trigger a stock transfer restriction. In these cases, however, it is likely that the agreement would provide for a mandatory purchase or sale upon the happening of the event. These mandatory agreements are discussed in detail later in this section.

Option to Purchase   The usual **option-to-purchase** share transfer restriction requires that an offer to sell be directed first to the corporation, which has a right of refusal, and then to the other shareholders, who also have the right of refusal to purchase the shares. If both the corporation and the shareholders decline to purchase the shares, then the selling shareholder may sell to the outsider. Alternatively, the restriction may run only to the corporation, or may bypass the corporation and grant the option to purchase only to the other shareholders. When the other shareholders are granted the option to purchase, the shares usually will be offered to them in the same proportion as their present ownership interests in the corporation.

An example of a provision granting a right of refusal to the corporation and then to the remaining shareholders follows.

Option to Purchase Shares

Should any shareholder wish to dispose of his or her stock, it shall first be offered to the corporation at a price no greater than a bona fide offer by any third person, and said stock shall be available to the corporation for a period of thirty days. In the event that any of the said stock is not purchased by the corporation, it shall be offered to the remaining shareholders of the same class of stock in the same proportion as their respective stock interests in said class of stock, for a like price and for a similar period of time. In the event any of the remaining shareholders declines to purchase his or her proportionate share of said stock, that share shall be offered to the then remaining shareholders of the same class of stock for a like price and for a similar period of time. In the event that any of said stock is not purchased by the corporation or the shareholders, the remaining stock may then be sold by the shareholder at the price of the bona fide offer of the third person.

By way of illustration, suppose the Nobles Company has three shareholders; Dworet, who owns 100 shares, Rezabeck, who owns 200 shares; and Weiler, who owns 300 shares. If Dworet desires to sell her shares and receives a bona fide offer for the purchase, she must first offer to sell the shares to the corporation at the price determined by the formula, and the corporation shall have thirty days to reject or accept the offer. If the corporation rejects the offer, Dworet must then offer the shares to Rezabeck and Weiler, who own the same class of stock in a 2:3 ratio, since Rezabeck owns 200 shares and Weiler owns 300 shares. Rezabeck and Weiler may then purchase in that ratio, meaning that Rezabeck can purchase 40 shares and

Weiler can purchase 60 shares. If Rezabeck declines to purchase the shares to which she is entitled, those shares must then be offered to Weiler, or vice versa, according to the sample provision. Only if the corporation and the other two shareholders decline to purchase the shares may Dworet sell the shares to the outsider.

Any variations in this scheme are permissible.

Considerations in Designating the Option to Purchase There are a couple of practical observations to consider in drafting the restriction. The first offer to the corporation is desirable because a solvent and profitable corporation will probably have funds legally available to purchase the shares. Moreover, it is more convenient to make the offer to the corporation through a single notice than to notify all of the other shareholders. The remaining shareholders also may prefer that the purchase funds come from internal corporate operations rather than attempting to raise funds individually. However, there may be situations when the corporation is not permitted to buy its own shares because of statutory restrictions on the funds that must be used for that purpose. If the corporation is unable to meet the statutory restrictions on distributions to shareholders, the corporation must refuse the offer, and to preserve the viability of the restriction, the offer should then run to the individual shareholders.

If the corporation is going to exercise an option to purchase or redeem its shares, it must do so in strict compliance with statutory restrictions on funds available for repurchase. Provided the corporation is solvent (and the purchase of shares will not render it insolvent), in many states the corporation may purchase its own shares only to the extent that it has unreserved and unrestricted surplus.[11] Under section 6.40 of the Model Business Corporation Act, the corporation may acquire its own shares as long as the funds distributed for the purchase will not reduce the corporation's net assets below the aggregate amount payable to shareholders with liquidation rights upon involuntary liquidation and dissolution of the corporation.[12] The surplus requirements under the applicable statute have nothing to do with the availability of cash to effect a repurchase, except insofar as the corporation must be able to pay its debts and liabilities as they fall due after distributing cash to the selling shareholder. The corporation may have sufficient cash for the stock purchase, but substantial current liabilities, or there may be only a few debts due on the corporation's books, but no ready cash.

The corporation may use life insurance as a method of funding a buyout agreement, especially when the event triggering the buyout is death. Life insurance funding also may be used when the triggering event is retirement, disability, or termination of employment. These funding options are discussed in detail later.

The remaining shareholders may find that raising funds to buy out a withdrawing shareholder is a difficult task, particularly if they must come up with the cash immediately on a shareholder's death or some other triggering event. The problem may be alleviated if the agreement provides for installment payments.

The agreement should permit those who elect to purchase more than their pro rata shares to divide equitably among themselves any shares not taken on the first division. If some shares still remain, the agreement should provide whether the original number or only the untaken shares may be sold to an outsider. Another question is whether the selling shareholder may break his or her stock holdings into small blocks and offer them to several people, thus obtaining a higher price per share. If the parties wish to eliminate these possibilities, the agreement should specifically prohibit such actions.

All or Nothing Purchase A choice must be made at the drafting stage between a restriction permitting a partial purchase of the offered stock or one requiring a purchase of **all or nothing.** Continuing with the example of the Nobles Company, presumably Dworet has received an offer from an outsider to buy her 100 shares at a price. The question now is whether the corporation or the other shareholders may purchase only a portion of her 100 shares in exercising the right of first refusal, or whether they must buy the entire block to exercise the option. Dworet is better protected if they must buy the entire block, since the outsider may not be interested in a purchase of only a portion of the 100 shares. However, the corporation and remaining shareholders have a greater guarantee against stock transfers if they are permitted to exercise their options in part, since they may then buy just enough of the stock to discourage the outsider, but they are not compelled to purchase all offered shares to prevent transfer. In the spirit of fairness, it is better practice to require the corporation to exercise its option in full or not at all. The restriction should further specify a procedure to prevent portion purchases, once the corporation has refused purchase and the offer is made to remaining shareholders, for the protection of the selling shareholder.

When more than one shareholder is entitled to an option to purchase, it is possible that some shareholders will exercise their options and others will not. In that case, a portion of the offered shares is available for sale to the outsider, but the outsider's interest in the purchase may dwindle after the number of shares has been reduced. To avoid this result, the restriction may provide that if all of the options are not exercised, none of them may be, which will preserve the block of stock intact. Alternatively, if the restriction permits some shareholders to refuse the option without impairing the rights of the other shareholders to exercise their options, it should further specify that the shares that have been refused will be offered to the shareholders who intend to exercise their options. These last shareholders have evidenced an interest in purchasing their quota of the offered stock; perhaps they will also purchase the remaining shares. This second chance for internal sale, which furthers the objectives of the remaining shareholders by granting another opportunity to avoid alienation of the shares, appears in the preceding example, "Option to Purchase Shares." Observe that if not all shares of the selling shareholder are purchased under the agreement, the amount paid by the corporation to the selling shareholder may be taxed as a dividend that is subject to ordinary income tax rates, while a complete redemption of all shares of the shareholder would be taxed at lower capital gain rates.[13]

In sum, the most fair and effective share transfer restriction first will grant the corporation the right to purchase all of the offered shares at a specified price; if the corporation refuses to buy all of the shares, then the other shareholders will have a right to purchase the offered shares according to their respective proportionate stock interests at a specified price; if some shareholders do not exercise their options, then none of them may, or the remaining unpurchased shares must be offered to the shareholders who have exercised their options before they may be sold to an outsider. All of these decisions should be made within a reasonably short time period so the shareholder and the outsider will have a prompt decision concerning whether the shares will be available for purchase by the outsider.

Mandatory Buyout or Sellout Provisions

The foregoing restrictions on transfer of shares are designed to avoid the alienation of shares and the potential loss of control of the corporation. Both goals are accomplished by granting the corporation or other shareholders the right of first refusal when shares are offered for sale. However, the shareholder may not be able to sell his or her shares to anybody (especially if the shareholder has invested in a small, closely held corporation), and then the shareholder deserves some protection. The shareholder agreement may require the corporation or the other shareholders to purchase the shares under certain circumstances. Conversely, the corporation may demand the right to purchase certain shares, such as when a shareholder-employee retires or quits. Thus, depending on the purpose to be served, mandatory buy or sell provisions may work both ways: the contract may require the corporation or other shareholders to purchase the shares, or it may require the shareholder to sell the shares.

Mandatory buyout agreements reflect an *obligation* on the part of the corporation and other shareholders to purchase the selling shareholder's stock, as distinguished from an option on their part to buy under the share transfer restriction. These mandatory provisions are designed to guarantee a market for the stock, which may be needed particularly by a minority shareholder. The minority shareholder cannot sell if no willing purchasers are available, and the minority shareholder is powerless to force dissolution to recoup invested capital if the majority shareholders resist. The majority shareholders also may need the guarantee. Willing purchasers may be difficult to find for a large block of stock, and while the majority shareholders can force dissolution, that may be an unwise business decision and may constitute oppression of the minority shareholders.

On the other hand, the mandatory buyout agreement also may impose the obligation on the part of the shareholder or the shareholder's representatives upon the occurrence of a triggering event to sell the shares to the corporation or to the other shareholders. The corporation and the other shareholders may thereby protect against the ownership of shares by persons who are strangers to the enterprise, such as the heirs of a deceased shareholder, a trustee in bankruptcy, or the representatives of a disabled shareholder.

Events Commonly Triggering Buyouts A mandatory buyout agreement is usually conditioned upon the death of a shareholder, the retirement of a shareholder at a certain age or after a specified length of service to the corporation, the disability of a shareholder, the bankruptcy of a shareholder, the loss of a shareholder's occupational license, or any attempt by a shareholder to force a dissolution of the corporation under statutory dissolution sections.[14]

The event triggering the buyout should be clearly defined; and if life insurance or other insurance is used to fund the buyout agreement, the definition of the contingent event should contain the same terms as the definition of that event under the insurance policies that are expected to fund the purchase. For example, if the disability of a shareholder will trigger a buyout, the agreement should define *disability* in the same method as the insurance policy defines the term, or the agreement should refer to the insurance policy definition. The agreement should further provide that after a specified period of time of continuous disability, again as defined in the insurance policy, a buyout will occur with the proceeds of the insurance policy.

Purchase on Death

EXAMPLE

The Company will have the option, for a period commencing with the death of any shareholder and ending 60 days following the qualification of his or her executor or administrator, to purchase all of the shares owned by the decedent, at the price and on the terms provided in this agreement. The option shall be exercised by giving notice to the decedent's estate or other successor in interest in accordance with this agreement. If the option is not exercised within such 60-day period as to all shares owned by the decedent, the surviving shareholders shall have the option, for a period of 30 days commencing with the end of that 60-day period, to purchase all of the shares owned by the decedent, at the price and on the terms provided in this agreement. The option shall be exercised by giving notice, in accordance with this agreement, to the executor or administrator, stating the number of shares as to which it is exercised. If notice of exercise from the surviving shareholders specify in the aggregate more shares than are available for purchase by the shareholders, each shareholder shall have priority, up to the number of shares specified in his or her notice, to such proportion of those available shares as the number of Company shares he or she holds bears to the number of the Company shares held by all shareholders electing to purchase. The shares not purchased on such a priority basis shall be allocated in one or more successive allocations to those shareholders electing to purchase more than the number of shares to which they have a priority right, up to the number of shares specified in their respective notices, in the proportion that the number of shares held by each of them bears to the number of shares held by all of them. In the event this option is not exercised as to all of the shares owned by the decedent, his or her estate will hold those shares subject to the provisions of this agreement.

Purchase on Other Events

EXAMPLE

In the event any shareholder is adjudicated a bankrupt (voluntary or involuntary), or makes an assignment for the benefit of his or her creditors, or is physically or mentally incapacitated for more than three months, the event of incapacity as described in an insurance policy now owned by the corporation with the Equitable Life Insurance Corporation, Policy No. 40-82-123, the Company and the remaining shareholders shall have the option for a period of 90 days following notice of any such event to purchase all of the shares owned by the shareholder. Notice shall be given to the shareholder or his or her representative in accordance with this agreement. The option shall be exercisable first by the Company and thereafter by the remaining shareholders, and the price, terms of purchase, and methods of exercise of the option shall be the same as are provided in this agreement to apply in the event of death. In the event this option is not exercised as to all of the shares owned by the shareholder, he or she or his or her successor in interest will own the shares subject to the provisions of this agreement.

The compelling reasons for these types of agreements are easy to appreciate. The shares of a close corporation are not generally marketable, and the beneficiaries or legatees of a deceased shareholder or the representatives of a disabled shareholder usually are not interested in holding shares in the business the shareholder enjoyed while the shareholder was productive in the business. Moreover, as an employee, the shareholder was probably receiving a salary instead of dividends, and dividends are rare in a small corporation anyway. Consequently, if the stock is not readily marketable, the salary is terminated, and there are no dividends or other benefits of share ownership, the beneficiaries or representatives of the shareholder will receive nothing from the share ownership, unless the corporation and the other shareholders are required to purchase the shares.

Mandatory sellout agreements are frequently used with employment contracts, the terms of which contemplate issuance of shares as an incentive to performance. If the employee was misjudged and is subsequently terminated, the corporation has the right to buy back the shares. The agreement also may be separately executed to prevent continued stock ownership by any person for whatever reason. The shareholder is required to sell the shares to the corporation or to the other shareholders if they insist on the sale, with appropriate notice. The price is usually established in the agreement, as discussed in detail later, and provisions for surrender of shares should be included.

EXAMPLE

Common Stock of One Leaving Employ of Corporation May Be Purchased

In the event that any holder of the common stock of this corporation who may now or hereafter be an officer or employee of this corporation ceases, for any reason, to be such officer or employee, and provided further that the Board of Directors shall require it, by resolution passed at a special meeting called for that express purpose on not less than 2 days' notice, the corporation or any officer or any common stockholder subscribing to this agreement shall have the option, within 30 days after such person shall cease to be an officer or employee, to purchase all of the common stock held by such person ceasing to be an officer or employee, at a price to be determined by the same method as hereinabove provided, and the tender of the amount of such purchase price shall operate to transfer and vest said shares of common stock in the corporation or officer or stockholder making such tender, and the common stockholder who has thus ceased to be an officer or employee shall, upon such payment or tender, transfer, assign, and set over his or her common stock to the officer or common stockholder exercising such option.

Considerations in Designating the Mandatory Purchase Requirement The agreement should bind the corporation and the other shareholders to the purchase. However, the corporation's ability to purchase shares, even though required by the agreement, is limited by most state statutes, and the corporation may not have funds legally available for the purchase. In that event, the agreement should obligate the other shareholders to purchase their proportionate share of the stock, or to vote in favor of dissolution of the corporation. The latter provision anticipates the possibility that the individual shareholders will not be able to afford the purchase.

If the other shareholders are to buy the shares under the agreement, a procedure should be specified to proportion the shares they are permitted to purchase among them in the same ratio as their existing share ownership. (See the earlier example "Purchase on Death.")

Forced Buyout Provisions

In many closely held corporations, partnerships, and limited liability companies, the owners seek to provide for a "back door" through which they can exit the business, even if another triggering event for a buyout has not occurred. If none of the owners has received a bona fide offer and they are all well, alive, and solvent, the equity owner of the company is trapped in the business. He or she may yearn for a fishing trip in the Rockies or may want to make a career change to further his or her professional endeavors, but there is no way out of the ownership of the business unless an agreement has anticipated this situation. On the dark side, the owners may have lost their compatibility and realize they can no longer work together; their adventure, and perhaps their relationship, may have lost the luster. The only manner in which they can salvage the value of the business may be to sever their relationship—but it may be the case that none of them wants to leave, and each believes that he or she is the most capable of advancing the business. In such cases, the agreement may provide a **forced buyout** procedure, a mechanism designed to require that the other owners purchase or sell the ownership interest at a fair price.

The forced buyout is usually found in a corporation with only two shareholders. It is most useful when the shareholders have elected equal ownership because each is an equal contributor to the business. Such shareholders are typically people who would have selected a partnership for the organization, but have formed a corporation because of its limited liability features. When two shareholders each own fifty percent of the outstanding stock, the possibility of deadlock is obvious and the likelihood of discord is predictable. Usually both shareholders are directors (of a two-person board) and both serve in important officer positions. A dissenting vote of one cancels the affirmative vote of the other. An agreement can provide a mechanism to resolve the dilemma of equal ownership when the owners of the entity cannot agree.

The commonly used forced buyout provisions have earned legendary names. The procedure by which the funds of the corporation are used to purchase the shares of one of the owners at the lowest possible cost is called a **"Jeopardy Auction,"** or a **"Wheel of Fortune."** The procedure by which one shareholder is forced to either buy or sell shares in a corporation is called the **"Deadwood Draw."** The names are descriptive of the process used in an agreement to permit any owner to elect to eliminate the other or to exit the business by engaging in certain agreed procedural steps to force the purchase or sale of shares.

The Auction The Jeopardy Auction, or the Wheel of Fortune, involves an election by one of the owners to require the corporation to purchase shares from a shareholder. The shareholders must agree to these terms, and the corporation must be a party to this agreement. The agreement must be adopted by the board of directors on the corporation's behalf. Thus, the agreement must be drafted and approved during the time when the shareholders (who usually are also the directors) are congenial and committed. This agreement requires the purchase of shares by the corporation with corporate funds and avoids the need for any shareholder to use personal funds to buy out the other shareholder. Because the corporation is purchasing the shares of any of its shareholders willing to sell at the lowest price, this agreement also may be used for corporations with multiple shareholders, unlike the Deadwood Draw agreement that is most useful with two relatively equal shareholders. However, as in the Deadwood Draw, the shareholder initiating the Jeopardy Auction procedure is subject to a risk that he or she may be forced to sell the shares and leave the company or may become the owner of a company struggling with an inadequate cash position while satisfying the terms of an expensive buyout of the other shareholders.

The Jeopardy Auction, or Wheel of Fortune, provisions begin with clauses permitting a shareholder to initiate a buy-sell procedure by giving written notice to the corporation that requires the corporation to solicit offers from all shareholders according to certain described terms. The procedure usually requires that each shareholder must offer to sell all of the shares owned by him or her, and provides certain boundaries for the transaction (such as the method by which the price will be paid or the basis upon which the payment of the price will be secured). Because the corporation is subject to statutory limitations on the repurchase of shares, the agreement must anticipate that the corporation may not meet the statutory criteria to purchase the shares. In addition, it is prudent to set limits on the use of the corporation's liquid assets for this purpose, since the corporation will continue to function with its normal business obligations while completing this transaction. In such cases, the agreement should require that if the corporation cannot satisfy the stated or statutory conditions, the shareholders will be obligated to purchase the shares or to contribute additional capital to permit the corporation to complete the purchase.

> ### EXAMPLE
>
> ## Initiation
>
> If, during the term of this Agreement, either Smith, on the one hand, or Jones, on the other hand ("Initiator"), wishes to initiate a buy-sell procedure, he or she will do so by giving written notice ("Initiating Notice") to the Corporation and to the Remaining Shareholders. The Initiating Notice shall state the terms under which the buy-sell procedure shall be conducted, within the following limitations:
>
> (1) The price for the Shares purchased shall be paid in cash or certified funds within ninety (90) days following the Acceptance;
>
> (2) The Offer must offer all Shares owned by Smith, on the one hand, and Jones, on the other hand; and
>
> (3) If the Corporation does not have legally available funds for the purchase of Shares in the buy-sell procedure, or if more than one-half of the Corporation's cash on hand as of the date of the Closing is required to pay the purchase price, each Shareholder must commit to purchase individually the Shares sold through the buy-sell procedure or to contribute to the Corporation any capital or cash (in addition to one-half of the Corporation's cash on hand at the Closing) necessary to purchase the Shares as in the event that such Shareholder retains his or her Shares following the buy-sell procedure.

Upon receipt of the notice initiating the procedure, the corporation solicits the shareholders to submit an offer to the corporation to sell their shares according to the terms in the solicitation. The solicitation states any restrictive terms required by the agreement (such as the fact that the offer must include all shares owned by a shareholder or that the selling shareholder must offer to commit to a covenant not to compete with the company for a period of time) and describes a procedure for the response (such as the submission of offers in sealed envelopes within a certain period of time). Similarly, any affirmative requirements for the sale (such as warranties against encumbrances or liens on the shares or resignations from officer and director positions) are described. There is always a possibility that one or more of the shareholders will not tender an offer as required by the solicitation, especially if the shareholders are not cooperating with each other and that is the catalyst for the use of the buyout procedure. The agreement must provide some penalty for failure to submit, such as providing that the shareholder so failing is deemed to have made the lowest offer and is thus subject to elimination by default.

> ### EXAMPLE
>
> ## Solicitation
>
> The Corporation shall, within a period of three (3) days after the Corporation's receipt of the Initiating Notice, give a written solicitation ("Solicitation"), stating the terms described in the Initiating Notice, to Smith and Jones to submit to the Corporation an offer to sell his or her Shares according to the terms stated in the Solicitation.

> ### EXAMPLE
>
> ## Offers
>
> Smith and Jones shall submit offers to sell his or her Shares ("Offer") to the Corporation in writing within ten (10) days after the date of the Solicitation. The Offer shall state the price upon which Smith and Jones, as the case may be, are willing to sell his or her Shares upon the terms stated in the Solicitation; shall contain a representation that the Offer is authorized by all necessary action on behalf of the Shareholder and that the Shares are free of any liens, encumbrances, or claims of any person; shall contain a written agreement to sell such Shares at the price stated in the Offer; shall contain the commitment by the Shareholders to purchase or contribute additional capital as required by this agreement; shall contain the resignations from all corporate offices held by the individuals represented by the Shareholders making the Offer; and shall be signed by all persons claiming an interest in the Shares. The failure to submit a timely, complete, and correct written Offer shall be deemed to be an offer to sell Shares owned by the person or entity failing to so submit an Offer at book value as of the date of the Solicitation.

The corporation is required to accept the lowest offer submitted by the shareholders, and thus is purchasing the shares at the lowest possible price. If the process works, the shareholders who desire to remain with the business will submit high bids for their shares, and the shareholders with other objectives will bid low. If some shareholders want to get rid of another shareholder, they will inflate their offers (to be sure their offers are not the lowest), allowing the departing shareholder to request and receive a wide range of possible values, some of which may be substantially higher than fair market value. On the other hand, if a shareholder wants to leave for other pursuits, he or she will submit a bid at the lowest amount that will allow an acceptable return of some of the investment, even if it is substantially below the actual value of the shares. The agreement should provide a procedure for the corporation to accept the lowest offer, and describe the position of the shareholder owning the shares to be purchased after the acceptance occurs.

> ### Acceptance
>
> The Corporation shall accept in writing the Offer containing the lowest price ("Acceptance") within three (3) days after receipt of the Offers, and shall notify the Shareholders in writing of the Acceptance. Following the Acceptance, the Shareholder whose Shares are being purchased (the "Selling Shareholder") shall be entitled only to payment of the purchase price according to the terms stated in the Offer and Acceptance, and shall not thereafter be entitled to any rights as a Shareholder, except to enforce the agreement to purchase the Shares as provided in this agreement.

EXAMPLE

After acceptance, the selling shareholder should only be entitled to receive the payment for the shares and should exercise no other shareholder rights. At this point, the shareholder is an outsider and is not likely to exercise his or her judgment in the best interests of the corporation. Thereafter, a closing of the transaction should occur. If the closing is not contemporaneous with the acceptance of the offer, the agreement must anticipate what will happen if the closing does not occur, since in the intervening period, the other shareholders may have adopted corporate action that is adverse to the interests or inclination of the departing shareholder, and if the shares are not purchased, the selling shareholder may still own an interest in a company that is traveling in the wrong direction, at least as far as that shareholder is concerned. It is typical to provide for a period of limbo between the acceptance and closing during which no corporate policies may be changed, or to require that all corporate action taken during that period is rescinded if the closing does not occur.

> ### Closing
>
> The agreement contemplated hereunder shall be closed and completely performed within ninety (90) days following the Acceptance. In the event that the agreement is not so closed, the Selling Shareholder shall be restored to the status of a Shareholder of the Corporation, all Corporation action taken during the ninety (90) day period pending the Closing shall be rescinded, and the Selling Shareholder shall retain an action against the Corporation for damages for breach of the agreement.

EXAMPLE

The Deadwood Draw As the name implies, this forced buyout provision contemplates a shoot-out at high noon (or any other time a shareholder decides to get out of the company). These provisions are most effective with equal or nearly equal shareholders who have similar financial abilities. If one shareholder owns a substantially greater number of shares than the other, or if one shareholder has substantially greater financial resources than the other, the lack of balance may produce oppressive and unwanted results from the Deadwood Draw provisions.

The process is simple. If one shareholder decides to leave or decides that the other shareholder has to go, a notice is served on the other shareholder that the buyout process is being initiated. The notice includes an offer to sell or buy shares of the corporation at a price and on certain terms and conditions. The shareholder receiving the notice may then elect, during the period specified in the offer or in the agreement, to either buy all the shares owned by the offering shareholder or sell all the shares owned by the responding shareholder to the offering shareholder. In the end, one of the shareholders will sell and the other shareholder will buy. Since each shareholder is likely to protect his or her own interests, the price and terms stated in the offer are likely to be fair. The offering shareholder does not want to risk having to sell his or her shares at a price below their actual value, so he or she will offer to buy the other shareholder's shares at a price that may be higher than their actual value. The other shareholder does not want to sell his or her shares below their actual value, so he or she will accept any offer that states a lower-than-actual price. Either way, the shareholder who wants to stay will buy at a price he or she is willing to pay, and the shareholder who wants to go will sell at a price he or she is willing to accept.

The agreement should provide for an initiation procedure and describe the requirements and conditions of the offer.

EXAMPLE

Initiation

If, during the term of this Agreement, either Smith, on the one hand, or Jones, on the other hand (the "Offering Shareholder"), desires to initiate a buy-sell procedure, he or she will do so by giving written notice (the "Offer") to the Corporation and to the Remaining Shareholder. The Offer shall specify the purchase price and the terms and conditions of sale, and shall constitute an offer to sell the Shares to the other Shareholder (the "Offeree Shareholder"). The Offer shall be subject to the following limitations:
(1) The price for the Shares purchased shall be paid in cash or certified funds within ninety (90) days following the acceptance; and
(2) The Offer must offer all Shares owned by the Offering Shareholder.

Once the offer is served, the receiving shareholder will have the option to purchase or sell. A period of time for this decision should be stated. If the receiving shareholder does not respond, a default provision should be included, preferably with a penalty for silence. The closing procedures and conditions also should be described.

EXAMPLE

Right to Purchase or Sell

For thirty (30) days after the receipt of the Offer, the Offeree Shareholder shall either:
(1) Purchase all of the shares owned by the Offering Shareholder on the terms and conditions as specified in the Offer; or
(2) Sell all of the Offeree Shareholder's Shares to the Offering Shareholder on the same terms and conditions as specified in the Offer.
The Offeree Shareholder must give notice of his or her choice of the options under this section within thirty (30) days following the receipt of the Offer from the Offering Shareholder. Failure to give notice of the choice shall be considered as an agreement by the Offeree Shareholder to purchase the Shares pursuant to Paragraph (1) above. A closing shall be held within thirty (30) days following the expiration of said thirty-day period or such earlier date as the parties shall agree.
At the closing, the selling Shareholder shall deliver a certificate for the shares, duly endorsed, and shall warrant the selling Shareholder has marketable title to the shares, free and clear of all encumbrances, and shall deliver all documents necessary to effectuate the transfer thereof. The purchasing Shareholder on shall deliver the payment as required.
In the event that the Offeree Shareholder has elected to sell all of his or her shares to the Offering Shareholder pursuant to the provisions of Paragraph (2) above, and the Offering Shareholder thereafter fails to purchase the Offeree's Shareholder's shares, the Offeree Shareholder shall have, for a period of ten business days after the passing of the closing date, the right to purchase the Offering Shareholder's shares at a price determined by calculating the book value of the Corporation's assets as of the last day of the preceding fiscal year. The book value of the Corporation shall be determined by a certified public accountant retained by the Corporation for this purpose, determined in accordance with generally accepted accounting principles.

Mechanics of the Agreement

Notice Procedure The agreement should always establish a notice procedure to advise the corporation and the other shareholders of the intended sale (in the case of the stock transfer restriction) or to advise the persons holding the shares of a shareholder subject to a mandatory buyout agreement that the option to purchase is being exercised. This notice procedure should further state a time period for a decision to purchase or refuse and for surrender of the shares.

Notice of Sale

The shareholder shall notify the directors of a desire to sell or transfer by notice in writing, which notice shall contain the price at which the shareholder is willing to sell. The directors shall within thirty days thereafter either accept or reject the offer by notice to the shareholder in writing. After the acceptance of the offer, the directors shall have thirty days within which to purchase the same at such valuation, but if at the expiration of thirty days, the corporation shall not have exercised the right to so purchase, the owner of the stock shall be at liberty to dispose of the same in any manner he or she may see fit.

EXAMPLE

Notice to Purchase

The Company shall have the option, for a period commencing with the death of any shareholder and ending 30 days following the death of the shareholder, to purchase any part of the shares owned by the decedent, at the price and on the terms provided in this agreement. The option shall be exercised by giving notice of it to the decedent's estate or other successor in interest in writing. Such notice shall be deemed to have been duly given on the date of service if served personally on the party to whom notice is to be given, or within 72 hours after mailing if mailed to the party to whom notice is to be given by first class mail, registered or certified, postage prepaid and properly addressed to the party at his or her address set forth on the signature page of this agreement, or any other address that that party may designate by written notice to the other parties of this agreement.

EXAMPLE

Price Provisions Any shareholder agreement involving the purchase and sale of stock must specify the price and payment terms applicable to the transaction. Restrictions on share transfer that require the offer of shares to the corporation and/or the remaining shareholders must establish a price for the offer. Similarly, mandatory buyout or sellout agreements must specify the price to be paid.

Competing interests frequently arise in the negotiation of the price term. The shareholder would usually prefer to receive the highest price in cash as soon as possible, while the purchaser would usually prefer to pay the lowest price over the longest period of time. Many practical considerations also arise. For one thing, extended payment provisions always involve some risk for the selling shareholder, since the purchaser may become insolvent, may be unable to pay for another reason, or may simply refuse to pay. However, immediate payment in cash may be unrealistic, depending upon the number of shares involved and the cash position of the purchaser.

The price provisions of the buyout or restrictive agreement may accomplish several objectives. Depending upon the clients' desires, the following questions should be considered.

1. What price will estimate most accurately the value of the stock in case of a buyout or sellout?
2. What price term will reflect most permanently the formula necessary to value the stock accurately?
3. What assets will be used to fund the stock purchase, and if insurance proceeds are anticipated, will the price vary from the availability of the proceeds, and if so, in what manner?
4. Is there a desire to use the price provision as a further restriction upon the transfer of the shares?
5. Will the price provision be so unrealistic that the entire agreement will be unenforceable?

To be fair, the price provision of the stock purchase agreement should attempt to accurately reflect the true value of the stock at the time of purchase. Even if the parties intend to use the price provision as an additional restriction on the stock, so that no shareholder will be motivated to attempt to sell the stock because the price at which it must be sold under the stock transfer restriction would be prohibitive, it should be noted that courts are reluctant to enforce a stock transfer restriction that contains an unrealistically low price for the transfer of the stock. The effect of such price provisions are to prohibit the sale of the stock, since no shareholder would attempt to locate a buyer if it were necessary to sell the stock to other shareholders or to the corporation at an unrealistically low price.

There are several ways to prescribe the price and method of payment for stock purchase agreements. These terms are always subject to negotiation by the parties. Moreover, counsel who represents the corporation may not be able to represent ethically the interests of the individual shareholders who are intended to be parties to the agreement. Each shareholder has an individual interest in maximizing the amount to be paid for his or her shares and minimizing the amount to be paid for any of the other shareholders' shares. The corporation has an interest in paying a fair value for the shares. These conflicting interests place the lawyer and paralegal in an ethical conflict if they attempt to accomplish the interests of all parties. Accordingly, corporate counsel should recommend that individual shareholders obtain their own legal counsel to review and advise them concerning the agreement.

Firm Price   The agreement may establish a **firm price** to be paid for shares, such as fifty dollars a share, which will be applied to any purchase of stock for the duration of the agreement. This practice should be discouraged except in extremely short-term agreements or at the early stages of the corporation (when the price is difficult to establish from other sources). It is probable that the stated price will become unrealistic one way or the other over an extended period of time.

EXAMPLE

Firm Price

The price at which the shares are to be offered to the corporation or to the remaining shareholders shall be $2.00 per share for the first year of this agreement.

Adjusted Stated Value   The agreement may provide for a **stated value** with a procedure for periodic adjustment. This method allows modifications in price to account for changed circumstances over an extended period of time. Usually a stated price will be coupled with a further agreement that the shareholders of the corporation will evaluate and reset the stated value on a periodic basis. As in any situation where people are negotiating a price, it is possible that the shareholders will not be able to agree on the adjustment. Therefore, the provision should include a certain formula to compute the adjustment to stated value in case the parties cannot agree upon an adjustment to the price. For example, in the absence of shareholder agreement, the stated value may be increased or decreased by a percentage of the net income or loss, or a reevaluation of the assets. Alternatively, arbitration or another dispute resolution technique may be used to resolve issues that prevent an agreement on the price of the shares.

EXAMPLE

Agreed Price with Arbitration

The purchase price to be paid for each of the shares subject to this agreement shall be equal to the agreed value of the Company divided by the total number of shares outstanding as of the date of the price to be determined. The initial agreed value of the Company is $185,000, and on January 20 of each year hereafter, the parties to this agreement shall review the Company's financial condition as of the end of the preceding fiscal year and shall determine by mutual agreement the Company's fair market value, which, if agreed upon, shall be the Company's value until a different value is agreed on or otherwise established under the provisions of this agreement. If the parties are able to reach mutual agreement, they shall evidence it by placing their written and executed agreement in the minute book of the Company.

If no valuation has been agreed upon within two years before the date of the event requiring determination of value, the value of a selling shareholder's interest shall be agreed upon by the selling shareholder or that shareholder's successor in interest and the remaining shareholders. If they do not mutually agree on a value within 60 days after the date of the event requiring the determination, the value of the selling shareholder's interest shall be determined by arbitration as follows: The remaining shareholders and the selling shareholder or that shareholder's successor in interest shall each name an arbitrator. If the two arbitrators cannot agree on a value, they shall appoint a third, and the decision of the majority shall be binding on all parties. Arbitration shall be in accordance with the rules of the American Arbitration Association that are in effect at the time of arbitration.

Earnings Multiple Formula A preferred method of determining the price of the stock is to specify a formula that will account for the success of the business, the value of the assets, and the desirability of the stock if a market existed for its sale. A common formula for evaluation of stock is a **multiple of earnings formula.**

An earnings multiple formula establishes the price of corporate stock by multiplying the earnings of the corporation by a stated figure, which is set when the agreement is negotiated. The multiplier may fluctuate in the agreement, depending upon the number of years the shares have been held, or upon the number of shares held. For example, a multiplier of 3 times earnings may apply to blocks of 100 shares or less, held less than 2 years; a multiplier of 4 times earnings may apply for blocks of 100 to 200 shares held more than 2 years; and so forth. The definition of *earnings* deserves attention in the agreement, which should specify whether earnings refers to net earnings before or after tax, and whether the earnings will be determined by an average of several years' earnings or a current income figure.

The earnings multiple formula probably has no relation to the actual market value of the stock, if one exists, or to the book value of the stock. It simply ensures that if the corporation has increased its earnings during the agreed period, the shareholder who desires to sell stock will realize some benefit from that increase. On the other hand, if earnings have decreased, the shareholder will have suffered by waiting to sell shares. In the event the corporation loses money and the earnings multiple produces a negative figure, the agreement may contain a **savings provision** that in no event will the stock be valued at any less than a stated amount. Such a provision ensures that the stock will always have some minimum value, and is obviously a desirable provision from the shareholder's standpoint.

The provisions that establish the earnings multiple formula should identify the person who will determine earnings conclusively from a specified source. The company's accountant, who has prepared the financial statements under generally accepted accounting principles, is often specified as the person who will determine and compute earnings as of the date of the buyout agreement. Moreover, it may be necessary, in small, closely held corporations, to specify certain adjustments to earnings that will more accurately reflect the true earnings of the corporation for the period averaged. In closely held corporations, it is common to pay shareholder-employees salaries that may be higher than those normally paid for similar employees. It is also common to provide for greater-than-normal lease payments for shareholder-owned equipment, and greater-than-normal interest payments for shareholder loans. These expense figures should be addressed and adjusted in the earnings formula computation in order to reflect more accurately the true value of the stock based upon earnings.

The determination of an earnings multiple is frequently a negotiated matter, and ultimately depends upon a reasonable rate of return in the industry. Rates of return for certain industries are published from time to time by economic marketing sources and business brokers, and they may be used as a guide in determining the appropriate rate of return to set the multiple for earnings. The shareholders themselves are frequently capable of estimating a reasonable rate of return, which, if agreed to, may be used as the multiple in the earnings formula.

EXAMPLE	**Capitalized Earnings Formula**

The purchase price to be paid for each of the shares subject to this agreement shall be determined as follows:

The net profits of the Company for each of the three complete fiscal years preceding the date of determination of price for purposes of this agreement shall be adjusted by deducting from the Company's profits state and federal income taxes, lease payments to shareholders, salary payments to shareholders, and interest payments on loans from shareholders. The net profit figures for the three years, thus adjusted, shall be added, and the total shall be divided by three. The average adjusted net profit figure so obtained shall be multiplied by 10, and the result shall be divided by the number of shares of the Company's capital stock then outstanding.

Book Value Formula A book value formula may be a more accurate estimate of the actual value of the shares, depending upon the definition of book value and the nature of the business. Usually book value is determined by dividing the net assets (total assets less total liabilities) by the number of the outstanding shares of the corporation. This means that each shareholder is entitled to a proportionate share of the assets, and the purchase price of the shares will be an amount equal to this proportionate interest. The purchase price will increase as net assets increase, and vice versa. The accuracy of the formula is affected by the nature of the business. A highly profitable organization may operate with few assets, in which case the book value will be considerably lower than the fair market value of the shares. Conversely, it may be possible for a business with many assets to have high book value for shares that are virtually worthless. For example, a highly profitable real estate brokerage may have only a few assets, such as some desks, computers, and telephones, but the income earned by the company makes its shares very valuable. If only the value of the assets are used to determine the value of the shares, the price will be too low. On the other hand, a manufacturing facility that makes an obsolete product has machines and equipment with a high book value, but the fact that the product cannot be sold makes the business valueless. In this case, a book value formula will overstate the value of the shares.

The book value should be determined by a specified person, and the clause containing the book value formula should provide some guidance for the computation of book value. Again, if an independent accountant is used to prepare the corporate balance sheets in accordance with generally accepted accounting principles, that person may make the sole determination of the book value at a specified time. In addition, if certain assets are undervalued on the balance sheet, such as real estate that has appreciated considerably from the time it was purchased, or if liabilities are overstated, such as contingent liabilities that are not likely to be realized by the corporation, the book value formula should direct the accountant to adjust those figures to reflect more accurately the true value or liability.

To minimize the cost of a determination of book value at any point in time, it is advisable to provide that book value will be determined as of the date of the last financial statement prepared before the occurrence of a contingent event. The financial statements are prepared on a regular basis, and it is much less expensive for the corporation to use a regular financial statement than to prepare a new balance sheet only for the purpose of estimating the value of the stock for the contingent event that has triggered a buyout. It may be provided that the values contained on the last financial statement should be adjusted, upward or downward, to reflect material changes in current operations.

Since book value includes all the assets of the corporation, care must be taken not to include the proceeds of insurance that may be payable to the corporation and were intended to be used to purchase the shares under the shareholder agreement. For example, if the corporation is expecting to use proceeds of life insurance to fund a buyout in case of a shareholder's death, the proceeds should be specifically excluded from a determination of book value, since the corporation will be entitled to them upon the death of the shareholder, and they will increase the corporation's net assets.

Book Value

The purchase price to be paid for the shares subject to this agreement shall be their book value determined as of the most recent financial statement prepared by the Company's accountants with additions or subtractions for current operations up to the end of the month preceding the month in which the event requiring determination of the purchase price occurs. Book value shall be determined from the books of the Company according to generally accepted principles of cash accounting applied in a consistent manner by the accountants of the Company who customarily prepare the Company's financial statements. The Company's book value shall be equal to its assets, excluding any proceeds of insurance policies, less its liabilities, and the amount thus determined shall be divided by all shares of the Company's capital stock then outstanding.

Combination of Formulas Since earnings multiple and book value formulas rarely reflect the true market value of the stock, it may be appropriate to combine these formulas with others to estimate accurately the true value of the stock at the time of the purchase.

Formula to Determine Value (Book Value with Earnings)

If any holder of any shares of the common stock of this Corporation desires to dispose of the same or any part thereof, that shareholder shall not transfer or otherwise dispose of the same to any person unless and until he or she has first complied with the provisions hereof and given the other common stockholders of the Corporation who are entitled to the benefits of this contract an opportunity to purchase the same, as herein provided. The common stockholder desiring to dispose of all or any of his or her stock shall give written notice of such desire to each of the officers of this Corporation within the State of Montana, stating the number of shares he or she desires to sell. Any officer or any other common stockholder of the Corporation entitled to the benefits of this contract may, within thirty days after the service of such notice upon the last officer to be served, elect to purchase any part or all of the common stock so offered, and in the event of the exercise of such option, the common stockholder so giving such notice of a desire to sell shall forthwith sell, assign, transfer, and set over said shares of common stock to the officer or common stockholder electing to purchase the same, and the officer or common stockholder to whom the shares are so transferred shall, at the same time, pay to the seller, as and for the purchase price thereof, the amount of the book value of said common stock as shown upon the last annual statement of the Corporation, and in addition thereto an amount equal to the stock's pro rata proportion of the net profits of the business of the Corporation for such fractional part of the fiscal year as has elapsed since the date as of which the last annual statement was made, less any dividends declared during said fractional period.

For the purpose of determining said profits, the amount of the average annual net profits of the Corporation for the two fiscal years preceding the last annual statement shall be assumed to be the amount of the net profits the Corporation shall earn during the current fiscal year, and the amount of the net profits of the Corporation for the fractional period of the year since the last annual statement shall be considered as that proportion of the average annual net profits of said two preceding years as the length of time which has lapsed since the last annual statement bears to the period of a full year. For the purposes of this contract, until the first annual statement of the Corporation is made, the book value shall be determined on the figures at which this Corporation has purchased the business and property of Everready Associates, a copartnership, and until this Corporation has completed two fiscal years which may be used as a basis for determining the average annual net profits, as aforesaid, the net earnings of the Corporation, for the purpose of this contract, shall be determined from the average net earnings during the preceding two fiscal years of the operation of said business either by this Corporation or by the copartnership from which its business was acquired, and for that purpose, reference shall be had to the books of said copartnership for a sufficient period prior to the organization of this Corporation to produce a two-year average. If it shall be necessary to use the net profits of the copartnership as a basis, proper adjustment and allowance shall be made for the fact that no salaries were paid by said copartnership, and that part of the capital of the Corporation is preferred stock. For the purposes of this contract, the annual statements of the Corporation shall be made up on the same plan and method as has heretofore been followed by said copartnership.

Several other formulas may be used for determining the value of the shares, but they are mostly a product of the imagination of the drafter. Any formula that will establish a value for the shares and will serve the purposes of the agreement may be used. Note that the choice of the formula may significantly assist the effect of share transfer restrictions. If a share transfer restriction requires that all shares must be offered to the corporation at book value, and the book value considerably understates market price, the shareholder will be less likely to attempt to sell shares because the shareholder risks having to accept the book value price in any case. This provision does not run afoul of the rule that a complete restriction on sale is prohibited, since the shareholder does have the right to sell the stock. However, as a practical matter the shareholder is not likely to do so.

Matching a Bona Fide Offer If a shareholder intends to sell stock and is subject to a share transfer restriction, the agreement may specify, in lieu of an agreed value, adjustable agreed value, or formula evaluation of price, that the corporation will be obliged to pay a price equal to that offered to the shareholder by the outsider investor. The selling shareholder benefits from this price determination, since the shares will be purchased by the corporation at exactly the same price as would have been received from the outsider. A **matching price provision** should be used only when the agreement also requires, as is usually the case, that the shareholder must have received a good faith offer from an outsider that is definite and provable to the corporation's satisfaction.

If one objective of the agreement is to discourage the transfer of shares to outsiders, the matching price provision is not the best alternative, because it ensures that the shareholder will receive the same consideration no matter who purchases the shares. Transfer is best discouraged by a clause giving the corporation or other shareholders the option to match the price, or to purchase at some other price, stated or determined by formula, whichever is lower.

EXAMPLE	**Matching Offer**

The price at which the shares are to be offered to the corporation or to the remaining shareholders shall be equal to the bona fide offer received from the offeror, or equal to book value as determined by the provisions of this agreement, whichever is lower.

Appraisal An **appraisal** at the time of purchase may provide the most accurate but also the most expensive determination of value. The person who is to make the appraisal should be named in the agreement, or a procedure for naming appraisers should be described. For example, the agreement can name a mutually agreeable appraiser or can provide for the selection of a panel of appraisers who will determine the value of the stock.

The clause providing for an appraiser should specify the appraiser's qualifications, which should indicate some familiarity with the particular industry in which the corporation conducts its business. The clause should provide for the method of payment of the appraiser's expenses, and it is fair to provide that these expenses will be paid by the corporation (thereby absorbing the cost of the appraisal among all shareholders). Note that if the corporation is paying the appraiser, however, the appraiser's independence in determining the actual market value of the stock may be impaired.

The method of appraisal should be specified, since business appraisers use various methods to determine the value of a business. A liquidation value may be unrealistic, since it would include only the value of the assets, less the payment of the liabilities, if the assets were immediately sold for a price. A preferable method is an appraisal based upon **going-concern value,** which should include consideration of goodwill, business reputation, expected useful life of the assets, and liquidity of the company (its cash and current asset position projected over a period of time considering potential expenses and liabilities). Most business appraisers apply a discount to the value of minority shares, since minority shareholders are rarely able to affect corporate policies. This potential discount for minority interests should be considered in the agreement; if a discount of shares simply because they represent a minority position is not desirable, the discount should be excluded in the instructions to the appraiser.

E X A M P L E

Appraisal

The purchase price to be paid for each of the shares subject to this agreement shall be determined by appraisal. Within ten days after the occurrence of the event requiring the determination of the purchase price under this agreement, the Company shall cause Levine & Company, independent appraisers, to appraise the Company and determine its value. The appraisal fee shall be paid by the Company. In making the appraisal, the appraisers shall value real estate and improvements at fair market value; machinery and equipment shall be valued at replacement costs or fair market value, whichever is lower; finished inventory shall be valued at cost or market, whichever is lower; goods in process shall be valued at cost, using cost accounting procedures customarily employed by the Company in preparing financial statements; receivables shall be valued at their face amount, less an allowance for uncollectable receivables that is reasonable in view of the past experience of the Company and the recent review of their collectability; all liabilities shall be deducted at their face value, and a reserve for contingent liabilities shall be established, if appropriate in the sole discretion of the appraiser. The value of other comparable companies, if known, shall also be considered. The value determined by appraisal shall be divided by the total number of shares of the Company's capital stock then outstanding. No discount shall be applied for the fact that the shares to be purchased under this agreement shall constitute less than 50% of the total shares then outstanding.

The appraisal provisions may be combined with other evaluation methods. The following clause uses a shareholder determination of stated value, but appraisal is used if the determination of the shareholders is not current.

E X A M P L E

Agreed Value or Appraisal to Determine Price

For the purposes of this agreement, each share of said stock shall be regarded as having a value of One hundred dollars ($100). The value of said stock as above determined may be changed from time to time by an endorsement over the signatures of the stockholders in the appendix to this agreement. A determination of value, whether made in this clause or in the appendix, shall remain vital and controlling for the period of one year from its effective date unless within such period it is superseded by a new determination. Should the death of a stockholder occur after one year from the effective date of the last determination of value, the value at the date of death shall be determined by three appraisers, one to be appointed by the surviving stockholder(s), one by the decedent's estate, and one by the two appraisers appointed as first provided. In their process of appraisement, the appraisers shall assume that the last valuation made by the stockholders, whether in this clause or in this appendix, was true and correct as of the date it was made, and with that assumption as a point of beginning, they shall proceed to redetermine such value with reference to the relevant facts and circumstances existing at the time of the decedent's death. Notwithstanding this provision for appraisement, the surviving stockholder(s) and the decedent's estate may elect to accept as controlling the last valuation made by the stockholders, even though such valuation was not made within the year preceding the date of the decedent's death.

The value of the stock as above stated or as same may be determined from time to time hereafter is or shall be inclusive of any value referable to the goodwill of the corporation as a going concern.

Arbitration Rather than appraisal, the agreement may provide for an **arbitration** among independent arbitrators, who will conduct whatever investigation may be necessary to ascertain the value of the stock. This objective determination by independent third parties may be desirable, but is usually expensive and only serves to resolve a dispute rather than establish a true reflection of the value of the Company's stock. If arbitration is to be used as a method of determining the value of shares, it is advisable to describe the qualifications of the arbitrator in the agreement. For example, if the shares of a medical professional corporation are being evaluated, it would be best to have an arbitrator who is familiar with and has experience in the business of running a medical practice. It is also important to provide that the parties agree to be bound by the decision of the arbitrator and that the decision can be enforced by a court, if necessary. Otherwise, it would be possible for a disappointed party to simply ignore the arbitrator's determination of value, thereby thwarting the purpose of this clause in the agreement.

EXAMPLE

Value Determined by Arbitration

The shareholder shall notify the corporation of the price at which he or she is willing to sell the stock, which notification shall contain the name of one arbitrator. The corporation shall, within thirty days thereafter, accept the offer, or by notice to the shareholder in writing, name a second arbitrator, and these two shall name a third. All arbitrators named must have at least five years experience in a business similar to the business of the corporation. It shall then be the duty of the arbitrators to ascertain the value of the stock, and if any arbitrator shall neglect or refuse to appear at any meeting appointed by the arbitrators, a majority may act in the absence of such arbitrator. The decision of the arbitrator(s) shall be binding upon all parties, and all parties agree that the decision may be enforced in any court of competent jurisdiction.

Terms of Payment The agreement should specify the procedure and terms of payment when the transfer of shares is accomplished. The purchasers may prefer to extend payment over a period of time, while the seller may prefer immediate cash. Full payment in cash rarely happens; the most common terms of payment provide for a cash down payment and installment payments for the balance, which may be represented by an interest-bearing promissory note. Installment payments may provide tax benefits to the seller, especially if a large block of valuable stock is the subject of the transfer and there are contingencies reflected that might change or eliminate the promised payments upon the occurrence of certain events. Whenever stock is sold, the seller is required to report any gain received in the year of the sale. A shareholder who sells a large block of stock at one time may incur considerable tax liability by receiving the payments in cash during the year of sale. However, if payments are to be made in installments, and future payments are contingent as to the amount (such as payments that vary depending on subsequent earnings or based upon asset levels of the corporation), the shareholder need report only the amount of the proportionate gain represented by the installments received during the year. This will spread the shareholder's profit on the shares being sold over the period of installments, which may be several years. The installment sale tax treatment now applies no matter how much of the purchase price is received during the year in which the sale is consummated and whether or not the payments extend over two or more installments.[15]

By agreeing to extend payments over a period of time, the selling shareholder risks the subsequent insolvency of the purchasers, or the purchasers' unwillingness to pay. This problem can be lessened by providing the selling shareholder with some **security** to protect the payments. The security may be any property pledged as collateral to secure the note, but usually consists of the stock being sold. This means that the selling shareholder may repossess the stock upon default of the obligation. The agreement may specify this right of repossession or may establish an escrow arrangement by placing the shares being transferred in the hands of a third party pending payment of the full purchase price. Escrow terms require the return of the shares to the seller if the obligation is defaulted. If the obligation is paid in full, the shares are delivered to the purchaser. A clause reciting the installment sale requirements and permitting a security interest in the stock follows.

Payment of Purchase Price

Not less than one-half the consideration required under the preceding clauses shall be paid in cash, and for the balance, a promissory note(s) of the kind hereinafter described may be given. On failure of the purchaser to settle in the manner required within the period of sixty (60) days from the election to purchase, the seller may rescind this agreement and reestablish the situation that would have existed had it never been made.

A note given for part of the consideration shall provide for annual payments on the principal over a period not to exceed five (5) years from the date of the purchase, at the end of which time the unpaid portion of the principal shall be due and payable, and shall provide for interest at the rate of ten percent (10%) per annum and for optional acceleration of maturity in event of a default in payment of principal or interest. The seller may require the purchaser to secure the payment of a note given for the purchase price by a pledge of all or a portion of the stock.

Whether the selling shareholder will have the right to vote the shares that are security for the installment purchase is a subject of negotiation. Usually, the selling shareholder is allowed to vote the shares only if there is a default in the payment of the installments of the purchase price. Shares of the corporation, as security for the installment payment, may represent worthless collateral, since if the corporation ceased to pay on the installments, it would be likely that the corporation's financial position would have deteriorated so much that the shares might be valueless. In representing a shareholder whose only security is the shares being sold, it is advisable to consider the following additional terms in the security agreement concerning the shares:

1. restrictions upon the payment of distributions or salaries during the time that the shares are held as security;
2. the imposition of an asset-to-liability ratio during the period that the shares are security, so that the corporation will maintain more assets than liabilities while making the installment payments, and the installment payments may be accelerated if the ratio is not maintained;
3. restriction on the corporation's ability to borrow money, sell substantially all of its assets outside of the ordinary course of business, merge, exchange shares, or dissolve during the period that the shares are subject to the restriction;
4. antidilution provisions that will adjust the shares held as security to reflect any stock splits, stock dividends, or other capital reorganization; and
5. terms that facilitate the priority of the security interest in the shares, such as a promise by the company to deliver necessary stock certificates or other documents that may be necessary to perfect the security interest in the particular jurisdiction.

Purchase with Security

The deferred portion of the purchase price for any shares purchased under this agreement shall be represented by a promissory note executed by all the purchasing shareholders providing for joint and several liability. Each maker agrees that he or she will pay his or her pro rata portion of each installment of principal and interest as it falls due. The note shall provide for payment of principal in 24 equal quarterly installments with interest on the unpaid balance at the rate of 18% per annum, with full privilege of prepayment of all or any part of the principal at any time without penalty or bonus. Any prepaid sums shall be applied against the installments thereafter falling due in inverse order of their maturity, or against all the remaining installments equally, at the option of the payers. The note shall provide that in case of default, at the election of the holder, the entire sum of principal and interest will be immediately due and payable, and that the makers shall pay reasonable attorneys' fees to the holder in the event that such suit is commenced because of default. The note shall be secured by a pledge of all the shares being purchased in the transaction to which the note relates, and of all other shares owned by the purchasing shareholders. The note shall further be secured by a deed of trust on the real property of the corporation, and a security interest in all

(continued)

> personal property owned by the corporation. The pledge agreements and other agreements required to effect and execute such pledges shall contain such other terms and provisions as may be customary and reasonable. As long as no default occurs in payments on the note, the purchaser shall be entitled to vote the shares; however, dividends shall be paid to the holder of the note as a prepayment of principal. The purchaser shall expressly waive demand, notice of default, and notice of sale, and shall consent to public or private sale of the shares in the event of default, in whole or in lots at the option of the pledge holder, and the seller shall have the right to purchase at the sale.

It is preferable for the shareholder to obtain security other than the shares being transferred as collateral for installment payments under a share transfer agreement. The preceding example illustrates a security interest in personal property of the corporation and a mortgage on the corporation's real estate. If the corporation is not the purchaser, other personal or real property of the purchasing shareholders should be considered. The terms of the security must be negotiated, and the corporation's counsel should be particularly sensitive to the impairment on the corporation's borrowing power by the grant of a security to the shareholder whose shares are being purchased. Appropriate subordination provisions may be included in the security documents to permit the corporation to borrow for normal operating reasons.

Funding of the Agreement through Insurance   The corporation may use life insurance, disability insurance, or other insurance contracts as a method of **funding** a buyout agreement. These funding techniques are especially effective if the event triggering the buyout is death or disability. Other insurance contracts are also available for retirement or termination of employment.

A principal determination is whether all or some of the shareholders should or can be insured. A problem may arise when there are differences in ages, such as when one shareholder is over sixty-five and others are under thirty, or when one or more of the shareholders is not insurable because of physical infirmities. When the corporation purchases the life insurance policies funding the buyout agreement, the shareholders automatically bear the cost in proportion to their ownership interests in the corporation. If the majority shareholder is the oldest, that shareholder has a disadvantage. If all of the shareholders are roughly in the same age category for insurance purposes, the cost of insurance is spread more equitably. Advantages of corporation ownership of the policies include having fewer policies and more easily ensuring that the premiums are timely paid and that the policies remain in effect. The shareholders have statutory rights to access to the corporation's books and can verify the information given to them about the status of the policies.[16]

A buyout agreement funded with life insurance usually causes the last survivor or survivors to come out ahead. The problem may be illustrated by the case of a corporation valued at $100,000 with four shareholders. The interest of each shareholder is worth $25,000, and the corporation purchases insurance policies for $25,000 on the life of each shareholder. The estate of the first shareholder to die receives $25,000, and each remaining shareholder then has a one-third interest, with a value of $33,333.33, in a corporation still worth $100,000. The last survivor gets the entire corporation. One way to avoid this problem is to increase the insurance on the survivors' lives, but this may be too expensive and does not entirely eliminate the windfall to the longer-surviving shareholders.

The corporation may not deduct life insurance premiums paid on policies on shareholders' lives if it is directly or indirectly a beneficiary under those policies.[17] This rule ordinarily prevents the corporation from deducting premiums for life insurance used to fund the corporation's purchase of its stock whether the corporation is the designated beneficiary or the indirect recipient of the proceeds through a trustee or a member of the decedent's family. If the shareholder is the beneficiary, some portion of the insurance proceeds may be included in the shareholder's gross estate for estate tax purposes.[18]

As alternative funding methods, the corporation may build up cash or liquid investments as a reserve with which to purchase the shareholder's interest. This creates an evaluation problem, especially when book value is considered the appropriate formula for determining the price of the purchased shares, in that the existence of the reserve enhances the value of the corporation and, therefore, may increase the amount to be paid at the buyout. In addition, the corporation's inability to use the money in the reserve may handicap its day-to-day operations, and the fund may be reachable by its creditors. There is further risk that the accumulated earnings tax will be imposed on such a reserve under the Internal Revenue Code.[19]

Life insurance may be used to fund a **cross-purchase agreement** of the shareholders, but the tax and nontax factors should be considered carefully. If the shareholders are employees, they may pay the premiums out of their corporate salaries, which are deductible by the corporation if the compensation is reasonable.[20] If the shareholders are using dividend income from the corporation to pay the premiums, the corporate deduction is not available. Direct payments of the insurance premiums by the corporation may be held to constitute dividends to a shareholder. To avoid estate tax problems, each shareholder should purchase insurance on the life of each other shareholder, but not on his or her own life.[21] A factor weighing against life insurance funding is the potential windfall for the surviving shareholders.

Especially when the cross-purchase agreement among shareholders is funded by life insurance, a trustee is often appointed to perform certain functions. Stock certificates may be deposited with the trustee, and the trustee may receive payments and handle the paperwork attendant to such transfers. The trustee also may send notices and perform calculations as to the number of shares the offeree may purchase. The shareholders may prefer that a disinterested person perform these functions, and the agreement should provide the manner in which the trustee will be selected. The agreement should also provide the manner in which the cost for the trustee's services will be paid.

Cross-Purchase Insurance Agreement

EXAMPLE

In order to fund the payment of the purchase price for the shares to be purchased under this agreement on the death of any shareholder, each shareholder shall maintain in full force and effect a policy of life insurance on the life of each other shareholder in the face amount shown on Exhibit A to this agreement. Each such policy is listed and described in the Exhibit, and any additional policies hereafter acquired for the same purpose shall also be listed in the Exhibit. Each policy belongs solely to the shareholder who applied for it and, subject to the provisions of this agreement, the owner of each policy reserves all the powers and rights of ownership of it. Each such owner shall be named as the primary beneficiary of his or her respective policies, and shall pay all premiums on them as they become due. No shareholder shall exercise any of the powers of ownership of any of the policies by changing the named beneficiary, canceling the policy, electing optional methods of payment, converting the policy, borrowing against it, or in any other way changing its nature, value, or the rights under the policy. Any dividends paid on any of the policies before maturity or the insured's death shall be paid to the policy owner and shall not be subject to this agreement. Receipts showing payment of premiums shall be delivered to the Secretary of the company no less than 20 days before each date upon which the respective premiums are due, and the receipts shall be held by the Secretary for inspection by all shareholders.

If one shareholder dies, that shareholder will have owned policies of insurance on the lives of fellow shareholders. Accordingly, it is desirable to provide for the disposition of any unneeded policies in the agreement.

Unneeded Insurance Policies

On the death of any shareholder, each of the surviving shareholders shall have the option for 90 days to purchase the policy of life insurance on the shareholder's life owned by the decedent. Each shareholder shall also have the right to purchase the policies on that shareholder's life within 90 days after the sale or transfer of all that shareholder's shares, or after termination of this agreement. This option shall be exercised by delivery of written notice of exercise to the decedent's personal representative or to the owner of the policy and by payment of the purchase price in cash. The purchase price shall be equal to the cash surrender value of the policy, reduced by any unpaid loans made against the policy. If the option is not exercised within that period, the policy owner may surrender the policy for its cash value or dispose of it in any other way he or she sees fit. The parties agree to execute any releases and assignments that may be necessary to effectuate the provisions of this paragraph.

Legend on Certificates To ensure that shareholders will not violate the agreement and provide a purchase of the shares with stock certificates free from the transfer restrictions, it is necessary to place a conspicuous **legend** on each certificate for the shares, the terms of which should be specified by the agreement. Section 8–204 of the Uniform Commercial Code states that a purchaser of stock that is subject to a stock transfer restriction will purchase the shares free from the transfer restriction unless the certificate contains a conspicuous notation of the restriction or unless the purchaser has actual knowledge of the restriction. Section 6.27 of the Model Business Corporation Act also contains this rule.

The agreement should require that each shareholder shall surrender the certificate representing the shares to permit the inscription of an appropriate legend. The legend may provide the actual terms of the restriction, or simply say that the shares shall not be transferred, encumbered, or in any way alienated except under the terms of the agreement, referring to the agreement by date and indicating a place at which the agreement may be inspected.

Legend

Each share certificate, when issued, shall have a conspicuously endorsed legend on its face with the following words: "Sale, transfer, or hypothecation of the shares represented by this certificate is restricted by the provisions of a buyout agreement among the shareholders and the Company dated November 28, 2005, a copy of which may be inspected at the principal office of the Company and all the provisions of which are incorporated by reference in this certificate." A copy of this agreement shall be delivered to the Secretary of the company, and shall be shown by the Secretary to any person making any inquiry about it.

Miscellaneous Provisions Several additional considerations must be reviewed in preparing an agreement regarding share ownership. Since the transfer of shares under the agreement may affect other corporate activities and may be regulated with respect to securities law aspects by state and federal agencies, special issues concerning transfer of shares must be reviewed with the client and considered in drafting the agreement. For example, it is typical to require that the corporation's counsel render an opinion that the transfer of the shares does not violate any federal or state securities laws as a condition to any transfer of the shares under the agreement.

If the corporation has previously elected Subchapter S status for taxation, it may be desirable to continue the Subchapter S election even though shares are being transferred under a stock transfer agreement. Each shareholder's consent is desirable to provide for taxation of the corporation under Subchapter S, and the agreement should provide that any transferee of the shares under the share transfer agreement will execute required documents and consent to the election.

EXAMPLE

Subchapter S Election

The Company and each of the shareholders agree to execute such documents and consents and to cause them to be delivered in a timely manner to the Internal Revenue Service in order to cause the Company to elect to be taxed as a small business corporation under section 1361 of the Internal Revenue Code of 1986. Each shareholder shall cause any transferee of any of his or her shares to file in a timely manner the required consent to the election. Notwithstanding any provision of this agreement to the contrary, no transfer of any of the Company's shares shall be made by any shareholder to any corporation, partnership, or trust, or to any other transferee, if the effect of the transfer would cause the election to be lost or revoked.

In the case of death or disability of a shareholder, the shareholder's spouse will have certain rights to assets of the shareholder. These assets include the shares of stock owned by the shareholder. The agreement should contemplate the potential claims to be made by spouses and heirs of the shareholder, which may be inconsistent with the terms of the agreement. For example, the spouse of a married shareholder who dies without a will is entitled in most states to receive the shares from the decedent's estate. The spouse may prefer to keep the shares even though the shareholder agreement requires that they be sold to the corporation or the other shareholders. Since the spouse is not a party to the agreement, it may not be possible to force the spouse to sell the shares without additional consent or waiver documents from the spouse. The shareholders should also be required to take any steps that may be necessary to reconcile personal estate documents, such as wills and trusts, with the shareholder agreement.

EXAMPLE

Spouse's Consent

I acknowledge that I have read the foregoing agreement and that I know its contents. I am aware that by its provisions my spouse agrees to sell all of his or her shares to the Company, including my community interest in them, if any, on the occurrence of certain events. I hereby consent to the sale, approve of the provisions of the agreement, and agree that those shares and my interest in them are subject to the provisions of the agreement and that I will take no action at any time to hinder operation of the agreement on those shares or my interest in them.

EXAMPLE

Wills

Each shareholder agrees to include in his or her will a direction and authorization to his or her executor to comply with the provisions of this agreement and to sell his or her shares in accordance with this agreement; however, the failure of any shareholder to do so shall not affect the validity or enforceability of this agreement.

KEY TERMS

share transfer restriction
shareholder voting agreement
voting trust
stock voting agreement
minority nominee
savings clause
mandatory buyout or sellout
   arrangements
good faith offer

option to purchase
all or nothing purchase
forced buyout provision
Jeopardy Auction/Wheel of Fortune
   provision
Deadwood Draw provision
firm price
adjusted stated value
multiple of earnings formula

savings provision
matching price provision
appraisal
going-concern value
arbitration
security
insurance funding
cross-purchase insurance agreement
legend on certificate

WEB RESOURCES

Access to state corporate laws relating to voting and share restriction agreements may be obtained through the Legal Information Institute maintained at the Cornell Law School:

<http://www.law.cornell.edu>

A variety of business forms and articles, including buy-sell agreements and other share transfer restrictions are available as Law Commerce™, a member of the LexisNexis Group. Several research pages and best-selling forms and agreements are available in an electronic marketplace at

<http://www.lawcommerce.com>

Various resources are available for sample forms and information about voting control agreements and share transfer restrictions or buy-sell agreements, including the following:

<http://www.toolkit.cch.com>
<http://www.findlaw.com>
<http://www.tannedfeet.com>
<http://www.lectlaw.com>
<http://www.ilrg.com>

 CASES

RINGLING BROS.-BARNUM & BAILEY COMBINED SHOWS, INC. v. RINGLING
53 A.2d 441 (Del. 1947)
PEARSON, JUDGE

The Court of Chancery was called upon to review an attempted election of directors at the 1946 annual stockholders meeting of the corporate defendant. The pivotal questions concern an agreement between two of the three present stockholders, and particularly the effect of this agreement with relation to the exercise of voting rights by these two stockholders. At the time of the meeting, the corporation had outstanding 1000 shares of capital stock held as follows: 315 by petitioner Edith Conway Ringling; 315 by defendant Aubrey B. Ringling Haley (individually or as executrix and legatee of a deceased husband); and 370 by defendant John Ringling North. The purpose of the meeting was to elect the entire board of seven directors. The shares could be voted cumulatively. Mrs. Ringling asserts that by virtue of the operation of an agreement between her and Mrs. Haley, the latter was bound to vote her shares for an adjournment of the meeting, or in the alternative, for a certain slate of directors. Mrs. Haley contends that she was not so bound for reason that the agreement was invalid, or at least revocable.

The two ladies entered into the agreement in 1941. It makes like provisions concerning stock of the corporate defendant and of another corporation, but in this case, we are concerned solely with the agreement as it affects the voting of stock of the corporate defendant. The agreement recites that each party was the owner "subject only to possible claims of creditors of the estates of Charles Ringling and Richard Ringling, respectively" (deceased husbands of the parties), of 300 shares of the capital stock of the defendant corporation; that in 1938 these shares had been deposited under a voting trust agreement which would terminate in 1947, or earlier, upon the elimination of certain liability of the corporation; that each party also owned 15 shares individually; that the parties had "entered into an agreement in April 1934 providing for joint action by them in matters affecting their ownership of stock and interest in" the corporate defendant; that the parties desired "to continue to act jointly in all matters relating to their stock ownership or interest in" the corporate defendant (and the other corporation). The agreement then provides as follows:

* * *

"2. In exercising any voting rights to which either party may be entitled by virtue of ownership of stock or voting trust certificates held by them in either of said corporation, each party will consult and confer with the other and the parties will act jointly in exercising such voting rights in accordance with such agreement as they may reach with respect to any matter calling for the exercise of such voting rights.

"3. In the event the parties fail to agree with respect to any matter covered by paragraph 2 above, the question in disagreement shall be submitted for arbitration to Karl D. Loos, of Washington, D.C. as arbitrator and his decision thereon shall be binding upon the parties hereto. Such arbitration shall be exercised to the end of assuring for the respective corporations good management and such participation therein by the members of the Ringling family as the experience, capacity and ability of each may warrant.

The parties may at any time by written agreement designate any other individual to act as arbitrator in lieu of said Loos."

* * *

The Mr. Loos mentioned in the agreement is an attorney and has represented both parties since 1937, and, before and after the voting trust was terminated in late 1942, advised them with respect to the exercise of their voting rights. At the annual meetings in 1943 and the two following years, the parties voted their shares in accordance with mutual understandings arrived at as a result of discussions. In each of these years, they elected five of the seven directors. Mrs. Ringling and Mrs. Haley each had sufficient votes, independently of the other, to elect two of the seven directors. By both voting for an additional candidate, they could be sure of his election regardless of how Mr. North, the remaining stockholder, might vote.[1]

Some weeks before the 1946 meeting, they discussed with Mr. Loos the matter of voting for directors. They were in accord that Mrs. Ringling should cast sufficient votes to elect herself and her son; and that Mrs. Haley should elect herself and her husband; but they did not agree upon a fifth director. The day before the meeting, the discussions were continued, Mrs. Haley being represented by her husband since she could not be present because of illness. In a conversation with Mr. Loos, Mr. Haley indicated that he would make a motion for an adjournment of the meeting for sixty days, in order to give the ladies additional time to come to an agreement about their voting. On the morning of the meeting, however, he stated that because of something Mrs. Ringling had done, he would not consent to a postponement. Mrs. Ringling then made a demand upon Mr. Loos to act under the third paragraph of the agreement "to arbitrate the disagreement" between her and Mrs. Haley in connection with the manner in which the stock of the two ladies should be voted. At the opening of the meeting, Mr. Loos read the written demand and stated that he determined and directed that the stock of both ladies be voted for an adjournment of sixty days. Mrs. Ringling then made a motion for adjournment and voted for it. Mr. Haley, as proxy for his wife, and Mr. North voted against the motion. Mrs. Ringling (herself or through her attorney, it is immaterial which), objected to the voting of Mrs. Haley's stock

in any manner other than in accordance with Mr. Loos' direction. The chairman ruled that the stock could not be voted contrary to such direction, and declared the motion for adjournment had carried. Nevertheless, the meeting proceeded to the election of directors. Mrs. Ringling stated that she would continue in the meeting "but without prejudice to her position with respect to the voting of the stock and the fact that adjournment had not been taken." Mr. Loos directed Mrs. Ringling to cast her votes

> 882 for Mrs. Ringling,
> 882 for her son, Robert, and
> 441 for a Mr. Dunn,

who had been a member of the board for several years. She complied. Mr. Loos directed that Mrs. Haley's votes be cast

> 882 for Mrs. Haley,
> 882 for Mr. Haley, and
> 441 for Mr. Dunn.

Instead of complying, Mr. Haley attempted to vote his wife's shares

> 1103 for Mrs. Haley, and
> 1102 for Mr. Haley.

Mr. North voted his shares

> 864 for a Mr. Woods,
> 863 for a Mr. Griffin, and
> 863 for Mr. North.

The chairman ruled that the five candidates proposed by Mr. Loos, together with Messrs. Woods and North, were elected. The Haley-North group disputed this ruling insofar as it declared the election of Mr. Dunn; and insisted that Mr. Griffin, instead, had been elected. A directors' meeting followed in which Mrs. Ringling participated after stating that she would do so "without prejudice to her position that the stockholders' meeting had been adjourned and that the directors' meeting was not properly held." Mr. Dunn and Mr. Griffin, although each was challenged by an opposing faction, attempted to join in voting as directors for different slates of officers. Soon after the meeting, Mrs. Ringling instituted this proceeding.

* * *

Having examined what the parties sought to provide by the agreement, we come now to defendants' contention that the voting provisions are illegal and revocable. They say that the courts of this state have definitely established the doctrine "that there can be no agreement, or any device whatsoever, by which the voting power of stock of a Delaware corporation may be irrevocably separated from the ownership of the stock, except by an agreement which complies with Section 18" of the Corporation Law, Rev.Code 1935, § 2050, and except by a proxy coupled with an interest.

* * *

---

1. *Each lady was entitled to cast 2205 votes (since each had the cumulative voting rights of 315 shares, and there were 7 vacancies in the directorate). The sum of the votes of both is 4410, which is sufficient to allow 882 votes for each of 5 persons. Mr. North, holding 370 shares, was entitled to cast 2590 votes, which obviously cannot be divided so as to give to more than two candidates as many as 882 votes each. It will be observed that in order for Mrs. Ringling and Mrs. Haley to be sure to elect five directors (regardless of how Mr. North might vote) they must act together in the sense that their combined votes must be divided among five different candidates and at least one of the five must be voted for by both Mrs. Ringling and Mrs. Haley.*

The statute reads, in part, as follows: "Sec. 18. Fiduciary Stockholders; Voting Power of; Voting Trusts:—Persons holding stock in a fiduciary capacity shall be entitled to vote the shares so held, and persons whose stock is pledged shall be entitled to vote, unless in the transfer by the pledgor on the books of the corporation he shall have expressly empowered the pledgee to vote thereon, in which case only the pledgee, or his proxy may represent said stock and vote thereon.

"One or more stockholders may by agreement in writing deposit capital stock of an original issue with or transfer capital stock to any person or persons, or corporation or corporations authorized to act as trustee, for the purpose of vesting in said person or persons, corporation or corporations, who may be designated Voting Trustee or Voting Trustees, the right to vote thereon for any period of time determined by such agreement, not exceeding ten years, upon the terms and conditions stated in such agreement. Such agreement may contain any other lawful provisions not inconsistent with said purpose. * * * Said Voting Trustees may vote upon the stock so issued or transferred during the period in such agreement specified; stock standing in the names of such Voting Trustees may be voted either in person or by proxy, and in voting said stock, such Voting Trustees shall incur no responsibility as stockholder, trustee or otherwise, except for their own individual malfeasance."

In our view, neither the cases nor the statute sustain the rule for which the defendants contend.

* * *

[T]he statute does not purport to deal with agreements whereby shareholders attempt to bind each other as to how they shall vote their shares. Various forms of such pooling agreements, as they are sometimes called, have been held valid and have been distinguished from voting trusts. [Citations omitted] We think the particular agreement before us does not violate Section 18 or constitute an attempted evasion of its requirements, and is not illegal for any other reason. Generally speaking, a shareholder may exercise wide liberality of judgment in the matter of voting, and it is not objectionable that his motives may be for personal profit, or determined by whims or caprice, so long as he violates no duty owed his fellow shareholders. Heil v. Standard G. & E. Co., 17 Del. Ch. 214, 151 A. 303. The ownership of voting stock imposes no legal duty to vote at all. A group of shareholders may, without impropriety, vote their respective shares so as to obtain advantages of concerted action. They may lawfully contract with each other to vote in the future in such way as they, or a majority of their group, from time to time determine. (See authorities listed above.) Reasonable provisions for cases of failure of the group to reach a determination because of an even division in their ranks seem unobjectionable. The provision here for submission to the arbitrator is plainly designed as a deadlock-breaking measure, and the arbitrator's decision cannot be enforced unless at least one of the parties (entitled to cast one-half of their combined votes) is willing that it be enforced. We find the provision reasonable. It does not appear that the agreement enables the parties to take any unlawful advantage of the outside shareholder, or of any other person. It offends no rule of law or public policy of this state of which we are aware.

Legal consideration for the promises of each party is supplied by the mutual promises of the other party. The undertaking to vote in accordance with the arbitrator's decision is a valid contract. The good faith of the arbitrator's action has not been challenged and, indeed, the record indicates that no such challenge could be supported. Accordingly, the failure of Mrs. Haley to exercise her voting rights in accordance with his decision was a breach of her contract. It is no extenuation of the breach that her votes were cast for two of the three candidates directed by the arbitrator. His directions to her were part of a single plan or course of action for the voting of the shares of both parties to the agreement, calculated to utilize an advantage of joint action by them which would bring about the election of an additional director. The actual voting of Mrs. Haley's shares frustrates that plan to such an extent that it should not be treated as a partial performance of her contract.

* * *

[W]e have concluded that the election should not be declared invalid, but that effect should be given to a rejection of the votes representing Mrs. Haley's shares. No other relief seems appropriate in this proceeding. Mr. North's vote against the motion for adjournment was sufficient to defeat it. With respect to the election of directors, the return of the inspectors should be corrected to show a rejection of Mrs. Haley's votes, and to declare the election of the six persons for whom Mr. North and Mrs. Ringling voted.

* * *

An order should be entered directing a modification of the order of the Court of Chancery in accordance with this opinion.

LING & CO., INC. v. TRINITY SAVINGS & LOAN ASSOCIATION

482 S.W.2d 841 (Texas 1972)

REAVLEY, JUSTICE

Trinity Savings and Loan Association sued Bruce W. Bowman for the balance owed on a promissory note and also to foreclose on a certificate for 1500 shares of Class A Common Stock in Ling & Company, Inc. pledged by Bowman to secure payment of the note. Ling & Company was made a party to the suit by Trinity Savings and Loan because of Ling & Company's insistence that the transfer of its stock was subject to restrictions that were unfulfilled. Bowman did not appear and has not appealed from the judgment against him. The trial court entered summary judgment in favor of Trinity Savings and Loan, against the contentions of Ling & Company, foreclosing the security interest in the stock and ordering it sold. The court of civil appeals affirmed. 470 S.W.2d 441. We reverse the judgments and remand the case to the trial court.

The objection to the foreclosure and public sale of this stock is based upon restrictions imposed upon the transfer of the stock by the articles of incorporation of Ling & Company. It is conceded that no offer of sale has been made to the other holders of this class of stock and that the approval of the pledge of the stock has not been obtained from the New York Stock Exchange. It is the position of Trinity Savings and Loan that all of the restrictions upon the transfer of any interest in this stock are invalid and of no effect. This has been the holding of the courts below.

The face and back of the stock certificate are reproduced and attached to this opinion.

The restrictions appear in Article Four of the Ling & Company articles of incorporation, as amended and filed with the Secretary of State in 1968. Section D requires the holder to obtain written approval of the New York Stock Exchange prior to the sale or encumbrance of the stock if, at the time, Ling & Company is a member corporation of the Exchange. Then Section E(4) prevents the sale of the stock without first affording the corporation the opportunity to buy and, if it fails to purchase, giving that opportunity to all holders of the same class of stock. The method of computation of the price, based upon the corporate books, is provided in this section of the articles.

The court of civil appeals struck down the restrictions for three reasons: the lack of conspicuous notice thereof on the stock certificate, the unreasonableness of the restrictions, and statutory prohibition against an option in favor of other stockholders whenever they number more than twenty. These objections will be examined in that order.

CONSPICUOUSNESS

The Texas Business Corporation Act as amended in 1957, V.A.T.S. Bus. Corp.Act, art. 2.22, subd. A, provides that a corporation may impose restrictions on the transfer of its stock if they are "expressly set forth in the articles of incorporation . . . and . . . copied at length or in summary form on the face or so copied on the back and referred to on the face of each certificate . . ." Article 2.19, subd. F, enacted by the Legislature at the same time, permits the incorporation by reference on the face or back of the certificate of the provision of the articles of incorporation which restricts the transfer of the stock. The court of civil appeals objected to the general reference to the articles of incorporation and the

failure to print the full conditions imposed upon the transfer of the shares. However, reference is made on the face of the certificate to the restrictions described on the reverse side; the notice on the reverse side refers to the particular article of the articles of incorporation as restricting the transfer or encumbrance and requiring "the holder hereof to grant options to purchase the shares represented hereby first to the Corporation and then pro rata to the other holders of the class A Common Stock . . ." We hold that the content of the certificate complies with the requirements of the Texas Business Corporation Act.

There remains the requirement of the Texas Business and Commerce Code that the restriction or reference thereto on the certificate must be conspicuous. Sec. 8.204, V.T.C.A. Bus. & C., requires that a restriction on transferability be "noted conspicuously on the security." Sec. 1.201(10) of the Business and Commerce Code defines "conspicuous" and makes the determination a question of law for the court to decide. It is provided that a conspicuous term is so written as to be noticed by a reasonable person. Examples of conspicuous matter are given there as a "printed heading in capitals . . . [or] larger or other contrasting type or color." This means that something must appear on the face of the certificate to attract the attention of a reasonable person when he looks at it. Hunt v. Perkins Machinery Co., 352 Mass. 535, 226 N.E.2d 228 (1967); Boeing Airplane Co. v. O'Malley, 329 F.2d 585 (8th Cir. 1964); 1 Anderson, Uniform Commercial Code 87 (2nd ed. 1970). The line of print on the face of the Ling & Company certificate does not stand out and cannot be considered conspicuous.

Our holding that the restriction is not noted conspicuously on the certificate does not entitle Trinity Savings and Loan to a summary judgment under this record. Sec. 8.204 of the Business and Commerce Code provides that the restriction is effective against a person with actual knowledge of it. The record does not establish conclusively that Trinity Savings and Loan lacked knowledge of the restriction on January 28, 1969, the date the record indicates when Bowman executed an assignment of this stock to Trinity Savings and Loan.

REASONABLENESS

Art. 2.22, subd. A of the Texas Business Corporation Act provides that a corporation may impose restrictions on disposition of its stock if the restrictions "do not unreasonably restrain or prohibit transferability." The court of civil appeals has held that the restrictions on the transferability of this stock are unreasonable for two reasons: because of the required approval of the New York Stock Exchange and because of successive options to purchase given the corporation and the other holders of the same class of stock.

Ling & Company in its brief states that it was a brokerage house member of the New York Stock Exchange at an earlier time and that Rule 315 of the Exchange required approval of any sale or pledge of the stock. Under these circumstances we must disagree with the court of civil appeals holding that this provision of article 4D of the articles of incorporation is "arbitrary, capricious, and unreasonable." Nothing appears in the summary judgment proof on this matter, and the mere provision in the article is no cause for vitiating the restrictions as a matter of law.

It was also held by the intermediate court that it is unreasonable to require a shareholder to notify all other record holders of Class A Common Stock of his intent to sell and to give the other holders a ten day option to buy. The record does not reveal the number of holders of this class of stock; we only know that there are more than twenty. We find nothing unusual or oppressive in these first option provisions. See Coleman v. Kettering, 289 S.W.2d 953 (Tex.Civ.App.1956, no writ); 2 O'Neal, Close Corporations, § 7.13 (1971). Conceivably the number of stock-

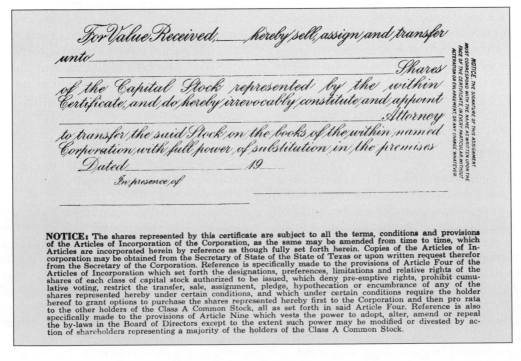

holders might be so great as to make the burden too heavy upon the stockholder who wishes to sell and, at the same time, dispel any justification for contending that there exists a reasonable corporate purpose in restricting the ownership. But there is no showing of that nature in this summary judgment record.

STATUTORY LIMIT ON OPTIONEES

Art. 2.22, subd. B of the Texas Business Corporation Act provides that, in addition to other reasonable restrictions, any of the following restrictions may be imposed upon the transfer of corporate shares:

(1) Restrictions reasonably defining pre-emptive or prior rights of the corporation or its shareholders of record, to purchase any of its shares offered for transfer.

(2) Restrictions reasonably defining rights and obligations of the holders of shares of any class, in connection with buy-and-sell agreements binding on all holders of shares of that class, so long as there are no more than twenty (20) holders of record of such class.

(3) Restrictions reasonably defining rights of the corporation or of any other person or persons, granted as an option or options or refusal or refusals on any shares.

The court of civil appeals regarded subsection (2) as being applicable to the stock restriction in this case. Since it was stipulated that there were more than twenty holders of record of Class A stock, it has been held that the restriction fails for this reason. We disagree. Subsection (2) is not applicable to the Ling & Company restriction. It seems that a "buy and sell agreement" usually refers to a contract between shareholders rather than a restriction imposed by the corporation. In any event, there is no obligation to purchase this stock placed upon anyone, and these restrictions can only be considered as options and not "buy and sell agreements." 2 O'Neal, Close Corporations, § 7.10 (1971); Fletcher Cyc. Corp. § 5461.1 (1971).

The summary judgment proof does not justify the holding that restrictions on the transfer of this stock were ineffective as to Trinity Savings and Loan Association. The judgment below is reversed and the cause is remanded to the trial court.

DANIEL, J., concurs in result.

PROBLEMS

1. What steps can be taken to warn a potential purchaser of shares in a corporation that the shares of stock are restricted by a shareholder ownership agreement? What are the consequences of failing to take such steps?

2. State the advantages and disadvantages of the following methods of determining a price for a shareholder's buy-sell agreement. Also indicate the type of business in which each method would be most useful and representative of the actual value of the stock:
   a. book value formula;
   b. capitalized earnings multiple formula;
   c. appraised method;
   d. arbitration; and
   e. firm price method.

3. State the reasons why you would recommend or discourage the following types of voting agreements or arrangements for a client:
   a. a voting trust;
   b. a stock voting agreement; and
   c. an irrevocable proxy.

4. When a stock is subject to a share transfer restriction, a third-party purchaser will take free from the restriction upon purchase of the stock unless
   a. the purchaser has actual knowledge of the restriction;
   b. the restriction is noted conspicuously on the certificate;
   c. the corporation is notified of the sale;
   d. a and b but not c;
   e. b and c but not a; or
   f. a and c but not b.

5. Which of the following clauses has the most restrictive effect on a shareholder attempting to sell shares?
   a. The price shall be paid in equal installments over a period of two months.
   b. The price shall be book value or the same as any bona fide offer, whichever is higher.
   c. The price shall be book value or the same as any bona fide offer, whichever is lower.
   d. The price shall be determined in the discretion of the shareholder.

6. Which of the following is a requirement for effectiveness of a voting trust?
   a. A voting trust certificate is issued.
   b. A copy of the agreement is deposited with the corporation.
   c. The other shareholders, not represented by the voting trust, are notified of the existence of the agreement.
   d. All of the above.

PRACTICE ASSIGNMENTS

1. Erika Bolsinger and Susan Stroud are equal share-holders of Glorified Technologies, Inc., a corporation they formed in 1990. The business is prospering, and Erika and Susan are concerned about the possibility of losing control of the business as it expands. They want to preserve their harmonious working relationship. Erika does not intend to leave the active participation in the business in the near future and does not suspect any such interest by Susan. If Susan were to leave, however, she would take with her considerable technical know-how and expertise in computer programming and software development. Susan would be very capable of competing with the corporation if she were to leave. Both women desire protection against the other party selling her shares to an outsider. They are willing to sign an agreement with each other, each promising to sell her shares to the other party before selling to a third party. Their primary objective is to discourage the sale of the shares, but if the shares are sold, they each want to be certain that the other receives a fair price. Either party would be satisfied if the selling shareholder's shares were purchased by the corporation and held as treasury shares or canceled. Erika cautions, however, that if the corporation were to buy the stock, it would be very important to avoid dilution of the available working capital, which could be accomplished by a long-term payout provision.

   Draft an agreement on Erika's behalf to accomplish the foregoing objectives, incorporating any suggestions you would make.

2. Draft a memorandum for a client stating the advantages and disadvantages of including agreed voting provisions in
   a. the articles of incorporation;
   b. the bylaws;
   c. a voting trust agreement;
   d. a stock voting agreement; and
   e. an employment agreement.

3. Review your state corporation code and list the statutory requirements for the formation of a voting trust.

ENDNOTES

1. See "Close Corporations" in Chapter 7.

2. See "The Articles of Incorporation" in Chapter 8;"Shareholder Business and Vote Required" in Chapter 10.

3. See Chapter 15.

4. See "Shareholder Meetings" in Chapter 10.

5. See Model Business Corporation Act (hereinafter M.B.C.A.) § 7.32 and Model Statutory Close Corporation Supplement § 20(c); Delaware's close corporation statute allows written shareholder agreements that interfere with the discretion of the directors, but the shareholders are responsible for acts controlled by the agreement. Del. Code Ann. tit. 8, § 350.

6. M.B.C.A. § 7.30.

7. E.g., Minnesota, Minn. Stat. Ann. § 302A.453 (West); Nevada, Nev. Rev. Stat. § 78.365.

8. New Jersey, N. J. Stat. Ann. § 14A:5-20 (West); Maine, Me. Rev. Stat. Ann. tit. 13A, § 619 (West).

9. M.B.C.A. § 7.30 (b).

10. See the example described in "Shareholder Business and Vote Required" in Chapter 10.

11. See "Corporation's Purchase of Its Own Shares" in Chapter 11.

12. See M.B.C.A. § 6.31.

13. Internal Revenue Code (hereafter I.R.C.) of 1986, 26 U.S.C.A. § 302.

14. See "Involuntary Dissolution" in Chapter 15.

15. I.R.C. of 1986, 26 U.S.C.A. § 453.

16. M.B.C.A. § 16.02.

17. See I.R.C. of 1986, 26 U.S.C.A. § 264 (a).

18. See I.R.C. of 1986, 26 U.S.C.A. § 2042.

19. See I.R.C. of 1986, 26 U.S.C.A. § 531.

20. See I.R.C. of 1986, 26 U.S.C.A. § 162 (a) (1).

21. See I.R.C. of 1986, 26 U.S.C.A. § 2042(2).

CORPORATIONS IN FOREIGN JURISDICTIONS

SELECTION OF JURISDICTION

Early in the formation stages of a corporation, a particular jurisdiction is selected as the situs of incorporation. The selection process is described in detail in an earlier chapter.[1] A multistate business has several jurisdictions to consider. A decision to form the multistate corporation in one particular state usually is made following a comparison of the permissiveness and flexibility of the various statutes. The state of incorporation is the domestic state, and the corporation is a foreign corporation to every other state. The rule to be considered in this chapter is that a foreign corporation must *qualify* to do business in any state in which it intends to conduct business.

Similarly, other entities and associations that will be conducting business in more than one state may be required to qualify to do business as a condition to exercising their powers and privileges in foreign jurisdictions. The limited liability statutes anticipate that these companies will have multistate operations, and most of the statutes provide qualification rules similar to those used for corporations.[2] Limited partnerships also need to qualify to do business in several states,[3] and in a few states, general partnerships must qualify to do business if they are not formed under the law of that state.[4] This chapter concentrates primarily on the corporate issues involved in the qualification to do business in foreign jurisdictions, but the procedures and forms applicable to the corporate process are similar to those used in the process of qualifying a limited liability company and a partnership.

CONSTITUTIONAL BASIS FOR QUALIFICATION

A brief overview of the history and legal theory of the corporate entity is important here. A corporation is a fictitious person created under the authority of a state statute and, consequently, is a citizen of the state in which it has incorporated. Under the early common law, the corporation existed only in the state in which it incorporated, and it was not permitted to do business in any other jurisdiction. When corporate businesses began to outgrow the boundaries of their domestic states, a legal question arose regarding whether a state could prevent a foreign corporation from doing business within its boundaries unless it became incorporated therein. Alternatively, if incorporation could not be required, could a state place restrictions upon the foreign corporation's business and require the foreign corporation to satisfy certain conditions before it was entitled to do business in the foreign state?

The Constitution of the United States guarantees to all persons the ability to move freely among the states without restriction, so the question then became whether a corporation could be considered to be a "person" under these provisions of the Constitution. The Supreme Court eventually decided that a corporation, whether or not it is a person in the constitutional sense, could not be prevented from entering another state, but could be reasonably regulated by the foreign state, under the guise of the state's power to prescribe regulations to protect its own residents. If the regulations imposed were reasonable and designed to protect the local citizenry, the regulations were permitted.

The current regulations on foreign corporations may be more easily understood with this history in mind. Most states require foreign corporations to disclose certain matters about their business structure by a public filing with a state official, so that the citizens of the state have access to necessary information about the organization with which they transact business. A separate area of regulation is concerned with litigation by and against the foreign corporation. These statutes are designed to subject the foreign organization to legal process within the state so that the citizens of the state may conveniently redress their complaints against the corporation. They further ensure compliance with qualification requirements before the corporation may use the state courts. In a constitutional sense, therefore, any state may impose regulations on foreign corporations, provided the regulations are reasonably directed to the state's responsibility and power to protect its own citizens.

AUTHORIZATION TO QUALIFY AS A FOREIGN CORPORATION

The authority to conduct business in a foreign state must come from within the corporation by official direction of the board of directors. Such management approval, which is usually accompanied by an enabling provision in the articles of incorporation, authorizes the corporation to submit to the necessary regulations in order to do business within a foreign jurisdiction.

The board of directors usually adopts a resolution authorizing qualification at its organizational meeting if the plans for expansion are solidified at that time. The resolution states that the corporation may qualify to do business under the laws of other states, and that the officers of the corporation are empowered to execute any necessary documents and to pay all necessary taxes and fees in order to qualify the corporation as a foreign corporation.[5]

STATUTORY PROHIBITION FROM DOING BUSINESS WITHOUT QUALIFICATION

Every state has a statute pertaining to qualification of foreign corporations. Several states have adopted the Model Business Corporation Act approach, prohibiting any foreign corporation from transacting business within the boundaries of the state without qualifying and receiving a certificate of authority from the appropriate state official.[6] This is a strict provision. Nearly half of the states do not condition the right to transact business on the receipt of the certificate of authority, but they do specify a procedure for obtaining a certificate of authority, and further specify sanctions for failure to qualify.

It is not necessary that the foreign corporation be incorporated in a state whose laws are substantially similar to the laws of the state in which it seeks authority to do business. Indeed, many state statutes specifically prohibit denial of a certificate of authority simply because the laws of the state under which the foreign corporation is organized differ from the laws of the particular state in which it intends to qualify. Therefore, a corporation established under the permissive laws of Delaware, where the regulation of corporate management is very flexible, cannot be denied admission to another state whose corporate statute restricts the activities of the intracorporate parties. However, the foreign corporation can be denied admission if it is organized for a purpose that is unlawful in the host state. For example, a Nevada corporation organized to conduct a gambling business may be denied admission to conduct gambling operations in a state where those activities are illegal. Otherwise, any corporation may qualify to do any business in any foreign jurisdiction.

TRANSACTING BUSINESS

The traditional statutory test for determining whether a corporation must qualify in a foreign jurisdiction is whether the corporation is **transacting business** within the foreign state. The transacting business test is not the most precise definition ever devised, and it has been responsible for considerable litigation. A sample of the cases illustrates the problem:

1. Would an Indiana corporation be doing business in Oklahoma by manufacturing equipment in Indiana, delivering it to Oklahoma, and installing it in Oklahoma?
2. Would a Delaware corporation be transacting business in New York by engaging an answering service and a soliciting salesman in New York?
3. Would an Arizona corporation be conducting business in Texas by sending salespeople and mechanics into Texas to solicit orders and to install and repair the machinery?
4. Would a Georgia corporation be doing business in Mississippi by hiring a local Mississippi mechanic to service an ice-cream dispenser for one year?

The answers from the cases that considered these questions are as follows: (1) no, (2) yes, (3) no, (4) yes.

The judicial uncertainty surrounding this test is particularly unfortunate when the sanctions for failure to qualify are considered. A corporation may suffer severe penalties if it is found to have been conducting business without qualification. To obviate the problem, section 15.01 of the Model Business Corporation Act enumerates certain activities that may be conducted by a foreign corporation without it being considered to be transacting business. These activities are

> (1) maintaining, defending, or settling any proceeding;
> (2) holding meetings of the board of directors or shareholders or carrying on other activities concerning internal corporate affairs;
> (3) maintaining bank accounts;
> (4) maintaining offices or agencies for the transfer, exchange, and registration of the corporation's own securities or maintaining trustees or depositaries with respect to those securities;
> (5) selling through independent contractors;
> (6) soliciting or obtaining orders, whether by mail or through employees or agents or otherwise, if the orders require acceptance outside this state before they become contracts;
> (7) creating or acquiring indebtedness, mortgages, and security interests in real or personal property;
> (8) securing or collecting debts or enforcing mortgages and security interests in property securing the debts;
> (9) owning, without more, real or personal property;
> (10) conducting an isolated transaction that is completed within 30 days and that is not one in the course of repeated transactions of a like nature;
> (11) transacting business in interstate commerce.

Only a few states detail such a comprehensive list, and many states have no list at all. Delaware provides a more specific list, which might be helpful in solving the illustrative cases described earlier. The Delaware statute states that a foreign corporation shall not be required to qualify in the state under the following circumstances:

> (1) If it is in the mail order or a similar business, merely receiving orders by mail or otherwise in pursuance of letters, circulars, catalogs, or other forms of advertising,

or solicitation, accepting the orders outside this State, and filling them with goods shipped into this State;

(2) If it employs salespersons, either resident or traveling, to solicit orders in this State, either by display of samples or otherwise (whether or not maintaining sales offices in this State), all orders being subject to approval at the offices of the corporation without this State, and all goods applicable to the orders being shipped in pursuance thereof from without this State to the vendee or to the seller or such seller's agent for delivery to the vendee, and if any samples kept within this State are for display or advertising purposes only, and no sales, repairs, or replacements are made from stock on hand in this State;

(3) If it sells, by contract consummated outside this State, and agrees, by the contract, to deliver into this State, machinery, plants or equipment, the construction, erection, or installation of which within this State requires the supervision of technical engineers or skilled employees performing services not generally available, and as a part of the contract of sale agrees to furnish such services, and such services only, to the vendee at the time of construction, erection, or installation;

(4) If its business operations within this State, although not falling within the terms of paragraphs (1), (2), and (3) of this subsection or any of them, are nevertheless wholly interstate in character;

(5) If it is an insurance company doing business in this State;

(6) If it creates, as borrower or lender, or acquires, evidences of debt, mortgages, or liens on real or personal property;

(7) If it secures or collects debts or enforces any rights in property securing the same.[7]

Some statutory guidance may be available, therefore, on what does *not* constitute the transaction of business within the state. However, that is not to say that everything not enumerated in the statute *is* transacting business so as to require qualification. There is still room for judicial interpretation of the other corporate activities.

The safe approach should be obvious: If there is any question about the scope of the corporation's activities in a foreign jurisdiction, the corporation should apply for admission as a foreign corporation and obtain a certificate of authority. Failure to do so may subject the corporation to the statutory sanctions for failing to qualify. The safe approach is not always the most practical, however. Qualification imposes certain burdens on the corporation, and corporate management may be unwilling to accept those burdens. Management should be fully advised on all ramifications of qualification and can then make the decision based on costs, formalities, taxes, and fees on the one hand, and the penalties for failure to qualify on the other.

SANCTIONS FOR NOT QUALIFYING

If a foreign corporation is transacting business within the state and has not received a certificate of authority from the host state, most state statutes impose certain interdictions and fines on the corporation or its management. Foreign corporations may be denied access to the local courts for any action, suit, or proceeding until a certificate of authority has been obtained. This sanction is found in the Model Business Corporation Act and in most jurisdictions. However, under the Model Business Corporation Act, the failure to qualify does not impair the validity of any contract or act of the corporation, and it does not prevent any corporation from *defending* any action in a court of the host state. Consequently, the practical drawback of failing to qualify under the Model Business Corporation Act is the inability of the corporation to maintain a suit in its own name. However, there are also pecuniary disadvantages. The failure to obtain a certificate renders the corporation liable to the state for all fees and taxes that would have been imposed had the corporation been qualified for the years during which it transacted business without a certificate of authority. In addition, the Model Business Corporation Act authorizes the imposition of any penalties normally levied for failure to pay the fees, and these fines also will be exacted from the foreign corporation. The attorney general is authorized to bring a suit to recover the amounts due under the statute.[8]

Although the prohibition from maintaining litigation and the collection of fees, taxes, and fines are severe sanctions, the Model Business Corporation Act is somewhat liberal by comparison with the sanctions imposed in some states. Alabama provides that all contracts of an unauthorized foreign corporation are void.[9] Certain jurisdictions impose fines, instead of the normal penalties for fees, and the amount of a fine may be as high as ten thousand dollars.[10] Fines also may be levied on corporate directors and officers. Other states authorize an action by the attorney general to enjoin the corporation from doing business.[11]

In the spirit of forgiveness, many states excuse the sanctions as soon as the corporation properly qualifies, although the relief may depend upon showing good cause for failure to qualify or obtaining court approval.

APPLICATION FOR CERTIFICATE OF AUTHORITY

All state statutes describe a procedure for the qualification of a foreign corporation. To acquire a certificate of authority in most states, the corporation must apply to the appropriate state official. The contents of the application vary among the jurisdictions, but there is a common purpose behind the qualification procedures. The applications reveal necessary information about the corporation's structure, its solvency, the location of its property, and its business potential. Foreign corporations are required to furnish essentially the same initial and periodic information as domestic corporations.

Section 15.03 of the Model Business Corporation Act includes the following items in an application for a certificate of authority:

1. the name of the foreign corporation;
2. the state or country under the laws of which the corporation is incorporated;
3. the date of incorporation and the period of duration;
4. the street address of the corporation's principal office;
5. the address of the corporation's registered office in the state, and the name of its registered agent at that office; and
6. the names and usual business addresses of the corporation's current directors and officers.

State statutes expand the previous list of disclosable items to include the following:

1. a statement of the purpose or purposes the corporation proposes to pursue in the transaction of business in the host state;
2. a statement of the aggregate number of shares the corporation has authority to issue, itemized by classes and series, if any, within a class;
3. a statement of the aggregate number of issued shares itemized by classes and series, if any, within a class;
4. an estimate, expressed in dollars, of the value of all property to be owned by the corporation for the following year, wherever located, and an estimate of the value of the property of the corporation to be located within the state during such year, and an estimate, expressed in dollars, of the gross amount of business that will be transacted by the corporation during such year, and an estimate of the gross amount thereof that will be transacted by the corporation at or from places of business in the state during such year; and
5. such additional information as may be necessary or appropriate in order to enable the secretary of state to determine whether such corporation is entitled to a certificate of authority to transact business in the state and to determine and assess the fees and franchise taxes payable as prescribed in the applicable act.

A study of the requirements of the application for authority should suggest that those requirements are designed to facilitate the discovery and evaluation of corporate property within the state and to gauge the local productivity of the foreign corporation. This information is used to estimate the tax potential of the foreign corporation, and may also assist local citizens in their litigation against the corporation.

Each state statute should be consulted for local application requirements. In addition to the information listed here, it may be necessary to state the purposes for the transaction of business in the foreign jurisdiction.[12] Statements of good standing may be required from the corporation's home state,[13] and nearly half of the states require filing of the articles of incorporation duly authenticated by the domestic state officials. In Pennsylvania it is necessary to officially publish notice of its name, principal address and local address.[14] Other unusual formalities include the following: the corporation may be required to state its assets and liabilities as of a recent date;[15] the corporation may have to stipulate an agent who is a local resident and a member of the local bar;[16] and statements regarding the amount of paid-in capital or paid-in surplus may be required.[17] Payment of fees and franchise taxes is almost always necessary, and some states require the filing of previous annual reports. To reiterate, as with other matters respecting corporate existence, it is necessary to carefully examine the statute of the state in which the corporation intends to do business, and to strictly comply with the statutory requirements.

The application for certificate of authority (see Exhibit 14–1, Application for Certificate of Authority) is prepared in duplicate or triplicate, as the statute requires, and is executed by the president and secretary or one of their assistants. In many states, the application must be verified by one of the signatories.

Most of the matters contained in the application for qualification are self-explanatory, but a couple of items deserve elaboration. The following material discusses requirements concerning the corporate name and the registered office and agent.

Corporate Name

The foreign corporation must comply with statutes regulating corporate names in the host state. The Model Business Corporation Act prescribes essentially the same name requirements for domestic and foreign corporations.[18] The name must contain the word *Corporation, Company, Incorporated,* or (in a few remaining states) *Limited,* or an abbreviation of one of these words, and it may not contain any word or phrase that indicates or implies that the corporation is organized for any purpose other than the purposes enumerated in its articles of incorporation. Moreover, the name cannot be the same as, or deceptively similar to, the name of any domestic corporation existing under the laws of the state or of any foreign corporation already authorized to transact business in the state.

If the name under which the corporation is organized is not available in the host state, the corporation may use a fictitious name to transact business. Alternatively, a foreign corporation will be allowed to use the name of an existing corporation, already organized in the host state, if

1. the other corporation consents to the use of the name and agrees to change its name to a distinguishable name; or
2. the applicant has a court order establishing the applicant's right to use the name in the state.[19]

Suppose American Can Company, a New York corporation, is seeking to qualify to do business in Tennessee, where there is an established domestic corporation by the same name. The name of the foreign corporation cannot be the same as that of a domestic corporation or a previously qualified foreign corporation. Therefore, the New York corporation cannot be qualified in Tennessee under the circumstances. However, if the board of directors of the New York corporation adopts a *fictitious* name that is not deceptively similar to an existing name, then the corporation may be qualified under that fictitious name.

The foreign corporation seeking to qualify to do business generally resists the fictitious name technique because the reputation of the corporate name, usually well-established in other states, is lost by the adoption of an assumed name. One can only speculate at the business success of Xerox Corporation if it had been required to use the fictitious name of Copying Machines, Inc., in some of the foreign jurisdictions where it qualified to do business. However, many state officials have adopted informal tests for variations in fictitious names that will be acceptable. For example, if a domestic corporation had reserved the name Xerox Corp. and the real Xerox Corporation attempted to qualify to do business, many states would permit the fictitious name to be Xerox Corporation of Delaware, simply adding the name of the state of incorporation.

Corporations also may buy the right to use a particular name from its owner, and that is usually what must be done to obtain written consent for its use under the consent alternative. Law

Exhibit 14–1.

Application for Certificate of Authority (North Carolina)

State of North Carolina
Department of the Secretary of State

APPLICATION FOR CERTIFICATE OF AUTHORITY

Pursuant to ß55-15-03 of the General Statutes of North Carolina, the undersigned corporation hereby applies for a Certificate of Authority to transact business in the State of North Carolina, and for that purpose submits the following:

1. The name of the corporation is _____ ; and if the corporate name is unavailable for use in the State of North Carolina, the name the corporation wishes to use is:
_____.

2. The state or country under whose laws the corporation was organized is: _____.

3. The date of incorporation was _____ ; its period of duration is: _____.

4. Principal office information: *(Select either a or b.)*

     a. ☐ The corporation has a principal office.

        The street address and county of the principal office of the corporation is:

        Number and Street_____

        City, State, Zip Code_____County_____

        The mailing address, *if different from the street address*, of the principal office of the corporation is:
        _____

     b. ☐ The corporation does not have a principal office.

5. The street address and county of the registered office in the State of North Carolina is:

    Number and Street _____

    City, State, Zip Code _____County_____

6. The mailing address, *if different from the street address*, of the registered office in the State of North Carolina is:
    _____

7. The name of the registered agent in the State of North Carolina is: _____

8. The names, titles, and usual business addresses of the current officers of the corporation are (attach if necessary):

Name	*Title*	*Business Address*
_____	_____	_____
_____	_____	_____
_____	_____	_____
_____	_____	_____

9. Attached is a Certificate of Existence (or document of similar import) duly authenticated by the Secretary of State or other official having custody of corporate records in the state or country of incorporation. ***The Certificate of Existence must be an original and less than six months old.***

CORPORATIONS DIVISION   P. O. BOX 29622   RALEIGH, NC 27626-0622
(Revised January, 2002)   *(Form B-09)*

(continued)

students who have studied this procedure have dreamed of making immediate and great fortunes by anticipating expansion of a large established corporation into their state, filing a reservation of the corporate name, and waiting to be approached for the consent.

The court order alternative is designed to give the corporation another choice if the price of the consent is excessive and a prior right to the name can be shown. For example, suppose Xerox Corporation had initially confined its business to the eastern states. Further suppose that an enterprising student of corporations, anticipating that Xerox would expand its business nationally, reserved the name Xerox Corporation in California, but did not actively conduct business under that name. Xerox probably could obtain a court order establishing its prior use of the name and eliminate the impediment of the name reservation in California.

The corporate name problem may be solved in advance with a little planning. Recall that all jurisdictions permit reservation of a corporate name, and several permit registration of the name.[20] Registration is specifically designed for use by foreign corporations. An organized and existing

Exhibit 14–1.

(continued)

APPLICATION FOR CERTIFICATE OF AUTHORITY
Page 2

10. If the corporation is required to use a fictitious name in order to transact business in this State, a copy of the resolution of its board of directors, certified by its secretary, adopting the fictitious name is attached.

11. This application will be effective upon filing, unless a delayed date and/or time is specified:

This is the ____ day of _____ , 20___

_____
Name of Corporation

_____
Signature

_____
Type or Print Name and Title

NOTES:
1. Filing fee is $250. This document must be filed with the Secretary of State.

CORPORATIONS DIVISION   P. O. BOX 29622   RALEIGH, NC 27626-0622
(Revised January, 2002)   *(Form B-09)*

(continued)

corporation may file an application for registration of its corporate name with the secretary of state for a small fee. The name may be registered for calendar years, and the registration may be renewed. Corporate management, foreseeing growth into foreign jurisdictions, is well advised to pursue registration of the corporate name in states where registration is permitted.[21]

Registered Office and Agent

Each state requires that a qualified foreign corporation must maintain a registered office and appoint a registered agent to receive legal documents addressed to the corporation. The registered office may be, but need not be, the same as the corporation's place of business in the state; the registered agent may be either an individual resident in the state or a domestic corporation, or another foreign corporation authorized to transact business in the state. As is required of a domestic corporation, any changes in the office or agent of the foreign corporation must be filed in the office of the secretary of state (see Exhibit 14–2, Statement of Change of Registered Office or Agent).[22]

Exhibit 14–1.

(continued)

Instructions for Filing

APPLICATION FOR CERTIFICATE OF AUTHORITY
(Form B-09)

Item 1   Enter the complete name of the corporation exactly as it appears in the records of the appropriate official in the state or country of incorporation. If the name cannot be used in North Carolina, enter the name (including a corporate ending) that it wishes to use in North Carolina.

Item 2   Enter the state or country of incorporation.

Item 3   Enter the date of incorporation and the period of duration.

Item 4   Select item ìaî if the corporation has a principal office. Enter the com plete street address of the principal office and the county in which it is located. If mail is not delivered to the street address of the principal office or if you prefer to receive mail at a P.O. Box or Drawer, enter the complete mailing address of the principal office.
Select item ìbî if the corporation does not have a principal office.

Item 5   Enter the complete street address of the corporationís registered office and the county in which it is located.

Item 6   Enter the complete mailing address of the corporationís registered agent, only if mail is not delivered to the street address above or if you prefer to receive mail at a P. O. Box or Drawer.

Item 7   Enter the name of the registered agent. The registered agent must be a North Carolina resident, an existing domestic business corporation, nonprofit corporation or limited liability company, or a foreign business corporation, nonprofit corporation or limited liability company authorized to transact business or conduct affairs in North Carolina.

Item 8   Enter the names, titles, and usual business address of the current officers of the corporation.

Item 9   See Form

Item 10   See Form

Item 11   The document will be effective on the date and at the time of filing, unless a delayed date or an effective time (on the date of filing) is specified. If a delayed effective date is specified without a time, it will be effective at 11:59:59 p.m. A delayed effective date may be specified up to and including the 90th day after the day of filing.

Date and Execution

Enter the date the document was executed.

In the blanks provided enter:

- The name of the corporation as it appears in Item 1
- The signature of the representative of the corporation executing the document (may be the chairman of the board of directors or any officer of the corporation).
- The name and title of the above-signed representative.

CORPORATIONS DIVISION	P. O. BOX 29622	RALEIGH, NC 27626-0622
(Revised January, 2002)		*(Form B-09)*

The purpose of the registered office and the agent is to facilitate the service of any process, notice, or demand required or permitted by law. A state may reasonably require a convenient way to notify a foreign corporation of any legal matters as a condition to its permission to do business in the state. For that reason, whenever a foreign corporation fails to appoint or maintain a registered agent in the state or whenever the registered agent cannot be found with due diligence, most statutes and the Model Business Corporation Act provides that the foreign corporation that has failed to maintain a registered agent within the host state may be served by registered or certified mail directly addressed to the secretary of the foreign corporation at its principal office.[23] This eliminates the burden placed upon the secretary of state to receive the document and to send it to the foreign corporation. Direct delivery is just as effective if the statute permits it. These provisions circumvent any potential escape from local complaints by failing to maintain a local agent and ensure the amenability of the foreign corporation to suit in local courts.

Exhibit 14–2.

Statement of Change of
Registered Office or Agent
(South Dakota)

SECRETARY OF STATE
STATE CAPITOL
500 E. CAPITOL AVE.
PIERRE, S.D. 57501
605-773-4845

STATEMENT OF CHANGE OF REGISTERED OFFICE, OR REGISTERED AGENT, OR BOTH
FILING FEE: $10

Pursuant to the provisions of the South Dakota Corporation Acts, the undersigned corporation submits the following statement for the purpose of changing its registered office and/or its registered agent in the state of South Dakota.

1. The name of the corporation is _____
_____

2. The previous street address <u>or</u> a statement that there is no street address, of its registered office _____
_____ ZIP _____

3. The street address, <u>or</u> a statement that there is no street address, to which the registered office is to be changed is_____
_____ ZIP _____

4. The name of its previous registered agent is _____
5. The name of its successor registered agent is * _____

* The Consent of Registered Agent below <u>must</u> be completed by the new agent.

6. The address of its registered office and the address of the business office of its registered agent, as changed, will be identical.

7. This change has been authorized by resolution duly adopted by the board of directors.

The statement may be signed by the chairman of the board of directors, by its president or by another of its officers in the presence of a notary public.

Date _____

_____
(Signature)
_____
(Title)

STATE OF _____

COUNTY OF _____

I, _____, a notary public, do hereby certify that on this _____ day of _____, 20____, personally appeared before me _____ who, being by me first duly sworn, declared that he/she is the _____ of _____, that he/she signed the foregoing document as officer of the corporation, and the statements therein contained are true.

_____   _____
My Commission Expires   (Notary Public)

Notarial Seal

CONSENT OF APPOINTMENT BY THE REGISTERED AGENT

I, _____, hereby give my consent to serve as the
(name of registered agent)

registered agent for _____
(corporate name)

Dated _____   _____
(signature of registered agent)

Several "registered agent" companies are available at the request of attorneys to act as registered agents for foreign corporations and to comply with the requirements of local laws on their behalf. They include the CT Corporation System; Prentice Hall, Inc.; and the United States Corporation Company.

CERTIFICATE OF AUTHORITY

Upon receipt of the application for a certificate of authority (see Exhibit 14–3, Certificate of Authority [Model Act]), the secretary of state or other appropriate official files the application and issues a certificate of authority. When the certificate is issued, the corporation is authorized to transact business in the state for the purposes set forth in its application as long as it remains in good standing.[24]

```
                    STATE OF_____
           OFFICE OF THE SECRETARY OF STATE
               CERTIFICATE OF AUTHORITY
                          OF
                 _____

        The undersigned, as Secretary of State of the State of _____hereby certifies
    that duplicate originals of an Application of_____
    for a Certificate of Authority to transact business in this State, duly signed and
    verified pursuant to the provisions of the _____Business Corporation Act,
    have been received in this office and are found to conform to law.
        ACCORDINGLY the undersigned, as such Secretary of State, and by virtue of
    the authority vested in him by law, hereby issues this Certificate of Authority
    to_____
    to transact business in this State under the name of_____
    and attaches hereto a duplicate original of the Application for such Certificate.
        Dated _____, 20___ .

                                              _____
                                                      Secretary of State
```

Exhibit 14–3.

Certificate of Authority
(Model Act)

EFFECT OF QUALIFICATION

Once a foreign corporation has received authority to do business within the foreign state, it is entitled to enjoy the same rights and privileges as a domestic corporation organized for the same purposes. In addition, it is subject to the same duties, restrictions, penalties, and liabilities as a domestic corporation. In the host state, therefore, the foreign corporation is treated like a native, receiving no better or worse treatment than the domestic corporations. The foreign corporation also remains subject to restrictions imposed by its home state, and it must observe those restrictions while operating in the host state.

Consider an Arkansas corporation that qualifies to do business in Pennsylvania. Suppose Arkansas law permits the corporation to be a general partner in another enterprise only if it is authorized to do so in the articles of incorporation or by vote of the shareholders. Pennsylvania law permits a corporation to be a general partner without any such authorization. If the articles of incorporation do not authorize the corporation's entry into a partnership and the shareholders have not approved such a transaction, the Arkansas corporation cannot become a general partner, even in Pennsylvania where otherwise it is treated like a domestic corporation. The restrictions placed upon the corporation in its home state are superimposed upon its operations in the foreign state.

The reverse is not exactly the same. Consider a Nevada corporation that qualifies to do business in Pennsylvania. The Nevada corporation is authorized to conduct gambling activities in its home state, but Pennsylvania law does not permit gambling operations in Pennsylvania. The Nevada corporation must abide by the local laws, and it has no greater privileges in Pennsylvania than does a domestic Pennsylvania corporation. However, the internal affairs of the Nevada corporation are always regulated by the law of Nevada. Thus, for example, if Pennsylvania law requires a shareholder vote to change the name of the corporation but Nevada law does not, the Nevada corporation is entitled to change its name in Pennsylvania without a shareholder vote, since that matter is an internal affair of the corporation.

In addition to the restrictions upon privileges and powers discussed here, a qualified foreign corporation accepts other responsibilities within the host state. It agrees to certain requirements concerning service of process, taxes, and annual reports.

Service of Process

A foreign corporation authorized to transact business in a state is subjected to the jurisdiction of the courts of the host state. Consequently, **service** of documents relating to litigation upon the registered agent of the corporation is as effective as if the corporation were incorporated within the state and had been served at its principal office.

Taxes

By qualifying to do business within a state, a foreign corporation agrees to pay taxes to the host state. A state is permitted to tax a foreign corporation under the Constitution if the corporation has **substantial contacts** within the state. The law is now quite clear that by qualifying to do business within the state, the corporation creates those substantial contacts. The individual tax structures of the states are dissimilar, but several typical types of taxes are imposed upon foreign corporations.

Some states impose an initial **franchise tax** upon the filing of the application for a certificate of authority. This tax is generally based upon the aggregate amount of authorized capital stock of the corporation, similar to the measure for taxes imposed on a domestic corporation when its articles of incorporation are filed. A fee is also charged for filing the application of a foreign corporation.

Annual income taxes are imposed upon foreign corporations. Generally, the tax formula used in any given state has been designed around the commercial character of the state and is intended to maximize tax revenues from foreign corporations. If the state is a recognized location for heavy industry, so that most foreign corporations have manufacturing or industrial plants there, the state will probably impose a tax on the value of the property of the foreign corporation located within the state. This tax formula maximizes revenue for states with an industrial character to their commerce. If the state is not heavily industrialized but has a large population, a tax may be imposed on the proportionate volume of business that the foreign corporation is transacting in the state. A tax on foreign corporations also may be computed by a formula based upon the total number of employees located within the state.

The tax provisions of each state play an important role in the selection of jurisdiction for a corporation anticipating a multistate business. At the formation stage, the choice between incorporating or qualifying to do business in a given jurisdiction is influenced by that state's tax attitude. For example, if a corporation plans to locate a manufacturing plant in State X and intends to sell its products to customers primarily located in State Y, it would be a mistake to incorporate in State X, where the plant is located, if that state bases its foreign corporation tax on the volume of sales transacted within the state. The corporation should operate as a foreign corporation in State X, because that state's tax base depends upon volume of sales and this corporation will be making most of its sales out of state.

Annual Reports

Like domestic corporations, qualified foreign corporations must file **annual reports** with the state. The Model Business Corporation Act requires that the annual reports of domestic and foreign corporations contain the same information.[25] Most states require that the annual report contain certain standard information regarding the corporation, its registered offices and agents, its directors and officers, and the character of its business. The reported items typically used to levy taxes include the following:

1. a statement of the aggregate number of shares the corporation has authority to issue, itemized by classes and series, if any, within a class;
2. a statement of the aggregate number of issued shares, itemized by classes and series;
3. a statement, expressed in dollars, of the value of all the property of the corporation, wherever located, and the value of the property of the corporation located within the state, and the statement of the gross amount of business transacted by the corporation for the period of the report; and
4. additional information as may be necessary or appropriate in order to enable the secretary of state to determine and assess the proper amount of franchise taxes payable by the corporation.

The annual reports are used to assist the secretary of state in enforcing the corporation statute and ensuring compliance with its provisions, in fixing responsibility for any corporate transgressions on the named officers and directors, and in evaluating the appropriate tax to be assessed. Most states have the same reporting requirements for foreign and domestic corporations. (See Exhibit 14–4, Annual Report.)

☐ **CORPORATION ANNUAL REPORT**
STATE OF TENNESSEE
SECRETARY OF STATE
SUITE 1800, JAMES K. POLK BUILDING
NASHVILLE, TN 37243-0306
AMOUNT DUE - $20.00

CURRENT FISCAL YEAR CLOSING MONTH:	IF DIFFERENT,	
CORRECT MONTH IS_____		THIS REPORT IS DUE ON OR BEFORE

(1) SECRETARY OF STATE CONTROL NUMBER: OR FEDERAL EMPLOYER IDENTIFICATION NUMBER:

(2A.) NAME AND MAILING ADDRESS OF CORPORATION:	(2B.) STATE OR COUNTRY OF INCORPORATION:
	(2C.) ADD OR CHANGE MAILING ADDRESS:

(3)   A. PRINCIPAL ADDRESS INCLUDING CITY, STATE, ZIP CODE:

   B. CHANGE OF PRINCIPAL ADDRESS:

STREET	CITY	STATE	ZIP CODE +4

❋❋ **BLOCKS 4A AND 4B MUST BE COMPLETED OR THE ANNUAL REPORT WILL BE RETURNED** ❋❋

(4) A. NAME AND BUSINESS ADDRESS, INCLUDING ZIP CODE, OF THE PRESIDENT, SECRETARY AND OTHER PRINCIPAL OFFICERS. (ATTACH ADDITIONAL SHEET IF NECESSARY.)

TITLE	NAME	BUSINESS ADDRESS	CITY, STATE, ZIP CODE + 4
PRESIDENT			
SECRETARY			

B. BOARD OF DIRECTORS (NAMES, BUSINESS ADDRESS INCLUDING ZIP CODE). (ATTACH ADDITIONAL SHEET IF NECESSARY.)
☐ SAME AS ABOVE
☐ NONE

OR LIST BELOW: NAME	BUSINESS ADDRESS	CITY, STATE, ZIP CODE + 4

(5) A. NAME OF REGISTERED AGENT AS APPEARS ON SECRETARY OF STATE RECORDS:

B. REGISTERED ADDRESS AS APPEARS ON SECRETARY OF STATE RECORDS:

(6) INDICATE BELOW ANY CHANGES TO THE REGISTERED AGENT NAME AND/OR REGISTERED OFFICE.
(BLOCK 5A AND/OR 5B.) THERE IS AN ADDITIONAL $20.00 REQUIRED FOR CHANGES MADE TO THIS INFORMATION.

   A. CHANGE OF REGISTERED AGENT:

   B. CHANGE OF REGISTERED OFFICE:

STREET	CITY	STATE TN	ZIP CODE + 4	COUNTY

(7) A. THIS BOX APPLIES **ONLY** TO NONPROFIT CORPORATIONS. OUR RECORDS REFLECT THAT YOUR NONPROFIT CORPORATION IS A PUBLIC BENEFIT OR A MUTUAL BENEFIT CORPORATION AS INDICATED BELOW:

IF BLANK OR CHANGE, PLEASE CHECK APPROPRIATE BOX:
☐ PUBLIC
☐ MUTUAL

B. IF A TENNESSEE RELIGIOUS CORPORATION, PLEASE CHECK BOX UNLESS OTHERWISE INDICATED.
☐ RELIGIOUS

(8) SIGNATURE	(9) DATE
(10) TYPE/PRINT NAME OF SIGNER:	(11) TITLE OF SIGNER

❋❋ THIS REPORT MUST BE DATED AND SIGNED ❋❋

SS4444 (Rev. 11-95)   RDA 1678

Exhibit 14–4.

Annual Report (Tennessee)

STRUCTURAL CHANGES
OF A FOREIGN CORPORATION

Every state requires domestic corporations to report all **corporate structural changes** such as mergers, share exchanges, sale or exchange of assets, or amendments to the articles of incorporation. Similarly, qualified foreign corporations must follow certain procedures in the host state whenever structural changes occur in the corporate organizations.

Amendment to the Articles of Incorporation

Model Business Corporation Act section 15.04 provides that a qualified foreign corporation must obtain an amended certificate of authority from the secretary of state of the host state if the corporation changes its name or the period of its duration. In addition, if the corporation changes the state or country in which it is incorporated, an amended certificate of authority must be obtained.

In most states, any amendment to the articles of incorporation of the foreign corporation requires the filing of a statement with the secretary of state in the foreign jurisdiction. The time period for filing copies or statements of amendments differs among the states. Most states require that such an amendment be filed within thirty days, several states permit as long as sixty days,[26] and a few states have no time limit.[27] Careful study of the appropriate state law is important.

The filing procedure for amendments to the articles of incorporation of a foreign corporation is amplified if the amendment changes the corporate name or the period of duration. Merely filing copies of the amended articles of incorporation will not suffice to authorize the foreign corporation to use another name or to extend its longevity. A foreign corporation may change its corporate name or its duration by filing an application for an amended certificate of authority. The Model Business Corporation Act requires the issuance of an amended certificate of authority to accomplish these changes (see Exhibit 14–5, Application for Amended Certificate of Authority, and Exhibit 14–6, Amended Certificate of Authority).[28] The form and contents of the application for an amended certificate and the procedure for issuance of the amended certificate are the same as those described for the original application for a certificate of authority.[29]

There is an obvious problem if a foreign corporation changes its name by amending its articles of incorporation and the new name is not available in the host state. The drafters of the Model Business Corporation Act took a fairly firm stand on this issue.[30] If the new name is not available, the certificate of authority for the corporation is suspended until the corporation again changes its name to one that is available. A few states soften the harshness of this rule by allowing an interim grace period of 180 days during which the corporation may transact business under its old name, but by the end of the period, the corporation must change its name to a name that is available under the laws of the state. If the corporation fails to change to an acceptable name and continues to transact business, its certificate of authority may be suspended.

Merger and Share Exchange with the Foreign Corporation

A merger of a foreign corporation requires additional filings in the host state when the foreign corporation is the surviving corporation after the merger. The legal consequences of a merger are considered in detail later,[31] but stated simply, a merger is a combination of two or more corporations into one corporate entity, whereby one of the corporate parties survives the transaction and the others cease to exist. In most state statutes, if the foreign corporation survives the merger, it must file a copy of the articles of merger with the secretary of state to make the merger effective.[32] It is not necessary for the surviving foreign corporation to procure an amended certificate of authority unless the corporation has changed its name under the merger or unless it has adopted a different period of duration than that authorized in its current cer-

State of North Carolina
Department of the Secretary of State

APPLICATION FOR AMENDED CERTIFICATE OF AUTHORITY

Pursuant to ß55-15-04 of the General Statutes of North Carolina, the undersigned corporation hereby applies for an Amended Certificate of Authority to transact business in the State of North Carolina and for that purpose submits the following statement.

1. The name of the corporation is:_____

2. The name the corporation is currently using in the State of North Carolina is:

_____

3. The state or country of incorporation is:_____

4. The date the corporation was authorized to transact business in the State of North Carolina is:

_____

5. This application is filed for the following reason (**complete all applicable items**):
   a. The corporation has changed its corporate name to:*

   _____

   b. The name the corporation will hereafter use in the State of North Carolina is changed to:

   _____

   c. The corporation has changed its period of duration to:_____

   d. The corporation has changed the state or country of its incorporation to:_____

6. Attached is a certificate attesting to the change, duly authenticated by the secretary of state or other official having custody of corporate records in the state of country of incorporation.

7. If the corporation is required to use a fictitious name in order to transact business in this State, a copy of the resolution of its board of directors, certified by its secretary, adopting the fictitious name is attached.

8. This application will be effective upon filing, unless a date and/or time is specified:_____

This the _____day of_____, 20_____

_____
Name of Corporation

_____
Signature

_____
Type or Print Name and Title

NOTES:
1. Filing fee is $75. One executed original and one exact or conformed copy of this application must be filed with the Secretary of State.
2. * If the name of the corporation as changed is unavailable for use in North Carolina, indicate this fact and state the name the corporation wishes to use in North Carolina on 5b. (See NCGS ß55-15-06)
(Revised January 2000) *(Form B-10)*

Instructions for Filing
CORPORATIONS DIVISION   P. O. BOX 29622   RALEIGH, NC 27626-0622

Exhibit 14–5.

Application for Amended Certificate of Authority (North Carolina)

(continued)

tificate of authority. If either of those results are produced by the merger, the amendment procedure described earlier must be followed.

If a qualified foreign corporation merges with another foreign corporation that is not authorized to transact business within the host state and the nonqualified corporation survives the merger, the surviving corporation must qualify in the foreign jurisdiction by filing an original application for a certificate of authority. The surviving corporation does not inherit the previously granted authority of the merged corporation through the merger.

If a foreign corporation merges with a domestic corporation and the domestic corporation survives the merger, the articles of merger must be filed by the domestic corporation pursuant to the laws of the state.[33] However, if the foreign corporation survives the merger,

Exhibit 14–5.

(continued)

APPLICATION FOR AMENDED CERTIFICATE OF AUTHORITY
(Form B-10)

Item 1   Enter the complete name of the corporation exactly as it appears on the Certificate of Authority.

Item 2   Enter the corporate name used in North Carolina exactly as it appears on the Certificate of Authority.

Item 3   Enter the state or country of incorporation.

Item 4   Enter the date the corporation was authorized to transact business in North Carolina.

Item 5   Complete the applicable items.

Item 6   See Form.

Item 7   See Form.

Item 8   The document will be effective on the date and at the time of filing, unless a delayed date or an effective time (on the day of filing) is specified. If a delayed effective date is specified without a time, the document will be effective at 11:59:59 p.m. on the day specified. If a delayed effective date is specified with a time, the document will be effective on the day and at the time specified. A delayed effective date may be specified up to and including the 90th day after the day of filing.

Date and Execution

Enter the date the document was executed.

In the blanks provided enter:
The name of the corporation as it appears in item 1.
The signature of the representative of the corporation executing the document (may be the chairman of the board of directors or any officer of the corporation).
The name and title of the representative.

CORPORATIONS DIVISION   P. O. BOX 29622   RALEIGH, NC 27626-0622

---

other filings are required. The surviving foreign corporation may not be authorized to transact business within the state, and if it intends to do so, it must file an original application for a certificate of authority. Even if it does not intend to do business within the state, the surviving foreign corporation is deemed, through the merger,

1. to appoint the secretary of state as its agent for service of process in a proceeding to enforce any obligation or the rights of dissenting shareholders of each domestic corporation that was a party to the merger or share exchange; and
2. to agree that it will promptly pay to the dissenting shareholders of each domestic corporation that was a party to the merger or share exchange the amount, if any, to which those shareholders are entitled under dissenting shareholders' rights.[34]

STATE OF_____
OFFICE OF THE SECRETARY OF STATE
AMENDED CERTIFICATE OF AUTHORITY
OF

_____

The undersigned, as Secretary of State of the State of _____hereby certifies
that duplicate originals of an Application of_____
for an Amended Certificate of Authority to transact business in this State, duly
signed and verified pursuant to the provisions of the _____Business Corporation Act, have been received in this office and are found to conform to law.

ACCORDINGLY the undersigned, as such Secretary of State, and by virtue of
the authority vested in him by law, hereby issues this Amended Certificate of
Authority to_____
to transact business in this State under the name of_____
and attaches hereto a duplicate original of the Application for such Amended
Certificate.

Dated _____, 20___ .

_____
Secretary of State

Many states require that the foreign corporation must file with the secretary of state a document that promises to perform these acts. However, if the surviving foreign corporation has
been authorized to do business within the state, the terms of the corporation's authority theoretically include each of these items, and no further filing should be required; the Model Business Corporation Act now makes these consequences automatic.

Finally, a foreign corporation can enter into a **share exchange** with another corporation, either domestic or foreign. A share exchange is a transaction in which one corporation exchanges
its shares for all or part of the shares of the other corporation. If the foreign corporation is the
acquiring corporation in a share exchange, the procedure is exactly the same as if the foreign
corporation were the surviving corporation in a merger.

WITHDRAWAL OF AUTHORITY

The management of a qualified foreign corporation may decide to discontinue business operations within the host state. However, this does not mean that they may simply pull up their
tent and steal away. State regulation of foreign corporations is designed to require payment
of fees and taxes and to ensure the availability of the foreign corporation for litigation commenced against it in the state. Consequently, the withdrawal of a foreign corporation is a formal procedure. The foreign corporation must file an application for withdrawal (see Exhibit
14–7, Application for Certificate of Withdrawal), which, under the Model Business Corporation Act, states that the corporation surrenders its authority to transact business in the state.
It must further specifically revoke the authority of its registered agent to accept service of
process, and consent to service of process on the secretary of state for any proceeding based
upon a cause of action arising during the time the corporation was operating within the state.
The withdrawal application also includes a post office address to which the state officials
may mail a copy of any process received for the corporation.[35] Many states require additional information necessary to enable the secretary of state to assess any unpaid fees or
franchise taxes.

Exhibit 14–7.

Application for Certificate of Withdrawal (Massachusetts)

MSC.4

Examiner

P.C.

FEDERAL IDENTIFICATION
NO. _____
Fee: $100.00

The Commonwealth of Massachusetts

William Francis Galvin
Secretary of the Commonwealth
One Ashburton Place, Boston, Massachusetts 02108-1512

CERTIFICATE OF WITHDRAWAL
(General Laws, Chapter 181, Section 16)

We, _____ , *President / *Vice President,

and _____ , *Clerk / *Assistant Clerk **or** *Secretary / *Asst. Secretary,

of _____ ,
(Exact name of corporation)

located at _____ ,
(Street address of corporation)

in compliance with the provisions of General Laws, Chapter 181, Section 16, certify as follows:

1. The corporation was organized under the laws of the state of:

2. The date of organization of the corporation is:

3. The date on which the corporation's fiscal year ends is:

4. The name and residential address of each director and officer of the corporation is as follows:

NAME	RESIDENTIAL ADDRESS

President:

Treasurer:

Clerk or Secretary:

Directors:

*Delete the inapplicable words.

181cwith 4/5/00

(continued)

State statutes governing withdrawal of foreign corporations are as varied as those pertaining to admission. Most statutes are directed toward full financial disclosure and amenability to service of process, and generally require that the foreign corporation tidy up its affairs before leaving the state. The statute may require that the corporation commit to notify the Secretary of State of any future address changes[36] or to provide the names and residence addresses of its corporate officers and directors.[37] In all cases, taxes and fees must be paid as a condition to the approval of withdrawal.

Upon the filing of the application and the satisfaction of all statutory conditions, the appropriate state official will issue a certificate of withdrawal (see Exhibit 14–8, Certificate of Withdrawal on page 515).

Exhibit 14–7.

(continued)

5. The corporation is no longer doing business in the Commonwealth of Massachusetts.

6. Attached to this certificate shall be a certificate from the Commissioner of Revenue that all taxes due and payable by the corporation to the Commonwealth have been paid or provided for.

SIGNED UNDER THE PENALTIES OF PERJURY, this _____ day of _____ , 20 _____ ,

_____ , *President / *Vice President,

_____ , *Clerk / *Assistant Clerk or *Secretary / * Asst. Secretary.

Delete the inapplicable words.

(continued)

REVOCATION OF CERTIFICATE OF AUTHORITY

A foreign corporation's authority to do business within a state may cease by the revocation of authority by the host state. Generally, the certificate may be revoked whenever the foreign corporation has failed to comply with the law. For example, the corporation may have failed to file annual reports, or may have failed to pay fees, franchise taxes, or penalties. Other grounds for revocation include the corporation's failure to appoint and maintain a registered agent; failure to notify the state of a change in the agent or office; failure to file amendments to its articles of incorporation or articles of merger within the time prescribed; or misrepresentation in the material matter in any application, report, affidavit, or other document filed with the state. In addition to these grounds, some states add abusing or exceeding the corporation's authority; violating a state law; using an unauthorized name; or

Exhibit 14–7.

(continued)

THE COMMONWEALTH OF MASSACHUSETTS

CERTIFICATE OF WITHDRAWAL
(General Laws, Chapter 181, Section 16)

I hereby approve the within Certificate of Withdrawal and, the filing fee in the amount of $ _____having been paid, said application is deemed to have been filed with me this _____ day of_____ , 20 ____ .

WILLIAM FRANCIS GALVIN
Secretary of the Commonwealth

TO BE FILLED IN BY CORPORATION
Photocopy of document to be sent to:

_____

_____

_____

Telephone: _____

STATE OF_____
OFFICE OF THE SECRETARY OF STATE
CERTIFICATE OF WITHDRAWAL
OF

_____

The undersigned, as Secretary of State of the State of _____, hereby certifies that duplicate originals of an Application of_____ for a Certificate of Withdrawal from this State, duly signed and verified pursuant to the provisions of the _____Business Corporation Act, have been received in this office and are found to conform to law.

ACCORDINGLY the undersigned, as such Secretary of State, and by virtue of the authority vested in him by law, hereby issues this Certificate of Withdrawal to _____, and attaches hereto a duplicate original of the Application for such Certificate.
Dated _____, 20__.

_____
Secretary of State

Exhibit 14–8.

Certificate of Withdrawal

STATE OF_____
OFFICE OF THE SECRETARY OF STATE
CERTIFICATE OF REVOCATION OF
CERTIFICATE OF AUTHORITY
OF

_____

The undersigned, as Secretary of State of the State of _____, and by virtue of the authority vested in him by Section 122 of the _____Business Corporation Act, hereby revokes the Certificate of Authority of_____ to transact business in this State, for the following reasons:_____
_____
_____
_____

Dated _____, 20__ .

_____
Secretary of State

Exhibit 14–9.

Certificate of Revocation of
Certificate of Authority

acting in a manner detrimental to the citizens of the state. The District of Columbia and Illinois have a revocation provision that looks like default: if the corporation does not conduct business or own tangible property within the state for a specified period, its certificate of authority may be revoked.

Most state statutes require notice to the corporation before the revocation of a certificate of authority. The Model Business Corporation Act directs the secretary of state to give the corporation sixty days' notice by mail addressed to the corporation's registered office in the state; if the corporation corrects the specified problem within the notice period, the certificate of authority may not be revoked. However, following the sixty-day period, if nothing has been done, the secretary of state may issue a certificate of revocation.[38] The minimum notice period among the individual state statutes is thirty days,[39] and the maximum is ninety days.[40] Many states permit the remedy of the defect during the intermediate period.

When the certificate of revocation of authority is issued (see Exhibit 14–9, Certificate of Revocation of Certificate of Authority), the corporation's authority to transact business in the state ceases.

KEY TERMS

transacting business
service of process
substantial contacts

franchise tax
annual report

corporate structural changes
share exchange

WEB RESOURCES

General information concerning formation and operation of foreign corporations in the various jurisdictions is available on every state Secretary of State's (or Department of Commerce) Web site. Most of the sites offer forms that are required for filing to apply for certificates of authority to do business and to maintain the accuracy of the corporate records in the foreign state. The National Association of Secretaries of State maintains links directly to the offices of the Secretaries of State in all states. These can be accessed through

<http://www.nass.org>

Access to state corporate laws for the specific requirements of applying for foreign authority to do business may be obtained through the Legal Information Institute maintained at the Cornell Law School:

<http://www.law.cornell.edu>

The specific sections of a state's corporate law applicable to foreign corporations may be located by a search site that directly ties to the corporate laws of the state. This search may be accessed at

<http://www.megalaw.com>

Several companies act as registered agents in foreign jurisdictions when the foreign corporation does not maintain an active presence in the foreign jurisdiction. These services charge a fee, but also assist the corporate personnel and their counsel in any unique requirements of the local law that may be applicable to the foreign corporation. They include

<http://www.corporate.com>
<http://www.inc-it-now.com>
<http://www.mycorporation.com>
<http://www.delaware-agents.com>
<http://www.nrai.com>
<http://www.superiorregisteredagents.com>

CASES

STATE OF MISSOURI v. MURRAY'S

767 S.W.2d 127 (Mo. App. 1989)
KAROHL, JUDGE

The issue on appeal is whether defendant Murray's business activities were business transactions within Missouri so as to subject Murray's to the registration requirements of § 351.570.1 RSMo 1986. Murray's, a California corporation, appeals a $20,000 fine for failure to comply with §§ 351.570 and 351.635 RSM. 1986. The trial court entered judgment after finding Murray's transacted intrastate business in the State of Missouri without procuring a certificate of authority on registering with the state in violation of § 351.570.1 RSM. 1986. On appeal, Murray's contends it

only engaged in interstate commerce, not intrastate commerce. The statute does not apply to interstate transactions. We find the evidence of Murray's business activities did not support a finding of intrastate transactions within Missouri so as to subject Murray's to the registration requirements of § 351.570 RSMo 1986. We reverse.

* * *

Chapter 351 provides in pertinent part: "No foreign corporation shall have the right to transact business in this state . . . until it shall have procured a certificate of authority so to do from the secretary of state." § 351.570.1 RSMo 1986. Failure to procure a certificate may result in a fine as provided in § 351.635 RSMo 1986. Transacting any business in interstate commerce by a foreign corporation is not considered to be transaction of business in this state. § 351.570.2(9) RSMo 1986.

The record discloses proof of the following facts. Murray's concedes it is a California corporation incorporated on September 30, 1977, with its principal place of business in Los Angeles, California. Murray's business includes brokering tickets for major sporting events. It solicits ticket purchasers and buyers by nationwide advertising. Customers purchase tickets by telephone and pay for them by supplying charge card numbers with their order. Murray's accepts orders and payment from its offices in California. Murray's delivers the tickets to purchasers at the site of the event.

In October of 1987, Murray's placed an advertisement in the St. Louis Post Dispatch soliciting potential buyers and sellers of World Series tickets. The advertisement listed two phone numbers which were located in California. The third number listed in the advertisement was a St. Louis number followed by the word "buying." Ticket orders were placed with Murray's office in California via the California phone numbers.

Tickets were distributed to customers in St. Louis, which was the site of several games of Major League Baseball's 1987 World Series. Murray's leased an apartment for one month and opened a checking account in St. Louis. While in St. Louis Murray's sold two tickets to Ms. McNamara, the leasing consultant of the apartment complex, and bought two tickets from a St. Louis city policeman. Except for proof of these two transactions, Murray's business in St. Louis consisted of distributing tickets to customers, the majority of whom were from outside Missouri and had purchased and paid for tickets by long distance telephone to California.

The trial court found that Murray's was a foreign corporation transacting business in Missouri without being registered to do business in the State of Missouri. It found Murray's to be in violation of § 351.570.1 RSMo 1986 and ordered Murray's to pay a $20,000 civil fine and costs pursuant to § 351.635 RSMo 1986.

Murray's claim of error is that the court erred in finding Murray's violated § 351.570 RSMo 1986 because the business conducted by Murray's was the transaction of business in interstate commerce which does not subject Murray's, a foreign corporation, to the registration requirements of § 351.570.1 RSMo 1986. We agree.

* * *

There is no definitive definition of what constitutes "doing business" within Missouri so as to subject a foreign corporation to the registration requirements of § 351.570 RSMo 1986. A finding of what constitutes "doing business" in the state is to be determined on the facts in each individual case. *Filmakers Releasing Organization,* 374 S.W.2d at 540. Thus, the cases interpreting § 351.570.1 establish no clear pattern of what business activities establish "transacting business" in Missouri so as to require registration of a foreign corporation. *American Trailers, Inc. v. Curry,* 480 F.Supp. 663, 665 (E.D.Mo.1979), *rev'd on other grounds,* 621 F.2d 918 (8th Cir.1980). "It is well-settled [however] that, in determining whether a particular movement of freight is interstate or intrastate . . ., the intention

existing at the time the movement starts governs and fixes the character of the shipment. . . ." [citations omitted].

The importation into one state from another is the indispensable element of interstate commerce. *Filmakers Releasing Organization,* 374 S.W.2d at 540. The usual dispute involving sale transactions develops when some part of an interstate sale occurs in the state. Where purchase, payment and delivery are done in Missouri the transactions are intrastate. Where all three elements are done outside the state, i.e., purchase and payment by telephone and delivery by mail, the transactions are purely interstate. With two exceptions the evidence supported only a finding all transactions involving Murray's were interstate sales with delivery intrastate. In such case the test is whether there exists: "continued dealing by the foreign corporation with the property after interstate commerce had wholly ceased, and whether that continued dealing [if any] was an isolated transaction or a continuing form of the business of the foreign corporation." *Western Outdoor Advertising Co. of Nebraska v. Berbiglia, Inc.,* 263 S.W.2d 205, 209 (Mo.App.1953).

Here, Murray's did not continue to deal with the tickets after the tickets were distributed to the purchasers in Missouri. The distribution of World Series tickets in Missouri was the final step in an interstate transaction where the first two steps in the sale of these tickets, ordering and payment, were made by telephone with Murray's in California. Because Murray's did not continue to deal with the tickets after interstate commerce had wholly ceased, Murray's did not change the character of the transaction from interstate commerce to intrastate commerce. Therefore, in completing the interstate sales Murray's was not transacting business within Missouri so as to subject it to the registration requirements of § 351.570 RSMo 1986. An apartment was rented for one month only to complete the interstate sales. There is no evidence to support a finding of how long Murray's occupied the apartment. These sales were the only business activities of Murray's, with two exceptions.

It was stipulated that Murray's engaged in two transactions which were intrastate in nature. One transaction consisted of Murray's selling two tickets to Ms. McNamara, the leasing consultant of the apartment complex, for $40 each. The face value of these tickets was not proven. The other transaction consisted of Murray's buying two tickets for more than face value from a St. Louis city police officer. Neither of these two intrastate transactions, nor the combination thereof, were sufficient to subject Murray's, a foreign corporation, to the registration requirements of § 351.570.1 RSMo 1986 because they were isolated transactions.

Section 351.570.2(10) RSMo 1986 specifically provides that a foreign corporation shall not be required to register as provided in § 351.570.1 RSMo 1986 where the foreign corporation's business transaction consists of: "Conducting an isolated transaction completed within a period of thirty days and not in the course of *a number of repeated transactions of like nature."* (Our emphasis). § 351.570.2(10) RSMo 1986.

In the instant case, the sale of two tickets for $40 each to Ms. McNamara was a "favored" sale to the leasing consultant. The evidence is insufficient to support a finding and the trial court did not find this to be a business transaction in the sense of a sale for economic gain or for profit. A sale of two tickets without profit was not a substantial part of Murray's ordinary business.

The purchase of tickets for above face value was a part of Murray's ordinary course of business. However, the purchase of two tickets above face value from the St. Louis city police officer was an isolated transaction. There is no evidence that Murray's purchased other tickets while in Missouri. This single transaction does not constitute a substantial part of Murray's ordinary business. *See Filmakers Releasing Organization,* 374 S.W.2d at 540. Murray's purchases a large number of tickets in its business. The purchase of the two tickets did not result in a profit sufficient to constitute a substantial part of Murray's ordinary business. Because Murray's did not transact a substantial part of its ordinary business in this state, the isolated purchase was insufficient to require registration.

The evidence would support a finding that Murray's performed one intrastate business transaction. It purchased two tickets above face value from a police officer. This was an isolated intrastate transaction because: (1) it was completed in a matter of minutes, not beyond the thirty day limit for such transactions in § 351.570.1 RSMo 1986; and, (2) it was not shown by evidence to be a purchase "in the course of a number of repeated transactions of like nature" as specified in § 351.570.2(10) RSMo 1986. Neither the interstate transactions nor the sale as a favor to the rental agent were intrastate business "transactions of like nature." There was no evidence of any previous or subsequent transactions by Murray's as intrastate transactions.

Accordingly, the court erred in applying the facts to § 351.570 RSMo 1986 and imposing a fine for failure of a foreign corporation to register in Missouri. On the facts, considered in a light most favorable to plaintiff state, the court erred as matter of law in applying the facts to the provisions of § 351.570 RSMo 1986. Murray's was not required to register as a foreign corporation to deliver tickets which were purchased interstate in Missouri. The single sale and the single isolated business purchase of tickets were insufficient to subject Murray's to the provisions of fine for violation.

We reverse.

SOUTH CAROLINA EQUIPMENT, INC. v. SHEEDY

353 N.W.2d 63 (Wis. App. 1984)

MOSER, JUDGE

[South Carolina Equipment, Inc. ("South Carolina") held a promissory note and a mortgage on some property owned by Ralph and June Jeka ("Jekas"). When Jekas defaulted on the mortgage, South Carolina commenced a foreclosure action in 1982. South Carolina had not previously qualified to do business in Wisconsin as a foreign corporation, but during the pendency of the action in 1983, South Carolina qualified and received a certificate of authority in September 1983.]

* * *

The trial court found that a foreign corporation must have standing to sue at the commencement of its suit, and that tardy filing of a certificate was not sufficient to give the trial court jurisdiction. The trial court therefore dismissed the complaint. It reasoned that since it had no jurisdiction over the subject matter of the original complaint then the "progeny" of cross complaints also should be dismissed. An order dismissing the complaints with the trial court's memorandum decision attached was entered. It is from that order that all parties appeal.

The issues on appeal are whether the trial court was correct in dismissing the complaint of South Carolina on jurisdictional grounds and whether after doing so it was correct in dismissing the cross complaints.

We must quickly lay to rest the jurisdiction error of the trial court. Our supreme court has previously held that the legislative purpose of sec. 180.847(1), Stats., was to facilitate the collection of Wisconsin foreign corporation registration fees, and that it had no function with respect to the jurisdiction of Wisconsin courts over foreign corporations.

The next logical question is how does one interpret the full meaning of the proscription that an unregistered foreign corporation cannot sue or defend suit until it has obtained registration. Commentators and the vast majority of courts have held that when an unregistered foreign corporation commences or defends a suit, and during the course of that suit complies with the registration law, that act is sufficient to allow it to maintain a court action or a defense. The courts that have made such findings have done so under controlling statutes, similar to Wisconsin's, that say a foreign corporation cannot maintain a suit until registered and certified.

Also, sec. 180.847, Stats., is substantially similar to sec. 124 of the Model Business Corporation Act. There is some difference of opinion in the jurisdictions following the Model Act provision as to when a corporation "maintains" an action. However, "[t]he trend of authority supports the proposition that the word 'maintain' merely means a continuation of a proceeding already begun and that a foreign corporation may qualify by obtaining a certificate of authority even after instituting an action."

We agree with the vast majority of courts' holdings in this field of law because our supreme court held in *Nagle Motors v. Volkswagen North Central Distributors, Inc.,* that this proscription is not jurisdictional and because the language of the statute specifically states:

Nor shall a civil action or special proceeding be *maintained* in any court of this state by any foreign corporation or a successor, assignee or grantee of such corporation on any right, claim or demand arising out of the transaction of business by such corporation in this state *at a time when such corporation was without such certificate of authority until a certificate of authority has been obtained by such corporation or, in the case of a successor, assignee or grantee of such corporation, until all fees which were payable by such corporation under this chapter not exceeding the maximum sum of $300 have been paid.* [Emphasis added.]

It is obvious from this clear and unambiguous language that once the Wisconsin certification fees are paid and the foreign corporation is registered, the impediments to sue and defend suits are immediately removed.

* * *

The trial court reasoned that regardless of South Carolina's certificate/registration impediment the validity of its mortgage contract was not impaired. What Lowe and Kaminski really sought in the trial court, and what they would have this court do, is to totally reject South Carolina's priority position because it was a non-certificate-holding foreign corporation. Neither court can accommodate Lowe and Kaminski.

Regardless of whether the trial court was incorrect in dismissing the various cross complaints, the court's priority listing, at least as far as placing South Carolina in a secondary position behind the Girard Bank claim and before the Lowe and Kaminski claims, was correct. An unregistered foreign corporation's inability to prosecute or defend court claims because of nonregistration does not impair the validity of its contracts or of its title to or interest in the property in this state. The legislature's adoption of sec. 180.847(2), Stats., by its clear and unequivocal language, voided all prior Wisconsin case law holding that all contracts of unregistered/uncertified foreign corporations were invalid. The contracts of and the interest in property of these types of corporations are now valid by statute. The determination of South Carolina's secondary priority claim position by its recorded mortgage is affirmed.

PROBLEMS

1. What is the difference between a foreign corporation and a domestic corporation?

2. A corporation doing business in a state other than that in which it is incorporated is subjected to
   a. service of process in the state in which it is doing business;
   b. taxation in the state in which it is doing business;
   c. qualification requirements of the state in which it is doing business; or
   d. all of the above.

3. The name of a corporation that wants to do business in another state may be
   a. reserved;
   b. registered;
   c. certificated;
   d. a and b but not c;
   e. b and c but not a; or
   f. a and c but not b.

4. Which of the following are *not* considered "transacting business within the state" under the Model Act?
   a. Operating a factory.
   b. Receiving orders for processing out of state.

   c. Holding meetings of directors and shareholders.
   d. Acting as an agent, contractor, or surety.
   e. Making loans secured by real estate.

5. State the typical sanction imposed upon a foreign corporation that has failed to qualify to do business in a foreign state.

6. What is the procedure required for a foreign corporation to stop doing business within a foreign state?

7. ABC Corporation is planning to do business in Montana only. Give three reasons why the incorporators should incorporate ABC Corporation in Montana rather than in Delaware.

8. Who signs an application for certificate of authority to do business?

9. Which of the following are responsible for deciding that a corporation will do business in a foreign state?
   a. Officers.
   b. Directors.
   c. Shareholders.
   d. Incorporators.

PRACTICE ASSIGNMENTS

1. Agri-Services, Inc., is a foreign corporation engaged in the purchase and sale of hay, feed yard chemicals, conditioners, and preservatives. Agri-Service is opening an office and storage facility in your city. It will invest $100,000 in this local operation, and it will employ seven persons in its office and warehouse. Agri-Services has 29,000 shares of common stock, $ .01 par value, issued and outstanding, and its principal place of business is 2309 South Elati Street, Metropolis, New State. Mary Naugle is the president and George Foreman is the secretary of the corporation. You will be the registered agent for Agri-Services in your state. Prepare all documents required for qualification under your local corporation code, inserting any assumed facts necessary to complete the forms.

2. Review your local corporation code and prepare a memorandum on the following issues:
   a. What are the penalties for a corporation conducting business without qualifying?
   b. What types of transactions do not constitute "doing business" for purposes of qualification?
   c. Under what circumstances must a corporation amend its qualification documents?
   d. What names are permitted to be used by a foreign corporation in your state?

3. Find a local business that is a foreign corporation and find out the state of its incorporation. Describe the reasons you believe the corporation was formed in the state of its domestication instead of being formed in your state.

4. Describe three reasons why you would incorporate a business in Delaware, even though its primary business activity is in your state.

ENDNOTES

1. "Selection of Jurisdiction" in Chapter 8.

2. See, e.g., Kan. Stat. Ann. § 17-7648.

3. See, e.g., W. Va. Code § 47-9-49.

4. See "Formation and Operation of a General Partnership" in Chapter 3.

5. See the sample resolution for organizational meetings of the board of directors in "Business Conducted at Organizational Meetings" in Chapter 10.

6. See Model Business Corporation Act (hereafter M.B.C.A.) § 15.01.

7. Del. Code Ann. tit. 8, § 373(a).

8. M.B.C.A. § 15.02.

9. Ala. Bus. Corp. Act § 10-2B-15.02.

10. See the schedule of penalties for doing business without qualifying, 1 Prentice-Hall, Corporations § 7103.

11. E.g., Delaware, Del. Code Ann. tit. 8, § 384; New York, N.Y. Bus. Corp. Law § 1303 (McKinney).

12. E.g., West Virginia, W. Va. Bus. Corp. Act § 31D-15-1503.

13. E.g., Nebraska, Neb. Rev. Stat. § 21-20.170.

14. 15 Pa. Stat. Ann. § 4124.

15. Oklahoma, Okla. Stat. Ann. tit. 18, § 1130 (West).

16. Virginia, Va. Code Ann. § 13.1-759 (Michie).

17. E.g., Wisconsin, Wis. Stat. Ann. § 180.1503 (West)(paid-in capital).

18. Compare M.B.C.A. §§ 4.01 and 15.06.

19. M.B.C.A. § 15.06.

20. See "Selection and Reservation or Corporate Name" in Chapter 8.

21. See M.B.C.A. § 4.03; and forms for registration and transfer of a corporate name in Chapter 8.

22. See M.B.C.A. §§ 15.07, 15.08.

23. M.B.C.A. § 15.10.

24. See M.B.C.A. § 15.05.

25. M.B.C.A. § 16.21.

26. E.g., Arizona, Ariz. Rev. Stat. Ann. § 10-1504(A).

27. E.g., Indiana, Ind. Code Ann. § 23-1-49-4 (Burns).

28. M.B.C.A. § 15.04.

29. See "Application for Certificate of Authority" and "Certificate of Authority" earlier in this chapter; M.B.C.A. § 15.04.

30. M.B.C.A. § 15.06.

31. See "Merger, Consolidation, and Exchange" in Chapter 15.

32. See M.B.C.A. § 11.06.

33. M.B.C.A. § 11.06.

34. M.B.C.A. § 11.07(d).

35. M.B.C.A. § 15.20.

36. E.g., Connecticut, Conn. Bus. Corp. Act § 33-932.

37. E.g., Massachusetts, Mass. Corp. Code Ch. 181 § 17.

38. M.B.C.A. § 15.31.

39. E.g., District of Columbia, D.C. Bus. Corp. Act § 29-101.115.

40. New Jersey, N.J. Stat. Ann. § 14A:13-10 (West).

CHANGES IN CORPORATE STRUCTURE AND DISSOLUTION

Previous chapters have considered corporate activities that occur in the ordinary course of business. The board of directors and the officers to whom the directors delegate authority are vested with continuing discretion in the management of business affairs; the shareholders exercise only indirect control over corporate operations through their election of the directors. This chapter is concerned with **extraordinary corporate activity** outside the scope of corporate business routine. Each extraordinary matter involves structural changes to the corporation and, in most cases, affects the ownership rights of the shareholders. Consequently, a common characteristic in each transaction is the requirement for shareholder approval. Moreover, the law governing extraordinary corporate activity grants special rights for shareholders in some cases, such as the right to have their shares appraised and purchased by the corporation if they disagree with the decision of management and their fellow shareholders. Special statutory procedures have been adopted by most states to regulate these structural changes.

AMENDMENT OF THE ARTICLES OF INCORPORATION

Any amendment of the articles of incorporation is a structural change of the corporation because the amendment changes the primary authorizing document for corporate existence. The corporation has the right to amend its articles of incorporation within the statutory guidelines established for the original articles of incorporation. Any provision may be inserted in an amendment if it would have been permitted in the original articles. Section 10.01 of the Model Business Corporation Act simply states that "a corporation may amend its articles of incorporation at any time to add or change a provision that is required or permitted in the articles of incorporation or to delete a provision not required in the articles of incorporation."

This broad statutory power to amend is typical of most modern state statutes on the subject of amendments to the articles of incorporation. The power to amend on any issue that may be permitted in the original articles of incorporation may be safely inferred from the general statutory authority.

Procedure

Section 10.05 of the Model Business Corporation Act permits the corporation's board of directors to adopt certain amendments to the articles of incorporation without shareholder action, including amendments to accomplish the following:

1. extend the duration of the corporation;
2. delete the names and addresses of the initial directors;
3. delete the name and address of the initial registered agent and registered office, if a statement of change is on file with the secretary of state;
4. change each issued and unissued authorized share of an outstanding class into a greater number of whole shares or increase the number of authorized shares to permit a share dividend if the corporation has only shares of that class outstanding;
5. change the corporate name by substituting the word *corporation, incorporated, company,* or *limited,* or the abbreviation *Corp., Inc., Co.,* or *Ltd.,* or a similar word or abbreviation in the name, or by adding, deleting, or changing a geographical attribution for the name; or
6. make any other changes permitted by the statute to be made without shareholder action (such as canceling shares reacquired by the corporation under section 6.31 or creating a series of shares under section 6.02).

If the incorporators would prefer that the shareholders always be involved in approving amendments to the articles, the power of the board of directors to adopt these amendments without shareholder action may be denied expressly in the articles themselves.

In the usual amendment procedure, the board of directors adopts a resolution that sets forth the proposed amendment and directs that it be submitted to a vote at an annual or special meeting of the shareholders.[1]

EXAMPLE

Resolution to Change Corporate Name

RESOLVED, that Article I of the Articles of Incorporation of The Nobles Company be amended to read as follows:

"The name of this corporation is The Nobility Company."

FURTHER RESOLVED, that this amendment shall be submitted to the vote of the shareholders at a special meeting called for the purpose of considering the amendment.

Some states permit the shareholders to propose an amendment to the articles of incorporation.[2] The concerted action of a specified number of shareholders—for example, the holders of one-tenth of the outstanding voting stock of the corporation—is required, and those shareholders may petition the board of directors to propose the amendment or may request that the president of the company call a meeting of shareholders to consider the proposed amendment.

Written notice of the proposed amendment must be given within the statutory period to each shareholder of record entitled to vote upon the proposal.[3] In many cases, the proposal is submitted to the shareholders at their annual meeting, and the written proposal may be included in the notice of the annual meeting. If a special meeting is called, the notice must state the reason for the meeting—that is, to consider a proposed amendment to the articles of incorporation.[4] In jurisdictions where the shareholders may unanimously consent in writing in lieu of a meeting, the consent procedure may be used to consider and approve the amendment.[5]

Adoption of the Amendment

The number of shareholder votes required to approve a proposed amendment to the articles of incorporation may be greater than the number required for routine shareholder matters. Moreover, if the amendment affects the rights of the shareholders of a certain class, those shareholders must approve the amendment, even if they otherwise have no voting rights.

The Model Business Corporation Act formerly required the affirmative vote of the holders of two-thirds of the shares entitled to vote, but a recent amendment to the act has reduced the vote to a majority. The reduced voting provision has been accepted in most of the jurisdictions that follow the act.

If a proposed amendment affects the rights of the holders of a certain class of shares, those shares are entitled to vote as a class on the amendment's adoption. An amendment is deemed to affect the rights of a particular class when it increases or decreases the aggregate number of authorized shares of the class, or modifies the number of shares held by shareholders of the class. Changing any of the designations, preferences, limitations, or rights of the shares of the class also qualifies for special approval. If the proposed amendment creates a new class having rights that are prior or superior to the rights of the class, provides for an exchange of shares of another class into shares of the class, or divides the class into series, class voting applies. Finally, any amendment that limits or denies the preemptive rights of the shares of the class, or affects accrued but undeclared dividends of the class, must be approved by the class.[6] In most states, a change in the par value of the shares of the class also requires a class vote.

Some examples are appropriate. If the corporation has a class of common stock and a class of nonvoting 6% cumulative preferred stock with a par value of $100, the holders of the preferred shares would be entitled to vote on all amendments to accomplish the following:

1. increase par value to $200 per share;
2. change dividends from cumulative to noncumulative, but only if dividends have accrued at the time the amendment is proposed;
3. add a new class of preferred stock with equal, prior, or superior liquidation preferences to the existing preferred class;
4. permit the directors to issue the remaining authorized shares of the preferred class in series; and
5. add an additional one thousand authorized shares of the preferred class.

Each of these amendments would directly affect the preferred shareholders by diluting their ownership interest or altering their preferred status, and in order to pass such an amendment, the holders of a majority (or two-thirds, depending upon the jurisdiction) of the shares of the class must vote affirmatively. The class would not have a separate voice on other amendments, however. If the corporation were to change its stated purposes, or its name, the nonvoting class could not vote, even though these amendments might indirectly affect the value or quality of the shares.

Since shareholder approval is required for adoption of an amendment to the articles of incorporation, it would be difficult to amend the articles before any shares have been issued unless there were a separate procedure for that contingency. The Model Business Corporation Act provides such a procedure in section 10.02, and many states have comparable provisions. If shares have not been issued, an amendment to the articles of incorporation may be adopted by the resolution of the incorporators or the initial board of directors named in the articles of incorporation.

Articles of Amendment

The adopted amendment is set forth in the articles of amendment (see Exhibit 15–1, Articles of Amendment), which are filed with the appropriate state official. Additional fees and franchise taxes may be due under the state statute when the articles of amendment are filed.

In addition to the statement of the amendment, the Model Business Corporation Act requires that the articles of amendment contain information about the corporation, whether the amendment was duly approved by the incorporators, directors, or shareholders, and the date of adoption of the amendment.[7]

In most states the amendment becomes effective when it has been accepted for filing by the appropriate filing officer.[8] In some states, there may be conditions to the filing officer's acceptance for filing, such as consent of the state's taxing authorities when certain[9] tax consequences may result from the amendment. In most states and under the Model Business Corporation Act, it is now possible to specify a delayed effective time and date up to ninety days following the filing of the amendment.[10]

Exhibit 15–1.

Articles of Amendment
(Delaware)

STATE OF DELAWARE
CERTIFICATE OF AMENDMENT
OF CERTIFICATE OF INCORPORATION

_____

a corporation organized and existing under and by virtue of the General
Corporation Law of the State of Delaware.

DOES HEREBY CERTIFY:

FIRST: That at a meeting of the Board of Directors of_____

_____

resolutions were duly adopted setting forth a proposed amendment of the
Certificate of Incorporation of said corporation, declaring said amendment to
be advisable and calling a meeting of the stockholders of said corporation for
consideration thereof. The resolution setting forth the proposed amendment is
as follows:

RESOLVED, that the Certificate of Incorporation of this corporation be amended
by changing the Article thereof numbered "_____" so that, as
amended, said Article shall be and read as follows:

_____

_____

SECOND: That thereafter, pursuant to resolution of its Board of Directors, a
special meeting of the stockholders of said corporation was duly called and held
upon notice in accordance with Section 222 of the General Corporation Law of
the State of Delaware at which meeting the necessary number of shares as required
by statute were voted in favor of the amendment.

THIRD: That said amendment was duly adopted in accordance with the
provisions of Section 242 of the General Corporation Law of the State of
Delaware.

FOURTH: That the capital of said corporation shall not be reduced under or by
reason of said amendment.

IN WITNESS WHEREOF, said_____
has caused this certificate to be signed by
_____, an Authorized Officer,
this _____ day of _____, _____.

BY:_____
                    Authorized Officer

TITLE:_____

NAME:_____
                    Print or Type

Finally, the additional formalities for amendment of the articles of incorporation parallel the formalities for the articles of incorporation in each jurisdiction.[11] Thus, a jurisdiction that requires that the articles be filed with a county clerk in addition to the secretary of state will also require that an amendment to the articles be so filed. Similarly, if the state statute requires that the articles of incorporation be published in a newspaper, the amendment to the articles also must be published.

Restated Articles of Incorporation

If the original articles of incorporation have been amended several times, it may be difficult to determine the current status of the articles by studying the files of the secretary of state. Consequently, most statutes permit a **restatement** or composite of the articles of incorporation whereby all past amendments are consolidated with the original articles of incorporation into a new document, which supersedes the original articles and the filed amendments. This procedure is also used if the corporation was formed many years ago and several amendments to the articles of incorporation are required to conform to current law. Under section 10.07 of the Model Business Corporation Act, shareholder approval is not necessary to restate the articles of incorporation, since restatement is only a mechanical process of putting the corporation's file in order. If a new amendment is to be added in connection with the restatement, shareholder approval is required. The procedure for restatement is specified in the statute, and a restated certificate of incorporation is usually issued (see Exhibit 15–2, Restated Articles of Incorporation).[12]

MERGER AND EXCHANGE

Merger and share exchange are statutory devices for combining two or more corporations into one corporate entity or into a parent-subsidiary relationship. In a merger, the acquiring corporation takes over the assets, liabilities, and business of the merging corporation, and one of the corporations in the transaction ceases to exist. In a share exchange, the acquiring corporation exchanges some of its shares for some or all of the shares of the acquired corporation. If fewer than all of the acquired corporation's shares are exchanged, the corporations continue their businesses in a parent-subsidiary relationship. It is also possible for two corporations to form a new corporation, which exchanges its shares for all of the shares of both acquired corporations. That transaction has historically been called a consolidation. The corporate parties to these transactions are called **constituent corporations**, and that terminology is used in the discussion of these transactions.

A **merger** is a device whereby one or more constituent corporations merge into and become a part of another constituent corporation. The corporations that merge into the other corporation cease to exist after the merger. The **surviving corporation** continues to exist after the merger, and takes over the assets and liabilities of the merging corporations. The survivor also takes over the stockholders, personnel, business contacts, and other normal business activities of the terminated corporations. To illustrate, suppose the ABC Corporation and the XYZ Corporation agree to merge, and their agreement provides that the XYZ Corporation will survive the merger. When the merger is accomplished, the ABC Corporation will no longer exist, and all of its assets, liabilities, and other business incidents will belong to XYZ Corporation, which will maintain its original corporate structure throughout, unless the merger requires certain amendments to the structure.

In a **consolidation transaction**, one or more constituent corporations join together to form a new corporation, pooling their assets, liabilities, and business, and transferring them to a new consolidated entity. The hypothetical ABC and XYZ Corporations could consolidate by forming the LMN Corporation and by transferring all of their respective business to this new corporation. In a consolidation, all constituent corporations cease to exist, and the consolidation results with the combined businesses of the constituent corporations.

Exhibit 15–2.

Restated Articles of
Incorporation (Maine)

Filing Fee $80.00

**DOMESTIC
BUSINESS CORPORATION**

STATE OF MAINE

**RESTATED ARTICLES
OF INCORPORATION**

_____
Deputy Secretary of State

A True Copy When Attested By Signature

_____
Deputy Secretary of State

_____
(Name of Corporation)

Pursuant to 13-C MRSA ß1007, the undersigned corporation executes and delivers the following Restated Articles of Incorporation:

FIRST: The text of the restated articles of incorporation as set forth in Exhibit _____ attached contains the same information and provisions as are required for original articles.

SECOND: ("X" one box only.)

☐   The restated articles of incorporation consolidate all amendments into a single document **OR**

☐   If a new amendment is included in the restated articles of incorporation the following must be completed:

The text of the new amendment was adopted on (date) _____ and was duly approved as follows: ("X" one box only.)

☐   by the incorporators ñ shareholder approval was not required **OR**
☐   by the board of directors ñ shareholder approval was not required **OR**
☐   by the shareholders in the manner required by this Act and by the articles of incorporation.

THIRD: If the text of the new amendment provides for an exchange, reclassification or cancellation of issued shares, provisions for implementing the amendment, if not contained in the amendment itself, are set forth in Exhibit _____ or as follows:

FOURTH: The effective date of the restated articles of incorporation (if other than the date of filing of the restated articles of incorporation) is _____.

DATED _____   *By _____
                                                                         (signature of any duly authorized person)

                                                            _____
                                                                         (type or print name and capacity)

*This document **MUST** be signed by any duly authorized officer **OR** the clerk. (ß121.5)

Please remit your payment made payable to the Maine Secretary of State.

**SUBMIT COMPLETED FORMS TO: CORPORATE EXAMINING SECTION, SECRETARY OF STATE,
101 STATE HOUSE STATION, AUGUSTA, ME 04333-0101**
FORM NO. MBCA-6A   7/1/2003   **TEL. (207) 624-7740**

The revised Model Business Corporation Act has deleted all references to consolidation. In modern corporate practice, consolidation transactions are obsolete, since it is nearly always advantageous for one of the constituent corporations in the transaction to be the surviving corporation. If creation of a new entity is considered desirable, the new act provides that a new entity may be created for the merger and the disappearing constituent corporations are simply merged into it. Many state statutes still refer to consolidation transactions, however, and provide a statutory procedure by which to accomplish them. Consequently, this text still refers to the consolidation as a separate transaction, although it will have limited usefulness in the future.

A more cautious combination than a merger or consolidation is an **exchange**. Neither corporation ceases to exist in an exchange, but some or all of the shares of one corporation are exchanged for some or all of the shares of the other corporation. For example, the XYZ Corporation could exchange a certain number of its common shares for all of the preferred shares of ABC Corporation or all of the common shares of ABC Corporation, or it could complete some combination of those transactions. If XYZ Corporation exchanged shares of its common stock for *all* shares of ABC Corporation, common and preferred, the exchange would begin to look like a merger, and it might be necessary to follow merger rules. The charts on the next page illustrate how mergers, consolidations, and exchanges differ.

Merger, consolidation, and exchange involve structural changes and affect share ownership in the constituent corporations. Consider the shareholders of the ABC Corporation in a merger with the XYZ Corporation. After the merger, their corporation will no longer exist, and they will rightfully expect to be consulted for their approval of the transaction. The shareholders of the expiring constituent corporation usually receive a specified number of shares of the surviving corporation or cash in return for their original shares. The shareholders of the XYZ Corporation also should approve the transaction because their share ownership will be diluted when shares are issued to all of the shareholders of the late ABC Corporation. Consolidation

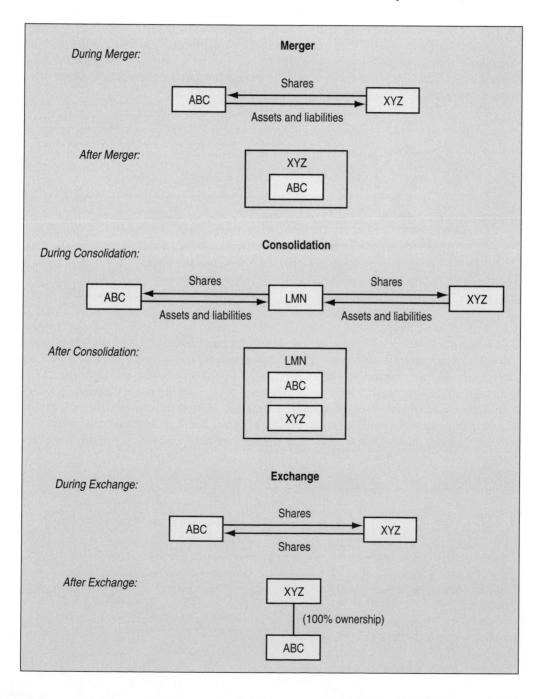

and exchange transactions involve the same equities, since shareholders of both constituent corporations will probably receive shares of the new consolidated corporation or receive them in exchange for their original shares.

Variations on the Merger Transaction

In many merger transactions, a newly formed subsidiary is used to accomplish the transaction. Say, for instance, that ABC Corporation and XYZ Corporation desire to merge. Because ABC Corporation is involved in a high-risk business (such as manufacturing potentially dangerous products that may cause injuries to consumers), the managers of XYZ Corporation decide to insulate the assets of their corporation by forming a new corporation to accomplish the merger. When the subsidiary is formed, XYZ Corporation owns all of its stock, so it has complete control over the subsidiary's activities. The new corporation will be entitled to limited liability when it is formed, so the potential products liability problems of ABC that will transfer in the merger will not expose the assets of the parent corporation, XYZ Corporation, after the merger. The merger is accomplished by merging ABC Corporation with the subsidiary. In the transaction, the shareholders of ABC Corporation will receive shares of XYZ Corporation, and the assets and liabilities of ABC Corporation will be transferred to the wholly owned subsidiary corporation of XYZ. This transaction is called a **triangular merger** because of the three-way transaction by which it is accomplished.

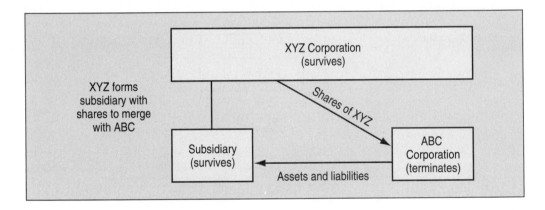

Another three-way merger is called a **reverse triangular merger**. This is the same transaction as a triangular merger, except the newly formed subsidiary is merged into the target corporation. In this transaction, ABC Corporation would become the wholly owned subsidiary of XYZ Corporation. This type of merger is used when the target corporation, ABC Corporation, has valuable licenses or other contractual arrangements that might terminate if the corporation ceases to exist. Accordingly, the effect of this transaction is to allow the target corporation to continue to survive, but as a wholly owned subsidiary of the acquiring corporation, XYZ Corporation.

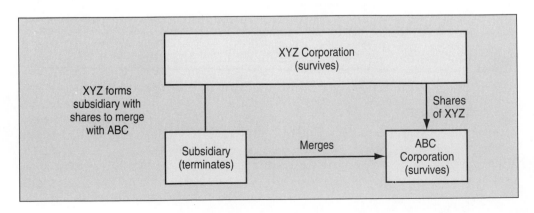

Tax Terminology

In tax terminology, the merger, consolidation, or exchange may be referred to as a **reorganization**. Several different types of reorganizations follow:

A. **Reorganization**—a statutory merger or consolidation accomplished under the state corporate statutes, as described in this section.

B. **Reorganization**—the acquisition of one corporation by another or a combination of two corporations through a share exchange, but not a complete corporate law merger or consolidation. In a type B reorganization, one corporation swaps its voting shares for a controlling block (80% to 100%) of the shares of another corporation. Both corporations continue to exist, so a complete merger or consolidation is not accomplished. The acquired corporation becomes a subsidiary of the acquiring corporation, which maintains at least an 80% controlling interest in the subsidiary's stock.

C. **Reorganization**—the exchange of voting shares of the acquiring corporation for substantially all of the assets of the acquired corporation. Since both corporations continue to exist, this transaction is not a true merger or consolidation, but neither is it an exchange, because the stock was traded for assets, not for other stock.

Procedure

The board of directors' resolution is the procedural starting point for a merger, consolidation, or exchange. The boards of directors of both corporations approve the transaction, stating the names of the constituent corporations; the terms of the proposed combination; and the manner and basis for converting the shares of the constituent corporations into shares of the exchanging corporation in an exchange, or shares or cash of the surviving corporation in a merger. The plan approved by resolution also must state changes to be made in the articles of incorporation of the surviving corporations. The plan may include any other terms necessary to accomplish the transaction.[13]

The resolution of the board of directors is the first statutory step toward approval of these transactions, but it is only the tip of the iceberg. Notice that the resolution must contain the terms and conditions of the proposed transaction. This unassuming requirement represents the culmination of several months (maybe years) of planning, drafting, and negotiation between the parties to establish those terms. Corporate management will have labored over a lengthy agreement containing the terms of the structural changes that it believes will be acceptable to the shareholders and in the best business interests of all corporate parties. New corporate purposes must be drafted to account for the expanded business; the positions of the directors and officers of the constituent corporations must be placed or abandoned in the surviving or new corporation; the accounts of all corporate parties must be combined and reconciled; and bylaws must be harmonized. Certain restrictions regarding dividends, sales of stock, issuance of options, or other activities out of the ordinary course of business are usually placed on the constituent corporations during the pendency of the transaction. At various stages of these negotiations, the corporate parties usually exchange **letters of intent**, which express in writing their respective understandings of the terms of the proposed agreement. Further negotiations are conducted based upon these stated positions, and eventually the negotiations result in the final agreement, or in abandonment of the transaction if the negotiations reach an impasse. After acceptable terms are drafted, a proposed closing date is set, considering the other preparatory procedures that must be accomplished before closing. Rulings on the tax ramifications of the transaction are usually required, and the impact of the securities laws on the transfers of stock should be examined. Current accounting opinions should be scheduled, and financial reports are supplemented with current information. Documents must be reviewed by the attorneys, accountants, and other experts for all parties, and appropriate directors' and shareholders' meetings must be held in accordance with state law. That brings us back to the statutory requirements, which begin with the directors' resolution to approve the merger or exchange plan.

The resolution should reflect that the plan for the combination has been presented to the meeting of directors and approved by the directors, should authorize appropriate corporate officers to call a meeting of shareholders to consider the plan, and should further authorize the officers to file the necessary documents to accomplish the plan if the shareholders of the constituent corporations approve it.

| EXAMPLE | **Resolution to Approve Merger** |

RESOLVED, that the board of directors hereby recommends and approves the proposed Plan of Merger between this corporation and The Nobles Company, a Colorado corporation, substantially in the form presented to this meeting, and the directors and officers of this corporation are hereby authorized to enter into said plan by executing the same, under the seal of this corporation, and

FURTHER RESOLVED, that said plan as entered into by the directors and officers of this corporation be submitted to the holders of the common stock of this corporation at a special meeting to be called for the purpose of considering and adopting said plan on August 15, 2005, at 2:00 P.M., at the offices of the corporation, and

FURTHER RESOLVED, that July 15, 2005, is hereby fixed as the record date for the determination of the holders of the common stock entitled to notice of and to vote at such special meeting, and

FURTHER RESOLVED, that in the event said plan shall be approved and adopted at the special meeting of the shareholders of this corporation in accordance with the statutory requirements of the State of Colorado, and shall also be approved and adopted by the shareholders of The Nobles Company in accordance with the statutory requirements of the State of Colorado, then the Secretary of this corporation is hereby authorized to certify upon said plan that it has been adopted, and the President and Secretary of this corporation are hereby authorized to execute articles of merger in the name and on behalf of this corporation and under its seal and to cause the same to be filed in the Office of the Secretary of State of the State of Colorado.

The Model Business Corporation Act requires shareholder approval by the shareholders of both corporations. Some states limit the approval of an exchange to only the shareholders of the corporation whose shares are being exchanged.

With respect to mergers, there are two important exceptions to the requirement or shareholder vote. The first exception is that under the revised Model Business Corporation Act, a shareholder vote of the surviving corporation on a merger is not required if

1. the corporation will survive the merger;
2. the corporation's articles will not be changed in the transaction;
3. each shareholder of the surviving corporation will have the same number of shares with the same rights after the merger;
4. the issuance of shares in the merger will not cause an increase in the outstanding shares above 20% of the voting power of the shares.[14]

This transaction is called a **small-impact merger**; the shareholders of the surviving corporation are not required to vote on the plan because it has such a small impact on their ownership rights. Following the merger, the shareholders of the surviving corporation have essentially the same rights and shares, subject to a dissolution of up to 20%, but they are otherwise unaffected by the transaction.

The second exception is contained in section 11.05 of the Model Business Corporation Act. If a parent corporation owns at least 90% of the voting power of a subsidiary corporation, the parent may merge the subsidiary into itself without shareholder approval of either corporation. This is called a **short-form merger**. Since the parent corporation already owns at least 90% of the voting power of the subsidiary, the two respective business organizations are practically merged anyway. In addition, a shareholder vote at the subsidiary corporation level would be useless, since the parent already owns 90% of the voting power, and everyone knows how the parent corporation would vote.

Shareholder approval of a plan of merger, consolidation, or exchange is very similar to that required for amendment of the articles of incorporation and other structural changes. The plan may be considered at either a special or an annual meeting of shareholders. The Model Business Corporation Act requires notice to be given to every shareholder, whether or not entitled to vote, and the notice must always state that the plan of merger, consolidation, or exchange is to be considered at the meeting.[15] Most states require that notice be sent to every shareholder and that it contain a statement of the purpose of the meeting. Further, the notice may have to inform shareholders of their dissenting rights.

Because these transactions affect all corporate shares, many jurisdictions permit all shares to vote on the plan, whether or not they have the right to vote on other corporate matters. The Model Business Corporation Act originally demanded these expanded voting rights but later was amended to include only regular voting shares on the theory that shareholders with non-voting stock had waived the right to vote unless the shares of their particular class would be directly affected by the plan. Presently, section 11.04 of the act requires the affirmative vote of the holders of the majority of voting stock and the affirmative vote of the holders of shares of each class entitled to vote, based upon the same tests for class voting as those applied to amendments to the articles of incorporation.[16] Many states require the affirmative vote of the holders of two-thirds of the voting shares.

Shareholders are almost uniformly granted the right to dissent to these transactions and to demand payment for their shares.[17]

Articles of Merger, Consolidation, or Exchange

Following the shareholder approval, articles of merger, consolidation, or share exchange are prepared and filed with the appropriate state official (see Exhibit 15–3, Articles of Merger). Many state statutes have no provision for separate articles and instead require that the plan of merger or exchange, duly certified as having been approved, be filed. Publication also may be required, paralleling the formalities for the original articles of incorporation.[18]

Section 11.06 of the Model Business Corporation Act establishes the contents of the articles of merger or share exchange, including

1. the names of the parties to the merger;
2. the amendments, if any, to the articles of incorporation of the surviving corporation;
3. a statement whether or not shareholder approval was required, and, if so, that the merger was duly approved by the shareholders and by each voting group whose approval was required;
4. for foreign corporations that are parties to the merger, a statement that the participation of the foreign corporation in the transaction was authorized by the law of the state of its formation.

As with other filings, the articles of merger or share exchange will be effective when they are accepted for filing by the secretary of state or other appropriate filing officer.[19] In addition, most states and the Model Business Corporation Act provide that the effectiveness of the transaction may be delayed until a date fixed in the plan, not longer than 90 days after filing.[20]

The delayed effectiveness alternative is particularly desirable where filings are required in several states and simultaneous filing is impracticable. The effective date may be set at a specified time, and all the filings may be completed before that date. For example, if a corporation in New York is acquiring two corporations, one in Florida and one in California, the merger will require filings in all three states. The companies may want the merger to be effective as of 12:01 A.M. January 1 (so the three companies will be fully combined at the beginning of the year). It will not be possible to be physically in New York, Florida, and California at that time and date to make the required filings. The delayed effective date permits the filing of all necessary documents with the appropriate state filing offices in December. If the documents state that the merger will be effective at the agreed time, it will be effective as stated.

Statutory Effect

When the merger or consolidation becomes effective, all constituent corporate parties to the plan become a single corporation (the designated survivor in a merger or the new corporation

Exhibit 15–3.

Articles of Merger
(Massachusetts)

FEDERAL IDENTIFICATION   FEDERAL IDENTIFICATION
NO. _____   NO. _____

Examiner

The Commonwealth of Massachusetts

William Francis Galvin
Secretary of the Commonwealth
One Ashburton Place, Boston, Massachusetts 02108-1512

ARTICLES OF *CONSOLIDATION / *MERGER
(General Laws, Chapter 156B, Section 78)

*Consolidation / *merger of

_____

_____

_____

_____

_____ ,

the constituent corporations, into

_____ ,

*a new corporation / *one of the constituent corporations.

The undersigned officers of each of the constituent corporations certify under the penalties of perjury as follows:

1. An agreement of *consolidation / *merger has been duly adopted in compliance with the requirements of General Laws, Chapter 156B, Section 78, and will be kept as provided by Subsection (d) thereof. The *resulting / *surviving corporation will furnish a copy of said agreement to any of its stockholders, or to any person who was a stockholder of any constituent corporation, upon written request and without charge.

2. The effective date of the *consolidation / *merger determined pursuant to the agreement of *consolidation / *merger shall be the date approved and filed by the Secretary of the Commonwealth. If a *later* effective date is desired, specify such date which shall not be more than *thirty days* after the date of filing:

3. (For a merger)
**The following amendments to the Articles of Organization of the *surviving* corporation have been effected pursuant to the agreement of merger:

C   ☐
P   ☐
M   ☐
R.A. ☐

*Delete the inapplicable word.   **If there are no provisions state "None".
Note: If the space provided under any article or item on this form is insufficient, additions shall be set forth on separate 8 1/2 x 11 sheets of paper with a left margin of at least 1 inch. Additions to more than one article may be made on a single sheet as long as each article requiring each addition is clearly indicated.

156b78m 4/4/00

P.C.

---

in a consolidation), and the other corporations cease to exist. The surviving or new corporation has all the rights and privileges, is vested with all the assets, and is responsible for all liabilities and obligations of the constituent corporations. The articles of incorporation of the surviving corporation are deemed amended to the extent provided in the merger plan, filed as a part of the articles of merger. Thus, if the plan requires modifications to the structure of the surviving corporation, there is no need to comply separately with the statutory procedure for amendments to the articles of incorporation.[21] In the case of consolidation, the articles of consolidation are deemed to be the articles of incorporation of the new consolidated corporation.

Exhibit 15–3.

(continued)

(For a consolidation)

(a) The purpose of the *resulting* corporation is to engage in the following business activities:

(b) State the total number of shares and the par value, if any, of each class of stock which the *resulting* corporation is authorized to issue.

WITHOUT PAR VALUE		WITH PAR VALUE		
TYPE	NUMBER OF SHARES	TYPE	NUMBER OF SHARES	PAR VALUE
Common:		Common:		
Preferred:		Preferred:		

**(c) If more than one class of stock is authorized, state a distinguishing designation for each class and provide a description of the preferences, voting powers, qualifications, and special or relative rights or privileges of each class and of each series then established.

**(d) The restrictions, if any, on the transfer of stock contained in the agreement of consolidation are:

**(e) Other lawful provisions, if any, for the conduct and regulation of the business and affairs of the corporation, for its voluntary dissolution, or for limiting, defining, or regulating the powers of the corporation, or of its directors or stockholders, or of any class of stockholders:

**If there are no provisions state "None".*

(continued)

Hostile Takeovers

Not all business combination transactions are friendly. While many mergers and share exchanges result from negotiations among corporations that desire to combine their businesses, in some cases a corporation or individual will attempt to take over the operations of another corporation by using these statutory combinations against the will of the other corporation and its shareholders.

Exhibit 15–3.

(continued)

4. The information contained in Item 4 is *not* a *permanent* part of the Articles of Organization of the *resulting / *surviving corporation.

(a) The street address of the *resulting / *surviving corporation in Massachusetts is: *(post office boxes are not acceptable)*

(b) The name, residential address, and post office address of each director and officer of the *resulting / *surviving corporation is:

NAME	RESIDENTIAL ADDRESS	POST OFFICE ADDRESS

President:

Treasurer:

Clerk:

Directors:

(c) The fiscal year (i.e. tax year) of the *resulting / *surviving corporation shall end on the last day of the month of:

(d) The name and business address of the resident agent, if any, of the *resulting / *surviving corporation is:

The undersigned officers of the several constituent corporations listed above further state under the penalties of perjury as to their respective corporations that the agreement of *consolidation / *merger has been duly executed on behalf of such corporation and duly approved by the stockholders of such corporation in the manner required by General Laws, Chapter 156B, Section 78.

_____ , *President / *Vice President,

_____ , *Clerk / *Assistant Clerk,

of _____ .
                                    (Name of constituent corporation)

_____ , *President / *Vice President,

_____ , *Clerk / *Assistant Clerk,

of _____ .
                                    (Name of constituent corporation)

Delete the inapplicable words.

One corporation may perceive a profitable area for business expansion, but rather than develop its own operations for this purpose, it may attempt to take over another corporation that is already successfully engaged in that type of business. Another corporation's business may be deteriorating because management has lost interest or has been protecting its own expensive, personal objectives (such as high salaries or generous benefit plans). The performance of this corporation may be mediocre. Other companies or individuals may believe that if this corporation's management is replaced, the corporation would be substantially more profitable. These outsiders may see an opportunity to acquire control of the corporation, eliminate its existing management, and replace its management with more effective persons who will make the business profitable. In this situation, the prospect of a business combination becomes an adversary transaction. Existing management circles its wagons to protect its position and resist the potential takeover, while the acquiring parties aggressively attempt to secure control of

Exhibit 15–3.

(continued)

THE COMMONWEALTH OF MASSACHUSETTS

ARTICLES OF *CONSOLIDATION / *MERGER
(General Laws, Chapter 156B, Section 78)

I hereby approve the within Articles of *Consolidation / *Merger and,
the filing fee in the amount of $ _____ , having been paid,
said articles are deemed to have been filed with me this _____
day of _____ , 20 _____ .

Effective date: _____

WILLIAM FRANCIS GALVIN
Secretary of the Commonwealth

TO BE FILLED IN BY CORPORATION
Contact information:

_____

_____

_____

Telephone: _____

Email: _____

A copy this filing will be available on-line at www.state.ma.us/sec/cor
once the document is filed.

the corporation to modify its business structure and objectives. Note that this situation may create a conflict of interest for the management of the target corporation, since they have fiduciary duties to the shareholders of the corporation who should want the corporation to be more profitable, but members of management also want to save their jobs and preserve their benefits. The extent to which management resists a takeover attempt must be carefully reviewed by counsel to ensure that the fiduciary duties to shareholders are not abandoned in favor of management's self-interest.

The aggressors will attempt to use statutory procedures to acquire the business operations for their own gain. With public corporations, stock is readily available for purchase in the market. Consequently, a purchaser can buy enough shares of a publicly held corporation in the market to control the shareholder vote on a merger or similar transaction. Even in a closely held corporation, an outsider can acquire a substantial block of stock that will allow that outsider to control corporate activities. It is for this reason that close corporations usually have shareholder agreements in place that prevent the sale of stock to outsiders without a first offering of the shares to other shareholders or to the company.

Not all acquisitions are for the altruistic business reason of improving the company. Many investors search for stock in companies that may be underpriced either because the market has responded negatively to publicity concerning the company or because the business of the company is in trouble and the market is reflecting uncertainty about the future of the company. These investors may purchase substantial blocks of stock to acquire control, and then use the stock as a basis upon which to make a personal profit. An investor may sell control back to the company when the directors seek to protect their own positions without having to deal with new shareholders who may threaten their future. The term **greenmail** describes situations in which investors profit from their newly acquired control by selling it back to the corporation or to other interested shareholders at a premium.

Several corporate procedures and statutory rules have been developed to avoid abuses that are likely to occur in a hostile takeover.

Corporate Structure Defenses When management of a corporation perceives that the corporation is vulnerable to a hostile takeover, certain structural changes can be made to the corporation to discourage the possibility of a takeover. The structure of the corporation can be changed only with the approval of the shareholders, but management frequently can convince the shareholders that the company's vulnerability may result in a substantial loss of the value of its shares if an outsider acquires control of the company through discount purchases of the company stock in a depressed market.

Management usually proposes that the stock structure be altered to provide for special rights to existing stockholders in case of a potential takeover. These special rights are frequently called **"poison pills,"** because existing stockholders can exercise them in the event of a takeover to make the takeover ineffective. A new class of shares is created that has rights that are superior to those of all other shares in the corporation. The corporation declares a dividend and distributes either the newly created shares or rights to purchase the newly created shares to its existing shareholders. These shares provide that in the event of a proposed merger or share exchange, the existing shareholders will have greater rights than any shareholder who has purchased without having the newly created rights or shares. These plans come in various forms, but the general approach of each is to permit the existing shareholders to dilute an interest or acquire a substantially greater interest in the corporation as soon as a triggering event, such as a merger, consolidation, or share exchange, is proposed. Management of the corporation is given the right to redeem these special shares (and thereby neutralize the poison) in the event of a friendly takeover.

Management may be able to devise its own defense to a hostile takeover without involving its shareholders. All the officers of a public company recently announced a **people pill**, or *"suicide pact,"* where these officers agreed that if *any* of them were demoted or fired after a change of control of their company, they would *all* resign. Any purchaser would have to choose between retaining all the existing management without change or losing the entire executive staff at once. Again, such an agreement may not be consistent with the fiduciary duties of these officers, and the conflict of interest inherent in such an agreement would undoubtedly require that it be prepared and reviewed by lawyers other than the corporate counsel.

Statutory Rules Many states have adopted statutes designed to discourage hostile takeovers of their local corporations. These statutes recognize that a hostile takeover usually starts by a market acquisition of controlling shares. Once the **control shares** have been acquired by an investor, the investor usually can cause corporate action to be taken to merge, consolidate, or exchange shares with another company. Investors who purchase shares with this objective are called **"sharks,"** and many of the statutory provisions and corporate structures that can be developed to prevent these takeovers are called **"shark repellant."** The effect of these statutory provisions is to place any persons who acquire control shares at a disadvantage as long as they do not have the consensus of the other shareholders on their plans for the business.

One example of such statutory provisions is the procedures for control share acquisitions found in several states, such as Florida and Indiana. Control shares are defined to mean the shares that would have voting power sufficient to entitle the owner to control the affairs of the corporation. They usually are described in terms of thresholds of percentage of voting power. For example, in Florida, the restrictions on control shares are triggered whenever a shareholder acquires 20% of all voting power in a corporation. A second trigger occurs at the acquisition of 30%, and a third occurs when 50% of the voting power is acquired. In a publicly held corporation, only 20% of the entire voting power of the corporation may substantially control the outcome of a vote on a merger or consolidation, but 50% certainly will control the vote.

Whenever a person acquires sufficient control shares, the acquiring shareholder will not be entitled to vote the shares unless the other shareholders affirmatively decide to permit the shareholder to exercise voting power. Voting power is lost and must be affirmatively restored at each triggering event. In other words, the effect of the statute is to take away all votes of the shares acquired until the acquiring shareholder has been able to convince the other shareholders (and probably management) that his or her motives with respect to the control of the corporation are not adverse to the interests of the corporation and the other shareholders. The statute also allows the corporation's articles of incorporation or bylaws to provide that control shares acquired can be redeemed by the corporation at the fair value of the shares, permitting the corporation to buy out a hostile investor, rather than permit the investor to vote the shares in a manner that will cause harm to other shareholders.

Another approach to statutory protection involves statutory rules relating to mergers and share exchanges with **affiliated corporations**. In a hostile takeover context, one corporation may acquire a substantial number of shares in another corporation. Once the corporation has acquired those shares, it may then elect to vote to merge the acquired corporation into its own operations. Such an action may be against the business policies or best interests of the management and shareholders of the acquired corporation. Several state statutes provide that once a corporation acquires a certain percentage of the shares in another corporation, the corporations become affiliated. Then, the shareholder vote required to accomplish a business combination among the affiliated corporations is automatically increased from a majority to a two-thirds vote for that purpose. This requirement gives the existing shareholders statutory protection, since a potential shark will have to acquire a substantially larger number of shares to accomplish a business combination transaction if the other shareholders are not persuaded that the combination is in their best interests.

The Model Business Corporation Act offers a form of statutory protection to existing shareholders when the corporation is undertaking a transaction that will result in the voting power of shares to be issued to comprise more than 20% of the voting power outstanding immediately before the transaction. In such a case, section 6.21(f) requires shareholder approval of such a transaction by a majority vote. Thus, if a potential acquirer with enough votes to influence the board of directors convinced the board to issue a block of shares that increased the voting power by 20% or more, the shareholders would have to vote on the transaction. The act anticipates the potential manipulation of such transactions to avoid a shareholder vote by providing that a series of transactions will be integrated (and considered as one transaction) if one transaction is contingent on the consummation of other similar transactions. If an acquirer entered into an agreement to purchase 16%, then 16% more, and 19.999% more shares, with all transactions contingent on the others (as they should be if the acquirer wants to obtain control of the voting power), shareholder approval would be required for the entire transaction.

SALE, MORTGAGE, OR OTHER DISPOSITION OF ASSETS

If the corporation disposes of substantially all of its assets, a **corporate shell** results; while the basic corporate structure remains the same, the corporation becomes an organization without normal business assets. The sale, mortgage, lease, exchange, or other disposition of substantially all corporate assets is considered by most states to be a structural change in the corporation that requires shareholder approval.

This type of transaction may be, in tax language, part of a type C reorganization, where an acquiring corporation exchanges its voting stock for substantially all of the assets of the acquired corporation, or a type D reorganization, where substantially all of the assets are transferred to a corporation controlled by the transferring corporation or its shareholders.[22] These transactions are not statutory mergers or exchanges, since all corporations survive the transaction; however, instead of owning business assets, the transferring corporation will own voting stock of the acquiring corporation. The management of the corporation also may sell the entire corporate business to a purchaser for cash and subsequently dissolve the corporation, distributing the cash to its shareholders.

Statutes regulating these dispositions of assets are designed to secure shareholder approval if substantially all of the assets of the corporation are to be alienated from the business. To illustrate the equities of these statutes, suppose that the Nobles Company is engaged in the business of manufacturing and selling sporting goods. Its assets include all the machinery used for manufacture; the manufacturing plant; its inventory of skis, bicycles, and other sporting goods; accounts receivable; goodwill; and so forth. If substantially all of these assets are sold to another company for cash or stock, the Nobles Company shareholders will have an entirely different investment. Instead of owning an investment in a growing, successful sporting goods company, they may own a corporation holding cash, which will probably be distributed to them in exchange for their shares. Alternatively, their corporation may receive stock of the purchasing corporation, and while the business may be continued by the purchaser, it will operate under different management, which probably has different policies and interests. The character of the investment is thus changed. The law recognizes the fairness of consulting shareholders for their approval of such transactions.

The Model Business Corporation Act makes several distinctions regarding these transactions in sections 12.01 and 12.02:

1. The mortgage or pledge of corporate property never requires shareholder approval. If the corporation borrows money from its bank and secures the loan with all of the corporate assets, the shareholders do not need to be consulted.
2. The sale, exchange, lease, or other disposition of substantially all of the property and assets in the usual and regular course of business (such as a company with a cyclical business that disposes of substantially all of its inventory to its customers in the summer) does not require shareholder approval.
3. No shareholder approval is required for a corporation to transfer all of its assets to another corporation when the transferring corporation already owns all of the other corporation's shares (such as when a parent corporation transfers all of its assets to a wholly owned subsidiary).
4. Shareholder approval is required if substantially all of the corporate assets are sold, leased, exchanged, or disposed of in a transaction *not* within the ordinary course of business if the disposition would leave the corporation without a significant continuing business activity.

Most states permit the mortgage or pledge of corporate property without shareholder approval. In these transactions, the corporation continues to use the property, but has granted an interest in the property as collateral to secure a loan or other obligation. Business should continue as usual, and the property will be lost only if the corporation defaults on the obligation. The character of the shareholder's investment will not be affected if all goes as planned—that is, the corporate business will generate enough income to pay the obligation, the mortgage or pledge will be removed, and the corporate assets will remain intact. Consequently, there is no pressing need for shareholder protection here.

Several jurisdictions provide, as does the Model Business Corporation Act, that a sale or other disposition of substantially all of the corporate assets, if within the usual and regular course of corporate business, may be accomplished by action of the board of directors without shareholder approval. The theory behind this rule is that if the transaction is within the ordinary course of corporate business, the board of directors is already authorized to proceed with it, and shareholder approval is never required for normal business transactions. On the other hand, other state statutes do not attempt to distinguish between transactions in or out of the ordinary course of business, perhaps because the distinction is difficult to apply. However, where the distinction exists, the normalcy of the transaction may be determined by the statement of purposes in the articles of incorporation. Suppose a corporation is organized for the purpose of purchasing and selling a single parcel of real estate, anticipating a profit from the sale. When the property is sold, the transaction is within the ordinary course of business, since that is exactly what the corporation was organized to do. Most cases are not that clear, however. If the articles of incorporation of the Nobles Company stated that one purpose of the corporation is to "sell, lease, transfer, exchange, or otherwise deal in the assets of the corporation," the broad enabling authority may make a transfer of substantially all assets a normal corporate event, but that certainly would be subject to interpretation. From the standpoint of better corporate practice, any questionable transaction should be approved by the shareholders.

The transfer of all of the assets of a parent corporation to its subsidiary need not involve shareholder approval. The shareholders own the shares of the parent, which already owns all of the shares of the subsidiary. When the parent's assets are distributed to the subsidiary, the same shareholders still own the assets through their ownership of the parent.

Procedure

The sale or other disposition of assets is characterized as a structural change when the transaction is not within the usual and regular course of the corporation's business, and the disposition would leave the corporation without a significant continuing business activity. The Model Business Corporation Act provides some guidance about what would constitute a "significant continuing business activity" by providing that a corporation is conclusively deemed to have it if it retains a business that uses at least 25% of the total assets used at the end of the most recent fiscal year, and is producing income or revenues of at least 25% of the prior fiscal year.

EXAMPLE

Resolution for Sale of Assets Outside the Ordinary Course of Business

RESOLVED, that this Board hereby declares that the consideration in the form of capital stock of The Nobles Company to be received in exchange for the hereinabove described properties and interests, is a full, fair, and adequate consideration; that this Board hereby ratifies, confirms, and approves all of the acts of its officers in making said agreement with The Nobles Company; and that this Board hereby recommends to the stockholders of this Company that said agreement be approved by said stockholders; and

FURTHER RESOLVED, that the question of approval of said agreement with The Nobles Company be submitted to the stockholders of this Company in a special meeting called for that purpose; and to that end it is

FURTHER RESOLVED, that a special meeting of the stockholders of this Company be called to be held at the principal office of this Company in the City of Des Moines, State of Iowa, at 10:00 A.M. on the 10th day of October, 2005; that the secretary of this Company be and hereby is authorized and directed to give all the stockholders of this Company proper, timely, and adequate notice of the time, place, and purpose of said meeting; and that books for the transfer of stock will close at the conclusion of business on September 15, 2005, and will reopen on the day following the adjournment of said meeting.

If a structural change is involved in the disposition of assets transaction, the procedure for approval of the transaction parallels the approval of a merger or share exchange. The board of directors adopts a resolution recommending the transaction and directing the submission of its terms to the shareholders for their approval.

The shareholders may consider the transaction at either an annual or special meeting.[23] Every shareholder, whether or not otherwise entitled to vote, must receive such notice. The period of notice may be different in the various states, and most states require a statement of the shareholders' rights if they have the right to dissent to the transaction.[24] The Model Business Corporation Act requires an affirmative vote of the majority of the voting shares to approve the transaction, and authorizes class voting if the transaction affects the rights of the particular class.

DOMESTICATION AND CONVERSION

Whenever a corporation has been formed in one state and prefers to be governed by the laws of another state, it is possible to change the state of **domestication**. Of course, any corporation formed in any state may qualify to do business in other states and be entitled to the benefits of the laws of the foreign jurisdiction for the business conducted there.[25] Although qualifying to do business as a foreign corporation authorizes a corporation to enter into transactions and have a presence in the foreign state, it remains subject to any limitations on its operations as a result of being domesticated in its state of formation. There may be good reasons for a corporation to be domesticated in a state other than where it was formed. For example, suppose a corporation were formed in State X but does most of its business in State Y. The corporation may be subject to taxation by State Y on sales of its products in State Y and may also be subject to tax on its income in State X, because it is domesticated there. If the corporation domesticated itself as a corporation in State Y, its income would not be subject to taxation in State X. Another common occurrence involves state laws that favor local contractors. Many states' laws provide that local corporations are to be given a priority for state projects or are entitled to special financial incentives because they are local corporations. Thus, a corporation formed in State A seeking to do a highway project in State B will not receive the local preference to which contractors in State B are entitled. The corporation could domesticate itself in State B and become a local corporation for that project. Finally, many corporations that have been formed in various states will review the possibility of domesticating in Delaware or another permissive corporate state before offering shares to the public, so that the entity will have the benefit of the permissive statutory provisions favoring management and the ample precedents in the cases interpreting the corporate statutes to regulate the internal affairs of the corporation.

Historically, corporations could domesticate in a new jurisdiction by using a merger procedure. A new domestic corporation was formed in the new state and the existing corporation was merged into it. Merger of a foreign corporation with a domestic corporation is authorized in the laws of every state.[26] Modern corporation statutes are now permitting domestication by a more direct method, authorizing a procedure whereby the corporation can simply domesticate itself in a new jurisdiction.

The Model Business Corporation Act permits a foreign corporation to become a domestic corporation if the process is permitted by the laws of the state of formation. Thus, a corporation in State X will be allowed to domesticate itself in State Y only if the laws of State X authorize this procedure. The domestication procedure in the Model Business Corporation Act is very similar to other fundamental changes in the corporate structure.[27] A plan of domestication is adopted by the board of directors and is submitted to the shareholders for their approval. The plan must include

1. the new jurisdiction in which the corporation is to be domesticated;
2. any amendments to articles of incorporation that are necessary or desired;
3. the manner and basis of reclassifying shares of the corporation based upon the laws of the new state of domestication;
4. any other terms and conditions of the domestication.

The plan must be approved by the shareholders by a majority vote, and, like the cases of a merger or share exchange, if there are provisions of the domestication that will affect the rights of a particular class of shares, such a class must be allowed to approve the plan as a separate voting group.

Exhibit 15–4.

Articles of Domestication (Maine)

**FOREIGN
BUSINESS CORPORATION**

STATE OF MAINE

ARTICLES OF DOMESTICATION

Filing Fee $125.00

_____
Deputy Secretary of State

A True Copy When Attested By Signature

_____
Deputy Secretary of State

_____
(Name of Corporation in Jurisdiction of Incorporation)

Pursuant to 13-C MRSA §923, the undersigned corporation executes and delivers the following Articles of Domestication:

FIRST: If the true corporate name is not available or the corporation desires to change its name in connection with the domestication, the name it proposes to use in the State of Maine:

_____.

The corporation was originally incorporated in _____ (state or country)

and the original date of incorporation was _____.

SECOND: The domestication of the corporation in this State was duly authorized as required by the laws of the jurisdiction in which the corporation was incorporated.

THIRD: All the statements required to be set forth in Articles of Incorporation (Form MBCA-6-1) are attached as Exhibit

_____.

FOURTH: The effective date of the articles of domestication (if other than the date of filing of the articles of domestication):

_____.

DATED _____   *By _____
(signature of an officer or other duly authorized representative)

_____
(type or print name and capacity)

*This document **MUST** be signed by an officer or other duly authorized representative. (§923.1)

Please remit your payment made payable to the Maine Secretary of State.

**SUBMIT COMPLETED FORMS TO: CORPORATE EXAMINING SECTION, SECRETARY OF STATE,
101 STATE HOUSE STATION, AUGUSTA, ME 04333-0101**

FORM NO. MBCA-19   7-1-2003   **TEL. (207) 624-7740**

Upon approval of the plan, articles of domestication are prepared and are delivered to the Secretary of State or other public filing officer in the new domestic state. These articles of domestication include

1. the name of the corporation (which must satisfy the requirements of the corporate name statute in the new state);
2. the jurisdiction of incorporation before filing the articles and the date of initial incorporation;
3. a statement that domestication of the corporation was duly authorized under the laws of the initial state of formation. (See Exhibit 15–4, Articles of Domestication).

At the same time, the corporation is required to file articles of charter surrender in the state of its formation. The articles of charter surrender state that the corporation is now being domesticated in a foreign jurisdiction and that the shareholders have appropriately approved the procedure. (See Exhibit 15–5, Articles of Charter Surrender)

Upon completion of the process, the corporation becomes a domesticated corporation in the new state. Title to its property and its rights and obligations are unaffected, and, except

Exhibit 15–5.

Articles of Charter
Surrender for
Domestication (Maine)

Filing Fee $70.00

**DOMESTIC
BUSINESS CORPORATION**

STATE OF MAINE

ARTICLES OF CHARTER SURRENDER
(Upon Domestication)

_____
Deputy Secretary of State

A True Copy When Attested By Signature

_____
Deputy Secretary of State

_____
(Name of Corporation)

Pursuant to 13-C MRSA §§924 and 925, the undersigned corporation executes and delivers the following Articles of Charter Surrender:

FIRST: The articles of charter surrender are being filed in connection with the domestication of the corporation in a foreign jurisdiction and the effective date of the domestication is (date) _____.

SECOND: The domestication was duly approved by the shareholders and, if voting by any separate voting group was required, by each such separate voting group, in the manner required by this Act and the corporation's articles of incorporation.

THIRD: The corporation's new jurisdiction of incorporation is _____.

FOURTH: The corporation shall appoint the Secretary of State as its agent for service of process in a proceeding to enforce the rights of shareholders who exercise appraisal rights in connection with the domestication and that the foreign business corporation shall provide a mailing address to which the Secretary of State may mail a copy of any process served on the Secretary of State.

_____
(mailing address)

FIFTH: The corporation agrees that it will promptly pay the amount, if any, to which the shareholders are entitled under **chapter** 13.

DATED _____   *By _____
(signature of an officer or other duly authorized representative)

_____
(type or print name and capacity)

*This document **MUST** be signed by an officer or other duly authorized representative. (§924.1)

Please remit your payment made payable to the Maine Secretary of State.

SUBMIT COMPLETED FORMS TO: CORPORATE EXAMINING SECTION, SECRETARY OF STATE,
101 STATE HOUSE STATION, AUGUSTA, ME 04333-0101
TEL. (207) 624-7740

FORM NO. MBCA-19A   7-1-2003

---

for any amendments it has chosen to adopt or that were required by the new state's laws, nothing will have changed but the jurisdiction in which it is now considered a domestic corporation. The corporation is the same corporation as it was originally, and it has not been necessary to maneuver domestication through a merger or share exchange transaction for whatever other consequences such a transaction might have. The new laws permit the entire procedure to be accomplished within the existing corporation, and, to the extent not changed in the domestication process by specific amendments and express provisions adopted by the shareholders, preserve the status quo within the corporation. It just has a new home state.

A **conversion** is a procedure that allows a corporation to become a different type of entity, such as a limited liability company or partnership. Modern corporate laws have begun to recognize that the corporate form is rigid and inflexible compared with the features of a limited liability company or a limited liability partnership. In these entity structures, a variety of rights and obligations may be created in the operating or partnership agreements to tailor the operation of the company to suit the needs of the managers, members, partners, and other investors. The corporation, on the other hand, still requires considerable separation in the responsibilities and rights of the owners (the shareholders), the policy makers (the directors), and other management (the officers). The corporation also requires that distributions of profits and assets must occur in the proportion of stock ownership and the only techniques that permit variety and diversion from the standard proportionate ownership will be express agreements with shareholders and investors that permit payments to them for other reasons, such as employment with the corporation or payments under separately agreed loans and leases. Consequently, many managers of corporations have considered whether the limited liability company or partnership structure may be better suited to the current operations of the business.

Historically, the conversion of a corporation into another form of entity was accomplished through other fundamental change procedures, such as the sale of substantially all of the assets to a new entity. If a corporation desired to become a limited liability company, it could sell all of its assets to a newly formed limited liability company or partnership in exchange for all of the ownership interests of the company. The corporation could then distribute the ownership interests of the new entity to its shareholders in exchange for their shares in the corporation. At the end of this transaction, the shareholders were members or partners of a new entity that owned the assets formerly owned by the corporation. A variation on such a transaction would involve the corporation distributing all of its assets to its shareholders, who then contribute the assets to a limited liability company or partnership in exchange for the ownership interests of the new entity. There were problems with all of these procedures, depending on the flexibility of the local state's laws. When the corporation sold all of its assets to a new entity and tried to distribute the ownership interests received in exchange for the assets, the taxing authorities considered that to be a distribution of all of the assets to the shareholders and a taxable event at that time, even though the assets were simply going into another company. In addition, if the corporation distributed all of its assets to shareholders so they could contribute them to a new entity, the tax problems were compounded by the fact that most states permit such a distribution only if creditor claims have been satisfied or provided for. The assumption by the new entity of all corporate obligations may not have been enough to satisfy creditor's rights under the local corporate statute. Moreover, limited liability companies and partnerships function under agreements with all members and partners. Somewhere in this process, the shareholders of the corporation that was converting to the new entity had to agree to the terms of the operating or partnership agreement that was to govern it.

Modern statutes are now authorizing conversion by a corporation (and other entities) into different entities. The conversions authorized in the Model Business Corporation Act now include

1. a conversion of a domestic business corporation to become a domestic nonprofit corporation;[28]
2. a conversion of a foreign nonprofit corporation to a domestic business corporation;[29]
3. a conversion by entities generally, such as a domestic or foreign business corporation to a domestic or foreign unincorporated entity or a domestic or foreign unincorporated entity into a domestic or foreign corporation.[30]

The procedures for these various conversions are similar to each other and to the normal procedure for fundamental corporation changes. The conversions must be permitted by the laws of the various states governing the entities that are being converted. If the statute under which the entity was formed does not permit a conversion, the Model Business Corporation Act treats the owners and managers of the entity as if they were shareholders and directors, respectively, of a corporation, so that they can follow a procedure that converts the unincorporated association into a corporate form. Similarly, the act gives shareholders and directors a method to convert the business corporation to a non-profit corporation or an unincorporated entity.

The entity must adopt a plan of conversion that includes

1. the type of entity that the surviving entity will be;
2. the terms and conditions of conversion;

Filing Fee $125.00

**DOMESTIC
BUSINESS CORPORATION**

STATE OF MAINE

ARTICLES OF ENTITY CONVERSION

_____
Deputy Secretary of State

A True Copy When Attested By Signature

_____
Deputy Secretary of State

_____
(Name of Corporation Prior to Conversion)

Pursuant to 13-C MRSA §955.1, the undersigned corporation executes and delivers the following Articles of Entity Conversion:

FIRST: The name of the corporation is changed as follows (the name must satisfy the organic law of the surviving entity):

_____

SECOND: The type of unincorporated entity that the surviving entity will be: _____.

THIRD: The plan of entity conversion was duly approved by the shareholders in the manner required by this Act and the corporation's articles of incorporation.

FOURTH: If the surviving entity is a filing entity, attached is Exhibit _____ which contains all the provisions required to be set forth in its public organic document with any other desired provisions that are permitted.

For a Domestic Limited Liability Company, attach form MLLC-6-1.
For a Domestic Limited Partnership, attach form MLPA-6-1.

FIFTH: The effective date of the articles of entity conversion (if other than the date of filing of the articles of entity conversion) is _____.

DATED _____   *By _____
                                        (signature of an officer or other duly authorized representative)

                                     _____
                                        (type or print name and capacity)

*This document **MUST** be signed by an officer or other duly authorized representative. (§955.1)

Please remit your payment made payable to the Maine Secretary of State.

**SUBMIT COMPLETED FORMS TO: CORPORATE EXAMINING SECTION, SECRETARY OF STATE,
101 STATE HOUSE STATION, AUGUSTA, ME 04333-0101**
FORM NO. MBCA-21   7-1-2003   **TEL. (207) 624-7740**

3. the manner and basis of converting shares to new ownership interests;
4. the full text of the organic documents of the surviving entity (such as the articles of organization and the operating agreement for a limited liability company or the partnership agreement and registration of a limited liability partnership).

The board of directors must adopt the plan and submit it to the shareholders, who must approve it by a majority vote. As in the case of other fundamental corporate changes, if the rights of any class of shares will be affected, that class must affirmatively approve the plan as a separate voting group.

Following approval by the intracorporate groups, articles of entity conversion are adopted and filed with the following information:

1. the name of the corporation before filing the conversion, and the name of the new entity;
2. the type of entity that the new entity will be;
3. a statement that the plan of entity conversion was approved by the shareholders as required;
4. all of the provisions that are required to be set forth in the new entity's filing requirements (such as the provisions that are required for articles of organization to form a limited liability company) (See Exhibit 15–6, Articles of Entity Conversion).

Exhibit 15–7.

Articles of Charter
Surrender for Entity
Conversion (Maine)

Filing Fee $70.00

**DOMESTIC
BUSINESS CORPORATION**

STATE OF MAINE

ARTICLES OF CHARTER SURRENDER
(Upon Entity Conversion)

_____
Deputy Secretary of State

A True Copy When Attested By Signature

_____
Deputy Secretary of State

_____
(Name of Corporation Prior to Conversion)

Pursuant to 13-C MRSA §§956 and 957, the undersigned corporation executes and delivers the following Articles of Charter Surrender:

FIRST: The articles of charter surrender are being filed in connection with the conversion of the corporation to a foreign unincorporated entity and the effective date of the conversion is (date) _____.

SECOND: The conversion was duly approved by the shareholders in the manner required by this Act and the corporation's articles of incorporation.

THIRD: The jurisdiction under the laws of which the surviving entity is organized is _____.

FOURTH: If the surviving entity is a nonfiling entity, the address of its executive office immediately after the conversion.

_____

FIFTH: The surviving entity shall appoint the Secretary of State as its agent for service of process in a proceeding to enforce the rights of shareholders who exercise appraisal rights in connection with the conversion and shall provide a mailing address to which the Secretary of State may mail a copy of any process served on the Secretary of State.

_____
(mailing address)

SIXTH: The corporation agrees that it will promptly pay the amount, if any, to which the shareholders are entitled under **chapter** 13.

DATED _____   *By _____
(signature of an officer or other duly authorized representative)

_____
(type or print name and capacity)

*This document **MUST** be signed by an officer or other duly authorized representative. (§956.1)

Please remit your payment made payable to the Maine Secretary of State.

**SUBMIT COMPLETED FORMS TO: CORPORATE EXAMINING SECTION, SECRETARY OF STATE,
101 STATE HOUSE STATION, AUGUSTA, ME 04333-0101
TEL. (207) 624-7740**

FORM NO. MBCA-21B   7-1-2003

Similar provisions are contained in the Model Business Corporation Act to accomplish the reverse of this transaction: the conversion of an unincorporated entity into a domestic business corporation. Of course, the statutory authority for conversions of one entity to another must be scrupulously followed, and each local variation must be observed.

Upon the delivery of the articles of entity conversion to the appropriate filing officer, and, if necessary, the delivery of articles of charter surrender in any foreign jurisdictions in which the converting entity was formed, the conversion results in the title to property and all rights and obligations of the converted entity to be vested in the surviving entity, and the surviving entity is deemed to be the same company as the corporation from which it was converted without interruption (See Exhibit 15–7, Articles of Charter Surrender).

One of the primary purposes and advantages of the domestication and conversion provisions of the Model Business Corporation Act is that the entity remains the same for all legal purposes (except for its home state or its business form), and, consequently, the company does not risk a violation of contractual provisions, licensing requirements, or other issues that might have been affected by a fundamental change transaction that involved a merger or share exchange.

RIGHTS OF DISSENTING SHAREHOLDERS

Under the Model Business Corporation Act and several statues, nearly half of the outstanding shares may be voted *against* a merger, share exchange, sale of assets domestication, or conversion and the transaction will still be approved. The majority rule controls the holders of the dissenting shares, who must live with the decision of the majority, despite the effect the transaction may have on their shares. The statutory solution to this problem is to grant the dissenting shareholders the right to have their shares appraised and purchased, with limited exceptions, if they do not want to continue as investors in the corporation. In some states, this right is called the "shareholder's **right of appraisal**" or the "shareholder's right to demand payment of the value of the stock." Every state includes some rights of dissent and payment in its corporate statute.

Circumstances Giving Rise to Appraisal Rights

The Model Business Corporation Act grants the right to dissent in cases of mergers, share exchanges, and sales or exchange of substantially all assets outside the ordinary course of business. In addition, **dissenters' rights** will apply if the articles of incorporation are amended to materially affect the rights of a shareholder (such as by abolishing a preferential right, a preemptive right, a redemption right, or a voting right); and if the articles, bylaws, or resolutions of the board of directors so provide, dissenters' rights may apply to any transaction designated therein.[31]

Dissenters' rights will apply to a domestication transaction in which the shareholders receive shares in the corporation with terms that are not as favorable to the shareholders in all material respects, including voting rights, as before the transaction. Finally, the conversion of a corporation to another type of entity (such as non-profit corporation, limited liability company, or partnership) certainly results in a fundamental change of the owner's rights and, consequently, appraisal rights are triggered by any conversion transaction.

The dissent and appraisal rights are limited by two important exceptions. They do not apply to shareholders of a surviving corporation whose votes were not necessary to approve the transaction. This rule covers a merger that will have a small impact upon the surviving corporation.[32] The Model Business Corporation Act formerly excluded holders of shares registered on a national securities exchange at the time the shareholders entitled to vote were identified, unless the articles of incorporation provided otherwise. Delaware and several other states have adopted such a rule, excepting holders of shares listed on a national exchange and holders of a class of shares that has 2,000 or more shareholders of record (or a market value of more than $20 million). The assumption that forms the basis for these rules is that the shares are readily salable if they are registered on a national securities exchange (or if 2,000 other shareholders exist or the shares are so valuable), so the cumbersome appraisal procedure is not necessary to satisfy the dissenting shareholder. A shareholder should be able to sell shares at market if he or she decides to terminate an investment.

The Model Business Corporation Act includes another interesting provision allowing a shareholder to dissent as to less than all shares registered in the shareholder's name, in which case the dissenter's rights are to be determined as to the shares dissenting, and the remaining shares are treated as if they belonged to different shareholders. On its face, the provision seems to be directed to an indecisive shareholder who is uncertain about the transaction and who will dissent as to some shares to recoup some of an investment, but will keep other shares in case the structural change turns out to be successful. Theoretically, this could happen, but the rule was designed to permit brokers, trustees, and agents holding shares for their clients to split the shares into approving and disapproving groups, depending upon their clients' wishes.

Some states are more generous with dissenting shareholders' appraisal rights than is the Model Business Corporation Act. They extend the rights to certain other amendments to the articles of incorporation, such as changes in the corporate purposes, extension of corporate life, and changes in the capital stock structure.

Procedure

Statutory procedures for perfecting the shareholder's right to payment after dissent are quite complex.[33] The first step is the notice of the shareholders meeting, which, when dissenters' rights apply, must state that shareholders may be entitled to assert dissenters' rights and must be accompanied by a copy of the statute that grants the rights.

Then comes the dissent itself. The shareholder must file *written* notice of an intention to demand payment for shares before the vote is taken at the meeting of shareholders called to consider the transaction. The objection must be made before the meeting in some states, and a few states require that the objection include a demand for appraisal and purchase of the shares.

Of course, the shareholder must not vote in favor of the transaction at the meeting.

Next, assume the transaction is approved by the other shareholders and eventually will be consummated by the corporation. In most states, after approval, the shareholder has a certain period of time within which to demand payment of the fair value of the shares. This time period varies. The demand is addressed to the corporation in a sale of assets or a share exchange; or to the surviving or new corporation in a merger. If the shareholder fails to object, to vote against the action, or to demand payment within the time provided, he or she loses the right to payment for shares and is bound by the corporate action.

The revised Model Business Corporation Act takes a little different approach. If the transaction is approved, the corporation must send notice of that fact to the shareholder who has demanded payment and voted properly (against or abstaining from the transaction), together with a form to use to demand payment and a copy of the statute, stating when the demand must be made and where the shares must be deposited. The time period in the notice cannot be less than forty days or more than sixty days from the date the notice was delivered. Failure to return the demand on time, with the shares, forfeits the shareholder's rights to dissent and sell shares to the corporation. If the shareholder demands payment and deposits the share certificates within the time period required by the notice, the shareholder will be entitled to continue to exercise shareholder rights until the rights are canceled or modified by the taking of the proposed corporate action.[34]

The **fair value** of the shares is defined by the Model Business Corporation Act to be the value immediately before the effectuation of the corporate transaction, using customary and current valuation concepts and techniques generally employed for similar businesses in this context, and without discounting for lack of marketability or minority status.[35] In most state statutes, the appraiser is not given that much guidance. Most states simply require that "fair value" should exclude appreciation or depreciation in anticipation of the transaction. This test requires an evaluation of the impact of the publicity surrounding the transaction in the appraisal of the shares and is extremely difficult to apply. For that reason, many states ignore appreciation or depreciation in value determination, or set the date for the appraisal at some time farther removed from shareholder approval. The Model Business Corporation Act leaves it to the appraiser to determine and apply customary and current valuation concepts and directs that they be applied as they would be to similar businesses in the context of the transaction requiring appraisal. This is a more subtle way of saying to ignore appreciation and depreciation from the transaction if it would be appropriate to do that for similar businesses in such a corporate transaction. If customary and current appraisal policies would consider the appreciation or depreciation from certain businesses engaged in a merger, then such factors should be taken into account. In addition, the Model Business Corporation Act excludes any consideration of a "marketability" discount (a reduction in value because there is no public market upon which the shares could be rapidly sold) or a "minority" discount (a reduction in value because the number of shares being valued is insufficient to effect voting control over the corporation). Modern corporate practice and case law have also confirmed that these discounts should not apply in the context of appraising shares held by dissenters to these fundamental corporate transactions.

The corporation and the shareholder are encouraged to agree upon the value of the shares, but if fair value is disputed, the Model Business Corporation Act prescribes an elaborate procedure for resolving the issue. Once the corporation has delivered the dissenters' notice (no later than ten days after the corporate action has been taken), the shareholders who wish to sell their shares must demand payment, certify their ownership of the shares, and deposit their certificates in accordance with the terms of the notice. The reason for the certification of ownership is to allow the corporation to determine whether a shareholder owned the shares before the public announcement of the proposed corporate action. If the shareholder purchased the shares after information concerning the proposed corporate action was available, the corporation may withhold payment for that shareholder's shares. This provision prevents shareholders from purchasing shares just before a corporation enters into a fundamental transaction so that they have an automatic market for the sale of their stock through dissenters' rights.[36]

Except for shares acquired after public information is available, the corporation must pay each dissenter the amount the corporation estimates to be a fair value of the shares, plus accrued interest. This payment must be accompanied by the corporation's recent financial statements, an estimate of the fair value from the corporation, an explanation of how the interest was calculated, and a statement of the dissenters' rights (usually including a copy of the statute itself).[37]

If a shareholder disagrees with the estimate of fair value, the shareholder may file his or her own estimate with the corporation within thirty days. If the corporation cannot settle with the shareholder within sixty days after the shareholder's demand, the question of fair value will be referred to a court. The corporation must file the petition, and if it fails to do so, the corporation must pay the shareholder the price the shareholder demanded. If an action is filed with a court, all dissenters who dispute fair value are made parties to the action. The court may appoint appraisers to determine the fair value of the shares, and the court will enter a judgment for the value set by those appraisers.[38] The corporation is usually required to pay the expenses of the proceedings, but the court may assess the expenses against the dissenting shareholders if it finds that their rejection of the corporation's offered amount was arbitrary, vexatious, or not in good faith, and was without justification.[39] This table illustrates the differences between the former act and the revised act:

Timetable #1	Number of Days	Former Model Business Corporation Act	Revised Model Business Corporation Act
	−10	Date notice is sent to shareholders	Date corporation notifies shareholders of right to dissent
	−1	Date fair value determined	Date fair value determined
Date of meeting for shareholder approval	0	Latest date for written objection to action; shareholder must vote against action	Latest date for filing written objection; shareholder must not vote in favor of transaction
	10	Latest dates for written demand for payment	If transaction is approved, date corporation sends notice to dissenters
	30	Latest date for submitting certificates representing shares to corporation for notation	Earliest date that corporation may require shareholder to demand payment and deposit certificates
	60		If transaction is not effected by now, date the corporation must return certificates

Timetable #2

Date action is effected	0		Date corporation remits payment of fair value with information required by statute
	10	Latest date for corporation notice to shareholders with an offer at a specified price	
	30	Latest date for agreement	Latest date for dissenter's demand for estimate of fair value
	60	Latest date for corporation to file petition on its own	
	90	Latest date for corporation to file petition on shareholder demand; date of payment if agreement reached on fair value	Latest date for corporation to settle with shareholder or file petition with the court; failure to do one or the other requires payment to the dissenter at dissenter's price

In some states, it is necessary to file an agreement to pay dissenting shareholders and to appoint the secretary of state as an agent to receive process for the corporation if it is not a domestic corporation (see Exhibit 15–8, Agreement to Pay Dissenting Shareholders).

Once a shareholder exercises the right to dissent and obtain an appraisal of the shares, the shareholder's rights as such are forfeited except to pursue this remedy, which is said to be "exclusive," meaning that a demand for payment for shares is the only remedy a shareholder has if dissatisfied with the transaction. When the demand for payment is made, the shareholder loses the right to vote or to exercise any other rights as a shareholder. The shareholder usually cannot withdraw the demand unless the corporation consents, and shareholder status is regained only upon withdrawal and consent, or if the corporation abandons the transaction, or if a court decides that the shareholder is not entitled to the right of payment for the shares.

VOLUNTARY DISSOLUTION

The dissolution of the corporation is a structural change that will affect the shareholders, and the shareholders must be consulted for their approval.

Procedure

The corporation may be dissolved at any time after it is formed by the appropriate concurrence of its aggregate membership. A decision to dissolve may be made immediately after formation, before the corporation commences business and before shares are issued. The incorporators (or the initial directors, if named in the articles of incorporation) constitute the total aggregate membership at this point, and an admission that the corporation was a bad idea is theirs to make. The Model Business Corporation Act procedure for dissolution before commencement of business and before the issuance of shares is very simple. The majority of the incorporators (or the initial directors) may execute and file articles of dissolution.[40]

A corporation that has commenced business and has issued shares may be dissolved through two typical procedures, which may originate with either the shareholders or the directors of the corporation. If the shareholders take the initiative, many states allow voluntary dissolution by the shareholders' unanimous written consent. All shareholders, whether or not they are otherwise entitled to vote, normally must join the consent, but a few states allow the holders of only the voting shares to make the decision.[41]

Exhibit 15–8.

Agreement to Pay
Dissenting Shareholders
(Maine)

---

*(To be filed with Articles of Merger when the surviving corporation
is to be governed by the laws of any jurisdiction other than Maine.)*

AGREEMENT BY

_____
surviving corporation

**TO PAY DISSENTING SHAREHOLDERS OF DOMESTIC CORPORATIONS
AND APPOINTMENT OF SECRETARY OF STATE AS AGENT**

Pursuant to 13-A MRSA §906.4, the undersigned corporation submits the following agreement and appointment of agent to accept service of process.

FIRST: The corporation agrees that it will promptly pay to the dissenting shareholders of any participating domestic corporation the amount, if any, to which they are entitled under 13-A MRSA (Maine Business Corporation Act) with respect to the rights of dissenting shareholders.

SECOND: The corporation agrees that it may be served with process in the State of Maine in any proceeding to enforce any obligation of a participating domestic corporation or any participating foreign corporation previously subject to suit in the State of Maine, or to enforce the right of dissenting shareholders of any participating domestic corporation against the surviving corporation.

THIRD: The corporation irrevocably appoints the Secretary of State of Maine as its agent to accept service of process in any such proceedings.

FOURTH: The address to which the Secretary of State shall mail a copy of any process in such proceeding is _____

_____

FIFTH: The address of the registered office of the corporation is* _____

_____
(street, city, state and zip code)

DATED _____   _____
                                                              (surviving corporation)

                                        By _____
                                                              (signature)

                                        _____
                                                              (type or print name and capacity)

                                        By _____
                                                              (signature)

                                        _____
                                                              (type or print name and capacity)

*Give address of registered office in Maine. If the corporation does not have a registered office in Maine, the address given should be the principal or registered office in the State of incorporation.

This document **MUST be signed by (1) the **Clerk OR** (2) the **President** or a vice-president *and* the **Secretary** or an assistant secretary, or such other officer as the bylaws may designate as a 2nd certifying officer **OR** (3) if there are no such officers, then a majority of the **Directors** or such directors as may be designated by a majority of directors then in office **OR** (4) if there are no such directors, then the **Holders**, or such of them as may be designated by the holders, **of record of a *majority* of all outstanding shares** entitled to vote thereon **OR** (5) the **Holders of all of the outstanding shares** of the corporation.

SUBMIT COMPLETED FORMS TO: CORPORATE EXAMINING SECTION, SECRETARY OF STATE,
101 STATE HOUSE STATION, AUGUSTA, ME 04333-0101
TEL. (207) 287-4195

FORM NO. MBCA-10Ma Rev. 96

If dissolution is recommended by the board of directors (as it must under the Model Business Corporation Act), or if unanimous shareholder consent to the dissolution is not feasible, the corporation may be dissolved by the usual procedure for corporate structural changes—that is, by the directors and the shareholders acting in their respective meetings. The board of directors adopts a resolution recommending that the corporation be dissolved and submits this resolution to the vote of the shareholders at either an annual or a special meeting.[42]

EXAMPLE

Resolution to Dissolve

The president made a statement as to the present plight of the Corporation, and after a confirmatory statement by the treasurer, it was unanimously

RESOLVED, that the Board of Directors hereby recommends to the stockholders that in their interest, this Corporation be dissolved and its affairs wound up; and

FURTHER RESOLVED, that a special meeting of the stockholders of the Corporation be held at the offices of the Corporation, on the 3rd day of December, 2005, at 3:00 P.M., to vote on the question of whether this Corporation be dissolved, and that the secretary is hereby directed to give due notice of said meeting.

The Model Business Corporation Act does not specify any unusual time period within which notice must be given, but the notice must state that the meeting will be for the purpose of considering the dissolution of the corporation.[43]

Notice of a Meeting for Dissolution

The stockholders of The Nobles Company are hereby notified that a special meeting of the stockholders of said Company will be held at the corporation's offices, 200 West 14th Avenue, Denver, Colorado, on the 3rd day of December, 2005, at 3:00 P.M., to vote on the question of whether said Company should be dissolved.

Dated November 18, 2005.

_____ , Secretary

The shareholders must approve dissolution by a designated percentage of the vote. The Model Business Corporation Act originally required the affirmative vote of the holders of two-thirds of the outstanding shares entitled to vote on the issue, but the percentage currently is a majority of the voting shares. Class voting is also authorized under the act. Many states continue to adhere to the two-thirds vote requirement, and several jurisdictions allow every share to vote on the dissolution question, whether or not otherwise entitled to vote. The minutes of the shareholders' meeting would reflect the approval of the dissolution.

Resolution to Dissolve

WHEREAS, the Board of Directors believe this Corporation should be dissolved, and have called this special meeting of the stockholders to consider the matter; and

WHEREAS, after considering the statements of officers and a report of a committee of the stockholders, it appears to be for the best interests of the stockholders of this Corporation that its business should be terminated, the Corporation dissolved, and its assets distributed according to law:

NOW, THEREFORE, whereas the holders of record of two-thirds of the outstanding shares of this Corporation entitled to vote therein concur therein:

RESOLVED, that this Corporation hereby elects to dissolve, and that pursuant to the Colorado Corporation Law, the president and secretary, or other proper officers, are hereby authorized to execute and file the proper certificate of dissolution with the Secretary of State, that they duly publish the certificate of the Secretary of State of said filing, and that they and the other officers of this Corporation are hereby authorized and directed to take the steps prescribed by law to complete the dissolution and to wind up the affairs of this Corporation.

The result of a dissolution will be to distribute the assets of the corporation (after creditors are paid) to the shareholders, so the shareholders will receive their proportionate share of the value of the corporation. Consequently, a dissenting shareholder's appraisal remedy is rare in dissolution, and even if authorized, it is usually limited to special circumstances surrounding the manner in which the dissolution and liquidation is conducted.

Statement of Intent to Dissolve

The dissolution procedure in many states has two sections designed to give advance public and private notice to outsiders that the corporation has initiated dissolution proceedings. These notices are intended to facilitate orderly liquidation of the corporation.

The statement or notice of intent to dissolve, the first notice filed for dissolution of a going concern, is not required for dissolution by the incorporators, since one prerequisite to that dissolution procedure is that the corporation has not yet commenced business, and thus protection of the public is not deemed to be necessary.

The statement or notice of intent to dissolve must be executed and filed with the secretary of state if the dissolution has been approved by the vote or consent of the shareholders or by

Exhibit 15–9.

Statement of Intent to
Dissolve (Shareholders)

Filing Fee $20.00

**DOMESTIC
BUSINESS CORPORATION**

STATE OF MAINE

STATEMENT OF INTENT TO DISSOLVE

(Written Consent of All Shareholders)

_____
Deputy Secretary of State

A True Copy When Attested By Signature

_____
Deputy Secretary of State

_____
(Name of Corporation)

Pursuant to 13-A MRSA §1102, the undersigned corporation intends to dissolve the corporation.

FIRST: The names and respective addresses of its officers and directors are:

Title	Name	Address
President	_____	_____
Treasurer	_____	_____
Secretary	_____	_____
Clerk	_____	_____
Directors:	_____	_____
	_____	_____
	_____	_____

SECOND: Exhibit A attached hereto is a copy of the written consent signed by all shareholders of the corporation, or signed in their names by their duly authorized attorneys.

THIRD: All required Annual Reports have been filed with the Secretary of State. (Note: If the dissolution process is completed on or before June 1st, then the Annual Report covering the previous calendar year is not required.)

FOURTH: The undersigned corporation understands that the filing of this document _**DOES NOT**_ complete the dissolution process. You must _**ALSO FILE**_ Articles of Dissolution.

FIFTH: The address of the registered office of the corporation in the State of Maine is _____

_____
(street, city, state and zip code)

---

resolution of the board of directors with subsequent shareholder approval (see Exhibit 15–9, Statement of Intent to Dissolve). Many states require this first notice of the dissolution, although the statement may have to be published rather than filed (see Exhibit 15–10, Affidavit to Dissolve Corporation on page 554).

Upon filing the statement, or beginning other specified statutory requirements for dissolution, the corporation must cease all normal business activity, and it may continue in business only for the purpose of winding up its affairs. The filing of the statement of intent does not terminate corporate existence. The corporate existence usually continues until a certificate of dissolution has been issued by the secretary of state or until a court has declared the corporation to be dissolved.

Exhibit 15–9.

(continued)

DATED _____   *By _____
                                          (signature)

MUST BE COMPLETED FOR VOTE OF SHAREHOLDERS
I certify that I have custody of the minutes showing the above action by the shareholders.
_____
(signature of clerk, secretary or asst. secretary)

_____
(type or print name and capacity)

*By _____
        (signature)

_____
(type or print name and capacity)

Notice of the filing of this statement shall be mailed to each known creditor of the corporation and to the State Tax Assessor pursuant to 13-A MRSA §1106.2.

*This document **MUST** be signed by (1) the **Clerk** **OR** (2) the **President** or a vice-president *and* the **Secretary** or an assistant secretary, or such other officer as the bylaws may designate as a 2nd certifying officer **OR** (3) if there are no such officers, then a majority of the **Directors** or such directors as may be designated by a majority of directors then in office **OR** (4) if there are no such directors, then the **Holders**, or such of them as may be designated by the holders, **of record of a *majority* of all outstanding shares** entitled to vote thereon **OR** (5) the **Holders of all of the outstanding shares** of the corporation.

SUBMIT COMPLETED FORMS TO: CORPORATE EXAMINING SECTION, SECRETARY OF STATE,
101 STATE HOUSE STATION, AUGUSTA, ME 04333-0101

FORM NO. MBCA-11 Rev. 96   TEL. (207) 287-4195

Notice to Creditors

After filing a statement of intent to dissolve, the corporation will proceed to collect its assets and to liquidate its business. As a part of the liquidation process, the corporation gives to each known creditor notice of its intent to dissolve, which is the private notice that complements the filed statement. Through these notices, everyone who cares about the corporation should learn about the dissolution before it becomes effective. Some states require that the corporation advertise its intention to dissolve in a newspaper, rather than sending notices directly to creditors.

Exhibit 15–10.

Affidavit to Dissolve
Corporation (Louisiana)

**W. Fox McKeithen
Secretary of State**

AFFIDAVIT TO DISSOLVE CORPORATION
(R.S. 12:142.1 & 12:250.1)

| Domestic Corporation (Business or Non-Profit) Enclose $60.00 filing fee Make remittance payable to Secretary of State *Do Not Send Cash* | Return to: | Commercial Division P. O. Box 94125 Baton Rouge, LA 70804-9125 Phone (225) 925-4704 Web Site: www.sec.state.la.us |

STATE OF _____

PARISH/COUNTY OF _____

BEFORE ME, the undersigned Notary Public in and for the parish/county herein above shown, personally came and appeared the undersigned who, after being duly sworn, did depose and say that:

_____
Corporation Name

_____

is no longer doing business, owes no debts and is dissolved by filing this affidavit with the Secretary of State, executed by the shareholder(s), or incorporator(s) if no shares have been issued, attesting to such facts.

The undersigned further declared that they are: (check one)

( )   The shareholders of the above named corporation.

( )   The incorporators of the above named corporation and no shares have been issued.

_____

_____

_____

_____
Incorporator(s) or Shareholder(s)

Sworn to and subscribed before me, the undersigned Notary Public, on this date: _____

_____
Notary

339 Rev. 5/00   (See instructions on back)

Articles of Dissolution

The Model Business Corporation Act eliminates the prior requirements of filing a statement of intent to dissolve and giving notice to creditors, and provides simply that after the dissolution is authorized, the corporation must deliver articles of dissolution to the secretary of state (see Exhibit 15–11, Articles of Dissolution). In most states, these articles of dissolution will be filed only after payment of all corporate debts, liabilities, and obligations and after distribution of the remaining corporate property and assets to the shareholders. The articles of dissolution are executed and filed with the Secretary of State

Exhibit 15–11.

Articles of Dissolution
(Massachusetts)

FEDERAL IDENTIFICATION
NO. _____

Examiner

The Commonwealth of Massachusetts

William Francis Galvin
Secretary of the Commonwealth
One Ashburton Place, Boston, Massachusetts 02108-1512

ARTICLES OF DISSOLUTION
(General Laws, Chapter 156B, Section 100)

We, _____ , *President / *Vice President,

and _____ , *Clerk / *Assistant Clerk,

of _____ ,
(Exact name of corporation)

located at: _____ ,
(Street address of corporation in Massachusetts)

certify as follows:

1. The name and post office address of each director and officer of the corporation is:

	NAME	POST OFFICE ADDRESS
President:		
Treasurer:		
Clerk:		
Directors:		

P.C.   *Delete the inapplicable words.

156badis 4/5/00

(continued)

with the same formality as are the original articles of incorporation. Although the articles of dissolution described in the Model Business Corporation Act only must state the name of the corporation and the date and manner that the dissolution was authorized, in many states the article of dissolution must state that the corporation has been liquidated; that its debts, obligations, and liabilities have been paid and discharged or that adequate provisions have been made therefor, and that all the remaining property and assets of the corporation have been distributed among the shareholders in accordance with their respective rights and interests. If the voluntary dissolution occurs before the issuance of shares and commencement of business, the incorporators file articles of dissolution declaring those

Exhibit 15–11.

(continued)

2. On _____ , 20 _____ , the dissolution of the corporation was duly authorized in the manner required by General Laws, Chapter 156B, Section 100, and notice of the proposed dissolution was duly given to the Commissioner of Revenue as required by said section.

3. The effective date of dissolution of the corporation shall be the date approved and filed by the Secretary of the Commonwealth. If a *later* effective date is desired, specify such date which shall not be more than *thirty days* after the date of filing.

**4. Other provisions deemed necessary by the corporation for its dissolution.

SIGNED UNDER THE PENALTIES OF PERJURY, this _____ day of _____ , 20 _____ ,

_____ , *President / *Vice President,

_____ , *Clerk / *Assistant Clerk.

*Delete the inapplicable words.
**If there are no such provisions, state "None".
Note: Provisions for which the space provided above is not sufficient should be made on one side of separate 8 1/2 x 11 sheets of white paper, numbered 2A, 2B, etc., with a left margin of at least 1 inch.

facts and confirming the return of amounts paid for subscriptions (see Exhibit 15–12, Articles of Dissolution by Incorporators on page 558).

The corporation is dissolved on the effective date stated in its articles of dissolution.[44]

A dissolved corporation continues its corporate existence but may not carry on any business except to wind up its business affairs. Dissolution of the corporation does not affect title to the corporation's property, prevent transfer of the corporation's shares or securities, subject the corporation's directors and officers to personal liability, prevent commencement of a proceeding by or against the corporation in its name, or affect any proceedings that have been commenced by or against the corporation.[45] Thus, the corporation remains in existence to complete its business, including transferring title to property and finishing litigation that may have been started by it or against it, and the persons

Exhibit 15–11.

(continued)

THE COMMONWEALTH OF MASSACHUSETTS

ARTICLES OF DISSOLUTION
(General Laws, Chapter 156B, Section 100)

I hereby approve the within Articles of Dissolution and, the filing fee in the amount of $ _____ having been paid, said application is deemed to have been filed with me this _____ day of _____ , 20 _____ .

Effective date: _____

WILLIAM FRANCIS GALVIN
Secretary of the Commonwealth

TO BE FILLED IN BY CORPORATION
Contact information:

_____

_____

_____

Telephone: _____

Email: _____

A copy this filing will be available on-line at www.state.ma.us/sec/cor once the document is filed.

acting on behalf of the corporation are still insulated from personal liability. All of these activities must be directed toward terminating the corporation's affairs. Section 14.06 of the Model Business Corporation Act requires that the dissolved corporation must notify any creditors or other claimants of the dissolution in writing after the dissolution has occurred. This notice will state a deadline, which cannot be fewer than 120 days from the date of the notice, by which claims will be considered. If a creditor does not make a claim within the stated time, the creditor may be barred from ever asserting the claim.[46] The dissolved corporation also may publish a notice of its dissolution for any persons who have claims that are not known to the corporation. This publication may state that any claim against the corporation will be barred after three years from the publication of the notice. Any timely filed claim may be enforced against the corporation (to the extent of

Exhibit 15–12.

Articles of Dissolution by
Incorporators

Filing fee: $_____

ARTICLES OF DISSOLUTION
BY INCORPORATOR(S)
OF

_____

 Pursuant to the provisions of Section 82 of the _____Business Corporation
Act, the undersigned of the corporation hereinafter named, adopt the following
Articles of Dissolution:
 FIRST: The name of the corporation is_____
 SECOND: The date of issuance of its certificate of incorporation was_____
 THIRD: None of its shares has been issued.
 FOURTH: The corporation has not commenced business.
 FIFTH: The amount, if any, actually paid in on subscriptions for its shares, less
any part thereof disposed of for necessary expenses, has been returned to those
entitled thereto.
 SIXTH: No debts of the corporation remain unpaid.
 SEVENTH: The sole incorporator or a majority of the incorporators elects that
the corporation be dissolved.
 Dated _____, 20__.

_____
_____
_____
             Incorporator(s)

its undistributed assets) or, if the assets have been distributed, against the shareholders
who have received those assets on a pro rata basis.

Revocation of Voluntary Dissolution Proceedings

Just as the shareholders and the corporation approve voluntary dissolution, so may they
revoke it. This indecision is expensive and time-consuming, but every statute gives the
intracorporate parties the right to change their minds. The procedure for revocation usually duplicates the procedure for approval. If the shareholders consented to the dissolution (where permitted under local law), they may, by written consent any time before the
issuance of a certificate of dissolution, revoke the dissolution proceedings by submitting
a statement of revocation to the secretary of state (see Exhibit 15–13, Articles of Revocation of Voluntary Dissolution). The revocation also may be accomplished by act of the
corporation. The board of directors may submit to the vote of the shareholders a resolution revoking voluntary dissolution proceedings. Shareholder approval of revocation of
voluntary dissolution requires the same vote (either majority or two-thirds) as that required for approval of dissolution.[47] When the statement of revocation is filed with the
secretary of state, the corporation may again conduct business as though nothing ever
happened. The revocation of voluntary dissolution proceedings must occur within
120 days of the effective date of dissolution under the Model Business Corporation Act,
but most jurisdictions require the decision to be made before the articles of dissolution
are filed.

INVOLUNTARY DISSOLUTION

By the State

A wayward corporation may be dragged, perhaps kicking and screaming, into dissolution by
its creator, the state. The state is always entitled to enforce its laws, and if a corporation has
failed to comply with the statutory requirements, the secretary of state or the attorney general

Office of the Secretary of State
Corporations Section
P.O. Box 13697
Austin, Texas 78711-3697

ARTICLES OF REVOCATION OF DISSOLUTION

Pursuant to the provisions of article 6.05 of the Texas Business Corporation Act, the undersigned corporation adopts the following articles of revocation of dissolution:

1.   The name of the corporation is _____

2.   The file number is _____

3.   The date on which the dissolution became effective was _____

4.   The date on which the revocation of dissolution was authorized was _____

    Check either A or B in item 5 below:

5.   ☐ **A. A written consent to revoke voluntary dissolution proceedings, A COPY OF WHICH IS ATTACHED, was signed by all the shareholders of the corporation, or was signed in their names by their attorneys thereunto duly authorized.**

or   ☐ **B. A resolution to revoke was adopted by the shareholders of the corporation on the following date: _____ The number of shares outstanding and entitled to vote, and voting for and against the revocation were as follows:**

CLASS	SERIES	OUTSTANDING AND ENTITLED TO VOTE	TOTAL VOTED FOR	TOTAL VOTED AGAINST
_____	_____	_____	_____	_____
_____	_____	_____	_____	_____

By _____
                  Signature

_____
                  Officer Title

(continued)

may bring an action to force dissolution of the corporation. Typical corporate abuses that will justify **involuntary dissolution** include failing to file annual reports, failing to pay franchise taxes, procuring articles of incorporation through fraud, or abusing or exceeding authority granted by law.[48] Some jurisdictions add failure to appoint a registered agent or to notify regarding a change of the corporation's registered office within thirty days, insolvency, unfair competition or restraint of trade, persistent violations of state laws, or an existence that is detrimental to the public interest.

Most corporations never run afoul of state law or commit acts that support involuntary dissolution, but a few of the provisions in this area require caution on the part of the corporation. Even otherwise conscientious corporate officers may delay annual reports, overlook payment of franchise taxes, or neglect to report changes of the registered office or registered agent. The procedures for involuntary dissolution should be explored, therefore, in an effort to save the corporate creation from untimely demise because of a mere oversight.

The Model Business Corporation Act provisions appear to take the fairest approach to the problem. Under sections 14.20 and 14.21, the secretary of state sends notice of any alleged transgressions to the corporation at its registered office or, if it no longer maintains

Exhibit 15–13.

(continued)

INSTRUCTIONS FOR FILING
ARTICLES OF REVOCATION OF DISSOLUTION

1. The articles of revocation must be signed by an officer of the corporation. <u>Prior to signing, please read the statements on this form carefully. A person commits an offense under the Texas Business Corporation Act if the person signs a document the person knows is false in any material respect with the intent that the document be delivered to the secretary of state for filing. The offense is a Class A misdemeanor</u>

2. If the articles of dissolution have been filed but have not become effective by reason of a noted future effective date, note "NOT APPLICABLE" in item number 3.

3. If item 5A is checked, a copy of the consent of all shareholders to revoke the dissolution proceedings must be attached.

4. This document must be received within 120 days of the date the certificate of dissolution was issued to the corporation by the secretary of state.

5. Enclose $15.00 remittance for the filing fee for the articles of revocation of dissolution. The check should be made payable to the secretary of state.

6. Two copies of the form along with the filing fee should be mailed to the address shown in the heading of this form. The delivery address is James Earl Rudder Office Building, 1019 Brazos, Austin, Texas 78701. We will place one document on record and, *if a duplicate copy has been provided for such purpose*, return a file stamped copy. The telephone number is (512) 463-5555, TDD: (800) 735-2989, FAX: (512) 463-5709.

7. Before filing articles of revocation of dissolution, the secretary of state must determine that the corporation's name is still available. A preliminary determination of availability may be obtained by telephone at (512) 463-5555 or by e-mail at corpinfo.sos.state.tx.us/ This is only a preliminary clearance. The final decision on the name will be made when the document is submitted for filing. If the corporation name is unavailable, it will be necessary to file articles of amendment changing the name in order to file the articles of revocation of dissolution.

8. Corporations which have dissolved under article 6.01 of the Texas Business Corporation Act cannot file articles of revocation of dissolution since revocation requires adoption by shareholders.

9. Upon issuance of the certificate of revocation, the existence of the corporation shall be deemed to have continued without interruption.

10. The corporation should inquire of the comptroller of public accounts whether any tax returns or payments are due following revocation. Questions should be directed to the Comptroller of Public Accounts, Tax Assistance Section, Austin, Texas 78774-0100. The telephone number is (512) 463-4600. The toll-free number is (800) 252-1381. TDD: (800) 248-4099 or (512) 463-4621.

11. The foregoing form promulgated by the secretary of state is designed to meet minimum statutory filing requirements and no warranty is made regarding the suitability of this form. This form and the information provided are not substitutes for the advice of an attorney and it is recommended that the services of an attorney be obtained before preparation of the articles of revocation of dissolution.

Form No. 606
Revised 9/99

a registered office within the state, at its principal place of business. This notice may be sent if the corporation does not pay taxes, deliver its annual report, or maintain current information concerning its registered agent or registered office, or if the corporation's period of duration expires. Within sixty days after service of the notice, the corporation may satisfy the secretary of state that the matter has been resolved or that the grounds for the notice did not exist. If the corporation fails to respond to the notice, the secretary of state may administratively dissolve the corporation by issuing a certificate of dissolution. After the certificate of dissolution has been issued, the corporation may not carry on any business except to wind up and liquidate its affairs. At any time within two years after the effective date of an administrative dissolution, the corporation may apply to the secretary of state to be reinstated. A condition to reinstatement is the resolution or elimination of any grounds that existed for dissolution at the time of the issuance of the certificate. If the secretary of state permits a reinstatement (or if a court orders reinstatement on appeal from the secretary of state's denial of an application for reinstatement), the reinstatement is retroactive, and the corporation may resume its business as though the administrative dissolution never occurred.[49]

Not all the states are so forgiving. Although many states require notice to the corporation, only about half of the jurisdictions allow the corporation to cure the defect after dissolution proceedings have actually been commenced.

By Shareholders

If corporate management refuses to consider dissolution and the unanimous consent of the shareholders cannot be obtained, voluntary dissolution is impossible, but an involuntary dissolution procedure may be invoked in special circumstances. For example, under the Model Business Corporation Act, if the board of directors does not recommend a voluntary dissolution to the shareholders, the shareholders have no independent authority to dissolve the corporation alone. Even under jurisdictions that permit the shareholders to voluntarily dissolve their own corporation by unanimous consent, if the majority of the directors are also shareholders and oppose dissolution, no matter how many other shareholders favor dissolution, dissolution cannot be accomplished voluntarily. The approval of the directors-shareholders is necessary for unanimous shareholder consent and for a director resolution for dissolution. Dissolution by voluntary proceedings also is impossible if the directors or shareholders are deadlocked.

The statutory escape is the shareholders' application to a court for liquidation of the business and a decree of dissolution. Section 14.30 of the Model Business Corporation Act grants liquidation power to a court upon application of a shareholder who can establish an unbreakable director deadlock threatening irreparable injury to the corporation; oppressive, illegal, or fraudulent acts of those in control of the corporation; a shareholder deadlock in failing to elect new directors for a period of two years; or misapplication or waste of the corporate assets. These grounds are typical among corporate statutes granting the shareholders the right to bring an action for involuntary liquidation and dissolution. Abandonment of the corporate business or persistent commission of ultra vires acts also are frequently specified grounds.

Some states have expanded the shareholders' authority to obtain a judicial decree of dissolution. In doing so, they have recognized that majority shareholders or directors may take action against certain minority shareholders that may, at the least, put pressure on the minority shareholders to go along with the policies of the majority and, at the worst, actually oppress the minority shareholders so that the corporation is not acting in their best interests. Under these statutes, the shareholders may obtain a decree of dissolution by showing that the directors or those in control of the corporation are acting in a manner "unfairly prejudicial" to the shareholders in their capacity as shareholders, directors, or officers, or as employees of closely held corporations. These statutes also empower a court to order that the corporation buy out the complaining shareholders at a fair price, rather than dissolve the corporation.[50] The Model Business Corporation Act's Close Corporation Supplement provides for a similar remedy in section 42 that would apply to closely held corporations.

If the shareholders prove the allegations in the action, the court proceeds to a judicially supervised liquidation ending in a decree of dissolution.[51] However, if the problem is solved during the course of the liquidation proceedings, most state statutes require that the proceedings be discontinued and all corporate property be returned to the corporation.[52]

By a Creditor

A creditor may force involuntary dissolution if the corporation is insolvent and the creditor's claim is undisputed. The Model Business Corporation Act deems claims that have been reduced to judgment and claims that have been admitted by the corporation in writing to be undisputed.[53] The creditor may be in the frustrating position of owning an uncontested debt that corporate management cannot pay because the corporation is insolvent, but management may be resisting dissolution and liquidation whereby the creditor would receive some satisfaction from the assets. In such a case, the creditor may force judicial liquidation and involuntary dissolution.

LIQUIDATION

Closely associated with dissolution, whether voluntary or involuntary, is the process of collecting all corporate assets, completing or terminating unexecuted contracts, paying creditors and expenses, and distributing the remains to the owners. These activities are collectively referred to as **liquidation**. Under the Model Business Corporation Act, normal corporate business ceases when a decree of dissolution is entered by a court or when the secretary of state issues a certificate of dissolution.[54] The only corporate activities that may follow a dissolution are those necessary to wind up and liquidate the business and affairs of the corporation. Consequently, liquidation and winding up precede final dissolution.

Nonjudicial Liquidation

When dissolution is voluntary and does not involve judicial proceedings, corporate management is responsible for winding up and liquidating the corporate business. In most states, this process is commenced after the statement of intent to dissolve is filed and must be completed before the articles of dissolution are filed, since the articles usually recite that all debts, obligations, and liabilities have been paid or provided for, and that the remaining assets have been distributed among the shareholders. There is no time limit on the liquidation process, but practical considerations encourage management to proceed as expeditiously as possible.

Nonjudicial liquidation may be conducted as informally as desired, as long as all creditors are paid and remaining assets are distributed. Special safeguards are inserted for creditors: The directors of the corporation may be personally liable if they distribute assets to the shareholders without providing for creditors,[55] and a forgotten creditor may enforce its claim against the corporation, directors, or shareholders for a period of time after dissolution.[56]

The Model Business Corporation Act has expanded creditor protection in the dissolution of a corporation. Known creditors must receive notice of the dissolution instructing them about submitting claims within a period of time, no less than 120 days from the effective date of the notice. If a creditor does not deliver the claim, or if the claim is rejected and the creditor does not promptly commence a proceeding to enforce the claim, the claim will be barred.[57] For persons who may have a claim against the corporation but are not known at the time of dissolution, the dissolved corporation may publish notice of dissolution and request that persons with claims present them in accordance with the notice. Any person who does not respond to the published notice within five years after the publication date will not be entitled to assert a claim against the corporation.[58]

In connection with the liquidation of a corporation, it may also be necessary to obtain releases or termination certificates from various state agencies, such as workers' compensation administrations or sales tax licensing authorities. In some states, the shareholder may assume personal liability related to obligations that may arise through these agencies (such as workers' compensation claims or unpaid tax liabilities) instead of obtaining the agency's release certificates.

If the directors or officers become immersed in liquidation and discover dissatisfied shareholders or hostile creditors, they may apply to have the liquidation supervised by a court.

Judicial Liquidation

Court-supervised liquidation is available to corporate management in voluntary dissolution proceedings and is also used when involuntary proceedings have been commenced by the state, the shareholders, or creditors of a corporation. The court may enjoin any person who threatens to interfere with orderly proceedings, and may appoint a receiver who will carry on the corporate business and preserve the corporation's assets during the proceedings. Creditors usually are required to file their claims under oath within a prescribed time, and a hearing is held to finally determine the claims of all parties. A liquidating receiver is then appointed with authority to collect and sell the assets of the corporation, to apply the proceeds to the expenses of the liquidation and to creditors' claims, and then to distribute remaining funds to shareholders.[59]

Liquidation Distributions

In any liquidation of a corporation, judicially supervised or conducted by management, the corporate assets will be collected and may be sold, and the proceeds are used to pay first the expenses of liquidation and then the creditors of the corporation. Whatever remains belongs to the shareholders of the corporation. The remnants of the stockholders' corporation are distributed to them in accordance with their liquidation preferences.[60]

KEY TERMS

extraordinary corporate activity	short-form merger	conversion
restatement of articles	hostile takeover	appraisal right
constituent corporations	greenmail	dissenter's rights
merger	poison pills	fair value
surviving corporation	people pill	voluntary dissolution
consolidation	control shares	revocation of voluntary dissolution
share exchange	sharks	involuntary dissolution
triangular merger	shark repellant	liquidation
reverse triangular merger	affiliated corporation	nonjudicial liquidation
reorganization	corporate shell	judicial liquidation
letter of intent	domestication	liquidating distributions
small-impact merger		

WEB RESOURCES

General information concerning local statutes governing fundamental changes such as amendments, mergers, share exchanges, sales of substantially all of the assets outside the ordinary course of business, and dissolution is available on every state's Secretary of State's (or Department of Commerce) Web site. Most of the sites offer forms that are required for filing to accomplish these transactions. The National Association of Secretaries of State maintains links directly to the offices of the Secretaries of State in all states. These can be accessed through

<http://www.nass.org>

Access to state corporate laws governing fundamental corporate changes may be obtained through the Legal

Information Institute maintained at the Cornell Law School:

<http://www.law.cornell.edu>

The specific sections of a state's corporate law may be located through a search site that directly ties to the corporate laws of the state. This search may be accessed at

<http://www.megalaw.com>

Various forms of notices to creditors for purposes of dissolution of a corporation are available from the following:

<http://www.toolkit.cch.com>
<http://www.findlaw.com>
<http://www.lectlaw.com>
<http://www.ilrg.com>

CASES

BECKER v. GRABER BUILDERS, INC.

149 N.C. App. 787, 561 S.E.2d 905 (2002)
THOMAS, J.

[Pamela Becker contracted with Graber Builders, Inc. to build a house and alleges that the septic system was inadequate. Graber Builders, Inc. was administratively dissolved. Dwight E. Graber continued the construction business under the name Graber Homes, Inc., with the same assets of the dissolved corporation. Ms. Becker sued both Graber Builders, Inc. and Graber Homes, Inc. to recover her damages for breach of contract].

The general rule is that a corporation that purchases all, or substantially all, of the assets of another corporation is not liable for the old corporation's debts. *G.P. Publica-*

tions, Inc. v. Quebecor Printing-St. Paul, Inc., 125 N.C.App. 424, 432, 481 S.E.2d 674, 679, *disc. review denied,* 346 N.C. 546, 488 S.E.2d 800 (1997). Plaintiff alleges no facts supporting one of the four well-settled exceptions to this general rule against successor liability. *See id.* at 432-33, 481 S.E.2d at 679 (setting forth the four exceptions: "(1) where there is an express or implied agreement by the purchasing corporation to assume the debt or liability; (2) where the transfer amounts to a *de facto* merger of the two corporations; (3) where the transfer of assets was done for the purpose of defrauding the corporation's creditors; or (4) where the purchasing corporation is a 'mere continuation' of the selling corporation in that the purchasing corporation has some of the same shareholders, directors, and officers.").

Consequently, plaintiff fails to allege a claim upon which relief may be granted against Graber Homes, Inc.

* * *

[The motion to dismiss is sustained].

CORPORATE EXPRESS OFFICE PRODUCTS, INC. v. PHILLIPS

Florida Supreme Court
847 S. 2d 406 (2003)
PARIENTE, J.

This case involves the enforceability of noncompete agreements against former employees. Corporate Express Office Products, Inc. (Corporate Express) sought to enforce noncompete agreements against respondents Edward Goff, Doug Phillips, and Lori Farrell. The former employees raised as a defense that the noncompete agreements had been entered into with prior employers and not with Corporate Express. Because one corporate acquisition by Corporate Express was initially accomplished through a 100 percent stock purchase . . . and the other corporate acquisition occurred through a sale of assets, we explain the facts of each acquisition separately.

The first factual scenario involved employees Phillips and Farrell. In 1986, Phillips signed a noncompete agreement with his employer, Bishop Office Furniture Company (Bishop). In 1989, Farrell signed a noncompete agreement with Bishop. Neither agreement included an assignment clause. In 1997, Corporate Express of the South, Inc. (CES) purchased 100 percent of Bishop's stock. The stock purchase agreement between Bishop and CES listed the noncompete agreements with Phillips and Farrell. CES operated the business under the Bishop name until 1998, when

Bishop was merged into CES. Shortly thereafter, CES merged into Corporate Express of the East, Inc. (CEE). CEE then changed its name to Corporate Express Office Products, Inc.

The second scenario began in 1986 when Goff signed a noncompete agreement with his employer, Ciera Office Products (Ciera). In 1996, Ciera sold its assets, including the noncompete agreement with Goff, to CES. Goff executed a consent to Ciera's assignment of his noncompete agreement to CES. Goff did not execute any additional consents to assignment after CES merged with CEE and then changed its name to Corporate Express.

Like Bishop and Ciera, Corporate Express is engaged in the business of selling office furniture and business equipment. Phillips, Farrell, and Goff remained continuously employed with CES from the time of the corporate acquisition through the merger into CEE and the renaming of CEE as Corporate Express. In 2000, the employees terminated their employment with Corporate Express and joined a different employer, allegedly in violation of their noncompete agreements.

The terms of the noncompete agreements precluded the employees from competing against their employers or soliciting the employers' customers for one year following the termination of employment. Further, the agreements covered seven Florida counties, which were the territories serviced by respondents. Corporate Express sued Goff, Phillips, and Farrell and their new employer for unlawful use of trade secrets and breach of the noncompete agreements.

Corporate Express sought a preliminary injunction to enforce the agreements.

The former employees asserted that because the noncompete agreements did not contain a clause authorizing assignment and were in fact never assigned to Corporate Express, the noncompete agreements could not be enforced. * * *

The 1986 noncompete agreements between Goff and Ciera, and Phillips and Bishop, and the 1989 noncompete agreement between Farrell and Bishop, are governed by section 542.33, Florida Statutes (1985), which states in pertinent part:

> (2)(a) . . . [O]ne who is employed as an agent or employee may agree with his employer to refrain from carrying on or engaging in a similar business and from soliciting old customers of such employer within a reasonably limited time and area, . . . so long as such employer continues to carry on a like business therein. Said agreements may, in the discretion of a court of competent jurisdiction, be enforced by injunction.

* * *

The question in this case is whether the nature of the business transaction affects whether a consent to an assignment of a noncompete agreement is necessary either in the original agreement or in connection with the subsequent transactions. The types of transactions relevant to this case are an asset sale, a 100 percent stock sale, a merger, and a name change.

* * *

We begin with a discussion of the effect of a 100 percent stock purchase on a corporation's existence. Unlike partnerships, a corporate entity is not dissolved by a change of ownership. *See St. Petersburg Sheraton Corp. v. Stuart,* 242 So.2d 185, 190 (Fla. 2d DCA 1970) ("Ownership by one corporation of all the stock of another corporation does not destroy the identity of the latter as a distinct legal entity. . . ."). In fact, a foundation of corporate law is that, unlike a partnership or a sole proprietorship, the existence of a corporate entity is not affected by changes in its ownership or changes in management. *See Cedric Kushner Promotions, Ltd. v. King,* 533 U.S. 158, 163, 121 S.Ct. 2087, 150 L.Ed.2d 198 (2001) ("The corporate owner/employee, a natural person, is distinct from the corporation itself, a legally different entity with different rights and responsibilities due to its different legal status."); *see also Am. States Inc. Co. v. Kelley,* 446 So.2d 1085, 1086 (Fla. 4th DCA 1984) ("The general rule is that corporations are legal entities separate and distinct from the persons comprising them."). Moreover, there is a "clear distinction between the transfer of an asset or a corporation, such as a franchise agreement, and a transfer of the stock in a corporation itself." *Hawkins v. Ford Motor Co.,* 748 So.2d 993, 1000 (Fla.1999). *Cf. Cruising World, Inc. v. Westermeyer,* 351 So.2d 371, 373 (Fla. 2d DCA 1977) (stating that a share of stock does not vest owner with any right or title to any of corporation's property). With a stock purchase, the corporation

whose stock is acquired continues in existence, even though there may be a change in its management. As explained in *Sears Termite,* the "fact that there is a change in ownership of corporate stock does not affect the corporation's existence or its contract rights, or its liabilities." 745 So.2d at 486.

In contrast to a sale of corporate stock, in a sale of corporate assets the transaction introduces into the equation an entirely different entity, the acquiring business. The asset sale to that entity may include some or all of the corporate assets, and the transferred assets may include tangibles such as machinery and intangibles such as accounts receivable. *See* § 607.1202(1), Fla. Stat. (2002) ("A corporation may sell, lease, exchange, or otherwise dispose of all, or substantially all, of its property. . . ."). A corporation that sells its assets may continue in existence, may dissolve, or may merge with the entity that purchased its assets. *See Best Towing & Recovery, Inc. v. Beggs,* 531 So.2d 243, 245 (Fla. 2d DCA 1988) (noting that pursuant to an agreement, a transfer of assets may immediately dissolve a corporation).

A corporation that acquires the assets of another business entity does not as a matter of law assume the liabilities of the prior business. *See Bernard v. Kee Mfg. Co.,* 409 So.2d 1047, 1049 (Fla.1982). In *Bernard,* this Court declined to impose product liability on a successor corporation that purchased the assets of the manufacturer of a defective product and continued the product line under the same trade name, but discontinued the allegedly defective model. *See id.* at 1048. This Court set out the generally accepted rule applicable to an asset purchase:

The vast majority of jurisdictions follow the traditional corporate law rule which does not impose the liabilities of the selling predecessor upon the buying successor company unless (1) the successor expressly or impliedly assumes obligations of the predecessor, (2) the transaction is a de facto merger, (3) the successor is a mere continuation of the predecessor, or (4) the transaction is a fraudulent effort to avoid liabilities of the predecessor.

[Citations omitted]

In an asset purchase, the liabilities and responsibilities of each party would be set forth in the parties' agreement. *See* William Meade Fletcher et al., *Fletcher Cyclopedia of the Law of Private Corporations,* § 7122 (perm.ed., rev.vol.1990) ("The general rule . . . is that where one company sells or otherwise transfers all its assets to another company, the latter is not liable for the debts and liabilities of the transferor. . . . An express agreement, or one that can be implied, to assume the other company's debts and obligations, is necessary. . . ."). Thus, when the sale of the assets includes a personal service contract that contains a noncompete agreement, the purchaser can enforce its terms only with the employee's consent to an assignment. *See, e.g., Pino v. Spanish Broad. Sys. of Fla., Inc.,* 564 So.2d 186, 189 (Fla. 3d DCA 1990) (holding that because contract containing covenant not to compete included a provision permitting assignment, the covenant was assignable and enforceable by business that bought assets of employee's former employer).

We next address a corporate merger, which is also involved in this case. Under longstanding precedent, on the date of a merger the surviving corporation becomes "liable for the debts, contracts and torts" of the former corporation. *Barnes v. Liebig,* 146 Fla. 219, 1 So.2d 247, 253 (1941). This principle is codified in section 607.1106, Florida Statutes (2002), which provides in pertinent part:

(1) When a merger becomes effective:

(a) Every other corporation party to the merger merges into the surviving corporation and the separate existence of every corporation except the surviving corporation ceases;

(b) The title to all real estate and other property, or any interest therein, owned by each corporation party to the merger is vested in the surviving corporation without reversion or impairment;

(c) The surviving corporation shall thenceforth be responsible and liable for all the liabilities and obligations of each corporation party to the merger[.]

This provision has remained unchanged since its 1989 enactment and thus contains the statutory language applicable at the time of the mergers in this case. Prior to the enactment of section 607.1106, section 607.231(3), Florida Statutes (1987), similarly provided that the surviving corporation of a merger "shall have all the rights, privileges, immunities and powers, and shall be subject to all of the duties and liabilities" of the merged corporation.

Precedent applying these provisions demonstrates the passage of the obligations and rights of a merged corporation to the survivor of the merger. In *Celotex Corp. v. Pickett,* 490 So.2d 35, 37 (Fla.1986), this Court construed section 607.231(3) to hold Celotex liable for punitive damages stemming from a shipyard worker's exposure to asbestos manufactured by a corporation it had absorbed in a merger. This Court stated:

Where two corporations have truly merged, a corporate tortfeasor by any other name is still a tortfeasor, to paraphrase Shakespeare. *See, e.g., Moe v. Transamerica Title Insurance Co.,* 21 Cal.App.3d 289, 98 Cal.Rpt[r]. 547, 556-57 (1971) (merger "merely directs the blood of the old corporation into the veins of the new, the old living in the new"); *Atlanta Newspapers, Inc. v. Doyal,* 84 Ga.App. 122, 128, 65 S.E.2d 432, 437 (1951) (merger "is like the uniting of two or more rivers, neither stream is annihilated, but all continue in existence").

[Citations omitted]

Based on the language in Florida's statute as well as the decisions in *Barnes* and *Celotex,* we conclude that the surviving corporation in a merger assumes the right to enforce a noncompete agreement entered into with an employee of the merged corporation by operation of law, and no assignment is necessary. This is because in a merger, the two corporations in essence unite into a single corporate existence.

Accordingly, based on fundamental principles of commercial transactions and the applicable statutes, we hold that, in contrast to an asset purchase, neither a 100 percent purchase of corporate stock nor a corporate merger affects the enforceability of a noncompete agreement. This holding is in accord with our decisions in both *Bernard* and *Celotex* where we have followed the traditional principles of corporate law in determining the obligations and liabilities of a successor corporation. This holding also "conforms with the policy of preserving the sanctity of contract and providing uniformity and certainty in commercial transactions." *Pino,* 564 So.2d at 189.

* * *

PROBLEMS

1. A shareholder of LMN Corporation does *not* have a right to dissent and appraisal of shares under the Model Act when:
   a. LMN Corporation is the surviving corporation to a merger and LMN owns all the outstanding shares of the other corporate party to the merger;
   b. LMN Corporation is selling substantially all its assets to XYZ Corporation;
   c. LMN Corporation is exchanging its shares with XYZ Corporation shareholders; or
   d. LMN Corporation is being merged in XYZ Corporation.

2. When two corporations continue by forming a new corporation into which both of their businesses are combined, it is a
   a. merger;
   b. consolidation;
   c. dissolution; or
   d. transfer of assets outside the ordinary course of business.

3. Name the intracorporate parties who must approve a merger.

4. XYZ Corporation has 100,000 shares of common stock outstanding. ABC Corporation has 200,000 shares of common stock outstanding. The corporations are planning to merge. If XYZ Corporation already owns 185,000 shares of ABC Corporation, the transaction is called a _____ merger.

5. Under the facts of problem 4, the following parties must approve the merger:
   a. the shareholders of XYZ Corporation;
   b. the shareholders of ABC Corporation;
   c. the board of directors of XYZ Corporation;
   d. b and c but not a;
   e. a and b but not c; or
   f. a and c but not b.

6. Ignoring the facts of problems 4 and 5, if XYZ Corporation is planning to issue 15,000 shares of its common stock to the shareholders of ABC Corporation in exchange for all of their shares of ABC Corporation, the transaction is called a _____ merger.

7. Under the facts of problem 6, the following parties must approve the merger:
   a. the shareholders of XYZ Corporation;
   b. the shareholders of ABC Corporation;
   c. the board of directors of XYZ Corporation;
   d. a and b but not c;
   e. b and c but not a; or
   f. a and c but not b.

8. A "poison pill" is
   a. a bitter thing to swallow;
   b. a corporate structure designed to prevent a takeover;
   c. a corporate structure designed to make a takeover undesirable; or
   d. a compensation agreement among management.

9. State three ways in which a corporation may be voluntarily dissolved.

10. Dissenters' rights are usually permitted for:
    a. amendments of the articles of incorporation;
    b. dissolution;
    c. changes to the bylaws; or
    d. mergers.

PRACTICE ASSIGNMENTS

1. Allstate Corporation has been doing business in your state for forty years, but now, after significant economic reversals, the board of directors has decided to terminate the business. Allstate has creditor claims of $1,086,789 and assets of $2,345,098. It will eliminate its offices at 37856 South Wadsworth Boulevard in your city. All the employees will be fired, and the officers and directors will resign. Shareholders own 34,980 shares of common stock. Prepare the necessary documents to dissolve Allstate.

2. Sara Smith is a shareholder of Righteous Corporation and has received a notice that Righteous Corporation is going to merge with Humble Company. Ms. Smith does not want to be a shareholder of Humble, and regards its business policies as meek and timid. Prepare a letter to Ms. Smith describing her right to dissent to the transaction under your local law. Include all advice necessary for her exercise of dissenters' rights, and describe what she will receive as a result.

3. Review your local corporation code and describe in a memorandum the circumstances under which a corporation may be involuntarily dissolved.

4. Describe the advantages and disadvantages of a judicially supervised dissolution and liquidation of the corporation to the following persons:
   a. directors of the corporation;
   b. officers of the corporation;
   c. creditors of the corporation;
   d. shareholders of the corporation; and
   e. attorneys for the corporation.

END NOTES

1. Model Business Corporation Act (hereafter M.B.C.A.) § 10.03.

2. E.g., Pennsylvania, 15 Pa. Stat. Ann. § 1912.

3. See "Shareholder Meetings" in Chapter 10.

4. See M.B.C.A. § 7.04.

5. See "Action without a Meeting" in Chapter 10.

6. See M.B.C.A. § 10.04.

7. M.B.C.A. § 10.06.

8. This is also the rule under the Model Business Corporation Act. See M.B.C.A. § 1.23.

9. E.g., New York requires consent of the state tax commission for amendments reviving an administratively dissolved corporation, N.Y. Bus. Corp. Law § 806 (McKinney).

10. See M.B.C.A.§ 1.23.

11. See "Filing and Other Formalities" in Chapter 8.

12. See M.B.C.A. § 10.07.

13. See M.B.C.A. §§ 11.01, 11.02.

14. M.B.C.A. § 11.04(g).

15. M.B.C.A. § 11.04.

16. See "Amendment of the Articles of Incorporation" earlier in this chapter.

17. See "Rights of Dissenting Shareholders" later in this chapter.

18. See "Filing and Other Formalities" in Chapter 8.

19. See M.B.C.A. §§ 11.06(b) and 1.23.

20. E.g. Georgia, Ga. Bus. Corp. Act § 14-2-123.

21. M.B.C.A. § 11.07.

22. I.R.C. of 1986, 26 U.S.C.A. § 368(1)(a).

23. M.B.C.A. § 12.02.

24. See "Rights of Dissenting Shareholders" later in this chapter.

25. See "Effect of Qualification" in Chapter 14.

26. See "Structural Changes in the Foreign Corporation" in Chapter 14.

27. See M..B.C.A. §§ 9.20-9.25.

28. M.B.C.A. §§ 9.30-9.35.

29. M.B.C.A. §§ 9.40-9.43.

30. M.B.C.A. §§ 9.50-9.56.

31. M.B.C.A. § 13.02.

32. M.B.C.A. §§ 11.04, 13.02.

33. M.B.C.A. §§ 13.20-13.23.

34. M.B.C.A. § 13.23.

35. M.B.C.A. § 13.01(4).

36. M.B.C.A. § 13.23.

37. M.B.C.A. § 13.24.

38. M.B.C.A. § 13.30.

39. M.B.C.A. § 13.31

40. M.B.C.A. § 14.01.

41. E.g., Delaware, Del. Code Ann. tit. 8, § 275(c).

42. M.B.C.A. § 14.02.

43. M.B.C.A. § 14.02.

44. M.B.C.A. § 14.03.

45. M.B.C.A. § 14.05.

46. M.B.C.A. § 14.06.

47. M.B.C.A. § 14.04.

48. M.B.C.A. § 14.30.

49. M.B.C.A. §§ 14.22, 14.23.

50. E.g., Minnesota, Minn. Stat. Ann. § 3201A.751 (West).

51. M.B.C.A. §§ 14.31–14.33.

52. See M.B.C.A. § 14.32.

53. M.B.C.A. § 14.30(3).

54. M.B.C.A. §§ 14.21, 14.33.

55. M.B.C.A. § 8.33.

56. See, e.g., Nevada, Nev. Rev. Stat. § 78.585 (permitting creditor claims within two years after dissolution).

57. M.B.C.A. § 14.06.

58. M.B.C.A. § 14.07.

59. M.B.C.A. § 14.32.

60. See "Dissolution and Liquidation" in Chapter 11.

UNIFORM PARTNERSHIP ACT (ORIGINAL)

(Adopted in 48 States, all except Georgia and Louisiana; the District of Columbia, the Virgin Islands, and Guam. The adoptions by Alabama and Nebraska do not follow the official text in every respect, but are substantially similar, with local variations.)

The Act consists of 7 Parts as follows:

I. Preliminary Provisions
II. Nature of Partnership
III. Relations of Partners to Persons Dealing with the Partnership
IV. Relations of Partners to One Another
V. Property Rights of a Partner
VI. Dissolution and Winding Up
VII. Miscellaneous Provisions

An Act to make uniform the Law of Partnerships

Be it enacted, etc.:

PART I PRELIMINARY PROVISIONS

SECTION 1. NAME OF ACT.
THIS ACT MAY BE CITED AS UNIFORM PARTNERSHIP ACT.

SECTION 2. DEFINITION OF TERMS.
In this act, "Court" includes every court and judge having jurisdiction in the case.

"Business" includes every trade, occupation, or profession.

"Person" includes individuals, partnerships, corporations, and other associations.

"Bankrupt" includes bankrupt under the Federal Bankruptcy Act or insolvent under any state insolvent act.

"Conveyance" includes every assignment, lease, mortgage, or encumbrance.

"Real property" includes land and any interest or estate in land.

SECTION 3. INTERPRETATION OF KNOWLEDGE AND NOTICE.
(1) A person has "knowledge" of a fact within the meaning of this act not only when he has actual knowledge thereof, but also when he has knowledge of such other facts as in the circumstances shows bad faith.

(2) A person has "notice" of a fact within the meaning of this act when the person who claims the benefit of the notice

(a) States the fact to such person, or

(b) Delivers through the mail, or by other means of communication, a written statement of the fact to such person or to a proper person at his place of business or residence.

SECTION 4. RULES OF CONSTRUCTION.

(1) The rule that statutes in derogation of the common law are to be strictly construed shall have no application to this act.

(2) The law of estoppel shall apply under this act.

(3) The law of agency shall apply under this act.

(4) This act shall be so interpreted and construed as to effect its general purpose to make uniform the law of those states which enact it.

(5) This act shall not be construed so as to impair the obligations of any contract existing when the act goes into effect, nor to affect any action or proceedings begun or right accrued before this act takes effect.

SECTION 5. RULES FOR CASES NOT PROVIDED FOR IN THIS ACT.

In any case not provided for in this act the rules of law and equity, including the law merchant, shall govern.

PART II   NATURE OF PARTNERSHIP

SECTION 6. PARTNERSHIP DEFINED.

(1) A partnership is an association of two or more persons to carry on as co-owners a business for profit.

(2) But any association formed under any other statute of this state, or any statute adopted by authority, other than the authority of this state, is not a partnership under this act, unless such association would have been a partnership in this state prior to the adoption of this act; but this act shall apply to limited partnerships except in so far as the statutes relating to such partnerships are inconsistent herewith.

SECTION 7. RULES FOR DETERMINING THE EXISTENCE OF A PARTNERSHIP.

In determining whether a partnership exists, these rules shall apply:

(1) Except as provided by Section 16 persons who are not partners as to each other are not partners as to third persons.

(2) Joint tenancy, tenancy in common, tenancy by the entireties, joint property, common property, or part ownership does not of itself establish a partnership, whether such co-owners do or do not share any profits made by the use of the property.

(3) The sharing of gross returns does not of itself establish a partnership, whether or not the persons sharing them have a joint or common right or interest in any property from which the returns are derived.

(4) The receipt by a person of a share of the profits of a business is prima facie evidence that he is a partner in the business, but no such inference shall be drawn if such profits were received in payment:

(a) As a debt by installments or otherwise,

(b) As wages of an employee or rent to a landlord,

(c) As an annuity to a widow or representative of a deceased partner,

(d) As interest on a loan, though the amount of payment varies with the profits of the business,

(e) As the consideration for the sale of a good-will of a business or other property by installments or otherwise.

SECTION 8. PARTNERSHIP PROPERTY.

(1) All property originally brought into the partnership stock or subsequently acquired by purchase or otherwise, on account of the partnership, is partnership property.

(2) Unless the contrary intention appears, property acquired with partnership funds is partnership property.

(3) Any estate in real property may be acquired in the partnership name. Title so acquired can be conveyed only in the partnership name.

(4) A conveyance to a partnership in the partnership name, though without words of inheritance, passes the entire estate of the grantor unless a contrary intent appears.

PART III   RELATIONS OF PARTNERS TO PERSONS DEALING WITH THE PARTNERSHIP

SECTION 9. PARTNER AGENT OF PARTNERSHIP AS TO PARTNERSHIP BUSINESS.

(1) Every partner is an agent of the partnership for the purpose of its business, and the act of every partner, including the execution in the partnership name of any instrument, for apparently carrying on in the usual way the business of the partnership of which he is a member binds the partnership, unless the partner so acting has in fact no authority to act for the partnership in the particular matter, and the person with whom he is dealing has knowledge of the fact that he has no such authority.

(2) An act of a partner which is not apparently for the carrying on of the business of the partnership in the usual way does not bind the partnership unless authorized by the other partners.

(3) Unless authorized by the other partners or unless they have abandoned the business, one or more but less than all the partners have no authority to:

(a) Assign the partnership property in trust for creditors or on the assignee's promise to pay the debts of the partnership,

(b) Dispose of the good-will of the business,

(c) Do any other act which would make it impossible to carry on the ordinary business of a partnership,

(d) Confess a judgment,

(e) Submit a partnership claim or liability to arbitration or reference.

(4) No act of a partner in contravention of a restriction on authority shall bind the partnership to persons having knowledge of the restriction.

SECTION 10. CONVEYANCE OF REAL PROPERTY OF THE PARTNERSHIP.

(1) Where title to real property is in the partnership name, any partner may convey title to such property by a conveyance executed in the partnership name; but the partnership may recover such property unless the partner's act binds the partnership under the provisions of paragraph (1) of section 9 or unless such property has been conveyed by the grantee or a person claiming through such grantee to a holder for value without knowledge that the partner, in making the conveyance, has exceeded his authority.

(2) Where title to real property is in the name of the partnership, a conveyance executed by a partner, in his own name, passes the equitable interest of the partnership, provided the act is one within the authority of the partner under the provisions of paragraph (1) of section 9.

(3) Where title to real property is in the name of one or more but not all the partners, and the record does not disclose the right of the partnership, the partners in whose name the title stands may convey title to such property, but the partnership may recover such property if the partners' act does not bind the partnership under the provisions of paragraph (1) of section 9, unless the purchaser or his assignee, is a holder for value, without knowledge.

(4) Where the title to real property is in the name of one or more or all the partners, or in a third person in trust for the partnership, a conveyance executed by a partner in the partnership name, or in his own name, passes the equitable interest of the partnership, provided the act is one within the authority of the partner under the provisions of paragraph (1) of section 9.

(5) Where the title to real property is in the names of all the partners a conveyance executed by all the partners passes all their rights in such property.

SECTION 11. PARTNERSHIP BOUND BY ADMISSION OF PARTNER.

An admission or representation made by any partner concerning partnership affairs within the scope of his authority as conferred by this act is evidence against the partnership.

SECTION 12. PARTNERSHIP CHARGED WITH KNOWLEDGE OF OR NOTICE TO PARTNER.

Notice to any partner of any matter relating to partnership affairs, and the knowledge of the partner acting in the particular matter, acquired while a partner or then present to his mind, and the knowledge of any other partner who reasonably could and should have communicated it to the acting partner, operate as notice to or knowledge of the partnership, except in the case of a fraud on the partnership committed by or with the consent of that partner.

SECTION 13. PARTNERSHIP BOUND BY PARTNER'S WRONGFUL ACT.

Where, by any wrongful act or omission of any partner acting in the ordinary course of the business of the partnership or with the authority of his copartners, loss or injury is caused to any person, not being a partner in the partnership, or any penalty is incurred, the partnership is liable therefor to the same extent as the partner so acting or omitting to act.

SECTION 14. PARTNERSHIP BOUND BY PARTNER'S BREACH OF TRUST.

The partnership is bound to make good the loss:

(a) Where one partner acting within the scope of his apparent authority receives money or property of a third person and misapplies it; and

(b) Where the partnership in the course of its business receives money or property of a third person and the money or property so received is misapplied by any partner while it is in the custody of the partnership.

SECTION 15. NATURE OF PARTNER'S LIABILITY.

All partners are liable

(a) Jointly and severally for everything chargeable to the partnership under sections 13 and 14.

(b) Jointly for all other debts and obligations of the partnership; but any partner may enter into a separate obligation to perform a partnership contract.

SECTION 16. PARTNER BY ESTOPPEL.

(1) When a person, by words spoken or written or by conduct, represents himself, or consents to another representing him to any one, as a partner in an existing partnership or with one or more persons not actual partners, he is liable to any such person to whom such representation has been made, who has, on the faith of such representation, given credit to the actual or apparent partnership, and if he has made such representation or consented to its being made in a public manner he is liable to such person, whether the representation has or has not been made or communicated to such person so giving credit by or with the knowledge of the apparent partner making the representation or consenting to its being made.

(a) When a partnership liability results, he is liable as though he were an actual member of the partnership.

(b) When no partnership liability results, he is liable jointly with the other persons, if any, so consenting to the contract or representation as to incur liability, otherwise separately.

(2) When a person has been thus represented to be a partner in an existing partnership, or with one or more persons not actual partners, he is an agent of the persons consenting to such representation to bind them to the same extent and in the same manner as though he were a partner in fact, with respect to persons who rely upon the representation. Where all the members of the existing partnership consent to the representation, a partnership act or obligation results; but in all other cases it is the joint act or obligation of the person acting and the persons consenting to the representation.

SECTION 17. LIABILITY OF INCOMING PARTNER.

A person admitted as a partner into an existing partnership is liable for all the obligations of the partnership arising before his admission as though he had been a partner when such obligations were incurred, except that this liability shall be satisfied only out of partnership property.

PART IV   RELATIONS OF PARTNERS TO ONE ANOTHER

SECTION 18. RULES DETERMINING RIGHTS AND DUTIES OF PARTNERS.

The rights and duties of the partners in relation to the partnership shall be determined, subject to any agreement between them, by the following rules:

(a) Each partner shall be repaid his contributions, whether by way of capital or advances to the partnership property and share equally in the profits and surplus remaining after all liabilities, including those to partners, are satisfied; and must contribute towards the losses, whether of capital or otherwise, sustained by the partnership according to his share in the profits.

(b) The partnership must indemnify every partner in respect of payments made and personal liabilities reasonably incurred by him in the ordinary and proper conduct of its business, or for the preservation of its business or property.

(c) A partner, who in aid of the partnership makes any payment or advance beyond the amount of capital which he agreed to contribute, shall be paid interest from the date of the payment or advance.

(d) A partner shall receive interest on the capital contributed by him only from the date when repayment should be made.

(e) All partners have equal rights in the management and conduct of the partnership business.

(f) No partner is entitled to remuneration for acting in the partnership business, except that a surviving partner is entitled to reasonable compensation for his services in winding up the partnership affairs.

(g) No person can become a member of a partnership without the consent of all the partners.

(h) Any difference arising as to ordinary matters connected with the partnership business may be decided by a majority of the partners; but no act in contravention of any agreement between the partners may be done rightfully without the consent of all the partners.

SECTION 19. PARTNERSHIP BOOKS.

The partnership books shall be kept, subject to any agreement between the partners, at the principal place of business of the partnership, and every partner shall at all times have access to and may inspect and copy any of them.

SECTION 20. DUTY OF PARTNERS TO RENDER INFORMATION.

Partners shall render on demand true and full information of all things affecting the partnership to any partner or the legal representative of any deceased partner or partner under legal disability.

SECTION 21. PARTNER ACCOUNTABLE AS A FIDUCIARY.

(1) Every partner must account to the partnership for any benefit, and hold as trustee for it any profits derived by him without the consent of the other partners from any transaction connected with the formation, conduct, or liquidation of the partnership or from any use by him of its property.

(2) This section applies also to the representatives of a deceased partner engaged in the liquidation of the affairs of the partnership as the personal representatives of the last surviving partner.

SECTION 22. RIGHT TO AN ACCOUNT.

Any partner shall have the right to a formal account as to partnership affairs:

(a) If he is wrongfully excluded from the partnership business or possession of its property by his copartners,

(b) If the right exists under the terms of any agreement,

(c) As provided by section 21,

(d) Whenever other circumstances render it just and reasonable.

SECTION 23. CONTINUATION OF PARTNERSHIP BEYOND FIXED TERM.

(1) When a partnership for a fixed term or particular undertaking is continued after the termination of such term or particular undertaking without any express agreement, the rights and duties of the partners remain the same as they were at such termination, so far as is consistent with a partnership at will.

(2) A continuation of the business by the partners or such of them as habitually acted therein during the term, without any settlement or liquidation of the partnership affairs, is prima facie evidence of a continuation of the partnership.

PART V   PROPERTY RIGHTS OF A PARTNER

SECTION 24. EXTENT OF PROPERTY RIGHTS OF A PARTNER.

The property rights of a partner are (1) his rights in specific partnership property, (2) his interest in the partnership, and (3) his right to participate in the management.

SECTION 25. NATURE OF A PARTNER'S RIGHT IN SPECIFIC PARTNERSHIP PROPERTY.

(1) A partner is co-owner with his partners of specific partnership property holding as a tenant in partnership.

(2) The incidents of this tenancy are such that:

(a) A partner, subject to the provisions of this act and to any agreement between the partners, has an equal right with his partners to possess specific partnership property for partnership purposes; but he has no right to possess such property for any other purpose without the consent of his partners.

(b) A partner's right in specific partnership property is not assignable except in connection with the assignment of rights of all the partners in the same property.

(c) A partner's right in specific partnership property is not subject to attachment or execution, except on a claim against the partnership. When partnership property is attached for a partnership debt the partners, or any of them, or the representatives of a deceased partner, cannot claim any right under the homestead or exemption laws.

(d) On the death of a partner his right in specific partnership property vests in the surviving partner or partners, except where the deceased was the last surviving partner, when his right in such property vests in his legal representative. Such surviving partner or partners, or the legal representative of the last surviving partner, has no right to possess the partnership property for any but a partnership purpose.

(e) A partner's right in specific partnership property is not subject to dower, curtesy, or allowances to widows, heirs, or next of kin.

SECTION 26. NATURE OF PARTNER'S INTEREST IN THE PARTNERSHIP.

A partner's interest in the partnership is his share of the profits and surplus, and the same is personal property.

SECTION 27. ASSIGNMENT OF PARTNER'S INTEREST.

(1) A conveyance by a partner of his interest in the partnership does not of itself dissolve the partnership, nor, as against the other partners in the absence of agreement, entitle the assignee, during the continuance of the partnership to interfere in the management or administration of the partnership business or affairs, or to require any information or account of partnership transactions, or to inspect the partnership books; but it merely entitles the assignee to receive in accordance with his contract the profits to which the assigning partner would otherwise be entitled.

(2) In case of a dissolution of the partnership, the assignee is entitled to receive his assignor's interest and may require an account from the date only of the last account agreed to by all the partners.

SECTION 28. PARTNER'S INTEREST SUBJECT TO CHARGING ORDER.

(1) On due application to a competent court by any judgment creditor of a partner, the court which entered the judgment, order, or decree, or any other court, may charge the interest of the debtor partner with payment of the unsatisfied amount of such judgment debt with interest thereon; and may then or later appoint a receiver of his share of the profits, and of any other money due or to fall due to him in respect of the partnership, and make all other orders, directions, accounts and inquiries which the debtor partner might have made, or which the circumstances of the case may require.

(2) The interest charged may be redeemed at any time before foreclosure, or in case of a sale being directed by the court may be purchased without thereby causing a dissolution:

(a) With separate property, by any one or more of the partners, or

(b) With partnership property, by any one or more of the partners with the consent of all the partners whose interests are not so charged or sold.

(3) Nothing in this act shall be held to deprive a partner of his right, if any, under the exemption laws, as regards his interest in the partnership.

PART VI DISSOLUTION AND WINDING UP

SECTION 29. DISSOLUTION DEFINED.

The dissolution of a partnership is the change in the relation of the partners caused by any partner ceasing to be associated in the carrying on as distinguished from the winding up of the business.

SECTION 30. PARTNERSHIP NOT TERMINATED BY DISSOLUTION.

On dissolution the partnership is not terminated, but continues until the winding up of partnership affairs is completed.

SECTION 31. CAUSES OF DISSOLUTION.

Dissolution is caused:

(1) Without violation of the agreement between the partners,

(a) By the termination of the definite term or particular undertaking specified in the agreement,

(b) By the express will of any partner when no definite term or particular undertaking is specified,

(c) By the express will of all the partners who have not assigned their interests or suffered them to be charged for their separate debts, either before or after the termination of any specified term or particular undertaking.

(d) By the expulsion of any partner from the business bona fide in accordance with such a power conferred by the agreement between the partners;

(2) In contravention of the agreement between the partners, where the circumstances do not permit a dissolution under any other provision of this section, by the express will of any partner at any time;

(3) By any event which makes it unlawful for the business of the partnership to be carried on or for the members to carry it on in partnership;

(4) By the death of any partner;

(5) By the bankruptcy of any partner or the partnership;

(6) By decree of court under section 32.

SECTION 32. DISSOLUTION BY DECREE OF COURT.

(1) On application by or for a partner the court shall decree a dissolution whenever:

(a) A partner has been declared a lunatic in any judicial proceeding or is shown to be of unsound mind,

(b) A partner becomes in any other way incapable of performing his part of the partnership contract,

(c) A partner has been guilty of such conduct as tends to affect prejudicially the carrying on of the business,

(d) A partner wilfully or persistently commits a breach of the partnership agreement, or otherwise so conducts himself in matters relating to the partnership business that it is not reasonably practicable to carry on the business in partnership with him,

(e) The business of the partnership can only be carried on at a loss,

(f) Other circumstances render a dissolution equitable.

(2) On the application of the purchaser of a partner's interest under section 27 or 28:

(a) After the termination of the specified term or particular undertaking,

(b) At any time if the partnership was a partnership at will when the interest was assigned or when the charging order was issued.

SECTION 33. GENERAL EFFECT OF DISSOLUTION ON AUTHORITY OF PARTNER.

Except so far as may be necessary to wind up partnership affairs or to complete transactions begun but not then finished, dissolution terminates all authority of any partner to act for the partnership,

(1) With respect to the partners,

(a) When the dissolution is not by the act, bankruptcy or death of a partner; or

(b) When the dissolution is by such act, bankruptcy or death of a partner, in cases where section 34 so requires.

(2) With respect to persons not partners, as declared in section 35.

SECTION 34. RIGHT OF PARTNER TO CONTRIBUTION FROM COPARTNERS AFTER DISSOLUTION.

Where the dissolution is caused by the act, death or bankruptcy of a partner, each partner is liable to his copartners for his share of any liability created by any partner acting for the partnership as if the partnership had not been dissolved unless

(a) The dissolution being by act of any partner, the partner acting for the partnership had knowledge of the dissolution, or

(b) The dissolution being by the death or bankruptcy of a partner, the partner acting for the partnership had knowledge or notice of the death or bankruptcy.

SECTION 35. POWER OF PARTNER TO BIND PARTNERSHIP TO THIRD PERSONS AFTER DISSOLUTION.

(1) After dissolution a partner can bind the partnership except as provided in paragraph (3)

(a) By any act appropriate for winding up partnership affairs or completing transactions unfinished at dissolution;

(b) By any transaction which would bind the partnership if dissolution had not taken place, provided the other party to the transaction

(I) Had extended credit to the partnership prior to dissolution and had no knowledge or notice of the dissolution; or
(II) Though he had not so extended credit, had nevertheless known of the partnership prior to dissolution, and, having no knowledge or notice of dissolution, the fact of dissolution had not been advertised in a newspaper of general circulation in the place (or in each place if more than one) at which the partnership business was regularly carried on.

(2) The liability of a partner under paragraph (1b) shall be satisfied out of partnership assets alone when such partner had been prior to dissolution

(a) Unknown as a partner to the person with whom the contract is made; and

(b) So far unknown and inactive in partnership affairs that the business reputation of the partnership could not be said to have been in any degree due to his connection with it.

(3) The partnership is in no case bound by any act of a partner after dissolution

(a) Where the partnership is dissolved because it is unlawful to carry on the business, unless the act is appropriate for winding up partnership affairs; or

(b) Where the partner has become bankrupt; or

(c) Where the partner has no authority to wind up partnership affairs; except by a transaction with one who

(I) Had extended credit to the partnership prior to dissolution and had no knowledge or notice of his want of authority; or

(II) Had not extended credit to the partnership prior to dissolution, and, having no knowledge or notice of his want of authority, the fact of his want of authority has not been advertised in the manner provided for advertising the fact of dissolution in paragraph (1bII).

(4) Nothing in this section shall affect the liability under section 16 of any person who after dissolution represents himself or consents to another representing him as a partner in a partnership engaged in carrying on business.

SECTION 36. EFFECT OF DISSOLUTION ON PARTNER'S EXISTING LIABILITY.

(1) The dissolution of the partnership does not of itself discharge the existing liability of any partner.

(2) A partner is discharged from any existing liability upon dissolution of the partnership by an agreement to that effect between himself, the partnership creditor and the person or partnership continuing the business; and such agreement may be inferred from the course of dealing between the creditor having knowledge of the dissolution and the person or partnership continuing the business.

(3) Where a person agrees to assume the existing obligations of a dissolved partnership, the partners whose obligations have been assumed shall be discharged from any liability to any creditor of the partnership who, knowing of the agreement, consents to a material alteration in the nature or time of payment of such obligations.

(4) The individual property of a deceased partner shall be liable for all obligations of the partnership incurred while he was a partner but subject to the prior payment of his separate debts.

SECTION 37. RIGHT TO WIND UP.

Unless otherwise agreed the partners who have not wrongfully dissolved the partnership or the legal representative of the last surviving partner, not bankrupt, has the right to wind up the partnership affairs; provided, however, that any partner, his legal representative or his assignee, upon cause shown, may obtain winding up by the court.

SECTION 38. RIGHTS OF PARTNERS TO APPLICATION OF PARTNERSHIP PROPERTY.

(1) When dissolution is caused in any way, except in contravention of the partnership agreement, each partner as against his copartners and all persons claiming through them in respect of their interests in the partnership, unless otherwise agreed, may have the partnership property applied to discharge its liabilities, and the surplus applied to pay in cash the net amount owing to the respective partners. But if dissolution is caused by expulsion of a partner, bona fide under the partnership agreement and if the expelled partner is discharged from all partnership liabilities, either by payment or agreement under section 36(2), he shall receive in cash only the net amount due him from the partnership.

(2) When dissolution is caused in contravention of the partnership agreement the rights of the partners shall be as follows:

(a) Each partner who has not caused dissolution wrongfully shall have,

(I) All the rights specified in paragraph (1) of this section, and

(II) The right, as against each partner who has caused the dissolution wrongfully, to damages for breach of the agreement.

(b) The partners who have not caused the dissolution wrongfully, if they all desire to continue the business in the same name, either by themselves or jointly with others, may do so, during the agreed term for the partnership and for that purpose may possess the partnership property, provided they secure the payment by bond approved by the court, or pay to any partner who has caused the dissolution wrongfully, the value of his interest in the partnership at the dissolution, less any damages recoverable under clause (2aII) of the section, and in like manner indemnify him against all present or future partnership liabilities.

(c) A partner who has caused the dissolution wrongfully shall have:

(I) If the business is not continued under the provisions of paragraph (2b) all the rights of a partner under paragraph (1), subject to clause (2aII), of this section,

(II) If the business is continued under paragraph (2b) of this section the right as against his co-partners and all claiming through them in respect of their interests in the partnership, to have the value of his interest in the partnership, less any damages caused to his copartners by the dissolution, ascertained and paid to him in cash, or the payment secured by bond approved by the court, and to be released from all existing liabilities of the partnership; but in ascertaining the value of the partner's interest the value of the good-will of the business shall not be considered.

SECTION 39. RIGHTS WHERE PARTNERSHIP IS DISSOLVED FOR FRAUD OR MISREPRESENTATION.

Where a partnership contract is rescinded on the ground of the fraud or misrepresentation of one of the parties thereto, the party entitled to rescind is, without prejudice to any other right, entitled,

(a) To a lien on, or right of retention of, the surplus of the partnership property after satisfying the partnership liabilities to third persons for any sum of money paid by him for the purchase of an interest in the partnership and for any capital or advances contributed by him; and

(b) To stand, after all liabilities to third person have been satisfied, in the place of the creditors of the partnership for any payments made by him in respect of the partnership liabilities; and

(c) To be indemnified by the person guilty of the fraud or making the representation against all debts and liabilities of the partnership.

SECTION 40. RULES FOR DISTRIBUTION.

In settling accounts between the partners after dissolution, the following rules shall be observed, subject to any agreement to the contrary:

(a) The assets of the partnership are:

(I) The partnership property,

(II) The contributions of the partners necessary for the payment of all the liabilities specified in clause (b) of this paragraph.

(b) The liabilities of the partnership shall rank in order of payment, as follows:

(I) Those owing to creditors other than partners,

(II) Those owing to partners other than for capital and profits,

(III) Those owing to partners in respect of capital,

(IV) Those owing to partners in respect of profits.

(c) The assets shall be applied in the order of their declaration in clause (a) of this paragraph to the satisfaction of the liabilities.

(d) The partners shall contribute, as provided by section 18(a) the amount necessary to satisfy the liabilities; but if any, but not all, of the partners are insolvent, or, not being subject to process, refuse to contribute, the other parties shall contribute their share of the liabilities, and, in the relative proportions in which they share the profits, the additional amount necessary to pay the liabilities.

(e) An assignee for the benefit of creditors or any person appointed by the court shall have the right to enforce the contributions specified in clause (d) of this paragraph.

(f) Any partner or his legal representative shall have the right to enforce the contributions specified in clause (d) of this paragraph, to the extent of the amount which he has paid in excess of his share of the liability.

(g) The individual property of a deceased partner shall be liable for the contributions specified in clause (d) of this paragraph.

(h) When partnership property and the individual properties of the partners are in possession of a court for distribution, partnership creditors shall have priority on partnership property and separate creditors on individual property, saving the rights of lien or secured creditors as heretofore.

(i) Where a partner has become bankrupt or his estate is insolvent the claims against his separate property shall rank in the following order:

(I) Those owing to separate creditors,

(II) Those owing to partnership creditors,

(III) Those owing to partners by way of contribution.

SECTION 41. LIABILITY OF PERSONS CONTINUING THE BUSINESS IN CERTAIN CASES.

(1) When any new partner is admitted into an existing partnership, or when any partner retires and assigns (or the representative of the deceased partner assigns) his rights in partnership property to two or more of the partners, or to one or more of the partners and one or more third persons, if the business is continued without liquidation of the partnership affairs, creditors of the first or dissolved partnership are also creditors of the partnership so continuing the business.

(2) When all but one partner retire and assign (or the representative of a deceased partner assigns) their rights in partnership property to the remaining partner, who continues the business without liquidation of partnership affairs, either alone or with others, creditors of the dissolved partnership are also creditors of the person or partnership so continuing the business.

(3) When any partner retires or dies and the business of the dissolved partnership is continued as set forth in paragraphs (1) and (2) of this section, with the consent of the retired partners or the representative of the deceased partner, but without any assignment of his right in partnership property, rights of creditors of the dissolved partnership and of the creditors of the person or partnership continuing the business shall be as if such assignment had been made.

(4) When all the partners or their representatives assign their rights in partnership property to one or more third persons who promise to pay the debts and who continue the business of the dissolved partnership, creditors of the dissolved partnership are also creditors of the person or partnership continuing the business.

(5) When any partner wrongfully causes a dissolution and the remaining partners continue the business under the provisions of section 38(2b), either alone or with others, and without liquidation of the partnership affairs, creditors of the dissolved partnership are also creditors of the person or partnership continuing the business.

(6) When a partner is expelled and the remaining partners continue the business either alone or with others, without liquidation of the partnership affairs, creditors of the dissolved partnership are also creditors of the person or partnership continuing the business.

(7) The liability of a third person becoming a partner in the partnership continuing the business, under this section, to the creditors of the dissolved partnership shall be satisfied out of partnership property only.

(8) When the business of a partnership after dissolution is continued under any conditions set forth in this section the creditors of the dissolved partnership, as against the separate creditors of the retiring or deceased partner or the representative of the deceased partner, have a prior right to any claim of the retired partner or the representative of the deceased partner against the person or partnership continuing the business, on account of the retired or deceased partner's interest in the dissolved partnership or on account of any consideration promised for such interest or for his right in partnership property.

(9) Nothing in this section shall be held to modify any right of creditors to set aside any assignment on the ground of fraud.

(10) The use by the person or partnership continuing the business of the partnership name, or the name of a deceased partner as part thereof, shall not of itself make the individual property of the deceased partner liable for any debts contracted by such person or partnership.

SECTION 42. RIGHTS OF RETIRING OR ESTATE OF DECEASED PARTNER WHEN THE BUSINESS IS CONTINUED.

When any partner retires or dies, and the business is continued under any of the conditions set forth in section 41 (1, 2, 3, 5, 6), or section 38(2b), without any settlement of accounts as between him or his estate and the person or partnership continuing the business, unless otherwise agreed, he or his legal representative as against such persons or partnership may have the value of his interest at the date of dissolution ascertained, and shall receive as an ordinary creditor an amount equal to the value of his interest in the dissolved partnership with interest, or, at his option or at the option of his legal representative, in lieu of interest, the profits attributable to the use of his right in the property of the dissolved partnership; provided that the creditors of the dissolved partnership as against the separate creditors, or the representative of the retired or deceased partner, shall have priority on any claim arising under this section, as provided by section 41(8) of this act.

SECTION 43. ACCRUAL OF ACTIONS.

The right to an account of his interest shall accrue to any partner, or his legal representative, as against the winding up partners or the surviving partners or the person or partnership continuing the business, at the date of dissolution, in the absence of any agreement to the contrary.

PART VII   MISCELLANEOUS PROVISIONS

SECTION 44. WHEN ACT TAKES EFFECT.

This act shall take effect on the _____ day of _____ one thousand nine hundred and _____ .

SECTION 45. LEGISLATION REPEALED.

All acts or parts of acts inconsistent with this act are hereby repealed.

UNIFORM PARTNERSHIP ACT (1997)

[ARTICLE] 1
GENERAL PROVISIONS

SECTION 101. DEFINITIONS.

In this [Act]:

(1) "Business" includes every trade, occupation, and profession.

(2) "Debtor in bankruptcy" means a person who is the subject of:

(i) an order for relief under Title 11 of the United States Code or a comparable order under a successor statute of general application; or

(ii) a comparable order under federal, state, or foreign law governing insolvency.

(3) "Distribution" means a transfer of money or other property from a partnership to a partner in the partner's capacity as a partner or to the partner's transferee.

(4) "Foreign limited liability partnership" means a partnership that:

(i) is formed under laws other than the laws of this State; and

(ii) has the status of a limited liability partnership under those laws.

(5) "Limited liability partnership" means a partnership that has filed a statement of qualification under Section 1001 and does not have a similar statement in effect in any other jurisdiction.

(6) "Partnership" means an association of two or more persons to carry on as co-owners a business for profit formed under Section 202, predecessor law, or comparable law of another jurisdiction.

(7) "Partnership agreement" means the agreement, whether written, oral, or implied, among the partners concerning the partnership, including amendments to the partnership agreement.

(8) "Partnership at will" means a partnership in which the partners have not agreed to remain partners until the expiration of a definite term or the completion of a particular undertaking.

(9) "Partnership interest" or "partner's interest in the partnership" means all of a partner's interests in the partnership, including the partner's transferable interest and all management and other rights.

(10) "Person" means an individual, corporation, business trust, estate, trust, partnership, association, joint venture, government, governmental subdivision, agency, or instrumentality, or any other legal or commercial entity.

(11) "Property" means all property, real, personal, or mixed, tangible or intangible, or any interest therein.

(12) "State" means a State of the United States, the District of Columbia, the Commonwealth of Puerto Rico, or any territory or insular possession subject to the jurisdiction of the United States.

(13) "Statement" means a statement of partnership authority under Section 303, a statement of denial under Section 304, a statement of dissociation under Section 704, a statement of dissolution under Section 805, a statement of merger under Section 907, a statement of qualification under Section 1001, a statement of foreign qualification under Section 1102, or an amendment or cancellation of any of the foregoing.

(14) "Transfer" includes an assignment, conveyance, lease, mortgage, deed, and encumbrance.

SECTION 102. KNOWLEDGE AND NOTICE.

(a) A person knows a fact if the person has actual knowledge of it.

(b) A person has notice of a fact if the person:

(1) knows of it;

(2) has received a notification of it; or

(3) has reason to know it exists from all of the facts known to the person at the time in question.

(c) A person notifies or gives a notification to another by taking steps reasonably required to inform the other person in ordinary course, whether or not the other person learns of it.

(d) A person receives a notification when the notification:

(1) comes to the person's attention; or

(2) is duly delivered at the person's place of business or at any other place held out by the person as a place for receiving communications.

(e) Except as otherwise provided in subsection (f), a person other than an individual knows, has notice, or receives a notification of a fact for purposes of a particular transaction when the individual conducting the transaction knows, has notice, or receives a notification of the fact, or in any event when the fact would have been brought to the individual's attention if the person had exercised reasonable diligence. The person exercises reasonable diligence if it maintains reasonable routines for communicating significant information to the individual conducting the transaction and there is reasonable compliance with the routines. Reasonable diligence does not require an individual acting for the person to communicate information unless the communication is part of the individual's regular duties or the individual has reason to know of the transaction and that the transaction would be materially affected by the information.

(f) A partner's knowledge, notice, or receipt of a notification of a fact relating to the partnership is effective immediately as knowledge by, notice to, or receipt of a notification by the partnership, except in the case of a fraud on the partnership committed by or with the consent of that partner.

SECTION 103. EFFECT OF PARTNERSHIP AGREEMENT; NONWAIVABLE PROVISIONS.

(a) Except as otherwise provided in subsection (b), relations among the partners and between the partners and the partnership are governed by the partnership agreement. To the extent the partnership agreement does not otherwise provide, this [Act] governs relations among the partners and between the partners and the partnership.

(b) The partnership agreement may not:

(1) vary the rights and duties under Section 105 except to eliminate the duty to provide copies of statements to all of the partners;

(2) unreasonably restrict the right of access to books and records under Section 403(b);

(3) eliminate the duty of loyalty under Section 404(b) or 603(b)(3), but:

(i) the partnership agreement may identify specific types or categories of activities that do not violate the duty of loyalty, if not manifestly unreasonable; or

(ii) all of the partners or a number or percentage specified in the partnership agreement may authorize or ratify, after full disclosure of all material facts, a specific act or transaction that otherwise would violate the duty of loyalty;

(4) unreasonably reduce the duty of care under Section 404(c) or 603(b)(3);

(5) eliminate the obligation of good faith and fair dealing under Section 404(d), but the partnership agreement may prescribe the standards by which the performance of the obligation is to be measured, if the standards are not manifestly unreasonable;

(6) vary the power to dissociate as a partner under Section 602(a), except to require the notice under Section 601(1) to be in writing;

(7) vary the right of a court to expel a partner in the events specified in Section 601(5);

(8) vary the requirement to wind up the partnership business in cases specified in Section 801(4), (5), or (6);

(9) vary the law applicable to a limited liability partnership under Section 106(b); or

(10) restrict rights of third parties under this [Act].

SECTION 104.   SUPPLEMENTAL PRINCIPLES OF LAW.

(a) Unless displaced by particular provisions of this [Act], the principles of law and equity supplement this [Act].

(b) If an obligation to pay interest arises under this [Act] and the rate is not specified, the rate is that specified in [applicable statute].

SECTION 105.   EXECUTION, FILING, AND RECORDING OF STATEMENTS.

(a) A statement may be filed in the office of [the Secretary of State]. A certified copy of a statement that is filed in an office in another State may be filed in the office of [the Secretary of State]. Either filing has the effect provided in this [Act] with respect to partnership property located in or transactions that occur in this State.

(b) A certified copy of a statement that has been filed in the office of the [Secretary of State] and recorded in the office for recording transfers of real property has the effect provided for recorded statements in this [Act]. A recorded statement that is not a certified copy of a statement filed in the office of the [Secretary of State] does not have the effect provided for recorded statements in this [Act].

(c) A statement filed by a partnership must be executed by at least two partners. Other statements must be executed by a partner or other person authorized by this [Act]. An individual who executes a statement as, or on behalf of, a partner or other person named as a partner in a statement shall personally declare under penalty of perjury that the contents of the statement are accurate.

(d) A person authorized by this [Act] to file a statement may amend or cancel the statement by filing an amendment or cancellation that names the partnership, identifies the statement, and states the substance of the amendment or cancellation.

(e) A person who files a statement pursuant to this section shall promptly send a copy of the statement to every nonfiling partner and to any other person named as a partner in the statement. Failure to send a copy of a statement to a partner or other person does not limit the effectiveness of the statement as to a person not a partner.

(f) The [Secretary of State] may collect a fee for filing or providing a certified copy of a statement. The [officer responsible for recording transfers of real property] may collect a fee for recording a statement.

SECTION 106.   GOVERNING LAW.

(a) Except as otherwise provided in subsection (b), the law of the jurisdiction in which a partnership has its chief executive office governs relations among the partners and between the partners and the partnership.

(b) The law of this State governs relations among the partners and between the partners and the partnership and the liability of partners for an obligation of a limited liability partnership.

SECTION 107.   PARTNERSHIP SUBJECT TO AMENDMENT OR REPEAL OF [ACT].

A partnership governed by this [Act] is subject to any amendment to or repeal of this [Act].

[ARTICLE] 2
NATURE OF PARTNERSHIP

SECTION 201.   PARTNERSHIP AS ENTITY.

(a) A partnership is an entity distinct from its partners.

(b) A limited liability partnership continues to be the same entity that existed before the filing of a statement of qualification under Section 1001.

SECTION 202.   FORMATION OF PARTNERSHIP.

(a) Except as otherwise provided in subsection (b), the association of two or more persons to carry on as co-owners a business for profit forms a partnership, whether or not the persons intend to form a partnership.

(b) An association formed under a statute other than this [Act], a predecessor statute, or a comparable statute of another jurisdiction is not a partnership under this [Act].

(c) In determining whether a partnership is formed, the following rules apply:

(1) Joint tenancy, tenancy in common, tenancy by the entireties, joint property, common property, or part ownership does not by itself establish a partnership, even if the co-owners share profits made by the use of the property.

(2) The sharing of gross returns does not by itself establish a partnership, even if the persons sharing them have a joint or common right or interest in property from which the returns are derived.

(3) A person who receives a share of the profits of a business is presumed to be a partner in the business, unless the profits were received in payment:

(i) of a debt by installments or otherwise;

(ii) for services as an independent contractor or of wages or other compensation to an employee;

(iii) of rent;

(iv) of an annuity or other retirement or health benefit to a beneficiary, representative, or designee of a deceased or retired partner;

(v) of interest or other charge on a loan, even if the amount of payment varies with the profits of the business, including a direct or indirect present or future ownership of the collateral, or rights to income, proceeds, or increase in value derived from the collateral; or

(vi) for the sale of the goodwill of a business or other property by installments or otherwise.

SECTION 203. PARTNERSHIP PROPERTY.
Property acquired by a partnership is property of the partnership and not of the partners individually.

SECTION 204. WHEN PROPERTY IS PARTNERSHIP PROPERTY.
(a) Property is partnership property if acquired in the name of:
   (1) the partnership; or
   (2) one or more partners with an indication in the instrument transferring title to the property of the person's capacity as a partner or of the existence of a partnership but without an indication of the name of the partnership.
(b) Property is acquired in the name of the partnership by a transfer to:
   (1) the partnership in its name; or
   (2) one or more partners in their capacity as partners in the partnership, if the name of the partnership is indicated in the instrument transferring title to the property.
(c) Property is presumed to be partnership property if purchased with partnership assets, even if not acquired in the name of the partnership or of one or more partners with an indication in the instrument transferring title to the property of the person's capacity as a partner or of the existence of a partnership.
(d) Property acquired in the name of one or more of the partners, without an indication in the instrument transferring title to the property of the person's capacity as a partner or of the existence of a partnership and without use of partnership assets, is presumed to be separate property, even if used for partnership purposes.

[ARTICLE] 3
RELATIONS OF PARTNERS TO PERSONS DEALING WITH PARTNERSHIP

SECTION 301. PARTNER AGENT OF PARTNERSHIP.
Subject to the effect of a statement of partnership authority under Section 303:
(1) Each partner is an agent of the partnership for the purpose of its business. An act of a partner, including the execution of an instrument in the partnership name, for apparently carrying on in the ordinary course the partnership business or business of the kind carried on by the partnership binds the partnership, unless the partner had no authority to act for the partnership in the particular matter and the person with whom the partner was dealing knew or had received a notification that the partner lacked authority.
(2) An act of a partner which is not apparently for carrying on in the ordinary course the partnership business or business of the kind carried on by the partnership binds the partnership only if the act was authorized by the other partners.

SECTION 302. TRANSFER OF PARTNERSHIP PROPERTY.
(a) Partnership property may be transferred as follows:
   (1) Subject to the effect of a statement of partnership authority under Section 303, partnership property held in the name of the partnership may be transferred by an instrument of transfer executed by a partner in the partnership name.
   (2) Partnership property held in the name of one or more partners with an indication in the instrument transferring the property to them of their capacity as partners or of the existence of a partnership, but without an indication of the name

of the partnership, may be transferred by an instrument of transfer executed by the persons in whose name the property is held.
   (3) Partnership property held in the name of one or more persons other than the partnership, without an indication in the instrument transferring the property to them of their capacity as partners or of the existence of a partnership, may be transferred by an instrument of transfer executed by the persons in whose name the property is held.
(b) A partnership may recover partnership property from a transferee only if it proves that execution of the instrument of initial transfer did not bind the partnership under Section 301 and:
   (1) as to a subsequent transferee who gave value for property transferred under subsection (a)(1) and (2), proves that the subsequent transferee knew or had received a notification that the person who executed the instrument of initial transfer lacked authority to bind the partnership; or
   (2) as to a transferee who gave value for property transferred under subsection (a)(3), proves that the transferee knew or had received a notification that the property was partnership property and that the person who executed the instrument of initial transfer lacked authority to bind the partnership.
(c) A partnership may not recover partnership property from a subsequent transferee if the partnership would not have been entitled to recover the property, under subsection (b), from any earlier transferee of the property.
(d) If a person holds all of the partners' interests in the partnership, all of the partnership property vests in that person. The person may execute a document in the name of the partnership to evidence vesting of the property in that person and may file or record the document.

SECTION 303. STATEMENT OF PARTNERSHIP AUTHORITY.
(a) A partnership may file a statement of partnership authority, which:
   (1) must include:
      (i) the name of the partnership;
      (ii) the street address of its chief executive office and of one office in this State, if there is one;
      (iii) the names and mailing addresses of all of the partners or of an agent appointed and maintained by the partnership for the purpose of subsection (b); and
      (iv) the names of the partners authorized to execute an instrument transferring real property held in the name of the partnership; and
   (2) may state the authority, or limitations on the authority, of some or all of the partners to enter into other transactions on behalf of the partnership and any other matter.
(b) If a statement of partnership authority names an agent, the agent shall maintain a list of the names and mailing addresses of all of the partners and make it available to any person on request for good cause shown.
(c) If a filed statement of partnership authority is executed pursuant to Section 105(c) and states the name of the partnership but does not contain all of the other information required by subsection (a), the statement nevertheless operates with respect to a person not a partner as provided in subsections (d) and (e).
(d) Except as otherwise provided in subsection (g), a filed statement of partnership authority supplements the authority of a

partner to enter into transactions on behalf of the partnership as follows:

(1) Except for transfers of real property, a grant of authority contained in a filed statement of partnership authority is conclusive in favor of a person who gives value without knowledge to the contrary, so long as and to the extent that a limitation on that authority is not then contained in another filed statement. A filed cancellation of a limitation on authority revives the previous grant of authority.

(2) A grant of authority to transfer real property held in the name of the partnership contained in a certified copy of a filed statement of partnership authority recorded in the office for recording transfers of that real property is conclusive in favor of a person who gives value without knowledge to the contrary, so long as and to the extent that a certified copy of a filed statement containing a limitation on that authority is not then of record in the office for recording transfers of that real property. The recording in the office for recording transfers of that real property of a certified copy of a filed cancellation of a limitation on authority revives the previous grant of authority.

(e) A person not a partner is deemed to know of a limitation on the authority of a partner to transfer real property held in the name of the partnership if a certified copy of the filed statement containing the limitation on authority is of record in the office for recording transfers of that real property.

(f) Except as otherwise provided in subsections (d) and (e) and Sections 704 and 805, a person not a partner is not deemed to know of a limitation on the authority of a partner merely because the limitation is contained in a filed statement.

(g) Unless earlier canceled, a filed statement of partnership authority is canceled by operation of law five years after the date on which the statement, or the most recent amendment, was filed with the [Secretary of State].

SECTION 304.   STATEMENT OF DENIAL.

A partner or other person named as a partner in a filed statement of partnership authority or in a list maintained by an agent pursuant to Section 303(b) may file a statement of denial stating the name of the partnership and the fact that is being denied, which may include denial of a person's authority or status as a partner. A statement of denial is a limitation on authority as provided in Section 303(d) and (e).

SECTION 305.   PARTNERSHIP LIABLE FOR PARTNER'S ACTIONABLE CONDUCT.

(a) A partnership is liable for loss or injury caused to a person, or for a penalty incurred, as a result of a wrongful act or omission, or other actionable conduct, of a partner acting in the ordinary course of business of the partnership or with authority of the partnership.

(b) If, in the course of the partnership's business or while acting with authority of the partnership, a partner receives or causes the partnership to receive money or property of a person not a partner, and the money or property is misapplied by a partner, the partnership is liable for the loss.

SECTION 306.   PARTNER'S LIABILITY.

(a) Except as otherwise provided in subsections (b) and (c), all partners are liable jointly and severally for all obligations of the partnership unless otherwise agreed by the claimant or provided by law.

(b) A person admitted as a partner into an existing partnership is not personally liable for any partnership obligation incurred before the person's admission as a partner.

(c) An obligation of a partnership incurred while the partnership is a limited liability partnership, whether arising in contract, tort, or otherwise, is solely the obligation of the partnership. A partner is not personally liable, directly or indirectly, by way of contribution or otherwise, for such an obligation solely by reason of being or so acting as a partner. This subsection applies notwithstanding anything inconsistent in the partnership agreement that existed immediately before the vote required to become a limited liability partnership under Section 1001(b).

SECTION 307.   ACTIONS BY AND AGAINST PARTNERSHIP AND PARTNERS.

(a) A partnership may sue and be sued in the name of the partnership.

(b) An action may be brought against the partnership and, to the extent not inconsistent with Section 306, any or all of the partners in the same action or in separate actions.

(c) A judgment against a partnership is not by itself a judgment against a partner. A judgment against a partnership may not be satisfied from a partner's assets unless there is also a judgment against the partner.

(d) A judgment creditor of a partner may not levy execution against the assets of the partner to satisfy a judgment based on a claim against the partnership unless the partner is personally liable for the claim under Section 306 and:

(1) a judgment based on the same claim has been obtained against the partnership and a writ of execution on the judgment has been returned unsatisfied in whole or in part;

(2) the partnership is a debtor in bankruptcy;

(3) the partner has agreed that the creditor need not exhaust partnership assets;

(4) a court grants permission to the judgment creditor to levy execution against the assets of a partner based on a finding that partnership assets subject to execution are clearly insufficient to satisfy the judgment, that exhaustion of partnership assets is excessively burdensome, or that the grant of permission is an appropriate exercise of the court's equitable powers; or

(5) liability is imposed on the partner by law or contract independent of the existence of the partnership.

(e) This section applies to any partnership liability or obligation resulting from a representation by a partner or purported partner under Section 308.

SECTION 308.   LIABILITY OF PURPORTED PARTNER.

(a) If a person, by words or conduct, purports to be a partner, or consents to being represented by another as a partner, in a partnership or with one or more persons not partners, the purported partner is liable to a person to whom the representation is made, if that person, relying on the representation, enters into a transaction with the actual or purported partnership. If the representation, either by the purported partner or by a person with the purported partner's consent, is made in a public manner, the purported partner is liable to a person who relies upon the purported partnership even if the purported partner is not aware of being held out as a partner to the claimant. If partnership liability results, the purported partner is liable with respect to that liability as if the purported partner were a partner. If no partnership liability results, the purported partner is liable with respect to that liability jointly and severally with any other person consenting to the representation.

(b) If a person is thus represented to be a partner in an existing partnership, or with one or more persons not partners, the purported partner is an agent of persons consenting to the representation to bind them to the same extent and in the same manner as if the purported partner were a partner, with respect to persons who enter into transactions in reliance upon the representation. If all of the partners of the existing partnership consent to the representation, a partnership act or obligation results. If fewer than all of the partners of the existing partnership consent to the representation, the person acting and the partners consenting to the representation are jointly and severally liable.

(c) A person is not liable as a partner merely because the person is named by another in a statement of partnership authority.

(d) A person does not continue to be liable as a partner merely because of a failure to file a statement of dissociation or to amend a statement of partnership authority to indicate the partner's dissociation from the partnership.

(e) Except as otherwise provided in subsections (a) and (b), persons who are not partners as to each other are not liable as partners to other persons.

[ARTICLE] 4
RELATIONS OF PARTNERS TO EACH OTHER AND TO PARTNERSHIP

SECTION 401.   PARTNER'S RIGHTS AND DUTIES.

(a) Each partner is deemed to have an account that is:

(1) credited with an amount equal to the money plus the value of any other property, net of the amount of any liabilities, the partner contributes to the partnership and the partner's share of the partnership profits; and

(2) charged with an amount equal to the money plus the value of any other property, net of the amount of any liabilities, distributed by the partnership to the partner and the partner's share of the partnership losses.

(b) Each partner is entitled to an equal share of the partnership profits and is chargeable with a share of the partnership losses in proportion to the partner's share of the profits.

(c) A partnership shall reimburse a partner for payments made and indemnify a partner for liabilities incurred by the partner in the ordinary course of the business of the partnership or for the preservation of its business or property.

(d) A partnership shall reimburse a partner for an advance to the partnership beyond the amount of capital the partner agreed to contribute.

(e) A payment or advance made by a partner which gives rise to a partnership obligation under subsection (c) or (d) constitutes a loan to the partnership which accrues interest from the date of the payment or advance.

(f) Each partner has equal rights in the management and conduct of the partnership business.

(g) A partner may use or possess partnership property only on behalf of the partnership.

(h) A partner is not entitled to remuneration for services performed for the partnership, except for reasonable compensation for services rendered in winding up the business of the partnership.

(i) A person may become a partner only with the consent of all of the partners.

(j) A difference arising as to a matter in the ordinary course of business of a partnership may be decided by a majority of the partners. An act outside the ordinary course of business of a partnership and an amendment to the partnership agreement may be undertaken only with the consent of all of the partners.

(k) This section does not affect the obligations of a partnership to other persons under Section 301.

SECTION 402.   DISTRIBUTIONS IN KIND.

A partner has no right to receive, and may not be required to accept, a distribution in kind.

SECTION .403.   PARTNER'S RIGHTS AND DUTIES WITH RESPECT TO INFORMATION.

(a) A partnership shall keep its books and records, if any, at its chief executive office.

(b) A partnership shall provide partners and their agents and attorneys access to its books and records. It shall provide former partners and their agents and attorneys access to books and records pertaining to the period during which they were partners. The right of access provides the opportunity to inspect and copy books and records during ordinary business hours. A partnership may impose a reasonable charge, covering the costs of labor and material, for copies of documents furnished.

(c) Each partner and the partnership shall furnish to a partner, and to the legal representative of a deceased partner or partner under legal disability:

(1) without demand, any information concerning the partnership's business and affairs reasonably required for the proper exercise of the partner's rights and duties under the partnership agreement or this [Act]; and

(2) on demand, any other information concerning the partnership's business and affairs, except to the extent the demand or the information demanded is unreasonable or otherwise improper under the circumstances.

SECTION 404.   GENERAL STANDARDS OF PARTNER'S CONDUCT.

(a) The only fiduciary duties a partner owes to the partnership and the other partners are the duty of loyalty and the duty of care set forth in subsections (b) and (c).

(b) A partner's duty of loyalty to the partnership and the other partners is limited to the following:

(1) to account to the partnership and hold as trustee for it any property, profit, or benefit derived by the partner in the conduct and winding up of the partnership business or derived from a use by the partner of partnership property, including the appropriation of a partnership opportunity;

(2) to refrain from dealing with the partnership in the conduct or winding up of the partnership business as or on behalf of a party having an interest adverse to the partnership; and

(3) to refrain from competing with the partnership in the conduct of the partnership business before the dissolution of the partnership.

(c) A partner's duty of care to the partnership and the other partners in the conduct and winding up of the partnership business is limited to refraining from engaging in grossly negligent or reckless conduct, intentional misconduct, or a knowing violation of law.

(d) A partner shall discharge the duties to the partnership and the other partners under this [Act] or under the partnership agreement and exercise any rights consistently with the obligation of good faith and fair dealing.

(e) A partner does not violate a duty or obligation under this [Act] or under the partnership agreement merely because the partner's conduct furthers the partner's own interest.

(f) A partner may lend money to and transact other business with the partnership, and as to each loan or transaction the rights and obligations of the partner are the same as those of a person who is not a partner, subject to other applicable law.

(g) This section applies to a person winding up the partnership business as the personal or legal representative of the last surviving partner as if the person were a partner.

SECTION 405.   ACTIONS BY PARTNERSHIP AND PARTNERS.

(a) A partnership may maintain an action against a partner for a breach of the partnership agreement, or for the violation of a duty to the partnership, causing harm to the partnership.

(b) A partner may maintain an action against the partnership or another partner for legal or equitable relief, with or without an accounting as to partnership business, to:

(1) enforce the partner's rights under the partnership agreement;

(2) enforce the partner's rights under this [Act], including:

(i) the partner's rights under Sections 401, 403, or 404;

(ii) the partner's right on dissociation to have the partner's interest in the partnership purchased pursuant to Section 701 or enforce any other right under [Article] 6 or 7; or

(iii) the partner's right to compel a dissolution and winding up of the partnership business under Section 801 or enforce any other right under [Article] 8; or

(3) enforce the rights and otherwise protect the interests of the partner, including rights and interests arising independently of the partnership relationship.

(c) The accrual of, and any time limitation on, a right of action for a remedy under this section is governed by other law. A right to an accounting upon a dissolution and winding up does not revive a claim barred by law.

SECTION 406.   CONTINUATION OF PARTNERSHIP BEYOND DEFINITE TERM OR PARTICULAR UNDERTAKING.

(a) If a partnership for a definite term or particular undertaking is continued, without an express agreement, after the expiration of the term or completion of the undertaking, the rights and duties of the partners remain the same as they were at the expiration or completion, so far as is consistent with a partnership at will.

(b) If the partners, or those of them who habitually acted in the business during the term or undertaking, continue the business without any settlement or liquidation of the partnership, they are presumed to have agreed that the partnership will continue.

[ARTICLE] 5
TRANSFEREES AND CREDITORS OF PARTNER

SECTION 501.   PARTNER NOT CO-OWNER OF PARTNERSHIP PROPERTY.

A partner is not a co-owner of partnership property and has no interest in partnership property which can be transferred, either voluntarily or involuntarily.

SECTION 502.   PARTNER'S TRANSFERABLE INTEREST IN PARTNERSHIP.

The only transferable interest of a partner in the partnership is the partner's share of the profits and losses of the partnership and the partner's right to receive distributions. The interest is personal property.

SECTION 503.   TRANSFER OF PARTNER'S TRANSFERABLE INTEREST.

(a) A transfer, in whole or in part, of a partner's transferable interest in the partnership:

(1) is permissible;

(2) does not by itself cause the partner's dissociation or a dissolution and winding up of the partnership business; and

(3) does not, as against the other partners or the partnership, entitle the transferee, during the continuance of the partnership, to participate in the management or conduct of the partnership business, to require access to information concerning partnership transactions, or to inspect or copy the partnership books or records.

(b) A transferee of a partner's transferable interest in the partnership has a right:

(1) to receive, in accordance with the transfer, distributions to which the transferor would otherwise be entitled;

(2) to receive upon the dissolution and winding up of the partnership business, in accordance with the transfer, the net amount otherwise distributable to the transferor; and

(3) to seek under Section 801(6) a judicial determination that it is equitable to wind up the partnership business.

(c) In a dissolution and winding up, a transferee is entitled to an account of partnership transactions only from the date of the latest account agreed to by all of the partners.

(d) Upon transfer, the transferor retains the rights and duties of a partner other than the interest in distributions transferred.

(e) A partnership need not give effect to a transferee's rights under this section until it has notice of the transfer.

(f) A transfer of a partner's transferable interest in the partnership in violation of a restriction on transfer contained in the partnership agreement is ineffective as to a person having notice of the restriction at the time of transfer.

SECTION 504.   PARTNER'S TRANSFERABLE INTEREST SUBJECT TO CHARGING ORDER.

(a) On application by a judgment creditor of a partner or of a partner's transferee, a court having jurisdiction may charge the transferable interest of the judgment debtor to satisfy the judgment. The court may appoint a receiver of the share of the distributions due or to become due to the judgment debtor in respect of the partnership and make all other orders, directions, accounts, and inquiries the judgment debtor might have made or which the circumstances of the case may require.

(b) A charging order constitutes a lien on the judgment debtor's transferable interest in the partnership. The court may order a foreclosure of the interest subject to the charging order at any time. The purchaser at the foreclosure sale has the rights of a transferee.

(c) At any time before foreclosure, an interest charged may be redeemed:

(1) by the judgment debtor;

(2) with property other than partnership property, by one or more of the other partners; or

(3) with partnership property, by one or more of the other partners with the consent of all of the partners whose interests are not so charged.

(d) This [Act] does not deprive a partner of a right under exemption laws with respect to the partner's interest in the partnership.

(e) This section provides the exclusive remedy by which a judgment creditor of a partner or partner's transferee may satisfy a judgment out of the judgment debtor's transferable interest in the partnership.

[ARTICLE] 6
PARTNER'S DISSOCIATION

SECTION 601.   EVENTS CAUSING PARTNER'S DISSOCIATION.

A partner is dissociated from a partnership upon the occurrence of any of the following events:

(1) the partnership's having notice of the partner's express will to withdraw as a partner or on a later date specified by the partner;

(2) an event agreed to in the partnership agreement as causing the partner's dissociation;

(3) the partner's expulsion pursuant to the partnership agreement;

(4) the partner's expulsion by the unanimous vote of the other partners if:

(i) it is unlawful to carry on the partnership business with that partner;

(ii) there has been a transfer of all or substantially all of that partner's transferable interest in the partnership, other than a transfer for security purposes, or a court order charging the partner's interest, which has not been foreclosed;

(iii) within 90 days after the partnership notifies a corporate partner that it will be expelled because it has filed a certificate of dissolution or the equivalent, its charter has been revoked, or its right to conduct business has been suspended by the jurisdiction of its incorporation, there is no revocation of the certificate of dissolution or no reinstatement of its charter or its right to conduct business; or

(iv) a partnership that is a partner has been dissolved and its business is being wound up;

(5) on application by the partnership or another partner, the partner's expulsion by judicial determination because:

(i) the partner engaged in wrongful conduct that adversely and materially affected the partnership business;

(ii) the partner willfully or persistently committed a material breach of the partnership agreement or of a duty owed to the partnership or the other partners under Section 404; or

(iii) the partner engaged in conduct relating to the partnership business which makes it not reasonably practicable to carry on the business in partnership with the partner;

(6) the partner's:

(i) becoming a debtor in bankruptcy;

(ii) executing an assignment for the benefit of creditors;

(iii) seeking, consenting to, or acquiescing in the appointment of a trustee, receiver, or liquidator of that partner or of all or substantially all of that partner's property; or

(iv) failing, within 90 days after the appointment, to have vacated or stayed the appointment of a trustee, receiver, or liquidator of the partner or of all or substantially all of the partner's property obtained without the partner's consent or acquiescence, or failing within 90 days after the expiration of a stay to have the appointment vacated;

(7) in the case of a partner who is an individual:

(i) the partner's death;

(ii) the appointment of a guardian or general conservator for the partner; or

(iii) a judicial determination that the partner has otherwise become incapable of performing the partner's duties under the partnership agreement;

(8) in the case of a partner that is a trust or is acting as a partner by virtue of being a trustee of a trust, distribution of the trust's entire transferable interest in the partnership, but not merely by reason of the substitution of a successor trustee;

(9) in the case of a partner that is an estate or is acting as a partner by virtue of being a personal representative of an estate, distribution of the estate's entire transferable interest in the partnership, but not merely by reason of the substitution of a successor personal representative; or

(10) termination of a partner who is not an individual, partnership, corporation, trust, or estate.

SECTION 602.   PARTNER'S POWER TO DISSOCIATE; WRONGFUL DISSOCIATION.

(a) A partner has the power to dissociate at any time, rightfully or wrongfully, by express will pursuant to Section 601(1).

(b) A partner's dissociation is wrongful only if:

(1) it is in breach of an express provision of the partnership agreement; or

(2) in the case of a partnership for a definite term or particular undertaking, before the expiration of the term or the completion of the undertaking:

(i) the partner withdraws by express will, unless the withdrawal follows within 90 days after another partner's dissociation by death or otherwise under Section 601(6) through (10) or wrongful dissociation under this subsection;

(ii) the partner is expelled by judicial determination under Section 601(5);

(iii) the partner is dissociated by becoming a debtor in bankruptcy; or

(iv) in the case of a partner who is not an individual, trust other than a business trust, or estate, the partner is expelled or otherwise dissociated because it willfully dissolved or terminated.

(c) A partner who wrongfully dissociates is liable to the partnership and to the other partners for damages caused by the dissociation. The liability is in addition to any other obligation of the partner to the partnership or to the other partners.

SECTION 603.   EFFECT OF PARTNER'S DISSOCIATION.

(a) If a partner's dissociation results in a dissolution and winding up of the partnership business, [Article] 8 applies; otherwise, [Article] 7 applies.

(b) Upon a partner's dissociation:

(1) the partner's right to participate in the management and conduct of the partnership business terminates, except as otherwise provided in Section 803;

(2) the partner's duty of loyalty under Section 404(b)(3) terminates; and

(3) the partner's duty of loyalty under Section 404(b)(1) and (2) and duty of care under Section 404(c) continue only with regard to matters arising and events occurring before the partner's dissociation, unless the partner participates in winding up the partnership's business pursuant to Section 803.

[ARTICLE] 7
PARTNER'S DISSOCIATION WHEN BUSINESS NOT WOUND UP

SECTION 701.   PURCHASE OF DISSOCIATED PARTNER'S INTEREST.

(a) If a partner is dissociated from a partnership without resulting in a dissolution and winding up of the partnership business under

Section 801, the partnership shall cause the dissociated partner's interest in the partnership to be purchased for a buyout price determined pursuant to subsection (b).

(b) The buyout price of a dissociated partner's interest is the amount that would have been distributable to the dissociating partner under Section 807(b) if, on the date of dissociation, the assets of the partnership were sold at a price equal to the greater of the liquidation value or the value based on a sale of the entire business as a going concern without the dissociated partner and the partnership were wound up as of that date. Interest must be paid from the date of dissociation to the date of payment.

(c) Damages for wrongful dissociation under Section 602(b), and all other amounts owing, whether or not presently due, from the dissociated partner to the partnership, must be offset against the buyout price. Interest must be paid from the date the amount owed becomes due to the date of payment.

(d) A partnership shall indemnify a dissociated partner whose interest is being purchased against all partnership liabilities, whether incurred before or after the dissociation, except liabilities incurred by an act of the dissociated partner under Section 702.

(e) If no agreement for the purchase of a dissociated partner's interest is reached within 120 days after a written demand for payment, the partnership shall pay, or cause to be paid, in cash to the dissociated partner the amount the partnership estimates to be the buyout price and accrued interest, reduced by any offsets and accrued interest under subsection (c).

(f) If a deferred payment is authorized under subsection (h), the partnership may tender a written offer to pay the amount it estimates to be the buyout price and accrued interest, reduced by any offsets under subsection (c), stating the time of payment, the amount and type of security for payment, and the other terms and conditions of the obligation.

(g) The payment or tender required by subsection (e) or (f) must be accompanied by the following:

(1) a statement of partnership assets and liabilities as of the date of dissociation;

(2) the latest available partnership balance sheet and income statement, if any;

(3) an explanation of how the estimated amount of the payment was calculated; and

(4) written notice that the payment is in full satisfaction of the obligation to purchase unless, within 120 days after the written notice, the dissociated partner commences an action to determine the buyout price, any offsets under subsection (c), or other terms of the obligation to purchase.

(h) A partner who wrongfully dissociates before the expiration of a definite term or the completion of a particular undertaking is not entitled to payment of any portion of the buyout price until the expiration of the term or completion of the undertaking, unless the partner establishes to the satisfaction of the court that earlier payment will not cause undue hardship to the business of the partnership. A deferred payment must be adequately secured and bear interest.

(i) A dissociated partner may maintain an action against the partnership, pursuant to Section 405(b)(2)(ii), to determine the buyout price of that partner's interest, any offsets under subsection (c), or other terms of the obligation to purchase. The action must be commenced within 120 days after the partnership has tendered payment or an offer to pay or within one year after written demand for payment if no payment or offer to pay is tendered. The court shall determine the buyout price of the dissociated partner's interest, any offset due under subsection (c), and accrued interest, and enter judgment for any additional payment or refund. If deferred payment is authorized under subsection (h), the court shall also determine the security for payment and other terms of the obligation to purchase. The court may assess reasonable attorney's fees and the fees and expenses of appraisers or other experts for a party to the action, in amounts the court finds equitable, against a party that the court finds acted arbitrarily, vexatiously, or not in good faith. The finding may be based on the partnership's failure to tender payment or an offer to pay or to comply with subsection (g).

SECTION 702.   DISSOCIATED PARTNER'S POWER TO BIND AND LIABILITY TO PARTNERSHIP.

(a) For two years after a partner dissociates without resulting in a dissolution and winding up of the partnership business, the partnership, including a surviving partnership under [Article] 9, is bound by an act of the dissociated partner which would have bound the partnership under Section 301 before dissociation only if at the time of entering into the transaction the other party:

(1) reasonably believed that the dissociated partner was then a partner;

(2) did not have notice of the partner's dissociation; and

(3) is not deemed to have had knowledge under Section 303(e) or notice under Section 704(c).

(b) A dissociated partner is liable to the partnership for any damage caused to the partnership arising from an obligation incurred by the dissociated partner after dissociation for which the partnership is liable under subsection (a).

SECTION 703.   DISSOCIATED PARTNER'S LIABILITY TO OTHER PERSONS.

(a) A partner's dissociation does not of itself discharge the partner's liability for a partnership obligation incurred before dissociation. A dissociated partner is not liable for a partnership obligation incurred after dissociation, except as otherwise provided in subsection (b).

(b) A partner who dissociates without resulting in a dissolution and winding up of the partnership business is liable as a partner to the other party in a transaction entered into by the partnership, or a surviving partnership under [Article] 9, within two years after the partner's dissociation, only if the partner is liable for the obligation under Section 306 and at the time of entering into the transaction the other party:

(1) reasonably believed that the dissociated partner was then a partner;

(2) did not have notice of the partner's dissociation; and

(3) is not deemed to have had knowledge under Section 303(e) or notice under Section 704(c).

(c) By agreement with the partnership creditor and the partners continuing the business, a dissociated partner may be released from liability for a partnership obligation.

(d) A dissociated partner is released from liability for a partnership obligation if a partnership creditor, with notice of the partner's dissociation but without the partner's consent, agrees to a material alteration in the nature or time of payment of a partnership obligation.

SECTION 704.   STATEMENT OF DISSOCIATION.

(a) A dissociated partner or the partnership may file a statement of dissociation stating the name of the partnership and that the partner is dissociated from the partnership.

(b) A statement of dissociation is a limitation on the authority of a dissociated partner for the purposes of Section 303(d) and (e).

(c) For the purposes of Sections 702(a)(3) and 703(b)(3), a person not a partner is deemed to have notice of the dissociation 90 days after the statement of dissociation is filed.

SECTION 705.   CONTINUED USE OF PARTNERSHIP NAME.

Continued use of a partnership name, or a dissociated partner's name as part thereof, by partners continuing the business does not of itself make the dissociated partner liable for an obligation of the partners or the partnership continuing the business.

[ARTICLE] 8
WINDING UP PARTNERSHIP BUSINESS

SECTION 801.   EVENTS CAUSING DISSOLUTION AND WINDING UP OF PARTNERSHIP BUSINESS.

A partnership is dissolved, and its business must be wound up, only upon the occurrence of any of the following events:

(1) in a partnership at will, the partnership's having notice from a partner, other than a partner who is dissociated under Section 601(2) through (10), of that partner's express will to withdraw as a partner, or on a later date specified by the partner;

(2) in a partnership for a definite term or particular undertaking:

(i) within 90 days after a partner's dissociation by death or otherwise under Section 601(6) through (10) or wrongful dissociation under Section 602(b), the express will of at least half of the remaining partners to wind up the partnership business, for which purpose a partner's rightful dissociation pursuant to Section 602(b)(2)(i) constitutes the expression of that partner's will to wind up the partnership business;

(ii) the express will of all of the partners to wind up the partnership business; or

(iii) the expiration of the term or the completion of the undertaking;

(3) an event agreed to in the partnership agreement resulting in the winding up of the partnership business;

(4) an event that makes it unlawful for all or substantially all of the business of the partnership to be continued, but a cure of illegality within 90 days after notice to the partnership of the event is effective retroactively to the date of the event for purposes of this section;

(5) on application by a partner, a judicial determination that:

(i) the economic purpose of the partnership is likely to be unreasonably frustrated;

(ii) another partner has engaged in conduct relating to the partnership business which makes it not reasonably practicable to carry on the business in partnership with that partner; or

(iii) it is not otherwise reasonably practicable to carry on the partnership business in conformity with the partnership agreement; or

(6) on application by a transferee of a partner's transferable interest, a judicial determination that it is equitable to wind up the partnership business:

(i) after the expiration of the term or completion of the undertaking, if the partnership was for a definite term or particular undertaking at the time of the transfer or entry of the charging order that gave rise to the transfer; or

(ii) at any time, if the partnership was a partnership at will at the time of the transfer or entry of the charging order that gave rise to the transfer.

SECTION 802.   PARTNERSHIP CONTINUES AFTER DISSOLUTION.

(a) Subject to subsection (b), a partnership continues after dissolution only for the purpose of winding up its business. The partnership is terminated when the winding up of its business is completed.

(b) At any time after the dissolution of a partnership and before the winding up of its business is completed, all of the partners, including any dissociating partner other than a wrongfully dissociating partner, may waive the right to have the partnership's business wound up and the partnership terminated. In that event:

(1) the partnership resumes carrying on its business as if dissolution had never occurred, and any liability incurred by the partnership or a partner after the dissolution and before the waiver is determined as if dissolution had never occurred; and

(2) the rights of a third party accruing under Section 804(1) or arising out of conduct in reliance on the dissolution before the third party knew or received a notification of the waiver may not be adversely affected.

SECTION 803.   RIGHT TO WIND UP PARTNERSHIP BUSINESS.

(a) After dissolution, a partner who has not wrongfully dissociated may participate in winding up the partnership's business, but on application of any partner, partner's legal representative, or transferee, the [designate the appropriate court], for good cause shown, may order judicial supervision of the winding up.

(b) The legal representative of the last surviving partner may wind up a partnership's business.

(c) A person winding up a partnership's business may preserve the partnership business or property as a going concern for a reasonable time, prosecute and defend actions and proceedings, whether civil, criminal, or administrative, settle and close the partnership's business, dispose of and transfer the partnership's property, discharge the partnership's liabilities, distribute the assets of the partnership pursuant to Section 807, settle disputes by mediation or arbitration, and perform other necessary acts.

SECTION 804.   PARTNER'S POWER TO BIND PARTNERSHIP AFTER DISSOLUTION.

Subject to Section 805, a partnership is bound by a partner's act after dissolution that:

(1) is appropriate for winding up the partnership business; or

(2) would have bound the partnership under Section 301 before dissolution, if the other party to the transaction did not have notice of the dissolution.

SECTION 805.   STATEMENT OF DISSOLUTION.

(a) After dissolution, a partner who has not wrongfully dissociated may file a statement of dissolution stating the name of the partnership and that the partnership has dissolved and is winding up its business.

(b) A statement of dissolution cancels a filed statement of partnership authority for the purposes of Section 303(d) and is a limitation on authority for the purposes of Section 303(e).

(c) For the purposes of Sections 301 and 804, a person not a partner is deemed to have notice of the dissolution and the limitation on the partners' authority as a result of the statement of dissolution 90 days after it is filed.

(d) After filing and, if appropriate, recording a statement of dissolution, a dissolved partnership may file and, if appropriate, record a statement of partnership authority which will operate with respect to a person not a partner as provided in Section 303(d) and

(e) in any transaction, whether or not the transaction is appropriate for winding up the partnership business.

SECTION 806.   PARTNER'S LIABILITY TO OTHER PARTNERS AFTER DISSOLUTION.

(a) Except as otherwise provided in subsection (b) and Section 306, after dissolution a partner is liable to the other partners for the partner's share of any partnership liability incurred under Section 804.

(b) A partner who, with knowledge of the dissolution, incurs a partnership liability under Section 804(2) by an act that is not appropriate for winding up the partnership business is liable to the partnership for any damage caused to the partnership arising from the liability.

SECTION 807.   SETTLEMENT OF ACCOUNTS AND CONTRIBUTIONS AMONG PARTNERS.

(a) In winding up a partnership's business, the assets of the partnership, including the contributions of the partners required by this section, must be applied to discharge its obligations to creditors, including, to the extent permitted by law, partners who are creditors. Any surplus must be applied to pay in cash the net amount distributable to partners in accordance with their right to distributions under subsection (b).

(b) Each partner is entitled to a settlement of all partnership accounts upon winding up the partnership business. In settling accounts among the partners, profits and losses that result from the liquidation of the partnership assets must be credited and charged to the partners' accounts. The partnership shall make a distribution to a partner in an amount equal to any excess of the credits over the charges in the partner's account. A partner shall contribute to the partnership an amount equal to any excess of the charges over the credits in the partner's account but excluding from the calculation charges attributable to an obligation for which the partner is not personally liable under Section 306.

(c) If a partner fails to contribute the full amount required under subsection (b), all of the other partners shall contribute, in the proportions in which those partners share partnership losses, the additional amount necessary to satisfy the partnership obligations for which they are personally liable under Section 306. A partner or partner's legal representative may recover from the other partners any contributions the partner makes to the extent the amount contributed exceeds that partner's share of the partnership obligations for which the partner is personally liable under Section 306.

(d) After the settlement of accounts, each partner shall contribute, in the proportion in which the partner shares partnership losses, the amount necessary to satisfy partnership obligations that were not known at the time of the settlement and for which the partner is personally liable under Section 306.

(e) The estate of a deceased partner is liable for the partner's obligation to contribute to the partnership.

(f) An assignee for the benefit of creditors of a partnership or a partner, or a person appointed by a court to represent creditors of a partnership or a partner, may enforce a partner's obligation to contribute to the partnership.

[ARTICLE] 9
CONVERSIONS AND MERGERS

SECTION 901.   DEFINITIONS.

In this [Article]:

(1) "General partner" means a partner in a partnership and a general partner in a limited partnership.

(2) "Limited partner" means a limited partner in a limited partnership.

(3) "Limited partnership" means a limited partnership created under the [State Limited Partnership Act], predecessor law, or comparable law of another jurisdiction.

(4) "Partner" includes both a general partner and a limited partner.

SECTION 902.   CONVERSION OF PARTNERSHIP TO LIMITED PARTNERSHIP.

(a) A partnership may be converted to a limited partnership pursuant to this section.

(b) The terms and conditions of a conversion of a partnership to a limited partnership must be approved by all of the partners or by a number or percentage specified for conversion in the partnership agreement.

(c) After the conversion is approved by the partners, the partnership shall file a certificate of limited partnership in the jurisdiction in which the limited partnership is to be formed. The certificate must include:

> (1) a statement that the partnership was converted to a limited partnership from a partnership;

> (2) its former name; and

> (3) a statement of the number of votes cast by the partners for and against the conversion and, if the vote is less than unanimous, the number or percentage required to approve the conversion under the partnership agreement.

(d) The conversion takes effect when the certificate of limited partnership is filed or at any later date specified in the certificate.

(e) A general partner who becomes a limited partner as a result of the conversion remains liable as a general partner for an obligation incurred by the partnership before the conversion takes effect. If the other party to a transaction with the limited partnership reasonably believes when entering the transaction that the limited partner is a general partner, the limited partner is liable for an obligation incurred by the limited partnership within 90 days after the conversion takes effect. The limited partner's liability for all other obligations of the limited partnership incurred after the conversion takes effect is that of a limited partner as provided in the [State Limited Partnership Act].

SECTION 903.   CONVERSION OF LIMITED PARTNERSHIP TO PARTNERSHIP.

(a) A limited partnership may be converted to a partnership pursuant to this section.

(b) Notwithstanding a provision to the contrary in a limited partnership agreement, the terms and conditions of a conversion of a limited partnership to a partnership must be approved by all of the partners.

(c) After the conversion is approved by the partners, the limited partnership shall cancel its certificate of limited partnership.

(d) The conversion takes effect when the certificate of limited partnership is canceled.

(e) A limited partner who becomes a general partner as a result of the conversion remains liable only as a limited partner for an obligation incurred by the limited partnership before the conversion takes effect. Except as otherwise provided in Section 306, the partner is liable as a general partner for an obligation of the partnership incurred after the conversion takes effect.

SECTION 904. EFFECT OF CONVERSION; ENTITY UNCHANGED.

(a) A partnership or limited partnership that has been converted pursuant to this [ARTICLE] is for all purposes the same entity that existed before the conversion.

(b) When a conversion takes effect:

(1) all property owned by the converting partnership or limited partnership remains vested in the converted entity;

(2) all obligations of the converting partnership or limited partnership continue as obligations of the converted entity; and

(3) an action or proceeding pending against the converting partnership or limited partnership may be continued as if the conversion had not occurred.

SECTION 905. MERGER OF PARTNERSHIPS.

(a) Pursuant to a plan of merger approved as provided in subsection (c), a partnership may be merged with one or more partnerships or limited partnerships.

(b) The plan of merger must set forth:

(1) the name of each partnership or limited partnership that is a party to the merger;

(2) the name of the surviving entity into which the other partnerships or limited partnerships will merge;

(3) whether the surviving entity is a partnership or a limited partnership and the status of each partner;

(4) the terms and conditions of the merger;

(5) the manner and basis of converting the interests of each party to the merger into interests or obligations of the surviving entity, or into money or other property in whole or part; and

(6) the street address of the surviving entity's chief executive office.

(c) The plan of merger must be approved:

(1) in the case of a partnership that is a party to the merger, by all of the partners, or a number or percentage specified for merger in the partnership agreement; and

(2) in the case of a limited partnership that is a party to the merger, by the vote required for approval of a merger by the law of the State or foreign jurisdiction in which the limited partnership is organized and, in the absence of such a specifically applicable law, by all of the partners, notwithstanding a provision to the contrary in the partnership agreement.

(d) After a plan of merger is approved and before the merger takes effect, the plan may be amended or abandoned as provided in the plan.

(e) The merger takes effect on the later of:

(1) the approval of the plan of merger by all parties to the merger, as provided in subsection (c);

(2) the filing of all documents required by law to be filed as a condition to the effectiveness of the merger; or

(3) any effective date specified in the plan of merger.

SECTION 906. EFFECT OF MERGER.

(a) When a merger takes effect:

(1) the separate existence of every partnership or limited partnership that is a party to the merger, other than the surviving entity, ceases;

(2) all property owned by each of the merged partnerships or limited partnerships vests in the surviving entity;

(3) all obligations of every partnership or limited partnership that is a party to the merger become the obligations of the surviving entity; and

(4) an action or proceeding pending against a partnership or limited partnership that is a party to the merger may be continued as if the merger had not occurred, or the surviving entity may be substituted as a party to the action or proceeding.

(b) The [Secretary of State] of this State is the agent for service of process in an action or proceeding against a surviving foreign partnership or limited partnership to enforce an obligation of a domestic partnership or limited partnership that is a party to a merger. The surviving entity shall promptly notify the [Secretary of State] of the mailing address of its chief executive office and of any change of address. Upon receipt of process, the [Secretary of State] shall mail a copy of the process to the surviving foreign partnership or limited partnership.

(c) A partner of the surviving partnership or limited partnership is liable for:

(1) all obligations of a party to the merger for which the partner was personally liable before the merger;

(2) all other obligations of the surviving entity incurred before the merger by a party to the merger, but those obligations may be satisfied only out of property of the entity; and

(3) except as otherwise provided in Section 306, all obligations of the surviving entity incurred after the merger takes effect, but those obligations may be satisfied only out of property of the entity if the partner is a limited partner.

(d) If the obligations incurred before the merger by a party to the merger are not satisfied out of the property of the surviving partnership or limited partnership, the general partners of that party immediately before the effective date of the merger shall contribute the amount necessary to satisfy that party's obligations to the surviving entity, in the manner provided in Section 807 or in the [Limited Partnership Act] of the jurisdiction in which the party was formed, as the case may be, as if the merged party were dissolved.

(e) A partner of a party to a merger who does not become a partner of the surviving partnership or limited partnership is dissociated from the entity, of which that partner was a partner, as of the date the merger takes effect. The surviving entity shall cause the partner's interest in the entity to be purchased under Section 701 or another statute specifically applicable to that partner's interest with respect to a merger. The surviving entity is bound under Section 702 by an act of a general partner dissociated under this subsection, and the partner is liable under Section 703 for transactions entered into by the surviving entity after the merger takes effect.

SECTION 907. STATEMENT OF MERGER.

(a) After a merger, the surviving partnership or limited partnership may file a statement that one or more partnerships or limited partnerships have merged into the surviving entity.

(b) A statement of merger must contain:

(1) the name of each partnership or limited partnership that is a party to the merger;

(2) the name of the surviving entity into which the other partnerships or limited partnership were merged;

(3) the street address of the surviving entity's chief executive office and of an office in this State, if any; and

(4) whether the surviving entity is a partnership or a limited partnership.

(c) Except as otherwise provided in subsection (d), for the purposes of Section 302, property of the surviving partnership or limited partnership which before the merger was held in the name of another party to the merger is property held in the name of the surviving entity upon filing a statement of merger.

(d) For the purposes of Section 302, real property of the surviving partnership or limited partnership which before the merger was held in the name of another party to the merger is property held in the name of the surviving entity upon recording a certified copy of the statement of merger in the office for recording transfers of that real property.

(e) A filed and, if appropriate, recorded statement of merger, executed and declared to be accurate pursuant to Section 105(c), stating the name of a partnership or limited partnership that is a party to the merger in whose name property was held before the merger and the name of the surviving entity, but not containing all of the other information required by subsection (b), operates with respect to the partnerships or limited partnerships named to the extent provided in subsections (c) and (d).

SECTION 908.   NONEXCLUSIVE.

This [article] is not exclusive. Partnerships or limited partnerships may be converted or merged in any other manner provided by law.

[ARTICLE] 10
LIMITED LIABILITY PARTNERSHIP

SECTION 1001. STATEMENT OF QUALIFICATION.

(a) A partnership may become a limited liability partnership pursuant to this section.

(b) The terms and conditions on which a partnership becomes a limited liability partnership must be approved by the vote necessary to amend the partnership agreement except, in the case of a partnership agreement that expressly considers obligations to contribute to the partnership, the vote necessary to amend those provisions.

(c) After the approval required by subsection (b), a partnership may become a limited liability partnership by filing a statement of qualification. The statement must contain:

(1) the name of the partnership;

(2) the street address of the partnership's chief executive office and, if different, the street address of an office in this State, if any;

(3) if the partnership does not have an office in this State, the name and street address of the partnership's agent for service of process;

(4) a statement that the partnership elects to be a limited liability partnership; and

(5) a deferred effective date, if any.

(d) The agent of a limited liability partnership for service of process must be an individual who is a resident of this State or other person authorized to do business in this State.

(e) The status of a partnership as a limited liability partnership is effective on the later of the filing of the statement or a date specified in the statement. The status remains effective, regardless of changes in the partnership, until it is canceled pursuant to Section 105(d) or revoked pursuant to Section 1003.

(f) The status of a partnership as a limited liability partnership and the liability of its partners is not affected by errors or later changes in the information required to be contained in the statement of qualification under subsection (c).

(g) The filing of a statement of qualification establishes that a partnership has satisfied all conditions precedent to the qualification of the partnership as a limited liability partnership.

(h) An amendment or cancellation of a statement of qualification is effective when it is filed or on a deferred effective date specified in the amendment or cancellation.

SECTION 1002. NAME.

The name of a limited liability partnership must end with "Registered Limited Liability Partnership," "Limited Liability Partnership," "R.L.L.P.," "L.L.P.," "RLLP," or "LLP."

SECTION 1003. ANNUAL REPORT.

(a) A limited liability partnership, and a foreign limited liability partnership authorized to transact business in this State, shall file an annual report in the office of the [Secretary of State] which contains:

(1) the name of the limited liability partnership and the State or other jurisdiction under whose laws the foreign limited liability partnership is formed;

(2) the street address of the partnership's chief executive office and, if different, the street address of an office of the partnership in this State, if any; and

(3) if the partnership does not have an office in this State, the name and street address of the partnership's current agent for service of process.

(b) An annual report must be filed between [January 1 and April 1] of each year following the calendar year in which a partnership files a statement of qualification or a foreign partnership becomes authorized to transact business in this State.

(c) The [Secretary of State] may revoke the statement of qualification of a partnership that fails to file an annual report when due or pay the required filing fee. To do so, the [Secretary of State] shall provide the partnership at least 60 days' written notice of intent to revoke the statement. The notice must be mailed to the partnership at its chief executive office set forth in the last filed statement of qualification or annual report. The notice must specify the annual report that has not been filed, the fee that has not been paid, and the effective date of the revocation. The revocation is not effective if the annual report is filed and the fee is paid before the effective date of the revocation.

(d) A revocation under subsection (c) only affects a partnership's status as a limited liability partnership and is not an event of dissolution of the partnership.

(e) A partnership whose statement of qualification has been revoked may apply to the [Secretary of State] for reinstatement within two years after the effective date of the revocation. The application must state:

(1) the name of the partnership and the effective date of the revocation; and

(2) that the ground for revocation either did not exist or has been corrected.

(f) A reinstatement under subsection (e) relates back to and takes effect as of the effective date of the revocation, and the partnership's status as a limited liability partnership continues as if the revocation had never occurred.

[ARTICLE] 11
FOREIGN LIMITED LIABILITY PARTNERSHIP

SECTION 1101. LAW GOVERNING FOREIGN LIMITED LIABILITY PARTNERSHIP.

(a) The law under which a foreign limited liability partnership is formed governs relations among the partners and between the partners and the partnership and the liability of partners for obligations of the partnership.

(b) A foreign limited liability partnership may not be denied a statement of foreign qualification by reason of any difference between the law under which the partnership was formed and the law of this State.

(c) A statement of foreign qualification does not authorize a foreign limited liability partnership to engage in any business or exercise any power that a partnership may not engage in or exercise in this State as a limited liability partnership.

SECTION 1102. STATEMENT OF FOREIGN QUALIFICATION.

(a) Before transacting business in this State, a foreign limited liability partnership must file a statement of foreign qualification. The statement must contain:

(1) the name of the foreign limited liability partnership which satisfies the requirements of the State or other jurisdiction under whose law it is formed and ends with "Registered Limited Liability Partnership," "Limited Liability Partnership," "R.L.L.P.," "L.L.P.," "RLLP," or "LLP";

(2) the street address of the partnership's chief executive office and, if different, the street address of an office of the partnership in this State, if any;

(3) if there is no office of the partnership in this State, the name and street address of the partnership's agent for service of process; and

(4) a deferred effective date, if any.

(b) The agent of a foreign limited liability company for service of process must be an individual who is a resident of this State or other person authorized to do business in this State.

(c) The status of a partnership as a foreign limited liability partnership is effective on the later of the filing of the statement of foreign qualification or a date specified in the statement. The status remains effective, regardless of changes in the partnership, until it is canceled pursuant to Section 105(d) or revoked pursuant to Section 1003.

(d) An amendment or cancellation of a statement of foreign qualification is effective when it is filed or on a deferred effective date specified in the amendment or cancellation.

SECTION 1103. EFFECT OF FAILURE TO QUALIFY.

(a) A foreign limited liability partnership transacting business in this State may not maintain an action or proceeding in this State unless it has in effect a statement of foreign qualification.

(b) The failure of a foreign limited liability partnership to have in effect a statement of foreign qualification does not impair the validity of a contract or act of the foreign limited liability partnership or preclude it from defending an action or proceeding in this State.

(c) A limitation on personal liability of a partner is not waived solely by transacting business in this State without a statement of foreign qualification.

(d) If a foreign limited liability partnership transacts business in this State without a statement of foreign qualification, the [Secretary of State] is its agent for service of process with respect to a right of action arising out of the transaction of business in this State.

SECTION 1104. ACTIVITIES NOT CONSTITUTING TRANSACTING BUSINESS.

(a) Activities of a foreign limited liability partnership which do not constitute transacting business for the purpose of this [article] include:

(1) maintaining, defending, or settling an action or proceeding;

(2) holding meetings of its partners or carrying on any other activity concerning its internal affairs;

(3) maintaining bank accounts;

(4) maintaining offices or agencies for the transfer, exchange, and registration of the partnership's own securities or maintaining trustees or depositories with respect to those securities;

(5) selling through independent contractors;

(6) soliciting or obtaining orders, whether by mail or through employees or agents or otherwise, if the orders require acceptance outside this State before they become contracts;

(7) creating or acquiring indebtedness, with or without a mortgage, or other security interest in property;

(8) collecting debts or foreclosing mortgages or other security interests in property securing the debts, and holding, protecting, and maintaining property so acquired;

(9) conducting an isolated transaction that is completed within 30 days and is not one in the course of similar transactions; and

(10) transacting business in interstate commerce.

(b) For purposes of this [article], the ownership in this State of income-producing real property or tangible personal property, other than property excluded under subsection (a), constitutes transacting business in this State.

(c) This section does not apply in determining the contacts or activities that may subject a foreign limited liability partnership to service of process, taxation, or regulation under any other law of this State.

SECTION 1105. ACTION BY [ATTORNEY GENERAL].

The [Attorney General] may maintain an action to restrain a foreign limited liability partnership from transacting business in this State in violation of this [article].

[ARTICLE] 12
MISCELLANEOUS PROVISIONS

SECTION 1201. UNIFORMITY OF APPLICATION AND CONSTRUCTION.

This [Act] shall be applied and construed to effectuate its general purpose to make uniform the law with respect to the subject of this [Act] among States enacting it.

SECTION 1202. SHORT TITLE.

This [Act] may be cited as the Uniform Partnership Act (1997).

SECTION 1203. SEVERABILITY CLAUSE.

If any provision of this [Act] or its application to any person or circumstance is held invalid, the invalidity does not affect other provisions or applications of this [Act] which can be given effect without the invalid provision or application, and to this end the provisions of this [Act] are severable.

SECTION 1204. EFFECTIVE DATE.

This [Act] takes effect . . . .

SECTION 1205. REPEALS.

Effective January 1, 199____, the following acts and parts of acts are repealed: [the State Partnership Act as amended and in effect immediately before the effective date of this [Act]].

SECTION 1206. APPLICABILITY.

(a) Before January 1, 199____, this [Act] governs only a partnership formed:

(1) after the effective date of this [Act], except a partnership that is continuing the business of a dissolved partnership under [Section 41 of the superseded Uniform Partnership Act]; and

(2) before the effective date of this [Act], that elects, as provided by subsection (c), to be governed by this [Act].

(b) On and after January 1, 199____, this [Act] governs all partnerships.

(c) Before January 1, 199____, a partnership voluntarily may elect, in the manner provided in its partnership agreement or by law for amending the partnership agreement, to be governed by this [Act]. The provisions of this [Act] relating to the liability of the partnership's partners to third parties apply to limit those partners' liability to a third party who had done business with the partnership within one year before the partnership's election to be governed by this [Act] only if the third party knows or has received a notification of the partnership's election to be governed by this [Act].

SECTION 1207. SAVINGS CLAUSE.

This [Act] does not affect an action or proceeding commenced or right accrued before this [Act] takes effect.

SECTION 1208. EFFECTIVE DATE.

These [Amendments] take effect . . . .

SECTION 1209. REPEALS.

Effective January 1, 199__, the following acts and parts of acts are repealed: [the Limited Liability Partnership amendments to the State Partnership Act as amended and in effect immediately before the effective date of these [Amendments]].

SECTION 1210. APPLICABILITY.

(a) Before January 1, 199__, these [Amendments] govern only a limited liability partnership formed:

(1) on or after the effective date of these [Amendments], unless that partnership is continuing the business of a dissolved limited liability partnership; and

(2) before the effective date of these [Amendments], that elects, as provided by subsection (c), to be governed by these [Amendments].

(b) On and after January 1, 199__, these [Amendments] govern all partnerships.

(c) Before January 1, 199__, a partnership voluntarily may elect, in the manner provided in its partnership agreement or by law for amending the partnership agreement, to be governed by these [Amendments]. The provisions of these [Amendments] relating to the liability of the partnership's partners to third parties apply to limit those partners' liability to a third party who had done business with the partnership within one year before the partnership's election to be governed by these [Amendments], only if the third party knows or has received a notification of the partnership's election to be governed by these [Amendments].

(d) The existing provisions for execution and filing a statement of qualification of a limited liability partnership continue until either the limited liability partnership elects to have this [Act] apply or January 1, 199__.

SECTION 1211. SAVINGS CLAUSE.

These [Amendments] do not affect an action or proceeding commenced or right accrued before these [Amendments] take effect.

APPENDIX C

UNIFORM LIMITED PARTNERSHIP ACT*

(Adopted in 46 states, all except Connecticut, Minnesota, Wyoming and Louisiana; also in the District of Columbia, and the Virgin Islands.) An Act to Make Uniform the Law Relating to Limited Partnerships Be it enacted, etc., as follows:

SECTION 1.   LIMITED PARTNERSHIP DEFINED.

A limited partnership is a partnership formed by two or more persons under the provisions of Section 2, having as members one or more general partners and one or more limited partners. The lim-ited partners as such shall not be bound by the obligations of the partnership.

SECTION 2.   FORMATION.

(1) Two or more persons desiring to form a limited partnership shall
   (a) Sign and swear to a certificate, which shall state
       I. The name of the partnership,
       II. The character of the business,
       III. The location of the principal place of business,
       IV. The name and place of residence of each member; general and limited partners being respectively designated,
       V. The term for which the partnership is to exist,
       VI. The amount of cash and a description of and the agreed value of the other property contributed by each limited partner,
       VII. The additional contributions, if any, agreed to be made by each limited partner and the times at which or events on the happening of which they shall be made,
       VIII. The time, if agreed upon, when the contribution of each limited partner is to be returned,
       IX. The share of the profits or the other compensation by way of income which each limited partner shall receive by reason of his contribution,
       X. The right, if given, of a limited partner to substitute an assignee as contributor in his place, and the terms and conditions of the substitution,
       XI. The right, if given, of the partners to admit additional limited partners,
       XII. The right, if given, of one or more of the limited partners to priority over other limited partners, as to contributions or as to compensation by way of income, and the nature of such priority,
       XIII. The right, if given, of the remaining general partner or partners to continue the business on the death, retirement or insanity of a general partner, and
       XIV. The right, if given, of a limited partner to demand and receive property other than cash in return for his contribution.
   (b) File for record the certificate in the office of (here designate the proper office).
       (2) A limited partnership is formed if there has been substantial compliance in good faith with the requirements of paragraph (1).

SECTION 3.   BUSINESS WHICH MAY BE CARRIED ON.

A limited partnership may carry on any business which a partnership without limited partners may carry on, except (here designate the business to be prohibited).

SECTION 4.   CHARACTER OF LIMITED PARTNER'S CONTRIBUTION.

The contributions of a limited partner may be cash or other property, but not services.

*The Uniform Limited Partnership Act was revised in 1976 and amended in 1985, but several states base their state statutes on the original version of the act. This is the original version; the revised act with amendments follows.

SECTION 5.   A NAME NOT TO CONTAIN SURNAME OF
LIMITED PARTNER, EXCEPTIONS.

(1) The surname of a limited partner shall not appear in the partnership name, unless

(a) It is also the surname of a general partner, or

(b) Prior to the time when the limited partner became such the
business had been carried on under a name in which his surname appeared.

(2) A limited partner whose name appears in a partnership name
contrary to the provisions of paragraph (1) is liable as a general
partner to partnership creditors who extend credit to the partnership without actual knowledge that he is not a general partner.

SECTION 6.   LIABILITY FOR FALSE STATEMENTS IN
CERTIFICATE.

If the certificate contains a false statement, one who suffers loss
by reliance on such statement may hold liable any party to the certificate who knew the statement to be false

(a) At the time he signed the certificate, or

(b) Subsequently, but within a sufficient time before the statement was relied upon to enable him to cancel or amend the
certificate, or to file a petition for its cancellation or amendment as provided in Section 25(3).

SECTION 7.   LIMITED PARTNER NOT LIABLE TO
CREDITORS.

A limited partner shall not become liable as a general partner unless, in addition to the exercise of his rights and powers as a limited partner, he takes part in the control of the business.

SECTION 8.   ADMISSION OF ADDITIONAL LIMITED
PARTNERS.

After the formation of a limited partnership, additional limited
partners may be admitted upon filing an amendment to the original certificate in accordance with the requirements of Section 25.

SECTION 9.   RIGHTS, POWERS AND LIABILITIES OF A
GENERAL PARTNER.

(1) A general partner shall have all the rights and powers and be
subject to all the restrictions and liabilities of a partner in a partnership without limited partners, except that without the written
consent or ratification of the specific act by all the limited partners, a general partner or all of the general partners have no authority to

(a) Do any act in contravention of the certificate,

(b) Do any act which would make it impossible to carry on the
ordinary business of the partnership,

(c) Confess a judgment against the partnership,

(d) Possess partnership property, or assign their rights in specific partnership property, for other than a partnership purpose,

(e) Admit a person as a general partner,

(f) Admit a person as a limited partner, unless the right so to
do is given in the certificate,

(g) Continue the business with partnership property on the
death, retirement or insanity of a general partner, unless the
right so to do is given in the certificate.

SECTION 10.   RIGHTS OF A LIMITED PARTNER.

(1) A limited partner shall have the same rights as a general
partner to

(a) Have the partnership books kept at the principal place of
business of the partnership, and at all times to inspect and
copy any of them,

(b) Have on demand true and full information of all things affecting the partnership, and a formal account of partnership
affairs, whenever circumstances render it just and reasonable, and

(c) Have dissolution and winding up by decree of court.

(2) A limited partner shall have the right to receive a share of the
profits or other compensation by way of income, and to the return
of his contribution as provided in Sections 15 and 16.

SECTION 11.   STATUS OF PERSON ERRONEOUSLY
BELIEVING HIMSELF A LIMITED
PARTNER.

A person who has contributed to the capital of a business conducted by a person or partnership erroneously believing that he
has become a limited partner in a limited partnership, is not, by
reason of his exercise of the rights of a limited partner, a general
partner with the person or in the partnership carrying on the business, or bound by the obligations of such person or partnership;
provided that on ascertaining the mistake he promptly renounces
his interest in the profits of the business, or other compensation by
way of income.

SECTION 12.   ONE PERSON BOTH GENERAL AND
LIMITED PARTNER.

(1) A person may be a general partner and a limited partner in the
same partnership at the same time.

(2) A person who is a general, and also at the same time a limited
partner, shall have all the rights and powers and be subject to all
the restrictions of a general partner; except that, in respect to his
contribution, he shall have the rights against the other members
which he would have had if he were not also a general partner.

SECTION 13.   LOANS AND OTHER BUSINESS
TRANSACTIONS WITH LIMITED
PARTNER.

(1) A limited partner also may loan money to and transact other
business with the partnership, and, unless he is also a general partner, receive on account of resulting claims against the partnership,
with general creditors, a pro rata share of the assets. No limited
partner shall in respect to any such claim

(a) Receive or hold as collateral security any partnership
property, or

(b) Receive from a general partner or the partnership any payment, conveyance, or release from liability, if at the time the
assets of the partnership are not sufficient to discharge partnership liabilities to persons not claiming as general or limited partners.

(2) The receiving of collateral security, or a payment, conveyance,
or release in violation of the provisions of paragraph (1) is a fraud
on the creditors of the partnership.

SECTION 14.   RELATION OF LIMITED PARTNERS INTER SE.

Where there are several limited partners the members may agree
that one or more of the limited partners shall have a priority over
other limited partners as to the return of their contributions, as to
their compensation by way of income, or as to any other matter. If
such an agreement is made it shall be stated in the certificate, and

in the absence of such a statement all the limited partners shall stand upon equal footing.

SECTION 15. COMPENSATION OF LIMITED PARTNER.

A limited partner may receive from the partnership the share of the profits or the compensation by way of income stipulated for in the certificate; provided, that after such payment is made, whether from the property of the partnership or that of a general partner, the partnership assets are in excess of all liabilities of the partnership except liabilities to limited partners on account of their contributions and to general partners.

SECTION 16. WITHDRAWAL OR REDUCTION OF LIMITED PARTNER'S CONTRIBUTION.

(1) A limited partner shall not receive from a general partner or out of partnership property any part of his contribution until

(a) All liabilities of the partnership, except liabilities to general partners and to limited partners on account of their contributions, have been paid or there remains property of the partnership sufficient to pay them,

(b) The consent of all members is had, unless the return of the contribution may be rightfully demanded under the provisions of paragraph (2), and

(c) The certificate is cancelled or so amended as to set forth the withdrawal or reduction.

(2) Subject to the provisions of paragraph (1) a limited partner may rightfully demand the return of his contribution

(a) On the dissolution of a partnership, or

(b) When the date specified in the certificate for its return has arrived, or

(c) After he has given six months' notice in writing to all other members, if no time is specified in the certificate either for the return of the contribution or for the dissolution of the partnership.

(3) In the absence of any statement in the certificate to the contrary or the consent of all members, a limited partner, irrespective of the nature of his contribution, has only the right to demand and receive cash in return for his contribution.

(4) A limited partner may have the partnership dissolved and its affairs wound up when

(a) He rightfully but unsuccessfully demands the return of his contribution, or

(b) The other liabilities of the partnership have not been paid, or the partnership property is insufficient for their payment as required by paragraph (1a) and the limited partner would otherwise be entitled to the return of his contribution.

SECTION 17. LIABILITY OF LIMITED PARTNER TO PARTNERSHIP.

(1) A limited partner is liable to the partnership

(a) For the difference between his contribution as actually made and that stated in the certificate as having been made, and

(b) For any unpaid contribution which he agreed in the certificate to make in the future at the time and on the conditions stated in the certificate.

(2) A limited partner holds as trustee for the partnership

(a) Specific property stated in the certificate as contributed by him, but which was not contributed or which has been wrongfully returned, and

(b) Money or other property wrongfully paid or conveyed to him on account of his contribution.

(3) The liabilities of a limited partner as set forth in this section can be waived or compromised only by the consent of all members; but a waiver or compromise shall not affect the right of a creditor of a partnership, who extended credit or whose claim arose after the filing and before a cancellation or amendment of the certificate, to enforce such liabilities.

(4) When a contributor has rightfully received the return in whole or in part of the capital of his contribution, he is nevertheless liable to the partnership for any sum, not in excess of such return with interest, necessary to discharge its liabilities to all creditors who extended credit or whose claims arose before such return.

SECTION 18. NATURE OF LIMITED PARTNER'S INTEREST IN PARTNERSHIP.

A limited partner's interest in the partnership is personal property.

SECTION 19. ASSIGNMENT OF LIMITED PARTNER'S INTEREST.

(1) A limited partner's interest is assignable.

(2) A substituted limited partner is a person admitted to all the rights of a limited partner who has died or has assigned his interest in a partnership.

(3) An assignee, who does not become a substituted limited partner, has no right to require any information or account of the partnership transactions or to inspect the partnership books; he is only entitled to receive the share of the profits or other compensation by way of income, or the return of his contribution, to which his assignor would otherwise be entitled.

(4) An assignee shall have the right to become a substituted limited partner if all the members (except the assignor) consent thereto or if the assignor, being thereunto empowered by the certificate, gives the assignee that right.

(5) An assignee becomes a substituted limited partner when the certificate is appropriately amended in accordance with Section 25.

(6) The substituted limited partner has all the rights and powers, and is subject to all the restrictions and liabilities of his assignor, except those liabilities of which he was ignorant at the time he became a limited partner and which could not be ascertained from the certificate.

(7) The substitution of the assignee as a limited partner does not release the assignor from liability to the partnership under Sections 6 and 17.

SECTION 20. EFFECT OF RETIREMENT, DEATH OR INSANITY OF A GENERAL PARTNER.

The retirement, death or insanity of a general partner dissolves the partnership, unless the business is continued by the remaining general partners

(a) Under a right so to do stated in the certificate, or

(b) With the consent of all members.

SECTION 21. DEATH OF LIMITED PARTNER.

(1) On the death of a limited partner his executor or administrator shall have all the rights of a limited partner for the purpose of settling his estate, and such power as the deceased had to constitute his assignee a substituted limited partner.

(2) The estate of a deceased limited partner shall be liable for all his liabilities as a limited partner.

SECTION 22.   RIGHTS OF CREDITORS OF LIMITED PARTNER.

(1) On due application to a court of competent jurisdiction by any judgment creditor of a limited partner, the court may charge the interest of the indebted limited partner with payment of the unsatisfied amount of the judgment debt; and may appoint a receiver, and make all other orders, directions, and inquiries which the circumstances of the case may require.

In those states where a creditor on beginning an action can attach debts due the defendant before he has obtained a judgment against the defendant it is recommended that paragraph (1) of this section read as follows:

On due application to a court of competent jurisdiction by any creditor of a limited partner, the court may charge the interest of the indebted limited partner with payment of the unsatisfied amount of such claim; and may appoint a receiver, and make all other orders, directions, and inquiries which the circumstances of the case may require.

(2) The interest may be redeemed with the separate property of any general partner, but may not be redeemed with partnership property.

(3) The remedies conferred by paragraph (1) shall not be deemed exclusive of others which may exist.

(4) Nothing in this act shall be held to deprive a limited partner of his statutory exemption.

SECTION 23.   DISTRIBUTION OF ASSETS.

(1) In settling accounts after dissolution the liabilities of the partnership shall be entitled to payment in the following order:

(a) Those to creditors, in the order of priority as provided by law, except those to limited partners on account of their contributions, and to general partners,

(b) Those to limited partners in respect to their share of the profits and other compensation by way of income on their contributions,

(c) Those to limited partners in respect to the capital of their contributions,

(d) Those to general partners other than for capital and profits,

(e) Those to general partners in respect to profits,

(f) Those to general partners in respect to capital.

(2) Subject to any statement in the certificate or to subsequent agreement, limited partners share in the partnership assets in respect to their claims for capital, and in respect to their claims for profits or for compensation by way of income on their contributions respectively, in proportion to the respective amounts of such claims.

SECTION 24.   WHEN CERTIFICATE SHALL BE CANCELLED OR AMENDED.

(1) The certificate shall be cancelled when the partnership is dissolved or all limited partners cease to be such.

(2) A certificate shall be amended when

(a) There is a change in the name of the partnership or in the amount or character of the contribution of any limited partner,

(b) A person is substituted as a limited partner,

(c) An additional limited partner is admitted,

(d) A person is admitted as a general partner,

(e) A general partner retires, dies or becomes insane, and the business is continued under section 20,

(f) There is a change in the character of the business of the partnership,

(g) There is a false or erroneous statement in the certificate,

(h) There is a change in the time as stated in the certificate for the dissolution of the partnership or for the return of a contribution,

(i) A time is fixed for the dissolution of the partnership, or the return of a contribution, no time having been specified in the certificate, or

(j) The members desire to make a change in any other statement in the certificate in order that it shall accurately represent the agreement between them.

SECTION 25.   REQUIREMENTS FOR AMENDMENT AND FOR CANCELLATION OF CERTIFICATE.

(1) The writing to amend a certificate shall

(a) Conform to the requirements of Section 2(1a) as far as necessary to set forth clearly the change in the certificate which it is desired to make, and

(b) Be signed and sworn to by all members, and an amendment substituting a limited partner or adding a limited or general partner shall be signed also by the member to be substituted or added, and when a limited partner is to be substituted, the amendment shall also be signed by the assigning limited partner.

(2) The writing to cancel a certificate shall be signed by all members.

(3) A person desiring the cancellation or amendment of a certificate, if any person designated in paragraphs (1) and (2) as a person who must execute the writing refuses to do so, may petition the [here designate the proper court] to direct a cancellation or amendment thereof.

(4) If the court finds that the petitioner has a right to have the writing executed by a person who refuses to do so, it shall order the [here designate the responsible official in the office designated in Section 2] in the office where the certificate is recorded to record the cancellation or amendment of the certificate; and where the certificate is to be amended, the court shall also cause to be filed for record in said office a certified copy of its decree setting forth the amendment.

(5) A certificate is amended or cancelled when there is filed for record in the office [here designate the office designated in Section 2] where the certificate is recorded

(a) A writing in accordance with the provisions of paragraph (1), or (2) or

(b) A certified copy of the order of court in accordance with the provisions of paragraph (4).

(6) After the certificate is duly amended in accordance with this section, the amended certificate shall thereafter be for all purposes the certificate provided for by this act.

SECTION 26.   PARTIES TO ACTIONS.

A contributor, unless he is a general partner, is not a proper party to proceedings by or against a partnership, except where the object is to enforce a limited partner's right against or liability to the partnership.

SECTION 27.   NAME OF ACT.

This act may be cited as The Uniform Limited Partnership Act.

SECTION 28.   RULES OF CONSTRUCTION.

(1) The rule that statutes in derogation of the common law are to be strictly construed shall have no application to this act.

(2) This act shall be so interpreted and construed as to effect its general purpose to make uniform the law of those states which enact it.
(3) This act shall not be so construed as to impair the obligations of any contract existing when the act goes into effect, nor to affect any action on proceedings begun or right accrued before this act takes effect.

SECTION 29.   RULES FOR CASES NOT PROVIDED FOR IN THIS ACT.

In any case not provided for in this act the rules of law and equity, including the law merchant, shall govern.

SECTION 30.[1]   PROVISIONS FOR EXISTING LIMITED PARTNERSHIPS.

(1) A limited partnership formed under any statute of this state prior to the adoption of this act, may become a limited partnership under this act by complying with the provisions of Section 2; provided the certificate sets forth

    (a) The amount of the original contribution of each limited partner, and the time when the contribution was made, and

    (b) That the property of the partnership exceeds the amount sufficient to discharge its liabilities to persons not claiming as general or limited partners by an amount greater than the sum of the contributions of its limited partners.

(2) A limited partnership formed under any statute of this state prior to the adoption of this act, until or unless it becomes a limited partnership under this act, shall continue to be governed by the provisions of [here insert proper reference to the existing limited partnership act or acts], except that such partnership shall not be renewed unless so provided in the original agreement.

SECTION 31.[1]   ACT [ACTS] REPEALED.

Except as affecting existing limited partnerships to the extent set forth in Section 30, the act (acts) of [here designate the existing limited partnership act or acts] is (are) hereby repealed.

---

[1]Section 30, 31, will be omitted in any state which has not previously had a limited partnership act.

REVISED UNIFORM LIMITED PARTNERSHIP ACT, 1976, WITH 1985 AMENDMENTS

ARTICLE 1
GENERAL PROVISIONS

SECTION 101.   DEFINITIONS.
As used in this [Act], unless the context otherwise requires:
(1) "Certificate of limited partnership" means the certificate referred to in Section 201, and the certificate as amended or restated.
(2) "Contribution" means any cash, property, services rendered, or a promissory note or other binding obligation to contribute cash or property or to perform services, which a partner contributes to a limited partnership in his capacity as a partner.
(3) "Event of withdrawal of a general partner" means an event that causes a person to cease to be a general partner as provided in Section 402.
(4) "Foreign limited partnership" means a partnership formed under the laws of any state other than this State and having as partners one or more general partners and one or more limited partners.
(5) "General partner" means a person who has been admitted to a limited partnership as a general partner in accordance with the

partnership agreement and named in the certificate of limited partnership as a general partner.

(6) "Limited partner" means a person who has been admitted to a limited partnership as a limited partner in accordance with the partnership agreement.

(7) "Limited partnership" and "domestic limited partnership" mean a partnership formed by two or more persons under the laws of this State and having one or more general partners and one or more limited partners.

(8) "Partner" means a limited or general partner.

(9) "Partnership agreement" means any valid agreement, written or oral, of the partners as to the affairs of a limited partnership and the conduct of its business.

(10) "Partnership interest" means a partner's share of the profits and losses of a limited partnership and the right to receive distributions of partnership assets.

(11) "Person" means a natural person, partnership, limited partnership (domestic or foreign), trust, estate, association, or corporation.

(12) "State" means a state, territory, or possession of the United States, the District of Columbia, or the Commonwealth of Puerto Rico.

SECTION 102. NAME.

The name of each limited partnership as set forth in its certificate of limited partnership:

(1) shall contain without abbreviation the words "limited partnership";

(2) may not contain the name of a limited partner unless (i) it is also the name of a general partner or the corporate name of a corporate general partner, or (ii) the business of the limited partnership had been carried on under that name before the admission of that limited partner;

(3) may not be the same as, or deceptively similar to, the name of any corporation or limited partnership organized under the laws of this State or licensed or registered as a foreign corporation or limited partnership in this State; and

(4) may not contain the following words [here insert prohibited words].

SECTION 103. RESERVATION OF NAME.

(a) The exclusive right to the use of a name may be reserved by:

(1) any person intending to organize a limited partnership under this [Act] and to adopt that name;

(2) any domestic limited partnership or any foreign limited partnership registered in this State which, in either case, intends to adopt that name;

(3) any foreign limited partnership intending to register in this State and adopt that name; and

(4) any person intending to organize a foreign limited partnership and intending to have it register in this State and adopt that name.

(b) The reservation shall be made by filing with the Secretary of State an application, executed by the applicant, to reserve a specified name. If the Secretary of State finds that the name is available for use by a domestic or foreign limited partnership, he [or she] shall reserve the name for the exclusive use of the applicant for a period of 120 days. Once having so reserved a name, the same applicant may not again reserve the same name until more than 60 days after the expiration of the last 120-day period for which that applicant reserved that name. The right to the exclusive use of a reserved name may be transferred to any

other person by filing in the office of the Secretary of State a notice of the transfer, executed by the applicant for whom the name was reserved and specifying the name and address of the transferee.

SECTION 104. SPECIFIED OFFICE AND AGENT.

Each limited partnership shall continuously maintain in this State:

(1) an office, which may but need not be a place of its business in this State, at which shall be kept the records required by Section 105 to be maintained; and

(2) an agent for service of process on the limited partnership, which agent must be an individual resident of this State, a domestic corporation, or a foreign corporation authorized to do business in this State.

SECTION 105. RECORDS TO BE KEPT.

(a) Each limited partnership shall keep at the office referred to in Section 104(1) the following:

(1) a current list of the full name and last known business address of each partner, separately identifying the general partners (in alphabetical order) and the limited partners (in alphabetical order);

(2) a copy of the certificate of limited partnership and all certificates of amendment thereto, together with executed copies of any powers of attorney pursuant to which any certificate has been executed;

(3) copies of the limited partnership's federal, state and local income tax returns and reports, if any, for the three most recent years;

(4) copies of any then effective written partnership agreements and of any financial statements of the limited partnership for the three most recent years; and

(5) unless contained in written partnership agreement, a writing setting out:

(i) the amount of cash and a description and statement of the agreed value of the other property or services contributed by each partner and which each partner has agreed to contribute;

(ii) the times at which or events on the happening of which any additional contributions agreed to be made by each partner are to be made;

(iii) any right of a partner to receive, or of a general partner to make, distributions to a partner which include a return of all or any part of the partner's contribution; and

(iv) any events upon the happening of which the limited partnership is to be dissolved and its affairs wound up.

(b) Records kept under this section are subject to inspection and copying at the reasonable request and at the expense, of any partner during ordinary business hours.

SECTION 106. NATURE OF BUSINESS.

A limited partnership may carry on any business that a partnership without limited partners may carry on except [here designate prohibited activities].

SECTION 107. BUSINESS TRANSACTIONS OF PARTNER WITH PARTNERSHIP.

Except as provided in the partnership agreement, a partner may lend money to and transact other business with the limited partnership and, subject to other applicable law, has the same rights and obligations with respect thereto as a person who is not a partner.

ARTICLE 2
FORMATION; CERTIFICATE OF LIMITED PARTNERSHIP

SECTION 201.   CERTIFICATE OF LIMITED
                              PARTNERSHIP.

(a) In order to form a limited partnership, a certificate of limited partnership must be executed and filed in the office of the Secretary of State. The certificate shall set forth:

(1) the name of the limited partnership;

(2) the address of the office and the name and address of the agent for service of process required to be maintained by Section 104;

(3) the name and the business address of each general partner;

(4) the latest date upon which the limited partnership is to dissolve; and

(5) any other matters the general partners determine to include therein.

(b) A limited partnership is formed at the time of the filing of the certificate of limited partnership in the office of the Secretary of State or at any later time specified in the certificate of limited partnership if, in either case, there has been substantial compliance with the requirements of this section.

SECTION 202.   AMENDMENT TO CERTIFICATE.

(a) A certificate of limited partnership is amended by filing a certificate of amendment thereto in the office of the Secretary of State. The certificate shall set forth:

(1) the name of the limited partnership;

(2) the date of filing the certificate; and

(3) the amendment to the certificate.

(b) Within 30 days after the happening of any of the following events, an amendment to a certificate of limited partnership reflecting the occurrence of the event or events shall be filed:

(1) the admission of a new general partner;

(2) the withdrawal of a general partner; or

(3) the continuation of the business under Section 801 after an event of withdrawal of a general partner.

(c) A general partner who becomes aware that any statement in a certificate of limited partnership was false when made or that any arrangements or other facts described have changed, making the certificate inaccurate in any respect, shall promptly amend the certificate.

(d) A certificate of limited partnership may be amended at any time for any other proper purpose the general partners determine.

(e) No person has any liability because an amendment to a certificate of limited partnership has not been filed to reflect the occurrence of any event referred to in subsection (b) of this section if the amendment is filed within the 30-day period specified in subsection (b).

(f) A restated certificate of limited partnership may be executed and filed in the same manner as a certificate of amendment.

SECTION 203.   CANCELLATION OF CERTIFICATE.

A certificate of limited partnership shall be cancelled upon the dissolution and the commencement of winding up of the partnership or at any other time there are no limited partners. A certificate of cancellation shall be filed in the office of the Secretary of State and set forth:

(1) the name of the limited partnership;

(2) the date of filing of its certificate of limited partnership;

(3) the reason for filing the certificate of cancellation;

(4) the effective date (which shall be a date certain) of cancellation if it is not to be effective upon the filing of the certificate; and

(5) any other information the general partners filing the certificate determine.

SECTION 204.   EXECUTION OF CERTIFICATES.

(a) Each certificate required by this Article to be filed in the office of the Secretary of State shall be executed in the following manner:

(1) an original certificate of limited partnership must be signed by all general partners;

(2) a certificate of amendment must be signed by at least one general partner and by each other general partner designated in the certificate as a new general partner; and

(3) a certificate of cancellation must be signed by all general partners.

(b) Any person may sign a certificate by an attorney-in-fact, but a power of attorney to sign a certificate relating to the admission of a general partner must specifically describe the admission.

(c) The execution of a certificate by a general partner constitutes an affirmation under the penalties of perjury that the facts stated therein are true.

SECTION 205.   EXECUTION BY JUDICIAL ACT.

If a person required by Section 204 to execute any certificate fails or refuses to do so, any other person who is adversely affected by the failure or refusal, may petition the [designate the appropriate court] to direct the execution of the certificate. If the court finds that it is proper for the certificate to be executed and that any person so designated has failed or refused to execute the certificate, it shall order the Secretary of State to record an appropriate certificate.

SECTION 206.   FILING IN OFFICE OF SECRETARY OF
                              STATE.

(a) Two signed copies of the certificate of limited partnership and of any certificates of amendment or cancellation (or of any judicial decree of amendment or cancellation) shall be delivered to the Secretary of State. A person who executes a certificate as an agent or fiduciary need not exhibit evidence of his [or her] authority as a prerequisite to filing. Unless the Secretary of State finds that any certificate does not conform to law, upon receipt of all filing fees required by law he [or she] shall:

(1) endorse on each duplicate original the word "Filed" and the day, month and year of the filing thereof;

(2) file one duplicate original in his [or her] office; and

(3) return the other duplicate original to the person who filed it or his [or her] representative.

(b) Upon the filing of a certificate of amendment (or judicial decree of amendment) in the office of the Secretary of State, the certificate of limited partnership shall be amended as set forth therein, and upon the effective date of a certificate of cancellation (or a judicial decree thereof), the certificate of limited partnership is cancelled.

SECTION 207.   LIABILITY FOR FALSE STATEMENT IN CERTIFICATE.

If any certificate of limited partnership or certificate of amendment or cancellation contains a false statement, one who suffers loss by reliance on the statement may recover damages for the loss from:

(1) any person who executes the certificate, or causes another to execute it on his behalf, and knew, and any general partner who knew or should have known; the statement to be false at the time the certificate was executed; and

(2) Any general partner who thereafter knows or should have known that any arrangement or other fact described in the certificate has changed, making the statement inaccurate in any respect within a sufficient time before the statement was relied upon reasonably to have enabled that general partner to cancel or amend the certificate, or to file a petition for its cancellation or amendment under Section 205.

SECTION 208.   SCOPE OF NOTICE.

The fact that a certificate of limited partnership is on file in the office of the Secretary of State is notice that the partnership is a limited partnership and the persons designated therein as general partners are general partners, but it is not notice of any other fact.

SECTION 209.   DELIVERY OF CERTIFICATES TO LIMITED PARTNERS.

Upon the return by the Secretary of State pursuant to Section 206 of a certificate marked "Filed," the general partners shall promptly deliver or mail a copy of the certificate of limited partnership and each certificate of amendment or cancellation to each limited partner unless the partnership agreement provides otherwise.

ARTICLE 3
LIMITED PARTNERS

SECTION 301.   ADMISSION OF ADDITIONAL LIMITED PARTNERS.

(a) A person becomes a limited partner on the later of:

(1) the date the original certificate of limited partnership is filed; or

(2) the date stated in the records of the limited partnership as the date that person becomes a limited partner.

(b) After the filing of a limited partnership's original certificate of limited partnership, a person may be admitted as an additional limited partner:

(1) in the case of a person acquiring a partnership interest directly from the limited partnership, upon compliance with the partnership agreement or, if the partnership agreement does not so provide, upon the written consent of all partners; and

(2) in the case of an assignee of a partnership interest of a partner who has the power, as provided in Section 704, to grant the assignee the right to become a limited partner, upon the exercise of that power and compliance with any conditions limiting the grant or exercise of the power.

SECTION 302.   VOTING.

Subject to Section 303, the partnership agreement may grant to all or a specified group of the limited partners the right to vote (on a per capita or other basis) upon any matter.

SECTION 303.   LIABILITY TO THIRD PARTIES.

(a) Except as provided in subsection (d), a limited partner is not liable for the obligations of a limited partnership unless he [or she] is also a general partner or, in addition to the exercise of his [or her] rights and powers as a limited partner, he [or she] participates in the control of the business. However, if the limited partner participates in the control of the business, he [or she] is liable only to persons who transact business with the limited partnership reasonably believing, based upon the limited partner's conduct, that the limited partner is a general partner.

(b) A limited partner does not participate in the control of the business within the meaning of subsection (a) solely by doing one or more of the following:

(1) being a contractor for or an agent or employee of the limited partnership or of a general partner or being an officer, director, or shareholder of a general partner that is a corporation;

(2) consulting with and advising a general partner with respect to the business of the limited partnership;

(3) acting as surety for the limited partnership or guaranteeing or assuming one or more specific obligations of the limited partnership;

(4) taking any action required or permitted by law to bring or pursue a derivative action in the right of the limited partnership;

(5) requesting or attending a meeting of partners;

(6) proposing, approving, or disapproving, by voting or otherwise, one or more of the following matters:

(i) the dissolution and winding up of the limited partnership;

(ii) the sale, exchange, lease, mortgage, pledge, or other transfer of all or substantially all of the assets of the limited partnership;

(iii) the incurrence of indebtedness by the limited partnership other than in the ordinary course of its business;

(iv) a change in the nature of the business;

(v) the admission or removal of a general partner;

(vi) the admission or removal of a limited partner;

(vii) a transaction involving an actual or potential conflict of interest between a general partner and the limited partnership or the limited partners;

(viii) an amendment to the partnership agreement or certificate of limited partnership; or

(ix) matters related to the business of the limited partnership not otherwise enumerated in this subsection (b), which the partnership agreement states in writing may be subject to the approval or disapproval of limited partners;

(7) winding up the limited partnership pursuant to Section 803; or

(8) exercising any right or power permitted to limited partners under this [Act] and not specifically enumerated in this subsection (b).

(c) The enumeration in subsection (b) does not mean that the possession or exercise of any other powers by a limited partner constitutes participation by him [or her] in the business of the limited partnership.

(d) A limited partner who knowingly permits his [or her] name to be used in the name of the limited partnership, except under circumstances permitted by Section 102(2), is liable to creditors who extend credit to the limited partnership without actual knowledge that the limited partner is not a general partner.

SECTION 304. ERRONEOUSLY BELIEVING HIMSELF [OR HERSELF] LIMITED PARTNER.

(a) Except as provided in subsection (b), a person who makes a contribution to a business enterprise and erroneously but in good faith believes that he [or she] has become a limited partner in the enterprise is not a general partner in the enterprise and is not bound by its obligations by reason of making the contribution, receiving distributions from the enterprise, or exercising any rights of a limited partner, if, on ascertaining the mistake, he [or she]:

(1) causes an appropriate certificate of limited partnership or a certificate of amendment to be executed and filed; or

(2) withdraws from future equity participation in the enterprise by executing and filing in the office of the Secretary of State a certificate declaring withdrawal under this section.

(b) A person who makes a contribution of the kind described in subsection (a) is liable as a general partner to any third party who transacts business with the enterprise (i) before the person withdraws and an appropriate certificate is filed to show withdrawal, or (ii) before an appropriate certificate is filed to show that he [or she] is not a general partner, but in either case only if the third party actually believed in good faith that the person was a general partner at the time of the transaction.

SECTION 305. INFORMATION.

Each limited partner has the right to:

(1) inspect and copy any of the partnership records required to be maintained by Section 105; and

(2) obtain from the general partners from time to time upon reasonable demand (i) true and full information regarding the state of the business and financial condition of the limited partnership, (ii) promptly after becoming available, a copy of the limited partnership's federal, state and local income tax returns for each year, and (iii) other information regarding the affairs of the limited partnership as is just and reasonable.

ARTICLE 4
GENERAL PARTNERS

SECTION 401. ADMISSION OF ADDITIONAL GENERAL PARTNERS.

After the filing of a limited partnership's original certificate of limited partnership, additional general partners may be admitted as provided in writing in the partnership agreement or, if the partnership agreement does not provide in writing for the admission of additional general partners, with the written consent of all partners.

SECTION 402. EVENTS OF WITHDRAWAL.

Except as approved by the specific written consent of all partners at the time, a person ceases to be a general partner of a limited partnership upon the happening of any of the following events:

(1) the general partner withdraws from the limited partnership as provided in Section 602;

(2) the general partner ceases to be a member of the limited partnership as provided in Section 702;

(3) the general partner is removed as a general partner in accordance with the partnership agreement;

(4) unless otherwise provided in writing in the partnership agreement, the general partner: (i) makes an assignment for the benefit of creditors; (ii) files a voluntary petition in bankruptcy; (iii) is adjudicated a bankrupt or insolvent; (iv) files a petition or answer seeking for himself [or herself] any reor-

ganization, arrangement, composition, readjustment, liquidation, dissolution or similar relief under any statute, law, or regulation; (v) files an answer or other pleading admitting or failing to contest the material allegations of a petition filed against him [or her] in any proceeding of this nature; or (vi) seeks, consents to, or acquiesces in the appointment of a trustee, receiver, or liquidator of the general partner or of all or any substantial part of his [or her] properties;

(5) unless otherwise provided in writing in the partnership agreement, [120] days after the commencement of any proceeding against the general partner seeking reorganization, arrangement, composition, readjustment, liquidation, dissolution or similar relief under any statute, law, or regulation, the proceeding has not been dismissed, or if within [90] days after the appointment without his [or her] consent or acquiescence of a trustee, receiver, or liquidator of the general partner or of all or any substantial part of his [or her] properties, the appointment is not vacated or stayed or within [90] days after the expiration of any such stay, the appointment is not vacated;

(6) in the case of a general partner who is a natural person,

(i) his [or her] death; or

(ii) the entry by a court of competent jurisdiction adjudicating him [or her] incompetent to manage his [or her] person or his [or her] estate;

(7) in the case of a general partner who is acting as a general partner by virtue of being a trustee of a trust, the termination of the trust (but not merely the substitution of a new trustee);

(8) in the case of a general partner that is a separate partnership, the dissolution and commencement of winding up of the separate partnership;

(9) in the case of a general partner that is a corporation, the filing of a certificate of dissolution, or its equivalent, for the corporation or the revocation of its charter; or

(10) in the case of an estate, the distribution by the fiduciary of the estate's entire interest in the partnership.

SECTION 403. GENERAL POWERS AND LIABILITIES.

(a) Except as provided in this [Act] or in the partnership agreement, a general partner of a limited partnership has the rights and powers and is subject to the restrictions of a partner in a partnership without limited partners.

(b) Except as provided in this [Act], a general partner of a limited partnership has the liabilities of a partner in a partnership without limited partners to persons other than the partnership and the other partners. Except as provided in this [Act] or in the partnership agreement, a general partner of a limited partnership has the liabilities of a partner in a partnership without limited partners to the partnership and to the other partners.

SECTION 404. CONTRIBUTIONS BY GENERAL PARTNER.

A general partner of a limited partnership may make contributions to the partnership and share in the profits and losses of, and in distributions from, the limited partnership as a general partner. A general partner also may make contributions to and share in profits, losses, and distributions as a limited partner. A person who is both a general partner and a limited partner has the rights and powers, and is subject to the restrictions and liabilities, of a general partner and, except as provided in the partnership agreement, also has the powers, and is subject to the restrictions, of a limited partner to the extent of his [or her] participation in the partnership as a limited partner.

SECTION 405.   VOTING.

The partnership agreement may grant to all or certain identified general partners the right to vote (on a per capita or any other basis), separately or with all or any class of the limited partners, on any matter.

ARTICLE 5
FINANCE

SECTION 501.   FORM OF CONTRIBUTION.

The contribution of a partner may be in cash, property, or services rendered, or a promissory note or other obligation to contribute cash or property or to perform services

SECTION 502.   LIABILITY FOR CONTRIBUTION.

(a) A promise by a limited partner to contribute to the limited partnership is not enforceable unless set out in a writing signed by the limited partner.

(b) Except as provided in the partnership agreement, a partner is obligated to the limited partnership to perform any enforceable promise to contribute cash or property or to perform services, even if he [or she] is unable to perform because of death, disability, or any other reason. If a partner does not make the required contribution of property or services, he [or she] is obligated at the option of the limited partnership to contribute cash equal to that portion of the value, as stated in the partnership records required to be kept pursuant to Section 105, of the stated contribution which has not been made.

(c) Unless otherwise provided in the partnership agreement, the obligation of a partner to make a contribution or return money or other property paid or distributed in violation of this [Act] may be compromised only by consent of all partners. Notwithstanding the compromise, a creditor of a limited partnership who extends credit or otherwise acts in reliance on that obligation after the partner signs a writing which reflects the obligation and before the amendment or cancellation thereof to reflect the compromise may enforce the original obligation.

SECTION 503.   SHARING OF PROFITS AND LOSSES.

The profits and losses of a limited partnership shall be allocated among the partners, and among classes of partners, in the manner provided in writing in the partnership agreement. If the partnership agreement does not so provide in writing, profits and losses shall be allocated on the basis of the value, as stated in the partnership records required to be kept pursuant to Section 105, of the contributions made by each partner to the extent they have been received by the partnership and have not been returned.

SECTION 504.   SHARING OF DISTRIBUTIONS.

Distributions of cash or other assets of a limited partnership shall be allocated among the partners and among classes of partners in the manner provided in writing in the partnership agreement. If the partnership agreement does not so provide in writing, distributions shall be made on the basis of the value, as stated in the partnership records required to be kept pursuant to Section 105, of the contributions made by each partner to the extent they have been received by the partnership and have not been returned.

ARTICLE 6
DISTRIBUTIONS AND WITHDRAWAL

SECTION 601.   INTERIM DISTRIBUTIONS.

Except as provided in this Article, a partner is entitled to receive distributions from a limited partnership before his [or her] withdrawal from the limited partnership and before the dissolution and winding up thereof.

To the extent and at the times or upon the happening of the events specified in the partnership agreement.

SECTION 602.   WITHDRAWAL OF GENERAL PARTNER.

A general partner may withdraw from a limited partnership at any time by giving written notice to the other partners, but if the withdrawal violates the partnership agreement, the limited partnership may recover from the withdrawal general partner damages for breach of the partnership agreement and offset the damages against the amount otherwise distributable to him [or her].

SECTION 603.   WITHDRAWAL OF LIMITED PARTNER.

A limited partner may withdraw from a limited partnership at the time or upon the happening of events specified in writing in the partnership agreement. If the agreement does not specify in writing the time or the events upon the happening of which a limited partner may withdraw or a definite time for the dissolution and winding up of the limited partnership, a limited partner may withdraw upon not less than six months' prior written notice to each general partner at his [or her] address on the books of the limited partnership at its office in this State.

SECTION 604.   DISTRIBUTION UPON WITHDRAWAL.

Except as provided in this Article, upon withdrawal any withdrawing partner is entitled to receive any distribution to which he [or she] is entitled under the partnership agreement and, if not otherwise provided in the agreement, he [or she] is entitled to receive, within a reasonable time after withdrawal, the fair value of his [or her] interest in the limited partnership as of the date of withdrawal based upon his [or her] right to share in distributions from the limited partnership.

SECTION 605.   DISTRIBUTION IN KIND.

Except as provided in writing in the partnership agreement, a partner, regardless of the nature of his [or her] contribution, has no right to demand and receive any distribution from the limited partnership in any form other than cash. Except as provided in writing in the partnership agreement, a partner may not be compelled to accept a distribution of any asset in kind from a limited partnership to the extent that the percentage of the asset distributed to him [or her] exceeds a percentage of that asset which is equal to the percentage in which he [or she] shares in distributions from the limited partnership.

SECTION 606.   RIGHT TO DISTRIBUTION.

At the time a partner becomes entitled to receive a distribution, he [or she] has the status of, and is entitled to all remedies available to, a creditor of the limited partnership with respect to the distribution.

SECTION 607.   LIMITATIONS ON DISTRIBUTION.

A partner may not receive a distribution from a limited partnership to the extent that, after giving effect to the distribution, all liabilities of the limited partnership, other than liabilities to partners on account of their partnership interest, exceed the fair value of the partnership assets.

SECTION 608.   LIABILITY UPON RETURN OF
                         CONTRIBUTION.

(a) If a partner has received the return of any part of his [or her] contribution without violation of the partnership agreement or this

[Act], he [or she] is liable to the limited partnership for a period of one year thereafter for the amount of the returned contribution, but only to the extent necessary to discharge the limited partnership's liabilities to creditors who extended credit to the limited partnership during the period the contribution was held by the partnership.

(b) If a partner has received the return of any part of his [or her] contribution in violation of the partnership agreement or this [Act], he [or she] is liable to the limited partnership for a period of six years thereafter for the amount of the contribution wrongfully returned.

(c) A partner receives a return of his [or her] contribution to the extent that a distribution to him [or her] reduces his [or her] share of the fair value of the net assets of the limited partnership below the value, as set forth in the partnership records required to be kept pursuant to Section 105, of his [or her] contribution which has not been distributed to him [or her].

ARTICLE 7
ASSIGNMENT OF PARTNERSHIP INTERESTS

SECTION 701.   NATURE OF PARTNERSHIP INTEREST.
A partnership interest is personal property.

SECTION 702.   ASSIGNMENT OF PARTNERSHIP
                         INTEREST.
Except as provided in the partnership agreement, a partnership interest is assignable in whole or in part. An assignment of a partnership interest does not dissolve a limited partnership or entitle the assignee to become or to exercise any rights of a partner. An assignment entitles the assignee to receive, to the extent assigned, only the distribution to which the assignor would be entitled. Except as provided in the partnership agreement, a partner ceases to be a partner upon assignment of all his [or her] partnership interest.

SECTION 703.   RIGHTS OF CREDITOR.
On application to a court of competent jurisdiction by any judgment creditor of a partner, the court may charge the partnership interest of the partner with payment of the unsatisfied amount of the judgment with interest. To the extent so charged, the judgment creditor has only the rights of an assignee of the partnership interest. This [Act] does not deprive any partner of the benefit of any exemption laws applicable to his [or her] partnership interest.

SECTION 704.   RIGHT OF ASSIGNEE TO BECOME
                         LIMITED PARTNER.
(a) An assignee of a partnership interest, including an assignee of a general partner, may become a limited partner if and to the extent that (i) the assignor gives the assignee that right in accordance with authority described in the partnership agreement, or (ii) all other partners consent.

(b) An assignee who has become a limited partner has, to the extent assigned, the rights and powers, and is subject to the restrictions and liabilities, of a limited partner under the partnership agreement and this [Act]. An assignee who becomes a limited partner also is liable for the obligations of his [or her] assignor to make and return contributions as provided in Articles 5 and 6. However, the assignee is not obligated for liabilities unknown to the assignee at the time he [or she] became a limited partner.

(c) If an assignee of a partnership interest becomes a limited partner, the assignor is not released from his [or her] liability to the limited partnership under Sections 207 and 502.

SECTION 705.   POWER OF ESTATE OF DECEASED OR
                         INCOMPETENT PARTNER.
If a partner who is an individual dies or a court of competent jurisdiction adjudges him [or her] to be incompetent to manage his [or her] person or his [or her] property, the partner's executor, administrator, guardian, conservator, or other legal representative may exercise all the partner's rights for the purpose of settling his [or her] estate or administering his [or her] property, including any power the partner had to give an assignee the right to become a limited partner. If a partner is a corporation, trust, or other entity and is dissolved or terminated, the powers of that partner may be exercised by its legal representative or successor.

ARTICLE 8
DISSOLUTION

SECTION 801.   NONJUDICIAL DISSOLUTION.
A limited partnership is dissolved and its affairs shall be wound up upon the happening of the first to occur of the following:
   (1) at the time specified in the certificate of limited partnership;
   (2) upon the happening of events specified in writing in the partnership agreement;
   (3) written consent of all partners;
   (4) an event of withdrawal of a general partner unless at the time there is at least one other general partner and the written provisions of the partnership agreement permit the business of the limited partnership to be carried on by the remaining general partner and that partner does so, but the limited partnership is not dissolved and is not required to be wound up by reason of any event of withdrawal, if within 90 days after the withdrawal, all partners agree in writing to continue the business of the limited partnership and to the appointment of one or more additional general partners if necessary or desired; or (5) entry of a decree of judicial dissolution under Section 802.

SECTION 802.   JUDICIAL DISSOLUTION.
On application by or for a partner the [designate the proper court] court may decree dissolution of a limited partnership whenever it is not reasonably practicable to carry on the business in conformity with the partnership agreement.

SECTION 803.   WINDING UP.
Except as provided in the partnership agreement, the general partners who have not wrongfully dissolved a limited partnership or, if none, the limited partners, may wind up the limited partnership's affairs; but the [designate the proper court] court may wind up the limited partnership's affairs upon application of any partner, his [or her] legal representative, or assignee.

SECTION 804.   DISTRIBUTION OF ASSETS.
Upon the winding up of a limited partnership, the assets shall be distributed as follows:
   (1) to creditors, including partners who are creditors, to the extent permitted by law, in satisfaction of liabilities of the limited partnership other than liabilities for distributions to partners under Section 601 or 604;

(2) except as provided in the partnership agreement, to partners and former partners in satisfaction of liabilities for distributions under Section 601 or 604; and

(3) except as provided in the partnership agreement, to partners first for the return of their contributions and secondly respecting their partnership interests, in the proportions in which the partners share in distributions.

ARTICLE 9
FOREIGN LIMITED PARTNERSHIPS

SECTION 901.   LAW GOVERNING.
Subject to the Constitution of this State, (i) the laws of the state under which a foreign limited partnership is organized govern its organization and internal affairs and the liability of its limited partners, and (ii) a foreign limited partnership may not be denied registration by reason of any difference between those laws and the laws of this State.

SECTION 902.   REGISTRATION.
Before transacting business in this State, a foreign limited partnership shall register with the Secretary of State. In order to register, a foreign limited partnership shall submit to the Secretary of State, in duplicate, an application for registration as a foreign limited partnership, signed and sworn to by a general partner and setting forth:

(1) the name of the foreign limited partnership and, if different, the name under which it proposes to register and transact business in this State;

(2) the State and date of its formation;

(3) the name and address of any agent for service of process on the foreign limited partnership whom the foreign limited partnership elects to appoint; the agent must be an individual resident of this State, a domestic corporation, or a foreign corporation having a place of business in, and authorized to do business in, this State;

(4) a statement that the Secretary of State is appointed the agent of the foreign limited partnership for service of process if no agent has been appointed under paragraph (3) or, if appointed, the agent's authority has been revoked or if the agent cannot be found or served with the exercise of reasonable diligence;

(5) the address of the office required to be maintained in the state of its organization by the laws of that state or, if not so required, of the principal office of the foreign limited partnership;

(6) the name and business address of each general partner; and

(7) the address of the office at which is kept a list of the names and addresses of the limited partners and their capital contributions, together with an undertaking by the foreign limited partnership to keep those records until the foreign limited partnership's registration in this State is cancelled or withdrawn.

SECTION 903.   ISSUANCE OF REGISTRATION.
(a) If the Secretary of State finds that an application for registration conforms to law and all requisite fees have been paid, he [or she] shall:

(1) endorse on the application the word "Filed," and the month, day and year of the filing thereof;

(2) file in his [or her] office a duplicate original of the application; and

(3) issue a certificate of registration to transact business in this State.

(b) The certificate of registration, together with a duplicate original of the application, shall be returned to the person who filed the application or his [or her] representative.

SECTION 904.   NAME.
A foreign limited partnership may register with the Secretary of State under any name, whether or not it is the name under which it is registered in its state of organization, that includes without abbreviation the words "limited partnership" and that could be registered by a domestic limited partnership.

SECTION 905.   CHANGES AND AMENDMENTS.
If any statement in the application for registration of a foreign limited partnership was false when made or any arrangements or other facts described have changed, making the application inaccurate in any respect, the foreign limited partnership shall promptly file in the office of the Secretary of State a certificate, signed and sworn to by a general partner, correcting such statement.

SECTION 906.   CANCELLATION OF REGISTRATION.
A foreign limited partnership may cancel its registration by filing with the Secretary of State a certificate of cancellation signed and sworn to by a general partner. A cancellation does not terminate the authority of the Secretary of State to accept service of process on the foreign limited partnership with respect to [claims for relief] [causes of action] arising out of the transactions of business in this State.

SECTION 907.   TRANSACTION OF BUSINESS WITHOUT
REGISTRATION.
(a) A foreign limited partnership transacting business in this State may not maintain any action, suit, or proceeding in any court of this State until it has registered in this State.
(b) The failure of a foreign limited partnership to register in this State does not impair the validity of any contract or act of the foreign limited partnership or prevent the foreign limited partnership from defending any action, suit, or proceeding in any court of this State.
(c) A limited partner of a foreign limited partnership is not liable as a general partner of the foreign limited partnership solely by reason of having transacted business in this State without registration.
(d) A foreign limited partnership, by transacting business in this State without registration, appoints the Secretary of State as its agent for service of process with respect to [claims for relief] [causes of action] arising out of the transaction of business in this State.

SECTION 908.   ACTION BY [APPROPRIATE OFFICIAL].
The [designate the appropriate official] may bring an action to restrain a foreign limited partnership from transacting business in this State in violation of this Article.

ARTICLE 10
DERIVATIVE ACTIONS

SECTION 1001.   RIGHT OF ACTION.
A limited partner may bring an action in the right of a limited partnership to recover a judgment in its favor if general partners with

authority to do so have refused to bring the action or if an effort to cause those general partners to bring the action is not likely to succeed.

SECTION 1002.   PROPER PLAINTIFF.
In a derivative action, the plaintiff must be a partner at the time of bringing the action and (i) must have been a partner at the time of the transaction of which he [or she] complains or (ii) his [or her] status as a partner must have had devolved upon him [or her] by operation of law or pursuant to the terms of the partnership agreement from a person who was a partner at the time of the transaction.

SECTION 1003.   PLEADING.
In a derivative action, the complaint shall set forth with particularity the effort of the plaintiff to secure initiation of the action by a general partner or the reasons for not making the effort.

SECTION 1004.   EXPENSES.
If a derivative action is successful, in whole or in part, or if anything is received by the plaintiff as a result of a judgment, compromise or settlement of an action or claim, the court may award the plaintiff reasonable expenses, including reasonable attorney's fees, and shall direct him [or her] to remit to the limited partnership the remainder of those proceeds received by him [or her].

ARTICLE 11
MISCELLANEOUS

SECTION 1101.   CONSTRUCTION AND APPLICATION.
This [Act] shall be so applied and construed to effectuate its general purpose to make uniform the law with respect to the subject of this [Act] among states enacting it.

SECTION 1102.   SHORT TITLE.
This [Act] may be cited as the Uniform Limited Partnership Act.

SECTION 1103.   SEVERABILITY.
If any provision of this [Act] or its application to any person or circumstance is held invalid, the invalidity does not affect other provisions or applications of the [Act] which can be given effect without the invalid provision or application, and to this end the provisions of this Act are severable.

SECTION 1104.   EFFECTIVE DATE, EXTENDED
EFFECTIVE DATE, AND REPEAL.
Except as set forth below, the effective date of this [Act] _____ is and the following Acts [list existing limited partnership acts] are hereby repealed:

(1) The existing provisions for execution and filing of certificates of limited partnerships and amendments thereunder and cancellations thereof continue in effect until [specify time required to create central filing system], the extended effective date, and Sections 102, 103, 104, 105, 201, 202, 203, 204 and 206 are not effective until the extended effective date.

(2) Section 402, specifying the conditions under which a general partner ceases to be a member of a limited partnership, is not effective until the extended effective date, and the applicable provisions of existing law continue to govern until the extended effective date.

(3) Sections 501, 502 and 608 apply only to contributions and distributions made after the effective date of this [Act].

(4) Section 704 applies only to assignments made after the effective date of this [Act].

(5) Article 9, dealing with registration of foreign limited partnerships, is not effective until the extended effective date.

(6) Unless otherwise agreed by the partners, the applicable provisions of existing law governing allocation of profits and losses (rather than the provisions of Section 503), distributions to a withdrawing partner (rather than the provisions of Section 604), and distribution of assets upon the winding up of a limited partnership (rather than the provisions of Section 804) govern limited partnerships formed before the effective date of this [Act].

SECTION 1105.   RULES FOR CASES NOT PROVIDED
FOR IN THIS [ACT].
In any case not provided for in this [Act] the provisions of the Uniform Partnership Act govern.

SECTION 1106.   SAVINGS CLAUSE.
The repeal of any statutory provision by this Act does not impair, or otherwise affect, the organization or the continued existence of a limited partnership existing at the effective date of this Act, nor does the repeal of any existing statutory provision by this Act impair any contract or affect any right accrued before the effective date of this Act.

UNIFORM LIMITED PARTNERSHIP ACT (2001)

[ARTICLE] 1
GENERAL PROVISIONS

SECTION 101.   SHORT TITLE.

This [Act] may be cited as the Uniform Limited Partnership Act [year of enactment].

SECTION 102.   DEFINITIONS.

In this [Act]:

(1) "Certificate of limited partnership" means the certificate required by Section 201. The term includes the certificate as amended or restated.

(2) "Contribution," except in the phrase "right of contribution," means any benefit provided by a person to a limited partnership in order to become a partner or in the person's capacity as a partner.

(3) "Debtor in bankruptcy" means a person that is the subject of:

(A) an order for relief under Title 11 of the United States Code or a comparable order under a successor statute of general application; or

(B) a comparable order under federal, state, or foreign law governing insolvency.

(4) "Designated office" means:

(A) with respect to a limited partnership, the office that the limited partnership is required to designate and maintain under Section 114; and

(B) with respect to a foreign limited partnership, its principal office.

(5) "Distribution" means a transfer of money or other property from a limited partnership to a partner in the partner's capacity as a partner or to a transferee on account of a transferable interest owned by the transferee.

(6) "Foreign limited liability limited partnership" means a foreign limited partnership whose general partners have limited liability for the obligations of the foreign limited partnership under a provision similar to Section 404(c).

(7) "Foreign limited partnership" means a partnership formed under the laws of a jurisdiction other than this State and required by those laws to have one or more general partners and one or more limited partners. The term includes a foreign limited liability limited partnership.

(8) "General partner" means:

(A) with respect to a limited partnership, a person that:

(i) becomes a general partner under Section 401; or

(ii) was a general partner in a limited partnership when the limited partnership became subject to this [Act] under Section 1206(a) or (b); and

(B) with respect to a foreign limited partnership, a person that has rights, powers, and obligations similar to those of a general partner in a limited partnership.

(9) "Limited liability limited partnership," except in the phrase "foreign limited liability limited partnership," means a limited partnership whose certificate of limited partnership states that the limited partnership is a limited liability limited partnership.

(10) "Limited partner" means:

(A) with respect to a limited partnership, a person that:

(i) becomes a limited partner under Section 301; or

(ii) was a limited partner in a limited partnership when the limited partnership became subject to this [Act] under Section 1206(a) or (b); and

(B) with respect to a foreign limited partnership, a person that has rights, powers, and obligations similar to those of a limited partner in a limited partnership.

(11) "Limited partnership," except in the phrases "foreign limited partnership" and "foreign limited liability limited partnership," means an entity, having one or more general partners and one or more limited partners, which is formed under this [Act] by two or more persons or becomes subject to this [Act] under [Article] 11 or Section 1206(a) or (b). The term includes a limited liability limited partnership.

(12) "Partner" means a limited partner or general partner.

(13) "Partnership agreement" means the partners' agreement, whether oral, implied, in a record, or in any combination, concerning the limited partnership. The term includes the agreement as amended.

(14) "Person" means an individual, corporation, business trust, estate, trust, partnership, limited liability company, association, joint venture, government; governmental subdivision, agency, or instrumentality; public corporation, or any other legal or commercial entity.

(15) "Person dissociated as a general partner" means a person dissociated as a general partner of a limited partnership.

(16) "Principal office" means the office where the principal executive office of a limited partnership or foreign limited partnership is located, whether or not the office is located in this State.

(17) "Record" means information that is inscribed on a tangible medium or that is stored in an electronic or other medium and is retrievable in perceivable form.

(18) "Required information" means the information that a limited partnership is required to maintain under Section 111.

(19) "Sign" means:

(A) to execute or adopt a tangible symbol with the present intent to authenticate a record; or

(B) to attach or logically associate an electronic symbol, sound, or process to or with a record with the present intent to authenticate the record.

(20) "State" means a State of the United States, the District of Columbia, Puerto Rico, the United States Virgin Islands, or any territory or insular possession subject to the jurisdiction of the United States.

(21) "Transfer" includes an assignment, conveyance, deed, bill of sale, lease, mortgage, security interest, encumbrance, gift, and transfer by operation of law.

(22) "Transferable interest" means a partner's right to receive distributions.

(23) "Transferee" means a person to which all or part of a transferable interest has been transferred, whether or not the transferor is a partner.

SECTION 103.   KNOWLEDGE AND NOTICE.

(a) A person knows a fact if the person has actual knowledge of it.

(b) A person has notice of a fact if the person:

(1) knows of it;

(2) has received a notification of it;

(3) has reason to know it exists from all of the facts known to the person at the time in question; or

(4) has notice of it under subsection (c) or (d).

(c) A certificate of limited partnership on file in the [office of the Secretary of State] is notice that the partnership is a limited partnership and the persons designated in the certificate as general partners are general partners. Except as otherwise provided in subsection (d), the certificate is not notice of any other fact.

(d) A person has notice of:

(1) another person's dissociation as a general partner, 90 days after the effective date of an amendment to the certificate of limited partnership which states that the other person has dissociated or 90 days after the effective date of a statement of dissociation pertaining to the other person, whichever occurs first;

(2) a limited partnership's dissolution, 90 days after the effective date of an amendment to the certificate of limited partnership stating that the limited partnership is dissolved;

(3) a limited partnership's termination, 90 days after the effective date of a statement of termination;

(4) a limited partnership's conversion under [Article] 11, 90 days after the effective date of the articles of conversion; or

(5) a merger under [Article] 11, 90 days after the effective date of the articles of merger.

(e) A person notifies or gives a notification to another person by taking steps reasonably required to inform the other person in ordinary course, whether or not the other person learns of it.

(f) A person receives a notification when the notification:

(1) comes to the person's attention; or

(2) is delivered at the person's place of business or at any other place held out by the person as a place for receiving communications.

(g) Except as otherwise provided in subsection (h), a person other than an individual knows, has notice, or receives a notification of a fact for purposes of a particular transaction when the individual conducting the transaction for the person knows, has notice, or receives a notification of the fact, or in any event when the fact would have been brought to the individual's attention if the person had exercised reasonable diligence. A person other than an individual exercises reasonable diligence if it maintains reasonable routines for communicating significant information to the individual conducting the transaction for the person and there is reasonable compliance with the routines. Reasonable diligence does not require an individual acting for the person to communicate information unless the communication is part of the individual's regular duties or the individual has reason to know of the transaction and that the transaction would be materially affected by the information.

(h) A general partner's knowledge, notice, or receipt of a notification of a fact relating to the limited partnership is effective immediately as knowledge of, notice to, or receipt of a notification by the limited partnership, except in the case of a fraud on the limited partnership committed by or with the consent of the general partner. A limited partner's knowledge, notice, or receipt of a notifi-cation of a fact relating to the limited partnership is not effective as knowledge of, notice to, or receipt of a notification by the limited partnership.

SECTION 104.   NATURE, PURPOSE, AND DURATION OF ENTITY.

(a) A limited partnership is an entity distinct from its partners. A limited partnership is the same entity regardless of whether its certificate states that the limited partnership is a limited liability limited partnership.

(b) A limited partnership may be organized under this [Act] for any lawful purpose.

(c) A limited partnership has a perpetual duration.

SECTION 105.   POWERS.

A limited partnership has the powers to do all things necessary or convenient to carry on its activities, including the power to sue, be sued, and defend in its own name and to maintain an action against a partner for harm caused to the limited partnership by a breach of the partnership agreement or violation of a duty to the partnership.

SECTION 106.   GOVERNING LAW.

The law of this State governs relations among the partners of a limited partnership and between the partners and the limited partnership and the liability of partners as partners for an obligation of the limited partnership.

SECTION 107.   SUPPLEMENTAL PRINCIPLES OF LAW; RATE OF INTEREST.

(a) Unless displaced by particular provisions of this [Act], the principles of law and equity supplement this [Act].

(b) If an obligation to pay interest arises under this [Act] and the rate is not specified, the rate is that specified in [applicable statute].

SECTION 108.   NAME.

(a) The name of a limited partnership may contain the name of any partner.

(b) The name of a limited partnership that is not a limited liability limited partnership must contain the phrase "limited partnership" or the abbreviation "L.P." or "LP" and may not contain the phrase "limited liability limited partnership" or the abbreviation "LLLP" or "L.L.L.P."

(c) The name of a limited liability limited partnership must contain the phrase "limited liability limited partnership" or the abbreviation "LLLP" or "L.L.L.P." and must not contain the abbreviation "L.P." or "LP."

(d) Unless authorized by subsection (e), the name of a limited partnership must be distinguishable in the records of the [Secretary of State] from:

(1) the name of each person other than an individual incorporated, organized, or authorized to transact business in this State; and

(2) each name reserved under Section 109 [or other state laws allowing the reservation or registration of business names, including fictitious name statutes].

(e) A limited partnership may apply to the [Secretary of State] for authorization to use a name that does not comply with subsection (d). The [Secretary of State] shall authorize use of the name applied for if, as to each conflicting name:

(1) the present user, registrant, or owner of the conflicting name consents in a signed record to the use and submits an undertaking in a form satisfactory to the [Secretary of State] to change the conflicting name to a name that complies with subsection (d) and is distinguishable in the records of the [Secretary of State] from the name applied for;

(2) the applicant delivers to the [Secretary of State] a certified copy of the final judgment of a court of competent jurisdiction establishing the applicant's right to use in this State the name applied for; or

(3) the applicant delivers to the [Secretary of State] proof satisfactory to the [Secretary of State] that the present user, registrant, or owner of the conflicting name:

(A) has merged into the applicant;

(B) has been converted into the applicant; or

(C) has transferred substantially all of its assets, including the conflicting name, to the applicant.

(f) Subject to Section 905, this section applies to any foreign limited partnership transacting business in this State, having a certificate of authority to transact business in this State, or applying for a certificate of authority.

SECTION 109.   RESERVATION OF NAME.

(a) The exclusive right to the use of a name that complies with Section 108 may be reserved by:

(1) a person intending to organize a limited partnership under this [Act] and to adopt the name;

(2) a limited partnership or a foreign limited partnership authorized to transact business in this State intending to adopt the name;

(3) a foreign limited partnership intending to obtain a certificate of authority to transact business in this State and adopt the name;

(4) a person intending to organize a foreign limited partnership and intending to have it obtain a certificate of authority to transact business in this State and adopt the name;

(5) a foreign limited partnership formed under the name; or

(6) a foreign limited partnership formed under a name that does not comply with Section 108(b) or (c), but the name reserved under this paragraph may differ from the foreign limited partnership's name only to the extent necessary to comply with Section 108(b) and (c).

(b) A person may apply to reserve a name under subsection (a) by delivering to the [Secretary of State] for filing an application that states the name to be reserved and the paragraph of subsection (a) which applies. If the [Secretary of State] finds that the name is available for use by the applicant, the [Secretary of State] shall file a statement of name reservation and thereby reserve the name for the exclusive use of the applicant for 120 days.

(c) An applicant that has reserved a name pursuant to subsection (b) may reserve the same name for additional 120-day periods. A person having a current reservation for a name may not apply for another 120-day period for the same name until 90 days have elapsed in the current reservation.

(d) A person that has reserved a name under this section may deliver to the [Secretary of State] for filing a notice of transfer that states the reserved name, the name and street and mailing address of some other person to which the reservation is to be transferred, and the paragraph of subsection (a) which applies to the other person. Subject to Section 206(c), the transfer is effective when the [Secretary of State] files the notice of transfer.

SECTION 110.   EFFECT OF PARTNERSHIP AGREEMENT; NONWAIVABLE PROVISIONS.

(a) Except as otherwise provided in subsection (b), the partnership agreement governs relations among the partners and between the partners and the partnership. To the extent the partnership agreement does not otherwise provide, this [Act] governs relations among the partners and between the partners and the partnership.

(b) A partnership agreement may not:

(1) vary a limited partnership's power under Section 105 to sue, be sued, and defend in its own name;

(2) vary the law applicable to a limited partnership under Section 106;

(3) vary the requirements of Section 204;

(4) vary the information required under Section 111 or unreasonably restrict the right to information under Sections 304 or 407, but the partnership agreement may impose reasonable restrictions on the availability and use of information obtained under those sections and may define appropriate remedies, including liquidated damages, for a breach of any reasonable restriction on use;

(5) eliminate the duty of loyalty under Section 408, but the partnership agreement may:

(A) identify specific types or categories of activities that do not violate the duty of loyalty, if not manifestly unreasonable; and

(B) specify the number or percentage of partners which may authorize or ratify, after full disclosure to all partners of all material facts, a specific act or transaction that otherwise would violate the duty of loyalty;

(6) unreasonably reduce the duty of care under Section 408(c);

(7) eliminate the obligation of good faith and fair dealing under Sections 305(b) and 408(d), but the partnership agreement may prescribe the standards by which the performance of the obligation is to be measured, if the standards are not manifestly unreasonable;

(8) vary the power of a person to dissociate as a general partner under Section 604(a) except to require that the notice under Section 603(1) be in a record;

(9) vary the power of a court to decree dissolution in the circumstances specified in Section 802;

(10) vary the requirement to wind up the partnership's business as specified in Section 803;

(11) unreasonably restrict the right to maintain an action under [Article] 10;

(12) restrict the right of a partner under Section 1110(a) to approve a conversion or merger or the right of a general partner under Section 1110(b) to consent to an amendment to the certificate of limited partnership which deletes a statement that the limited partnership is a limited liability limited partnership; or

(13) restrict rights under this [Act] of a person other than a partner or a transferee.

SECTION 111.   REQUIRED INFORMATION.

A limited partnership shall maintain at its designated office the following information:

(1) a current list showing the full name and last known street and mailing address of each partner, separately identifying the general partners, in alphabetical order, and the limited partners, in alphabetical order;

(2) a copy of the initial certificate of limited partnership and all amendments to and restatements of the certificate, together with signed copies of any powers of attorney under which any certificate, amendment, or restatement has been signed;

(3) a copy of any filed articles of conversion or merger;

(4) a copy of the limited partnership's federal, state, and local income tax returns and reports, if any, for the three most recent years;

(5) a copy of any partnership agreement made in a record and any amendment made in a record to any partnership agreement;

(6) a copy of any financial statement of the limited partnership for the three most recent years;

(7) a copy of the three most recent annual reports delivered by the limited partnership to the [Secretary of State] pursuant to Section 210;

(8) a copy of any record made by the limited partnership during the past three years of any consent given by or vote taken of any partner pursuant to this [Act] or the partnership agreement; and

(9) unless contained in a partnership agreement made in a record, a record stating:

> (A) the amount of cash, and a description and statement of the agreed value of the other benefits, contributed and agreed to be contributed by each partner;
>
> (B) the times at which, or events on the happening of which, any additional contributions agreed to be made by each partner are to be made;
>
> (C) for any person that is both a general partner and a limited partner, a specification of what transferable interest the person owns in each capacity; and
>
> (D) any events upon the happening of which the limited partnership is to be dissolved and its activities wound up.

SECTION 112.   BUSINESS TRANSACTIONS OF PARTNER WITH PARTNERSHIP.

A partner may lend money to and transact other business with the limited partnership and has the same rights and obligations with respect to the loan or other transaction as a person that is not a partner.

SECTION 113.   DUAL CAPACITY.

A person may be both a general partner and a limited partner. A person that is both a general and limited partner has the rights, powers, duties, and obligations provided by this [Act] and the partnership agreement in each of those capacities. When the person acts as a general partner, the person is subject to the obligations, duties and restrictions under this [Act] and the partnership agreement for general partners. When the person acts as a limited partner, the person is subject to the obligations, duties and restrictions under this [Act] and the partnership agreement for limited partners.

SECTION 114.   OFFICE AND AGENT FOR SERVICE OF PROCESS.

(a) A limited partnership shall designate and continuously maintain in this State:

> (1) an office, which need not be a place of its activity in this State; and
>
> (2) an agent for service of process.

(b) A foreign limited partnership shall designate and continuously maintain in this State an agent for service of process.

(c) An agent for service of process of a limited partnership or foreign limited partnership must be an individual who is a resident of this State or other person authorized to do business in this State.

SECTION 115.   CHANGE OF DESIGNATED OFFICE OR AGENT FOR SERVICE OF PROCESS.

(a) In order to change its designated office, agent for service of process, or the address of its agent for service of process, a limited partnership or a foreign limited partnership may deliver to the [Secretary of State] for filing a statement of change containing:

> (1) the name of the limited partnership or foreign limited partnership;
>
> (2) the street and mailing address of its current designated office;
>
> (3) if the current designated office is to be changed, the street and mailing address of the new designated office;
>
> (4) the name and street and mailing address of its current agent for service of process; and
>
> (5) if the current agent for service of process or an address of the agent is to be changed, the new information.

(b) Subject to Section 206(c), a statement of change is effective when filed by the [Secretary of State].

SECTION 116.   RESIGNATION OF AGENT FOR SERVICE OF PROCESS.

(a) In order to resign as an agent for service of process of a limited partnership or foreign limited partnership, the agent must deliver to the [Secretary of State] for filing a statement of resignation containing the name of the limited partnership or foreign limited partnership.

(b) After receiving a statement of resignation, the [Secretary of State] shall file it and mail a copy to the designated office of the limited partnership or foreign limited partnership and another copy to the principal office if the address of the office appears in the records of the [Secretary of State] and is different from the address of the designated office.

(c) An agency for service of process is terminated on the 31st day after the [Secretary of State] files the statement of resignation.

SECTION 117.   SERVICE OF PROCESS.

(a) An agent for service of process appointed by a limited partnership or foreign limited partnership is an agent of the limited partnership or foreign limited partnership for service of any process, notice, or demand required or permitted by law to be served upon the limited partnership or foreign limited partnership.

(b) If a limited partnership or foreign limited partnership does not appoint or maintain an agent for service of process in this State or the agent for service of process cannot with reasonable diligence be found at the agent's address, the [Secretary of State] is an agent of the limited partnership or foreign limited partnership upon whom process, notice, or demand may be served.

(c) Service of any process, notice, or demand on the [Secretary of State] may be made by delivering to and leaving with the [Secretary of State] duplicate copies of the process, notice, or demand. If a process, notice, or demand is served on the [Secretary of State], the [Secretary of State] shall forward one of the copies by registered or certified mail, return receipt requested, to the limited partnership or foreign limited partnership at its designated office.

(d) Service is effected under subsection (c) at the earliest of:

> (1) the date the limited partnership or foreign limited partnership receives the process, notice, or demand;
>
> (2) the date shown on the return receipt, if signed on behalf of the limited partnership or foreign limited partnership; or
>
> (3) five days after the process, notice, or demand is deposited in the mail, if mailed postpaid and correctly addressed.

(e) The [Secretary of State] shall keep a record of each process, notice, and demand served pursuant to this section and record the time of, and the action taken regarding, the service.

(f) This section does not affect the right to serve process, notice, or demand in any other manner provided by law.

SECTION 118.   CONSENT AND PROXIES OF PARTNERS.

Action requiring the consent of partners under this [Act] may be taken without a meeting, and a partner may appoint a proxy to consent or otherwise act for the partner by signing an appointment record, either personally or by the partner's attorney in fact.

[ARTICLE] 2
FORMATION; CERTIFICATE OF
LIMITED PARTNERSHIP AND OTHER FILINGS

SECTION 201.   FORMATION OF LIMITED PARTNERSHIP; CERTIFICATE OF LIMITED PARTNERSHIP.

(a) In order for a limited partnership to be formed, a certificate of limited partnership must be delivered to the [Secretary of State] for filing. The certificate must state:

(1) the name of the limited partnership, which must comply with Section 108;

(2) the street and mailing address of the initial designated office and the name and street and mailing address of the initial agent for service of process;

(3) the name and the street and mailing address of each general partner;

(4) whether the limited partnership is a limited liability limited partnership; and

(5) any additional information required by [Article] 11.

(b) A certificate of limited partnership may also contain any other matters but may not vary or otherwise affect the provisions specified in Section 110(b) in a manner inconsistent with that section.

(c) If there has been substantial compliance with subsection (a), subject to Section 206(c) a limited partnership is formed when the [Secretary of State] files the certificate of limited partnership.

(d) Subject to subsection (b), if any provision of a partnership agreement is inconsistent with the filed certificate of limited partnership or with a filed statement of dissociation, termination, or change or filed articles of conversion or merger:

(1) the partnership agreement prevails as to partners and transferees; and

(2) the filed certificate of limited partnership, statement of dissociation, termination, or change or articles of conversion or merger prevail as to persons, other than partners and transferees, that reasonably rely on the filed record to their detriment.

SECTION 202.   AMENDMENT OR RESTATEMENT OF CERTIFICATE.

(a) In order to amend its certificate of limited partnership, a limited partnership must deliver to the [Secretary of State] for filing an amendment or, pursuant to [Article] 11, articles of merger stating:

(1) the name of the limited partnership;

(2) the date of filing of its initial certificate; and

(3) the changes the amendment makes to the certificate as most recently amended or restated.

(b) A limited partnership shall promptly deliver to the [Secretary of State] for filing an amendment to a certificate of limited partnership to reflect:

(1) the admission of a new general partner;

(2) the dissociation of a person as a general partner; or

(3) the appointment of a person to wind up the limited partnership's activities under Section 803(c) or (d).

(c) A general partner that knows that any information in a filed certificate of limited partnership was false when the certificate was filed or has become false due to changed circumstances shall promptly:

(1) cause the certificate to be amended; or

(2) if appropriate, deliver to the [Secretary of State] for filing a statement of change pursuant to Section 115 or a statement of correction pursuant to Section 207.

(d) A certificate of limited partnership may be amended at any time for any other proper purpose as determined by the limited partnership.

(e) A restated certificate of limited partnership may be delivered to the [Secretary of State] for filing in the same manner as an amendment.

(f) Subject to Section 206(c), an amendment or restated certificate is effective when filed by the [Secretary of State].

SECTION 203.   STATEMENT OF TERMINATION.

A dissolved limited partnership that has completed winding up may deliver to the [Secretary of State] for filing a statement of termination that states:

(1) the name of the limited partnership;

(2) the date of filing of its initial certificate of limited partnership; and

(3) any other information as determined by the general partners filing the statement or by a person appointed pursuant to Section 803(c) or (d).

SECTION 204.   SIGNING OF RECORDS.

(a) Each record delivered to the [Secretary of State] for filing pursuant to this [Act] must be signed in the following manner:

(1) An initial certificate of limited partnership must be signed by all general partners listed in the certificate.

(2) An amendment adding or deleting a statement that the limited partnership is a limited liability limited partnership must be signed by all general partners listed in the certificate.

(3) An amendment designating as general partner a person admitted under Section 801(3)(B) following the dissociation of a limited partnership's last general partner must be signed by that person.

(4) An amendment required by Section 803(c) following the appointment of a person to wind up the dissolved limited partnership's activities must be signed by that person.

(5) Any other amendment must be signed by:

(A) at least one general partner listed in the certificate;

(B) each other person designated in the amendment as a new general partner; and

(C) each person that the amendment indicates has dissociated as a general partner, unless:

(i) the person is deceased or a guardian or general conservator has been appointed for the person and the amendment so states; or

(ii) the person has previously delivered to the [Secretary of State] for filing a statement of dissociation.

(6) A restated certificate of limited partnership must be signed by at least one general partner listed in the certificate, and, to the extent the restated certificate effects a change under any

other paragraph of this subsection, the certificate must be signed in a manner that satisfies that paragraph.

(7) A statement of termination must be signed by all general partners listed in the certificate or, if the certificate of a dissolved limited partnership lists no general partners, by the person appointed pursuant to Section 803(c) or (d) to wind up the dissolved limited partnership's activities.

(8) Articles of conversion must be signed by each general partner listed in the certificate of limited partnership.

(9) Articles of merger must be signed as provided in Section 1108(a).

(10) Any other record delivered on behalf of a limited partnership to the [Secretary of State] for filing must be signed by at least one general partner listed in the certificate.

(11) A statement by a person pursuant to Section 605(a)(4) stating that the person has dissociated as a general partner must be signed by that person.

(12) A statement of withdrawal by a person pursuant to Section 306 must be signed by that person.

(13) A record delivered on behalf of a foreign limited partnership to the [Secretary of State] for filing must be signed by at least one general partner of the foreign limited partnership.

(14) Any other record delivered on behalf of any person to the [Secretary of State] for filing must be signed by that person.

(b) Any person may sign by an attorney in fact any record to be filed pursuant to this [Act].

SECTION 205.   SIGNING AND FILING PURSUANT TO JUDICIAL ORDER.

(a) If a person required by this [Act] to sign a record or deliver a record to the [Secretary of State] for filing does not do so, any other person that is aggrieved may petition the [appropriate court] to order:

(1) the person to sign the record;

(2) deliver the record to the [Secretary of State] for filing; or

(3) the [Secretary of State] to file the record unsigned.

(b) If the person aggrieved under subsection (a) is not the limited partnership or foreign limited partnership to which the record pertains, the aggrieved person shall make the limited partnership or foreign limited partnership a party to the action. A person aggrieved under subsection (a) may seek the remedies provided in subsection (a) in the same action in combination or in the alternative.

(c) A record filed unsigned pursuant to this section is effective without being signed.

SECTION 206.   DELIVERY TO AND FILING OF RECORDS BY [SECRETARY OF STATE]; EFFECTIVE TIME AND DATE.

(a) A record authorized or required to be delivered to the [Secretary of State] for filing under this [Act] must be captioned to describe the record's purpose, be in a medium permitted by the [Secretary of State], and be delivered to the [Secretary of State]. Unless the [Secretary of State] determines that a record does not comply with the filing requirements of this [Act], and if all filing fees have been paid, the [Secretary of State] shall file the record and:

(1) for a statement of dissociation, send:

(A) a copy of the filed statement and a receipt for the fees to the person which the statement indicates has dissociated as a general partner; and

(B) a copy of the filed statement and receipt to the limited partnership;

(2) for a statement of withdrawal, send:

(A) a copy of the filed statement and a receipt for the fees to the person on whose behalf the record was filed; and

(B) if the statement refers to an existing limited partnership, a copy of the filed statement and receipt to the limited partnership; and

(3) for all other records, send a copy of the filed record and a receipt for the fees to the person on whose behalf the record was filed.

(b) Upon request and payment of a fee, the [Secretary of State] shall send to the requester a certified copy of the requested record.

(c) Except as otherwise provided in Sections 116 and 207, a record delivered to the [Secretary of State] for filing under this [Act] may specify an effective time and a delayed effective date. Except as otherwise provided in this [Act], a record filed by the [Secretary of State] is effective:

(1) if the record does not specify an effective time and does not specify a delayed effective date, on the date and at the time the record is filed as evidenced by the [Secretary of State's] endorsement of the date and time on the record;

(2) if the record specifies an effective time but not a delayed effective date, on the date the record is filed at the time specified in the record;

(3) if the record specifies a delayed effective date but not an effective time, at 12:01 A.M. on the earlier of:

(A) the specified date; or

(B) the 90th day after the record is filed; or

(4) if the record specifies an effective time and a delayed effective date, at the specified time on the earlier of:

(A) the specified date; or

(B) the 90th day after the record is filed.

SECTION 207.   CORRECTING FILED RECORD.

(a) A limited partnership or foreign limited partnership may deliver to the [Secretary of State] for filing a statement of correction to correct a record previously delivered by the limited partnership or foreign limited partnership to the [Secretary of State] and filed by the [Secretary of State], if at the time of filing the record contained false or erroneous information or was defectively signed.

(b) A statement of correction may not state a delayed effective date and must:

(1) describe the record to be corrected, including its filing date, or attach a copy of the record as filed;

(2) specify the incorrect information and the reason it is incorrect or the manner in which the signing was defective; and

(3) correct the incorrect information or defective signature.

(c) When filed by the [Secretary of State], a statement of correction is effective retroactively as of the effective date of the record the statement corrects, but the statement is effective when filed:

(1) for the purposes of Section 103(c) and (d); and

(2) as to persons relying on the uncorrected record and adversely affected by the correction.

SECTION 208.   LIABILITY FOR FALSE INFORMATION IN FILED RECORD.

(a) If a record delivered to the [Secretary of State] for filing under this [Act] and filed by the [Secretary of State] contains false information, a person that suffers loss by reliance on the information may recover damages for the loss from:

(1) a person that signed the record, or caused another to sign it on the person's behalf, and knew the information to be false at the time the record was signed; and

(2) a general partner that has notice that the information was false when the record was filed or has become false because of changed circumstances, if the general partner has notice for a reasonably sufficient time before the information is relied upon to enable the general partner to effect an amendment under Section 202, file a petition pursuant to Section 205, or deliver to the [Secretary of State] for filing a statement of change pursuant to Section 115 or a statement of correction pursuant to Section 207.

(b) Signing a record authorized or required to be filed under this [Act] constitutes an affirmation under the penalties of perjury that the facts stated in the record are true.

SECTION 209.   CERTIFICATE OF EXISTENCE OR AUTHORIZATION.

(a) The [Secretary of State], upon request and payment of the requisite fee, shall furnish a certificate of existence for a limited partnership if the records filed in the [office of the Secretary of State] show that the [Secretary of State] has filed a certificate of limited partnership and has not filed a statement of termination. A certificate of existence must state:

(1) the limited partnership's name;

(2) that it was duly formed under the laws of this State and the date of formation;

(3) whether all fees, taxes, and penalties due to the [Secretary of State] under this [Act] or other law have been paid;

(4) whether the limited partnership's most recent annual report required by Section 210 has been filed by the [Secretary of State];

(5) whether the [Secretary of State] has administratively dissolved the limited partnership;

(6) whether the limited partnership's certificate of limited partnership has been amended to state that the limited partnership is dissolved;

(7) that a statement of termination has not been filed by the [Secretary of State]; and

(8) other facts of record in the [office of the Secretary of State] which may be requested by the applicant.

(b) The [Secretary of State], upon request and payment of the requisite fee, shall furnish a certificate of authorization for a foreign limited partnership if the records filed in the [office of the Secretary of State] show that the [Secretary of State] has filed a certificate of authority, has not revoked the certificate of authority, and has not filed a notice of cancellation. A certificate of authorization must state:

(1) the foreign limited partnership's name and any alternate name adopted under Section 905(a) for use in this State;

(2) that it is authorized to transact business in this State;

(3) whether all fees, taxes, and penalties due to the [Secretary of State] under this [Act] or other law have been paid;

(4) whether the foreign limited partnership's most recent annual report required by Section 210 has been filed by the [Secretary of State];

(5) that the [Secretary of State] has not revoked its certificate of authority and has not filed a notice of cancellation; and

(6) other facts of record in the [office of the Secretary of State] which may be requested by the applicant.

(c) Subject to any qualification stated in the certificate, a certificate of existence or authorization issued by the [Secretary of State] may be relied upon as conclusive evidence that the limited partnership or foreign limited partnership is in existence or is authorized to transact business in this State.

SECTION 210.   ANNUAL REPORT FOR [SECRETARY OF STATE].

(a) A limited partnership or a foreign limited partnership authorized to transact business in this State shall deliver to the [Secretary of State] for filing an annual report that states:

(1) the name of the limited partnership or foreign limited partnership;

(2) the street and mailing address of its designated office and the name and street and mailing address of its agent for service of process in this State;

(3) in the case of a limited partnership, the street and mailing address of its principal office; and

(4) in the case of a foreign limited partnership, the State or other jurisdiction under whose law the foreign limited partnership is formed and any alternate name adopted under Section 905(a).

(b) Information in an annual report must be current as of the date the annual report is delivered to the [Secretary of State] for filing.

(c) The first annual report must be delivered to the [Secretary of State] between [January 1 and April 1] of the year following the calendar year in which a limited partnership was formed or a foreign limited partnership was authorized to transact business. An annual report must be delivered to the [Secretary of State] between [January 1 and April 1] of each subsequent calendar year.

(d) If an annual report does not contain the information required in subsection (a), the [Secretary of State] shall promptly notify the reporting limited partnership or foreign limited partnership and return the report to it for correction. If the report is corrected to contain the information required in subsection (a) and delivered to the [Secretary of State] within 30 days after the effective date of the notice, it is timely delivered.

(e) If a filed annual report contains an address of a designated office or the name or address of an agent for service of process which differs from the information shown in the records of the [Secretary of State] immediately before the filing, the differing information in the annual report is considered a statement of change under Section 115.

[ARTICLE] 3
LIMITED PARTNERS

SECTION 301.   BECOMING LIMITED PARTNER.

A person becomes a limited partner:

(1) as provided in the partnership agreement;

(2) as the result of a conversion or merger under [Article] 11; or

(3) with the consent of all the partners.

SECTION 302.   NO RIGHT OR POWER AS LIMITED PARTNER TO BIND LIMITED PARTNERSHIP.

A limited partner does not have the right or the power as a limited partner to act for or bind the limited partnership.

SECTION 303. NO LIABILITY AS LIMITED PARTNER FOR LIMITED PARTNERSHIP OBLIGATIONS.

An obligation of a limited partnership, whether arising in contract, tort, or otherwise, is not the obligation of a limited partner. A limited partner is not personally liable, directly or indirectly, by way of contribution or otherwise, for an obligation of the limited partnership solely by reason of being a limited partner, even if the limited partner participates in the management and control of the limited partnership.

SECTION 304. RIGHT OF LIMITED PARTNER AND FORMER LIMITED PARTNER TO INFORMATION.

(a) On 10 days' demand, made in a record received by the limited partnership, a limited partner may inspect and copy required information during regular business hours in the limited partnership's designated office. The limited partner need not have any particular purpose for seeking the information.

(b) During regular business hours and at a reasonable location specified by the limited partnership, a limited partner may obtain from the limited partnership and inspect and copy true and full information regarding the state of the activities and financial condition of the limited partnership and other information regarding the activities of the limited partnership as is just and reasonable if:

    (1) the limited partner seeks the information for a purpose reasonably related to the partner's interest as a limited partner;

    (2) the limited partner makes a demand in a record received by the limited partnership, describing with reasonable particularity the information sought and the purpose for seeking the information; and

    (3) the information sought is directly connected to the limited partner's purpose.

(c) Within 10 days after receiving a demand pursuant to subsection (b), the limited partnership in a record shall inform the limited partner that made the demand:

    (1) what information the limited partnership will provide in response to the demand;

    (2) when and where the limited partnership will provide the information; and

    (3) if the limited partnership declines to provide any demanded information, the limited partnership's reasons for declining.

(d) Subject to subsection (f), a person dissociated as a limited partner may inspect and copy required information during regular business hours in the limited partnership's designated office if:

    (1) the information pertains to the period during which the person was a limited partner;

    (2) the person seeks the information in good faith; and

    (3) the person meets the requirements of subsection (b).

(e) The limited partnership shall respond to a demand made pursuant to subsection (d) in the same manner as provided in subsection (c).

(f) If a limited partner dies, Section 704 applies.

(g) The limited partnership may impose reasonable restrictions on the use of information obtained under this section. In a dispute concerning the reasonableness of a restriction under this subsection, the limited partnership has the burden of proving reasonableness.

(h) A limited partnership may charge a person that makes a demand under this section reasonable costs of copying, limited to the costs of labor and material.

(i) Whenever this [Act] or a partnership agreement provides for a limited partner to give or withhold consent to a matter, before the consent is given or withheld, the limited partnership shall, without demand, provide the limited partner with all information material to the limited partner's decision that the limited partnership knows.

(j) A limited partner or person dissociated as a limited partner may exercise the rights under this section through an attorney or other agent. Any restriction imposed under subsection (g) or by the partnership agreement applies both to the attorney or other agent and to the limited partner or person dissociated as a limited partner.

(k) The rights stated in this section do not extend to a person as transferee, but may be exercised by the legal representative of an individual under legal disability who is a limited partner or person dissociated as a limited partner.

SECTION 305. LIMITED DUTIES OF LIMITED PARTNERS.

(a) A limited partner does not have any fiduciary duty to the limited partnership or to any other partner solely by reason of being a limited partner.

(b) A limited partner shall discharge the duties to the partnership and the other partners under this [Act] or under the partnership agreement and exercise any rights consistently with the obligation of good faith and fair dealing.

(c) A limited partner does not violate a duty or obligation under this [Act] or under the partnership agreement merely because the limited partner's conduct furthers the limited partner's own interest.

SECTION 306. PERSON ERRONEOUSLY BELIEVING SELF TO BE LIMITED PARTNER.

(a) Except as otherwise provided in subsection (b), a person that makes an investment in a business enterprise and erroneously but in good faith believes that the person has become a limited partner in the enterprise is not liable for the enterprise's obligations by reason of making the investment, receiving distributions from the enterprise, or exercising any rights of or appropriate to a limited partner, if, on ascertaining the mistake, the person:

    (1) causes an appropriate certificate of limited partnership, amendment, or statement of correction to be signed and delivered to the [Secretary of State] for filing; or

    (2) withdraws from future participation as an owner in the enterprise by signing and delivering to the [Secretary of State] for filing a statement of withdrawal under this section.

(b) A person that makes an investment described in subsection (a) is liable to the same extent as a general partner to any third party that enters into a transaction with the enterprise, believing in good faith that the person is a general partner, before the [Secretary of State] files a statement of withdrawal, certificate of limited partnership, amendment, or statement of correction to show that the person is not a general partner.

(c) If a person makes a diligent effort in good faith to comply with subsection (a)(1) and is unable to cause the appropriate certificate of limited partnership, amendment, or statement of correction to be signed and delivered to the [Secretary of State] for filing, the person has the right to withdraw from the enterprise pursuant to subsection (a)(2) even if the withdrawal would otherwise breach an agreement with others that are or have agreed to become co-owners of the enterprise.

[ARTICLE] 4
GENERAL PARTNERS

SECTION 401.   BECOMING GENERAL PARTNER.

A person becomes a general partner:

(1) as provided in the partnership agreement:

(2) under Section 801(3)(B) following the dissociation of a limited partnership's last general partner;

(3) as the result of a conversion or merger under [Article] 11; or

(4) with the consent of all the partners.

SECTION 402.   GENERAL PARTNER AGENT OF LIMITED PARTNERSHIP.

(a) Each general partner is an agent of the limited partnership for the purposes of its activities. An act of a general partner, including the signing of a record in the partnership's name, for apparently carrying on in the ordinary course the limited partnership's activities or activities of the kind carried on by the limited partnership binds the limited partnership, unless the general partner did not have authority to act for the limited partnership in the particular matter and the person with which the general partner was dealing knew, had received a notification, or had notice under Section 103(d) that the general partner lacked authority.

(b) An act of a general partner which is not apparently for carrying on in the ordinary course the limited partnership's activities or activities of the kind carried on by the limited partnership binds the limited partnership only if the act was actually authorized by all the other partners.

SECTION 403.   LIMITED PARTNERSHIP LIABLE FOR GENERAL PARTNER'S ACTIONABLE CONDUCT.

(a) A limited partnership is liable for loss or injury caused to a person, or for a penalty incurred, as a result of a wrongful act or omission, or other actionable conduct, of a general partner acting in the ordinary course of activities of the limited partnership or with authority of the limited partnership.

(b) If, in the course of the limited partnership's activities or while acting with authority of the limited partnership, a general partner receives or causes the limited partnership to receive money or property of a person not a partner, and the money or property is misapplied by a general partner, the limited partnership is liable for the loss.

SECTION 404.   GENERAL PARTNER'S LIABILITY.

(a) Except as otherwise provided in subsections (b) and (c), all general partners are liable jointly and severally for all obligations of the limited partnership unless otherwise agreed by the claimant or provided by law.

(b) A person that becomes a general partner of an existing limited partnership is not personally liable for an obligation of a limited partnership incurred before the person became a general partner.

(c) An obligation of a limited partnership incurred while the limited partnership is a limited liability limited partnership, whether arising in contract, tort, or otherwise, is solely the obligation of the limited partnership. A general partner is not personally liable, directly or indirectly, by way of contribution or otherwise, for such an obligation solely by reason of being or acting as a general partner. This subsection applies despite anything inconsistent in the partnership agreement that existed immediately before the consent required to become a limited liability limited partnership under Section 406(b)(2).

SECTION 405.   ACTIONS BY AND AGAINST PARTNERSHIP AND PARTNERS.

(a) To the extent not inconsistent with Section 404, a general partner may be joined in an action against the limited partnership or named in a separate action.

(b) A judgment against a limited partnership is not by itself a judgment against a general partner. A judgment against a limited partnership may not be satisfied from a general partner's assets unless there is also a judgment against the general partner.

(c) A judgment creditor of a general partner may not levy execution against the assets of the general partner to satisfy a judgment based on a claim against the limited partnership, unless the partner is personally liable for the claim under Section 404 and:

(1) a judgment based on the same claim has been obtained against the limited partnership and a writ of execution on the judgment has been returned unsatisfied in whole or in part;

(2) the limited partnership is a debtor in bankruptcy;

(3) the general partner has agreed that the creditor need not exhaust limited partnership assets;

(4) a court grants permission to the judgment creditor to levy execution against the assets of a general partner based on a finding that limited partnership assets subject to execution are clearly insufficient to satisfy the judgment, that exhaustion of limited partnership assets is excessively burdensome, or that the grant of permission is an appropriate exercise of the court's equitable powers; or

(5) liability is imposed on the general partner by law or contract independent of the existence of the limited partnership.

SECTION 406.   MANAGEMENT RIGHTS OF GENERAL PARTNER.

(a) Each general partner has equal rights in the management and conduct of the limited partnership's activities. Except as expressly provided in this [Act], any matter relating to the activities of the limited partnership may be exclusively decided by the general partner or, if there is more than one general partner, by a majority of the general partners.

(b) The consent of each partner is necessary to:

(1) amend the partnership agreement;

(2) amend the certificate of limited partnership to add or, subject to Section 1110, delete a statement that the limited partnership is a limited liability limited partnership; and

(3) sell, lease, exchange, or otherwise dispose of all, or substantially all, of the limited partnership's property, with or without the good will, other than in the usual and regular course of the limited partnership's activities.

(c) A limited partnership shall reimburse a general partner for payments made and indemnify a general partner for liabilities incurred by the general partner in the ordinary course of the activities of the partnership or for the preservation of its activities or property.

(d) A limited partnership shall reimburse a general partner for an advance to the limited partnership beyond the amount of capital the general partner agreed to contribute.

(e) A payment or advance made by a general partner which gives rise to an obligation of the limited partnership under subsection (c) or (d) constitutes a loan to the limited partnership which accrues interest from the date of the payment or advance.

(f) A general partner is not entitled to remuneration for services performed for the partnership.

SECTION 407.   RIGHT OF GENERAL PARTNER AND FORMER GENERAL PARTNER TO INFORMATION.

(a) A general partner, without having any particular purpose for seeking the information, may inspect and copy during regular business hours:

(1) in the limited partnership's designated office, required information; and

(2) at a reasonable location specified by the limited partnership, any other records maintained by the limited partnership regarding the limited partnership's activities and financial condition.

(b) Each general partner and the limited partnership shall furnish to a general partner:

(1) without demand, any information concerning the limited partnership's activities and activities reasonably required for the proper exercise of the general partner's rights and duties under the partnership agreement or this [Act]; and

(2) on demand, any other information concerning the limited partnership's activities, except to the extent the demand or the information demanded is unreasonable or otherwise improper under the circumstances.

(c) Subject to subsection (e), on 10 days' demand made in a record received by the limited partnership, a person dissociated as a general partner may have access to the information and records described in subsection (a) at the location specified in subsection (a) if:

(1) the information or record pertains to the period during which the person was a general partner;

(2) the person seeks the information or record in good faith; and

(3) the person satisfies the requirements imposed on a limited partner by Section 304(b).

(d) The limited partnership shall respond to a demand made pursuant to subsection (c) in the same manner as provided in Section 304(c).

(e) If a general partner dies, Section 704 applies.

(f) The limited partnership may impose reasonable restrictions on the use of information under this section. In any dispute concerning the reasonableness of a restriction under this subsection, the limited partnership has the burden of proving reasonableness.

(g) A limited partnership may charge a person dissociated as a general partner that makes a demand under this section reasonable costs of copying, limited to the costs of labor and material.

(h) A general partner or person dissociated as a general partner may exercise the rights under this section through an attorney or other agent. Any restriction imposed under subsection (f) or by the partnership agreement applies both to the attorney or other agent and to the general partner or person dissociated as a general partner.

(i) The rights under this section do not extend to a person as transferee, but the rights under subsection (c) of a person dissociated as a general may be exercised by the legal representative of an individual who dissociated as a general partner under Section 603(7)(B) or (C).

SECTION 408.   GENERAL STANDARDS OF GENERAL PARTNER'S CONDUCT.

(a) The only fiduciary duties that a general partner has to the limited partnership and the other partners are the duties of loyalty and care under subsections (b) and (c).

(b) A general partner's duty of loyalty to the limited partnership and the other partners is limited to the following:

(1) to account to the limited partnership and hold as trustee for it any property, profit, or benefit derived by the general partner in the conduct and winding up of the limited partnership's activities or derived from a use by the general partner of limited partnership property, including the appropriation of a limited partnership opportunity;

(2) to refrain from dealing with the limited partnership in the conduct or winding up of the limited partnership's activities as or on behalf of a party having an interest adverse to the limited partnership; and

(3) to refrain from competing with the limited partnership in the conduct or winding up of the limited partnership's activities.

(c) A general partner's duty of care to the limited partnership and the other partners in the conduct and winding up of the limited partnership's activities is limited to refraining from engaging in grossly negligent or reckless conduct, intentional misconduct, or a knowing violation of law.

(d) A general partner shall discharge the duties to the partnership and the other partners under this [Act] or under the partnership agreement and exercise any rights consistently with the obligation of good faith and fair dealing.

(e) A general partner does not violate a duty or obligation under this [Act] or under the partnership agreement merely because the general partner's conduct furthers the general partner's own interest.

[ARTICLE] 5
CONTRIBUTIONS AND DISTRIBUTIONS

SECTION 501.   FORM OF CONTRIBUTION.

A contribution of a partner may consist of tangible or intangible property or other benefit to the limited partnership, including money, services performed, promissory notes, other agreements to contribute cash or property, and contracts for services to be performed.

SECTION 502.   LIABILITY FOR CONTRIBUTION.

(a) A partner's obligation to contribute money or other property or other benefit to, or to perform services for, a limited partnership is not excused by the partner's death, disability, or other inability to perform personally.

(b) If a partner does not make a promised non-monetary contribution, the partner is obligated at the option of the limited partnership to contribute money equal to that portion of the value, as stated in the required information, of the stated contribution which has not been made.

(c) The obligation of a partner to make a contribution or return money or other property paid or distributed in violation of this [Act] may be compromised only by consent of all partners. A creditor of a limited partnership which extends credit or otherwise acts in reliance on an obligation described in subsection (a), without notice of any compromise under this subsection, may enforce the original obligation.

SECTION 503.   SHARING OF DISTRIBUTIONS.

A distribution by a limited partnership must be shared among the partners on the basis of the value, as stated in the required records when the limited partnership decides to make the distribution, of the contributions the limited partnership has received from each partner.

SECTION 504.   INTERIM DISTRIBUTIONS.

A partner does not have a right to any distribution before the dissolution and winding up of the limited partnership unless the limited partnership decides to make an interim distribution.

SECTION 505.   NO DISTRIBUTION ON ACCOUNT OF DISSOCIATION.

A person does not have a right to receive a distribution on account of dissociation.

SECTION 506.   DISTRIBUTION IN KIND.

A partner does not have a right to demand or receive any distribution from a limited partnership in any form other than cash. Subject to Section 812(b), a limited partnership may distribute an asset in kind to the extent each partner receives a percentage of the asset equal to the partner's share of distributions.

SECTION 507.   RIGHT TO DISTRIBUTION.

When a partner or transferee becomes entitled to receive a distribution, the partner or transferee has the status of, and is entitled to all remedies available to, a creditor of the limited partnership with respect to the distribution. However, the limited partnership's obligation to make a distribution is subject to offset for any amount owed to the limited partnership by the partner or dissociated partner on whose account the distribution is made.

SECTION 508.   LIMITATIONS ON DISTRIBUTION.

(a) A limited partnership may not make a distribution in violation of the partnership agreement.

(b) A limited partnership may not make a distribution if after the distribution:

> (1) the limited partnership would not be able to pay its debts as they become due in the ordinary course of the limited partnership's activities; or

> (2) the limited partnership's total assets would be less than the sum of its total liabilities plus the amount that would be needed, if the limited partnership were to be dissolved, wound up, and terminated at the time of the distribution, to satisfy the preferential rights upon dissolution, winding up, and termination of partners whose preferential rights are superior to those of persons receiving the distribution.

(c) A limited partnership may base a determination that a distribution is not prohibited under subsection (b) on financial statements prepared on the basis of accounting practices and principles that are reasonable in the circumstances or on a fair valuation or other method that is reasonable in the circumstances.

(d) Except as otherwise provided in subsection (g), the effect of a distribution under subsection (b) is measured:

> (1) in the case of distribution by purchase, redemption, or other acquisition of a transferable interest in the limited partnership, as of the date money or other property is transferred or debt incurred by the limited partnership; and

> (2) in all other cases, as of the date:

>> (A) the distribution is authorized, if the payment occurs within 120 days after that date; or

>> (B) the payment is made, if payment occurs more than 120 days after the distribution is authorized.

(e) A limited partnership's indebtedness to a partner incurred by reason of a distribution made in accordance with this section is at parity with the limited partnership's indebtedness to its general, unsecured creditors.

(f) A limited partnership's indebtedness, including indebtedness issued in connection with or as part of a distribution, is not considered a liability for purposes of subsection (b) if the terms of the indebtedness provide that payment of principal and interest are made only to the extent that a distribution could then be made to partners under this section.

(g) If indebtedness is issued as a distribution, each payment of principal or interest on the indebtedness is treated as a distribution, the effect of which is measured on the date the payment is made.

SECTION 509.   LIABILITY FOR IMPROPER DISTRIBUTIONS.

(a) A general partner that consents to a distribution made in violation of Section 508 is personally liable to the limited partnership for the amount of the distribution which exceeds the amount that could have been distributed without the violation if it is established that in consenting to the distribution the general partner failed to comply with Section 408.

(b) A partner or transferee that received a distribution knowing that the distribution to that partner or transferee was made in violation of Section 508 is personally liable to the limited partnership but only to the extent that the distribution received by the partner or transferee exceeded the amount that could have been properly paid under Section 508.

(c) A general partner against which an action is commenced under subsection (a) may:

> (1) implead in the action any other person that is liable under subsection (a) and compel contribution from the person; and

> (2) implead in the action any person that received a distribution in violation of subsection (b) and compel contribution from the person in the amount the person received in violation of subsection (b).

(d) An action under this section is barred if it is not commenced within two years after the distribution.

[ARTICLE] 6
DISSOCIATION

SECTION 601.   DISSOCIATION AS LIMITED PARTNER.

(a) A person does not have a right to dissociate as a limited partner before the termination of the limited partnership.

(b) A person is dissociated from a limited partnership as a limited partner upon the occurrence of any of the following events:

> (1) the limited partnership's having notice of the person's express will to withdraw as a limited partner or on a later date specified by the person;

> (2) an event agreed to in the partnership agreement as causing the person's dissociation as a limited partner;

> (3) the person's expulsion as a limited partner pursuant to the partnership agreement;

> (4) the person's expulsion as a limited partner by the unanimous consent of the other partners if:

>> (A) it is unlawful to carry on the limited partnership's activities with the person as a limited partner;

>> (B) there has been a transfer of all of the person's transferable interest in the limited partnership, other than a

transfer for security purposes, or a court order charging the person's interest, which has not been foreclosed;

(C) the person is a corporation and, within 90 days after the limited partnership notifies the person that it will be expelled as a limited partner because it has filed a certificate of dissolution or the equivalent, its charter has been revoked, or its right to conduct business has been suspended by the jurisdiction of its incorporation, there is no revocation of the certificate of dissolution or no reinstatement of its charter or its right to conduct business; or

(D) the person is a limited liability company or partnership that has been dissolved and whose business is being wound up;

(5) on application by the limited partnership, the person's expulsion as a limited partner by judicial order because:

(A) the person engaged in wrongful conduct that adversely and materially affected the limited partnership's activities;

(B) the person willfully or persistently committed a material breach of the partnership agreement or of the obligation of good faith and fair dealing under Section 305(b); or

(C) the person engaged in conduct relating to the limited partnership's activities which makes it not reasonably practicable to carry on the activities with the person as limited partner;

(6) in the case of a person who is an individual, the person's death;

(7) in the case of a person that is a trust or is acting as a limited partner by virtue of being a trustee of a trust, distribution of the trust's entire transferable interest in the limited partnership, but not merely by reason of the substitution of a successor trustee;

(8) in the case of a person that is an estate or is acting as a limited partner by virtue of being a personal representative of an estate, distribution of the estate's entire transferable interest in the limited partnership, but not merely by reason of the substitution of a successor personal representative;

(9) termination of a limited partner that is not an individual, partnership, limited liability company, corporation, trust, or estate;

(10) the limited partnership's participation in a conversion or merger under [Article] 11, if the limited partnership:

(A) is not the converted or surviving entity; or

(B) is the converted or surviving entity but, as a result of the conversion or merger, the person ceases to be a limited partner.

SECTION 602.   EFFECT OF DISSOCIATION AS LIMITED PARTNER.

(a) Upon a person's dissociation as a limited partner:

(1) subject to Section 704, the person does not have further rights as a limited partner;

(2) the person's obligation of good faith and fair dealing as a limited partner under Section 305(b) continues only as to matters arising and events occurring before the dissociation; and

(3) subject to Section 704 and [Article] 11, any transferable interest owned by the person in the person's capacity as a limited partner immediately before dissociation is owned by the person as a mere transferee.

(b) A person's dissociation as a limited partner does not of itself discharge the person from any obligation to the limited partnership or the other partners which the person incurred while a limited partner.

SECTION 603.   DISSOCIATION AS GENERAL PARTNER.

A person is dissociated from a limited partnership as a general partner upon the occurrence of any of the following events:

(1) the limited partnership's having notice of the person's express will to withdraw as a general partner or on a later date specified by the person;

(2) an event agreed to in the partnership agreement as causing the person's dissociation as a general partner;

(3) the person's expulsion as a general partner pursuant to the partnership agreement;

(4) the person's expulsion as a general partner by the unanimous consent of the other partners if:

(A) it is unlawful to carry on the limited partnership's activities with the person as a general partner;

(B) there has been a transfer of all or substantially all of the person's transferable interest in the limited partnership, other than a transfer for security purposes, or a court order charging the person's interest, which has not been foreclosed;

(C) the person is a corporation and, within 90 days after the limited partnership notifies the person that it will be expelled as a general partner because it has filed a certificate of dissolution or the equivalent, its charter has been revoked, or its right to conduct business has been suspended by the jurisdiction of its incorporation, there is no revocation of the certificate of dissolution or no reinstatement of its charter or its right to conduct business; or

(D) the person is a limited liability company or partnership that has been dissolved and whose business is being wound up;

(5) on application by the limited partnership, the person's expulsion as a general partner by judicial determination because:

(A) the person engaged in wrongful conduct that adversely and materially affected the limited partnership activities;

(B) the person willfully or persistently committed a material breach of the partnership agreement or of a duty owed to the partnership or the other partners under Section 408; or

(C) the person engaged in conduct relating to the limited partnership's activities which makes it not reasonably practicable to carry on the activities of the limited partnership with the person as a general partner;

(6) the person's:

(A) becoming a debtor in bankruptcy;

(B) execution of an assignment for the benefit of creditors;

(C) seeking, consenting to, or acquiescing in the appointment of a trustee, receiver, or liquidator of the person or of all or substantially all of the person's property; or

(D) failure, within 90 days after the appointment, to have vacated or stayed the appointment of a trustee, receiver, or liquidator of the general partner or of all or substantially all of the person's property obtained without the person's consent or acquiescence, or failing within 90 days after the expiration of a stay to have the appointment vacated;

(7) in the case of a person who is an individual:

(A) the person's death;

(B) the appointment of a guardian or general conservator for the person; or

(C) a judicial determination that the person has otherwise become incapable of performing the person's duties as a general partner under the partnership agreement;

(8) in the case of a person that is a trust or is acting as a general partner by virtue of being a trustee of a trust, distribution of the trust's entire transferable interest in the limited partnership, but not merely by reason of the substitution of a successor trustee;

(9) in the case of a person that is an estate or is acting as a general partner by virtue of being a personal representative of an estate, distribution of the estate's entire transferable interest in the limited partnership, but not merely by reason of the substitution of a successor personal representative;

(10) termination of a general partner that is not an individual, partnership, limited liability company, corporation, trust, or estate; or

(11) the limited partnership's participation in a conversion or merger under [Article] 11, if the limited partnership:

(A) is not the converted or surviving entity; or

(B) is the converted or surviving entity but, as a result of the conversion or merger, the person ceases to be a general partner.

SECTION 604. PERSON'S POWER TO DISSOCIATE AS GENERAL PARTNER; WRONGFUL DISSOCIATION.

(a) A person has the power to dissociate as a general partner at any time, rightfully or wrongfully, by express will pursuant to Section 603(1).

(b) A person's dissociation as a general partner is wrongful only if:

(1) it is in breach of an express provision of the partnership agreement; or

(2) it occurs before the termination of the limited partnership, and:

(A) the person withdraws as a general partner by express will;

(B) the person is expelled as a general partner by judicial determination under Section 603(5);

(C) the person is dissociated as a general partner by becoming a debtor in bankruptcy; or

(D) in the case of a person that is not an individual, trust other than a business trust, or estate, the person is expelled or otherwise dissociated as a general partner because it willfully dissolved or terminated.

(c) A person that wrongfully dissociates as a general partner is liable to the limited partnership and, subject to Section 1001, to the other partners for damages caused by the dissociation. The liability is in addition to any other obligation of the general partner to the limited partnership or to the other partners.

SECTION 605. EFFECT OF DISSOCIATION AS GENERAL PARTNER.

(a) Upon a person's dissociation as a general partner:

(1) the person's right to participate as a general partner in the management and conduct of the partnership's activities terminates;

(2) the person's duty of loyalty as a general partner under Section 408(b)(3) terminates;

(3) the person's duty of loyalty as a general partner under Section 408(b)(1) and (2) and duty of care under Section 408(c) continue only with regard to matters arising and events occurring before the person's dissociation as a general partner;

(4) the person may sign and deliver to the [Secretary of State] for filing a statement of dissociation pertaining to the person and, at the request of the limited partnership, shall sign an amendment to the certificate of limited partnership which states that the person has dissociated; and

(5) subject to Section 704 and [Article] 11, any transferable interest owned by the person immediately before dissociation in the person's capacity as a general partner is owned by the person as a mere transferee.

(b) A person's dissociation as a general partner does not of itself discharge the person from any obligation to the limited partnership or the other partners which the person incurred while a general partner.

SECTION 606. POWER TO BIND AND LIABILITY TO LIMITED PARTNERSHIP BEFORE DISSOLUTION OF PARTNERSHIP OF PERSON DISSOCIATED AS GENERAL PARTNER.

(a) After a person is dissociated as a general partner and before the limited partnership is dissolved, converted under [Article] 11, or merged out of existence under [Article] 11, the limited partnership is bound by an act of the person only if:

(1) the act would have bound the limited partnership under Section 402 before the dissociation; and

(2) at the time the other party enters into the transaction:

(A) less than two years has passed since the dissociation; and

(B) the other party does not have notice of the dissociation and reasonably believes that the person is a general partner.

(b) If a limited partnership is bound under subsection (a), the person dissociated as a general partner which caused the limited partnership to be bound is liable:

(1) to the limited partnership for any damage caused to the limited partnership arising from the obligation incurred under subsection (a); and

(2) if a general partner or another person dissociated as a general partner is liable for the obligation, to the general partner or other person for any damage caused to the general partner or other person arising from the liability.

SECTION 607. LIABILITY TO OTHER PERSONS OF PERSON DISSOCIATED AS GENERAL PARTNER.

(a) A person's dissociation as a general partner does not of itself discharge the person's liability as a general partner for an obligation of the limited partnership incurred before dissociation. Except as otherwise provided in subsections (b) and (c), the person is not liable for a limited partnership's obligation incurred after dissociation.

(b) A person whose dissociation as a general partner resulted in a dissolution and winding up of the limited partnership's activities is liable to the same extent as a general partner under Section 404 on an obligation incurred by the limited partnership under Section 804.

(c) A person that has dissociated as a general partner but whose dissociation did not result in a dissolution and winding up of the limited partnership's activities is liable on a transaction entered into by the limited partnership after the dissociation only if:

(1) a general partner would be liable on the transaction; and

(2) at the time the other party enters into the transaction:

    (A) less than two years has passed since the dissociation; and

    (B) the other party does not have notice of the dissociation and reasonably believes that the person is a general partner.

(d) By agreement with a creditor of a limited partnership and the limited partnership, a person dissociated as a general partner may be released from liability for an obligation of the limited partnership.

(e) A person dissociated as a general partner is released from liability for an obligation of the limited partnership if the limited partnership's creditor, with notice of the person's dissociation as a general partner but without the person's consent, agrees to a material alteration in the nature or time of payment of the obligation.

[ARTICLE] 7
TRANSFERABLE INTERESTS AND RIGHTS OF TRANSFEREES AND CREDITORS

SECTION 701. PARTNER'S TRANSFERABLE INTEREST.
The only interest of a partner which is transferable is the partner's transferable interest. A transferable interest is personal property.

SECTION 702. TRANSFER OF PARTNER'S TRANSFERABLE INTEREST.
(a) A transfer, in whole or in part, of a partner's transferable interest:

    (1) is permissible;

    (2) does not by itself cause the partner's dissociation or a dissolution and winding up of the limited partnership's activities; and

    (3) does not, as against the other partners or the limited partnership, entitle the transferee to participate in the management or conduct of the limited partnership's activities, to require access to information concerning the limited partnership's transactions except as otherwise provided in subsection (c), or to inspect or copy the required information or the limited partnership's other records.

(b) A transferee has a right to receive, in accordance with the transfer:

    (1) distributions to which the transferor would otherwise be entitled; and

    (2) upon the dissolution and winding up of the limited partnership's activities the net amount otherwise distributable to the transferor.

(c) In a dissolution and winding up, a transferee is entitled to an account of the limited partnership's transactions only from the date of dissolution.

(d) Upon transfer, the transferor retains the rights of a partner other than the interest in distributions transferred and retains all duties and obligations of a partner.

(e) A limited partnership need not give effect to a transferee's rights under this section until the limited partnership has notice of the transfer.

(f) A transfer of a partner's transferable interest in the limited partnership in violation of a restriction on transfer contained in the partnership agreement is ineffective as to a person having notice of the restriction at the time of transfer.

(g) A transferee that becomes a partner with respect to a transferable interest is liable for the transferor's obligations under Sections 502 and 509. However, the transferee is not obligated for liabilities unknown to the transferee at the time the transferee became a partner.

SECTION 703. RIGHTS OF CREDITOR OF PARTNER OR TRANSFEREE.
(a) On application to a court of competent jurisdiction by any judgment creditor of a partner or transferee, the court may charge the transferable interest of the judgment debtor with payment of the unsatisfied amount of the judgment with interest. To the extent so charged, the judgment creditor has only the rights of a transferee. The court may appoint a receiver of the share of the distributions due or to become due to the judgment debtor in respect of the partnership and make all other orders, directions, accounts, and inquiries the judgment debtor might have made or which the circumstances of the case may require to give effect to the charging order.

(b) A charging order constitutes a lien on the judgment debtor's transferable interest. The court may order a foreclosure upon the interest subject to the charging order at any time. The purchaser at the foreclosure sale has the rights of a transferee.

(c) At any time before foreclosure, an interest charged may be redeemed:

    (1) by the judgment debtor;

    (2) with property other than limited partnership property, by one or more of the other partners; or

    (3) with limited partnership property, by the limited partnership with the consent of all partners whose interests are not so charged.

(d) This [Act] does not deprive any partner or transferee of the benefit of any exemption laws applicable to the partner's or transferee's transferable interest.

(e) This section provides the exclusive remedy by which a judgment creditor of a partner or transferee may satisfy a judgment out of the judgment debtor's transferable interest.

SECTION 704. POWER OF ESTATE OF DECEASED PARTNER.
If a partner dies, the deceased partner's personal representative or other legal representative may exercise the rights of a transferee as provided in Section 702 and, for the purposes of settling the estate, may exercise the rights of a current limited partner under Section 304.

[ARTICLE] 8
DISSOLUTION

SECTION 801. NONJUDICIAL DISSOLUTION.
Except as otherwise provided in Section 802, a limited partnership is dissolved, and its activities must be wound up, only upon the occurrence of any of the following:

(1) the happening of an event specified in the partnership agreement;

(2) the consent of all general partners and of limited partners owning a majority of the rights to receive distributions as limited partners at the time the consent is to be effective;

(3) after the dissociation of a person as a general partner:

    (A) if the limited partnership has at least one remaining general partner, the consent to dissolve the limited partnership given within 90 days after the dissociation by partners owning a majority of the rights to receive distributions as partners at the time the consent is to be effective; or

(B) if the limited partnership does not have a remaining general partner, the passage of 90 days after the dissociation, unless before the end of the period:

(i) consent to continue the activities of the limited partnership and admit at least one general partner is given by limited partners owning a majority of the rights to receive distributions as limited partners at the time the consent is to be effective; and

(ii) at least one person is admitted as a general partner in accordance with the consent;

(4) the passage of 90 days after the dissociation of the limited partnership's last limited partner, unless before the end of the period the limited partnership admits at least one limited partner; or

(5) the signing and filing of a declaration of dissolution by the [Secretary of State] under Section 809(c).

SECTION 802.   JUDICIAL DISSOLUTION.

On application by a partner the [appropriate court] may order dissolution of a limited partnership if it is not reasonably practicable to carry on the activities of the limited partnership in conformity with the partnership agreement.

SECTION 803.   WINDING UP.

(a) A limited partnership continues after dissolution only for the purpose of winding up its activities.

(b) In winding up its activities, the limited partnership:

(1) may amend its certificate of limited partnership to state that the limited partnership is dissolved, preserve the limited partnership business or property as a going concern for a reasonable time, prosecute and defend actions and proceedings, whether civil, criminal, or administrative, transfer the limited partnership's property, settle disputes by mediation or arbitration, file a statement of termination as provided in Section 203, and perform other necessary acts; and

(2) shall discharge the limited partnership's liabilities, settle and close the limited partnership's activities, and marshal and distribute the assets of the partnership.

(c) If a dissolved limited partnership does not have a general partner, a person to wind up the dissolved limited partnership's activities may be appointed by the consent of limited partners owning a majority of the rights to receive distributions as limited partners at the time the consent is to be effective. A person appointed under this subsection:

(1) has the powers of a general partner under Section 804; and

(2) shall promptly amend the certificate of limited partnership to state:

(A) that the limited partnership does not have a general partner;

(B) the name of the person that has been appointed to wind up the limited partnership; and

(C) the street and mailing address of the person.

(d) On the application of any partner, the [appropriate court] may order judicial supervision of the winding up, including the appointment of a person to wind up the dissolved limited partnership's activities, if:

(1) a limited partnership does not have a general partner and within a reasonable time following the dissolution no person has been appointed pursuant to subsection (c); or

(2) the applicant establishes other good cause.

SECTION 804.   POWER OF GENERAL PARTNER AND PERSON DISSOCIATED AS GENERAL PARTNER TO BIND PARTNERSHIP AFTER DISSOLUTION.

(a) A limited partnership is bound by a general partner's act after dissolution which:

(1) is appropriate for winding up the limited partnership's activities; or

(2) would have bound the limited partnership under Section 402 before dissolution, if, at the time the other party enters into the transaction, the other party does not have notice of the dissolution.

(b) A person dissociated as a general partner binds a limited partnership through an act occurring after dissolution if:

(1) at the time the other party enters into the transaction:

(A) less than two years has passed since the dissociation; and

(B) the other party does not have notice of the dissociation and reasonably believes that the person is a general partner; and

(2) the act:

(A) is appropriate for winding up the limited partnership's activities; or

(B) would have bound the limited partnership under Section 402 before dissolution and at the time the other party enters into the transaction the other party does not have notice of the dissolution.

SECTION 805.   LIABILITY AFTER DISSOLUTION OF GENERAL PARTNER AND PERSON DISSOCIATED AS GENERAL PARTNER TO LIMITED PARTNERSHIP, OTHER GENERAL PARTNERS, AND PERSONS DISSOCIATED AS GENERAL PARTNER.

(a) If a general partner having knowledge of the dissolution causes a limited partnership to incur an obligation under Section 804(a) by an act that is not appropriate for winding up the partnership's activities, the general partner is liable:

(1) to the limited partnership for any damage caused to the limited partnership arising from the obligation; and

(2) if another general partner or a person dissociated as a general partner is liable for the obligation, to that other general partner or person for any damage caused to that other general partner or person arising from the liability.

(b) If a person dissociated as a general partner causes a limited partnership to incur an obligation under Section 804(b), the person is liable:

(1) to the limited partnership for any damage caused to the limited partnership arising from the obligation; and

(2) if a general partner or another person dissociated as a general partner is liable for the obligation, to the general partner or other person for any damage caused to the general partner or other person arising from the liability.

SECTION 806.   KNOWN CLAIMS AGAINST DISSOLVED LIMITED PARTNERSHIP.

(a) A dissolved limited partnership may dispose of the known claims against it by following the procedure described in subsection (b).

(b) A dissolved limited partnership may notify its known claimants of the dissolution in a record. The notice must:

(1) specify the information required to be included in a claim;

(2) provide a mailing address to which the claim is to be sent;

(3) state the deadline for receipt of the claim, which may not be less than 120 days after the date the notice is received by the claimant;

(4) state that the claim will be barred if not received by the deadline; and

(5) unless the limited partnership has been throughout its existence a limited liability limited partnership, state that the barring of a claim against the limited partnership will also bar any corresponding claim against any general partner or person dissociated as a general partner which is based on Section 404.

(c) A claim against a dissolved limited partnership is barred if the requirements of subsection (b) are met and:

(1) the claim is not received by the specified deadline; or

(2) in the case of a claim that is timely received but rejected by the dissolved limited partnership, the claimant does not commence an action to enforce the claim against the limited partnership within 90 days after the receipt of the notice of the rejection.

(d) This section does not apply to a claim based on an event occurring after the effective date of dissolution or a liability that is contingent on that date.

SECTION 807.   OTHER CLAIMS AGAINST DISSOLVED LIMITED PARTNERSHIP.

(a) A dissolved limited partnership may publish notice of its dissolution and request persons having claims against the limited partnership to present them in accordance with the notice.

(b) The notice must:

(1) be published at least once in a newspaper of general circulation in the [county] in which the dissolved limited partnership's principal office is located or, if it has none in this State, in the [county] in which the limited partnership's designated office is or was last located;

(2) describe the information required to be contained in a claim and provide a mailing address to which the claim is to be sent;

(3) state that a claim against the limited partnership is barred unless an action to enforce the claim is commenced within five years after publication of the notice; and

(4) unless the limited partnership has been throughout its existence a limited liability limited partnership, state that the barring of a claim against the limited partnership will also bar any corresponding claim against any general partner or person dissociated as a general partner which is based on Section 404.

(c) If a dissolved limited partnership publishes a notice in accordance with subsection (b), the claim of each of the following claimants is barred unless the claimant commences an action to enforce the claim against the dissolved limited partnership within five years after the publication date of the notice:

(1) a claimant that did not receive notice in a record under Section 806;

(2) a claimant whose claim was timely sent to the dissolved limited partnership but not acted on; and

(3) a claimant whose claim is contingent or based on an event occurring after the effective date of dissolution.

(d) A claim not barred under this section may be enforced:

(1) against the dissolved limited partnership, to the extent of its undistributed assets;

(2) if the assets have been distributed in liquidation, against a partner or transferee to the extent of that person's proportionate share of the claim or the limited partnership's assets distributed to the partner or transferee in liquidation, whichever is less, but a person's total liability for all claims under this paragraph does not exceed the total amount of assets distributed to the person as part of the winding up of the dissolved limited partnership; or

(3) against any person liable on the claim under Section 404.

SECTION 808.   LIABILITY OF GENERAL PARTNER AND PERSON DISSOCIATED AS GENERAL PARTNER WHEN CLAIM AGAINST LIMITED PARTNERSHIP BARRED.

If a claim against a dissolved limited partnership is barred under Section 806 or 807, any corresponding claim under Section 404 is also barred.

SECTION 809.   ADMINISTRATIVE DISSOLUTION.

(a) The [Secretary of State] may dissolve a limited partnership administratively if the limited partnership does not, within 60 days after the due date:

(1) pay any fee, tax, or penalty due to the [Secretary of State] under this [Act] or other law; or

(2) deliver its annual report to the [Secretary of State].

(b) If the [Secretary of State] determines that a ground exists for administratively dissolving a limited partnership, the [Secretary of State] shall file a record of the determination and serve the limited partnership with a copy of the filed record.

(c) If within 60 days after service of the copy the limited partnership does not correct each ground for dissolution or demonstrate to the reasonable satisfaction of the [Secretary of State] that each ground determined by the [Secretary of State] does not exist, the [Secretary of State] shall administratively dissolve the limited partnership by preparing, signing and filing a declaration of dissolution that states the grounds for dissolution. The [Secretary of State] shall serve the limited partnership with a copy of the filed declaration.

(d) A limited partnership administratively dissolved continues its existence but may carry on only activities necessary to wind up its activities and liquidate its assets under Sections 803 and 812 and to notify claimants under Sections 806 and 807.

(e) The administrative dissolution of a limited partnership does not terminate the authority of its agent for service of process.

SECTION 810.   REINSTATEMENT FOLLOWING ADMINISTRATIVE DISSOLUTION.

(a) A limited partnership that has been administratively dissolved may apply to the [Secretary of State] for reinstatement within two years after the effective date of dissolution. The application must be delivered to the [Secretary of State] for filing and state:

(1) the name of the limited partnership and the effective date of its administrative dissolution;

(2) that the grounds for dissolution either did not exist or have been eliminated; and

(3) that the limited partnership's name satisfies the requirements of Section 108.

(b) If the [Secretary of State] determines that an application contains the information required by subsection (a) and that the information is correct, the [Secretary of State] shall prepare a declaration of reinstatement that states this determination, sign, and file the original of the declaration of reinstatement, and serve the limited partnership with a copy.

(c) When reinstatement becomes effective, it relates back to and takes effect as of the effective date of the administrative dissolution and the limited partnership may resume its activities as if the administrative dissolution had never occurred.

SECTION 811. APPEAL FROM DENIAL OF REINSTATEMENT.

(a) If the [Secretary of State] denies a limited partnership's application for reinstatement following administrative dissolution, the [Secretary of State] shall prepare, sign and file a notice that explains the reason or reasons for denial and serve the limited partnership with a copy of the notice.

(b) Within 30 days after service of the notice of denial, the limited partnership may appeal from the denial of reinstatement by petitioning the [appropriate court] to set aside the dissolution. The petition must be served on the [Secretary of State] and contain a copy of the [Secretary of State's] declaration of dissolution, the limited partnership's application for reinstatement, and the [Secretary of State's] notice of denial.

(c) The court may summarily order the [Secretary of State] to reinstate the dissolved limited partnership or may take other action the court considers appropriate.

SECTION 812. DISPOSITION OF ASSETS; WHEN CONTRIBUTIONS REQUIRED.

(a) In winding up a limited partnership's activities, the assets of the limited partnership, including the contributions required by this section, must be applied to satisfy the limited partnership's obligations to creditors, including, to the extent permitted by law, partners that are creditors.

(b) Any surplus remaining after the limited partnership complies with subsection (a) must be paid in cash as a distribution.

(c) If a limited partnership's assets are insufficient to satisfy all of its obligations under subsection (a), with respect to each unsatisfied obligation incurred when the limited partnership was not a limited liability limited partnership, the following rules apply:

(1) Each person that was a general partner when the obligation was incurred and that has not been released from the obligation under Section 607 shall contribute to the limited partnership for the purpose of enabling the limited partnership to satisfy the obligation. The contribution due from each of those persons is in proportion to the right to receive distributions in the capacity of general partner in effect for each of those persons when the obligation was incurred.

(2) If a person does not contribute the full amount required under paragraph (1) with respect to an unsatisfied obligation of the limited partnership, the other persons required to contribute by paragraph (1) on account of the obligation shall contribute the additional amount necessary to discharge the obligation. The additional contribution due from each of those other persons is in proportion to the right to receive distributions in the capacity of general partner in effect for each of those other persons when the obligation was incurred.

(3) If a person does not make the additional contribution required by paragraph (2), further additional contributions are determined and due in the same manner as provided in that paragraph.

(d) A person that makes an additional contribution under subsection (c)(2) or (3) may recover from any person whose failure to contribute under subsection (c)(1) or (2) necessitated the additional contribution. A person may not recover under this subsection more than the amount additionally contributed. A person's liability under this subsection may not exceed the amount the person failed to contribute.

(e) The estate of a deceased individual is liable for the person's obligations under this section.

(f) An assignee for the benefit of creditors of a limited partnership or a partner, or a person appointed by a court to represent creditors of a limited partnership or a partner, may enforce a person's obligation to contribute under subsection (c).

[ARTICLE] 9
FOREIGN LIMITED PARTNERSHIPS

SECTION 901. GOVERNING LAW.

(a) The laws of the State or other jurisdiction under which a foreign limited partnership is organized govern relations among the partners of the foreign limited partnership and between the partners and the foreign limited partnership and the liability of partners as partners for an obligation of the foreign limited partnership.

(b) A foreign limited partnership may not be denied a certificate of authority by reason of any difference between the laws of the jurisdiction under which the foreign limited partnership is organized and the laws of this State.

(c) A certificate of authority does not authorize a foreign limited partnership to engage in any business or exercise any power that a limited partnership may not engage in or exercise in this State.

SECTION 902. APPLICATION FOR CERTIFICATE OF AUTHORITY.

(a) A foreign limited partnership may apply for a certificate of authority to transact business in this State by delivering an application to the [Secretary of State] for filing. The application must state:

(1) the name of the foreign limited partnership and, if the name does not comply with Section 108, an alternate name adopted pursuant to Section 905(a);

(2) the name of the State or other jurisdiction under whose law the foreign limited partnership is organized;

(3) the street and mailing address of the foreign limited partnership's principal office and, if the laws of the jurisdiction under which the foreign limited partnership is organized require the foreign limited partnership to maintain an office in that jurisdiction, the street and mailing address of the required office;

(4) the name and street and mailing address of the foreign limited partnership's initial agent for service of process in this State;

(5) the name and street and mailing address of each of the foreign limited partnership's general partners; and

(6) whether the foreign limited partnership is a foreign limited liability limited partnership.

(b) A foreign limited partnership shall deliver with the completed application a certificate of existence or a record of similar import signed by the [Secretary of State] or other official having custody of the foreign limited partnership's publicly filed records in the

State or other jurisdiction under whose law the foreign limited partnership is organized.

SECTION 903. ACTIVITIES NOT CONSTITUTING TRANSACTING BUSINESS.

(a) Activities of a foreign limited partnership which do not constitute transacting business in this State within the meaning of this [article] include:

(1) maintaining, defending, and settling an action or proceeding;

(2) holding meetings of its partners or carrying on any other activity concerning its internal affairs;

(3) maintaining accounts in financial institutions;

(4) maintaining offices or agencies for the transfer, exchange, and registration of the foreign limited partnership's own securities or maintaining trustees or depositories with respect to those securities;

(5) selling through independent contractors;

(6) soliciting or obtaining orders, whether by mail or electronic means or through employees or agents or otherwise, if the orders require acceptance outside this State before they become contracts;

(7) creating or acquiring indebtedness, mortgages, or security interests in real or personal property;

(8) securing or collecting debts or enforcing mortgages or other security interests in property securing the debts, and holding, protecting, and maintaining property so acquired;

(9) conducting an isolated transaction that is completed within 30 days and is not one in the course of similar transactions of a like manner; and

(10) transacting business in interstate commerce.

(b) For purposes of this [article], the ownership in this State of income-producing real property or tangible personal property, other than property excluded under subsection (a), constitutes transacting business in this State.

(c) This section does not apply in determining the contacts or activities that may subject a foreign limited partnership to service of process, taxation, or regulation under any other law of this State.

SECTION 904. FILING OF CERTIFICATE OF AUTHORITY.

Unless the [Secretary of State] determines that an application for a certificate of authority does not comply with the filing requirements of this [Act], the [Secretary of State], upon payment of all filing fees, shall file the application, prepare, sign, and file a certificate of authority to transact business in this State, and send a copy of the filed certificate, together with a receipt for the fees, to the foreign limited partnership or its representative.

SECTION 905. NONCOMPLYING NAME OF FOREIGN LIMITED PARTNERSHIP.

(a) A foreign limited partnership whose name does not comply with Section 108 may not obtain a certificate of authority until it adopts, for the purpose of transacting business in this State, an alternate name that complies with Section 108. A foreign limited partnership that adopts an alternate name under this subsection and then obtains a certificate of authority with the name need not comply with [fictitious name statute]. After obtaining a certificate of authority with an alternate name, a foreign limited partnership shall transact business in this State under the name unless the for-

eign limited partnership is authorized under [fictitious name statute] to transact business in this State under another name.

(b) If a foreign limited partnership authorized to transact business in this State changes its name to one that does not comply with Section 108, it may not thereafter transact business in this State until it complies with subsection (a) and obtains an amended certificate of authority.

SECTION 906. REVOCATION OF CERTIFICATE OF AUTHORITY.

(a) A certificate of authority of a foreign limited partnership to transact business in this State may be revoked by the [Secretary of State] in the manner provided in subsections (b) and (c) if the foreign limited partnership does not:

(1) pay, within 60 days after the due date, any fee, tax or penalty due to the [Secretary of State] under this [Act] or other law;

(2) deliver, within 60 days after the due date, its annual report required under Section 210;

(3) appoint and maintain an agent for service of process as required by Section 114(b); or

(4) deliver for filing a statement of a change under Section 115 within 30 days after a change has occurred in the name or address of the agent.

(b) In order to revoke a certificate of authority, the [Secretary of State] must prepare, sign, and file a notice of revocation and send a copy to the foreign limited partnership's agent for service of process in this State, or if the foreign limited partnership does not appoint and maintain a proper agent in this State, to the foreign limited partnership's designated office. The notice must state:

(1) the revocation's effective date, which must be at least 60 days after the date the [Secretary of State] sends the copy; and

(2) the foreign limited partnership's failures to comply with subsection (a) which are the reason for the revocation.

(c) The authority of the foreign limited partnership to transact business in this State ceases on the effective date of the notice of revocation unless before that date the foreign limited partnership cures each failure to comply with subsection (a) stated in the notice. If the foreign limited partnership cures the failures, the [Secretary of State] shall so indicate on the filed notice.

SECTION 907. CANCELLATION OF CERTIFICATE OF AUTHORITY; EFFECT OF FAILURE TO HAVE CERTIFICATE.

(a) In order to cancel its certificate of authority to transact business in this State, a foreign limited partnership must deliver to the [Secretary of State] for filing a notice of cancellation. The certificate is canceled when the notice becomes effective under Section 206.

(b) A foreign limited partnership transacting business in this State may not maintain an action or proceeding in this State unless it has a certificate of authority to transact business in this State.

(c) The failure of a foreign limited partnership to have a certificate of authority to transact business in this State does not impair the validity of a contract or act of the foreign limited partnership or prevent the foreign limited partnership from defending an action or proceeding in this State.

(d) A partner of a foreign limited partnership is not liable for the obligations of the foreign limited partnership solely by reason of the foreign limited partnership's having transacted business in this State without a certificate of authority.

(e) If a foreign limited partnership transacts business in this State without a certificate of authority or cancels its certificate of authority, it appoints the [Secretary of State] as its agent for service of process for rights of action arising out of the transaction of business in this State.

SECTION 908.   ACTION BY [ATTORNEY GENERAL].

The [Attorney General] may maintain an action to restrain a foreign limited partnership from transacting business in this State in violation of this [article].

[ARTICLE] 10
ACTIONS BY PARTNERS

SECTION 1001.   DIRECT ACTION BY PARTNER.

(a) Subject to subsection (b), a partner may maintain a direct action against the limited partnership or another partner for legal or equitable relief, with or without an accounting as to the partnership's activities, to enforce the rights and otherwise protect the interests of the partner, including rights and interests under the partnership agreement or this [Act] or arising independently of the partnership relationship.

(b) A partner commencing a direct action under this section is required to plead and prove an actual or threatened injury that is not solely the result of an injury suffered or threatened to be suffered by the limited partnership.

(c) The accrual of, and any time limitation on, a right of action for a remedy under this section is governed by other law. A right to an accounting upon a dissolution and winding up does not revive a claim barred by law.

SECTION 1002.   DERIVATIVE ACTION.

A partner may maintain a derivative action to enforce a right of a limited partnership if:

(1) the partner first makes a demand on the general partners, requesting that they cause the limited partnership to bring an action to enforce the right, and the general partners do not bring the action within a reasonable time; or

(2) a demand would be futile.

SECTION 1003.   PROPER PLAINTIFF.

A derivative action may be maintained only by a person that is a partner at the time the action is commenced and:

(1) that was a partner when the conduct giving rise to the action occurred; or

(2) whose status as a partner devolved upon the person by operation of law or pursuant to the terms of the partnership agreement from a person that was a partner at the time of the conduct.

SECTION 1004.   PLEADING.

In a derivative action, the complaint must state with particularity:

(1) the date and content of plaintiff's demand and the general partners' response to the demand; or

(2) why demand should be excused as futile.

SECTION 1005.   PROCEEDS AND EXPENSES.

(a) Except as otherwise provided in subsection (b):

    (1) any proceeds or other benefits of a derivative action, whether by judgment, compromise, or settlement, belong to the limited partnership and not to the derivative plaintiff;

    (2) if the derivative plaintiff receives any proceeds, the derivative plaintiff shall immediately remit them to the limited partnership.

(b) If a derivative action is successful in whole or in part, the court may award the plaintiff reasonable expenses, including reasonable attorney's fees, from the recovery of the limited partnership.

[ARTICLE] 11
CONVERSION AND MERGER

SECTION 1101.   DEFINITIONS.

In this [article]:

(1) "Constituent limited partnership" means a constituent organization that is a limited partnership.

(2) "Constituent organization" means an organization that is party to a merger.

(3) "Converted organization" means the organization into which a converting organization converts pursuant to Sections 1102 through 1105.

(4) "Converting limited partnership" means a converting organization that is a limited partnership.

(5) "Converting organization" means an organization that converts into another organization pursuant to Section 1102.

(6) "General partner" means a general partner of a limited partnership.

(7) "Governing statute" of an organization means the statute that governs the organization's internal affairs.

(8) "Organization" means a general partnership, including a limited liability partnership; limited partnership, including a limited liability limited partnership; limited liability company; business trust; corporation; or any other person having a governing statute. The term includes domestic and foreign organizations whether or not organized for profit.

(9) "Organizational documents" means:

    (A) for a domestic or foreign general partnership, its partnership agreement;

    (B) for a limited partnership or foreign limited partnership, its certificate of limited partnership and partnership agreement;

    (C) for a domestic or foreign limited liability company, its articles of organization and operating agreement, or comparable records as provided in its governing statute;

    (D) for a business trust, its agreement of trust and declaration of trust;

    (E) for a domestic or foreign corporation for profit, its articles of incorporation, bylaws, and other agreements among its shareholders which are authorized by its governing statute, or comparable records as provided in its governing statute; and

    (F) for any other organization, the basic records that create the organization and determine its internal governance and the relations among the persons that own it, have an interest in it, or are members of it.

(10) "Personal liability" means personal liability for a debt, liability, or other obligation of an organization which is imposed on a person that co-owns, has an interest in, or is a member of the organization:

    (A) by the organization's governing statute solely by reason of the person co-owning, having an interest in, or being a member of the organization; or

    (B) by the organization's organizational documents under a provision of the organization's governing statute authorizing those documents to make one or more specified persons liable for all or specified debts, liabilities, and other obligations of the organization solely by reason of the person or persons co-owning, having an interest in, or being a member of the organization.

(11) "Surviving organization" means an organization into which one or more other organizations are merged. A surviving organization may preexist the merger or be created by the merger.

SECTION 1102.   CONVERSION.

(a) An organization other than a limited partnership may convert to a limited partnership, and a limited partnership may convert to another organization pursuant to this section and Sections 1103 through 1105 and a plan of conversion, if:

(1) the other organization's governing statute authorizes the conversion;

(2) the conversion is not prohibited by the law of the jurisdiction that enacted the governing statute; and

(3) the other organization complies with its governing statute in effecting the conversion.

(b) A plan of conversion must be in a record and must include:

(1) the name and form of the organization before conversion;

(2) the name and form of the organization after conversion; and

(3) the terms and conditions of the conversion, including the manner and basis for converting interests in the converting organization into any combination of money, interests in the converted organization, and other consideration; and

(4) the organizational documents of the converted organization.

SECTION 1103.   ACTION ON PLAN OF CONVERSION BY CONVERTING LIMITED PARTNERSHIP.

(a) Subject to Section 1110, a plan of conversion must be consented to by all the partners of a converting limited partnership.

(b) Subject to Section 1110 and any contractual rights, after a conversion is approved, and at any time before a filing is made under Section 1104, a converting limited partnership may amend the plan or abandon the planned conversion:

(1) as provided in the plan; and

(2) except as prohibited by the plan, by the same consent as was required to approve the plan.

SECTION 1104.   FILINGS REQUIRED FOR CONVERSION; EFFECTIVE DATE.

(a) After a plan of conversion is approved:

(1) a converting limited partnership shall deliver to the [Secretary of State] for filing articles of conversion, which must include:

(A) a statement that the limited partnership has been converted into another organization;

(B) the name and form of the organization and the jurisdiction of its governing statute;

(C) the date the conversion is effective under the governing statute of the converted organization;

(D) a statement that the conversion was approved as required by this [Act];

(E) a statement that the conversion was approved as required by the governing statute of the converted organization; and

(F) if the converted organization is a foreign organization not authorized to transact business in this State, the street and mailing address of an office which the [Secretary of State] may use for the purposes of Section 1105(c); and

(2) if the converting organization is not a converting limited partnership, the converting organization shall deliver to the [Secretary of State] for filing a certificate of limited partnership, which must include, in addition to the information required by Section 201:

(A) a statement that the limited partnership was converted from another organization;

(B) the name and form of the organization and the jurisdiction of its governing statute; and

(C) a statement that the conversion was approved in a manner that complied with the organization's governing statute.

(b) A conversion becomes effective:

(1) if the converted organization is a limited partnership, when the certificate of limited partnership takes effect; and

(2) if the converted organization is not a limited partnership, as provided by the governing statute of the converted organization.

SECTION 1105.   EFFECT OF CONVERSION.

(a) An organization that has been converted pursuant to this [article] is for all purposes the same entity that existed before the conversion.

(b) When a conversion takes effect:

(1) all property owned by the converting organization remains vested in the converted organization;

(2) all debts, liabilities, and other obligations of the converting organization continue as obligations of the converted organization;

(3) an action or proceeding pending by or against the converting organization may be continued as if the conversion had not occurred;

(4) except as prohibited by other law, all of the rights, privileges, immunities, powers, and purposes of the converting organization remain vested in the converted organization;

(5) except as otherwise provided in the plan of conversion, the terms and conditions of the plan of conversion take effect; and

(6) except as otherwise agreed, the conversion does not dissolve a converting limited partnership for the purposes of [Article] 8.

(c) A converted organization that is a foreign organization consents to the jurisdiction of the courts of this State to enforce any obligation owed by the converting limited partnership, if before the conversion the converting limited partnership was subject to suit in this State on the obligation. A converted organization that is a foreign organization and not authorized to transact business in this State appoints the [Secretary of State] as its agent for service of process for purposes of enforcing an obligation under this subsection. Service on the [Secretary of State] under this subsection is made in the same manner and with the same consequences as in Section 117(c) and (d).

SECTION 1106.   MERGER.

(a) A limited partnership may merge with one or more other constituent organizations pursuant to this section and Sections 1107 through 1109 and a plan of merger, if:

(1) the governing statute of each the other organizations authorizes the merger;

(2) the merger is not prohibited by the law of a jurisdiction that enacted any of those governing statutes; and

(3) each of the other organizations complies with its governing statute in effecting the merger.

(b) A plan of merger must be in a record and must include:

(1) the name and form of each constituent organization;

(2) the name and form of the surviving organization and, if the surviving organization is to be created by the merger, a statement to that effect;

(3) the terms and conditions of the merger, including the manner and basis for converting the interests in each constituent organization into any combination of money, interests in the surviving organization, and other consideration;

(4) if the surviving organization is to be created by the merger, the surviving organization's organizational documents; and

(5) if the surviving organization is not to be created by the merger, any amendments to be made by the merger to the surviving organization's organizational documents.

SECTION 1107. ACTION ON PLAN OF MERGER BY CONSTITUENT LIMITED PARTNERSHIP.

(a) Subject to Section 1110, a plan of merger must be consented to by all the partners of a constituent limited partnership.

(b) Subject to Section 1110 and any contractual rights, after a merger is approved, and at any time before a filing is made under Section 1108, a constituent limited partnership may amend the plan or abandon the planned merger:

(1) as provided in the plan; and

(2) except as prohibited by the plan, with the same consent as was required to approve the plan.

SECTION 1108. FILINGS REQUIRED FOR MERGER; EFFECTIVE DATE.

(a) After each constituent organization has approved a merger, articles of merger must be signed on behalf of:

(1) each preexisting constituent limited partnership, by each general partner listed in the certificate of limited partnership; and

(2) each other preexisting constituent organization, by an authorized representative.

(b) The articles of merger must include:

(1) the name and form of each constituent organization and the jurisdiction of its governing statute;

(2) the name and form of the surviving organization, the jurisdiction of its governing statute, and, if the surviving organization is created by the merger, a statement to that effect;

(3) the date the merger is effective under the governing statute of the surviving organization;

(4) if the surviving organization is to be created by the merger:

(A) if it will be a limited partnership, the limited partnership's certificate of limited partnership; or

(B) if it will be an organization other than a limited partnership, the organizational document that creates the organization;

(5) if the surviving organization preexists the merger, any amendments provided for in the plan of merger for the organizational document that created the organization;

(6) a statement as to each constituent organization that the merger was approved as required by the organization's governing statute;

(7) if the surviving organization is a foreign organization not authorized to transact business in this State, the street and mailing address of an office which the [Secretary of State] may use for the purposes of Section 1109(b); and

(8) any additional information required by the governing statute of any constituent organization.

(c) Each constituent limited partnership shall deliver the articles of merger for filing in the [office of the Secretary of State].

(d) A merger becomes effective under this [article]:

(1) if the surviving organization is a limited partnership, upon the later of:

(i) compliance with subsection (c); or

(ii) subject to Section 206(c), as specified in the articles of merger; or

(2) if the surviving organization is not a limited partnership, as provided by the governing statute of the surviving organization.

SECTION 1109. EFFECT OF MERGER.

(a) When a merger becomes effective:

(1) the surviving organization continues or comes into existence;

(2) each constituent organization that merges into the surviving organization ceases to exist as a separate entity;

(3) all property owned by each constituent organization that ceases to exist vests in the surviving organization;

(4) all debts, liabilities, and other obligations of each constituent organization that ceases to exist continue as obligations of the surviving organization;

(5) an action or proceeding pending by or against any constituent organization that ceases to exist may be continued as if the merger had not occurred;

(6) except as prohibited by other law, all of the rights, privileges, immunities, powers, and purposes of each constituent organization that ceases to exist vest in the surviving organization;

(7) except as otherwise provided in the plan of merger, the terms and conditions of the plan of merger take effect; and

(8) except as otherwise agreed, if a constituent limited partnership ceases to exist, the merger does not dissolve the limited partnership for the purposes of [Article] 8;

(9) if the surviving organization is created by the merger:

(A) if it is a limited partnership, the certificate of limited partnership becomes effective; or

(B) if it is an organization other than a limited partnership, the organizational document that creates the organization becomes effective; and

(10) if the surviving organization preexists the merger, any amendments provided for in the articles of merger for the organizational document that created the organization become effective.

(b) A surviving organization that is a foreign organization consents to the jurisdiction of the courts of this State to enforce any obligation owed by a constituent organization, if before the merger the constituent organization was subject to suit in this State on the obligation. A surviving organization that is a foreign organization and not authorized to transact business in this State appoints the [Secretary of State] as its agent for service of process for the purposes of enforcing an obligation under this subsection. Service on the [Secretary of State] under this subsection is made in the same manner and with the same consequences as in Section 117(c) and (d).

SECTION 1110. RESTRICTIONS ON APPROVAL OF CONVERSIONS AND MERGERS AND ON RELINQUISHING LLLP STATUS.

(a) If a partner of a converting or constituent limited partnership will have personal liability with respect to a converted or surviving organization, approval and amendment of a plan of conversion or merger are ineffective without the consent of the partner, unless:

(1) the limited partnership's partnership agreement provides for the approval of the conversion or merger with the consent of fewer than all the partners; and

(2) the partner has consented to the provision of the partnership agreement.

(b) An amendment to a certificate of limited partnership which deletes a statement that the limited partnership is a limited liability limited partnership is ineffective without the consent of each general partner unless:

(1) the limited partnership's partnership agreement provides for the amendment with the consent of less than all the general partners; and

(2) each general partner that does not consent to the amendment has consented to the provision of the partnership agreement.

(c) A partner does not give the consent required by subsection (a) or (b) merely by consenting to a provision of the partnership agreement which permits the partnership agreement to be amended with the consent of fewer than all the partners.

SECTION 1111.   LIABILITY OF GENERAL PARTNER AFTER CONVERSION OR MERGER.

(a) A conversion or merger under this [article] does not discharge any liability under Sections 404 and 607 of a person that was a general partner in or dissociated as a general partner from a converting or constituent limited partnership, but:

(1) the provisions of this [Act] pertaining to the collection or discharge of the liability continue to apply to the liability;

(2) for the purposes of applying those provisions, the converted or surviving organization is deemed to be the converting or constituent limited partnership; and

(3) if a person is required to pay any amount under this subsection:

(A) the person has a right of contribution from each other person that was liable as a general partner under Section 404 when the obligation was incurred and has not been released from the obligation under Section 607; and

(B) the contribution due from each of those persons is in proportion to the right to receive distributions in the capacity of general partner in effect for each of those persons when the obligation was incurred.

(b) In addition to any other liability provided by law:

(1) a person that immediately before a conversion or merger became effective was a general partner in a converting or constituent limited partnership that was not a limited liability limited partnership is personally liable for each obligation of the converted or surviving organization arising from a transaction with a third party after the conversion or merger becomes effective, if, at the time the third party enters into the transaction, the third party:

(A) does not have notice of the conversion or merger; and

(B) reasonably believes that:

(i) the converted or surviving business is the converting or constituent limited partnership;

(ii) the converting or constituent limited partnership is not a limited liability limited partnership; and

(iii) the person is a general partner in the converting or constituent limited partnership; and

(2) a person that was dissociated as a general partner from a converting or constituent limited partnership before the conversion or merger became effective is personally liable for each obligation of the converted or surviving organization arising from a transaction with a third party after the conversion or merger becomes effective, if:

(A) immediately before the conversion or merger became effective the converting or surviving limited partnership was a not a limited liability limited partnership; and

(B) at the time the third party enters into the transaction less than two years have passed since the person dissociated as a general partner and the third party:

(i) does not have notice of the dissociation;

(ii) does not have notice of the conversion or merger; and

(iii) reasonably believes that the converted or surviving organization is the converting or constituent limited partnership, the converting or constituent limited partnership is not a limited liability limited partnership, and the person is a general partner in the converting or constituent limited partnership.

SECTION 1112.   POWER OF GENERAL PARTNERS AND PERSONS DISSOCIATED AS GENERAL PARTNERS TO BIND ORGANIZATION AFTER CONVERSION OR MERGER.

(a) An act of a person that immediately before a conversion or merger became effective was a general partner in a converting or constituent limited partnership binds the converted or surviving organization after the conversion or merger becomes effective, if:

(1) before the conversion or merger became effective, the act would have bound the converting or constituent limited partnership under Section 402; and

(2) at the time the third party enters into the transaction, the third party:

(A) does not have notice of the conversion or merger; and

(B) reasonably believes that the converted or surviving business is the converting or constituent limited partnership and that the person is a general partner in the converting or constituent limited partnership.

(b) An act of a person that before a conversion or merger became effective was dissociated as a general partner from a converting or constituent limited partnership binds the converted or surviving organization after the conversion or merger becomes effective, if:

(1) before the conversion or merger became effective, the act would have bound the converting or constituent limited partnership under Section 402 if the person had been a general partner; and

(2) at the time the third party enters into the transaction, less than two years have passed since the person dissociated as a general partner and the third party:

(A) does not have notice of the dissociation;

(B) does not have notice of the conversion or merger; and

(C) reasonably believes that the converted or surviving organization is the converting or constituent limited partnership and that the person is a general partner in the converting or constituent limited partnership.

(c) If a person having knowledge of the conversion or merger causes a converted or surviving organization to incur an obligation under subsection (a) or (b), the person is liable:

(1) to the converted or surviving organization for any damage caused to the organization arising from the obligation; and

(2) if another person is liable for the obligation, to that other person for any damage caused to that other person arising from the liability.

SECTION 1113.   [ARTICLE] NOT EXCLUSIVE.

This [article] does not preclude an entity from being converted or merged under other law.

[ARTICLE] 12
MISCELLANEOUS PROVISIONS

SECTION 1201.   UNIFORMITY OF APPLICATION AND CONSTRUCTION.

In applying and construing this Uniform Act, consideration must be given to the need to promote uniformity of the law with respect to its subject matter among States that enact it.

SECTION 1202.   SEVERABILITY CLAUSE.

If any provision of this [Act] or its application to any person or circumstance is held invalid, the invalidity does not affect other provisions or applications of this [Act] which can be given effect without the invalid provision or application, and to this end the provisions of this [Act] are severable.

SECTION 1203.   RELATION TO ELECTRONIC SIGNATURES IN GLOBAL AND NATIONAL COMMERCE ACT.

This [Act] modifies, limits, or supersedes the federal Electronic Signatures in Global and National Commerce Act, 15 U.S.C. Section 7001 et seq., but this [Act] does not modify, limit, or supersede Section 101(c) of that Act or authorize electronic delivery of any of the notices described in Section 103(b) of that Act.

SECTION 1204.   EFFECTIVE DATE.

This [Act] takes effect [effective date].

SECTION 1205.   REPEALS.

Effective [all-inclusive date], the following acts and parts of acts are repealed: [the State Limited Partnership Act as amended and in effect immediately before the effective date of this [Act]].

SECTION 1206.   APPLICATION TO EXISTING RELATIONSHIPS.

(a) Before [all-inclusive date], this [Act] governs only:

(1) a limited partnership formed on or after [the effective date of this [Act]]; and

(2) except as otherwise provided in subsections (c) and (d), a limited partnership formed before [the effective date of this [Act]] which elects, in the manner provided in its partnership agreement or by law for amending the partnership agreement, to be subject to this [Act].

(b) Except as otherwise provided in subsection (c), on and after [all-inclusive date] this [Act] governs all limited partnerships.

(c) With respect to a limited partnership formed before [the effective date of this [Act]], the following rules apply except as the partners otherwise elect in the manner provided in the partnership agreement or by law for amending the partnership agreement:

(1) Section 104(c) does not apply and the limited partnership has whatever duration it had under the law applicable immediately before [the effective date of this [Act]].

(2) the limited partnership is not required to amend its certificate of limited partnership to comply with Section 201(a)(4).

(3) Sections 601 and 602 do not apply and a limited partner has the same right and power to dissociate from the limited partnership, with the same consequences, as existed immediately before [the effective date of this [Act]].

(4) Section 603(4) does not apply.

(5) Section 603(5) does not apply and a court has the same power to expel a general partner as the court had immediately before [the effective date of this [Act]].

(6) Section 801(3) does not apply and the connection between a person's dissociation as a general partner and the dissolution of the limited partnership is the same as existed immediately before [the effective date of this [Act]].

(d) With respect to a limited partnership that elects pursuant to subsection (a)(2) to be subject to this [Act], after the election takes effect the provisions of this [Act] relating to the liability of the limited partnership's general partners to third parties apply:

(1) before [all-inclusive date], to:

(A) a third party that had not done business with the limited partnership in the year before the election took effect; and

(B) a third party that had done business with the limited partnership in the year before the election took effect only if the third party knows or has received a notification of the election; and

(2) on and after [all-inclusive date], to all third parties, but those provisions remain inapplicable to any obligation incurred while those provisions were inapplicable under paragraph (1)(B).

SECTION 1207.   SAVINGS CLAUSE. This [Act] does not affect an action commenced, proceeding brought, or right accrued before this [Act] takes effect.

UNIFORM LIMITED LIABILITY COMPANY ACT (1996)

[ARTICLE] 1
GENERAL PROVISIONS

SECTION 101.   DEFINITIONS.

(1) "Articles of organization" means initial, amended, and restated articles of organization and articles of merger. In the case of a foreign limited liability company, the term includes all records serving a similar function required to be filed in the office of the [Secretary of State] or other official having custody of company records in the State or country under whose law it is organized.

(2) "At-will company" means a limited liability company other than a term company.

(3) "Business" includes every trade, occupation, profession, and other lawful purpose, whether or not carried on for profit.

(4) "Debtor in bankruptcy" means a person who is the subject of an order for relief under Title 11 of the United States Code or a comparable order under a successor statute of general application or a comparable order under federal, state, or foreign law governing insolvency.

(5) "Distribution" means a transfer of money, property, or other benefit from a limited liability company to a member in the member's capacity as a member or to a transferee of the member's distributional interest.

(6) "Distributional interest" means all of a member's interest in distributions by the limited liability company.

(7) "Entity" means a person other than an individual.

(8) "Foreign limited liability company" means an unincorporated entity organized under laws other than the laws of this State which afford limited liability to its owners comparable to the liability under Section 303 and is not required to obtain a certificate of authority to transact business under any law of this State other than this [Act].

(9) "Limited liability company" means a limited liability company organized under this [Act].

(10) "Manager" means a person, whether or not a member of a manager-managed company, who is vested with authority under Section 301.

(11) "Manager-managed company" means a limited liability company which is so designated in its articles of organization.

(12) "Member-managed company" means a limited liability company other than a manager-managed company.

(13) "Operating agreement" means the agreement under Section 103 concerning the relations among the members, managers, and limited liability company. The term includes amendments to the agreement.

(14) "Person" means an individual, corporation, business trust, estate, trust, partnership, limited liability company, association, joint venture, government, governmental subdivision, agency, or instrumentality, or any other legal or commercial entity.

(15) "Principal office" means the office, whether or not in this State, where the principal executive office of a domestic or foreign limited liability company is located.

(16) "Record" means information that is inscribed on a tangible medium or that is stored in an electronic or other medium and is retrievable in perceivable form.

(17) "Sign" means to identify a record by means of a signature, mark, or other symbol, with intent to authenticate it.

(18) "State" means a State of the United States, the District of Columbia, the Commonwealth of Puerto Rico, or any territory or insular possession subject to the jurisdiction of the United States.

(19) "Term company" means a limited liability company in which its members have agreed to remain members until the expiration of a term specified in the articles of organization.

(20) "Transfer" includes an assignment, conveyance, deed, bill of sale, lease, mortgage, security interest, encumbrance, and gift.

SECTION 102.   KNOWLEDGE AND NOTICE.

(a) A person knows a fact if the person has actual knowledge of it.

(b) A person has notice of a fact if the person:

(1) knows the fact;

(2) has received a notification of the fact; or

(3) has reason to know the fact exists from all of the facts known to the person at the time in question.

(c) A person notifies or gives a notification of a fact to another by taking steps reasonably required to inform the other person in ordinary course, whether or not the other person knows the fact.

(d) A person receives a notification when the notification:

(1) comes to the person's attention; or

(2) is duly delivered at the person's place of business or at any other place held out by the person as a place for receiving communications.

(e) An entity knows, has notice, or receives a notification of a fact for purposes of a particular transaction when the individual conducting the transaction for the entity knows, has notice, or receives a notification of the fact, or in any event when the fact would have been brought to the individual's attention had the entity exercised reasonable diligence. An entity exercises reasonable diligence if it maintains reasonable routines for communicating significant information to the individual conducting the transaction for the entity and there is reasonable compliance with the routines. Reasonable diligence does not require an individual acting for the entity to communicate information unless the communication is part of the individual's regular duties or the individual has reason to know of the transaction and that the transaction would be materially affected by the information.

SECTION 103. EFFECT OF OPERATING AGREEMENT; NONWAIVABLE PROVISIONS.

(a) Except as otherwise provided in subsection (b), all members of a limited liability company may enter into an operating agreement, which need not be in writing, to regulate the affairs of the company and the conduct of its business, and to govern relations among the members, managers, and company. To the extent the operating agreement does not otherwise provide, this [Act] governs relations among the members, managers, and company.

(b) The operating agreement may not:

(1) unreasonably restrict a right to information or access to records under Section 408;

(2) eliminate the duty of loyalty under Section 409(b) or 603(b)(3), but the agreement may:

(i) identify specific types or categories of activities that do not violate the duty of loyalty, if not manifestly unreasonable; and

(ii) specify the number or percentage of members or disinterested managers that may authorize or ratify, after full disclosure of all material facts, a specific act or transaction that otherwise would violate the duty of loyalty;

(3) unreasonably reduce the duty of care under Section 409(c) or 603(b)(3);

(4) eliminate the obligation of good faith and fair dealing under Section 409(d), but the operating agreement may determine the standards by which the performance of the obligation is to be measured, if the standards are not manifestly unreasonable;

(5) vary the right to expel a member in an event specified in Section 601(6);

(6) vary the requirement to wind up the limited liability company's business in a case specified in Section 801(a)(3) or(a)(4); or

(7) restrict rights of a person, other than a manager, member, and transferee of a member's distributional interest, under this [Act].

SECTION 104. SUPPLEMENTAL PRINCIPLES OF LAW.

(a) Unless displaced by particular provisions of this [Act], the principles of law and equity supplement this [Act].

(b) If an obligation to pay interest arises under this [Act] and the rate is not specified, the rate is that specified in [applicable statute].

SECTION 105. NAME.

(a) The name of a limited liability company must contain "limited liability company" or "limited company" or the abbreviation "L.L.C.," "LLC," "L.C.," or "LC." "Limited" may be abbreviated as "Ltd.," and "company" may be abbreviated as "Co."

(b) Except as authorized by subsections (c) and (d), the name of a limited liability company must be distinguishable upon the records of the [Secretary of State] from:

(1) the name of any corporation, limited partnership, or company incorporated, organized or authorized to transact business, in this State;

(2) a name reserved or registered under Section 106 or 107;

(3) a fictitious name approved under Section 1005 for a foreign company authorized to transact business in this State because its real name is unavailable.

(c) A limited liability company may apply to the [Secretary of State] for authorization to use a name that is not distinguishable upon the records of the [Secretary of State] from one or more of the names described in subsection (b). The [Secretary of State] shall authorize use of the name applied for if:

(1) the present user, registrant, or owner of a reserved name consents to the use in a record and submits an undertaking in form satisfactory to the [Secretary of State] to change the name to a name that is distinguishable upon the records of the [Secretary of State] from the name applied for; or

(2) the applicant delivers to the [Secretary of State] a certified copy of the final judgment of a court of competent jurisdiction establishing the applicant's right to use the name applied for in this State.

(d) A limited liability company may use the name, including a fictitious name, of another domestic or foreign company which is used in this State if the other company is organized or authorized to transact business in this State and the company proposing to use the name has:

(1) merged with the other company;

(2) been formed by reorganization with the other company; or

(3) acquired substantially all of the assets, including the name, of the other company.

SECTION 106. RESERVED NAME.

(a) A person may reserve the exclusive use of the name of a limited liability company, including a fictitious name for a foreign company whose name is not available, by delivering an application to the [Secretary of State] for filing. The application must set forth the name and address of the applicant and the name proposed to be reserved. If the [Secretary of State] finds that the name applied for is available, it must be reserved for the applicant's exclusive use for a nonrenewable 120-day period.

(b) The owner of a name reserved for a limited liability company may transfer the reservation to another person by delivering to the [Secretary of State] a signed notice of the transfer which states the name and address of the transferee.

SECTION 107. REGISTERED NAME.

(a) A foreign limited liability company may register its name subject to the requirements of Section 1005, if the name is distinguishable upon the records of the [Secretary of State] from names that are not available under Section 105(b).

(b) A foreign limited liability company registers its name, or its name with any addition required by Section 1005, by delivering to the [Secretary of State] for filing an application:

(1) setting forth its name, or its name with any addition required by Section 1005, the State or country and date of its organization, and a brief description of the nature of the business in which it is engaged; and

(2) accompanied by a certificate of existence, or a record of similar import, from the State or country of organization.

(c) A foreign limited liability company whose registration is effective may renew it for successive years by delivering for filing in the office of the [Secretary of State] a renewal application complying with subsection (b) between October 1 and December 31 of the preceding year. The renewal application renews the registration for the following calendar year.

(d) A foreign limited liability company whose registration is effective may qualify as a foreign company under its name or consent in writing to the use of its name by a limited liability company later organized under this [Act] or by another foreign company later authorized to transact business in this State. The registered name terminates when the limited liability company is organized or the foreign company qualifies or consents to the qualification of another foreign company under the registered name.

SECTION 108. DESIGNATED OFFICE AND AGENT FOR SERVICE OF PROCESS.

(a) A limited liability company and a foreign limited liability company authorized to do business in this State shall designate and continuously maintain in this State:

(1) an office, which need not be a place of its business in this State; and

(2) an agent and street address of the agent for service of process on the company.

(b) An agent must be an individual resident of this State, a domestic corporation, another limited liability company, or a foreign corporation or foreign company authorized to do business in this State.

SECTION 109. CHANGE OF DESIGNATED OFFICE OR AGENT FOR SERVICE OF PROCESS.

A limited liability company may change its designated office or agent for service of process by delivering to the [Secretary of State] for filing a statement of change which sets forth:

(1) the name of the company;

(2) the street address of its current designated office;

(3) if the current designated office is to be changed, the street address of the new designated office;

(4) the name and address of its current agent for service of process; and

(5) if the current agent for service of process or street address of that agent is to be changed, the new address or the name and street address of the new agent for service of process.

SECTION 110. RESIGNATION OF AGENT FOR SERVICE OF PROCESS.

(a) An agent for service of process of a limited liability company may resign by delivering to the [Secretary of State] for filing a record of the statement of resignation.

(b) After filing a statement of resignation, the [Secretary of State] shall mail a copy to the designated office and another copy to the limited liability company at its principal office.

(c) An agency is terminated on the 31st day after the statement is filed in the office of the [Secretary of State].

SECTION 111. SERVICE OF PROCESS.

(a) An agent for service of process appointed by a limited liability company or a foreign limited liability company is an agent of the company for service of any process, notice, or demand required or permitted by law to be served upon the company.

(b) If a limited liability company or foreign limited liability company fails to appoint or maintain an agent for service of process in this State or the agent for service of process cannot with reasonable diligence be found at the agent's address, the [Secretary of State] is an agent of the company upon whom process, notice, or demand may be served.

(c) Service of any process, notice, or demand on the [Secretary of State] may be made by delivering to and leaving with the [Secretary of State], the [Assistant Secretary of State], or clerk having charge of the limited liability company department of the [Secretary of State's] office duplicate copies of the process, notice, or demand. If the process, notice, or demand is served on the [Secretary of State], the [Secretary of State] shall forward one of the copies by registered or certified mail, return receipt requested, to the company at its designated office. Service is effected under this subsection at the earliest of:

(1) the date the company receives the process, notice, or demand;

(2) the date shown on the return receipt, if signed on behalf of the company; or

(3) five days after its deposit in the mail, if mailed postpaid and correctly addressed.

(d) The [Secretary of State] shall keep a record of all processes, notices, and demands served pursuant to this section and record the time of and the action taken regarding the service.

(e) This section does not affect the right to serve process, notice, or demand in any manner otherwise provided by law.

SECTION 112. NATURE OF BUSINESS AND POWERS.

(a) A limited liability company may be organized under this [Act] for any lawful purpose, subject to any law of this State governing or regulating business.

(b) Unless its articles of organization provide otherwise, a limited liability company has the same powers as an individual to do all things necessary or convenient to carry on its business or affairs, including power to:

(1) sue and be sued, and defend in its name;

(2) purchase, receive, lease, or otherwise acquire, and own, hold, improve, use, and otherwise deal with real or personal property, or any legal or equitable interest in property, wherever located;

(3) sell, convey, mortgage, grant a security interest in, lease, exchange, and otherwise encumber or dispose of all or any part of its property;

(4) purchase, receive, subscribe for, or otherwise acquire, own, hold, vote, use, sell, mortgage, lend, grant a security interest in, or otherwise dispose of and deal in and with, shares or other interests in or obligations of any other entity;

(5) make contracts and guarantees, incur liabilities, borrow money, issue its notes, bonds, and other obligations, which may be convertible into or include the option to purchase other securities of the limited liability company, and secure any of its obligations by a mortgage on or a security interest in any of its property, franchises, or income;

(6) lend money, invest and reinvest its funds, and receive and hold real and personal property as security for repayment;

(7) be a promoter, partner, member, associate, or manager of any partnership, joint venture, trust, or other entity;

(8) conduct its business, locate offices, and exercise the powers granted by this [Act] within or without this State;

(9) elect managers and appoint officers, employees, and agents of the limited liability company, define their duties, fix their compensation, and lend them money and credit;

(10) pay pensions and establish pension plans, pension trusts, profit sharing plans, bonus plans, option plans, and benefit or incentive plans for any or all of its current or former members, managers, officers, employees, and agents;

(11) make donations for the public welfare or for charitable, scientific, or educational purposes; and

(12) make payments or donations, or do any other act, not inconsistent with law, that furthers the business of the limited liability company.

[ARTICLE] 2
ORGANIZATION

SECTION 201.   LIMITED LIABILITY COMPANY AS LEGAL ENTITY.

A limited liability company is a legal entity distinct from its members.

SECTION 202.   ORGANIZATION.

(a) One or more persons may organize a limited liability company, consisting of one or more members, by delivering articles of organization to the office of the [Secretary of State] for filing.

(b) Unless a delayed effective date is specified, the existence of a limited liability company begins when the articles of organization are filed.

(c) The filing of the articles of organization by the [Secretary of State] is conclusive proof that the organizers satisfied all conditions precedent to the creation of a limited liability company.

SECTION 203.   ARTICLES OF ORGANIZATION.

(a) Articles of organization of a limited liability company must set forth:

(1) the name of the company;

(2) the address of the initial designated office;

(3) the name and street address of the initial agent for service of process;

(4) the name and address of each organizer;

(5) whether the company is to be a term company and, if so, the term specified;

(6) whether the company is to be manager-managed, and, if so, the name and address of each initial manager; and

(7) whether one or more of the members of the company are to be liable for its debts and obligations under Section 303(c).

(b) Articles of organization of a limited liability company may set forth:

(1) provisions permitted to be set forth in an operating agreement; or

(2) other matters not inconsistent with law.

(c) Articles of organization of a limited liability company may not vary the nonwaivable provisions of Section 103(b). As to all other matters, if any provision of an operating agreement is inconsistent with the articles of organization:

(1) the operating agreement controls as to managers, members, and members' transferees; and

(2) the articles of organization control as to persons, other than managers, members and their transferees, who reasonably rely on the articles to their detriment.

SECTION 204.   AMENDMENT OR RESTATEMENT OF ARTICLES OF ORGANIZATION.

(a) Articles of organization of a limited liability company may be amended at any time by delivering articles of amendment to the [Secretary of State] for filing. The articles of amendment must set forth the:

(1) name of the limited liability company;

(2) date of filing of the articles of organization; and

(3) amendment to the articles.

(b) A limited liability company may restate its articles of organization at any time. Restated articles of organization must be signed and filed in the same manner as articles of amendment. Restated articles of organization must be designated as such in the heading and state in the heading or in an introductory paragraph the limited liability company's present name and, if it has been changed, all of its former names and the date of the filing of its initial articles of organization.

SECTION 205.   SIGNING OF RECORDS.

(a) Except as otherwise provided in this [Act], a record to be filed by or on behalf of a limited liability company in the office of the [Secretary of State] must be signed in the name of the company by a:

(1) manager of a manager-managed company;

(2) member of a member-managed company;

(3) person organizing the company, if the company has not been formed; or

(4) fiduciary, if the company is in the hands of a receiver, trustee, or other court-appointed fiduciary.

(b) A record signed under subsection (a) must state adjacent to the signature the name and capacity of the signer.

(c) Any person may sign a record to be filed under subsection (a) by an attorney-in-fact. Powers of attorney relating to the signing of records to be filed under subsection (a) by an attorney-in-fact need not be filed in the office of the [Secretary of State] as evidence of authority by the person filing but must be retained by the company.

SECTION 206.   FILING IN OFFICE OF [SECRETARY OF STATE].

(a) Articles of organization or any other record authorized to be filed under this [Act] must be in a medium permitted by the [Secretary of State] and must be delivered to the office of the [Secretary of State]. Unless the [Secretary of State] determines that a record fails to comply as to form with the filing requirements of this [Act], and if all filing fees have been paid, the [Secretary of State] shall file the record and send a receipt for the record and the fees to the limited liability company or its representative.

(b) Upon request and payment of a fee, the [Secretary of State] shall send to the requester a certified copy of the requested record.

(c) Except as otherwise provided in subsection (d) and Section 207(c), a record accepted for filing by the [Secretary of State] is effective:

(1) at the time of filing on the date it is filed, as evidenced by the [Secretary of State's] date and time endorsement on the original record; or

(2) at the time specified in the record as its effective time on the date it is filed.

(d) A record may specify a delayed effective time and date, and if it does so the record becomes effective at the time and date specified. If a delayed effective date but no time is specified, the record is effective at the close of business on that date. If a delayed effective date is later than the 90th day after the record is filed, the record is effective on the 90th day.

SECTION 207.   CORRECTING FILED RECORD.

(a) A limited liability company or foreign limited liability company may correct a record filed by the [Secretary of State] if the record contains a false or erroneous statement or was defectively signed.

(b) A record is corrected:

(1) by preparing articles of correction that:

(i) describe the record, including its filing date, or attach a copy of it to the articles of correction;

(ii) specify the incorrect statement and the reason it is incorrect or the manner in which the signing was defective; and

(iii) correct the incorrect statement or defective signing; and

(2) by delivering the corrected record to the [Secretary of State] for filing.

(c) Articles of correction are effective retroactively on the effective date of the record they correct except as to persons relying on the uncorrected record and adversely affected by the correction. As to those persons, articles of correction are effective when filed.

SECTION 208.   CERTIFICATE OF EXISTENCE OR AUTHORIZATION.

(a) A person may request the [Secretary of State] to furnish a certificate of existence for a limited liability company or a certificate of authorization for a foreign limited liability company.

(b) A certificate of existence for a limited liability company must set forth:

(1) the company's name;

(2) that it is duly organized under the laws of this State, the date of organization, whether its duration is at-will or for a specified term, and, if the latter, the period specified;

(3) if payment is reflected in the records of the [Secretary of State] and if nonpayment affects the existence of the company, that all fees, taxes, and penalties owed to this State have been paid;

(4) whether its most recent annual report required by Section 211 has been filed with the [Secretary of State];

(5) that articles of termination have not been filed; and

(6) other facts of record in the office of the [Secretary of State] which may be requested by the applicant.

(c) A certificate of authorization for a foreign limited liability company must set forth:

(1) the company's name used in this State;

(2) that it is authorized to transact business in this State;

(3) if payment is reflected in the records of the [Secretary of State] and if nonpayment affects the authorization of the company, that all fees, taxes, and penalties owed to this State have been paid;

(4) whether its most recent annual report required by Section 211 has been filed with the [Secretary of State];

(5) that a certificate of cancellation has not been filed; and

(6) other facts of record in the office of the [Secretary of State] which may be requested by the applicant.

(d) Subject to any qualification stated in the certificate, a certificate of existence or authorization issued by the [Secretary of State] may be relied upon as conclusive evidence that the domestic or foreign limited liability company is in existence or is authorized to transact business in this State.

SECTION 209.   LIABILITY FOR FALSE STATEMENT IN FILED RECORD.

If a record authorized or required to be filed under this [Act] contains a false statement, one who suffers loss by reliance on the statement may recover damages for the loss from a person who signed the record or caused another to sign it on the person's behalf and knew the statement to be false at the time the record was signed.

SECTION 210.   FILING BY JUDICIAL ACT.

If a person required by Section 205 to sign any record fails or refuses to do so, any other person who is adversely affected by the failure or refusal may petition the [designate the appropriate court] to direct the signing of the record.   If the court finds that it is proper for the record to be signed and that a person so designated has failed or refused to sign the record, it shall order the [Secretary of State] to sign and file an appropriate record.

SECTION 211.   ANNUAL REPORT FOR [SECRETARY OF STATE].

(a) A limited liability company, and a foreign limited liability company authorized to transact business in this State, shall deliver to the [Secretary of State] for filing an annual report that sets forth:

(1) the name of the company and the State or country under whose law it is organized;

(2) the address of its designated office and the name and address of its agent for service of process in this State;

(3) the address of its principal office; and

(4) the names and business addresses of any managers.

(b) Information in an annual report must be current as of the date the annual report is signed on behalf of the limited liability company.

(c) The first annual report must be delivered to the [Secretary of State] between [January 1 and April 1] of the year following the calendar year in which a limited liability company was organized or a foreign company was authorized to transact business. Subsequent annual reports must be delivered to the [Secretary of State] between [January 1 and April 1] of the ensuing calendar years.

(d) If an annual report does not contain the information required in subsection (a), the [Secretary of State] shall promptly notify the reporting limited liability company or foreign limited liability company and return the report to it for correction. If the report is corrected to contain the information required in subsection (a) and delivered to the [Secretary of State] within 30 days after the effective date of the notice, it is timely filed.

[ARTICLE] 3
RELATIONS OF MEMBERS AND MANAGERS TO PERSONS DEALING WITH LIMITED LIABILITY COMPANY

Section 301. Agency of Members and Managers.
Section 302. Limited Liability Company Liable for Member's or Manager's Actionable Conduct.
Section 303. Liability of Members and Managers.

SECTION 301.   AGENCY OF MEMBERS AND MANAGERS.

(a) Subject to subsections (b) and (c):

(1) Each member is an agent of the limited liability company for the purpose of its business, and an act of a member, including the signing of an instrument in the company's name, for apparently carrying on in the ordinary course the company's business or business of the kind carried on by the company binds the company, unless the member had no authority to act for the company in the particular matter and the person with whom the member was dealing knew or had notice that the member lacked authority.

(2) An act of a member which is not apparently for carrying on in the ordinary course the company's business or business of the kind carried on by the company binds the company only if the act was authorized by the other members.

(b) Subject to subsection (c), in a manager-managed company:

(1) A member is not an agent of the company for the purpose of its business solely by reason of being a member. Each manager is an agent of the company for the purpose of its business, and an act of a manager, including the signing of an instrument in the company's name, for apparently carrying on in the ordinary course the company's business or business of the kind carried on by the company binds the company, unless the manager had no authority to act for the company in the particular matter and the person with whom the manager was dealing knew or had notice that the manager lacked authority.

(2) An act of a manager which is not apparently for carrying on in the ordinary course the company's business or business of the kind carried on by the company binds the company only if the act was authorized under Section 404.

(c) Unless the articles of organization limit their authority, any member of a member-managed company or manager of a manager-managed company may sign and deliver any instrument transferring or affecting the company's interest in real property. The instrument is conclusive in favor of a person who gives value without knowledge of the lack of the authority of the person signing and delivering the instrument.

SECTION 302.   LIMITED LIABILITY COMPANY LIABLE FOR MEMBER'S OR MANAGER'S ACTIONABLE CONDUCT.

A limited liability company is liable for loss or injury caused to a person, or for a penalty incurred, as a result of a wrongful act or omission, or other actionable conduct, of a member or manager acting in the ordinary course of business of the company or with authority of the company.

SECTION 303.   LIABILITY OF MEMBERS AND MANAGERS.

(a) Except as otherwise provided in subsection (c), the debts, obligations, and liabilities of a limited liability company, whether arising in contract, tort, or otherwise, are solely the debts, obligations, and liabilities of the company. A member or manager is not personally liable for a debt, obligation, or liability of the company solely by reason of being or acting as a member or manager.

(b) The failure of a limited liability company to observe the usual company formalities or requirements relating to the exercise of its company powers or management of its business is not a ground for imposing personal liability on the members or managers for liabilities of the company.

(c) All or specified members of a limited liability company are liable in their capacity as members for all or specified debts, obligations, or liabilities of the company if:

(1) a provision to that effect is contained in the articles of organization; and

(2) a member so liable has consented in writing to the adoption of the provision or to be bound by the provision.

[ARTICLE] 4
RELATIONS OF MEMBERS TO EACH OTHER AND TO LIMITED LIABILITY COMPANY

Section 401. Form of Contribution.
Section 402. Member's Liability for Contributions.
Section 403. Member's and Manager's Rights to Payments and Reimbursement.
Section 404. Management of Limited Liability Company.
Section 405. Sharing of and Right to Distributions.
Section 406. Limitations on Distributions.
Section 407. Liability for Unlawful Distributions.
Section 408. Member's Right to Information.
Section 409. General Standards of Member's and Manager's Conduct.
Section 410. Actions by Members.
Section 411. Continuation of Term Company After Expiration of Specified Term.

SECTION 401.   FORM OF CONTRIBUTION.

A contribution of a member of a limited liability company may consist of tangible or intangible property or other benefit to the company, including money, promissory notes, services performed, or other agreements to contribute cash or property, or contracts for services to be performed.

SECTION 402.   MEMBER'S LIABILITY FOR CONTRIBUTIONS.

(a) A member's obligation to contribute money, property, or other benefit to, or to perform services for, a limited liability company is not excused by the member's death, disability, or other inability to perform personally. If a member does not make the required contribution of property or services, the member is obligated at the option of the company to contribute money equal to the value of that portion of the stated contribution which has not been made.

(b) A creditor of a limited liability company who extends credit or otherwise acts in reliance on an obligation described in subsection (a), and without notice of any compromise under Section 404(c)(5), may enforce the original obligation.

SECTION 403.   MEMBER'S AND MANAGER'S RIGHTS TO PAYMENTS AND REIMBURSEMENT.

(a) A limited liability company shall reimburse a member or manager for payments made and indemnify a member or manager for liabilities incurred by the member or manager in the ordinary course of the business of the company or for the preservation of its business or property.

(b) A limited liability company shall reimburse a member for an advance to the company beyond the amount of contribution the member agreed to make.

(c) A payment or advance made by a member which gives rise to an obligation of a limited liability company under subsection (a) or (b) constitutes a loan to the company upon which interest accrues from the date of the payment or advance.

(d) A member is not entitled to remuneration for services performed for a limited liability company, except for reasonable compensation for services rendered in winding up the business of the company.

SECTION 404. MANAGEMENT OF LIMITED LIABILITY COMPANY.

(a) In a member-managed company:

(1) each member has equal rights in the management and conduct of the company's business; and

(2) except as otherwise provided in subsection (c), any matter relating to the business of the company may be decided by a majority of the members.

(b) In a manager-managed company:

(1) each manager has equal rights in the management and conduct of the company's business;

(2) except as otherwise provided in subsection (c), any matter relating to the business of the company may be exclusively decided by the manager or, if there is more than one manager, by a majority of the managers; and

(3) a manager:

(i) must be designated, appointed, elected, removed, or replaced by a vote, approval, or consent of a majority of the members; and

(ii) holds office until a successor has been elected and qualified, unless the manager sooner resigns or is removed.

(c) The only matters of a member or manager-managed company's business requiring the consent of all of the members are:

(1) the amendment of the operating agreement under Section 103;

(2) the authorization or ratification of acts or transactions under Section 103(b)(2)(ii) which would otherwise violate the duty of loyalty;

(3) an amendment to the articles of organization under Section 204;

(4) the compromise of an obligation to make a contribution under Section 402(b);

(5) the compromise, as among members, of an obligation of a member to make a contribution or return money or other property paid or distributed in violation of this [Act];

(6) the making of interim distributions under Section 405(a), including the redemption of an interest;

(7) the admission of a new member;

(8) the use of the company's property to redeem an interest subject to a charging order;

(9) the consent to dissolve the company under Section 801(b)(2);

(10) a waiver of the right to have the company's business wound up and the company terminated under Section 802(b);

(11) the consent of members to merge with another entity under Section 904(c)(1); and

(12) the sale, lease, exchange, or other disposal of all, or substantially all, of the company's property with or without goodwill.

(d) Action requiring the consent of members or managers under this [Act] may be taken without a meeting.

(e) A member or manager may appoint a proxy to vote or otherwise act for the member or manager by signing an appointment instrument, either personally or by the member's or manager's attorney-in-fact.

SECTION 405. SHARING OF AND RIGHT TO DISTRIBUTIONS.

(a) Any distributions made by a limited liability company before its dissolution and winding up must be in equal shares.

(b) A member has no right to receive, and may not be required to accept, a distribution in kind.

(c) If a member becomes entitled to receive a distribution, the member has the status of, and is entitled to all remedies available to, a creditor of the limited liability company with respect to the distribution.

SECTION 406. LIMITATIONS ON DISTRIBUTIONS.

(a) A distribution may not be made if:

(1) the limited liability company would not be able to pay its debts as they become due in the ordinary course of business; or

(2) the company's total assets would be less than the sum of its total liabilities plus the amount that would be needed, if the company were to be dissolved, wound up, and terminated at the time of the distribution, to satisfy the preferential rights upon dissolution, winding up, and termination of members whose preferential rights are superior to those receiving the distribution.

(b) A limited liability company may base a determination that a distribution is not prohibited under subsection (a) on financial statements prepared on the basis of accounting practices and principles that are reasonable in the circumstances or on a fair valuation or other method that is reasonable in the circumstances.

(c) Except as otherwise provided in subsection (e), the effect of a distribution under subsection (a) is measured:

(1) in the case of distribution by purchase, redemption, or other acquisition of a distributional interest in a limited liability company, as of the date money or other property is transferred or debt incurred by the company; and

(2) in all other cases, as of the date the:

(i) distribution is authorized if the payment occurs within 120 days after the date of authorization; or

(ii) payment is made if it occurs more than 120 days after the date of authorization.

(d) A limited liability company's indebtedness to a member incurred by reason of a distribution made in accordance with this section is at parity with the company's indebtedness to its general, unsecured creditors.

(e) Indebtedness of a limited liability company, including indebtedness issued in connection with or as part of a distribution, is not considered a liability for purposes of determinations under subsection (a) if its terms provide that payment of principal and interest are made only if and to the extent that payment of a distribution to members could then be made under this section. If the indebtedness is issued as a distribution, each payment of principal or interest on the indebtedness is treated as a distribution, the effect of which is measured on the date the payment is made.

SECTION 407.   LIABILITY FOR UNLAWFUL DISTRIBUTIONS.

(a) A member of a member-managed company or a member or manager of a manager-managed company who votes for or assents to a distribution made in violation of Section 406, the articles of organization, or the operating agreement is personally liable to the company for the amount of the distribution which exceeds the amount that could have been distributed without violating Section 406, the articles of organization, or the operating agreement if it is established that the member or manager did not perform the member's or manager's duties in compliance with Section 409.

(b) A member of a manager-managed company who knew a distribution was made in violation of Section 406, the articles of organization, or the operating agreement is personally liable to the company, but only to the extent that the distribution received by the member exceeded the amount that could have been properly paid under Section 406.

(c) A member or manager against whom an action is brought under this section may implead in the action all:

(1) other members or managers who voted for or assented to the distribution in violation of subsection (a) and may compel contribution from them; and

(2) members who received a distribution in violation of subsection (b) and may compel contribution from the member in the amount received in violation of subsection (b).

(d) A proceeding under this section is barred unless it is commenced within two years after the distribution.

SECTION 408.   MEMBER'S RIGHT TO INFORMATION.

(a) A limited liability company shall provide members and their agents and attorneys access to its records, if any, at the company's principal office or other reasonable locations specified in the operating agreement. The company shall provide former members and their agents and attorneys access for proper purposes to records pertaining to the period during which they were members. The right of access provides the opportunity to inspect and copy records during ordinary business hours. The company may impose a reasonable charge, limited to the costs of labor and material, for copies of records furnished.

(b) A limited liability company shall furnish to a member, and to the legal representative of a deceased member or member under legal disability:

(1) without demand, information concerning the company's business or affairs reasonably required for the proper exercise of the member's rights and performance of the member's duties under the operating agreement or this [Act]; and

(2) on demand, other information concerning the company's business or affairs, except to the extent the demand or the information demanded is unreasonable or otherwise improper under the circumstances.

(c) A member has the right upon written demand given to the limited liability company to obtain at the company's expense a copy of any written operating agreement.

SECTION 409.   GENERAL STANDARDS OF MEMBER'S AND MANAGER'S CONDUCT.

(a) The only fiduciary duties a member owes to a member-managed company and its other members are the duty of loyalty and the duty of care imposed by subsections (b) and (c).

(b) A member's duty of loyalty to a member-managed company and its other members is limited to the following:

(1) to account to the company and to hold as trustee for it any property, profit, or benefit derived by the member in the conduct or winding up of the company's business or derived from a use by the member of the company's property, including the appropriation of a company's opportunity;

(2) to refrain from dealing with the company in the conduct or winding up of the company's business as or on behalf of a party having an interest adverse to the company; and

(3) to refrain from competing with the company in the conduct of the company's business before the dissolution of the company.

(c) A member's duty of care to a member-managed company and its other members in the conduct of and winding up of the company's business is limited to refraining from engaging in grossly negligent or reckless conduct, intentional misconduct, or a knowing violation of law.

(d) A member shall discharge the duties to a member-managed company and its other members under this [Act] or under the operating agreement and exercise any rights consistently with the obligation of good faith and fair dealing.

(e) A member of a member-managed company does not violate a duty or obligation under this [Act] or under the operating agreement merely because the member's conduct furthers the member's own interest.

(f) A member of a member-managed company may lend money to and transact other business with the company. As to each loan or transaction, the rights and obligations of the member are the same as those of a person who is not a member, subject to other applicable law.

(g) This section applies to a person winding up the limited liability company's business as the personal or legal representative of the last surviving member as if the person were a member.

(h) In a manager-managed company:

(1) a member who is not also a manager owes no duties to the company or to the other members solely by reason of being a member;

(2) a manager is held to the same standards of conduct prescribed for members in subsections (b) through (f);

(3) a member who pursuant to the operating agreement exercises some or all of the rights of a manager in the management and conduct of the company's business is held to the standards of conduct in subsections (b) through (f) to the extent that the member exercises the managerial authority vested in a manager by this [Act]; and

(4) a manager is relieved of liability imposed by law for violation of the standards prescribed by subsections (b) through (f) to the extent of the managerial authority delegated to the members by the operating agreement.

SECTION 410.   ACTIONS BY MEMBERS.

(a) A member may maintain an action against a limited liability company or another member for legal or equitable relief, with or without an accounting as to the company's business, to enforce:

(1) the member's rights under the operating agreement;

(2) the member's rights under this [Act]; and

(3) the rights and otherwise protect the interests of the member, including rights and interests arising independently of the member's relationship to the company.

(b) The accrual, and any time limited for the assertion, of a right of action for a remedy under this section is governed by other law. A right to an accounting upon a dissolution and winding up does not revive a claim barred by law.

SECTION 411.   CONTINUATION OF TERM COMPANY AFTER EXPIRATION OF SPECIFIED TERM.

(a) If a term company is continued after the expiration of the specified term, the rights and duties of the members and managers remain the same as they were at the expiration of the term except to the extent inconsistent with rights and duties of members and managers of an at-will company.

(b) If the members in a member-managed company or the managers in a manager-managed company continue the business without any winding up of the business of the company, it continues as an at-will company.

[ARTICLE] 5
TRANSFEREES AND CREDITORS OF MEMBER

Section 501. Member's Distributional Interest.

Section 502. Transfer of Distributional Interest.

Section 503. Rights of Transferee.

Section 504. Rights of Creditor.

SECTION 501.   MEMBER'S DISTRIBUTIONAL INTEREST.

(a) A member is not a co-owner of, and has no transferable interest in, property of a limited liability company.

(b) A distributional interest in a limited liability company is personal property and, subject to Sections 502 and 503, may be transferred in whole or in part.

(c) An operating agreement may provide that a distributional interest may be evidenced by a certificate of the interest issued by the limited liability company and, subject to Section 503, may also provide for the transfer of any interest represented by the certificate.

SECTION 502.   TRANSFER OF DISTRIBUTIONAL INTEREST.

A transfer of a distributional interest does not entitle the transferee to become or to exercise any rights of a member.   A transfer entitles the transferee to receive, to the extent transferred, only the distributions to which the transferor would be entitled.

SECTION 503.   RIGHTS OF TRANSFEREE.

(a) A transferee of a distributional interest may become a member of a limited liability company if and to the extent that the transferor gives the transferee the right in accordance with authority described in the operating agreement or all other members consent.

(b) A transferee who has become a member, to the extent transferred, has the rights and powers, and is subject to the restrictions and liabilities, of a member under the operating agreement of a limited liability company and this [Act]. A transferee who becomes a member also is liable for the transferor member's obligations to make contributions under Section 402 and for obligations under Section 407 to return unlawful distributions, but the transferee is not obligated for the transferor member's liabilities unknown to the transferee at the time the transferee becomes a member.

(c) Whether or not a transferee of a distributional interest becomes a member under subsection (a), the transferor is not released from liability to the limited liability company under the operating agreement or this [Act].

(d) A transferee who does not become a member is not entitled to participate in the management or conduct of the limited liability company's business, require access to information concerning the company's transactions, or inspect or copy any of the company's records.

(e) A transferee who does not become a member is entitled to:

(1) receive, in accordance with the transfer, distributions to which the transferor would otherwise be entitled;

(2) receive, upon dissolution and winding up of the limited liability company's business:

(i) in accordance with the transfer, the net amount otherwise distributable to the transferor;

(ii) a statement of account only from the date of the latest statement of account agreed to by all the members;

(3) seek under Section 801(a)(5) a judicial determination that it is equitable to dissolve and wind up the company's business.

(f) A limited liability company need not give effect to a transfer until it has notice of the transfer.

SECTION 504.   RIGHTS OF CREDITOR.

(a) On application by a judgment creditor of a member of a limited liability company or of a member's transferee, a court having jurisdiction may charge the distributional interest of the judgment debtor to satisfy the judgment. The court may appoint a receiver of the share of the distributions due or to become due to the judgment debtor and make all other orders, directions, accounts, and inquiries the judgment debtor might have made or which the circumstances may require to give effect to the charging order.

(b) A charging order constitutes a lien on the judgment debtor's distributional interest. The court may order a foreclosure of a lien on a distributional interest subject to the charging order at any time. A purchaser at the foreclosure sale has the rights of a transferee.

(c) At any time before foreclosure, a distributional interest in a limited liability company which is charged may be redeemed:

(1) by the judgment debtor;

(2) with property other than the company's property, by one or more of the other members; or

(3) with the company's property, but only if permitted by the operating agreement.

(d) This [Act] does not affect a member's right under exemption laws with respect to the member's distributional interest in a limited liability company.

(e) This section provides the exclusive remedy by which a judgment creditor of a member or a transferee may satisfy a judgment out of the judgment debtor's distributional interest in a limited liability company.

[ARTICLE] 6
MEMBER'S DISSOCIATION

Section 601. Events Causing Member's Dissociation.
Section 602. Member's Power to Dissociate; Wrongful Dissociation.
Section 603. Effect of Member's Dissociation.

SECTION 601. EVENTS CAUSING MEMBER'S DISSOCIATION.

A member is dissociated from a limited liability company upon the occurrence of any of the following events:

(1) the company's having notice of the member's express will to withdraw upon the date of notice or on a later date specified by the member;

(2) an event agreed to in the operating agreement as causing the member's dissociation;

(3) upon transfer of all of a member's distributional interest, other than a transfer for security purposes or a court order charging the member's distributional interest which has not been foreclosed;

(4) the member's expulsion pursuant to the operating agreement;

(5) the member's expulsion by unanimous vote of the other members if:

   (i) it is unlawful to carry on the company's business with the member;

   (ii) there has been a transfer of substantially all of the member's distributional interest, other than a transfer for security purposes or a court order charging the member's distributional interest which has not been foreclosed;

   (iii) within 90 days after the company notifies a corporate member that it will be expelled because it has filed a certificate of dissolution or the equivalent, its charter has been revoked, or its right to conduct business has been suspended by the jurisdiction of its incorporation, the member fails to obtain a revocation of the certificate of dissolution or a reinstatement of its charter or its right to conduct business; or

   (iv) a partnership or a limited liability company that is a member has been dissolved and its business is being wound up;

(6) on application by the company or another member, the member's expulsion by judicial determination because the member:

   (i) engaged in wrongful conduct that adversely and materially affected the company's business;

   (ii) willfully or persistently committed a material breach of the operating agreement or of a duty owed to the company or the other members under Section 409; or

   (iii) engaged in conduct relating to the company's business which makes it not reasonably practicable to carry on the business with the member;

(7) the member's:

   (i) becoming a debtor in bankruptcy;

   (ii) executing an assignment for the benefit of creditors;

   (iii) seeking, consenting to, or acquiescing in the appointment of a trustee, receiver, or liquidator of the member or of all or substantially all of the member's property; or

   (iv) failing, within 90 days after the appointment, to have vacated or stayed the appointment of a trustee, receiver, or liquidator of the member or of all or substantially all of the member's property obtained without the member's consent or acquiescence, or failing within 90 days after the expiration of a stay to have the appointment vacated;

(8) in the case of a member who is an individual:

   (i) the member's death;

   (ii) the appointment of a guardian or general conservator for the member; or

   (iii) a judicial determination that the member has otherwise become incapable of performing the member's duties under the operating agreement;

(9) in the case of a member that is a trust or is acting as a member by virtue of being a trustee of a trust, distribution of the trust's entire rights to receive distributions from the company, but not merely by reason of the substitution of a successor trustee;

(10) in the case of a member that is an estate or is acting as a member by virtue of being a personal representative of an estate, distribution of the estate's entire rights to receive distributions from the company, but not merely the substitution of a successor personal representative; or

(11) termination of the existence of a member if the member is not an individual, estate, or trust other than a business trust.

SECTION 602. MEMBER'S POWER TO DISSOCIATE; WRONGFUL DISSOCIATION.

(a) Unless otherwise provided in the operating agreement, a member has the power to dissociate from a limited liability company at any time, rightfully or wrongfully, by express will pursuant to Section 601(1).

(b) If the operating agreement has not eliminated a member's power to dissociate, the member's dissociation from a limited liability company is wrongful only if:

   (1) it is in breach of an express provision of the agreement; or

   (2) before the expiration of the specified term of a term company:

      (i) the member withdraws by express will;

      (ii) the member is expelled by judicial determination under Section 601(6);

      (iii) the member is dissociated by becoming a debtor in bankruptcy; or

      (iv) in the case of a member who is not an individual, trust other than a business trust, or estate, the member is expelled or otherwise dissociated because it willfully dissolved or terminated its existence.

(c) A member who wrongfully dissociates from a limited liability company is liable to the company and to the other members for damages caused by the dissociation. The liability is in addition to any other obligation of the member to the company or to the other members.

(d) If a limited liability company does not dissolve and wind up its business as a result of a member's wrongful dissociation under subsection (b), damages sustained by the company for the wrongful dissociation must be offset against distributions otherwise due the member after the dissociation.

SECTION 603. EFFECT OF MEMBER'S DISSOCIATION.

(a) Upon a member's dissociation:

   (1) in an at-will company, the company must cause the dissociated member's distributional interest to be purchased under [Article] 7; and

   (2) in a term company:

      (i) if the company dissolves and winds up its business on or before the expiration of its specified term, [Article] 8 applies to determine the dissociated member's rights to distributions; and

(ii) if the company does not dissolve and wind up its business on or before the expiration of its specified term, the company must cause the dissociated member's distributional interest to be purchased under [Article] 7 on the date of the expiration of the term specified at the time of the member's dissociation.

(b) Upon a member's dissociation from a limited liability company:

(1) the member's right to participate in the management and conduct of the company's business terminates, except as otherwise provided in Section 803, and the member ceases to be a member and is treated the same as a transferee of a member;

(2) the member's duty of loyalty under Section 409(b)(3) terminates; and

(3) the member's duty of loyalty under Section 409(b)(1) and (2) and duty of care under Section 409(c) continue only with regard to matters arising and events occurring before the member's dissociation, unless the member participates in winding up the company's business pursuant to Section 803.

[ARTICLE] 7
MEMBER'S DISSOCIATION WHEN BUSINESS NOT WOUND UP

Section 701. Company Purchase of Distributional Interest.
Section 702. Court Action to Determine Fair Value of Distributional Interest.
Section 703. Dissociated Member's Power to Bind Limited Liability Company.
Section 704. Statement of Dissociation.

SECTION 701.   COMPANY PURCHASE OF DISTRIBUTIONAL INTEREST.

(a) A limited liability company shall purchase a distributional interest of a:

(1) member of an at-will company for its fair value determined as of the date of the member's dissociation if the member's dissociation does not result in a dissolution and winding up of the company's business under Section 801; or

(2) member of a term company for its fair value determined as of the date of the expiration of the specified term that existed on the date of the member's dissociation if the expiration of the specified term does not result in a dissolution and winding up of the company's business under Section 801.

(b) A limited liability company must deliver a purchase offer to the dissociated member whose distributional interest is entitled to be purchased not later than 30 days after the date determined under subsection (a). The purchase offer must be accompanied by:

(1) a statement of the company's assets and liabilities as of the date determined under subsection (a);

(2) the latest available balance sheet and income statement, if any; and

(3) an explanation of how the estimated amount of the payment was calculated.

(c) If the price and other terms of a purchase of a distributional interest are fixed or are to be determined by the operating agreement, the price and terms so fixed or determined govern the purchase unless the purchaser defaults. If a default occurs, the dis-

sociated member is entitled to commence a proceeding to have the company dissolved under Section 801(a)(4)(iv).

(d) If an agreement to purchase the distributional interest is not made within 120 days after the date determined under subsection (a), the dissociated member, within another 120 days, may commence a proceeding against the limited liability company to enforce the purchase. The company at its expense shall notify in writing all of the remaining members, and any other person the court directs, of the commencement of the proceeding. The jurisdiction of the court in which the proceeding is commenced under this subsection is plenary and exclusive.

(e) The court shall determine the fair value of the distributional interest in accordance with the standards set forth in Section 702 together with the terms for the purchase. Upon making these determinations, the court shall order the limited liability company to purchase or cause the purchase of the interest.

(f) Damages for wrongful dissociation under Section 602(b), and all other amounts owing, whether or not currently due, from the dissociated member to a limited liability company, must be offset against the purchase price.

SECTION 702.   COURT ACTION TO DETERMINE FAIR VALUE OF DISTRIBUTIONAL INTEREST.

(a) In an action brought to determine the fair value of a distributional interest in a limited liability company, the court shall:

(1) determine the fair value of the interest, considering among other relevant evidence the going concern value of the company, any agreement among some or all of the members fixing the price or specifying a formula for determining value of distributional interests for any other purpose, the recommendations of any appraiser appointed by the court, and any legal constraints on the company's ability to purchase the interest;

(2) specify the terms of the purchase, including, if appropriate, terms for installment payments, subordination of the purchase obligation to the rights of the company's other creditors, security for a deferred purchase price, and a covenant not to compete or other restriction on a dissociated member; and

(3) require the dissociated member to deliver an assignment of the interest to the purchaser upon receipt of the purchase price or the first installment of the purchase price.

(b) After the dissociated member delivers the assignment, the dissociated member has no further claim against the company, its members, officers, or managers, if any, other than a claim to any unpaid balance of the purchase price and a claim under any agreement with the company or the remaining members that is not terminated by the court.

(c) If the purchase is not completed in accordance with the specified terms, the company is to be dissolved upon application under Sectio 801(b)(5)(iv). If a limited liability company is so dissolved, the dissociated member has the same rights and priorities in the company's assets as if the sale had not been ordered.

(d) If the court finds that a party to the proceeding acted arbitrarily, vexatiously, or not in good faith, it may award one or more other parties their reasonable expenses, including attorney's fees and the expenses of appraisers or other experts, incurred in the proceeding. The finding may be based on the company's failure to make an offer to pay or to comply with Section 701(b).

(e) Interest must be paid on the amount awarded from the date determined under Section 701(a) to the date of payment.

SECTION 703.   DISSOCIATED MEMBER'S POWER TO BIND LIMITED LIABILITY COMPANY.

For two years after a member dissociates without the dissociation resulting in a dissolution and winding up of a limited liability company's business, the company, including a surviving company under [Article] 9, is bound by an act of the dissociated member which would have bound the company under Section 301 before dissociation only if at the time of entering into the transaction the other party:

(1) reasonably believed that the dissociated member was then a member;

(2) did not have notice of the member's dissociation; and

(3) is not deemed to have had notice under Section 704.

SECTION 704.   STATEMENT OF DISSOCIATION.

(a) A dissociated member or a limited liability company may file in the office of the [Secretary of State] a statement of dissociation stating the name of the company and that the member is dissociated from the company.

(b) For the purposes of Sections 301 and 703, a person not a member is deemed to have notice of the dissociation 90 days after the statement of dissociation is filed.

[ARTICLE] 8
WINDING UP COMPANY'S BUSINESS

Section 801.   Events Causing Dissolution and Winding Up of Company's Business.

Section 802.   Limited Liability Company Continues After Dissolution.

Section 803.   Right to Wind Up Limited Liability Company's Business.

Section 804.   Member's or Manager's Power and Liability as Agent After Dissolution.

Section 805.   Articles of Termination.

Section 806.   Distribution of Assets in Winding Up Limited Liability Company's Business.

Section 807.   Known Claims Against Dissolved Limited Liability Company.

Section 808.   Other Claims Against Dissolved Limited Liability Company.

Section 809.   Grounds for Administrative Dissolution.

Section 810.   Procedure for and Effect of Administrative Dissolution.

Section 811.   Restatement Following Administrative Dissolution.

Section 812.   Appeal from Denial of Reinstatement.

SECTION 801.   EVENTS CAUSING DISSOLUTION AND WINDING UP OF COMPANY'S BUSINESS.

(a) A limited liability company is dissolved, and its business must be wound up, upon the occurrence of any of the following events:

(1) an event specified in the operating agreement;

(2) consent of the number or percentage of members specified in the operating agreement;

(3) an event that makes it unlawful for all or substantially all of the business of the company to be continued, but any cure of illegality within 90 days after notice to the company of the

event is effective retroactively to the date of the event for purposes of this section;

(4) on application by a member or a dissociated member, upon entry of a judicial decree that:

(i) the economic purpose of the company is likely to be unreasonably frustrated;

(ii) another member has engaged in conduct relating to the company's business that makes it not reasonably practicable to carry on the company's business with that member;

(iii) it is not otherwise reasonably practicable to carry on the company's business in conformity with the articles of organization and the operating agreement;

(iv) the company failed to purchase the petitioner's distributional interest as required by Section 701; or

(v) the managers or members in control of the company have acted, are acting, or will act in a manner that is illegal, oppressive, fraudulent, or unfairly prejudicial to the petitioner; or

(5) on application by a transferee of a member's interest, a judicial determination that it is equitable to wind up the company's business:

(i) after the expiration of the specified term, if the company was for a specified term at the time the applicant became a transferee by member dissociation, transfer, or entry of a charging order that gave rise to the transfer; or

(ii) at any time, if the company was at will at the time the applicant became a transferee by member dissociation, transfer, or entry of a charging order that gave rise to the transfer.

SECTION 802.   LIMITED LIABILITY COMPANY CONTINUES AFTER DISSOLUTION.

(a) Subject to subsection (b), a limited liability company continues after dissolution only for the purpose of winding up its business.

(b) At any time after the dissolution of a limited liability company and before the winding up of its business is completed, the members, including a dissociated member whose dissociation caused the dissolution, may unanimously waive the right to have the company's business wound up and the company terminated. In that case:

(1) the limited liability company resumes carrying on its business as if dissolution had never occurred and any liability incurred by the company or a member after the dissolution and before the waiver is determined as if the dissolution had never occurred; and

(2) the rights of a third party accruing under Section 804(a) or arising out of conduct in reliance on the dissolution before the third party knew or received a notification of the waiver are not adversely affected.

SECTION 803.   RIGHT TO WIND UP LIMITED LIABILITY COMPANY'S BUSINESS.

(a) After dissolution, a member who has not wrongfully dissociated may participate in winding up a limited liability company's business, but on application of any member, member's legal representative, or transferee, the [designate the appropriate court], for good cause shown, may order judicial supervision of the winding up.

(b) A legal representative of the last surviving member may wind up a limited liability company's business.

(c) A person winding up a limited liability company's business may preserve the company's business or property as a going concern for a reasonable time, prosecute and defend actions and proceedings, whether civil, criminal, or administrative, settle and close the company's business, dispose of and transfer the company's property, discharge the company's liabilities, distribute the assets of the company pursuant to Section 806, settle disputes by mediation or arbitration, and perform other necessary acts.

SECTION 804.   MEMBER'S OR MANAGER'S POWER AND LIABILITY AS AGENT AFTER DISSOLUTION.

(a) A limited liability company is bound by a member's or manager's act after dissolution that:

(1) is appropriate for winding up the company's business; or

(2) would have bound the company under Section 301 before dissolution, if the other party to the transaction did not have notice of the dissolution.

(b) A member or manager who, with knowledge of the dissolution, subjects a limited liability company to liability by an act that is not appropriate for winding up the company's business is liable to the company for any damage caused to the company arising from the liability.

SECTION 805.   ARTICLES OF TERMINATION.

(a) At any time after dissolution and winding up, a limited liability company may terminate its existence by filing with the [Secretary of State] articles of termination stating:

(1) the name of the company;

(2) the date of the dissolution; and

(3) that the company's business has been wound up and the legal existence of the company has been terminated.

(b) The existence of a limited liability company is terminated upon the filing of the articles of termination, or upon a later effective date, if specified in the articles of termination.

SECTION 806.   DISTRIBUTION OF ASSETS IN WINDING UP LIMITED LIABILITY COMPANY'S BUSINESS.

(a) In winding up a limited liability company's business, the assets of the company must be applied to discharge its obligations to creditors, including members who are creditors. Any surplus must be applied to pay in money the net amount distributable to members in accordance with their right to distributions under subsection (b).

(b) Each member is entitled to a distribution upon the winding up of the limited liability company's business consisting of a return of all contributions which have not previously been returned and a distribution of any remainder in equal shares.

SECTION 807.   KNOWN CLAIMS AGAINST DISSOLVED LIMITED LIABILITY COMPANY.

(a) A dissolved limited liability company may dispose of the known claims against it by following the procedure described in this section.

(b) A dissolved limited liability company shall notify its known claimants in writing of the dissolution. The notice must:

(1) specify the information required to be included in a claim;

(2) provide a mailing address where the claim is to be sent;

(3) state the deadline for receipt of the claim, which may not be less than 120 days after the date the written notice is received by the claimant; and

(4) state that the claim will be barred if not received by the deadline.

(c) A claim against a dissolved limited liability company is barred if the requirements of subsection (b) are met, and:

(1) the claim is not received by the specified deadline; or

(2) in the case of a claim that is timely received but rejected by the dissolved company, the claimant does not commence a proceeding to enforce the claim within 90 days after the receipt of the notice of the rejection.

(d) For purposes of this section, "claim" does not include a contingent liability or a claim based on an event occurring after the effective date of dissolution.

SECTION 808.   OTHER CLAIMS AGAINST DISSOLVED LIMITED LIABILITY COMPANY.

(a) A dissolved limited liability company may publish notice of its dissolution and request persons having claims against the company to present them in accordance with the notice.

(b) The notice must:

(1) be published at least once in a newspaper of general circulation in the [county] in which the dissolved limited liability company's principal office is located or, if none in this State, in which its designated office is or was last located;

(2) describe the information required to be contained in a claim and provide a mailing address where the claim is to be sent; and

(3) state that a claim against the limited liability company is barred unless a proceeding to enforce the claim is commenced within five years after publication of the notice.

(c) If a dissolved limited liability company publishes a notice in accordance with subsection (b), the claim of each of the following claimants is barred unless the claimant commences a proceeding to enforce the claim against the dissolved company within five years after the publication date of the notice:

(1) a claimant who did not receive written notice under Section 807;

(2) a claimant whose claim was timely sent to the dissolved company but not acted on; and

(3) a claimant whose claim is contingent or based on an event occurring after the effective date of dissolution.

(d) A claim not barred under this section may be enforced:

(1) against the dissolved limited liability company, to the extent of its undistributed assets; or

(2) if the assets have been distributed in liquidation, against a member of the dissolved company to the extent of the member's proportionate share of the claim or the company's assets distributed to the member in liquidation, whichever is less, but a member's total liability for all claims under this section may not exceed the total amount of assets distributed to the member.

SECTION 809.   GROUNDS FOR ADMINISTRATIVE DISSOLUTION.

The [Secretary of State] may commence a proceeding to dissolve a limited liability company administratively if the company does not:

(1) pay any fees, taxes, or penalties imposed by this [Act] or other law within 60 days after they are due; or

(2) deliver its annual report to the [Secretary of State] within 60 days after it is due.

SECTION 810. PROCEDURE FOR AND EFFECT OF ADMINISTRATIVE DISSOLUTION.

(a) If the [Secretary of State] determines that a ground exists for administratively dissolving a limited liability company, the [Secretary of State] shall enter a record of the determination and serve the company with a copy of the record.

(b) If the company does not correct each ground for dissolution or demonstrate to the reasonable satisfaction of the [Secretary of State] that each ground determined by the [Secretary of State] does not exist within 60 days after service of the notice, the [Secretary of State] shall administratively dissolve the company by signing a certification of the dissolution that recites the ground for dissolution and its effective date. The [Secretary of State] shall file the original of the certificate and serve the company with a copy of the certificate.

(c) A company administratively dissolved continues its existence but may carry on only business necessary to wind up and liquidate its business and affairs under Section 802 and to notify claimants under Sections 807 and 808.

(d) The administrative dissolution of a company does not terminate the authority of its agent for service of process.

SECTION 811. REINSTATEMENT FOLLOWING ADMINISTRATIVE DISSOLUTION.

(a) A limited liability company administratively dissolved may apply to the [Secretary of State] for reinstatement within two years after the effective date of dissolution. The application must:

(1) recite the name of the company and the effective date of its administrative dissolution;

(2) state that the ground for dissolution either did not exist or have been eliminated;

(3) state that the company's name satisfies the requirements of Section 105; and

(4) contain a certificate from the [taxing authority] reciting that all taxes owed by the company have been paid.

(b) If the [Secretary of State] determines that the application contains the information required by subsection (a) and that the information is correct, the [Secretary of State] shall cancel the certificate of dissolution and prepare a certificate of reinstatement that recites this determination and the effective date of reinstatement, file the original of the certificate, and serve the company with a copy of the certificate.

(c) When reinstatement is effective, it relates back to and takes effect as of the effective date of the administrative dissolution and the company may resume its business as if the administrative dissolution had never occurred.

SECTION 812. APPEAL FROM DENIAL OF REINSTATEMENT.

(a) If the [Secretary of State] denies a limited liability company's application for reinstatement following administrative dissolution, the [Secretary of State] shall serve the company with a record that explains the reason or reasons for denial.

(b) The company may appeal the denial of reinstatement to the [name appropriate] court within 30 days after service of the notice of denial is perfected. The company appeals by petitioning the court to set aside the dissolution and attaching to the petition copies of the [Secretary of State's] certificate of dissolution, the company's application for reinstatement, and the [Secretary of State's] notice of denial.

(c) The court may summarily order the [Secretary of State] to reinstate the dissolved company or may take other action the court considers appropriate.

(d) The court's final decision may be appealed as in other civil proceedings.

[ARTICLE] 9
CONVERSIONS AND MERGERS

SECTION 901. DEFINITIONS.

In this [article]:

(1) "Corporation" means a corporation under [the State Corporation Act], a predecessor law, or comparable law of another jurisdiction.

(2) "General partner" means a partner in a partnership and a general partner in a limited partnership.

(3) "Limited partner" means a limited partner in a limited partnership.

(4) "Limited partnership" means a limited partnership created under [the State Limited Partnership Act], a predecessor law, or comparable law of another jurisdiction.

(5) "Partner" includes a general partner and a limited partner.

(6) "Partnership" means a general partnership under [the State Partnership Act], a predecessor law, or comparable law of another jurisdiction.

(7) "Partnership agreement" means an agreement among the partners concerning the partnership or limited partnership.

(8) "Shareholder" means a shareholder in a corporation.

SECTION 902. CONVERSION OF PARTNERSHIP OR LIMITED PARTNERSHIP TO LIMITED LIABILITY COMPANY.

(a) A partnership or limited partnership may be converted to a limited liability company pursuant to this section.

(b) The terms and conditions of a conversion of a partnership or limited partnership to a limited liability company must be approved by all of the partners or by a number or percentage of the partners required for conversion in the partnership agreement.

(c) An agreement of conversion must set forth the terms and conditions of the conversion of the interests of partners of a partnership or of a limited partnership, as the case may be, into interests in the converted limited liability company or the cash or other consideration to be paid or delivered as a result of the conversion of the interests of the partners, or a combination thereof.

(d) After a conversion is approved under subsection (b), the partnership or limited partnership shall file articles of organization in the office of the [Secretary of State] which satisfy the requirements of Section 203 and contain:

(1) a statement that the partnership or limited partnership was converted to a limited liability company from a partnership or limited partnership, as the case may be;

(2) its former name;

(3) a statement of the number of votes cast by the partners entitled to vote for and against the conversion and, if the vote is less than unanimous, the number or percentage required to approve the conversion under subsection (b); and

(4) in the case of a limited partnership, a statement that the certificate of limited partnership is to be canceled as of the date the conversion took effect.

(e) In the case of a limited partnership, the filing of articles of organization under subsection (d) cancels its certificate of limited partnership as of the date the conversion took effect.

(f) A conversion takes effect when the articles of organization are filed in the office of the [Secretary of State] or at any later date specified in the articles of organization.

(g) A general partner who becomes a member of a limited liability company as a result of a conversion remains liable as a partner for an obligation incurred by the partnership or limited partnership before the conversion takes effect.

(h) A general partner's liability for all obligations of the limited liability company incurred after the conversion takes effect is that of a member of the company. A limited partner who becomes a member as a result of a conversion remains liable only to the extent the limited partner was liable for an obligation incurred by the limited partnership before the conversion takes effect.

SECTION 903.   EFFECT OF CONVERSION; ENTITY UNCHANGED.

(a) A partnership or limited partnership that has been converted pursuant to this [article] is for all purposes the same entity that existed before the conversion.

(b) When a conversion takes effect:

(1) all property owned by the converting partnership or limited partnership vests in the limited liability company;

(2) all debts, liabilities, and other obligations of the converting partnership or limited partnership continue as obligations of the limited liability company;

(3) an action or proceeding pending by or against the converting partnership or limited partnership may be continued as if the conversion had not occurred;

(4) except as prohibited by other law, all of the rights, privileges, immunities, powers, and purposes of the converting partnership or limited partnership vest in the limited liability company; and

(5) except as otherwise provided in the agreement of conversion under Section 902(c), all of the partners of the converting partnership continue as members of the limited liability company.

SECTION 904.   MERGER OF ENTITIES.

(a) Pursuant to a plan of merger approved under subsection (c), a limited liability company may be merged with or into one or more limited liability companies, foreign limited liability companies, corporations, foreign corporations, partnerships, foreign partnerships, limited partnerships, foreign limited partnerships, or other domestic or foreign entities.

(b) A plan of merger must set forth:

(1) the name of each entity that is a party to the merger;

(2) the name of the surviving entity into which the other entities will merge;

(3) the type of organization of the surviving entity;

(4) the terms and conditions of the merger;

(5) the manner and basis for converting the interests of each party to the merger into interests or obligations of the surviving entity, or into money or other property in whole or in part; and

(6) the street address of the surviving entity's principal place of business.

(c) A plan of merger must be approved:

(1) in the case of a limited liability company that is a party to the merger, by all of the members or by a number or percentage of members specified in the operating agreement;

(2) in the case of a foreign limited liability company that is a party to the merger, by the vote required for approval of a merger by the law of the State or foreign jurisdiction in which the foreign limited liability company is organized;

(3) in the case of a partnership or domestic limited partnership that is a party to the merger, by the vote required for approval of a conversion under Section 902(b); and

(4) in the case of any other entities that are parties to the merger, by the vote required for approval of a merger by the law of this State or of the State or foreign jurisdiction in which the entity is organized and, in the absence of such a requirement, by all the owners of interests in the entity.

(d) After a plan of merger is approved and before the merger takes effect, the plan may be amended or abandoned as provided in the plan.

(e) The merger is effective upon the filing of the articles of merger with the [Secretary of State], or at such later date as the articles may provide.

SECTION 905.   ARTICLES OF MERGER.

(a) After approval of the plan of merger under Section 904(c), unless the merger is abandoned under Section 904(d), articles of merger must be signed on behalf of each limited liability company and other entity that is a party to the merger and delivered to the [Secretary of State] for filing. The articles must set forth:

(1) the name and jurisdiction of formation or organization of each of the limited liability companies and other entities that are parties to the merger;

(2) for each limited liability company that is to merge, the date its articles of organization were filed with the [Secretary of State];

(3) that a plan of merger has been approved and signed by each limited liability company and other entity that is to merge;

(4) the name and address of the surviving limited liability company or other surviving entity;

(5) the effective date of the merger;

(6) if a limited liability company is the surviving entity, such changes in its articles of organization as are necessary by reason of the merger;

(7) if a party to a merger is a foreign limited liability company, the jurisdiction and date of filing of its initial articles of or-

ganization and the date when its application for authority was filed by the [Secretary of State] or, if an application has not been filed, a statement to that effect; and

(8) if the surviving entity is not a limited liability company, an agreement that the surviving entity may be served with process in this State and is subject to liability in any action or proceeding for the enforcement of any liability or obligation of any limited liability company previously subject to suit in this State which is to merge, and for the enforcement, as provided in this [Act], of the right of members of any limited liability company to receive payment for their interest against the surviving entity.

(b) If a foreign limited liability company is the surviving entity of a merger, it may not do business in this State until an application for that authority is filed with the [Secretary of State].

(c) The surviving limited liability company or other entity shall furnish a copy of the plan of merger, on request and without cost, to any member of any limited liability company or any person holding an interest in any other entity that is to merge.

(d) Articles of merger operate as an amendment to the limited liability company's articles of organization.

SECTION 906.   EFFECT OF MERGER.

(a) When a merger takes effect:

(1) the separate existence of each limited liability company and other entity that is a party to the merger, other than the surviving entity, terminates;

(2) all property owned by each of the limited liability companies and other entities that are party to the merger vests in the surviving entity;

(3) all debts, liabilities, and other obligations of each limited liability company and other entity that is party to the merger become the obligations of the surviving entity;

(4) an action or proceeding pending by or against a limited liability company or other party to a merger may be continued as if the merger had not occurred or the surviving entity may be substituted as a party to the action or proceeding; and

(5) except as prohibited by other law, all the rights, privileges, immunities, powers, and purposes of every limited liability company and other entity that is a party to a merger vest in the surviving entity.

(b) The [Secretary of State] is an agent for service of process in an action or proceeding against the surviving foreign entity to enforce an obligation of any party to a merger if the surviving foreign entity fails to appoint or maintain an agent designated for service of process in this State or the agent for service of process cannot with reasonable diligence be found at the designated office. Upon receipt of process, the [Secretary of State] shall send a copy of the process by registered or certified mail, return receipt requested, to the surviving entity at the address set forth in the articles of merger. Service is effected under this subsection at the earliest of:

(1) the date the company receives the process, notice, or demand;

(2) the date shown on the return receipt, if signed on behalf of the company; or

(3) five days after its deposit in the mail, if mailed postpaid and correctly addressed.

(c) A member of the surviving limited liability company is liable for all obligations of a party to the merger for which the member was personally liable before the merger.

(d) Unless otherwise agreed, a merger of a limited liability company that is not the surviving entity in the merger does not require the limited liability company to wind up its business under this [Act] or pay its liabilities and distribute its assets pursuant to this [Act].

(e) Articles of merger serve as articles of dissolution for a limited liability company that is not the surviving entity in the merger.

SECTION 907.   [ARTICLE] NOT EXCLUSIVE.

This [article] does not preclude an entity from being converted or merged under other law.

[ARTICLE] 10
FOREIGN LIMITED LIABILITY COMPANIES

SECTION 1001.   LAW GOVERNING FOREIGN LIMITED LIABILITY COMPANIES.

(a) The laws of the State or other jurisdiction under which a foreign limited liability company is organized govern its organization and internal affairs and the liability of its managers, members, and their transferees.

(b) A foreign limited liability company may not be denied a certificate of authority by reason of any difference between the laws of another jurisdiction under which the foreign company is organized and the laws of this State.

(c) A certificate of authority does not authorize a foreign limited liability company to engage in any business or exercise any power that a limited liability company may not engage in or exercise in this State.

SECTION 1002.   APPLICATION FOR CERTIFICATE OF AUTHORITY.

(a) A foreign limited liability company may apply for a certificate of authority to transact business in this State by delivering an application to the [Secretary of State] for filing. The application must set forth:

(1) the name of the foreign company or, if its name is unavailable for use in this State, a name that satisfies the requirements of Section 1005;

(2) the name of the State or country under whose law it is organized;

(3) the street address of its principal office;

(4) the address of its initial designated office in this State;

(5) the name and street address of its initial agent for service of process in this State;

(6) whether the duration of the company is for a specified term and, if so, the period specified;

(7) whether the company is manager-managed, and, if so, the name and address of each initial manager; and

(8) whether the members of the company are to be liable for its debts and obligations under a provision similar to Section 303(c).

(b) A foreign limited liability company shall deliver with the completed application a certificate of existence or a record of similar import authenticated by the secretary of state or other official having custody of company records in the State or country under whose law it is organized.

SECTION 1003. ACTIVITIES NOT CONSTITUTING TRANSACTING BUSINESS.

(a) Activities of a foreign limited liability company that do not constitute transacting business in this State within the meaning of this [article] include:

(1) maintaining, defending, or settling an action or proceeding;

(2) holding meetings of its members or managers or carrying on any other activity concerning its internal affairs;

(3) maintaining bank accounts;

(4) maintaining offices or agencies for the transfer, exchange, and registration of the foreign company's own securities or maintaining trustees or depositories with respect to those securities;

(5) selling through independent contractors;

(6) soliciting or obtaining orders, whether by mail or through employees or agents or otherwise, if the orders require acceptance outside this State before they become contracts;

(7) creating or acquiring indebtedness, mortgages, or security interests in real or personal property;

(8) securing or collecting debts or enforcing mortgages or other security interests in property securing the debts, and holding, protecting, and maintaining property so acquired;

(9) conducting an isolated transaction that is completed within 30 days and is not one in the course of similar transactions of a like manner; and

(10) transacting business in interstate commerce.

(b) For purposes of this [article], the ownership in this State of income-producing real property or tangible personal property, other than property excluded under subsection (a), constitutes transacting business in this State.

(c) This section does not apply in determining the contacts or activities that may subject a foreign limited liability company to service of process, taxation, or regulation under any other law of this State.

SECTION 1004. ISSUANCE OF CERTIFICATE OF AUTHORITY.

Unless the [Secretary of State] determines that an application for a certificate of authority fails to comply as to form with the filing requirements of this [Act], the [Secretary of State], upon payment of all filing fees, shall file the application and send a receipt for it and the fees to the limited liability company or its representative.

SECTION 1005. NAME OF FOREIGN LIMITED LIABILITY COMPANY.

(a) If the name of a foreign limited liability company does not satisfy the requirements of Section 105, the company, to obtain or maintain a certificate of authority to transact business in this State, must use a fictitious name to transact business in this State if its real name is unavailable and it delivers to the [Secretary of State] for filing a copy of the resolution of its managers, in the case of a manager-managed company, or of its members, in the case of a member-managed company, adopting the fictitious name.

(b) Except as authorized by subsections (c) and (d), the name, including a fictitious name to be used to transact business in this State, of a foreign limited liability company must be distinguishable upon the records of the [Secretary of State] from:

(1) the name of any corporation, limited partnership, or company incorporated, organized, or authorized to transact business in this State;

(2) a name reserved or registered under Section 106 or 107; and

(3) the fictitious name of another foreign limited liability company authorized to transact business in this State.

(c) A foreign limited liability company may apply to the [Secretary of State] for authority to use in this State a name that is not distinguishable upon the records of the [Secretary of State] from a name described in subsection (b). The [Secretary of State] shall authorize use of the name applied for if:

(1) the present user, registrant, or owner of a reserved name consents to the use in a record and submits an undertaking in form satisfactory to the [Secretary of State] to change its name to a name that is distinguishable upon the records of the [Secretary of State] from the name of the foreign applying limited liability company; or

(2) the applicant delivers to the [Secretary of State] a certified copy of a final judgment of a court establishing the applicant's right to use the name applied for in this State.

(d) A foreign limited liability company may use in this State the name, including the fictitious name, of another domestic or foreign entity that is used in this State if the other entity is incorporated, organized, or authorized to transact business in this State and the foreign limited liability company:

(1) has merged with the other entity;

(2) has been formed by reorganization of the other entity; or

(3) has acquired all or substantially all of the assets, including the name, of the other entity.

(e) If a foreign limited liability company authorized to transact business in this State changes its name to one that does not satisfy the requirements of Section 105, it may not transact business in this State under the name as changed until it adopts a name satisfying the requirements of Section 105 and obtains an amended certificate of authority.

SECTION 1006. REVOCATION OF CERTIFICATE OF AUTHORITY.

(a) A certificate of authority of a foreign limited liability company to transact business in this State may be revoked by the [Secretary of State] in the manner provided in subsection (b) if:

(1) the company fails to:

(i) pay any fees, taxes, and penalties owed to this State;

(ii) deliver its annual report required under Section 211 to the [Secretary of State] within 60 days after it is due;

(iii) appoint and maintain an agent for service of process as required by this [article]; or

(iv) file a statement of a change in the name or business address of the agent as required by this [article]; or

(2) a misrepresentation has been made of any material matter in any application, report, affidavit, or other record submitted by the company pursuant to this [article].

(b) The [Secretary of State] may not revoke a certificate of authority of a foreign limited liability company unless the [Secretary of State] sends the company notice of the revocation, at least 60 days before its effective date, by a record addressed to its agent for service of process in this State, or if the company fails to appoint and maintain a proper agent in this State, addressed to the office required to be maintained by Section 108. The notice must specify the cause for the revocation of the certificate of authority. The authority of the company to transact business in this

State ceases on the effective date of the revocation unless the foreign limited liability company cures the failure before that date.

SECTION 1007.   CANCELLATION OF AUTHORITY.

A foreign limited liability company may cancel its authority to transact business in this State by filing in the office of the [Secretary of State] a certificate of cancellation.   Cancellation does not terminate the authority of the [Secretary of State] to accept service of process on the company for [claims for relief] arising out of the transactions of business in this State.

SECTION 1008.   EFFECT OF FAILURE TO OBTAIN CERTIFICATE OF AUTHORITY.

(a) A foreign limited liability company transacting business in this State may not maintain an action or proceeding in this State unless it has a certificate of authority to transact business in this State.

(b) The failure of a foreign limited liability company to have a certificate of authority to transact business in this State does not impair the validity of a contract or act of the company or prevent the foreign limited liability company from defending an action or proceeding in this State.

(c) Limitations on personal liability of managers, members, and their transferees are not waived solely by transacting business in this State without a certificate of authority.

(d) If a foreign limited liability company transacts business in this State without a certificate of authority, it appoints the [Secretary of State] as its agent for service of process for [claims for relief] arising out of the transaction of business in this State.

SECTION 1009.   ACTION BY [ATTORNEY GENERAL].

The [Attorney General] may maintain an action to restrain a foreign limited liability company from transacting business in this State in violation of this [article].

[ARTICLE] 11
DERIVATIVE ACTIONS

SECTION 1101.   RIGHT OF ACTION.

A member of a limited liability company may maintain an action in the right of the company if the members or managers having authority to do so have refused to commence the action or an effort to cause those members or managers to commence the action is not likely to succeed.

SECTION 1102.   PROPER PLAINTIFF.

In a derivative action for a limited liability company, the plaintiff must be a member of the company when the action is commenced; and:

(1) must have been a member at the time of the transaction of which the plaintiff complains; or

(2) the plaintiff's status as a member must have devolved upon the plaintiff by operation of law or pursuant to the terms of the operating agreement from a person who was a member at the time of the transaction.

SECTION 1103.   PLEADING.

In a derivative action for a limited liability company, the complaint must set forth with particularity the effort of the plaintiff to secure initiation of the action by a member or manager or the reasons for not making the effort.

SECTION 1104.   EXPENSES.

If a derivative action for a limited liability company is successful, in whole or in part, or if anything is received by the plaintiff as a result of a judgment, compromise, or settlement of an action or claim, the court may award the plaintiff reasonable expenses, including reasonable attorney's fees, and shall direct the plaintiff to remit to the limited liability company the remainder of the proceeds received.

[ARTICLE] 12
MISCELLANEOUS PROVISIONS

SECTION 1201.   UNIFORMITY OF APPLICATION AND CONSTRUCTION.

This [Act] shall be applied and construed to effectuate its general purpose to make uniform the law with respect to the subject of this [Act] among States enacting it.

SECTION 1202.   SHORT TITLE.

This [Act] may be cited as the Uniform Limited Liability Company Act (1996).

SECTION 1203.   SEVERABILITY CLAUSE.

If any provision of this [Act] or its application to any person or circumstance is held invalid, the invalidity does not affect other provisions or applications of this [Act] which can be given effect without the invalid provision or application, and to this end the provisions of this [Act] are severable.

SECTION 1204.   EFFECTIVE DATE.

This [Act] takes effect [_____].

SECTION 1205.   TRANSITIONAL PROVISIONS.

(a) Before January 1, 199__, this [Act] governs only a limited liability company organized:

(1) after the effective date of this [Act], unless the company is continuing the business of a dissolved limited liability company under [Section of the existing Limited Liability Company Act]; and

(2) before the effective date of this [Act], which elects, as provided by subsection (c), to be governed by this [Act].

(b) On and after January 1, 199__, this [Act] governs all limited liability companies.

(c) Before January 1, 199__, a limited liability company voluntarily may elect, in the manner provided in its operating agreement or by law for amending the operating agreement, to be governed by this [Act].

SECTION 1206.   SAVINGS CLAUSE.

This [Act] does not affect an action or proceeding commenced or right accrued before the effective date of this [Act].

MODEL BUSINESS CORPORATION ACT

CHAPTER 1. GENERAL PROVISIONS
Subchapter A. Short Title and Reservation of Power

§ 1.01. Short Title.
This Act shall be known and may be cited as the "[name of state] Business Corporation Act."

§ 1.02. Reservation of Power to Amend or Repeal.
The [name of state legislature] has power to amend or repeal all or part of this Act at any time and all domestic and foreign corporations subject to this Act are governed by the amendment or repeal.

Subchapter B. Filing Documents

§ 1.20. Requirements for Documents; Extrinsic Facts.
(a) A document must satisfy the requirements of this section, and of any other section that adds to or varies these requirements, to be entitled to filing by the secretary of state.

(b) This Act must require or permit filing the document in the office of the secretary of state.

(c) The document must contain the information required by this Act. It may contain other information as well.

(d) The document must be typewritten or printed or, if electronically transmitted, it must be in a format that can be retrieved or reproduced in typewritten or printed form.

(e) The document must be in the English language. A corporate name need not be in English if written in English letters or Arabic or Roman numerals, and the certificate of existence required of foreign corporations need not be in English if accompanied by a reasonably authenticated English translation.

(f) The document must be executed:

    (1) by the chairman of the board of directors of a domestic or foreign corporation, by its president, or by another of its officers;

    (2) if directors have not been selected or the corporation has not been formed, by an incorporator; or

    (3) if the corporation is in the hands of a receiver, trustee, or other court-appointed fiduciary, by that fiduciary.

(g) The person executing the document shall sign it and state beneath or opposite his signature his name and the capacity in which he signs. The document may but need not contain a corporate seal, attestation, acknowledgment or verification.

(h) If the secretary of state has prescribed a mandatory form for the document under § 1.21, the document must be in or on the prescribed form.

(i) The document must be delivered to the office of the secretary of state for filing. Delivery may be made by electronic transmission if and to the extent permitted by the secretary of state. If it is filed in typewritten or printed form and not transmitted electronically, the secretary of state may require one exact or conformed copy to be delivered with the document (except as provided in §§ 5.03 and 15.09).

(j) When the document is delivered to the office of the secretary of state for filing, the correct filing fee, and any franchise tax, license fee, or penalty required to be paid therewith by this Act or other law must be paid or provision for payment made in a manner permitted by the secretary of state.

(k) Whenever a provision of this Act permits any of the terms of a plan or a filed document to be dependent on facts objectively ascertainable outside the plan or filed document, the following provisions apply:

    (1) The manner in which the facts will operate upon the terms of the plan or filed document shall be set forth in the plan or filed document.

    (2) The facts may include, but are not limited to:

        (i) any of the following that is available in a nationally recognized news or information medium either in print or electronically: statistical or market indices, market prices of any security or group of securities, interest rates, currency exchange rates, or similar economic or financial data;

        (ii) a determination or action by any person or body, including the corporation or any other party to a plan or filed document; or

        (iii) the terms of, or actions taken under, an agreement to which the corporation is a party, or any other agreement or document.

    (3) As used in this subsection:

        (i) "filed document " means a document filed with the secretary of state under any provision of this Act except chapter 15 or § 16.21; and

        (ii) "plan" means a plan of domestication, nonprofit conversion, entity conversion, merger or share exchange.

    (4) The following provisions of a plan or filed document may not be made dependent on facts outside the plan or filed document:

        (i) The name and address of any person required in a filed document.

        (ii) The registered office of any entity required in a filed document.

        (iii) The registered agent of any entity required in a filed document.

        (iv) The number of authorized shares and designation of each class or series of shares.

        (v) The effective date of a filed document.

        (vi) Any required statement in a filed document of the date on which the underlying transaction was approved or the manner in which that approval was given.

(5) If a provision of a filed document is made dependent on a fact ascertainable outside of the filed document, and that fact is not ascertainable by reference to a source described in subsection (k)(2)(i) or a document that is a matter of public record, or the affected shareholders have not received notice of the fact from the corporation, then the corporation shall file with the secretary of state articles of amendment setting forth the fact promptly after the time when the fact referred to is first ascertainable or thereafter changes. Articles of amendment under this subsection (k)(5) are deemed to be authorized by the authorization of the original filed document or plan to which they relate and may be filed by the corporation without further action by the board of directors or the shareholders.

§ 1.21. Forms.

(a) The secretary of state may prescribe and furnish on request forms for: (1) an application for a certificate of existence, (2) a foreign corporation's application for a certificate of authority to transact business in this state, (3) a foreign corporation's application for a certificate of withdrawal, and (4) the annual report. If the secretary of state so requires, use of these forms is mandatory.

(b) The secretary of state may prescribe and furnish on request forms for other documents required or permitted to be filed by this Act but their use is not mandatory.

§ 1.22. Filing, Service, and Copying Fees.

(a) The secretary of state shall collect the following fees when the documents described in this subsection are delivered to him for filing:

Document Fee

    (1) Articles of incorporation $_____

    (2) Application for use of indistinguishable name $_____

    (3) Application for reserved name $_____

    (4) Notice of transfer of reserved name $_____

    (5) Application for registered name $_____

    (6) Application for renewal of registered name $_____

    (7) Corporation's statement of change of registered agent or registered office or both $_____

    (8) Agent's statement of change of registered office for each affected corporation not to exceed a total of $_____

    (9) Agent's statement of resignation No fee

        (9A) Articles of domestication $_____

        (9B) Articles of charter surrender $_____

        (9C) Articles of nonprofit conversion $_____

        (9D) Articles of domestication and conversion $_____

        (9E) Articles of entity conversion $_____

    (10) Amendment of articles of incorporation $_____

    (11) Restatement of articles of incorporation with amendment of articles $_____

    (12) Articles of merger or share exchange $_____

    (13) Articles of dissolution $_____

    (14) Articles of revocation of dissolution $_____

(15) Certificate of administrative dissolution No fee

(16) Application for reinstatement following administrative dissolution $_____

(17) Certificate of reinstatement No fee

(18) Certificate of judicial dissolution No fee

(19) Application for certificate of authority $_____

(20) Application for amended certificate of authority $_____

(21) Application for certificate of withdrawal $_____

(21A) Application for transfer or authority $_____

(22) Certificate of revocation of authority to transact business No fee

(23) Annual report $_____

(24) Articles of correction $_____

(25) Application for certificate of existence or authorization $_____

(26) Any other document required or permitted to be filed by this Act $_____

(b) The secretary of state shall collect a fee of $_____ each time process is served on him under this Act. The party to a proceeding causing service of process is entitled to recover this fee as costs if he prevails in the proceeding.

(c) The secretary of state shall collect the following fees for copying and certifying the copy of any filed document relating to a domestic or foreign corporation:

(1) $_____ a page for copying; and

(2) $_____ for the certificate.

§ 1.23. Effective Time and Date of Document.

(a) Except as provided in subsection (b) and § 1.24(c), a document accepted for filing is effective:

(1) at the date and time of filing, as evidenced by such means as the secretary of state may use for the purpose of recording the date and time of filing; or

(2) at the time specified in the document as its effective time on the date it is filed.

(b) A document may specify a delayed effective time and date, and if it does so the document becomes effective at the time and date specified. If a delayed effective date but no time is specified, the document is effective at the close of business on that date. A delayed effective date for a document may not be later than the 90th day after the date it is filed.

§ 1.24. Correcting Filed Document.

(a) A domestic or foreign corporation may correct a document filed by the secretary of state if

(1) the document contains an inaccuracy, or (2) the document was defectively executed, attested, sealed, verified or acknowledged, or (3) the electronic transmission was defective.

(b) A document is corrected:

(1) by preparing articles of correction that

(i) describe the document (including its filing date) or attach a copy of it to the articles,

(ii) specify the inaccuracy or defect to be corrected, and

(iii) correct the inaccuracy or defect; and

(2) by delivering the articles to the secretary of state for filing.

(c) Articles of correction are effective on the effective date of the document they correct except as to persons relying on the uncorrected document and adversely affected by the correction. As to those persons, articles of correction are effective when filed.

§ 1.25. Filing Duty of Secretary of State.

(a) If a document delivered to the office of the secretary of state for filing satisfies the requirements of § 1.20, the secretary of state shall file it.

(b) The secretary of state files a document by recording it as filed on the date and time of receipt. After filing a document, except as provided in §§ 5.03 and 15.10, the secretary of state shall deliver to the domestic or foreign corporation or its representative a copy of the document with an acknowledgement of the date and time of filing.

(c) If the secretary of state refuses to file a document, he shall return it to the domestic or foreign corporation or its representative within five days after the document was delivered, together with a brief, written explanation of the reason for his refusal.

(d) The secretary of state's duty to file documents under this section is ministerial. His filing or refusing to file a document does not:

(1) affect the validity or invalidity of the document in whole or part;

(2) relate to the correctness or incorrectness of information contained in the document;

(3) create a presumption that the document is valid or invalid or that information contained in the document is correct or incorrect.

§ 1.26. Appeal from Secretary of State's Refusal To File Document.

(a) If the secretary of state refuses to file a document delivered to his office for filing, the domestic or foreign corporation may appeal the refusal within 30 days after the return of the document to the [name or describe] court [of the county where the corporation's principal office (or, if none in this state, its registered office) is or will be located] [of __ county]. The appeal is commenced by petitioning the court to compel filing the document and by attaching to the petition the document and the secretary of state's explanation of his refusal to file.

(b) The court may summarily order the secretary of state to file the document or take other action the court considers appropriate.

(c) The court's final decision may be appealed as in other civil proceedings.

§ 1.27. Evidentiary Effect of Copy of Filed Document.

A certificate from the secretary of state delivered with a copy of a document filed by the secretary of state, is conclusive evidence that the original document is on file with the secretary of state.

§ 1.28. Certificate of Existence.

(a) Anyone may apply to the secretary of state to furnish a certificate of existence for a domestic corporation or a certificate of authorization for a foreign corporation.

(b) A certificate of existence or authorization sets forth:

(1) the domestic corporation's corporate name or the foreign corporation's corporate name used in this state;

(2) that

(i) the domestic corporation is duly incorporated under the law of this state, the date of its incorporation, and the period of its duration if less than perpetual; or

(ii) that the foreign corporation is authorized to transact business in this state;

(3) that all fees, taxes, and penalties owed to this state have been paid, if

(i) payment is reflected in the records of the secretary of state and

(ii) nonpayment affects the existence or authorization of the domestic or foreign corporation;

(4) that its most recent annual report required by § 16.21 has been delivered to the secretary of state;

(5) that articles of dissolution have not been filed; and

(6) other facts of record in the office of the secretary of state that may be requested by the applicant.

(c) Subject to any qualification stated in the certificate, a certificate of existence or authorization issued by the secretary of state may be relied upon as conclusive evidence that the domestic or foreign corporation is in existence or is authorized to transact business in this state.

§ 1.29. Penalty for Signing False Document.

(a) A person commits an offense if he signs a document he knows is false in any material respect with intent that the document be delivered to the secretary of state for filing.

(b) An offense under this section is a [__] misdemeanor [punishable by a fine of not to exceed $__].

Subchapter C. Secretary of State

§ 1.30. Powers.

The secretary of state has the power reasonably necessary to perform the duties required of him by this Act.

Subchapter D. Definitions

§ 1.40. Act Definitions. In this Act:

(1) "Articles of incorporation" means the original articles of incorporation, all amendments thereof, and any other documents permitted or required to be filed by a domestic business corporation with the secretary of state under any provision of this Act except § 16.21. If an amendment of the articles or any other document filed under this Act restates the articles in their entirety, thenceforth the "articles" shall not include any prior documents.

(2) "Authorized shares" means the shares of all classes a domestic or foreign corporation is authorized to issue.

(3) "Conspicuous" means so written that a reasonable person against whom the writing is to operate should have noticed it. For example, printing in italics or boldface or contrasting color, or typing in capitals or underlined, is conspicuous.

(4) "Corporation," "domestic corporation" or "domestic business corporation" means a corporation for profit, which is not a foreign corporation, incorporated under or subject to the provisions of this Act.

(5) "Deliver" or "delivery" means any method of delivery used in conventional commercial practice, including delivery by hand, mail, commercial delivery, and electronic transmission.

(6) "Distribution" means a direct or indirect transfer of money or other property (except its own shares) or incurrence of indebtedness by a corporation to or for the benefit of its shareholders in respect of any of its shares. A distribution may be in the form of a declaration or payment of a dividend; a purchase, redemption, or other acquisition of shares; a distribution of indebtedness; or otherwise.

(6A) "Domestic unincorporated entity" means an unincorporated entity whose internal affairs are governed by the laws of this state.

(7) "Effective date of notice" is defined in § 1.41.

(7A) "Electronic transmission" or "electronically transmitted" means any process of communication not directly involving the physical transfer of paper that is suitable for the retention, retrieval, and reproduction of information by the recipient.

(7B) "Eligible entity" means a domestic or foreign unincorporated entity or a domestic or foreign nonprofit corporation.

(7C) "Eligible interests" means interests or memberships.

(8) "Employee" includes an officer but not a director. A director may accept duties that make him also an employee.

(9) "Entity" includes domestic and foreign business corporation; domestic and foreign nonprofit corporation; estate; trust; domestic and foreign unincorporated entity; and state, United States, and foreign government.

(9A) The phrase "facts objectively ascertainable" outside of a filed document or plan is defined in § 1.20(k).

(9B) "Filing entity" means an unincorporated entity that is of a type that is created by filing a public organic document.

(10) "Foreign corporation" means a corporation incorporated under a law other than the law of this state; which would be a business corporation if incorporated under the laws of this state.

(10A) "Foreign nonprofit corporation" means a corporation incorporated under a law other than the law of this state, which would be a nonprofit corporation if incorporated under the laws of this state.

(10B) "Foreign unincorporated entity" means an unincorporated entity whose internal affairs are governed by an organic law of a jurisdiction other than this state.

(11) "Governmental subdivision" includes authority, county, district, and municipality.

(12) "Includes" denotes a partial definition.

(13) "Individual" means a natural person.

(13A) "Interest" means either or both of the following rights under the organic law of an unincorporated entity:

(i) the right to receive distributions from the entity either in the ordinary course or upon liquidation; or

(ii) the right to receive notice or vote on issues involving its internal affairs, other than as an agent, assignee, proxy or person responsible for managing its business and affairs.

(13B) "Interest holder" means a person who holds of record an interest.

(14) "Means" denotes an exhaustive definition.

(14A) "Membership" means the rights of a member in a domestic or foreign nonprofit corporation.

(14B) "Nonfiling entity's" means an unincorporated entity that is of a type that is not created by filing a public organic document.

(14C) "Nonprofit corporation" or "domestic nonprofit corporation" means a corporation incorporated under the laws of this state and subject to the provisions of the Model Nonprofit Corporation Act.

(15) "Notice" is defined in § 1.41.

(15A) "Organic document" means a public organic document or a private organic document.

(15B) "Organic law" means the statute governing the internal affairs of a domestic or foreign business or nonprofit corporation or unincorporated entity.

(15C) "Owner liability" means personal liability for a debt, obligation or liability of a domestic or foreign business or nonprofit corporation or unincorporated entity that is imposed on a person:

(i) solely by reason of the person's status as a shareholder, member or interest holder; or

(ii) by the articles of incorporation, bylaws or an organic document under a provision of the organic law of an entity authorizing the articles of incorporation, bylaws or an organic document to make one or more specified shareholders, members or interest holders liable in their capacity as shareholders, members or interest holders for all or specified debts, obligations or liabilities of the entity.

(16) "Person" includes an individual and an entity.

(17) "Principal office" means the office (in or out of this state) so designated in the annual report where the principle executive offices of a domestic or foreign corporation are located.

(17A) "Private organic document" means any document (other than the public organic document, if any) that determines the internal governance of an unincorporated entity. Where a private organic document has been amended or restated, the term means the private organic document as last amended or restated.

(17B) "Public organic document" means the document, if any, that is filed of public record to create an unincorporated entity. Where a public organic document has been amended or restated, the term means the public organic document as last amended or restated.

(18) "Proceeding" includes civil suit and criminal, administrative, and investigatory action.

(19) "Record date" means the date established under chapter 6 or 7 on which a corporation determines the identity of its shareholders and their shareholdings for purposes of this Act. The determinations shall be made as of the close of business on the record date unless another time for doing so is specified when the record date is fixed.

(20) "Secretary" means the corporate officer to whom the board of directors has delegated responsibility under § 8.40(c) for custody of the minutes of the meetings of the board of directors and of the shareholders and for authenticating records of the corporation.

(21) "Shareholder" means the person in whose name shares are registered in the records of a corporation or the beneficial owner of shares to the extent of the rights granted by a nominee certificate on file with a corporation.

(22) "Shares" means the units into which the proprietary interests in a corporation are divided.

(22A) "Sign" or "signature" includes any manual, facsimile, conformed or electronic signature.

(23) "State," when referring to a part of the United States, includes a state and commonwealth (and their agencies and governmental subdivisions) and a territory and insular possession (and their agencies and governmental subdivisions) of the United States.

(24) "Subscriber" means a person who subscribes for shares in a corporation, whether before or after incorporation.

(24A) "Unincorporated entity" means an organization or artificial legal person that either has a separate legal existence or has the power to acquire an estate in real property in its own name and that is not any of the following: a domestic or foreign business or nonprofit corporation, an estate, a trust, a

state, the United States, or a foreign government. The term includes a general partnership, limited liability company, limited partnership, business trust, joint stock association and incorporated nonprofit association.

(25) "United States" includes district, authority, bureau, commission, department, and any other agency of the United States.

(26) "Voting group" means all shares of one or more classes or series that under the articles of incorporation or this Act are entitled to vote and be counted together collectively on a matter at a meeting of shareholders. All shares entitled by the articles of incorporation or this Act to vote generally on the matter are for that purpose a single voting group.

(27) "Voting power" means the current power to vote in the election of directors.

§ 1.41. Notice.

(a) Notice under this Act must be in writing unless oral notice is reasonable under the circumstances. Notice by electronic transmission is written notice.

(b) Notice may be communicated in person; by mail or other method of delivery; or by telephone, voice mail or other electronic means. If these forms of personal notice are impracticable, notice may be communicated by a newspaper of general circulation in the area where published, or by radio, television, or other form of public broadcast communication.

(c) Written notice by a domestic or foreign corporation to its shareholder, if in a comprehensible form, is effective

(i) upon deposit in the United States mail, if mailed postpaid and correctly addressed to the shareholder's address shown in the corporation's current record of shareholders, or

(ii) when electronically transmitted to the shareholder in a manner authorized by the shareholder.

(d) Written notice to a domestic or foreign corporation (authorized to transact business in this state) may be addressed to its registered agent at its registered office or to the corporation or its secretary at its principal office shown in its most recent annual report or, in the case of a foreign corporation that has not yet delivered an annual report, in its application for a certificate of authority.

(e) Except as provided in subsection (c), written notice, if in a comprehensible form, is effective at the earliest of the following:

(1) when received;

(2) five days after its deposit in the United States Mail, as evidenced by the postmark, if mailed postpaid and correctly addressed;

(3) on the date shown on the return receipt, if sent by registered or certified mail, return receipt requested, and the receipt is signed by or on behalf of the addressee.

(f) Oral notice is effective when communicated, if communicated in a comprehensible manner.

(g) If this Act prescribes notice requirements for particular circumstances, those requirements govern. If articles of incorporation or bylaws prescribe notice requirements, not inconsistent with this section or other provisions of this Act, those requirements govern.

§ 1.42. Number of Shareholders.

(a) For purposes of this Act, the following identified as a shareholder in a corporation's current record of shareholders constitutes one shareholder:

(1) three or fewer co-owners;

(2) a corporation, partnership, trust, estate, or other entity;

(3) the trustees, guardians, custodians, or other fiduciaries of a single trust, estate, or account.

(b) For purposes of this Act, shareholdings registered in substantially similar names constitute one shareholder if it is reasonable to believe that the names represent the same person.

CHAPTER 2. INCORPORATION

§ 2.01. Incorporators.

One or more persons may act as the incorporator or incorporators of a corporation by delivering articles of incorporation to the secretary of state for filing.

§ 2.02. Articles of Incorporation.

(a) The articles of incorporation must set forth:

(1) a corporate name for the corporation that satisfies the requirements of § 4.01;

(2) the number of shares the corporation is authorized to issue;

(3) the street address of the corporation's initial registered office and the name of its initial registered agent at that office; and

(4) the name and address of each incorporator.

(b) The articles of incorporation may set forth:

(1) the names and addresses of the individuals who are to serve as the initial directors;

(2) provisions not inconsistent with law regarding:

(i) the purpose or purposes for which the corporation is organized;

(ii) managing the business and regulating the affairs of the corporation;

(iii) defining, limiting, and regulating the powers of the corporation, its board of directors, and shareholders;

(iv) a par value for authorized shares or classes of shares;

(v) the imposition of personal liability on shareholders for the debts of the corporation to a specified extent and upon specified conditions;

(3) any provision that under this Act is required or permitted to be set forth in the bylaws;

(4) a provision eliminating or limiting the liability of a director to the corporation or its shareholders for money damages for any action taken, or any failure to take any action, as a director, except liability for

(A) the amount of a financial benefit received by a director to which he is not entitled;

(B) an intentional infliction of harm on the corporation or the shareholders;

(C) a violation of § 8.33; or

(D) an intentional violation of criminal law; and

(5) a provision permitting or making obligatory indemnification of a director for liability (as defined in § 8.50(5)) to any person for any action taken, or any failure to take any action, as a director, except liability for

(A) receipt of a financial benefit to which he is not entitled,

(B) an intentional infliction of harm on the corporation or its shareholders,

(C) a violation of § 8.33, or

(D) an intentional violation of criminal law.

(c) The articles of incorporation need not set forth any of the corporate powers enumerated in this Act.

(d) Provisions of the articles of incorporation may be made dependent upon facts objectively ascertainable outside the articles of incorporation in accordance with § 1.20(k).

§ 2.03. Incorporation.

(a) Unless a delayed effective date is specified, the corporate existence begins when the articles of incorporation are filed.

(b) The secretary of state's filing of the articles of incorporation is conclusive proof that the incorporators satisfied all conditions precedent to incorporation except in a proceeding by the state to cancel or revoke the incorporation or involuntarily dissolve the corporation.

§ 2.04. Liability for Preincorporation Transactions.
All persons purporting to act as or on behalf of a corporation, knowing there was no incorporation under this Act, are jointly and severally liable for all liabilities created while so acting.

§ 2.05. Organization of Corporation.

(a) After incorporation:

(1) if initial directors are named in the articles of incorporation, the initial directors shall hold an organizational meeting, at the call of a majority of the directors, to complete the organization of the corporation by appointing officers, adopting bylaws, and carrying on any other business brought before the meeting;

(2) if initial directors are not named in the articles, the incorporator or incorporators shall hold an organizational meeting at the call of a majority of the incorporators:

(i) to elect directors and complete the organization of the corporation; or

(ii) to elect a board of directors who shall complete the organization of the corporation.

(b) Action required or permitted by this Act to be taken by incorporators at an organizational meeting may be taken without a meeting if the action taken is evidenced by one or more written consents describing the action taken and signed by each incorporator.

(c) An organizational meeting may be held in or out of this state.

§ 2.06. Bylaws.

(a) The incorporators or board of directors of a corporation shall adopt initial bylaws for the corporation.

(b) The bylaws of a corporation may contain any provision for managing the business and regulating the affairs of the corporation that is not inconsistent with law or the articles of incorporation.

§ 2.07. Emergency Bylaws.

(a) Unless the articles of incorporation provide otherwise, the board of directors of a corporation may adopt bylaws to be effective only in an emergency defined in subsection (d). The emergency bylaws, which are subject to amendment or repeal by the shareholders, may make all provisions necessary for managing the corporation during the emergency, including:

(1) procedures for calling a meeting of the board of directors;

(2) quorum requirements for the meeting; and

(3) designation of additional or substitute directors.

(b) All provisions of the regular bylaws consistent with the emergency bylaws remain effective during the emergency. The emergency bylaws are not effective after the emergency ends.

(c) Corporate action taken in good faith in accordance with the emergency bylaws:

    (1) binds the corporation; and

    (2) may not be used to impose liability on a corporate director, officer, employee, or agent.

(d) An emergency exists for purposes of this section if a quorum of the corporation's directors cannot readily be assembled because of some catastrophic event.

CHAPTER 3. PURPOSES AND POWERS

§ 3.01. Purposes.

(a) Every corporation incorporated under this Act has the purpose of engaging in any lawful business unless a more limited purpose is set forth in the articles of incorporation.

(b) A corporation engaging in a business that is subject to regulation under another statute of this state may incorporate under this Act only if permitted by, and subject to all limitations of, the other statute.

§ 3.02. General Powers.

Unless its articles of incorporation provide otherwise, every corporation has perpetual duration and succession in its corporate name and has the same powers as an individual to do all things necessary or convenient to carry out its business and affairs, including without limitation power:

(1) to sue and be sued, complain and defend in its corporate name;

(2) to have a corporate seal, which may be altered at will, and to use it, or a facsimile of it, by impressing or affixing it or in any other manner reproducing it;

(3) to make and amend bylaws, not inconsistent with its articles of incorporation or with the laws of this state, for managing the business and regulating the affairs of the corporation;

(4) to purchase, receive, lease, or otherwise acquire, and own, hold, improve, use, and otherwise deal with, real or personal property, or any legal or equitable interest in property, wherever located;

(5) to sell, convey, mortgage, pledge, lease, exchange, and otherwise dispose of all or any part of its property;

(6) to purchase, receive, subscribe for, or otherwise acquire; own, hold, vote, use, sell, mortgage, lend, pledge, or otherwise dispose of and deal in and with shares or other interests in, or obligations of, any other entity;

(7) to make contracts and guarantees, incur liabilities, borrow money, issue its notes, bonds, and other obligations (which may be convertible into or include the option to purchase other securities of the corporation), and secure any of its obligations by mortgage or pledge of any of its property, franchises, or income;

(8) to lend money, invest and reinvest its funds, and receive and hold real and personal property as security for repayment;

(9) to be a promoter, partner, member, associate, or manager of any partnership, joint venture, trust, or other entity;

(10) to conduct its business, locate offices, and exercise the powers granted by this Act within or without this state;

(11) to elect directors and appoint officers, employees, and agents of the corporation, define their duties, fix their compensation, and lend them money and credit;

(12) to pay pensions and establish pension plans, pension trusts, profit sharing plans, share bonus plans, share option plans, and benefit or incentive plans for any or all of its current or former directors, officers, employees, and agents;

(13) to make donations for the public welfare or for charitable, scientific, or educational purposes;

(14) to transact any lawful business that will aid governmental policy;

(15) to make payments or donations, or do any other act, not inconsistent with law, that furthers the business and affairs of the corporation.

§ 3.03. Emergency Powers.

(a) In anticipation of or during an emergency defined in subsection (d), the board of directors of a corporation may:

    (1) modify lines of succession to accommodate the incapacity of any director, officer, employee, or agent; and

    (2) relocate the principal office, designate alternative principal offices or regional offices, or authorize the officers to do so.

(b) During an emergency defined in subsection (d), unless emergency bylaws provide otherwise:

    (1) notice of a meeting of the board of directors need be given only to those directors whom it is practicable to reach and may be given in any practicable manner, including by publication and radio; and

    (2) one or more officers of the corporation present at a meeting of the board of directors may be deemed to be directors for the meeting, in order of rank and within the same rank in order of seniority, as necessary to achieve a quorum.

(c) Corporate action taken in good faith during an emergency under this section to further the ordinary business affairs of the corporation:

    (1) binds the corporation; and

    (2) may not be used to impose liability on a corporate director, officer, employee, or agent.

(d) An emergency exists for purposes of this section if a quorum of the corporation's directors cannot readily be assembled because of some catastrophic event.

§ 3.04. Ultra Vires.

(a) Except as provided in subsection (b), the validity of corporate action may not be challenged on the ground that the corporation lacks or lacked power to act.

(b) A corporation's power to act may be challenged:

    (1) in a proceeding by a shareholder against the corporation to enjoin the act;

    (2) in a proceeding by the corporation, directly, derivatively, or through a receiver, trustee, or other legal representative, against an incumbent or former director, officer, employee, or agent of the corporation; or

    (3) in a proceeding by the attorney general under § 14.30.

(c) In a shareholder's proceeding under subsection (b)(1) to enjoin an unauthorized corporate act, the court may enjoin or set aside the act, if equitable and if all affected persons are parties to the proceeding, and may award damages for loss (other than anticipated profits) suffered by the corporation or another party because of enjoining the unauthorized act.

CHAPTER 4. NAME

§ 4.01. Corporate Name.

(a) A corporate name:

    (1) must contain the word "corporation," "incorporated," "company," or "limited," or the abbreviation "corp.," "inc.,"

"co.," or "ltd.," or words or abbreviations of like import in another language; and

(2) may not contain language stating or implying that the corporation is organized for a purpose other than that permitted by § 3.01 and its articles of incorporation.

(b) Except as authorized by subsections (c) and (d), a corporate name must be distinguishable upon the records of the secretary of state from:

(1) the corporate name of a corporation incorporated or authorized to transact business in this state;

(2) a corporate name reserved or registered under § 4.02 or 4.03;

(3) the fictitious name adopted by a foreign corporation authorized to transact business in this state because its real name is unavailable; and

(4) the corporate name of a not-for-profit corporation incorporated or authorized to transact business in this state.

(c) A corporation may apply to the secretary of state for authorization to use a name that is not distinguishable upon his records from one or more of the names described in subsection (b). The secretary of state shall authorize use of the name applied for if:

(1) the other corporation consents to the use in writing and submits an undertaking in form satisfactory to the secretary of state to change its name to a name that is distinguishable upon the records of the secretary of state from the name of the applying corporation; or

(2) the applicant delivers to the secretary of state a certified copy of the final judgment of a court of competent jurisdiction establishing the applicant's right to use the name applied for in this state.

(d) A corporation may use the name (including the fictitious name) of another domestic or foreign corporation that is used in this state if the other corporation is incorporated or authorized to transact business in this state and the proposed user corporation:

(1) has merged with the other corporation;

(2) has been formed by reorganization of the other corporation; or

(3) has acquired all or substantially all of the assets, including the corporate name, of the other corporation.

(e) This Act does not control the use of fictitious names.

§ 4.02. Reserved Name.

(a) A person may reserve the exclusive use of a corporate name, including a fictitious name for a foreign corporation whose corporate name is not available, by delivering an application to the secretary of state for filing. The application must set forth the name and address of the applicant and the name proposed to be reserved. If the secretary of state finds that the corporate name applied for is available, he shall reserve the name for the applicant's exclusive use for a nonrenewable 120-day period.

(b) The owner of a reserved corporate name may transfer the reservation to another person by delivering to the secretary of state a signed notice of the transfer that states the name and address of the transferee.

§ 4.03. Registered Name.

(a) A foreign corporation may register its corporate name, or its corporate name with any addition required by § 15.06, if the name is distinguishable upon the records of the secretary of state from the corporate names that are not available under § 4.01(b).

(b) A foreign corporation registers its corporate name, or its corporate name with any addition required by § 15.06, by delivering to the secretary of state for filing an application:

(1) setting forth its corporate name, or its corporate name with any addition required by § 15.06, the state or country and date of its incorporation, and a brief description of the nature of the business in which it is engaged; and

(2) accompanied by a certificate of existence (or a document of similar import) from the state or country of incorporation.

(c) The name is registered for the applicant's exclusive use upon the effective date of the application.

(d) A foreign corporation whose registration is effective may renew it for successive years by delivering to the secretary of state for filing a renewal application, which complies with the requirements of subsection (b), between October 1 and December 31 of the preceding year. The renewal application when filed renews the registration for the following calendar year.

(e) A foreign corporation whose registration is effective may thereafter qualify as a foreign corporation under the registered name or consent in writing to the use of that name by a corporation thereafter incorporated under this Act or by another foreign corporation thereafter authorized to transact business in this state. The registration terminates when the domestic corporation is incorporated or the foreign corporation qualifies or consents to the qualification of another foreign corporation under the registered name.

CHAPTER 5. OFFICE AND AGENT

§ 5.01. Registered Office and Registered Agent.

Each corporation must continuously maintain in this state:

(1) a registered office that may be the same as any of its places of business; and

(2) a registered agent, who may be:

(i) individual who resides in this state and whose business office is identical with the registered office;

(ii) a domestic corporation or not-for-profit domestic corporation whose business office is identical with the registered office; or

(iii) a foreign corporation or not-for-profit foreign corporation authorized to transact business in this state whose business office is identical with the registered office.

§ 5.02. Change of Registered Office or Registered Agent.

(a) A corporation may change its registered office or registered agent by delivering to the secretary of state for filing a statement of change that sets forth:

(1) the name of the corporation,

(2) the street address of its current registered office;

(3) if the current registered office is to be changed, the street address of the new registered office;

(4) the name of its current registered agent;

(5) if the current registered agent is to be changed, the name of the new registered agent and the new agent's written consent (either on the statement or attached to it) to the appointment; and

(6) that after the change or changes are made, the street addresses of its registered office and the business office of its registered agent will be identical.

(b) If a registered agent changes the street address of his business office, he may change the street address of the registered office of any corporation for which he is the registered agent by notifying the corporation in writing of the change and signing (either manually or in facsimile) and delivering to the secretary of state for filing a statement that complies with the requirements of subsection (a) and recites that the corporation has been notified of the change.

§ 5.03. Resignation of Registered Agent.

(a) A registered agent may resign his agency appointment by signing and delivering to the secretary of state for filing the signed original and two exact or conformed copies of a statement of resignation. The statement may include a statement that the registered office is also discontinued.

(b) After filing the statement the secretary of state shall mail one copy to the registered office (if not discontinued) and the other copy to the corporation at its principal office.

(c) The agency appointment is terminated, and the registered office discontinued if so provided, on the 31st day after the date on which the statement was filed.

§ 5.04 Service on Corporation.

(a) A corporation's registered agent is the corporation's agent for service of process, notice, or demand required or permitted by law to be served on the corporation.

(b) If a corporation has no registered agent, or the agent cannot with reasonable diligence be served, the corporation may be served by registered or certified mail, return receipt requested, addressed to the secretary of the corporation at its principal office. Service is perfected under this subsection at the earliest of:

(1) the date the corporation receives the mail;

(2) the date shown on the return receipt, if signed on behalf of the corporation; or

(3) five days after its deposit in the United States Mail, as evidenced by the postmark, if mailed postpaid and correctly addressed.

(c) This section does not prescribe the only means, or necessarily the required means of serving a corporation.

CHAPTER 6. SHARES AND DISTRIBUTIONS
Subchapter A. Shares

§ 6.01. Authorized Shares.

(a) The articles of incorporation must set forth any classes of shares and series of shares within a class, and the number of shares of each class and series, that the corporation is authorized to issue. If more than one class or series of shares is authorized, the articles of incorporation must prescribe a distinguishing designation for each class or series and must describe, prior to the issuance of shares of a class or series, the terms, including the preferences, rights, and limitations, of that class or series. Except to the extent varied as permitted by this section, all shares of a class or series must have terms, including preferences, rights and limitations, that are identical with those of other shares of the same class or series

(b) The articles of incorporation must authorize:

(1) one or more classes or series of shares that together have unlimited voting rights, and

(2) one or more classes or series of shares (which may be the same class or classes as those with voting rights) that together are entitled to receive the net assets of the corporation upon dissolution.

(c) The articles of incorporation may authorize one or more classes or series of shares that:

(1) have special, conditional, or limited voting rights, or no right to vote, except to the extent otherwise provided by this Act;

(2) are redeemable or convertible as specified in the articles of incorporation:

(i) at the option of the corporation, the shareholder, or another person or upon the occurrence of a specified event;

(ii) for cash, indebtedness, securities, or other property; and

(iii) at prices and in amounts specified, or determined in accordance with a formula;

(3) entitle the holders to distributions calculated in any manner, including dividends that may be cumulative, noncumulative, or partially cumulative; or

(4) have preference over any other class or series of shares with respect to distributions, including distributions upon the dissolution of the corporation.

(d) Terms of shares may be made dependent upon facts objectively ascertainable outside the articles of incorporation in accordance with § 1.20(k).

(e) Any of the terms of shares may vary among holders of the same class or series so long as such variations are expressly set forth in the articles of incorporation.

(f) The description of the preferences, rights and limitations of classes or series of shares in subsection (c) is not exhaustive.

§ 6.02. Terms of Class or Series Determined by Board of Directors.

(a) If the articles of incorporation so provide, the board of directors is authorized, without shareholder approval, to:

(1) classify any unissued shares into one or more classes or into one or more series within a class,

(2) reclassify any unissued shares of any class into one or more classes or into one or more series within one or more classes, or

(3) reclassify any unissued shares of any series of any class into one or more classes or into one or more series within a class.

(b) If the board of directors acts pursuant to subsection (a), it must determine the terms, including the preferences, rights and limitations, to the same extent permitted under § 6.01, of:

(1) any class of shares before the issuance of any shares of that class, or

(2) any series within a class before the issuance of any shares of that series.

(c) Before issuing any shares of a class or series created under this section, the corporation must deliver to the secretary of state for filing articles of amendment setting forth the terms determined under subsection (a).

§ 6.03. Issued and Outstanding Shares.

(a) A corporation may issue the number of shares of each class or series authorized by the articles of incorporation. Shares that are issued are outstanding shares until they are reacquired, redeemed, converted, or cancelled.

(b) The reacquisition, redemption, or conversion of outstanding shares is subject to the limitations of subsection (c) of this section and to § 6.40.

(c) At all times that shares of the corporation are outstanding, one or more shares that together have unlimited voting rights and one or more shares that together are entitled to receive the net assets of the corporation upon dissolution must be outstanding.

§ 6.04. Fractional Shares.

(a) A corporation may:

(1) issue fractions of a share or pay in money the value of fractions of a share;

(2) arrange for disposition of fractional shares by the shareholders;

(3) issue scrip in registered or bearer form entitling the holder to receive a full share upon surrendering enough scrip to equal a full share.

(b) Each certificate representing scrip must be conspicuously labeled "scrip" and must contain the information required by § 6.25(b).

(c) The holder of a fractional share is entitled to exercise the rights of a shareholder, including the right to vote, to receive dividends, and to participate in the assets of the corporation upon liquidation. The holder of scrip is not entitled to any of these rights unless the scrip provides for them.

(d) The board of directors may authorize the issuance of scrip subject to any condition considered desirable, including:

(1) that the scrip will become void if not exchanged for full shares before a specified date; and

(2) that the shares, for which the scrip is exchangeable may be sold and the proceeds paid to the scripholders.

Subchapter B. Issuance of Shares

§ 6.20. Subscription for Shares Before Incorporation.

(a) A subscription for shares entered into before incorporation is irrevocable for six months unless the subscription agreement provides a longer or shorter period or all the subscribers agree to revocation.

(b) The board of directors may determine the payment terms of subscription for shares that were entered into before incorporation, unless the subscription agreement specifies them. A call for payment by the board of directors must be uniform so far as practicable as to all shares of the same class or series, unless the subscription agreement specifies otherwise.

(c) Shares issued pursuant to subscriptions entered into before incorporation are fully paid and nonassessable when the corporation receives the consideration specified in the subscription agreement.

(d) If a subscriber defaults in payment of money or property under a subscription agreement entered into before incorporation, the corporation may collect the amount owed as any other debt. Alternatively, unless the subscription agreement provides otherwise, the corporation may rescind the agreement and may sell the shares if the debt remains unpaid for more than 20 days after the corporation sends written demand for payment to the subscriber.

(e) A subscription agreement entered into after incorporation is a contract between the subscriber and the corporation subject to § 6.21.

§ 6.21. Issuance of Shares.

(a) The powers granted in this section to the board of directors may be reserved to the shareholders by the articles of incorporation.

(b) The board of directors may authorize shares to be issued for consideration consisting of any tangible or intangible property or benefit to the corporation, including cash, promissory notes, services performed, contracts for services to be performed, or other securities of the corporation.

(c) Before the corporation issues shares, the board of directors must determine that the consideration received or to be received for shares to be issued is adequate. That determination by the board of directors is conclusive insofar as the adequacy of consideration for the issuance of shares relates to whether the shares are validly issued, fully paid, and nonassessable.

(d) When the corporation receives the consideration for which the board of directors authorized the issuance of shares, the shares issued therefore are fully paid and nonassessable.

(e) The corporation may place in escrow shares issued for a contract for future services or benefits or a promissory note, or make other arrangements to restrict the transfer of the shares, and may credit distributions in respect of the shares against their purchase price, until the services are performed, the note is paid, or the benefits received. If the services are not performed, the note is not paid, or the benefits are not received, the shares escrowed or restricted and the distributions credited may be cancelled in whole or part.

(1) An issuance of shares or other securities convertible into or rights exercisable for shares, in a transaction or a series of integrated transactions, requires approval of the shareholders, at a meeting at which a quorum consisting of at least a majority of the votes entitled to be cast on the matter exists if:

(i) the shares, other securities, or rights are issued for consideration other than cash or cash equivalents, and

(ii) the voting power of shares that are issued and issuable as a result of the transaction or series of integrated transactions will comprise more than 20 percent of the voting power of the shares of the corporation that were outstanding immediately before the transaction.

(2) In this subsection:

(i) For purposes of determining the voting power of shares issued and issuable as a result of a transaction or series of integrated transactions, the voting power of shares shall be the greater of

(A) the voting power of the shares to be issued, or

(B) the voting power of the shares that would be outstanding after giving effect to the conversion of convertible shares and other securities and the exercise of rights to be issued.

(ii) A series of transactions is integrated if consummation of one transaction is made contingent on consummation of one or more of the other transactions.

§ 6.22. Liability of Shareholders.

(a) A purchaser from a corporation of its own shares is not liable to the corporation or its creditors with respect to the shares except to pay the consideration for which the shares were authorized to be issued (§ 6.21) or specified in the subscription agreement (§ 6.20).

(b) Unless otherwise provided in the articles of incorporation, a shareholder of a corporation is not personally liable for the acts or debts of the corporation except that he may become personally liable by reason of his own acts or conduct.

§ 6.23. Share Dividends.

(a) Unless the articles of incorporation provide otherwise, shares may be issued pro rata and without consideration to the corporation's shareholders or to the shareholders of one or more classes or series. An issuance of shares under this subsection is a share dividend.

(b) Shares of one class or series may not be issued as a share dividend in respect of shares of another class or series unless

(1) the articles of incorporation so authorize,

(2) a majority of the votes entitled to be cast by the class or series to be issued approve the issue, or

(3) there are no outstanding shares of the class or series to be issued.

(c) If the board of directors does not fix the record date for determining shareholders entitled to a share dividend, it is the date the board of directors authorizes the share dividend.

§ 6.24. Share Options.

(a) A corporation may issue rights, options, or warrants for the purchase of shares or other securities of the corporation. The board of directors shall determine

(i) the terms upon which the rights, options, or warrants are issued and

(ii) the terms, including the consideration for which the shares or other securities are to be issued. The authorization by the board of directors for the corporation to issue such rights, options, or warrants constitutes authorization of the issuance of the shares or other securities for which the rights, options or warrants are exercisable.

(b) The terms and conditions of such rights, options or warrants, including those outstanding on the effective date of this section, may include, without limitation, restrictions or conditions that:

(1) preclude or limit the exercise, transfer or receipt of such rights, options or warrants by any person or persons owning or offering to acquire a specified number or percentage of the outstanding shares or other securities of the corporation or by any transferee or transferees of any such person or persons, or

(2) invalidate or void such rights, options or warrants held by any such person or persons or any such transferee or transferees.

§ 6.25. Form and Content of Certificates.

(a) Shares may but need not be represented by certificates. Unless this Act or another statute expressly provides otherwise, the rights and obligations of shareholders are identical whether or not their shares are represented by certificates.

(b) At a minimum each share certificate must state on its face:

(1) the name of the issuing corporation and that it is organized under the law of this state;

(2) the name of the person to whom issued; and

(3) the number and class of shares and the designation of the series, if any, the certificate represents.

(c) If the issuing corporation is authorized to issue different classes of shares or different series within a class, the designations, relative rights, preferences, and limitations applicable to each class and the variations in rights, preferences, and limitations determined for each series (and the authority of the board of directors to determine variations for future series) must be summarized on the front or back of each certificate. Alternatively, each certificate may state conspicuously on its front or back that the corporation will furnish the shareholder this information on request in writing and without charge.

(d) Each share certificate (1) must be signed (either manually or in facsimile) by two officers designated in the bylaws or by the board of directors and (2) may bear the corporate seal or its facsimile.

(e) If the person who signed (either manually or in facsimile) a share certificate no longer holds office when the certificate is issued, the certificate is nevertheless valid.

§ 6.26. Shares Without Certificates.

(a) Unless the articles of incorporation or bylaws provide otherwise, the board of directors of a corporation may authorize the issue of some or all of the shares of any or all of its classes or series without certificates. The authorization does not affect shares already represented by certificates until they are surrendered to the corporation.

(b) Within a reasonable time after the issue or transfer of shares without certificates, the corporation shall send the shareholder a written statement of the information required on certificates by § 6.25(b) and (c), and, if applicable, § 6.27.

§ 6.27. Restriction on Transfer of Shares and Other Securities.

(a) The articles of incorporation, bylaws, an agreement among shareholders, or an agreement between shareholders and the corporation may impose restrictions on the transfer or registration of transfer of shares of the corporation. A restriction does not affect shares issued before the restriction was adopted unless the holders of the shares are parties to the restriction agreement or voted in favor of the restriction.

(b) A restriction on the transfer or registration of transfer of shares is valid and enforceable against the holder or a transferee of the holder if the restriction is authorized by this section and its existence is noted conspicuously on the front or back of the certificate or is contained in the information statement required by § 6.26(b). Unless so noted, a restriction is not enforceable against a person without knowledge of the restriction.

(c) A restriction on the transfer or registration of transfer of shares is authorized:

(1) to maintain the corporation's status when it is dependent on the number or identity of its shareholders;

(2) to preserve exemptions under federal or state securities law;

(3) for any other reasonable purpose.

(d) A restriction on the transfer or registration of transfer of shares may:

(1) obligate the shareholder first to offer the corporation or other persons (separately, consecutively, or simultaneously) an opportunity to acquire the restricted shares;

(2) obligate the corporation or other persons (separately, consecutively, or simultaneously) to acquire the restricted shares;

(3) require the corporation, the holders of any class of its shares, or another person to approve the transfer of the restricted shares, if the requirement is not manifestly unreasonable;

(4) prohibit the transfer of the restricted shares to designated persons or classes of persons, if the prohibition is not manifestly unreasonable.

(e) For purposes of this section, "shares" includes a security convertible into or carrying a right to subscribe for or acquire shares.

§ 6.28. Expense of Issue.

A corporation may pay the expenses of selling or underwriting its shares, and of organizing or reorganizing the corporation, from the consideration received for shares.

Subchapter C. Subsequent Acquisition of Shares by Shareholders and Corporation

6.30. Shareholders' Preemptive Rights.

(a) The shareholders of a corporation do not have a preemptive right to acquire the corporation's unissued shares except to the extent the articles of incorporation so provide.

(b) A statement included in the articles of incorporation that "the corporation elects to have preemptive rights" (or words of similar import) means that the following principles apply except to the extent the articles of incorporation expressly provide otherwise:

(1) The shareholders of the corporation have a preemptive right, granted on uniform terms and conditions prescribed by the board of directors to provide a fair and reasonable opportunity to exercise the right, to acquire proportional amounts of the corporation's unissued shares upon the decision of the board of directors to issue them.

(2) A shareholder may waive his preemptive right. A waiver evidenced by a writing is irrevocable even though it is not supported by consideration.

(3) There is no preemptive right with respect to:

(i) shares issued as compensation to directors, officers, agents, or employees of the corporation, its subsidiaries or affiliates;

(ii) shares issued to satisfy conversion or option rights created to provide compensation to directors, officers, agents, or employees of the corporation, its subsidiaries or affiliates;

(iii) shares authorized in articles of incorporation that are issued within six months from the effective date of incorporation;

(iv) shares sold otherwise than for money.

(4) Holders of shares of any class without general voting rights but with preferential rights to distributions or assets have no preemptive rights with respect to shares of any class.

(5) Holders of shares of any class with general voting rights but without preferential rights to distributions or assets have no preemptive rights with respect to shares of any class with preferential rights to distributions or assets unless the shares with preferential rights are convertible into or carry a right to subscribe for or acquire shares without preferential rights.

(6) Shares subject to preemptive rights that are not acquired by shareholders may be issued to any person for a period of one year after being offered to shareholders at a consideration set by the board of directors that is not lower than the consideration set for the exercise of preemptive rights. An offer at a lower consideration or after the expiration of one year is subject to the shareholders' preemptive rights.

(c) For purposes of this section, "shares" includes a security convertible into or carrying a right to subscribe for or acquire shares.

§ 6.31. Corporation's Acquisition of its Own Shares.

(a) A corporation may acquire its own shares, and shares so acquired constitute authorized but unissued shares.

(b) If the articles of incorporation prohibit the reissue of the acquired shares, the number of authorized shares is reduced by the number of shares acquired.

Subchapter D. Distributions

§ 6.40. Distributions to Shareholders.

(a) A board of directors may authorize and the corporation may make distributions to its shareholders subject to restriction by the articles of incorporation and the limitation in subsection (c).

(b) If the board of directors does not fix the record date for determining shareholders entitled to a distribution (other than one involving a purchase, redemption, or other acquisition of the corporation's shares), it is the date the board of directors authorizes the distribution.

(c) No distribution may be made if, after giving it effect:

(1) the corporation would not be able to pay its debts as they become due in the usual course of business; or

(2) the corporation's total assets would be less than the sum of its total liabilities plus (unless the articles of incorporation permit otherwise) the amount that would be needed, if the corporation were to be dissolved at the time of the distribution, to satisfy the preferential rights upon dissolution of shareholders whose preferential rights are superior to those receiving the distribution.

(d) The board of directors may base a determination that a distribution is not prohibited under subsection (c) either on financial statements prepared on the basis of accounting practices and principles that are reasonable in the circumstances or on a fair valuation or other method that is reasonable in the circumstances.

(e) Except as provided in subsection (g), the effect of a distribution under subsection (c) is measured:

(1) in the case of distribution by purchase, redemption, or other acquisition of the corporation's shares, as of the earlier of

(i) the date money or other property is transferred or debt incurred by the corporation or

(ii) the date the shareholder ceases to be a shareholder with respect to the acquired shares;

(2) in the case of any other distribution of indebtedness, as of the date the indebtedness is distributed; and

(3) in all other cases, as of

(i) the date the distribution is authorized if the payment occurs within 120 days after the date of authorization or

(ii) the date the payment is made if it occurs more than 120 days after the date of authorization.

(f) A corporation's indebtedness to a shareholder incurred by reason of a distribution made in accordance with this section is at parity with the corporation's indebtedness to its general, unsecured creditors except to the extent subordinated by agreement.

(g) Indebtedness of a corporation, including indebtedness issued as a distribution, is not considered a liability for purposes of determinations under subsection (c) if its terms provide that payment of principal and interest are made only if and to the extent that payment of a distribution to shareholders could then be made under this section. If the indebtedness is issued as a distribution, each payment of principal or interest is treated as a distribution, the effect of which is measured on the date the payment is actually made.

(h) This section shall not apply to distributions in liquidation under chapter 14.

CHAPTER 7. SHAREHOLDERS
Subchapter A. Meetings

§ 7.01. Annual Meeting.

(a) A corporation shall hold a meeting of shareholders annually at a time stated in or fixed in accordance with the bylaws.

(b) Annual shareholders' meetings may be held in or out of this state at the place stated in or fixed in accordance with the bylaws. If no place is stated in or fixed in accordance with the bylaws, annual meetings shall be held at the corporation's principal office.

(c) The failure to hold an annual meeting at the time stated in or fixed in accordance with a corporation's bylaws does not affect the validity of any corporate action.

§ 7.02. Special Meeting.

(a) A corporation shall hold a special meeting of shareholders:

(1) on call of its board of directors or the person or persons authorized to do so by the articles of incorporation or bylaws; or

(2) if the holders of at least 10 percent of all the votes entitled to be cast on an issue proposed to be considered at the proposed special meeting sign, date, and deliver to the corporation one or more written demands for the meeting describing the purpose or purposes for which it is to be held, provided that the articles of incorporation may fix a lower percentage or a higher percentage not exceeding 25 percent of all the votes entitled to be cast on any issue proposed to be considered. Unless otherwise provided in the articles of incorporation, a written demand for a special meeting may be revoked by a writing to that effect received by the corporation prior to the receipt by the corporation of demands sufficient in number to require the holding of a special meeting.

(b) If not otherwise fixed under § 7.03 or 7.07, the record date for determining shareholders entitled to demand a special meeting is the date the first shareholder signs the demand.

(c) Special shareholders' meetings may be held in or out of this state at the place stated in or fixed in accordance with the bylaws. If no place is stated or fixed in accordance with the bylaws, special meetings shall be held at the corporation's principal office.

(d) Only business within the purpose or purposes described in the meeting notice required by § 7.05(c) may be conducted at a special shareholders' meeting.

§ 7.03. Court-Ordered Meeting.

(a) The "name or describe" court of the county where a corporation's principal office (or, if none in this state, its registered office) is located may summarily order a meeting to be held:

(1) on application of any shareholder of the corporation entitled to participate in an annual meeting if an annual meeting was not held within the earlier of 6 months after the end of the corporation's fiscal year or 15 months after its last annual meeting; or

(2) on application of a shareholder who signed a demand for a special meeting valid under § 7.02, if:

(i) notice of the special meeting was not given within 30 days after the date the demand was delivered to the corporation's secretary; or

(ii) the special meeting was not held in accordance with the notice.

(b) The court may fix the time and place of the meeting, determine the shares entitled to participate in the meeting, specify a record date for determining shareholders entitled to notice of and to vote at the meeting, prescribe the form and content of the meeting notice, fix the quorum required for specific matters to be considered at the meeting (or direct that the votes represented at the meeting constitute a quorum for action on those matters), and enter other orders necessary to accomplish the purpose or purposes of the meeting.

§ 7.04. Action Without Meeting.

(a) Action required or permitted by this Act to be taken at a shareholders' meeting may be taken without a meeting if the action is taken by all the shareholders entitled to vote on the action. The action must be evidenced by one or more written consents bearing the date of signature and describing the action taken, signed by all the shareholders entitled to vote on the action, and delivered to the corporation for inclusion in the minutes or filing with the corporate records.

(b) If not otherwise fixed under § 7.03 or 7.07, the record date for determining shareholders entitled to take action without a meeting is the date the first shareholder signs the consent under subsection (a). No written consent shall be effective to take the corporate action referred to therein unless, within 60 days of the earliest date appearing on a consent delivered to the corporation in the manner required by this section, written consents signed by all shareholders entitled to vote on the action are received by the corporation. A written consent may be revoked by a writing to that effect received by the corporation prior to receipt by the corporation of unrevoked written consents sufficient in number to take corporate action.

(c) A consent signed under this section has the effect of a meeting vote and may be described as such in any document.

(d) If this Act requires that notice of proposed action be given to nonvoting shareholders and the action is to be taken by unanimous consent of the voting shareholders, the corporation must give its nonvoting shareholders written notice of the proposed action at least 10 days before the action is taken. The notice must contain or be accompanied by the same material that, under this Act, would have been required to be sent to nonvoting shareholders in a notice of meeting at which the proposed action would have been submitted to the shareholders for action.

§ 7.05. Notice of Meeting.

(a) A corporation shall notify shareholders of the date, time, and place of each annual and special shareholders' meeting no fewer than 10 nor more than 60 days before the meeting date. Unless this Act or the articles of incorporation require otherwise, the corporation is required to give notice only to shareholders entitled to vote at the meeting.

(b) Unless this Act or the articles of incorporation require otherwise, notice of an annual meeting need not include a description of the purpose or purposes for which the meeting is called.

(c) Notice of a special meeting must include a description of the purpose or purposes for which the meeting is called.

(d) If not otherwise fixed under § 7.03 or 7.07, the record date for determining shareholders entitled to notice of and to vote at an annual or special shareholders' meeting is the day before the first notice is delivered to shareholders.

(e) Unless the bylaws require otherwise, if an annual or special shareholders' meeting is adjourned to a different date, time, or place, notice need not be given of the new date, time, or place if the new date, time, or place is announced at the meeting before adjournment. If a new record date for the adjourned meeting is or must be fixed under § 7.07, however, notice of the adjourned meeting must be given under this section to persons who are shareholders as of the new record date.

§ 7.06. Waiver of Notice.

(a) A shareholder may waive any notice required by this Act, the articles of incorporation, or bylaws before or after the date and time stated in the notice. The waiver must be in writing, be signed by the shareholder entitled to the notice, and be delivered to the corporation for inclusion in the minutes or filing with the corporate records.

(b) A shareholder's attendance at a meeting:

(1) waives objection to lack of notice or defective notice of the meeting, unless the shareholder at the beginning of the meeting objects to holding the meeting or transacting business at the meeting;

(2) waives objection to consideration of a particular matter at the meeting that is not within the purpose or purposes described in the meeting notice, unless the shareholder objects to considering the matter when it is presented.

§ 7.07. Record Date.

(a) The bylaws may fix or provide the manner of fixing the record date for one or more voting groups in order to determine the shareholders entitled to notice of a shareholders' meeting, to demand a special meeting, to vote, or to take any other action. If the bylaws do not fix or provide for fixing a record date, the board of directors of the corporation may fix a future date as the record date.

(b) A record date fixed under this section may not be more than 70 days before the meeting or action requiring a determination of shareholders.

(c) A determination of shareholders entitled to notice of or to vote at a shareholders' meeting is effective for any adjournment of the meeting unless the board of directors fixes a new record date, which it must do if the meeting is adjourned to a date more than 120 days after the date fixed for the original meeting.

(d) If a court orders a meeting adjourned to a date more than 120 days after the date fixed for the original meeting, it may provide that the original record date continues in effect or it may fix a new record date.

§ 7.08. Conduct of the Meeting.

(a) At each meeting of shareholders, a chair shall preside. The chair shall be appointed as provided in the bylaws or, in the absence of such provision, by the board.

(b) The chair, unless the articles of incorporation or bylaws provide otherwise, shall determine the order of business and shall have the authority to establish rules for the conduct of the meeting.

(c) Any rules adopted for, and the conduct of, the meeting shall be fair to shareholders.

(d) The chair of the meeting shall announce at the meeting when the polls close for each matter voted upon. If no announcement is made, the polls shall be deemed to have closed upon the final adjournment of the meeting. After the polls close, no ballots, proxies or votes nor any revocations or changes thereto may be accepted.

Subchapter B. Voting

§ 7.20. Shareholders' List for Meeting.

(a) After fixing a record date for a meeting, a corporation shall prepare an alphabetical list of the names of all its shareholders who are entitled to notice of a shareholders' meeting. The list must be arranged by voting group (and within each voting group by class or series of shares) and show the address of and number of shares held by each shareholder.

(b) The shareholders' list must be available for inspection by any shareholder, beginning two business days after notice of the meeting is given for which the list was prepared and continuing through the meeting, at the corporation's principal office or at a place identified in the meeting notice in the city where the meeting will be held. A shareholder, his agent, or attorney is entitled on written demand to inspect and, subject to the requirements of § 16.02(c), to copy the list, during regular business hours and at his expense, during the period it is available for inspection.

(c) The corporation shall make the shareholders' list available at the meeting, and any shareholder, his agent, or attorney is entitled to inspect the list at any time during the meeting or any adjournment.

(d) If the corporation refuses to allow a shareholder, his agent, or attorney to inspect the shareholders' list before or at the meeting (or copy the list as permitted by subsection (b)), the [name or describe] court of the county where a corporation's principal office (or, if none in this state, its registered office) is located, on application of the shareholder, may summarily order the inspection or copying at the corporation's expense and may postpone the meeting for which the list was prepared until the inspection or copying is complete.

(e) Refusal or failure to prepare or make available the shareholders' list does not affect the validity of action taken at the meeting.

§ 7.21. Voting Entitlement of Shares.

(a) Except as provided in subsections (b) and (d) or unless the articles of incorporation provide otherwise, each outstanding share, regardless of class, is entitled to one vote on each matter voted on at a shareholders' meeting. Only shares are entitled to vote.

(b) Absent special circumstances, the shares of a corporation are not entitled to vote if they are owned, directly or indirectly, by a second corporation, domestic or foreign, and the first corporation owns, directly or indirectly, a majority of the shares entitled to vote for directors of the second corporation.

(c) Subsection (b) does not limit the power of a corporation to vote any shares, including its own shares, held by it in a fiduciary capacity.

(d) Redeemable shares are not entitled to vote after notice of redemption is mailed to the holders and a sum sufficient to redeem the shares has been deposited with a bank, trust company, or other financial institution under an irrevocable obligation to pay the holders the redemption price on surrender of the shares.

§ 7.22. Proxies.

(a) A shareholder may vote his shares in person or by proxy.

(b) A shareholder or his agent or attorney-in-fact may appoint a proxy to vote or otherwise act for the shareholder by signing an appointment form, or by an electronic transmission. An electronic transmission must contain or be accompanied by information from which one can determine that the shareholder, the shareholder's agent, or the shareholder's attorney-in-fact authorized the transmission.

(c) An appointment of a proxy is effective when a signed appointment form or an electronic transmission of the appointment is received by the inspector of election or the officer or agent of the corporation authorized to tabulate votes. An appointment is valid for 11 months unless a longer period is expressly provided in the appointment form.

(d) An appointment of a proxy is revocable unless the appointment form or electronic transmission states that it is irrevocable and the appointment is coupled with an interest. Appointments coupled with an interest include the appointment of:

(1) a pledgee;

(2) a person who purchased or agreed to purchase the shares;

(3) a creditor of the corporation who extended it credit under terms requiring the appointment;

(4) an employee of the corporation whose employment contract requires the appointment; or

(5) a party to a voting agreement created under § 7.31.

(e) The death or incapacity of the shareholder appointing a proxy does not affect the right of the corporation to accept the proxy's authority unless notice of the death or incapacity is received by the secretary or other officer or agent authorized to tabulate votes before the proxy exercises his authority under the appointment.

(f) An appointment made irrevocable under subsection (d) is revoked when the interest with which it is coupled is extinguished.

(g) A transferee for value of shares subject to an irrevocable appointment may revoke the appointment if he did not know of its existence when he acquired the shares and the existence of the irrevocable appointment was not noted conspicuously on the certificate representing the shares or on the information statement for shares without certificates.

(h) Subject to § 7.24 and to any express limitation on the proxy's authority stated in the appointment form or electronic transmission, a corporation is entitled to accept the proxy's vote or other action as that of the shareholder making the appointment.

§ 7.23. Shares Held by Nominees.

(a) A corporation may establish a procedure by which the beneficial owner of shares that are registered in the name of a nominee is recognized by the corporation as the shareholder. The extent of this recognition may be determined in the procedure.

(b) The procedure may set forth:

(1) the types of nominees to which it applies;

(2) the rights or privileges that the corporation recognizes in a beneficial owner;

(3) the manner in which the procedure is selected by the nominee;

(4) the information that must be provided when the procedure is selected;

(5) the period for which selection of the procedure is effective; and

(6) other aspects of the rights and duties created.

§ 7.24. Corporation's Acceptance of Votes.

(a) If the name signed on a vote, consent, waiver, or proxy appointment corresponds to the name of a shareholder, the corporation if acting in good faith is entitled to accept the vote, consent, waiver, or proxy appointment and give it effect as the act of the shareholder.

(b) If the name signed on a vote, consent, waiver, or proxy appointment does not correspond to the name of its shareholder, the corporation if acting in good faith is nevertheless entitled to accept the vote, consent, waiver, or proxy appointment and give it effect as the act of the shareholder if:

(1) the shareholder is an entity and the name signed purports to be that of an officer or agent of the entity;

(2) the name signed purports to be that of an administrator, executor, guardian, or conservator representing the shareholder and, if the corporation requests, evidence of fiduciary status acceptable to the corporation has been presented with respect to the vote, consent, waiver, or proxy appointment;

(3) the name signed purports to be that of a receiver or trustee in bankruptcy of the shareholder and, if the corporation requests, evidence of this status acceptable to the corporation has been presented with respect to the vote, consent, waiver, or proxy appointment;

(4) the name signed purports to be that of a pledgee, beneficial owner, or attorney-in-fact of the shareholder and, if the corporation requests, evidence acceptable to the corporation of the signatory's authority to sign for the shareholder has been presented with respect to the vote, consent, waiver, or proxy appointment;

(5) two or more persons are the shareholder as co-tenants or fiduciaries and the name signed purports to be the name of at least one of the co-owners and the person signing appears to be acting on behalf of all the co-owners.

(c) The corporation is entitled to reject a vote, consent, waiver, or proxy appointment if the secretary or other officer or agent authorized to tabulate votes, acting in good faith, has reasonable basis for doubt about the validity of the signature on it or about the signatory's authority to sign for the shareholder.

(d) The corporation and its officer or agent who accepts or rejects a vote, consent, waiver, or proxy appointment in good faith and in accordance with the standards of this section or § 7.22(b) are not liable in damages to the shareholder for the consequences of the acceptance or rejection.

(e) Corporate action based on the acceptance or rejection of a vote, consent, waiver, or proxy appointment under this section is valid unless a court of competent jurisdiction determines otherwise.

§ 7.25. Quorum and Voting Requirements for Voting Groups.

(a) Shares entitled to vote as a separate voting group may take action on a matter at a meeting only if a quorum of those shares exists with respect to that matter. Unless the articles of incorporation or this Act provide otherwise, a majority of the votes entitled to be cast on the matter by the voting group constitutes a quorum of that voting group for action on that matter.

(b) Once a share is represented for any purpose at a meeting, it is deemed present for quorum purposes for the remainder of the meeting and for any adjournment of that meeting unless a new record date is or must be set for that adjourned meeting.

(c) If a quorum exists, action on a matter (other than the election of directors) by a voting group is approved if the votes cast within the voting group favoring the action exceed the votes cast opposing the action, unless the articles of incorporation or this Act require a greater number of affirmative votes.

(d) An amendment of articles of incorporation adding, changing, or deleting a quorum or voting requirement for a voting group greater than specified in subsection (a) or (c) is governed by § 7.27.

(e) The election of directors is governed by § 7.28.

§ 7.26. Action by Single and Multiple Voting Groups.

(a) If the articles of incorporation or this Act provide for voting by a single voting group on a matter, action on that matter is taken when voted upon by that voting group as provided in § 7.25.

(b) If the articles of incorporation or this act provide for voting by two or more voting groups on a matter, action on that matter is taken only when voted upon by each of those voting groups counted separately as provided in § 7.25. Action may be taken by one voting group on a matter even though no action is taken by another voting group entitled to vote on the matter.

§ 7.27. Greater Quorum or Voting Requirements.

(a) The articles of incorporation may provide for a greater quorum or voting requirement for shareholders (or voting groups of shareholders) than is provided for by this Act.

(b) An amendment to the articles of incorporation that adds, changes, or deletes a greater quorum or voting requirement must meet the same quorum requirement and be adopted by the same vote and voting groups required to take action under the quorum and voting requirements then in effect or proposed to be adopted, whichever is greater.

§ 7.28. Voting for Directors; Cumulative Voting.

(a) Unless otherwise provided in the articles of incorporation, directors are elected by a plurality of the votes cast by the shares entitled to vote in the election at a meeting at which a quorum is present.

(b) Shareholders do not have a right to cumulate their votes for directors unless the articles of incorporation so provide.

(c) A statement included in the articles of incorporation that "[all] [a designated voting group of] shareholders are entitled to cumulate their votes for directors" (or words of similar import) means that the shareholders designated are entitled to multiply the number of votes they are entitled to cast by the number of directors for whom they are entitled to vote and cast he product for a single candidate or distribute the product among two or more candidates.

(d) Shares otherwise entitled to vote cumulatively may not be voted cumulatively at a particular meeting unless:

(1) the meeting notice or proxy statement accompanying the notice states conspicuously that cumulative voting is authorized; or

(2) a shareholder who has the right to cumulate his votes gives notice to the corporation not less than 48 hours before the time set for the meeting of his intent to cumulate his votes during the meeting, and if one shareholder gives this notice all other shareholders in the same voting group participating in the election are entitled to cumulate their votes without giving further notice.

§ 7.29. Inspectors of Election.

(a) A corporation having any shares listed on a national securities exchange or regularly traded in a market maintained by one or more members of a national or affiliated securities association shall, and any other corporation may, appoint one or more inspectors to act at a meeting of shareholders and make a written report of the inspectors' determinations. Each inspector shall take and sign an oath faithfully to execute the duties of inspector with strict impartiality and according to the best of the inspector's ability.

(b) The inspectors shall

(1) ascertain the number of shares outstanding and the voting power of each;

(2) determine the shares represented at a meeting;

(3) determine the validity of proxies and ballots;

(4) count all votes; and

(5) determine the result.

(c) An inspector may be an officer or employee of the corporation.

Subchapter C. Voting Trusts and Agreements

§ 7.30. Voting Trusts.

(a) One or more shareholders may create a voting trust, conferring on a trustee the right to vote or otherwise act for them, by signing an agreement setting out the provisions of the trust (which may include anything consistent with its purpose) and transferring their shares to the trustee. When a voting trust agreement is signed, the trustee shall prepare a list of the names and addresses of all owners of beneficial interests in the trust, together with the number and class of shares each transferred to the trust, and deliver copies of the list and agreement to the corporation's principal office.

(b) A voting trust becomes effective on the date the first shares subject to the trust are registered in the trustee's name. A voting trust is valid for not more than 10 years after its effective date unless extended under subsection (c).

(c) All or some of the parties to a voting trust may extend it for additional terms of not more than 10 years each by signing written consent to the extension. An extension is valid for 10 years from the date the first shareholder signs the extension agreement. The voting trustee must deliver copies of the extension agreement and list of beneficial owners to the corporation's principal office. An extension agreement binds only those parties signing it.

§ 7.31. Voting Agreements.

(a) Two or more shareholders may provide for the manner in which they will vote their shares by signing an agreement for that purpose. A voting agreement created under this section is not subject to the provisions of § 7.30.

(b) A voting agreement created under this section is specifically enforceable.

§ 7.32. Shareholder Agreements.

(a) An agreement among the shareholders of a corporation that complies with this section is effective among the shareholders and the corporation even though it is inconsistent with one or more other provisions of this Act in that it:

(1) eliminates the board of directors or restricts the discretion or powers of the board of directors;

(2) governs the authorization or making of distributions whether or not in proportion to ownership of shares, subject to the limitations in § 6.40;

(3) establishes who shall be directors or officers of the corporation, or their terms of office or manner of selection or removal;

(4) governs, in general or in regard to specific matters, the exercise or division of voting power by or between the shareholders and directors or by or among any of them, including use of weighted voting rights or director proxies;

(5) establishes the terms and conditions of any agreement for the transfer or use of property or the provision of services between the corporation and any shareholder, director, officer or employee of the corporation or among any of them;

(6) transfers to one or more shareholders or other persons all or part of the authority to exercise the corporate powers or to manage the business and affairs of the corporation, including the resolution of any issue about which there exists a deadlock among directors or shareholders;

(7) requires dissolution of the corporation at the request of one or more of the shareholders or upon the occurrence of a specified event or contingency; or

(8) otherwise governs the exercise of the corporate powers or the management of the business and affairs of the corporation or the relationship among the shareholders, the directors and the corporation, or among any of them, and is not contrary to public policy.

(b) An agreement authorized by this section shall be:

(1) set forth (A) in the articles of incorporation or bylaws and approved by all persons who are shareholders at the time of the agreement or (B) in a written agreement that is signed by all persons who are shareholders at the time of the agreement and is made known to the corporation;

(2) subject to amendment only by all persons who are shareholders at the time of the amendment, unless the agreement provides otherwise; and

(3) valid for 10 years, unless the agreement provides otherwise.

(c) The existence of an agreement authorized by this section shall be noted conspicuously on the front or back of each certificate for outstanding shares or on the information statement required by § 6.26(b). If at the time of the agreement the corporation has shares outstanding represented by certificates, the corporation shall recall the outstanding certificates and issue substitute certificates that comply with this subsection. The failure to note the existence of the agreement on the certificate or information statement shall not affect the validity of the agreement or any action taken pursuant to it. Any purchaser of shares who, at the time of purchase, did not have knowledge of the existence of the agreement shall be entitled to rescission of the purchase. A purchaser shall be deemed to have knowledge of the existence of the agreement if its existence is noted on the certificate or information statement for the shares in compliance with this subsection and, if the shares are not represented by a certificate, the information statement is delivered to the purchaser at or prior to the time of purchase of the shares. An action to enforce the right of rescission authorized by this subsection must be commenced within the earlier of 90 days after discovery of the existence of the agreement or two years after the time of purchase of the shares.

(d) An agreement authorized by this section shall cease to be effective when shares of the corporation are listed on a national securities exchange or regularly traded in a market maintained by one or more members of a national or affiliated securities association. If the agreement ceases to be effective for any reason, the board of directors may, if the agreement is contained or referred to in the corporation's articles of incorporation or bylaws, adopt an amendment to the articles of incorporation or bylaws, without shareholder action, to delete the agreement and any references to it.

(e) An agreement authorized by this section that limits the discretion or powers of the board of directors shall relieve the directors of, and impose upon the person or persons in whom such discretion or powers are vested, liability for acts or omissions imposed by law on directors to the extent that the discretion or powers of the directors are limited by the agreement.

(f) The existence or performance of an agreement authorized by this section shall not be a ground for imposing personal liability on any shareholder for the acts or debts of the corporation even if the agreement or its performance treats the corporation as if it were a partnership or results in failure to observe the corporate formalities otherwise applicable to the matters governed by the agreement.

(g) Incorporators or subscribers for shares may act as shareholders with respect to an agreement authorized by this section if no shares have been issued when the agreement is made.

Subchapter D. Derivative Proceedings

§ 7.40. Subchapter Definitions.

In this subchapter:

(1) "Derivative proceeding" means a civil suit in the right of a domestic corporation or, to the extent provided in § 7.47, in the right of a foreign corporation.

(2) "Shareholder" includes a beneficial owner whose shares are held in a voting trust or held by a nominee on the beneficial owner's behalf.

§ 7.41. Standing.

A shareholder may not commence or maintain a derivative proceeding unless the shareholder:

(1) was a shareholder of the corporation at the time of the act or omission complained of or became a shareholder through transfer by operation of law from one who was a shareholder at that time; and

(2) fairly and adequately represents the interests of the corporation in enforcing the right of the corporation.

§ 7.42. Demand.

No shareholder may commence a derivative proceeding until:

(1) a written demand has been made upon the corporation to take suitable action; and

(2) 90 days have expired from the date the demand was made unless the shareholder has earlier been notified that the demand has been rejected by the corporation or unless irreparable injury to the corporation would result by waiting for the expiration of the 90-day period.

§ 7.43. Stay of Proceedings.

If the corporation commences an inquiry into the allegations made in the demand or complaint, the court may stay any derivative proceeding for such period as the court deems appropriate.

§ 7.44. Dismissal.

(a) A derivative proceeding shall be dismissed by the court on motion by the corporation if one of the groups specified in subsections (b) or (f) has determined in good faith after conducting a reasonable inquiry upon which its conclusions are based that the maintenance of the derivative proceeding is not in the best interests of the corporation.

(b) Unless a panel is appointed pursuant to subsection (f), the determination in subsection (a) shall be made by:

(1) a majority vote of independent directors present at a meeting of the board of directors if the Independent directors constitute a quorum; or

(2) a majority vote of a committee consisting of two or more independent directors appointed by majority vote of independent directors present at a meeting of the board of directors, whether or not such independent directors constituted a quorum.

(c) None of the following shall by itself cause a director to be considered not independent for purposes of this section:

(1) the nomination or election of the director by persons who are defendants in the derivative proceeding or against whom action is demanded;

(2) the naming of the director as a defendant in the derivative proceeding or as a person against whom action is demanded; or

(3) the approval by the director of the act being challenged in the derivative proceeding or demand if the act resulted in no personal benefit to the director.

(d) If a derivative proceeding is commenced after a determination has been made rejecting a demand by a shareholder, the complaint shall allege with particularity facts establishing either

(1) that a majority of the board of directors did not consist of independent directors at the time the determination was made or

(2) that the requirements of subsection (a) have not been met.

(e) If a majority of the board of directors does not consist of independent directors at the time the determination is made, the corporation shall have the burden of proving that the requirements of subsection (a) have been met. If a majority of the board of directors consists of independent directors at the time the determination is made, the plaintiff shall have the burden of proving that the requirements of subsection (a) have not been met.

(f) The court may appoint a panel of one or more independent persons upon motion by the corporation to make a determination whether the maintenance of the derivative proceeding is in the best interests of the corporation. In such case, the plaintiff shall have the burden of proving that the requirements of subsection (a) have not been met.

§ 7.45. Discontinuance or Settlement.

A derivative proceeding may not be discontinued or settled without the court's approval. If the court determines that a proposed discontinuance or settlement will substantially affect the interests of the corporation's shareholders or a class of shareholders, the court shall direct that notice be given to the shareholders affected.

§ 7.46. Payment of Expenses.

On termination of the derivative proceeding the court may:

(1) order the corporation to pay the plaintiff's reasonable expenses (including counsel fees) incurred in the proceeding if it finds that the proceeding has resulted in a substantial benefit to the corporation;

(2) order the plaintiff to pay any defendant's reasonable expenses (including counsel fees) incurred in defending the proceeding if it finds that the proceeding was commenced or maintained without reasonable cause or for an improper purpose; or

(3) order a party to pay an opposing party's reasonable expenses (including counsel fees) incurred because of the filing of a pleading, motion or other paper, if it finds that the pleading, motion or other paper was not well grounded in fact, after reasonable inquiry, or warranted by existing law or a good faith argument for the extension, modification or reversal of existing law and was interposed for an improper purpose, such as to harass or cause unnecessary delay or needless increase in the cost of litigation.

§ 7.47. Applicability to Foreign Corporations.

In any derivative proceeding in the right of a foreign corporation, the matters covered by this subchapter shall be governed by the laws of the jurisdiction of incorporation of the foreign corporation except for §§ 7.43, 7.45, and 7.46.

CHAPTER 8. DIRECTORS AND OFFICERS
Subchapter A. Board of Directors

§ 8.01. Requirement for and Duties of Board of Directors.

(a) Except as provided in § 7.32, each corporation must have a board of directors.

(b) All corporate powers shall be exercised by or under the authority of, and the business and affairs of the corporation managed by or under the direction of, its board of directors, subject to any limitation set forth in the articles of incorporation or in an agreement authorized under § 7.32.

§ 8.02. Qualifications of Directors.

The articles of incorporation or bylaws may prescribe qualifications for directors. A director need not be a resident of this state or a shareholder of the corporation unless the articles of incorporation or bylaws so prescribe.

§ 8.03. Number and Election of Directors.

(a) A board of directors must consist of one or more individuals, with the number specified in or fixed in accordance with the articles of incorporation or bylaws.

(b) The number of directors may be increased or decreased from time to time by amendment to, or in the manner provided in the articles of incorporation or the bylaws.

(c) Directors are elected at the first annual shareholders' meeting and at each annual meeting thereafter unless their terms are staggered under § 8.06.

§ 8.04. Election of Directors by Certain Classes of Shareholders.

If the articles of incorporation authorize dividing the shares into classes, the articles may also authorize the election of all or a specified number of directors by the holders of one or more authorized classes of shares. A class (or classes) of shares entitled to elect one or more directors is a separate voting group for purposes of the election of directors.

§ 8.05. Terms of Directors Generally.

(a) The terms of the initial directors of a corporation expire at the first shareholders' meeting at which directors are elected.

(b) The terms of all other directors expire at the next annual shareholders' meeting following their election unless their terms are staggered under § 8.06.

(c) A decrease in the number of directors does not shorten an incumbent director's term.

(d) The term of a director elected to fill a vacancy expires at the next shareholders' meeting at which directors are elected.

(e) Despite the expiration of a director's term, he continues to serve until his successor is elected and qualifies or until there is a decrease in the number of directors.

§ 8.06. Staggered Terms for Directors.

The articles of incorporation may provide for staggering the terms of directors by dividing the total number of directors into two or three groups, with each group containing one-half or one-third of the total, as near as may be. In that event, the terms of directors in the first group expire at the first annual shareholders' meeting after their election, the terms of the second group expire at the second annual shareholders' meeting after their election, and the terms of the third group, if any, expire at the third annual shareholders' meeting after their election. At each annual shareholders' meeting held thereafter, directors shall be chosen for a term of two years or three years, as the case may be, to succeed those whose terms expire.

§ 8.07. Resignation of Directors.

(a) A director may resign at any time by delivering written notice to the board of directors, its chairman, or to the corporation.

(b) A resignation is effective when the notice is delivered unless the notice specifies a later effective date.

§ 8.08. Removal of Directors by Shareholders.

(a) The shareholders may remove one or more directors with or without cause unless the articles of incorporation provide that directors may be removed only for cause.

(b) If a director is elected by a voting group of shareholders, only the shareholders of that voting group may participate in the vote to remove him.

(c) If cumulative voting is authorized, a director may not be removed if the number of votes sufficient to elect him under cumulative voting is voted against his removal. If cumulative voting is not authorized, a director may be removed only if the number of votes cast to remove him exceeds the number of votes cast not to remove him.

(d) A director may be removed by the shareholders only at a meeting called for the purpose of removing him and the meeting notice must state that the purpose, or one of the purposes, of the meeting is removal of the director.

§ 8.09. Removal of Directors by Judicial Proceeding.

(a) The [name or describe] court of the county where a corporation's principal office (or, if none in this state, its registered office) is located may remove a director of the corporation from office in a proceeding commenced by or in the right of the corporation if the court finds that

> (1) the director engaged in fraudulent conduct with respect to the corporation or its shareholders, grossly abused the position of director, or intentionally inflicted harm on the corporation; and

> (2) considering the director's course of conduct and the inadequacy of other available remedies, removal would be in the best interest of the corporation.

(b) A shareholder proceeding on behalf of the corporation under subsection (a) shall comply with all of the requirements of subchapter 7D, except § 7.41(1).

(c) The court, in addition to removing the director, may bar the director from reelection for a period prescribed by the court.

(d) Nothing in this section limits the equitable powers of the court to order other relief.

§ 8.10. Vacancy on Board.

(a) Unless the articles of incorporation provide otherwise, if a vacancy occurs on a board of directors, including a vacancy resulting from an increase in the number of directors:

> (1) the shareholders may fill the vacancy;

> (2) the board of directors may fill the vacancy; or

> (3) if the directors remaining in office constitute fewer than a quorum of the board, they may fill the vacancy by the affirmative vote of a majority of all the directors remaining in office.

(b) If the vacant office was held by a director elected by a voting group of shareholders, only the holders of shares of that voting group are entitled to vote to fill the vacancy if it is filled by the shareholders.

(c) A vacancy that will occur at a specific later date (by reason of a resignation effective at a later date under § 8.07(b) or otherwise) may be filled before the vacancy occurs but the new director may not take office until the vacancy occurs.

§ 8.11. Compensation of Directors.

Unless the articles of incorporation or bylaws provide otherwise, the board of directors may fix the compensation of directors.

Subchapter B. Meetings and Action of the Board

§ 8.20. Meetings.

(a) The board of directors may hold regular or special meetings in or out of this state.

(b) Unless the articles of incorporation or bylaws provide otherwise, the board of directors may permit any or all directors to participate in a regular or special meeting by, or conduct the meeting through the use of, any means of communication by which all directors participating may simultaneously hear each other during the meeting. A director participating in a meeting by this means is deemed to be present in person at the meeting.

§ 8.21. Action Without Meeting.

(a) Except to the extent that the articles of incorporation or bylaws require that action by the board of directors be taken at a meeting, action required or permitted by this Act to be taken by the board of directors may be taken without a meeting if each director signs a consent describing the action to be taken and delivers it to the corporation.

(b) Action taken under this section is the act of the board of directors when one or more consents signed by all the directors are delivered to the corporation. The consent may specify the time at which the action taken thereunder is to be effective. A director's consent may be withdrawn by a revocation signed by the director and delivered to the corporation prior to delivery to the corporation of unrevoked written consents signed by all the directors.

(c) A consent signed under this section has the effect of action taken at a meeting of the board of directors and may be described as such in any document.

§ 8.22. Notice of Meeting.

(a) Unless the articles of incorporation or bylaws provide otherwise, regular meetings of the board of directors may be held without notice of the date, time, place, or purpose of the meeting.

(b) Unless the articles of incorporation or bylaws provide for a longer or shorter period, special meetings of the board of directors must be preceded by at least two days' notice of the date, time, and place of the meeting. The notice need not describe the purpose of the special meeting unless required by the articles of incorporation or bylaws.

§ 8.23. Waiver of Notice.

(a) A director may waive any notice required by this Act, the articles of incorporation, or bylaws before or after the date and time stated in the notice. Except as provided by subsection (b), the waiver must be in writing, signed by the director entitled to the notice, and filed with the minutes or corporate records.

(b) A director's attendance at or participation in a meeting waives any required notice to him of the meeting unless the director at the beginning of the meeting (or promptly upon his arrival) objects to holding the meeting or transacting business at the meeting and does not thereafter vote for or assent to action taken at the meeting.

§ 8.24. Quorum and Voting.

(a) Unless the articles of incorporation or bylaws require a greater number or unless otherwise specifically provided in this Act, a quorum of a board of directors consists of:

> (1) a majority of the fixed number of directors if the corporation has a fixed board size; or

(2) a majority of the number of directors prescribed, or if no number is prescribed the number in office immediately before the meeting begins, if the corporation has a variable-range size board.

(b) The articles of incorporation or bylaws may authorize a quorum of a board of directors to consist of no fewer than one-third of the fixed or prescribed number of directors determined under subsection (a).

(c) If a quorum is present when a vote is taken, the affirmative vote of a majority of directors present is the act of the board of directors unless the articles of incorporation or bylaws require the vote of a greater number of directors.

(d) A director who is present at a meeting of the board of directors or a committee of the board of directors when corporate action is taken is deemed to have assented to the action taken unless:

(1) he objects at the beginning of the meeting (or promptly upon his arrival) to holding it or transacting business at the meeting;

(2) his dissent or abstention from the action taken is entered in the minutes of the meeting; or

(3) he delivers written notice of his dissent or abstention to the presiding officer of the meeting before its adjournment or to the corporation immediately after adjournment of the meeting. The right of dissent or abstention is not available to a director who votes in favor of the action taken.

§ 8.25. Committees.

(a) Unless this Act, the articles of incorporation or the bylaws provide otherwise, a board of directors may create one or more committees and appoint one or more members of the board of directors to serve on any such committee.

(b) Unless this Act otherwise provides, the creation of a committee and appointment of members to it must be approved by the greater of

(1) a majority of all the directors in office when the action is taken or

(2) the number of directors required by the articles of incorporation or bylaws to take action under § 8.24.

(c) Sections 8.20 through 8.24 apply both to committees of the board and to their members.

(d) To the extent specified by the board of directors or in the articles of incorporation or bylaws, each committee may exercise the powers of the board of directors under § 8.01.

(e) A committee may not, however:

(1) authorize or approve distributions, except according to a formula or method, or within limits, prescribed by the board of directors;

(2) approve or propose to shareholders action that this Act requires be approved by shareholders;

(3) fill vacancies on the board of directors or, subject to subsection (g), on any of its committees; or

(4) adopt, amend, or repeal bylaws.

(f) The creation of, delegation of authority to, or action by a committee does not alone constitute compliance by a director with the standards of conduct described in § 8.30.

(g) The board of directors may appoint one or more directors as alternate members of any committee to replace any absent or disqualified member during the member's absence or disqualification. Unless the articles of incorporation or the bylaws or the resolution creating the committee provide otherwise, in the event

of the absence or disqualification of a member of a committee, the member or members present at any meeting and not disqualified from voting, unanimously, may appoint another director to act in place of the absent or disqualified member.

Subchapter C. Directors

§ 8.30. Standards of Conduct for Directors.

(a) Each member of the board of directors, when discharging the duties of a director, shall act:

(i) in good faith, and

(ii) in a manner the director reasonably believes to be in the best interests of the corporation.

(b) The members of the board of directors or a committee of the board, when becoming informed in connection with their decision-making function or devoting attention to their oversight function, shall discharge their duties with the care that a person in a like position would reasonably believe appropriate under similar circumstances.

(c) In discharging board or committee duties a director, who does not have knowledge that makes reliance unwarranted, is entitled to rely on the performance by any of the persons specified in subsection (e)(1) or subsection (e)(3) to whom the board may have delegated, formally or informally by course of conduct, the authority or duty to perform one or more of the board's functions that are delegable under applicable law.

(d) In discharging board or committee duties a director, who does not have knowledge that makes reliance unwarranted, is entitled to rely on information, opinions, reports or statements, including financial statements and other financial data, prepared or presented by any of the persons specified in subsection (e).

(e) A director is entitled to rely, in accordance with subsection (c) or (d), on:

(A) one or more officers or employees of the corporation whom the director reasonably believes to be reliable and competent in the functions performed or the information, opinions, reports or statements provided;

(B) legal counsel, public accountants, or other persons retained by the corporation as to matters involving skills or expertise the director reasonably believes are matters

(i) within the particular person's professional or expert competence or

(ii) as to which the particular person merits confidence; or

(iii) a committee of the board of directors of which the director is not a member if the director reasonably believes the committee merits confidence.

§ 8.31. Standards of Liability for Directors.

I. A director shall not be liable to the corporation or its shareholders for any decision to take or not to take action, or any failure to take any action, as a director, unless the party asserting liability in a proceeding establishes that:

A. any provision in the articles of incorporation authorized by § 2.02(b)(4) or the protection afforded by § 8.61 for action taken in compliance with § 8.62 or 8.63, if interposed as a bar to the proceeding by the director, does not preclude liability; and

B. the challenged conduct consisted or was the result of:

(1) action not in good faith; or

(2) a decision a. which the director did not reasonably believe to be in the best interests of the corporation, or as to

which the director was not informed to an extent the director reasonably believed appropriate in the circumstances; or

(3) a lack of objectivity due to the director's familial, financial or business relationship with, or a lack of independence due to the director's domination or control by, another person having a material interest in the challenged conduct

(a) which relationship or which domination or control could reasonably be expected to have affected the director's judgment respecting the challenged conduct in a manner adverse to the corporation, and

(b) after a reasonable expectation to such effect has been established, the director shall not have established that the challenged conduct was reasonably believed by the director to be in the best interests of the corporation; or

(4) a sustained failure of the director to devote attention to ongoing oversight of the business and affairs of the corporation, or a failure to devote timely attention, by making (or causing to be made) appropriate inquiry, when particular facts and circumstances of significant concern materialize that would alert a reasonably attentive director to the need therefore; or

(5) receipt of a financial benefit to which the director was not entitled or any other breach of the director's duties to deal fairly with the corporation and its shareholders that is actionable under applicable law.

II. The party seeking to hold the director liable:

A. for money damages, shall also have the burden of establishing that:

(1) harm to the corporation or its shareholders has been suffered, and

(2) the harm suffered was proximately caused by the director's challenged conduct; or

B. for other money payment under a legal remedy, such as compensation for the unauthorized use of corporate assets, shall also have whatever persuasion burden may be called for to establish that the payment sought is appropriate in the circumstances; or

C. for other money payment under an equitable remedy, such as profit recovery by or disgorgement to the corporation, shall also have whatever persuasion burden may be called for to establish that the equitable remedy sought is appropriate in the circumstances.

III. Nothing contained in this section shall (1) in any instance where fairness is at issue, such as consideration of the fairness of a transaction to the corporation under § 8.61(b)(3), alter the burden of proving the fact or lack of fairness otherwise applicable, (2) alter the fact or lack of liability of a director under another section of this Act, such as the provisions governing the consequences of an unlawful distribution under § 8.33 or a transactional interest under § 8.61, or (3) affect any rights to which the corporation or a shareholder may be entitled under another statute of this state or the United States.

§ 8.32. [Reserved]

§ 8.33. Directors' Liability for Unlawful Distributions.

I. A director who votes for or assents to a distribution in excess of what may be authorized and made pursuant to § 6.40(a) or

14.09(a) is personally liable to the corporation for the amount of the distribution that exceeds what could have been distributed without violating § 6.40(a) or 14.09(a) if the party asserting liability establishes that when taking the action the director did not comply with § 8.30

II. A director held liable under subsection (a) for an unlawful distribution is entitled to:

A. contribution from every other director who could be held liable under subsection (a) for the unlawful distribution; and

B. recoupment from each shareholder of the pro-rata portion of the amount of the unlawful distribution the shareholder accepted, knowing the distribution was made in violation of § 6.40(a) or 14.09(a).

III. A proceeding to enforce:

A. the liability of a director under subsection (a) is barred unless it is commenced within two years after the date (i) on which the effect of the distribution was measured under § 6.40(e) or (g), (ii) as of which the violation of § 6.40(a) occurred as the consequence of disregard of a restriction in the articles of incorporation or (iii) on which the distribution of assets to Shareholders under § 14.09(a) was made; or

B. contribution or recoupment under subsection (b) is barred unless it is commenced within one year after the liability of the claimant has been finally adjudicated under subsection (a).

Subchapter D. Officers

§ 8.40. Officers.

(a) A corporation has the officers described in its bylaws or appointed by the board of directors in accordance with the bylaws

(b) The board of directors may elect individuals to fill one or more offices of the corporation. An officer may appoint one or more officers if authorized by the bylaws or the board of directors.

(c) The bylaws or the board of directors shall assign to one of the officers responsibility for preparing the minutes of the directors' and shareholders' meetings and for maintaining and authenticating the records of the corporation required to be kept under §§ 16.01(a) and 16.01(e).

(d) The same individual may simultaneously hold more than one office in a corporation.

§ 8.41. Duties of Officers.
Each officer has the authority and shall perform the duties set forth in the bylaws or, to the extent consistent with the bylaws, the duties prescribed by the board of directors or by direction of an officer authorized by the board of directors to prescribe the duties of other officers.

§ 8.42. Standards of Conduct for Officers.

(a) An officer, when performing in such capacity, shall act:

(1) in good faith;

(2) with the care that a person in a like position would reasonably exercise under similar circumstances; and

(3) in a manner the officer reasonably believes to be in the best interests of the corporation.

(b) In discharging those duties an officer, who does not have knowledge that makes reliance unwarranted, is entitled to rely on:

(1) the performance of properly delegated responsibilities by one or more employees of the corporation whom the officer reasonably believes to be reliable and competent in performing the responsibilities delegated; or

(2) information, opinions, reports or statements, including financial statements and other financial data, prepared or presented by one or more employees of the corporation whom the officer reasonably believes to be reliable and competent in the matters presented or by legal counsel, public accountants, or other persons retained by the corporation as to matters involving skills or expertise the officer reasonably believes are matters (i) within the particular person's professional or expert competence or (ii) as to which the particular person merits confidence. (c) An officer shall not be liable to the corporation or its shareholders for any decision to take or not to take action, or any failure to take any action, as an officer, if the duties of the office are performed in compliance with this section. Whether an officer who does not comply with this section shall have liability will depend in such instance on applicable law, including those principles of § 8.31 that have relevance.

§ 8.43. Resignation and Removal of Officers.

(a) An officer may resign at any time by delivering notice to the corporation. A resignation is effective when the notice is delivered unless the notice specifies a later effective time. If a resignation is made effective at a later time and the board or the appointing officer accepts the future effective time, the board or the appointing officer may fill the pending vacancy before the effective time if the board or the appointing officer provides that the successor does not take office until the effective time.

(b) An officer may be removed at any time with or without cause by:

    (i) the board of directors;

    (ii) the officer who appointed such officer, unless the bylaws or the board of directors provide otherwise; or

    (iii) any other officer if authorized by the bylaws or the board of directors.

(c) In this section, "appointing officer" means the officer (including any successor to that officer) who appointed the officer resigning or being removed.

§ 8.44. Contract Rights of Officers.

(a) The appointment of an officer does not itself create contract rights.

(b) An officer's removal does not affect the officer's contract rights, if any, with the corporation.

An officer's resignation does not affect the corporation's contract rights, if any, with the officer.

Subchapter E. Indemnification and Advance for Expenses

§ 8.50. Subchapter Definitions. In this subchapter:

(1) "Corporation" includes any domestic or foreign predecessor entity of a corporation in a merger.

(2) "Director" or "officer" means an individual who is or was a director or officer, respectively, of a corporation or who, while a director or officer of the corporation, is or was serving at the corporation's request as a director, officer, partner, trustee, employee, or agent of another domestic or foreign corporation, partnership, joint venture, trust, employee benefit plan, or other entity. A director or officer is considered to be serving an employee benefit plan at the corporation's request if his duties to the corporation also impose duties on, or otherwise involve services by, him to the plan or to participants in or beneficiaries of the plan. "Director" or "officer" includes, unless the context

requires otherwise, the estate or personal representative of a director or officer.

(3) "Disinterested director" means a director who, at the time of a vote referred to in § 8.53(c) or a vote or selection referred to in § 8.55(b) or (c), is not (i) a party to the proceeding, or (ii) an individual having a familial, financial, professional or employment relationship with the director whose indemnification or advance for expenses is the subject of the decision being made, which relationship would, in the circumstances, reasonably be expected to exert an influence on the director's judgment when voting on the decision being made.

(4) "Expenses" includes counsel fees.

(5) "Liability" means the obligation to pay a judgment, settlement, penalty, fine (including an excise tax assessed with respect to an employee benefit plan), or reasonable expenses incurred with respect to a proceeding.

(6) "Official capacity" means: (i) when used with respect to a director, the office of director in a corporation; and (ii) when used with respect to an officer, as contemplated in § 8.56, the office in a corporation held by the officer. "Official capacity" does not include service for any other domestic or foreign corporation or any partnership, joint venture, trust, employee benefit plan, or other entity.

(7) "Party" means an individual who was, is, or is threatened to be made, a defendant or respondent in a proceeding.

(8) "Proceeding" means any threatened, pending, or completed action, suit, or proceeding, whether civil, criminal, administrative, arbitrative, or investigative and whether formal or informal.

§ 8.51. Permissible Indemnification.

(a) Except as otherwise provided in this section, a corporation may indemnify an individual who is a party to a proceeding because he is a director against liability incurred in the proceeding if:

    (1) (i) he conducted himself in good faith; and

        (ii) he reasonably believed:

            (A) in the case of conduct in his official capacity, that his conduct was in the best interests of the corporation; and

            (B) in all other cases, that his conduct was at least not opposed to the best interests of the corporation; and

        (iii) in the case of any criminal proceeding, he had no reasonable cause to believe his conduct was unlawful; or

    (2) he engaged in conduct for which broader indemnification has been made permissible or obligatory under a provision of the articles of incorporation (as authorized by § 2.02(b)(5)).

(b) A director's conduct with respect to an employee benefit plan for a purpose he reasonably believed to be in the interests of the participants in, and the beneficiaries of, the plan is conduct that satisfies the requirement of subsection (a)(1)(ii)(B).

(c) The termination of a proceeding by judgment, order, settlement, or conviction, or upon a plea of nolo contendere or its equivalent, is not, of itself, determinative that the director did not meet the relevant standard of conduct described in this section.

(d) Unless ordered by a court under § 8.54(a)(3), a corporation may not indemnify a director:

    (1) in connection with a proceeding by or in the right of the corporation, except for reasonable expenses incurred in connection with the proceeding if it is determined that the director has met the relevant standard of conduct under subsection (a); or

(2) in connection with any proceeding with respect to conduct for which he was adjudged liable on the basis that he received a financial benefit to which he was not entitled, whether or not involving action in his official capacity.

§ 8.52. Mandatory Indemnification.

A corporation shall indemnify a director who was wholly successful, on the merits or otherwise, in the defense of any proceeding to which he was a party because he was a director of the corporation against reasonable expenses incurred by him in connection with the proceeding.

§ 8.53. Advance for Expenses.

(a) A corporation may, before final disposition of a proceeding, advance funds to pay for or reimburse the reasonable expenses incurred by a director who is a party to a proceeding because he is a director if he delivers to the corporation:

> (1) a written affirmation of his good faith belief that he has met the relevant standard of conduct described in § 8.51 or that the proceeding involves conduct for which liability has been eliminated under a provision of the articles of incorporation as authorized by § 2.02(b)(4); and
>
> (2) his written undertaking to repay any funds advanced if he is not entitled to mandatory indemnification under §8.52 and it is ultimately determined under § 8.54 or 8.55 that he has not met the relevant standard of conduct described in § 8.51.

(b) The undertaking required by subsection (a)(2) must be an unlimited general obligation of the director but need not be secured and may be accepted without reference to the financial ability of the director to make repayment.

(c) Authorizations under this section shall be made:

> (1) by the board of directors:
>
>> (i) if there are two or more disinterested directors, by a majority vote of all the disinterested directors (a majority of whom shall for such purpose constitute a quorum) or by a majority of the members of a committee of two or more disinterested directors appointed by such a vote; or
>>
>> (ii) if there are fewer than two disinterested directors, by the vote necessary for action by the board in accordance with § 8.24(c), in which authorization directors who do not qualify as disinterested directors may participate; or
>
> (2) by the shareholders, but shares owned by or voted under the control of a director who at the time does not qualify as a disinterested director may not be voted on the authorization.

§ 8.54. Court-Ordered Indemnification and Advance for Expenses.

(a) A director who is a party to a proceeding because he is a director may apply for indemnification or an advance for expenses to the court conducting the proceeding or to another court of competent jurisdiction. After receipt of an application and after giving any notice it considers necessary, the court shall:

> (1) order indemnification if the court determines that the director is entitled to mandatory indemnification under § 8.52;
>
> (2) order indemnification or advance for expenses if the court determines that the director is entitled to indemnification or advance for expenses pursuant to a provision authorized by § 8.58(a); or

> (3) order indemnification or advance for expenses if the court determines, in view of all the relevant circumstances, that it is fair and reasonable
>
>> (i) to indemnify the director, or
>>
>> (ii) to advance expenses to the director, even if he has not met the relevant standard of conduct set forth in §8.51(a), failed to comply with § 8.53 or was adjudged liable in a proceeding referred to in subsection 8.51(d)(1) or (d)(2), but if he was adjudged so liable his indemnification shall be limited to reasonable expenses incurred in connection with the proceeding.

(b) If the court determines that the director is entitled to indemnification under subsection (a)(b) or to indemnification or advance for expenses under subsection (a)(2), it shall also order the corporation to pay the director's reasonable expenses incurred in connection with obtaining court-ordered indemnification or advance for expenses. If the court determines that the director is entitled to indemnification or advance for expenses under subsection (a)(3), it may also order the corporation to pay the director's reasonable expenses to obtain court-ordered indemnification or advance for expenses.

§ 8.55. Determination and Authorization of Indemnification.

(a) A corporation may not indemnify a director under § 8.51 unless authorized for a specific proceeding after a determination has been made that indemnification of the director is permissible because he has met the relevant standard of conduct set forth in § 8.51.

(b) The determination shall be made:

> (1) if there are two or more disinterested directors, by the board of directors by a majority vote of all the disinterested directors (a majority of whom shall for such purpose constitute a quorum), or by a majority of the members of a committee of two or more disinterested directors appointed by such a vote;
>
> (2) by special legal counsel:
>
>> (i) selected in the manner prescribed in subdivision (1); or
>>
>> (ii) if there are fewer than two disinterested directors, selected by the board of directors (in which selection directors who do not qualify as disinterested directors may participate); or
>
> (3) by the shareholders, but shares owned by or voted under the control of a director who at the time does not qualify as a disinterested director may not be voted on the determination.

(c) Authorization of indemnification shall be made in the same manner as the determination that indemnification is permissible, except that if there are fewer than two disinterested directors or if the determination is made by special legal counsel, authorization of indemnification shall be made by those entitled under subsection (b)(2)(ii) to select special legal counsel.

§ 8.56. Indemnification of Officers.

(a) A corporation may indemnify and advance expenses under this subchapter to an officer of the corporation who is a party to a proceeding because he is an officer of the corporation

> (1) to the same extent as a director; and
>
> (2) if he is an officer but not a director, to such further extent as may be provided by the articles of incorporation, the bylaws, a resolution of the board of directors, or contract except for
>
>> (A) liability in connection with a proceeding by or in the right of the corporation other than for reasonable expenses incurred in connection with the proceeding or

(B) liability arising out of conduct that constitutes
    (i) receipt by him of a financial benefit to which he is not entitled,
    (ii) an intentional infliction of harm on the corporation or the shareholders, or
    (iii) an intentional violation of criminal law.

(b) The provisions of subsection (a)(2) shall apply to an officer who is also a director if the basis on which he is made a party to the proceeding is an act or omission solely as an officer.

(c) An officer of a corporation who is not a director is entitled to mandatory indemnification under § 8.52, and may apply to a court under § 8.54 for indemnification or an advance for expenses, in each case to the same extent to which a director may be entitled to indemnification or advance for expenses under those provisions.

§ 8.57. Insurance.

A corporation may purchase and maintain insurance on behalf of an individual who is a director or officer of the corporation, or who, while a director or officer of the corporation, serves at the corporation's request as a director, officer, partner, trustee, employee, or agent of another domestic or foreign corporation, partnership, joint venture, trust, employee benefit plan, or other entity, against liability asserted against or incurred by him in that capacity or arising from his status as a director or officer, whether or not the corporation would have power to indemnify or advance expenses to him against the same liability under this subchapter.

§ 8.58. Variation by Corporate Action; Application of Subchapter.

(a) A corporation may, by a provision in its articles of incorporation or bylaws or in a resolution adopted or a contract approved by its board of directors or shareholders, obligate itself in advance of the act or omission giving rise to a proceeding to provide indemnification in accordance with § 8.51 or advance funds to pay for or reimburse expenses in accordance with §8.53. Any such obligatory provision shall be deemed to satisfy the requirements for authorization referred to in § 8.53(c) and in § 8.55(c). Any such provision that obligates the corporation to provide indemnification to the fullest extent permitted by law shall be deemed to obligate the corporation to advance funds to pay for or reimburse expenses in accordance with § 8.53 to the fullest extent permitted by law, unless the provision specifically provides otherwise.

(b) Any provision pursuant to subsection (a) shall not obligate the corporation to indemnify or advance expenses to a director of a predecessor of the corporation, pertaining to conduct with respect to the predecessor, unless otherwise specifically provided. Any provision for indemnification or advance for expenses in the articles of incorporation, bylaws, or a resolution of the board of directors or shareholders of a predecessor of the corporation in a merger or in a contract to which the predecessor is a party, existing at the time the merger takes effect, shall be governed by § 11.07(a)(4).

(c) A corporation may, by a provision in its articles of incorporation, limit any of the rights to indemnification or advance for expenses created by or pursuant to this subchapter.

(d) This subchapter does not limit a corporation's power to pay or reimburse expenses incurred by a director or an officer in connection with his appearance as a witness in a proceeding at a time when he is not a party.

(e) This subchapter does not limit a corporation's power to indemnify, advance expenses to or provide or maintain insurance on behalf of an employee or agent.

§ 8.59. Exclusivity of Subchapter.

A corporation may provide indemnification or advance expenses to a director or an officer only as permitted by this subchapter.

Subchapter F. Directors' Conflicting Interest Transactions Introductory Comment

§ 8.60. Subchapter Definitions.

In this subchapter:

(1) "Conflicting interest" with respect to a corporation means the interest a director of the corporation has respecting a transaction effected or proposed to be effected by the corporation (or by a subsidiary of the corporation or any other entity in which the corporation has a controlling interest) if (i) whether or not the transaction is brought before the board of directors of the corporation for action, the director knows at the time of commitment that he or a related person is a party to the transaction or has a beneficial financial interest in or so closely linked to the transaction and of such financial significance to the director or a related person that the interest would reasonably be expected to exert an influence on the director's judgment if he were called upon to vote on the transaction; or (ii) the transaction is brought (or is of such character and significance to the corporation that it would in the normal course be brought) before the board of directors of the corporation for action, and the director knows at the time of commitment that any of the following persons is either a party to the transaction or has a beneficial financial interest in or so closely linked to the transaction and of such financial significance to the person that the interest would reasonably be expected to exert an influence on the director's judgment if he were called upon to vote on the transaction: (A) an entity (other than the corporation) of which the director is a director, general partner, agent, or employee; (B) a person that controls one or more of the entities specified in subclause (A) or an entity that is controlled by, or is under common control with, one or more of the entities specified in subclause (A); or (C) an individual who is a general partner, principal, or employer of the director.

(2) "Director's conflicting interest transaction" with respect to a corporation means a transaction effected or proposed to be effected by the corporation (or by a subsidiary of the corporation or any other entity in which the corporation has a controlling interest) respecting which a director of the corporation has a conflicting interest.

(3) "Related person" of a director means (i) the spouse (or a parent or sibling thereof) of the director, or a child, grandchild, sibling, parent (or spouse of any thereof) of the director, or an individual having the same home as the director, or a trust or estate of which an individual specified in this clause (i) is a substantial beneficiary; or (ii) a trust, estate, incompetent, conservatee, or minor of which the director is a fiduciary.

(4) "Required disclosure" means disclosure by the director who has a conflicting interest of (i) the existence and nature of his conflicting interest, and (ii) all facts known to him respecting the subject matter of the transaction that an ordinarily prudent person would reasonably believe to be material to a judgment about whether or not to proceed with the transaction.

(5) "Time of commitment" respecting a transaction means the time when the transaction is consummated or, if made pursuant to contract, the time when the corporation (or its subsidiary or the entity in which it has a controlling interest) becomes contractually obligated so that its unilateral withdrawal from the transaction would entail significant loss, liability, or other damage.

§ 8.61. Judicial Action.

(a) A transaction effected or proposed to be effected by a corporation (or by a subsidiary of the corporation or any other entity in which the corporation has a controlling interest) that is not a director's conflicting interest transaction may not be enjoined, set aside, or give rise to an award of damages or other sanctions, in a proceeding by a shareholder or by or in the right of the corporation, because a director of the corporation, or any person with whom or which he has a personal, economic, or other association, has an interest in the transaction.

(b) A director's conflicting interest transaction may not be enjoined, set aside, or give rise to an award of damages or other sanctions, in a proceeding by a shareholder or by or in the right of the corporation, because the director, or any person with whom or which he has a personal, economic, or other association, has an interest in the transaction, if:

    (1) directors' action respecting the transaction was at any time taken in compliance with § 8.62;

    (2) shareholders' action respecting the transaction was at any time taken in compliance with § 8.63; or

    (3) the transaction, judged according to the circumstances at the time of commitment, is established to have been fair to the corporation.

§ 8.62. Directors' Action.

(a) Directors' action respecting a transaction is effective for purposes of § 8.61(b)(1) if the transaction received the affirmative vote of a majority (but no fewer than two) of those qualified directors on the board of directors or on a duly empowered committee of the board who voted on the transaction after either required disclosure to them (to the extent the information was not known by them) or compliance with subsection (b); provided that action by a committee is so effective only if:

    (1) all its members are qualified directors, and

    (2) its members are either all the qualified directors on the board or are appointed by the affirmative vote of a majority of the qualified directors on the board.

(b) If a director has a conflicting interest respecting a transaction, but neither he nor a related person of the director specified in § 8.60(3)(i) is a party to the transaction, and if the director has a duty under law or professional canon, or a duty of confidentiality to another person, respecting information relating to the transaction such that the director may not make the disclosure described in § 8.60(4)(ii), then disclosure is sufficient for purposes of subsection (a) if the director (1) discloses to the directors voting on the transaction the existence and nature of his conflicting interest and informs them of the character and limitations imposed by that duty before their vote on the transaction, and (2) plays no part, directly or indirectly, in their deliberations or vote.

(c) A majority (but no fewer than two) of all the qualified directors on the board of directors, or on the committee, constitutes a quorum for purposes of action that complies with this section. Directors' action that otherwise complies with this section is not af-

fected by the presence or vote of a director who is not a qualified director.

(d) For purposes of this section, "qualified director" means, with respect to a director's conflicting interest transaction, any director who does not have either (1) a conflicting interest respecting the transaction, or (2) a familial, financial, professional, or employment relationship with a second director who does have a conflicting interest respecting the transaction, which relationship would, in the circumstances, reasonably be expected to exert an influence on the first director's judgment when voting on the transaction.

§ 8.63. Shareholders' Action.

(a) Shareholders' action respecting a transaction is effective for purposes of § 8.61(b)(2) if a majority of the votes entitled to be cast by the holders of all qualified shares were cast in favor of the transaction after (1) notice to shareholders describing the director's conflicting interest transaction, (2) provision of the information referred to in subsection (d), and (3) required disclosure to the shareholders who voted on the transaction (to the extent the information was not known by them).

(b) For purposes of this section, "qualified shares" means any shares entitled to vote with respect to the director's conflicting interest transaction except shares that, to the knowledge, before the vote, of the secretary (or other officer or agent of the corporation authorized to tabulate votes), are beneficially owned (or the voting of which is controlled) by a director who has a conflicting interest respecting the transaction or by a related person of the director, or both.

(c) A majority of the votes entitled to be cast by the holders of all qualified shares constitutes a quorum for purposes of action that complies with this section. Subject to the provisions of subsections (d) and (e), shareholders' action that otherwise complies with this section is not affected by the presence of holders, or the voting, of shares that are not qualified shares.

(d) For purposes of compliance with subsection (a), a director who has a conflicting interest respecting the transaction shall, before the shareholders' vote, inform the secretary (or other office or agent of the corporation authorized to tabulate votes) of the number, and the identity of persons holding or controlling the vote, of all shares that the director knows are beneficially owned (or the voting of which is controlled) by the director or by a related person of the director, or both.

(e) If a shareholders' vote does not comply with subsection (a) solely because of a failure of a director to comply with subsection (d), and if the director establishes that his failure did not determine and was not intended by him to influence the outcome of the vote, the court may, with or without further proceedings respecting § 8.61 (b)(3), take such action respecting the transaction and the director, and give such effect, if any, to the shareholders' vote, as it considers appropriate in the circumstances.

CHAPTER 9. DOMESTICATION AND CONVERSION
Subchapter A. Preliminary Provisions

§ 9.01. Excluded Transactions.

This chapter may not be used to effect a transaction that:

(1) [converts an insurance company organized on the mutual principle to one organized on a stock-share basis];

(2) [Reserved]

(3) [Reserved]

§ 9.02. Required Approvals [Optional].

(a) If a domestic or foreign business corporation or eligible entity may not be a party to a merger without the approval of the [attorney general], the [department of banking], the [department of insurance] or the [public utility commission], the corporation or eligible entity shall not be a party to a transaction under this chapter without the prior approval of that agency.

(b) Property held in trust or for charitable purposes under the laws of this state by a domestic or foreign eligible entity shall not, by any transaction under this chapter, be diverted from the objects for which it was donated, granted or devised, unless and until the eligible entity obtains an order of [court] [the attorney general] specifying the disposition of the property to the extent required by and pursuant to [cite state statutory cy pres or other nondiversion statute].

Subchapter B. Domestication

§ 9.20. Domestication.

(a) A foreign business corporation may become a domestic business corporation only if the domestication is permitted by the organic law of the foreign corporation.

(b) A domestic business corporation may become a foreign business corporation if the domestication is permitted by the laws of the foreign jurisdiction. Regardless of whether the laws of the foreign jurisdiction require the adoption of a plan of domestication, the domestication shall be approved by the adoption by the corporation of a plan of domestication in the manner provided in this subchapter.

(c) The plan of domestication must include:

(1) a statement of the jurisdiction in which the corporation is to be domesticated;

(2) the terms and conditions of the domestication;

(3) the manner and basis of reclassifying the shares of the corporation following its domestication into shares or other securities, obligations, rights to acquire shares or other securities, cash, other property, or any combination of the foregoing; and

(4) any desired amendments to the articles of incorporation of the corporation following its domestication.

(d) The plan of domestication may also include a provision that the plan may be amended prior to filing the document required by the laws of this state or the other jurisdiction to consummate the domestication, except that subsequent to approval of the plan by the shareholders the plan may not be amended to change: (1) the amount or kind of shares or other securities, obligations, rights to acquire shares or other securities, cash, or other property to be received by the shareholders under the plan; (2) the articles of incorporation as they will be in effect immediately following the domestication, except for changes permitted by § 10.05 or by comparable provisions of the laws of the other jurisdiction; or (3) any of the other terms or conditions of the plan if the change would adversely affect any of the shareholders in any material respect.

(e) Terms of a plan of domestication may be made dependent upon facts objectively ascertainable outside the plan in accordance with § 1.20(k).

(f) If any debt security, note or similar evidence of indebtedness for money borrowed, whether secured or unsecured, or a contract of any kind, issued, incurred or executed by a domestic business corporation before [the effective date of this subchapter] contains a provision applying to a merger of the corporation and the document does not refer to a domestication of the corporation, the provision shall be deemed to apply to a domestication of the corporation until such time as the provision is amended subsequent to that date.

§ 9.21. Action on a Plan of Domestication.

In the case of a domestication of a domestic business corporation in a foreign jurisdiction:

(1) The plan of domestication must be adopted by the board of directors.

(2) After adopting the plan of domestication the board of directors must submit the plan to the shareholders for their approval. The board of directors must also transmit to the shareholders a recommendation that the shareholders approve the plan, unless the board of directors makes a determination that because of conflicts of interest or other special circumstances it should not make such a recommendation, in which case the board of directors must transmit to the shareholders the basis for that determination.

(3) The board of directors may condition its submission of the plan of domestication to the shareholders on any basis.

(4) If the approval of the shareholders is to be given at a meeting, the corporation must notify each shareholder, whether or not entitled to vote, of the meeting of shareholders at which the plan of domestication is to be submitted for approval. The notice must state that the purpose, or one of the purposes, of the meeting is to consider the plan and must contain or be accompanied by a copy or summary of the plan. The notice shall include or be accompanied by a copy of the articles of incorporation as they will be in effect immediately after the domestication.

(5) Unless the articles of incorporation, or the board of directors acting pursuant to paragraph (3), requires a greater vote or a greater number of votes to be present, approval of the plan of domestication requires the approval of the shareholders at a meeting at which a quorum consisting of at least a majority of the votes entitled to be cast on the plan exists, and, if any class or series of shares is entitled to vote as a separate group on the plan, the approval of each such separate voting group at a meeting at which a quorum of the voting group consisting of at least a majority of the votes entitled to be cast on the domestication by that voting group exists.

(6) Separate voting by voting groups is required by each class or series of shares that:

(i) are to be reclassified under the plan of domestication into other securities, obligations, rights to acquire shares or other securities, cash, other property, or any combination of the foregoing;

(ii) would be entitled to vote as a separate group on a provision of the plan that, if contained in a proposed amendment to articles of incorporation, would require action by separate voting groups under § 10.04; or

(iii) is entitled under the articles of incorporation to vote as a voting group to approve an amendment of the articles.

(7) If any provision of the articles of incorporation, bylaws or an agreement to which any of the directors or shareholders are parties, adopted or entered into before [the effective date of this subchapter], applies to a merger of the corporation and that document does not refer to a domestication of the corporation, the provision shall be deemed to apply to a domestication of the corporation until such time as the provision is amended subsequent to that date.

§ 9.22. Articles of Domestication.

(a) After the domestication of a foreign business corporation has been authorized as required by the laws of the foreign jurisdiction, articles of domestication shall be executed by any officer or other duly authorized representative. The articles shall set forth:

(1) the name of the corporation immediately before the filing of the articles of domestication and, if that name is unavailable for use in this state or the corporation desires to change its name in connection with the domestication, a name that satisfies the requirements of § 4.01;

(2) the jurisdiction of incorporation of the corporation immediately before the filing of the articles of domestication and the date the corporation was incorporated in that jurisdiction; and

(3) a statement that the domestication of the corporation in this state was duly authorized as required by the laws of the jurisdiction in which the corporation was incorporated immediately before its domestication in this state.

(b) The articles of domestication shall either contain all of the provisions that § 2.02(a) requires to be set forth in articles of incorporation and any other desired provisions that § 2.02(b) permits to be included in articles of incorporation, or shall have attached articles of incorporation. In either case, provisions that would not be required to be included in restated articles of incorporation may be omitted.

(c) The articles of domestication shall be delivered to the secretary of state for filing, and shall take effect at the effective time provided in § 1.23.

(d) If the foreign corporation is authorized to transact business in this state under chapter 15, its certificate of authority shall be cancelled automatically on the effective date of its domestication.

§ 9.23. Surrender of Charter upon Domestication.

(a) Whenever a domestic business corporation has adopted and approved, in the manner required by this subchapter, a plan of domestication providing for the corporation to be domesticated in a foreign jurisdiction, articles of charter surrender shall be executed on behalf of the corporation by any officer or other duly authorized representative. The articles of charter surrender shall set forth:

(1) the name of the corporation;

(2) a statement that the articles of charter surrender are being filed in connection with the domestication of the corporation in a foreign jurisdiction;

(3) a statement that the domestication was duly approved by the shareholders and, if voting by any separate voting group was required, by each such separate voting group, in the manner required by this Act and the articles of incorporation;

(4) the corporation's new jurisdiction of incorporation.

(b) The articles of charter surrender shall be delivered by the corporation to the secretary of state for filing. The articles of charter surrender shall take effect on the effective time provided in § 1.23.

§ 9.24. Effect of Domestication.

(a) When a domestication becomes effective:

(1) the title to all real and personal property, both tangible and intangible, of the corporation remains in the corporation without reversion or impairment;

(2) the liabilities of the corporation remain the liabilities of the corporation;

(3) an action or proceeding pending against the corporation continues against the corporation as if the domestication had not occurred;

(4) the articles of domestication, or the articles of incorporation attached to the articles of domestication, constitute the articles of incorporation of a foreign corporation domesticating in this state;

(5) the shares of the corporation are reclassified into shares, other securities, obligations, rights to acquire shares or other securities, or into cash or other property in accordance with the terms of the domestication, and the shareholders are entitled only to the rights provided by those terms and to any appraisal rights they may have under the organic law of the domesticating corporation; and

(6) the corporation is deemed to:

(i) be incorporated under and subject to the organic law of the domesticated corporation for all purposes;

(ii) be the same corporation without interruption as the domesticating corporation; and

(iii) have been incorporated on the date the domesticating corporation was originally incorporated.

(b) When a domestication of a domestic business corporation in a foreign jurisdiction becomes effective, the foreign business corporation is deemed to:

(1) appoint the secretary of state as its agent for service of process in a proceeding to enforce the rights of shareholders who exercise appraisal rights in connection with the domestication; and

(2) agree that it will promptly pay the amount, if any, to which such shareholders are entitled under chapter 13.

(c) The owner liability of a shareholder in a foreign corporation that is domesticated in this state shall be as follows:

(1) The domestication does not discharge any owner liability under the laws of the foreign jurisdiction to the extent any such owner liability arose before the effective time of the articles of domestication.

(2) The shareholder shall not have owner liability under the laws of the foreign jurisdiction for any debt, obligation or liability of the corporation that arises after the effective time of the articles of domestication.

(3) The provisions of the laws of the foreign jurisdiction shall continue to apply to the collection or discharge of any owner liability preserved by paragraph (1), as if the domestication had not occurred.

(4) The shareholder shall have whatever rights of contribution from other shareholders are provided by the laws of the foreign jurisdiction with respect to any owner liability preserved by paragraph (1), as if the domestication had not occurred.

[(d) A shareholder who becomes subject to owner liability for some or all of the debts, obligations or liabilities of the corporation as a result of its domestication in this state shall have owner liability only for those debts, obligations or liabilities of the corporation that arise after the effective time of the articles of domestication.]

§ 9.25. Abandonment of a Domestication.

(a) Unless otherwise provided in a plan of domestication of a domestic business corporation, after the plan has been adopted and approved as required by this subchapter, and at any time before the domestication has become effective, it may be abandoned by the board of directors without action by the shareholders.

(b) If a domestication is abandoned under subsection (a) after articles of charter surrender have been filed with the secretary of state but before the domestication has become effective, a statement that the domestication has been abandoned in accordance with this section, executed by an officer or other duly authorized representative, shall be delivered to the secretary of state for filing prior to the effective date of the domestication. The statement shall take effect upon filing and the domestication shall be deemed abandoned and shall not become effective.

(c) If the domestication of a foreign business corporation in this state is abandoned in accordance with the laws of the foreign jurisdiction after articles of domestication have been filed with the secretary of state, a statement that the domestication has been abandoned, executed by an officer or other duly authorized representative, shall be delivered to the secretary of state for filing. The statement shall take effect upon filing and the domestication shall be deemed abandoned and shall not become effective.

Subchapter C. Nonprofit Conversion

§ 9.30. Nonprofit Conversion.

(a) A domestic business corporation may become a domestic nonprofit corporation pursuant to a plan of nonprofit conversion.

(b) A domestic business corporation may become a foreign nonprofit corporation if the nonprofit conversion is permitted by the laws of the foreign jurisdiction. Regardless of whether the laws of the foreign jurisdiction require the adoption of a plan of nonprofit conversion, the foreign nonprofit conversion shall be approved by the adoption by the domestic business corporation of a plan of nonprofit conversion in the manner provided in this subchapter.

(c) The plan of nonprofit conversion must include:

(1) the terms and conditions of the conversion;

(2) the manner and basis of reclassifying the shares of the corporation following its conversion into memberships, if any, or securities, obligations, rights to acquire memberships or securities, cash, other property, or any combination of the foregoing;

(3) any desired amendments to the articles of incorporation of the corporation following its conversion; and

(4) if the domestic business corporation is to be converted to a foreign nonprofit corporation, a statement of the jurisdiction in which the corporation will be incorporated after the conversion.

(d) The plan of nonprofit conversion may also include a provision that the plan may be amended prior to filing articles of nonprofit conversion, except that subsequent to approval of the plan by the shareholders the plan may not be amended to change:

(1) the amount or kind of memberships or securities, obligations, rights to acquire memberships or securities, cash, or other property to be received by the shareholders under the plan;

(2) the articles of incorporation as they will be in effect immediately following the conversion, except for changes permitted by § 10.05; or

(3) any of the other terms or conditions of the plan if the change would adversely affect any of the shareholders in any material respect.

(e) Terms of a plan of nonprofit conversion may be made dependent upon facts objectively ascertainable outside the plan in accordance with § 1.20(k).

(f) If any debt security, note or similar evidence of indebtedness for money borrowed, whether secured or unsecured, or a contract of any kind, issued, incurred or executed by a domestic business corporation before [the effective date of this subchapter] contains a provision applying to a merger of the corporation and the document does not refer to a nonprofit conversion of the corporation, the provision shall be deemed to apply to a nonprofit conversion of the corporation until such time as the provision is amended subsequent to that date.

§ 9.31. Action on a Plan of Nonprofit Conversion.

In the case of a conversion of a domestic business corporation to a domestic or foreign nonprofit corporation:

(1) The plan of nonprofit conversion must be adopted by the board of directors.

(2) After adopting the plan of nonprofit conversion, the board of directors must submit the plan to the shareholders for their approval. The board of directors must also transmit to the shareholders a recommendation that the shareholders approve the plan, unless the board of directors makes a determination that because of conflicts of interest or other special circumstances it should not make such a recommendation, in which case the board of directors must transmit to the shareholders the basis for that determination.

(3) The board of directors may condition its submission of the plan of nonprofit conversion to the shareholders on any basis.

(4) If the approval of the shareholders is to be given at a meeting, the corporation must notify each shareholder of the meeting of shareholders at which the plan of nonprofit conversion is to be submitted for approval. The notice must state that the purpose, or one of the purposes, of the meeting is to consider the plan and must contain or be accompanied by a copy or summary of the plan. The notice shall include or be accompanied by a copy of the articles of incorporation as they will be in effect immediately after the nonprofit conversion.

(5) Unless the articles of incorporation, or the board of directors acting pursuant to paragraph (3), requires a greater vote or a greater number of votes to be present, approval of the plan of nonprofit conversion requires the approval of each class or series of shares of the corporation voting as a separate voting group at a meeting at which a quorum of the voting group consisting of at least a majority of the votes entitled to be cast on the nonprofit conversion by that voting group exists.

(6) If any provision of the articles of incorporation, bylaws or an agreement to which any of the directors or shareholders are parties, adopted or entered into before [the effective date of this subchapter], applies to a merger of the corporation and the document does not refer to a nonprofit conversion of the corporation, the provision shall be deemed to apply to a nonprofit conversion of the corporation until such time as the provision is amended subsequent to that date.

§ 9.32. Articles of Nonprofit Conversion.

(a) After a plan of nonprofit conversion providing for the conversion of a domestic business corporation to a domestic nonprofit corporation has been adopted and approved as required by this Act, articles of nonprofit conversion shall be executed on behalf of the corporation by any officer or other duly authorized representative. The articles shall set forth:

(1) the name of the corporation immediately before the filing of the articles of nonprofit conversion and if that name does not satisfy the requirements of [the Model Nonprofit Corporation

Act], or the corporation desires to change its name in connection with the conversion, a name that satisfies the requirements of [the Model Nonprofit Corporation Act];

(2) a statement that the plan of nonprofit conversion was duly approved by the shareholders in the manner required by this Act and the articles of incorporation.

(b) The articles of nonprofit conversion shall either contain all of the provisions that [the Model Nonprofit Corporation Act] requires to be set forth in articles of incorporation of a domestic nonprofit corporation and any other desired provisions permitted by [the Model Nonprofit Corporation Act], or shall have attached articles of incorporation that satisfy the requirements of [the Model Nonprofit Corporation Act]. In either case, provisions that would not be required to be included in restated articles of incorporation of a domestic nonprofit corporation may be omitted.

(c) The articles of nonprofit conversion shall be delivered to the secretary of state for filing, and shall take effect at the effective time provided in § 1.23.

§ 9.33. Surrender of Charter upon Foreign Nonprofit Conversion.

(a) Whenever a domestic business corporation has adopted and approved, in the manner required by this subchapter, a plan of nonprofit conversion providing for the corporation to be converted to a foreign nonprofit corporation, articles of charter surrender shall be executed on behalf of the corporation by any officer or other duly authorized representative. The articles of charter surrender shall set forth:

(1) the name of the corporation;

(2) a statement that the articles of charter surrender are being filed in connection with the conversion of the corporation to a foreign nonprofit corporation;

(3) a statement that the foreign nonprofit conversion was duly approved by the shareholders in the manner required by this Act and the articles of incorporation;

(4) the corporation's new jurisdiction of incorporation.

(b) The articles of charter surrender shall be delivered by the corporation to the secretary of state for filing. The articles of charter surrender shall take effect on the effective time provided in § 1.23.

§ 9.34. Effect of Nonprofit Conversion.

(a) When a conversion of a domestic business corporation to a domestic nonprofit corporation becomes effective:

(1) the title to all real and personal property, both tangible and intangible, of the corporation remains in the corporation without reversion or impairment;

(2) the liabilities of the corporation remain the liabilities of the corporation;

(3) an action or proceeding pending against the corporation continues against the corporation as if the conversion had not occurred;

(4) the articles of incorporation of the domestic or foreign nonprofit corporation become effective;

(5) the shares of the corporation are reclassified into memberships, securities, obligations, rights to acquire memberships or securities, or into cash or other property in accordance with the plan of conversion, and the shareholders are entitled only to the rights provided in the plan of nonprofit conversion or to any rights they may have under chapter 13; and

(6) the corporation is deemed to:

(i) be a domestic nonprofit corporation for all purposes;

(ii) be the same corporation without interruption as the corporation that existed prior to the conversion; and

(iii) have been incorporated on the date that it was originally incorporated as a domestic business corporation.

(b) When a conversion of a domestic business corporation to a foreign nonprofit corporation becomes effective, the foreign nonprofit corporation is deemed to:

(1) appoint the secretary of state as its agent for service of process in a proceeding to enforce the rights of shareholders who exercise appraisal rights in connection with the conversion; and

(2) agree that it will promptly pay the amount, if any, to which such shareholders are entitled under chapter 13

(c) The owner liability of a shareholder in a domestic business corporation that converts to a domestic nonprofit corporation shall be as follows:

(1) The conversion does not discharge any owner liability of the shareholder as a shareholder of the business corporation to the extent any such owner liability arose before the effective time of the articles of nonprofit conversion.

(2) The shareholder shall not have owner liability for any debt, obligation or liability of the nonprofit corporation that arises after the effective time of the articles of nonprofit conversion.

(3) The laws of this state shall continue to apply to the collection or discharge of any owner liability preserved by paragraph (1), as if the conversion had not occurred and the nonprofit corporation were still a business corporation.

(4) The shareholder shall have whatever rights of contribution from other shareholders are provided by the laws of this state with respect to any owner liability preserved by paragraph (1), as if the conversion had not occurred and the nonprofit corporation were still a business corporation.

(d) A shareholder who becomes subject to owner liability for some or all of the debts, obligations or liabilities of the nonprofit corporation shall have owner liability only for those debts, obligations or liabilities of the nonprofit corporation that arise after the effective time of the articles of nonprofit conversion.

§ 9.35. Abandonment of a Nonprofit Conversion.

(a) Unless otherwise provided in a plan of nonprofit conversion of a domestic business corporation, after the plan has been adopted and approved as required by this subchapter, and at any time before the nonprofit conversion has become effective, it may be abandoned by the board of directors without action by the shareholders.

(b) If a nonprofit conversion is abandoned under subsection (a) after articles of nonprofit conversion or articles of charter surrender have been filed with the secretary of state but before the nonprofit conversion has become effective, a statement that the nonprofit conversion has been abandoned in accordance with this section, executed by an officer or other duly authorized representative, shall be delivered to the secretary of state for filing prior to the effective date of the nonprofit conversion. The statement shall take effect upon filing and the nonprofit conversion shall be deemed abandoned and shall not become effective.

Subchapter D. Foreign Nonprofit Domestication and Conversion

§ 9.40. Foreign Nonprofit Domestication and Conversion. A foreign nonprofit corporation may become a domestic business corporation if the domestication and conversion is permitted by the organic law of the foreign nonprofit corporation.

§ 9.41. Articles of Domestication and Conversion.

(a) After the conversion of a foreign nonprofit corporation to a domestic business corporation has been authorized as required by the laws of the foreign jurisdiction, articles of domestication and conversion shall be executed by any officer or other duly authorized representative. The articles shall set forth:

(1) the name of the corporation immediately before the filing of the articles of domestication and conversion and, if that name is unavailable for use in this state or the corporation desires to change its name in connection with the domestication and conversion, a name that satisfies the requirements of § 4.01;

(2) the jurisdiction of incorporation of the corporation immediately before the filing of the articles of domestication and conversion and the date the corporation was incorporated in that jurisdiction; and

(3) a statement that the domestication and conversion of the corporation in this state was duly authorized as required by the laws of the jurisdiction in which the corporation was incorporated immediately before its domestication and conversion in this state.

(b) The articles of domestication and conversion shall either contain all of the provisions that § 2.02(a) requires to be set forth in articles of incorporation and any other desired provisions that § 2.02(b) permits to be included in articles of incorporation, or shall have attached articles of incorporation. In either case, provisions that would not be required to be included in restated articles of incorporation may be omitted.

(c) The articles of domestication and conversion shall be delivered to the secretary of state for filing, and shall take effect at the effective time provided in § 1.23.

(d) If the foreign nonprofit corporation is authorized to transact business in this state under [the foreign qualification provision of the Model Nonprofit Corporation Act], its certificate of authority shall be cancelled automatically on the effective date of its domestication and conversion.

§ 9.42. Effect of Foreign Nonprofit Domestication and Conversion.

(a) When a domestication and conversion of a foreign nonprofit corporation to a domestic business corporation becomes effective:

(1) the title to all real and personal property, both tangible and intangible, of the corporation remains in the corporation without reversion or impairment;

(2) the liabilities of the corporation remain the liabilities of the corporation;

(3) an action or proceeding pending against the corporation continues against the corporation as if the domestication and conversion had not occurred;

(4) the articles of domestication and conversion, or the articles of incorporation attached to the articles of domestication and conversion, constitute the articles of incorporation of the corporation;

(5) shares, other securities, obligations, rights to acquire shares or other securities of the corporation, or cash or other property shall be issued or paid as provided pursuant to the laws of the foreign jurisdiction, so long as at least one share is outstanding immediately after the effective time; and

(6) the corporation is deemed to:

(i) be a domestic corporation for all purposes;

(ii) be the same corporation without interruption as the foreign nonprofit corporation; and

(iii) have been incorporated on the date the foreign nonprofit corporation was originally incorporated.

(b) The owner liability of a member of a foreign nonprofit corporation that domesticates and converts to a domestic business corporation shall be as follows:

(1) The domestication and conversion does not discharge any owner liability under the laws of the foreign jurisdiction to the extent any such owner liability arose before the effective time of the articles of domestication and conversion.

(2) The member shall not have owner liability under the laws of the foreign jurisdiction for any debt, obligation or liability of the corporation that arises after the effective time of the articles of domestication and conversion.

(3) The provisions of the laws of the foreign jurisdiction shall continue to apply to the collection or discharge of any owner liability preserved by paragraph (1), as if the domestication and conversion had not occurred.

(4) The member shall have whatever rights of contribution from other members are provided by the laws of the foreign jurisdiction with respect to any owner liability preserved by paragraph (1), as if the domestication and conversion had not occurred.

(c) A member of a foreign nonprofit corporation who becomes subject to owner liability for some or all of the debts, obligations or liabilities of the corporation as a result of its domestication and conversion in this state shall have owner liability only for those debts, obligations or liabilities of the corporation that arise after the effective time of the articles of domestication and conversion.

§ 9.43. Abandonment of a Foreign Nonprofit Domestication and Conversion.

If the domestication and conversion of a foreign nonprofit corporation to a domestic business corporation is abandoned in accordance with the laws of the foreign jurisdiction after articles of domestication and conversion have been filed with the secretary of state, a statement that the domestication and conversion has been abandoned, executed by an officer or other duly authorized representative, shall be delivered to the secretary of state for filing. The statement shall take effect upon filing and the domestication and conversion shall be deemed abandoned and shall not become effective.

Subchapter E. Entity Conversion

§ 9.50. Entity Conversion Authorized; Definitions.

(a) A domestic business corporation may become a domestic unincorporated entity pursuant to a plan of entity conversion.

(b) A domestic business corporation may become a foreign unincorporated entity if the entity conversion is permitted by the laws of the foreign jurisdiction.

(c) A domestic unincorporated entity may become a domestic business corporation. If the organic law of a domestic unincorporated entity does not provide procedures for the approval of an entity conversion, the conversion shall be adopted and approved, and the entity conversion effectuated, in the same manner as a merger of the unincorporated entity. If the organic law of a domestic unincorporated entity does not provide procedures for the approval of either an entity conversion or a merger, a plan of entity conversion shall be adopted and approved, the entity conversion effectuated, and appraisal rights exercised, in accordance with the procedures in this subchapter and chapter 13. Without limiting the provisions of this subsection, a domestic unincorporated entity whose organic law does not provide procedures for the approval of an entity conversion shall be subject to subsection (e) and § 9.52(7). For purposes of applying this subchapter and chapter 13:

 (1) the unincorporated entity, its interest holders, interests and organic documents taken together, shall be deemed to be a domestic business corporation, shareholders, shares and articles of incorporation, respectively and vice versa, as the context may require; and

 (2) if the business and affairs of the unincorporated entity are managed by a group of persons that is not identical to the interest holders, that group shall be deemed to be the board of directors.

(d) A foreign unincorporated entity may become a domestic business corporation if the organic law of the foreign unincorporated entity authorizes it to become a corporation in another jurisdiction.

(e) If any debt security, note or similar evidence of indebtedness for money borrowed, whether secured or unsecured, or a contract of any kind, issued, incurred or executed by a domestic business corporation before [the effective date of this subchapter], applies to a merger of the corporation and the document does not refer to an entity conversion of the corporation, the provision shall be deemed to apply to an entity conversion of the corporation until such time as the provision is amended subsequent to that date.

(f) As used in this subchapter:

 (1) "Converting entity" means the domestic business corporation or domestic unincorporated entity that adopts a plan of entity conversion or the foreign unincorporated entity converting to a domestic business corporation.

 (2) "Surviving entity" means the corporation or unincorporated entity that is in existence immediately after consummation of an entity conversion pursuant to this subchapter.

§ 9.51. Plan of Entity Conversion.

(a) A plan of entity conversion must include:

 (1) a statement of the type of other entity the surviving entity will be and, if it will be a foreign other entity, its jurisdiction of organization;

 (2) the terms and conditions of the conversion;

 (3) the manner and basis of converting the shares of the domestic business corporation following its conversion into interests or other securities, obligations, rights to acquire interests or other securities, cash, other property, or any combination of the foregoing; and

 (4) the full text, as they will be in effect immediately after consummation of the conversion, of the organic documents of the surviving entity.

(b) The plan of entity conversion may also include a provision that the plan may be amended prior to filing articles of entity conversion, except that subsequent to approval of the plan by the shareholders the plan may not be amended to change:

 (1) the amount or kind of shares or other securities, interests, obligations, rights to acquire shares, other securities or interests, cash, or other property to be received under the plan by the shareholders;

 (2) the organic documents that will be in effect immediately following the conversion, except for changes permitted by a provision of the organic law of the surviving entity comparable to § 10.05; or

 (3) any of the other terms or conditions of the plan if the change would adversely affect any of the shareholders in any material respect.

(c) Terms of a plan of entity conversion may be made dependent upon facts objectively ascertainable outside the plan in accordance with § 1.20(k).

§ 9.52. Action on a Plan of Entity Conversion.
In the case of an entity conversion of a domestic business corporation to a domestic or foreign unincorporated entity:

(1) The plan of entity conversion must be adopted by the board of directors.

(2) After adopting the plan of entity conversion, the board of directors must submit the plan to the shareholders for their approval. The board of directors must also transmit to the shareholders a recommendation that the shareholders approve the plan, unless the board of directors makes a determination that because of conflicts of interest or other special circumstances it should not make such a recommendation, in which case the board of directors must transmit to the shareholders the basis for that determination.

(3) The board of directors may condition its submission of the plan of entity conversion to the shareholders on any basis.

(4) If the approval of the shareholders is to be given at a meeting, the corporation must notify each shareholder, whether or not entitled to vote, of the meeting of shareholders at which the plan of entity conversion is to be submitted for approval. The notice must state that the purpose, or one of the purposes, of the meeting is to consider the plan and must contain or be accompanied by a copy or summary of the plan. The notice shall include or be accompanied by a copy of the organic documents as they will be in effect immediately after the entity conversion.

(5) Unless the articles of incorporation, or the board of directors acting pursuant to paragraph (3), requires a greater vote or a greater number of votes to be present, approval of the plan of entity conversion requires the approval of each class or series of shares of the corporation voting as a separate voting group at a meeting at which a quorum of the voting group consisting of at least a majority of the votes entitled to be cast on the conversion by that voting group exists.

(6) If any provision of the articles of incorporation, bylaws or an agreement to which any of the directors or shareholders are parties, adopted or entered into before [the effective date of this subchapter], applies to a merger of the corporation and the document does not refer to an entity conversion of the corporation, the provision shall be deemed to apply to an entity conversion of the corporation until such time as the provision is subsequently amended.

(7) If as a result of the conversion one or more shareholders of the corporation would become subject to owner liability for the debts, obligations or liabilities of any other person or entity, approval of the plan of conversion shall require the execution, by each such shareholder, of a separate written consent to become subject to such owner liability.

§ 9.53. Articles of Entity Conversions.

(a) After the conversion of a domestic business corporation to a domestic unincorporated entity has been adopted and approved as required by this Act, articles of entity conversion shall be executed on behalf of the corporation by any officer or other duly authorized representative. The articles shall:

(1) set forth the name of the corporation immediately before the filing of the articles of entity conversion and the name to which the name of the corporation is to be changed, which shall be a name that satisfies the organic law of the surviving entity;

(2) state the type of unincorporated entity that the surviving entity will be;

(3) set forth a statement that the plan of entity conversion was duly approved by the shareholders in the manner required by this Act and the articles of incorporation;

(4) if the surviving entity is a filing entity, either contain all of the provisions required to be set forth in its public organic document and any other desired provisions that are permitted, or have attached a public organic document; except that, in either case, provisions that would not be required to be included in a restated public organic document may be omitted.

(b) After the conversion of a domestic unincorporated entity to a domestic business corporation has been adopted and approved as required by the organic law of the unincorporated entity, articles of entity conversion shall be executed on behalf of the unincorporated entity by any officer or other duly authorized representative. The articles shall:

(1) set forth the name of the unincorporated entity immediately before the filing of the articles of entity conversion and the name to which the name of the unincorporated entity is to be changed, which shall be a name that satisfies the requirements of § 4.01;

(2) set forth a statement that the plan of entity conversion was duly approved in accordance with the organic law of the unincorporated entity;

(3) either contain all of the provisions that § 2.02(a) requires to be set forth in articles of incorporation and any other desired provisions that § 2.02(b) permits to be included in articles of incorporation, or have attached articles of incorporation; except that, in either case, provisions that would not be required to be included in restated articles of incorporation of a domestic business corporation may be omitted.

(c) After the conversion of a foreign unincorporated entity to a domestic business corporation has been authorized as required by the laws of the foreign jurisdiction, articles of entity conversion shall be executed on behalf of the foreign unincorporated entity by any officer or other duly authorized representative. The articles shall:

(1) set forth the name of the unincorporated entity immediately before the filing of the articles of entity conversion and the name to which the name of the unincorporated entity is to be changed, which shall be a name that satisfies the requirements of § 4.01;

(2) set forth the jurisdiction under the laws of which the unincorporated entity was organized immediately before the filing of the articles of entity conversion and the date on which the unincorporated entity was organized in that jurisdiction;

(3) set forth a statement that the conversion of the unincorporated entity was duly approved in the manner required by its organic law; and

(4) either contain all of the provisions that § 2.02(a) requires to be set forth in articles of incorporation and any other desired provisions that § 2.02(b) permits to be included in articles of incorporation, or have attached articles of incorporation; except that, in either case, provisions that would not be required to be included in restated articles of incorporation of a domestic business corporation may be omitted.

(d) The articles of entity conversion shall be delivered to the secretary of state for filing, and shall take effect at the effective time provided in § 1.23. Articles of entity conversion filed under § 9.53(a) or (b) may be combined with any required conversion filing under the organic law of the domestic unincorporated entity if the combined filing satisfies the requirements of both this section and the other organic law.

(e) If the converting entity is a foreign unincorporated entity that is authorized to transact business in this state under a provision of law similar to chapter 15, its certificate of authority or other type of foreign qualification shall be cancelled automatically on the effective date of its conversion.

§ 9.54. Surrender of Charter Upon Conversion.

(a) Whenever a domestic business corporation has adopted and approved, in the manner required by this subchapter, a plan of entity conversion providing for the corporation to be converted to a foreign unincorporated entity, articles of charter surrender shall be executed on behalf of the corporation by any officer or other duly authorized representative. The articles of charter surrender shall set forth:

(1) the name of the corporation;

(2) a statement that the articles of charter surrender are being filed in connection with the conversion of the corporation to a foreign unincorporated entity;

(3) a statement that the conversion was duly approved by the shareholders in the manner required by this Act and the articles of incorporation;

(4) the jurisdiction under the laws of which the surviving entity will be organized;

(5) if the surviving entity will be a nonfiling entity, the address of its executive office immediately after the conversion.

(b) The articles of charter surrender shall be delivered by the corporation to the secretary of state for filing. The articles of charter surrender shall take effect on the effective time provided in § 1.23.

§ 9.55. Effect of Entity Conversion.

(a) When a conversion under this subchapter becomes effective:

(1) the title to all real and personal property, both tangible and intangible, of the converting entity remains in the surviving entity without reversion or impairment;

(2) the liabilities of the converting entity remain the liabilities of the surviving entity;

(3) an action or proceeding pending against the converting entity continues against the surviving entity as if the conversion had not occurred;

(4) in the case of a surviving entity that is a filing entity, its articles of incorporation or public organic document and its private organic document become effective;

(5) in the case of a surviving entity that is a nonfiling entity, its private organic document becomes effective;

(6) the shares or interests of the converting entity are reclassified into shares, interests, other securities, obligations, rights

to acquire shares, interests or other securities, or into cash or other property in accordance with the plan of conversion; and the shareholders or interest holders of the converting entity are entitled only to the rights provided to them under the terms of the conversion and to any appraisal rights they may have under the organic law of the converting entity; and

(7) the surviving entity is deemed to:

(i) be incorporated or organized under and subject to the organic law of the converting entity for all purposes;

(ii) be the same corporation or unincorporated entity without interruption as the converting entity; and

(iii) have been incorporated or otherwise organized on the date that the converting entity was originally incorporated or organized.

(b) When a conversion of a domestic business corporation to a foreign other entity becomes effective, the surviving entity is deemed to:

(1) appoint the secretary of state as its agent for service of process in a proceeding to enforce the rights of shareholders who exercise appraisal rights in connection with the conversion; and

(2) agree that it will promptly pay the amount, if any, to which such shareholders are entitled under chapter 13.

(c) A shareholder who becomes subject to owner liability for some or all of the debts, obligations or liabilities of the surviving entity shall be personally liable only for those debts, obligations or liabilities of the surviving entity that arise after the effective time of the articles of entity conversion.

(d) The owner liability of an interest holder in an unincorporated entity that converts to a domestic business corporation shall be as follows:

(1) The conversion does not discharge any owner liability under the organic law of the unincorporated entity to the extent any such owner liability arose before the effective time of the articles of entity conversion.

(2) The interest holder shall not have owner liability under the organic law of the unincorporated entity for any debt, obligation or liability of the corporation that arises after the effective time of the articles of entity conversion.

(3) The provisions of the organic law of the unincorporated entity shall continue to apply to the collection or discharge of any owner liability preserved by paragraph (1), as if the conversion had not occurred.

(4) The interest holder shall have whatever rights of contribution from other interest holders are provided by the organic law of the unincorporated entity with respect to any owner liability preserved by paragraph (1), as if the conversion had not occurred.

§ 9.56. Abandonment of an Entity Conversion.

(a) Unless otherwise provided in a plan of entity conversion of a domestic business corporation, after the plan has been adopted and approved as required by this subchapter, and at any time before the entity conversion has become effective, it may be abandoned by the board of directors without action by the shareholders.

(b) If an entity conversion is abandoned after articles of entity Conversion or articles of charter surrender have been filed with the secretary of state but before the entity conversion has become effective, a statement that the entity conversion has been abandoned in accordance with this section, executed by an officer or other duly authorized representative, shall be delivered to the secretary of state for filing prior to the effective date of the entity conversion. Upon filing, the statement shall take effect and the entity conversion shall be deemed abandoned and shall not become effective.

CHAPTER 10. AMENDMENT OF ARTICLES OF INCORPORATION AND BYLAWS
Subchapter A. Amendment of Articles of Incorporation

§ 10.01. Authority To Amend.

(a) A corporation may amend its articles of incorporation at any time to add or change a provision that is required or permitted in the articles of incorporation as of the effective date of the amendment or to delete a provision that is not required to be contained in the articles of incorporation.

(b) A shareholder of the corporation does not have a vested property right resulting from any provision in the articles of incorporation, including provisions relating to management, control, capital structure, dividend entitlement, or purpose or duration of the corporation.

§ 10.02. Amendment before Issuance of Shares.

If a corporation has not yet issued shares, its board of directors, or its incorporators if it has no board of directors, may adopt one or more amendments to the corporation's articles of incorporation.

§ 10.03. Amendment by Board of Directors and Shareholders.

If a corporation has issued shares, an amendment to the articles of incorporation shall be adopted in the following manner:

(a) The proposed amendment must be adopted by the board of directors.

(b) Except as provided in §§ 10.05, 10.07, and 10.08, after adopting the proposed amendment the board of directors must submit the amendment to the shareholders for their approval. The board of directors must also transmit to the shareholders a recommendation that the shareholders approve the amendment, unless the board of directors makes a determination that because of conflicts of interest or other special circumstances it should not make such a recommendation, in which case the board of directors must transmit to the shareholders the basis for that determination.

(c) The board of directors may condition its submission of the amendment to the shareholders on any basis.

(d) If the amendment is required to be approved by the shareholders, and the approval is to be given at a meeting, the corporation must notify each shareholder, whether or not entitled to vote, of the meeting of shareholders at which the amendment is to be submitted for approval. The notice must state that the purpose, or one of the purposes, of the meeting is to consider the amendment and must contain or be accompanied by a copy of the amendment.

(e) Unless the articles of incorporation, or the board of directors acting pursuant to subsection (c), requires a greater vote or a greater number of shares to be present, approval of the amendment requires the approval of the shareholders at a meeting at which a quorum consisting of at least a majority of the votes entitled to be cast on the amendment exists, and, if any class or series of shares is entitled to vote as a separate group on the amendment, except as provided in § 10.04(c), the approval of each such separate voting group at a meeting at which a quorum of the voting group consisting of at least a majority of the votes entitled to be cast on the amendment by that voting group exists.

§ 10.04. Voting on Amendments by Voting Groups.

(a) If a corporation has more than one class of shares outstanding, the holders of the outstanding shares of a class are entitled to vote as a separate voting group (if shareholder voting is otherwise required by this Act) on a proposed amendment to the articles of incorporation if the amendment would:

(1) effect an exchange or reclassification of all or part of the shares of the class into shares of another class;

(2) effect an exchange or reclassification, or create the right of exchange, of all or part of the shares of another class into shares of the class;

(3) change the rights, preferences, or limitations of all or part of the shares of the class;

(4) change the shares of all or part of the class into a different number of shares of the same class;

(5) create a new class of shares having rights or preferences with respect to distributions or to dissolution that are prior or superior to the shares of the class;

(6) increase the rights, preferences, or number of authorized shares of any class that, after giving effect to the amendment, have rights or preferences with respect to distributions or to dissolution that are prior or superior to the shares of the class;

(7) limit or deny an existing preemptive right of all or part of the shares of the class; or

(8) cancel or otherwise affect rights to distributions that have accumulated but not yet been authorized on all or part of the shares of the class.

(b) If a proposed amendment would affect a series of a class of shares in one or more of the ways described in subsection (a), the holders of shares of that series are entitled to vote as a separate voting group on the proposed amendment.

(c) If a proposed amendment that entitles the holders of two or more classes or series of shares to vote as separate voting groups under this section would affect those two or more classes or series in the same or a substantially similar way, the holders of shares of all the classes or series so affected must vote together as a single voting group on the proposed amendment, unless otherwise provided in the articles of incorporation or required by the board of directors.

(d) A class or series of shares is entitled to the voting rights granted by this section although the articles of incorporation provide that the shares are nonvoting shares.

§ 10.05. Amendment by Board of Directors.

Unless the articles of incorporation provide otherwise, a corporation's board of directors may adopt amendments to the corporation's articles of incorporation without shareholder approval:

(1) to extend the duration of the corporation if it was incorporated at a time when limited duration was required by law;

(2) to delete the names and addresses of the initial directors;

(3) to delete the name and address of the initial registered agent or registered office, if a statement of change is on file with the secretary of state;

(4) if the corporation has only one class of shares outstanding:

(a) to change each issued and unissued authorized share of the class into a greater number of whole shares of that class; or

(b) to increase the number of authorized shares of the class to the extent necessary to permit the issuance of shares as a share dividend;

(5) to change the corporate name by substituting the word "corporation," "incorporated," "company," "limited," or the abbreviation "corp.," "inc.," "co.," or "ltd.," for a similar word or abbreviation in the name, or by adding, deleting, or changing a geographical attribution for the name;

(6) to reflect a reduction in authorized shares, as a result of the operation of § 6.31(b), when the corporation has acquired its own shares and the articles of incorporation prohibit the reissue of the acquired shares;

(7) to delete a class of shares from the articles of incorporation, as a result of the operation of § 6.31(b), when there are no remaining shares of the class because the corporation has acquired all shares of the class and the articles of incorporation prohibit the reissue of the acquired shares; or

(8) to make any change expressly permitted by § 6.02(a) or (b) to be made without shareholder approval.

§ 10.06. Articles of Amendment.

After an amendment to the articles of incorporation has been adopted and approved in the manner required by this Act and by the articles of incorporation, the corporation shall deliver to the secretary of state, for filing, articles of amendment, which shall set forth:

(1) the name of the corporation;

(2) the text of each amendment adopted, or the information required by § 1.20(k)(5);

(3) if an amendment provides for an exchange, reclassification, or cancellation of issued shares, provisions for implementing the amendment if not contained in the amendment itself, (which may be made dependent upon facts objectively ascertainable outside the articles of amendment in accordance with § 1.20(k)(5);

(4) the date of each amendment's adoption; and

(5) if an amendment:

(a) was adopted by the incorporators or board of directors without shareholder approval, a statement that the amendment was duly approved by the incorporators or by the board of directors, as the case may be, and that shareholder approval was not required;

(b) required approval by the shareholders, a statement that the amendment was duly approved by the shareholders in the manner required by this Act and by the articles of incorporation; or

(c) is being filed pursuant to § 1.20(k)(5), a statement to that effect.

§ 10.07. Restated Articles of Incorporation.

(a) A corporation's board of directors may restate its articles of incorporation at any time, with or without shareholder approval, to consolidate all amendments into a single document.

(b) If the restated articles include one or more new amendments that require shareholder approval, the amendments must be adopted and approved as provided in § 10.03.

(c) A corporation that restates its articles of incorporation shall deliver to the secretary of state for filing articles of restatement setting forth the name of the corporation and the text of the restated articles of incorporation together with a certificate which states that the restated articles consolidate all amendments into a single document and, if a new amendment is included in the restated articles, which also includes the statements required under § 10.06.

(d) Duly adopted restated articles of incorporation supersede the original articles of incorporation and all amendments thereto.

(e) The secretary of state may certify restated articles of incorporation as the articles of incorporation currently in effect, without including the certificate information required by subsection (c).

§ 10.08. Amendment Pursuant to Reorganization.

(a) A corporation's articles of incorporation may be amended without action by the board of directors or shareholders to carry out a plan of reorganization ordered or decreed by a court of competent jurisdiction under the authority of a law of the United States.

(b) The individual or individuals designated by the court shall deliver to the secretary of state for filing articles of amendment setting forth:

(1) the name of the corporation;

(2) the text of each amendment approved by the court;

(3) the date of the court's order or decree approving the articles of amendment;

(4) the title of the reorganization proceeding in which the order or decree was entered; and

(5) a statement that the court had jurisdiction of the proceeding under federal statute.

(c) This section does not apply after entry of a final decree in the reorganization proceeding even though the court retains jurisdiction of the proceeding for limited purposes unrelated to consummation of the reorganization plan.

§ 10.09. Effect of Amendment.
An amendment to the articles of incorporation does not affect a cause of action existing against or in favor of the corporation, a proceeding to which the corporation is a party, or the existing rights of persons other than shareholders of the corporation. An amendment changing a corporation's name does not abate a proceeding brought by or against the corporation in its former name.

Subchapter B. Amendment of Bylaws

§ 10.20. Amendment by Board of Directors or Shareholders.

(a) A corporation's shareholders may amend or repeal the corporation's bylaws.

(b) A corporation's board of directors may amend or repeal the corporation's bylaws, unless:

(1) the articles of incorporation or § 10.21 reserve that power exclusively to the shareholders in whole or part; or

(2) the shareholders in amending, repealing, or adopting a bylaw expressly provide that the board of directors may not amend, repeal, or reinstate that bylaw.

§ 10.21. Bylaw Increasing Quorum or Voting Requirement for Directors.

(a) A bylaw that increases a quorum or voting requirement for the board of directors may be amended or repealed:

(1) if originally adopted by the shareholders, only by the shareholders, unless the bylaw otherwise provides;

(2) if adopted by the board of directors, either by the shareholders or by the board of directors.

(b) A bylaw adopted or amended by the shareholders that increases a quorum or voting requirement for the board of directors may provide that it can be amended or repealed only by a specified vote of either the shareholders or the board of directors.

(c) Action by the board of directors under subsection (a) to amend or repeal a bylaw that changes the quorum or voting requirement for the board of directors must meet the same quorum requirement and be adopted by the same vote required to take action under the quorum and voting requirement then in effect or proposed to be adopted, whichever is greater.

CHAPTER 11. MERGER AND SHARE EXCHANGES

§ 11.01. Definitions.
As used in this chapter:

(a) "Merger" means a business combination pursuant to § 11.02.

(b) "Party to a merger" or "party to a share exchange" means any domestic or foreign corporation or eligible entity that will:

(1) merge under a plan of merger;

(2) acquire shares or eligible interests of another corporation or an eligible entity in a share exchange; or

(3) have all of its shares or eligible interests or all of one or more classes or series of its shares or eligible interests acquired in a share exchange.

(c) "Share exchange" means a business combination pursuant to § 11.03.

(d) "Survivor" in a merger means the corporation or eligible entity into which one or more other corporations or eligible entities are merged. A survivor of a merger may preexist the merger or be created by the merger.

§ 11.02. Merger.

(a) One or more domestic business corporations may merge with one or more domestic or foreign business corporations or eligible entities pursuant to a plan of merger, or two or more foreign business corporations or domestic or foreign eligible entities may merge into a new domestic business corporation to be created in the merger in the manner provided in this chapter.

(b) A foreign business corporation, or a foreign eligible entity, may be a party to a merger with a domestic business corporation, or may be created by the terms of the plan of merger, only if the merger is permitted by the foreign business corporation or eligible entity.

(b.1) If the organic law of a domestic eligible entity does not provide procedures for the approval of a merger, a plan of merger may be adopted and approved, the merger effectuated, and appraisal rights exercised in accordance with the procedures in this chapter and chapter 13. For the purposes of applying this chapter and chapter 13:

(1) the eligible entity, its members or interest holders, eligible interests and organic documents taken together shall be deemed to be a domestic business corporation, shareholders, shares and articles of incorporation, respectively and vice versa as the context may require; and

(2) if the business and affairs of the eligible entity are managed by a group of persons that is not identical to the members or interest holders, that group shall be deemed to be the board of directors.

(c) The plan of merger must include:

(1) the name of each domestic or foreign business corporation or eligible entity that will merge and the name of the domestic or foreign business corporation or eligible entity that will be the survivor of the merger;

(2) the terms and conditions of the merger;

(3) the manner and basis of converting the shares of each merging domestic or foreign business corporation and eligible interests of each merging domestic or foreign eligible entity into shares or other securities, eligible interests, obligations, rights to acquire shares, other securities or eligible interests, cash, other property, or any combination of the foregoing;

(4) the articles of incorporation of any domestic or foreign business or nonprofit corporation, or the organic documents of any domestic or foreign unincorporated entity, to be created by the merger, or if a new domestic or foreign business or nonprofit corporation or unincorporated entity is not to be created by the merger, any amendments to the survivor's articles of incorporation or organic documents; and

(5) any other provisions required by the laws under which any party to the merger is organized or by which it is governed, or by the articles of incorporation or organic document of any such party.

(d) Terms of a plan of merger may be made dependent on facts objectively ascertainable outside the plan in accordance with § 1.20(k).

(e) The plan of merger may also include a provision that the plan may be amended prior to filing articles of merger, but if the shareholders of a domestic corporation that is a party to the merger are required or permitted to vote on the plan, the plan must provide that subsequent to approval of the plan by such shareholders the plan may not be amended to change:

(1) the amount or kind of shares or other securities, eligible interests, obligations, rights to acquire shares, other securities or eligible interests, cash, or other property to be received under the plan by the shareholders of or owners of eligible interests in any party to the merger;

(2) the articles of incorporation of any corporation, or the organic documents of any unincorporated entity, that will survive or be created as a result of the merger, except for changes permitted by § 10.05 or by comparable provisions of the organic laws of any such foreign corporation or domestic or foreign unincorporated entity; or

(3) any of the other terms or conditions of the plan if the change would adversely affect such shareholders in any material respect.

(f) Property held in trust or for charitable purposes under the laws of this state by a domestic or foreign eligible entity shall not be diverted by a merger from the objects for which it was donated, granted or devised, unless and until the eligible entity obtains an order of [court] [the attorney general] specifying the disposition of the property to the extent required by and pursuant to [cite state statutory cy pres or other nondiversion statute].

§ 11.03. Share Exchange.

(a) Through a share exchange:

(1) a domestic corporation may acquire all of the shares of one or more classes or series of shares of another domestic or foreign corporation, or all of the interests of one or more classes or series of interests of a domestic or foreign other entity, in exchange for shares or other securities, interests, obligations, rights to acquire shares or other securities, cash, other property, or any combination of the foregoing, pursuant to a plan of share exchange, or

(2) all of the shares of one or more classes or series of shares of a domestic corporation may be acquired by another domestic or foreign corporation or other entity, in exchange for shares or other securities, interests, obligations, rights to acquire shares or other securities, cash, other property, or any combination of the foregoing, pursuant to a plan of share exchange.

(b) A foreign corporation or eligible entity, may be a party to a share exchange only if the share exchange is permitted by the [organic law of the jurisdiction in which] corporation or other entity is organized or by which it is governed.

(b. 1) If the organic law of a domestic other entity does not provide procedures for the approval of a share exchange, a plan of share exchange may be adopted and approved, and the share exchange effectuated, in accordance with the procedures, if any, for a merger. If the organic law of a domestic other entity does not provide procedures for the approval of either a share exchange or a merger, a plan of share exchange may be adopted and approved, the share exchange effectuated, and appraisal rights exercised, in accordance with the procedures in this chapter and chapter 13. For the purposes of applying this chapter and chapter 13:

(1) the other entity, its interest holders, interests and organic documents taken together shall be deemed to be a domestic business corporation, shareholders, shares and articles of incorporation, respectively and vice versa as the context may require; and

(2) if the business and affairs of the other entity are managed by a group of persons that is not identical to the interest holders, that group shall be deemed to be the board of directors.

(c) The plan of share exchange must include:

(1) the name of each corporation or other entity whose shares or interests will be acquired and the name of the corporation or other entity that will acquire those shares or interests;

(2) the terms and conditions of the share exchange;

(3) the manner and basis of exchanging shares of a corporation or interests in an other entity whose shares or interests will be acquired under the share exchange into shares or other securities, interests, obligations, rights to acquire shares, other securities, or interests, cash, other property, or any combination of the foregoing; and

(4) any other provisions required by the laws under which any party to the share exchange is organized or by the articles of incorporation or organic document of any such party.

(d) Terms of a plan of share exchange may be made dependent on facts objectively ascertainable outside the plan in accordance with § 1.20(k).

(e) The plan of share exchange may also include a provision that the plan may be amended prior to filing articles of share exchange, but if the shareholders of a domestic corporation that is a party to the share exchange are required or permitted to vote on the plan, the plan must provide that subsequent to approval of the plan by such shareholders the plan may not be amended to change:

(1) the amount or kind of shares or other securities, interests, obligations, rights to acquire shares, other securities or interests, cash, or other property to be issued by the corporation or to be received under the plan by the shareholders of or owners of interests in any party to the share exchange; or

(2) any of the other terms or conditions of the plan if the change would adversely affect such shareholders in any material respect.

(f) Section 11.03 does not limit the power of a domestic corporation to acquire shares of another corporation or interests in another entity in a transaction other than a share exchange.

§ 11.04. Action on a Plan of Merger or Share Exchange.

In the case of a domestic corporation that is a party to a merger or share exchange:

(a) The plan of merger or share exchange must be adopted by the board of directors.

(b) Except as provided in subsection (g) and in § 11.05, after adopting the plan of merger or share exchange the board of directors must submit the plan to the shareholders for their approval. The board of directors must also transmit to the shareholders a recommendation that the shareholders approve the plan, unless the board of directors makes a determination that because of conflicts of interest or other special circumstances it should not make such a recommendation, in which case the board of directors must transmit to the shareholders the basis for that determination.

(c) The board of directors may condition its submission of the plan of merger or share exchange to the shareholders on any basis.

(d) If the plan of merger or share exchange is required to be approved by the shareholders, and if the approval is to be given at a meeting, the corporation must notify each shareholder, whether or not entitled to vote, of the meeting of shareholders at which the plan is to be submitted for approval. The notice must state that the purpose, or one of the purposes, of the meeting is to consider the plan and must contain or be accompanied by a copy or summary of the plan. If the corporation is to be merged into an existing corporation or other entity, the notice shall also include or be accompanied by a copy or summary of the articles of incorporation or organizational documents of that corporation or other entity. If the corporation is to be merged into a corporation or other entity that is to be created pursuant to the merger, the notice shall include or be accompanied by a copy or a summary of the articles of incorporation or organizational documents of the new corporation or other entity.

(e) Unless the articles of incorporation, or the board of directors acting pursuant to subsection (c), requires a greater vote or a greater number of votes to be present, approval of the plan of merger or share exchange requires the approval of the shareholders at a meeting at which a quorum consisting of at least a majority of the votes entitled to be cast on the plan exists, and, if any class or series of shares is entitled to vote as a separate group on the plan of merger or share exchange, the approval of each such separate voting group at a meeting at which a quorum of the voting group consisting of at least a majority of the votes entitled to be cast on the merger or share exchange by that voting group is present.

(f) Separate voting by voting groups is required:

(1) on a plan of merger, by each class or series of shares that:

(i) are to be converted under the plan of merger into other securities, interests, obligations, rights to acquire shares, other securities or interests, cash, other property, or any combination of the foregoing; or

(ii) would be entitled to vote as a separate group on a provision in the plan that, if contained in a proposed amendment to articles of incorporation, would require action by separate voting groups under § 10.04;

(2) on a plan of share exchange, by each class or series of shares included in the exchange, with each class or series constituting a separate voting group; and

(3) on a plan of merger or share exchange, if the voting group is entitled under the articles of incorporation to vote as a voting group to approve a plan of merger or share exchange.

(g) Unless the articles of incorporation otherwise provide, approval by the corporation's shareholders of a plan of merger or share exchange is not required if:

(1) the corporation will survive the merger or is the acquiring corporation in a share exchange;

(2) except for amendments permitted by § 10.05, its articles of incorporation will not be changed;

(3) each shareholder of the corporation whose shares were outstanding immediately before the effective date of the merger or share exchange will hold the same number of shares, with identical preferences, limitations, and relative rights, immediately after the effective date of change; and

(4) the issuance in the merger or share exchange of shares or other securities convertible into or rights exercisable for shares does not require a vote under § 6.21(f).

(h) If as a result of a merger or share exchange one or more shareholders of a domestic corporation would become subject to owner liability for the debts, obligations or liabilities of any other person or entity, approval of the plan of merger or share exchange shall require the execution, by each such shareholder, of a separate written consent to become subject to such owner liability.

§ 11.05. Merger Between Parent and Subsidiary or Between Subsidiaries.

(a) A domestic parent corporation that owns shares of a domestic or foreign subsidiary corporation that carry at least 90 percent of the voting power of each class and series of the outstanding shares of the subsidiary that have voting power may merge the subsidiary into itself or into another such subsidiary, or merge itself into the subsidiary, without the approval of the board of directors or shareholders of the subsidiary, unless the articles of incorporation of any of the corporations otherwise provide, and unless, in the case of a foreign subsidiary, approval by the subsidiary's board of directors or shareholders is required by the laws under which the subsidiary is organized.

(b) If under subsection (a) approval of a merger by the subsidiary's shareholders is not required, the parent corporation shall, within ten days after the effective date of the merger, notify each of the subsidiary's shareholders that the merger has become effective.

(c) Except as provided in subsections (a) and (b), a merger between a parent and a subsidiary shall be governed by the provisions of chapter 11 applicable to mergers generally.

§ 11.06. Articles of Merger or Share Exchange.

(a) After a plan of merger or share exchange has been adopted and approved as required by this Act, articles of merger or share exchange shall be executed on behalf of each party to the merger or share exchange by any officer or other duly authorized representative. The articles shall set forth:

(1) the names of the parties to the merger or share exchange;

(2) if the articles of incorporation of the survivor of a merger are amended, or if a new corporation is created as a result of a merger, the amendments to the survivor's articles of incorporation or the articles of incorporation of the new corporation;

(3) if the plan of merger or share exchange required approval by the shareholders of a domestic corporation that was a party to the merger or share exchange, a statement that the plan was duly approved by the shareholders and, if voting by any separate voting group was required, by each such separate voting group, in the manner required by this Act and the articles of incorporation;

(4) if the plan of merger or share exchange did not require approval by the shareholders of a domestic corporation that was a party to the merger or share exchange, a statement to that effect; and

(5) as to each foreign corporation or eligible entity that was a party to the merger or share exchange, a statement that the participation of the foreign corporation or eligible entity was duly authorized as required by the organic law of the corporation or eligible entity.

(b) Articles of merger or share exchange shall be delivered to the secretary of state for filing by the survivor of the merger or the acquiring corporation in a share exchange, and shall take effect at the effective time provided in § 1.23. Articles of merger or share exchange filed under this section may be combined with any filing required under the organic law of any domestic eligible entity involved in the transaction if the combined filing satisfies the requirements of both this section and the other organic law.

§ 11.07. Effect of Merger or Share Exchange.

(a) When a merger becomes effective:

(1) the corporation or eligible entity that is designated in the plan of merger as the survivor continues or comes into existence, as the case may be;

(2) the separate existence of every corporation or eligible entity that is merged into the survivor ceases;

(3) all property owned by, and every contract right possessed by, each corporation or eligible entity that merges into the survivor is vested in the survivor without reversion or impairment;

(4) all liabilities of each corporation or eligible entity that is merged into the survivor are vested in the survivor;

(5) the name of the survivor may, but need not be, substituted in any pending proceeding for the name of any party to the merger whose separate existence ceased in the merger;

(6) the articles of incorporation or organic documents of the survivor are amended to the extent provided in the plan of merger;

(7) the articles of incorporation or organic documents of a survivor that is created by the merger become effective; and

(8) the shares of each corporation that is a party to the merger, and the interests in an eligible entity that is a party to a merger, that are to be converted under the plan of merger into shares, eligible interests, obligations, rights to acquire securities, other securities, or eligible interests, cash, other property, or any combination of the foregoing, are converted, and the former holders of such shares or eligible interests are entitled only to the rights provided to them in the plan of merger or to any rights they may have under chapter 13 or the organic law of the eligible entity.

(b) When a share exchange becomes effective, the shares of each domestic corporation that are to be exchanged for shares or other securities, interests, obligations, rights to acquire shares or other securities, cash, other property, or any combination of the foregoing, are entitled only to the rights provided to them in the plan of share exchange or to any rights they may have under chapter 13.

(c) A person who becomes subject to owner liability for some or all of the debts, obligations or liabilities of any entity as a result of a merger or share exchange shall have owner liability only to the extent provided in the organic law of the entity and only for those debts, obligations and liabilities that arise after the effective time of the articles of merger or share exchange.

(d) Upon a merger becoming effective, a foreign corporation, or a foreign eligible entity, that is the survivor of the merger is deemed to:

(1) appoint the secretary of state as its agent for service of process in a proceeding to enforce the rights of shareholders of each domestic corporation that is a party to the merger who exercise appraisal rights, and

(2) agree that it will promptly pay the amount, if any, to which such shareholders are entitled under chapter 13.

(e) The effect of a merger or share exchange on the owner liability of a person who had owner liability for some or all of the debts, obligations or liabilities of a party to the merger or share exchange shall be as follows:

(1) The merger or share exchange does not discharge any owner liability under the organic law of the entity in which the person was a shareholder or interest holder to the extent any such owner liability arose before the effective time of the articles of merger or share exchange.

(2) The person shall not have owner liability under the organic law of the entity in which the person was a shareholder or interest holder prior to the merger or share exchange for any debt, obligation or liability that arises after the effective time of the articles of merger or share exchange.

(3) The provisions of the organic law of any entity for which the person had owner liability before the merger or share exchange shall continue to apply to the collection or discharge of any owner liability preserved by paragraph (1), as if the merger or share exchange had not occurred.

(4) The person shall have whatever rights of contribution from other persons are provided by the organic law of the entity for which the person had owner liability with respect to any owner liability preserved by paragraph (1), as if the merger or share exchange had not occurred.

§ 11.08. Abandonment of a Merger or Share Exchange.

(a) Unless otherwise provided in a plan of merger or share exchange or in the laws under which a foreign business corporation or a domestic or foreign eligible entity that is a party to a merger or a share exchange is organized or by which it is governed, after the plan has been adopted and approved as required by this chapter, and at any time before the merger or share exchange has become effective, it may be abandoned by a domestic business corporation that is a party thereto without action by its shareholders in accordance with any procedures set forth in the plan of merger or share exchange or, if no such procedures are set forth in the plan, in the manner determined by the board of directors, subject to any contractual rights of other parties to the merger or share exchange.

(b) If a merger or share exchange is abandoned under subsection (a) after articles of merger or share exchange have been filed with the secretary of state but before the merger or share exchange has become effective, a statement that the merger or share exchange has been abandoned in accordance with this section, executed on behalf of a party to the merger or share exchange by an officer or other duly authorized representative, shall be delivered to the secretary of state for filing prior to the effective date of the merger or share exchange. Upon filing, the statement shall take effect and the merger or share exchange shall be deemed abandoned and shall not become effective.

CHAPTER 12. DISPOSITION OF ASSETS

§ 12.01. Disposition of Assets Not Requiring Shareholder Approval.

No approval of the shareholders of a corporation is required, unless the articles of incorporation otherwise provide:

(1) to sell, lease, exchange, or otherwise dispose of any or all of the corporation's assets in the usual and regular course of business;

(2) to mortgage, pledge, dedicate to the repayment of indebtedness (whether with or without recourse), or otherwise encumber any or all of the corporation's assets, whether or not in the usual and regular course of business;

(3) to transfer any or all of the corporation's assets to one or more corporations or other entities all of the shares or interests of which are owned by the corporation; or

(4) to distribute assets pro rata to the holders of one or more classes or series of the corporation's shares.

§ 12.02. Shareholder Approval of Certain Dispositions.

(a) A sale, lease, exchange, or other disposition of assets, other than a disposition described in § 12.01, requires approval of the corporation's shareholders if the disposition would leave the corporation without a significant continuing business activity. If a corporation retains a business activity that represented at least 25 percent of total assets at the end of the most recently completed fiscal year, and 25 percent of either income from continuing operations before taxes or revenues from continuing operations for that fiscal year, in each case of the corporation and its subsidiaries on a consolidated basis, the corporation will conclusively be deemed to have retained a significant continuing business activity.

(b) A disposition that requires approval of the shareholders under subsection (a) shall be initiated by a resolution by the board of directors authorizing the disposition. After adoption of such a resolution, the board of directors shall submit the proposed disposition to the shareholders for their approval. The board of directors shall also transmit to the shareholders a recommendation that the shareholders approve the proposed disposition, unless the board of directors makes a determination that because of conflicts of interest or other special circumstances it should not make such a recommendation, in which case the board of directors shall transmit to the shareholders the basis for that determination.

(c) The board of directors may condition its submission of a disposition to the shareholders under subsection (b) on any basis.

(d) If a disposition is required to be approved by the shareholders under subsection (a), and if the approval is to be given at a meeting, the corporation shall notify each shareholder, whether or not entitled to vote, of the meeting of shareholders at which the disposition is to be submitted for approval. The notice shall state that the purpose, or one of the purposes, of the meeting is to consider the disposition and shall contain a description of the disposition, including the terms and conditions thereof and the consideration to be received by the corporation.

(e) Unless the articles of incorporation or the board of directors acting pursuant to subsection (c) requires a greater vote, or a greater number of votes to be present, the approval of a disposition by the shareholders shall require the approval of the shareholders at a meeting at which a quorum consisting of at least a majority of the votes entitled to be cast on the disposition exists.

(f) After a disposition has been approved by the shareholders under subsection (b), and at any time before the disposition has been consummated, it may be abandoned by the corporation without action by the shareholders, subject to any contractual rights of other parties to the disposition.

(g) A disposition of assets in the course of dissolution under chapter 14 is not governed by this section.

(h) The assets of a direct or indirect consolidated subsidiary shall be deemed the assets of the parent corporation for the purposes of this section.

CHAPTER 13. APPRAISAL RIGHTS
Subchapter A. Right to Appraisal and Payment for Shares

§ 13.01. Definitions. In this chapter:

(1) "Affiliate" means a person that directly or indirectly through one or more intermediaries controls, is controlled by, or is under common control with another person or is a senior executive thereof. For purposes of § 13.02(b)(4), a person is deemed to be an affiliate of its senior executives.

(2) "Beneficial shareholder" means a person who is the beneficial owner of shares held in a voting trust or by a nominee on the beneficial owner's behalf.

(3) "Corporation" means the issuer of the shares held by a shareholder demanding appraisal and, for matters covered in §§ 13.22 to 13.31, includes the surviving entity in a merger.

(4) "Fair value" means the value of the corporation's shares determined:

(i) immediately before the effectuation of the corporate action to which the shareholder objects;

(ii) using customary and current valuation concepts and techniques generally employed for similar businesses in the context of the transaction requiring appraisal; and

(iii) without discounting for lack of marketability or minority status except, if appropriate, for amendments to the articles pursuant to § 13.02(a)(5).

(5) "Interest" means interest from the effective date of the corporate action until the date of payment, at the rate of interest on judgments in this state on the effective date of the corporate action.

(6) "Preferred shares" means a class or series of shares whose holders have preference over any other class or series with respect to distributions.

(7) "Record shareholder" means the person in whose name shares are registered in the records of the corporation or the beneficial owner of shares to the extent of the rights granted by a nominee certificate on file with the corporation.

(8) "Senior executive" means the chief executive officer, chief operating officer, chief financial officer, and anyone in charge of a principal business unit or function.

(9) "Shareholder" means both a record shareholder and a beneficial shareholder.

§ 13.02. Right to Appraisal.

(a) A shareholder is entitled to appraisal rights, and to obtain payment of the fair value of that shareholder's shares, in the event of any of the following corporate actions:

    (1) consummation of a merger to which the corporation is a party

        (i) if shareholder approval is required for the merger by § 11.04 and the shareholder is entitled to vote on the merger, except that appraisal rights shall not be available to any shareholder of the corporation with respect to shares of any class or series that remain outstanding after consummation of the merger, or

        (ii) if the corporation is a subsidiary and the merger is governed by § 11.05;

    (2) consummation of a share exchange to which the corporation is a party as the corporation whose shares will be acquired if the shareholder is entitled to vote on the exchange, except that appraisal rights shall not be available to any shareholder of the corporation with respect to any class or series of shares of the corporation that is not exchanged;

    (3) consummation of a disposition of assets pursuant to § 12.02 if the shareholder is entitled to vote on the disposition;

    (4) an amendment of the articles of incorporation with respect to a class or series of shares that reduces the number of shares of a class or series owned by the shareholder to a fraction of a share if the corporation has the obligation or right to repurchase the fractional share so created;

    (5) any other amendment to the articles of incorporation, merger, share exchange or disposition of assets to the extent provided by the articles of incorporation, bylaws or a resolution of the board of directors;

    (6) consummation of a domestication if the shareholder does not receive shares in the foreign corporation resulting from the domestication that have terms as favorable to the shareholder in all material respects, and represent at least the same percentage interest of the total voting rights of the outstanding shares of the corporation, as the shares held by the shareholder before the domestication;

    (7) consummation of a conversion of the corporation to nonprofit status pursuant to subchapter 9C; or

    (8) consummation of a conversion of the corporation to an unincorporated entity pursuant to subchapter 9E.

(b) Notwithstanding subsection (a), the availability of appraisal rights under subsections (a)(1), (2), (3), (4), (6) and (8) shall be limited in accordance with the following provisions:

    (1) Appraisal rights shall not be available for the holders of shares of any class or series of shares which is:

        (i) listed on the New York Stock Exchange or the American Stock Exchange or designated as a national market system security on an interdealer quotation system by the National Association of Securities Dealers, Inc.; or

        (ii) not so listed or designated, but has at least 2,000 shareholders and the outstanding shares of such class or series has a market value of at least $20 million (exclusive of the value of such shares held by its subsidiaries, senior executives, directors and beneficial shareholders owning more than 10 percent of such shares).

    (2) The applicability of subsection (b)(l) shall be determined as of:

        (i) the record date fixed to determine the shareholders entitled to receive notice of, and to vote at, the meeting of shareholders to act upon the corporate action requiring appraisal rights; or

        (ii) the day before the effective date of such corporate action if there is no meeting of shareholders.

    (3) Subsection (b)(l) shall not be applicable and appraisal rights shall be available pursuant to subsection (a) for the holders of any class or series of shares who are required by the terms of the corporate action requiring appraisal rights to accept for such shares anything other than cash or shares of any class or any series of shares of any corporation, or any other proprietary interest of any other entity, that satisfies the standards set forth in subsection (b)(l) at the time the corporate action becomes effective.

    (4) Subsection (b)(1) shall not be applicable and appraisal rights shall be available pursuant to subsection (a) for the holders of any class or series of shares where:

        (i) any of the shares or assets of the corporation are being acquired or converted, whether by merger, share exchange or otherwise, pursuant to the corporate action by a person, or by an affiliate of a person, who:

           (A) is, or at any time in the one-year period immediately preceding approval by the board of directors of the corporate action requiring appraisal rights was, the beneficial owner of 20 percent or more of the voting power of the corporation, excluding any shares acquired pursuant to an offer for all shares having voting power if such offer was made within one year prior to the corporate action requiring appraisal rights for consideration of the same kind and of a value equal to or less than that paid in connection with the corporate action; or

           (B) directly or indirectly has, or at any time in the one-year period immediately preceding approval by the board of directors of the corporation of the corporate action requiring appraisal rights had, the power, contractually or otherwise, to cause the appointment or election of 25 percent or more of the directors to the board of directors of the corporation; or

        (ii) any of the shares or assets of the corporation are being acquired or converted, whether by merger, share exchange or otherwise, pursuant to such corporate action by a person, or by an affiliate of a person, who is, or at any time in the one-year period immediately preceding approval by the board of directors of the corporate action requiring appraisal rights was, a senior executive or director of the corporation or a senior executive of any affiliate thereof, and that senior executive or director will receive, as a result of the corporate action, a financial benefit not generally available to other shareholders as such, other than:

(A) employment, consulting, retirement or similar benefits established separately and not as part of or in contemplation of the corporate action; or

(B) employment, consulting, retirement or similar benefits established in contemplation of, or as part of, the corporate action that are not more favorable than those existing before the corporate action or, if more favorable, that have been approved on behalf of the corporation in the same manner as is provided in § 8.62; or

(C) in the case of a director of the corporation who will, in the corporate action, become a director of the acquiring entity in the corporate action or one of its affiliates, rights and benefits as a director that are provided on the same basis as those afforded by the acquiring entity generally to other directors of such entity or such affiliate.

(5) For the purposes of paragraph (4) only, the term "beneficial owner" means any person who, directly or indirectly, through any contract, arrangement, or understanding, other than a revocable proxy, has or shares the power to vote, or to direct the voting of, shares, provided that a member of a national securities exchange shall not be deemed to be a beneficial owner of securities held directly or indirectly by it on behalf of another person solely because such member is the record holder of such securities if the member is precluded by the rules of such exchange from voting without instruction on contested matters or matters that may affect substantially the rights or privileges of the holders of the securities to be voted. When two or more persons agree to act together for the purpose of voting their shares of the corporation, each member of the group formed thereby shall be deemed to have acquired beneficial ownership, as of the date of such agreement, of all voting shares of the corporation beneficially owned by any member of the group.

(c) Notwithstanding any other provision of § 13.02, the articles of incorporation as originally filed or any amendment thereto may limit or eliminate appraisal rights for any class or series of preferred shares, but any such limitation or elimination contained in an amendment to the articles of incorporation that limits or eliminates appraisal rights for any of such shares that are outstanding immediately prior to the effective date of such amendment or that the corporation is or may be required to issue or sell thereafter pursuant to any conversion, exchange or other right existing immediately before the effective date of such amendment shall not apply to any corporate action that becomes effective within one year of that date if such action would otherwise afford appraisal rights.

(d) A shareholder may not challenge a completed corporate action described in subsection (a), other than those subscribed in subsection (b)(3) and (4), unless such corporate action:

(1) was not effectuated in accordance with the applicable provisions of chapters 9, 10, 11 or 12 or the corporation's articles of incorporation, bylaws or board of directors' resolution authorizing the corporate action; or

(2) was procured as a result of fraud or material misrepresentation.

§ 13.03. Assertion of Rights by Nominees and Beneficial Owners.

(a) A record shareholder may assert appraisal rights as to fewer than all the shares registered in the record shareholder's name but owned by a beneficial shareholder only if the record shareholder objects with respect to all shares of the class or series owned by the beneficial shareholder and notifies the corporation in writing of the name and address of each beneficial shareholder on whose behalf appraisal rights are being asserted. The rights of a record shareholder who asserts appraisal rights for only part of the shares held of record in the record shareholder's name under this subsection shall be determined as if the shares as to which the record shareholder objects and the record shareholder's other shares were registered in the names of different record shareholders.

(b) A beneficial shareholder may assert appraisal rights as to shares of any class or series held on behalf of the shareholder only if such shareholder:

(1) submits to the corporation the record shareholder's written consent to the assertion of such rights no later than the date referred to in § 13.22(b)(2)(ii); and

(2) does so with respect to all shares of the class or series that are beneficially owned by the beneficial shareholder.

Subchapter B. Procedure for Exercise of Appraisal Rights

§ 13.20. Notice of Appraisal Rights.

(a) If proposed corporate action described in § 13.02(a) is to be submitted to a vote at a shareholders' meeting, the meeting notice must state that the corporation has concluded that shareholders are, are not or may be entitled to assert appraisal rights under this chapter. If the corporation concludes that appraisal rights are or may be available, a copy of this chapter must accompany the meeting notice sent to those record shareholders entitled to exercise appraisal rights.

(b) In a merger pursuant to § 11.05, the parent corporation must notify in writing all record shareholders of the subsidiary who are entitled to assert appraisal rights that the corporate action became effective. Such notice must be sent within ten days after the corporate action became effective and include the materials described in § 13.22.

§ 13.21. Notice of Intent To Demand Payment.

(a) If proposed corporate action requiring appraisal rights under § 13.02 is submitted to a vote at a shareholders' meeting, a shareholder who wishes to assert appraisal rights with respect to any class or series of shares:

(1) must deliver to the corporation before the vote is taken written notice of the shareholder's intent to demand payment if the proposed action is effectuated; and

(2) must not vote, or cause or permit to be voted, any shares of such class or series in favor of the proposed action.

(b) A shareholder who does not satisfy the requirements of subsection (a) is not entitled to payment under this chapter.

§ 13.22. Appraisal Notice and Form.

(a) If proposed corporate action requiring appraisal rights under § 13.02(a) becomes effective, the corporation must deliver a written appraisal notice and form required by subsection (b)(1) to all shareholders who satisfied the requirements of § 13.21. In the case of a merger under § 11.05, the parent must deliver a written appraisal notice and form to all record shareholders who may be entitled to assert appraisal rights.

(b) The appraisal notice must be sent no earlier than the date the corporate action became effective and no later than ten days after such date and must:

(1) supply a form that specifies the date of the first announcement to shareholders of the principal terms of the proposed

corporate action and requires the shareholder asserting appraisal rights to certify

> (i) whether or not beneficial ownership of those shares for which appraisal rights are asserted was acquired before that date and
> (ii) that the shareholder did not vote for the transaction;

(2) state:

> (i) where the form must be sent and where certificates for certificated shares must be deposited and the date by which those certificates must be deposited, which date may not be earlier than the date for receiving the required form under subsection (2)(ii);
> (ii) a date by which the corporation must receive the form which date may not be fewer than 40 nor more than 60 days after the date the subsection (a) appraisal notice and form are sent, and state that the shareholder shall have waived the right to demand appraisal with respect to the shares unless the form is received by the corporation by such specified date;
> (iii) the corporation's estimate of the fair value of the shares;
> (iv) that, if requested in writing, the corporation will provide, to the shareholder so requesting, within ten days after the date specified in subsection (2)(ii) the number of shareholders who return the forms by the specified date and the total number of shares owned by them; and
> (v) the date by which the notice to withdraw under § 13.23 must be received, which date must be within 20 days after the date specified in subsection (2)(ii); and

(3) be accompanied by a copy of this chapter.

§ 13.23. Perfection of Rights; Right to Withdraw.

(a) A shareholder who receives notice pursuant to § 13.22 and who wishes to exercise appraisal rights must certify on the form sent by the corporation whether the beneficial owner of such shares acquired beneficial ownership of the shares before the date required to be set forth in the notice pursuant to § 13.22(b)(1). If a shareholder fails to make this certification, the corporation may elect to treat the shareholder's shares as after-acquired shares under § 13.25. In addition, a shareholder who wishes to exercise appraisal rights must execute and return the form and, in the case of certificated shares, deposit the shareholder's certificates in accordance with the terms of the notice by the date referred to in the notice pursuant to §13.22(b)(2)(ii). Once a shareholder deposits that shareholder's certificates or, in the case of uncertificated shares, returns the executed forms, that shareholder loses all rights as a shareholder, unless the shareholder withdraws pursuant to subsection (b).

(b) A shareholder who has complied with subsection (a) may nevertheless decline to exercise appraisal rights and withdraw from the appraisal process by so notifying the corporation in writing by the date set forth in the appraisal notice pursuant to § 13.22(b)(2)(v). A shareholder who fails to so withdraw from the appraisal process may not thereafter withdraw without the corporation's written consent.

(c) A shareholder who does not execute and return the form and, in the case of certificated shares, deposit that shareholder's share certificates where required, each by the date set forth in the notice described in § 13.22(b), shall not be entitled to payment under this chapter.

§ 13.24. Payment.

(a) Except as provided in § 13.25, within 30 days after the form required by § 13.22(b)(2)(ii) is due, the corporation shall pay in cash to those shareholders who complied with § 13.23(a) the amount the corporation estimates to be the fair value of their shares, plus interest.

(b) The payment to each shareholder pursuant to subsection (a) must be accompanied by:

> (1) financial statements of the corporation that issued the shares to be appraised, consisting of a balance sheet as of the end of a fiscal year ending not more than 16 months before the date of payment, an income statement for that year, a statement of changes in shareholders' equity for that year, and the latest available interim financial statements, if any;
> (2) a statement of the corporation's estimate of the fair value of the shares, which estimate must equal or exceed the corporation's estimate given pursuant to § 13.22(b)(2)(iii);
> (3) a statement that shareholders described in subsection (a) have the right to demand further payment under § 13.26 and that if any such shareholder does not do so within the time period specified therein, such shareholder shall be deemed to have accepted such payment in full satisfaction of the corporation's obligations under this chapter.

§ 13.25. After-Acquired Shares.

(a) A corporation may elect to withhold payment required by § 13.24 from any shareholder who did not certify that beneficial ownership of all of the shareholder's shares for which appraisal rights are asserted was acquired before the date set forth in the appraisal notice sent pursuant to § 13.22(b)(1).

(b) If the corporation elected to withhold payment under subsection (a), it must, within 30 days after the form required by §13.22(b)(2)(ii) is due, notify all shareholders who are described in subsection (a):

> (1) of the information required by § 13.24(b)(1);
> (2) of the corporation's estimate of fair value pursuant to § 13.24(b)(2);
> (3) that they may accept the corporation's estimate of fair value, plus interest, in full satisfaction of their demands or demand appraisal under § 13.26;
> (4) that those shareholders who wish to accept such offer must so notify the corporation of their acceptance of the corporation's offer within 30 days after receiving the offer; and
> (5) that those shareholders who do not satisfy the requirements for demanding appraisal under § 13.26 shall be deemed to have accepted the corporation's offer.

(c) Within ten days after receiving the shareholder's acceptance pursuant to subsection (b), the corporation must pay in cash the amount it offered under subsection (b)(2) to each shareholder who agreed to accept the corporation's offer in full satisfaction of the shareholder's demand.

(d) Within 40 days after sending the notice described in subsection (b), the corporation must pay in cash the amount it offered to pay under subsection (b)(2) to each shareholder described in subsection (b)(5).

§ 13.26. Procedure if Shareholder Dissatisfied with Payment or Offer.

(a) A shareholder paid pursuant to § 13.24 who is dissatisfied with the amount of the payment must notify the corporation in writing of that shareholder's estimate of the fair value of the shares and demand payment of that estimate plus interest (less any payment under § 13.24). A shareholder offered payment under § 13.25 who is dissatisfied with that offer must reject the offer and demand payment of the shareholder's stated estimate of the fair value of the shares plus interest.

(b) A shareholder who fails to notify the corporation in writing of that shareholder's demand to be paid the shareholder's stated estimate of the fair value plus interest under subsection (a) within 30 days after receiving the corporation's payment or offer of payment under § 13.24 or § 13.25, respectively, waives the right to demand payment under this section and shall be entitled only to the payment made or offered pursuant to those respective sections.

Subchapter C. Judicial Appraisal of Shares

§ 13.30. Court Action.

(a) If a shareholder makes demand for payment under § 13.26 which remains unsettled, the corporation shall commence a proceeding within 60 days after receiving the payment demand and petition the court to determine the fair value of the shares and accrued interest. If the corporation does not commence the proceeding within the 60-day period, it shall pay in cash to each shareholder the amount the shareholder demanded pursuant to § 13.26 plus interest.

(b) The corporation shall commence the proceeding in the appropriate court of the county where the corporation's principal office (or, if none, its registered office) in this state is located. If the corporation is a foreign corporation without a registered office in this state, it shall commence the proceeding in the county in this state where the principal office or registered office of the domestic corporation merged with the foreign corporation was located at the time of the transaction.

(c) The corporation shall make all shareholders (whether or not residents of this state) whose demands remain unsettled parties to the proceeding as in an action against their shares, and all parties must be served with a copy of the petition. Nonresidents may be served by registered or certified mail or by publication as provided by law.

(d) The jurisdiction of the court in which the proceeding is commenced under subsection (b) is plenary and exclusive. The court may appoint one or more persons as appraisers to receive evidence and recommend a decision on the question of fair value. The appraisers shall have the powers described in the order appointing them, or in any amendment to it. The shareholders demanding appraisal rights are entitled to the same discovery rights as parties in other civil proceedings. There shall be no right to a jury trial.

(e) Each shareholder made a party to the proceeding is entitled to judgment (i) for the amount, if any, by which the court finds the fair value of the shareholder's shares, plus interest, exceeds the amount paid by the corporation to the shareholder for such shares or (ii) for the fair value, plus interest, of the shareholder's shares for which the corporation elected to withhold payment under § 13.25.

§ 13.31. Court Costs and Counsel Fees.

(a) The court in an appraisal proceeding commenced under § 13.30 shall determine all costs of the proceeding, including the reasonable compensation and expenses of appraisers appointed by the court. The court shall assess the costs against the corporation, except that the court may assess costs against all or some of the shareholders demanding appraisal, in amounts the court finds equitable, to the extent the court finds such shareholders acted arbitrarily, vexatiously, or not in good faith with respect to the rights provided by this chapter.

(b) The court in an appraisal proceeding may also assess the fees and expenses of counsel and experts for the respective parties, in amounts the court finds equitable:

(1) against the corporation and in favor of any or all shareholders demanding appraisal if the court finds the corporation did not substantially comply with the requirements of § 13.20, 13.22, 13.24 or 13.25; or

(2) against either the corporation or a shareholder demanding appraisal, in favor of any other party, if the court finds that the party against whom the fees and expenses are assessed acted arbitrarily, vexatiously, or not in good faith with respect to the rights provided by this chapter.

(c) If the court in an appraisal proceeding finds that the services of counsel for any shareholder were of substantial benefit to other shareholders similarly situated, and that the fees for those services should not be assessed against the corporation, the court may award to such counsel reasonable fees to be paid out of the amounts awarded the shareholders who were benefited.

(d) To the extent the corporation fails to make a required payment pursuant to § 13.24, 13.25, or 13.26, the shareholder may sue directly for the amount owed and, to the extent successful, shall be entitled to recover from the corporation all costs and expenses of the suit, including counsel fees.

CHAPTER 14. DISSOLUTION
Subchapter A. Voluntary Dissolution

§ 14.01. Dissolution by Incorporators or Initial Directors.
A majority of the incorporators or initial directors of a corporation that has not issued shares or has not commenced business may dissolve the corporation by delivering to the secretary of state for filing articles of dissolution that set forth:

(1) the name of the corporation;

(2) the date of its incorporation;

(3) either (i) that none of the corporation's shares has been issued or (ii) that the corporation has not commenced business;

(4) that no debt of the corporation remains unpaid;

(5) that the net assets of the corporation remaining after winding up have been distributed to the shareholders, if shares were issued; and

(6) that a majority of the incorporators or initial directors authorized the dissolution.

§ 14.02. Dissolution by Board of Directors and Shareholders.

(a) A corporation's board of directors may propose dissolution for submission to the shareholders.

(b) For a proposal to dissolve to be adopted:

(1) the board of directors must recommend dissolution to the shareholders unless the board of directors determines that because of conflict of interest or other special circumstances it should make no recommendation and communicates the basis for its determination to the shareholders; and

(2) the shareholders entitled to vote must approve the proposal to dissolve as provided in subsection (e).

(c) The board of directors may condition its submission of the proposal for dissolution on any basis.

(d) The corporation shall notify each shareholder, whether or not entitled to vote, of the proposed shareholders' meeting. The notice must also state that the purpose, or one of the purposes, of the meeting is to consider dissolving the corporation.

(e) Unless the articles of incorporation or the board of directors acting pursuant to subsection (c) require a greater vote, a greater number of shares to be present, or a vote by voting groups, adoption of the proposal to dissolve shall require the approval of the shareholders at a meeting at which a quorum consisting of at least a majority of the votes entitled to be cast exists.

§ 14.03. Articles of Dissolution.

(a) At any time after dissolution is authorized, the corporation may dissolve by delivering to the secretary of state for filing articles of dissolution setting forth:

(1) the name of the corporation;

(2) the date dissolution was authorized; and

(3) if dissolution was approved by the shareholders, a statement that the proposal to dissolve was duly approved by the shareholders in the manner required by this Act and by the articles of incorporation.

(b) A corporation is dissolved upon the effective date of its articles of dissolution.

(c) For purposes of this subchapter, "dissolved corporation" means a corporation whose articles of dissolution have become effective and includes a successor entity to which the remaining assets of the corporation are transferred subject to its liabilities for purposes of liquidation.

§ 14.04. Revocation of Dissolution.

(a) A corporation may revoke its dissolution within 120 days of its effective date.

(b) Revocation of dissolution must be authorized in the same manner as the dissolution was authorized unless that authorization permitted revocation by action of the board of directors alone, in which event the board of directors may revoke the dissolution without shareholder action.

(c) After the revocation of dissolution is authorized, the corporation may revoke the dissolution by delivering to the secretary of state for filing articles of revocation of dissolution, together with a copy of its articles of dissolution, that set forth:

(1) the name of the corporation;

(2) the effective date of the dissolution that was revoked;

(3) the date that the revocation of dissolution was authorized;

(4) if the corporation's board of directors (or incorporators) revoked the dissolution, a statement to that effect;

(5) if the corporation's board of directors revoked a dissolution authorized by the shareholders, a statement that revocation was permitted by action by the board of directors alone pursuant to that authorization; and

(6) if shareholder action was required to revoke the dissolution, the information required by § 14.03(a)(3) or (4).

(d) Revocation of dissolution is effective upon the effective date of the articles of revocation of dissolution.

(e) When the revocation of dissolution is effective, it relates back to and takes effect as of the effective date of the dissolution and the corporation resumes carrying on its business as if dissolution had never occurred.

§ 14.05. Effect of Dissolution.

(a) A dissolved corporation continues its corporate existence but may not carry on any business except that appropriate to wind up and liquidate its business and affairs, including:

(1) collecting its assets;

(2) disposing of its properties that will not be distributed in kind to its shareholders;

(3) discharging or making provision for discharging its liabilities;

(4) distributing its remaining property among its shareholders according to their interests; and

(5) doing every other act necessary to wind up and liquidate its business and affairs.

(b) Dissolution of a corporation does not:

(1) transfer title to the corporation's property;

(2) prevent transfer of its shares or securities, although the authorization to dissolve may provide for closing the corporation's share transfer records;

(3) subject its directors or officers to standards of conduct different from those prescribed in chapter 8;

(4) change quorum or voting requirements for its board of directors or shareholders; change provisions for selection, resignation, or removal of its directors or officers or both; or change provisions for amending its bylaws;

(5) prevent commencement of a proceeding by or against the corporation in its corporate name;

(6) abate or suspend a proceeding pending by or against the corporation on the effective date of dissolution; or

(7) terminate the authority of the registered agent of the corporation.

§ 14.06. Known Claims Against Dissolved Corporation.

(a) A dissolved corporation may dispose of the known claims against it by following the procedure described in this section.

(b) The dissolved corporation shall notify its known claimants in writing of the dissolution at any time after its effective date. The written notice must:

(1) describe information that must be included in a claim;

(2) provide a mailing address where a claim may be sent;

(3) state the deadline, which may not be fewer than 120 days from the effective date of the written notice, by which the dissolved corporation must receive the claim; and

(4) state that the claim will be barred if not received by the deadline.

(c) A claim against the dissolved corporation is barred:

(1) if a claimant who was given written notice under subsection (b) does not deliver the claim to the dissolved corporation by the deadline;

(2) if a claimant whose claim was rejected by the dissolved corporation does not commence a proceeding to enforce the claim within 90 days from the effective date of the rejection notice.

(d) For purposes of this section, "claim" does not include a contingent liability or a claim based on an event occurring after the effective date of dissolution.

§ 14.07. Other Claims Against Dissolved Corporation.

(a) A dissolved corporation may also publish notice of its dissolution and request that persons with claims against the dissolved corporation present them in accordance with the notice.

(b) The notice must:

(1) be published one time in a newspaper of general circulation in the county where the dissolved corporation's principal office (or, if none in this state, its registered office) is or was last located;

(2) describe the information that must be included in a claim and provide a mailing address where the claim may be sent; and

(3) state that a claim against the dissolved corporation will be barred unless a proceeding to enforce the claim is commenced within three years after the publication of the notice.

(c) If the dissolved corporation publishes a newspaper notice in accordance with subsection (b), the claim of each of the following claimants is barred unless the claimant commences a proceeding to enforce the claim against the dissolved corporation within three years after the publication date of the newspaper notice:

(1) a claimant who was not given written notice under § 14.06;

(2) a claimant whose claim was timely sent to the dissolved corporation but not acted on;

(3) a claimant whose claim is contingent or based on an event occurring after the effective date of dissolution.

(d) A claim that is not barred by § 14.06(b) or 14.07(c) may be enforced:

(1) against the dissolved corporation, to the extent of its undistributed assets; or

(2) except as provided in § 14.08(d), if the assets have been distributed in liquidation, against a shareholder of the dissolved corporation to the extent of the shareholder's pro rata share of the claim or the corporate assets distributed to the shareholder in liquidation, whichever is less, but a shareholder's total liability for all claims under this section may not exceed the total amount of assets distributed to the shareholder.

§ 14.08. Court Proceedings.

(a) A dissolved corporation that has published a notice under § 14.07 may file an application with the [name or describe] court of the county where the dissolved corporation's principal office (or, if none in this state, its registered office) is located for a determination of the amount and form of security to be provided for payment of claims that are contingent or have not been made known to the dissolved corporation or that are based on an event occurring after the effective date of dissolution but that, based on the facts known to the dissolved corporation, are reasonably estimated to arise after the effective date of dissolution. Provision need not be made for any claim that is or is reasonably anticipated to be barred under § 14.07(c).

(b) Within 10 days after the filing of the application, notice of the proceeding shall be given by the dissolved corporation to each claimant holding a contingent claim whose contingent claim is shown on the records of the dissolved corporation.

(c) The court may appoint a guardian ad litem to represent all claimants whose identities are unknown in any proceeding brought under this section. The reasonable fees and expenses of such guardian, including all reasonable expert witness fees, shall be paid by the dissolved corporation.

(d) Provision by the dissolved corporation for security in the amount and the form ordered by the court under § 14.08(a) shall satisfy the dissolved corporation's obligations with respect to claims that are contingent, have not been made known to the dissolved corporation or are based on an event occurring after the effective date of dissolution, and such claims may not be enforced against a shareholder who received assets in liquidation.

§ 14.09. Director Duties.

(a) Directors shall cause the dissolved corporation to discharge or make reasonable provision for the payment of claims and make distributions of assets to shareholders after payment or provision for claims.

(b) Directors of a dissolved corporation which has disposed of claims under § 14.06, 14.07, or 14.08 shall not be liable for breach of § 14.09(a) with respect to claims against the dissolved corporation that are barred or satisfied under § 14.06, 14.07, or 14.08.

Subchapter B. Administrative Dissolution

§ 14.20. Grounds for Administrative Dissolution.

The secretary of state may commence a proceeding under § 14.21 to administratively dissolve a corporation if:

(1) the corporation does not pay within 60 days after they are due any franchise taxes or penalties imposed by this Act or other law;

(2) the corporation does not deliver its annual report to the secretary of state within 60 days after it is due;

(3) the corporation is without a registered agent or registered office in this state for 60 days or more;

(4) the corporation does not notify the secretary of state within 60 days that its registered agent or registered office has been changed, that its registered agent has resigned, or that its registered office has been discontinued; or

(5) the corporation's period of duration stated in its articles of incorporation expires.

§ 14.21. Procedure for and Effect of Administrative Dissolution.

(a) If the secretary of state determines that one or more grounds exist under § 14.20 for dissolving a corporation, he shall serve the corporation with written notice of his determination under § 5.04.

(b) If the corporation does not correct each ground for dissolution or demonstrate to the reasonable satisfaction of the secretary of state that each ground determined by the secretary of state does not exist within 60 days after service of the notice is perfected under § 5.04, the secretary of state shall administratively dissolve the corporation by signing a certificate of dissolution that recites the ground or grounds for dissolution and its effective date. The secretary of state shall file the original of the certificate and serve a copy on the corporation under § 5.04.

(c) A corporation administratively dissolved continues its corporate existence but may not carry on any business except that necessary to wind up and liquidate its business and affairs under § 14.05 and notify claimants under §§ 14.06 and 14.07.

(d) The administrative dissolution of a corporation does not terminate the authority of its registered agent.

§ 14.22. Reinstatement Following Administrative Dissolution.

(a) A corporation administratively dissolved under § 14.21 may apply to the secretary of state for reinstatement within two years after the effective date of dissolution. The application must:

(1) recite the name of the corporation and the effective date of its administrative dissolution;

(2) state that the ground or grounds for dissolution either did not exist or have been eliminated;

(3) state that the corporation's name satisfies the requirements of § 4.01; and

(4) contain a certificate from the [taxing authority] reciting that all taxes owed by the corporation have been paid.

(b) If the secretary of state determines that the application contains the information required by subsection (a) and that the information is correct, he shall cancel the certificate of dissolution and prepare a certificate of reinstatement that recites his determination and the effective date of reinstatement, file the original of the certificate, and serve a copy on the corporation under § 5.04.

(c) When the reinstatement is effective, it relates back to and takes effect as of the effective date of the administrative dissolution and the corporation resumes carrying on its business as if the administrative dissolution had never occurred.

§ 14.23. Appeal from Denial of Reinstatement.

(a) If the secretary of state denies a corporation's application for reinstatement following administrative dissolution, he shall serve the corporation under § 5.04 with a written notice that explains the reason or reasons for denial.

(b) The corporation may appeal the denial of reinstatement to the [name or describe] court within 30 days after service of the notice of denial is perfected. The corporation appeals by petitioning the court to set aside the dissolution and attaching to the petition copies of the secretary of state's certificate of dissolution, the corporation's application for reinstatement, and the secretary of state's notice of denial.

(c) The court may summarily order the secretary of state to reinstate the dissolved corporation or may take other action the court considers appropriate.

(d) The court's final decision may be appealed as in other civil proceedings.

Subchapter C. Judicial Dissolution

§ 14.30. Grounds for Judicial Dissolution.

The [name or describe court or courts] may dissolve a corporation:

(1) in a proceeding by the attorney general if it is established that:

    (i) the corporation obtained its articles of incorporation through fraud; or

    (ii) the corporation has continued to exceed or abuse the authority conferred upon it by law;

(2) in a proceeding by a shareholder if it is established that:

    (i) the directors are deadlocked in the management of the corporate affairs, the shareholders are unable to break the deadlock, and irreparable injury to the corporation is threatened or being suffered, or the business and affairs of the corporation can no longer be conducted to the advantage of the shareholders generally, because of the deadlock;

    (ii) the directors or those in control of the corporation have acted, are acting, or will act in a manner that is illegal, oppressive, or fraudulent;

    (iii) the shareholders are deadlocked in voting power and have failed, for a period that includes at least two consecutive annual meeting dates, to elect successors to directors whose terms have expired; or

    (iv) the corporate assets are being misapplied or wasted;

(3) in a proceeding by a creditor if it is established that:

    (i) the creditor's claim has been reduced to judgment, the execution on the judgment returned unsatisfied, and the corporation is insolvent; or

    (ii) the corporation has admitted in writing that the creditor's claim is due and owing and the corporation is insolvent; or

(4) in a proceeding by the corporation to have its voluntary dissolution continued under court supervision.

§ 14.31. Procedure for Judicial Dissolution.

(a) Venue for a proceeding by the attorney general to dissolve a corporation lies in [name the county or counties]. Venue for a proceeding brought by any other party named in § 14.30 lies in the county where a corporation's principal office (or, if none in this state, its registered office) is or was last located.

(b) It is not necessary to make shareholders parties to a proceeding to dissolve a corporation unless relief is sought against them individually.

(c) A court in a proceeding brought to dissolve a corporation may issue injunctions, appoint a receiver or custodian pendente lite with all powers and duties the court directs, take other action required to preserve the corporate assets wherever located, and carry on the business of the corporation until a full hearing can be held.

(d) Within 10 days of the commencement of a proceeding under section 14.30(2) to dissolve a corporation that has no shares listed on a national securities exchange or regularly traded in a market maintained by one or more members of a national or affiliated securities association, the corporation must send to all shareholders, other than the petitioner, a notice stating that the shareholders are entitled to avoid the dissolution of the corporation by electing to purchase the petitioner's shares under section 14.34 and accompanied by a copy of section 14.34.

§ 14.32. Receivership or Custodianship.

(a) A court in a judicial proceeding brought to dissolve a corporation may appoint one or more receivers to wind up and liquidate, or one or more custodians to manage, the business and affairs of the corporation. The court shall hold a hearing, after notifying all parties to the proceeding and any interested persons designated by the court, before appointing a receiver or custodian. The court appointing a receiver or custodian has exclusive jurisdiction over the corporation and all of its property wherever located.

(b) The court may appoint an individual or a domestic or foreign corporation (authorized to transact business in this state) as a receiver or custodian. The court may require the receiver or custodian to post bond, with or without sureties, in an amount the court directs.

(c) The court shall describe the powers and duties of the receiver or custodian in its appointing order, which may be amended from time to time. Among other powers:

    (1) the receiver (i) may dispose of all or any part of the assets of the corporation wherever located, at a public or private sale, if authorized by the court; and (ii) may sue and defend in his own name as receiver of the corporation in all courts of this state;

    (2) the custodian may exercise all of the powers of the corporation, through or in place of its board of directors or officers, to the extent necessary to manage the affairs of the corporation in the best interests of its shareholders and creditors.

(d) The court during a receivership may redesignate the receiver a custodian, and during a custodianship may redesignate the custodian a receiver, if doing so is in the best interests of the corporation, its shareholders, and creditors.

(e) The court from time to time during the receivership or custodianship may order compensation paid and expense disbursements or reimbursements made to the receiver or custodian and his counsel from the assets of the corporation or proceeds from the sale of the assets.

§ 14.33. Decree of Dissolution.

(a) If after a hearing the court determines that one or more grounds for judicial dissolution described in § 14.30 exist, it may enter a decree dissolving the corporation and specifying the effective date of the dissolution, and the clerk of the court shall deliver a certified copy of the decree to the secretary of state, who shall file it.

(b) After entering the decree of dissolution, the court shall direct the winding up and liquidation of the corporation's business and affairs in accordance with § 14.05 and the notification of claimants in accordance with §§ 14.06 and 14.07.

§ 14.34. Election to Purchase in Lieu of Dissolution.

(a) In a proceeding under § 14.30(2) to dissolve a corporation that has no shares listed on a national securities exchange or regularly traded in a market maintained by one or more members of a national or affiliated securities association, the corporation may elect or, if it fails to elect, one or more shareholders may elect to purchase all shares owned by the petitioning shareholder at the fair value of the shares. An election pursuant to this section shall be irrevocable unless the court determines that it is equitable to set aside or modify the election.

(b) An election to purchase pursuant to this section may be filed with the court at any time within 90 days after the filing of the petition under § 14.30(2) or at such later time as the court in its discretion may allow. If the election to purchase is filed by one or more shareholders, the corporation shall, within 10 days thereafter, give written notice to all shareholders, other than the petitioner. The notice must state the name and number of shares owned by the petitioner and the name and number of shares owned by each electing shareholder and must advise the recipients of their right to join in the election to purchase shares in accordance with this section. Shareholders who wish to participate must file notice of their intention to join in the purchase no later than 30 days after the effective date of the notice to them. All shareholders who have filed an election or notice of their intention to participate in the election to purchase thereby become parties to the proceeding and shall participate in the purchase in proportion to their ownership of shares as of the date the first election was filed, unless they otherwise agree or the court otherwise directs. After an election has been filed by the corporation or one or more shareholders, the proceeding under § 14.30(2) may not be discontinued or settled, nor may the petitioning shareholder sell or otherwise dispose of his shares, unless the court determines that it would be equitable to the corporation and the shareholders, other than the petitioner, to permit such discontinuance, settlement, sale, or other disposition.

(c) If, within 60 days of the filing of the first election, the parties reach agreement as to the fair value and terms of purchase of the petitioner's shares, the court shall enter an order directing the purchase of petitioner's shares upon the terms and conditions agreed to by the parties.

(d) If the parties are unable to reach an agreement as provided for in subsection (c), the court, upon application of any party, shall stay the § 14.30(2) proceedings and determine the fair value of the petitioner's shares as of the day before the date on which the petition under § 14.30(2) was filed or as of such other date as the court deems appropriate under the circumstances.

(e) Upon determining the fair value of the shares, the court shall enter an order directing the purchase upon such terms and conditions as the court deems appropriate, which may include payment of the purchase price in installments, where necessary in the interests of equity, provision for security to assure payment of the purchase price and any additional costs, fees, and expenses as may have been awarded, and, if the shares are to be purchased by shareholders, the allocation of shares among them. In allocating petitioner's shares among holders of different classes of shares, the court should attempt to preserve the existing distribution of voting rights among holders of different classes insofar as practicable and may direct that holders of a specific class or classes shall not participate in the purchase. Interest may be allowed at the rate and from the date determined by the court to be equitable, but if the court finds that the refusal of the petitioning shareholder to accept an offer of payment was arbitrary or otherwise not in good faith, no interest shall be allowed. If the court finds that the petitioning shareholder had probable grounds for relief under paragraphs (ii) or (iv) of § 14.30(2), it may award to the petitioning shareholder reasonable fees and expenses of counsel and of any experts employed by him.

(f) Upon entry of an order under subsections (c) or (e), the court shall dismiss the petition to dissolve the corporation under § 14.30, and the petitioning shareholder shall no longer have any rights or status as a shareholder of the corporation, except the right to receive the amounts awarded to him by the order of the court which shall be enforceable in the same manner as any other judgment.

(g) The purchase ordered pursuant to subsection (e) shall be made within 10 days after the date the order becomes final unless before that time the corporation files with the court a notice of its intention to adopt articles of dissolution pursuant to §§ 14.02 and 14.03, which articles must then be adopted and filed within 50 days thereafter. Upon filing of such articles of dissolution, the corporation shall be dissolved in accordance with the provisions of §§ 14.05 through 14.07, and the order entered pursuant to subsection (e) shall no longer be of any force or effect, except that the court may award the petitioning shareholder reasonable fees and expenses in accordance with the provisions of the last sentence of subsection (e) and the petitioner may continue to pursue any claims previously asserted on behalf of the corporation.

(h) Any payment by the corporation pursuant to an order under subsections (c) or (e), other than an award of fees and expenses pursuant to subsection (e), is subject to the provisions of § 6.40.

Subchapter D. Miscellaneous

§ 14.40. Deposit with State Treasurer.

Assets of a dissolved corporation that should be transferred to a creditor, claimant, or shareholder of the corporation who cannot be found or who is not competent to receive them shall be reduced to cash and deposited with the state treasurer or other appropriate state official for safekeeping. When the creditor, claimant, or shareholder furnishes satisfactory proof of entitlement to the amount deposited, the state treasurer or other appropriate state official shall pay him or his representative that amount.

CHAPTER 15. FOREIGN CORPORATIONS
Subchapter A. Certificate of Authority

§ 15.01. Authority To Transact Business Required.

(a) A foreign corporation may not transact business in this state until it obtains a certificate of authority from the secretary of state.

(b) The following activities, among others, do not constitute transacting business within the meaning of subsection (a):

(1) maintaining, defending, or settling any proceeding;

(2) holding meetings of the board of directors or shareholders or carrying on other activities concerning internal corporate affairs;

(3) maintaining bank accounts;

(4) maintaining offices or agencies for the transfer, exchange, and registration of the corporation's own securities or maintaining trustees or depositaries with respect to those securities;

(5) selling through independent contractors;

(6) soliciting or obtaining orders, whether by mail or through employees or agents or otherwise, if the orders require acceptance outside this state before they become contracts;

(7) creating or acquiring indebtedness, mortgages, and security interests in real or personal property;

(8) securing or collecting debts or enforcing mortgages and security interests in property securing the debts;

(9) owning, without more, real or personal property;

(10) conducting an isolated transaction that is completed within 30 days and that is not one in the course of repeated transactions of a like nature;

(11) transacting business in interstate commerce.

(c) The list of activities in subsection (b) is not exhaustive.

§ 15.02. Consequences of Transacting Business Without Authority.

(a) A foreign corporation transacting business in this state without a certificate of authority may not maintain a proceeding in any court in this state until it obtains a certificate of authority.

(b) The successor to a foreign corporation that transacted business in this state without a certificate of authority and the assignee of a cause of action arising out of that business may not maintain a proceeding based on that cause of action in any court in this state until the foreign corporation or its successor obtains a certificate of authority.

(c) A court may stay a proceeding commenced by a foreign corporation, its successor, or assignee until it determines whether the foreign corporation or its successor requires a certificate of authority. If it so determines, the court may further stay the proceeding until the foreign corporation or its successor obtains the certificate.

(d) A foreign corporation is liable for a civil penalty of $__ for each day, but not to exceed a total of $__ for each year, it transacts business in this state without a certificate of authority. The attorney general may collect all penalties due under this subsection.

(e) Notwithstanding subsections (a) and (b), the failure of a foreign corporation to obtain a certificate of authority does not impair the validity of its corporate acts or prevent it from defending any proceeding in this state.

§ 15.03. Application for Certificate of Authority.

(a) A foreign corporation may apply for a certificate of authority to transact business in this state by delivering an application to the secretary of state for filing. The application must set forth:

(1) the name of the foreign corporation or, if its name is unavailable for use in this state, a corporate name that satisfies the requirements of § 15.06;

(2) the name of the state or country under whose law it is incorporated;

(3) its date of incorporation and period of duration;

(4) the street address of its principal office;

(5) the address of its registered office in this state and the name of its registered agent at that office; and

(6) the names and usual business addresses of its current directors and officers.

(b) The foreign corporation shall deliver with the completed application a certificate of existence (or a document of similar import) duly authenticated by the secretary of state or other official having custody of corporate records in the state or country under whose law it is incorporated.

§ 15.04. Amended Certificate of Authority.

(a) A foreign corporation authorized to transact business in this state must obtain an amended certificate of authority from the secretary of state if it changes:

(1) its corporate name;

(2) the period of its duration; or

(3) the state or country of its incorporation.

(b) The requirements of § 15.03 for obtaining an original certificate of authority apply to obtaining an amended certificate under this section.

§ 15.05. Effect of Certificate of Authority.

(a) A certificate of authority authorizes the foreign corporation to which it is issued to transact business in this state subject, however, to the right of the state to revoke the certificate as provided in this Act.

(b) A foreign corporation with a valid certificate of authority has the same but no greater rights and has the same but no greater privileges as, and except as otherwise provided by this Act is subject to the same duties, restrictions, penalties, and liabilities now or later imposed on, a domestic corporation of like character.

(c) This Act does not authorize this state to regulate the organization or internal affairs of a foreign corporation authorized to transact business in this state.

§ 15.06. Corporate Name of Foreign Corporation.

(a) If the corporate name of a foreign corporation does not satisfy the requirements of § 4.01, the foreign corporation to obtain or maintain a certificate of authority to transact business in this state:

(1) may add the word "corporation," "incorporated," "company," or "limited," or the abbreviation "corp.," "inc.," "co.," or "ltd.," to its corporate name for use in this state; or

(2) may use a fictitious name to transact business in this state if its real name is unavailable and it delivers to the secretary of state for filing a copy of the resolution of its board of directors, certified by its secretary, adopting the fictitious name.

(b) Except as authorized by subsections (c) and (d), the corporate name (including a fictitious name) of a foreign corporation must be distinguishable upon the records of the secretary of state from:

(1) the corporate name of a corporation incorporated or authorized to transact business in this state;

(2) a corporate name reserved or registered under § 4.02 or 4.03;

(3) the fictitious name of another foreign corporation authorized to transact business in this state; and

(4) the corporate name of a not-for-profit corporation incorporated or authorized to transact business in this state.

(c) A foreign corporation may apply to the secretary of state for authorization to use in this state the name of another corporation (incorporated or authorized to transact business in this state) that is not distinguishable upon his records from the name applied for. The secretary of state shall authorize use of the name applied for if:

(1) the other corporation consents to the use in writing and submits an undertaking in form satisfactory to the secretary of state to change its name to a name that is distinguishable upon the records of the secretary of state from the name of the applying corporation; or

(2) the applicant delivers to the secretary of state a certified copy of a final judgment of a court of competent jurisdiction establishing the applicant's right to use the name applied for in this state.

(d) A foreign corporation may use in this state the name (including the fictitious name) of another domestic or foreign corporation that is used in this state if the other corporation is incorporated or authorized to transact business in this state and the foreign corporation:

(1) has merged with the other corporation;

(2) has been formed by reorganization of the other corporation; or

(3) has acquired all or substantially all of the assets, including the corporate name, of the other corporation.

(e) If a foreign corporation authorized to transact business in this state changes its corporate name to one that does not satisfy the requirements of § 4.01, it may not transact business in this state under the changed name until it adopts a name satisfying the requirements of § 4.01 and obtains an amended certificate of authority under § 15.04.

§ 15.07. Registered Office and Registered Agent of Foreign Corporation.

Each foreign corporation authorized to transact business in this state must continuously maintain in this state:

(1) a registered office that may be the same as any of its places of business; and

(2) a registered agent, who may be:

(i) an individual who resides in this state and whose business office is identical with the registered office;

(ii) a domestic corporation or not-for-profit domestic corporation whose business office is identical with the registered office; or

(iii) a foreign corporation or foreign not-for-profit corporation authorized to transact business in this state whose business office is identical with the registered office.

§ 15.08. Change of Registered Office or Registered Agent of Foreign Corporation.

(a) A foreign corporation authorized to transact business in this state may change its registered office or registered agent by delivering to the secretary of state for filing a statement of change that sets forth:

(1) its name;

(2) the street address of its current registered office;

(3) if the current registered office is to be changed, the street address of its new registered office;

(4) the name of its current registered agent;

(5) if the current registered agent is to be changed, the name of its new registered agent and the new agent's written consent (either on the statement or attached to it) to the appointment; and

(6) that after the change or changes are made, the street addresses of its registered office and the business office of its registered agent will be identical.

(b) If a registered agent changes the street address of his business office, he may change the street address of the registered office of any foreign corporation for which he is the registered agent by notifying the corporation in writing of the change and signing (either manually or in facsimile) and delivering to the secretary of state for filing a statement of change that complies with the requirements of subsection (a) and recites that the corporation has been notified of the change.

§ 15.09. Resignation of Registered Agent of Foreign Corporation.

(a) The registered agent of a foreign corporation may resign his agency appointment by signing and delivering to the secretary of state for filing the original and two exact or conformed copies of a statement of resignation. The statement of resignation may include a statement that the registered office is also discontinued.

(b) After filing the statement, the secretary of state shall attach the filing receipt to one copy and mail the copy and receipt to the registered office if not discontinued. The secretary of state shall mail the other copy to the foreign corporation at its principal office address shown in its most recent annual report.

(c) The agency appointment is terminated, and the registered office discontinued if so provided, on the 31st day after the date on which the statement was filed.

§ 15.10. Service on Foreign Corporation.

(a) The registered agent of a foreign corporation authorized to transact business in this state is the corporation's agent for service of process, notice, or demand required or permitted by law to be served on the foreign corporation.

(b) A foreign corporation may be served by registered or certified mail, return receipt requested, addressed to the secretary of the foreign corporation at its principal office shown in its application for a certificate of authority or in its most recent annual report if the foreign corporation:

(1) has no registered agent or its registered agent cannot with reasonable diligence be served;

(2) has withdrawn from transacting business in this state under § 15.20; or

(3) has had its certificate of authority revoked under § 15.31.

(c) Service is perfected under subsection (b) at the earliest of:

(1) the date the foreign corporation receives the mail;

(2) the date shown on the return receipt, if signed on behalf of the foreign corporation; or

(3) five days after its deposit in the United States mail, as evidenced by the postmark, if mailed postpaid and correctly addressed.

(d) This section does not prescribe the only means, or necessarily the required means, of serving a foreign corporation.

Subchapter B. Withdrawal or Transfer of Authority

§ 15.20. Withdrawal of Foreign Corporation.

(a) A foreign corporation authorized to transact business in this state may not withdraw from this state until it obtains a certificate of withdrawal from the secretary of state.

(b) A foreign corporation authorized to transact business in this state may apply for a certificate of withdrawal by delivering an application to the secretary of state for filing. The application must set forth:

(1) the name of the foreign corporation and the name of the state or country under whose law it is incorporated;

(2) that it is not transacting business in this state and that it surrenders its authority to transact business in this state;

(3) that it revokes the authority of its registered agent to accept service on its behalf and appoints the secretary of state as its agent for service of process in any proceeding based on a cause of action arising during the time it was authorized to transact business in this state;

(4) a mailing address to which the secretary of state may mail a copy of any process served on him under subdivision (3); and

(5) a commitment to notify the secretary of state in the future of any change in its mailing address.

(c) After the withdrawal of the corporation is effective, service of process on the secretary of state under this section is service on the foreign corporation. Upon receipt of process, the secretary of state shall mail a copy of the process to the foreign corporation at the mailing address set forth under subsection (b).

§ 15.21. Automatic Withdrawal upon Certain Conversions.

A foreign business corporation authorized to transact business in this state that converts to a domestic nonprofit corporation or any form of domestic filing entity shall be deemed to have withdrawn on the effective date of the conversion.

§ 15.22. Withdrawal upon Conversion to a Nonfiling Entity.

(a) A foreign business corporation authorized to transact business in this state that converts to a domestic or foreign nonfiling entity shall apply for a certificate of withdrawal by delivering an application to the secretary of state for filing. The application must set forth:

(1) the name of the foreign business corporation and the name of the state or country under whose law it was incorporated before the conversion;

(2) that it surrenders its authority to transact business in this state as a foreign business corporation;

(3) the type of unincorporated entity to which it has been converted and the jurisdiction whose laws govern its internal affairs;

(4) if it has been converted to a foreign unincorporated entity:

(i) that it revokes the authority of its registered agent to accept service on its behalf and appoints the secretary of state as its agent for service of process in any proceeding based on a cause of action arising during the time it was authorized to transact business in this state;

(ii) a mailing address to which the secretary of state may mail a copy of any process served on him under paragraph (i); and

(iii) a commitment to notify the secretary of state in the future of any change in its mailing address.

(b) After the withdrawal under this section of a corporation that has converted to a foreign unincorporated entity is effective, service of process on the secretary of state is service on the foreign unincorporated entity. Upon receipt of process, the secretary of state shall mail a copy of the process to the foreign unincorporated entity at the mailing address set forth under subsection (a)(4).

(c) After the withdrawal under this section of a corporation that has converted to a domestic unincorporated entity is effective, service of process shall be made on the unincorporated entity in accordance with the regular procedures for service of process on the form of unincorporated entity to which the corporation was converted.

§ 15.23. Transfer of Authority.

(a) A foreign business corporation authorized to transact business in this state that converts to a foreign nonprofit corporation or to any form of foreign unincorporated entity that is required to obtain a certificate of authority or make a similar type of filing with the secretary of state if it transacts business in this state shall file with the secretary of state an application for transfer of authority executed by any officer or other duly authorized representative. The application shall set forth:

(1) the name of the corporation;

(2) the type of unincorporated entity to which it has been converted and the jurisdiction whose laws govern its internal affairs;

(3) any other information that would be required in a filing under the laws of this state by an unincorporated entity of the type the corporation has become seeking authority to transact business in this state.

(b) The application for transfer of authority shall be delivered to the secretary of state for filing and shall take effect at the effective time provided in § 1.23.

(c) Upon the effectiveness of the application for transfer of authority, the authority of the corporation under this chapter to transact business in this state shall be transferred without interruption to the converted entity which shall thereafter hold such authority subject to the provisions of the laws of this state applicable to that type of unincorporated entity.

Subchapter C. Revocation of Certificate of Authority

§ 15.30. Grounds for Revocation.

The secretary of state may commence a proceeding under § 15.31 to revoke the certificate of authority of a foreign corporation authorized to transact business in this state if:

(1) the foreign corporation does not deliver its annual report to the secretary of state within 60 days after it is due;

(2) the foreign corporation does not pay within 60 days after they are due any franchise taxes or penalties imposed by this Act or other law;

(3) the foreign corporation is without a registered agent or registered office in this state for 60 days or more;

(4) the foreign corporation does not inform the secretary of state under § 15.08 or 15.09 that its registered agent or registered office has changed, that its registered agent has resigned, or that its registered office has been discontinued within 60 days of the change, resignation, or discontinuance;

(5) an incorporator, director, officer, or agent of the foreign corporation signed a document he knew was false in any material respect with intent that the document be delivered to the secretary of state for filing;

(6) the secretary of state receives a duly authenticated certificate from the secretary of state or other official having custody of corporate records in the state or country under whose law the foreign corporation is incorporated stating that it has been dissolved or disappeared as the result of a merger.

§ 15.31. Procedure for and Effect of Revocation.

(a) If the secretary of state determines that one or more grounds exist under § 15.30 for revocation of a certificate of authority, he shall serve the foreign corporation with written notice of his determination under § 15.10.

(b) If the foreign corporation does not correct each ground for revocation or demonstrate to the reasonable satisfaction of the secretary of state that each ground determined by the secretary of state does not exist within 60 days after service of the notice is perfected under § 15.10, the secretary of state may revoke the foreign corporation's certificate of authority by signing a certificate of revocation that recites the ground or grounds for revocation and its effective date. The secretary of state shall file the original of the certificate and serve a copy on the foreign corporation under § 15.10.

(c) The authority of a foreign corporation to transact business in this state ceases on the date shown on the certificate revoking its certificate of authority.

(d) The secretary of state's revocation of a foreign corporation's certificate of authority appoints the secretary of state the foreign corporation's agent for service of process in any proceeding based on a cause of action which arose during the time the foreign corporation was authorized to transact business in this state. Service of process on the secretary of state under this subsection is service on the foreign corporation. Upon receipt of process, the secretary of state shall mail a copy of the process to the secretary of the foreign corporation at its principal office shown in its most recent annual report or in any subsequent communication received from the corporation stating the current mailing address of its principal office, or, if none are on file, in its application for a certificate of authority.

(e) Revocation of a foreign corporation's certificate of authority does not terminate the authority of the registered agent of the corporation.

§ 15.32. Appeal from Revocation.

(a) A foreign corporation may appeal the secretary of state's revocation of its certificate of authority to the [name or describe] court within 30 days after service of the certificate of revocation is perfected under § 15.10. The foreign corporation appeals by petitioning the court to set aside the revocation and attaching to the petition copies of its certificate of authority and the secretary of state's certificate of revocation.

(b) The court may summarily order the secretary of state to reinstate the certificate of authority or may take any other action the court considers appropriate.

(c) The court's final decision may be appealed as in other civil proceedings.

CHAPTER 16. RECORDS AND REPORTS
Subchapter A. Records

§ 16.01. Corporate Records.

(a) A corporation shall keep as permanent records minutes of all meetings of its shareholders and board of directors, a record of all actions taken by the shareholders or board of directors without a meeting, and a record of all actions taken by a committee of the board of directors in place of the board of directors on behalf of the corporation.

(b) A corporation shall maintain appropriate accounting records.

(c) A corporation or its agent shall maintain a record of its shareholders, in a form that permits preparation of a list of the names and addresses of all shareholders, in alphabetical order by class of shares showing the number and class of shares held by each.

(d) A corporation shall maintain its records in written form or in another form capable of conversion into written form within a reasonable time.

(e) A corporation shall keep a copy of the following records at its principal office:

(1) its articles or restated articles of incorporation, all amendments to them currently in effect, and any notices to shareholders referred to in § 1.20(k)(5) regarding facts on which a filed document is dependent;

(2) its bylaws or restated bylaws and all amendments to them currently in effect;

(3) resolutions adopted by its board of directors creating one or more classes or series of shares, and fixing their relative rights, preferences, and limitations, if shares issued pursuant to those resolutions are outstanding;

(4) the minutes of all shareholders' meetings, and records of all action taken by shareholders without a meeting, for the past three years;

(5) all written communications to shareholders generally within the past three years, including the financial statements furnished for the past three years under § 16.20;

(6) a list of the names and business addresses of its current directors and officers; and

(7) its most recent annual report delivered to the secretary of state under § 16.21.

§ 16.02. Inspection of Records by Shareholders.

(a) A shareholder of a corporation is entitled to inspect and copy, during regular business hours at the corporation's principal office, any of the records of the corporation described in § 16.01(e) if he gives the corporation written notice of his demand at least five business days before the date on which he wishes to inspect and copy.

(b) A shareholder of a corporation is entitled to inspect and copy, during regular business hours at a reasonable location specified by the corporation, any of the following records of the corporation if the shareholder meets the requirements of subsection (c) and gives the corporation written notice of his demand at least five business days before the date on which he wishes to inspect and copy:

(1) excerpts from minutes of any meeting of the board of directors, records of any action of a committee of the board of directors while acting in place of the board of directors on be-

half of the corporation, minutes of any meeting of the shareholders, and records of action taken by the shareholders or board of directors without a meeting, to the extent not subject to inspection under § 16.02(a);

(2) accounting records of the corporation; and

(3) the record of shareholders.

(c) A shareholder may inspect and copy the records described in subsection (b) only if:

(1) his demand is made in good faith and for a proper purpose;

(2) he describes with reasonable particularity his purpose and the records he desires to inspect; and

(3) the records are directly connected with his purpose.

(d) The right of inspection granted by this section may not be abolished or limited by a corporation's articles of incorporation or bylaws.

(e) This section does not affect:

(1) the right of a shareholder to inspect records under § 7.20 or, if the shareholder is in litigation with the corporation, to the same extent as any other litigant;

(2) the power of a court, independently of this Act, to compel the production of corporate records for examination.

(f) For purposes of this section, "shareholder" includes a beneficial owner whose shares are held in a voting trust or by a nominee on his behalf.

§ 16.03. Scope of Inspection Right.

(a) A shareholder's agent or attorney has the same inspection and copying rights as the shareholder represented.

(b) The right to copy records under § 16.02 includes, if reasonable, the right to receive copies by xerographic or other means, including copies through an electronic transmission if available and so requested by the shareholder.

(c) The corporation may comply at its expense with a shareholder's demand to inspect the record of shareholders under § 16.02(b)(3) by providing the shareholder with a list of shareholders that was compiled no earlier than the date of the shareholder's demand.

(d) The corporation may impose a reasonable charge, covering the costs of labor and material, for copies of any documents provided to the shareholder. The charge may not exceed the estimated cost of production, reproduction or transmission of the records.

§ 16.04. Court-ordered Inspection.

(a) If a corporation does not allow a shareholder who complies with § 16.02(a) to inspect and copy any records required by that subsection to be available for inspection, the [name or describe court] of the county where the corporation's principal office (or, if none in this state, its registered office) is located may summarily order inspection and copying of the records demanded at the corporation's expense upon application of the shareholder.

(b) If a corporation does not within a reasonable time allow a shareholder to inspect and copy any other record, the shareholder who complies with §§ 16.02(b) and (c) may apply to the [name or describe court] in the county where the corporation's principal office (or, if none in this state, its registered office) is located for an order to permit inspection and copying of the records demanded. The court shall dispose of an application under this subsection on an expedited basis.

(c) If the court orders inspection and copying of the records demanded, it shall also order the corporation to pay the shareholder's costs (including reasonable counsel fees) incurred to obtain the order unless the corporation proves that it refused inspection in good faith because it had a reasonable basis for doubt about the right of the shareholder to inspect the records demanded.

(d) If the court orders inspection and copying of the records demanded, it may impose reasonable restrictions on the use or distribution of the records by the demanding shareholder.

§ 16.05. Inspection of Records by Directors.

(a) A director of a corporation is entitled to inspect and copy the books, records and documents of the corporation at any reasonable time to the extent reasonably related to the performance of the director's duties as a director, including duties as a member of a committee, but not for any other purpose or in any manner that would violate any duty to the corporation.

(b) The [name or describe the court] of the county where the corporation's principal office (or if none in this state, its registered office) is located may order inspection and copying of the books, records and documents at the corporation's expense, upon application of a director who has been refused such inspection rights, unless the corporation establishes that the director is not entitled to such inspection rights. The court shall dispose of an application under this subsection on an expedited basis.

(c) If an order is issued, the court may include provisions protecting the corporation from undue burden or expense, and prohibiting the director from using information obtained upon exercise of the inspection rights in a manner that would violate a duty to the corporation, and may also order the corporation to reimburse the director for the director's costs (including reasonable counsel fees) incurred in connection with the application.

§ 16.06. Exception to Notice Requirement.

(a) Whenever notice is required to be given under any provision of this Act to any shareholder, such notice shall not be required to be given if:

(i) Notice of two consecutive annual meetings, and all notices of meetings during the period between such two consecutive annual meetings, have been sent to such shareholder at such shareholder's address as shown on the records of the corporation and have been returned undeliverable; or

(ii) All, but not less than two, payments of dividends on securities during a twelve month period, or two consecutive payments of dividends on securities during a period of more than twelve months, have been sent to such shareholder at such shareholder's address as shown on the records of the corporation and have been returned undeliverable.

(b) If any such shareholder shall deliver to the corporation a written notice setting forth such shareholder's then-current address, the requirement that notice be given to such shareholder shall be reinstated.

Subchapter B. Reports

§ 16.20. Financial Statements for Shareholders.

(a) A corporation shall furnish its shareholders annual financial statements, which may be consolidated or combined statements of the corporation and one or more of its subsidiaries, as appropriate, that include a balance sheet as of the end of the fiscal year, an income statement for that year, and a statement of changes in shareholders' equity for the year unless that information appears elsewhere in the financial statements. If financial statements are prepared for the corporation on the basis of generally accepted accounting principles, the annual financial statements must also be prepared on that basis.

(b) If the annual financial statements are reported upon by a public accountant, his report must accompany them. If not, the statements must be accompanied by a statement of the president or the person responsible for the corporation's accounting records:

(1) stating his reasonable belief whether the statements were prepared on the basis of generally accepted accounting principles and, if not, describing the basis of preparation; and

(2) describing any respects in which the statements were not prepared on a basis of accounting consistent with the statements prepared for the preceding year.

(c) A corporation shall mail the annual financial statements to each shareholder within 120 days after the close of each fiscal year. Thereafter, on written request from a shareholder who was not mailed the statements, the corporation shall mail him the latest financial statements.

§ 16.21. Annual Report for Secretary of State.

(a) Each domestic corporation, and each foreign corporation authorized to transact business in this state, shall deliver to the secretary of state for filing an annual report that sets forth:

(1) the name of the corporation and the state or country under whose law it is incorporated;

(2) the address of its registered office and the name of its registered agent at that office in this state;

(3) the address of its principal office;

(4) the names and business addresses of its directors and principal officers;

(5) a brief description of the nature of its business;

(6) the total number of authorized shares, itemized by class and series, if any, within each class; and

(7) the total number of issued and outstanding shares, itemized by class and series, if any, within each class.

(b) Information in the annual report must be current as of the date the annual report is executed on behalf of the corporation.

(c) The first annual report must be delivered to the secretary of state between January 1 and April 1 of the year following the calendar year in which a domestic corporation was incorporated or a foreign corporation was authorized to transact business. Subsequent annual reports must be delivered to the secretary of state between January 1 and April 1 of the following calendar years.

(d) If an annual report does not contain the information required by this section, the secretary of state shall promptly notify the reporting domestic or foreign corporation in writing and return the report to it for correction. If the report is corrected to contain the information required by this section and delivered to the secretary of state within 30 days after the effective date of notice, it is deemed to be timely filed.

CHAPTER 17. TRANSITION PROVISIONS

§ 17.01. Application to Existing Domestic Corporations.
This Act applies to all domestic corporations in existence on its effective date that were incorporated under any general statute of this state providing for incorporation of corporations for profit if power to amend or repeal the statute under which the corporation was incorporated was reserved.

§ 17.02. Application to Qualified Foreign Corporations.
A foreign corporation authorized to transact business in this state on the effective date of this Act is subject to this Act but is not required to obtain a new certificate of authority to transact business under this Act.

§ 17.03. Saving Provisions.
(a) Except as provided in subsection (b), the repeal of a statute by this Act does not affect:

(1) the operation of the statute or any action taken under it before its repeal;

(2) any ratification, right, remedy, privilege, obligation, or liability acquired, accrued, or incurred under the statute before its repeal;

(3) any violation of the statute, or any penalty, forfeiture, or punishment incurred because of the violation, before its repeal;

(4) any proceeding, reorganization, or dissolution commenced under the statute before its repeal, and the proceeding, reorganization, or dissolution may be completed in accordance with the statute as if it had not been repealed.

(b) If a penalty or punishment imposed for violation of a statute repealed by this Act is reduced by this Act, the penalty or punishment if not already imposed shall be imposed in accordance with this Act.

§ 17.04. Severability.
If any provision of this Act or its application to any person or circumstance is held invalid by a court of competent jurisdiction, the invalidity does not affect other provisions or applications of the Act that can be given effect without the invalid provision or application, and to this end the provisions of the Act are severable.

§ 17.05. Repeal. The following laws and parts of laws are repealed: [to be inserted].

§ 17.06. Effective Date. This Act takes effect _____.

MODEL STATUTORY CLOSE CORPORATION SUPPLEMENT

Creation

SECTION 1. SHORT TITLE

This Supplement shall be known and may be cited as the "[name of state] Statutory Close Corporation Supplement."

SECTION 2. APPLICATION OF [MODEL] BUSINESS CORPORATION ACT AND [MODEL] PROFESSIONAL CORPORATION SUPPLEMENT

(a) The [Model] Business Corporation Act applies to statutory close corporations to the extent not inconsistent with the provisions of this Supplement.

(b) This Supplement applies to a professional corporation organized under the [Model] Professional Corporation Supplement whose articles of incorporation contain the statement required by section 3(a), except insofar as the [Model] Professional Corporation Supplement contains inconsistent provisions.

(c) This Supplement does not repeal or modify any statute or rule of law that is or would apply to a corporation that is organized under the [Model] Business Corporation Act or the [Model] Professional Corporation Supplement and that does not elect to become a statutory close corporation under section 3.

SECTION 3. DEFINITION AND ELECTION OF STATUTORY CLOSE CORPORATION STATUS

(a) A statutory close corporation is a corporation whose articles of incorporation contain a statement that the corporation is a statutory close corporation.

(b) A corporation having 50 or fewer shareholders may become a statutory close corporation by amending its articles of incorporation to include the statement required by subsection (a). The amendment must be approved by the holders of at least two-thirds of the votes of each class or series of shares of the corporation, voting as separate voting groups, whether or not otherwise entitled to vote on amendments. If the amendment is adopted, a shareholder who voted against the amendment is entitled to assert dissenters' rights under [MBCA ch. 13].

Shares

SECTION 10. NOTICE OF STATUTORY CLOSE CORPORATION STATUS ON ISSUED SHARES

(a) The following statement must appear conspicuously on each share certificate issued by a statutory close corporation:

The rights of shareholders in a statutory close corporation may differ materially from the rights of shareholders in other corporations. Copies of the articles of incorporation and bylaws, shareholders' agreements, and other documents, any of which may restrict transfers and affect voting and other rights, may be obtained by a shareholder on written request to the corporation.

(b) Within a reasonable time after the issuance or transfer of uncertificated shares, the corporation shall send to the shareholders a written notice containing the information required by subsection (a).

(c) The notice required by this section satisfies all requirements of this Act and of [MBCA § 6.27] that notice of share transfer restrictions be given.

(d) A person claiming an interest in shares of a statutory close corporation which has complied with the notice requirement of this section is bound by the documents referred to in the notice. A person claiming an interest in shares of a statutory close corporation which has not complied with the notice requirement of this section is bound by any documents of which he, or a person through whom he claims, has knowledge or notice.

(e) A corporation shall provide to any shareholder upon his written request and without charge copies of provisions that restrict transfer or affect voting or other rights of shareholders appearing in articles of incorporation, bylaws, or shareholders' or voting trust agreements filed with the corporation.

SECTION 11. SHARE TRANSFER PROHIBITION

(a) An interest in shares of a statutory close corporation may not be voluntarily or involuntarily transferred, by operation of law or otherwise, except to the extent permitted by the articles of incorporation or under section 12.

(b) Except to the extent the articles of incorporation provide otherwise, this section does not apply to a transfer:

(1) to the corporation or to any other holder of the same class or series of shares;

(2) to members of the shareholder's immediate family (or to a trust, all of whose beneficiaries are members of the shareholder's immediate family), which immediate family consists of his spouse, parents, lineal descendants (including adopted children and stepchildren) and the spouse of any lineal descendant, and brothers and sisters;

(3) that has been approved in writing by all of the holders of the corporation's shares having general voting rights;

(4) to an executor or administrator upon the death of a shareholder or to a trustee or receiver as the result of a bankruptcy, insolvency, dissolution, or similar proceeding brought by or against a shareholder;

(5) by merger or share exchange [under MBCA ch. 11] or an exchange of existing shares for other shares of a different class or series in the corporation;

(6) by a pledge as collateral for a loan that does not grant the pledgee any voting rights possessed by the pledgor;

(7) made after termination of the corporation's status as a statutory close corporation.

SECTION 12. SHARE TRANSFER AFTER FIRST REFUSAL BY CORPORATION

(a) A person desiring to transfer shares of a statutory close corporation subject to the transfer prohibition of section 11 must first offer them to the corporation by obtaining an offer to purchase the shares for cash from a third person who is eligible to purchase the shares under subsection (b). The offer by the third person must be in writing and state the offeror's name and address, the number and class (or series) of shares offered, the offering price per share, and the other terms of the offer.

(b) A third person is eligible to purchase the shares if:

(1) he is eligible to become a qualified shareholder under any federal or state tax statute the corporation has adopted and he agrees in writing not to terminate his qualification without the approval of the remaining shareholders; and

(2) his purchase of the shares will not impose a personal holding company tax or similar federal or state penalty tax on the corporation.

(c) The person desiring to transfer shares shall deliver the offer to the corporation, and by doing so offers to sell the shares to the corporation on the terms of the offer. Within 20 days after the corporation receives the offer, the corporation shall call a special shareholders' meeting, to be held not more than 40 days after the call, to decide whether the corporation should purchase all (but not less than all) of the offered shares. The offer must be approved by the affirmative vote of the holders of a majority of votes entitled to be cast at the meeting, excluding votes in respect of the shares covered by the offer.

(d) The corporation must deliver to the offering shareholder written notice of acceptance within 75 days after receiving the offer or the offer is rejected. If the corporation makes a counteroffer, the shareholder must deliver to the corporation written notice of acceptance within 15 days after receiving the counteroffer or the counteroffer is rejected. If the corporation accepts the original offer or the shareholder accepts the corporation's counteroffer, the shareholder shall deliver to the corporation duly endorsed certificates for the shares, or instruct the corporation in writing to transfer the shares if uncertificated, within 20 days after the effective date of the notice of acceptance. The corporation may specifically enforce the shareholder's delivery or instruction obligation under this subsection.

(e) A corporation accepting an offer to purchase shares under this section may allocate some or all of the shares to one or more of its shareholders or to other persons if all the shareholders voting in favor of the purchase approve the allocation. If the corporation has more than one class (or series) of shares, however, the remaining holders of the class (or series) of shares being purchased are entitled to a first option to purchase the shares not purchased by the corporation in proportion to their shareholdings or in some other proportion agreed to by all the shareholders participating in the purchase.

(f) If an offer to purchase shares under this section is rejected, the offering shareholder, for a period of 120 days after the corporation received his offer, is entitled to transfer to the third person offeror all (but not less than all) of the offered shares in accordance with the terms of his offer to the corporation.

SECTION 13. ATTEMPTED SHARE TRANSFER IN BREACH OF PROHIBITION

(a) An attempt to transfer shares in a statutory close corporation in violation of a prohibition against transfer binding on the transferee is ineffective.

(b) An attempt to transfer shares in a statutory close corporation in violation of a prohibition against transfer that is not binding on the transferee, either because the notice required by section 10 was not given or because the prohibition is held unenforceable by a court, gives the corporation an option to purchase the shares from the transferee for the same price and on the same terms that he purchased them. To exercise its option, the corporation must give the transferee written notice within 30 days after they are presented for registration in the transferee's name. The corporation may specifically enforce the transferee's sale obligation upon exercise of its purchase option.

SECTION 14. COMPULSORY PURCHASE OF SHARES AFTER DEATH OF SHAREHOLDER

(a) This section, and sections 15 through 17, apply to a statutory close corporation only if so provided in its articles of incorporation.

If these sections apply, the executor or administrator of the estate of a deceased shareholder may require the corporation to purchase or cause to be purchased all (but not less than all) of the decedent's shares or to be dissolved.

(b) The provisions of sections 15 through 17 may be modified only if the modification is set forth or referred to in the articles of incorporation.

(c) An amendment to the articles of incorporation to provide for application of sections 15 through 17, or to modify or delete the provisions of these sections, must be approved by the holders of at least two-thirds of the votes of each class or series of shares of the statutory close corporation, voting as separate voting groups, whether or not otherwise entitled to vote on amendments. If the corporation has no shareholders when the amendment is proposed, it must be approved by at least two-thirds of the subscribers for shares, if any, or, if none, by all of the incorporators.

(d) A shareholder who votes against an amendment to modify or delete the provisions of sections 15 through 17 is entitled to dissenters' rights under [MBCA chapter 13] if the amendment upon adoption terminates or substantially alters his existing rights under these sections to have his shares purchased.

(e) A shareholder may waive his and his estate's rights under sections 15 through 17 by a signed writing.

(f) Sections 15 through 17 do not prohibit any other agreement providing for the purchase of shares upon a shareholder's death, nor do they prevent a shareholder from enforcing any remedy he has independently of these sections.

SECTION 15. EXERCISE OF COMPULSORY PURCHASE RIGHT

(a) A person entitled and desiring to exercise the compulsory purchase right described in section 14 must deliver a written notice to the corporation, within 120 days after the death of the shareholder, describing the number and class or series of shares beneficially owned by the decedent and requesting that the corporation offer to purchase the shares.

(b) Within 20 days after the effective date of the notice, the corporation shall call a special shareholders' meeting, to be held not more than 40 days after the call, to decide whether the corporation should offer to purchase the shares. A purchase offer must be approved by the affirmative vote of the holders of a majority of votes entitled to be cast at the meeting, excluding votes in respect of the shares covered by the notice.

(c) The corporation must deliver a purchase offer to the person requesting it within 75 days after the effective date of the request notice. A purchase offer must be accompanied by the corporation's balance sheet as of the end of a fiscal year ending not more than 16 months before the effective date of the request notice, an income statement for that year, a statement of changes in shareholders' equity for that year, and the latest available interim financial statements, if any. The person must accept the purchase offer in writing within 15 days after receiving it or the offer is rejected.

(d) A corporation agreeing to purchase shares under this section may allocate some or all of the shares to one or more of its shareholders or to other persons if all the shareholders voting in favor of the purchase offer approve the allocation. If the corporation has more than one class or series of shares, however, the remaining holders of the class or series of shares being purchased are entitled to a first option to purchase the shares not purchased by the

corporation in proportion to their shareholdings or in some other proportion agreed to by all the shareholders participating in the purchase.

(e) If price and other terms of a compulsory purchase of shares are fixed or are to be determined by the articles of incorporation, by-laws, or a written agreement, the price and terms so fixed or determined govern the compulsory purchase unless the purchaser defaults, in which event the buyer is entitled to commence a proceeding for dissolution under section 16.

SECTION 16. COURT ACTION TO COMPEL PURCHASE

(a) If an offer to purchase shares made under section 15 is rejected, or if no offer is made, the person exercising the compulsory purchase right may commence a proceeding against the corporation to compel the purchase in the [name or describe] court of the county where the corporation's principal office (or, if none in this state, its registered office) is located. The corporation at its expense shall notify in writing all of its shareholders, and any other person the court directs, of the commencement of the proceeding. The jurisdiction of the court in which the proceeding is commenced under this subsection is plenary and exclusive.

(b) The court shall determine the fair value of the shares subject to compulsory purchase in accordance with the standards set forth in section 42 together with terms for the purchase. Upon making these determinations the court shall order the corporation to purchase or cause the purchase of the shares or empower the person exercising the compulsory purchase right to have the corporation dissolved.

(c) After the purchase order is entered, the corporation may petition the court to modify the terms of purchase and the court may do so if it finds that changes in the financial or legal ability of the corporation or other purchaser to complete the purchase justify a modification.

(d) If the corporation or other purchaser does not make a payment required by the court's order within 30 days of its due date, the seller may petition the court to dissolve the corporation and, absent a showing of good cause for not making the payment, the court shall do so.

(e) A person making a payment to prevent or cure a default by the corporation or other purchaser is entitled to recover the payment from the defaulter.

SECTION 17. COURT COSTS AND OTHER EXPENSES

(a) The court in a proceeding commenced under section 16 shall determine the total costs of the proceeding, including the reasonable compensation and expenses of appraisers appointed by the court and of counsel and experts employed by the parties. Except as provided in subsection (b), the court shall assess these costs equally against the corporation and the party exercising the compulsory purchase right.

(b) The court may assess all or a portion of the total costs of the proceeding:

(1) against the person exercising the compulsory purchase right if the court finds that the fair value of the shares does not substantially exceed the corporation's last purchase offer made before commencement of the proceeding and that the person's failure to accept the offer was arbitrary, vexatious, or otherwise not in good faith; or

(2) against the corporation if the court finds that the fair value of the shares substantially exceeds the corporation's last sale offer made before commencement of the proceeding and that the offer was arbitrary, vexatious, or otherwise not made in good faith.

Governance

SECTION 20. SHAREHOLDER AGREEMENTS

(a) All the shareholders of a statutory close corporation may agree in writing to regulate the exercise of the corporate powers and the management of the business and affairs of the corporation or the relationship among the shareholders of the corporation.

(b) An agreement authorized by this section is effective although:

(1) it eliminates a board of directors;

(2) it restricts the discretion or powers of the board or authorizes director proxies or weighted voting rights;

(3) its effect is to treat the corporation as a partnership; or

(4) it creates a relationship among the shareholders or between the shareholders and the corporation that would otherwise be appropriate only among partners.

(c) If the corporation has a board of directors, an agreement authorized by this section restricting the discretion or powers of the board relieves directors of liability imposed by law, and imposes that liability on each person in whom the board's discretion or power is vested, to the extent that the discretion or powers of the board of directors are governed by the agreement.

(d) A provision eliminating a board of directors in an agreement authorized by this section is not effective unless the articles of incorporation contain a statement to that effect as required by section 21.

(e) A provision entitling one or more shareholders to dissolve the corporation under section 33 is effective only if a statement of this right is contained in the articles of incorporation.

(f) To amend an agreement authorized by this section, all the shareholders must approve the amendment in writing unless the agreement provides otherwise.

(g) Subscribers for shares may act as shareholders with respect to an agreement authorized by this section if shares are not issued when the agreement was made.

(h) This section does not prohibit any other agreement between or among shareholders in a statutory close corporation.

SECTION 21. ELIMINATION OF BOARD OF DIRECTORS

(a) A statutory close corporation may operate without a board of directors if its articles of incorporation contain a statement to that effect.

(b) An amendment to articles of incorporation eliminating a board of directors must be approved by all the shareholders of the corporation, whether or not otherwise entitled to vote on amendments, or if no shares have been issued, by all the subscribers for shares, if any, or if none, by all the incorporators.

(c) While a corporation is operating without a board of directors as authorized by subsection (a):

(1) all corporate powers shall be exercised by or under the authority of, and the business and affairs of the corporation managed under the direction of, the shareholders;

(2) unless the articles of incorporation provide otherwise, (i) action requiring director approval or both director and shareholder approval is authorized if approved by the shareholders and (ii) action requiring a majority or greater percentage vote of the board of directors is authorized if approved by the ma-

jority or greater percentage of the votes of shareholders entitled to vote on the action;

(3) a shareholder is not liable for his act or omission, although a director would be, unless the shareholder was entitled to vote on the action;

(4) a requirement by a state or the United States that a document delivered for filing contain a statement that specified action has been taken by the board of directors is satisfied by a statement that the corporation is a statutory close corporation without a board of directors and that the action was approved by the shareholders;

(5) the shareholders by resolution may appoint one or more shareholders to sign documents as "designated directors."

(d) An amendment to articles of incorporation deleting the statement eliminating a board of directors must be approved by the holders of at least two-thirds of the votes of each class or series of shares of the corporation, voting as separate voting groups, whether or not otherwise entitled to vote on amendments. The amendment must also specify the number, names, and addresses of the corporation's directors or describe who will perform the duties of a board under [MBCA § 8.01].

SECTION 22. BYLAWS

(a) A statutory close corporation need not adopt bylaws if provisions required by law to be contained in bylaws are contained in either the articles of incorporation or a shareholder agreement authorized by section 20.

(b) If a corporation does not have bylaws when its statutory close corporation status terminates under section 31, the corporation shall immediately adopt bylaws under [MBCA § 2.06].

SECTION 23. ANNUAL MEETING

(a) The annual meeting date for a statutory close corporation is the first business day after May 31st unless its articles of incorporation, bylaws, or a shareholder agreement authorized by section 20 fixes a different date.

(b) A statutory close corporation need not hold an annual meeting unless one or more shareholders deliver written notice to the corporation requesting a meeting at least 30 days before the meeting date determined under subsection (a).

SECTION 24. EXECUTION OF DOCUMENTS IN MORE THAN ONE CAPACITY

Notwithstanding any law to the contrary, an individual who holds more than one office in a statutory close corporation may execute, acknowledge, or verify in more than one capacity any document required to be executed, acknowledged, or verified by the holders of two or more offices.

SECTION 25. LIMITED LIABILITY

The failure of a statutory close corporation to observe the usual corporate formalities or requirements relating to the exercise of its corporate powers or management of its business and affairs is not a ground for imposing personal liability on the shareholders for liabilities of the corporation.

Reorganization and Termination

SECTION 30. MERGER, SHARE EXCHANGE, AND SALE OF ASSETS

(a) A plan of merger or share exchange:

(1) that if effected would terminate statutory close corporation status must be approved by the holders of at least two-thirds of the votes of each class or series of shares of the statutory close corporation, voting as separate voting groups, whether or not the holders are otherwise entitled to vote on the plan;

(2) that if effected would create the surviving corporation as a statutory close corporation must be approved by the holders of at least two-thirds of the votes of each class or series of shares of the surviving corporation, voting as separate voting groups, whether or not the holders are otherwise entitled to vote on the plan.

(b) A sale, lease, exchange, or other disposition of all or substantially all of the property (with or without the good will) of a statutory close corporation, if not made in the usual and regular course of business, must be approved by the holders of at least two-thirds of the votes of each class or series of shares of the corporation, voting as separate voting groups, whether or not the holders are otherwise entitled to vote on the transaction.

SECTION 31. TERMINATION OF STATUTORY CLOSE CORPORATION STATUS

(a) A statutory close corporation may terminate its statutory close corporation status by amending its articles of incorporation to delete the statement that it is a statutory close corporation. If the statutory close corporation has elected to operate without a board of directors under section 21, the amendment must either comply with [MBCA § 8.01] or delete the statement dispensing with the board of directors from its articles of incorporation.

(b) An amendment terminating statutory close corporation status must be approved by the holders of at least two-thirds of the votes of each class or series of shares of the corporation, voting as separate voting groups, whether or not the holders are otherwise entitled to vote on amendments.

(c) If an amendment to terminate statutory close corporation status is adopted, each shareholder who voted against the amendment is entitled to assert dissenters' rights under [MBCA ch. 13].

SECTION 32. EFFECT OF TERMINATION OF STATUTORY CLOSE CORPORATION STATUS

(a) A corporation that terminates its status as a statutory close corporation is thereafter subject to all provisions of the [Model] Business Corporation Act or, if incorporated under the [Model] Professional Corporation Supplement, to all provisions of that Supplement.

(b) Termination of statutory close corporation status does not affect any right of a shareholder or of the corporation under an agreement or the articles of incorporation unless this Act, the [Model] Business Corporation Act, or another law of this state invalidates the right.

SECTION 33. SHAREHOLDER OPTION TO DISSOLVE CORPORATION

(a) The articles of incorporation of a statutory close corporation may authorize one or more shareholders, or the holders of a specified number or percentage of shares of any class or series, to dissolve the corporation at will or upon the occurrence of a specified event or contingency. The shareholder or shareholders exercising this authority must give written notice of the intent to dissolve to all the other shareholders. Thirty-one days after the effective date of the notice, the corporation shall begin to wind up and liquidate its business and affairs and file articles of dissolution under [MBCA sections 14.03 through 14.07].

(b) Unless the articles of incorporation provide otherwise, an amendment to the articles of incorporation to add, change, or delete the authority to dissolve described in subsection (a) must be approved by the holders of all the outstanding shares, whether or not otherwise entitled to vote on amendments, or if no shares have been issued, by all the subscribers for shares, if any, or if none, by all the incorporators.

Judicial Supervision

SECTION 40. COURT ACTION TO PROTECT SHAREHOLDERS

(a) Subject to satisfying the conditions of subsections (c) and (d), a shareholder of a statutory close corporation may petition the [name or describe] court for any of the relief described in section 41, 42, or 43 if:

(1) the directors or those in control of the corporation have acted, or are acting, or will act in a manner that is illegal, oppressive, fraudulent, or unfairly prejudicial to the petitioner, whether in his capacity as shareholder, director, or officer, of the corporation;

(2) the directors or those in control of the corporation are deadlocked in the management of the corporation's affairs, the shareholders are unable to break the deadlock, and the corporation is suffering or will suffer irreparable injury or the business and affairs of the corporation can no longer be conducted to the advantage of the shareholders generally because of the deadlock; or

(3) there exists one or more grounds for judicial dissolution of the corporation under [MBCA § 14.30].

(b) A shareholder must commence a proceeding under subsection (a) in the [name or describe] court of the county where the corporation's principal office (or, if none in this state, its registered office) is located. The jurisdiction of the court in which the proceeding is commenced is plenary and exclusive.

(c) If a shareholder has agreed in writing to pursue a nonjudicial remedy to resolve disputed matters, he may not commence a proceeding under this section with respect to the matters until he has exhausted the nonjudicial remedy.

(d) If a shareholder has dissenters' rights under this Act or [MBCA ch. 13] with respect to proposed corporate action, he must commence a proceeding under this section before he is required to give notice of his intent to demand payment under [MBCA § 13.21] or to demand payment under [MBCA § 13.23] or the proceeding is barred.

(e) Except as provided in subsections (c) and (d), a shareholder's right to commence a proceeding under this section and the remedies available under sections 41 through 43 are in addition to any other right or remedy he may have.

SECTION 41. ORDINARY RELIEF

(a) If the court finds that one or more of the grounds for relief described in section 40(a) exist, it may order one or more of the following types of relief:

(1) the performance, prohibition, alteration, or setting aside of any action of the corporation or of its shareholders, directors, or officers of or any other party to the proceeding;

(2) the cancellation or alteration of any provision in the corporation's articles of incorporation or bylaws;

(3) the removal from office of any director or officer;

(4) the appointment of any individual as a director or officer;

(5) an accounting with respect to any matter in dispute;

(6) the appointment of a custodian to manage the business and affairs of the corporation;

(7) the appointment of a provisional director (who has all the rights, powers, and duties of a duly elected director) to serve for the term and under the conditions prescribed by the court;

(8) the payment of dividends;

(9) the award of damages to any aggrieved party.

(b) If the court finds that a party to the proceeding acted arbitrarily, vexatiously, or otherwise not in good faith, it may award one or more other parties their reasonable expenses, including counsel fees and the expenses of appraisers or other experts, incurred in the proceeding.

SECTION 42. EXTRAORDINARY RELIEF: SHARE PURCHASE

(a) If the court finds that the ordinary relief described in section 41(a) is or would be inadequate or inappropriate, it may order the corporation dissolved under section 43 unless the corporation or one or more of its shareholders purchases all the shares of the shareholder for their fair value and on terms determined under subsection (b).

(b) If the court orders a share purchase, it shall:

(1) determine the fair value of the shares, considering among other relevant evidence the going concern value of the corporation, any agreement among some or all of the shareholders fixing the price or specifying a formula for determining share value for any purpose, the recommendations of appraisers (if any) appointed by the court, and any legal constraints on the corporation's ability to purchase the shares;

(2) specify the terms of the purchase, including if appropriate terms for installment payments, subordination of the purchase obligation to the rights of the corporation's other creditors, security for a deferred purchase price, and a covenant not to compete or other restriction on the seller;

(3) require the seller to deliver all his shares to the purchaser upon receipt of the purchase price or the first installment of the purchase price;

(4) provide that after the seller delivers his shares he has no further claim against the corporation, its directors, officers, or shareholders, other than a claim to any unpaid balance of the purchase price and a claim under any agreement with the corporation or the remaining shareholders that is not terminated by the court; and

(5) provide that if the purchase is not completed in accordance with the specified terms, the corporation is to be dissolved under section 43.

(c) After the purchase order is entered, any party may petition the court to modify the terms of the purchase and the court may do so if it finds that changes in the financial or legal ability of the corporation or other purchaser to complete the purchase justify a modification.

(d) If the corporation is dissolved because the share purchase was not completed in accordance with the court's order, the selling shareholder has the same rights and priorities in the corporation's assets as if the sale had not been ordered.

SECTION 43. EXTRAORDINARY RELIEF: DISSOLUTION

(a) The court may dissolve the corporation if it finds:

(1) there are one or more grounds for judicial dissolution under [MBCA § 14.30]; or

(2) all other relief ordered by the court under section 41 or 42 has failed to resolve the matters in dispute.

(b) In determining whether to dissolve the corporation, the court shall consider among other relevant evidence the financial condition of the corporation but may not refuse to dissolve solely because the corporation has accumulated earnings or current operating profits.

Transition Provisions

SECTION 50. APPLICATION TO EXISTING CORPORATIONS

(a) This Supplement applies to all corporations electing statutory close corporation status under section 3 after its effective date.

(b) [If Sec. 54 repeals an integrated close corporation statute enacted before this Supplement, this and additional subsections should provide a cutoff date by which corporations qualified under the repealed statute must elect whether to be covered by this Supplement, the procedure for making the election, and the effect of the election on existing agreements among shareholders. Cf. MBCA ch. 17 and Model Professional Corporation Supplement sec. 70.]

SECTION 51. RESERVATION OF POWER TO AMEND OR REPEAL

The [name of state legislature] has power to amend or repeal all or part of this supplement at any time and all corporations subject to this supplement are governed by the amendment or repeal.

SECTION 52. SAVING PROVISIONS

(a) The repeal of a statute by this Supplement does not affect:

(1) the operation of the statute or any action taken under it before its repeal;

(2) any ratification, right, remedy, privilege, obligation, or liability acquired, accrued, or incurred under the statute before its repeal;

(3) any violation of the statute, or any penalty, forfeiture, or punishment incurred because of the violation, before its repeal;

(4) any proceeding, reorganization, or dissolution commenced under the statute before its repeal, and the proceeding, reorganization, or dissolution may be completed in accordance with the statute as if it had not been repealed.

SECTION 53. SEVERABILITY

If any provision of this Supplement or its application to any person or circumstance is held invalid by a court of competent jurisdiction, the invalidity does not affect other provisions or applications of the Supplement that can be given effect without the invalid provision or application, and to this end the provisions of the Supplement are severable.

SECTION 54. REPEAL

The following laws and parts of laws are repealed:
_____.

SECTION 55. EFFECTIVE DATE

This Supplement takes effect _____.

MODEL PROFESSIONAL CORPORATION SUPPLEMENT (1984)

GENERAL PROVISIONS

SECTION 1. SHORT TITLE

This Act shall be known and may be cited as the "[name of state] Professional Corporation Supplement."

SECTION 2. APPLICATION OF [MODEL] BUSINESS CORPORATION ACT

The [Model] Business Corporation Act applies to professional corporations, both domestic and foreign, to the extent not inconsistent with the provisions of this Supplement.

SECTION 3. SUPPLEMENT DEFINITIONS

In this supplement:

(1) "Disqualified person" means an individual or entity that for any reason is or becomes ineligible under this Supplement to be issued shares by a professional corporation.

(2) "Domestic professional corporation" means a professional corporation.

(3) "Foreign professional corporation" means a corporation or association for profit incorporated for the purpose of rendering professional services under a law other than the law of this state.

(4) "Law" includes rules promulgated in accordance with section 63.

(5) "Licensing authority" means the officer, board, agency, court, or other authority in this state empowered to license or otherwise authorize the rendition of a professional service.

(6) "Professional corporation" means a corporation for profit, other than a foreign professional corporation, subject to the provisions of this Supplement.

(7) "Professional service" means a service that may be lawfully rendered only by a person licensed or otherwise authorized by a licensing authority in this state to render the service and that may not be lawfully rendered by a corporation under the [Model] Business Corporation Act.

(8) "Qualified person" means an individual, general partnership, or professional corporation that is eligible under this Supplement to be issued shares by a professional corporation. [*Reviser's note:* the phrase "or professional corporation" should be deleted if Alternative 2 or 3 of section 34(c) or (c) and (d) is chosen.]

Creation

SECTION 10. ELECTION OF PROFESSIONAL CORPORATION STATUS

(a) One or more persons may incorporate a professional corporation by delivering to the secretary of state for filing articles of incorporation that state (1) it is a professional corporation and (2) its purpose is to render the specified professional services.

(b) A corporation incorporated under a general law of this state that is not repealed by this Supplement may elect professional corporation status by amending its articles of incorporation to comply with subsection (a) and section 15.

SECTION 11. PURPOSES

(a) Except to the extent authorized by subsection (b), a corporation may elect professional corporation status under section 10 solely for the purpose of rendering professional services (including services ancillary to them) and solely within a single profession.

(b) A corporation may elect professional corporation status under section 10 for the purpose of rendering professional services within two or more professions, and for the purpose of engaging in any lawful business authorized by [MBCA § 3.01], to the extent the combination of professional purposes or of professional and business purposes is authorized by the licensing law of this state applicable to each profession in the combination.

SECTION 12. GENERAL POWERS

(a) Except as provided in subsection (b), a professional corporation has the powers enumerated in [MBCA § 3.02].

(b) A professional corporation may be a promoter, general partner, member, associate, or manager of a partnership, joint venture, trust, or other entity only if the entity is engaged solely in rendering professional services or in carrying on business authorized by the professional corporation's articles of incorporation.

SECTION 13. RENDERING PROFESSIONAL SERVICES

(a) A domestic or foreign corporation may render professional services in this state only through individuals licensed or otherwise authorized in this state to render the services.

(b) Subsection (a) does not:

(1) require an individual employed by a professional corporation to be licensed to perform services for the corporation if a license is not otherwise required;

(2) prohibit a licensed individual from rendering professional services in his individual capacity although he is a shareholder, director, officer, employee, or agent of a domestic or foreign professional corporation;

(3) prohibit an individual licensed in another state from rendering professional services for a domestic or foreign professional corporation in this state if not prohibited by the licensing authority.

SECTION 14. PROHIBITED ACTIVITIES

(a) A professional corporation may not render any professional service or engage in any business other than the professional service and business authorized by its articles of incorporation.

(b) Subsection (a) does not prohibit a professional corporation from investing its funds in real estate, mortgages, securities, or any other type of investment.

SECTION 15. CORPORATE NAME

(a) The name of a domestic professional corporation and of a foreign professional corporation authorized to transact business in this state, in addition to satisfying the requirements of [MBCA § § 4.01 and 15.06]:

(1) must contain the words "professional corporation," "professional association," or "service corporation" or the abbreviation "P.C.," "P.A.," or "S.C.";

(2) may not contain language stating or implying that it is incorporated for a purpose other than that authorized by section 11 and its articles of incorporation; and

(3) must conform with any rule promulgated by the licensing authority having jurisdiction over a professional service described in the corporation's articles of incorporation.

(b) [MBCA § § 4.01 and 15.06] do not prevent the use of a name otherwise prohibited by those sections if it is the personal name of a shareholder or former shareholder of the domestic or foreign professional corporation or the name of an individual who was associated with a predecessor of the corporation.

Shares

SECTION 20. ISSUANCE OF SHARES

(a) A professional corporation may issue shares, fractional shares, and rights or options to purchase shares only to:

(1) individuals who are authorized by law in this or another state to render a professional service described in the corporation's articles of incorporation;

(2) general partnerships in which all the partners are qualified persons with respect to the professional corporation and in which at least one partner is authorized by law in this state to render a professional service described in the corporation's articles of incorporation;

(3) professional corporations, domestic or foreign, authorized by law in this state to render a professional service described in the corporation's articles of incorporation. [*Reviser's note:* Subsection (3) should be deleted if Alternative 2 or 3 of section 34(c) or (c) and (d) is chosen.]

(b) If a licensing authority with jurisdiction over a profession considers it necessary to prevent violation of the ethical standards of the profession, the authority may by rule restrict or condition, or revoke in part, the authority of professional corporations subject to its jurisdiction to issue shares. A rule promulgated under this section does not, of itself, make a shareholder of a professional corporation at the time the rule becomes effective a disqualified person.

(c) Shares issued in violation of this section or a rule promulgated under this section are void.

SECTION 21. NOTICE OF PROFESSIONAL
CORPORATION STATUS ON SHARES

(a) The following statement must appear conspicuously on each share certificate issued by a professional corporation:

The transfer of shares of a professional corporation is restricted by the [Model Professional Corporation Supplement] and is subject to further restriction imposed from time to time by the licensing authority. Shares of a professional corporation are also subject to a statutory compulsory repurchase obligation.

(b) Within a reasonable time after the issuance or transfer of uncertificated shares of a professional corporation, the corporation shall send the shareholders a written notice containing the statement required by subsection (a).

SECTION 22. SHARE TRANSFER RESTRICTION

(a) A shareholder of a professional corporation may transfer or pledge shares, fractional shares, and rights or options to purchase shares of the corporation only to individuals, general partnerships, and professional corporations qualified under section 20 to be issued shares. [*Reviser's note:* The phrase "and professional corporations" should be deleted if Alternative 2 or 3 of section 34(c) or (c) and (d) is chosen.]

(b) A transfer of shares made in violation of subsection (a), except one made by operation of law or court judgment, is void.

SECTION 23.   COMPULSORY ACQUISITION OF SHARES AFTER DEATH OR DISQUALIFICATION OF SHAREHOLDER

(a) A professional corporation must acquire (or cause to be acquired by a qualified person) the shares of its shareholder, at a price the corporation believes represents their fair value as of the date of death, disqualification, or transfer, if:

(1) the shareholder dies;

(2) the shareholder becomes a disqualified person, except as provided in subsection (c); or

(3) the shares are transferred by operation of law or court judgment to a disqualified person, except as provided in subsection (c).

(b) If a price for the shares is fixed in accordance with the articles of incorporation or bylaws or by private agreement, that price controls. If the price is not so fixed, the corporation shall acquire the shares in accordance with section 24. If the disqualified person rejects the corporation's purchase offer, either the person or the corporation may commence a proceeding under section 25 to determine the fair value of the shares.

(c) This section does not require the acquisition of shares in the event of disqualification if the disqualification lasts no more than five months from the date the disqualification or transfer occurs.

(d) This section, and section 24, do not prevent or relieve a professional corporation from paying pension benefits or other deferred compensation for services rendered to a former shareholder if otherwise permitted by law.

(e) A provision for the acquisition of shares contained in a professional corporation's articles of incorporation or bylaws, or in a private agreement, is specifically enforceable.

SECTION 24.   ACQUISITION PROCEDURE

(a) If shares must be acquired under section 23, the professional corporation shall deliver a written notice to the executor or administrator of the estate of its deceased shareholder, or to the disqualified person or transferee, offering to purchase the shares at a price the corporation believes represents their fair value as of the date of death, disqualification, or transfer. The offer notice must be accompanied by the corporation's balance sheet for a fiscal year ending not more than 16 months before the effective date of the offer notice, an income statement for that year, a statement of changes in shareholders' equity for that year, and the latest available interim financial statements, if any.

(b) The disqualified person has 30 days from the effective date of the notice to accept the corporation's offer or demand that the corporation commence a proceeding under section 25 to determine the fair value of his shares. If he accepts the offer, the corporation shall make payment for the shares within 60 days from the effective date of the offer notice (unless a later date is agreed on) upon the disqualified person's surrender of his shares to the corporation.

(c) After the corporation makes payment for the shares, the disqualified person has no further interest in them.

SECTION 25.   COURT ACTION TO APPRAISE SHARES

(a) If the disqualified shareholder does not accept the professional corporation's offer under section 24(b) within the 30 day period, the shareholder during the following 30 day period may deliver a written notice to the corporation demanding that it commence a proceeding to determine the fair value of the shares. The corporation may commence a proceeding at any time during the 60 days following the effective date of its offer notice. If it does not do so, the shareholder may commence a proceeding against the corporation to determine the fair value of his shares.

(b) The corporation or disqualified shareholder shall commence the proceeding in the [name or describe] court of the county where the corporation's principal office (or, if none in this state, its registered office) is located. The corporation shall make the disqualified shareholder a party to the proceeding as in an action against his shares. The jurisdiction of the court in which the proceeding is commenced is plenary and exclusive.

(c) The court may appoint one or more persons as appraisers to receive evidence and recommend decision on the question of fair value. The appraisers have the power described in the order appointing them, or in any amendment to it.

(d) The disqualified shareholder is entitled to judgment for the fair value of his shares determined by the court as of the date of death, disqualification, or transfer together with interest from that date at a rate found by the court to be fair and equitable.

(e) The court may order the judgment paid in installments determined by the court.

SECTION 26.   COURT COSTS AND FEES OF EXPERTS

(a) The court in an appraisal proceeding commenced under section 25 shall determine all costs of the proceeding, including the reasonable compensation and expenses of appraisers appointed by the court, and shall assess the costs against the professional corporation. But the court may assess costs against the disqualified shareholder, in an amount the court finds equitable, if the court finds the shareholder acted arbitrarily, vexatiously, or not in good faith in refusing to accept the corporation's offer.

(b) The court may also assess the fees and expenses of counsel and experts for the disqualified shareholder against the corporation and in favor of the shareholder if the court finds that the fair value of his shares substantially exceeded the amount offered by the corporation or that the corporation did not make an offer.

SECTION 27.   CANCELLATION OF DISQUALIFIED SHARES

If the shares of a disqualified person are not acquired under section 24 or 25 within 10 months after the death of the shareholder or within 5 months after the disqualification or transfer, the professional corporation shall immediately cancel the shares on its books and the disqualified person has no further interest as a shareholder in the corporation other than his right to payment of the fair value of the shares under section 24 or 25.

Governance

SECTION 30.   DIRECTORS AND OFFICERS

Not less than one-half of the directors of a professional corporation, and all of its officers except the secretary and treasurer (if any), must be qualified persons with respect to the corporation.

SECTION 31.   VOTING OF SHARES

(a) Only a qualified person may be appointed a proxy to vote shares of a professional corporation.

(b) A voting trust with respect to shares of a professional corporation is not valid [unless all of its trustees and beneficiaries are qualified persons. But if a beneficiary who is a qualified person dies or becomes disqualified, a voting trust valid under this subsection continues to be valid for 10 months after the date of death or for 5 months after the disqualification occurred.] [*Reviser's note:* The bracketed text should be deleted if Alternative 2 or 3 of section 34(c) or (c) and (d) is chosen.]

SECTION 32.   CONFIDENTIAL RELATIONSHIP

(a) The relationship between an individual rendering professional services as an employee of a domestic or foreign professional corporation and his client or patient is the same as if the individual were rendering the services as a sole practitioner.

(b) The relationship between a domestic or foreign professional corporation and the client or patient for whom its employee is rendering professional services is the same as that between the client or patient and the employee.

SECTION 33.   PRIVILEGED COMMUNICATIONS

A privilege applicable to communications between an individual rendering professional services and the person receiving the services recognized under the statute or common law of this state is not affected by this Supplement. The privilege applies to a domestic or foreign professional corporation and to its employees in all situations in which it applies to communications between an individual rendering professional services on behalf of the corporation and the person receiving the services.

SECTION 34.   RESPONSIBILITY FOR PROFESSIONAL
SERVICES

(a) Each individual who renders professional services as an employee of a domestic or foreign professional corporation is liable for a negligent or wrongful act or omission in which he personally participates to the same extent as if he rendered the services as a sole practitioner. An employee of a domestic or foreign professional corporation is not liable, however, for the conduct of other employees of the corporation unless he is at fault in appointing, supervising, or cooperating with them.

(b) A domestic or foreign professional corporation whose employees perform professional services within the scope of their employment or of their apparent authority to act for the corporation is liable to the same extent as its employees.

ALTERNATIVE 1

(c) Except as otherwise provided by statute, the personal liability of a shareholder of a domestic or foreign professional corporation is no greater in any respect than the liability of a shareholder of a corporation incorporated under the [Model] Business Corporation Act.

ALTERNATIVE 2

(c) Except as otherwise provided by statute, if a domestic or foreign professional corporation is liable under subsection (b), every shareholder of the corporation is liable to the same extent as if he were a partner in a partnership and the services creating liability were rendered on behalf of the partnership.

ALTERNATIVE 3

(c) If a domestic or foreign professional corporation is liable under subsection (b), every shareholder of the corporation is liable to the same extent as if he were a partner in a partnership and the services creating liability were rendered on behalf of the partnership:

(1) except as otherwise provided by statute; or

(2) unless the corporation has provided security for professional responsibility under subsection (d) and the liability is satisfied to the extent provided by the security.

(d) A domestic or foreign professional corporation may provide security for professional responsibility by obtaining insurance or a surety bond. The licensing authority with jurisdiction over a profession may determine by rule the amount, coverage, and form of insurance or bond required based on the number of shareholders, type of practice, and other variables considered appropriate by the authority for the profession. If a licensing authority has not determined the amount of security required for the profession, the amount is the product of $_____ multiplied by the number of shareholders of the corporation rendering services in that profession.

Reorganization and Termination

SECTION 40. MERGER

(a) If all the shareholders of the disappearing and surviving corporations are qualified to be shareholders of the surviving corporation, a professional corporation may merge with another domestic or foreign professional corporation or with a domestic or foreign business corporation.

(b) If the surviving corporation is to render professional services in this state, it must comply with this Supplement.

SECTION 41. TERMINATION OF PROFESSIONAL
ACTIVITIES

If a professional corporation ceases to render professional services, it must amend its articles of incorporation to delete references to rendering professional services and to conform its corporate name to the requirements of [MBCA § 4.01]. After the amendment becomes effective the corporation may continue in existence as a business corporation under the [MBCA] and it is no longer subject to this Supplement.

SECTION 42. JUDICIAL DISSOLUTION

The attorney general may commence a proceeding under [MBCA § § 14.30-14.33] to dissolve a professional corporation if:

(1) the secretary of state or a licensing authority with jurisdiction over a professional service described in the corporation's articles of incorporation serves written notice on the corporation under [MBCA § 5.04] that it has violated or is violating a provision of this Supplement;

(2) the corporation does not correct each alleged violation, or demonstrate to the reasonable satisfaction of the secretary of state or licensing authority that it did not occur, within 60 days after service of the notice is perfected under [MBCA § 5.04]; and

(3) the secretary of state or licensing authority certifies to the attorney general a description of the violation, that it notified the corporation of the violation, and that the corporation did not correct it, or demonstrate that it did not occur, within 60 days after perfection of service of the notice.

Foreign Professional Corporations

SECTION 50. AUTHORITY TO TRANSACT BUSINESS

(a) Except as provided in subsection (c), a foreign professional corporation may not transact business in this state until it obtains a certificate of authority from the secretary of state.

(b) A foreign professional corporation may not obtain a certificate of authority unless:

(1) its corporate name satisfies the requirements of section 15;

(2) it is incorporated for one or more of the purposes described in section 11; and

(3) all of its shareholders, not less than one-half of its directors, and all of its officers other than its secretary and treasurer (if any) are licensed in one or more states to render a professional service described in its articles of incorporation.

(c) A foreign professional corporation is not required to obtain a certificate of authority to transact business in this state unless it maintains or intends to maintain an office in this state for conduct of business or professional practice.

SECTION 51. APPLICATION FOR CERTIFICATE OF AUTHORITY

The application of a foreign professional corporation for a certificate of authority to render professional services in this state must contain the information called for by [MBCA § 15.03] and in addition include a statement that all of its shareholders, not less than one-half of its directors, and all of its officers other than its secretary and treasurer (if any), are licensed in one or more states to render a professional service described in its articles of incorporation.

SECTION 52. REVOCATION OF CERTIFICATE OF AUTHORITY

The secretary of state may administratively revoke under [MBCA § § 15.30-15.32] the certificate of authority of a foreign professional corporation authorized to transact business in this state if a licensing authority with jurisdiction over a professional service described in the corporation's articles of incorporation certifies to the secretary of state that the corporation has violated or is violating a provision of this Supplement and describes the violation in the certificate.

Miscellaneous Regulatory Provisions

SECTION 60. ARTICLES OF INCORPORATION FOR LICENSING AUTHORITY

A domestic or foreign professional corporation authorized to transact business in this state may not render professional services in this state until it delivers a certified copy of its articles of incorporation for filing to each licensing authority with jurisdiction over a professional service described in the articles.

SECTION 61. ANNUAL QUALIFICATION STATEMENT FOR LICENSING AUTHORITY

(a) Each domestic professional corporation, and each foreign professional corporation authorized to transact business in this state, shall deliver for filing to each licensing authority having jurisdiction over a professional service described in the corporation's articles of incorporation an annual statement of qualification setting forth:

(1) the names and usual business addresses of its directors and officers; and

(2) information required by rule promulgated by the licensing authority to determine compliance with this Supplement and other rules promulgated under it.

(b) The first qualification statement must be delivered to the licensing authority between January 1 and April 1 of the year following the calendar year in which a domestic corporation became a professional corporation or a foreign professional corporation

was authorized to transact business in this state. Subsequent qualification statements must be delivered to the licensing authority between January 1 and April 1 of the following calendar years.

(c) The licensing authority shall collect a fee of $___ when a qualification statement is delivered to it for filing.

SECTION 62. ANNUAL REPORT FOR SECRETARY OF STATE

The annual report required by [MBCA § 16.22] for each domestic professional corporation, and for each foreign professional corporation authorized to transact business in this state, must include a statement that all of its shareholders, not less than one-half of its directors, and all of its officers other than its secretary and treasurer (if any), are qualified persons with respect to the corporation.

SECTION 63. RULEMAKING BY LICENSING AUTHORITY

Each licensing authority is empowered to promulgate rules expressly authorized by this Supplement if the rules are consistent with the public interest or required by the public health or welfare or by generally recognized standards of professional conduct.

SECTION 64. LICENSING AUTHORITY'S REGULATORY JURISDICTION

This Supplement does not restrict the jurisdiction of a licensing authority over individuals rendering a professional service within the jurisdiction of the licensing authority, nor does it affect the interpretation or application of any law pertaining to standards of professional conduct.

SECTION 65. PENALTY FOR SIGNING FALSE DOCUMENT

(a) A person commits an offense if he signs a document he knows is false in any material respect with intent that the document be delivered to the licensing authority for filing.

(b) An offense under this section is a [____] misdemeanor [punishable by a fine of not to exceed $_____].

(c) The offense created by this section is in addition to any other offense created by law for the same conduct.

Transition Provisions

SECTION 70. APPLICATION TO EXISTING CORPORATIONS

(a) This Supplement applies to every corporation incorporated under a general law of this state that is repealed by this Supplement. If an existing corporation to which this Supplement applies must amend its articles of incorporation to comply with this Supplement, it shall do so within 90 days after the effective date of this Supplement.

(b) This Supplement does not apply to a corporation now existing or later incorporated under a law of this state that is not repealed by this Supplement unless the corporation elects professional corporation status under section 10.

(c) This Supplement does not affect an existing or future right or privilege to render professional services through the use of any other form of business entity.

SECTION 71. RESERVATION OF POWER TO AMEND OR REPEAL

The [name of state legislature] has power to amend or repeal all or part of this Supplement at any time and all domestic and foreign professional corporations subject to this Supplement are governed by the amendment or repeal.

SECTION 72. SAVING PROVISIONS

(a) Except as provided in subsection (b), the repeal of a statute by this Supplement does not affect:

(1) the operation of the statute or any action taken under it before its repeal;

(2) any ratification, right, remedy, privilege, obligation, or liability acquired, accrued, or incurred under the statute before its repeal;

(3) any violation of the statute, or any penalty, forfeiture, or punishment incurred because of the violation, before its repeal;

(4) any proceeding, reorganization, or dissolution commenced under the statute before its repeal, and the proceeding, reorganization, or dissolution may be completed in accordance with the statute as if it had not been repealed.

(b) If a penalty or punishment imposed for violation of a statute repealed by this Supplement is reduced by this Supplement, the penalty or punishment if not already imposed shall be imposed in accordance with this Supplement.

SECTION 73. SEVERABILITY

If any provision of this Supplement or its application to any person or circumstance is held invalid by a court of competent jurisdiction, the invalidity does not affect other provisions or applications of the Supplement that can be given effect without the invalid provision or application, and to this end the provisions of the Supplement are severable.

SECTION 74. REPEAL

THE FOLLOWING LAWS AND PARTS OF LAWS ARE RE-PEALED: _____.

SECTION 75. EFFECTIVE DATE

This Supplement takes effect _____.

FORMS

ARTICLE I.   GENERAL PROVISIONS
A.   Recitals.
B.   Parties.
C.   Purpose.
D.   Firm Name.
E.   Term.
F.   Location of Principal Place of Business.

ARTICLE II.   CAPITAL
A.   Original Capital Contributed by Partners.
B.   Annual Additional Contributions to Capital.
C.   Reserve for Capital Expenditures; Other Reserves.
D.   Annual Reimbursements on Contributions to Capital.

ARTICLE III. PROFITS AND LOSSES OF THE FIRM; PARTICIPATION OF PARTNERS THEREIN; DRAWINGS; BONUSES
A.   Units of Participation in Profits and Losses Held by the Respective Partners.
B.   Drawing Accounts of the Respective Partners and the Extent to Which Any Are Guaranteed.
C.   Reserve for Bonuses and Payments Therefrom.

ARTICLE IV.   MEETINGS AND VOTING OF PARTNERS
A.   Meetings of Partners; Voting at Such Meetings.
B.   Percentage of Votes Required for Certain Partnership Decisions; Requirement of Recommendation of the Management Committee in Advance of Certain Partnership Decisions.

ARTICLE V.   CHANGES AS TO PARTNERS
A.   No Classes of Partners.
B.   Addition of Partners.
C.   Death or Permanent Disability of a Partner.
   1.   Death.
   2.   Permanent Disability.
D.   Permanent Withdrawal of a Partner.
   1.   Notice of Withdrawal and Effective Date of Withdrawal.
   2.   Possible Termination of the Firm Superseding Withdrawal Notice.
   3.   Partition with and Payments to the Withdrawing Partner.
E.   Retirement of Partners; Gradual Steps toward Retirement; Retirement Plans for Partners.
   1.   Retired Partners; Plans for Their Compensation.
   2.   When a Partner Retires.
   3.   Gradual Steps toward Retirement.
F.   Expulsion of a Partner.
   1.   Expulsion for Cause.
   2.   Effects of Expulsion for Cause.
   3.   Expulsion without Determining Any Cause Therefor.
   4.   Effects of Expulsion without Determining Any Cause Therefor.

G. Temporary Incapacity; Leave of Absence; Temporary Withdrawal; Vacations.
    1. Temporary Incapacity or Illness.
    2. Leave of Absence.
    3. Temporary Withdrawal.
    4. Vacations.

ARTICLE VI. DUTIES OF PARTNERS
A. Devotion to Duty.
B. Charging for Services.

ARTICLE VII. MANAGEMENT
A. Authority and Membership of the Management Committee.
B. Functioning of the Management Committee and Its Subcommittees.
C. Membership in Subcommittees of the Management Committee.

ARTICLE VIII. INSURANCE; INVESTMENTS
A. Life Insurance.
B. Other Insurance.
C. Investments.

ARTICLE IX. PROPERTIES AND RECORDS
A. Firm Properties.
B. Accounting Records.

ARTICLE X. TERMINATION AND LIQUIDATION OF FIRM
A. Termination of the Firm by Voluntary Vote or Otherwise.
B. Pending Employments on Termination.
C. Liquidation of Assets.
D. Prior Opportunity of Partners to Bid for Purchase of Assets Being Liquidated.
E. Distribution of Proceeds from Liquidation.

ARTICLE XI. LEGAL EFFECT OF PROVISIONS; ARBITRATION
A. Governing Law.
B. Persons Bound.
C. Rights of Partners Not Assignable; Not to Be Pledged.
D. Finality of Decisions within the Firm; Effect of Diverse or Adverse Interest of Any Partner.
E. Arbitration.
F. Severability.

ARTICLE XII. AMENDMENTS

ARTICLES OF PARTNERSHIP FOR THE FIRM OF A, B & C
ARTICLE I. GENERAL PROVISIONS

Section A. Recitals. 1. The undersigned parties hereby agree this day of _____ , 20__, to organize a partnership under the name of A, B & C.

2. The effective date of this Agreement is the _____ day of _____, 20.

Section B. Parties. A, B, C, D, E and F constitute the original partners of the firm.

Section C. Purpose. The purpose of this partnership is to engage in [*here set out nature of the business*], and any other business related thereto.

Section D. Firm Name. The name of the partnership "A, B & C" shall continue until changed in accordance with the provisions of this Agreement.

Section E. Term. The partnership shall continue from the effective date of this Agreement until dissolved in accordance with the terms hereof.

Section F. Location of Principal Place of Business. The principal place of business of the partnership shall be at _____, or at such other place or places as the partners shall hereafter determine.

ARTICLE II. CAPITAL

Section A. Original Capital Contributed by Partners. The original capital contributions of the respective partners hereunder are shown on Exhibit A attached hereto. It reflects cash contributed and property, the title of which is transferred to the firm at the current agreed market value of each item. The firm agrees to repay to each partner, at the time and as hereinafter provided, the aggregate amount he or she has thus contributed as original capital plus interest thereon at the rate of _____ percent per annum on all unpaid balances.

Section B. Annual Additional Contributions to Capital. Five percent of the net income of the firm for each fiscal year shall be withheld from distribution and credited, as additional contributions to capital, to partners, in the amount that each would have received had that sum been distributed. Interest shall be paid by the firm on all unreimbursed balances of all these additional contributions to capital at the rate of _____ percent per annum until fully repaid.

Section C. Reserve for Capital Expenditures; Other Reserves.

1. Out of the sums contributed as additional contributions to capital for each fiscal year, there shall be set aside as of the beginning of the new fiscal year that amount, in addition to any unexpended balance in that reserve fund left over from the last year, estimated to be needed for capital expenditures of the firm during the new fiscal year. As such expenditures are incurred during that year they shall be paid for out of that reserve fund.

2. Out of the remainder of the sums contributed as additional contributions to the capital for each fiscal year, there shall be set aside that amount for any other reserve fund, or to add to any existing reserve fund, estimated to be needed to meet any other anticipated obligations or commitments of the firm. As such expenditures are incurred they may be paid out of the appropriate reserve fund.

Section D. Annual Reimbursements on Contributions to Capital.

1. At the end of each fiscal year there shall be charged to firm expense for that year the amount of depreciation accrued for the year, which the firm for federal income tax purposes is entitled to deduct from firm income, and the amount of interest accrued for the year on the unreimbursed balances of contributions to capital.

2. At the end of each fiscal year, (i) the amount of such interest shall be paid to the partners entitled thereto; and (ii) cash sums aggregating the amount of such depreciation shall be paid ratably in reimbursement of contributions to capital.

3. Any amounts remaining out of the annual contributions to capital provided for in Section B of this Article, after the deduction of the reserves as provided in Section C of this Article, shall be paid to partners to reimburse them for their contributions to capital. Such reimbursements shall be made for the oldest contributions first, all repayments for contributions as of the same time being made ratably as to them.

ARTICLE III. PROFITS AND LOSSES OF THE FIRM; PARTICIPATION OF PARTNERS THEREIN; DRAWINGS; BONUSES

Section A. Units of Participation in Profits and Losses Held by the Respective Partners. Except as otherwise expressly provided in this Article, participation of partners in net profits and losses shall be on the basis of the units of participation held by each partner, which shall be as follows:

A: 30 units
B: 20 units
C: 20 units
D: 12 units
E: 8 units
F: 5 units

Upon termination of all interest in the partnership as to any partner, his or her units of participation and all rights thereunder shall expire. No amendment of this Agreement shall be required therefor. Otherwise no change in the aggregate number of units held by partners or in the number held by any partner shall be effected except by an appropriate amendment of this Agreement.

Section B.   Drawing Accounts of the Respective Partners and the Extent to Which Any Are Guaranteed. 1. The firm shall carry on its books a drawing account for each partner. As of the end of each calendar month he or she shall be paid the sum indicated below; which shall thereupon be charged to his or her drawing account.

A: $2,400.00   per month
B: 1,600.00   per month
C: 1,600.00   per month
D: 1,000.00   per month
E: 800.00   per month
F: 800.00   per month

2.   As of close of each fiscal year there shall be credited to the drawing account of each partner his or her share of the net profits computed as provided in this Article III, less the amount of his or her annual contribution to capital of the firm; any reimbursements to him or her of contributions shall be so credited and all other debits and credits between the partner and the firm to date shall be included in the calculation. Any excess of credits over debits shall thereupon be paid to the partner.

3.   If at the end of the fiscal year, after crediting to the drawing accounts of partners E and F the participation of each such partner in the net profits, there remains a deficit in his or her drawing account, he or she shall not be required to pay the amount of that deficit to the firm, but as an expense of the firm (to be shared ratably by the remaining partners who do not have the benefit of this guaranty) his or her account shall be credited in the amount of such deficit. Thus E and F each is guaranteed that he or she shall receive as a minimum his or her drawing account for each month of the year. Moreover, if the net profits of the year aggregate as much as the total of the drawing accounts of all partners plus any amounts credited in balancing the drawing accounts of E and F, all of the other partners shall retain the amounts of their respective drawing accounts. But, if the net profits aggregate less than the total paid in the drawing accounts plus the said amounts credited to the accounts of E and F, then A, B, C and D shall share ratably all such deficits for the year in the proportion of their respective drawing accounts, except however that D shall not be required to pay back to the firm any more than the amount that he or she has received in excess of the stated amounts of the drawing accounts of E and F.

4.   If at the end of the fiscal year there are net profits for distribution over and above the aggregate of all the stipulated monthly drawings and payments made

as the agreed annual additional contributions to capital, then the portion of such net profits not transferred to the reserve for bonuses, as provided for in the next section hereof, shall be applied first to payments to those partners who have received in their monthly drawings less than their ratable share of net profits; and thereafter the balance of net profits shall be distributed ratably to all partners in proportion to their respective units of participation.

Section C.   Reserve for Bonuses and Payments Therefrom.   The net profits of the firm remaining for each fiscal year after paying (or setting aside funds for paying) all expenses of the year and after paying fully the stipulated monthly drawings and making the annual agreed additional contributions to capital, shall be distributed as follows: seventy-five percent of such remaining net profits shall be distributed as heretofore provided (Sections A and B of this Article) and the remaining twenty-five percent shall be placed in a "bonus reserve." The management committee shall as promptly as is convenient recommend to all partners the uses to which this fund of twenty-five percent shall be placed, and thereupon at a meeting of the firm it shall be determined to whom and in what amounts such reserved funds shall be paid. It is anticipated that normally, unless some anticipated need for the reserve fund seems to require other use of such funds in the new fiscal year immediately ahead, said reserve fund will be used for extra distributions to partners as achievement bonuses.

ARTICLE IV.   MEETINGS AND VOTING OF PARTNERS

Section A.   Meetings of Partners; Voting at Such Meetings.   1.   A meeting of partners shall be held at any time on call of the management committee or at any time after written notice at least 10 days in advance jointly signed by any three partners, specifying the hour and purposes of the meeting. The call by the management committee may be written or oral and need not be made any period of time in advance of the meeting, nor need it specify the purposes of the meeting; except, however, that in those instances where written notice for at least a specified period of time is required by any provision of these Articles, every call or notice of such meeting shall comply with such requirement.

2.   At each meeting of partners every partner shall have one vote for each unit of participation held by him or her, as specified in Section A of Article III of this document; a quorum for any issue at any meeting shall exist if partners holding a majority of such units are present in person or voting by proxy or written instruction. Any partner may vote on any matter (subject to provisions of paragraph 3, this Section) if not present, by general or specific proxy to a partner present or by specific instructions in writing.

3.   A partner shall not vote, however, and the number of outstanding units shall be deemed to be reduced by the number he or she holds (for the purposes of determining on any such issue whether quorum exists or whether the requisite percentage of outstanding units have been voted in the affirmative), when he or she is the partner affected by any of the following issues:

(a)   If the partner has given a notice of withdrawal from the firm and the partnership meeting is voting on a proposal to terminate the firm and liquidate its affairs (see Article V, Section D), the person whose notice of withdrawal is pending shall not vote and the percentage of votes for termination and liquidation shall be determined as though that partner's units of participation did not exist.

(b)   If the issue before the partnership is whether a partner (i) is under permanent disability, or (ii) should be expelled from the firm, whether for cause or without determining that a cause exists, or (iii) should be permitted to retire or to attain retirement by gradual steps, or (iv) should be granted a temporary withdrawal from the firm (see Article V, Sections C, E, F and G), then as to each such issue the partner involved shall not vote and the percentage of votes shall be determined as though his or her units of participation did not exist.

4. Excepting only as provided in paragraph 3 of this Section A of Article IV or in Section D of Article XI of this Agreement, no partner shall be disqualified from voting on any issue, notwithstanding any interest he or she may have therein which differs from the interest of the firm or the other partners.

Section B.   Percentage of Votes Required for Certain Partnership Decisions; Requirement of Recommendation of the Management Committee in Advance of Certain Partnership Decisions.

1. As provided by Article V of this Agreement, it may be determined by partnership vote that one presently a partner (i) is under permanent disability, (ii) should be expelled from the firm, (iii) should be permitted to retire or to attain retirement by gradual steps, or (iv) should be granted temporary withdrawal from the firm; or that one not a partner presently be added as a partner (see Article V, Sections B, C, E, F and G). As to each such issue (subject in each instance to the provisions of paragraph 3 of Section A of this Article), it is required that for so determining that issue in the affirmative, affirmative votes shall be cast by partners holding at least two-thirds of the outstanding units of participation that can be voted on that issue. An affirmative recommendation of the management committee in advance is required for a vote of the partners on the addition of a new partner (see Article V, Section B) or for a vote on payments out of the bonus reserve (see Article III, Section C).

2. As provided by Article X of this Agreement, decision may be made that the firm be terminated and its affairs liquidated at any meeting held for the specific purpose of determining whether this shall be done, on the written call of the management committee or of any three partners stating the purpose of the meeting and giving at least three days' notice. For determining this issue in the affirmative (subject to the provisions of paragraph 3(a) of Section A of this Article), votes in the affirmative of partners holding at least two-thirds of the outstanding units of participation that can be voted on that issue shall be required.

3. As provided in Article XII of this Agreement, these Articles of Partnership may be amended upon affirmative votes of partners holding at least two-thirds of the outstanding units of participation that can be voted on that issue, provided that the proposed amendment and the recommendation of the management committee with reference thereto are attached to the written notice of the meeting at which the proposed amendment is to be considered.

4. A majority of the votes cast, a quorum being present, may determine any other issue at a partnership meeting, provided no such determination shall be contrary to a provision of law or of this Agreement.

ARTICLE V.   CHANGES AS TO PARTNERS

Section A.   No Classes of Partners. Though their contractual rights differ, as provided in this instrument, all partners are of the same class and have identical and equal rights except as herein otherwise provided.

Section B.   Addition of Partners. The management committee may from time to time propose that additional partners be invited to join the partnership, and may propose the units of participation and the drawing accounts for each, together with the proposed amendment to the Articles of Partnership, specifically providing for any drawing account, guaranties and other provisions. In each such instance:

1.   There shall be given to each partner a notice of at least ten days of a meeting for all partners at which each partner shall be entitled to discuss the proposal fully; each partner shall be entitled to a postponement of that meeting up to a date not less than thirty days after the giving of the ten-day notice.

2.   At that meeting the partners may by their affirmative votes (as provided in paragraph 1 of Section B of Article IV) determine that the invitation shall be extended as proposed by the management committee or with such revisions as are determined upon.

3.   If the invitation is accepted, the new partner and prior partners holding at least two-thirds of the participating units entitled to vote at the meeting referred to in paragraphs 1 and 2 of this Section B, shall join in executing an amendment to these Articles of Partnership providing for the change in the partnership thus effected.

Section C.   Death or Permanent Disability of a Partner.

1.   *Death.* The death of a partner shall terminate all his or her interest in the partnership, its property and assets. The continuing firm shall pay in cash to his or her estate (or to his or her nominee or nominees in accordance with the provisions of any separate agreement entered into between that partner and the management committee acting for the firm) the following amounts to be paid in installments at the times indicated:

(a)   On or before thirty days after the date of death, the net amount of his or her capital in the firm as of the date of death plus interest on the capital to that date.

(b)   Within ninety days from the date of death, an amount computed as follows:

(i)   Start with his or her pro rata share of seventy-five percent of the net profits (after reducing said profits by interest on the capital accounts of all partners to date of death) of the firm for that portion of its then current year ending with the date of death;

(ii)   Add thereto any part of the remaining twenty-five percent of the firm's net profits which the management committee in its discretion determines to be his or her fair share of such net profits as a bonus payment to him or her, based on the same considerations for that part of the year as are provided for any full year in Section C of Article III hereof;

(iii)   Deduct from the total arrived at in (ii) above, all distributions the deceased partner had received from the firm on account of net earnings during the year; and

(iv)   Adjust the remaining balance by debiting and crediting all sums owing to the firm by the deceased partner or by the firm to him or her immediately prior to death. If the result is a minus balance, it shall be deducted from the aggregate amount payable in monthly installments as provided in subparagraph (c) of Section C, paragraph 1.

(c)   In a series of forty-two consecutive monthly installments, beginning on or before one hundred twenty days after the date of death, a further amount which (except as otherwise herein provided) shall be the average of the sums paid to him or her as a partner of the firm during each of the last three complete fiscal years of the firm during which he or she was a partner.

(i)   The computation of the sums so paid to him or her each year shall include all distributions to him or her out of net income of the firm, but without any deductions for contributions to its capital or any additions for reimbursements therefor or interest on unreimbursed contributions. If he or she became a retired partner or temporarily withdrawn partner, the years of retirement or of temporary withdrawal are not to be included in the computation. If he or she had not been a member of the firm for as long as three complete fiscal years, then there shall be paid the average of sums paid to him or her for two such years, and if not a member for as long as two such years, then the sums so paid to him or her for one year. If he or she had not been a member one full year, no sums shall be paid under this subparagraph (c).

(ii)   The first six installments of the amount thus to be paid by the continuing firm shall each be as much as decedent's current agreed monthly drawing at the time of death and may, at the option of the firm, be as much more as the firm shall elect. The remainder of the sum payable by the continuing firm, if any (after the payment of the first six installments) shall be paid in thirty-six monthly installments, approximately equal, beginning three hundred days after death, with interest added to each of these installments at the rate of five percent per annum from date of death until paid.

2.   *Permanent Disability.*   (a)   The determination that a partner is permanently disabled shall terminate all his or her interests in the partnership and his or her units of participation as a partner. That determination shall be made only upon the affirmative vote by partners holding at least two-thirds of all units of participation, not including the partner whose disability is in issue or the units held by him or her, all in accordance with the provisions of Article IV of this agreement.

(b)   As of the time of the determination of permanent disability of a partner, he or she shall no longer be a partner and shall no longer have any duties to perform with respect to any professional employment of the firm, nor shall he or she be privileged to perform any services in any such matter. His or her units of participation shall expire as of that time, and hence no votes at any partnership meeting may thereafter be cast by him or her, and he or she shall not be entitled to any share of profits or losses thereafter. Except for sums to be paid to him or her by the continuing firm as provided for in subparagraph (c) of this paragraph 2, he or she shall not be entitled to any payments from the firm and shall have no rights or interests in any of its properties or assets from the time of such determination. However, the partners in their discretion may vote to bestow upon him or her some purely honorary title such as "Partner Emeritus," without compensation.

(c)   The amounts payable by the continuing firm to or for the account of a partner determined to be permanently disabled shall be computed in the same way and paid in the same manner as though the partner had died on the date of the determination of permanent disability. His or her death before all such payments have been made shall not interrupt the continued payments by the continuing firm; but no further sums shall be owing by the firm because of his or her death.

Section D.   Permanent Withdrawal of a Partner.

1.   *Notice of Withdrawal and Effective Date of Withdrawal.* Any partner may voluntarily withdraw from the partnership at any time on notice of thirty days to the other partners. As of the expiration of the thirty-day period, or sooner if mutually agreed upon, the withdrawal shall be effective.

2.   *Possible Termination of the Firm Superseding Withdrawal Notice.* At any time during the pendency of a withdrawal notice and before the effective date of withdrawal, a termination of the firm may be voted in accordance with the provisions of Article X of this Agreement. If this is done, the dissolution proceedings, the liquidation of assets, and the distribution of proceeds shall ensue, and the notice of withdrawal shall be of no effect.

3.   *Partition with and Payments to the Withdrawing Partner.* The withdrawing partner's right, title, and interest in the firm shall be extinguished in consideration of the partition with and the payments to him or her by the continuing firm on the following bases:

(a)   On the effective date of withdrawal he or she shall be paid the amount of his or her net capital in the firm plus interest thereon to that date. This payment shall be in cash unless the firm at its option elects to set aside and deliver in kind his or her pro rata share of all its capital assets. In the event the firm sets aside property for him or her, it shall have a discretion as to what items to set aside, all items being valued for the purposes of partition, either by agreement between the firm and the withdrawing partner or by an independent appraisal, at current market prices.

(b)   Within ninety days after the effective date of withdrawal an amount in cash shall be paid computed as follows:

(i)   Start with the pro rata share of seventy-five percent of the net profits (after reducing said profits by interest on the capital accounts of all partners to the effective date of withdrawal) of the firm for that portion of its then current year ending on the effective date of withdrawal;

(ii)   Add thereto any part of the twenty-five percent of the firm's net profits for said portion of its then current year, which the management committee fairly determines to be his or her fair share of such net profits as a bonus payment to him or her based on the same considerations for that portion of the year that are provided in Section C of Article III for any full year, and bearing in mind that the same part of twenty-five percent of the profits from receipts of the portion of the current year will be applied to future receipts from fees charged for services rendered before the withdrawal, pursuant to the provisions of subparagraph (c) (ii) of this paragraph 3;

(iii)   Deduct from the total arrived at in (ii) above all distributions the withdrawing partner had received from the firm on account of net earnings during the year;

(iv)   Adjust the balance thus arrived at by debiting the discounted value at that time of his or her ratable share of payments yet to accrue against the firm on account of the prior death or permanent disability of a partner; and

(v)   Adjust the balance thus arrived at by debiting and crediting all sums owing to the firm by him or her or by the firm to him or her immediately prior to the effective date of withdrawal.

If the foregoing computations result in a minus balance it shall be debited against each quarterly payment later accruing to him or her under the provisions of subparagraphs (c) and (d); and if the debt is not thus discharged, it shall be owing by the withdrawing partner to the continuing firm.

(c)   In quarter-annual installments following the withdrawal, a share of the fees collected by the firm during each quarter thereafter for services rendered by the firm prior to the effective date of withdrawal shall be paid, the amount of these quarter-annual payments to be computed as follows:

(i)   Start with the pro rata share of seventy-five percent of the gross amount of such fees collected during such quarter (after reducing same by the amount, if any, which the management committee of the continuing firm fairly determines to represent the share of all fees earned during that quarter by the firm which were prepaid by the client prior to the effective date of withdrawal);

(ii)   Add thereto an amount which is that percentage of the figure computed under (i) immediately above, which the amount computed under (b) (ii) of this paragraph 3 bears to the figure computed under paragraph (b) (i) of this paragraph 3; and

(iii)   The total amount thus arrived at shall be paid to the withdrawing partner with an accounting to him or her at that time of how the amount is arrived at, provided he or she then makes a like accounting and payment if any is due by him or her to the firm, in accordance with the provisions of subparagraph (d) immediately following.

(d)   Subject to the right of each client to direct that any or all of his or her pending matters in which the firm is employed on the effective date of withdrawal shall be handled for him or her by the continuing firm rather than the withdrawing partner, the withdrawing partner, at his or her option, as to each of the current employments of the firm pending on that date for which he or she was the responsible partner in charge, shall then be entitled (provided he or she then pays the firm for all its expenditures on behalf of the client in connection with such matter for which the client then is or would later be indebted to the firm) to assume all further responsibilities to the client for that matter and to take with him or her all files and documents pertaining wholly to that employment. Thereafter, the withdrawing partner shall bill the client for and be entitled to collect for disbursements theretofore made and services theretofore rendered in connection with that matter as well as for subsequent services and disbursements. The withdrawing partner shall account to the continuing firm with respect to his or her gross collections of fees for services rendered on each such matter by the firm prior to the effective date of withdrawal, and shall pay the firm in cash, in quarter-annual installments from such collections, amounts calculated on the same basis, or as nearly as possible on the same basis, as the firm shall be accounting to the withdrawing partner and paying him or her in accordance with the provisions of subparagraph (c) immediately above.

Agreement as to Tax Effects

In view of the differences in tax results dependent upon distinctions which may not be readily apparent to lawyers outside the tax field, it is quite important that contracts with reference to the liquidation or sale of the interest of a withdrawing or disabled partner, and especially of a deceased partner, should clearly express the intention of the parties as to the tax effects anticipated by the parties to flow from their agreement. Naturally, they should be careful to see that the agreement does what they think it does. As an addition to the agreement, therefore, we suggest a paragraph pertinent to all provisions of Sections C and D of Article V:

It is contemplated by the parties to this Agreement that any payments hereunder for the interest in the firm of a withdrawing or permanently disabled or deceased partner are, to the extent that they represent payment for partnership properties, capital payments falling under Section 736(b) of the Internal Revenue Code. All other payments for the interests of such persons, including so-called "interest" payments on capital invested, are intended by the partners as payments of partnership income under Section 736(a) of the Internal Revenue Code. Each partner covenants for himself or herself and his or her heirs and assigns that he or she will make no claims or representations with reference to the income tax nature of any such amounts that are inconsistent with the intent expressed in this subparagraph.

Section E.   Retirement of Partners; Gradual Steps toward Retirement; Retirement Plans for Partners.

1.   *Retired Partners; Plans for Their Compensation.* (a) A retired partner shall receive no current compensation from the firm in payment for current services, either by way of participation in distribution of net profits of the firm or agreed monthly drawings. He or she may receive bonuses or specifically agreed fees or shares of fees. He or she shall be offered, at the expense of the firm, so long as he or she is able and wishes to use same for at least twenty percent of the business time of each year, an office in the offices of the firm and a secretary to give him or her such secretarial assistance as he or she may require; in consideration of which he or she shall, whenever convenient to him or her, advise with and serve

as consultant to any of the partners or associates of the firm. His or her name shall be carried on firm letterheads, in legal directories and otherwise not as an active partner of the firm but under the heading, "Of Counsel."

(b)   The management committee in its discretion is authorized to pay during any year, to each retired partner as a "retirement bonus," up to twenty-five percent of his or her average annual income for the last three full years during which he or she was an active partner of the firm.

2. *When a Partner Retires.* Any partner may retire at any time upon approval by the partners, in accordance with provisions of Article IV of this Agreement, of his or her request to retire. Any partner who has attained the age of seventy-five shall retire if and when requested to do so by partners holding at least two-thirds of the units or participation entitled to vote.

3. *Gradual Steps toward Retirement.* If the request of a partner that he or she be permitted to enter upon and carry out a plan for gradual retirement is approved by vote of the partners in accordance with the provisions of Article IV of this Agreement, a program of gradual steps toward retirement shall be entered into and consummated, as agreed between him or her and the firm. Such a plan may be required of any partner at any time after the partner attains the age of seventy. The adoption of such a plan as to any partner will involve a program over a period of the following ten years (provided his or her interest in the firm is not meanwhile terminated by death, total disability, withdrawal, or expulsion; and provided said interest is not modified by an agreement between him or her and the firm approved by vote of the partners). During that ten-year period his or her duties shall be gradually reduced and, hence, his or her units of participation, and thus his or her share of net profits or losses, and his or her voting rights shall be reduced from what they are at the start of the period by eight percent at the end of each of the first nine fiscal years of the period, and his or her remaining interest in the firm shall be terminated by effecting his or her retirement at the end of the tenth year.

Section F.   Expulsion of a Partner.

1.   *Expulsion for Cause.* A partner shall be expelled for cause when it has been determined by vote of partners in accordance with the provisions of Article IV of this Agreement, that any of the following reasons for expulsion exist:

(a)   Disbarment, suspension or other major disciplinary action of any duly constituted authority.

(b)   Professional misconduct or violation of the canons of professional ethics, if such misconduct continues after its desistance has been requested by the management committee.

(c)   Action that injures the professional standing of the firm, if such action continues after its desistance is requested by the management committee.

(d)   Insolvency or bankruptcy or assignment of assets for the benefit of creditors.

(e)   Breach of any provision of the Articles of Partnership of the firm, which all other partners expressly agree is a major provision, if, after the breach has been specified as a prospective ground for expulsion by written notice given by the management committee, the same breach continues or occurs again.

(f)   Any other reason which the other partners unanimously agree warrants expulsion.

2.   *Effects of Expulsion for Cause.* Upon a determination that a partner be expelled for cause, he or she shall thereby be so expelled and shall have no right or interest thereafter in the firm or any of its assets, clientele, files or records, or affairs. He or she shall have thereafter no further duties to the firm or any of its clients and shall be privileged to serve none of them thereafter. He or she shall

immediately remove himself or herself and all personal effects from the firm offices. Upon any such expulsion, the expelled partner shall be obligated not to accept employments for services from any who have been clients of the firm during the last five years preceding the determination of expulsion, the obligation not to accept such employments being a continuing one for a term of the next ensuing five years. From the time of the expulsion, the expelled partner shall have no participation whatever in the income or losses of the firm or any distribution or drawings from the net income. Realizing that the existence of any such cause for expulsion may bring disgrace on the firm and damage the firm in amounts and ways that cannot be calculated or become liquidated in amount, each partner agrees that the firm shall succeed to all of the rights of the expelled partner as hereinabove set forth and shall retain all sums unpaid by it to the expelled partner, whether accrued or not at that time; further, that the receipt and retention by the firm of all such rights and sums shall satisfy and discharge the damages of the firm, being retained as and thereby determined to be liquidated damages; no other indebtedness of the expelled partner to the firm being discharged.

3. *Expulsion without Determining Any Cause Therefor.* A partner shall be expelled immediately when, on recommendation of the management committee, it is determined by a vote of the partners as provided in Article IV that he or she shall be expelled without determination of any cause therefor. This method of expulsion may be employed notwithstanding the fact that grounds may exist for expulsion for cause.

4. *Effects of Expulsion without Determining Any Cause Therefor.* Upon such expulsion without determining a cause therefor, the partner so expelled shall have no right or interest thereafter in the firm or any of its assets, clientele, files or records, or affairs. He or she shall have thereafter no further duties to the firm or any of its clients and shall be privileged to serve none of them thereafter. He or she shall immediately remove himself or herself and all personal effects from the firm offices. Except as otherwise provided in this paragraph, a partner so expelled shall be entitled to the same rights, the same payments by, and be subject to the same duties to the continuing firm as though he or she were then voluntarily withdrawing from the firm.

Section G. Temporary Incapacity; Leave of Absence; Temporary Withdrawal; Vacations.

1. *Temporary Incapacity or Illness.* In the event of any interruption of the performance of any partner's services to the firm or to its clients on account of any temporary incapacity or illness, or any other reason not voluntary with the partner, the management committee may, in its complete discretion, make any arrangements it deems fair to the partner and to the firm, as to the period of his or her absence and compensation during that period.

2. *Leave of Absence.* In the event any partner desires an interruption of the performance of his or her services to the firm or its clients, for any reason voluntary with the partner, the request shall be submitted to and may be approved by the management committee which, if the interruption shall not be for more than one year, may in its complete discretion make any arrangements it deems fair to the partner and to the firm, as to the period of his or her absence and compensation during that period.

3. *Temporary Withdrawal.* If any partner desires an interruption of his or her services to the firm and its clients for a period longer than the management committee can, or feels that it should, approve under either of the last two paragraphs of this instrument, the partner may apply to the firm for a temporary withdrawal. The firm, by vote of the partners in accordance with provisions of

Article IV of this document, shall determine whether the request shall be granted and, if so, on what terms and conditions. During the period of any temporary withdrawal, there shall be a suspension and not a termination of the units of participation of the partner involved. Such a temporary withdrawal, unless extended under the same procedure by which it was originally granted, shall be for a specific time, at the expiration of which the temporarily withdrawing partner shall resume his or her services.

4. *Vacations.* All decisions of the firm with reference to vacations of partners in excess of _____weeks a year for each partner are to be wholly within the discretion of the management committee.

ARTICLE VI.   DUTIES OF PARTNERS

Section A.   Devotion to Duty. Each partner shall devote his or her best efforts to serving professionally the firm and its clients. Subject to any exceptions provided in rules of the firm adopted in accordance with the provisions of Article VII, Section A of this Agreement, or any other exceptions consented to by the management committee, each partner shall devote substantially all his or her normal business time to such services.

Section B.   Charging for Services. 1. Each partner shall charge reasonably for all services rendered by that partner, following generally the policies of the firm as to fees charged. However, each partner may serve without charge any member of his or her own family, and with the consent of the management committee any partner may serve without charge, or at less than regular charge, any civic, educational, religious, or charitable organization or project.

2. Each partner will follow rules and policies of the firm adopted in accordance with the provisions of Section A of Article VII of this Agreement relating to consideration by the firm, rather than one partner only, of fees on substantial services rendered by the firm.

3. No salaries, commissions, fees or gratuities of any substantial significance shall be accepted, directly or indirectly, by any partner personally from any client or prospective client of the firm, unless with the express consent in advance of the management committee, and the fair value of any such item received with such consent, though retained by the partner, shall be treated for accounting purposes as compensation to the firm and shall be charged against such partner as an advance on the next maturing installment or installments of his or her drawing account. The management committee may agree, however, to any exception to any provision of this paragraph.

ARTICLE VII.   MANAGEMENT

Section A.   Authority and Membership of the Management Committee.

1.   Subject to the express terms of this Agreement, which as to certain specific matters provides that decisions of the firm shall be determined by the vote of the partners holding required units of participation, the complete and sole management of the firm is hereby vested in the management committee.

2.   Any part or parts of the power, right, and authority vested in the management committee may, at any time and from time to time, be delegated by it to a subcommittee of one or more chosen by it. Such authority may be delegated with power in the subcommittee only to recommend to the management committee what action should be taken, or with power to act; in the latter event, action of the subcommittee shall be the action of the management committee. Any delegation may be terminated by the management committee at any time.

3. It may from time to time cause a set of the rules and policies of the firm to be distributed in an office manual to all partners, associated attorneys and employees of the firm.

4. The management committee shall consist of three partners. No one of them shall be retired (though they may be participating in gradual steps toward retirement) or the subject of pending action for expulsion. Partners subject to any of the stated disabilities shall be disqualified from election to or from acting on the management committee. Upon any such event that disqualifies from continued service a member of the committee, he or she shall automatically cease to be a member of the committee and shall not serve thereafter unless and until (when qualified) reelected to fill a vacancy on the committee. There shall be an alternate member elected by the partners, and if there is a vacancy on the committee because of death, resignation, or disqualification, the alternate shall become a member of the committee. In the event of any temporary absence of a member, the alternate may serve as a member of the committee during the period of the absence. As soon as is convenient the partners shall meet and choose a successor to fill any vacancy (other than a vacancy resulting from a temporary absence of one of the four elected). In the event of any vacancy not yet filled by vote of the partners, the management committee may on its own account call on any qualified partner of its choice to serve temporarily with the committee. The tenure of one so chosen shall expire when the partners elect a successor.

5. The management committee, from the effective date of this instrument, shall consist of A, C and E. The named alternate shall be B. Each of the four shall serve respectively until his or her tenure is terminated by death, resignation, disqualification, or a determination by vote of the partners that the term shall expire.

6. The tenure of every member of the committee and every alternate member shall be subject to termination without cause, by requisite vote of the partners in accordance with the provisions of Article IV of this document.

Section B. Functioning of the Management Committee and Its Subcommittees. 1. Members of the management committee shall make every reasonable effort to keep each other and the alternate advised of all pending problems, prospective decisions, and actions taken. Action of the committee shall be by majority vote. It shall not be necessary that any notice be given of the time or place of decision or of the matter to be decided. Any decision of the committee may be reversed prospectively by any subsequent action of the committee.

2. Though the committee has no obligation so to do, it may refer any matter on which all members of the committee are not in agreement to a meeting of the partners for decision.

Section C. Membership in Subcommittees of the Management Committee. The management committee shall decide what subcommittees there shall be from time to time, how many members (one or more) there shall be of each subcommittee, who the members shall be, and what the subcommittee's functions and authority shall be. The management committee may at any time modify or revise prospectively any authorized decision of any subcommittee. Any partner or any full-time employee may be a member of any subcommittee.

ARTICLE VIII. INSURANCE; INVESTMENTS

Section A. Life Insurance. The management committee in its discretion shall determine from time to time what life insurance, if any, shall be carried on the lives of partners for benefit of the firm.

Section B. Other Insurance. The management committee in its discretion shall determine from time to time what other insurance, if any, the firm shall carry.

Section C.   Investments. The management committee in its discretion shall determine from time to time what investments, if any, the firm shall make and all matters with reference to the proceeds of such investments, and with reference to reinvestments or changes in investment policies.

ARTICLE IX. PROPERTIES AND RECORDS

The management committee in its discretion shall make all decisions of the firm from time to time on the following subjects:

Section A.   Firm Properties. [Some firms in their Articles limit the authority of the management committee or its equivalent with respect to properties. Examples:

(i)   Require that the purchase of all properties, except supplies, be approved by partnership vote; or

(ii)   Require such a vote for purchase of properties costing more than a specific amount; or

(iii)   Require such a vote for purchase of an office site or office building or any property not deemed necessary to the practice of law; or

(iv)   Limit the amount to be spent in a year, without a partnership vote for replacements, repairs or upkeep.]

Section B.   Accounting Records. [Many firms have express provisions in their partnership agreements covering one or more of the following points on this subject.

(i)   Specifically requiring that the books of account be kept on a cash basis;

(ii)   Specifically defining the fiscal year of the firm;

(iii)   Specifically defining what financial statements shall be prepared with copies given to each partner;

(iv)   Specifically requiring that partnership income tax returns be prepared and filed regularly and a copy of the same given to each partner a specific period, say at least one week, before each return is filed, and a specific period, say at least two weeks, before his or her personal return is due;

(v)   Specifically requiring that all accounting records of the firm shall be open to inspection by each partner at any time during business hours;

(vi)   Specifically requiring that the financial records of the firm shall be retained for an agreed period and shall be available for inspection or copying by anyone who was a partner at the time that such records were prepared, including one who at the time of the inspection is a former partner.]

ARTICLE X. TERMINATION AND LIQUIDATION OF FIRM

Section A.   Termination of the Firm by Voluntary Vote or Otherwise. The partnership may be terminated at any time by affirmative vote of the partners at a partnership meeting, in accordance with the provisions of Article IV of this Agreement.

Section B.   Pending Employments on Termination. In the event of termination of the partnership, no further services shall be rendered in the partnership name and no further business transacted for the partnership except action necessary for the winding up of its affairs, the distribution or liquidation of its assets, and the distribution of the proceeds of the liquidation. Maintenance of offices to effectuate or facilitate the winding up of the partnership affairs shall not be construed to involve a continuation of the partnership. In advance of the effective date of the termination of the partnership the management committee shall assign every uncompleted service to one or another of the partners on such terms as shall be agreeable to the clients involved and the partners to whom such matters are assigned; and the rendition of services from the effective date of the termination shall henceforth be by such individuals and other law firms, if any, in which they may respectively become partners.

Section C.   Liquidation of Assets. The members of the management committee (but not including alternate members) on the effective date of the termination of the partnership, shall be the agents of the terminated partnership in liquidation, and of the individual partners, for winding up all its affairs and all business transactions of the partnership, other than the performance of incomplete professional services referred to in Section B above. Said members of the management committee shall continue to serve (unless death, incapacity or resignation shall intervene) until the completion of the winding up and liquidation. The committee shall act by majority vote or votes. In the event of any temporary or permanent vacancy in the committee, the remaining members shall choose a third member of the committee. Members of the management committee shall not be paid for their services after the termination of the partnership in the winding up or liquidation operations. They may, out of the assets and proceeds of the assets on hand, employ such assistants as they determine appropriate, and the committee may so employ and pay any one of its members to take any such actions and render any such services in the winding up and liquidation.

Section D.   Prior Opportunity of Partners to Bid for Purchase of Assets Being Liquidated. The partners holding units of participation immediately prior to the termination of the partnership may, in the discretion of the management committee, be given first opportunity over any other prospective bidder for the purchase of any of the assets, all such partners being given an equal opportunity, so that they respectively as individuals or jointly or in groups, may bid; and if the best bid by any of them, in the opinion of the management committee, is at least ninety-five percent of the highest and best bid otherwise received, then such best bid by any partner or partners may be accepted.

Section E.   Distribution of Proceeds from Liquidation. The business affairs of the partnership, in the event of the termination of the partnership, shall be wound up and liquidated as promptly as business circumstances and orderly business practices will permit. After payment of expenses incurred, the net assets and the proceeds of the liquidation shall be applied in the following order:

1.   To the payment of the debts and liabilities of the partnership owing to the creditors other than partners, and the expenses of liquidation.

2.   To the payment of the debts and liabilities owing to the partners other than for (i) capital, (ii) profits and (iii) any unmatured installments yet to be paid on account of the death, permanent disability, retirement (or death following retirement) or withdrawal of a partner. It is agreed that all sums to become due on installments referred to in (iii) shall be assumed ratably by each partner at the date of termination and that each shall thereafter pay his or her ratable share of each such installment as it becomes due.

3.   To the repayment to each of the partners of his or her capital contributions to the firm.

4.   To the payment to partners (computed on the basis of their respective units of participation at the date of termination of the firm) of all the remaining net of assets and proceeds, if any, first in whatever amounts are necessary to complete a ratable distribution for the current year, to each partner to the full extent of distributions previously received by each other partner; and second, to ratable distributions to all partners.

5.   If the assets and proceeds of the liquidation are insufficient to pay all of the items referred to in paragraphs 1 and 2, but not including (i), (ii) and (iii) referred to in paragraph 2, then the management committee shall make an

assessment against the partners to cover net losses of the firm and such assessments shall be paid and applied to the satisfaction of the items covered by paragraphs 1 and 2.

ARTICLE XI. LEGAL EFFECT OF PROVISIONS; ARBITRATION

Section A. Governing Law. All provisions of this Agreement shall be construed, shall be given effect and shall be enforced according to the laws of the State of _____ .

Section B. Persons Bound. Each of the partners executes this Agreement with the understanding and agreement that each has hereby bound and obligated himself or herself, his or her estate, and any and all claiming by, through, or under him or her.

Section C. Rights of Partners Not Assignable; Not to Be Pledged. No partner and no one acting by authority of or for a partner may pledge, hypothecate, or in any manner transfer the partner's interest in the partnership, or the partner's interest in any of its assets, receivables, records, documents, files, or clientele, all such rights and interests of each partner being personal to him or her and nontransferable and nonassignable (except that other partners of the firm may succeed to such rights or some of them in accordance with the terms of this Agreement).

Section D. Finality of Decisions within the Firm; Effect of Diverse or Adverse Interest of Any Partner. Every final decision of the firm on any matter affecting any party hereto or anyone claiming by, through or under any party, by vote of the partners or by decision of the management committee, when in accordance with the terms and provisions of this Agreement, shall be binding and conclusive. Except where it is expressly provided in this Agreement that one shall not be permitted to vote as to any such decision, there shall be no disqualification of anyone from voting who shall be entitled to vote according to the terms and provisions of this Agreement, notwithstanding any adverse or divergent interest that he or she may personally have in the decision; and the decision shall, nevertheless, be binding and final notwithstanding any such adverse or divergent interest held by anyone so voting. It is understood that individual partners and that members of the management committee will doubtless have divergent and may have adverse, or arguably adverse, personal interests from one another on some matters that are to be determined according to the provisions of this Agreement and have diverse or adverse interests personally from those of some party affected by the decision; all this is agreed to and waived as a disqualification. Nonetheless, anyone entitled to such a vote on any such matter may recuse himself or herself from voting, and thereupon the decision shall be made on the computation of votes to the same effect as if the one so recusing himself or herself had, as to that matter, no right to vote; and if the vote is by the partners, as though he or she held no units of participation. Each party having any vote on any such matters shall recuse himself or herself on any vote if requested so to do by joint action of partners holding a majority of the units of participation then outstanding.

Section E. Arbitration. Any controversy or claim arising out of or relating to any provision of this Agreement or the breach thereof, shall be settled by arbitration in accordance with the rules then in effect of the American Arbitration Association, to the extent consistent with the laws of the State of. It is agreed that any party to any award rendered in any such arbitration proceedings may seek a judgment upon the award and that judgment may be entered thereon by any court having jurisdiction.

EXHIBIT J–1.

(continued)

Section F.   Severability. It is agreed that the invalidity or unenforceability of any Article, Section, paragraph or provision of this Agreement shall not affect the validity or enforceability of any one or more of the other Articles, Sections, paragraphs or provisions; and that the parties hereto will execute any further instruments or perform any acts which are or may be necessary to effectuate all and each of the terms and provisions of this agreement.

ARTICLE XII.   AMENDMENTS

An amendment hereto may alter, revise, delete or add to any provision or provisions of this agreement. No amendment to this instrument shall be adopted or become effective unless and until it (i) has been voted in accordance with the provisions of paragraph 3 of Section B of Article IV of this Agreement; and (ii) has been executed and attached to this Agreement as a part of same.

In Witness Whereof, the parties have signed this Agreement.

[Signatures]*

*Adapted from West's Modern Legal Forms § 6257. The original agreement was prepared by Paul Carrington and William A. Sutherland for the American Bar Association Standing Committee on Economics of Law Practice, and was printed in the ABA Economics of Law Practice Series Pamphlet Number 6, November 1961. The authors emphasized the need to tailor each partnership agreement to the clients, and cautioned their readers to consider the various provisions of this agreement as merely suggestions for comparison and study.

EXHIBIT J–2.

Limited Partnership Agreement

Agreement of Limited Partnership made this _____day of _____, 20_____, between _____and _____, both of _____(herein referred to as general partners), and _____of _____, and _____of _____(herein referred to as limited partners).

1.   **Formation.** The parties hereby form a limited partnership pursuant to sections _____of the [Revised Statutes] of the State of _____, known as the Uniform Limited Partnership Act.

2.   **Certificate.** The parties shall forthwith sign and swear to a certificate prepared in accordance with the provisions of the Uniform Limited Partnership Act cited above, and cause the same to be filed for record in the office of [*here designate the proper office*].

3.   **Name.** The name of the partnership is _____.

4.   **Business.** The purpose of the partnership shall be to engage in the business of _____, and in any other business necessary and related to it.

5.   **Place of Business.** The principal place of business of the partnership shall be at _____, but additional places of business may be established as the general partners shall determine.

6.   **Term.** The partnership shall commence on _____, 20_____, and shall continue until terminated as herein provided.

7.   **Capital.** The initial capital of the partnership shall be $_____. Each of the partners shall contribute in cash or in property the amount set opposite the partner's name.

General Partners	Cash Contributions	Agreed Value of Property Contributions
_____	$_____	$_____
_____	_____	_____
Limited Partners	_____	_____
_____	_____	_____

The property contributed is described in a separate instrument attached hereto as Exhibit A.

8. **Additional Contributions to Capital.** The general partners shall make, and the limited partners shall each have the option of making, additional contributions to the capital of the partnership in such amount as the general partners deem necessary to carry on the business of the partnership.

9. **Withdrawal of Capital.** Neither a general nor a limited partner may withdraw all or any part of his or her capital contribution without the consent of all the general partners, provided that each limited partner may rightfully demand the return of all or part of his or her contribution after he or she has given six months' notice in writing to all the other partners. Upon any withdrawal by a limited partner the certificate of limited partnership shall be amended to reflect this change in his or her capital contribution.

10. **Profits and Losses.** The net profits of the partnership during each fiscal year shall be credited, and the net losses incurred by the partnership during any fiscal year shall be debited, as of the close thereof, to the capital accounts of the partners in the proportions set opposite their respective names.

General Partners	Percentage
_____	_____ %
_____	_____ %
Limited Partners	
_____	_____ %
_____	_____ %

Notwithstanding anything to the contrary herein contained, no limited partner shall be liable for any of the debts of the partnership or any of its losses in excess of his or her capital contributions to the partnership.

11. **Capital Accounts.** An individual capital account shall be maintained for each partner, to which shall be credited his or her contributions to capital and to which shall be debited his or her withdrawals from capital and his or her share of partnership losses.

12. **Salaries.** Each of the general partners shall receive such reasonable salaries as may from time to time be agreed upon by the general partners. These salaries shall be treated as an expense of the partnership in determining the net profit or loss in any fiscal year.

13. **Drawing Accounts.** An individual drawing account may be maintained for each partner in an amount fixed by the general partners, but such drawing accounts shall be in the proportion to which the partners are entitled to share in the profits of the partnership.

14. **Management.** The general partners shall have equal rights in the management of the partnership business.

15. **Devotion to Business.** Each general partner shall devote all his or her normal business time and best efforts to the conduct of the business of the partnership.

16. **Limitations on General Partners' Powers.** No general partner shall, without the written consent or ratification of the specific act by all the other partners:

(a) Assign, transfer, or pledge any of the claims of or debts due to the partnership except upon payment in full, or arbitrate or consent to the arbitration of any disputes or controversies of the partnership;

(b) Make, execute, or deliver any assignment for the benefit of creditors, or sign any bond, confession of judgment, security agreement, deed, guarantee, indemnity bond, surety bond, or contract to sell or contract of sale of all or substantially all profit of the partnership;

(c) Lease or mortgage any part of partnership real estate or any interest therein, or enter into any contract for any such purpose;

(d) Pledge or hypothecate or in any manner transfer his or her interest in the partnership, except to the parties of this agreement;

(e) Become a surety, guarantor, or accommodation party to any obligation except for partnership business;

(f) Do any act prohibited by law to be done by a single partner.

17. **Books of Account.** The partnership shall maintain adequate accounting records. All books, records, and accounts of the partnership shall be kept at its principal place of business and shall be open at all times to inspection by all the partners.

18. **Accounting Basis.** The books of account shall be kept on a cash [*or an accrual*] basis.

19. **Fiscal Year.** The fiscal year of the partnership shall be the calendar year. The net profit or net loss of the partnership shall be determined in accordance with generally accepted accounting principles as soon as practicable after the close of each fiscal year.

20. **Annual Audit.** The books of account shall be audited as of the close of each fiscal year by a certified public accountant chosen by all the partners.

21. **Banking.** All the funds of the partnership shall be deposited in its name in such checking account or accounts as shall be designated by the general partners. Checks shall be drawn on such accounts for partnership purposes only and shall be signed by any of the general partners.

22. **Assignment by Limited Partner.** Each limited partner may assign his or her interest in the partnership, and the assignee shall have the right to become a substituted limited partner and entitled to all the rights of the assignor if all the partners (except the assignor) consent thereto. Otherwise the assignee is only entitled to receive the share of the profits to which his or her assignor would be entitled.

23. **Retirement of a General Partner.** A general partner may retire from the partnership at the end of any fiscal year by giving at least 90 days' notice in writing to all the other partners.

24. **Effect of Retirement, Death, or Insanity of a General Partner.** The retirement, death, or insanity of a general partner dissolves the partnership, unless the business is continued by the remaining partners as herein provided.

25. **Distribution of Assets on Dissolution.** Upon dissolution of the partnership by mutual agreement or for any other reason its liabilities to creditors shall be paid in the order of priority provided by law, and the remaining assets, or the proceeds of their sale, shall be distributed in the following order:

(a) To the limited partners in proportion to their share of the profits;

(b) To the limited partners in proportion to their capital contributions;

(c) To the general partners other than for capital and profits;

(d) To the general partners in proportion to their share of the profits;

(e) To the general partners in proportion to their capital contributions.

26. **Election of Remaining Partners to Continue Business.** In the event of the retirement, death, or insanity of a general partner, the remaining partners shall have the right to continue the business of the partnership under its present name either by themselves or in conjunction with any other person or persons they may select, but they shall pay to the retiring partner, or to the legal representatives of the deceased or insane partner, as the case may be, the value of his or her interest in the partnership, as provided in paragraph 28.

27. **Notice of Election to Continue Business.** If the remaining partners elect to continue the business of the partnership, they shall serve notice in writing of

such election upon the retiring partner within two months after receipt of his or her notice of intention to retire, or upon the legal representatives of the deceased or insane partner within three months after the death of the decedent or the adjudication of insanity, as the case may be. If at the time of such election no legal representative has been appointed, notice shall be sent to the last known address of the decedent or insane partner.

28. **Valuation of Partner's Interest.** The value of the interest of a retiring, deceased, or insane partner shall be the sum of the partner's: (a) capital account, (b) drawing account, and (c) proportionate share of accrued net profits. If a net loss has been incurred to the date of dissolution, his or her share of such net loss shall be deducted. The assets of the partnership shall be valued at book value and no value shall be attributed to goodwill.

29. **Payment of Purchase Price.** The value of the partner's interest as determined in the above paragraph shall be paid without interest to the retiring partner, or to the legal representatives of the deceased or insane partner, as the case may be, in _____monthly installments, commencing on the first day of the second month after the effective date of the purchase.

30. **Death of a Limited Partner.** In the event of the death of a limited partner, his or her personal representative during the period of administration of his or her estate shall succeed to his or her rights hereunder as a limited partner, and this interest as a limited partner may be assigned to any member of the family of the limited partner in distribution of his or her estate, or to any person in pursuance of a bequest in his or her last will and testament, and such member of the family [or person, if made by will] to whom such assignment or bequest is made, shall thereupon succeed to his or her interest as a limited partner and have all the rights of a substituted limited partner.

In Witness Whereof, the parties have signed and sealed this agreement.

*[Signatures and seals]**

*Adapted from West's Modern Legal Forms § 6452.

Client: _____

File Number: _____

Date: _____

1. Originating Attorney: _____

    Lead Working Attorney: _____

    Assisting: _____

    Client Contact:

      Name: _____

      Address: _____

      Telephone Number: _____

2. State of Formation: _____

3. Proposed Date of Formation: _____

4. Organizer:

    Name   *Address*

    _____   _____

                            _____

                            _____

NOTE: Only one organizer is necessary for a Colorado limited liability company. To simplify matters, suggest using a firm attorney.

EXHIBIT J–3.

(continued)

5. Name of Limited Liability Company: _____
_____
Alternate Name: _____
Trade Name: _____
6. Should name be reserved? Yes (_____) No(_____)
7. Is going business being formed? Yes(_____) No(_____)
If so, describe additional documents needed (e.g., bill of sale, assignment of liabilities, etc.):_____
_____
_____

8. Principal purpose of Limited Liability Company: _____
_____
_____
_____
_____
_____

9. Principal place of business: _____
_____/_____/ Own /_____/ Lease
10. Qualification in other states required? Yes (_____) No (_____)
If so, what states: _____
_____
_____Check qualification costs
_____Check annual fees and taxes
11. Registered Agent and Office in Colorado: _____
_____
Registered Agent and Office in states in which qualified: _____
_____
_____

NOTE: If a firm attorney not to be registered agent, recommend CT Corporation System. A post office box number is not acceptable as the registered office address.
12. Membership Interests (must be at least two upon formation):
    Name of Member   *Percentage of Profits, Losses, Etc.*
    _____   _____
    _____   _____
    _____   _____

13. Indicate the percentage vote required for the following actions by Members, if other than the standard statutory requirement of majority:
    _____ 1. Amendment to Articles of Organization
    _____ 2. Election of Managers
    _____ 3. Other Voting of Members
    NOTE: Cannot be less than a majority.
14. Managers:
        Name   *Address*
    _____   _____
                                 _____
    _____   _____
                                 _____
    _____   _____
                                 _____

15. Bank: _____
    Signatories: _____
    Limitations: _____
    _____

16. Should the firm obtain banking resolutions? Yes (_____) No (_____)

17. Should the firm obtain employer identification number? Yes (_____)
    No (_____)

18. Date of first meeting of Managers: _____
    _____

19. Annual meeting date and time: _____

20. Fiscal Year:
    Calendar Year? Yes (_____) No (_____) Other (_____)
    To be determined by the Managers: Yes (_____) No (_____)

21. Accountant: _____
    Address: _____
    Telephone: _____

22. Should the firm prepare employment agreement? Yes (_____) No (_____)

23. Should the firm prepare long-form transmittal letter? Yes (_____) No (__)

24. Membership Transfer Restrictions? Yes (_____) No (_____)
    Special Provisions:
      Restriction Covers:
        Sales to outsiders: _____
        Withdrawal or retirement: _____
        Bankruptcy: _____
        Resignation: _____
        Termination of employment: _____ or other
        Death: _____
          Insurance Funded Yes (_____) No (_____)
        Disability: _____
          Insurance Funded Yes (_____) No (_____)
        Insurance Company or Agent: _____
      Option:
        Limited Liability Company: _____
        Other members: _____
        Residual option: _____
      Price:
        Book value: _____
        Earnings multiple: _____
        Appraisal: _____
        Other: _____

[NAME]
A [STATE] LIMITED LIABILITY COMPANY

THIS OPERATING AGREEMENT is made as of this _____day of _____,
20___, by and among the members of _____[Name]_____, a [State] Limited
Liability Company (the "Company"), who have signed this Operating Agreement or have signed a Subscription Agreement agreeing to be obligated by the
terms of this Operating Agreement.

EXHIBIT J–4.

(continued)

EXPLANATORY STATEMENT

This Operating Agreement governs the relationship among members of the Company and between the Company and the members, pursuant to the [State] Limited Liability Company Act, as amended from time to time (the "Act").

In consideration of their mutual promises, covenants, and agreements, and the Explanatory Statement, which Explanatory Statement is incorporated by reference herein and made a substantive part of this Operating Agreement, the parties hereto do hereby promise, covenant, and agree as follows:

DEFINITIONS

Throughout this Operating Agreement, and unless the context otherwise requires, the word or words set forth below within the quotation marks shall be deemed to mean the words which follow them:

A.   "Agreement"—This Operating Agreement.

B.   "Bankruptcy"—The filing by a Member of a petition commencing a voluntary case under the Bankruptcy Code; a general assignment by a Member for the benefit of creditors; an admission in writing by a Member of his or her inability to pay his or her debts as they become due; the filing by a Member of any petition or answer in any proceeding seeking for himself or herself, or consenting to, or acquiescing in, any insolvency, receivership, composition, readjustment, liquidation, dissolution, or similar relief under any present or future statute, law, or regulation, or the filing by a Member of an answer or other pleading admitting or failing to deny, or to contest, the material allegations of the petition filed against him or her in any such proceeding; the seeking or consenting to, or acquiescence by a Member in, the appointment of any trustee, receiver, or liquidator of him or her, or any part of his or her property; and the commencement against a Member of an involuntary case under the Bankruptcy Code, or a proceeding under any receivership, composition, readjustment, liquidation, insolvency, dissolution, or like law or statute, which case or proceeding is not dismissed or vacated within 60 days.

C.   "Company"—___[Name]___, a [State] Limited Liability Company.

D.   "Dissolution"—(1)   In the case of a Member who is acting as a Member by virtue of being a trustee of a trust, the termination of the trust (but not merely the substitution of a new trustee); (2)   in the case of a Member that is a partnership, the dissolution and commencement of winding up of the partnership; (3)   in the case of a Member that is a corporation, the filing of a Certificate of Dissolution, or its equivalent, for the corporation or the revocation of its charter; (4)   in the case of a limited liability company, the filing of Articles of Dissolution, or its equivalent, for the limited liability company, or the involuntary dissolution by a nonappealable order of the district court; or (5)   in the case of an estate, the distribution by the fiduciary of the estate's entire Membership Interest.

E.   "Expulsion"—The final decision of expulsion of a Member as provided in this Operating Agreement.

F.   "Member"—Each of the persons signatory hereto either by signing this Agreement or a Subscription Agreement agreeing to be obligated by the terms of this Agreement and any other person or persons who may subsequently be designated as a Member of this Company pursuant to the further terms of this Agreement.

G.   "Membership Interest"—The share of profits and losses, gains, deductions, credits, cash, assets, and other distributions of a Member.

H.   "Membership Rights"—The rights of a Member which are comprised of a Member's: (1)   Membership Interest, and (2)   right to participate in the management of the Company.

I. "Persons"—Individuals, partnerships, corporations, limited liability companies, unincorporated associations, trusts, estates, and any other types of entities.

J. "Resignation"—The decision or determination of a Member to no longer continue as a Member, upon written notice to the Company.

K. "Retirement"—The withdrawal from the Company upon such times and events as are provided in this Operating Agreement which will permit withdrawal of a Member without violating or breaching the terms of this Operating Agreement.

Section 1.   *Articles of Organization.*

The Articles of Organization of this Company are hereby adopted and incorporated by reference in this Operating Agreement. In the event of any inconsistency between the Articles of Organization and this Operating Agreement, the terms of the [Articles of Organization] or [this Operating Agreement] shall govern.

Section 2.   *Term of This Agreement.*

The term of this Operating Agreement shall be coterminus with the term of the Company. This Operating Agreement shall terminate upon the voluntary or involuntary dissolution of the Company or the expiration of its term as provided in the Articles of Organization.

Section 3.   *Contributions.*

3.1   *Original Contributions.* The original capital contributions to the Company of each of the Members shall be made [in accordance with their respective Subscription Agreements, which shall be effective with their respective execution and delivery of the Subscription Agreements, the terms of which are hereby incorporated by reference as if fully set forth herein] or [concurrently with their respective execution and delivery of this Operating Agreement] in the following dollar amounts set forth after their respective names:

_____	$_____
_____	$_____
_____	$_____]

3.2   *Capital Accounts.* An individual capital account shall be maintained for each Member. The capital account of each Member shall consist of his or her original capital contribution, increased by (a) additional capital contributions made by him or her, and (b) his or her share of Company gains and profits, and decreased by (i) distributions of such profits and capital to him or her, and (ii) his or her share of Company losses.

3.3   *Liability for Contributions.* Each Member is obligated to the Company to perform his or her Subscription Agreement, and any other promise contained in this Operating Agreement to contribute cash or property or perform services, even if he or she is unable to perform because of death, disability, or any other reason. If a Member does not make the contribution required by the Subscription Agreement or this Operating Agreement, the Member is obligated at the option of the Company to contribute cash equal to that portion of the value, as stated in the Subscription Agreement, of such contribution that has not been made.

3.4   *Compromise of a Member's Liability.* The obligation of a Member to make a contribution to the Company may be compromised only by a consent in writing of all of the Members of the Company.

Section 4.   *Profit and Loss.*

4.1   *Percentages.* The percentages of Membership Rights and Membership Interest of each of the Members in the Company shall be as follows:

_____	_____%
_____	_____%
_____	_____%

4.2   *Allocation of Taxable Items.* Except as provided in Section 4.1 of this Agreement, for purposes of Sections 702 and 704 of the Internal Revenue Code of 1986, or the corresponding provisions of any future federal internal revenue law, or any similar tax law of any state or jurisdiction, the determination of each Member's distributive share of all items of income, gain, loss, deduction, credit, or allowance of the Company for any period or year shall be made in accordance with, and in proportion to, such Member's percentage of Membership Interest as it may then exist.

Section 5.   *Distributions.*

5.1   *Cash.* The Net Cash from Operations of the Company shall be distributed at such times as may be determined by the Managers in accordance with Section 8 of this Agreement among the Members in proportion to their respective percentages of Membership Interest.

5.2   *"Net Cash from Operations."* As used in this Section 5, the term "Net Cash from Operations" shall mean:

5.2.1   The taxable income of the Company for federal income tax purposes as shown on the books of the Company increased by (a) the amount of depreciation and amortization deductions taken in computing such taxable income and (b) any nontaxable income or receipts of the Company, and reduced by (i) payments upon the principal of any installment obligations, mortgages, or deeds of trust respecting Company assets or of other Company debts, and (ii) such expenditures for capital improvements or replacements, such reserves for said improvements and replacements, and such reserves for repairs and to meet anticipated expenses and for working capital as the Managers, in accordance with Section 8 of this Agreement, shall deem to be reasonably necessary in the efficient conduct of the business; plus

5.2.2   Any excess funds resulting from the placement, or excess or refinancing of, any mortgages or deeds of trust on Company property or the encumbrancing or financing of such property in any other manner; plus

5.2.3   Any other funds (including amounts previously set aside for reserves by the Managers, in accordance with Section 8 of this Agreement, to the extent the Managers, in accordance with Section 8 of this Agreement, no longer regard such reserves as reasonably necessary in the efficient conduct of the Company business) deemed available for the distribution by the Managers, in accordance with Section 8 of this Agreement.

5.2.4   In determining the amount of Net Cash from Operations, any negative balances in any category described in Sections 5.2.1, 5.2.2, and 5.2.3 shall be netted against the positive balances in the other such categories. Cumulative negative or positive balances shall be carried forward.

5.3   *Other Assets.* In addition to the distributions pursuant to Section 5.1 of this Agreement, upon any sale, transfer, or other disposition of any capital asset of the Company (hereinafter referred to as a "Disposition"), the proceeds of such Disposition shall first be applied to the payment or repayment of any selling or other expenses incurred in connection with the Disposition and to the payment of any indebtedness secured by the asset subject to the Disposition immediately prior thereto; all proceeds remaining thereafter (the "Net Proceeds") shall be retained by the Company or be distributed, at such time or times as shall be determined by the Managers in accordance with Section 8 of this Agreement, to the Members in proportion to their respective percentages of Membership Interest; provided, however, that for purposes of Sections 702 and 704 of the Internal Revenue Code of 1986, or the corresponding provisions of any future federal internal revenue law, or any similar tax law of any state or jurisdiction, each Member's distributive share of all items of income, gain, loss, deduction, credit, or allowance in respect of any such Disposition shall be made and based upon such Member's basis in such capital asset.

Section 6.   *Distributions upon Resignation.*

Upon resignation of a Member, a resigning Member shall be entitled to receive only the distributions to which he or she is entitled under this Operating Agreement, as provided in Section 15.

Section 7.   *Distributions in Kind.*

A Member, regardless of the nature of his or her contribution, has no right to demand and receive any distribution from the Company in any form other than cash. However, a Member shall be required and compelled to accept the distribution of any asset in kind from the Company, as determined from time to time by the Managers, in accordance with Section 8 of this Agreement, regardless of whether the percentage of the asset distributed to him or her exceeds the percentage of that asset which is equal to that Member's Membership Interest in the Company.

Section 8.   *Management of the Company.*

8.1   *Managers.* The business and affairs of the Company shall be managed by its Managers.

8.2   *Duties of Managers.* A Manager of the Company shall perform his or her duties as a Manager, including his or her duties as a member of any committee upon which he or she may serve, in good faith, in a manner he or she reasonably believes to be in the best interests of the Company, and with such care as an ordinarily prudent person in a like position would use under similar circumstances. In performing his or her duties, a Manager shall be entitled to rely on information, opinions, reports, or statements, including financial statements and other financial data, in each case prepared or presented by persons and groups listed in paragraphs (a), (b), and (c) of this Section 8.2; but he or she shall not be considered to be acting in good faith if he or she has knowledge concerning the matter in question that would cause such reliance to be unwarranted. A person who so performs his or her duties shall not have any liability by reason of being or having been a Manager of the Company. Those persons and groups whose information, opinions, reports, and statements a Manager is entitled to rely upon are:

(a)   One or more employees or other agents of the Company whom the Manager reasonably believes to be reliable and competent in the matters presented;

(b)   Counsel, public accountants, or other persons as to matters which the Manager reasonably believes to be within such persons' professional or expert competence; and

(c)   A committee appointed by the Managers upon which he or she does not serve, duly designated in accordance with the provision of this Operating Agreement, as to matters within its designated authority, which committee the Manager reasonably believes to merit confidence.

8.3   *Number of Managers.* The number of Managers of the Company shall be _____. Each Manager shall hold office until the next annual meeting of Members or until his or her successor shall have been elected and qualified. Managers need not be residents of the State of [State] or Members of the Company.

8.4   *Regular Meetings.* A regular meeting of the Managers shall be held without the requirement of any other notice immediately after, and at the same place as, the annual meeting of Members. The Managers may provide, by resolution, the time and place, either within or without the State of [State], for the holding of additional regular meetings without other notice than such resolution.

8.5   *Special Meetings.* Special meetings of the Managers may be called by or at the request of any two Managers. The persons calling the special meetings of the Managers may fix any place, either within or without the State of [State], as the place for holding any special meeting of the Managers called by them.

8.6   *Notice.* Written notice of any special meeting of Managers shall be given as follows:

(a)   By mail to each Manager at his or her business address at least three days prior to the meeting; or

(b)   By personal delivery, telegram, or telecopy at least twenty-four hours prior to the meeting to the business address of each Manager, or in the event such notice is given on a Saturday, Sunday, or holiday, to the residence address of each Manager.

If mailed, such notice shall be deemed to be delivered when deposited in the United States mail, so addressed, with postage thereon prepaid. If given by telegram, such notice shall be deemed to be delivered when the telegram is delivered to the telegraph company. If delivered by telecopy, such notice shall be deemed to be delivered when a confirmation of receipt of the telecopy is printed by the sending telecopier. Any Manager may waive notice of any meeting. The attendance of a Manager at any meeting shall constitute a waiver of notice of such meeting, except where a Manager attends a meeting for the express purpose of objecting to the transaction of any business because the meeting is not lawfully called or convened. Neither the business to be transacted at, nor the purpose of, any regular of special meeting of the Managers need be specified in the notice or waiver of notice of such meeting. When any notice is required to be given to a Manager, a waiver thereof in writing signed by such Manager, whether before, at or after the time stated therein, shall constitute the giving of such notice.

8.7   *Quorum.* A majority of the number of Managers fixed by or pursuant to Section 8.3 of this Agreement shall constitute a quorum for the transaction of business at any meeting of the Managers, but if less than such majority is present at a meeting, a majority of the Managers present may adjourn the meeting from time to time without further notice.

8.8   *Manner of Acting.* The act of the majority of the Managers present at a meeting at which a quorum is present shall be the act of the Managers.

8.9   *Informal Action by Managers.* Any action required or permitted to be taken at a meeting of the Managers or any committee designated by the Managers may be taken without a meeting if the action is evidenced by one or more written consents describing the action taken, signed by each Manager or committee member, and delivered to the person having custody of the Company records for inclusion in the minutes or for filing with the records. Action taken under this section is effective when all Managers or committee members have signed the consent, unless the consent specifies a different effective date. Such consent has the same force and effect as an unanimous vote of the Managers or committee members and may be stated as such in any document.

8.10   *Participation by Electronic Means.* Any Manager or any committee designated by the Managers may participate in a meeting of the Managers or committee by means of telephone conference or similar communications equipment by which all persons participating in the meeting can hear each other at the same time. Such participation shall constitute presence in person at the meeting.

8.11   *Vacancies.* Any vacancy occurring in the Managers may be filled by the affirmative vote of a majority of the remaining Managers though less than a quorum of the Managers. A Manager elected to fill a vacancy shall be elected for the unexpired term of his or her predecessor in office. Any Manager position to be filled by reason of an increase in the number of Managers may be filled by election by the Managers for a term of office continuing only until the next election of Managers by the Members.

8.12 *Resignation.* Any Manager of the Company may resign at any time by giving written notice to the Company. The resignation of any Manager shall take effect upon receipt of notice thereof or at such later time as shall be specified in such notice; and, unless otherwise specified therein, the acceptance of such resignation shall not be necessary to make it effective. When one or more Managers shall resign, effective at a future date, a majority of the Managers then in office, including those who have so resigned, shall have power to fill such vacancy or vacancies, the vote thereon to take effect when such resignation or resignations shall become effective.

8.13 *Removal.* Any Manager or Managers of the Company may be removed at any time, with or without cause, by a vote of the majority of the Members then entitled to vote at an election of Managers.

8.14 *Committees.* By resolution adopted by a majority of the Managers, the Managers may designate two or more Managers to constitute a committee, any of which shall have such authority in the management of the Company as the Managers shall designate.

8.15 *Compensation.* By resolution of the Managers and irrespective of any personal interest of any of the Managers, each Manager may be paid his or her expenses, if any, of attendance at each meeting of the Managers, and may be paid a stated salary as Manager or a fixed sum for attendance at each meeting of the Managers or both. No such payment shall preclude any Manager from serving the Company in any other capacity and receiving compensation therefor.

8.16 *Presumption of Assent.* A Manager of the Company who is present at a meeting of the Managers or committee thereof, at which action on any matter is taken, shall be presumed to have assented to the action taken unless such Manager objects at the beginning of such meeting to the holding of the meeting or to the transacting of business at the meeting, unless his or her dissent is entered in the minutes of the meeting, or unless he or she shall file a written dissent to such action with the presiding officer of the meeting before the adjournment thereof or shall forward such dissent by registered mail to the Company immediately after the adjournment of the meeting. Such right to dissent shall not apply to a Manager who voted in favor of such action.

8.17 *Transactions with Company and Otherwise.* Any of the Managers, or any agent, servant, or employee of any of the Managers, may engage in and possess any interest in other businesses or ventures of every nature and description, independently or with other persons, whether or not, directly or indirectly, in competition with the business or purpose of the Company, and neither the Company nor any of the Members shall have any rights, by virtue of this Agreement or otherwise, in and to such independent ventures or the income or profits derived therefrom, or any rights, duties, or obligations in respect thereof. A Manager may lend money to, act as surety for, and transact other business with the Company and shall have the same rights and obligations with respect thereto as a person who is not a Manager of the Company, except that nothing contained in this section shall be construed to relieve a Manager from any of his or her duties to the Company.

Section 9. *Members.*

9.1 *Original Members.* The Original Members of this Company shall be those persons who [signed subscription agreements, adopting and agreeing to be bound by this Operating Agreement, prior to or contemporaneous with the date of this Operating Agreement] or [those persons who have signed this Operating Agreement].

9.2   *Admission of New Members.* After the filing of this Company's original Articles of Organization, a person may be admitted as an additional member upon the written consent of all Members.

9.3   *Annual Meeting.* [The annual meeting of the Members shall be held on the _____day of _____in each year, commencing with the year 20__ , at the hour of _____ , or at such other time on such other day as shall be fixed by the Managers,] or [The annual meeting of the shareholders shall be held at such time on such day as shall be fixed by the Managers, commencing with the year 20__ ,] for the purpose of electing Managers and for the transaction of such other business as may come before the meeting. If the day fixed for the annual meeting shall be a legal holiday in the State of [State], such meeting shall be held on the next succeeding business day. If the election of Managers shall not be held on the day designated herein for any annual meeting of the Members, or at any adjournment thereof, the Managers shall cause the election to be held at a special meeting of the Members as soon thereafter as may be convenient.

9.4   *Special Meetings.* Special meetings of the Members, for any purpose or purposes, unless otherwise prescribed by statute, may be called by the Managers, and by not less than one-tenth of all Members entitled to vote at the meeting.

9.5   *Place of Meetings.* The Managers may designate any place, either within or outside of the State of [State], as the place of meeting for any annual meeting or for any special meeting called by the Managers. If no designation is made, or if a special meeting is otherwise called, the place of meeting shall be the principal office of the Company in the State of [State].

9.6   *Notice of Meeting.* Written notice stating the place, day, and hour of the meeting of Members and, in case of a special meeting, the purpose or purposes for which the meeting is called, shall be delivered not less than ten nor more than fifty days before the date of the meeting, either personally or by mail, by or at the direction of the Managers or other persons calling the meeting, to each Member of record entitled to vote at such meeting. If mailed, such notice shall be deemed to be delivered when deposited in the United States mail, addressed to the Member at his or her address as it appears on the books of the Company, with postage thereon prepaid. If three successive letters mailed to the last-known address of any Member of record are returned as undeliverable, no further notices to such Member shall be necessary until another address for such Member is delivered in writing to the Company.

9.7   *Meeting of All Members.* If all of the Members shall meet at any time and place, either within or outside of the State of [State], and consent to the holding of a meeting at such time and place, such meeting shall be valid without call or notice, and at such meeting any action of the Members may be taken.

9.8   *Quorum.* A majority of the Members entitled to vote, represented in person or by proxy, shall constitute a quorum at any meeting of Members. In the absence of a quorum at any such meeting, a majority of the Members so represented may adjourn the meeting from time to time for a period not to exceed thirty days without further notice. However, if the adjournment is for more than thirty days, a notice of the adjourned meeting shall be given to each Member of record entitled to vote at the meeting. At such adjourned meeting at which a quorum shall be present or represented, any business may be transacted which might have been transacted at the meeting as originally noticed. The

Members present at a duly organized meeting may continue to transact business until adjournment, notwithstanding the withdrawal during such meeting of that number of Members whose absence would cause there to be less than a quorum.

9.9 *Manner of Acting.* If a quorum is present, the affirmative vote of the majority of the Members represented at the meeting and entitled to vote on the subject matter shall be the act of the Members.

9.10 *Proxies.* At all meetings of Members, a Member may vote in person or by proxy executed in writing by the Member or by a duly authorized attorney-in-fact. Such proxy shall be filed with the Company before or at the time of the meeting. No proxy shall be valid after eleven months from the date of its execution, unless otherwise provided in the proxy.

9.11 *Voting of Members.* Each Member entitled to vote shall be entitled to one vote upon each matter submitted to a vote at a meeting of Members.

9.12 *Voting by Certain Members.*

9.12.1 Membership Interests owned in the name of a corporation may be voted by such officer, agent, or proxy as the Bylaws of such corporation may prescribe or, in the absence of such provision, as the Board of Directors of such corporation may determine.

9.12.2 Membership Interests owned in the name of a deceased person, a minor ward, or an incompetent person may be voted by an administrator, executor, court-appointed guardian, or conservator, either in person or by proxy, without a transfer of such Membership Interests into the name of such administrator, executor, court-appointed guardian, or conservator. Membership Interests owned in the name of a trustee may be voted by him or her, either in person or by proxy, but no trustee shall be entitled to vote Membership Interests held by him or her without a transfer of such Membership Interests into his or her name.

9.12.3 Membership Interests owned in the name of a receiver may be voted by such receiver and Membership Interests held by or under the control of a receiver may be voted by such receiver, either in person or by proxy, but no receiver shall be entitled to vote Membership Interests without a transfer thereof into the receiver's name.

9.12.4 A Member whose Membership Interests are pledged shall be entitled to vote such Membership Interests until the Membership Interests have been transferred into the name of the pledgee, and thereafter the pledgee shall be entitled to vote the Membership Interests so transferred.

9.12.5 If Membership Interests are owned in the names of two or more persons, whether fiduciaries, members of a partnership, joint tenants, tenants in common, tenants by the entirety, or otherwise, or if two or more persons have the same fiduciary relationship respecting the same Membership Interests, voting with respect to the Membership Interests shall have the following effect:

(a) If only one person votes, his or her act binds all;

(b) If two or more persons vote, the act of the majority so voting binds all;

(c) If two or more persons vote but the vote is evenly split on any particular matter, each faction may vote the Membership Interest in question proportionately, or any person voting the Membership Interest of a beneficiary, if any, may apply to any court of competent jurisdiction in the State of [State] to appoint an additional person to act with the persons so voting the Membership Interest. The Membership Interest shall then be voted as determined by a majority of such persons and the person appointed by the court. If a tenancy is held in unequal interests, a majority or even split for the purpose of this subparagraph (c) shall be a majority or even split in interest.

9.13   *Action by Members without a Meeting.* Action required or permitted to be taken at a meeting of Members may be taken without a meeting if the action is evidenced by one or more written consents describing the action taken, signed by each Member entitled to vote, and delivered to the Managers for filing with the Company records. Action taken under this section is effective when all Members entitled to vote have signed the consent, unless the consent specifies a different effective date.

9.14   *Voting by Ballot.* Voting on any question or in any election may be by voice vote unless the Managers or any Member shall demand that voting be by ballot.

9.15   *Waiver of Notice.* When any notice is required to be given to any Member, a waiver thereof in writing signed by the person entitled to such notice, whether before, at, or after the time stated therein, shall be equivalent to the giving of such notice. The attendance of a Member at any meeting shall constitute a waiver of notice, waiver of objection to defective notice of such meeting, and a waiver of objection to the consideration of a particular matter at the meeting unless the Member, at the beginning of the meeting, objects to the holding of the meeting, the transaction of business at the meeting, or the consideration of a particular matter at the time it is presented at the meeting.

Section 10.   *Banking.*

All revenues of the Company shall be deposited regularly in the Company savings and checking accounts at such bank or banks as shall be selected by the Managers in accordance with Section 8 of this Agreement, and the signatures of such Managers as shall be determined in accordance with Section 8 of this Agreement shall be honored for banking purposes, including other than the extension of credit to, or the borrowing of money by or on behalf of, the Company.

Section 11.   *Books; Fiscal Year; Audits.*

Accurate and complete books of account shall be kept by the Managers and entries promptly made therein of all of the transactions of the Company, and such books of account shall be open at all times to the inspection and examination of the Managers and Members. The books shall be kept on the basis of accounting selected by the accountant regularly servicing the Company, and the fiscal year of the Company shall be the calendar year. A compilation, review, or audit of the Company, as shall be determined by the Managers in accordance with Section 8 of this Agreement, shall be made as of the closing of each fiscal year of the Company by the accountants who shall then be engaged by the Company.

Section 12.   *Membership Interest and Membership Rights of a Deceased, Incompetent, or Dissolved Member.*

If a Member who is an individual dies or a court of competent jurisdiction adjudges him or her to be incompetent to manage his or her person or his or her property, the Member's executor, administrator, guardian, conservator, or other legal representative may exercise all of the Member's rights and receive the benefits of the Member's Membership Interest for the purpose of settling the Member's estate or administering the Member's property. If a Member is a corporation, trust, partnership, limited liability company, or other entity and is dissolved or terminated, the powers of that Member may be exercised by its legal representative or successor.

Section 13.   *Transfer of Membership Interest and Membership Rights.*

Except as otherwise provided in Sections 14, 15, and 16 hereof, no Member (the "Offering Member") shall sell, hypothecate, pledge, assign, or otherwise transfer with or without consideration ("Transfer") any part or all of his or her Membership Interest or Membership Rights in the Company to any other person (a "Transferee"), without first offering (the "Offer") that portion of his or her Membership Interest and Membership Rights in the Company subject to the contemplated transfer (the "Offered Interest") first to the Company, and secondly, to the other Members, at a purchase price (hereinafter referred to as the "Transfer Purchase Price") and in a manner as follows:

13.1   *Transfer Purchase Price.* The Transfer Purchase Price shall be the Appraised Value (as defined in Section 18.1).

13.2   *Offer.*

13.2.1   The Offer shall be made by the Offering Member first to the Company by written notice (hereinafter referred to as the "Offering Notice"). Within twenty (20) days (the "Company Offer Period") after receipt by the Company of the Offering Notice, the Company shall notify the Offering Member in writing (the "Company Notice"), whether or not the Company shall accept the Offer and shall purchase all but not less than all of the Offered Interest. If the Company accepts the Offer to purchase the Offered Interest, the Company Notice shall fix a closing date not more than twenty-five (25) days (the "Company Closing Date") after the expiration of the Company Offer Period.

13.2.2   In the event the Company decides not to accept the Offer, the Offering Member or the Company, at his or her or its election, shall, by written notice (the "Remaining Member Notice") given within that period (the "Member Offer Period") terminating ten (10) days after the expiration of the Company Offer Period, make the Offer of the Offered Interest to the other Members, each of whom shall then have a period of twenty-five (25) days (the "Member Acceptance Period") after the expiration of the Member Offer Period within which to notify in writing the Offering Member whether or not he or she intends to purchase all but not less than all of the Offered Interest. If two (2) or more Members of the Company desire to accept the Offer to purchase the Offered Interest, then, in the absence of an agreement between them, such Members shall have the right to purchase the Offered Interest in the proportion which their respective percentage of Membership Interest in the Membership bears to the percentage of Membership Interest of all of the Members who desire to accept the Offer. If the other Members intend to accept the Offer and to purchase the Offered Interest, the written notice required to be given by them shall fix a closing date not more than ten (10) days after the expiration of the Member Acceptance Period (hereinafter referred to as the "Member Closing Date").

13.3   *Payment.* The aggregate dollar amount of the Transfer Purchase Price shall be payable in cash on the Company Closing Date or on the Member Closing Date, as the case may be, unless the Company or the purchasing Members shall elect prior to or on the Company Closing Date or the Member Closing Date, as the case may be, to purchase such Offered Interest in installments pursuant to the provisions of Section 19 hereof.

13.4   *Free Transfer Period.* If the Company or the other Members fail to accept the Offer or, if the Offer is accepted by the Company or the other Members and the Company or the other Members fail to purchase all of the Offered Interest at the Transfer Purchase Price within the time and in the manner specified in this Section 13, then the Offering Member shall be free, for a period (hereinafter referred to as the "Free Transfer Period") of sixty (60) days from the occurrence of such failure, to transfer the Offered Interest to a Transferee; provided, however, that if all of the other Members other than the Offering Member do not approve of the proposed transfer by unanimous written consent, the Transferee of the Offered Interest shall have no right to participate in the management of the business and affairs of the Company or to become a Member. The Transferee shall only be entitled to receive the share of profits or other compensation by way of income and the return of contributions to which the Offering Member would otherwise have been entitled. In the event that the other Members approve the Transfer by unanimous written consent, any such Transferee, upon acquiring the Offered Interest, shall automatically be bound by the terms of this Agreement and shall be required to join in, execute, acknowledge, seal, and deliver a copy of this Agreement as a result of which he or she shall become a substituted Member. If the Offering Member shall not transfer the Offered Interest within the Free Transfer Period, his or her right to transfer the Offered Interest free of the foregoing restrictions shall thereupon cease and terminate.

13.5   *No Dissolution.* No transfer made pursuant to this Section 13 shall dissolve or terminate the Company or cause the Company to be dissolved, but, instead, the business of the Company shall be continued as if such Transfer had not occurred.

Section 14.   *Death of a Member.*

14.1   *Purchase of Decedent's Interest.* Upon the death of any Member (the "Decedent") so long as there are at least two surviving Members who consent to do so, the Company shall neither be dissolved nor wound up, but, instead, the business of the Company shall be continued as if such death had not occurred. Each Member shall have the right by testamentary disposition to bequeath all or any portion of his or her percentage of Membership Interest and Membership Rights in the Company to a member of his or her immediate family (as defined in Section 21) or to any trust in which any one or more members of his or her immediate family (as defined in Section 21) retain the full beneficial interest; provided, however, that in the case of any such bequest, the legatee or legatees shall hold the percentage of Membership Interest and Membership Rights received as a result of such bequest subject to the terms of this Agreement and, if the other Members unanimously consent in writing, shall be required to join in and execute, acknowledge, seal, and deliver a copy of this Agreement as a substituted Member. In the event that: (a) all or any portion of the percentage of Membership Interest and Membership Rights owned by a Decedent at the time of his or her death shall not be bequeathed by testamentary disposition or shall be bequeathed to one or more persons other than those persons to whom such a bequest is permitted under the foregoing provisions of this Section 14.1; or (b) all or any portion of the percentage of Membership Interest and Membership Rights owned by a Decedent at the time of his or her death shall be bequeathed by testamentary disposition to one or more persons (collectively the "Heir") to whom such a bequest is permitted under the foregoing provisions of this Section 14.1, and (i) the Heir shall notify in writing the Company within six months of the date of death of the Decedent that the Heir desires to sell to the Company the said percentage of Membership Interest and Membership Rights so bequeathed to the Heir or (ii) the Heir shall die (hereinafter all or any portion of the percentage of Membership Interest and Membership Rights referred to in Section 14.1(a) and (b) shall be collectively referred to as the "Decedent Interest"), then the Company shall purchase and the Decedent's personal representatives, the Heir, or the personal representatives of the Heir, as the case may be, shall sell the Decedent Interest. The Company shall, by written notice addressed to the Decedent's personal representatives, the Heir, or the personal representatives of the Heir, as the case may be, fix a closing date for such purchase; the closing date shall not be less than ten (10) days after the appointment of such personal representatives, but in no event longer than one (1) year after the date of death of the Decedent or of the Heir, as the case may be. The Company shall purchase the Decedent Interest on the closing date at a price (hereinafter referred to as the "Decedent Purchase Price") which shall be the Appraised Value (as defined in Section 18.1).

14.2 *Payment.* The aggregate dollar amount of the Decedent Purchase Price shall be payable in cash on the closing date, unless the Company shall elect prior to or on the closing date to purchase the Decedent Interest in installments as provided in Section 19 hereof.

Section 15.   *Bankruptcy, Retirement, or Resignation of a Member.*

15.1 *Purchase of Membership Interest.* Upon the Bankruptcy, Retirement, or Resignation of any Member (the "Withdrawing Member"), the Company shall neither be terminated nor wound up, but, instead, the business of the Company shall be continued as if such Bankruptcy, Retirement, or Resignation, as the case may be, had not occurred, and the Company shall purchase and the Withdrawing Member shall sell all of the Membership Interest and Membership Rights (the "Withdrawing Member's Interest") owned by the Withdrawing Member in the Company on the date of such Bankruptcy, Retirement, or Resignation (the "Withdrawal Date"). The Company shall, by written notice addressed to the Withdrawing Member or to the legal representative of a bankrupt Member, fix a closing date for such purchase which shall be not less than seventy-five (75) days after the Withdrawal Date. The Withdrawing Member's Interest shall be purchased by the Company on such closing date at a price (the "Withdrawing Purchase Price") which shall be the Appraised Value (as defined in Section 18.1 of this Agreement).

15.2 *Payment.* The aggregate dollar amount of the Withdrawing Purchase Price shall be payable in cash on the closing date, unless the Company shall elect prior to or on the closing date to purchase the Withdrawing Member's Interest in installments as provided in Section 19 of this Agreement.

15.3 *Consequences of Bankruptcy, Retirement, or Resignation.* Retirement of a Member shall not be considered to be a breach or default of this Agreement so long as a Member meets the following criteria: [state the qualifications for Permitted Retirement] ("Permitted Retirement"). Bankruptcy, Resignation, and Retirement, other than Permitted Retirement, of a Member shall be regarded as a breach and default of this Agreement, and the Company may withhold and set off from the Withdrawing Purchase Price any damages incurred by the Company, including, but not limited to, the costs of complying with the provisions of this Agreement to determine and fix the Withdrawing Purchase Price, from the amount paid to the Withdrawing Member.

Section 16.   *Expulsion of a Member.*

16.1 *Basis for Expulsion and Purchase.* A Member shall be expelled (the "Expelled Member"), if the Member:

16.1.1   Shall have filed against him or her any tax lien respecting all or substantially all of his or her property and such tax lien shall not be discharged, removed, or bonded within sixty (60) days of the date on which it was filed; or

16.1.2 Shall subject his or her Membership Interest or Membership Rights or any part thereof or interest therein to a charging order entered by any court of competent jurisdiction;

[state other reasons]

Then, so long as there are at least two or more remaining Members who consent to the continuation of the business of the Company, immediately upon the occurrence of any of the said events (the "Occurrence Date"), the Company shall have the right and option, exercisable by written notice to the Expelled Member, within thirty (30) days of the Occurrence Date, to purchase from the Expelled Member, who shall sell to the Company, all of the Membership Interest and Membership Rights (the "Expelled Member's Interest") owned by the Expelled Member in the Company on the Occurrence Date. The Company shall, by written notice delivered to the Expelled Member or his or her successors, fix a closing date for such purchase which shall be not less than forty (40) days after the Occurrence Date, but in no event longer than seventy-five (75) days after the Occurrence Date. The Expelled Member's Interest shall be purchased by the Company on such closing date at a price (the "Expelled Member's Purchase Price") which shall be the Appraised Value (as defined in Section 18.1 of this Agreement).

16.2   *Payment.* The aggregate dollar amount of the Expelled Member's Purchase Price shall be payable in cash on the closing date, unless the Company shall elect prior to or on the closing date to purchase the Expelled Member's Interest in installments as provided in Section 19 of this Agreement.

Section 17.   *Certain Tax Aspects Incident to Transactions Contemplated by This Agreement.*

It is the intention of the parties that the Transfer Purchase Price, the Decedent Purchase Price, the Withdrawing Purchase Price, and the Expelled Member's Purchase Price shall constitute and be considered as made in exchange for the interest of a partner in partnership property, including goodwill, within the meaning of Section 736(b) of the Internal Revenue Code of 1986, as amended.

Section 18.   *The Appraised Value.*

18.1   *"Appraised Value."* The term "Appraised Value," as used in this Agreement, shall be the dollar amount equal to the product obtained by multiplying (a)   the percentage of Membership Interest and Membership Rights owned by a Member by (b)   the Fair Market Value of the Company's assets, as determined in accordance with Section 18.2, minus the liabilities of the Company.

18.2   *Fair Market Value.* The Fair Market Value of the Company's assets shall be determined in the following manner:

18.2.1   Within thirty (30) days of the date of the Offering Notice, date of death of Decedent, the Withdrawal Date, or the Occurrence Date, as the case may be, the Managers shall select an appraiser (the "Company Appraiser") to determine the Fair Market Value of the Company's assets, and the Company Appraiser shall submit his or her determination thereof within thirty (30) days after the date of his or her selection (the "Appraisal Due Date").

18.2.2   If the appraisal made by the Company Appraiser is unsatisfactory to the Offering Member, the personal representatives of the Decedent or Heir, the Withdrawing Member, or the Expelled Member, as the case may be, then within fifteen (15) days after the date of the Appraisal Due Date, the Offering Member, the personal representatives of the Decedent or Heir, the Withdrawing Member, or the Expelled Member, as the case may be, shall select an appraiser (the "Member's Appraiser") to determine the Fair Market Value of the Company's assets, and such appraiser shall submit his or her determination thereof within thirty (30) days after the date of his or her selection.

18.2.3   If the appraisal made by the Member's Appraiser is unsatisfactory to the Managers, then the Company Appraiser and the Member's Appraiser shall select a third appraiser (the "Appraiser") to determine the Fair Market Value of the Company's assets, and such Appraiser shall submit his or her determination thereof within thirty (30) days after the date of his or her selection. The Appraiser's determination thereof shall be binding upon the

Company, the remaining Members and the Offering Member, the personal representatives of the Decedent or Heir, the Withdrawing Member, or the Expelled Member, as the case may be.

18.3   *Qualifications of Appraiser.* Any and all appraisers selected in accordance with the provisions of this Section 18 shall be appraisers who conduct their business in the same location as the Company property is located, who shall conduct appraisals provided for in this Section 18 in accordance with generally accepted appraising standards. Any and all costs incurred in connection with any of the appraisals provided for in this Section 18 shall be borne equally by the Company, and the Offering Member, the personal representatives of the Decedent or Heir, or the Withdrawing or Expelled Member, as the case may be.

Section 19.   *Installment of Payments.*

19.1   *Election to Pay by Installment.* In the event that there shall be an election pursuant to the provisions of Sections 13.2, 14.2, 15.2, or 16.2 hereof to purchase (the Member or the Company so purchasing shall be hereinafter, where appropriate, referred to as the "Purchasing Person") the Offering Member's Interest, the Decedent's Interest, the Withdrawing Member's Interest, or the Expelled Member's Interest, as the case may be (hereinafter, where appropriate, referred to as the "Interest"), on an installment basis, then the terms and conditions of such installment purchase shall be as set forth in Sections 19.1.1 and 19.1.2 in the case of an election pursuant to Section 13.2 or 14.2 and as set forth in Sections 19.1.3 and 19.1.4 in the case of an election pursuant to Section 15.2 or 16.2 hereof.

19.1.1   Twenty-nine percent (29%) of the aggregate purchase price due for such Interest (hereinafter, where appropriate, referred to as the "Aggregate Purchase Price") shall be paid on the closing date; and

19.1.2   The remainder of the Aggregate Purchase Price shall be paid in three (3) equal consecutive annual installments on each anniversary of the closing date over a period, beginning with the year following the calendar year in which the sale occurred (hereinafter referred to as the "Installment Payment Period").

19.1.3   _____ percent (__%) of the aggregate purchase price due for such Interest (hereinafter, where appropriate, referred to as the "Special Aggregate Purchase Price") shall be paid on the closing date; and

19.1.4   The remainder of the Special Aggregate Purchase Price shall be paid in _____(_____) equal consecutive installments on each anniversary of the closing date over a period, beginning with the year following the calendar year in which the sale occurred (hereinafter referred to as the "Special Installment Payment Period").

19.1.4.1   Anything contained in this Section 19 to the contrary notwithstanding, the entire unpaid balance of the Aggregate Purchase Price and Special Aggregate Purchase Price shall become immediately due and payable upon the sale, exchange, transfer, or other disposition of all or substantially all of the property or assets of the Company.

19.1.5   The Purchasing Person shall pay simple interest at a rate that shall be equal to the prime rate of interest then being charged by United Bank of Denver, N.A. to its highest credit-rated corporate borrowers on short-term unsecured commercial borrowings on the unpaid balance of the Aggregate Purchase Price or Special Aggregate Purchase Price on each anniversary of the closing date during the Installment Period or Special Installment Period, as the case may be.

19.2   *Rights of Members under Installment Payments.* So long as any part of the Aggregate Purchase Price or Special Aggregate Purchase Price remains unpaid, the Company shall permit the Offering Member, the personal representatives of the Decedent or the Heir, the Withdrawing Member (or the legal representative of the Withdrawing Member in the event of the bankruptcy of the Withdrawing Member), or the Expelled Member, as the case may be, and the attorneys and the accountants of each of the foregoing Persons, to examine the books and records of the Company and its business following the event that shall have given rise to the election referred to in Section 19.1 hereof during regular business hours from time to time upon reasonable prior notice and to receive copies of the annual accounting reports and tax returns of the Company.

Section 20.   *Delivery of Evidence of Interest.*

On the closing date, upon payment of the Aggregate Purchase Price for the purchase of the Interest hereunder or, if payment is to be made in installments pursuant to the provisions of Section 19 hereof, upon the first payment, the Offering Member, the personal representatives of the Decedent or the Heir, the Withdrawing Member, the personal representative of the Withdrawing Member (in the event of the bankruptcy of the Withdrawing Member), or the Expelled Member, as the case may be, shall execute, acknowledge, seal, and deliver to the Purchasing Person such instrument or instruments of transfer to evidence the purchase of the Interest (the "Instrument of Transfer") that shall be reasonably requested by counsel to the Purchasing Person in form and substance reasonably satisfactory to such counsel. If a tender of the Aggregate Purchase Price or Special Aggregate Purchase Price or, if payment is to be made in installments pursuant to the provisions of Section 19.1 hereof, the tender of the first payment thereof, shall be refused, or if the Instrument of Transfer shall not be delivered contemporaneously with the tender of the Aggregate Purchase Price or Special Aggregate Purchase Price or of the first payment thereof, as aforesaid, then the purchasing person shall be appointed, and the same is hereby irrevocably constituted and appointed, the attorney-in-fact with full power and authority to execute, acknowledge, seal, and deliver the Instrument of Transfer.

Section 21.   *Family Members.*

For purposes of this Agreement, members of the "immediate family" of a Member are hereby defined to be such person's spouse or children.

Section 22.   *Notices.*

Any and all notices, offers, acceptances, requests, certifications, and consents provided for in this Agreement shall be in writing and shall be given and be deemed to have been given when personally delivered against a signed receipt or mailed by registered or certified mail, return receipt requested, to the last address which the addressee has given to the Company. The address of each Member is set forth [on his or her Subscription Agreement adopting and agreeing to be bound by the terms of this Agreement] or [under his or her signature at the end of this Agreement], and each Member agrees to notify the Company of any change of address. The address of the Company shall be its principal office.

Section 23.   *Governing Law.*

It is the intent of the parties hereto that all questions with respect to the construction of this Agreement and the rights, duties, obligations, and liabilities of the parties shall be determined in accordance with the applicable provisions of the laws of the State of [State].

Section 24.   *Miscellaneous Provisions.*

24.1   *Inurement.* This Agreement shall be binding upon, and inure to the benefit of, all parties hereto, their personal and legal representatives, guardians, successors, and assigns to the extent, but only to the extent, that assignment is provided for in accordance with, and permitted by, the provisions of this Agreement.

24.2 *No Limit on Personal Activities.* Nothing herein contained shall be construed to limit in any manner the Members or their respective agents, servants, and employees, in carrying out their own respective businesses or activities.

24.3 *Further Assurances.* The Members and the Company agree that they and each of them will take whatever action or actions are deemed by counsel to the Company to be reasonably necessary or desirable from time to time to effectuate the provisions or intent of this Agreement, and to that end the Members and the Company agree that they will execute, acknowledge, seal, and deliver any further instruments or documents which may be necessary to give force and effect to this Agreement or any of the provisions hereof, or to carry out the intent of this Agreement, or any of the provisions hereof.

24.4 *Gender and Headings.* Throughout this Agreement, where such meanings would be appropriate: (a) the masculine gender shall be deemed to include the feminine and the neuter, and vice versa, and (b) the singular shall be deemed to include the plural, and vice versa. The headings herein are inserted only as a matter of convenience and reference, and in no way define or describe the scope of the Agreement or the intent of any provisions thereof.

24.5 *Entire Agreement.* This Agreement and the Subscription Agreements of each of the Members and exhibits attached hereto and thereto set forth all (and are intended by all parties hereto to be an integration of all) of the promises, agreements, conditions, understandings, warranties, and representations among the parties hereto with respect to the Company, and there are no promises, agreements, conditions, understandings, warranties, or representations, oral or written, express or implied, among them other than as set forth herein.

24.6 *Severability.* Nothing contained in this Agreement shall be construed as requiring the commission of any act contrary to law. In the event there is any conflict between any provision of this Agreement and any statute, law, ordinance, or regulation contrary to which the Members or the Company have no legal right to contract, the latter shall prevail, but in such event the provisions of this Agreement thus affected shall be curtailed and limited only to the extent necessary to conform with said requirement of law. In the event that any part, article, section, paragraph, or clause of this Agreement shall be held to be indefinite, invalid, or otherwise unenforceable, the entire Agreement shall not fail on account thereof, and the balance of the Agreement shall continue in full force and effect.

24.7 *Consent of Spouses.* Each married party to this Agreement agrees to obtain the consent and approval of his or her spouse, by the execution hereof by such spouse, to all the terms and provisions of this Agreement; provided, however, that such execution shall be for the sole purpose of acknowledging such spouse's consent and approval, as aforesaid, and nothing contained in this Section 24.7 shall be deemed to have constituted any such spouse a Member of the Company.

24.8 *Wills.* Each Member agrees to insert in his or her Will or to execute a Codicil thereto directing and authorizing his or her personal representatives to fulfill and comply with the provisions hereof and to sell and transfer his or her percentage of Membership Interest and Membership Rights in accordance herewith.

24.9 *Insurance.* The Company shall have the right to make application for, take out, and maintain in effect such policies of life insurance on the lives of any or all of the Members, whenever and in such amounts as the Members shall determine in accordance with Section 8 of this Agreement. Each Member shall exert his or her best efforts and fully assist and cooperate with the Company in obtaining any such policies of life insurance.

EXHIBIT J–4.

(continued)

IN WITNESS WHEREOF, the parties have hereunto set their hands and seals and acknowledged this Agreement as of the date first above written.

Membership Interest and Membership Rights

_____ (SEAL)   ___%

_____

_____

_____

Residence Address

_____ (SEAL)   ___%

_____

_____

_____

Residence Address

_____ (SEAL)   ___%

_____

_____

_____

Residence Address

__[Name]__ , a [State] Limited Liability Company

By:_____

Manager

EXHIBIT J–5.

Contract Between Stockholders Organizing a Close Corporation

Agreement, made this _____day of _____, 20__, between A_____ B_____ of _____, and C_____ D_____ of _____(hereinafter referred to as the "Shareholders").

Whereas, the Shareholders have caused _____Corporation to be organized as a corporation under the laws of the State of _____, and have agreed that it shall be financed and its business conducted subject to the provisions of this agreement.

Now, therefore, in consideration of the mutual covenants herein contained, it is agreed:

1. **Subscription to Stock.** The Shareholders each subscribe for and agree to purchase _____shares each of the capital stock of the Corporation at $_____ per share. These shares shall be issued and paid for within _____days after the organization of the Corporation.

2. **Loan to Corporation.** The Shareholders each agree to loan to the Corporation the sum of $_____, to be used for the purposes of the business of the Corporation, such loan to be repaid at the convenience of the Corporation, with interest thereon at _____percent per annum.

3. **Employment.** The Corporation shall employ A_____ B_____ and C_____ D_____ each at a salary of $_____ per week. A_____ B_____ and C_____ D_____ each agree to accept such employment, to devote their full time and best efforts to the business of the Corporation, and not to engage in any other competing business, directly or indirectly. Such salary shall be subject to increase or decrease and the term of employment of A_____ B_____ and C_____ D_____ may be terminated only by vote of the Board of Directors of the Corporation in accordance with the provisions contained in the Certificate of Incorporation.

4. **First Option on Termination of Employment.** In the event that either A_____ B_____ or C_____ D_____ shall at any time, for any reason whatsoever, leave the employ of the Corporation or cease to be actively engaged in the

business of the Corporation, all of the shares owned by such Shareholder shall be offered for sale to the other Shareholder, who is hereby given an option for a period of _____days from the date on which such employment or activity shall terminate, to purchase all of such shares at a price equal to the book value thereof. Book value of shares shall be computed from the books of the Corporation maintained by its regular accountant in accordance with generally accepted principles of accounting. The option hereby given shall relate to all of such shares of the offeror, and the offeree shall not have the right to purchase only part thereof. If the aforesaid offer is accepted, notwithstanding any of the foregoing provisions of this paragraph, the offeror shall receive from the offeree not less than the value of his or her investment in the Corporation plus the amount of any unpaid loan theretofore made by the offeror to the Corporation, with appropriate interest thereon to the date of purchase. Payments to be made under this paragraph shall be made as follows: _____upon the acceptance of the offer; _____ _____ months thereafter; and the final_____ _____ months thereafter. Title to the shares shall pass to the offeree only upon the completion of all payments. After the payment of the first installment, the offeror shall hold such shares only as security for payment of the remaining installments, and the offeree shall have the sole right to vote the shares and to collect all dividends and other distributions thereon. Upon payment of the last installments, the shares shall be transferred of record to the offeree.

5. **Restriction on Transfer of Stock.** Each of the Shareholders expressly agrees not to transfer, sell, assign, pledge, or otherwise in any manner dispose of or encumber any of his or her shares unless and until he or she shall have offered to sell all of his or her shares to the other Shareholder at a price to be computed and to be paid as specified in paragraph 4 above. Such offer shall be made in writing and shall continue for _____days from the date thereof.

6. **Legend on Stock Certificates.** All stock certificates issued by the Corporation shall have marked on the face thereof "Subject to provisions of Stockholders' Agreement dated _____, 20__, restricting transfer." No dividend shall be paid on any shares transferred, pledged, assigned, or encumbered in breach of this agreement.

7. **Death and Disability.** Upon the death of any Shareholder who is also an employee, his or her salary shall be paid to the widow or widower or next of kin for _____weeks following such death. If any Shareholder shall become physically incapacitated and unable to attend to his or her duties as an employee of the Corporation, he or she shall continue to receive his or her full salary (less the sum required to employ a substitute in his or her place) for a period of _____months after the commencement of such incapacity. In the event of the death or incapacity of any shareholder-employee for more than _____months, the other Shareholder shall have the option, for _____days after such death or expiration of said _____month period, to purchase his or her shares at the price and on the terms provided for in paragraph 4 hereof. The life of the other Shareholder shall be insured for the benefit of the other Shareholder for $_____, or for such other amount as the Shareholders may jointly agree upon. If the proceeds of such insurance payable to any Shareholder are equal to at least _____percent of the purchase price of the stock of the deceased Shareholder as computed in accordance with the provisions of paragraph 4, such Shareholder agrees that he or she will exercise his or her option to purchase all of the shares from the estate of the deceased Shareholder as herein provided. Upon the receipt of any such proceeds, any then remaining unpaid installments of such purchase price shall be prepaid by the purchaser, to at least the extent of such proceeds.

EXHIBIT J–5.

(continued)

8. **Election of Directors.** Each Shareholder agrees, so long as he or she shall remain a Shareholder, to vote his or her shares for the election of the following four persons as Directors of the Corporation:

A_____ B_____ (or such other person as is designated by A_____ B_____)

C_____ D_____ (or such other person as is designated by C_____ D_____)

and generally to so vote at directors' and stockholders' meetings of the Corporation as to carry out and make effective all the terms and provisions of this agreement.

9. **Appointment of Officers.** So long as they are faithful, efficient, and competent in the performance of their duties, the following persons shall be supported by the Shareholders for election to offices of the Corporation:

President and Treasurer   A_____ B_____

Vice President and Secretary C_____ D_____

10. **Arbitration.** All disputes, differences, and controversies arising under and in connection with this agreement shall be settled and finally determined by arbitration in the City of _____ according to the rules of the American Arbitration Association now in force or hereafter adopted.

11. **Duration.** This agreement shall continue in force during the entire period of the life of the Corporation.

12. **Successors.** This agreement and all provisions hereof shall inure to the benefit of and shall be binding upon the heirs, executors, legal representatives, next of kin, transferees, and assigns of the parties hereto.

13. **Severability.** If for any reason any provision hereof shall be inoperative, the validity and effect of all other provisions shall not be affected thereby.

14. **Modifications.** No modification or waiver of any provision of this agreement shall be valid unless in writing signed by all of the parties.

In witness whereof, the parties have signed this agreement on the day and year first above written.

_____

_____

Confirmed and Agreed to:
_____Corporation

_____
                President
Attest:
_____ *
                Secretary

*Adapted from West's Modern Legal Forms §   2432.15.

EXHIBIT J–6.

Articles of Incorporation of
a Medical Corporation

ARTICLES OF INCORPORATION
OF

_____

We, the undersigned, hereby associate ourselves together for the purpose of becoming a professional corporation for profit under the provisions of _____, Statutes, as amended by "The Professional Service Corporation Act" of the State of _____, and pursuant to the following Articles of Incorporation:

ARTICLE I.   NAME

The name of this corporation shall be _____.

ARTICLE II.   PURPOSE

The general nature of the business to be transacted by the corporation shall be and is to engage in every aspect of the general practice of medicine. The professional services involved in the corporation's practice of medicine may be rendered only through its officers, agents, and employees who are duly authorized and licensed to practice medicine in the State of _____.

This corporation shall not engage in any business other than the practice of medicine. However, this corporation may invest its funds in real estate, mortgages, stocks, bonds, and other types of investments, and may own real and personal property necessary for the rendering of the professional services authorized hereby.

ARTICLE III.   CAPITAL STOCK

The maximum number of shares of stock that the corporation is authorized to have outstanding at any time shall be _____ shares of the par value of one dollar ($1.00) per share, all of which shall be common stock of the same class. All stock issued shall be fully paid and nonassessable. The stockholders shall have no preemptive rights with respect to the stock of the corporation, and the corporation may issue and sell its common stock from time to time without offering such shares to the stockholders then holding shares of common stock. Shares of the corporation's stock and certificates therefore shall be issued only to doctors authorized and licensed to practice medicine in the State of _____.

ARTICLE IV.   INITIAL CAPITAL

The amount of capital with which this corporation will begin business shall be and is the sum of _____ dollars.

ARTICLE V.   DURATION

The corporation shall have perpetual existence.

ARTICLE VI.   PRINCIPAL OFFICE

The principal office of this corporation shall be located in the City of _____, County of _____, State of _____, and the post office address of said principal office of the corporation shall be _____.

ARTICLE VII.   NUMBER OF DIRECTORS

The number of directors of this corporation shall be not less than three (3) nor more than five (5).

ARTICLE VIII.   INITIAL BOARD OF DIRECTORS

The names and post office addresses of the members of the first Board of Directors, who, subject to the provisions of the Bylaws and these Articles of Incorporation, shall hold office for the first year of the corporation's existence or until their successors are elected and have qualified, are as follows:

Names	Addresses
_____	_____
_____	_____
_____	_____
_____	_____
_____	_____

ARTICLE IX.   SUBSCRIBERS

The name and post office address of each subscriber of these Articles of Incorporation are as follows:

Names	Addresses
_____	_____
_____	_____
_____	_____
_____	_____
_____	_____

The subscribers certify that the proceeds of the stock subscribed for will not be less than the amount of capital with which the corporation will begin business, as set forth in Article IV hereinabove.

ARTICLE X.   STOCKHOLDERS

The stock of this corporation may be issued, owned, and registered only in the name or names of an individual or individuals who are duly authorized and licensed to practice medicine in the State of _____and who are employees, officers, or agents of this corporation. In the event that a stockholder:

(a)   becomes disqualified to practice medicine in this State; or

(b)   is elected to a public office or accepts employment that, pursuant to law, places restrictions or limitations upon his or her continued rendering of professional services as a medical doctor; or

(c)   ceases to be an employee, officer, or agent of the corporation; or

(d)   sells, transfers, hypothecates, or pledges, or attempts to sell, transfer, hypothecate, or pledge, any shares of stock in this corporation to any person ineligible by law or by virtue of these Articles to be a shareholder in this corporation, or if such sale, transfer, hypothecation, or pledge or attempt to sell, transfer, hypothecate, or pledge is made in a manner prohibited by law, or in a manner inconsistent with the provisions of these Articles or the Bylaws of this corporation; or

(e)   suffers an execution to be levied upon his or her stock, or such stock is subjected to judicial sale or other process, the effect of which is to vest any legal or equitable interest in such stock in some person other than the stockholder, then the stock of such stockholder shall immediately stand forfeited, such stock shall be immediately canceled by this corporation, and the stockholder or other person in possession of such stock shall be entitled only to receive payment for the value of such stock, which said value shall be the book value thereof as of the last day of the month preceding the month in which any of the events above enumerated occurs. The stockholder whose stock so becomes forfeit and is canceled by the corporation shall forthwith cease to be an employee, officer, director, or agent of the corporation and except to receive payment for his or her stock in accordance with the foregoing and payment of any other sums then lawfully due and owing to said stockholder by the corporation, such stockholder shall then and thereafter have no further financial interest of any kind in this corporation.

ARTICLE XI.   DEATH OF STOCKHOLDER

Upon the death of a stockholder, his or her stock shall be subject to purchase by the corporation or by the other stockholders at such price and upon such terms and conditions and in such manner as may be provided for in the Bylaws of this corporation, in a manner consistent with law and these Articles.

ARTICLE XII.   SALE OF STOCK

No stockholder of this corporation may sell or transfer any of such stockholder's shares of stock in this corporation except to another individual who is then duly authorized and licensed to practice medicine in the State of _____and then only after the proposed sale or transfer shall have been first approved, at a stockholders' meeting specially called for such purpose, by such proportion, not less than a majority, of the outstanding stock excluding the shares of stock proposed to be sold or transferred, as may be provided from time to time in the Bylaws. In such stockholders' meeting, the shares of stock proposed to be sold or transferred may not be voted or counted for any purpose.

The corporation's shareholders are specifically authorized from time to time to adopt Bylaws not inconsistent herewith restraining the alienation of shares of stock of this corporation and providing for the purchase or redemption by the corporation of its shares of stock.

ARTICLE XIII.   REGULATION OF BUSINESS

In furtherance of and not in limitation of the powers conferred by statute, the following specific provisions are made for the regulation of the business and the conduct of the affairs of the corporation:

1.   **Management.** Subject to such restrictions, if any, as are herein expressed and such further restrictions, if any, as may be set forth in the Bylaws, the Board of Directors shall have the general management and control of the business and may exercise all of the powers of the corporation except such as may be by statute, or by the articles of incorporation or amendment thereto, or by the Bylaws as constituted from time to time, expressly conferred upon or reserved to the stockholders.

2.   **Officers.** The corporation shall have such officers as may from time to time be provided in the Bylaws and such officers shall be designated in such manner and shall hold their offices for such terms and shall have such powers and duties as may be prescribed by the Bylaws or as may be determined from time to time by the Board of Directors subject to the Bylaws.

3.   **Contracts.** No contract or other transaction between the corporation and any other firm, association, or corporation shall be affected or invalidated by the fact that any one or more of the directors of the corporation is or are interested in or is a member, director, or officer or are members, directors, or officers of such firm or corporation and any director or directors individually or jointly may be a party or parties to or may be interested in any contract or transaction of the corporation or in which the corporation is interested; and no contract, act, or transaction of the corporation with any person, firm, association, or corporation shall be affected or invalidated by the fact that any director or directors of the corporation is a party or are parties to or interested in such contract, act, or transaction or in any way connected with such person, firm, association, or corporation, and each and every person who may become a director of the corporation is hereby relieved from any liability that might otherwise exist from contracting with the corporation for the benefit of himself or herself or any firm, association, or corporation in which he or she may in any way be interested.

ARTICLE XIV.   AMENDMENTS

This corporation reserves the right to amend, alter, change, or repeal any provision contained herein in the manner now or hereafter prescribed by law, and all rights conferred on stockholders herein are granted subject to this reservation.

EXHIBIT J–6.

(continued)

In Witness Whereof, each subscriber has signed these Articles of Incorporation.

_____
_____
_____
_____
_____

[*Acknowledgment*]*

*Adapted from West's Modern Legal Forms § 3158.7.

EXHIBIT J–7.

Application for Registration
of Professional Corporation
(California)

File No._____
(To be filled in by Board)
Fee: $100.00

APPLICATION
for issuance of
CERTIFICATE OF REGISTRATION AS A MEDICAL CORPORATION
(Section 2501 of the Business and Professions Code)

1. _____
(Name of Applicant)
a professional corporation, hereby requests issuance to it of a Certificate of Registration as a medical corporation.

2. Applicant will do business as (fictitious name) _____

_____
(See Section 2393 of the Business and Professions Code and Section 13409 of the Corporations Code.)

3. The corporation number assigned to the applicant by the California Secretary of State is _____.

4. Date of incorporation _____.

5. A. The address of applicant's principal office is:
_____

B. The address of all other offices of applicant are:
_____

_____

C. Applicant's telephone number is: _____
(Area Code)   (Number)

6. The directors of the applicant are:
NAME   ADDRESS   PROFESSIONAL LICENSE NUMBER
(1) _____
(2) _____
(3) _____
(4) _____
(File supplemental sheet if more space required)

7. The officers of the applicant are:
(If any officers are not licensed persons, so indicate. See Section 13403 of the Corporations Code.)

NAME   *ADDRESS*   *PROFESSIONAL LICENSE NUMBER*

President _____

Vice President _____

Secretary _____

Treasurer _____

Asst. Secretary _____

           (Need not be a licensed person. See Section 2501 of the Business and Professions Code.)

Asst. Treasurer _____

(Need not be a licensed person. See Section 2501 of the Business and Professions Code.)

8. The shareholders of the applicant are:

    NAME   *ADDRESS*   *PROFESSIONAL LICENSE NUMBER*

    (1) _____

    (2) _____

    (3) _____

    (4) _____

    (5) _____

    (File supplemental sheet if more space required)

9. The employees of the applicant rendering professional services are:

    NAME   *ADDRESS*   *PROFESSIONAL LICENSE NUMBER*

    (1) _____

    (2) _____

    (3) _____

    (4) _____

    (5) _____

    (File supplemental sheet if more space required)

10. The bylaws of the applicant adopted on _____comply with Medical Corporation Rule 1378.6 in that:

    (a) Shares of the applicant may be owned only by a medical corporation or by a licensed physician, surgeon, or podiatrist, as the case may be.

    (b) The income of the applicant attributable to medical services rendered while a shareholder is a disqualified person shall not in any manner accrue to the benefit of such shareholder or his or her shares.

    (c) The share certificates of the applicant contain a legend setting forth the restrictions of sections (a) and (b) above and, where applicable, the restrictions of section (d) below.

    and, where applicable:

    (d) Where there are two or more shareholders in the corporation and one of the shareholders:

        (1) dies;

        (2) ceases to be an eligible shareholder; or

        (3) becomes a disqualified person as defined in Section 13401(d) of the Corporations Code, for a period exceeding ninety (90) days,

    his or her shares shall be sold and transferred to the corporation, its shareholders, or other eligible persons, on such terms as are agreed upon. Such sale or transfer shall be not later than six (6) months after any such death and not later than ninety (90) days after the date he or she ceases to be an eligible shareholder, or ninety (90) days after the date he or she becomes a disqualified person. The requirements of subsections (a) and (b) of this section shall be set forth in the medical corporation's articles of incorporation or by-

EXHIBIT J–7.

(continued)

laws, except that the terms of the sale or transfer provided for in said subsection (b) need not be set forth in said articles or bylaws if they are set forth in a written agreement.

(e)   The applicant and its shareholders may, but need not, agree that shares sold to it by a person who becomes a disqualified person may be resold to such person if and when he or she again becomes an eligible shareholder.

11.   Security for claims against applicant.
(Check one)

☐   Applicant is insured as provided in Section 1378.5(a) of the Medical Corporation Rules as evidenced by the Certificate of Insurance attached as Exhibit C.

☐   Applicant is not insured.
(NOTE: Under Section 1378.5(b) of the Medical Corporation Rules, all shareholders of the corporation shall be jointly and severally liable for all claims established against the corporation by its patients arising out of the rendering of, or failure to render, medical services up to the minimum amounts specified for insurance under subsection (a) hereof except during periods of time when the corporation shall provide and maintain insurance for claims against it by its patients arising out of the rendering of, or failure to render, medical services.)

12.   Applicant is an existing corporation and its organization, bylaws, articles of incorporation, and general plan of operation are such that its affairs will be conducted in compliance with the Medical Practice Act, the Professional Corporations Act, and other applicable provisions of the Corporations Code, the Medical Corporation Rules of the Board of Medical Examiners, and such other law, rules, and regulations as may be applicable.

13.   Enclosed herewith are the following exhibits:

A.   Articles of Incorporation, certified by the Secretary of State. (Section 2501 of the Business and Professions Code.)

B.   Bylaws certified by the Secretary of the applicant corporation. (Section 2501 of the Business and Professions Code.)

C.   Certificate of insurance.
(Must be filed if applicant is insured. Section 1378.5(a) of the Medical Corporation Rules.)

D.   Notice of Liability of Shareholders (Section 1378.5(b) of the Medical Corporation Rules.)
Executed this _____day of _____, 20___.

_____
[*Name of Corporation*]
By_____
[*Type name*]

_____
[*Title of person executing*]

_____
[*Signature*]

DECLARATION

I am an officer of _____, (Name of Applicant) and as such make this declaration for and on behalf of said corporation. I have read the foregoing application and all attachments thereto and know the contents thereof, and the same are true of my own knowledge. I declare, under penalty of perjury, that the foregoing is true and correct.

Executed at _____, California, this _____day of _____, 20__.

_____
(Signature)

_____ *
(Title)

*Adapted from West's Modern Legal Forms § 3158.4.

These forms are intended for use at an initial client interview as information gathering forms, and as external checklists to assist the attorney in following up with the client, the accountant, the insurance agent, and others so that all aspects of the incorporation are accomplished in a timely fashion and without duplication of effort.

These forms should be filled out during the client interview and reviewed with the legal assistant when the assignment is made. A copy is to be mailed to the client, the accountant, and the insurance agent when acknowledging the engagement.

The Agenda should be kept in the file and reviewed periodically during the incorporation process; follow-up letters may be generated by these reviews.

PREINCORPORATION AGENDA
FOR

_____

Item	Responsibility	To Be Completed	Date Completed
1. Reserve Corporate Name			
2. Draft and File Articles of Incorporation			
3. Prepare Initial Organizational Consent or Minutes			
4. Prepare Bylaws			
5. Additional Organization Documents:			
a) Employment Agreements			
b) Service Agreements			
c) Medical and Dental Expense Reimbursement Plan			
d) Shareholders' Agreement			
e) Share Certificates			
f) Transfer Documents			
g) Bank Resolution			
h) Subchapter S Election			
6. Order Corporate Kit			
7. Send Explanatory Transmittal Letter			
8. Other:			

EXHIBIT J–8.

(continued)

Client: _____

File No.: _____

PREINCORPORATION INFORMATION SHEET

1. Date Information Supplied: _____

   Parties Present: _____

      Lawyer: _____

      Client: _____

   Other Parties: _____

2. State of Incorporation: _____

3. Proposed Date of Incorporation: _____

4. Name of Corporation: _____

   Alternative Name: _____ /

   Trade Name: _____

5. Name Reserved? YES (__) NO (__) SHOULD BE (__)

6. Will Be Incorporating a Going Business?_____

   If so, describe generally: _____

   Any Patents, Copyrights, or Trademarks to Be Registered or Transferred: _

   _____

7. Principal Purpose of Corporation: _____

   _____

   (State broadly, but with sufficient specificity to meet statutory requirements.)

8. Principal Place of Business: _____

   ☐ Own   ☐ Lease_____

   _____

   Other places of significant business activity or presence:

Address	Description	Own/Lease

9. Qualification in other states required. YES (__) NO (__)

   If so, what states: _____

10. Registered Agent and Office in State: _____

    _____

    Registered Agent and Office in states in which qualified:

    _____

    _____

    (Do not commit lawyer to be registered agent.)

11. Common Stock (if preferred, explain details):

Class	Number of Shares	Par Value	Issue Price

    Explain details: _____

    Will there be a formal stock subscription agreement:_____

    If no par value, amount of consideration to be allocated to capital surplus:

    _____

    Note: If stock is no par value, stated capital of the company will be equal to actual consideration paid for issued stock except that part of consideration that directors may allocate to capital surplus.

12. Anticipated Shareholders:

Name and Phone	Address	Zip Code
(1)		
(2)		
(3)		
(4)		

13. Section 1244 Plan: _____
    Date of Commencement of Offer: _____
Note: Section 1244 stock permits deduction of capital losses, if any, upon sale of
      such stock as ordinary losses against ordinary income of Section 1244
      stock owner. See Section 1244 of the Internal Revenue Code for details.
14. Share Ownership and Consideration (corresponding to above stockholders):

Number of Shares	Consideration	Date to be Paid
(1) _____	_____	_____
(2) _____	_____	_____
(3) _____	_____	_____
(4) _____	_____	_____

15. Initial Indebtedness: Secured $_____ Unsecured $_____
Note: (1) If capital structure of the company will involve debt, advised debt
      equity ratio should not be in excess of 3/1, and recommend 2/1 if
      workable for participants. Point out that any debt must specifically be
      treated as debt by the company, or the IRS is likely to characterize any
      such debt securities as stock.
Note: (2) If prospective contributor to corporate capital will take back note to
      secure corporate debt, make sure note will qualify as a "long-term
      security" under § 351 of the Internal Revenue Code. Otherwise, transfer of
      property to company may constitute a taxable event (i.e., a "sale") which
      will cause realization of probable capital gain to taxpayer-transferor.
16. Incorporators:

Name	Address (if not shown above)	Zip Code
_____	_____	_____
_____	_____	_____
_____	_____	_____
_____	_____	_____
_____	_____	_____

17. Directors:

Name and Phone	Address (if not shown above)	Zip Code
_____	_____	_____
_____	_____	_____
_____	_____	_____
_____	_____	_____

18. Officers:

Name	Office	Address
_____	President	_____
_____	Treasurer	_____
_____	Secretary	_____
_____	_____	_____

19. Preemptive Rights. YES (_____) NO (_____) Restrictions_____
    Note: See explanatory material in Corporate Law Notebook or in B. M.
          Miller, *Manual and Guide for the Corporate Secretary* 815–844 (1969), for
          background prior to client conference.
20. Cumulative Voting. YES (_____) NO (_____)
    Note: See explanatory material in Corporate Law Notebook or in B. M.
          Miller, *supra* at 89–94, for background prior to client conference.
21. Date and Time of Annual Meeting: _____
    (e.g., "_____ days following close of fiscal year" or "held each year prior to
    the _____day of _____").
    For provision in Bylaws: "In the event the Board of Directors fails to so fix
    the date and time of such meeting, it shall be held on the _____in_____
    at _____A.M. (e.g., on the first Tuesday in March at 10:00 A.M.)

22. Bank: _____
Signatories: _____
Limitations: _____
Should we obtain banking resolutions: YES (_____) NO (_____)
23. Commencement of Employment, if any: _____
Note: If business is already in progress, obtain Employer Identification
Number: _____
24. Date of First Meeting of Board of Directors: _____
25. Stock Transfer Restrictions? YES (_____) NO (_____) Special provisions:

_____

Insurance Funded: YES (_____) NO (_____)
Insurance Company or Agent _____
26. Ownership of Real Property (list states and counties):

_____
_____

Ownership of Personal Property:

_____
_____

27. Custody of Corporate Minute Book, Stock Book, and Seal:
Client (_____) Us (_____)
Other Custodian: _____
28. Supplemental Checklist
☐ COMPARE FEATURES OF CORPORATION LAWS OF FOLLOWING
STATES: _____
☐ COMPARE ORGANIZATION FEES AND TAXES
☐ CHECK COSTS OF QUALIFICATION IN FOREIGN STATES
☐ CHECK ANNUAL FEES AND TAXES
☐ CHECK STATE TAX SAVINGS WHICH MAY BE EFFECTED BY SCHED-
ULING INCORPORATION (AND ANY QUALIFICATIONS) BEFORE
OR AFTER CERTAIN DATES
29. Miscellaneous Advice to Include in Cover Letter to Client:
(a) Securities Laws Considerations (i.e., investment letter): _____
_____
(b) Retail Sales Tax, Use Tax, and Store Licenses: _____
_____
(c) State License to Do Business Compliance: _____
_____
(d) Qualification in Other States: _____
_____
(e) State Workers' Compensation Insurance Compliance: _____
_____
(f) State Unemployment Insurance Compliance: _____
_____
(g) Obtain Federal Employer Identification Number: _____
_____
(h) Employer's Tax Guide re Withholding Requirements (Federal and
State): _____
_____
(i) State Consumer Credit Compliance (Notification): _____
_____
(j) Local Retail Sales Tax License: _____
_____
(k) Local Use Tax License: _____
_____

(l)   Local Occupational Privilege Tax Compliance: _____

(m) "Tax Information on Subchapter S Corporations" (IRS Publication 589): __

(n)   "Corporations and the Federal Income Tax" (IRS Publication 542): _____

(o)   Other Matters: _____

_____

NOTES AND COMMENTS

_____

_____

_____

_____

_____

_____

_____

_____

_____

_____

_____

Attorney handling
incorporation

CERTIFICATE OF INCORPORATION
OF
FINE FABRICS CORPORATION

1.   **Name.** The name of the Corporation is Fine Fabrics Corporation.

2.   **Registered Office and Registered Agent.** The address of the Corporation's registered office in Delaware is 100 _____Street in the City of Wilmington and County of New Castle, and the name of its registered agent at such address is _____Trust Company.

3.   **Purposes.** The purpose of the Corporation is to engage in any lawful act or activity for which corporations may be now or hereafter organized under the General Corporation Law of Delaware.

4.   **Capital Stock** [*providing for one class of par value stock*]. The Corporation is authorized to issue only one class of stock. The total number of such shares is ten thousand and the par value of each of such shares is ten dollars.

[Alternate] 4.   Capital Stock [*providing for two classes of stock, one voting and one nonvoting*]. The total number of shares of all classes of stock which the Corporation shall have authority to issue is ten thousand, all of which are to be without par value. Five thousand of such shares shall be Class A voting shares and five thousand of such shares shall be Class B nonvoting shares. The Class A shares and the Class B shares shall have identical rights except that the Class B shares shall not entitle the holder thereof to vote on any matter unless specifically required by law.

[Alternate] 4.   Capital Stock [*providing for two classes of stock, preferred and common*]. The total number of shares of all classes of capital stock which the

Corporation shall have authority to issue is twenty-six million shares, of which one million shares shall be shares of Preferred Stock without par value (hereinafter called "Preferred Stock"), and twenty-five million shares shall be shares of Common Stock of the par value of $5 per share (hereinafter called "Common Stock").

Any amendment to the Certificate of Incorporation which shall increase or decrease the authorized capital stock of the Corporation may be adopted by the affirmative vote of the holders of a majority of the outstanding shares of stock of the Corporation entitled to vote.

The designations and the powers, preferences and rights, and the qualifications, limitations or restrictions thereof, of the Preferred Stock shall be as follows:

(1)   The Board of Directors is expressly authorized at any time, and from time to time, to provide for the issuance of shares of Preferred Stock in one or more series, with such voting powers, full or limited but not to exceed one vote per share, or without voting powers and with such designations, preferences, and relative, participating, optional, or other special rights, and qualifications, limitations, or restrictions thereof, as shall be expressed in the resolution or resolutions providing for the issue thereof adopted by the Board of Directors and as are not expressed in this Certificate of Incorporation or any amendment thereto, including (but without limiting the generality of the foregoing) the following:

(a) the designation of such series;

(b) the dividend rate of such series, the conditions and dates upon which such dividends shall be payable, the preference or relation which such dividends shall bear to the dividends payable on any other class or classes or on any other series of any class or classes of capital stock of the Corporation, and whether such dividends shall be cumulative or noncumulative;

(c) whether the shares of such series shall be subject to redemption by the Corporation and, if made subject to such redemption, the times, prices, and other terms and conditions of such redemption;

(d) the terms and amount of any sinking fund provided for the purchase or redemption of the shares of such series;

(e) whether the shares of such series shall be convertible into or exchangeable for shares of any other class or classes or of any other series of any class or classes of capital stock of the Corporation and, if provision is made for conversion one exchange, the times, prices, rates, adjustments, and other terms and conditions of such conversion or exchange;

(f) the extent, if any, to which the holders of the shares of such series shall be entitled to vote as a class or otherwise with respect to the election of directors or otherwise; provided, however, that in no event shall any holder of any series of Preferred Stock be entitled to more than one vote for each share of such Preferred Stock held by him or her;

(g) the restrictions and conditions, if any, upon the issue or reissue of any additional Preferred Stock ranking on a parity with or prior to such shares as to dividends or upon dissolution;

(h) the rights of the holders of the shares of such series upon the dissolution of, or upon the distribution of assets of, the Corporation, which rights may be different in the case of a voluntary dissolution than in the case of an involuntary dissolution.

(2)   Except as otherwise required by law and except for such voting powers with respect to the election of directors or other matters as may be

stated in the resolutions of the Board of Directors creating any series of   Preferred Stock, the holders of any such series shall have no voting power   whatsoever.

5. **Incorporators.** The names and mailing addresses of the incorporations are:

Name	Mailing Address
_____	_____

[Optional] 6. Initial Directors [*If the powers of the incorporator or incorporators are to terminate upon the filing of the certificate of incorporation*]. The names and mailing addresses of the persons who are to serve as directors until the first annual meeting of stockholders or until their successors are elected and qualify are:

Name	Mailing Address
_____	_____

[Optional] 7. Regulatory Provisions. The following additional provisions are inserted for the management of the business and for the conduct of the affairs of the Corporation, and creating, defining, limiting, and regulating the powers of the Corporation, the directors, and the stockholders, or any class of stockholders:

(a) *Power of Directors to Amend Bylaws.* The Board of Directors is authorized and empowered from time to time in its discretion to make, alter, or repeal the bylaws of the Corporation, except as such power may be limited by any one or more bylaws of the Corporation adopted by the stockholders.

(b) *Books.* The books of the Corporation (subject to the provisions of the laws of the State of Delaware) may be kept outside of the State of Delaware at such places as from time to time may be designated by the Board of Directors.

(c) *Cumulative Voting.* At all elections of directors of the Corporation, each stockholder shall be entitled to as many votes as shall equal the number of votes which he or she would be entitled to cast for the election of directors with respect to his or her shares of stock multiplied by the number of directors to be elected, and that he or she may cast all of such votes for a single director or may distribute them among the number to be voted for, or for any two or more of them as he or she may see fit.

(d) *Consent of Stockholders in Lieu of Meeting.* Whenever the vote of stockholders at a meeting thereof is required or permitted to be taken for or in connection with any corporate action by any provision of the General Corporation Law of the State of Delaware, the meeting and vote of stockholders may be dispensed with if such action is taken with the written consent of the holders of not less than a majority of all the stock entitled to be voted upon such action if a meeting were held; provided that in no case shall the written consent be by the holders of stock having less than the minimum percentage of the vote required by statute for such action, and provided that prompt notice is given to all stockholders of the taking of corporate action without a meeting and by less than unanimous written consent.

(e) *Elections of Directors.* Elections of directors need not be by written ballot.

(f) *Removal of Directors.* The stockholders may at any time, at a meeting expressly called for that purpose, remove any or all of the directors, with or without cause, by a vote of the holders of a majority of the shares then entitled to vote at an election of directors. No director may be removed when the votes cast against his or her removal would be sufficient to elect him or her if voted cumulatively at an election at which the same total number of votes were cast and the entire board were then being elected. [When by the provisions of the certificate of incorporation the holders of the shares of any class or series, voting as a class, are entitled to elect one or more directors, any director so elected may

EXHIBIT J–9.

(continued)

be removed only by the applicable vote of the holders of the shares of that class or series, voting as a class.]

[Optional] 8. **Creditor Arrangements.** Whenever a compromise or arrangement is proposed between this corporation and its creditors or any class of them and/or between this corporation and its stockholders or any class of them, any court of equitable jurisdiction within the State of Delaware may, on the application in a summary way of this corporation or of any creditor or stockholder thereof or on the application of any receiver or receivers appointed for this corporation under the provisions of section 291 of Title 8 of the Delaware Code or on the application of trustees in dissolution or of any receiver or receivers appointed for this corporation under the provisions of section 279 of Title 8 of the Delaware Code order a meeting of the creditors or class of creditors, and/or of the stockholders or class of stockholders of this corporation, as the case may be, to be summoned in such manner as the said court directs. If a majority in number representing three-fourths in value of the creditors or class of creditors, and/or of the stockholders or class of stockholders of this corporation, as the case may be, agree to any compromise or arrangement and to any reorganization of this corporation as consequence of such compromise or arrangement, the said compromise or arrangement and the said reorganization shall, if sanctioned by the court to which the said application has been made, be binding on all the creditors or class of creditors, and/or on all the stockholders or class of stockholders, of this corporation, as the case may be, and also on this corporation.

[Optional] 9. **Preemptive Rights.** The holders from time to time of the shares of the Corporation shall have the preemptive right to purchase, at such respective equitable prices, terms, and conditions as shall be fixed by the Board of Directors, such of the shares of the Corporation as may be issued, from time to time, over and above the issue of the first 5,000 shares of the Corporation which have never previously been sold. Such preemptive right shall apply to all shares issued after such first 5,000 shares, whether such additional shares constitute a part of the shares presently or subsequently authorized or constitute shares held in the treasury of the Corporation, and shall be exercised in the respective ratio which the number of shares held by each stockholder at the time of such issue bears to the total number of shares outstanding in the names of all stockholders at such time.

[Optional] 10. **Greater Voting Requirements.** The affirmative vote of a majority of the directors shall be necessary for the transaction of any business at any meeting of directors, except in the case of a proposal to borrow money on the Corporation's credit, in which case the favorable vote of all of the directors shall be necessary.

[Optional] 11. **Duration.** The duration of the Corporation's existence shall extend for the period beginning on the date the certificate of incorporation of the Corporation is filed with the Secretary of State of Delaware, and ending December 31, 2020.

[Optional] 12. **Personal Liability.** The stockholders shall be liable for the debts of the Corporation in the proportion that their stock bears to the total outstanding stock of the Corporation.

13. **Amendment.** The Corporation reserves the right to amend, alter, change, or repeal any provision contained in the Certificate of Incorporation, in the manner now or hereafter prescribed by statute, and all rights conferred upon stockholders herein are granted subject to this reservation.

We, the undersigned, being all of the incorporators above named, for the purpose of forming a corporation pursuant to the General Corporation Law of

Delaware, sign and acknowledge this certificate of incorporation this 1st day of September, 2020.

_____

_____

Acknowledgment

State of_____

County of _____ . ss

On this 1st day of September, 2020, before me personally came _____ , one of the persons who signed the foregoing certificate of incorporation, known to me personally to be such, and acknowledged that the said certificate is his or her act and deed and that the facts stated therein are true.

_____*

Notary Public

[*Seal*]

*Adapted from West's Modern Legal Forms § 2509.1.

**BYLAWS
OF
FINE FABRICS CORPORATION**
A Delaware Corporation

ARTICLE I   Offices

The principal office of the Corporation shall be in Wilmington, Delaware. The Corporation may have offices at such other places within or without the State of Delaware as the Board of Directors may from time to time establish.

ARTICLE II
Meetings of Stockholders

Section 1. *Annual Meetings.* The annual meeting of the stockholders for the election of directors and for the transaction of such other business as properly may come before such meeting shall be held at two o'clock in the afternoon on the second Wednesday of March in each year, if not a legal holiday, or, if a legal holiday, then on the next succeeding day not a legal holiday.

Section 2. *Special Meetings.* A special meeting of the stockholders may be called at any time by the President or the Board of Directors, and shall be called by the President upon the written request of stockholders of record holding in the aggregate one-fifth or more of the outstanding shares of stock of the Corporation entitled to vote, such written request to state the purpose or purposes of the meeting and to be delivered to the President.

Section 3. *Place of Meetings.* All meetings of the stockholders shall be held at the office of the Corporation in Lincoln, Nebraska, or at such other place, within or without the State of Delaware, as shall be determined from time to time by the Board of Directors of the stockholders of the Corporation.

Section 4. *Change in Time or Place of Meetings.* The time and place specified in this Article II for the meetings of stockholders for the election of directors shall not be changed within sixty days next before the day on which such election is to be held. A notice of any such change shall be given to each stockholder at least twenty days before the election is held, in person or by letter mailed to his or her last known post office address.

Section 5.   *Notice of Meetings.* Except as otherwise required by statute, written or printed notice of each meeting of the stockholders, whether annual or special, stating the place, day, and hour thereof and the purposes for which the meeting is called, shall be given by or under the direction of the Secretary at least ten but not more than fifty days before the date fixed for such meeting, to each stockholder entitled to vote at such meeting, of record at the close of business on the day fixed by the Board of Directors as a record date for the determination of the stockholders entitled to vote at such meetings, or if no such date has been fixed, of record at the close of business on the day next preceding the day on which notice is given, by leaving such notice with the stockholder or at his or her residence or usual place of business or by mailing it, postage prepaid and addressed to the stockholder at his or her post office address as it appears on the books of the Corporation. A waiver of such notice in writing, signed by the person or persons entitled to said notice, whether before or after the time stated therein, shall be deemed equivalent to such notice. Except as otherwise required by statute, notice of any adjourned meeting of the stockholders shall not be required.

Section 6.   *Quorum.* Except as otherwise required by statute, the presence at any meeting, in person or by proxy, of the holders of record of a majority of the shares then issued and outstanding and entitled to vote shall be necessary and sufficient to constitute a quorum for the transaction of business. In the absence of a quorum, a majority in interest of the stockholders entitled to vote, present in person or by proxy, or, if no stockholder entitled to vote is present in person or by proxy, any officer entitled to preside or act as secretary of such meeting, may adjourn the meeting from time to time for a period not exceeding twenty days in any one case. At any such adjourned meeting at which a quorum may be present, any business may be transacted which might have been transacted at the meeting as originally called.

Section 7.   *List of Stockholders Entitled to Vote.* The officer who has charge of the stock ledger of the Corporation shall prepare and make, at least ten days before every election of directors, a complete list of the stockholders entitled to vote at said election, arranged in alphabetical order, and showing the address of each stockholder and the number of shares registered in the name of each stockholder. Such list shall be open to the examination of any stockholder during ordinary business hours, for a period of at least ten days prior to the election, either at a place within the city, town, or village where the election is to be held and which place shall be specified in the notice of the meeting, or, if not so specified, at the place where said meeting is to be held, and the list shall be produced and kept at the time and place of election during the whole time thereof, and subject to the inspection of any stockholder who may be present.

Section 8.   *Voting.* Except as otherwise provided by statute or by the Certificate of Incorporation, and subject to the provisions of Section 4 of Article VIII of these Bylaws, each stockholder shall at every meeting of the stockholders be entitled to one vote in person or by proxy for each share of the capital stock having voting power held by such stockholder, but no proxy shall be voted on after three years from its date, unless the proxy provides for a longer period.

At all meetings of the stockholders, except as otherwise required by statute, by the Certificate of Incorporation, or by these Bylaws, all matters shall be decided by the vote of a majority in interest of the stockholders entitled to vote present in person or by proxy.

Persons holding stock in a fiduciary capacity shall be entitled to vote the shares so held, and persons whose stock is pledged shall be entitled to vote, unless in the transfer by the pledgor on the books of the Corporation he or she shall have expressly empowered the pledgee to vote thereon, in which case only the pledgee or his or her proxy may represent said stock and vote thereon.

Shares of the capital stock of the Corporation belonging to the Corporation shall not be voted upon directly or indirectly.

Section 9. *Consent of Stockholders in Lieu of Meeting.* Whenever the vote of stockholders at a meeting thereof is required or permitted to be taken in connection with any corporate action, by any provisions of the statutes or of the Certificate of Incorporation, the meeting and vote of stockholders may be dispensed with, if all the stockholders who would have been entitled to vote upon the action if such meeting were held, shall consent in writing to such corporate action being taken.

ARTICLE III
Board of Directors

Section 1. *General Powers.* The business of the Corporation shall be managed by the Board of Directors, except as otherwise provided by statute or by the Certificate of Incorporation.

Section 2. *Number and Qualifications.* The Board of Directors shall consist of five members. Except as provided in the Certificate of Incorporation this number can be changed only by the vote or written consent of the holders of 90 percent of the stock of the Corporation outstanding and entitled to vote. This number cannot be changed by amendment of the Bylaws of the Corporation. No director need be a stockholder.

[Alternative Clause: Indefinite Number of Directors]

Section 2. *Number and Qualifications.* The number of directors shall be not less than three nor more than fifteen, except that in case all the shares of the Corporation are owned beneficially and of record by either one or two stockholders, the number of directors may be less than three but not less than the number of stockholders. Within the limits specified, the number of directors for each corporate year shall be fixed by vote at the meeting at which they are elected. No director need be a stockholder.

Section 3. *Election and Term of Office.* The directors shall be elected annually by the stockholders, and shall hold office until their successors are respectively elected and qualified.

At all elections for directors, each stockholder shall be entitled to as many votes as shall equal the number of his or her shares of stock multiplied by the number of directors to be elected, and he or she may cast all of such votes for a single director, or may distribute them among the number to be voted for, or any two or more of them, as he or she may see fit.

Elections of directors need not be by ballot.

Section 4. *Compensation.* The members of the Board of Directors shall be paid a fee of $_____ for attendance at all annual, regular, special, and adjourned meetings of the Board. No such fee shall be paid any director if absent. Any director of the Corporation may also serve the Corporation in any other capacity, and receive compensation therefor in any form. Members of special or standing committees may be allowed like compensation for attending committee meetings.

Section 5. *Removals and Resignations.* The stockholders may, at any meeting called for the purpose, by vote of two-thirds of the capital stock issued and outstanding, remove any director from office, with or without cause; provided, however, that no director shall be removed in case the votes of a sufficient number of shares are cast against his or her removal, which if cumulatively voted at an election of directors would be sufficient to elect him or her.

The stockholders may, at any meeting, by vote of a majority of such stock represented at such meeting, accept the resignation of any director.

Section 6. *Vacancies.* Any vacancy occurring in the office of director may be filled by a majority of the directors then in office, though less than a quorum, and the directors so chosen shall hold office until the next annual election and until their successors are duly elected and qualified, unless sooner displaced.

When one or more directors resign from the Board, effective at a future date, a majority of the directors then in office, including those who have so resigned, shall have power to fill such vacancy or vacancies, the vote thereon to take effect when such resignation or resignations shall become effective, and each director so chosen shall hold office as herein provided in the filling of other vacancies.

ARTICLE IV
Meetings of Board of Directors

Section 1.   *Regular Meetings.* A regular meeting of the Board of Directors may be held without call or formal notice immediately after and at the same place as the annual meeting of the stockholders or any special meeting of the stockholders at which a Board of Directors is elected. Other regular meetings of the Board of Directors may be held without call or formal notice at such places within or without the State of Delaware and at such times as the Board may by vote from time to time determine.

Section 2.   *Special Meetings.* Special meetings of the Board of Directors may be held at any place either within or without the State of Delaware at any time when called by the President, Treasurer, Secretary, or two or more directors. Notice of the time and place thereof shall be given to each director at least three days before the meeting if by mail or at least twenty-four hours if in person or by telephone or telegraph. A waiver of such notice in writing, signed by the person or persons entitled to said notice, either before or after the time stated therein, shall be deemed equivalent to such notice. Notice of any adjourned meeting of the Board of Directors need not be given.

Section 3.   *Quorum.* The presence, at any meeting, of one-third of the total number of directors, but in no case less than two directors, shall be necessary and sufficient to constitute a quorum for the transaction of business except that when a Board of one director is authorized, then one director shall constitute a quorum. Except as otherwise required by statute or by the Certificate of Incorporation, the act of a majority of the directors present at a meeting at which a quorum is present shall be the act of the Board of Directors. In the absence of a quorum, a majority of the directors present at the time and place of any meeting may adjourn such meeting from time to time until a quorum is present.

Section 4.   *Consent of Directors in Lieu of Meeting.* Unless otherwise restricted by the Certificate of Incorporation, any action required or permitted to be taken at any meeting of the Board of Directors or any committee thereof may be taken without a meeting, if prior to such action a written consent thereto is signed by all members of the Board or committee, and such written consent is filed with the minutes of proceedings of the Board or committee.

ARTICLE V
Committees of Board of Directors

The Board of Directors may, by resolution passed by a majority of the whole Board, designate one or more committees, each committee to consist of two or more of the directors of the Corporation, which, to the extent provided in the resolution, shall have and may exercise the powers of the Board of Directors in the management of the business and affairs of the Corporation, and may authorize the seal of the Corporation to be affixed to all papers which may require it. Such committee or committees shall have such name or names as may be determined from time to time by resolution adopted by the Board of Directors.

The committees of the Board of Directors shall keep regular minutes of their proceedings and report the same to the Board of Directors when required.

ARTICLE VI
Officers

Section 1.   *Number.* The corporation shall have a President, one or more Vice Presidents, a Secretary, and a Treasurer, and such other officers, agents, and factors as may be deemed necessary. One person may hold any two offices except the offices of President and Vice President and the offices of President and Secretary.

Section 2.   *Election, Term of Office, and Qualifications.* The officers specifically designated in Section 1 of this Article VI shall be chosen annually by the Board of Directors and shall hold office until their successors are chosen and qualified. No officer need be a director.

Section 3.   *Subordinate Officers.* The Board of Directors from time to time may appoint other officers and agents, including one or more Assistant Secretaries and one or more Assistant Treasurers, each of whom shall hold office for such period, have such authority, and perform such duties as are provided in these Bylaws or as the Board of Directors from time to time may determine. The Board of Directors may delegate to any officer the power to appoint any such subordinate officers, agents, and factors and to prescribe their respective authorities and duties.

Section 4.   *Removals and Resignations.* The Board of Directors may at any meeting called for the purpose, by vote of a majority of their entire number, remove from office any officer or agent of the Corporation, or any member of any committee appointed by the Board of Directors.

The Board of Directors may at any meeting, by vote of a majority of the directors present at such meeting, accept the resignation of any officer of the Corporation.

Section 5.   *Vacancies.* Any vacancy occurring in the office of President, Vice President, Secretary, Treasurer, or any other office by death, resignation, removal, or otherwise shall be filled for the unexpired portion of the term in the manner prescribed by these Bylaws for the regular election or appointment to such office.

Section 6.   *The President.* The President shall be the chief executive officer of the Corporation and, subject to the direction and under the supervision of the Board of Directors, shall have general charge of the business, affairs, and property of the Corporation, and control over its officers, agents, and employees. The President shall preside at all meetings of the stockholders and of the Board of Directors at which he or she is present. The President shall do and perform such other duties and may exercise such other powers as from time to time may be assigned to him or her by these Bylaws or by the Board of Directors.

Section 7.   *The Vice President.* At the request of the President or in the event of his or her absence or disability, the Vice President, or in case there shall be more than one Vice President, the Vice President designated by the President, or in the absence of such designation, the Vice President designated by the Board of Directors, shall perform all the duties of the President, and when so acting, shall have all the powers of, and be subject to all the restrictions upon, the President. Any Vice President shall perform such other duties and may exercise such other powers as from time to time may be assigned to him or her by these Bylaws or by the Board of Directors or the President.

Section 8.   *The Secretary.* The Secretary shall

(a)   record all the proceedings of the meetings of the Corporation and directors in a book to be kept for that purpose;

(b)   have charge of the stock ledger (which may, however, be kept by any transfer agent or agents of the Corporation under the direction of the Secretary), an original or duplicate of which shall be kept at the principal office or place of business of the Corporation in the State of _____ ;

(c)   prepare and make, at least ten days before every election of directors, a complete list of the stockholders entitled to vote at said election, arranged in alphabetical order;

(d)   see that all notices are duly given in accordance with the provisions of these Bylaws or as required by statute;

(e)   be custodian of the records of the Corporation and the Board of Directors, and of the seal of the Corporation, and see that the seal is affixed to all stock certificates prior to their issuance and to all documents the execution of which on behalf of the Corporation under its seal shall have been duly authorized;

(f)   see that all books, reports, statements, certificates, and the other documents and records required by law to be kept or filed are properly kept or filed; and

(g)   in general, perform all duties and have all powers incident to the office of Secretary and perform such other duties and have such other powers as from time to time may be assigned to him or her by these Bylaws or by the Board of Directors or the President.

Section 9.   *The Treasurer.* The Treasurer shall

(a)   have supervision over the funds, securities, receipts, and disbursements of the Corporation;

(b)   cause all moneys and other valuable effects of the Corporation to be deposited in its name and to its credit, in such depositaries as shall be selected by the Board of Directors or pursuant to authority conferred by the Board of Directors;

(c)   cause the funds of the Corporation to be disbursed by checks or drafts upon the authorized depositaries of the Corporation, when such disbursements shall have been duly authorized;

(d)   cause to be taken and preserved proper vouchers for all moneys disbursed;

(e)   cause to be kept at the principal office of the Corporation correct books of account of all its business and transactions;

(f)   render to the President or the Board of Directors, whenever requested, an account of the financial condition of the Corporation and of his or her transactions as Treasurer;

(g)   be empowered to require from the officers or agents of the Corporation reports or statements giving such information as he or she may desire with respect to any and all financial transactions of the Corporation; and

(h)   in general, perform all duties and have all powers incident to the office of Treasurer and perform such other duties and have such other powers as from time to time may be assigned to him or her by these Bylaws or by the Board of Directors or the President.

Section 10.   *Assistant Secretaries and Assistant Treasurers.* The Assistant Secretaries and Assistant Treasurers shall have such duties as from time to time may be assigned to them by the Board of Directors or the President.

Section 11.   *Salaries.* The salaries of the officers of the Corporation shall be fixed from time to time by the Board of Directors, except that the Board of Directors may delegate to any person the power to fix the salaries or other compensation of any officers or agents appointed in accordance with the provisions of Section 3 of this Article VI. No officer shall be prevented from receiving such salary by reason of the fact that he or she is also a director of the Corporation.

Section 12.   *Surety Bond.* The Board of Directors may secure the fidelity of any or all of the officers of the Corporation by bond or otherwise.

ARTICLE VII
Execution of Instruments

Section 1.   *Execution of Instruments Generally.* All documents, instruments, or writings of any nature shall be signed, executed, verified, acknowledged, and delivered by such officer or officers or such agent or agents of the Corporation and in such manner as the Board of Directors from time to time may determine.

Section 2.   *Checks, Drafts, Etc.* All notes, drafts, acceptances, checks, endorsements, and all evidence of indebtedness of the Corporation whatsoever, shall be signed by such officer or officers or such agent or agents of the Corporation and in such manner as the Board of Directors from time to time may determine. Endorsements for deposit to the credit of the Corporation in any of its duly authorized depositaries shall be made in such manner as the Board of Directors from time to time may determine.

Section 3.   *Proxies.* Proxies to vote with respect to shares of stock of other corporations owned by or standing in the name of the Corporation may be executed and delivered from time to time on behalf of the Corporation by the President or a Vice President and the Secretary or an Assistant Secretary of the Corporation or by any other person or persons duly authorized by the Board of Directors.

ARTICLE VIII
Capital Stock

Section 1.   *Certificates of Stock.* Every holder of stock in the Corporation shall be entitled to have a certificate, signed in the name of the Corporation by the Chair or Vice Chair of the Board of Directors, the President or a Vice President, and by the Treasurer or an Assistant Treasurer, or the Secretary or an Assistant Secretary of the Corporation, certifying the number of shares owned by him or her in the Corporation; provided, however, that where such certificate is signed by a transfer agent or an assistant transfer agent or by a transfer clerk acting on behalf of the Corporation and a registrar, the signature of any such Chair or Vice Chair of the Board of Directors, President, Vice President, Treasurer, Assistant Treasurer, Secretary, or Assistant Secretary may be facsimile. In case any officer or officers who shall have signed, or whose facsimile signature or signatures shall have been used on, any such certificate or certificates shall cease to be such officer or officers of the Corporation, whether because of death, resignation, or otherwise, before such certificate or certificates shall have been delivered by the Corporation, such certificate or certificates may nevertheless be adopted by the Corporation and be issued and delivered as though the person or persons who signed such certificate or certificates, or whose facsimile signature or signatures shall have been used thereon, had not ceased to be such officer or officers of the Corporation, and any such delivery shall be regarded as an adoption by the Corporation of such certificate or certificates.

Certificates of stock shall be in such form as shall, in conformity to law, be prescribed from time to time by the Board of Directors.

Section 2.   *Transfer of Stock.* Shares of stock of the Corporation shall only be transferred on the books of the Corporation by the holder of record thereof or by his or her attorney duly authorized in writing, upon surrender to the Corporation of the certificates for such shares endorsed by the appropriate person or persons, with such evidence of the authenticity of such endorsement, transfer, authorization, and other matters as the Corporation may reasonably require, and accompanied by all necessary stock transfer tax stamps. In that event it shall be the duty of the Corporation to issue a new certificate to the person entitled thereto, cancel the old certificate, and record the transaction on its books.

Section 3.   *Rights of Corporation with Respect to Registered Owners.* Prior to the surrender to the Corporation of the certificates for shares of stock with a request to record the transfer of such shares, the Corporation may treat the registered owner as the person entitled to receive dividends, to vote, to receive notifications, and otherwise to exercise all the rights and powers of an owner.

Section 4.   *Closing Stock Transfer Book.* The Board of Directors may close the Stock Transfer Book of the Corporation for a period not exceeding fifty days preceding the date of any meeting of stockholders or the date for payment of any dividend or the date for the allotment of rights or the date when any change or conversion or exchange of capital stock shall go into effect or for a period of not exceeding fifty days in connection with obtaining the consent of stockholders for any purpose. However, in lieu of closing the Stock Transfer Book, the Board of Directors may fix in advance a date, not exceeding fifty days preceding the date of any meeting of stockholders, or the date for the payment of any dividend, or the date for the allotment of rights, or the date when any change or conversion or exchange of capital stock shall go into effect, or a date in connection with obtaining such consent, as a record date for the determination of the stockholders entitled to notice of, and to vote at, any such meeting and any adjournment thereof, or entitled to receive payment of any such dividend, or to any such allotment of rights, or to exercise the rights in respect of any such change, conversion, or exchange of capital stock, or to give such consent, and in such case such stockholders, and only such stockholders as shall be stockholders of record on the date so fixed, shall be entitled to such notice of, and to vote at, such meeting and any adjournment thereof, or to receive payment of such dividend, or to receive such allotment of rights, or to exercise such rights, or to give such consent, as the case may be, notwithstanding any transfer of any stock on the books of the Corporation after any such record date fixed as aforesaid.

Section 5.   *Lost, Destroyed, and Stolen Certificates.* Where the owner of a certificate for shares claims that such certificate has been lost, destroyed, or wrongfully taken, the Corporation shall issue a new certificate in place of the original certificate if the owner (a) so requests before the Corporation has notice that the shares have been acquired by a bona fide purchaser; (b) files with the Corporation a sufficient indemnity bond; and (c) satisfies such other reasonable requirements, including evidence of such loss, destruction, or wrongful taking, as may be imposed by the Corporation.

ARTICLE IX
Dividends

Section 1.   *Sources of Dividends.* The directors of the Corporation, subject to any restrictions contained in the statutes and Certificate of Incorporation, may declare and pay dividends upon the shares of the capital stock of the Corporation either (a) out of its net assets in excess of its capital, or (b) in case there shall be no such excess, out of its net profits for the fiscal year then current or the current and preceding fiscal year.

Section 2.   *Reserves.* Before the payment of any dividend, the directors of the Corporation may set apart out of any of the funds of the Corporation available for dividends a reserve or reserves for any proper purpose, and the directors may abolish any such reserve in the manner in which it was created.

Section 3.   *Reliance on Corporate Records.* A director shall be fully protected in relying in good faith upon the books of account of the Corporation or statements prepared by any of its officials as to the value and amount of the assets, liabilities, and net profits of the Corporation, or any other facts pertinent to the existence and amount of surplus or other funds from which dividends might properly be declared and paid.

Section 4. *Manner of Payment.* Dividends may be paid in cash, in property, or in shares of the capital stock of the Corporation at par.

ARTICLE X
Seal

The corporate seal, subject to alteration by the Board of Directors, shall be in the form of a circle and shall bear the name of the Corporation and the year of its incorporation and shall indicate its formation under the laws of the State of Delaware. Such seal may be used by causing it or a facsimile thereof to be impressed or affixed or reproduced or otherwise.

ARTICLE XI
Fiscal Year

Except as from time to time otherwise provided by the Board of Directors, the fiscal year of the Corporation shall be the calendar year.

ARTICLE XII
Amendments

Section 1. *By the Stockholders.* Except as otherwise provided in the Certificate of Incorporation or in these Bylaws, these Bylaws may be amended or repealed, or new Bylaws may be made and adopted, by a majority vote of all the stock of the Corporation issued and outstanding and entitled to vote at any annual or special meeting of the stockholders, provided that notice of intention to amend shall have been contained in the notice of meeting.

Section 2. *By the Directors.* Except as otherwise provided in the Certificate of Incorporation or in these Bylaws, these Bylaws, including amendments adopted by the stockholders, may be amended or repealed by a majority vote of the whole Board of Directors at any regular or special meeting of the Board, provided that the stockholders may from time to time specify particular provisions of the Bylaws which shall not be amended by the Board of Directors.*

*Adapted from West's Modern Legal Forms § 2793.

This Indenture, dated _____ _____ , 20__ , between _____Corporation, a corporation organized and existing under the laws of the State of _____(hereinafter called the Corporation), and the _____Trust Company of _____ , a corporation organized and existing under the laws of the State of _____ , as Trustee (hereinafter called the Trustee), Witnesseth:

Whereas, the Corporation, in the exercise of its corporate powers and for the purpose of furthering and accomplishing its corporate objects and purposes and pursuant to due corporate action, has determined to create an issue of First Mortgage Bonds, in an aggregate principal amount not exceeding $_____ at any one time outstanding, and to secure the same by this Indenture; and

Whereas, the Corporation has determined to create an initial series of Bonds hereunder and to issue forthwith $_____ in principal amount of said initial series of Bonds to be known as "First Mortgage Bonds, _____ % Series, due _____ , 20__", to contain such provisions as are hereinafter specified; and

WHEREAS, the text of all the First Mortgage Bonds, _____ % Series, due _____ _____ , 20__ , of the coupons for interest to be attached thereto and of the Trustee's certificate to be endorsed thereon, is to be substantially as follows:

[*Here insert full form of bond;*] and

WHEREAS, all the requirements of law relating to the authorization of the Bonds and the execution of this Indenture and the mortgage and pledge hereby evidenced have been complied with; and all things necessary to make the Bonds, when authenticated by the Trustee and issued as in this Indenture provided, the valid and binding obligations of the Corporation, and all things necessary to constitute this Indenture a valid and binding mortgage for the security of said Bonds have been done and performed and the issue of said Bonds subject to the terms hereof and the execution of this Indenture have been in all respects duly authorized;

NOW, THEREFORE, In order to secure the payment of the principal and interest of all the Bonds at any time issued and outstanding under this Indenture, according to their tenor, purport and effect, and the performance and observance of all the covenants, agreements and conditions therein and herein contained, and to declare the terms and conditions upon which said Bonds are to be issued, authenticated, secured and held, and for and in consideration of the premises and of the purchase and acceptance of the Bonds by the holders thereof, and of the sum of _____dollar(s) duly paid by the Trustee to the Corporation at or before the ensealing and delivery of these presents, the receipt whereof is hereby acknowledged, the Corporation has mortgaged, pledged, assigned, transferred, granted, bargained, sold, aliened, remised, released, conveyed, confirmed and set over, unto the Trustee, and its successor or successors, in the trusts hereby created, and its and their assigns, the following described properties:

[*Insert full description of properties. This usually includes all land, plants, offices and other buildings, together with all improvements and fixtures, etc., and a clause providing for after-acquired property. This is followed by the "Habendum clause":*]

TO HAVE AND TO HOLD the lands and interest in lands, estates, plants and appurtenances and other property hereby conveyed, mortgaged, pledged or transferred unto the Trustee, its successors and assigns forever;

[*There follows a clause excepting any specific property from the mortgage. This is followed by the "Trust" clause:*]

IN TRUST NEVERTHELESS, under and subject to the conditions herein set forth, for the common and equal benefit and security of all the holders of Bonds and coupons issued and to be issued under this Indenture.

[*The remainder of the indenture is divided into articles, as indicated below, each article being further divided into a number of sections and subsections:*]

Article 1:   Form, Execution, Delivery and Registration of the Bonds

[Authentication by Trustee; aggregate amount outstanding; recording of indenture.—Date of initial series; interest; place of payment of principal and interest; denominations.—Terms of later series.—Title of initial series; identification of later series; numbering of bonds.—Execution of supplemental indenture upon request for authentication and delivery of later series.—Registration and transfer of bonds.—Signature of bonds; use of facsimile signatures; seal; effect of Trustee's certificate.—Evidence of ownership of bonds.—Issuance of temporary bonds.—Mutilated, lost, destroyed or stolen bonds.]

Article 2:   Issue of Bonds

[Authentication and delivery of initial series of bonds.—Use of deposited funds for capital expenditures.—Limitation on amount of bonds authenticated and moneys paid out for capital expenditures.—Sale of bonds reserved for authentication.—Documents required before paying out deposited moneys and

authenticating and delivering bonds.—Discharge of prior lien on property.—
Trustee not liable for use of bonds or deposited moneys.—Delivery of bonds in
exchange for bonds cancelled.—Delivery of bonds upon surrender of bonds about
to mature or called for redemption.—Cancellation of bonds converted into stock or
retired through sinking fund.]

Article 3: Redemption of Bonds

[Premium paid on redemption.—Notice of redemption.—Cancellation of indenture
on redemption of all outstanding bonds.—Cancellation of redeemed or reacquired
bonds.]

*Article 4: Sinking fund for First Mortgage Bonds, ___% Series, due _____ _____,
20___ .*

[Amounts to be paid into sinking fund.—Additional sinking fund equal to percentage of net profits.—Fund payments in bonds purchased by Corporation.—
Application of fund to redemption of bonds.—Notice of redemption through
fund.—Cancellation of bonds redeemed.]

Article 5: Particular Covenants of the Corporation

[Covenants to pay principal and interest—not to extend time for payment of
interest—to subject present and after-acquired property to lien of indenture and to
execute further instruments of conveyance—not to permit prior lien on property
and to discharge liens—to discharge taxes and assessments—not to merge or sell
assets unless purchaser assumes payment of bonds—to maintain property—to
preserve corporate existence—to keep property insured—to pay expenses of
Trustee—to record and file indenture—not to dispose of bonds contrary to indenture provisions—to restrict declaration of dividends, distributions and redemption
of stock—to restrict purchase of stock—to maintain office for payment of principal
and interest—to deliver to Trustee annual financial statements—to furnish opinion
of expert as to fair value of property.]

Article 6: Release of Property Included in the Trust Estate

[Power of Corporation to sell obsolete property.—Power of Corporation to remove
property.—Power of Corporation to sell limited amount of property.—Obligations
in satisfaction of debt not to be subject to lien of indenture.—Power of Corporation
to move, alter or remodel buildings.—Power of Corporation to amend, alter or
cancel lease, license or easement.—Power of Corporation to sell or exchange for
other property.—Release of trust property taken by eminent domain.—Method of
release of mortgaged properties.—Application of moneys received by Trustee.—
Powers of Corporation to be exercised by receiver or Trustee.]

Article 7: Events of Default—Remedies of Trust and Bondholders

[Events of default: default in payment of principal, payment of interest or sinking
fund payment—involuntary bankruptcy or receivership—voluntary bankruptcy,
reorganization, assignment for benefit of creditors—default in performance of
covenants.—Acceleration of due date of principal; waiver of default.—Power of
Trustee to take possession.—Power of Trustee to sell trust estate.—Notice of sale.—
Execution of instruments and transfer to purchaser at sale.—Divesting of Corporation's title upon sale.—Suit by Trustee to enforce payment of bonds; foreclosure.—
Power of bondholders to decide on remedy sought.—Payment by Corporation to
Trustee for benefit of bondholders on default.—Restrictions on suits by
bondholders.—Application of proceeds of sale of trust estate.—Principal of all
bonds to become due on sale.—Appointment of receiver upon default.—Covenant
of Corporation to waive service of process, enter appearance and consent to entry
of judgment.—Waiver of Corporation of benefits of laws for stay or appraisal of trust
estate.—Remedies cumulative.—Delay or omission to exercise right not waiver.—
Restrictions against remedies which would surrender lien of indenture.—Power of
Trustee to restrain compliance with invalid law.]

EXHIBIT J–11.

(continued)

Article 8: Immunity of Incorporators, Stockholders, Officers and Directors
Article 9: Merger, Consolidation or Sale
[Covenant of Corporation not to merge, consolidate or sell assets unless new company can meet provisions of indenture.—Successor company to assume conditions of bonds and indentures.—Successor company to succeed to rights of Corporation.—Indenture to become lien on improvements by successor company and on after-acquired property.]
Article 10: Concerning the Trustee
[Power of Trustee to employ agents and attorneys.—Limitation on liability of Trustee.—Indemnification of Trustee by bondholders.—Form of request, notice or authorization to Trustee by Corporation.—Compensation of Trustee; lien for payment.—Return of moneys deposited with Trustee.—Advances by Trustee to preserve trust estate.—Conflicting interests of Trustee.—Removal of Trustee.—Appointment of successor Trustee.—Effect of merger or consolidation of Trustee.—Appointment of co-trustee.]
Article 11: Bondholders' Lists and Reports by the Corporation and the Trustee
[Corporation to furnish list of bondholders; Trustee to preserve list.—Application by bondholders for list.—Corporation to file annual and other reports.—Reports by Trustee to bondholders.—Notice by Trustee to bondholders of defaults.]
Article 12: Supplemental Indentures, Bondholders' Acts, Holdings and Apparent Authority
[Purposes for execution of supplemental indenture.—Consent to execution by proportion of bondholders.—Binding effect of supplemental indenture on non-consenting bondholders.—Revocation of consent by bondholders.—Trustee to join in supplemental indenture.—Proof of ownership of registered and bearer bonds.—Supplemental indenture to be considered part of original indenture.]
Article 13: Possession Until Default
[Corporation to retain possession until default, use income and dispose of profits.—Reversion of property to Corporation on payment of principal and interest; discharge of indenture.]
Article 14: Definitions and Miscellaneous Provisions
[Agreements binding on successors and assigns.—Definitions.—Provisions conflicting with Trust Indenture Act of 1939.—Agreements to be for exclusive benefit of parties and bondholders.—Notices to Corporation or Trustee.—Acceptance of trust by Trustee.—Appointment of attorneys for acknowledgment of indenture.]

IN WITNESS WHEREOF, _____Corporation has caused this instrument to be signed in its corporate name and its corporate seal to be affixed by its President and its Secretary, and its corporate seal to be attested by its Secretary, by order of its Board of Directors, and the _____Trust Company of__, in token of its acceptance of the trusts created hereby, has caused this instrument to be signed in its corporate name and its corporate seal to be affixed by its President and its Secretary, and its corporate seal to be attested by its Secretary, by order of the Executive Committee of its Board of Directors, as of the date given at the beginning of this indenture.

_____Corporation

[Corporate Seal]   by _____President

Attest:

_____Secretary   _____ Secretary

The _____Trust Company of

_____ , Trustee

[Corporate Seal]   by _____President

Attest:

_____Secretary   _____ Secretary*

*Prentice Hall, Corporations, Forms § 60351. Reprinted with the permission of Prentice Hall.

Agreement, made this _____day of _____ , 20___ , between _____ , _____ , _____ , _____ , and _____ , hereinafter designated as Trustees, and the undersigned shareholders of _____Company, hereinafter designated as the Beneficiaries.

Whereas, the parties do hereby agree and declare that the intent and purpose of this Agreement is to provide a means whereby the parties hereto may initiate or maintain in effect any general policy, plan, or program affecting _____Company which the parties should determine to be to their joint benefit, interest, and advantage, and to the best interests of all stockholders of _____Company, and to that end to elect or retain or replace any officer, executive, or employee of said corporation;

Now, therefore, the parties do hereby agree with each other as follows:

1. **Delivery of Shares to Trustees, Term of Trust.** Upon the signing of this agreement, the Beneficiaries shall deliver to the Trustees the certificate or certificates representing all the shares of _____Company now owned or controlled by them, said certificates to be endorsed in blank or accompanied by proper instruments of assignment and transfer thereof in blank. Said shares will be held by the Trustees for a period of ten years from _____, 20___ (unless this trust is sooner terminated, as hereinafter provided) in trust, however, for the Beneficiaries, their heirs, executors, administrators, successors, and assigns, and at all times subject to the terms and conditions herein set forth.

2. **Additional Shares.** Any and all certificates for additional shares of _____Company that shall hereafter during said ten-year period be issued to any of the Beneficiaries shall be in like manner endorsed and delivered to the Trustees, to be held by them under the terms hereof.

3. **Voting.** During the term of this Agreement the Trustees or their successors in trust shall have the sole and exclusive voting power of the stock standing in their names as such. They shall have the power to vote the stock at all regular and special meetings of the stockholders and may vote for, do, or assent or consent to any act or proceeding which the shareholders of said corporation might or could vote for, do, or assent or consent to and shall have all the powers, rights, and privileges of a shareholder of said corporation. The Trustees shall consult and confer with each other and shall make every effort to agree on how their votes are cast. The Trustees, as soon as this Agreement becomes effective, shall appoint a chair. In any case where shareholder action is required, the chair may, or upon the request of any two Trustees, shall, call a meeting of the Trustees, on reasonable notice, for the purpose of reaching an agreement on the manner of voting the stock held by the Trustees, or for any other purpose deemed to be in the best interests of _____Company. The vote of the Trustees shall always be exercised as a unit, as any four of said Trustees shall direct and determine. If any four Trustees fail to agree on any matter on which a vote of the stockholders is called for, then the question in disagreement shall be submitted for arbitration to some disinterested person (i.e., one having no financial interest in _____Company) chosen by the affirmative vote of four of the Trustees, as sole arbitrator. If four of the Trustees are unable to agree on an arbitrator, then each of the Trustees shall nominate a similarly disinterested person as a candidate and the arbitrator shall be selected by the affirmative vote of four of the Trustees from the panel of such candidates. If any candidate receives the affirmative vote of four of the Trustees, he or she shall be elected sole arbitrator. If no candidate receives the affirmative vote of four of the Trustees, then the candidate receives the vote of four of the Trustees, then those two candidates receiving the lowest number of votes shall be eliminated from the panel (or if there should be a tie among the low candidates, or among all the candidates, if more than two, one of such candidates shall be eliminated by lot) and the

Trustees shall continue the process of voting among those remaining on the panel until one has been selected by the affirmative vote of four of the Trustees. If the voting continues to the point where no candidate receives the vote of four of the Trustees, then those two candidates receiving the highest number of votes respectively from those who voted with the majority and those who voted with the minority on the issue to be submitted to arbitration (ties among the majority and minority candidates to be decided by lot) shall be appointed arbitrators and these two shall appoint a third disinterested person as arbitrator. The decision of the arbitrator or, if more than one, a majority thereof, shall be binding upon the parties hereto and the vote of all the stock in trust shall be cast in accordance with such decision. The Beneficiaries may by unanimous written agreement designate any person as sole arbitrator who shall act during the life of this agreement.

4. **Proxies.** Any Trustee may vote in person or by proxy and a proxy in writing signed by any four of the Trustees shall be sufficient authority to the person named therein to vote all the stock held by the Trustees hereunder at any meeting, regular or special, of the stockholders of _____Company. If at any such meeting less than four Trustees shall be present either in person or by proxy, then all of the stock held by the Trustees may be voted in accordance with the unanimous decision of those trustees present in person or by proxy.

5. **Appointment of Successor Trustees.** In the event of the death, resignation, removal, or incapacity of any of the Trustees, his or her successor shall be named by an instrument in writing signed by a majority of the remaining Trustees. All Successor Trustees shall be clothed with all the rights, privileges, duties, and powers herein conferred upon the Trustees herein named.

6. **Voting Trust Certificates.** Upon the delivery to the Trustees of said certificates representing the shares of _____Company, the Trustees will cause the same to be transferred on the books of the corporation to themselves as Trustees and will deliver to each of the Beneficiaries a Trustees' Certificate for the number of shares delivered to said Trustees, substantially in the form hereinafter set out. Upon receipt of certificates for additional shares of _____Company issued to any of the Beneficiaries, and upon receipt of certificates for such shares issued to other persons and which may be issued to future subscribers for shares of _____Company, and upon compliance with the terms of this agreement by the owners of such shares, the Trustees will cause said shares to be transferred on the books of said corporation to their names as trustees, and shall deliver to each of the persons so depositing said certificates a Trustees' Certificate for the number of shares so deposited by said person.

The Trustees' Certificate shall be substantially in the following form:

Trustees' Certificate

This is to certify that the undersigned Trustees have received a certificate or certificates issued in the name of _____ , evidencing the ownership of shares of _____Company, a _____corporation, and that said shares are held subject to all the terms and conditions of that certain agreement, dated _____ , 20___ , by and between _____ , _____ , _____ , _____ , and _____ , as Trustees, and certain shareholders of _____Company. During the period of ten years from and after _____ , 20___ , the said Trustees, or their successors, shall, as provided in said agreement, possess and be entitled to exercise the right to vote and otherwise represent all of said shares for all purposes, it being agreed that no voting right shall pass to the holder hereof by virtue of the ownership of this certificate.

This certificate is assignable with the right of issuance of a new certificate of like tenor only upon the surrender to the undersigned or their successors of this certificate properly endorsed. Upon the termination of said Trust this certificate shall be surrendered to the Trustees by the holder hereof upon delivery to such holder of a stock certificate representing a like number of said shares.

In witness whereof, the undersigned Trustees have executed this Certificate this _____ day of _____ , 20___ .

_____
_____
_____
_____
_____
                                                  Trustees

Said Trustee's Certificate, subject to the conditions hereof, may be transferred by endorsement by the person to whom issued, or by his or her attorney in fact, or by the administrator, executor, or guardian of his or her estate, and delivery of the same to said Trustees; but said transfer shall not be evidence to or be binding upon said Trustees until the certificate is surrendered to them and the transfer is so entered upon their "Trustees' Certificate Book," which shall be kept by them to show the names of the parties by whom and to whom transferred, the numbers of the certificates, the number of shares, and the date of transfer. No new Trustees' Certificate shall be issued until the former Trustees' Certificate for the shares represented thereby shall have been surrendered to and canceled by said Trustees, and they shall preserve the certificates so canceled as vouchers. In case any Trustees' Certificate shall be claimed to be lost or destroyed, a new Trustees' Certificate may be issued in lieu thereof, upon such proof of loss and such security as may be required by said Trustees.

7. **Restrictions on Transfer of Voting Trust Certificates.** Each of the Beneficiaries agrees that during the term of this agreement said Trustees' Certificates will not be sold or transferred except in accordance with Paragraph _____ of the Organization Agreement of _____ Company, dated _____ , 20___ , relating to the sale of shares of _____ Company, so long as said Organization Agreement remains in effect. Said Trustees' Certificates shall be regarded as stock of the _____ Company within the meaning of any provision of the Bylaws of said corporation imposing conditions or restrictions upon the sale of stock of said corporation.

8. **Dividends.** Before declaring any dividend the Board of Directors of _____ Company shall request the Trustees to certify to the Board the names of all persons who are the owners and holders of Trustees' Certificates, and the number of shares to which each of such persons is or may then be entitled as shown by the books of the Trustees and no dividend shall be declared and paid by said corporation until reasonable opportunity has been given the Trustees to submit such certificate. Said corporation is hereby irrevocably authorized and directed (a) to accept such certificate of the Trustees as true; and (b) to pay any and all dividends upon the shares enumerated in such certificate directly to the holders of the Trustees' Certificates.

In the event that any dividend paid in capital stock of the Company shall be received by the Trustees, the respective holders of Trustees' Certificates issued hereunder shall be entitled to the delivery of new or additional Trustees' Certificates to the amount of the stock received by the Trustees as such dividend upon the number of such shares of the Company represented by their respective Trustees' Certificates theretofore outstanding.

9. **Termination.** Except as herein otherwise provided the trust hereby created shall not be revoked and the powers herein delegated to the Trustees shall be irrevocable during said period of ten years from and after _____ , 20___ . This

trust, however, shall terminate upon the vote of any four of the Trustees and their declaration in writing that said trust is terminated. Unless the Trustees by unanimous vote otherwise determine, this trust shall also terminate if and when less than 50% of the outstanding shares of _____Company remain subject to this Trust Agreement. Upon the termination of said trust the certificates representing all of the shares so held under this agreement and then remaining in the hands of the Trustees or their successors shall be assigned to the parties then entitled thereto as shown by Trustees' Certificates then outstanding, upon surrender to the Trustees of the Trustees' Certificates representing said shares.

10. **Compensation of Trustees.** The Beneficiaries may pay a reasonable compensation to the Trustees for their service hereunder and all expenses and costs incurred by them in executing said trusts, and the Beneficiaries do agree to save and hold harmless said Trustees from any and all liability arising out of the holding by them of any of the shares of said _____Company hereunder.

11. **Exculpatory Clause.** The Trustees shall not be liable or incur any responsibility by reason of their acts of omission or commission in the premises except for wilful misconduct or gross negligence in the execution of the trusts hereby created.

12. **Extension of Term.** At any time within one year prior to the time of expiration of this agreement, one or more Beneficiaries hereunder may, by agreement in writing and with the written consent of all of the Trustees, extend the duration of this agreement for an additional period not exceeding ten years; provided, however, that no such extension agreement shall affect the rights or obligations of persons not parties thereto.

13. **Counterparts.** This agreement may be executed in several counterparts, each of which so executed shall be deemed to be the original, and such counterparts shall together constitute one and the same instrument.

In witness whereof, the parties have hereunto set their hands or have caused their corporate names to be hereunto affixed by their officers thereunto duly authorized, the day and year first above written.

_____

_____

_____

_____

_____

                   Trustees

_____holding _____shares

_____holding _____shares

_____holding _____shares

_____holding _____shares

_____holding _____shares

_____holding _____shares

                Stockholders of _____Company

                Beneficiaries*

*Adapted from West's Modern Legal Forms § 3012.1.

GLOSSARY

absence of fraud rule Property or services contributed for a share of stock are presumed to be equal to the par value or the stated value of no par value share.

actual authority Authority expressly or implicitly conferred by a principal to permit an agent to perform an assigned task.

adjusted stated value A price stated in an agreement that has a periodic adjustment based upon certain conditions or processes.

affiliated corporation A corporation that owns a sufficient number of shares in another corporation to control the vote of the shareholders.

agency A voluntary consensual relationship between two persons.

agent The person acting on behalf of a principal.

aggregate theory A partnership is only an aggregation of persons who own and conduct a partnership business; the partnership is not a separate entity.

all or nothing purchase A provision requiring that all shares subject to an option be purchased or none of them may be purchased.

annual report A report required by statute to be filed annually with a public official.

apparent authority A third party's reasonable belief in the authority of an agent, based upon a manifestation of the principal.

appraisal A determination of the value of the shares by a professional appraiser based upon agreed or customary industry valuation techniques.

appraisal right A shareholder's right to demand payment for the fair value of stock as a result of an extraordinary corporate transaction.

arbitration A procedure for an objective determination of a dispute.

articles of incorporation The document filed with a public official to form a corporation.

articles of organization The document filed to form a limited liability company.

articles of partnership The partnership agreement.

articles of termination Document filed to terminate the existence of a limited liability company.

assessable Additional consideration is required to be paid.

assignment of interest Transfer of a partner's interest in the partnership to another.

assumed name A name under which the corporation is operating other than its organized name.

at-will company A limited liability company without a specified duration or term.

attachments to minutes Documents appended to the minutes of a corporation.

authorized shares The shares of a corporation permitted to be sold in the articles of incorporation.

average benefits test Plan coverage of average benefits for highly compensated employees compared to non-highly compensated employees.

balance sheet A financial statement showing assets, liabilities, and shareholder equity.

basis for shares The cost of shares.

beneficial owner A person entitled to the benefits of ownership without having legal title.

best efforts An agreement between the corporation and the underwriter that the underwriter will use its best efforts to sell the securities to public investors.

blank stock Series shares.

"Blue-sky" requirements Laws of a state regulating the purchase and sale of stock in a business entity.

bonus plan A plan for additional compensation related to performance standards.

book value The value of a share of stock equal to the proportionate share of shareholder equity as shown on the corporation's balance sheet.

book value formula A formula based upon the assets less the liabilities of a business.

bulk transfer The sale or transfer of a major part of a company's assets outside the scope of ordinary business activities.

business corporation An artificial person or legal entity created under the law of the state to conduct business.

bylaws Regulations and rules adopted by an association or organization for its governance.

call for consideration due A determination by a board of directors to require payment of some or all of the consideration to be paid for stock.

cancellation of redeemable shares The procedure to restore redeemed shares to authorized by unissued status or to eliminate redeemed shares.

cancellation of repurchased shares The elimination of reacquired shares in a corporation.

capital account An account in which the capital contribution of a member or partner is recorded.

capital contributions The value of cash or property contributed to an entity by an owner.

capital gain and losses Profit or loss from the purchase and sale of an asset.

capital surplus An account in which a corporation records funds received from sales of stock in excess of par value and to which funds received from sales of no par value shares are allocated; the amount of consideration paid for stock without par value or in excess of its par value.

capitalization of earnings   A transfer of surplus to stated capital.

cash subscription   An offer to buy shares in a corporation for cash.

certificate of authority   The authorization to do business in a state other than the state in which the corporation is formed.

certificates   Instruments representing the ownership of shares of stock in a corporation.

circular holdings   A parent corporation that owns a majority of stock in a subsidiary and the subsidiary owns a majority of stock in the parent corporation.

classification   The grouping together of managers in a limited liability company to elect the group in different years.

classify   To designate certain positions on the board of directors to represent certain shareholders or groups of shareholders.

close corporation   A corporation owned by a small group of shareholders whose shares are not traded on an exchange.

commission   An amount paid to an employee based upon completion of transactions on behalf of the employer.

common stock   The ownership interests in a corporation with equal rights to voting, distributions and liquidation of assets.

comp time   Time off allowed to an employee in substitution for extra time worked for which overtime would normally be paid.

compensation   Amounts paid to employees for services.

consolidation   A combination of two or more corporations into a new corporation, whereby the new corporation survives the transaction and the others cease to exist.

constituent corporations   The corporate parties to a merger, consolidation, exchange or sale of assets.

constructive receipt   The right to receive a benefit that will be actually received later.

continuity of life   The continuous existence of a business entity.

control shares   A sufficient number of shares in a corporation to control voting decisions by the shareholders.

conversion of stock   The right of a holder of one class of stock to convert the shares owned to shares of another class of stock.

convertible shares   Shares that may be converted from one class of stock to another.

corporate powers   The powers of the corporation as authorized by the statute under which it is organized.

corporate purposes   The business objectives of a corporation.

corporate seal   An imprint signifying the official act of the corporation.

corporate shell   A corporation that has disposed of substantially all of its assets.

corporate structural changes   Transactions that have a significant impact on the structure or existence of the corporation.

covenant not to compete, noncompetition agreement   Provisions in an employment agreement restricting an employee's activities in competition with the employer's business.

cross purchase plan   The purchase of life insurance on the lives of the partners by each of the other partners.

cross-purchase insurance agreement   An agreement by each shareholder to purchase insurance relating to other shareholders to pay obligations that will be created under buy-out agreements upon the occurrence of certain events.

cumulative distribution preference   An accrued entitlement to a preferred payment of distributions from a corporation.

"cumulative to the extent earned" distribution preference   An entitlement to a preferred payment of distributions from a corporation that will accrue in any period in which the corporate operations are profitable.

cumulative voting   A system of voting allowing a person to concentrate the whole number of votes for one or more nominees to a board of directors.

current incentive program   A program to provide compensation related directly to current performance.

Deadwood draw provision   An agreement in which a shareholder offers to buy or sell shares at a price and on certain terms and the other shareholder may determine whether to buy or sell according to the offer.

death benefit compensation program   A program to pay benefits to an employee's heirs or estate upon death.

debenture   An unsecured corporate obligation to repay money borrowed from an investor.

debt securities   Loans to a business entity.

deferred compensation plan   A plan to provide an incentive to employees by deferring compensation until a later event.

deferred dissolution   A dissolution of a partnership delayed for ninety days following a partner's withdrawal from the partnership.

de jure corporation   A corporation formed in accordance with the appropriate law.

depletion reserve   A reserve of funds to account for assets that deplete over time.

derivative action   A suit brought by an owner of a business on behalf of the business.

diluted shares   Shares sold at a price higher than the most recent price charged for shares.

dilution   The reduction of a shareholder's percentage ownership by the issuance of additional shares of stock in a corporation.

director   A person elected to manage and direct the affairs of the corporation.

director and officer liability insurance   Insurance policies protecting directors and officers from liability.

disclosed principal   The existence and identity of the principal is known to a third party.

discount   A market price lower than the principal amount repayable on a bond.

disproportionate allocation   An agreed percentage to be shared with a partner that is not in the same proportion as capital contributions or the share of other benefits from the partnership.

dissenter's rights   The appraisal rights given to a dissenter in an extraordinary corporate transaction.

dissociate   A member's withdrawal from a company by resignation, expulsion, death, or bankruptcy.

dissociated partner   A partner who has withdrawn or retired from the partnership.

distributional interest   A member's right to distributions of cash or property from the company.

dissolution   Termination of the right to do business, except to wind up the affairs of the business.

dissolution distribution   A distribution of assets of a corporation to the shareholders when the corporation is terminated.

distribution   A transfer of money or property from a corporation to or for the benefit of a shareholder.

dividend   Income distributions to shareholders.

dividend arrearages   Accumulated unpaid accounts of dividend preferences.

dividend preference   A prior right to payment of dividend.

domestic corporation   A corporation organized under the laws of the state in which it is operating.

double taxation   The taxation of a corporation's income at the corporate level and also at the shareholder level when distributions of the income are made to the shareholders.

draws against compensation   Advance payments of anticipated compensation.

due diligence   The review and confirmation of all documentation and factual material information stated in a registration statement.

earned surplus   An account in which a corporation records accumulated earnings from operations.

earnings multiple formula   A formula based upon historical earnings of a business.

emergency powers   The power of a corporation to act in an emergency.

employee expense reimbursement plan   A plan whereby an employer reimburses an employee for certain expenses.

employee handbook/manual   A publication of the administrative rules and procedures relating to employment.

employment agreement/contract   An agreement between an employer and an employee.

employment at will   An employment relationship in which the employee may be terminated at any time and for any reason.

Employment Retirement Income Security Act (ERISA)   A federal law regulating employment benefits.

enterprise   A business that sells merchandise from stock (including one that manufactures what it sells).

entity   A separate organization having an existence apart from its members or owners.

entity purchase plan   The purchase of life insurance on the lives of partners by the partnership.

entity theory   A partnership is a separate business entity that operates independently of the individual partners.

equity securities   The ownership interest in a corporation, representing a right to vote, to receive distributions, and to receive assets in liquidation.

escrow of shares   An agreement to hold shares until they have been paid for in full.

event of withdrawal   The circumstance under which a general partner is deemed to have withdrawn from a limited partnership.

ex-dividend   A term used to describe shares of stock in a corporation in which a dividend has been declared and will be paid to the shareholder of record on the record date.

exempt employees   Salaried executive or professional employees who are employed for completion of the job, regardless of the number of hours they work.

exercise limitation   A restriction on the amount of options exercised during a period.

expulsion   The involuntary termination of a partner in a partnership.

extraordinary corporate activity   Transactions outside of the scope of normal corporate business routine.

extraordinary corporate matter   A decision affecting the organization of the corporation.

facsimile signature   A copy of an original signature affixed by a stamp or copy device.

fair-cross-section test   Plan coverage of employees on a nondiscriminating basis.

fair market value   The value of a share of stock based upon a transaction between a willing buyer and a willing seller.

fair value   Value of shares determined to be fair in connection with an extraordinary corporate transaction.

fiduciaries   Persons who have a duty to act primarily for another's benefit in matters connected with the operation of the corporation.

fiduciary duty   An obligation owed by a person in a position of trust or confidence to another.

fiduciary relationship   A relationship of trust or confidence based upon integrity and fidelity.

firm commitment   An agreement between the corporation and the managing underwriter that the underwriter will purchase the securities to be offered to the public and resell them to investors.

firm price   A price stated in an agreement that does not change.

fiscal year The annual accounting period for a business.

five-year cliff vesting An employee is entitled to all benefits after five years of service.

forced buyout provision Provision requiring a shareholder to sell or buy shares in a corporation.

foreign corporation A corporation formed under the laws of a state other than that in which it is operating.

foreign limited partnership A limited partnership organized in another state.

foreign partnership A partnership organized in another state.

foreign professional corporation A professional corporation formed in a state other than that in which it is operating.

forfeiture clause Provisions eliminating benefits or compensation upon certain conditions.

fractional share A certificate or notation that represents a percentage of one full share of stock in a corporation.

franchise fee A fee charged by some states to maintain the existence and good standing of a corporation.

franchise tax A tax imposed for the right to maintain an entity or a franchise in a state.

funding of plan Payments of money to a plan for employees.

general agent A person continuously employed to conduct a series of transactions for a principal.

general partnership An association of two or more persons to carry on as co-owners a business for profit.

going-concern value The value of the business assuming it continues carrying on its business as it is currently conducted.

golden parachute provision Provision for continuation of compensation and benefits after termination of employment.

good faith offer A valid and sincere offer to purchase shares in a corporation.

grant limitation A restriction on the amount of options granted during a period.

greenmail The sale of control of a corporation back to the corporation or to other shareholders at a premium.

group incentive plan Compensation and benefit provisions to provide compensation to members of a group related directly to the performance of the group.

guaranty A promise by one to pay the debt of another.

holder of record A shareholder who owns stock on a record date.

hostile takeover A person taking over the operations of corporation using statutory rules against the will of the corporation and its shareholders.

implied covenant of good faith and fair dealing An implied obligation to exercise legal rights honestly and equitably.

income account The account in which the income allocated to a member is recorded.

incorporator The person(s) who sign the Articles of Incorporation.

indemnification Reimbursement of a person who has paid another's debt or obligation.

indemnify To protect another from possible liability or expense.

indenture An agreement between a corporation, a trustee, and investors concerning the rights and obligations of a bond.

independent contractor An agent whose actions are not subject to the control of the principal.

informational reports Reports to the Internal Revenue Service showing dividends paid to shareholders.

inherent authority Authority of an agent to perform tasks typically performed by that type of agent.

initial public offering The first offering of a corporation's securities to the public.

inside shareholders Initial investors in a corporation before the corporation's shares are sold to the public.

insolvent The inability to pay debts as they come due in the usual course of business.

insurance funding The purchase of insurance policies to pay obligations created by certain events under a buy-out agreement.

interest in partnership A partner's equity in the partnership, comprising a proportionate share of assets and liabilities, a right to proportionate distributions, and a right to manage.

interlocking director A director who has been elected to serve on the board of more than one corporation.

intrastate offering A public offering of securities of a corporation for sale only within the boundaries of a particular state.

involuntary dissolution A dissolution of a corporation caused by the state, a creditor or a shareholder through judicial action.

irrevocable proxies An authorization for another to vote on behalf of a shareholder that may not be revoked.

issued shares The shares of a corporation sold to shareholders.

Jeopardy Auction/Wheel of fortune provision Provision permitting any shareholder to require that all shareholders offer to sell their shares to the corporation and to require the corporation to purchase the shares most favorably offered.

joint venture An association of two or more persons to conduct a specific transaction or project for a profit.

judicial liquidation The process of liquidating and winding up a corporation conducted by a court.

key employee Person employed in positions that are critical to the successful operations of a business.

legend on certificate Statement on a certificate for shares concerning restrictions on the transfer of the shares represented by the certificate.

letter of intent The initial formal writing expressing the understandings of parties to a proposed extraordinary corporate transaction.

limited liability   The concept by which corporate debts are limited to recovery from corporate assets, including capital contributed by shareholders.

limited partnership   An association of two or more persons carrying on business as co-owners for profit with one or more general partners and one or more limited partners.

liquidated damage clause   Provisions in an employment agreement specifying agreed amounts for damages for breach of the agreement.

liquidating distributions   The amount to be distributed to the shareholders of the corporation after creditors of the corporation have been paid.

liquidation   The process of collecting all corporate assets, completing or terminating unexecuted contracts, paying creditors and expenses, and distributing the remaining assets to the shareholders.

liquidation preference   A prior right to payment of assets in liquidation.

manager   A person responsible for management of a limited liability company, elected by the members.

mandatory buyout or sellout arrangements   Provisions in an agreement that require a purchaser to buy or a seller to sell shares in a corporation.

marshaling of assets   The procedure by which creditors of the partnership have priority to partnership assets and creditors of an individual partner have priority to the partner's personal assets.

master   A principal who employs another and who has the right to control the conduct of the agent in the performance of services.

matching price provision   An agreement that the corporation or the other shareholders are obligated to pay a price equal to that offered to a shareholder by an outside investor.

members   Owners of a limited liability company.

membership   An ownership interest in a limited liability company.

merge   Two or more entities combine by the transfer of property of all to one of them, which continues an existence, the others being terminated.

minority nominee   A person nominated for election to the board of directors by the minority shareholders.

minute book   The record of minutes of meetings and consents of the incorporators, directors, and shareholders.

mortgage bonds   A secured corporate obligation to repay money borrowed from an investor.

multiple of earnings formula   A price of corporate shares determined by multiplying the earnings of a corporation by a stated or determined figure.

"name-saver corporation"   A corporation formed only for the purpose of reserving the corporate name in a particular state.

negotiable   The transfer of a certificate for value and without notice of any defense by which the holder becomes entitled to the rights represented by the certificate.

net assets   The amount by which total assets exceed total liabilities.

net distributable profit   The amount of revenue to be distributed after deducting specified expenses and reserves for business purposes.

net worth   The shareholder's equity.

no par value   A term describing shares that do not have any minimum amount for which the shares can be sold to an investor.

nominal, or dummy, directors   Directors named in the articles of incorporation who are not intended to remain as directors after the organizational meeting.

nominee certificate   A certificate for shares in the name of another.

nonassessable   No additional consideration is required to be paid.

noncumulative distribution preference   An entitlement to a preferred payment of distributions from a corporation that does not accrue.

nondisclosure agreement   Provisions in an employment agreement preventing disclosure or use of proprietary and confidential information.

nonexempt employees   Hourly and salaried employees who are not executive or professional employees and are paid based upon the number of hours they work.

nonjudicial liquidation   The process of liquidating and winding up a corporation conducted by corporate management.

officer   Person(s) elected to administer a corporation by the board of directors.

operating agreement   The agreement governing the rights and obligations of members and managers in a limited liability company.

option price   The price at which stock may be purchased under a stock option.

option to purchase   An agreed right to purchase shares in a corporation, the exercise of which is at the election of the holder.

organizational meeting   The initial meeting of a group in a corporation.

outstanding shares   The shares of a corporation currently owned by shareholders.

over the counter   The exchange of securities of public corporations that involves computer communications among brokerage companies.

paid-in capital   The amount of capital required to be paid into a corporation.

par value   An arbitrary value placed upon shares of stock in a corporation to limit sale of the shares to at least the amount stated.

partial liquidation   The distribution of assets from a segment of a corporation's business after liabilities relating to that segment are paid.

partially disclosed principal   The existence of the principal is known to a third party, but the identity of the principal is not known.

participation (of preferred stockholder in other stocks) The right of a preferred stockholder to share in distributions made to other stockholders in addition to any preferred distributions received.

partition The right of a tenant in common to divide and sever his or her proportionate interest in property.

partnership agreement A contract among partners describing the administration of the partnership business.

pension plan A plan to pay benefits to an employee upon retirement.

people pill An agreement among members of management that if any of them are demoted or fired after a change of control, all will resign.

percentage test Plan coverage for a specified statutory percentage of employees.

piercing the corporate veil A judicial theory used to ignore the separate entity of the corporation and hold individual shareholders liable.

poison pills Provisions in the stock structure of a corporation that allow existing shareholders to have superior rights in the event an outsider attempts to acquire control of the corporation.

pool or syndicate A group of underwriters that agree to join together to sell securities of a public corporation.

preemptive rights The shareholder's rights to purchase a proportionate share of newly issued stock.

preferences Priority rights to distributions of cash or property from a corporation granted to a particular group of shareholders before any distribution can be received by the other shareholders.

preferred stock An ownership interest in a corporation with a preference to voting, distributions or liquidation of assets.

preincorporation share subscription An offer to purchase shares in a corporation to be formed.

premium A market price higher than the principal amount repayable on a loan.

principal The person empowering an agent to act on his or her behalf.

professional corporation An artificial person or legal entity created under the law of the state to conduct a profession.

profit sharing plan A plan to share profits with an employee.

promissory note An instrument promising to repay a debt.

promoters The persons responsible for organizing a corporation.

property subscription An offer to buy shares in a corporation for property.

prospectus The written disclosure of information about a corporation that must be furnished to a public investor before the sale of securities.

proxy A written authorization of a shareholder to another to vote the shareholder's shares at a meeting.

proxy statement A statement disclosing information concerning matters to be considered at a shareholder meeting of a public corporation.

public corporation A corporation that has sold shares to investors through public stock markets.

public offering Securities of a corporation offered for sale to public investors.

qualification Formal registration of a business formed in one jurisdiction for permission to do business in another.

qualification of plan Satisfying statutory requirements for tax benefits of an employee benefit plan.

quorum The minimum number of shares required to be represented at a meeting to conduct business.

ratification Retroactive authority for a transaction given by a principal with full knowledge of all material facts.

ratio test Plan coverage comparison of highly compensated employees with non-highly compensated employees.

record date A date set within a defined statutory period for determining shareholders entitled to notice of and to vote at a meeting.

redeemable shares Shares subject to a repurchase option in favor of the corporation.

redemption of shares The corporation's right to reacquire shares of stock according to the provisions under which the stock was issued.

red herring A preliminary prospectus for a public offering of securities that does not contain the price of the securities.

registered agent A person who officially acts on behalf of the corporation to receive official notices.

registered office The office of the corporation at which official papers are to be served or mailed.

registrar A person who records and signs certificates for securities.

registration by coordination The procedure to register securities with state securities administrators when a company is filing a registration statement with the SEC.

registration by filing The procedure to register securities with state securities administrators when a company is already registered with the SEC under the 1934 Act and meets minimum net worth and trading requirements.

registration by qualification The procedure to register securities with state securities administrators when no federal registration is required.

registration of corporate name The act of registering a corporate name for a defined period with a public official.

registration statement The statement of disclosure of all material activities and financial information of the corporation that is filed with the SEC prior to public offering of securities of the corporation.

regular meetings Periodic meetings of directors as specified in the articles of incorporation or bylaws of a corporation.

renewal provision Terms in an employment contract providing for an extension of the employment period.

reorganization An extraordinary corporate transaction that may occur without tax consequences under definitions in the Internal Revenue Code.

reservation of corporate name The act of reserving the corporate name with a public official.

restatement of articles A composite of the original articles of incorporation and all past amendments consolidated into a new document.

restrictive or proprietary covenant Provision in an employment agreement preventing an employee from exploiting the employer's business or assets.

retained earnings Accumulated profits of a corporation.

Revenue Act of 1978 A federal law regulating discrimination in uninsured employee expense reimbursement plans.

reverse triangular merger A merger transaction involving three corporations in which the acquiring corporation forms a subsidiary and funds it with shares to accomplish the merger of a target corporation; the target subsidiary merges into the target; and the target corporation becomes the wholly owned subsidiary of the acquiring corporation.

revocation of voluntary dissolution A decision by the incorporator, directors, and shareholders of a corporation to revoke a voluntary dissolution proceeding.

safe harbor activities Activities in which the limited partner may participate without risking loss of limited liability.

salary Periodic agreed payments to employees for services.

savings clause A clause that makes the election of a director obligatory only if that person is competent to serve in that position.

savings provision A provision in an earnings multiple formula that states a minimum amount for the stock regardless of the product of the formula.

scrip A certificate of ownership in a corporation (issued for less than a full share).

Section 1244 plan A plan to issue shares in a corporation according to the provisions of Section 1244 of the Internal Revenue Code.

Section 1244 stock Shares issued by a small business corporation that qualify for ordinary loss treatment under Section 1244 of the Internal Revenue Code.

secured debt A loan that is repayable either through the promise of the debtor to repay or through the sale of property securing the loan.

securities A contractual ownership obligation between a business and an investor.

Securities Act of 1933 A federal law regulating the issuance and sale of securities.

Securities Exchange Act of 1934 A federal law regulating the disclosure of information and trading of securities.

security A right to recover and sell assets in the event an obligation is not paid as agreed.

selected dealers Investment bankers or brokerage companies that agree to sell securities of a public corporation to their customers.

senior securities Securities that have preferential rights to payment before payments on other securities.

separate voting group Shares of stock entitled to vote as a group on certain issues described in the articles of incorporation or statute.

series of shares Shares of stock in a corporation, the rights for which are determined by the board of directors as authorized in the articles of incorporation.

servant An agent whose actions are subject to the control of the principal.

service of process The act of delivering court documents to a party to litigation.

severability provision Provision in an employment agreement allowing objectionable or illegal terms to be removed from the agreement.

severance compensation Compensation paid upon termination of employment.

share exchange A transaction in which one corporation exchanges its shares for all or part of the shares of another corporation.

share subscription An offer to buy shares in a corporation.

share transfer restriction An agreement among shareholders to restrict or require the sale of stock under certain circumstances stated in the agreement.

shareholder voting agreement An agreement among shareholders concerning the manner in which their shares will be voted on certain issues.

shareholders The owners of a corporation.

shark repellant Statutory provisions and corporate structures that prevent outsiders from causing an extraordinary corporate transaction to be approved for their personal benefit.

sharks Investors who purchase shares in a corporation to cause an extraordinary corporate transaction to be approved for their personal benefit.

short-form merger A merger between a parent corporation and a subsidiary corporation in which the parent corporation owns at least ninety shares of the subsidiary.

short swing profits The profit made through purchase and sale of a public corporation's securities by an officer, director, or ten percent shareholder during any six-month period.

silent partners Partners without any management authority.

sinking fund A reserve account for the redemption of stock into which periodic installments are deposited to fund the payment for redemption.

small-impact merger A merger transaction in which the surviving corporation will not change its articles of incorporation or the shares owned by its shareholders, and will not increase its outstanding stock by more than 20 as a result of the merger.

sole proprietorship   A business owned by an individual.

special agent   A person employed to conduct a limited number of transactions for a principal.

special meetings   Meetings of the directors that are called at times other than the periodic meeting specified in the articles of incorporation or bylaws.

split-dollar insurance   An insurance policy in which the employer and employee each pay a portion of the premium.

stagger   To elect only a portion of the board of directors each year.

stated capital   An account in which a corporation records the par value of share of stock or to which funds received from sales of no par value shares are allocated.

Stated value   The value established for no par stock by the board of directors of a corporation.

statement of denial   A filed statement denying an individual's authority or status as a partner.

statement of partnership authority   A filed statement identifying partners authorized to perform certain acts for the partnership and describing the extent of a partner's authority.

sticker   An amendment to the final prospectus to state current information about the public corporation.

stock exchange   A place of business that conducts the marketing of securities of public corporations.

stock option   A right to purchase shares in a corporation at a specified price.

stock option, incentive stock option   An option granted to an employee to buy stock that has tax benefits under federal law.

stock split   A division of the ownership interest of shareholders into a greater number of shares.

stock transfer agent   An independent company that administers the registration and transfer of a corporation's stock.

stock transfer ledger   The record of ownership and transfer of shares of a corporation.

stock voting agreement   An agreement among shareholders concerning the manner in which their shares will be voted on certain issues.

street name   The process of registering securities in the name of broker or bank to hold for an account of a particular investor.

subagent   An agent hired by another agent who has authority to do so.

Subchapter S corporation   A corporation the income of which is taxed to the individual shareholders.

Subchapter S election   An election to permit the income of a corporation to be treated and taxed as ordinary income of the shareholders.

subordination of bonds   An agreement to permit the payment of other indebtedness before payment of the obligation on a bond.

subsidiary corporation   A corporation whose shares are owned in whole or in part by another corporation.

substantial contacts   Participation in transactions or events that subject an individual or company to local regulation.

surplus   The excess of net assets over stated capital.

surviving corporation   The acquiring corporation in a corporate merger.

surviving partner   A partner still living after the death of a partner.

tax preference   Income subject to a surtax under federal law.

tenancy in common   Ownership of property by more than one person with each owner entitled to an undivided share of the property.

tenancy in partnership   The property classification used in the original Uniform Partnership Act generally requiring all partners to act together in using or disposing of partnership property.

thin incorporation   The term describing a situation in which a corporation's debt is disproportionately higher than its equity.

timetable   A schedule of tasks to be completed in preparation for a corporate meeting.

tombstone ad   Notice to publicize forthcoming sales of public securities.

trademark   A name protected from use by others by registration under federal or state law.

trade name   A name used by a business in promoting its products and services.

trade secrets   Proprietary and confidential business information.

transacting business   The test to determine whether a corporation must qualify to do business in a foreign jurisdiction.

transfer agent   A person who administers the transfers and issuance certificates for securities.

transfer of corporate name   The act of transferring a reserved corporate name from one person to another.

treasury shares   Shares of the corporation that have been purchased by the corporation from a shareholder.

triangular merger   A merger transaction involving three corporations in which the acquiring corporation forms a subsidiary and funds it with shares to accomplish the merger of a target corporation; the target merges into the subsidiary.

true value rule   The actual value of property or services contributed for a share of stock is equal to the par value or the stated value of no par value share.

trust indenture   An agreement between a corporation, a trustee, and investors concerning the rights and obligations of a bond.

Trust Indenture Act of 1939   A federal law regulating the contents of and rights under a trust indenture.

ultra vires doctrine   A corporation acting without authority to do so.

uncertificated securities   Stock of a corporation that is registered in the corporation records but is not represented by a stock certificate.

underwriter   An investment banker or brokerage company that offers and sells securities of a public corporation.

underwriter manager   The underwriter primarily responsible for supervision of the registration of securities and distribution of the securities to investors.

undisclosed principal   Neither the existence nor identity of the principal is known to the third party.

Uniform Commercial Code   A state statute regulating commercial transactions, including the sale and transfer of goods.

unlimited liability   The sole proprietor's personal liability for business debts.

unsecured debt   A loan that is repayable only through the promise of the debtor to repay.

vesting   The time at which an employee is entitled to the benefits of a plan.

vicarious liability or respondeat superior   Liability imposed on one person for the acts or omissions of another.

voluntary dissolution   A decision by the incorporator, directors, or shareholders of the corporation to dissolve the corporation.

voting group   Specified shareholders entitled to vote on specified issues.

voting list   A list of shareholders entitled to vote at a shareholder's meeting.

voting trust   A trust agreement that separates legal and beneficial ownership of shares and authorizes a voting trustee to vote shares for the term of the trust.

waiting period   The period of time after a registration statement has been filed with the SEC but before it becomes effective.

"wasting assets" provisions   A financial reserve established for assets that deteriorate over time.

watered, or discount, shares   Par value shares sold by a corporation for less than par value.

weighted voting   Specifying more than one vote per share for a certain class of stock.

winding-up   The act of liquidating the assets of an entity, paying creditors and distributing any surplus and profits to its owners.

work product protection clause   Provision in an employment agreement providing ownership by the employer of an employee's ideas and inventions.

wrongful dissolution   The termination of a partnership by a partner without having a right to do so.

INDEX

Members of limited liability
        company, 124
    admission of, 125
    contributions of, 124
    dissociation of, 125
    distributional interest to
        dissociated, 125
    right to information by, 125–126
    right to vote, 124–125
Membership interest, transferability of,
    128–129
Merger, 132, 372, 525–537
    articles of, 531
    defined, 525
    hostile takeovers, 532, 534–537
    notice to shareholders, 530–531
    procedure for, 529
    reverse triangular, 528
    short-form, 530
    small-impact, 530
    statutory effect of, 531–532
    surviving corporation in, 525
    tax terminology for, 529
    triangular, 528
    types of reorganizations, 529
    variations on transaction, 528
Merger of foreign corporation, 508–511
*Meyer v. Oklahoma Alcoholic Beverage
    Laws Enforcement Commission,*
    152–153
Minority discount of shares, 547–548
Minority nominee, 463
Minority representation, 462
Minority voting power, concentration of,
    462–463
Minute book, 273
Minutes of meetings, 375–377
    guidelines for, 376–377
Misconduct by limited partner, 94
Model Act, 298
Model Business Corporation Act, 32, 121,
    159, 164, 165, 166, 167, 169, 171,
    173, 178, 213, 214, 216, 217, 234,
    241, 242, 243, 258, 261, 263, 266,
    267, 271, 273, 274, 296, 303, 304,
    307, 308, 309, 314, 316, 343, 350,
    358, 360, 361, 362, 364, 367, 369,
    373, 374, 384, 387, 388, 392, 393,
    395, 397
    and restrictive agreements, 464–465
    close corporations and, 209, 210
    corporate powers in, 160, 161,
        162, 163
    foreign corporation and, 508
    foreign corporation sanctions in,
        498–499
    shareholder voting agreements in, 459
    voting trust and, 460
Model Professional Corporation Act, 214,
    215, 216, 217, 218
Model Professional Corporation
    Supplement, 214
Mortgage bond, 294, 322
Mortgage of assets, 537–540
    See also Assets, sale, mortgage,
        disposition of.

Multiple of earnings formula, 477
Murphy v. Crosland, 287–288
Myhre v. Myhre, 381

N
Name-saver subsidiaries, 246
Naming general partnership, 55, 57
NASDAQ, *See* National Association of
    Securities Dealers Automatic
    Quotation system.
National Association of Securities Dealers
    Automatic Quotation system
    (NASDAQ), 196
National Securities Trading System, 196
Negotiable share certificates, 297
Net assets, 385, 386, 387
Net distributable profit, 42
Net worth, 387
New York Stock Exchange, 196
No par value, 307, 391, 394
No par value shares, 255, 256, 296–297
Nominal directors, 344
Nominee certificate, 172
Nonassessable shares, 308
Non-competition clause, 51
Noncompetition agreements, 427, 428
    enforcing, 428
Noncumulative distribution, 310
Nondisclosure agreements, 424
Nonexempt employees, 407
Nonjudicial liquidation, 563
Nonsmoking ordinances, 406
Notice procedure for buyout, 475

O
Obedience, agent's duty to principal, 4
Office procedures, in employee
    handbooks, 418
Operating agreement, 130
Operating agreement for limited liability
    company, 135, 138, 139–149
    See also Limited liability company
        operating agreement checklist.
    checklist for preparing, 140–149
    filing procedure for, 149
    items addressed in, 139–140
    provisions not allowed in, 139
Operation of general partnership, 55–73
Operation of law, 6
Option price, 439, 442
Option to purchase, 466–467
    considerations in designating, 467
Organization of company, in employee
    handbooks, 418
Organizational meeting, 272–273
    See also Business conducted at
        organizational meetings.
    business at, 344–358
    director's, 343–342
    incorporator's, 344
    requirement for, 343
Original ideas, employers rights to, 421
Outstanding shares, 295
Over-the-counter market, 196

Overtime, 407–408
    records, 407
Ownership of corporation, 164–176

P
Paid-in capital, 232
Par value, 307, 391
Par value shares, 255, 296–297
Parent-subsidiary corporations, 180
Partial liquidations, 398
Partially disclosed principal, 2
Participation by preferred stockholder, 311
Partition ownership, 34
Partner,
    bankruptcy of, 71
    death of, 71
    devotion of duty by, 40
    dissociated, 45
    duties and compensation of, 40
    expulsion of, 70
    liability of, 44–46
    life insurance for, 50
    standards of conduct of, 41–42
    surviving, 35
Partner's interest in partnership, 35–36
Partnership, 9
    continuing despite dissolution, 49–51, 72
    definition of, 32
    dissolution of, 46–51
    doing business in foreign
        jurisdictions, 495
    management of, 36–42, 65–69
    partner's interest in, 35–36
    profits and losses in, 42–43
    technical dissolution of, 45
    termination of, 51–52
Partnership, general, *See* General
    partnership.
Partnership agreement, 30, 57–73
Partnership authority, statement of, 37
Partnership conversion to limited liability
    company, 131
Partnership creditors, 91
Partnership differentiated from limited
    liability company, 139
Partnership property, 33–35, 69
    loaned, 33–34
Passive partnership losses, 96
Pass-through tax consequences, 122–123
Pass-through taxation, 130, 213
Patentable inventions, company's right
    to, 422
Pay, defined, 407–408
Payment, terms in buyout, 482–484
Pension plans, 433–438
    contribution limits, 438
    formalities of, 438
    funding, 438
    qualification of, 435
    tax ramifications of, 434–435
People pill, 536
Percentage test, 436
Personal liability, 44, 74
Personnel policies, in employee
    handbooks, 418